1,000 BOOKS TO READ BEFORE YOU DIE

1,000 BOOKS TO READ

A LIFE-CHANGING LIST

BEFORE YOU DIE

JAMES MUSTICH

with Margot Greenbaum Mustich, Thomas Meagher,
and Karen Templer

WORKMAN PUBLISHING • NEW YORK

Library of Congress Cataloging-in-Publication Data is available.
ISBN 978-1-5235-0445-9

Design by Janet Vicario
Photo research by Aaron Clendening
Author photo by Trisha Keeler Photography

Workman books are available at special discounts when purchased in bulk for premiums
and sales promotions as well as for fund-raising or educational use. Special editions or
book excerpts can also be created to specification. For details, contact the Special Sales Director
at the address below, or send an email to specialmarkets@workman.com.

Workman Publishing Co., Inc.
225 Varick Street
New York, NY 10014-4381
workman.com

Printed in China
First printing September 2018

10 9 8 7 6 5 4 3 2

The only advice, indeed, that one person can give another about reading is to take no advice, to follow your own instincts, to use your own reason, to come to your own conclusions. If this is agreed between us, then I feel at liberty to put forward a few ideas and suggestions because you will not allow them to fetter that independence which is the most important quality that a reader can possess.

—*Virginia Woolf, "How Should One Read a Book?"*

To my parents, Annette and Jim Mustich,
for a thousand and one books and
the home that held them.

To Emma and Iris,
so they might explore the landscape
in which their father found his way.

To Margot Greenbaum Mustich,
whose intellect and diligence have ensured this book a life,
and whose love has enriched mine.

And to the memory of Peter Workman,
whose inspiration engendered this volume
and countless others.

Contents

Introduction

IN THE COMPANY OF BOOKS

I caught the reading bug as a child from my mother, who is still, at eighty-nine, the most constant reader I know. As library hound, student, English major, aspiring writer, and then, and enduringly, bookseller, I surrounded myself with books, which spontaneously sprouted and grew into piles in whatever room I inhabited. Parenthood only compounded the circumstance, and the house I share with my wife, Margot, remains filled with the picture books, chapter books, and YA novels that accompanied our two daughters on their journey to adulthood. Books are everywhere I look, and I like it that way; I suspect you share something of the feeling, or you wouldn't have picked up this one.

Naturally enough, one of my first jobs was working at the local bookstore in Briarcliff Manor, New York, that had fed so many of my fledgling literary enthusiasms. There I unpacked shipments from publishers, stocked front-of-store displays with new releases, and found room for backlist titles on the always crammed shelves. I learned to listen to customers and, eventually, to make useful, interesting, and potentially life-changing recommendations. That last hyphenated adjective may sound grandiose, but as Roger Mifflin, the protagonist of Christopher Morley's *The Haunted Bookshop*, puts it, steadfast booksellers are missionaries who seek "to spread good books about, to sow them on fertile minds, to propagate understanding and a carefulness of life and beauty."

With that mission in mind, in 1986 I cofounded a mail-order catalog called *A Common Reader*, and spent the next two decades running that venture, which, luckily for me, consisted of writing about books old and new, of every subject and style. Supported by a small band of colleagues, I managed to grow the enterprise until we were mailing rich commentary on scores of titles every three weeks to hundreds of thousands of readers across the United States.

In the early 2000s, Peter Workman—founder of Workman Publishing and to me both mentor and friend—and I began talking about the book you are now reading. Over the course of many book-soaked conversations, the idea of *1,000 Books to Read Before You Die* took shape. Again fate had pointed my simple desire to be immersed in written words toward a new destination. It turned out to be farther away than either of us thought—the book has been fourteen years in the making, and I regret that Peter is not alive to see it published.

Any exercise in curation provokes questions of discernment, epistemology, and even philosophy that can easily lead to befuddlement, and in the case of books, since they are carriers of such varied knowledge in themselves, it can be paralyzing. A book about 1,000 books could take so many different shapes. It could be a canon of classics; it could be a history of human thought and a tour of its significant disciplines; it might be a record of popular delights (or even delusions). But the crux of the difficulty was a less complicated truth: Readers read in so many different ways, any one standard of measure is inadequate. No matter their pedigree, inveterate readers read the way they eat—for pleasure as well as nourishment, indulgence as much as education, and sometimes for transcendence, too. Hot dogs one day, haute cuisine the next.

Keeping such diversity of appetite in mind, and hoping to have something to satisfy every kind of reading yen, I wanted to make *1,000 Books to Read Before You Die* expansive in its tastes, encompassing revered classics and commercial favorites, flights of escapist entertainment and enlightening works of erudition.

There had to be room for novels of imaginative reach and histories with intellectual grasp. And since the project in its title invoked a lifetime, there had to be room for books for children and adolescents. What criteria could I apply to accommodate such a menagerie, to give plausibility to the idea that *Where the Wild Things Are* belongs in the same collection as *In Search of Lost Time*, that Aeneas and Sherlock Holmes could be companions, that a persuasive collection could begin, in chronological terms, with *The Epic of Gilgamesh*, inscribed on Babylonian tablets more than four thousand years ago, and end with Ellen Ullman's personal history of technology, *Life in Code*, published in 2017?

I came upon the clue I needed in a passage written by the critic Edmund Wilson, describing "the miscellaneous learning of the bookstore, unorganized by any larger purpose, the undisciplined undirected curiosity of the indolent lover of reading." There, I knew instinctively, was a workable conceit: What if I had a bookstore that could hold only 1,000 volumes, and I wanted to ensure it held not only books for all time but also books for the moment, books to be savored or devoured in a night? A shop where any reading inclination—be it for thrillers or theology, or theological thrillers—might find reward. In the end, I was back in my favorite haunt, a browser's version of paradise.

That end, of course, was only the beginning. I still had to wrangle with myriad knotty concerns. I spent months—was it years?—arranging and rearranging lists of several thousand titles. What classics were compelling enough to earn a spot? Which kids' books so timeless they made the grade? What currents of thought retained their currency? Which life stories were larger than their protagonist's life span? Not least, what authors did I love so much that they might be ushered in without their credentials being subject to too much scrutiny?

Marcel Proust

Zadie Smith

My answers to all the above questions almost certainly will not be yours. Even where we agree, my description of a book might not highlight the things that have made you love it. A text is never static: Every sentence wends its way into the ear and mind of one reader differently than it is welcomed, or invites itself, into those of another. Just as a musician brings a score to life, so a reader animates an author's pages; as Emerson said, "'Tis the good reader that makes the good book." And true readers talk and listen to one another, recommend and contend, make lists in the service of their search for another volume; it's all part of the dance of serendipity and conversation that sweeps up all genuine book lovers time and again.

Once people know you are writing a book called *1,000 Books to Read Before You Die*, you can never enjoy a dinner party in quite the way you did before. No matter how many books you've managed to consider, and no matter how many pages you've written, every conversation with a fellow reader is almost sure to provide new titles to seek out, or, more worryingly, to expose an egregious omission or a gap in your knowledge—to say nothing of revealing privileges and prejudices, however unwitting, underlying your points of reference.

Although the choice of books that follows has been informed across the years by the generosity of other readers in the guise of teachers, friends, work colleagues, literary collaborators, correspondents, customers, and acquaintances, it is in the end mine, and as such personal and sometimes peculiar. At its core is an informed itinerary through literary culture, from Aeschylus to Zadie Smith, *Gilgamesh* to *Gilead*. *1,000 Books* is not a survey course in literature, although one could easily chart one through its entries, just as one could also map a journey in ideas from Plato to Darwin to Simone de Beauvoir, or in religious thinking from Saint Augustine to Simone Weil, in diaries from Samuel Pepys to Sarah Manguso, or in history from the Trojan War to Vietnam.

Whatever route you set out on, you'll find tempting distractions in every direction. You'll come upon books about insects, fish, and race horses; perspectives on revolutions political and scientific; profound thoughts on food as well as philosophy. More than a few of my selections may strike you as arguable, and some may provoke you to exclaim, "Are you kidding me?" Although I hope you'll be inspired to track your own reading against the works I've written about, I know for certain that you'll be making a list of all the books you love that I've left out.

For years a thousand books felt like far too many to get my head around, but now it seems too few by several multiples. So let me say what already should be obvious: *1,000 Books to Read Before You Die* is neither comprehensive nor authoritative, even if a good number of the titles assembled here would be on most lists of essential reading. It is meant to be an invitation to a conversation—even a merry argument— about the books and authors that are missing as well as the books and authors included, because the question of what to read next is the best prelude to even more important ones, like who to be, and how to live. Such faith in reading's power, and the learning and imagination it nourishes, is something I've been lucky enough to take for granted as both fact and freedom; it's something I fear may be forgotten in the great amnesia of our in-the-moment newsfeeds and algorithmically defined identities, which hide from our view the complexity of feelings and ideas that books demand we quietly, and determinedly, engage.

To get lost in a story, or even a study, is inherently to acknowledge the voice of another, to broaden one's perspective beyond the confines of one's own understanding. A good book is the opposite of a selfie; the right book at the right time can expand our lives in the way love does, making us more thoughtful, more generous, more brave, more alert to the world's wonders and more pained by its inequities, more wise, more kind. In the metaphorical bookshop you are about to enter, I hope you'll discover a few to add to those you already cherish.

Happy reading.

How the Book Is Organized

For ease of browsing and to foster serendipity, the entries are for the most part arranged alphabetically by author. Exceptions include works of scripture and books not attributable with confidence to any one author, which appear in alphabetical order by title. These are:

- *The Arabian Nights*, page 21
- *Beowulf*, page 68
- Bhagavad Gita, page 75
- The Bible, page 76
- The Book of Common Prayer, page 87
- *The Epic of Gilgamesh*, page 255
- *The 9/11 Commission Report*, page 589
- The Qur'an, page 652
- *The Sagas of Icelanders*, page 692
- Tao Te Ching, page 774

Other exceptions to the alphabetical listing are the titles in the **More to Explore** (books grouped by theme) and **Booknote** (a book appended to a relevant entry) features. A cross-reference for each of these titles appears where it would normally occur alphabetically by the author's last name, directing readers to the appropriate page.

Of the 1,000 books represented, roughly half are fiction and half nonfiction. Nine hundred and forty-eight have individual entries or, in the case of series or some multivolume works, are treated together with their complementary volumes in one essay. Appended to each of these are endnotes, whose components are described below. The other fifty-two appear in **More to Explore** and **Booknotes**. In the text of the entries and the endnotes, more than 6,000 additional titles are referenced, as are more than 3,000 authors beyond those in the core selection.

A Few Notes on the Endnotes

The endnotes that follow the entries display all or some of the following information, depending upon the book.

• *What:* Genre and/or subject matter.

• *When:* Date of first publication. If only one date is given for a book written in a language other than English, this is the date the work was published in the original language; wherever possible, we also give date of first publication in English (in either a British or an American edition). Some dates, especially for ancient works, are given as ranges based on current scholarly consensus or to indicate serial publication.

• *Edition(s):* Specific editions of merit or historical interest.

• *Award(s):* Major literary awards earned by the work and/or the author.

• *Also By:* Notable works by the author not mentioned in the text of the entry, followed by publication date (applying the rules described in *When*). These listings are not comprehensive, but are meant to point readers to signal works.

• *Further Reading:* Titles that shed additional light on the author's life and work, or on the subject treated by the main entry.

• *Try:* Works by other authors for readers to look for if they have enjoyed the featured book.

• *Adaptation(s):* Films, television productions, plays, musical compositions, audiobooks, and/or works in other media based on or inspired by the subject entry that are worth seeking out.

• *Footnote:* Special or surprising information we just couldn't bear to leave out!

Lists and Indexes

On page 885 you'll find **A Miscellany of Special Lists,** which presents groupings that are curated by subject or style, or with a particular audience in mind. After that is a comprehensive **General Index,** which is followed by a checklist of the 1,000 books. Indexes of the books by genre and by chronology can be found at 1000BookstoRead.com.

"Read at whim!
Read at whim!"

—Randall Jarrell

A, B, C

Desert Solitaire

A SEASON IN THE WILDERNESS

Edward Abbey (1927–1989)

An Earthly Prophet in the Wilderness

Written in the middle of the 1960s, yet composed largely from journals kept a decade earlier during the author's summers as a backcountry ranger at the Arches National Monument ("among," as he puts it, "the hoodoo rocks and voodoo silence of the Utah wilderness"), *Desert Solitaire* evokes the paradoxical loveliness of the harsh, hostile landscape with awestruck exactitude and visceral intensity. Edward Abbey's attention to the desert flora and fauna, to the ancient rock formations and the ever-present weather, to the pleasures of both solitude and company, brings a bracing alertness to the episodes he describes in the linked essays that organize his narrative. The discrete chapters are filled with discoveries gruesome, elegiac, and glorious. In "The Dead Man at Grandview Point," he joins the search for an unfortunate photographer who has lost his way in the unforgiving terrain; in "Down the River," he journeys with a companion along the Colorado River through Glen Canyon, soon to be flooded by the technological hubris of a hydroelectric dam; in "Terra Incognita: Into the Maze," he exults in the labyrinthine wonders of a last bit of unmapped wild, a haven he

Arches National Park, Utah

welcomes for its lack of any hint of hospitality. How long will it be safe from the "industrial tourism" that has tamed the surrounding country and that Abbey indicts, again and again, with mordant vehemence?

Despite its canonization as something of a backpacker's bible, *Desert Solitaire* is too quirky, cranky, and idiosyncratic to be stereotyped as a nature lover's handbook. While the spare majesty of its setting provides a stunning inspiration for Abbey's work, his meditations have as much to say about society, civilization, and culture as they do about nature; each of these dimensions of human life, the irascible author might proclaim, is nourished and sustained by wilderness. In this, of course, he echoes the gentler voice of the sage of Walden Pond, Henry David Thoreau: "In Wildness is the preservation of the World."

What: Nature. Memoir. **When:** 1968.
Also By: Best known among Abbey's many additional books is the controversial novel *The Monkey Wrench Gang* (1975). *Good News* (1980). *The Fool's Progress* (1988). *Further Reading: Escalante: The Best Kind of Nothing* by Brooke Williams, photographs by Chris Noble. *Try: My First Summer in the Sierra* by John Muir (see page 570). *A Sand County Almanac* by Aldo Leopold.

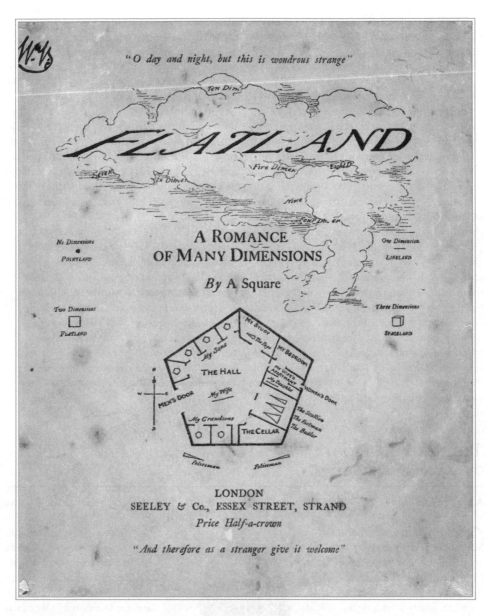

"O day and night, but this is wondrous strange"

Ten Dim

FLATLAND

Seven   Six Dimen   Five Dimen   Eight D

Nine

Four Di en

No Dimensions
●
POINTLAND

A ROMANCE
OF MANY DIMENSIONS

By A Square

One Dimension
―
LINELAND

Two Dimensions
□
FLATLAND

My Study
The Page   My Bedroom
My Sons
My Wife's
Apartment
My Daughter   Women's Door
THE HALL
N
W   E
S
MEN'S DOOR   My Wife
The Scullion
The Footman
The Butler
My Grandsons
THE CELLAR

Three Dimensions
▱
SPACELAND

Policeman   Policeman

LONDON
SEELEY & Co., ESSEX STREET, STRAND
Price Half-a-crown

"And therefore as a stranger give it welcome"

Flatland

A ROMANCE OF MANY DIMENSIONS
Edwin A. Abbott (1838–1926)

A Mathematical Dystopia

The Reverend Edwin Abbott Abbott was a schoolmaster and philologist whose writings comprise an eclectic collection, including a volume called *A Shakespearian Grammar*, a biography of Francis Bacon, three religious romances, a study of *The Anglican Career of Cardinal Newman*, the entry on "The Gospels" in the ninth edition of the *Encyclopedia Britannica*, and a school text called *Via Latina: First Latin Book*. All of these works are forgotten today, and Abbott would be, too, were it not for a slim book he published in 1884 called *Flatland: A Romance of Many Dimensions*.

A novel of mathematical whimsy, *Flatland* is set in the peculiar world that provides the book's name and is home to its putative author, A. Square, a two-dimensional being in a world inhabited by lines, triangles, circles, and polygons. Ingeniously composed as a kind of dystopian memoir, *Flatland* is a stunning piece of social satire, depicting with great acuity the gender and class distinctions of Victorian Britain. The mathematical surface of the tale (which is illustrated with Abbott's own diagrams) hides the fierce precision of the author's insight into the prejudices of his time. The male figures—triangular laborers, middle-class squares, and aristocratic polygons—have more volume than the women, who, no matter their class, are never more than straight lines (which, while limiting their reach, gives them a definite, and dangerous, sharpness when approached head on). Abbott starkly represents the risks of nonconformity through the society's treatment of irregular shapes: Figures lacking proper angles or embodying disproportions of one kind or another are consigned to a disadvantaged underclass.

What happens when a Sphere appears to initiate A. Square into the mysteries of three dimensions? Well, all hell breaks loose for our protagonist, and nothing ever looks the same. Abbott's notions about the larger conundrums posed by different dimensions and their relationships to one another were ahead of their time, mathematically speaking, but the enduring fascination of his fable is its depiction of the perils of making the world simpler than it is, no matter how elegantly provable that simplicity may seem.

What: Novel. Mathematics. *When:* 1884. *Edition: The Annotated Flatland* (2002) amplifies the text with a treasure trove of enlightening commentary by Ian Stewart. *Also By: How to Write Clearly* (1876). *Try: Sphereland* by Dionys Burger. *The Dot and the Line: A Romance in Lower Mathematics* by Norton Juster. *Flatterland* by Ian Stewart. *Adaptations:* 2007 saw the release of both a short animated film, *Flatland: The Movie*, and a feature-length computer animated updating of the story, *Flatland: The Film*.

Things Fall Apart
Chinua Achebe (1930–2013)

A Tragedy of Tribal Life

C omposed in English and published in 1958, two years before Nigeria declared independence, *Things Fall Apart* was the first African novel to attain a wide international readership. Set at the end of the nineteenth century on the cusp of Nigeria's British colonial era, it is the story of Okonkwo, a physically imposing man who has risen to prominence in his village through his prowess as a wrestler and warrior and his quantifiable success as a farmer (he has two barns full of yams)

and husband (as the book opens, he has just taken his third wife).

Okonkwo's achievements have been hard won, a direct result of his resolve to distinguish himself from his ne'er-do-well father. Yet for all his accomplishments, Okonkwo cannot quell his doubts as to his own worth, nor contain the furies that torment him. His anger is a constant threat to his family; his fear of appearing weak compels him to take part in the ritual killing of an adopted son, despite the caution of a respected elder; his accidental murder of the son of another tribesman leads to his banishment from the village for seven years. His exile coincides with the arrival of British colonial administrators and Christian missionaries, whose influence shatters the certainties and coherence of traditional tribal life, infiltrating even Okonkwo's family circle. His ultimate return home proves to be a flashpoint in the clash of cultures.

Things Fall Apart is a short, sparely told tale that nevertheless embraces themes of enormous import: fate and will, the determining influences of familial inheritance, the consequences and consolations of custom, the legacy of colonialism. It also illuminates the personal and political crises provoked by the failure of individuals and societies to grow while maintaining their identities in the face of change. And while the novel is steeped in Achebe's native Igbo culture and alert to the conflicts inherent in the historical moment it depicts, its action seems to unfold on a universal stage; it is as rich in human substance as Greek tragedy, and just as mysteriously powerful in its effect.

What: Novel. *When:* 1958. *Also By: No Longer at Ease* (1960). *Arrow of God* (1964). *A Man of the People* (1966). *Anthills of the Savannah* (1987). *Try: Houseboy* by Ferdinand Oyono. *Maps* by Nuruddin Farah. *Half of a Yellow Sun* by Chimamanda Ngozi Adichie (see page 8).

My Dog Tulip
J. R. Ackerley (1896–1967)

"One of the greatest masterpieces of animal literature."—*Christopher Isherwood*

A lively pack of "me and my dog" memoirs crowd bookstore shelves. Indeed, it's more than likely one sits atop bestseller lists this very moment. ("Stay!" its author has no doubt commanded it.) *My Dog Tulip* was one of the first noteworthy examples of this thriving genre, and it remains one of the best: honest, amusing, elegantly written, and emphatically canine-centric.

When first published in England in 1956, *Tulip* was considered shocking because of what one reviewer called its "scatological and gynaecological detail." But while the messy details are certainly present in abundance (Chapter Two, for example, is entitled "Liquids and Solids"), to be put off by them is to miss the forest for the trees. For it is precisely J. R. Ackerley's frank, unashamed, and often hilarious discussions of his beloved Alsatian's bodily functions, her insistent animality, which bring this particular dog to such vivid and unforgettable life. As E. M. Forster, one

of *Tulip*'s more perceptive early readers, noted, what was unprecedented about the book was the way its central character demanded recognition "as a creature in her own right, as a dog of dogdom and not as an appendage of man."

Ackerley observes Tulip's canine world with an artfully uncomplicated sense of wonder and delight, portraying himself in these pages as a comic figure; his fretful, bumbling attempts to "find a husband" for Tulip are especially funny. In reality, though, J. R. Ackerley was an accomplished and widely admired man of letters, best known as the long-serving editor of *The Listener*, the magazine of the British Broadcasting Corporation. His 1968 memoir, *My Father and Myself*, is another idiosyncratic gem.

What: Animals. Memoir. *When:* 1956. *Also By: Hindoo Holiday: An Indian Journal* (1932). *My Father and Myself* (1968). *Try: All the Dogs of My Life* by Elizabeth von Arnim. *Bandit* by Vicki Hearne. *My Dog Skip* by Willie Morris. *Adaptation:* The 2009 animated feature film, by Paul Fierlinger and Sandra Fierlinger, features the voices of Christopher Plummer and Lynn Redgrave.

The Hitchhiker's Guide to the Galaxy
Douglas Adams (1952–2001)

Lost in the Stars—and Laughing All the Way

To say that Douglas Adams's *The Hitchhiker's Guide to the Galaxy* is a book that captured the zeitgeist of the late 1970s and the 1980s is an understatement. Beginning as a BBC comedy radio series, it would mutate into versions in print, on stage, in comics, and on screens small and big, becoming an international sensation. Published as a novel in 1979, it was an immediate bestseller, and its reach with readers only grew as it was expanded by its author into a "trilogy" of five volumes.

Douglas Adams's insouciant way with the definition of "trilogy" is par for his book's course through outer space, and an emblem of the book's appeal: It's silly—cleverly, brilliantly, gloriously, ingeniously, and at times profoundly silly. Despite its technological trimmings and intergalactic itinerary, *The Hitchhiker's Guide to the Galaxy* is a virtuoso performance on the core instruments of British humor, from *Three Men in a Boat* to Monty Python. Think P. G. Wodehouse in space, complete with the zany names, and you'll get the idea.

The story begins with Arthur Dent in a panic because his modest home in a West Country village is about to be demolished to make way for a traffic bypass. While Arthur is lying in the mud in front of a bulldozer to prevent the machine's progress, he's approached by his friend Ford Prefect, who asks, ". . . look, are you busy?" Unbeknownst to Arthur, Ford has bigger things on his mind than the destruction of Arthur's house, because, also unbeknownst to Arthur, Ford is not an unemployed actor, as he has long claimed, but rather a stranded alien researcher originally sent to Earth to update *The Hitchhiker's Guide to the Galaxy*, the book-within-the-book that is an essential *vade mecum* for wanderers through deep space. ("It's a sort of electronic book. It tells you everything you need to know about anything. That's its job," Ford will later explain. Surprisingly, or perhaps not, the first extended excerpt from the guide we get to read concerns the critical importance of towels for the interstellar thumb-rider.) What's on Ford's mind while Arthur lies in the mud is the fact that in fifteen minutes or so, Earth will be destroyed to make way for a *galactic* traffic bypass, which makes the issue of West Country road construction moot.

That's just the launch pad for the laugh-out-loud literary journey that will carry Arthur, Ford, and the reader across millions of miles of space—and oceans of *Hitchhiker* invention and arcana—as they pursue the answer to the riddle of "life, the universe, and everything" (which turns out to be—but why spoil it?).

What: Science Fiction. *When:* 1979. *Also By:* Adams's four other books in the Hitchhiker "trilogy" are *The Restaurant at the End of the Universe* (1980); *Life, the Universe and Everything* (1982); *So Long, and Thanks for All the Fish* (1984); *Mostly Harmless* (1992). *Further Reading: Don't Panic: The Official Hitchhiker's Guide to the Galaxy Companion* by Neil Gaiman. *Try: Another Fine Myth* by Robert Asprin. *The Color of Magic* by Terry Pratchett. *Adaptations:* In every medium, including a feature film, which premiered in 2005. *Footnote:* The sixth book in the series, *And Another Thing . . .* (2009), was written by Eoin Colfer.

The Education of Henry Adams
Henry Adams (1838–1918)

The Man Who Wouldn't Be President

Henry Adams belonged to one of America's most prominent political families. Both his great-grandfather, John Adams (1735–1826), and his grandfather, John Quincy Adams (1767–1848), served as presidents of the United States. His father, Charles Francis Adams Sr. (1807–1886), was a congressman and US ambassador to Britain. Fate seemed to have set Henry on the path to power, yet he stayed out of politics, acting as his father's secretary for several years, teaching medieval history at Harvard, and writing journalism, fiction, and history. And although, given the public identity he had inherited, he viewed his life as a failure (a fact expressed with a rueful poise throughout this autobiography), he nurtured a private intelligence both idiosyncratic and profound; his two masterpieces, this *Education* and *Mont Saint Michel and Chartres*, are the products of a writing mind as curious and as complicated as America has ever produced.

In the first chapter of his *Education*, Adams writes:

Probably no child, born in the [same] year, held better cards than he. Whether life was an honest game of chance, or whether the cards were marked and forced, he could not refuse to play his excellent hand....

As it happened, he never got to the point of playing the game at all; he lost himself in the study of it, watching the errors of the players; but this is the only interest in the story, which otherwise has no moral and little incident.

You'll note that Adams writes of himself in the third person. While on the one hand this device suggests the weight of the legacy the Adams name embodied, on the other it affords the author the perspective needed to examine his own experience through seven decades with the detached, skeptical, witty, and ironic sensibility these pages so richly exhibit.

Surveying national events from his birth through the era of the Civil War and the subsequent economic expansion of the United States, Adams's distinctive autobiography is also a brilliant work of historical acumen. It depicts, with imaginative aplomb, the cultural transformations set in motion as the onrushing realities of the twentieth century overwhelmed the stately expectations of the nineteenth. Similarly, the accelerating complexities of the booming new America outpaced the author's ability to keep up with them ("the difficulties of education had gone on doubling with the coal output," Adams drolly explains).

Privately printed in 1907, *The Education of Henry Adams* was publicly issued after the author's death eleven years later. An immediate popular and critical success, it became a bestseller and won a Pulitzer Prize. Its reputation has only increased in the intervening decades; in 1998 the Modern Library placed it in the number one spot on its list of the Best Nonfiction Books of the Twentieth Century. A work of extraordinary eloquence and discernment, it has earned its author a place in literary history worthy of his illustrious pedigree.

What: Autobiography. History. *When:* Privately printed, 1907; first trade publication, 1918. *Award:* Pulitzer Prize for Biography or Autobiography, 1919. *Also By: Democracy: An American Novel* (1880). *Esther: A Novel* (1884). *History of the United States of America, 1801–1817* (9 volumes; 1884–91). *Mont Saint Michel and Chartres* (privately printed, 1904; revised trade edition, 1913). *Further Reading: The Five of Hearts: An Intimate Portrait of Henry Adams and His Friends, 1880–1918* by Patricia O'Toole. *Henry Adams and the Making of America* by Garry Wills. *Try:* A credible Henry Adams is an intriguing presence in Gore Vidal's splendid historical novel, *Empire.*

Watership Down
Richard Adams (1920–2016)

An Unputdownable Adventure Tale

One of the most phenomenal international bestsellers of the 1970s, *Watership Down* is an immersive saga that traverses great themes and feelings—courage, frailty, community, ecology, responsibility, friendship, love—while holding readers on the edge of their metaphorical seats. And oh, yes—it's a 500-page novel about rabbits.

You could call Richard Adams's beloved creation a children's book, but its expressive subtlety, emotional depth, and sophisticated narrative seduction work their magic on adults as well. The novel relates the exploits of a small band of unsure but intrepid rabbits who, under threat from encroaching human development, leave their familiar warren and set out across the English Downs in search of a new home. The characters of the rabbit protagonists are convincingly drawn, and the sweep of the action that carries them through encounters with predators, unfriendly terrain, and bad weather—to say nothing of fear, fatigue, despair, and other dangerous states of body and mind—is irresistible. Adams nourished his tale with a vivid depiction of rabbit culture, and spiced it with an occasional dose of "Lapine," a rabbit language, he would later explain, "invented word by word in the course of the writing" (*silflay*, for example, means "to go above ground to feed"). His small glossary of judiciously deployed vocabulary adds linguistic grace notes to the enthralling narrative melody.

Explaining the book's origins in his attempts to entertain his children on family trips, Adams described *Watership Down* as neither fable nor allegory, but "simply the story about rabbits made up and told in the car." That statement is too modest, as any reader of the novel soon learns; but it's true at its core, for between the lines of Adams's heroic adventure one can hear the voice of a father weaving a tale for his daughters, whose rapt attention seems to emanate from every page.

What: Novel. *When:* 1972. *Award:* Carnegie Medal, 1972. *Also By: Shardik* (1974). *The Plague Dogs* (1977). *Traveller* (1988). *The Day Gone By* (1990). *Try: The Wind in the Willows* by Kenneth Grahame (see page 328). *The Mouse and His Child* by Russell Hoban (see page 378). *Mrs. Frisby and the Rats of NIMH* by Robert C. O'Brien. *Adaptations:* The 1978 animated film achieved great popularity. The audiobook, read by Ralph Cosham, is superb.

Half of a Yellow Sun
Chimamanda Ngozi Adichie (born 1977)

A Harrowing, Life-Affirming Novel of the Nigerian Civil War

Set in Nigeria during the decade culminating in the 1967–70 Biafran war, a secession conflict that left more than a million dead from violence and famine, *Half of a Yellow Sun* is at once a historical drama and a tale of family struggles and romances gone right and wrong. Olanna and Kainene, twin sisters who come from the nation's Igbo elite, have taken different paths in life. Olanna, beautiful but stubborn, has left the country and become the mistress of a haughty academic; Kainene, ingenious but plain, has stayed in Nigeria. We see the painful creation of postcolonial Nigeria through their contrasting narratives, as well as

through the eyes of two men: Kainene's partner Richard, a British scholar who comes to think of himself as Biafran, and Ugwu, the young houseboy of Olanna's lover, whose fierce loyalty to his employer turns into something dark as the war gets underway.

As the novel shuttles back and forth in time, it bears witness to the massive upheaval of Nigeria's civil war and the horrors of the Biafran famine. When Kainene sees a young girl with a swollen stomach, she can't tell whether the girl is pregnant or suffering from kwashiorkor, the medical condition that causes starving children's bellies to inflate. Yet, amid the violence, the author paints riveting scenes of love and humor—persistent reminders that the courses of individual lives have their own itineraries of meaningful moments, destinies that historical timelines cannot comprehend. Midway through the book, Olanna and her lover agree to have a child, and her reaction is emblematic of the novelist's revelations of how grace can infiltrate our days: "She looked at him in wonder. This was love: a string of coincidences that gathered significance and became miracles."

Half of a Yellow Sun established Adichie, who hadn't been born when the war took place, as one of the most talented young writers of the twenty-first century. She now travels between the United States and Nigeria, and so, one might say, does her work; in both her essays and her fiction, she charts how ordinary lives span continents, carrying their own truths and consequences every measure of the way.

What: Novel. *When:* 2006. *Also By: Purple Hibiscus* (2003). *The Thing Around Your Neck* (2009). *Americanah* (2013). *Further Reading: There Was a Country: A Personal History of Biafra* by Chinua Achebe. *Try: De Niro's Game* by Rawi Hage. *The Blind Man's Garden* by Nadeem Aslam. *Adaptation:* A Nigerian film, directed by Biyi Bandele, premiered in 2013.

The Oresteia
Aeschylus (ca. 524 BC–ca. 456 BC)

The Wisdom That Precedes Philosophy

If you seek between covers an education in the trials and tribulations, the hopes and fears, the terrors and triumphs of the human spirit, the majestic tragedies of the ancient Greeks are the place to begin, and perhaps the place to end as well. In their beautiful, haunting, unsparing plays, Aeschylus, Sophocles (see page 739), and Euripides (see page 258)—these, alas, are the only tragedians whose works have weathered the centuries—expose the skeleton of human experience with preternatural vision. Freud was right to look for keys to our nature in the elemental confrontations the plays depict; the legacy of these works seems a gift from the gods, a mysterious clue to the puzzles of our hearts and minds.

Written for state-sponsored annual religious festivals held in spring in honor of the god Dionysus, the tragedies were ceremonial as well as dramatic, invoking the strife of legendary heroes—most often Homeric—to steep the community in the grief of individual destinies, the unfathomable energies of the gods, and the agonizing emergence of civilizing impulses. Zeus, the chorus warns us early in Aeschylus's *Agamemnon*, "lays it down as law / that we must suffer, suffer into truth." Such suffering is the stuff tragedies are made of.

Interestingly, the performance of the tragedies was competitive, enacting a contest among a trio of playwrights, who would each present a trilogy of tragic plays, plus a concluding, unrelated comic entertainment called a satyr play, over a three-day period. *The Oresteia* is the only trilogy that has come down to us complete (although its satyr play has not survived). Its three plays—*Agamemnon, The Libation Bearers,* and *The Eumenides*—depict the murderous intrigues of the royal family of Argos, a cycle of violence that the characters of *The Oresteia* inherit and expand. In *Agamemnon*, the title character's wife, Clytaemnestra, kills him for having sacrificed their daughter, Iphigeneia, to win the gods' favor for his expedition to Troy. In *The Libation Bearers*, Clytaemnestra is killed by her only son, Orestes, who acts to avenge his father's death; deities avenging his matricide—the Furies—drive him mad. In the final play, the goddess Athena empowers a group of men to judge Orestes's case, instituting a court of law in which the ideal of justice can prevail over the visceral impulses of vendetta; she enlists Orestes's pursuers, too, in this transformation, changing their names from Furies to Eumenides (Kindly Ones) and inducing them to protect Athens and its people.

No summary can convey the elemental forces that animate Aeschylus's work. "The

Oresteia is our rite of passage from savagery to civilization," write Robert Fagles and W. B. Stanford in the essay that introduces the former's majestic translation. Even on the page, the trilogy's vivifying alertness to the terrifying possibilities of human nature and culture is evoked with a stark and indelible power; we can only imagine what it was like in ancient performance. Informed by the imaginative richness of the myths and epics that preceded it, the trilogy's wisdom looms like an awesome natural wonder over the philosophical reasoning that Plato and Aristotle would leave in its wake. The truths *The Oresteia* tells are as ineluctable as fate, and just as enduring.

What: Drama. Antiquity. *When:* 458 BC. *Edition:* The translation by Robert Fagles, complemented by a brilliant introductory essay and notes by Fagles and W. B. Stanford, is peerless. If you can find a copy of the beautifully produced original Viking hardcover (1975), it is worth the effort. *Also By: The Persians* (472 BC). *Seven Against Thebes* (467 BC). *The Suppliants* (463 BC). *Further Reading: Tragedy and Philosophy* by Walter Kaufmann. *Try:* Plays of Sophocles (see page 739) and Euripides (see page 258). *Mourning Becomes Electra* by Eugene O'Neill. *The Flies* by Jean-Paul Sartre. *An Oresteia* by Anne Carson.

Let Us Now Praise Famous Men
James Agee (1909–1955) and Walker Evans (1903–1975)

An Inspired Testament in Words and Pictures

In the summer of 1936, *Fortune* magazine commissioned James Agee and Walker Evans to report on the lives of sharecroppers in the Deep South. Agee was a twenty-six-year-old journalist who'd published a volume of poems two years earlier; Evans was a thirty-two-year-old photographer. The assignment took them to Hale County, Alabama, where they spent eight weeks with three families of tenant farmers. *Fortune* chose not to run the article that resulted from Agee's and Evans's two-month stay, but in 1941 a more significant record of their collaboration finally saw the light: *Let Us Now Praise Famous Men*, a landmark volume of photographs and prose that has since been recognized as one of the most remarkable books of the twentieth century. A work of inspiration as much as reportage, its combination of impassioned attention to social conditions and sympathetic embrace of the families' experiences is both singular and unforgettable.

Evans's black-and-white portraits of the "Gudger," "Woods," and "Ricketts" families—their real names were Tingle, Fields, and Burroughs—are iconic images of the Great Depression, some of the best-known photographs ever taken, and they give the book an enduring power all by themselves. Yet Agee's text, so various in its styles and concerns, is a constant surprise, continually belying the impression many people have that this is a work of merely documentary import. While he captures in intimate detail the farmers' hardscrabble existence, he also treats common objects, from furniture to fireplaces, with almost sacramental attention. Exploring what can only be called the essences of everything from hallways to hats to the patch of ground where a house meets the dirt, his writing is by turns descriptive, rhapsodic, confessional, and meditative, conveying a strange communion with labor, time, and landscape. Walker Evans himself caught its arresting and mysterious character very well in the foreword to the expanded 1960 edition of the book: "Agee prose . . . was hardly a twentieth century style; it had Elizabethan colors."

The book does not need to be read sequentially or continuously; in fact, it repays a serendipitous approach. And, odd though it is to say it, "some of the sections read best at night, far in the night," as Evans aptly noted of his colleague's work. Again and again, Agee's sentences reach beyond the boundaries of everyday perception to create a conversation between observation and reverie that is deeply subjective and hauntingly human. He invests simple realities—and the struggling lives of sharecroppers—with beauty and moral gravity.

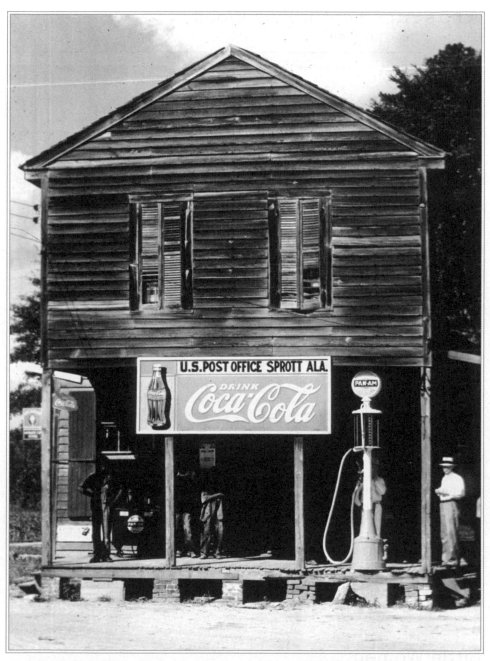

1930s Walker Evans photograph of Sprott, Alabama, post office, from Let Us Now Praise Famous Men

What: Essays. Photography. Sociology. *When:* 1941; expanded edition, 1960. *Edition:* For the 2000 Houghton Mifflin reissue, the photographs were reshot from archival negatives. *Also By:* James Agee: *The Morning Watch* (1951); *A Death in the Family* (1957); *Letters of James Agee to Father Flye* (1962); *Film Writing and Selected Journalism* (2005). Walker Evans: *Many Are Called* (1966); *Message from the Interior* (1966). *Further Reading: And Their Children After Them: The Legacy of Let Us Now Praise Famous Men* by Dale Maharidge and Michael Williamson. *Try: Hard Times: An Oral History of the Great Depression* by Studs Terkel.

Who's Afraid of Virginia Woolf?
Edward Albee (1928–2016)

Fear and Loathing in the Living Room

At the outset of his long, ever-evolving career as a dramatist, Edward Albee was an American heir to the intellectual energies of the European Theater of the Absurd. In the plays of Samuel Beckett and Eugène Ionesco, leading proponents of that movement, images and ideas were arrayed on the stage like characters, and artistic reasoning was plotted with a kind of geometric precision along axes of skepticism and incongruity. Albee would take this framework and electrify it with a savage comedy more terrifying than funny, fiercely rending the tenuous veil of convention and etiquette that hides our dread and disguises our despair. The result is drama in which setting and language are deployed in a kind of sentient, shocking, fearless laboratory to prove by experiment that things are seldom what they seem.

In *Who's Afraid of Virginia Woolf?*, first staged in 1962, Albee moved his ferocity out of the absurd into a more realistic setting, a faculty home in which an embittered husband and wife unleash their demons with a venomous urgency that spotlights the disturbing characteristics of the author's vision of family pathology. In a single night of drinking, taunting, and spouse-baiting, this older couple—George, a disappointed history professor, and Martha, daughter of the college president—lures a younger one into an emotional minefield. Every vicious line is like a lit fuse, and the searing experience of reading—or, even more, of watching—it is radical in the extreme. Albee

Richard Burton and Elizabeth Taylor in the 1966 film adaptation

goes to the root of primal anxieties and psychological dread with a vengeance that makes not only *Father Knows Best* but even Tennessee Williams look quaint. It's like Albee has staged *The Bacchae* in our living room: We see the violence that simmers beneath the veneer of our lives erupt among familiar furnishings.

What: Drama. *When:* 1962. *Award:* Tony Award for Best Play, 1963. *Also By: A Delicate Balance* (1966). *Seascape* (1974). *The Play About the Baby* (1997). *The Goat, or Who Is Sylvia?* (2002). *Try: Long Day's Journey into Night* by Eugene O'Neill (see page 604). *A Streetcar Named Desire* by Tennessee Williams (see page 857). *The Homecoming* by Harold Pinter. *Adaptation:* Mike Nichols directed the 1966 film starring Richard Burton and Elizabeth Taylor.

Little Women
Louisa May Alcott (1832–1888)

The Girls Next Door

Louisa May Alcott grew up in Concord, Massachusetts, the second of four daughters of a noted proponent of Transcendentalism, Bronson Alcott. Ralph Waldo Emerson was a friend of the family, as were Henry David Thoreau and Nathaniel Hawthorne. Sharing the ideals of many in their circle, the Alcotts devoted themselves to "plain living and high thinking." Despite her transcendentalist pedigree, however, Louisa May Alcott always kept her feet on the ground, working as a seamstress, a governess, a nurse, and, eventually, an author to contribute to the household income. Her most famous work, *Little Women*, is drawn from her own family life; it is among the most cherished and popular children's books of all time. Within its comfortable domestic compass, many readers first discover the import of the largest questions: Who am I, and who do I want to be?

The central figure of the novel is Alcott's alter ego, Jo March, a spirited fifteen-year-old tomboy who yearns to become a writer the way other girls dream of getting married. It's Christmastime as the book opens, and Jo and her three sisters—Meg is the oldest at sixteen, and Beth and Amy are thirteen and twelve, respectively—are at home with their beloved mother, Marmee, while Mr. March is off serving as a chaplain in the Civil War. Initially, the girls pity themselves for being poor at Christmas, but a letter from their father prompts a pledge to improve themselves by working variously on their faults—vanity, temper, shyness—in order to make him proud when he returns: "'I'll try and be what he loves to call me, "a little woman," and not be rough and wild; but do my duty here instead of wanting to be somewhere else,' said Jo, thinking that keeping her temper at home was a much harder task than facing a rebel or two down South."

From the first line—"'Christmas won't be Christmas without any presents,' grumbled Jo, lying on the rug"—Alcott taps a vein of realism and colloquial expression that was ahead of its time and that still retains its attraction. What follows is a tale of life, love, friendship, illness, and coming-of-age, one in which the "little women" prove to have more courage, resourcefulness, and character than the adults who ostensibly hold sway over them. More tellingly, *Little Women* is the story of four archetypal girls whose personalities remain familiar today; rare is the reader who

doesn't see herself, if only for an episode, as a Meg, a Jo, a Beth, or an Amy, fascinated by her reflection.

What: Children's. *When:* 1868. *Edition:* The novel is usually published with its first sequel, *Good Wives* (1869), appearing as part two. *Also By:* Sequels: *Little Men* (1871); *Jo's Boys* (1886). Other fiction: *Eight Cousins* (1875); *Rose in Bloom* (1876). *Further Reading:* *Louisa May Alcott: The Woman Behind Little Women* by Harriet Reisen. *Try: Five Little Peppers and How They Grew* by Margaret Sidney. *Anne of Green Gables* by L. M. Montgomery (see page 564). *A Tree Grows in Brooklyn* by Betty Smith (see page 729). *Adaptations:* Of the several screen versions of the novel, most famous is the 1933 version starring Katharine Hepburn as Jo; the most recent was released in 1994, with Winona Ryder in the role. *Footnote:* There are two twenty-first-century novels inspired by Alcott's book: *The Little Women* by Katharine Weber, a postmodern reimagining of Alcott's tale, and the Pulitzer Prize-winning *March* by Geraldine Brooks, which imagines Mr. March's Civil War experiences.

Illustration by M. V. Wheelhouse for a 1934 edition of Little Women

■ For Lloyd Alexander's *The Book of Three*, see page 795.

The Absolutely True Diary of a Part-Time Indian
Sherman Alexie (born 1966)

Growing Up On and Off the Reservation

Drawing on Sherman Alexie's personal experience growing up on the Spokane Indian Reservation, *The Absolutely True Diary of a Part-Time Indian* is a young adult novel that has more to say about big virtues like tolerance than a whole shelf of earnest adult tomes could ever manage. It has lots to tell readers about the hard truths of the Native American experience—the diminishments of poverty, the ravages of alcoholism on individuals and families, institutionalized bigotry, and the servitude engendered by low expectations and few opportunities. Also well drawn are the smaller but ever-present concerns of adolescence, such as popularity, awkwardness, masturbation, friendship, and proving one's mettle in the classroom or on the playground. That Alexie is able to encompass all of this in the narrative voice of Arnold Spirit Jr., better known as just "Junior," gives every element of his character's experience an integrity, and thereby a dignity, that runs like a current beneath the surface of events.

The depiction of events, from tragic deaths to triumphant basketball games, is, if not absolutely true, absolutely honest. Alexie imagines one Native American's coming to grips with coming of age as he follows his talents and ambitions off the reservation to assimilate into the white world of Reardan High School, becoming the "part-time Indian" of the title. Just as Junior learns to understand that parents can be both loving and imperfect, and that low expectations foster destructive habits, so too does he learn to see through the markers of identity and privilege that mask both the insecurities and kindnesses of his new friends at Reardan. Again and again, Alexie takes elements of Junior's personal distinction, from hydrocephalus to intellectual facility to a good jump shot, and makes them shareable with family, friends, teachers, teammates, and, most of all, readers. Similarly, Junior's understanding of others evolves from caricature to individuality in a kind of narrative real time that teaches us, unwittingly, lessons in generosity and joy.

The book's unflinching candor, irreverent comedy, and fierce alertness to difficult issues have made it a subject of controversy and a frequent target for book-banning school boards. But what's most valuable about it is that Alexie's novel is controversial in the way life itself is controversial: unsettled, uneasy, of two minds about itself and nevertheless ongoing, devastating one day and comic the next.

What: Novel. *When:* 2007. *Award:* National Book Award for Young People's Literature, 2007. *Also By: The Lone Ranger and Tonto Fistfight in Heaven* (1993). *Reservation Blues* (1995). *Flight* (2007). *War Dances* (2009). *Try: The House on Mango Street* by Sandra Cisneros. *American Born Chinese* by Gene Luen Yang. *Adaptation:* The author's own reading won the 2009 Odyssey Award as the year's best audiobook for children or young adults.

> "I grabbed my book and opened it up. I wanted to smell it. Heck, I wanted to kiss it. Yes, kiss it. That's right, I am a book kisser. Maybe that's kind of perverted or maybe it's just romantic and highly intelligent."—*The Absolutely True Diary of a Part-Time Indian*

Workers en route to the contaminated Chernobyl site

Voices from Chernobyl
THE ORAL HISTORY OF A NUCLEAR DISASTER
Svetlana Alexievich (born 1948)

Chronicle of a Nuclear Disaster—and History of the Soul

This book is an oral history of the nuclear reactor accident at Chernobyl in 1986, and of the suffering, death, and contamination—biological, environmental, psychological, existential—left in its wake. It is constructed from the testimony of dozens of people whose lives were transformed by the disaster: plant workers and first responders and their families; members of the clean-up brigades and service providers who coped with the unprecedented scope and severity of the radiation; former inhabitants of the land within thirty kilometers of the power plant that, after evacuation, would come to be designated as the Zone of Exclusion.

The testimony comes to us in a series of monologues. The first belongs to Lyudmilla Ignatenko, wife of a deceased fireman, and it begins with these words: "I don't know what I should talk about—about death or about love? Or are they the same? Which one should I talk about?" She describes her life with Vasily—"We were newlyweds"—and the night of the explosion, and then the nightmarish weeks that followed, as she watched him die a gruesome death from radiation. Love and death—and pain, disease, grief, anger, and fear—are each stripped bare and set naked on the page, as if breathing, animated by the witness of a solitary human voice.

The distillation of Svetlana Alexievich's interviews with Lyudmilla Ignatenko and the scores of other people represented in the pages that follow—Alexievich gives herself no voice in the book, except in the epilogue—is an intense feat of strange and harrowing eloquence. It's not writing, exactly, but a kind of expressive listening that is made more resonant by each monologue's setting within a polyphonic sequence. In the brief epilogue to the book, Alexievich explains:

Why repeat the facts—they cover up our feelings. The development of these feelings, the spilling of these feelings past the facts, is what fascinates me. I try to find them, collect them, protect them.

And this is what she does not only in *Voices from Chernobyl*, but also in her book about Soviet women's experience of World War II, *The Unwomanly Face of War* (1985), and in *Secondhand Time* (2013), which chronicles, again in private voices, the decline of communism and the dissolution of the Soviet Union.

The Swedish Academy may well have been correct when, awarding the author the

Nobel Prize in Literature in 2015, it suggested Alexievich has invented a new literary genre; it was certainly right when it called her work "a history of the emotions—a history of the soul, if you wish." With an imaginative reach Tolstoy might admire, Alexievich assembles evidence voice by voice in the service not of realism, but of the deeper human realities that both history and realism all too often mask.

What: Literature. History. *When:* 1997. *Editions:* First English translation (quoted here) by Keith Gessen, 2005. A new translation by Anna Gunin and Arch Tait, based on a revised 2013 text, was published as *Chernobyl Prayer* in 2016. *Award:* Nobel Prize in Literature, 2015. *Also By: Zinky Boys: Soviet Voices from the Afghanistan War* (1991). *Try: Khatyn* by Ales Adamovich. *Kolyma Tales* by Varlam Shalamov.

The House of the Spirits
Isabel Allende (born 1942)

A Hidden History of Love, Passion, and Politics

On January 8, 1981, journalist and former television host Isabel Allende, a Chilean political exile, sat down in Venezuela to write a letter to her nearly 100-year-old grandfather in an attempt to bridge the distance between her present and her family's past. She began with an anecdote he had told her when she was a child, about his fiancée, Rosa, who'd been mistakenly poisoned. As she wrote, she has explained elsewhere, "other characters stepped in," and the unsent letter grew into the manuscript of her first novel, *The House of the Spirits*.

Vividly charting the personal experience of three generations of women against the backdrop of Chile's volatile, violent twentieth-century political landscape, the book introduces us to seven-year-old Clara, who foretells fates and levitates objects, much to the chagrin of her parents, who worry about the repercussions of having a "bewitched" child in the family. When Clara's older sister, "Rosa the Beautiful," dies unexpectedly, Clara spends nine years without speaking, breaking her silence to announce that she plans to marry Rosa's fiancé, Esteban Trueba, who will loom with patriarchal obduracy over Clara's future and the fates of her daughter, Blanca, and granddaughter, Alba. The passion, love, and political commitment with which the women illuminate their lives in Esteban's shadow provide the absorbing narrative matter of Allende's richly peopled novel. Vibrant strands of magic realism heighten the color of a sweeping tapestry of romance, betrayal, revenge, social upheaval, and reconciliation.

The house of the book's title is the capacious dwelling that Esteban builds for Clara, which grows to accommodate family, friends, and rivals—spiritualists, artists, politicians, and children—across the decades of the novel's drama. Like the novel itself, it seems to have room for everything, even forgiveness.

What: Novel. *When:* 1982; English translation by Magda Bogin, 1985. *Also By: Of Love and Shadows* (1984). *Eva Luna* (1987). *Paula* (1994). *My Invented Country: A Nostalgic Journey Through Chile* (2003). *Try: One Hundred Years of Solitude* by Gabriel García Márquez (see page 308). *In the Time of the Butterflies* by Julia Alvarez. *Adaptation:* A 1993 Hollywood film stars Jeremy Irons and Meryl Streep.

Skellig
David Almond (born 1951)

A Modern Fairy Tale

Some books are like talismans, compact in their power, possessed of an aura mysterious and meaningful, even if—especially if—the precise nature of its mystery and meaning eludes us. Such a work is David Almond's *Skellig*, which won the Carnegie Medal as best children's book by a British author when it was published in 1998. While it's perfectly tuned for readers of ages eight to ten, the book's haunting music is captivating for audiences well beyond that range in years. The story is a swift read, seductive without being obviously dramatic; it's told by a ten-year-old named Michael, whose world has been turned upside down by a move to a new house and the birth of a sister. The new house is the ultimate fixer-upper, disorienting in its state of flux, and the baby's survival—she was born prematurely—is touch and go. One plus of the new neighborhood for Michael is a budding friendship with Mina, a girl with a passion for birds and the poetry of William Blake.

Drawn to the rickety garage on the new property, Michael is fascinated by its palpable and dilapidated sense of someone else's past. Despite his parents' repeated warnings to steer clear of it, Michael cannot resist his exploratory impulses: "I stood daring myself to go in." And inside he eventually goes, where he discovers— hidden within a cobwebbed clutter of broken tools and discarded furnishings—the strange man in the black suit:

I thought he was dead. He was sitting with his legs stretched out, and his head tipped back against the wall. He was covered in dust and webs like everything else and his face was thin and pale. Dead bluebottles were scattered on his hair and shoulders. I shone the torch on his white face and black suit.

The figure seems somehow ancient, otherworldly, and on the verge of expiring, although his familiarity with the menu of the local Chinese takeaway belies his supernatural mien (he has a particular penchant for menu items 23 and 57). He sits still amid the refuse of the garage like a character escaped from a Samuel Beckett play, answering Michael's questions with a litany of "nowhere" and "nothing." He is inscrutable and without tenderness, arthritic and in need of aspirin. And, under the cover of his shabby black jacket, he has wings.

Could he, given Michael's sister's state, be the angel of death? Or perhaps a fantastic incarnation of Mina's beloved birdness? Whatever he is—and Almond never makes it clear—his mystery brings fear, and hope, and strange poetry into the rag and bone shop of forgotten life that the garage houses—and into the consciousnesses of Michael and Mina. Blake hovers over the tale like an animating spirit, and what higher praise could there be than that Almond's book does that spirit—mystical, dangerous, gritty, joyful—justice?

What: Children's. *When:* 1998. *Awards:* Carnegie Medal, 1998. Whitbread Children's Book of the Year, 1998. *Also By: Kit's Wilderness* (1999). *The Fire-Eaters* (2003). *My Name Is Mina* (prequel to *Skellig*; 2010). *Try: Tom's Midnight Garden* by Philippa Pearce. *The Folk Keeper* by Franny Billingsley. *Adaptations:* Almond's story was adapted into a play in 2003, an opera by Tod Machover in 2008, and a film, starring Tim Roth, in 2009.

A Coffin for Dimitrios
Eric Ambler (1909–1998)

An Intricate Puzzle from a Pioneer of the Modern Suspense Novel

"To the master from one of his disciples," read a cable from Graham Greene to the author of *A Coffin for Dimitrios*, in acknowledgment of the latter's influence not only on Greene's own literary achievement, but also on the development of the international novel of intrigue. From Greene to John le Carré and Frederick Forsyth, most celebrated

practitioners of the modern thriller have plotted their way down paths first cut by Eric Ambler.

While *A Coffin for Dimitrios* was Ambler's fifth novel, it was the first in which his mature talent was fully displayed. It tells the story of Charles Latimer, a British mystery writer who is given the opportunity, by a Turkish officer with a taste for crime novels, to view a corpse in the Istanbul morgue. Intrigued by intimations of the dead man's criminal history, Latimer begins to investigate Dimitrios's past, hoping to uncover material for his next book. He ends up entangled in a plot more perilous than any he could dream up on his own. Pursuing the ghost of Dimitrios through an ever-expanding web of evil, Latimer discovers treachery of every sort—from theft and drug dealing to assassination and treason. Most chillingly, death has not diminished the dead man's power; Dimitrios's sinister influence is felt far beyond the grave.

In its depiction of an amateur's embroilment in unsuspected villainy, its attention to the nefarious predilections of government and business interests, its immersion in the seedy attractions of decadence, and—last but by no means least—its sheer page-turning pleasure, *A Coffin for Dimitrios* is a perfect example of Ambler's contributions to the genre that has flourished in his wake.

What: Mystery & Suspense. *When:* 1939. *Edition:* Published in England as *The Mask of Dimitrios. Also By:* Novels: *Journey into Fear* (1940); *Judgment on Deltchev* (1951); *The Schirmer Inheritance* (1953); *State of Siege* (1956); *Passage of Arms* (1959); *The Light of Day* (also published as *Topkapi,* 1962). Autobiography: *Here Lies* (1985). *Try:* The suspense novels of Graham Greene, John le Carré, and Lionel Davidson. *Adaptation:* Jean Negulesco's 1944 film, *The Mask of Dimitrios,* stars Peter Lorre and Sydney Greenstreet.

Lucky Jim
Kingsley Amis (1922–1995)

A Comic Storm in the Groves of Academe

Jim Dixon is a junior lecturer in history at a provincial British university in the 1950s. His job hangs by a thread. Part of the problem is that he can't stand his supervisor, Professor Welch, who is a boring and pompous twit—"no other professor in Great Britain," Jim realizes, "set such store by being called Professor." Further complicating matters are Jim's reluctant romance with Margaret Peel, a departmental colleague, and the crush he's developed on Welch's daughter, the seemingly unattainable Christine. All Jim's troubles come to a head when, drunk as a skunk, he turns his well-attended, end-of-term lecture on "Merrie England" into a mocking and contemptuous biting of the hands that feed him.

A riotous satire of English university life, the engaging and high-spirited *Lucky Jim* had a huge impact in its time, setting the style for postwar fiction and helping to define the generation of "Angry Young Men" in 1950s Britain. But *this* Angry Young Man is as funny as they come, and the novel's send-up—its explosion, really—of the codes and constraints of both British and academic snobbery has a reckless verve that is both entertaining and exhilarating. The award-winning book was Kingsley Amis's first novel, and it is laced with the same sort of unapologetic political incorrectness that would make the later Amis, after he had undergone the transformation from angry youngster to cranky old fogey, such a controversial figure in transatlantic literary circles.

What: Novel. Humor. *When:* 1954. *Award:* Britain's Society of Authors' Somerset Maugham Award for fiction, 1955. *Also By: One Fat Englishman* (1963). *The Green Man* (1969). *Ending Up* (1974). *Jake's Thing* (1978). *Stanley and the Women* (1984). *The Old Devils* (1986). *Memoirs* (1991). *Letters* (2000). *Further Reading: The Life of Kingsley Amis* by Zachary Leader. *Try: Pictures from an Institution* by Randall Jarrell. *The History Man* by Malcolm Bradbury. *Changing Places* by David Lodge. *Adaptations:* Ian Carmichael plays Jim Dixon in the 1957 film of *Lucky Jim.* The 2003 television remake stars Stephen Tompkinson.

Illustrations for two of Andersen's beloved tales: "The Little Mermaid" by Monro S. Orr (left); "The Princess and the Pea" by Edmund Dulac (right)

Fairy Tales
Hans Christian Andersen (1805–1875)

Once Upon a Time, and Again and Again

Hans Christian Andersen wrote some of the most treasured stories of the past two centuries, but his life was more like a Dickens novel than a fairy tale. Born poor in Denmark, the son of a cobbler and a washerwoman, he was an awkward, dreamy youth who imagined a theatrical career for himself and left home for Copenhagen when he was fourteen. He suffered a period of privation before being rescued by patrons who sponsored his education and allowed him to immerse himself in two transformative activities: travel and writing. The latter brought him acclaim, first as a novelist and later, resoundingly and lastingly, as an author of tales for children, the first volume of which he published in 1835.

Despite his success as a writer, Andersen remained something of a social misfit with a gift for alienating even his friends (including Dickens himself, with whom he overstayed his welcome on an 1857 visit to England: Dickens's daughter Katey would recall the author of "The Little Mermaid" as a "boney bore who stayed on and on"; her father reputedly used Andersen as the model for the character Uriah Heep in *David Copperfield*). No doubt Andersen's loneliness inspired the affection for outcasts and sorry souls that distinguishes many of his most beloved tales, such as "The Ugly Duckling," "The Little Match Girl," and "The Steadfast Tin Soldier."

While the emotional sophistication of such stories can make them seem darker than their child-friendly frames at first suggest, there is no shortage of humor or high spirits in Andersen's fanciful canon. Only a dozen or so of his more than 150 tales were drawn from existing folktales, in the manner of the Brothers Grimm; the rest came straight from his own imagination, enlivened by the vernacular ease and immediacy that made their telling innovative. Despite their relatively recent invention, Andersen's best tales—"The Emperor's New Clothes," "The Princess and the Pea," "The Snow Queen," "The

Nightingale," and "Thumbelina," to mention a few—have taken such strong root in our collective imagination that many readers fail to recognize that they have an author. Famously insecure in life, Andersen would almost certainly be stung by this failure to recognize his genius; but what better tribute to his stories than the assumption that they're as old as time?

What: Children's. *When:* 1835–72. *Editions:* Start with the Penguin Classics edition of thirty tales translated by Tiina Nunnally, then turn to *The Complete Tales and*

Stories in the Anchor Folktale Library. In addition to collections, there are countless, sumptuously illustrated versions of the individual tales. *Further Reading: Hans Christian Andersen: The Life of a Storyteller* by Jackie Wullschläger. *The Annotated Hans Christian Andersen* edited by Maria Tatar. *Try: Grimms' Tales for Young and Old* (see page 336). *The Little Bookroom* by Eleanor Farjeon. *Adaptations:* Too numerous to detail, in all media. The 1952 Hollywood film *Hans Christian Andersen,* starring Danny Kaye, is a romantic fantasia on the storyteller's life, notable for the lovely songs by Frank Loesser.

I Know Why the Caged Bird Sings
Maya Angelou (1928–2014)

The Radiant First Chapter of an Incomparable Life

When you discover that a person has written six books of autobiography, you're bound to wonder: Is she just a prolific narcissist, or has she really lived a six-volume life? If she's Maya Angelou, there's no doubt that the latter is the case: So compelling is her private story, so extravagant her public gifts, so generous her embrace of every level of experience that six volumes hardly seem enough.

It might well take a shelf of novels to encompass Angelou's decades of transformation and growth. Consider her professions and accomplishments: night club dancer; cable car conductor (the first woman in San Francisco to hold that job); madam; award-winning stage and screen actor; student of Martha Graham; newspaper editor in Cairo; administrator at the University of Ghana; educator; pioneering film writer and director; International Woman of the Year; and, last but by no means least, mother. She was invited to read her work at a presidential inauguration (Bill Clinton's), worked with both Martin Luther King Jr. and Malcolm X, and even put her name on a line of goods for Hallmark. Along the way, she published acclaimed volumes of poetry and several books for children, and somehow found time to compose the aforementioned six volumes of her life story. Of these, the best loved and most influential is the first, *I Know Why the Caged Bird Sings.*

Maya Angelou, 1970

Beginning when she is a three-year-old traveling by train from California to Arkansas with her four-year-old brother, their tickets pinned to the inside of his coat, it's an eloquent, funny, tragic, unapologetically revealing survey of her youth—including the terror of being raped as an eight-year-old and the five years she spent without speaking in the aftermath of that trauma. During this period of silence, Angleou discovered the power of literature, reveling in the work of authors from Shakespeare to Langston Hughes, Dickens to W. E. B. Du Bois. She writes with great affection about the woman—Mrs. Flowers—who encouraged her to speak again and inspired Angelou's enduring love of poetry and the spoken word. The book, which follows the author through her teenage years back in California, is as much about the people as the events that shaped Angelou's life; it honors the abiding lessons each one taught her in prose that bears a personal stamp and a music all its own.

The title is the first line of a poem called "Sympathy" by Harlem Renaissance poet Paul Laurence Dunbar. The last line of the same poem provides the title for the final volume in Angelou's autobiographical series, *A Song Flung Up to Heaven*. With the four volumes in between, these books—written over a span of thirty years—cover only half of the author's remarkable life. In fact, the last volume ends with her just beginning to write the first.

What: Autobiography. Memoir. **When:** 1969. **Also By:** Angelou's other autobiographical titles are *Gather Together in My Name* (1974), *Singin' and Swingin' and Gettin' Merry Like Christmas* (1976), *The Heart of a Woman* (1981), *All God's Children Need Traveling Shoes* (1986), and *A Song Flung Up to Heaven* (2002). *Mrs. Flowers: A Moment of Friendship* (1986) retells for young readers the episode detailing Angelou's struggle to regain her voice after five years of silence. **Try:** *The Autobiography of Malcolm X* (see page 876). **Adaptation:** A television movie aired in 1979.

The Arabian Nights

The Enchantment of Storytelling

I s there an entry in the annals of story more charming than the tale of the brave and brilliant Shahrazad, who, by dint of cunning and invention, puts off her death at the hands of King Shahryār for a thousand and one nights? Bewitching the king with a nightly dose of suspenseful storytelling, she subverts his custom of killing his consorts at dawn by leaving him yearning to discover what comes next. The stories she unfolds to assuage the violent passions of the king add to our enchantment with her own fate as we pass through the boxes within boxes that make up *The Arabian Nights*.

The tales gathered under this title do not really add up to one thousand and one, and a study of the several traditions that feed the various incarnations of the texts would lead one into forests of Indian and Persian folklore as well as ancient Arabic and Egyptian sources. Suffice it to say here that the earliest known references to the collection surfaced in the Arab world in the ninth century, and that the *Nights'* spell was first cast on the West through the French translation of Antoine Galland in the early 1700s, which informed near-contemporary English versions. Translations and embellishments continued to enrich the literary life of the tales in subsequent centuries.

There are myriad alternatives currently available, from retellings for children by Andrew Lang and W. Heath Robinson to Sir

19th-century illustration of Sinbad's ship fleeing enormous roc birds

Richard Burton's notoriously unbowdlerized nineteenth-century rendering, which relished the erotic exuberance of the tales. The best introduction for modern English readers is found in the two volumes of translations made by Husain Haddawy in the 1990s. The first volume, based on a reconstruction by Muhsin Mahdi of the oldest extant text, a fourteenth-century Syrian manuscript, presents an assortment of authentic tales in which magic, love, learning, and mischief fuel adventures both mundane and supernatural for demons and viziers, kings and thieves, maids and merchants. In his second volume, Haddawy offers faithful, fresh versions of the most popular later stories—including those of Sindbad the Sailor, Ali Baba and the Forty Thieves, and Aladdin and the Magic Lamp—that were added to the original constellation of stories as the

scope of the *Nights* grew in later centuries. Each of Haddawy's volumes provides fodder for a thousand dreams.

What: Literature. Fantasy. *When:* Probably early 8th century. The first English language translation was published in 1706. *Editions:* Haddawy's two volumes appeared in 1990 and 1995, respectively. Each is currently available in paperback from W. W. Norton, the first as *The Arabian Nights*, the second as *Sindbad and Other Stories from the Arabian Nights. Further Reading: The Arabian Nights: A Companion* by Robert Irwin. *Try: Arabian Nights and Days* by Naguib Mahfouz. *Haroun and the Sea of Stories* by Salman Rushdie. *Adaptations:* From Rimsky-Korsakov's 1888 symphonic suite *Scheherazade* to Alexander Korda's technicolor spectacular *The Thief of Bagdad* (1940) and Disney's animated *Aladdin* (1992), the *Nights* have inspired countless musical, theatrical, and cinematic adaptations.

The Clouds
Aristophanes (ca. 446 BC–ca. 386 BC)

The World's Oldest Comic

He wrote as many as fifty plays; nobody is sure exactly how many, and only eleven survive today. But Aristophanes established some principles of comedy (and even, if truth be told, some jokes) that have survived for more than two-and-a-half millennia. Though the distance of time and topic is of course considerable, there is much familiar in the playwright's repertoire: biting social satire, ridicule of public figures, wacky physical slapstick, gross-out gags, wordplay, and a message that goes beyond the laughs. Except for that last item, the plays of Aristophanes are more than a bit like Marx Brothers movies. In fact, the best way to appreciate *The Clouds* may be to imagine the antics of those modern siblings on the ancient stage.

The Clouds begins as a story of father and son: Strepsiades (think Groucho), a moderately prosperous country gentleman, is panicking that the young Pheidippides (think Zeppo) has racked up a mountain of debt betting on race

horses. ("Pheidippides" means "thrifty with horses" in Greek; Pheidippides is anything but.) Strepsiades has the idea to send his son to the fancy new philosophy academy in Athens to keep him away from the track and, perhaps, to learn some rhetorical tricks that will help outwit their creditors. The son refuses, so the father enrolls himself, and Socrates's academy turns out to be a madhouse (enter Chico and Harpo). Socrates is so haughty that he floats aloft in a basket, the better to see the meteorological phenomena he's studying, while the students are on their hands and knees, investigating the earth with their eyes and the heavens with their backsides. Strepsiades might be a buffoon, but Socrates comes off even worse: as a fraud and a trickster, using the tools of philosophy in deceptive, dangerous ways. The play ends with a hilarious bonfire of the academy, with Socrates going up in flames.

Intervening at regular breaks in the action is a chorus—a group of observers that stands apart from the play and comments on the proceedings, a standard feature of classical Greek theater. This chorus, though, isn't a group of citizens or soldiers, but a chorus of clouds: semi-divine beings who don't just make observations on the themes of the play, but actively berate the audience for not praising Aristophanes enough. (*The Clouds*, like all Greek plays of its era, was performed first in a drama competition; it lost.) Those interjections—here comes Harpo again, wielding sound effects!—remind us that *The Clouds*, for all the present laughter it can still provoke, is also an artifact of its author's life and times in the Athenian golden age.

What: Drama. Comedy. Antiquity. *When:* 423 BC; revised 420-417 BC. *Edition:* Among many fine translations, William Arrowsmith's 1962 version stands out. *Also By: The Wasps* (422 BC). *The Birds* (414 BC). *Lysistrata* (411 BC). *Try: Gargantua and Pantagruel* by François Rabelais (see page 656). *Candide* by Voltaire (see page 824).

Nicomachean Ethics
Aristotle (384 BC–322 BC)

How Do We Live Well?

Student of Plato, tutor of Alexander the Great, founder of the Athenian Lyceum, Aristotle possessed a pedigree every bit as singular as his influence would prove to be. As *The Oxford Companion to Classical Literature* asserts, "Aristotelian logic more than any other single influence formed the European mind." More broadly, his ideas, instruments of investigation, and observations of nature both loom over and underlie much intellectual endeavor. He can be credited with inventing the syllogism and defining key conceptual distinctions: universal and particular, premise and conclusion, subject and attribute. He named catharsis as the purpose of dramatic art. His unprecedented studies in natural history earned him the sobriquet of "Father of Biology," and his techniques presaged empirical modes of science. His works had profound authority for medieval thinkers from Muslim mathematicians to Catholic scholastics such as Thomas Aquinas.

But, to be honest, it's not much fun to turn his pages. Where Plato is a pleasure to read, Aristotle is a chore. This is in large part because most of the texts that have come down to us are in fact Aristotle's notes for the lectures he delivered in the Lyceum. While they lack expressive modulation and animation, they remain astonishing in the comprehensive range of their intellectual effort. He creates valuable and often enlightening systems of approach to subjects as varied as zoology, physics, metaphysics,

Statue of Aristotle at Stagira, Greece, the philosopher's birthplace

rhetoric, poetics, ethics, politics, and, of course, logic itself.

Still, it's well worth encountering Aristotle's thinking at its source, and the best place is the *Nicomachean Ethics*, in which he asks what makes people happy and offers instruction on living a successful life. You might even go directly to books II through V in order to concentrate on the Aristotelian idea of the behavioral golden mean—the need to conduct oneself between extremes—and the philosopher's annotated catalogue of the necessary moral virtues—courage, temperance, generosity, magnanimity, gentleness, friendliness, truthfulness, charm—and how best to measure them in our own behavior. There's plenty more of value in the rest of the volume, of course, as there is throughout Aristotle's oeuvre; yet this short course in how to live is a perfect introduction to the integration of meticulous precision and conceptual majesty that makes his thought enduringly resonant, relevant, and even beautiful.

What: Philosophy. Antiquity. *When:* ca. 350 BC. *Edition:* The translation by Robert C. Bartlett and Susan D. Collins (2011) is excellent, with valuable notes and commentary. *Also By: The Basic Works of Aristotle*, edited by Richard McKeon (1941), is the best compendium of the philosopher's essential texts, including excerpts from *Rhetoric* and *Metaphysics*, *Poetics*, *Politics* and the *Nicomachean Ethics* in their entirety, all in the standard Oxford translation. *Further Reading: Aristotle: A Very Short Introduction* by Jonathan Barnes. *Aristotle: The Desire to Understand* by Jonathan Lear. *The Lagoon: How Aristotle Invented Science* by Armand Marie Leroi. *Try: A Short History of Ethics* by Alasdair C. MacIntyre. *Love's Knowledge: Essays on Philosophy and Literature* by Martha C. Nussbaum.

Old Herbaceous
Reginald Arkell (1882–1959)

Goodbye, Mr. Chips in a Country House Garden

As the protagonist of a novel, Herbert Pinnegar is a rare breed: a gardener. Even the most green-thumbed reader of fiction would have to dig for a very long time before coming upon another example of a horticultural hero. The creation of British playwright and garden poet Reginald Arkell, *Old Herbaceous* marries the comic propriety of Jeeves to the poignant sentiment of Mr. Chips, setting the nuptials in the flowerbeds of a country house garden.

Arkell's 1950 tale chronicles Pinnegar's eight decades in the employ of an English manor, from his youth as a flower-loving orphan to his old age as an estimable master of the plots. When his boyhood enchantment with wildflowers leads to an unexpected, and accidental, win at the annual flower show, one of the judges—the lady of the manor house—takes notice and arranges a job for him on her estate. Once there, Bert plants himself and grows, gradually working his way up through the ranks to head gardener, making a national name for himself as a competition judge and hanging on long enough to earn the nickname "Old Herbaceous" from those who ultimately supplant him. In recounting Bert's life in episodes that encompass stolen orchids, April strawberries, and a running border of gardening wisdom, the narrator treats the reader to a nostalgic, wholly entertaining narrative. Slender in size and humorous in tone, *Old Herbaceous* is at root a social novel, reflecting the changes, challenges, and eccentricities of English country life from the late Victorian era to the age of the world wars.

What: House & Garden. Novel. *When:* 1950. *Edition:* The Modern Library Gardening series edition includes an introduction by Penelope Hobhouse. *Also By: A Cottage in the Country* (1934). *Collected Green Fingers* (1956; poems). *Try: Merry Hall* by Beverley Nichols (see page 586). *We Made a Garden* by Margery Fish.

Study Is Hard Work
William H. Armstrong (1911–1999)

How to Learn

I t is most often the habits of our minds, and not our inspirations, that define our accomplishments; aspiration is short breath indeed without some application of discipline. In this genuinely helpful manual on the development of study skills, William H. Armstrong persuasively asserts that the acquisition of knowledge is no exception. Study—and the learning it nourishes—is hard work indeed.

Best known for his Newbery Medal-winning 1969 novel *Sounder*, Armstrong was an educator by profession, spending more than five decades teaching teenagers at the Kent School in Connecticut. Much of what his vocation taught him is contained in *Study Is Hard Work*, an elegant, eloquently written series of lessons on, among other subjects, listening and the efficient use of time; the art of attentive reading; the expansion of vocabulary, the ordering of ideas, and the execution of written work; the specific study of languages, mathematics, science, and history; and the practice and purpose of tests and examinations. He delivers focused instruction on the development of effective mental habits and the proper conduct of one's own education. He is a splendid teacher: supportive yet blunt, hopeful but honest.

Although schoolwork in this digital age may require new generations to pursue the spirit rather than the letter of Armstrong's directives, there is no doubt that the qualities of mind that his book fosters will be relevant to readers for as long as thought remains the currency of learning. Whatever your age or circumstance, *Study Is Hard Work* is bound to enhance your attentions to learning—and to life.

What: Education. When: 1956. Also By: Word Power in Five Easy Lessons (1969). Sour Land (1971). Try: How to Read a Book by Mortimer J. Adler. Becoming a Writer by Dorothea Brande.

THE FOUNDATION TRILOGY
FOUNDATION • FOUNDATION AND EMPIRE • SECOND FOUNDATION
Isaac Asimov (1920–1992)

An Imperial Space Opera

I n his lifetime, Isaac Asimov was known as one of the "Big Three" of science fiction, a designation he shared with Arthur C. Clarke (see page 161) and Robert A. Heinlein (see page 360). It's fair to say, however, that through his work as editor and advocate he seemed to preside over the growth of the genre in the public imagination (the fact that the Asimov name seemed, for decades, to be everywhere in the library and the bookstore—he wrote or edited more than 500 volumes on a dizzying array of topics, from fantasy to mathematics, Bible study to nearly every branch of science—only cemented his standing in the popular mind).

As a writer, his reputation rests solidly on his ambitious Foundation Trilogy, which was awarded a special Hugo Award in 1966 as best science fiction series of all time. And although he would bow to fan pressure and resume the franchise nearly thirty years after publishing its initial installments, the seminal impact of Asimov's imaginative enterprise relies on the original three books composed in the 1940s and early 1950s: *Foundation, Foundation and Empire*, and *Second Foundation*. First published in bits and pieces in John W. Campbell's *Astounding* magazine, the premier showcase of its era, the Foundation stories chronicled "the decline and fall of Rome, writ large," using Edward Gibbon's classic books on that subject

Isaac Asimov, 1989

omniscience from a vantage point even further forward in the stream of time.

While Asimov's saga nowadays seems less original than when it first appeared, the sweep of its conception maintains a thrilling freshness. Humanity spreads throughout the galaxy (there are, notably, no aliens to contend with) and reaches a developmental peak after 12,000 years, typified by the uber-civilized steel-clad planet Trantor. Yet one man, Hari Seldon, foresees collapse, thanks to his immersion in the science of "psychohistory," and sets up a secret long-range buffer—the "Second Foundation"—against permanent downfall. The Dark Ages duly arrive, but the dead Seldon's proleptic plans are bent by the unpredictable appearance of a rogue mutant who seeks to undo all of the psychohistorian's safeguards. Asimov's penchant for discursive logic and brains over brawn does not prevent the Foundation series from being enthralling. Even today, ranked against all that has followed, it glows with quiet majesty.

as a template, as Asimov himself confessed. But the interstellar scope and temporal span of this history of the future, the intense melancholy engendered for the failure of an era yet unborn, the quiet heroism and intellectual byplay, the elements of mystery and detection—all of these components unite to create a sense that the writer (and the reader) is not anticipating things to come. Instead, we look back with providential

What: Science Fiction. *When:* 1951–53. *Award:* Hugo Award for Best All-Time Series, 1966. *Also By: Pebble in the Sky* (1950). *The Stars, Like Dust* (1951). *The Currents of Space* (1952). *Try: The Voyage of the Space Beagle* by A. E. van Vogt. *Primary Inversion* by Catherine Asaro. *Revelation Space* by Alastair Reynolds.

||||||||||||||||||||||||||||||||||||||||| M O R E   T O   E X P L O R E |||||||||||||||||||||||||||||||||||||||||

SPACE OPERA

With the debut of *Star Trek* in 1966, the general viewing public acquired its first real taste of what hardcore fans of the science fiction pulps had come to know as "space opera," a term coined by author Wilson Tucker in 1941. Postulating highly advanced civilizations and technologies that would spread across the galaxy and beyond, the genre had existed at least since the early novels of E. E. Smith (*The Skylark of Space*) written twenty years earlier.

Packed with melodrama, often violating scientific probabilities despite being replete with arcane detail, space opera—of which Asimov's Foundation series is a prime example—frequently employs dynastic and imperial templates from Earth's history, supersizing them to accommodate action across entire star systems. Here are three more highlights from the venerable and ever-growing operatic repertory of outer space.

Judgment Night
C. L. Moore (1911–1987)

Although C. L. Moore first won fame for turning out superlatively compelling stories with her first husband, Henry Kuttner, this stand-alone space opera reveals her solo mastery. It is set in the star empire of the Lyonese, whose central world is Ericon, where ancient patron gods live, remote from the day-to-day affairs of the empire. The present Emperor's heir is Juille, a daughter determined her dynasty will continue. Against the machinations of Ericon's living deities, to say nothing of the wishes of her doddering father, she wages a one-woman campaign to save all that her ancestors built. Moore veers from the cosmic to the intimate with breathtaking authority, amplifying the enveloping power of her storytelling—and the compelling character of her heroine.

Ringworld
Larry Niven (born 1938)

"Hard" science fiction—heavy on technical detail and informed with scientific precision—reached a pinnacle in the best work of Larry Niven, who, in his heyday, seemed to occupy a galaxy all his own. His headlong and engrossing

novel *Ringworld*, which spawned several sequels, illustrates his most captivating qualities as a novelist. While the protagonists' quest is Grail-like and dangerous, the real star is the boldly conceptualized venue itself: Picture a fat hula-hoop in orbit, with its sun at the empty center of the ring; the habitable portion of the engineered "planet" is the curved inner surface of the hoop, and it provides a make-believe realm for deliciously transporting adventure.

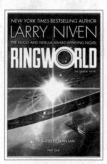

Vacuum Diagrams
Stephen Baxter (born 1957)

Stephen Baxter is a member of a new, ambitious cohort that has brought fresh vigor and reach to the old mode of space opera, fitting it for the needs and tastes of the twenty-first century. *Vacuum Diagrams*, a collection of connected stories, is part of Baxter's Xeelee sequence, which encompasses events from the birth of the universe to its destruction twenty billion years later. Baxter's style is direct, precise, and sparse, capturing the physicality of cosmic reality with both crispness and poetry. He compresses more thought and action into most of his short tales than other writers can squeeze into entire novels, and his tragic sense of life is both mysterious and inspiriting.

Instead of a Letter
Diana Athill (born 1917)

The Detours of Disappointed Love

There are many pleasures to be found in the pages of a memoir: the achievements of the author, if they be splendid; his or her sophistication, intellect, or humor; the insight that comes from sharing one person's perspective on a particular time or place. What is more rare, and what one gets from this book, is the alternately uncomfortable and exhilarating revelation of another's experience, in all its day-by-day, year-to-year uncertainty.

Written in the author's mid-forties, *Instead of a Letter* tells a story of childhood in the English countryside, high times at Oxford during the 1930s, bleak times during the war; of adolescent romance imagined into being, carried to the brink of adulthood, then lost with crushing effect. The ensuing sadness shadows Athill's emerging career at the BBC and in the book world—she was one of the founding members of the distinguished publishing firm André Deutsch—until she learns, through the

wisdom of work and words, to conjure something like happiness from the vagaries of love and the verities of time.

Beginning with an evocation of her grandmother's last days, Athill's narrative unfolds within the worrying embrace of that matriarch's memory: "What have I lived for?" the dying woman asks the young Diana. Asking the same question of herself in these pages, the author answers with startling alertness to the equivocations of emotion and intention that shape the weather of our waking hours. Beautifully honest in its self-portrait, *Instead of a Letter* captures, with paradoxical exactitude, the tentative aura every pilgrim bears on her progress toward maturity.

What: Memoir. *When:* 1963. *Also By: Stet: An Editor's Life* (2000). *Yesterday Morning: A Very English Childhood* (2002). *Somewhere Towards the End* (2008). *Try: The Perfect Stranger* by P. J. Kavanagh (see page 430). *Nothing to Be Frightened Of* by Julian Barnes. *The Three of Us* by Julia Blackburn.

Cat's Eye
Margaret Atwood (born 1939)

Self-Portrait of the Artist in Middle Age

There are few reading pleasures more delightful than the feeling of instant rapport a narrative voice can conjure, an intimacy that quickly becomes immersive as you are drawn into a confidence both close and resonant. Such is the case with Margaret Atwood's 1988 novel *Cat's Eye*, which shares qualities with a strand of her fiction—books like *Surfacing* (1972) and *Bodily Harm* (1981)— that casts a spell on the reader through first-person avowal, direct in address but clearly complicated in import: You can't help yourself from wanting to know more about the spinner of the sentences. Atwood, of course, is also adept at different kinds of fictional enchantment, as evidenced by the virtuosic shape-shifting of genres she has deployed in such acclaimed works as *The Handmaid's Tale* (1985) and *The Blind Assassin* (2000).

Margaret Atwood, 1981

In *Cat's Eye*, the voice belongs to Elaine Risley, a painter who has come back to her native Toronto for a retrospective exhibition of her art. On that return from a self-imposed and apparently necessary exile, she is tempted— with the inevitability that makes all real temptation worthy of the name—to unlayer her past: lost time, lost friends, lost luck, lost meaning. From the outset, Elaine's voice is capacious, curious, and personal: ". . . I began then to think of time as having a shape, something you could see, like a series of liquid transparencies, one laid on top of another. You don't look back along time but down through it, like water."

She gives her childhood as the daughter of an entomologist a vivid, almost organic presence, and writes vividly about her teenaged friendship with Cordelia. There may be no other single sentence that better captures the energy of adolescence than the one in which Elaine describes the rambunctious innocence with which she and Cordelia disrupt the sedate fatigue of elders on a city bus: "We're impervious, we scintillate, we are thirteen." Her recollections of Cordelia are also imbued with longing and an ominous undertone of elegy, for it is their relationship that introduces Elaine to the confusions of loyalty and love, the effects of cruelty and betrayal, and the contradictory repercussions of liberty.

Atwood is just as sensitive insinuating all the aches of adulthood and the pains of love, the fleeting truths of creativity and the hard consequences of big ambitions not quite big enough. Throughout the book, time is not only a bewildering dimension, it's a familiarly bewildering experience:

This is the middle of my life. I think of it as a place, like the middle of a river, the middle of a bridge, halfway across, halfway over. I'm supposed to have accumulated things by now: possessions, responsibilities, achievements, experience and wisdom. I'm supposed to be a person of substance.

There's something validating about hearing your thoughts in the voice of another, even when you've never been able to find your own words for them, as the reader is likely to discover again and again in the pages of this remarkable novel; it's like being given absolution for sins you haven't confessed—no penance, all blessing.

What: Novel. *When:* 1988. *Also By: Life Before Man* (1979). *The Robber Bride* (1993). *Alias Grace* (1996). *Oryx and Crake* (2003). *Try: The Golden Notebook* by Doris Lessing (see page 477). *The Stone Diaries* by Carol Shields (see page 720).

Aubrey's Brief Lives
John Aubrey (1626–1697)
Edited by Oliver Lawson Dick

"One of the most enchanting books ever written."—*Ogden Nash*

Thanks to the jumbled manuscripts that are now known as *Brief Lives*, John Aubrey deserves to be considered Britain's first genuine biographer. He is also one of the liveliest, most colorful, and most likable presences in all of English literature. Hopeless with his tangled finances, incorrigibly convivial, interested in everything and everyone, Aubrey led a rackety life as an "antiquary," which might be defined as a cross between historian, archaeologist, and gossip columnist. The *Lives*, like his other writings, were composed haphazardly: Hodgepodges of picturesque anecdote and deftly concise portraiture, they were "tumultuarily stitched up" by Aubrey for the benefit of a fellow scholar. Some of the 426 *Lives* are only a few words long—here, for example, in its entirety, is the "life" of John Holywood: "Dr. Pell is positive that his name was Holybushe"; others run to tens of thousands of words. In general, though, Aubrey's knack for the telling detail, and his ability to choose just the right incident that captures the essence of a personality, give an unexcelled piquancy and vigor to his sketches of eminent sixteenth- and seventeenth-century figures including Shakespeare, Erasmus, Descartes, Hobbes, William Penn, Milton, and Francis Bacon.

For centuries, the chaos of Aubrey's papers awaited an inspired editor. He finally arrived in 1949: Oliver Lawson Dick selected, or, more accurately, assembled, 134 *Lives*, and introduced them along with a superb ninety-page essay on Aubrey's own life and times. The result was published as *Aubrey's Brief Lives*, and it opened both a new window on the past and a perspective on human nature nonetheless fresh for being timeless.

What: Biography. Literature. *When:* ca. 1660s–80s. *Also By: Monumenta Britannica, Or a Miscellany of British Antiquities* (ca. 1663–93). *Further Reading: John Aubrey: My Own Life* by Ruth Scurr. *Try: The Anatomy of Melancholy* by Robert Burton (see page 113).

"His feeling for the significant scrap is so unerring that he can tell us more about a person in a sentence than most writers in a page."
—*W. H. Auden on John Aubrey*

Confessions
Saint Augustine (AD 354–AD 430)

The Story of a Soul

Of all the saints of the early Christian church, Saint Augustine of Hippo possesses, for the modern reader at least, the most interesting mind. His ideas on language, time, and the mysteries of personality, humanity, and divinity are still provocative—after sixteen centuries!—and his genius for expression remains vivid, even startling. "What is time? If nobody's asking me, I know. If I try to explain it to somebody who asks me, I don't know." And it's unlikely there has ever been a more telling embodiment of the desires that drive us to distraction from the straight and narrow than his youthful prayer: "Give me chastity and self-restraint, but don't do it just yet."

Speaking of prayer, it's important to remember that, as a sacrament in Catholicism, confession is an active engagement of one's sins,

Saints Augustine (right) and Cyril in a 16th-century miniature

rather than a tranquil recollection of them. So, too, Augustine's book is more prayer than memoir, even though its acute self-awareness has led many to call this book the first autobiography. What's true in that assessment is the recognition of Augustine's originality in inventing upon the page the interior space in which a personal narrative unfolds.

Augustine, as the *Confessions* relate, was born in Algeria to a pagan father and a Christian mother. Christianity was just one young religion among many in the fourth century AD, and for much of his young life Augustine was an adherent of Manichaeism, a syncretic religion spreading widely throughout the crumbling Roman Empire. He steals pears as a child, and he paints himself as something of a sex addict in his adolescence and early twenties. Only slowly does he turn to Christianity—a risky move for a professor in Milan and one that blocks his advancement in Roman society—but when he does, he comes to understand his entire life as a metaphor for humankind's journey to salvation. The tipping point of his conversion is the pinnacle of Augustine's dramatic scene-setting: In a garden in Milan, a mysterious voice directs him to scripture, saying "Pick it up! Read it! Pick it up! Read it!"

The *Confessions*, in its pulsing orchestration of metaphysical chords and personal melodies, is both a religious meditation and a cracking good read. At once an autobiography and a work of biblical exegesis, a philosophical text and a guide to living, it remains one of the most influential books ever published.

What: Autobiography. Religion. *When:* AD 397–AD 400. *Editions:* Sarah Ruden's 2017 translation is superbly readable and often revelatory. Other excellent modern translations include those by Henry Chadwick and R. S. Pine-Coffin. *Also By: On Christian Doctrine* (AD 397–AD 426). *City of God* (AD 426). *Further Reading: Augustine's Confessions: A Biography* (Lives of Great Religious Books series) by Garry Wills. *Augustine: Conversions to Confessions* by Robin Lane Fox. *Try: Pensées* by Blaise Pascal (see page 617). *The Seven Storey Mountain* by Thomas Merton (see page 547). *Surprised by Joy: The Shape of My Early Life* by C. S. Lewis.

||||||||||||||||||||||||||||||||||||||| B O O K N O T E |||||||||||||||||||||||||||||||||||||||||

A MODERN SAINT'S LIFE

The Long Loneliness
Dorothy Day (1897–1980)

The *Long Loneliness*, published in 1952, is the autobiography of Dorothy Day, the American political activist, pacifist, and cofounder of *The Catholic Worker* newspaper and movement. While Day has lately been put forth for canonization by the church, she might bridle at that idea: "Don't call me a saint," she once wrote, "I don't want to be dismissed that easily." In any case, like Saint Augustine, she spent her early years in the embrace of worldly pursuits—"the wisdom of the flesh is treacherous indeed" she would later reflect—before a conversion led her to focus her considerable energy on "[making] it a little simpler for people to feed, clothe and shelter themselves as God intended them to do." Her personal testament is as revelatory as Augustine's *Confessions*, although the difference in the two books' perspectives is striking: Where Augustine's autobiography is a conversation with God, Day's narrative is a conversation with the world. From its title on down, *The Long Loneliness* is about the struggle to nurture a spiritual life in the context of community. Her quest is to find her soul's place on earth rather than in heaven, to seek an answer to the question of what it means to be *human*—a state of being never pure nor simple—rather than what it might mean to be sanctified. There is womanly as well as saintly wisdom in this human vocation, wisdom that cannot be gainsaid no matter what divine laws one might invoke to transcend it. Day prayed in time as Augustine strove to pray in eternity; as he dreamed of a city of God, she tossed and turned in a city of women and men.

Meditations
Marcus Aurelius (AD 121–AD 180)

An Emperor's Enduring Wisdom

Perhaps even more than the great Athenian statesman Pericles, the Roman emperor Marcus Aurelius fulfilled Plato's notion of the philosopher-king. He was well trained for the role, having been handpicked by Hadrian at the age of eight to succeed that imperial luminary. The beneficiary of the finest education the ancient world could offer, Aurelius was drawn to the study of moral philosophy, and his every move as a man of action seems to have been judged according to its lights, as his *Meditations* attest.

A student of the Stoicism of Epictetus, Aurelius embraced that philosophical school's ideas of providence, endurance, restraint, and equanimity in the face of adversity. His two-decade reign, encompassing barbarian invasions, rebellion, plagues, and other assorted catastrophes, would turn out to be a proving ground for his convictions. Indeed, his

Meditations, written—in Greek—during his military and administrative travels throughout the empire, contain passages of self-encouragement that might be right at home in a twenty-first-century self-help book:

Everything you're trying to reach—by taking the long way round—you could have right now, this moment. If you'd only stop thwarting your own attempts. If you'd only let go of the past . . .

But the aphoristic reflections this volume collects are also shot through with a deep wisdom that is both consoling and inspiring, and pitched to catch the inner ear of any seeker of the meaning of existence. Aurelius's long view of the insignificance of human affairs ("The first step: Don't be anxious. Nature controls it all. And before long you'll be no one, nowhere—like Hadrian, like Augustus") is tempered by his affirmation of the value of the human soul and the need for its character to reveal itself in compassion and right conduct ("The best revenge is not to be like that"). Talking to himself in the pages of his *Meditations*, he has spoken to countless generations across the centuries, showing that retreat into the contemplative chambers of the self can stimulate a brave passage to a truer life, available to us all no matter what our station: "Anywhere you can lead your life, you can lead a good one."

What: Philosophy. Antiquity. *When:* ca. AD 165–AD 180. *Editions:* Gregory Hays's translation, in the Modern Library edition, is excellent, and quoted here. Earlier translations, such as that by George Long, lack Hays's exactitude and modern idiom, but are often more mellifluous and memorable. *Also By: Marcus Aurelius in Love*, edited and translated by Amy Richlin, collects the young Aurelius's correspondence with his teacher, Marcus Cornelius Fronto. *Further Reading:* "Homage to Marcus Aurelius" in the essay collection *On Grief and Reason*, by Joseph Brodsky. *Marcus Aurelius: A Life* by Frank McLynn. *Try: The Enchiridion of Epictetus*, compiled by Arrian. *Letters from a Stoic* by Seneca. *The Myth of Sisyphus* by Albert Camus.

JANE AUSTEN
(1775–1817)

But tell Jane Austen, that is, if you dare,
How much her novels are beloved down here.
She wrote them for posterity, she said;
'Twas rash, but by posterity she's read.

S o wrote W. H. Auden in his delightful 1937 verse epistle, *Letter to Lord Byron*, addressed to the poet in paradise. And beloved Jane Austen's books certainly have remained. Even in twenty-first-century America, her star is undimmed: Festivals summon devotees in period dress to celebrate the style and decorum of her world; novelists invoke her spirit in works like Shannon Hale's *Austenland*, which imagines a Jane Austen–themed resort, or such unembarrassed (but sometimes embarrassing) riffs on her most famous work as *Prada and Prejudice*, *Pride and Prejudice and Zombies*, and, yes, *Undressing Mr. Darcy*. Bumper stickers reading "I'd rather be reading Jane Austen" can even be glimpsed in the blur of our highway traffic. More seriously, her books continue to inform the inner lives and moral sensibilities of countless readers. The title of William Deresiewicz's 2011 volume, *A Jane Austen Education: How Six Novels Taught Me about Love, Friendship, and the Things That Really Matter*, sums up the profound influence of Austen's tutelage on the men and women who read her.

Austen's enduring popularity should be no surprise; her books, to quote another English paragon, are "practically perfect in every way." Although the novel was still a very young art form when Austen was born in the late eighteenth century, her works would become models for its maturity. She lived quietly in Hampshire among a loving family; she never married and rarely traveled. Although her sister Cassandra is alleged to have culled the crop judiciously, nothing in the novelist's extant correspondence suggests any upheaval or crisis of note. Nevertheless, Austen's outwardly quiet life produced a legacy that established the gold standard for English fiction.

Portrait of Jane Austen, ca. 1790

Always courteous to the reader, toward her characters Austen shows a sympathy that remains fond even when she is exposing their foolishness, a task from which she never shies: No foible escapes her attention, nor the sharp point with which her sentences can pin them to the page. Yet she also evinces an underlying compassion for the heroines whose course through a difficult world she plots. She astutely sets the glitter of romance in the cold light of economics, without ever forgetting that love can carry more in its ledgers than cash. (While Fitzwilliam Darcy, the haughty hero of *Pride*

and Prejudice, may be handsome, what really gets people's attention is "the report which was in general circulation within five minutes after his entrance, of his having ten thousand a year.") All the same, Austen makes sure we remember that the young women at the center of her novels will have neither money nor property if they don't find suitable husbands. The inequities of a daughter's inheritance in nineteenth-century England are felt and fretted over by her characters, and by Austen herself: The marriage contract is both boon and bind.

Pride and Prejudice
In a Class by Itself

The best introduction to Austen's work is surely the second of the six novels she wrote before her death at only forty-one, *Pride and Prejudice*, in which she introduces us to Elizabeth Bennet, the wittiest and most vivacious of five sisters on the hunt—if their mother has her way, at least—for husbands. A pair of wealthy young men arrive in the neighborhood—gentle Charles Bingley and arrogant Fitzwilliam Darcy—and Mrs. Bennet quickly sets her sights on one marriage, if not two. While Bingley falls for Elizabeth's sister Jane, Darcy and Elizabeth are opposites that don't attract, at least not instantly. When another man intimates that Darcy isn't such a scrupulous fellow, Elizabeth feels vindicated in her dislike of him; Darcy, in turn, is both infuriated and, against his better judgment, infatuated with her. Not until Elizabeth puts aside her prejudices and Darcy his pride are the two united. It's the plot that launched a thousand romantic comedies.

Pride and Prejudice is a marvel of vivid dialogue, winning characters, and lavish settings, but it is by no means frivolous. Austen's droll observation of the manners and mores of her characters and their society is throughout inscribed with a stately eloquence and poise, a note struck in the book's very first words: "It is a truth universally acknowledged, that a single man in possession of a good fortune, must be in want of a wife." From that famous first sentence to the last happy turns of amorous choreography for Elizabeth and Darcy, a deeply intelligent music carries the reader along.

To make art out of universally acknowledged truths and the compromises of social convention, both petty and pretty, is a rare gift, and no writer displays it more consistently than Austen. Sir Walter Scott, the big dog of contemporary fiction in Austen's day, acknowledged her mastery in his journal:

...read again, and for the third time at least, Miss Austen's finely written novel of Pride and Prejudice. *That young lady had a talent for describing the involvements and feelings and characters of ordinary life, which is to me the most wonderful I ever met with. The Big Bow-wow strain I can do myself like any now going; but the exquisite touch, which renders ordinary commonplace things and characters interesting, from truth of the description and the sentiment, is denied to me.*

But let's not forget the romance. Inventing the romantic comedy, in the most expansive meanings of both those words, Austen shaped the popular imagination in a way few writers have ever done. In a reading history of the world, Elizabeth Bennet, the heroine who overcomes her initial prejudice to conquer the heart of Mr. Darcy, may well be a more lively and influential model than Achilles or Quixote. While the seeds of the species of love story that Jane Austen planted have grown like kudzu—you can't turn on the television or go to the movies without seeing her shadow in the undergrowth—her own tending of them still makes her books the most enchanting of cultivated gardens, in which ordinary life, foolish attachments, and the hesitations of hope in which we live are rendered delicate and beautiful—and yes, capable of a moment's happiness. What Jane Austen teaches us is how much a life of feeling, however small and circumscribed, matters to the feeler—and, through the vital etiquette of her art, to readers as well.

What: Novel. **When:** 1813. *Further Reading: My Dear Cassandra: The Letters of Jane Austen,* edited by Penelope Hughes-Hallett. *Jane Austen: A Life* by Claire Tomalin. *The Real Jane Austen: A Life in Small Things* by Paula Byrne. *Try: Wives and Daughters* by

Elizabeth Gaskell. *Jane Eyre* by Charlotte Brontë (see page 97). *Some Tame Gazelle* by Barbara Pym. *Death Comes to Pemberley* by P. D. James (see page 411). *Adaptations: Pride and Prejudice* has been filmed several times. A 2005 movie stars Keira Knightley and Matthew Macfadyen, while a notable 1995 television miniseries features Jennifer Ehle and Colin Firth. But, validating both the seductive allure of star power and the brilliance of the old Hollywood studio system at its best, the most memorable screen adaptation is the 1940 film starring Greer Garson and Laurence Olivier.

Sense and Sensibility
Two Sisters v. Society

Austen's first published novel, which appeared under the pseudonym "A Lady," is the story of two sisters, Elinor and Marianne Dashwood, and of the tension between private passions and public decorum. Where Elinor is prudent and cautious, Marianne follows her heart where it leads—though the difference doesn't stop either from having her heart broken. This is Austen's most social novel, and in both town and country, she depicts a privileged class rife with vulgarity and vindictiveness, where falsehoods can go undetected or might as easily be rewarded. For the upstanding women of *Sense and Sensibility*, society can be a treacherous place, demanding the engagement of both head *and* heart.

What: Novel. **When:** 1811. *Try: The Semi-Attached Couple* by Emily Eden. *Sense and Sensibility* by Joanna Trollope. *Adaptations:* Of the several television and film versions, the best is the 1995 film directed by Ang Lee and starring Emma Thompson and Kate Winslet.

Mansfield Park
Money, Manners, and Marriage

From a large and not too wealthy family, bashful Fanny Price is sent to live with her rich aunt and uncle at the house that gives this book its name. She finds herself intimidated by everyone there, except her kind cousin Edmund; constantly bursting into tears, she won't even take part in her coevals' racy amateur theatricals. Despite the fact that Fanny

Letter from Jane Austen to her sister Cassandra

can be priggish, by following her convictions she ultimately finds true love. *Mansfield Park* stands at a distance from Austen's other novels: Although less lustrous than *Emma* or *Sense and Sensibility*, and less vibrant than *Pride and Prejudice*, it's probably her most substantial book. While some of her fans find it hard to love, it was actually the author's favorite.

What: Novel. **When:** 1814. **Try:** *North and South* by Elizabeth Gaskell.

Emma
Learning Life's Lessons

At twenty, Emma Woodhouse—"handsome, clever, and rich"—knows that she's the most fantastic woman in Highbury, and nothing amuses her more than meddling in other people's affairs. But although she has good intentions, her matchmaking goes seriously awry, wrecking a perfectly good engagement for her friend Harriet. Only after a spate

19th-century frontispiece for Emma, *engraved by William Greatbatch (based on a painting by George Pickering)*

of social disasters does Emma realize both her own failings and her love for her dashing neighbor. *Emma* is one of English literature's most sparkling comedies of manners, and one of the most telling depictions we have of the limits of charm and the shock of self-recognition.

What: Novel. **When:** 1815. **Try:** *Miss Marjoribanks* by Margaret Oliphant. *Daniel Deronda* by George Eliot. *Adaptations:* Loosely based on *Emma, Clueless* (1995), directed by Amy Heckerling and starring Alicia Silverstone, resets the story with some cleverness in Beverly Hills. Douglas McGrath's more faithful 1996 period version stars Gwyneth Paltrow.

Northanger Abbey
An Austen Curiosity

The first written of Austen's novels, *Northanger Abbey* was not published until after her death. It is a parody of Gothic fiction— a wildly popular genre in Austen's day, and one with which Catherine Morland, the novel's teenage protagonist, is unhealthily obsessed. She can hardly contain her excitement when Henry Tilney and his sister Eleanor invite her to stay at the titular home. For Catherine, an "abbey" must have been the site of all sorts of Gothic excesses; she even fools herself into thinking that Henry's father, the General, has killed his wife. Soon Gothic fantasies give way to actual struggles, but while Catherine learns that real life is not a fiction, *Northanger Abbey* also passionately defends the importance of literature—an art which offers "the most thorough knowledge of human nature, the happiest delineation of its varieties."

What: Novel. **When:** 1818. **Try:** *The Mysteries of Udolpho* by Ann Radcliffe. *Northanger Abbey* by Val McDermid.

Persuasion
A Tale of Second Chances

At age nineteen, high-born Anne Elliott was all set to marry her true love, the handsome, poor naval captain Frederick Wentworth, but she broke off the engagement on the advice of her officious godmother. Now twenty-seven, she seems resigned to spinsterhood. But when Anne's indebted father has to rent out the family estate, Wentworth comes back into Anne's life—and she discovers that her youthful love has lasted despite its ill-starred interruption. Though its plot may be less intricate than those of Austen's earlier works, *Persuasion* is a captivating tale, and Anne is one of her most enduring creations. The last novel Austen wrote in her short life, it points toward an expansion of her extraordinary talents; in the pages of *Persuasion*, Virginia Woolf would astutely write a century after its publication, Austen "is beginning to discover that the world is larger, more mysterious, and more romantic than she had supposed." It is a discovery the reader is happy to share.

What: Novel. **When:** 1818. **Try:** *Middlemarch* by George Eliot (see page 248). *Adaptation:* The 1995 film starring Amanda Root is very appealing.

Tuck Everlasting
Natalie Babbitt (1932–2016)

A Fable of a Girl's Escape from Forever

Age has its despairs, yet without its dimension, our lives lose their shape: A timeless life, without growth or change, would be drearier than the day is long. That's the profound truth that illuminates this extraordinary fable, in which a young girl named Winnie finds herself catapulted into great adventure by her discovery of a potion more powerful than time. So if you think you might want to live forever, never growing old, you'd do well to think again, as Angus Tuck, whose family is blessed (or cursed) with eternal life, has learned. "Living's heavy work," Angus tells the ten-year-old Winnie after she's stumbled upon the Tucks' secret, "but off to one side, the way we are, it's useless, too. It don't make sense. If I knowed how to climb back on the wheel, I'd do it in a minute. You can't have living without dying. So you can't call it living what we got. We just *are*, we just *be*, like rocks beside the road."

As Winnie wrestles with the implications of the Tucks' dilemma, the reader is led by Babbitt's alluring voice through a plot replete with action—there's a kidnapping, a murder, and a jailbreak—to an unexpected and deeply moving resting place. This enchanting novel for young people is filled with enough wit, suspense, and imagination to inform the hearts and minds of elders, too. It is a beautiful, luminous, and very wise tale conjured by a storytelling sorceress.

What: Children's. *When:* 1975. *Reading Note:* Age nine and up, and a perfect book for a family to read aloud. *Also By: The Search for Delicious* (1969). *The Devil's Storybook* (1974). *Herbert Rowbarge* (1982). *Bub: Or, the Very Best Thing* (1994). *Try: Tom's Midnight Garden* by Philippa Pearce. *The Wanderer* by Sharon Creech. *Adaptation:* A 2002 feature film stars Alexis Bledel, William Hurt, Sissy Spacek, and Jonathan Jackson.

The Baburnama
MEMOIRS OF BABUR, PRINCE AND EMPEROR
Babur (1483–1530)

The First Autobiography in Islamic Literature

"In the month of Ramadan in the year 899 [June 1494], in the province of Fergana, in my twelfth year, I became king." So begin the memoirs of Zahiruddin Muhammad Babur (1483–1530), descendant of Tamerlane and Genghis Khan. While the author spent his early years engaged in an unsuccessful effort to retain his inheritance and recover the city of Samarkand, he went on to establish a kingdom in Afghanistan in 1504. In his last decade, Babur was invited by the governor of the Punjab to invade India and overthrow the sultan of Delhi;

1589 painting of Babur holding court by Farrukh Beg

he accepted, subjugating Agra and Delhi and founding the fabled Mughal Empire.

Astonishingly, given its sophistication in both style and substance, the *Baburnama* was the first real autobiography in Islamic literature: With no literary precedent, and, as it were, between battles, Babur created a form and discovered a self within it. The result makes absorbing reading, presenting an engrossing account of the emperor's adventures as warrior and potentate; it is filled with evocative attentions to the natural world as well, and with glimpses of the gifts of expression that inspired the emperor's poetry (he was a man of many parts). One of the most fascinating features of the *Baburnama* is the juxtaposition of the author's active and contemplative selves; thus, on the same page, we get a description of the gruesome end of the storming of the Chanderi citadel ("Two to three hundred infidels . . . killed each other almost to the last by having one man hold a sword while the others willingly bent their necks. And thus most of them went to hell") and a scenic travelogue ("Chanderi is a superb place. All around the area are many flowing streams. . . . The lake, called the Betwa, is renowned throughout Hindustan for its good, sweet water. It is truly a nice little lake . . .").

In an essay on the *Baburnama*, Salman Rushdie asks:

Who, then, was Babur—scholar or barbarian, nature-loving poet or terror-inspiring warlord? The answer is . . . an uncomfortable one: he was both. It could be said that the struggle taking place within Islam in our own era . . . between Islam's male-dominated, aggressive, ruthless aspect and its gentler, deeply sophisticated culture of books, philosophers, musicians, and artists, that same, contradictory doubleness which modern commentators have found so hard to understand, was, in the case of Babur, an internal conflict.

As a result, the memoirs of this multifaceted Mughal remain intriguing reading as—all at once—personal narrative, historical chronicle, literary landmark, and enduring cultural artifact.

What: History. Autobiography. **When:** Written in Chaghatay Turkish during the author's lifetime. Persian translation, 1589. First English translation, 1826. *Edition:* Wheeler M. Thackston's superb, annotated 1996 translation is available in a Modern Library paperback; Rushdie's essay introduces this volume. *Further Reading:* "The Emperor Babur" by E. M. Forster, in *Abinger Harvest. The Mughal Throne* by Abraham Eraly. *Try: The Last Mughal* by William Dalrymple. *The Enchantress of Florence* by Salman Rushdie.

....

The Poetics of Space
Gaston Bachelard (1884–1962)

Phenomenology of the Daydream

This book is beloved by readers and writers, thinkers and dreamers the world over, despite its sometimes recondite rhetoric and its always French intellectual élan. A philosopher of science who occupied a chair at the Sorbonne in Paris, Gaston Bachelard employed his training in an original way, devoting himself in his later years to a groundbreaking exploration of that most unscientific of phenomena, the poetic imagination. He lectured and wrote extensively about psychology and the elements (earth, air, fire, water), before composing *The Poetics of Space*, the book for which he is best remembered.

Metaphorically and metaphysically rich, *Poetics* follows the imagination into spaces that nourish and inspire it, "inside" realms within the world's immensities that promise safe haven for the reveries that both define and enrich our lives. "Thought and experience are not the only things that sanction human values," Bachelard writes. "The values that belong to daydreaming mark humanity in its depths." He begins with a philosophical anatomy of the house and a consideration of how inhabited space has a profound subconscious influence on how we perceive reality (houses, he explains, "are in us as much as we are in them"). He then goes on to evoke the virtues of drawers and wardrobes, closets and corners, nests

Gaston Bachelard, 1960

and shells, quoting liberally from writers and philosophers to illustrate his points. In the end, the book itself becomes a valuable analogue of the charged spaces it so ingeniously explores.

What: Philosophy. *When:* First French publication, 1957; English translation by Maria Jolas, 1964. *Also By: The Psychoanalysis of Fire* (1938). *The Poetics of* *Reverie* (1960). *Try: The Practice of Everyday Life* by Michel de Certeau. *A Hut of One's Own* by Ann Cline. *Footnote:* Sandra Cisneros cites Bachelard's book as a sort of reverse influence. A feeling of alienation during a discussion of *The Poetics of Space* (particularly the "house of memory") at the Iowa Writers' Workshop led her to conceive and write her acclaimed novel *The House on Mango Street.*

....

The Ideological Origins of the American Revolution
Bernard Bailyn (born 1922)

Ideas That Launched a Nation

There was nothing inevitable about the American Revolution. But, looking back from the perspective of more than two centuries, that can be hard to tell. Historians themselves have contributed to this feeling of retrospective certainty. As one, quoted by Bernard Bailyn, wrote about a different historical episode, "by our explanations, interpretations, assumptions we gradually make [the event] seem automatic, natural, inevitable; we remove from it the sense of wonder, the unpredictability, and therefore the freshness it ought to have."

Bailyn's lively and award-winning study restores these qualities to the American Revolution and especially to the battle of ideas that was at the heart of the struggle for independence from Great Britain. Focusing on the extensive pamphlet literature of the colonial era, which ranged from theoretical treatises to sermons and even poems, Bailyn examines the vivid political rhetoric of the time and follows it "back into the unpredictable reality of the Revolution." By doing so, he reveals just what his title suggests: the fervent struggle of ideas that set the stage for the military battles. As he analyzes the eloquent, vigorous debates the pamphlets recorded, Bailyn illuminates the radical beliefs that inspired the unprecedented effort to champion individual liberty against the power of the state. Tracing the animating principles of the revolutionary movement back to eighteenth-century European thought, Bailyn provides an insightful education in the Enlightenment roots of the Founders' conception of law, government, and the Rights of Man.

What: History. *When:* 1967. *Edition:* The 1992 Twenty-fifth Anniversary "Enlarged Edition" adds a substantial postscript. *Awards:* Pulitzer Prize for History, 1968, and the Bancroft Prize, 1968. *Also By: The Origins of American Politics* (1968). *Voyagers to the West: A Passage in the Peopling of America on the Eve of the Revolution* (1986). *To Begin the World Anew: The Genius and Ambiguities of the American Founders* (2003). *Further Reading:* Bailyn has edited two superb volumes in the Library of America series; the primary sources they collect provide fascinating background to his arguments: *The Debate on the Constitution: Volume One: September 1787 to February 1788; Volume Two: January to August 1788. Try: American Creation* by Joseph J. Ellis.

· ·

The Birthday Boys
Beryl Bainbridge (1932–2010)

Adventure—and Love—in a Cold Climate
· ·

Captain Robert Falcon Scott's ill-fated 1912 Antarctic expedition is one of the great adventure stories of all time, and the mythic resonance of its misfortunes seems to deepen with each passing decade. In her novel *The Birthday Boys*, Beryl Bainbridge envisions the unfolding tragedy through the eyes of Captain Scott and the four men who died alongside him.

Hewing close to the facts, she begins her book in June 1910, when the sixty-man team left London for Antarctica. Although the expedition had many scientific purposes, its primary goal was to reach the South Pole—something that hadn't been previously accomplished (at least by representatives of "civilized" societies). The journey to the Pole began in earnest in November 1911. Two months into the grueling 800-mile trek, Scott selected four men to accompany him on the final push: Petty Officer Edgar Evans, Dr. Edward Wilson, Lieutenant "Birdie" Bowers, and Captain "Titus" Oates. They eventually reached their goal, only to discover that a rival expedition led by Roald Amundsen had beaten them to it. Their heartbroken return journey was beset by unimaginably fierce weather. Evans was the first to die; then Titus Oates wandered off into a blizzard, uttering the immortal words, "I am just going outside and may be some time"; finally Scott, Wilson, and Bowers succumbed in their tent in March 1912, a mere eleven miles from a depot where life-saving supplies awaited them.

The "boys" of the title are Scott and his polar companions, each of whom the author allows to recount a stage of the expedition. Through these evocative first-person narratives,

Captain Robert Falcon Scott and his companions pull a supply sled through the snow during their ill-fated expedition to Antarctica.

Bainbridge memorably captures the humanity of the explorers. Amid the beauty and terror of their surroundings, and under cruel and incredible sufferings, their admiration, affection, and their love for one another become the most remarkable revelations of this gripping tale. The author illuminates the power of male bonding as tellingly as any novelist ever has. As she has "Birdie" Bowers note: "It may be that the purpose of the worst journey in the world had been to collect eggs which might prove a scientific theory, but we'd unravelled a far greater

mystery on the way—the missing link between God and man is brotherly love."

What: Novel. When: 1991. Also By: The Bottle Factory Outing (1974). Young Adolf (1978). An Awfully Big Adventure (1989). Every Man for Himself (1996). Master Georgie (1998). Further Reading: Scott's Last Expedition: The Journals of Robert Falcon Scott. The Last Place on Earth: Scott and Amundsen's Race to the South Pole by Roland Huntford. Try: The Worst Journey in the World by Apsley Cherry-Garrard (see page 156). Endurance by Alfred Lansing (see page 463).

The Mezzanine
Nicholson Baker (born 1957)

Anatomy of a Lunch Hour

The plot of Nicholson Baker's debut novel is simple: A man, returning to his office building from a lunch hour that included milk, a cookie, a small errand, and a stroll, goes up an escalator. That's it. Yet as the narrator muses about milk and milk cartons, the shoelaces he bought and the small catastrophe that led to their need, and the thousands of other small thoughts that occupy his mind as he goes about routine business, we are treated to a disguised ascent into the wonderland of the seemingly automatic, insignificant perceptions that, more than most of our actions, shape our days. Only 135 pages long, and graced with numerous lengthy and absorbingly digressive footnotes, this is a wise, patient exploration of that unseen mental space in which we pass our time—and it's very funny to boot.

The author's slow attention to "the grain of events," combined with his deft prose, introduces the reader to one of the most inviting and offbeat voices in contemporary American writing. His book-length homage to John Updike, *U and I*, and his essays, collected in *The Size of Thoughts*, are as delightful as his several other acclaimed novels.

What: Novel. When: 1988. Also By: Room Temperature (1990). Vox (1992). The Fermata (1994). The Everlasting Story of Nory (1998). The Anthologist (2009). Try: A Journey Around My Room by Xavier de Maistre.

Growing Up
Russell Baker (born 1925)

A Satirist Comes of Age

In 1979, *New York Times* reporter and commentator Russell Baker won the Pulitzer Prize for his "Observer" column; three years later he won another for this autobiographical book. As the title suggests, *Growing Up* focuses on his childhood, Depression-era years spent in Virginia, New Jersey, and Baltimore under the watchful influence of his mother (his alcoholic father died when Baker was five). Lucy Elizabeth was "a formidable woman. Determined to speak her mind, determined to have her way, determined to bend those who opposed her. In that time when I had known her best, my mother had hurled herself at life with chin thrust forward, eyes blazing, and an energy that made her seem always on the run."

She couldn't stand a quitter and wouldn't be one, even when her husband's death meant giving up one of her children to the care of relatives.

As much as this is a book about the author growing up, it is also a book about Lucy growing old, and the son frames the bulk of the chapters—vibrantly drawn, good-humored scenes of hard times, adventures with the extended family of aunts and uncles, boyhood and adolescent antics, and eventual graduation to college and the military—with affecting portrayals of his aged mother adrift in senility. The clear-eyed honesty of the opening and closing pages does not disguise the enduring love he feels toward the woman he remembers so vividly throughout the book, "a warrior mother fighting to protect her children in a world run by sons-of-bitches." She was determined that her son Russell would make something of himself, as indeed he did through every stage of his distinguished career as a writer, which reached a culmination of sorts in *Growing Up*. In his apprenticeship as a newspaper reporter, he learned how to find a story and tell it; in his heyday as a satirist, he perfected the ability to illuminate the private and public vanities of the tumultuous times in which he lived; as a memoirist, he added a new dimension to his already considerable skill set. It's best called wisdom, and it makes this generous remembrance of things past a delight from start to finish.

What: Memoir. *When:* 1982. *Award:* Pulitzer Prize for Biography or Autobiography, 1983. *Also By:* Collections of Baker's newspaper columns include *Poor Russell's Almanac* (1972) and *So This Is Depravity* (1980). *The Good Times* (1989) is a memoir of his years as a mid-century newspaperman. *Try: Happy Days: 1880–1892* by H. L. Mencken. *One Man's Meat* by E. B. White. *The Florist's Daughter* by Patricia Hampl.

Collected Essays
James Baldwin (1924–1987)

Evidence and Eloquence

It can be a little too easy to pin labels on James Baldwin: black, gay, expatriate, aesthete. But every label sells him short, diminishing the singularity of his work. That he wrote specifically of his time and place—America in the middle of the twentieth century—and engaged its most dangerous themes—race, Civil Rights, the persisting degradations of history—does not limit the reach of his sentences into the past and the future: They are, and will remain, acute inquiries into the moral and political quandaries of our being, regardless of the age in which they're read. While the books are indeed indelible documents of their era, they ponder questions of inheritance, race, and social justice with a sense of perplexity and purpose that resonates far beyond their contemporary context.

His essays especially are provocative exercises for the reader. The volumes that first gathered them—*Notes of a Native Son, Nobody Knows My Name, The Fire Next Time, No Name in the Street*—made his reputation as a refulgent if often recalcitrant prophet of the Civil Rights era, landing him on the cover of *Time* magazine and keeping him in the public eye. In every paragraph, Baldwin's language reaches forward and back in time with a tragic sense of continuity and consequence. His deep well of evolving private memory enriches his—and our—perspective on current events. His writing is as challenging as it is rewarding exactly because his probing of complex realities realizes that their complexity emanates from contradictions at their cores. Truths, he'd learned, were never singular, and seldom in agreement; yet he remained unrelenting in his pursuit of them. This commitment to capturing the contradictions of lived experience imbued his explorations with an equivocal ferocity that revealed both the naïveté and the arrogance of others' certainties. If America, as he wrote in *Notes of a Native Son*, is a "country devoted to the death of the paradox," Baldwin realized that such devotion was a kind of suicide.

His essays move with restlessness and agility and, now as then, they offer his readers not solace but a kind of education in sorrow, teaching us that morality is far more fatal, and perhaps more unforgiving, than our sentimental narratives of reconciliation and redemption allow us to believe. And more personal as well: Baldwin knew that the subject of race in America was also the story of *him* in America, and his essays make of his insights and bewilderments a tortured light. As he writes in *No Name in the Street*, "the moral of the story (and the hope of the world) lies in what one demands, not of others, but of oneself."

James Baldwin, 1963

What: Essays. **When:** Published by the Library of America, 1998, collecting *Notes of a Native Son* (1955), *Nobody Knows My Name* (1961), *The Fire Next Time* (1963), *No Name in the Street* (1972), *The Evidence of Things Not Seen* (1985), and other essays. **Also By:** *Go Tell It on the Mountain* (1953). *Giovanni's Room* (1956). *Another Country* (1962). **Further Reading:** *James Baldwin: A Biography* by David Leeming. **Try:** *Shadow and Act* by Ralph Ellison. *After Henry* by Joan Didion. *Between the World and Me* by Ta-Nehisi Coates (see page 162).

....

Slaves in the Family
Edward Ball (born 1959)

Flesh and Blood Secrets in the Family Closet
....

My father had a little joke that made light of our legacy as a family that had once owned slaves.

"There are five things we don't talk about in the Ball family," he would say. "Religion, sex, death, money, and the Negroes."

"What does that leave to talk about?" my mother asked once.

"That's another of the family secrets," Dad said, smiling.

So begins Edward Ball's compelling family memoir, a narrative that reaches far beyond the realm of his own kin to explore the legacy of slavery in America, an inheritance at the heart of the nation's most obvious and most hidden history. Exploring its deep roots and intricate branches, Ball illuminates the subject with an uncommon blend of intelligence, empathy, and prodigious research; still, it is his personal perspective—shared, ultimately, with descendants of the Ball slaves—that gives his tale its startling inspiration and reverberating power.

Descended from Elias Ball, who emigrated from Devon, England, to Charleston, South Carolina, in 1698, the Ball family owned nearly 4,000 human beings during their 167 years as a slave dynasty. More than a hundred years after the end of the Civil War, the author's clergyman father gave him a copy of a 1909 family history, planting in twelve-year-old Edward the notion that the past might require further examination. But it was not until two decades later, when he was working as a journalist in New York in 1993, that he was ready to "face the plantation."

Moving to a dilapidated ancestral home in Charleston, Ball began an ambitious quest, charting not only his own genealogy but also that of the family's slaves, tracing their ancestry back to the first African captives. The book details Ball's subsequent travels throughout the United States to meet their descendants, some of whom are his distant cousins. His encounters are fraught with tension

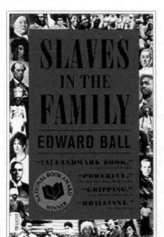

and emotion, yet Ball succeeds in making his testament a collective tale. Revealing who and what he found in his research, as well as how he made his discoveries, Ball creates what *Booklist* aptly described as "an informative, ruminative, and inspirational page-turner."

What: History. Memoir. *When:* 1998. *Award:* National Book Award, 1998. *Also By: The Sweet Hell Inside: The Rise of an Elite Black Family in the Segregated South* (2001). *Peninsula of Lies* (2004). *The Genetic Strand: Exploring a Family History Through DNA* (2007). *Try: Somerset Homecoming* by Dorothy Spruill Redford with Michael D'Orso. *The Hairstons* by Henry Wiencek. *Inheriting the Trade* by Thomas Norman DeWolf.

The Drowned World
J. G. Ballard (1930–2009)

The Future Primeval

The *Drowned World* first appeared in America as a mass-market paperback, somewhat indistinguishable from the paperback reprint of *Armageddon 2419 A.D.* by Philip Francis Nowlan—basis of the Buck Rogers franchise—that appeared on drugstore racks beside it. Over the next three decades, J. G. Ballard's works would move up in the world of literary reputation as he came to be recognized, even revered, as one of the most unconventional visionaries in modern fiction.

Even when his novels were drugstore fare, however, his work revealed an inspiration different in kind from its sci-fi rack mates. Having originally intended to study psychiatry, Ballard viewed individuals and society with a clinician's precision and a novelist's synthetic imagination. And given that his first four novels all dealt with apocalypses, he plainly felt bent on destroying the future world before he moved on to anatomizing the contemporary one, as he would do to startling effect in later acclaimed

works such as *Crash* (1973) and *High-Rise* (1975). The sense of impending disaster that haunts his work may have its roots in his Shanghai childhood during that city's destruction by the invading Japanese (a period powerfully evoked in Ballard's *Empire of the Sun*). His stories "tick like time bombs," Ali Smith has said, and she's right: The world is always ending, or could be, not with a bang or a whimper, but with a kind of ineluctable, eerie algorithmic calm.

The Drowned World begins with the Earth reverting to conditions approaching those of its ancient Triassic past—imagine climate change on steroids. After seventy years of increased solar radiation due to persistent anomalous flares, flora and fauna have devolved to primeval forms, and human psychology is backtracking too, regressing into an "archaeopsychic" realm beneath the layers of defenses, mechanisms, and sophistication civilization has bestowed upon the mind.

In the remnants of a London drowned by seas swollen by the melting ice caps, a scientific expedition tries to gather environmental data that might help humanity survive, and we follow the adventures of three participants—two men and one woman—who cut themselves off from their colleagues and stake their futures on adapting to the new conditions. Soon they encounter a piratical band—the leader, Strangman, has a flock of pet crocodiles—and what follows is a Conradian excursion into an increasingly desperate landscape (narratively speaking, *The Drowned World* is a missing link between *Heart of Darkness* and *Apocalypse Now*).

The Drowned World reaches into the future and the past at the same time, portraying an invented world that is both fantastic and strangely literal in its marshaling of detail. As Ballard developed as a writer, he would increasingly turn his attention to naturalistic incidents and settings—traffic accidents, apartment blocks—and reverse that effect, turning realism strangely fantastic in order to provide an uncanny high-definition portrait of the way we live now. No other writer of our time has been able to measure thousands of years of our biological past, hundreds of years of our projected future, and what might happen in the next five minutes into such remarkable imaginative tableaux.

What: Science Fiction. *When:* 1962. *Also By: The Crystal World* (1966). *Super-Cannes* (2000). *Try: After London* by Richard Jefferies. *The Purple Cloud* by M. P. Shiel. *Damnation Alley* by Roger Zelazny.

HONORÉ DE BALZAC
(1799–1850)

"I think you will come to Balzac yet," wrote Sylvia Townsend Warner in a 1961 letter to her *New Yorker* editor and friend William Maxwell. "When one has disproved all one's theories, outgrown all of one's standards, discarded all one's criterions, and left off minding about one's appearance, one comes to Balzac. And there he is, waiting outside his canvas tent—with such a circus going on inside."

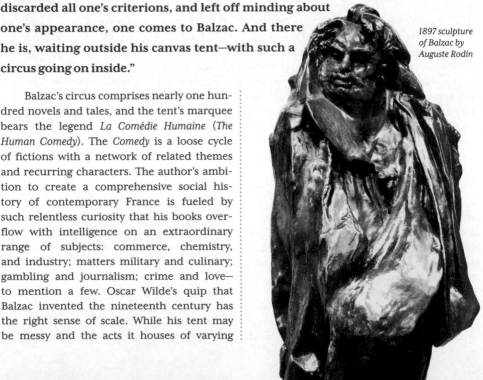

1897 sculpture
of Balzac by
Auguste Rodin

Balzac's circus comprises nearly one hundred novels and tales, and the tent's marquee bears the legend *La Comédie Humaine* (*The Human Comedy*). The *Comedy* is a loose cycle of fictions with a network of related themes and recurring characters. The author's ambition to create a comprehensive social history of contemporary France is fueled by such relentless curiosity that his books overflow with intelligence on an extraordinary range of subjects: commerce, chemistry, and industry; matters military and culinary; gambling and journalism; crime and love—to mention a few. Oscar Wilde's quip that Balzac invented the nineteenth century has the right sense of scale. While his tent may be messy and the acts it houses of varying degrees of fascination, an exhilarating elixir perfumes the air that permeates it, always luring us back for more.

What Austrian poet and essayist Hugo von Hofmannsthal said of one Balzac novel in particular (*Cousin Bette*) can also be applied to his work in general: While it may contain only "ugly, sad, and terrible facts," it nevertheless "glows with fire, life, and wisdom." Through *The Human Comedy*, Hofmannsthal writes, "vibrates an absolute joyfulness that is untouched by the gloom of its theme, as the divine joyousness of the sounds in a symphony by Beethoven can at no moment be perturbed by the fearful nature of its musical expression." No single book does justice to the reach and grasp of Balzac's genius, and the three chosen here merely suggest the scope of his achievement. There are plenty more where these came from, and a reader would do well to follow Sylvia Townsend Warner's advice to Maxwell on how to approach them: "I have an idea . . . that one should aim to read at the tempo at which the author wrote. Balzac wrote fast and recklessly, and read that way he emerges very much himself."

Lost Illusions
A Poet's Progress

Lost Illusions is a massive novel—more than six hundred pages. Written in three parts between 1837 and 1843, its several story lines conspire to display most of the author's abiding concerns: the claustrophobic dullness of provincial society and the ruthless snobbery of its Parisian counterpart; the wounds inflicted by every class distinction; the corruption of love and art by money and intrigue; the tawdry expediencies of the literary world; the cynicism of the press; the energies of commerce and industry; youth's endless capacity for delusion.

The main story revolves around the poet Lucien Chardon, a callow and ambitious youth who escapes the provinces only to be snubbed in Paris by the woman he had followed there. Balzac calibrates with a precision both tender and merciless each cut to Lucien's self-esteem, surveying the manners of country and city with a vigilance that misses no mordant phrase or dismissive glance. Lucien's poetic aspirations fare no better than his social ambitions, as he learns the dirty truth that talent counts for little compared to a venturesome venality: "The key to success in literature," a friendly editor advises him, "is not to work oneself, but to exploit others' work. . . . And so, the more mediocre a man is, the sooner he arrives at success."

Balzac no doubt poured his own youthful disenchantments into *Lost Illusions* (as he did his prodigious knowledge of printing and papermaking, through the secondary tale of Lucien's provincial companion and brother-in-law, the inventor David Séchard). But he filters these disappointments through an intelligence so alert to every nuance of physical, social, and commercial experience that his novel exudes a loyalty to life that no amount of disillusion can diminish.

What: Novel. *When:* 1837–43. *Edition:* The translations by Herbert J. Hunt, quoted here, and Kathleen Raine are both good. *Also By:* Lucien's story is continued in *A Harlot High and Low*, also known as *The Splendors and Miseries of Courtesans* (1847). *Further Reading:* V. S. Pritchett's *Balzac* and Graham Robb's *Balzac: A Biography* are both excellent. *Try: The Charterhouse of Parma* by Stendhal. *Look Homeward, Angel* by Thomas Wolfe (see page 865).

Père Goriot
A Father's Story

One of the more remarkable byproducts of Balzac's prodigious literary career is the *Repertory of the Comédie Humaine*, prepared by Anatole Cerfberr and Jules François Christophe toward the end of the nineteenth century. In this annotated alphabetical guide to the *dramatis personae* of the master's imaginative realm, Cerfberr and Christophe cull from the novels the biographies and Balzacian pedigrees of the hundreds upon hundreds of characters the *Comedy* contains. It makes fascinating browsing, for its five hundred pages constitute something like a seed catalog for stories. Of all the characters the *Repertory* references, perhaps none is more haunting than the unfortunate father whose fate is explored in the novel *Père Goriot* (*Goriot the Father*, sometimes rendered as *Old Goriot*).

In simple outline, the book sounds like a poor man's *King Lear*: A retired businessman is done in by the greed and callousness of his ungrateful daughters. What distinguishes the tale in the fullness of its telling, however, is the way in which Balzac uses Goriot's sad circumstances to paint a dynamic portrait of a society so entangled with venal motives that even the most fundamental human emotions are perverted. The novelist ironically traces Goriot's descent from prosperity to poverty by sending him ever higher in Madame Vauquer's boarding house. One floor at a time, he progresses from the best rooms down below to a hovel three floors up, his fortune and his spirit sapped by his married daughters' relentless need to fund their appetites and aspirations. His stylish offspring pay the occasional visit, arousing the suspicions of Goriot's fellow boarders, who are unaware of the nature of the young women's relationship to the old man. He befriends the ambitious but impoverished law student Eugène de Rastignac, who, becoming a lover of Goriot's daughter Delphine, soon finds his desires so far outstripping his means that he is drawn into the web of the criminal Vautrin. As Goriot's life declines into squalor, the brilliance of the world of Rastignac's social adventures is revealed to be nothing more than glitter from the chains of money and influence that imprison its inhabitants.

In the end, our sympathy for old Goriot is mitigated by our awareness that he has been complicit in his own misery, ruined by the monomania that twists his parental affection into a desperate avarice. Like the fatal flaw of many of Balzac's memorable protagonists, his obsession is neither unimaginable nor obscure, and all the more terrible for its familiarity.

Père Goriot was the first novel in which Balzac began to systematically color the fabric of his *Comedy* with people, families, and settings that would reappear, under lights of varying intensity, from one story to the next. In a portent of things to come, Goriot's private tragedy is given greater resonance by the reverberations of the teeming milieu that surrounds it.

What: Novel. **When:** 1835. **Edition:** Henry Reed's translation, in Signet paperback, is especially good. **Also By:** Other seminal works in Balzac's enterprise are *Eugénie Grandet* (1833), *Cousin Bette* (1847), and *Cousin Pons* (1847). **Try:** *King Lear* by William Shakespeare (see page 716). "A Father's Story" by Andre Dubus. **Footnote:** It is from *Père Goriot* that Balzac's most famous aphorism—"Behind every great fortune is a great crime"—comes to us, albeit indirectly; the novelist never actually says it in quite that way, although he might well admire the eloquent paraphrase of his meaning.

The Wild Ass's Skin
Melodrama as Metaphysics

The *Wild Ass's Skin*, a novel that Balzac revised repeatedly, issuing seven different editions in a period of fourteen years, begins in bravura fashion, with an extended description of a young man's entrance into a gambling house in the Palais-Royal. Commencing with a careful consideration of the social, cultural, legal, and providential ramifications of a patron checking his hat upon entrance, it proceeds to describe the physical and psychological atmosphere of the casino with preternatural sensitivity. The scene culminates with the hatless young man (we do not yet know him as Raphael de Valentin) placing, and losing, his last gold coin in a desperate wager. He leaves the gaming room—a place "where even despair must behave in a seemly fashion"—intent on committing unseemly suicide by drowning himself in the Seine.

Along the way, however, he is distracted by the allure of an antique shop, whose contents—

furnishings, objets d'art, souvenirs, weapons, china, paintings, and mirrors, assorted "relics of civilizations and religions" from around the world—Balzac catalogs with relish. At last the owner of this old curiosity shop shows Raphael an unimagined treasure: a piece of shagreen (untanned leather) with the power of granting its owner's every craving. And yet, as the shop-keeper warns his young customer, each wish granted will shrink the shagreen and diminish the days of its possessor. But Raphael is reck-less: "I want to live to excess!" he exclaims as he grasps the skin.

Thus the scene is set for one of Balzac's most telling philosophical explorations. In the foreground is the realism of the author's vivid descriptions of gambling den and curio shop (and subsequent episodes of equally astute observation). In the background is the overriding riddle posed by the supernatural skin and the reflections of the antiquary who proffers it: Do our desires use us up? Moving backward and forward in time, Balzac follows Raphael's fate through a dynamic panorama of contemporary society, illuminating, through the compulsions of a deliciously melodramatic plot, the metaphysical conundrums that thwart and thrill our souls.

What: Novel. *When:* First published in 1831, with several subsequent editions through 1845. *Edition:* The Penguin translation is by Herbert J. Hunt; other versions in English have used the title *The Magic Skin. Also By: Louis Lambert* (1832) and *Séraphita* (1835) are other examples of Balzac's philosophical fictions. *Further Reading: The Melodramatic Imagination: Balzac, Henry James, Melodrama, and the Mode of Excess* by Peter Brooks. *Try: An American Dream* by Norman Mailer.

The Sweet Hereafter
Russell Banks (born 1940)

When Bad Things Happen to Good People

" Well, most of us stopped learning very early, and spend the rest of our lives defending that point at which we stopped learning," novelist Russell Banks once said in an interview. "It's funny, you know, most of the characters I've written about only learn anything as adults as a result of a terrible calamity...."

Banks writes books about ordinary people trying to live decent lives in less than ideal cir-cumstances. They are stories about race, class, family, and keeping one's head above water, but as Cynthia Joyce wrote on Salon.com in 1998, "there's a redeeming wisdom to them, a sense of hopefulness found in the details that he so diligently draws out of his characters' mundane realities."

In the case of *The Sweet Hereafter*, the ter-rible calamity is a school bus accident in an upstate New York town; the mundane reality is that the town's life must go on after its children have been killed in the crash. The book begins with the driver, Dolores Driscoll, describing how she swerved to miss a dog and the bus got away from her, sliding off the snowy road and down the embankment. By turns, it shifts from Dolores's story to those of three others: a Vietnam vet who lost his two children, a law-yer from New York City who wants the families to sue the state for negligence, and a beautiful fourteen-year-old girl who survived the crash but now faces life in a wheelchair. The shifting viewpoints reveal Banks's gift for communi-cating how the inner lives of outwardly simple people are as rich and complex as those who wear sophistication on their sleeves. Providing different perspectives on events, the overlap-ping stories also portray how each narrator must process grief, and struggle for meaning, in his or her own way.

More than the sum of its parts, Banks's novel allows us to see into the heart of a com-munity that is speechless with sorrow. With the same magnanimity through which he imparts the lessons of calamity, Banks imparts the les-sons of community as well. As Dolores Driscoll puts it toward the end of the book: "The acci-dent had ruined a lot of lives. Or, to be exact, it had busted apart the structures on which those lives had depended—depended, I guess, to a greater degree than we had originally believed. A town needs its children for a lot more than it thinks."

What: Novel. *When:* 1991. *Also By: Continental Drift* (1985). *Affliction* (1989). *Rule of the Bone* (1995). *Cloudsplitter* (1998). *Lost Memory of Skin* (2011). *Try: Selected Stories* by Andre Dubus. *Nobody's Fool* by Richard Russo. *Adaptation:* Atom Egoyan's acclaimed film adaptation appeared in 1997.

The Journal of a Disappointed Man
W. N. P. Barbellion (1889–1919)

" . . . among the most moving diaries ever created."—*Ronald Blythe*

I llness is usually a private matter; a diary, too. But *The Journal of a Disappointed Man*, a wrenching but deeply humane diary by a young Edwardian suffering from a terminal condition, places the most private ordeal in public view—with extraordinary consequences. For anyone who has ever suffered, or seen a loved one suffer, Bruce Frederick Cummings—who, two years before his death, published his diaries under the pseudonym W. N. P. Barbellion—offers a candid but ultimately uplifting portrayal of the ravages of disease and the larger mysteries of mortality. In its unsparing recapitulation of a life cut short, his diary stands as one of literature's great monuments to endurance in the face of adversity; it is also, as Noel Perrin calls it, "one of the great affirmations in our literature."

Cummings, born into a family of journalists, starts keeping a diary at age thirteen, and its early entries—"Went out with L—to try to see the squirrels again"—show his keen interest in zoology and nature. Despite no formal scientific education, he eventually lands a job at London's Natural History Museum. Yet among the early entries on newts and frogs—and on girls, whom he chases with only moderate success—Cummings records coughs and sweats, palpitations, and worse. Soon his doctor concludes that

he suffers from multiple sclerosis (although the disease is not named in the book). But the doctor doesn't tell him. Though this now sounds shocking, it was standard practice at the time for doctors not to disclose mortal illnesses to their patients; the belief was that ignorance of one's lot was better for one's peace of mind. Only in November of 1915, after being exempted from military service, does Cummings unseal a letter his doctor provided for the inspectors: He has been suffering from MS for more than a year, and has not much longer to live. Unbeknownst to him, and as he would only discover sometime later, his wife already knew his diagnosis.

From this point on, the diary turns more and more to interior, emotional terrain, even as the descriptions of his worsening illness are inscribed with a naturalist's attention: "I become dreadfully emaciated," he writes in August 1917. "This morning, before getting off the bed I lifted my leg and gazed wistfully along all its length. My flabby gastrocnemius swung suspended from the tibia like a gondola from a Zeppelin. I touched it gently with the tip of my index finger and it oscillated."

Yet *The Journal of a Disappointed Man* is neither dismal nor disheartened. In fact, Cummings's descriptions of his failing health give greater force to his benevolent, even transcendent meditations on life, and love. His time on earth compressed into just thirty years,

"If there be no loving God to watch us it's a pity for His sake as much as for our own."

—*W. N. P. Barbellion*

Cummings nevertheless has no sense of injustice, and as his condition worsens he comes to see what we should all see: that every day is a gift, that we exist for one another and not just ourselves, and that our tendency to see such truths as clichés stands in the way of our fuller humanity.

What: Diaries & Letters. *When:* 1919. *Also By: Enjoying Life and Other Literary Remains* (1919). *A Last Diary* (1920). *Further Reading: A Reader's Delight* by Noel Perrin (see page 209). *The Pleasure of Diaries: Four Centuries of Private Writing*, edited by Ronald Blythe. *Try: Part of a Journey* and *End of a Journey* by Philip Toynbee. *Until Further Notice I Am Alive* by Tom Lubbock.

Laughing in the Hills
Bill Barich (born 1943)

Ruminations Around the Racetrack

Bill Barich started playing the horses out of the desperation bred by his mother's battle with cancer. Other family sadnesses followed, and to escape their shadow, he decided to spend a season at Golden Gate Fields, a thoroughbred racetrack outside San Francisco. "The track seemed circumscribed and manageable, especially when compared to the complex filigree of nature, hydrogen intertwined with embryos and tumors." He sought renewal and, if this perfectly cut gem of a book is any proof, he found it.

Barich's attentive, anecdotal account of track life is keenly observed and placed in intriguingly wider contexts by his off-track learning; you'll discover a good deal in these pages about the city of Florence and its Renaissance culture, for instance, and the author is ingenious enough to place his reading in conversation with the racing life around him:

I came to think of trainers as Renaissance princes who ruled the backstretch. Walking the shedrows I saw that each barn resembled a principality, embodying a unique blend of laws and mores,

an individuated style. Brightly colored placards bearing trainers' names or initials or devices shone in the sun, and it was possible to intuit the flesh of a prince from the sign he displayed.

What Barich absorbs about track life (from touts and handicappers, trainers and jockeys, grooms and breeders, and, not least, from the horses themselves) reveals itself to the reader as a short but deep course in the yearnings and resources of human nature. That his education unfolds before us in discerning, careful prose while taking the often eccentric measure of a cast of colorful characters makes reading *Laughing in the Hills* a surprising and wholly delightful experience. It is the kind of book that, once you've finished it, will make you long to be asked, "Read anything good lately?" You don't need to love horse racing to fall in love with this book.

What: Sports. Memoir. *When:* 1980. *Also By: Traveling Light* (1984). *Big Dreams: Into the Heart of California* (1994). *A Fine Place to Daydream* (2006). *Try: The Track* by William Surface. *The Wrong Horse* by William Murray. *The Sweet Science* by A. J. Liebling.

THE REGENERATION TRILOGY
REGENERATION • THE EYE IN THE DOOR • THE GHOST ROAD
Pat Barker (born 1943)

Ghosts in the Making

In 1917, Siegfried Sassoon—poet, friend of the celebrated Bloomsbury circle, and decorated military hero—had a crisis of conscience about the war he was fighting and penned a letter of protest that was sent to Parliament and published in *The Times* of London. For this very public refusal to fight he might have been court-martialed, but was instead sent to

Craiglockhart War Hospital, in Scotland, to be treated for "shell shock." His months there have been recounted in autobiographical works by at least three men: Sassoon himself (*Sherston's Progress*, 1936; see page 699), fellow poet Robert Graves (*Good-bye to All That*, 1929; see page 332), and Sassoon's doctor at Craiglockhart, noted psychiatrist and anthropologist W. H. R. Rivers (*Conflict and Dream*, 1923). They have also, more recently, been brilliantly imagined by Pat Barker in her award-winning Regeneration Trilogy.

In these meticulously researched novels, as in life, Sassoon is surrounded by genuine shell shock victims—men who have variously lost the ability to sleep, eat, or speak. The trilogy's central figure, Dr. Rivers, has the increasingly troubling job of "fixing" these men so they can be sent back to the trenches for more of the infernal combat that broke them. Sassoon and others—some invented, like the unforgettable amnesiac Billy Prior, who plays a crucial role in the novels—struggle with their own conflicting impulses, feeling a responsibility toward the soldiers despite recognizing the insanity and futility of the war. Outside the hospital, pacifists are treated brutally, and women weigh their losses against their liberation.

Barker's trilogy has earned reams of praise over the years, but Samuel Hynes might have said it best when reviewing the first volume, *Regeneration*, for the *New York Times*: "[Literary] fashions change, theories emerge and fade, but the realistic writer goes on believing that plain writing, energized by the named things of the world, can make imagined places actual and open other lives to the responsive reader, and that by living those lives through words a reader might be changed. Pat Barker must believe that, or she wouldn't write as she does." If not mightier than the savage sword that inflicted the wounds of World War I, the pen, in Barker's hand, bears powerful witness to the scars it left behind.

What: Novels. *When: Regeneration*, 1991; *The Eye in the Door*, 1993; *The Ghost Road*, 1995. *Awards: The Eye in the Door* won the Guardian Fiction Prize, 1993; *The Ghost Road* won the Booker Prize, 1995. *Reading Notes: Regeneration* succeeds splendidly as a stand-alone novel. *Also By: Union Street* (1982). *Blow Your House Down* (1984). *Border Crossing* (2001). *Life Class* (2007). *Further Reading:* In addition to the books mentioned above, Sassoon, Graves, and Wilfred Owen, each of whom is a character in Barker's trilogy, published numerous powerful poems about their combat experiences. *Try: Birdsong* by Sebastian Faulks. *Adaptation:* A 1997 British film, starring Jonathan Pryce as Rivers, is available in the US as *Behind the Lines.*

Flaubert's Parrot
Julian Barnes (born 1946)

A Stuffed Bird Takes Wing

Sophisticated literary inventions are seldom as charming as this one, an intricately composed but inviting exploration of the nature of desire. The intricacy of the composition comes from the author's playful orchestration of a variety of styles, combining fiction with literary criticism, biography, diversions scholarly and reflective, a chronology, even a mock exam; the charm comes from the unfailing tunefulness of Barnes's sentences—they are shaped with a confidence, clarity, and concentrated energy that give great pleasure.

What's the novel about? On the surface, it's about a retired British doctor's obsession with Gustave Flaubert, the author of *Madame Bovary* (see page 282). An amateur student of the work of the nineteenth-century French master, Geoffrey Braithwaite travels to France to investigate the settings and trappings of his idol's life. Specifically, he is seeking to determine which of several stuffed parrots is the one that Flaubert actually kept on his desk while composing "A Simple Heart," a marvelous tale of a peasant woman's devotion to her bird. In the course of his narration, Braithwaite puts before the reader anecdotes from Flaubert's life, analyses of his work, and even offers a chapter presenting a point-by-point rebuttal of the writer's numerous character flaws. The doctor's passion for Flaubert's work expands into a worship of the man, revealing one of Barnes's overriding themes: the irreconcilable differences between art and life.

Another love story deepens the plot, that between Braithwaite and his wife, recently deceased, for whom he grieves despite her unfaithfulness. The physician's version of their marital romance is at odds with its unrequited reality, just as his idealized image of Flaubert conflicts with the at times tawdry truth of the revered author's behavior. The objects of Braithwaite's desire slip away from him,

and yet the impulse to hold them remains. With digressive progress, Barnes leads us on a delightfully comic pursuit of large questions: Is love, like art, finally unknowable, except in the imaginative experience of it? Is memory itself an art, in which we shape, in story, our subjectivity? Filled with literary fun of a very high order, *Flaubert's Parrot* is a seriously delicious confection.

What: Novel. *When:* 1984. *Also By:* Novels: *A History of the World in 10½ Chapters* (1989); *England, England* (1998); *The Sense of an Ending* (2011). Memoir: *Nothing to Be Frightened Of* (2008). *Further Reading: Three Tales* (includes "A Simple Heart") by Gustave Flaubert. *Try: Pale Fire* by Vladimir Nabokov.

Peter and Wendy
J. M. Barrie (1860–1937)

The Boy Who Wouldn't Grow Up

You almost certainly know the story of Peter Pan and the Darling children—to say nothing of Peter's loyal fairy, Tinker Bell, or his mates in Neverland, the Lost Boys, or their fierce foe, Captain Hook—through the many justly popular stage or screen adaptations of J. M. Barrie's tale. The novel was, in fact, elaborated from the author's original, wildly successful 1904 theatrical presentation, and its winning mix of drama and fantasy has fueled many subsequent productions, including a perennially appealing Disney animated film; a Mary Martin television special featuring a joyous, tender, and unforgettable score by Jule Styne; a musical by Leonard Bernstein; and cinematic variations by Steven Spielberg and others. Like its flying protagonist, *Peter Pan* is a story that may revel forever in never growing up.

Despite your familiarity with the outline of the tale, a reading of the novel *Peter and Wendy* is likely to astonish you with its sophistication, allusiveness, and compelling, yet paradoxically reflective, storytelling. For all its fantasy and adventure, the book is very much written from an adult perspective: It is, in a way, a long

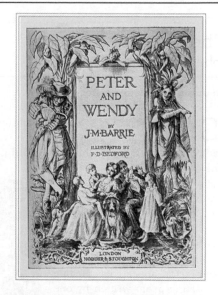

meditation on the inevitability of leaving the magical precincts of childhood. "All children, except one, grow up," it begins, and while Peter is the ageless wonder who soon charms us, his endless youth is married at the start to Wendy Darling's realization that childhood is a state of expansive desires but diminishing returns: "Two is the beginning of the end," Barrie writes of her precocious understanding.

The tale is filled with excitements. Who can forget Peter's search for his errant shadow, or the Darling children's first flight to Neverland, or the Lost Boys' battles, in alliance with the "redskin" Tiger Lily, with the sinister Hook? Yet all the amusement, delight, and suspense are bathed in the author's nostalgia and enlivened by his extraordinarily fanciful fidelity to the experience of not only children, but parents, too:

Mrs. Darling first heard of Peter when she was tidying up her children's minds. It is the nightly custom of every good mother after her children are asleep to rummage in their minds and put things straight for next morning, repacking into their proper places the many articles that have wandered during the day.

There follows an extraordinary disquisition on the "map of a person's mind" that will amuse young readers with its whimsy and fill older ones with wonder, and probably a few tears, as they reach its conclusion: ". . . it is all rather confusing, especially as nothing will stand still."

Uniquely targeted, with perfect aim, at both kids and adults, Barrie's masterpiece is the perfect vehicle to introduce a family to the pleasures of reading long tales aloud, for it allows each audience to lose itself in its own transporting reverie.

What: Children's. *When:* 1911; originally published as *Peter and Wendy*, later as both *Peter Pan and Wendy* and *Peter Pan*. *Edition:* There are countless editions, many with lovely illustrations. Look for one that includes Barrie's forerunner to the full story, *Peter Pan in Kensington Gardens* (1906). *Also By:* Plays: *Quality Street* (1901); *The Admirable Crichton* (1902). *Further Reading: J. M. Barrie and the Lost Boys* by Andrew Birkin. *Try: The Golden Age* by Kenneth Grahame. *Five Children and It* by E. Nesbit. *Adaptation:* No home with children should be without the Mary Martin recording of the Jule Styne score.

The Sot-Weed Factor
John Barth (born 1930)

An Uproarious Historical Romp

"Sot-weed" was colonial American slang for tobacco; a "factor," in the same era, was a trading agent. And so, as John Barth explains, "the sot-weed factor . . . was the man who exchanged consignments of English manufactured goods for hogsheads of tobacco from the tidewater plantations." Nearly 260 years before the publication of Barth's novel, "The Sot-Weed Factor" appeared as the title of a satiric poem written by one Ebenezer Cook and published in London. The subtitle of this 1706 burlesque read, in part, "A Voyage to Maryland . . . In which is describ'd, The Laws, Government, Courts and Institutions of the Country; and also the Buildings, Feasts, Frolics, Entertainments and Drunken Humours of the Inhabitants of that Part of America."

Coming upon Mr. Cook's poem in the course of his researches into the local history of his native Maryland, Barth's imagination took flight, and, turning poet into protagonist, he conceived his own comic extravaganza—an enormous, rambunctious, ribald, screamingly funny novel written in the exuberant narrative and literary style of eighteenth-century English fiction (think Henry Fielding's *The History of Tom Jones, a Foundling;* see page 273). Set in the late 1600s, Barth's *Sot-Weed Factor* chronicles Ebenezer's picaresque exploits as he voyages to America to supervise his father's tobacco business and to immortalize, in epic verse, the destiny of Maryland. The marvelously involved plot leads the awkward young innocent through uncounted attempts by innumerable rogues to divest him of his wits, his fortune, and his virginity. Barth's imaginative virtuosity in detailing these treacherous adventures animates every page of this huge tale with such rollicking delight that, despite its length, one is very sorry to reach its end.

What: Novel. *When:* 1960; revised 1967. *Edition:* Barth prefers his 1967 revision of the novel, "a slightly slimmed-down edition . . . about sixty pages shorter

than the original. No plot protein was removed," Barth writes, "only some excess verbal calories." The original 1960 edition boasted a jacket by Edward Gorey (see opposite page). *Also By: The Floating Opera* (1956). *The End of the Road* (1958). *Giles Goat-Boy* (1966). *Lost in the Funhouse* (1968). *Chimera* (1972). *Try: Mason & Dixon* by Thomas Pynchon. *Daisy Buchanan's Daughter* by Tom Carson.

....

■ For Matsuo Bashō's *The Narrow Road to the Deep North and Other Travel Sketches*, see page 356.

■ For W. Jackson Bate's *Samuel Johnson*, see page 418.

....

The Flowers of Evil
Charles Baudelaire (1821–1867)

Taking Poetry Out of the Ivory Tower

B audelaire is the great pathologist of shades: Beauty, death, melancholy, desire—all are led into his poetic laboratory for observation, dissection, autopsy. There, he turns abstractions, in one critic's apt phrase, into existential intimacies. His stanzas stand like dark prisms of hard light, decadent monuments in the sensible streets of his symbolic Paris. To walk among them is to enter a realm of mythological mystery and power, a netherworld that in some ways spawned the aesthetic embrace of excess, shock, and willful perversity that would come to shape—and, in lesser hands than Baudelaire's, to disfigure—so much of modern literature.

The *Flowers of Evil* was Baudelaire's first volume of poems, and it announces its sumptuous depravity right from the start. Here, in Richard Howard's translation, is the first stanza of the introductory "To the Reader":

Stupidity, delusion, selfishness and lust
torment our bodies and possess our minds,
and we sustain our affable remorse
the way a beggar nourishes his lice.

Charles Baudelaire, 1857

On account of its descriptions of "unnatural" sex, its fiendish insistence on the connection between sexuality and death, and its vivid portraits of urban seediness, *The Flowers of Evil* led to Baudelaire's prosecution for public indecency upon its original publication in 1857. Six poems were banned, and Baudelaire was fined three hundred francs. But as Victor Hugo, nineteenth-century France's most influential writer, noted at the time, Baudelaire's work had unquestionably created a new *frisson* (a shudder, a thrill) in French literature. If the shudder came from the poet's caress of corruption, drunkenness, and melancholy, the lasting thrill came from his unabashed conviction that the dignity of art and even beauty fell outside the borders of morality.

What: Poetry. *When: Les Fleurs du mal* was first published in 1857; a second edition appeared in 1861. *Editions:* Notable English language editions include Richard Howard's translation, which won a National Book Award in 1983, and the New Directions volume edited by Marthiel and Jackson Mathews, which collects versions from several hands, including Stanley Kunitz, Robert Lowell, Richard Wilbur, Anthony Hecht, and Edna St. Vincent Millay; both of these editions include the French text as well. *Also By: The Painter of Modern Life* (1863). *Paris Spleen* (1869). *My Heart Laid Bare* (1897). *Further Reading: Baudelaire* by Jean-Paul Sartre. *Try: Selected Writings* by Gérard de Nerval. *A Season in Hell* and *Illuminations* by Arthur Rimbaud.

The Wonderful Wizard of Oz
L. Frank Baum (1856–1919)

Adventures with Scarecrow, Tin Woodman, and Cowardly Lion

There's no greater tribute to the pleasures of L. Frank Baum's book than to say that the story is so good that it isn't overwhelmed by the images from the wonderful Judy Garland movie. Dorothy and her dog, Toto; the terrible cyclone that transports them from Kansas to a land of witches and an evasive wizard; the loyal trio lacking, respectively, brains, heart, and courage; the perils of every stripe in the company of Munchkins and Winged Monkeys; the gadgets galore, the yellow brick road and the City of Emeralds—all of it is every bit as rich, scary, bewitching, and happy in the reading, when we can linger among the marvels to our hearts' content. The pleasures of the film, with its marvelous songs, are only enhanced by acquaintance with the book.

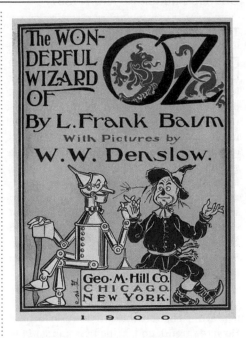

You may be shocked to discover that the ruby slippers whose heels Judy clicks to make her way home are Silver Shoes in the original, or that nobody says "I have a feeling we're not in Kansas anymore" or "Pay no attention to that man behind the curtain" in so many words, but in recompense you'll be treated to extra adventures that the movie lacks (like those among the Quadlings). More tellingly, especially if you share the book with youngsters on the cusp of being able to tackle its simple prose themselves, you'll witness Baum's narrative genius in pitching his language to that open-minded audience. The story unfolds with a declarative matter-of-factness that puts no barrier between the real and the imagined; because the author invites them to, young listeners and readers will take the fantasy at face value, indulging their sense of fancy with a concentration that's both liberating and

Judy Garland, Jack Haley, and Ray Bolger in the beloved 1939 film adaptation. Inset: illustration from the first edition by W. W. Denslow

beneficial. The magic works for adults, too, if they'll let it.

Surprisingly, no one has written about the empowering allure of the Oz books (Baum would go on to write several sequels) with more insight and affection than the generally unaffectionate Gore Vidal, who traces his addiction to reading to Baum's creations in a 1977 essay:

I still remember the look and the feel of those dark blue covers, the evocative smell of dust and old ink. I also remember that I could not stop reading and rereading the book. But "reading" is not the right word. In some mysterious way, I was translating myself to Oz, a place which I was to inhabit for many years while, simultaneously, visiting other fictional worlds as well as maintaining my cover in that dangerous one known as "real."

Baum's fables of Dorothy and friends encourage the imagination in a way that is essential to any true education. Young readers are apt to return to the real world, Vidal argues eloquently, as enhanced people: "imaginative, tolerant, alert to wonders, life." What more can one ask of a book?

What: Children's. **When:** 1900. **Edition:** Look for the original W. W. Denslow illustrations—you can't do better than the lovely Books of Wonder editions for any of Baum's classics. **Also By:** Baum wrote thirteen sequel novels, including *The Marvelous Land of Oz* (1904), *Ozma of Oz* (1907), and *Tik-Tok of Oz* (1914). **Try:** *Five Children and It* by E. Nesbit. *The Wonderful Flight to the Mushroom Planet* by Eleanor Cameron. **Adaptations:** You know about the 1939 film, with songs by Harold Arlen and Yip Harburg. Of the countless other adaptations, two Broadway musicals are worth noting: *The Wiz* (1975), which recasts the story in an African American milieu, and *Wicked* (2003), based on Gregory Maguire's 1995 novel, *Wicked: The Life and Times of the Wicked Witch of the West*, the first of several Oz-themed works Maguire has penned.

The Feast of Love
Charles Baxter (born 1947)

A Playful, Profound Novel of Love in All Its Guises

Set in Ann Arbor, Michigan, *The Feast of Love* relates the intertwining yet wildly divergent stories of several men and women who range across the generations and yet are pulled together, apart, and together again by strands of desire, sex, marriage, pain, and plain old human sympathy. With a sleight-of-hand that is literally thrilling, Baxter summons a community into being, investing every character with so much bewitching emotion that we quickly come to care about each one.

There is Bradley W. Smith, who first catches the ear of the insomniac narrator, a writer named Charlie Baxter. And Bradley's first and second wives. And the body-pierced, good-hearted young renegades Chloé and Oscar, who like to sneak into the University of Michigan football stadium and engage their passion on the fifty-yard-line. And Bradley's neighbors Esther and Harry Ginsberg, an elderly couple unable to cut the cord of affection that binds them to a hateful son. Taking up pieces of the tale in their own voices, the characters of Baxter's novel assume an imaginative presence that reaches far beyond the shortcomings, dissatisfactions, and fleeting joys of their Ann Arbor lives. Even Diana, Bradley's cold and secretive second wife, wins our affection, as she stumbles—pushed by life—into a revelation that is an emblem of the book's unexpected generosities:

And then we were making love ... and my soul—I can't believe I'm saying this, but it's what happened—became visible to me. My soul was a large and not particularly attractive waiting room, just like in a Victorian train station with people going in and out. In this waiting room were feelings I hadn't known I had, discarded feelings, feelings with nowhere to go, no ticket to a destination. It turned out that I was larger than I had known myself to be. ... My soul was not particularly attractive, but the surprise was that it was there, that I had one.

The Feast of Love is an extraordinarily satisfying novel. As we watch the ordinary world's fits and starts glide into the choreography of art, the happy surprise of what we witness transforms the mundane sorrows of disparate lives into a miraculous communion of the living.

What: Novel. *When:* 2000. *Also By:* Novels: *First Light* (1987); *The Soul Thief* (2008). Short story collections: *Through the Safety Net* (1985); *A Relative Stranger* (1990); *There's Something I Want You to Do* (2015). *Try: Jamesland* and *Round Rock* by Michelle Huneven. *Adaptation:* The 2007 film, starring Morgan Freeman and Greg Kinnear, was directed by Robert Benton.

■ For Stephen Baxter's *Vacuum Diagrams*, see page 27.

SIMONE DE BEAUVOIR
(1908–1986)

That Simone de Beauvoir was an intellect of the first rank, a writer of similar distinction, and a major figure in twentieth-century European culture is increasingly beyond dispute. She possessed a prodigious ability to synthesize matter and meaning across disciplines in ways that prove revelatory and profound.

Simone de Beauvoir, 1947

A protean woman of letters, she produced what seemed an unending stream of prose: novels, philosophical essays and inquiries, travel diaries, treatises, and autobiographical investigations. If Jean-Paul Sartre was the king of the existentialist ethos that dominated French intellectual debate in the decades after the Second World War, Beauvoir was the queen. Her reputation was inextricably linked to him as lover, companion, and colleague; much analytical ink has been spilled on their relationship and every tendril of scandal—sexual, political, personal—that trailed in its wake. As a result, Beauvoir's private predilections and pursuit of a liberated mode of conduct have distracted readers from her extraordinary achievements, as if there is something missing in her work that her behavior is required to supply.

No one ever expects the same justification of Voltaire, whose liaisons were every bit as intricately indecorous, for, generally speaking, complex women do not fare well in the history of ideas (just ask Madame de Staël or George Sand). This, of course, would have been a fine theme for Beauvoir, who famously sought a new understanding of the experience of women in *The Second Sex*. Not as notoriously, but just as thoroughly and courageously, she

dealt with the lives of the old in *The Coming of Age*. Those two books, together with her autobiography and several superb novels, secure their author a shelf of her own in the permanent library.

The Second Sex
An Exhaustive and Intimate Study of Human Experience

By Beauvoir's own account, Sartre had a critical role in the genesis of *The Second Sex*. When she told him that she was about to embark upon a memoir of her childhood, he suggested she consider how being a woman had shaped her upbringing and engagement with the world. After some resistance, she took his advice; more than a year and a half of research and reflection—and some eight hundred pages of prose—later, *The Second Sex* was completed. Its publication in 1949 sent waves of influence through subsequent decades as its arguments and insights disrupted, redirected, and recalibrated conventional thinking about the lives of women. Both formative and transformative, Beauvoir's scrutiny of the physical, social, and existential experience of women in the West is a groundbreaking work of feminism—and humanism, too.

"One is not born, but rather becomes, woman," Beauvoir writes, and her conception that "woman" is, experientially speaking, an idea constructed by the powers that be in society and culture (read: men) is advanced and validated across the book's two parts, "Facts and Myths" and "Lived Experience." In the first, Beauvoir examines biology and physiology and the cultural contexts that interpret them; psychology and political theory; historical and religious perspectives; and the myths that male culture has created from the physical truths of women's lives: menstruation, virginity, copulation, marriage, motherhood. The impact of this mythology is probed in the second part, in which Beauvoir explores situations of life— childhood, puberty, sexual initiation, family, and social circumstances—and how the cultural construction of "woman" is a box that becomes impossible to think outside of.

But this is exactly what Beauvoir does in *The Second Sex*, choosing not to dramatize women's lives but to *think* about them, with rigor, vigor, and a combination of clinical attention and imaginative resourcefulness. Filled with an awareness both domestic—"Few tasks are more similar to the torment of Sisyphus than those of the housewife; day after day, one must wash dishes, dust furniture, mend clothes that will be dirty, dusty, and torn again. . . . "—and universal—"And without doubt it is more comfortable to endure blind bondage than to work for one's liberation; the dead, too, are better suited to the earth than the living"—*The Second Sex* is singular in myriad ways.

What: Feminism. Sociology. Culture. *When:* 1949. *Edition:* The original 1953 American edition, translated by H. M. Parshley, was both flawed and abridged; a new, complete translation, by Constance Borde and Shelia Malovany-Chevalier, was issued in 2009. *Also By:* Fiction: *She Came to Stay* (1943); *The Mandarins* (1954). Philosophy: *Pyrrhus and Cineas* (1944); *The Ethics of Ambiguity* (1947). *Further Reading: Simone de Beauvoir: A Biography* by Deirdre Bair. *Tête-à-Tête: The Tumultuous Lives and Loves of Simone de Beauvoir and Jean-Paul Sartre* by Hazel Rowley. *Try: The Feminine Mystique* by Betty Friedan (see page 300). *Sexual Politics* by Kate Millett. *The Female Eunuch* by Germaine Greer.

Memoirs of a Dutiful Daughter
The Child Is Mother to the Woman

"The ability to pass over in silence events which I felt so keenly is one of the things which strike me most when I remember my childhood," writes Beauvoir early in *Memoirs of a Dutiful Daughter*; the length and density of her four volumes of autobiography make it clear that this youthful ability is one she would later abandon with a vengeance. Detailing her developmental years in a bourgeois family, her adolescent rebellion against religion and other conventions, and her initial foray into the academic and intellectual ferment of Paris in the 1920s, *Memoirs*, the first volume, is infused with an almost tactile rendering of perception:

I would crack between my teeth the candied shell of an artificial fruit, and a burst of light would illuminate my palate with a taste of black-currant or pineapple: all the colours, all the lights were mine, the gauzy scarves, the diamonds, the laces; I held the whole party in my mouth.

As she plays her well-tempered memory across the chords of her past, the music is orchestrated with richness of observation that adds resonance to her rumination.

Her affections and friendships, uncertainties and confidences, infatuations and intense attachments to ideas as well as people—including her nascent relationship with her brilliant fellow student Sartre—are lushly remembered and related with a decidedly literary complexion. Just as her most famous novel, *The Mandarins*, a roman à clef of her and Sartre's postwar circle, is fiction laced with reality, so her autobiography is fact that leverages the ways and means of fiction, a deliberate construction that allows her—with true existentialist agency—to create a portrait of the person she has chosen to be.

What: Autobiography. *When:* 1958; English edition, translated by James Kirkup, 1959. *Also By:* Other volumes of autobiography: *The Prime of Life* (1960); *Force of Circumstance* (1963); *All Said and Done* (1972). *Try: At the Existentialist Café: Freedom, Being, and Apricot Cocktails* by Sarah Bakewell.

The Coming of Age
A Rare Illumination of the Shadows of Old Age

All men are mortal: they reflect upon this fact. A great many of them become old: almost none ever foresees this state before it is upon him. Nothing should be more expected than old age: nothing is more unforeseen.

"**O**ld age is an island surrounded by death," the nineteenth-century Ecuadorean essayist Juan Montalvo wrote. In her impassioned book, which spans a thousand years and a variety of nations and cultures, Simone de Beauvoir asserts that all too often the inhabitants of that island are left to their own devices, ignored by the denizens of the mainland, distanced from community by the busy arrogance of youth and separated from it by the misapprehensions of policy and popular thought. It is a remote territory to be visited, as if the life upon it—physical, emotional, existential—is static and displaced, animated by none of the desires and feelings of the rest of our existence. "Until the moment it is upon us," Beauvoir writes, "old age is something that only affects other people."

With erudition, fierce intelligence, and a gracefulness of expression that is eloquent even when polemical, the author surveys old age biologically, ethnologically, historically, and philosophically. As brave as *The Second Sex* in its confrontation of the fundamental struggles of existence, *The Coming of Age* illustrates that Beauvoir's analytical intellect encompasses an intense and enlightening empathy.

What: Sociology. Culture. **When:** 1970. *Also By: A Very Easy Death* (1964), Beauvoir's wrenching account of her mother's last days, is a sort of personal prelude to the intellectual exertions of *The Coming of Age. Try: Growing Old in America* by David Hackett Fischer. *Footnote: The Coming of Age,* and many other books by Beauvoir, were translated into English by Patrick O'Brian, author of the Aubrey-Maturin seafaring novels (see page 593).

Fun Home
A FAMILY TRAGICOMIC
Alison Bechdel (born 1960)

A House of Many Mansions

One might expect a graphic narrative to be lean, wry, linear. Yet the pioneering triumph of Alison Bechdel's *Fun Home* is that it's resonantly rich in thought and theme, nuanced in its framing and feeling, contrapuntal in its treatment of chronology, character, and incident. Bechdel imbues her story with an expressive pulse that moves from words to pictures and back again like an intricate melody passed between the instruments of a string quartet.

The memoir is the story of a pre-adolescent girl with two brothers who comes to certain realizations about herself and her family. Her father, an English teacher who also runs a funeral parlor (the "fun home" in family parlance), is a stifled artist and a gay man pursuing his sexuality covertly. Her mother, who finds solace in amateur acting roles, struggles

to maintain normality in the household, having surrendered most of her early blisses to the obsessions of her dominant mate. Young Alison observes all this acutely, piecing together the reality behind the facades, while simultaneously puzzling out her own nascent lesbianism. She eventually goes off to college, awakes to her own nature, and then receives the news that her father has died—run over by a truck in what might plausibly be either accident or suicide.

Closure remains elusive, even decades later, yet Bechdel weaves all these matters of pain, growth, and mortality into a work of art vivid in both form and substance. A labyrinthine web of literary echoes and mythological invocations capture the emerging complexity of her intelligence, and you have to read her images with as much attention as her allusive, probing, and alert prose. Employing well-honed, powerful techniques developed over decades in mainstream comic books, Bechdel incorporates renderings of family photos, maps, and other found imagery into her panels, painstakingly transcribing the emblems of experience that both worry and honor memory. More than metaphorically, it's a handmade book, and lived time is layered into every panel.

All of which combines to make this graphic novel about gender identity, sexual orientation, and domestic dysfunction also about the mysterious anguish of our emotions; about the fears and tremblings of self-discovery, family, and personal destiny; about the intractable tragicomicness of being alive.

What: Graphic Novel. *When:* 2006. *Also By: The Essential Dykes to Watch Out For* (2008). *Are You My Mother?* (2012). *Try: The Contract with God Trilogy: Life on Dropsie Avenue* by Will Eisner. *The Quitter* by Harvey Pekar. *The Complete Wimmen's Comix* by Trina Robbins. *Adaptation: Fun Home* has succeeded on the stage in a musical adaptation by Lisa Kron and Jeanine Tesori, earning numerous honors, including the 2015 Tony Award for Best Musical.

Love, Loss, and What I Wore
Ilene Beckerman (born 1935)

A Life in Outfits

In this charming, unusual book, Ilene Beckerman uses sixty-odd outfits—from pinafore to prom dress, maternity clothes to Pucci knock-offs—to trace her life from the 1940s through the 1990s. Each memory is articulated in an unpretentious paragraph or two that serves, ostensibly, as a caption to Beckerman's drawing on the facing page. Taken together, the items in her illustrated wardrobe chart the author's uncertain progress on her journey from innocent youth (white dickey with Peter Pan collar) to elegant age (Donna Karan white silk shirt). Simple in concept, modest in execution, Beckerman's gallery of what she wore reveals with astonishing poignancy and good humor the fabric of a woman's years. Her clothes—the Brownie uniform, the scarf she's thinking of buying to satisfy her granddaughter's eye—are filled with life (and love and loss), and colored by the deep, true dyes in which experience steeps our days.

"Never has the love of beautiful clothes seemed less frivolous."
—The New Yorker

Love, Loss, and What I Wore

written and illustrated by
Ilene Beckerman

What: Memoir. *When:* 1995. *Reading Note:* You can read this in an hour. And then you'll have the pleasure of reading it again. *Also By: What We Do For Love* (1997). *Mother of the Bride* (2000). *Makeovers at the Beauty Counter of Happiness* (2005). *Try: Manhattan, When I Was Young* by Mary Cantwell. *The Clothes on Their Backs* by Linda Grant.

SAMUEL BECKETT
(1906–1989)

The plays, stories, and novels of the 1969 Nobel Laureate in Literature are, in a sense, all of a piece. Their style and demeanor are more significant than details of plot, cast, or setting, which, in every case, are spare to the point of comedy—or despair. This is not to diminish the individuality of specific works, but rather to identify the continuity of character that runs through them. Every page, and nearly every sentence, of Samuel Beckett wears the genetic imprint of its maker.

Beckett's prose—in which, quite often, his verbal genius is given the thankless task of expressing the futility of expression itself—is one of the most resonant instruments in modern letters, possessed of a somber musicality and a lapidary eloquence that can startle the reader with its haunting beauty. (This is all the more remarkable considering he alternated between English and French in composing his mature works, translating from one to the other upon completion with painstaking attention.) Even

Samuel Beckett, ca. 1950

when, or rather especially when, the sentiment expressed is bleak and pessimistic the phrasing is fraught with the hallowing power even the most halting words invoke. And how comic it can be—really—in its dry depiction of human relentlessness in the face of cosmic indifference.

His work can be forbidding, admittedly, and the best way at it may be in reverse, starting with one of his last short prose pieces and moving backward toward his longer fiction with an evening in the theater in between.

Company
Invitation to a Modern Master

Toward the end of his career, Beckett published in English a series of slender volumes, their austere proportions leavened by

the stoic comedy that coursed beneath every text he ever set upon a page.

The prose of these works—*Fizzles, Company, Ill Seen Ill Said*, and *Worstward Ho* among them—reads like writing stripped to a kind of current, a cable unraveled to a single filament that still carries an electric charge: on, off, shock, silence. It makes the writing of the earlier laconic masterpieces—*Murphy, Molloy, Malone Dies, The Unnamable*—seem loquacious. Yet despite this, or because of it, the cadences engrave themselves within one's hearing with a permanent, peculiar beauty.

Till finally you hear how words are coming to an end. With every inane word a little nearer to the last. And how the fable too. The fable of one with you in the dark. The fable of one fabling of one with you in the dark. And how better in the end labour lost and silence. And you as you always were.

Alone.

That passage marks the end of *Company*, a short work that stands as an almost perfect memorial to his peculiar and passionate weighing of words. Indeed, its beginning might well be an emblem for Beckett's works entire, for it sums up the legacy of his literary labor, which had begun in absorption in Joyce and Proust and wrung itself out into pregnant quiet: "A voice comes to one in the dark. Imagine."

His verbal genius, his unparalleled invocation of the destiny of language, even as he shuttled back and forth between English and French, restored to diction an almost sacramental gravity. In *Company* especially, he's like a composer who has scraped from his scores all orchestration, all melody, indeed, almost every instrument. He pares his music back to plainchant, a voice in the dark that might find some resonance in what we think and say, and, ultimately, feel: "A voice comes to one in the dark. Imagine."

What: Short Stories. **When:** 1970. **Award:** Beckett won the Nobel Prize in Literature, 1969. **Reading Note:** Beckett's prose is often incantatory and intricate with repetition; resist the temptation to gather speed, for appreciation of the verbal music requires a measured pace. **Also By:** Other short fiction: *Stories and Texts for Nothing* (1955); *The Lost Ones* (1970); *First Love and Other Shorts* (1970). **Further Reading:** *Beckett's Dying Words* by Christopher Ricks. *Damned to Fame: The Life of Samuel Beckett* by James Knowlson. **Try:** *On the Mountain* by Thomas Bernhard.

Waiting for Godot
"A country road. A tree. Evening."

Waiting for Godot was Samuel Beckett's first performed play, written in French and then translated by the author into English. It is one of the signal accomplishments in twentieth-century theater and one of the touchstones of modern literature. It is also, as one contemporary critic said of its two acts, "a play in which nothing happens, twice."

The play opens with what would become one of the most famous stage directions in all drama: "A country road. A tree. Evening." That's all the description Beckett gives us to set the scene for Vladimir and Estragon, two shabby and seemingly homeless men who wait—and wait, and wait—for the arrival of a certain Godot. While they bide their time, they try to amuse each other, enigmatically debate the nature of

religion, and talk about whether they should hang themselves. They are like two vaudevillians who have no act, but whose waiting evokes a cosmic routine beyond their ken, a joke in which the punch line never comes.

Of course—here is the most unnecessary spoiler alert in literature—Godot never comes either. Eventually someone does show up: not the mysterious Godot, but the arrogant Pozzo and his servant Lucky, the latter of whom speaks only in gibberish. Vladimir and Estragon make plans to leave, and even make plans to die, but all through the first act, and then the second, they just keep waiting.

Thematically, *Waiting for Godot* was not unprecedented. From Anton Chekhov's *Three Sisters* (see page 154) to Eugene O'Neill's *The Iceman Cometh*, several important plays from the early twentieth century had depicted characters who hope for change or salvation but end up lingering exactly where they started. What was revolutionary about *Waiting for Godot* was its extreme minimalism, from the starkness of its setting to the spareness of its speech. Paradoxically, Beckett's paring down of existence to just two tramps by a tree has given the play both emotional resonance and enduring relevance. From Sarajevo in the 1990s to New Orleans after Hurricane Katrina, performers and audiences in places of crisis keep turning to Beckett's masterpiece, which, with acuity and humor, reveals the hopes and fears of human life like few other literary exposés.

What: Drama. **When:** Original French version published in 1952; first performance 1953. First English publication, 1954; first performance 1955. **Also By:** Plays: *Endgame* (1957); *Krapp's Last Tape* (1958); *Happy Days* (1961). **Further Reading:** *Notes on a Cowardly Lion* by John Lahr (see page 461; Lahr's father, Bert, famous for his portrayal of the Cowardly Lion in *The Wizard of Oz*, played Estragon in the original Broadway production of *Godot*). **Try:** *The Cherry Orchard* by Anton Chekhov (see page 154). *No Exit* by Jean-Paul Sartre (see page 698). *Rosencrantz and Guildenstern are Dead* by Tom Stoppard.

Molloy

A Choreography of Consciousness

F our years before he was awarded the Nobel Prize, Samuel Beckett directed his only movie. It starred the silent film comedian Buster Keaton, for whom Beckett had conceived the project. While the austere author's fascination with the star of early cinema, then long past his prime, may seem odd on the surface, it becomes ingeniously obvious at depth. For just as Keaton in his heyday used kinetic movement—pratfalls, of course, but also determined nuances of gesture and gait—so Beckett took the familiar momentum of language—syntax, rhythm, cadence—and turned it to expressive and comic as well as philosophical effect. Take, for example, this passage from his novel *Molloy*, a diptych of two long interior monologues that are part existential rumination, all shaggy dog story:

He looks old and it is a sorry sight to see him solitary after so many years, so many days and nights unthinkingly given to that rumour rising at birth and even earlier, What shall I do? What shall I do? now low, a murmur, now precise as the headwaiter's And to follow? and often rising to a scream. And in the end, or almost, to be abroad alone, by unknown ways, in the gathering night, with a stick.

We never find out exactly who the man with the stick is; or why Molloy, the book's first narrator, seems confined in a room writing pages that another mysterious man arrives weekly to pick up; or why exactly the second narrator, named Jacques Moran, is on the trail of the first. All of their actions, peregrinations (real or imagined), and suppositions are enigmatic to the reader, indeterminate in both import and significance, and yet the prose leads us down labyrinthine paths that promise—and ultimately deliver—a carefully described perspective into the thicket of consciousness. By anatomizing thought and syncopating the progress of sentences with obsessive attention, Beckett creates, as Keaton did on screen, a kind of awkward poise—an anomalous grace—on the stage of narrative. It is both precise and riveting, reveling in the humors and movements of language as it explores, with comic impulse and tragic obstinacy, "the crass tenacity of life and its diligent pains."

What: Novel. **When:** Published in French, 1951; English version, 1955 (translated by Beckett and Patrick Bowles). *Also By: Molloy* is often regarded, although not by the author, as the first volume in a trilogy completed by *Malone Dies* (1951) and *The Unnamable* (1953). Other novels: *Murphy* (1938); *Watt* (1953); *How It Is* (1961); *Mercier and Camier* (1970). **Try:** *Correction* by Thomas Bernhard. *The Third Policeman* by Flann O'Brien. *House Mother Normal* by B. S. Johnson. *Footnote:* Beckett's 1965 short film starring Buster Keaton is called, plainly enough, *Film*.

The Hills is Lonely
Lillian Beckwith (1916–2004)

An Eventful Escape to the Hebrides

T *he Hills is Lonely* tells a simple tale. Needing to recuperate from an illness and in possession of a small annuity, the author gives up her teaching post in "a smoky North of England town" and advertises for a suitable retreat where she might, per her doctor's prescription, "rest without being too lazy, and laze without being too restive."

A pile of tempting offers is crowned by one she finds too intriguing to resist. The letter has come from the Hebrides, and it exudes a flinty hospitality that seems a native characteristic of that archipelago off the west coast of Scotland:

I live by myself, and you could have the room that is not a kitchen and bedroom reasonable. . . . You would be very welcomed. I have a cow for milk and eggs and the minister at the manse will be referee if you wish.

So, despite the imprecations—"Don't be a fool!"—of her flat mate, off our narrator sets for a primitive croft in Bruach on the Isle of Skye. There, under the aegis of her resourceful and well-connected landlady, Morag McDugan, she is initiated into the works and days of island life.

Beckwith's gentle, slightly fictionalized memoir describes—with humor (often hilarity), surprise (sometimes shock), tolerance (at times sorely stretched), affection (genuine and ever-deeper), and keen observance—the routines and rituals, traditions and ceremonies of life in Bruach. From her arrival in heavy weather through a cattle sale and a *ceilidh* (an evening of traditional tunes, tales, and dancing), a funeral

and a culminating wedding, Beckwith's island experience is restorative in every way, peopled with characters as eccentric and endearing as any reader could wish.

What: Memoir. *When:* 1959. *Also By:* Beckwith's Hebridean adventures continue in *The Sea for Breakfast* (1961), *The Loud Halo* (1964), *A Rope—In Case* (1968), and several other volumes. *Try: We Bought an Island* by Evelyn E. Atkins. *Seasons on Harris* by David Yeadon.

The Adventures of Augie March
Saul Bellow (1915–2005)

**"The Great American Novel.
Search no further."—*Martin Amis***

The title of Saul Bellow's third novel evokes Tom Sawyer and Huck Finn, and the voice that tells it—like the one Mark Twain created for Huck—is alive with the rhythms and energies of speech. From the outset, Augie March grabs our ear and yanks it exuberantly:

I am an American, Chicago born—Chicago, that somber city—and go at things as I have taught myself, free-style, and will make the record in my own way: first to knock, first admitted; sometimes an innocent knock, sometimes a not so innocent. But a man's character is his fate, says Heraclitus, and in the end there isn't any way to disguise the nature of the knocks by acoustical work on the door or gloving the knuckles.

The book's irrepressible hero grows up in a poor Jewish household during the Great Depression. He ventures out from the family circle to find his way in the world, trying his hand at a motley assortment of jobs and encountering a host of colorful schemers, scammers, dreamers, and lovers. Ever restless, always hungering for experience, Augie roams from Chicago to Mexico and on into postwar Europe—"Look at me, going everywhere!" he taunts himself—where he's wheeling and dealing at story's end, still searching "for the right thing to do, for a fate good enough." The worlds through which he passes and the characters he

Saul Bellow, 1962

meets are rendered with a richness and a density that is true to life rather than to art; and Augie's ardent inner life—fueled by the philosophies, plans, and passions he embraces and discards—plays out in pool rooms, department stores, apartment houses, and conversations, just like our own soulful enthusiasms.

For six hundred pages, Saul Bellow wrestles Augie's buoyant encounters with experience into sentences that are extraordinary in their capacity: "They are like hall closets;" Joan Acocella has written, "you open them and everything falls out. All of Chicago seems gathered into the book, and eventually all of America, and much of human history as well." The prose is dazzling indeed, capturing, in an admiring Philip Roth's words, "the dynamism of living without driving mentalness out." It pulses with the unresolved yet ineluctable hopefulness with which Augie March meets the facts of life that come his way.

What: Novel. **When:** 1953. **Awards:** National Book Award for Fiction, 1954. In 1976, Bellow was awarded the Nobel Prize in Literature. **Also By:** *Dangling Man* (1944). *The Victim* (1947). *Henderson the Rain King* (1959). *Seize the Day* (1956). *Herzog* (1964). *Mr. Sammler's Planet* (1970). *Humboldt's Gift* (1975). *The Dean's December* (1982). *More Die of Heartbreak* (1987). **Further Reading:** *Bellow: A Biography* by James Atlas. **Try:** *The Man Who Was Not With It* by Herbert Gold. *A New Life* by Bernard Malamud. The novels of Philip Roth (see page 676) and Salman Rushdie (see page 683), who, to different purposes, tapped into the literary energy unlocked by Bellow's prose.

■ For Ludwig Bemelmans's *Madeline*, see page 785.

The Uncommon Reader
Alan Bennett (born 1934)

Reading Royalty

Alan Bennett's charming and wryly hilarious celebration of the pleasures and powers of reading is a flawlessly pitched, perfectly proportioned novella. Its heroine is the Queen of England, who one day finds herself, while chasing an errant Corgi, wandering into the mobile library parked outside of Buckingham Palace. After exchanging pleasantries with the librarian and a palace kitchen employee named Norman, she borrows a book by Ivy Compton-Burnett. "She's not a popular author, ma'am," says the librarian. "Why, I wonder?" muses the queen. "I made her a dame."

Enticed by the diversion even the somewhat dry Compton-Burnett novel supplies, she progresses to *The Pursuit of Love* (see page 559) by Nancy Mitford ("Now," the queen quizzes the librarian, "didn't her sister marry the Mosley man? . . . And the mother-in-law of another sister was my mistress of the robes?"); J. R. Ackerley's *My Dog Tulip* (see page 5); and other volumes, under the improvised tutelage of the now-promoted Norman. Soon her eagerness to lose herself in books is disrupting the finely calibrated machinery of royal protocol, to the bafflement of her husband, the Duke of Edinburgh, the consternation of her private

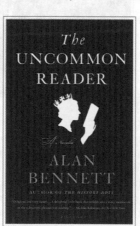

secretary, Sir Kevin, and the annoyance of the prime minister, who is put out at being quizzed on the books she lends him.

The court conspires to derail her literary education, but the queen is too clever to be caught in their stratagems, and continues to explore the commonwealth of letters with increasing admiration, devouring everything from showbiz memoirs—Lauren Bacall!—to the works of Jean Genet and Henry James. Bennett unspools his joke with a deft touch, gleefully skewering palace pretensions as he drops one witty literary reference after another into his narrative of a monarch's happy humbling by the majesty of books. Uncommonly funny, his little fable offers pleasures no book lover should forego.

What: Novella. **When:** 2007. **Reading Note:** Short and sweet, an evening's reading. **Also By:** *Writing Home* (1994). *The Clothes They Stood Up In* (2001). *Untold Stories* (2005). Among Bennett's plays are *The Madness of King George III* (1991) and *The History Boys* (2004). **Try:** *Seven Men* by Max Beerbohm. *Black Mischief* by Evelyn Waugh. **Adaptation:** Bennett's impeccably performed, unabridged audiobook is priceless. **Footnote:** Bennett first found fame with Dudley Moore, Jonathan Miller, and Peter Cook in the satirical revue *Beyond the Fringe*.

No Picnic on Mount Kenya

Felice Benuzzi (1910–1988)

A Flight of Fancy and Adventure in a Time of War

What a wonderful story: Three Italian prisoners of war, held in Kenya by the British during World War II, decide to alleviate the doldrums of their captivity by climbing the mountain—Africa's second highest—that looms over them. While it sounds like a plot concocted for a high-spirited film comedy, it is in fact entirely true, and Felice Benuzzi's firsthand account of his wartime exploit is an amusing, gripping, and singular narrative.

Having conceived the climb as a diversion from monotony, Benuzzi recruits two colleagues from among his Italian compatriots and then begins the arduous process of surreptitiously manufacturing the equipment they would need—no easy task under the circumstances. Yet the three manage to gather enough scrap metal and other materials to make crampons, ice axes, and other necessities at the same time as they squirrel away provisions. Setting out at last, they escape their confinement, elude capture, dodge rhinoceroses and other wild beasts, weather the onslaught of the elements, and, with resourcefulness and courage, master the taxing mountaineering

conditions Mount Kenya presents. As Benuzzi deftly tells it, their ascent of more than 16,000 feet is both perilous and exhilarating.

Upon completion of their mission—the way down is no easy trek, and it provides some of the book's best reading—the author and his two colleagues break back into the internment camp from which they had so ingeniously sprung themselves some two hundred pages earlier. Upon their reappearance, they are only half-heartedly punished for their escapade; the British commandant, in fact, expresses appreciation for their "sporting effort." As will the reader, for between the prisoners' departure and return, Benuzzi has treated us to a true-life tale filled with suspense, humor, bravery, and all the drama any armchair adventurer could desire. His book is a most unusual tale of escape, and a climbing classic to boot.

What: Adventure. War. *When:* 1947 in Italian; first English language edition, 1952. *Try: We Die Alone* by David Howarth (see page 391). *I Was a Stranger* by Sir John Winthrop Hackett (see page 343). *Nanda Devi* by Eric Shipton. *The Ascent of Rum Doodle* by W. E. Bowman (see page 90). *Love and War in the Apennines* by Eric Newby.

Beowulf

An Old English Action Hero

Surviving in one manuscript dating from around AD 1000, and believed to have been composed some two or three hundred years earlier, *Beowulf* is a poem composed in Old English, also known as Anglo-Saxon, a language worlds apart from even Chaucer's Middle English. Although written in England, the poem's action is set in Scandinavia; it centers

on the human warrior Beowulf's courageous encounters with three foes: the beast Grendel, whose fierce attacks have been terrifying the Danes; Grendel's mother, whom Beowulf battles in an underwater cavern; and, some fifty years on, an unnamed dragon who threatens Beowulf's homeland in southern Sweden and whom the hero dies defeating. The drama of these battles enlivens the heroic atmosphere the poet conjures: Beowulf's adventures unfold against a backdrop of stories and loyalties that, together with the monstrous nature of his adversaries, give this tale an ahistorical strangeness and power.

A large part of its force comes from the elemental fears the monsters summon, unnerving human pride by confronting it with the brute senselessness of death. The savage reality of Beowulf's antagonists—these fiends are never fanciful—inhabits what can only be described as a prescient psychological landscape: States of heart and mind are present as natural formations. Like the enigmatic rock wisdom of Stonehenge, terror looms with an expressive strength that is beyond our ability to explicate. "His fate hovered near, unknowable but certain."

Due to its singularity and antiquity, *Beowulf* was for generations a schoolroom staple, and untold numbers of students dutifully struggled to engage with the arcane text while glimpsing the tale's heraldry and drama. Nevertheless, it was not until 1936, when the poem was championed by Oxford don (and creator of *The Lord of the Rings*) J. R. R. Tolkien, that its stature as a work of literature, rather than a historical artifact, was widely recognized. While it has been translated into modern English scores of times, the poem's inherent character is perhaps most vividly captured in the version by Irish poet and Nobel Laureate Seamus Heaney. Heaney's lines lift their themes with a muscular music that echoes the original Anglo-Saxon alliterative form and four-beat metrics:

In off the moors, down through the mist bands
God-cursed Grendel came greedily loping.
The bane of the race of men roamed forth,
hunting for a prey in the high hall.
Under the cloud-murk he moved towards it
until it shone above him, a sheer keep
of fortified gold.

True to the sweep of the narrative and its heroic tenor, Heaney's language is also equal to the more reflective glory of the protagonist's old age, as in his evocation of

... the misery felt by an old man
who has lived to see his son's body
swing on the gallows. He begins to keen
and weep for his boy, watching the raven
gloat where he hangs: he can be of no help.
The wisdom of age is worthless to him.

Throughout his marvelous rendering, Heaney captures and holds fast the human feelings that animate this stirring saga.

What: Poetry. Antiquity. *When:* ca. 700-750. *Edition:* Seamus Heaney's version, 1999. *Further Reading:* Tolkien's essay, "*Beowulf:* The Monsters and the Critics." John Gardner's 1971 novel, *Grendel,* tells the monster's side of the story. *Try: The Sagas of Icelanders* (see page 692). *Adaptations:* There have been numerous adaptations of *Beowulf,* both live-action and animated, over the years. The latest, directed by Robert Zemeckis, was released in 2007.

Midnight in the Garden of Good and Evil
John Berendt (born 1939)

The Antiques Dealer, in the Study, with a Pistol

When *Esquire* columnist John Berendt began dividing his time between Manhattan and Savannah in the early 1980s, it wasn't with the idea of writing a book, much less breaking publishing records or single-handedly reinvigorating the tourist industry of the southern city. Savannah was simply an interesting, and much cheaper, place to hang out. Once there, charmed by the eccentric locals, the journalist in him began to sense something intriguing in a murder trial then in progress (for the second of what would ultimately be four times). By 1985, he'd taken up residence in Savannah and committed to writing a book about the city, and the sensibility and sensationalism that compelled his move: the aged mansions, the moss-laden trees, the gossip, the voodoo, and, of course, the murder.

The locals thought it sounded implausible—a book about them—and wondered who would buy it. But the result of Berendt's labors turned out to be just about as captivating as any book has ever been, and it spent four years on the *New York Times* bestseller list (in hardcover no less) thanks to its depiction of those very people: the malevolently stylish antiques dealer, Jim Williams, charged with the murder of a young hustler; the inventor who keeps pet flies on leashes and threatens to contaminate the city's water with a bottle of poison he possesses; the drag queen, known as the Lady Chablis, who uses Berendt as a chauffeur of sorts; the voodoo priestess Williams enlists to influence his trial with her powers; the list goes on. Published as "nonfiction," *Midnight in the Garden of Good and Evil* owes a heavy debt to the imaginative ambitions and techniques of fiction (for instance, Berendt begins his story before the murder happened and writes as if he'd been in Savannah at the time). No matter what's factual and what's fudged, it's all, truly, stranger than fiction, and more entertaining than most truth.

What: Memoir. **When:** 1994. **Also By:** *The City of Falling Angels* (2005). **Try:** *The Orchid Thief* by Susan Orlean. *The Devil in the White City* by Erik Larson. **Adaptation:** The 1997 movie, directed by Clint Eastwood and starring John Cusack and Kevin Spacey, was a box office disappointment after the bestselling success of the book.

A Fortunate Man
John Berger (1926–2017)
Photographs by Jean Mohr (born 1925)

The Story of a Country Doctor

John Berger produced a shelf of books that are curious in both senses of the word. He wrote a Booker Prize-winning novel (*G.*; 1972), an influential consideration of the power of visual images (*Ways of Seeing*; 1972), a searching correspondence with the painter John Christie (*I Send You This Cadmium Red . . .*; 2000), and a host of stories, essays, and documentaries that speak eloquently of his creative and political engagement.

A Fortunate Man is one of several volumes Berger made in collaboration with the photographer Jean Mohr. An assemblage of narrative episodes, passages of biographical profile, and both poetic and philosophical speculation on the labors of an English country doctor named John Sassall, its quiet power is amplified by Mohr's black-and-white images of Sassall, his patients, and the landscape in which they dwell. Whether depicting Sassall at the scene of an emergency ("His hands are at home on a body. Even these new wounds which had not existed twenty minutes before were familiar to him. . . . But now his very sureness made it seem to [the onlookers] that he was part of the accident: almost its accomplice") or evoking Sassall's concern for a young woman despairing of her prospects ("She is nubile in everything except her education and her chances"), Berger sensitively portrayed the human drama of the doctor-patient relationship. He was alert not only to his subject's empathy, but also, more tellingly, to the imagination and fitness of mind Sassall brought to the task of understanding the unvoiced feelings of the sick and their families. A carefully observed attempt to take the measure of the doctor's influence on an impoverished community's experience, *A Fortunate Man* is a probing meditation on medicine and meaning, conscience and commitment, and other matters of life and death.

What: Medicine. Anthropology. **When:** 1967. **Also By:** Nonfiction: *The Success and Failure of Picasso* (1965); *Another Way of Telling* (1982). Fiction: *Pig Earth* (1979); *To the Wedding* (1995); *From A to X* (2008). **Try:** *The Doctor Stories* by William Carlos Williams. *My Own Country* by Abraham Verghese. *The Soul of Medicine* by Sherwin B. Nuland. **Footnote:** Berger wrote screenplays for several films, including Alain Tanner's *Jonah Who Will Be 25 in the Year 2000*.

The Memoirs of Hector Berlioz
Hector Berlioz (1803–1869)

A Life of Love and Music

No other composer has been as accomplished in prose as Hector Berlioz. While his scores—among them the *Symphonie fantastique*, *Harold en Italie*, a spectacular requiem (*Grande Messe des morts*), and *Les Troyens*, an opera drawn from Virgil's *Aeneid*—prove him a musical master, his literary efforts—criticism, memoirs, letters—are imbued with a wit, passion, and intelligence that make them sheer pleasure to read. The delightful *Evenings with the Orchestra* (1852) is a treasury of tall tales, gossip, and musical critiques alleged by the author to have been read or recounted by the musicians of an unnamed orchestra "during the performance of bad operas." The reader's nights in the pit with these distracted musicians are wonderfully entertaining, but time spent with Berlioz's *Memoirs* is even more rewarding.

Beginning with the author's birth in a small French town, the memoir chronicles with leisurely but lively attention his education in music and in love, both of which, despite his talents and achievements, would lead more to disillusion than fulfillment. Yet he is an incurable Romantic in every sense, and a marvelous raconteur, as is soon made clear by his descriptions of his first encounter with the great Cherubini, who in a rage chases the young Berlioz from the library of the Paris Conservatoire, or his reaction to a trombone player's praise of a passage in his first full-scale orchestral work: "I was so elated that I went home with my head in the clouds and, not looking where I was going, twisted my ankle. I get a pain in my foot whenever I hear the piece. Others, perhaps, get a pain in the head."

He writes with fervor of his discovery of the artistic brilliance of both Shakespeare and Beethoven, and more fervor still of the passion that struck him when he watched the actress Harriet Smithson play the role of Ophelia in an English theater company's performance of *Hamlet* at the Odéon in 1827. The heartache

1892 advertisement for Berlioz's Les Troyens *(above)*

Caricature of Berlioz by Étienne Carjat (left)

caused by Berlioz's ardor for Smithson, and the couple's on-again, off-again liaison (their eventual marriage did not lead them to live happily ever after), runs like a leitmotif through the composer's reminiscences—as does his abundant creative energy and his bottomless disappointment at the unfavorable reception of his most ambitious later works, such as *La damnation de Faust* and *Les Troyens*.

Nonetheless, he narrates his tribulations, be they amorous or professional, with unflagging wit and inspiration, and his accounts of performances and travels (in Italy and Germany, in particular) are shot through with the emotional intensity of the Romantic sensibility his music expresses with such power and glory. Imagine a novel by Balzac or Dickens whose protagonist is as great a genius as the author, and you'll have some idea of the riches of these *Memoirs*.

What: Memoir. Music. *When:* 1870 in French; first translated into English in 1884. *Edition:* David Cairns's translation, first issued in 1969, is the one to look for. *Further Reading:* Cairns's superb two-volume biography, *The Making of an Artist, 1803–1832*

and *Servitude and Greatness, 1832–1869,* is highly recommended, as is Jacques Barzun's magnificent *Berlioz and the Romantic Century,* also in two volumes. *Try: Verdi: His Music, Life and Times* by George Martin.

The Diary of a Country Priest
Georges Bernanos (1888–1948)

A Novel That Explores the Enigma of Faith

One of the most intuitive and inspired explorations of religious faith in modern literature, Georges Bernanos's 1936 novel is a portrait of a humble and uncertain priest going quietly about the most significant business. The uncertainty of Bernanos's protagonist—an unnamed cleric in a village in rural France—is the key to the book's power and luminous beauty, for it is the author's achievement to depict faith in all its struggling hesitancy and inherent risk, dramatizing the truth that if faith were certitude, it wouldn't be faith.

Recording his daily rounds in his journal, the priest shares with us his visits to the families of his parish, his attendance on the sick, his distress that his parishioners' lives are not informed by spiritual concerns but rather by the earthly energies of money and pleasure. His relationships with an atheist physician, a rumor-mongering youth, and a local grandee

in despair at the death of her son are all fraught with his growing sense of his own failure. With his body succumbing to cancer, his soul thirsts for grace as he makes his way through this disenchanted world, a realm that seems stripped of divine presence and its consolations. And yet, through the quiet feeling with which the author suffuses his simple tale, the reader recognizes the providential blessings the priest has embodied, and the grand themes—good and evil, faith and fortitude, the pain and puzzle of mortality—that haunt even the landscapes of unbelief.

What: Novel. *When:* In French, 1936; English translation by Pamela Morris, 1937. *Also By: Under the Sun of Satan* (1926). *The Impostor* (1927). *Mouchette* (1937). *Monsieur Ouine* (1943). *Try: The Power and the Glory* by Graham Greene (see page 335). *Lying Awake* by Mark Salzman. *Gilead* by Marilynne Robinson (see page 670). *Adaptation:* Adapted for the screen in 1951 by Robert Bresson.

All the President's Men
Carl Bernstein (born 1944) and Bob Woodward (born 1943)

Two Reporters Chase the Story of Their Lives

June 17, 1972. Nine o'clock Saturday morning. Early for the telephone. Woodward fumbled for the receiver and snapped awake. The city editor of the Washington Post was on the line. Five men had been arrested earlier that morning in a burglary at Democratic headquarters, carrying photographic equipment and electronic gear. Could he come in?

Bob Woodward—twenty-nine, clean-cut Yale graduate, former Navy officer—had been

at the *Post* nine months and was finally getting bigger stories than a two-bit burglary like this one. Dejected by the assignment, he took it nonetheless, only to find that it wasn't the local HQ that had been burgled, but the Democratic National Committee offices, ironically located in the seat of Republican ruling-class opulence: the Watergate apartment complex. He also found Carl Bernstein—twenty-eight, shaggy-haired college dropout, full-time reporter since age nineteen—already working the story. That Saturday eight reporters contributed to

Sunday's front-page police-beat article about the five men in business suits (most of them Cuban, one of them a recently retired CIA security consultant) who sought to bug the offices of the DNC—why, nobody knew. Then the national staff went back to their usual beat, and Woodward and Bernstein were left to follow-up on what would turn out to be the investigative news story of the century; their reporting of it would lead to the downfall of President Richard Nixon (and a Pulitzer Prize for the two journalists).

Two years later they wrote the story again, this time between hard covers. *All the President's Men* follows their investigation from start to finish, this time taking readers behind the scenes, describing in detail their dogged efforts to uncover sources, pursue leads, and—as their most famous informant, "Deep Throat," had

THE MOST DEVASTATING DETECTIVE STORY OF THIS CENTURY

All The President's Men

CARL BERNSTEIN AND BOB WOODWARD

Now a film from Warner Bros. starring ROBERT REDFORD AND DUSTIN HOFFMAN

counseled them—follow the trail marked by money. The result is a vital historical document that also happens to be a riveting page-turner.

What: History. Journalism. Politics. *When:* 1974. *Also By:* The pair also co-authored *The Final Days* (1976), a behind-the-scenes account of the end of the Nixon presidency. *Try: Personal History* by Katharine Graham (see page 327). *Watergate: A Novel* by Thomas Mallon. *Adaptation:* The award-winning 1976 film stars Robert Redford and Dustin Hoffman. *Footnote:* Deep Throat unmasked himself in 2005: He was Mark Felt, who was Associate Director of the FBI at the time of the events described in *All the President's Men*. Soon after Felt's revelation, Woodward published *The Secret Man: The Story of Watergate's Deep Throat*, which included an essay by Bernstein.

The Stars My Destination
Alfred Bester (1913–1987)

A "Jaunte" into the Future

For science fiction, the 1950s represent a peak of achievement seldom matched before or since—a combination of innocence and ambition never quite equaled in decades to come, despite the dawning of a plethora of more sophisticated and elaborate speculative worlds. Certainly the preeminent author of the period, Alfred Bester, never subsequently reached the heights of his two milestone books, *The Demolished Man* (1953) and *The Stars My Destination* (1955). The latter novel in particular, arising from the imagination of a fellow who had been steeped since adolescence in the genre, remains an almost unduplicated example of the ramified intellectual and stylistic summits that science fiction can reach.

As the author related nearly twenty years after its publication, the book was inspired by the juxtaposition of his idea for a story following the betrayal, exile, and revenge-upon-return pattern of *The Count of Monte Cristo* (see page 238) with a *National Geographic* account of the survival of torpedoed sailors at sea. The real-life castaway who attracted Bester's "magpie mind" when reading that article was a cook's helper from the Philippines who was stranded for months on an open raft; crews of passing ships refused to rescue him because they thought him a decoy deployed by a Nazi submarine. The castaway was soon transformed into the protagonist of *The Stars My Destination*, the hopeful monster Gully Foyle, who is devil and savior rolled into one.

The first thing that hits the reader about this book is its commanding, jazzy voice—a bravura style which the author clearly relishes, and which his hero as clearly embodies: "Blasphemy came easily to him: it was half his speech, all his life. He had been raised in the gutter school of the twenty-fifth century and spoke nothing but the gutter tongue. Of all the brutes in the world he was among the least valuable alive and most likely to survive." The writing is a high-wire act balancing impatient exposition with a sort of baroque improvisation—sentences ricochet across the pages with a thrilling abandon that makes our progress along the taut plot line dizzyingly invigorating.

In the book's freakish and, in Gully's experience, feverish future, teleportation by strictly mental means (beautifully labeled "jaunting" by Bester) is a daily action open to all. The ability to "jaunte" gives everyone a kind of private power of social disruption; it's the catalyst and cornerstone of an imagined century of marvels and horrors, where ruling clans have adopted corporate identities, the outer solar system is at war with the inner planets, and one simple-minded plebeian spaceman holds the key to the conquest of all time and space. As Gully Foyle moves from outcast and hunted criminal to self-assured avenger and redeemer, the reader is treated to suspense in a hundred astonishing milieus, from lunar bacteria farms to cavernous prisons. Like Foyle in his famous bout of maddened synesthesia in chapter 15, we learn that ideas can pummel. *The Stars My Destination* is science fiction as a stunning assault on the reader's senses: bracing, vehement, breathtaking, and exhilarating fun every step of the way.

Despite his early success, Bester ultimately abandoned science fiction and worked at *Holiday* magazine for many years. At the end of his life, he consigned his estate to his favorite bartender, which some might see as a mark of his isolation and despair, but which others—Gully Foyle among them, perhaps—might consider a sign of world-weary grace.

What: Science Fiction. *When:* 1956. *Also By: Starlight: The Great Short Fiction of Alfred Bester* (1976). *Try: Saturn's Children* and *Neptune's Brood* by Charles Stross. *The Quantum Thief* and *The Fractal Prince* by Hannu Rajaniemi.

The Outermost House
Henry Beston (1888–1968)

A Year on a Cape Cod Beach

Henry Beston's account of a year spent in a small house at Eastham Beach on Cape Cod is a stirring evocation of nature and of solitude. His chapter "The Headlong Wave" articulates the grandeur and mystery of a roaring surf with as much beauty and accuracy as prose can muster, while his reports on aspects of the shore we seldom experience, such as the beach in winter or at night, are startling and visionary (don't miss his description of the "primeval ferocity and intensity of life" embodied by crowds of fish—predators and prey—swarming under a full moon).

It is just as rewarding to encounter the other phenomena he observes from his perch in the little house overlooking the North Atlantic and the dunes: the migration of shore and sea birds; the daily dramas of light and weather; the choreography of wind, sand, and ocean; the pageant of the changing seasons. Though it first appeared in 1928, *The Outermost House* remains vivid and satisfying, with an imaginative reach and stylistic eloquence that set it apart from most nature writing.

What: Nature. *When:* 1928. *Also By: The Book of Gallant Vagabonds* (1925). *Herbs and the Earth* (1935). *Northern Farm: A Chronicle of Maine* (1948). *Try: Cape Cod* by Henry David Thoreau. *The House on Nauset Marsh* by Wyman Richardson. *The Primal Place* by Robert Finch. *Adaptation:* In 1991, composer Ronald Perera set passages from *The Outermost House* to music in a piece for chorus, soprano soloist, narrator, and small instrumental ensemble. *Footnote:* In 1964, Beston's Outermost House was officially proclaimed a National Literary Landmark by the Governor of Massachusetts and the Secretary of the Interior. In the great hurricane of February 6–7, 1978, it was destroyed and washed out to sea.

Circa 1830 painting of Arjuna speaking with the god Krishna

Bhagavad Gita

The Battle for Meaning in Earthly Existence

" Every seeker has, at one time or another, to pass through a conflict of duties, a heart-churning," writes Mohandas K. Gandhi near the beginning of his commentary on the Hindu scripture called the Bhagavad Gita, and it is just such a moment that this ancient poem captures with dramatic force and philosophical power. The seeker in question is the warrior prince Arjuna, whose failure of nerve on the cusp of battle—he is paralyzed at the thought of killing his cousins and uncles in the internecine dynastic conflict being waged—prompts a dialogue with his charioteer, an incarnation of the god Krishna, who expounds profound lessons on duty and action, illusion and truth, attachment to the things of this world versus devotion to timeless spirituality.

There is no certainty about who wrote the Gita, or when; scholars have dated it anywhere between the third century BC and the sixth century of the modern era. At some point, it was incorporated into Hinduism's mammoth epic, the Mahabharata, but it appears to have been written later than the rest of the larger work. In any case, the Gita is a self-contained, complete, and wholly satisfying reading experience in its own right, and is often published separately. Replete with quotable wisdom, its verses have traveled far and wide: Thoreau brought a copy with him to Walden Pond, and when physicist J. Robert Oppenheimer recalled observing the explosion of the first atomic bomb outside of Alamogordo, New Mexico, in 1945, he invoked Krishna's description of himself as "the destroyer of worlds." The poem possesses an epigrammatic eloquence that makes its guidance applicable cross-culturally: "Set thy heart upon thy work, but never on its reward," is a key precept of its teaching, as is " . . . do thy duty, even if it be humble, rather than another's, even if it be great."

But, as Gandhi also pointed out, the Bhagavad Gita is not just an aphoristic work, but also a magnificent religious poem; it comprehends in its short but intense unfolding both the human anxieties of life and death and the divine continuities that should shape our response to them. Reading it closely is a harrowing experience, for its shifting dimensions reveal how transient our individual experience must always be. Yet there is also comfort in the poem's assurance of an eternal sincerity in the universe that offers fulfillment, if not reward.

What: Scripture. *When:* ca. 250 BC–AD 550. *Edition:* Recommended among the many translations are those by Juan Mascaró (quoted here), Eknath Easwaran, Barbara Stoler Miller, and, most recently, Amit Majmuder. *Further Reading: The Bhagavad Gita According to Gandhi* by Mohandas K. Gandhi. *The Bhagavad Gita: A Biography* by Richard H. Davis. *Try:* Composed centuries before the Gita, and more mystical and speculative in its themes, *The Upanishads* represent another seminal work of Hindu spirituality.

The Bible

Book Without End, Amen

....

In the beginning God created the heaven and the earth.

And the earth was without form, and void; and darkness was upon the face of the deep. And the Spirit of God moved upon the face of the waters.

And God said, Let there be light: and there was light.

And God saw the light, that it was good: and God divided the light from the darkness.

And God called the light Day, and the darkness he called Night. And the evening and the morning were the first day.

In the first chapter of the Book of Genesis—in just thirty-one short verses—the world is given form, light is summoned into being, Day and Night are named, Heaven hatched, the stars invoked, and Earth fashioned into land and sea, seeded with plants and populated with creatures. All in less than eight hundred words.

That the authority of the language in the most majestic English translation, the King James Version of 1611, seems commensurate with what it describes is astonishing. The confidence of the declarative eloquence—its cadenced sonorousness—evokes the eons that the stated chronology of seven days denies. The time is so deep only a spell can evince it, and the phrases resonate—albeit after years of echoing in churches and chambers of the imagination—like uncanny music conjuring a landscape equal to life's mysteries.

Genesis, of course, is the first of the nearly forty books in the Hebrew scripture or Old Testament that, combined with the four gospels—Matthew, Mark, Luke, and John—and the apostolic writings of the Christian New Testament, make up what is called the Bible. (Another set of books, known as the Apocrypha, are gathered outside the canonical testaments but often printed along with them.) One could write page upon page upon page without ever achieving clarity about the history, authorship, or composition of the great book, and that would be before one attempted to engage the religious, theological, and moral complexities it poses for this world and the next. One could read a thousand books about the Bible, covering subjects from archaeology to zoology, without beginning to exhaust the richness of its influence on civilization, culture, law, and literature.

But what's it like to read the Bible? Not puzzle over its provenance nor interpret its meaning, not make peace with its traditions nor argue with the inheritances they inform, not evangelize its teachings nor submit to its commandments, but simply *read* the narratives, poetry, historical chronicles, legends, observances, and revelations it encompasses? If we start with the first week of creation and make our way from the story of Adam and Eve through the tales of Abraham and Isaac, Noah and the flood, and Moses and the exodus of the Israelites from Egypt, we wander through a mythological realm that seems to be waiting at the back of our minds; there are battles and brave deeds (think David and Goliath) as well as figurative evocations of human realities (think the Tower of Babel) as memorable as any in literature. There are descriptions of rituals, admonitions to right conduct, and lists of strictures to govern body and soul. There are lamentations and prophecies, historical events and scenes of disaster as stark and terrifying as those conjured in dystopian fantasy or science fiction. Providence is often demanding and inscrutable, and divine retribution flows like a kind of supernatural resource, so much so that the territory of faith sometimes recalls the Theater of the Absurd. Supplications of enormous beauty (the Psalms) and poetry of romantic sensuality (the Song of Songs) in the Old Testament herald different kinds of comfort and love in the New. In relating the life of Jesus, from birth in a manger to Sermon on the Mount and death on the cross, the gospels deploy narrative methods—wonder tale, parable, passion play—as unconventional as the teachings they were meant to spread.

In short, reading the Bible is eerie, dramatic, beautiful, equivocal, infuriating, strange, for it is filled with knowledge that is inspired,

The Seven Plagues of Egypt *by Gustave Doré, 1866*

practical, mystical, and sometimes unintelligible. In its chapters and verses we discover a fathomless universe of character and circumstance rendered in literary modes that are varied and surprising, and often cryptic and oblique. The meanings of what we read in the Bible seem to change their color, if not their substance, depending on the context in which we consider them; this is by no means to say biblical truths are malleable, but rather that life is.

Reading the Bible is also, in long stretches, boring, and since even the most devout reader's life is not eternal, there is no reason not to skip what doesn't speak to you and dwell longer on what does. But don't miss the following books in the Old Testament: Genesis, Exodus, Ruth, the Book of Job (see page 78), Psalms, Proverbs, Ecclesiastes, the Song of Songs, Isaiah, Lamentations, and the Book of Daniel; and in the New: the four gospels, the Acts of the Apostles, and the Revelation of Saint John. While there are myriad translations available, try first the stately and blessedly archaic King James Version. Composed by a committee of churchmen and scholars led by Lancelot Andrewes (1555–1626), it is one of the most beautiful and influential works in English literature. Its language, by inspiration and accumulated lore, opens endlessly, like a door swinging wide on hinges of phrase, fable, and faith to reveal the profundity of human experience without supposing to explain it.

What: Scripture. *When:* The components of the Old Testament were written over a span of roughly one thousand years, beginning in the twelfth century BC. The New Testament was set down in the second half of the first century AD. *Reading Note:* If the King James Version proves too knotty in places, turn to a contemporary version, such as *The Revised English Bible* for smoother passages; there are many options, ranging from the scholarly to the evangelical to the vernacular. *Further Reading:* On the composition and compilation of the Bible, turn to Richard Elliott Friedman's *Who Wrote the Bible?* for the Old Testament, and Burton L. Mack's *Who Wrote the New Testament?* for the New. For the story of the Bible's place in culture and belief, try Christopher de Hamel's *The Book: A History of the Bible* and Karen Armstrong's *The Bible: A Biography*. *The Book of God: A Response to the Bible* by Gabriel Josipovici revealingly considers the whole as more than the sum of its parts, and *God's Secretaries: The Making of the King James Bible*, by Adam Nicolson, is a sprightly and informative narrative.

||||||||||||||||||||||||||||||||||||||||| B O O K N O T E |||||||||||||||||||||||||||||||||||||||||

WHAT DID I DO TO DESERVE THIS?

The Book of Job
As translated by Stephen Mitchell

We all know the story of patient, long-suffering Job. Or think we do: A blameless man undergoes tribulations for no apparent reason, losing all his worldly possessions, suffering great physical pain and indignity, being pushed to the very edge of endurance before cursing the day he was born, if not the God who allows him to be afflicted with such torments. At last, his reversed fortunes are set right, and his prosperity and good health restored—but that, frankly, seems small comfort given the trials he has undergone.

Job's tale is the Bible's profound and unsettling meditation on suffering, justice, and the inscrutability of life. It begins in prose (as it will close), introducing the legend of the pious man from the land of Uz and revealing what Job himself never knows: that the miseries visited upon him result from a bet between God and the Accusing Angel (whom we might as well call Satan), who is sure Job's piety is a consequence of the blessings bestowed upon him rather than true love of the Lord. What would happen if those blessings disappeared?

Disappear they will, and with a vengeance, as the heavenly kibitzers look on. The narrative turns to verse to detail the horrible events that bring Job low and to record the conversations he takes up with friends in an attempt to explain his misfortunes. These exchanges are animated with speculations on the state of Job's soul and the motivations of what can only be construed as an angry Almighty; they are lively with caustic argument and complaint—the parry and thrust of the dialogue gives this ancient legend a bracingly modern air.

When God finally deigns to respond to Job's plea for a stay against his confusion, the voice that comes from "within the whirlwind" speaks with an authority that is otherworldly, resonant with strength, terror, and beauty; it offers not consolation, but rather a vision of the awesome dimensions of creation that render futile any earthly demand for understanding:

> Have you ever commanded the morning
>   or guided dawn to its place—
> to hold the corners of the sky
>   and shake off the last few stars?
> All things are touched with color;
>   the whole world is changed.

You can read the Book of Job in countless translations, but through Stephen Mitchell's particular eloquence (abetted by his insightful introductory essay) the reader is powerfully reminded that the tale is prayer as well as story; its words are infused with the searching, impulsive expressiveness of need. In no other writing save the Greek tragedies is the sheer challenge of human existence (to say nothing of the dark majesty of divinity) so boldly assayed.

American Prometheus

THE TRIUMPH AND TRAGEDY OF J. ROBERT OPPENHEIMER

Kai Bird (born 1951) and Martin J. Sherwin (born 1937)

A Hamlet of the Atomic Age

After J. Robert Oppenheimer's death in 1967, his longtime colleague Isidor Rabi remembered him in this way: "In Oppenheimer, the element of earthiness was feeble. Yet it was essentially this spiritual quality, this refinement as expressed in speech and manner, that was the basis of his charisma. He never expressed himself completely. He always left a feeling that there were depths of sensibility and insight not yet revealed."

Kai Bird and Martin J. Sherwin are well aware of the mysteries surrounding the brilliant man most famous for his role as director of the Manhattan Project, which built the first atomic bomb. It is a paradoxical but undeniable measure of their achievement in this magnificent biography that their scholarship informs our understanding of Oppenheimer's private and public lives—indeed, our understanding of twentieth-century science, politics, and warfare as well—without reducing their subject to a figure less complicated and enigmatic than he was. Like a scientific Hamlet, Oppenheimer was pressed by circumstance and unresolved ambition to assume roles fraught with discomfort and moral ambiguity, so much so that his immense intellectual capacity became, like the Danish prince's, a dark chamber echoing with questions, ruminations, and contradictory truths. Describing his reaction to the successful explosion of the first test bomb in the New Mexican desert, he would invoke a line from the Bhagavad Gita (see page 75): "Now I am become death, the destroyer of worlds." That the man who led the scientific mobilization to create a weapon of unparalleled destructive power could also call Hindu scripture readily to mind gives some inkling of the puzzling figure brought to life in American Prometheus.

Oppenheimer knew the Bhagavad Gita because he had taught himself Sanskrit as a student, and Bird and Sherwin do justice to his cultural omnivorousness as well as his scientific genius. Their depiction of his alternately

Oppenheimer (left) and Leslie Groves at the Trinity Bomb site

brilliant and troubled training at Cambridge and Göttingen—he left a poisoned apple on the desk of a rival in England, and his fellow students in Germany (including a future Nobel Prize-winner) signed a petition threatening to boycott a seminar on quantum mechanics unless the professor stopped the American from interrupting—is compelling, as is their attention to both his tangled emotional commitments and his role in the charged network of modern physicists. Most importantly, of course, the authors chronicle with insight and judiciousness Oppenheimer's extraordinary achievements at Los Alamos and the political machinations that led to his being stripped of top-security clearance in the mid-1950s. A vivid depiction of many of the twentieth century's most telling themes, American Prometheus is a riveting narrative and a moving portrait of an individual of tempered, even tortured, nobility.

What: Biography. History. **When:** 2005. **Award:** Pulitzer Prize for Biography, 2006. **Further Reading:** The Making of the Atomic Bomb by Richard Rhodes. 109 East Palace: Robert Oppenheimer and the Secret City of Los Alamos by Jennet Conant. **Try:** Heisenberg's War: The Secret History of the German Bomb by Thomas Powers (see page 639).

The Complete Poems, 1927–1979
Elizabeth Bishop (1911–1979)

A Poet's Poet and a Reader's Delight

Elizabeth Bishop served as Poet Laureate of the United States, won a Pulitzer Prize and a National Book Award, and taught at Harvard and MIT. Yet upon her death in 1979, her achievement was still little known outside of literary circles. She produced a concentrated body of verse over the course of her long career, and all of it is collected in this volume. And while it's rather slim as collected works go, it is rich with unassuming splendor.

Bishop's poetry revels in place, and single stanzas can conjure entire geographies. She lived in Brazil for fifteen years (she also translated several volumes of Portuguese literature), and in many of her poems the South American landscape comes into view, as does the Nova Scotian landscape of her early childhood. Her depictions of the world around her are unadorned and exact, alert to mundane and local facts—fish scales, the oil-soaked surfaces of a filling station, a moose in the middle of a road—in a way which suggests that even the smallest realities are infinitely bigger than one might guess.

In her letters (magnificent reading in themselves), Bishop often confessed to uncertainty and fear, and her poetry is infused with a peculiar and remarkable diffidence. Her lines proceed with a sense of apprehension that the poem as a whole transforms into a permanent awareness that is unassuming, inevitable, and profoundly surprising—often all at the same time. She distills essences of Wordsworth, Emily Dickinson, and even William Carlos Williams into something completely her own, and quite unforgettable.

What: Poetry. *When:* 1983. *Awards:* Bishop was awarded the Pulitzer Prize for Poetry in 1956 and the National Book Award in 1970 for earlier books containing the poetry collected in this volume. *Also By: The Collected Prose* (1984). *One Art: Letters* (1994). *Words in Air: The Complete Correspondence Between Elizabeth Bishop and Robert Lowell* (2008). *Further Reading: Becoming a Poet: Elizabeth Bishop with Marianne Moore and Robert Lowell* by David Kalstone. *Try: The Poems of Marianne Moore. Water Street* by James Merrill. *The Blue Estuaries* by Louise Bogan.

Friday Night Lights
A TOWN, A TEAM, AND A DREAM
H. G. Bissinger (born 1954)

All Hopes on High School Football

It was his instinct for a good story that brought Philadelphia-based investigative reporter H. G. Bissinger to Odessa, Texas. He was intrigued by the fact that crowds of twenty thousand attended the Friday night football games of the Permian High School "Mojo" Panthers. Twenty thousand fans at a high school football game? What could that be about? Bissinger found out, studying "Mojo madness" by living with the Permian players, coaches, fans, and other townspeople during the 1988 season, in which, after a rough start, the team made a run at the state championship.

Even readers with no interest in football are likely to be fascinated by the surprising world that Bissinger describes so well—a world in which a lot of adults have a big stake in whether teenage football players win or lose. Those players, in turn, enjoy the indulgence of teachers and the adulation of the crowd, but soon find themselves lost in the off-field shadows once their youthful season is done; as the Permian coach, Gary Gaines, at one point tells them, "Gentlemen, the hopes and dreams of an entire town are riding on your shoulders. You may never matter again in your life as much as you do right now." Gaines certainly knows the stakes: Two tough losses lead townsmen to plant "For Sale" signs on his front lawn.

If the burdens the young athletes bear are symptomatic of America's consuming obsession with sports, there's no denying that their gridiron efforts nourish the life of their community. Bissinger carefully balances cultural concerns with human interest in his portrayal of a communal passion that is both seductive and scary; the result is a book that is compelling in every way.

What: Sports. *When:* 1990. *Edition:* The 2000 paperback edition includes "a new afterword on the town and players ten years later." *Also By: A Prayer for the City* (1997). *Three Nights in August: Strategy, Heartbreak, and Joy Inside the Mind of a Manager* (2005). *Try: Twelve Mighty Orphans* by Jim Dent. *Adaptations:* A movie version of *Friday Night Lights* starring Billy Bob Thornton was released in 2004. A television series loosely based on the book and movie ran on NBC for five seasons, beginning in 2006.

The Emperor's Last Island
A JOURNEY TO ST. HELENA
Julia Blackburn (born 1948)

A Mesmerizing Exploration of Napoleon's Final Act

What a beguiling journey through history and geography this is. Its emperor is Napoleon and his island is St. Helena, "further away from anywhere than anywhere else in all the world." In a manner deceptively offhand and in a voice immediately engaging, Julia Blackburn leads us to the fortress-like dot in the middle of the South Atlantic to which Bonaparte was exiled after the Battle of Waterloo. Tracking the last six years of the emperor's life, Blackburn depicts their peculiar setting and surreal circumstances with thoughtful scrutiny, sorting through the tangle of legend, testimony, and invention that still surrounds Napoleon's captivity and death. Her portrait of the great man of action—plump, middle-aged, drifting through the days, held in thrall by the extremities of nature and the precautions of his enemies—is filled with a bewildering, affecting sadness as she bears witness to his circumscribed routine of gardening, working on his memoirs, and cheating at cards. A small retinue of loyal companions (including a pastry chef) compete for his attention. Blackburn's own expedition to the distant redoubt adds a

Napoleon in exile

resonating intelligence to her unconventional research.

Personal, quirky, unpredictable, this book puts us on the receiving end of a rich and delightfully curious set of dispatches; so quiet is its originality, so supple its intuition, that readers may be slow to recognize that they are being addressed by a writer of no small genius. Fortunately for them, any doubt on that score can be erased by acquaintance with Blackburn's subsequent books, which include *Daisy Bates in the Desert* (1994), a stunning account of the legendary figure who in 1913, at fifty-four years of age, went to live among the Aborigines in South Australia; *The Leper's Companions* (1999), a daring novel that magically follows a modern woman's melancholy to a medieval English village and on a pilgrimage to the Holy Land; and *The Three of Us* (2008), the harrowing, generous story of the author's upbringing by deeply troubled parents. But start with a voyage to *The Emperor's Last Island.*

What: History. Geography. Travel. *When:* 1991. *Also By: The Book of Color* (1995). *Old Man Goya* (2002). *With Billie* (2005). *Further Reading: Napoleon: A Life* by Andrew Roberts is an excellent biography. *Try: Napoleon Symphony* by Anthony Burgess. *In Patagonia* by Bruce Chatwin.

Songs of Innocence and of Experience
William Blake (1757–1827)

A Visionary's Testament—in Words and Pictures

The remarkable thing about William Blake is that he was a visionary genius twice over—he is one of Britain's greatest visual artists and one of the greatest poets in the English language. He was also a fiercely independent and rebellious thinker: "I must Create a System or be enslaved by another Man's." His twofold artistry and unyielding individuality are seen to best effect in his illuminated books, the first of which was *Songs of Innocence and of Experience*. It is among the most beautiful books ever produced, an unparalleled marriage of word and image. Blake handcrafted the book himself, creating illuminated plates using a singular process that was partly his own invention. According to a scholar of Blake's work, "he covered a copper plate with acid-proof wax, engraved away the wax from a design that incorporated both text and pictorial illustration, then applied acid so that the design was left in relief. With this plate he printed a page, which he later colored with watercolors by hand and bound with the other pages to make up a volume." The result, as anyone who has seen the originals knows, is breathtaking.

Blake intended *Songs of Innocence and of Experience* to show "the two contrary states of the human soul." The innocent verses are "happy songs / Every child may joy to hear." Perhaps the best known of these short lyrics is "The Lamb," with its nursery-rhyme description of Christ ("He is meek & he is mild, / He became a little child"). The songs of experience are dark, pessimistic, even a bit terrifying. They include several well-known poems, such as "London" and, perhaps most famous of all, "The Tyger":

> Tyger! Tyger! burning bright
> In the forests of the night,
> What immortal hand or eye
> Could frame thy fearful symmetry?

Blake's illumination for "The Lamb" from Songs of Innocence and of Experience

Blake created fifty-four illuminated plates for *Songs of Innocence and of Experience*. Editions containing full-color reproductions are readily available and obviously preferred.

What: Poetry. Art. *When:* Songs of Innocence, 1789; *Songs of Innocence and of Experience*, 1794. *Also By:* Poetical Sketches (1783). The Marriage of Heaven and Hell (1790–93). America: A Prophecy (1793). Milton: A Poem (ca. 1804–20). Jerusalem: The Emanation of the Giant Albion (ca. 1804–20). The Complete Poetry and Prose of William Blake (edited by Erdman and Bloom; revised edition, 1982). *Further Reading: Blake* by Peter Ackroyd. *Eternity's Sunrise: The Imaginative World of William Blake* by Leo Damrosch. *Try:* The poetry of Samuel Taylor Coleridge. *Adaptation:* Don't miss William Bolcom's magnificent, complete, and stylistically eclectic musical setting, composed over a twenty-five-year period and recorded in 2004.

The Wilder Shores of Love
Lesley Blanch (1904–2007)

The Adventures of Four "Realists of Romance"

Adventure presents itself more often than we acknowledge, and in many guises: as accident, as disaster, as longing, or as love. What distinguishes adventurers from the rest of us is the courage that compels them to take up the reins when excitement beckons and ride where it leads without any map. The four nineteenth-century women profiled in this book were adventurers indeed, following their hearts, misfortunes, and desires right out of their own time and place, into an East that promised fruits forbidden in their native Europe.

Lesley Blanch's pioneering group biography tells their stories with scholarly attention, literary style, and romantic panache. It's hard not to get swept up in her narrative of the travails of French heiress Aimée Dubucq de Rivery, "a convent girl captured by corsairs and flung into the harem of the Grand Turk," or the travels of Jane Digby, also known as Lady Ellenborough, a society beauty who "smashed all the taboos of her time," fleeing midlife sorrow to live in the Syrian desert with a Bedouin sheik. Then there's the Victorian Catholic Isabel Burton, who abandoned the conformity suggested by those two descriptors when she wed the iconoclastic explorer Richard Burton,

Isabelle Eberhardt in Arabian guise, ca. 1899

whose exploits in Arabia and Africa provided his devoted spouse with tantalizing tastes of vicarious transgression. The last member of Blanch's venturesome quartet, Isabelle Eberhardt, was a Russian-born woman who, disguised as a man, went to live among the Arabs; her haunting stories and diaries are filled with a strangely prophetic sense of the emptiness that would be invoked some decades later by writers as different as Albert Camus and Paul Bowles.

"Each of them, in her own way," Blanch writes, "used love as a means of individual expression, of liberation. . . ." In an exotic landscape, far across the borders of the manners and mores of their age, these women—lured onward by "glowing horizons of emotion and daring"—imagined unconventional destinies, and for both good and ill, embraced them. Blanch relates their lives with intelligence and captivating sympathy.

What: Biography. *When:* 1954. *Also By: The Sabres of Paradise* (1960). *Journey into the Mind's Eye: Fragments of an Autobiography* (1968). *Pierre Loti* (1983). *Further Reading: The Oblivion Seekers* by Isabelle Eberhardt. *The Romance of Isabel Lady Burton* (autobiography). *Try: The Destiny of Isabelle Eberhardt* by Cecily Mackworth. *Rebel Heart: The Scandalous Life of Jane Digby* and *A Rage to Live: A Biography of Richard and Isabel Burton* by Mary S. Lovell.

Are You There God? It's Me, Margaret.
Judy Blume (born 1938)

A Still Small Voice—in Farbrook, New Jersey

If, as the adage goes, history is written by the victors, fiction of the first-person variety is usually written by the wise guys, especially if the fiction in question concerns adolescents or teenagers (think Holden Caulfield). Or at least it was until Judy Blume wrote *Are You There, God? It's Me, Margaret* at the end of the 1960s. Narrated by Margaret Simon, an almost twelve-year-old who moves from New York City to the Jersey suburbs, Blume's novel for young readers engages, with directness and a strong dose of appropriate preteen bewilderment, themes seldom treated so familiarly at the time. Top of the list is the perplexity Margaret feels—abetted by her grandparents' unhelpful meddling—over her lack of religious affiliation due to her parents' interfaith marriage; following close behind are the mysteries of menstruation, the awkwardness of buying her first bra, fear of not fitting in with her new classmates, and envy of more popular and more well-developed friends.

While these subjects may seem tame today, they weren't back then. Nonetheless, it's not the topical bravery of Blume's book that delivers its real distinction, but rather a deeper insight that she gives expression to through Margaret's diary and prayers: that the urgent secrets of adolescence are not rebelliousness and precociousness, but timidity and confusion. By making her book not an escape from these anxious states, but rather a stage for their articulation, Blume gave both Margaret and countless other preteen readers an agency that was a form of liberation, a license to explore the interiority that is at the heart of growing up—and of reading, too. Teaching kids to recognize the value of their inner voice when all the outer ones are shouting more loudly is no small gift, which explains in part why Blume's book is so beloved. Its influence on the minds of readers may be as deep as that of any book published in its era, and the many shelves of diary fiction that are produced each year are a tribute to its lasting influence on our collective imagination.

What: Children's. *When:* 1970. *Also By:* *Tales of a Fourth Grade Nothing* (1972). *Otherwise Known as Sheila the Great* (1972). *Forever* (1975). *Superfudge* (1980). *Tiger Eyes* (1981). *Try: The Great Gilly Hopkins* by Katherine Paterson. *Anastasia Krupnik* by Lois Lowry. *This One Summer* by Mariko Tamaki and Jillian Tamaki (see page 772).

Akenfield
PORTRAIT OF AN ENGLISH VILLAGE
Ronald Blythe (born 1922)

An Autobiography in the Words of Others

A blacksmith and a bellringer, schoolmasters and a magistrate, farmers and clergy, the district nurse and the local vet, a samaritan and a grave-digger (who is given, of course, the last word): such are the forty-nine men and women, ranging in age from seventeen to eighty-eight, whose voices animate this rich, rare book, speaking to us directly of their works and days in the rural county of Suffolk. The fiftieth voice, belonging to Ronald Blythe, himself born and raised in these East Anglian precincts, links the narratives with sensitive intelligence. "The book is more the work of a poet than a trained oral historian," Blythe has explained, "a profession I had never heard of when I wrote it. My only real credential for having written it was that I was native to its situation in nearly every way and had only to listen to hear my own world talking. Thus a thread of autobiography runs strongly through it. . . . I was able to structure their talk over farming, education, welfare, class, religion and indeed life and death in terms such as I myself was experiencing these things, although now with a writer's vision of them."

While the names of village and villagers have been changed, the honest and evocative monologues ring with authenticity. The collective testimony, captured in the mid-1960s, paints a vivid picture of a community in which the vast changes of the twentieth century are met by deep continuities of history, tradition, and nature. The chorus of voices lingers in the mind long after one has finished reading. Indeed, *Akenfield*, in the sum of its unassuming parts, transcends its disguise as a reportorial study to reveal a great poetic drama shaped with character and care. What Blythe has painted is the landscape of human fate itself, in the common colors of labor and experience, and in the hues of individual memory and meaning.

What: History. Place. **When:** 1969. *Also By: The View in Winter: Reflections on Old Age* (1979; another oral history). *Divine Landscapes* (1986). *First Friends* (1997). *Word from Wormingford: A Parish Year* (1997). *Going to Meet George and Other Outings* (1999). *Try: Passing the Time in Ballymenone* by Henry Glassie (see page 317).

> **"I have a lot of my grandfather's features, although I'm not so tall as he was. I have his hands. Hands last a long time, you know. A village sees the same hands century after century. It is a marvelous thing but it's true."**
> —*Gregory Gladwell, Blacksmith*

....

The Decameron
Giovanni Boccaccio (1313–1375)

An Early Renaissance Human Comedy

The storytelling of Boccaccio's *Decameron* takes place under a fierce deadline, as in another fabled compendium of tales, *The Arabian Nights* (see page 21). While the princess Shahrazad spins her nightly enchantments to avoid the fatal violence of King Shahryār, the Florentine aristocrats—seven women and three men—who narrate the one hundred stories of *The Decameron* fashion a more relaxed but no less desperate response to gruesome terror. Fleeing their native city to escape the ravages of the Black Death (the bubonic plague that claimed the lives of more than half of Florence's denizens in the middle of the fourteenth century), Boccaccio's elegant evacuees have retreated to a villa in the countryside. Having taken their bodies out of harm's way, they devote their minds to a round-robin of story, telling one tale apiece on each of ten nights devoted to diversion. Like Shahrazad, they discover that storytelling offers more than escape from harsh realities: In the leisurely urgency of their invention, stories provide the most beguiling way of embracing—and extending—the hardiness of life.

Portrait of Giovanni Boccaccio, likely created in the 17th century

Many of the narratives in *The Decameron* are famously, and scandalously, ribald, and all the more life-affirming for their avowal of the pleasures of the flesh. Boccaccio's endlessly ingenious euphemistic evocation of sexual activity—"grinding at the mill," "giving the wool a good whacking," "[she] lay in his arms and taught him how to sing a good half-dozen of her husband's hymns"—enlivens his accounts of lovers faithful or conniving, clergy faithless *and* conniving, and all manner of practical jokers and passionate schemers. The vitality of his writing exhibits for the first time in prose, really, the literary vigor of the Italian vernacular, roughly three decades after Dante had done the same in poetry by eschewing Latin in the composition of *The Divine Comedy* (see page 194).

Interestingly, it was Boccaccio who appended the adjective *divina* to the work Dante himself called merely *la commedia. The Decameron*, in contrast, is very much a *human* comedy. Where Dante articulates medieval ideals, encompassing both sin and love in a theological vision calibrated in one hundred carefully wrought verse cantos, Boccaccio celebrates, in one hundred prose narratives, the more worldly urges—

mercantile, calculating, crafty, erotic—of the dawning Renaissance, unashamedly rescuing sin from hell and love from heaven. What Dante sends spinning into ethereal realms, Boccaccio gleefully brings back to earth for readers to recognize as their own worldly, incorrigible, and often happy inheritance.

What: Literature. *When:* 1353. *Edition:* Wayne A. Rebhorn's lively 2013 translation of the complete *Decameron* is recommended. *Further Reading:* The Norton Critical Edition, which features a selection of the tales in excellent translations by Mark Musa and Peter Bondanella, provides valuable critical and historical context. *Try: The Canterbury Tales* by Geoffrey Chaucer (see page 150). *The Fabliaux,* translated by Nathaniel E. Dubin. *Adaptation:* Pier Paolo Pasolini's *The Decameron* (1971) is the most notable of several film adaptations.

2666
Roberto Bolaño (1953–2003)

Last Testament of an Unquiet Imagination

There's no point trying to summarize the plot of *2666*, the enigmatic, apocalyptic, gloriously messy final novel by the madly brilliant Chilean novelist Roberto Bolaño. It's five books in one, really, and each of those contains multitudes in itself. Set mostly in "Santa Teresa," a fictional Mexican town that stands in for the dangerous border city of Ciudad Juárez, the five novellas grafted together into one engulfing narrative feature countless intertwining plot lines. Literary critics pursue a reclusive writer (one of his books is about seaweed); a professor is haunted by voices and panicking about his daughter's safety; and a former Black Panther turns hard-boiled American journalist. All of their stories are circling around the central horror of the novel, which is based on a real crime wave: the grisly murders of hundreds of women, for no clear reason and with no resolution.

Like one of his own capacious and indefinable literary inventions, Bolaño's life is an amalgam of promise, mystery, achievement, surprise, and baffling yet tantalizing significance; in a word, it's fascinating. The son of a truck driver, he lived in Mexico as a teenager, returned to Chile to support the socialist president Salvador Allende ahead of the 1973 coup, and spent the rest of his life in exile, mostly in Spain. In his later years, he became a giant of Spanish-language literature, but it wasn't until after his premature death at the age of fifty that the English-speaking world began to grasp the luxuriant urgency of his unique style, which forgoes neat plots and safe resolutions for high-wire experimentation. *2666*, his last and greatest book, is too slippery to capture. This labyrinthine work of fiction, one of the first great novels of the new century, simply has to be read: Inspiring itself (and the reader) as it goes along, it explodes the idea of the novel as a careful construction to create a work of impulsive energy and expressionism.

What: Novel. *When:* 2004. *Edition:* Translated from the Spanish by Natasha Wimmer (2008). *Also By: Nazi Literature in the Americas* (1996). *The Savage Detectives* (1998). *By Night in Chile* (2000). *Antwerp* (2002). *Try: On Heroes and Tombs* by Ernesto Sabato. *Gravity's Rainbow* by Thomas Pynchon (see page 650). *Your Face Tomorrow* by Javier Marías.

The Book of Common Prayer

Faith in Language

The Church of England's Book of Common Prayer was first published in 1549, and, while it has gone through several revisions in response to shifts in political power and fluctuations in ecclesiastical fashion, it has been in continuous use ever since. Issued under the steward-ship of Thomas Cranmer, who served as Archbishop of Canterbury during and after the reign of Henry VIII (and so through the tumultuous years of the English Reformation), it was the first manual of worship in English, making available to ordinary people the words of the rituals and observances that had previously been the province of priests, formulated in Latin.

The Book of Common Prayer encompasses daily services, annual liturgical festivals and holidays, baptism, marriage, the burial of the dead, prayers for rain and fair weather, and prayers for safety from famine, war, and sickness. It provides a prayerful passage through the calendar year as well as through the milestones of a lifetime. As such, it composed a framework for the language of belief that soon reached beyond Anglicanism to other denominations, and beyond England to other shores.

Perhaps more enduringly, Cranmer's words and his inspired editing and recasting of other sources (including the Roman missal) represent an eternally rich vein in English speech and literature, reflecting the most meaningful moments of experience in brilliant and precious phrases, from "to have and to hold from this day forward" to "ashes to ashes, dust to dust."

To be sure, one wouldn't *read* the Book of Common Prayer in the same way one reads most other books; for all its beauty and significance, it is a devotional, purpose-built to help believers mark the year and find consolation for their private tribulations in the common measure of a public language. Like poetry, the prayers this book contains describe a space in which thoughts can congregate and gather strength, a stillness that even non-believers can visit time and again to refresh their spirits amidst an eloquence filled with both humility and grandeur.

What: Religion & Spirituality. *When:* First edition, 1549, with notable revisions in 1552, 1662, and 1928. *Further Reading: The Book of Common Prayer: Past, Present and Future,* edited by Prudence Dailey. *Try: Four Quartets* by T. S. Eliot (see page 249).

■ For *The Book of Job*, see page 78.

Ficciones
Jorge Luis Borges (1899–1986)

A 20th-Century Fabulist

Born in Argentina, Jorge Luis Borges began to receive international literary attention in the 1960s, and quickly came to be regarded as a modern master, one of the most original and influential writers of the twentieth century. "Borges [ranks] among the few fresh dreamers since Poe and Baudelaire," declared critic George Steiner when the Argentinian writer

was still living. "He has, that being the mark of a truly major artist, deepened the landscape of our memories."

Although he worked in many forms, Borges's lasting fame rests on his short stories. They are usually unconventional examples of the genre, often masquerading as learned essays. For example, one of Borges's best-known works is "Pierre Menard, Author of *Don Quixote.*" It takes the form of a bibliographic "note" about a remarkable literary undertaking: As we learn to our dizzied amazement, Pierre Menard, a twentieth-century man of letters, set himself the task of writing the sixteenth-century masterpiece *Don Quixote*. It's not what you first think; let Borges explain: "He did not want to compose another *Don Quixote*—which would be easy—but *the Don Quixote*. It is unnecessary to add that his aim was never to produce a mechanical transcription of the original; he did not propose to copy it. His admirable ambition was to produce pages which would coincide—word for word and line for line—with those of Miguel de Cervantes." Borges plays with this beguiling premise for a mere ten pages, but the result is endlessly ponderable, mind-expanding in an exhilarating and mysterious way.

Jorge Luis Borges

Because Borges's uncanny fables seldom resemble typical short stories, his works are frequently called "fictions"—which is precisely what *Ficciones* means. In addition to "Pierre Menard," the volume includes sixteen pieces, including several masterpieces, such as "The Library of Babel," "Tlön, Uqbar, Orbis Tertius," "The Garden of the Forking Paths," and "Funes, the Memorious." The latter is a brief, haunting memoir of a man who, after an accident, finds himself possessed by cripplingly acute mental powers. His "implacable memory" makes life literally unforgettable. That's also the word for Borges's intricate, erudite, playfully dream-weaving work.

What: Short Stories. **When:** *Ficciones,* was published in Spanish in Buenos Aires in 1944; in 1962, it became the first Borges collection available in English. *Edition:* A new translation, by Andrew Hurley, appears in the volume *Collected Fictions,* issued in 1998. *Also By: Selected Non-Fictions* (1999). *Selected Poems* (1999). *A Personal Anthology* (1967) is an excellent cross-genre selection. *Further Reading: With Borges,* by Alberto Manguel, is an evocative memoir of the hours Manguel—at the time a sixteen-year-old bookstore clerk—spent reading aloud to the blind Borges, who was then in his sixties. *Try: The Invention of Morel* by Adolfo Bioy Casares.

■ For James Boswell's *The Life of Samuel Johnson*, see page 418.

The Death of the Heart
Elizabeth Bowen (1899–1973)

A Gem from a Jeweler of Emotions

The opening of *The Death of the Heart,* Elizabeth Bowen's discerning portrayal of one woman's coming-of-age and another's realization that her own period of becoming has come and gone, reveals the power of perception this author calibrates with words. The sentences follow one another like facts in a natural history of sensibility.

That morning's ice, no more than a brittle film, had cracked and was now floating in segments.

These tapped together or, parting, left channels of dark water, down which swans in slow indignation swam. The islands stood in frozen woody brown dusk: it was now between three and four in the afternoon. . . . There is something momentous about the height of winter. Steps rang on the bridges, and along the black walks. This weather had set in; it would freeze harder tonight.

Here it's a lake, but throughout the book—indeed, throughout her body of work—Bowen imbues settings with an uncanny presence. Her rooms and houses take on nuances of living usually carried by characters, standing in plot and memory not as symbols but as organic and resonant elements of the story. Bowen's prose is precise, but it sets off vibrations like the strings of a viola; the resulting music is seductive, compelling, often haunted by the evocation of unresolved, and unresolvable, emotions.

What happens in *The Death of the Heart*? After the death of her father, sixteen-year-old Portia goes to live with her half-brother and his wife. The latter, Anna Quayne, resents Portia for the girl's innocence and lack of social graces. Anna's resentment is quickened by her envy of the youth's, well, *youth*, because the older woman cannot come to terms with time's indifferent squandering of her own. When Anna discovers and reads Portia's diary, the portrait of adulthood that emerges stirs a plot in which experience will shock the innocent, as expected, but also—and this is Bowen's distinction—innocence will deface experience with equally disruptive force. Like all heartbreaks, the ones depicted in *The Death of the*

Heart are part domestic tragedy, part emotionally fraught farce, and it is a measure of Bowen's art—and wisdom—that she depicts them with such penetrating tenderness:

One's sentiments—call them that—one's fidelities are so instinctive that one hardly knows they exist: only when they are betrayed or, worse still, when one betrays them does one realize their power. That betrayal is the end of an inner life, without which the everyday becomes threatening or meaningless.

If you've ever been bewildered by the deliciously tortured delicacy of consciousness that defines the later novels of Henry James and wondered what he is trying to get at, you might read Elizabeth Bowen to find out.

What: Novel. **When:** 1938. **Also By:** *The Last September* (1929). *The House In Paris* (1935). *The Heat of the Day* (1948). *Eva Trout* (1968). **Further Reading:** *Elizabeth Bowen: Portrait of a Writer* by Victoria Glendinning. **Try:** *Mrs. Palfrey at the Claremont* by Elizabeth Taylor. *Hotel du Lac* by Anita Brookner.

The Sheltering Sky
Paul Bowles (1910–1999)

A Searing Journey into Awayness

Paul Bowles began his writing life with poetry, seeing his first publication at the age of sixteen, but he was dissuaded from pursuit of the poetic muse by Gertrude Stein, whom he remembered telling him that he was "not a poet *at all*." Bowles went on to launch a career as a composer—he studied with Aaron Copland—before turning his creative energies, in his late thirties, to fiction. His first novel, *The Sheltering Sky*, immediately marked him as one of the most distinctive literary talents of the twentieth century.

Bowles was born in Queens, New York, and left home for stints in Berlin and Paris before choosing to live his adult life in Tangier, Morocco, as far from his birthplace—as much figuratively as literally—as he could get. Perhaps it should be no surprise then that his novels and stories are consistently (although

unintentionally, he maintained) about isolation and the separateness that, as much as connection, can define human relations: No one has better evoked the psychological resonance of empty landscapes.

The Sheltering Sky is the story of a New York married couple, Port and Kit Moresby, who bear some resemblance to Bowles and his brilliant, troubled wife, Jane, whose long physical and mental decline would occupy the author for years. Traveling in the Sahara with a friend, hoping the journey will impart some emotional momentum to their inert relationship, the Moresbys fall further and further away from each other, both losing themselves in a kind of primal surrender. Bowles described the book as "an adventure story in which the adventures take place on two planes simultaneously: in the actual desert and in the inner desert of the spirit." He describes both planes with a sensitivity that connects these distant travelers to our imaginations with startling immediacy. He is especially good at capturing the human limits that confound our grasp of time and experience, as in these words spoken by Port:

How many more times will you remember a certain afternoon of your childhood, some afternoon that's so deeply a part of your being that you can't even conceive of your life without it? Perhaps four or five times more. Perhaps not even that. How many more times will you watch the full moon rise? Perhaps twenty. And yet it all seems limitless.

The extremes of detachment and mortification Bowles's characters pursue and endure give their story the horrific beauty and otherness that other eras might have found in the lives of the saints. His unsaintly couple, neither holy nor blessed, lead our thoughts toward first and last things with an eerie surety.

What: Novel. *When:* 1949. *Edition:* The 50th anniversary edition contains a preface Bowles wrote just before his death. *Also By:* Bowles's copious works include the novels *Let It Come Down* (1952), *The Spider's House* (1955), *Up Above the World* (1966), several short story collections, a memoir, travelogues, poetry, and translations. *Further Reading: In Touch: The Letters of Paul Bowles,* edited by Jeffrey Miller. *A Little Original Sin: The Life and Work of Jane Bowles* by Millicent Dillon. *Try: The Tartar Steppe* by Dino Buzzati (see page 117). *My Sister's Hand in Mine: The Collected Work of Jane Bowles. Adaptation:* The 1990 Bernardo Bertolucci film stars Debra Winger and John Malkovich (Bowles found it "awful").

The Ascent of Rum Doodle
W. E. Bowman (1911–1985)

Up, Up, and Away with a Band of Bumbling Climbers

When a volume unknown to you is called "one of the funniest books you will ever read" by one of the funniest writers you know (that would be Bill Bryson), and when it appears on a list headlined "10 Great Books You've Probably Never Heard Of" (*Outside* magazine, January 2003), you're bound to seek out a copy. Originally published in Britain in the 1950s at the peak of mountaineering's prominence in the public eye—Everest, after all, had just been conquered in 1953—*The Ascent of Rum Doodle* is an inspired send-up of expedition books in general, and of climbing and its literature in particular.

A comic chronicle of an invented expedition up "Rum Doodle," a forty-thousand-and-one-half-foot peak in the Himalayas (slightly taller than

its neighbor, the aforementioned Everest), Bowman's tale is narrated by a stodgy old duffer named Binder, who has assembled an extraordinary team to conquer the summit, including Humphrey Jungle, the guide adept at getting lost; Christopher Wish, who has a thing about measuring things; Pong, a sadistic native cook; and Lancelot Constant, the language expert who manages to upset practically every one of the expedition's three thousand Yogistani porters (who, you'll be interested to know, speak their incomprehensible tongue by grunting through their stomachs). Binder's bumblers—can they, will they climb? Oh, indeed they can, and do: higher and higher until . . . but let's not spoil their moment of "triumph."

Imagine *Three Men in a Boat Go Mountaineering* or *Monty Python Climbs the Matterhorn,* and you'll get some idea of the hilarity Bowman provokes in this small gem of literary comedy.

What: Novel. Humor. *When:* 1956. *Reading Note:* While not required for enjoyment, a familiarity with classic climbing literature—Maurice Herzog's *Annapurna,* for example, or *Nanda Devi* by Eric Shipton—makes Bowman's parody even funnier. *Also By: The Cruise of the Talking Fish* (1957). *Try: No Picnic on Mount Kenya* by Felice Benuzzi (see page 68). *A Walk in the Woods* by Bill Bryson (see page 10). *Footnote:* In 1959, the Australian Antarctic Expedition named a small peak near Mawson Base "Mount Rumdoodle" in homage to the book.

Fahrenheit 451
Ray Bradbury (1920–2012)

A Thrilling Parable of the Power of Reading

Guy Montag is a fireman. But, in the dystopian future of Ray Bradbury's 1953 classic, a fireman's duty is not to put out fires, but to start them. His job, in fact, is to burn books, a task that requires the temperature of 451° Fahrenheit.

The world Montag inhabits is filled with features that may have once been far-fetched, but which are now worryingly familiar, from technologies such as wall-sized televisions and "Seashell Radios" that fit onto one's ear like prophetic smartphones to ubiquitous, unrelenting advertising. Political correctness has run rampant, constricting liberties by masking dilemmas that politics, in an ideal state, is meant to resolve.

As the book opens, Montag does his work well—even with relish: "It was a pleasure to burn. It was a special pleasure to see things eaten, to see things blackened and *changed.*" But his unquestioning acceptance of the status quo starts to melt when Guy meets a seventeen-year-old free spirit with an unconventional allegiance to curiosity and an unsettling, easy happiness. It further unravels when he responds to an alarm that an old woman has a hidden library; he is stunned when she chooses to be burned alive with her books. He wonders why books are forbidden, and why he has spent ten years destroying them with pleasure and without a second thought. He hides a cache of volumes he was meant to burn, and upon discovery, is given twenty-four hours by his superior to investigate their contents, with the explanation that it's natural for a fireman to be curious. Before he knows it, a different kind of spark has been lit, and he's on the run from his old life—with a new job to do.

It's natural to see *Fahrenheit 451* as an allegory about censorship, but that would be to limit Bradbury's purpose and accomplishment. What the tale really celebrates are the freedoms reading fosters—freedoms of thought, emotion, individuality, engagement with others and with nature—which are under threat from mass media, homogenization of public discourse, and the mediated experience technology promotes. But its function as a parable is only made possible by its power as a story: From first page to last, through Montag's personal perils and larger societal upheavals, the reader follows Bradbury's fireman on a journey that evokes more questions than it answers—one that is thrilling, satisfying, and deeply haunting.

60TH ANNIVERSARY EDITION

FAHRENHEIT 451

RAY BRADBURY

What: Science Fiction. *When:* 1953. *Also By: The Martian Chronicles* (1950). *The Illustrated Man* (1951). *Dandelion Wine* (1957). *Something Wicked This Way Comes* (1962). *Further Reading: A Universal History of the Destruction of Books* by Fernando Báez. *Try: 1984* by George Orwell (see page 606). *Brave New World* by Aldous Huxley (see page 398). *Adaptation:* François Truffaut made the first film version in 1966.

The Chaneysville Incident
David Bradley (born 1950)

A Riveting Novel of Slavery's Legacy

The *Chaneysville Incident* had its imaginative genesis in the uncovering of the graves of a band of runaway slaves in Bedford County, Pennsylvania, where novelist David Bradley was born. According to legend, they killed themselves rather than be recaptured and returned to slavery. Their legacy animates both the contemporary and historical aspects of Bradley's gripping novel, which weaves several threads of experience into a fictional fabric that is vivid and furious—both emotionally draining and emotionally satisfying.

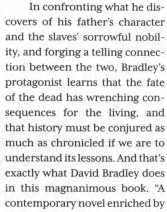

At the center of *The Chaneysville Incident* is John Washington, a late-twentieth-century historian who leaves his academic perch to return home in the hope of unraveling the mystery of his father's death. Beginning in conversations with keepers of local lore, his research continues through the study of historical documents and, ultimately, intense engagement with the history of his own heart. While his education has trained him to decipher the encoded messages of the former, experience has done little to prepare him for the latter, and Washington's turmoil adds a poignant personal drama to the larger tale Bradley tells.

In confronting what he discovers of his father's character and the slaves' sorrowful nobility, and forging a telling connection between the two, Bradley's protagonist learns that the fate of the dead has wrenching consequences for the living, and that history must be conjured as much as chronicled if we are to understand its lessons. And that's exactly what David Bradley does in this magnanimous book. "A contemporary novel enriched by historic and mythic appointments, and finally made tragic by them," wrote a reviewer when the book first appeared. Like most tragic works, *The Chaneysville Incident* bears witness to horrible sins as it testifies that humankind must suffer into truth; like only a few, it's a terrifically good read.

What: Novel. *When:* 1981. *Award:* PEN/Faulkner Award, 1982. *Also By: South Street* (1975). *Try: Angle of Repose* by Wallace Stegner (see page 749). *Beloved* by Toni Morrison (see page 569). *The Known World* by Edward P. Jones.

A Bullet in the Ballet
Caryl Brahms (1901–1982) and S. J. Simon (1904–1948)

A Wildly Choreographed Comic Mystery

This distinctively funny British novel—the first in a series of four centering on the fortunes of impresario Vladimir Stroganoff and his rambunctious ballet troupe—delivers comedy in high style. As readers will soon gather, Stroganoff and his dancers are remarkable largely for their off-stage antics and their unbridled eccentricities. Lovers of ballet will find the work of Brahms and Simon doubly delightful; the former was a dance critic in the London press, the latter a journalist who was also a master bridge player (which taught him, evidently, exactly when to hold and when to play his jokes).

Yet there is more than enough wit, hilarity, and abandon to bring great pleasure to any reader, even a confirmed balletophobe. The plot begins to unfold when Stroganoff's lead dancer, Anton Palook, is shot through the head during a performance of *Petrouchka*. Two unflappable Scotland Yard detectives are flapped indeed by the fact that everyone who knew Palook—ballerinas, stage mothers, the conductor, the company's financial backers, a wide web of lovers—seems to have a credible motive. Still, the show must go on, as always. After all, ticket sales soar on the scandal, especially when the detectives' best suspect reprises Palook's performance in *Petrouchka*, including taking a bullet himself.

While *A Bullet in the Ballet* is a murder mystery replete with corpses, suspects, interrogations, and revelations, suspense plays second fiddle to the decidedly screwball melody. This reader would have it no other way.

What: Mystery. Humor. *When:* 1937. *Also By:* Other Stroganoff novels: *Casino for Sale* (aka *Murder à la Stroganoff*, 1938); *Envoy on Excursion* (1940); *Six Curtains for Stroganova* (1945). *Try: Swan Song* by Edmund Crispin. *Hamlet, Revenge!* by Michael Innes. *Corpse de Ballet* by Ellen Pall.

AMERICA IN THE KING YEARS

PARTING THE WATERS, 1954–63 • PILLAR OF FIRE, 1963–65 • AT CANAAN'S EDGE, 1965–68

Taylor Branch (born 1947)

Martin Luther King and the Making of a Movement

As a biography of Martin Luther King, Taylor Branch's nearly 3,000-page trilogy stands alone in its understanding of King's place at the center of a pulsing network of moral convictions, political pressures, practical demands, historical committed people—from the powerless to the prominent—arrayed on both sides of his cause. As a history of that cause, it is both meticulous and majestic in its attention to the strategy and tactics—as well as the suffering and bravery—of a generation of civil rights advocates as it battled brutal proponents of bigotry and the entrenched cowardice and cruelty of local and national institutions. As a portrait of the United States in the tumultuous era from 1954 through 1968, it has few if any rivals in its scope, significance, and emotional force.

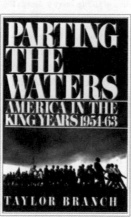

Branch did not begin his narrative biographical exploration of America in the King years with the intention of devoting a quarter-century of his own life to it, but the material demanded no less. In May 1954, two weeks before the Supreme Court handed down its landmark decision in *Brown v. Board of Education*, Martin Luther King gave his first sermon as pastor-designate of the Dexter Avenue Baptist Church in Montgomery, Alabama; from that month forward, Branch traces in tandem the path of King's career and the spread of the civil rights movement. His first volume, *Parting the Waters*, details, among myriad other events, the arrest of Rosa Parks and the launch of the Montgomery bus boycott, which King was drafted to lead; the lunch counter sit-ins and the bloody Freedom Rides; King's unswerving commitment to nonviolence and his imprisonment during a demonstration in Birmingham; his "I Have a Dream" speech at the 1963 March on Washington; and the KKK's bombing of Birmingham's 16th Street Baptist Church, killing four young girls. As the movement and resistance to it grow, Branch's broad focus continues, in *Pillar of Fire* and *At Canaan's Edge*, to illuminate the character and contributions of King's growing—and increasingly fractious—band of allies, while his close examination of federal documents and records affords insight into the roles played by presidents and power brokers in aiding or thwarting the activists in the South. From the hesitant support of the Kennedys to the nefarious subterfuge of FBI

Martin Luther King Jr. leading the march from Selma to Montgomery in March 1965

director J. Edgar Hoover, Branch reveals King's relations with Washington as alternately hopeful, unreliable, and desperate.

Despite the historical sweep of the material and the monumental scale of the research he marshals, Branch's hold on the reader's attention never loosens its grip. His narrative is often propelled by a page-turning suspense, as in the first hundred-odd pages of the third volume, which describe an astonishing two-week period in early 1965. When marchers attempting to cross Selma's Pettus Bridge are savagely beaten by Alabama state troopers, King is moved to summon help from around the country for a second confrontation. Ministers who heed King's call and journey to Selma are ambushed and murdered. Inspired at last to action, President Johnson delivers his stirring "We Shall Overcome" speech, calling upon Congress to immediately set in motion historic voting rights legislation. The reader—chased by feelings that run the gamut from revulsion toward hatemongers to awe of the desperate nobility of King and his followers—races through Branch's chapters with breathless anticipation; it is hard to imagine a more compelling portrayal of the public life of the nation, or the motives, fears, and faith of public figures.

Individually rewarding, together Branch's three volumes deliver an unparalleled portrait of America in the twentieth century, as reflected in the looking-glass of the fateful life and times of one remarkable man. The view is upsetting and uplifting, troubling in what it reveals about the often benighted history of a country born of the Enlightenment, inspiring in its testimony to the force of visionary dreams, despite—or perhaps because of—the responsibilities they entail.

What: Biography. History. *When: Parting the Waters,* 1988; *Pillar of Fire,* 1998; *At Canaan's Edge,* 2006. *Awards: Parting the Waters* was awarded both the National Book Critics Circle Award, 1988, and the Pulitzer Prize for History, 1989. *Further Reading:* For those seeking an introduction before diving into the Branch trilogy, Marshall Frady's *Martin Luther King, Jr.,* in the Penguin Lives series, is a good brief biography. In the same series, Douglas Brinkley's *Rosa Parks* also melds biography and civil rights history, with a bit more about the role women played. *Bearing the Cross: Martin Luther King, Jr., and the Southern Christian Leadership Conference*, by David J. Garrow, is another excellent, detailed biography of Dr. King, with closer attention to his personal life and spiritual and philosophical ideas. *Adaptation:* An eight-hour miniseries of *Parting the Waters* was made in 2000. *Try: Collected Essays* by James Baldwin (see page 43). *The Children* by David Halberstam.

How Buildings Learn
WHAT HAPPENS AFTER THEY'RE BUILT
Stewart Brand (born 1938)

A Surprising Course in Continuing Education

Inventor, designer, and influencer extraordinaire, Stewart Brand has spent his career as author and editor channeling a cascade of inspirations. Trained as a biologist and army officer, he has explored the culture of Native Americans, hung out with Ken Kesey's Merry Pranksters (as you can discover in Tom Wolfe's *The Electric Kool-Aid Acid Test*), created *The Whole Earth Catalog* and *CoEvolution Quarterly*, and been instrumental in the founding of such far-thinking organizations as the seminal online community The Well, the Global Business Network, and the Long Now Foundation. He has also written a handful of books, the best of which is *How Buildings Learn*, a volume that, in addition to its architectural insight, illustrates how close attention to a theme can broadly enhance the way we think, work, and live.

Beginning with an anecdote about the predictable long line for the ladies' room at the San Francisco Opera House, Brand argues that too many buildings are built in rigid adherence to long-held notions. Despite the assumptions of many planners, architects, and builders, he continues, time means more to most architecture than space; as a corollary, then, it's clear that design is not as important as the way that design adapts to use as use changes. "The building learns from its occupants, and they learn from it," writes Brand, and, in twelve absorbing chapters, he surveys and celebrates this process as it occurs in movie theaters and cathedrals, country homes and tenements, banks and bungalows. His book is extensively illustrated with buildings drawn and/or photographed at varying stages of their history—which makes for an uncommon, persuasive, and absorbing visual counterpoint to the text. (An especially intriguing metamorphosis is documented in photos showing how the author transformed a Sea-Land shipping container into the library/office in which he composed this book.)

Along the way, Brand picks the brains of architects, historians and theorists, facilities managers and real estate professionals, preservationists and inhabitants to see just how buildings learn, or fail to. What starts out as a treatise on architectural adaptability ends up delivering to the reader a host of new inspirations for exploring other "permanent" things—from cities to selves—that are layered in time. *How Buildings Learn* is a capacious toolbox of ideas, filled with surprising compartments. You'll learn a lot no matter where you open it.

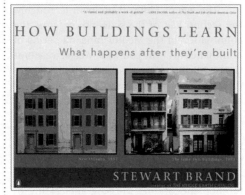

What: Architecture. **When:** 1994. **Also By: The Last Whole Earth Catalog** (1971). **The Media Lab: Inventing the Future at MIT** (1987). **The Clock of the Long Now: Time and Responsibility** (1999). **Try: Edge City** by Joel Garreau. **What Time Is This Place?** by Kevin Lynch. **The House: Portrait of Chatsworth** by Deborah Cavendish, Duchess of Devonshire.

The Mediterranean and the Mediterranean World in the Age of Philip II
Fernand Braudel (1902–1985)

Digging Deeper into History

In the history of historians, few modern figures loom as large as Fernand Braudel, who played a seminal role in revolutionizing his field of study, shifting its focus from strictly political narratives to the lasting patterns (the *longue durée*) of the geographic, social, and economic structures that shaped them. For Braudel and his fellow members of the French Annales school (including Marc Bloch, Lucien Febvre, Georges Duby, and Emmanuel Le Roy Ladurie), history's patterns are revealed through an almost microscopic attention to undramatic details, such as topographical features, trade figures, matters of climate, social themes, and modes of communication. Braudel approaches historical realities with the same kind of intelligence—rigorous, curious, and capacious, imbued with orderly ingenuity—that Darwin brought to his study of life forms. And like Darwin's *Origin of Species*, Braudel's masterpiece, *The Mediterranean and the Mediterranean World in the Age of Philip II*, is a book in which the patient accretion of small facts gradually opens the reader's mind to an extraordinary panorama.

The age of Philip II of Spain is, roughly, the second half of the sixteenth century—the culmination of the Mediterranean's period of dominance over the course of Western civilization. While Braudel's scholarship is highly concentrated, it is also animated with a breadth of active imagination that invigorates the reader's passage (don't let the 1,400 footnote-laden pages daunt you; the author's prose is filled with alluring pleasures). He reaches beyond the constraints of dates to explore the character and destiny of the Mediterranean in different planes of time: the geographical time of the environment, the social time of groups and their relations, the individual time of leaders and events.

Volume I examines the geography and economies of the Mediterranean; Volume II its empires, societies, and events. The work begins with mountains—"[H]ow can one ignore these

conspicuous actors, the half-wild mountains," Braudel ruminates, "where man has taken root like a hardy plant; always semi-deserted, for man is constantly leaving them? How can one ignore them when often their sheer slopes come right down to the sea's edge?"—and ends with an elegiac portrait of Philip, "applying himself to the work of a monarch, sitting at the centre, the intersection of the endless reports which combined to weave the great web of the Spanish Empire and the world." In between is a majestic work about everything under the Mediterranean sun. As a *New York Review of Books* critic wrote when the book was first released in the United States, "this is evocative history at its best, pursued with such richness of detail and example over space and time that it dazzles as well as illuminates."

Portrait of Phillip II by Titian, 1551

What: History. *When:* Published in France in 1949, revised in 1966; the first US edition, translated by Siân Reynolds, appeared in 1972. *Also By:* Braudel's magnificent trilogy *Civilization and Capitalism 15th-18th Century* (1979) is an illustrated marvel of erudition, ideal for those who would like to browse their way into Braudel's intellectual domain; it's packed with wonder and surprise. *Further Reading: The Mediterranean in History,* edited by David Abulafia. *Try: Montaillou: The Promised Land of Error* by Emmanuel Le Roy Ladurie.

Navigator of the Flood
Mario Brelich (1910–1982)

Scripture Rescripted

In his lifetime, Mario Brelich published only three books, each a distinctive, imaginative exploration of a biblical theme, and each a discovery of the first order. *The Work of Betrayal* (1975) is a novel (in every sense of the word) disquisition on "The Case of Judas Iscariot," conducted by none other than C. August Dupin—the prototypical amateur detective we meet in Edgar Allan Poe's "Murders in the Rue Morgue." *The Holy Embrace* (1972) details the exasperating marital discord between Abraham the patriarch and Sarah, "the most beautiful woman in the world"—discord that threatens to disrupt the Lord's design for his chosen people.

In *Navigator of the Flood*, Brelich's ingenuity is set to the task of explaining the drunkenness of Noah, the episode that concludes the ninth chapter of Genesis and stands as a peculiar coda to the story of the great flood. Explanation, of course, requires a detailed consideration of Noah's relations with the Lord, of the responsibilities—moral and practical—placed on Noah's shoulders by the Lord's directive to gather animals and build an ark, and of the uncertainties confronted by a man facing an incomprehensible but inevitable fate. Brelich takes the Bible at its word, turning each detail of its narrative under his penetrating and ironic intelligence with just enough reverence to make his ingenuity congenial. The result is a playful, trenchant, inspired, and funny meditation—a philosophical essay in the form of a novel—on the deep meanings we can still find hidden in the dusty folds of a familiar tale.

What: Novel. *When:* Written in Italian in 1954, not published in book form until 1979; English translation by John Shepley, 1991. *Try: Joseph and His Brothers* by Thomas Mann. *The Preservationist* by David Maine.

■ For Jean Anthelme Brillat-Savarin's *The Physiology of Taste*, see page 276.

Jane Eyre
AN AUTOBIOGRAPHY
Charlotte Brontë (1816–1855)

"Reader, I married him."

Destitute young woman leaves rotten boarding school for job as governess in sprawling mansion, falls in love with broodingly handsome employer with dark secret. In the twenty-first century, the plot of *Jane Eyre* might sound clichéd, yet Charlotte Brontë's 1847 novel, about a plain orphan girl exceeding her lot in life through righteousness and strong will tempered by desire, was and remains a true original. Not only might it be said to have inspired the imaginative atmosphere of countless fictions, movies, and television shows created in its wake, in a very real way *Jane Eyre* made available to readers modes of feeling that had never been articulated quite so tellingly before. As only the most powerful stories can, it seems to invent through expression the emotional truths it explores.

If Jane Austen charts the course of the coming of age and the coming of love in a social context that both defines her characters and to varying degrees determines their fates, Charlotte Brontë portrays a private life that struggles to maintain its shape and substance despite the buffetings of circumstance and the oppressions of social station. *Jane Eyre* tells one woman's story in her own compelling voice—not for nothing was it originally subtitled "An Autobiography." As she battles a stifling society and weathers storms of ardor and confusion, Jane must hold fast to the ideal of personal happiness in a world in which its denial is regarded not only as the norm, but as a moral imperative. Her narration of her passage from poor relation to self-possessed mistress of her destiny is, in its own way, as thrilling as any swashbuckling tale.

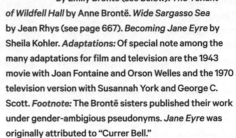

Portrait of Charlotte Brontë

That the story of Jane, Rochester, and his mad wife in the attic has been adapted, updated, and interpreted a thousand times over speaks to the power of the tale and its timeless appeal. Yet, for all the imitation, the exquisite passion of this most romantic of novels has never quite been equaled.

What: Novel. *When:* 1847. *Also By: Shirley* (1849). *Villette* (1853). *The Professor* (1857). *Further Reading: The Life of Charlotte Brontë* by Elizabeth Gaskell. *The Madwoman in the Attic: The Woman Writer and the Nineteenth-Century Literary Imagination* by Sandra M. Gilbert and Susan Gubar. *Try: Wuthering Heights* by Emily Brontë (see below). *The Tenant of Wildfell Hall* by Anne Brontë. *Wide Sargasso Sea* by Jean Rhys (see page 667). *Becoming Jane Eyre* by Sheila Kohler. *Adaptations:* Of special note among the many adaptations for film and television are the 1943 movie with Joan Fontaine and Orson Welles and the 1970 television version with Susannah York and George C. Scott. *Footnote:* The Brontë sisters published their work under gender-ambiguous pseudonyms. *Jane Eyre* was originally attributed to "Currer Bell."

Wuthering Heights
Emily Brontë (1818–1848)

Still Crazy After All These Years

When it was revealed that the "Ellis Bell" who was the author of *Wuthering Heights* was actually Emily Brontë, her contemporaries found it hard to imagine that this reclusive young woman, living in a dreary parsonage with her father and three surviving siblings (after the deaths of her mother, two eldest siblings, and aunt), could have written the scandalous tale of torrid, even violent, love between a landowner's daughter and the orphan who'd been raised as her brother. And while the life- and death-defying love of Catherine Earnshaw and Heathcliff, abetted by its cinematic retellings, has been domesticated, so to speak, into an archetypal tale of romantic passion, one

doesn't need to read more than twenty pages to recognize how weird and wild the novel itself remains. Indeed, it's so strange that the very fact of its composition by anyone in the middle of the nineteenth century is more astonishing than the gender of its creator. In its intense drama and disregard for orthodox morality, *Wuthering Heights* continues to surprise and challenge us today.

To attempt to chart the web of relationships of blood, marriage, social strata, economic dependence, love, envy, hatred, and revenge that bind Catherine and Heathcliff to the book's other characters would make *Wuthering Heights* sound like a story that somehow got drunk in Victorian England and ended up in the incestuous, jungly psychological

precincts of Faulkner's South. The plot is a tangle of primal feelings as palpable as the untamed landscape and tempestuous weather of the Yorkshire moors that Emily Brontë knew so well. As the couple's destiny is derailed by prevailing ideas of convention and class, their intense desire drives them to punish each other as passionately as they long to love. Their ardor doesn't prevail, but it does endure, with a grip on readers' imaginations that is as baffling, buffeting, and transporting as only the most powerful emotions can be.

What: Novel. *When:* 1847. *Also By: The Complete Poems of Emily Jane Brontë* (1908). *Further Reading: Emily Brontë: Her Life and Work* by Muriel Spark and Derek Stanford. *The Brontës: Wild Genius on the Moors* by Juliet Barker. *Try: Jane Eyre* by Charlotte Brontë (see page 97). *The Tenant of Wildfell Hall* by Anne Brontë. *Rebecca* by Daphne du Maurier (see page 236). *Adaptations:* Adapted too many ways and times to count; most famous is the 1939 film version starring Laurence Olivier and Merle Oberon.

The Da Vinci Code
Dan Brown (born 1964)

The Suspense of Belief—and Disbelief

Some books become popular phenomena of such extraordinary dimensions that it becomes impossible not to pick them up; usually this is because something about them makes them impossible to put down, no matter how hard we try. *The Da Vinci Code*, which dominated the bestseller list between 2003 and 2006, is a case in point. The second in Dan Brown's series of novels featuring Harvard symbologist Robert Langdon (after *Angels and Demons*, 2000), the novel is a conspiracy of crowd-pleasing themes, including religious espionage, alternative theological history, cryptography, ancient secret societies, and pagan rituals. There is murder in the Louvre and intrigue in the Vatican, to say nothing of schemes emanating endlessly from secret churchly cabals. The plot hinges on elements from the culturally sublime—the search

for the Holy Grail—to the cheesily ridiculous—a self-flagellating albino Catholic monk.

The whole framework is designed to intoxicate nominally skeptical readers with the possibility that history might mean more than it really does, at least for the space of a few hundred pages. The wild premise of the book—that the Merovingian dynasty of France is directly descended through the bloodline of Jesus and Mary Magdalene, a fact the powers-that-be will kill to keep clandestine—unfolds so swiftly, as Langdon races to and fro from Paris to Rome to Westminster Abbey, that readers more than willingly suspend disbelief, chasing the hero's breathless decoding of clues in a kind of ultra-logical but ultimately deranged scavenger hunt.

The vehemence of the critical response to the "historical inaccuracies" of Brown's book is in direct proportion to the seductiveness of the storytelling; why anyone would be looking for accuracy here is a bigger mystery than the one the plot weaves, and that one's pretty big. Brown's concoction may sound silly, but gleeful is perhaps a better word. The sheer energy of his invention is transporting. It is not that his critics are entirely wrong, but rather that their cavils are beside the point. Sometimes, a page-turner is all you want to get your hands on—holier grails being much too hard to find.

What: Novel. *When:* 2003. *Also By: The Lost Symbol* (2009). *Inferno* (2013). *Origin* (2017). *Try: The Eight* by Katherine Neville. *Adaptation:* Tom Hanks plays Robert Langdon in the 2006 film directed by Ron Howard.

Bury My Heart at Wounded Knee
AN INDIAN HISTORY OF THE AMERICAN WEST
Dee Brown (1908–2002)

How the West Was Really Won

"I have tried to fashion a narrative of the conquest of the American West as the victims experienced it, using their own words whenever possible." So Dee Brown announced his intention in this book, which fundamentally altered our perspective of the past. Published in 1971, Brown's unprecedented chronicle of the brutal campaigns that destroyed Native American culture and civilization—beginning in 1860 with the wars incited by the relocation of the Navajos and ending with the massacre of two hundred Sioux men, women, and children at Wounded Knee, South Dakota, in December 1890—overturned the prevailing mythology of "how the West was won."

Relying on contemporary sources including treaty council records, interviews, memoirs, pictographic accounts, and the words of leaders such as Chief Joseph, Geronimo, and Crazy Horse, Brown fashioned a rigorous history that is also a compelling story. On every page, that narrative is brought to vivid life by the fresh point of view, which is reflected, for example, in the use of the Native American names for historical figures, such as General George Armstrong Custer, who was "named Hard Backsides because he chased them over long distance for many hours without leaving his saddle." The frontier-following white settlers, habitually extolled for their bravery and pioneer spirit, are here revealed to be the beneficiaries of political treaties of convenience that were violated by the government almost as quickly as they were signed.

Displaced from their ancestral lands, the natives were hunted and herded onto reservations against their will, their traditional ways of life obliterated as the expanding nation pursued what it believed to be its manifest destiny. It is a disturbing, heartbreaking tale, told with both discipline and moral intensity in Brown's gripping pages.

What: History. *When:* 1971. *Also By: Creek Mary's Blood* (1980) engages, in fictional form, many of the themes of *Bury My Heart at Wounded Knee. Try: The Journey of Crazy Horse: A Lakota History* by Joseph M. Marshall III. *An Indigenous Peoples' History of the United States* by Roxanne Dunbar-Ortiz.

1887 photograph of Geronimo

MARGARET WISE BROWN
(1910–1952)

More exceptional than the books we label "read before we die" are those we've come to treasure before we learn to read. Within that rarefied category, *Goodnight Moon* has earned pride of place among generations of children since its original publication in 1947, and *The Runaway Bunny* and *Little Fur Family* are not far behind. What these three tales share, in addition to their family-friendly coziness, is a deep respect for the ritualistic aspects of the bedtime story, a respect evidenced by the unfixed but lilting, lulling cadences of their language; they're like books of common prayer for the comfort all children want, almost as much as their parents want to deliver it.

What these books also share is an author, Margaret Wise Brown. Brown was an educator and editor who combined in her own writing inspirations from classroom experiments (at the Bank Street School in New York) and literary innovation (she shepherded into print Gertrude Stein's only book for children, *The World is Round*, and Stein's style was an important influence). The little volumes Brown fashioned from these inspirations have proven to be enduring and ever-ready bedtime companions for generations of parents and children.

Goodnight Moon
Pictures by Clement Hurd (1908–1988)
The Quintessential Bedtime Book

How many bedtimes have commenced with a parent intoning the words

> In the great green room
> There was a telephone
> And a red balloon
> And a picture of—

and a child gazing at the accompanying picture, which depicts a bunny in bed in a room awash in bold green, red, and yellow?

As the pages are turned and the simplest of poems unfolds in casually rhymed lines, pictures of the cow jumping over the moon and of the three little bears are given their due, as are kittens and mittens and toyhouse and mouse, and the quiet old lady in the rocking chair whispering "hush." The contents of the room are enumerated, and then each element is bid goodnight in the simplest, sweetest evocation of a toddler's surrender to sleep that any reader is likely to find. Brown's conception is flawless, Clement Hurd's pictures are friendly and bright (till the lights go out!). Together they make a perfect bedtime tale: comforting, familiar, and possessed of a magic that never loses its charm—no matter how many times a parent is asked to read it again.

What: Children's. *When:* 1947. *Also By:* Brown and Hurd's *The Runaway Bunny* (1942) makes a happy companion volume, as does their *My World* (1949). *Try: The Carrot Seed* by Ruth Krauss. *The Very Hungry Caterpillar* by Eric Carle.

Little Fur Family
Pictures by Garth Williams (1912–1996)
Homeland Security

I s there a sweeter book in all the world than this simple tale of "a little fur family / warm as toast / smaller than most" who live in a warm wooden tree? It's hard to imagine one. Brown's mixture of rhyming lines and rhythmic prose follows the fur child as he ventures out to explore the woods about him, returning home at the end of the day to be tucked in and serenaded with a sleepy-time song by his parents. It's a perfect evocation of the security that children—and, if truth be told, parents—crave. The illustrations by Garth Williams capture the gentle spirit of the short and simple tale with winning art, helping to make *Little Fur Family* a bedtime essential that embodies the emotional power of books.

What: Children's. *When:* 1946. *Edition:* Some current editions are bound in imitation fur, replicating the feel of the original issue, which was reputedly bound in real rabbit fur. *Further Reading: Margaret Wise Brown: Awakened by the Moon* by Leonard S. Marcus. *Try: Pat the Bunny* by Dorothy Kunhardt. *Corduroy* by Don Freeman.

The Major Works
Sir Thomas Browne (1605–1682)

The Rarefied Pleasures of Rampant Prose

S ome books are clear streams of narrative that carry us easily along. Others are springs that inspire or refresh us; others still are lakes of calm and seductive capacities, or oceans that lure us to imaginative depths. But some books are composed with such exotic, even esoteric eloquence that they strike our readerly senses with the beauty, violence, and controlled intensity of a waterfall. We admire such writing before we understand it, and treasure it even when its language seems to keep its secrets. Such is the writing of Sir Thomas Browne.

Browne was a London-born physician who led, according to a scholar of his work, "a remarkably uneventful life." Yet his works have earned him recognition as an important seventeenth-century British literary figure and a virtuoso of English prose. He has awed and influenced a wide variety of other significant authors, from Herman Melville, who called him "a cracked archangel," to Samuel Taylor Coleridge, who praised him by saying "he has brains in his Head, which is all the more interesting for a *little Twist* in the Brains." Modern Argentine master Jorge Luis Borges translated him (into seventeenth-century Spanish, of course), and New England poet James Russell Lowell championed Browne as "our most imaginative mind since Shakespeare."

Browne's principal works are *Religio Medici* (*A Doctor's Religion*; 1643), a spiritual self-portrait; *Pseudodoxia Epidemica, or Vulgar Erros* (1646–72), a refutation of popular superstitions; and *Hydriotaphia, or Urn Burial* (1658), a contemplative work prompted by the discovery in an English field of burial urns that were believed to be of Roman origin. The texts prove to be as rich and strange as their titles. They are filled with unusual words, and their sentences have the intricate syntax and sonorous cadences one associates with the densest passages of the King James Bible. Yet the reader who persists will soon discover Browne's unmistakable singularity; his dramatic phrasing gives his observations a strikingly oracular power. Consider, for example, this sumptuously melancholy shard from *Hydriotaphia*:

Darknesse and light divide the course of time, and oblivion shares with memory a great part even of our living beings; we slightly remember our felicities, and the smartest stroaks of affliction leave but short smart upon us. Sense endureth no extremeties, and sorrows destroy us or themselves. To weep into stones are fables. Afflictions induce callosities, miseries are slippery, or fall like snow upon us. . . .

Not for everyone, perhaps. But connoisseurs of ornate and erudite prose will relish the astonishing sentences ("The created world is but a small parenthesis in eternity") that thrive herein.

What: Philosophy. Essays. *When: Religio Medici* was first published without his permission in 1642; an authorized edition appeared the following year. *Try: The Anatomy of Melancholy* by Robert Burton (see page 113). *Centuries of Meditations* by Thomas Traherne (see page 803). *Adaptation:* Tony Kushner's 1987 play *Hydriotaphia* is based on the life of Sir Thomas Browne.

The Story of Babar
Jean de Brunhoff (1899–1937)

An Elephant You'll Never Forget

S ome denizens of children's literature are so entrenched in our collective imagination, and Babar the elephant is certainly one, that they seem natural formations in the landscape of our fancy—timeless, enduring presences the world has always known. Not so, of course; even Babar was invented, making his first appearance in a bedtime tale told one summer evening in 1930 by Cécile de Brunhoff to her sons, five-year-old Laurent and four-year-old Mathieu. When the boys repeated the story to their father, the painter Jean de Brunhoff, he decided to write it down and illustrate it. In the next few years, before his untimely death in 1937, Jean de Brunhoff produced the seven original Babar tales, among the most wonderfully, wittily illustrated children's books ever produced.

One of Jean de Brunhoff's original Babar illustrations, 1931

In the first in the series, *The Story of Babar*, the young pachyderm, having lost his mother to a hunter's bullet, wanders from his homeland to a town that resembles Paris, where an elegant old lady befriends him. The excitement of his adventures there—shopping for clothes, dining with his new companion, taking a bath, touring in an automobile—are depicted by Brunhoff with marvelous élan, but are ultimately shadowed by Babar's homesickness. Soon enough, however, his little cousins Arthur and Céleste arrive to fetch him back to the forest; he returns home to be crowned king of the elephants, with Céleste as his queen.

To appreciate Babar in his full glory, one should seek out editions published in the original large format (with pages measuring approximately 10½ × 14 inches) which retain the hand-scripted, cursive lettering for the text (rather than replacing it with roman type); occasional affordable facsimiles have appeared. The large scale encourages readers young and old to climb right into Brunhoff's glorious two-page spreads and have a chat with the gentle beast he animates with simple lines and subtle colors. "No one before, and very few since," Maurice Sendak once wrote, "has utilized the double-spread illustration to such dazzling, dramatic effect." Take a look at the two spacious pages depicting Babar's purchase of a shirt, a smart green suit, a bowler hat, and shoes with spats, and you'll see exactly what Sendak means. It is hard to conjure a happier home for a child's imagination than between the covers of this capacious book.

What: Children's. *When:* First French edition, 1931; first English edition, 1933. *Also By: The Travels of Babar* (1932). *Babar the King* (1933). *Babar and His Children* (1938). *Babar and Father Christmas* (1940). *Further Reading: The Art of Babar: The Work of Jean and Laurent de Brunhoff* by Nicholas Fox Weber. *Try: Herbert the Lion* by Clare Turlay Newberry. *Madeline* by Ludwig Bemelmans (see page 785). *Adaptation:* A popular animated television series was launched in 1989. *Footnote:* In 1946, Brunhoff's son Laurent, by then an artist himself, resurrected his mother and father's creation and went on in subsequent decades to produce more than thirty Babar books of his own, with fidelity to the whimsy and invention that inspired the original volumes.

....

A Walk in the Woods
REDISCOVERING AMERICA ON THE APPALACHIAN TRAIL
Bill Bryson (born 1951)

America's Funniest Travel Writer Takes a Hike

....

Waddling slothfully through middle age, popular travel writer Bill Bryson decided one day that he could do with a walk in the woods—a lengthy walk, in fact: 2,100 rugged miles along the celebrated Appalachian Trail (AT), the longest continuous footpath in the world. The idea for the strenuous trek came to the self-confessedly flabby scribe when he discovered a portion of the AT running near the edge of the New Hampshire town to which he had recently moved with his family after decades in England. The little path inspired big dreams: a journey on foot from Georgia to Maine, through the Blue Ridge Mountains and the Smokies, the Shenandoah Valley and the Great North Woods, with the pen-pusher becoming a lean and hard-eyed outdoorsman en route, able to fend for himself in the perilous wild.

And yet: "Nearly everyone I talked to had some gruesome story involving a guileless acquaintance who had gone off hiking the trail with high hopes and new boots and come stumbling back two days later with a bobcat attached to his head or dripping blood from an armless sleeve and whispering 'Bear!' in a hoarse voice, before sinking into a troubled unconsciousness." Did Bryson dare? Well, not only did he dare, but so too did his old friend, the roisterous Stephen Katz, beside whom Bryson looked like a buffed triathlete ("[Katz] had always been kind of fleshy, but now he brought to mind Orson Welles after a very bad night"). The pair's steps and missteps along the AT are hilariously recounted, as is only to be expected from one of our funniest writers, while Bryson, with his usual offhand efficiency, imparts a great deal of knowledge about the landscapes he traverses and the lore and natural history they harbor. But there's something more at work here, a quality of heart arising from the fact that there's somebody else to look out for on these travels (despite Katz's comically aggravating ineptitudes); it's the depiction of their friendship that makes *A Walk in the Woods* the prolific author's most affecting and satisfying book.

What: Travel. Humor. *When:* 1998. *Also By: The Lost Continent: Travels in Small-Town America* (1989). *Neither Here Nor There: Travels in Europe* (1991). *In a Sunburned Country* (2000). *A Short History of Nearly Everything* (2003). *The Road to Little Dribbling* (2016). *Try: A Short Walk in the Hindu Kush* by Eric Newby (see page 585). *AWOL on the Appalachian Trail* by David Miller. *Adaptations:* Bryson's audiobook performance of *A Walk in the Woods* is marvelously entertaining. The 2015 film, starring Robert Redford and Nick Nolte, lacks most of the charm the book exhibits.

The Thirty-Nine Steps
John Buchan (1875–1940)

A Trailblazing Tale of International Intrigue

. . . .

I returned from the City about three o'clock on that May afternoon pretty well disgusted with life. I had been three months in the Old Country, and was fed up with it. . . . The weather made me liverish, the talk of the ordinary Englishman made me sick, I couldn't get enough exercise, and the amusements of London seemed as flat as soda-water that has been standing in the sun. "Richard Hannay," I kept telling myself, "you have got into the wrong ditch, my friend, and you had better climb out."

So our narrator introduces himself at the outset. Having returned to London after long residence in southern Africa, he finds himself stuck in a rut. Much to the reader's delight, he'll make his way out of it by falling into another ditch so deep that it hides in its dark recesses murder, espionage, and a plot to undermine the security of England on the eve of World War I. He'll climb to ultimate safety only by means of the mysterious thirty-nine steps that give this splendid adventure its title.

Inadvertently stumbling into a nest of intrigue, Hannay befriends an American who is in possession of information regarding a plan to assassinate the Greek premier on his imminent visit to London; within a matter of days, the American is the victim of homicide and Hannay is soon the authorities' chief suspect. Off he runs to Scotland, leading the police—as well as a band of German spies—on a merry and perilous chase. Piecing together the real danger as he cunningly eludes his pursuers, Hannay slips through close call after close call. All along, Buchan's crisp prose carries the narrative along briskly, and we follow at speed, invigorated by the rigors of the chase as we run with Hannay one step ahead of (or behind) his enemies. The first of Buchan's several Hannay adventures, *The Thirty-Nine Steps* is a precursor to the spy novel as later practiced by Graham Greene, Eric Ambler, and Ian Fleming; but it is the author's own storytelling inheritance from the likes of Robert Louis Stevenson and Arthur Conan Doyle that make this book an enduring joy.

What: Novel. *When:* 1915. *Also By:* Buchan wrote four additional Richard Hannay novels: *Greenmantle* (1916), *Mr. Standfast* (1919), *The Three Hostages* (1924), and *The Island of Sheep* (1936). Worth seeking out among his dozens of other books are the novels *John Macnab* (1925) and *Witch Wood* (1927), and the beautifully written autobiography, *Pilgrim's Way* (1940). *Try: Blind Corner* by Dornford Yates. *A Coffin for Dimitrios* by Eric Ambler (see page 17). *Rogue Male* by Geoffrey Household (see page 390). *Adaptations:* While more faithful to the book, the 1978 film version, directed by Don Sharp, can't hold a candle to Alfred Hitchcock's 1935 classic, starring Robert Donat as Hannay.

. . . .

The Good Earth
Pearl S. Buck (1892–1973)

An Old-Fashioned Tale of Timeless Experience

. . . .

Pearl S. Buck was the first American woman to win the Nobel Prize in Literature (it would be more than a half-century before there was a second). Through a long career, she published more than seventy volumes of fiction, biography, and tales for children, but her heyday as an author was in the 1930s and 1940s, when she was seldom off the bestseller lists. Her second novel, *The Good Earth*, remains the book for which she is best remembered. Published in 1931, while Modernism was turning fiction artfully on its ear, Buck's simple, plot-driven tale of the shifting fortunes of Chinese peasants Wang Lung and O-Lan was innovative in its own way, marking the introduction of Asian characters into mainstream Western literature. In its pages, readers witness the serenities of the ancient land being pulled into the confusions of the twentieth century.

Buck was the daughter of American missionaries. Raised in China, she returned as an adult and was living there when *The Good Earth* was published; her familiarity with its people and landscapes infuses her storytelling. Yet the enduring beauty and power of her tale stems from the universal resonance—evoked in part by Buck's mellifluous, unassumingly biblical prose—of Wang Lung's struggles with famine, drought, flood, and family as his fortunes ebb and flow.

A Pulitzer Prize winner, the book also held a place on bestseller lists for two years. In 1937, the story was turned into an Oscar-winning film; several decades later, in an unexpected and inspired choice, it became an Oprah's Book Club pick. And while literary critics may label the tale sentimental and its aesthetic merits suspect, they look too quickly past the pleasures—and, one might justly say, the profundities—that abide in the empathy an old-fashioned good read engenders. These pleasures have seldom been better caught than in this entirely apt conclusion from a contemporary review of *The Good Earth*: "To read this story of Wang Lung is to be slowly and deeply purified; and when the last page is finished it is as if some significant part of one's own days were over."

Pearl S. Buck, 1933

What: Novel. *When:* 1931. *Awards:* Pulitzer Prize for Fiction, 1932. Buck was also awarded the Nobel Prize in Literature, 1938. *Also By:* The book has two sequels: *Sons* (1932) and *A House Divided* (1935). Buck's biographies of her mother, *The Exile* (1936), and her father, *Fighting Angel* (1936), are also notable. *Further Reading: Pearl Buck in China: Journey to "The Good Earth"* by Hilary Spurling. *Try: Pearl of China: A Novel* by Anchee Min is a fine imagining of Buck's Chinese girlhood. *Adaptation:* The 1937 film stars Paul Muni and Luise Rainer.

Bulfinch's Mythology
Thomas Bulfinch (1796–1867)

A Storybook of Ancient Tales

Time was when mythology provided the learned with keys for deciphering fate: The figures of the ancient myths gave history, philosophy, psychology, and religion a human face, one that remains recognizable and beautiful, albeit somewhere beyond the reach of daily life. Familiarity with mythology's vivid features still serves as boon and ballast to any education in the enduring ways of the world, and *Bulfinch's Mythology* is as fine, and as fun, an introduction as you'll find.

Published in America in the middle of the nineteenth century, Thomas Bulfinch's retellings of Greek, Roman, and medieval myths have been popular since their first appearance, and deservedly so: They offer a splendid, leisurely tour through the landscape of fable on which so much of our literature, art, and culture are built. The son of the renowned Charles Bulfinch (who, after beginning his career in Boston, succeeded Benjamin Latrobe as architect of the Capitol in Washington, D.C.), Thomas was a businessman who wrote in his spare time. His fluent narratives cull treasures from the richest sources (Homer, Ovid, Virgil, the Mabinogion, Arthurian legends, and medieval sagas), acquainting readers with the characters and culture of the mythic past. No book has a grander cast: You'll meet Prometheus and Pandora, Cupid and Psyche, Daedalus and Icarus, Jason, Hercules, Orpheus, Orestes, Ulysses, Aeneas and Dido, Arthur and Merlin, Launcelot and Guenever, Cuchulain, Robin Hood, Charlemagne, and Rinaldo and Orlando, to name a few. Tempering the primal energies and ancient, often violent strangeness of the myths with a genteel, family-friendly narrative tone that seeks to give his work "the charm of a story-book," Bulfinch succeeds in imparting the infectious wonder of the tales,

planting seeds of imagination and insight that further reading, to say nothing of real life, will only nourish.

What: Mythology. *When: The Age of Fable* (1855); *The Age of Chivalry* (1858); *Legends of Charlemagne* (1863); combined in one volume as *Bulfinch's Mythology* in 1881. *Edition:* The volume edited by classicist Richard P. Martin offers an especially rich presentation of the tales. *Reading Note:* Marvelous reading aloud for family enjoyment. *Further Reading: Mythology* by Edith Hamilton. *The Complete World of Greek Mythology* by Richard Buxton. *Try: Metamorphoses* by Ovid (see page 609). *Adaptation:* There is an excellent audiobook of excerpts from Bulfinch, read by Richard Dreyfuss, Olympia Dukakis, and Cherry Jones.

The Master and Margarita
Mikhail Bulgakov (1891–1940)

The Devil in Moscow, Jesus in Jerusalem, and Stalin in the Background

The authors of Russian literature during the Soviet period have never inspired the same reverence among readers as Tolstoy, Dostoevsky, and other titans of the nineteenth century. Yet one Soviet writer has no shortage of admirers today: Mikhail Bulgakov, whose novel *The Master and Margarita* has become both a Russian phenomenon and cult classic in the West. At once a love story, a supernatural adventure, and a vicious satire of the USSR under Stalin, it bursts with a creative energy that propels the narrative forward at lightning speed.

The novel oscillates between two settings. The first is the Moscow of the 1930s, to which the Devil himself is paying a visit. He has come in the guise of a professor called Woland, a name borrowed from Goethe's *Faust* (see page 319), though in some ways Woland resembles Stalin even more than Mephistopheles. Accompanied by some shady factotums and

a wisecracking black cat, he is causing all sorts of havoc. When the head of the Soviet literature bureaucracy known as MASSOLIT crosses Woland's path, the functionary ends up dead under a streetcar. A poet trying to expose the Devil's treachery is committed to an insane asylum, where he meets the Master, an author in despair at the failure of his novel. The Master has burned his manuscript and abandoned Margarita, his lover and muse, who believes he's dead.

Interrupting this action are sections of the Master's novel, which retells the story of Christ's condemnation by Pontius Pilate and subsequent crucifixion. ("Manuscripts don't burn," one character says about the Master's supposedly destroyed novel—a phrase that has become an idiom in Russian.) While the Moscow sections of the novel are satiric and fantastical, the portions dealing with the life of Christ are painted in stunningly realist tones. This Jesus, whom Bulgakov gives the name "Yeshua Ha-Nostri," can be humorous or devious, and sometimes seems like a bit of a dolt; by contrast, Pontius Pilate, the procurator of Judea, is drawn as a deeply conflicted individual struggling with the legitimacy of law and the weight of power.

When Bulgakov read the manuscript of *The Master and Margarita* to his friends in 1939, they anxiously warned that he'd end up in serious trouble with the authorities if the book were published. He died soon after, and his masterpiece languished in a desk drawer until the death of Stalin. Issued in the Soviet Union in the late 1960s, it immediately made its way to the West, where it quickly developed a following (Mick Jagger of the Rolling Stones said that he wrote "Sympathy for the Devil" after Marianne Faithfull lent him her copy). In the decades since, as its black magic and biting humor attract new generations of readers, *The Master and Margarita* has become an ever more valuable document of the absurdities, dangers, and quandaries of life in the USSR and—all literature being more than local—beyond.

What: Novel. *When:* 1967 (posthumous). *Edition:* The English translation by Richard Pevear and Larissa Volokhonsky is complemented by superb annotations and commentary. *Also By: The White Guard* (1927). *A Country Doctor's Notebook* (1963; posthumous). *The Heart of a Dog* (1968; posthumous). *Try: Dead Souls* by Nikolai Gogol (see page 321). *Demons* by Fyodor Dostoevsky. *Adaptations:* Bulgakov's masterpiece has inspired a rich range of adaptations, including films, television shows, plays, graphic novels, ballets, songs, and operas.

The Civilization of the Renaissance in Italy
Jacob Burckhardt (1818–1897)

Inventing the Renaissance—and Cultural History, Too

The *Civilization of the Renaissance in Italy* is the epitome of a rare breed: the kind of book that, through the power of its fresh perspective, can shape for generations—perhaps forever—readers' understanding of history, ideas, or experience. Written by a Swiss historian who fell under the spell of Italian culture during a tour made when he was nineteen years old, the "essay"—as the author modestly called it—defined a seminal period in the development of the West in a way previously unimagined, and subsequently indispensable. While other writers, notably the French historian Jules Michelet, had characterized the period following the Middle Ages as a "Renaissance," it was Burckhardt who gave the word, and the era from 1350 to 1550, its enduring Italianate cast. One might even say that before the publication of his book in 1860, there was no Renaissance to speak of, at least not in the terms we are accustomed to today.

The insightfulness of Burckhardt's powerful vision is apparent in every chapter of his study, as he explores themes that have since become hallmarks of our understanding of the period: "The State as a Work of Art," "The Development of the Individual," "The Revival of Antiquity," "The Discovery of the World and of Man." His detailed treatment of public institutions, private life, fashion, science, superstition, religion, and manners is fascinating in its detail. Yet the enormous amount of information his scholarship comprehends is conveyed in a literary style both elegant and engaging, inviting readers not only to recognize but also to savor the fruits of the author's profound learning.

Rather than taking the conventional approach of chronicling strictly political or military history, Burckhardt considered the epic cultural transitions he studied as just that: cultural. By assessing the roles of religion, literature, art, and above all, the rebirth of individualism, along with the shift from superstition to science, Burckhardt fashioned a comprehensive account of perhaps the most influential period in the history of modern civilization. In so doing, he introduced the world not only to the Renaissance, but to the idea of cultural history—in a book that would define the field.

What: History. Culture. *When:* 1860. *Also By: The Architecture of the Italian Renaissance* (1867). *The*

Copy of Bartolomeo Ammannati's Fountain of Neptune, *which was completed in 1574 in Florence, Italy*

Greeks and Greek Civilization (1898–1902). *Force and Freedom: Reflections on History* (1905). *Footnote:* Revisionist historians may now question Burckhardt's largest claims regarding the meaning of the Renaissance and Italy's dominating role, yet the power of his intellectual vision remains exhilarating. As if anticipating the critiques of later scholars, Burckhardt himself emphasized the constructed nature of all historical perspectives: "In the wide ocean upon which [historians] venture, the possible ways and directions are many; and the same studies which have served for my work might easily, in other hands, not only receive a wholly different treatment and application, but lead to essentially different conclusions." *Try: The Collector of Lives: Giorgio Vasari and the Invention of Art* by Ingrid Rowland and Noah Charney.

A Clockwork Orange
Anthony Burgess (1917–1993)

A Savage and Violent Satire, and a Linguistic Tour de Force

There was me, that is Alex, and my three droogs, that is Pete, Georgie, and Dim, Dim being really dim, and we sat in the Korova Milkbar making up our rassoodocks what to do with the evening, a flip dark chill winter bastard though dry.

Alex, the frightening narrator of this brutal and brilliant novel, is an amoral, Beethoven-loving gang leader in a near-future dystopian Britain. The language he spouts is a street argot fabricated by the multilingual author from a mélange of elements—Russian vocabulary and cockney slang as well as antic inventions inspired by the entire spectrum of English literature, from Elizabethan verse to Beat poetry. Alex's twisted tongue reinforces the willful outsider stance of the gang (even though it's easy enough for the reader to pick up). What Alex and company will do with the evening is what they always do: commit random acts of violence. Whether adolescent girls or a schoolteacher returning from the library, their victims are treated with an exuberantly vicious disregard: They might as well be faceless, inhuman targets for the gratuitous venom of Alex and his thugs (sex, unsurprisingly, is reduced to its mechanical coordinates: "the old in-out-in-out").

The linguistic bravura of the book and the unbound rebellion that is described do not hide for long the philosophical inquiry into good and evil at the core of *A Clockwork Orange*. The turning point is Alex's prison stint, during which he submits to aversion therapy in exchange for early release. Although it does not last, the behavioral modification is "successful," making Alex nonviolent—which, Burgess makes clear, is not exactly the same as good. His return to brutal form prefaces the unexpected and disconcerting climax, in which a vision of affectionate human relations turns Alex's thoughts toward tenderness.

Though it's often compared to *1984* (see page 606) and *Brave New World* (see page 398), Burgess's book—in part a vision, both prescient and exaggerated, of the coming trauma of youth culture—has an extra layer of surreality and menace. He is more interested in invoking

ANTHONY BURGESS
A CLOCKWORK ORANGE

questions than answering them, and he puts his considerable imaginative powers to work in the service of his inquisition. The result for the reader is a vivid tour of an unforgettable future—a journey that remains both intellectually invigorating and deeply unsettling.

What: Novel. *When:* 1962. *Edition:* The book was initially published in the US without the final chapter of the British version, which details Alex's tender turnabout; most recent editions contain Burgess's complete original text. *Also By:* Burgess wrote dozens of books, both fiction and nonfiction. Among the former, look for *The Long Day Wanes: A Malayan Trilogy* (1965, comprising novels originally published 1956-59), *Nothing Like the Sun: A Story of Shakespeare's Love Life* (1964), and *Earthly Powers* (1980); among the latter, *Here Comes Everybody: An Introduction to James Joyce for the Ordinary Reader* (1965, revised 1982; also published as *Re Joyce*), *Shakespeare* (1970), and *Little Wilson and Big God* (1986). *Try: Riddley Walker* by Russell Hoban. *Adaptation:* Stanley Kubrick's controversial 1971 film, starring Malcolm McDowell as Alex, is based on the incomplete American edition.

Reflections on the Revolution in France
Edmund Burke (1729–1797)

Politics and Prophecy

Few dates in European history pulse as luminously—or throw such violent shadows—as July 14, 1789, when revolutionaries stormed the Bastille prison in central Paris, setting in motion an upheaval that swept away France's *ancien régime* and turned the established conception of political order on its head. The stability of the state based on the hierarchical empowerment of a few gave way to volatile freedom for the many. A new age of liberty, equality, and brotherhood was born.

That was the idea anyway: "Bliss was it in that dawn to be alive," wrote William Wordsworth speaking for a generation. But the

bright promise of the French Revolution would soon be darkened by the violence of the Reign of Terror, in which—with a blackly ironic egalitarianism—thousands of citizens would ultimately follow Louis XVI and Marie Antoinette to the guillotine.

Edmund Burke's *Reflections on the Revolution in France* is an unsparing denunciation of the *événements* of 1789, all the more remarkable when we realize it was published in 1790, nearly three years before the inauguration of the Terror that would drown the bliss of the Revolution in rivers of blood. While many Britons were still welcoming the tumult across the Channel—in the space of a few months, the entire French social structure had been dismantled, the authority of the king had been voided, and even the peasantry wanted a say in the political process—Burke, an Irish member of Parliament and one of Britain's most gifted orators, presciently imagined the horrors to come, including the eventual ascent of a Napoleon. His attack on the revolutionaries' theory of "natural, unalienable and sacred" rights, as enumerated in the Declaration of the Rights of Man and of the Citizen that the insurrectionist Assembly quickly adopted, argues that people are bound by "a fixed compact sanctioned by the inviolable oath which holds all physical and all moral natures, each in their appointed place." If faith in such social cohesion is ruptured, Burke averred, the only possible result is anarchy. He also stands up boldly for the despised Marie Antoinette, foreshadowing her incipient downfall:

... little did I dream that I should have lived to see such disasters fallen upon her in a nation of gallant men, in a nation of men of honor and of cavaliers! I thought ten thousand swords must have leaped from their scabbards to avenge even a look that threatened her with insult. But the age of chivalry is gone. That of sophisters, economists, and calculators has succeeded; and the glory of Europe is extinguished forever.

The contemporary success of Burke's *Reflections* unleashed a flurry of powerful defenses of republican ideals, among them Mary Wollstonecraft's *A Vindication of the Rights of Men* (1790) and Thomas Paine's *Rights of Man* (1791), which outsold Burke's pamphlet nearly ten to one. But as Robespierre and the Committee of Public Safety took power and the Revolution devolved into murderous spectacle, Burke's early warnings of the dangers of its ideological severity were vindicated in turn.

Burke is often held up as the forefather of modern Conservatism, and during the Cold War he was frequently trotted out in opposition to communist regimes and youthful protest movements. But he was never a reactionary, and would find little common cause with the radical conservatives who still claim his mantle today. He was a strong supporter of American

independence, for one thing; he also raged against corruption in the East India Company, and crusaded for years to reform Britain's imperial enterprise. Regardless of one's political orientation, reading Burke offers the welcome reminder that people are active agents in history, and that amid crisis and upheaval you can't just philosophize; you also have to act, and act with prudence as well as passion. The nuance of his thought, abetted by the pragmatism that governs his attention to the particular circumstances that shape any political situation, remains bracing—and slightly unsettling in its underlying attachment to values that must, in order to endure, be inscribed in custom, law, and statute.

The Radical's Arms, *a caricature of French revolutionaries by George Cruikshank, 1819*

What: History. Politics. *When:* 1790. *Also By:* *A Philosophical Enquiry into the Origin of Our Ideas of the Sublime and the Beautiful* (1756). *Thoughts on the Cause of the Present Discontents* (1770). *Letters on a Regicide Peace* (1796). *Further Reading: The Great Debate: Edmund Burke, Thomas Paine, and the Birth of Right and Left* by Yuval Levin. *Edmund Burke: The First Conservative* by Jesse Norman. *Try: The Theory of Moral Sentiments* by Adam Smith. *A Vindication of the Rights of Men* by Mary Wollstonecraft. *Rights of Man* by Thomas Paine.

FRANCES HODGSON BURNETT
(1849–1924)

Frances Hodgson (later Burnett) emigrated with her family from Manchester, England, to Knoxville, Tennessee, in 1865, when she was sixteen years old. She soon embarked on a writing career that would make her one of the most successful authors of the era and fund further peregrinations, resulting in her residence at one time or another in Paris, Washington, D.C., London and Kent in England, and Plandome, New York, where she died in 1924.

Although she wrote a number of popular novels and plays for adults, Burnett was most famous in her lifetime for *Little Lord Fauntleroy* (1886), a tale for young readers whose protagonist, an American boy in straitened circumstances, unexpectedly becomes heir to an English earldom and steps into the traditions—replete with velvet suits and flowing locks—his new position entails. While the little lord proved a sensation in print and on the stage on both sides of the Atlantic, he has not aged well. Burnett's considerable standing as a children's author now rightly rests on two later works, *A Little Princess* and *The Secret Garden,* each of which displays the gifts—vivid characterization of both virtue and villainy, atmospheric dramatization of fairy-tale-like reversals of fortune, a feel for the emotional pull of a sharply defined narrative arc (not to mention the happy ending)— that made their creator a precursor of the storytelling empire soon to assert its dominance: the movies.

through the power of fanciful identification, Sara Crewe possesses a poise that never deserts her, no matter what misfortunes are thrown her way. And make no mistake: *A Little Princess* is an adventure story as filled with bravery and resourcefulness as any episode in the *The Odyssey* or in J. K. Rowling's wizardly repertoire, even if Sara's story unfolds in the domesticated precincts of a Victorian era boarding school for girls in London, and even though her courage manifests itself in powers of imagination and empathy rather than cunning or magic.

Sent to Miss Minchin's school by her doting father, who has lavished on her the accoutrements of privilege that mark her as the royalty described by the book's title, Sara is stranded there upon his death, penniless and at the mercy of the hateful headmistress. Reduced to poverty and relegated to the position of an ill-treated servant, Sara summons not only a future, but also a brighter present for herself and her friend and new roommate, the scullery maid Becky, despite the bleakness of their circumstances. Readers, of course, are rooting for her all along, and we turn the pages with the fervent

A Little Princess
Once Upon a Heroine

Like most heroes whose trials and triumphs readers have loved to assume as their own belief that our wishes, as well as Sara's, can will a happy ending—and Miss Minchin's comeuppance—into being, as indeed they do, to our delight and satisfaction.

What: Children's. *When:* 1905. *Also By: The Fortunes of Philippa Fairfax* (1888). *The One I Knew the Best of All* (1893). *A Lady of Quality* (1896). *Further Reading: Waiting for the Party: The Life of Frances Hodgson Burnett* by Ann Thwaite. *Try: Heidi* by Johanna Spyri. *The Railway Children* by E. Nesbit. *Adaptations:* Shirley Temple stars as Sara in the 1939 Hollywood classic, which is not entirely faithful to Burnett's plot. The enjoyable 1995 film, directed by Alfonso Cuarón, transports the action to New York City during the First World War.

The Secret Garden
Mistress Mary, Quite Contrary, How Does Your Garden Grow?

The story begins in India, with sickly, plain, moody Mary Lennox. Unloved by her pretty mother, Mary has been raised by servants who've done nothing but indulge the child in order to appease her petulance. Orphaned by cholera, she is shipped off to England to live with her uncle, Archibald Craven, an equally ill-tempered person whose slight hunchback symbolizes his cramped heart, embittered by ceaseless mourning for his deceased wife. Craven's home, Misselthwaite Manor, is also an emblem of a closed and inhospitable existence: "The house is six hundred years old and it's on the edge of the moor," Mrs. Medlock, the head of the household staff, tells Mary, "and there's near a hundred rooms in it, though most of them's shut up and locked."

Soon after arriving on the estate, Mary stumbles upon a walled garden that's been locked and abandoned since the death of Mrs. Craven. Unbeknownst to anyone, Mr. Craven has buried the key; Mary, guided by a helpful robin (one of the story's several fairy-tale touches), unearths it and surreptitiously rejuvenates the dormant plot, creating—with the help of her maid Martha and Martha's resourceful young brother Dickon—an oasis in the midst of Misselthwaite's blight that will not only nurture Mary's emotional flowering, but restore the health of her invalid cousin and rouse her uncle from his profound grief. Ripe with metaphor and a heartwarming faith in the sympathetic magic of nature and friendship, *The Secret Garden* is a lovely fable of perseverance, restoration, and redemption.

What: Children's. *When:* 1911. *Try: Black Beauty* by Anna Sewell. *The Lion, the Witch and the Wardrobe* by C. S. Lewis (see page 485). *Adaptations: The Secret Garden* has been adapted often as play, musical, and movie. The 1991 Broadway production, with music by Lucy Simon and book and lyrics by Marsha Norman, was nominated for seven Tony awards, winning two. *Footnote:* In 1936, Frances Hodgson Burnett was paid tribute by the installation of a memorial fountain in Central Park's Conservatory Garden. In the middle of a reflecting pool, a reclining Dickon plays the flute for Mary, who holds a bowl that serves as a birdbath for three seasons out of the year.

The Anatomy of Melancholy
Robert Burton (1577–1640)

An Idiosyncratic and Indispensable Masterpiece

Robert Burton was a British scholar who spent virtually all of his adult life at Oxford University, first as a student and then as the librarian of Christ Church College. His vast erudition found expression in one of the most bookish books ever written: *The Anatomy of Melancholy.*

Burton and his time used the word "melancholy" in a more specialized sense than we use it today. According to theories dating back to the ancient Greeks, a person's temperament was determined by the distribution in the body of the four "humors." These were fluids—blood, phlegm, black bile, and yellow bile—that corresponded respectively to the basic elements of air, water, earth, and fire. When black bile predominated, the resultant temperament was

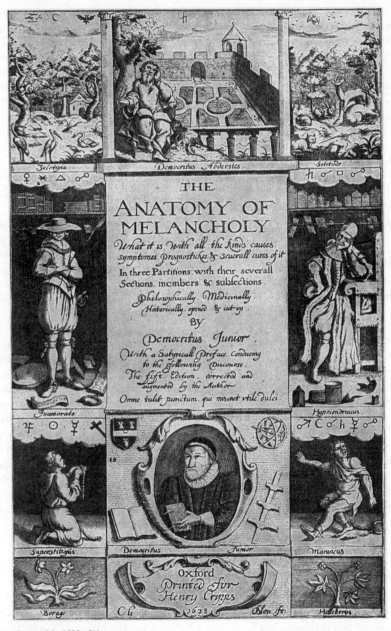

Cover of the 1638 edition

melancholic, the attendant mood one of pensive depression and enduring sadness.

Burton, the sedentary bookman, was melancholic himself, and on one level his *Anatomy* is a serious, encyclopedic attempt to understand melancholy and the various cures that had been proposed for it at one time or another; it has been called the first detailed psychological work in English. On another level, though, the work is a mischievous escapade—an insanely learned scholarly joke. The comedy derives from Burton's inexhaustible range of reference (more than 1,300 authors are cited) and his unstoppable loquacity (in his final version, there are more than 500,000 words). Weaving a tapestry of quotation, digression, contradiction, and mind-ful, ceaseless musing, Burton often reaches a pitch of giddy profundity that is nothing short of hilarious.

Anthony Burgess called *The Anatomy of Melancholy* "one of the great comic works of the world," while Llewelyn Powys, attuned to the author's peerless style, called it "the greatest work of prose of the greatest period of English prose-writing." A verbal city that is end-lessly fascinating in its attentions and design, Burton's elaborate construction repays a life-time's wandering. The caution and encourage-ment offered by M. A. Orthofer in the online *Complete Review* couldn't be more apt: "Densely packed, it defies reading as it is now generally practised. And yet it is the ultimate book, a vol-ume that one can not but return to over and over, constantly."

What: Philosophy. Psychology. *When:* First edition: 1621; Burton's later augmented editions: 1624, 1628, 1632, 1638, and 1651 (posthumous). *Edition:* The New York Review of Books Classics edition (2001), with an excellent introduction by William H. Gass, is a welcome if—at 1,400 pages—unwieldy paperback. For a full and appropriately dusty appreciation of Burton's antiquarian masterpiece, look for an old edition in several volumes. *Try: The Major Works* by Sir Thomas Browne (see page 102).

"This vast attic of a book is the strangest, funniest, and most consoling work I know."
—Philip Pullman

Independent Spirit
ESSAYS
Hubert Butler (1900–1991)

The Captivating Mind of a Profound Provincial

I n 1985, The Lilliput Press of Mullingar, County Westmeath, Ireland, published *Escape from the Anthill*, the first book to collect the essays of the then eighty-five-year-old Hubert Butler. The wide-ranging pieces, written over the preced-ing four decades, had previously appeared only in such disparate journals as *Ireland of the Welcomes*, *An Cosantóir* (The Irish Army Journal), and *The Irish Times*. Three years later, Lilliput issued a second volume, *The Children of Drancy*; a third and fourth followed in due course. *Independent Spirit*, the first American edition of Butler's work, presents in its nearly six hun-dred pages the best of the Lilliput quartet.

A native of Kilkenny, the Anglo-Irish Butler was a chronicler of local culture, an amateur archaeologist, an astute student of Irish history and politics, a traveler and peri-patetic conscience observing the tragedy of life in Central Europe in the abysmal middle of the last century. He was also a market farmer, a family man, a literary critic. Although rooted in his ancestral home ("When I was a boy of fourteen," he writes, "I decided I was going to live in the place where I was born and where my father, grandfather and great grandfa-ther had lived before me"), his essays spin out from a rich parochialism into a world as wide as curiosity allows. We learn the history of his home, Maidenhall, and of the eccentricities of his family; about the intrigues and desperations of neighborhood politics; about the ancient and festering sores of the Irish state; about a vast and brutal campaign in Croatia in 1941 to convert two million members of the Orthodox Church to Roman Catholicism. There are insightful essays as well on literature (Maria Edgeworth, D. H. Lawrence, Edmund Wilson), the discovery of prehistory, the decay of archae-ology, and other matters of the heart and mind.

Butler's overriding themes—that the les-sons of life and death are both local and moral; that culture withers without a dwelling place;

that conduct, like a compass, needs a fixed point to find its way—are put through eloquent variations. From his perch on the banks of the river Nore, Butler works his words toward wisdom in a way that is distinctive and remarkable. In a modest voice, he teaches us magnificently how to address what the poet James Merrill has called " . . . the dull need to make some kind of house / Out of the life lived, out of the love spent." His essays promise a lifetime's companionship to any reader lucky enough to discover them.

What: Essays. *When:* 1996, collecting essays written over the previous half-century. *Edition:* A British selection, *The Sub-Prefect Should Have Held His Tongue and Other Essays* (1990) offers fewer pieces, but has the virtues of a more alluring title and a more compact size. *Reading Note:* Open anywhere. *Also By:* The two Lilliput Press volumes not mentioned above are: *Grandmother and Wolfe Tone* (1990) and *In the Land of Nod* (1996). *Try: Bowen's Court* by Elizabeth Bowen. *Upstate* by Edmund Wilson. *From the Headlands* by Ronald Blythe.

The Way of All Flesh
Samuel Butler (1835–1902)

Coming of Age in Privilege and Pain

There are books we regard as indisputable classics that were ignored in their day, and whose original neglect we look back on with incomprehension—*Moby-Dick* (see page 542), for instance, or *The Great Gatsby* (see page 277). But what about the books whose reputations have evolved in the opposite direction: works once hailed as masterpieces that now are barely read? Samuel Butler's *The Way of All Flesh*, a scorching semiautobiographical novel, doesn't ring many bells today; you might struggle to find it in a bookstore (if you could first find a bookstore). Yet, at the dawn of the twentieth century, *The Way of All Flesh* crashed onto the English literary scene with the impact of a meteor; for the intellectual and artistic vanguard of a generation it stood as a brave, galvanizing indictment of a society the new breed was only too happy to see fading away.

Skewering the Anglican church, the bourgeoisie, the universities, and above all the sclerotic Victorian class system, Butler's novel follows several generations of the Pontifex family: prosperous, middle-class, religious, well-intentioned, and ultimately monstrous. Theobald Pontifex, an unimpressive boy driven into the church by a detached

Photograph of Samuel Butler, ca. 1898

father, is betrothed to Christina—after a bitterly comic scene in which she and her sisters play a game of cards to determine which of them must marry him. Christina is closer to a servant than a wife for Theobald, and their son Ernest (clearly modeled on the author) is subjected to a tyrannical upbringing, with frequent beatings and endless lectures on his own inferiority. Once out of the house, Ernest careers through a series of swindles and misfortunes, including a catastrophic marriage to a lower-class bride, before finally finding his calling as a writer.

Published posthumously in 1903, Butler's novel is of a piece with other bourgeois-shocking books of the period, from pens as diverse as those of Shaw and Ibsen, Nietzsche and Freud. Yet Butler had actually composed his bold fiction many years before, back in the 1870s and early 1880s. He declined to publish it, thinking it too dangerous an attack on the society of the day. Indeed, obscurity and hesitation run through his career, as does a certain crackpot brilliance; his earlier novel *Erewhon* (1872), a satire set in a seeming utopia that challenged the optimistic predictions of the future held by both Darwinists and socialists, was published anonymously; its ideas on both evolutionary thought and the prospective intelligence of machines remain arresting today. He also produced a work of literary criticism, *The Authoress of the Odyssey* (1897), which argues—with conviction and no little loopy persuasiveness—that Homer was a Sicilian woman.

While *The Way of All Flesh* has largely disappeared from view, its literary influence remains pervasive, from George Orwell, who was quite conscious of his debt to Butler, to any number of contemporary novelists who might not be aware of the roots of the irony in which they couch their tales. More importantly for readers, Butler's understanding of the perils of pious convention has much to teach our own impious age; indeed, many a twenty-first-century youth might do well to view the certainties of his or her privilege through the same sharp lens with which Butler comes to see Ernest's education, and his own: "an attempt, not so much to keep him in blinkers as to gouge his eyes out altogether."

What: Novel. *When:* 1903. *Also By: Erewhon Revisited* (1901). *Further Reading: Samuel Butler: A Biography* by Peter Raby. *Try: The Ambassadors* by Henry James. *Howards End* by E. M. Forster. *The Man Who Loved Children* by Christina Stead (see page 747).

"One of the world's great books."
—*George Bernard Shaw on* The Way of All Flesh

···

The Tartar Steppe
Dino Buzzati (1906–1972)

Waiting for the Barbarians

D ino Buzzati is one of modernity's most beguiling storytellers: His fictions are a cross between Kafka and the Brothers Grimm—fables and fantasies that are anxious, enchanting, exquisite, and elevated to an eerie sublimity by their reportorial matter-of-factness (the author spent his writing life in the employ of *Corriere della Sera*, Milan's leading newspaper). In one Buzzati tale, an elevator goes down, down, down, not crashing, not stopping; in another, a jacket's pockets miraculously—and malignantly—fill themselves with other people's money; in a third, an immense fist appears in the sky one morning ("It was God, and the end of the world").

Although his unforgettable short stories have only sporadically been available in English, his masterpiece, the 1940 novel *The Tartar Steppe*, has been more steadily in print (in Stuart Hood's translation). It spins the simplest of plots into a work that lodges in the reader's mind as an uncommonly persistent and apprehensive presence. A young military officer, Giovanni Drogo, posted to a remote outpost at the farthest reaches of an undefined empire, spends a lifetime on battlements overlooking a desert, waiting for the invasion of the legendary Tartars—an attack that will give him and his comrades a stage for martial glory. But, through years and then decades of anticipation, of investing his hope in the merest flicker of light on the horizon, of spending his vitality attending to the rigorous routines and elaborate password precautions of the isolated fort, the Tartars never come. While the soldier's friends back home marry, raise children, and lead more or less fulfilling lives, Drogo's own existence never quite begins; the promise of his days is dissipated in relentless, increasingly futile suspense.

Despite—or perhaps because of—its surreal stasis, *The Tartar Steppe* exerts a formidable spell. Buzzati refuses to reduce its force to a simple message, yet the novel suffuses our imaginations with a powerful sense of meaning nonetheless, for in its pages the author has fashioned a ghost story that is haunted by the most unnerving spirits of all: our own expectations.

What: Novel. *When:* 1940; English translation from the Italian by Stuart C. Hood, 1952. *Also By: The Bears' Famous Invasion of Sicily* (1945; children's book). *Restless Nights* (1971; in English, 1983) is a collection of stories edited and translated by Lawrence Venuti, as is *The Siren* (1984). *Try: The Castle* by Franz Kafka. *Waiting for the Barbarians* by J. M. Coetzee. *Adaptation:* Filmed as *The Desert of the Tartars* in 1976, with Vittorio Gassman, Jacques Perrin, and Max von Sydow.

Possession
A ROMANCE
A. S. Byatt (born 1936)

A Page-Turning Romance That Spans a Century

A feast of literary and storytelling invention, *Possession* is mysterious, layered, romantic, suspenseful—and nearly impossible to put down. It begins quietly enough, in September 1986, when British academic Roland Mitchell opens a long, undisturbed volume in the Reading Room of the London Library. Research into the sources of a work by the Victorian poet Randolph Henry Ash has led Mitchell to the book, Ash's own copy of an eighteenth-century Italian philosophical tome. His perusal of the poet's marginal notes is interrupted by his discovery—between pages 300 and 301—of drafts of a letter in Ash's hand to a woman not his wife. With some urgency, Ash writes that he enjoyed their recent encounter and hopes they might meet again. Sensing a scholarly windfall, Roland steals the evidence and sets out to uncover the truth about the correspondence. Was a letter ever sent? Who was the woman? Did she agree to see him again? And then what?

Quickly determining that the woman Ash addresses must have been the poetess Christabel LaMotte, Mitchell seeks out the preeminent LaMotte scholar, Maud Bailey, who is descended from the subject of her study. The two soon become literary detectives, uncovering and then retracing—with a pair of scholarly rivals on their heels—a clandestine voyage the Victorian poets had embarked upon. As they do so, the reader becomes absorbed in a pair of parallel love stories, one told in the extraordinarily accomplished letters, poems, and diaries that Byatt has invented for her nineteenth-century couple, the other in her contemporary tale of readerly revelation and romance.

It's hard to imagine that, before this novel won the Booker Prize and became an international bestseller in 1990, the author was working largely in the shadow of her sister, novelist Margaret Drabble. Byatt had published a handful of acclaimed books with somewhat narrow appeal, being what critics like to call "cerebral." But *Possession* found its way onto international bestseller lists because it appeals to readers' heads and hearts in equal measure. Byatt has said that, unlike her other books, it was "written out of pure literary pleasure." And that's precisely how it reads.

What: Novel. *When:* 1990. *Award:* Booker Prize, 1990. *Also By: The Virgin in the Garden* (1979). *Still Life* (1987). *Angels and Insects* (1992). *The Matisse Stories* (1993). *Babel Tower* (1996). *The Biographer's Tale* (2000). *The Children's Book* (2009). *Further Reading:* The essays in Byatt's *Passions of the Mind* (1991) bring a scholar's tools to bear on her ardent interests as reader and writer. *Try: The French Lieutenant's Woman* by John Fowles (see page 294). *The Name of the Rose* by Umberto Eco (see page 243). *Arcadia* by Tom Stoppard. *Adaptation:* The 2002 film stars Gwyneth Paltrow and Aaron Eckhart.

C

The Marriage of Cadmus and Harmony
Roberto Calasso (born 1941)

Greek Revival

Like a voluptuous soundscape emanating from the primordial deep, classical mythology haunts our imagination with mysterious chords, urgent harmonies, and frightening dissonances. The Greeks, Roberto Calasso might say, knew this music intimately, hearing its strains whenever risk or enthusiasm entered their lives: It meant that the gods were near. Throughout their existence, and especially at moments of passion or peril, the heroic ancients felt themselves "being sustained and imbued by something remote and whole."

Part storybook, part research into the wellsprings of our being, *The Marriage of Cadmus and Harmony* is a tour de force of invention and erudition. Not a novel, exactly, nor simply a collection of venerable tales retold, and certainly not a critical examination of our mythological legacy, it is rather an expert unraveling of the knots of story that bind human imagination to the divinities that shape its ends. With playful, eloquent, aphoristic variations on the mythic themes of Europa and the bull, the birth of Athens, Theseus and Ariadne, the Trojan War, and more, the author conjures Zeus and his cohorts in their vital, violent, and often erotic transformations. As we wander spellbound through Calasso's internationally bestselling symphony of storytelling and meditation, his narration illuminates the tragedy and mystery of our existence, enchanting us all the while.

What: Mythology. Literature. *When:* First Italian publication, 1988. English translation by Tim Parks, 1993. *Reading Note:* Although some familiarity with Greek mythology is helpful, adventurous readers will be able to follow Calasso's threads without it. *Also By: The Ruin of Kasch* (1983). *Ka: Stories of the Mind and Gods of India* (1996). *Tiepolo Pink* (2006). *Further Reading: Metamorphoses* by Ovid (see page 609). *Try: The Holy Embrace* by Mario Brelich. *The Songlines* by Bruce Chatwin (see page 149).

19th-century engraving of Ajax fighting the Trojans

Invisible Cities
Italo Calvino (1923–1985)

A Modern Book of Wonders

As light as a cloud and just as beautiful, Italo Calvino's *Invisible Cities* floats across the mind's sky and seduces our vision. Purporting to be a record of conversations between Marco Polo and Kublai Khan, in which the inveterate traveler describes the many extraordinary cities he has encountered in his wanderings, it is in fact a fiction of poetic and philosophical charm that unfolds in brief descriptions of fifty-five fantastic places, from Anastasia, "a city with concentric canals watering it and kites flying over it," to Zenobia, which, "though set on dry terrain . . . stands on high pilings, and the houses are of bamboo and zinc, with many platforms and balconies placed on stilts at various heights." In the colloquies that interrupt Marco Polo's catalog of urban curiosities, the Great Khan questions his interlocutor's purpose and veracity, but he cannot stop listening to the beguiling itinerary that leads him to cities named Diomira, Dorothea, Despina, Euphemia, Eutropia, and Eusapia, each with its own peculiar defining characteristic. "Cities, like dreams, are made of desires and fears," the Venetian voyager explains, "even if the thread of their discourse is secret, their rules are absurd, their perspectives deceitful, and everything conceals something else."

Calvino's cities, in other words, are emblems of the imagination—of memory, longing, expression, speculation, fancy. Each small scene the author draws invites us into a confluence of insight, enchantment, and intuition—a warren of streets we amble down, lost in thought but alert to marvels. To read *Invisible Cities* is to discover an unsuspected mythology whose truths are inexplicably recognizable; it is unlike nearly every other book you will ever open. A true master of the fabulous, Calvino succeeds by making his readers feel they are as imaginative as he is.

What: Novel. *When:* In Italian, 1972; the English translation by William Weaver appeared in 1974. *Also By: The Path to Spiders' Nests* (1947). *T Zero* (1967). *Cosmicomics* (1968). *The Castle of Crossed Destinies* (1973). *If on a Winter's Night a Traveler* (1979). *Six Memos for the Next Millennium* (1988). *Further Reading: The Travels of Marco Polo* (see page 635). *Try: The Tartar Steppe* (see page 117) and *Restless Nights* by Dino Buzzati. *Adaptations:* It is a mark of its singularity that, although it is impossible to imagine a film version of Calvino's book, *Invisible Cities* has inspired a hotel in Spain, computer programs, illustrations and installations by artists and architects, and music for rock bands, jazz combos, and string quartets.

Memorial
Ferdinando Camon (born 1935)

Requiem for a Mother and a Way of Life

Only 120 pages long, *Memorial* is a small book about a small life. Yet the reader who opens it will discover a story that is unforgettably moving in its sympathy, dignity, and desire to articulate the deepest human needs.

Written by one of the most notable of Italy's post–World War II writers, this enchanted autobiographical novel is steeped in the peasant culture of Camon's native Veneto, an ageless and all-but-vanished way of life the author has left behind for the city and the twentieth century. Relating the death of his mother and the building of an altar to her memory by his father, it mixes memory and meditation to evoke his people's spare, brutal, and profound intimacy with the earth and its animals, with mortality and generation.

"She knew nothing outside her house and those places where she worked," writes the narrator of his subject, "but those places she knew by heart." As he describes that house and her labors to nourish her family's life within it, Camon constructs an altar of words that, like his father's altar of copper and wood, bears witness to how much such a heart can hold.

What: Novel. Memoir. *When:* 1978; first American edition, translated by David Calicchio, 1983. *Also By: The Fifth Estate* (1970) and *Life Everlasting* (1972) are the first two volumes in Camon's Saga of Those Who Are Last (American editions, 1987). Although *Memorial* completes the trilogy, it is the best place to begin.

"A short novel of exceptional beauty set in an Italian peasant village—a sublime work of art."
—*Raymond Carver on* Memorial

THE MASKS OF GOD
PRIMITIVE MYTHOLOGY • ORIENTAL MYTHOLOGY • OCCIDENTAL MYTHOLOGY • CREATIVE MYTHOLOGY
Joseph Campbell (1904–1987)

From Here to Eternity, and Back Again

The sense that the world has a purpose more profound than its mere existence, and that we ourselves have a significance separate from our day-to-day experience, is the source of all myth. The mythic dimension is intuitive, inexact, yet vibrant: In its embrace we confront the things we *know* but can't explain, and tell stories about them. Joseph Campbell's great insight is that the seeds from which these stories grow share an imaginative DNA across time, space, and cultures, and that, accordingly, the various flowerings of myth are infused with universal themes.

Joseph Campbell

Drawing on researches in archaeology, anthropology, and psychology, and, not least, the author's inexhaustible enthusiasm, The Masks of God series celebrates the power of myth as a central mode of apprehension, surveying human testimony from the prehistoric and communal formulations of hunting tribes through the individual creations of modern artists.

Each of the four books that constitute The Masks of God is a fertile field of rumination, irrigated with an endless stream of mythological invention. *Primitive Mythology* examines the centrality of the human life cycle to the shape and substance of our earliest attempts at meaning making. *Oriental Mythology* delves into the rich traditions of Egypt, India, China, and Japan, and *Occidental Mythology* surveys the worship and literature of the West as they were fashioned under the influences of Zeus and the Olympians, Moses and Abraham, Jesus and Mohammed. The final book in the quartet, *Creative Mythology*, considers the artistic and aesthetic evolution of the mythic impulse from the early Middle Ages (Dante) to early Modernism (James Joyce and T. S. Eliot).

An inspiring guide to the landscape of insights that myths embody, Campbell leads us by the hand down its roads past creation, birth, love, and death, and toward eternity. He opens our ears to voices that call across cultures and centuries, singing life's secrets and surprises. The Masks of God is a comprehensive survey of his life's work, a stimulating treasury of learning, wisdom, and wonder.

What: Mythology. Anthropology. *When:* Four volumes: *Primitive Mythology* (1959); *Oriental Mythology* (1962); *Occidental Mythology* (1964); *Creative Mythology* (1968). *Also By: The Hero with a Thousand Faces* (1949). *The*

Mythic Image (with M. J. Abadie; 1974). *The Power of Myth* (with Bill Moyers; 1988). *Further Reading: A Joseph Campbell Companion: Reflections on the Art of Living*, edited by Diane K. Osbon. *Try: The Golden Bough* by James George Frazer. *The Myth of the Eternal Return* by Mircea Eliade. *Footnote:* Late in life, having retired after decades of teaching at Sarah Lawrence College, Campbell became something of a celebrity, partly as a result of the inspiration his work supplied to George Lucas's Star Wars saga, and partly because of the popularity of the 1988 public television series *The Power of Myth*, which he made with Bill Moyers.

ALBERT CAMUS
(1913–1960)

Through World War II and its aftermath, Albert Camus grew in stature as a representative of moral probity, literary achievement, and, if truth be told, intellectual glamour; in photographs, trench-coated and with ever-present cigarette, he seems to be the Parisian existentialist from central casting. But he wasn't really, strictly speaking, a philosopher, despite the aphoristic acumen—and international resonance—of his reflections on the human predicament. He was a lyrical rather than an analytical thinker, which would eventually lead to his belittlement by Jean-Paul Sartre and similarly severe savants of the time. For his part, Camus came to dub Sartre and his ilk the "professional humanists" of the "specialized cafés" of Paris; at their tables the author of *The Stranger*—born in Algeria to an impoverished family—would always be something of an outsider.

Yet what more academic sages saw as Camus's weakness —his lack of ruthless analytical rigor—was actually his great strength as a writer. His vision—one might better call it intuition—is rooted in the perception that lives validate many truths that are different in kind and substance, not only unequal in weight, measure, and proportion, but contradictory at their core. In other words, he understood that life is messier than philosophy can allow, and that

the compromises such messiness engenders demand that we treat others with tolerance, holding ourselves responsible for our own conduct even if— especially if—the full context of our actions is never entirely clear. It's a brave but uneasy position, and it gives his work a bracing provisionality and a sensory awareness that honor the exigencies—and the happy accidents—of our experience.

Albert Camus, 1946

The Plague
A Parable of Terror and Resistance

I t starts with one rodent, dead on the landing outside of Dr. Rieux's surgery: "something soft under his foot" that he kicks away without a second thought. But soon there are thousands of dead rats turning up in the streets of Oran, a port town in Algeria. The concierge in the doctor's building succumbs to a strange fever, then others in increasing numbers fall victim to the same fate, until contagion—and fear—have the entire city in their grip.

Welcome to the epidemic city: a place where rumors run wild, government can't coordinate relief, religious authorities rave ineffectually, and no one knows what today, much less tomorrow, holds in store. At first the citizens of Oran panic and revolt, but before long, as if numbed by the summer sun, their alarm gives way to despondency and resignation. Bodies are piled high in the streets, neighborhoods stink of pestilential flesh, homes are burned, and citizens wander in a hopeless daze. Yet somehow life goes on; in one astounding scene, Camus describes a performance of *Orpheus and Eurydice* at the local opera house, where the tenor collapses from the plague mid-aria.

The Plague has the intensity of a medical thriller, but it's more than that. As Camus intimated in his first and most famous novel, *The Stranger* (1942), and as he elucidated in philosophical works such as *The Myth of Sisyphus* (1942) and *The Rebel* (1951), he saw humankind as alone in an absurd, pointless universe. Quarantined Oran, in his novelist's hands, becomes a microcosm for society as a whole. Although the tale was written during the Nazi occupation of France, the infection it portrays is not just an allegorical stand-in for political oppression. What matters most to Camus is not the violence and lethality of the plague, but its random, meaningless force. As an old, asthmatic patient that Rieux treats frequently puts it, "But what does that mean—'plague'? Just life, no more than that." And yet, through his matter-of-fact narration of this book's horrifying events and their aftermath, the author manages to convey the lesson, as hopeful as it is simple, that he believes we are taught, not only by pestilence, but by existence itself, "that there are more things to admire in men than to despise."

What: Novel. *When:* 1947. First English translation by Stuart Gilbert, 1948. *Also By:* Fiction: *The Fall* (1956); *Exile and the Kingdom* (1957). *Further Reading: The Burden of Responsibility* by Tony Judt. *Try: Blindness* by José Saramago. *Year of Wonders* by Geraldine Brooks. *The Road* by Cormac McCarthy (see page 534).

Seven-year-old Albert Camus (at center, in black) in his uncle's workshop in Algiers, 1920

The First Man
Last Words of a 20th-Century Hero

C amus was awarded the Nobel Prize in Literature in 1957, when he was not yet forty-four; three years later, he was killed in an automobile accident. *The First Man* is the autobiographical novel in progress whose handwritten manuscript was discovered in the wreckage of the fatal crash; it would remain unpublished for thirty-five years after his death. It seems strangely fitting that this uncompleted project now stands as the most moving legacy of a man who devoted much of his creative energy to seeking meaning in the shadow of modernity's nihilism.

"Being pure," Camus wrote in one of his essays, "is recovering that spiritual home where one can feel the world's relationship, where one's pulse-beats coincide with the violent throbbing of the two o'clock sun." In the luminous pages of *The First Man*, the reader embarks with the protagonist on a quest for such purity, a journey through the landscape of memory, "back to the childhood from which he has never recovered," far from the sophisticated world in which he lived as a celebrated writer. The radiant episodes that reflect Camus's impoverished youth in Algeria—growing up fatherless with his illiterate, near-deaf mother and an extended family for whom words were blunt and awkward objects—are filled with a sensual affection and an immediacy of feeling that bears witness to the lessons that life, and love, can teach.

As a novel, *The First Man* stands unfinished, its ambitions apparent, abundant, rewarding, evocative yet unfulfilled. As a testament to the deep wells of emotion that haunted its author's

memory, from first man to last, it is, by any measure, an extraordinary monument.

What: Novel. *When:* Published posthumously in French in 1994, and in English, translated by David Hapgood, in 1995. *Also By:* In addition to titles listed above, the essays collected in *Resistance, Rebellion, and Death* (1957) and *Lyrical and Critical Essays* (1968), as well as the two-volume *Notebooks, 1935–1951* (1962 and 1964) are worth seeking out. *Further Reading: Albert Camus: A Life* by Olivier Todd. *Camus: A Romance* by Elizabeth Hawes. *Try: Hunger of Memory* by Richard Rodriguez (see page 671).

Slightly Out of Focus
Robert Capa (1913–1954)

A Peerless Photojournalist's Memoir of World War II

Capa was born in Budapest, Hungary. His real name was Endre Friedmann. The story of how he created the figure of "Robert Capa," a glamorous American photographer, to market his early work in 1930s Paris could be the seed of a perfect Eric Ambler thriller (see page 17). He spent the rest of his life living up to his invention.

By the time he was twenty-five, Capa was already being called "the greatest war photographer in the world." A few years later, his reputation as the most daring combat photojournalist alive was enhanced by the remarkable pictures he took during the June 6, 1944, D-Day landings, when he waded ashore, under blistering fire, with American troops at Omaha Beach in Normandy. ("I am a gambler," Capa acknowledged. "I decided to go in

Robert Capa photo of D-Day landings on Omaha Beach, June 6, 1944

with Company E in the first wave.") He died ten years later, not yet forty-one, when he stepped on an anti-personnel mine while covering the First Indochina War (1946–54). In all, he documented five conflicts, including, in addition to the two already mentioned, the Spanish Civil War (1936–39), the Second Sino-Japanese War (1937–45), and the 1948 Arab–Israeli War.

Slightly Out of Focus is Capa's personal take on World War II in Europe between 1942 and 1945. It is characterized from the outset by his congenial tone—"There was absolutely no reason to get up in the mornings any more," he begins, detailing a lazy morning in his New York studio—and his storytelling flair. In fleet and vivid prose, complemented by his arresting photographs, Capa recounts his intimate experience of fateful, fearsome events from London to Algiers, Sicily to Normandy. Describing battlefield experiences and reminiscing about people he met in the shadow of war, Capa's voice—compassionate, moving, and often very funny—proves as expressive as his camera.

His memoir takes its title from the wrongheaded phrase that *Life* magazine used to caption those amazing D-Day pictures: They were "slightly out of focus," *Life* claimed, because Capa's hands were shaking. But the truth was, as the author explains, "the excited darkroom assistant, while drying the negatives, had turned on too much heat and the emulsions had melted and run down before the eyes of the London office. Out of one hundred and six pictures in all, only eight were salvaged." All of them, plus dozens of other examples of Capa's contemporaneous work, are reproduced in recent editions of *Slightly Out of Focus*.

What: Memoir. War. Photography. *When:* 1947. *Edition:* The 2001 Modern Library paperback reissue contains more than 100 of Capa's black-and-white images. *Also By: A Russian Journal* (text by John Steinbeck; 1948). *Report on Israel* (text by Irwin Shaw; 1950). *Images of War* (1964). *Robert Capa: Photographs* (edited by Richard Whelan and Cornell Capa; 1985). *Further Reading: D-Day June 6, 1944* by Stephen E. Ambrose. *Blood and Champagne: The Life and Times of Robert Capa* by Alex Kershaw. *Try: Brave Men* by Ernie Pyle. *Up Front* by Bill Mauldin.

In Cold Blood
Truman Capote (1924–1984)

The True Crime Classic

Until one morning in mid-November of 1959, few Americans—in fact, few Kansans—had ever heard of Holcomb. Like the waters of the river, like the motorists on the highway, and like the yellow trains streaking down the Santa Fe tracks, drama, in the shape of exceptional happenings, had never stopped there.

So writes Truman Capote near the beginning of this "true account of a multiple murder and its consequences," after a quick but evocative sketch of the village in western Kansas—home to some 270 people—that would soon find its unexceptional, lonely quietude violently disturbed.

Among Holcomb's inhabitants lived Herbert William Clutter, along with his wife, sixteen-year-old daughter, and fifteen-year-old son. A college graduate and a successful farmer, Clutter was a prominent citizen, involved in agricultural affairs at both the state and the federal level. When he and his family were bound, gagged, and murdered on the night of November 15, 1959, there was little evidence of who'd done it, or why. The story of their gruesome end made the *New York Times*, where it was read by literary light Truman Capote, who determined almost immediately—even before the eventual suspects were arrested—that he would go to Kansas and write the story of the crime.

Capote traveled to Holcomb with his childhood friend Harper Lee (author of *To Kill a Mockingbird*, see page 469). The two conducted extensive interviews and recorded a wealth of notes, after which Capote devoted several years to work on the book. During that time, Capote closely monitored the case as arrests were made and a trial conducted.

Ultimately, the killers—Perry Smith and Dick Hickock—were hanged, freeing Capote to tell the tale as he wanted: in the form and style of a novel, complete with complex character study and scene-setting, moral tangles and ambiguities, suspense, and, not least, an empathetic, if unobtrusive, authorial intelligence. In this groundbreaking work of creative nonfiction, Capote reconstructs the homicides and their aftermath with stunning attention and a paradoxically expressive reticence; from the perpetrators' first knowledge of the well-to-do farmer, gleaned from a former jail mate, to the discovery of the murder scene and the subsequent investigation, capture, trial, and punishment, *In Cold Blood* is one of the most powerful true-crime dramas ever penned. It remains the gold standard of the genre it transfigured, and transcends.

Truman Capote in Holcomb, Kansas, 1966

What: True Crime. *When:* Serialized in *The New Yorker*, 1965; published in book form, 1966. *Also By: Other Voices, Other Rooms* (1948). *The Muses Are Heard* (1956). *Breakfast at Tiffany's* (1958). *The Dogs Bark* (1973). *Music for Chameleons* (1983). *Answered Prayers* (1987). *The Complete Stories of Truman Capote* (2004). *Further Reading: Capote* by Gerald Clarke. *Try: The Executioner's Song* by Norman Mailer (see page 514). *Helter Skelter: The True Story of the Manson Murders* by Vincent Bugliosi. *Adaptations:* The 1967 movie stars Robert Blake, Scott Wilson, and John Forsythe. The 1996 TV remake stars Eric Roberts, Anthony Edwards, and Sam Neill. The 2005 biopic *Capote*, starring Philip Seymour Hoffman, who won an Academy Award in the title role, depicts the author's time in Kansas researching *In Cold Blood*.

Ender's Game
Orson Scott Card (born 1951)

Unputdownable Science Fiction

The Wiggin children are unusual, even for the unusual world in which *Ender's Game* unfolds. There's the oldest, Peter, a power-mad sociopath; Valentine, the sister who turns her eloquence to Peter's service; and then there's Ender, their little brother, who is singled out by the authorities as the military genius who just might prove to be Earth's savior in its epic conflict with an alien enemy. Set at some indeterminate time in the planet's future, when humanity has been at war with the Formics, an insect-like alien race (familiarly dubbed "buggers") for a hundred years, *Ender's Game* might appear at first blush to be the most formulaic of science fiction novels.

But just try to put it down. Tracing Ender's path to Battle School—a space center in which the best and the brightest children are trained for high-tech war—and, ultimately, to Command School, on the edge of the interstellar front lines, Orson Scott Card's novel is riveting. While Peter and Valentine's machinations throw Earth-bound politics into crisis, Ender's fierce initiation reveals his unparalleled gifts for warfare. As the stakes mount, the simulated battles he dominates are transformed from complex and dangerous games into sinister—and spectacular—realities. Be you teen or adult, the plot will raise all sorts of questions in your mind about militarism, violence, xenophobia, and the grooming of young minds, but not until you've stopped racing to find out what happens next.

What: Science Fiction. *When:* 1986; revised by the author 1991. *Awards:* Nebula Award, 1995. Hugo Award,

1996. *Also By:* Sequels and related books include *Speaker for the Dead* (1986); *Xenocide* (1991); *Ender's Shadow* (1999); *A War of Gifts* (2007); *Ender in Exile* (2008). *Try:* The Foundation Trilogy by Isaac Asimov (see page 25). *Starship Troopers* by Robert A. Heinlein. *Old Man's War* by John Scalzi. *Adaptation:* A superb unabridged audiobook is read by Stefan Rudnicki, Harlan Ellison, and others.

Eyewitness to History
Edited by John Carey (born 1934)

You Are There

A treasured shelf in any personal library is dedicated to those books that can be picked up at whim, opened to any page, and enjoyed for three minutes or three hours as the spirit moves us or as our circumstances allow. An almanac can fill the bill, or a dictionary (John Ciardi's *A Browser's Dictionary* leaps to mind), or any number of diaries or collections of letters, but few volumes serve such serendipitous purpose as well as John Carey's delightful compendium, *Eyewitness to History*.

Beginning in 430 BC with a description by Thucydides of the plague in Athens, and concluding with James Fenton's account of the fall of President Ferdinand Marcos of the Philippines in 1986, Carey's addictive anthology delivers nearly two-and-a-half millennia of history in more than three hundred eyewitness reports, most just a few pages long (and nonetheless potent for that). You'll share Xenophon's fabled march to the sea and a dinner with Attila the Hun; delve into the Black Hole of Calcutta

and visit with Louis XVI and his family imprisoned in the Tuileries; be in the thick of battle at Trafalgar, Gettysburg, Gallipoli, and at Omaha Beach on D-Day. You'll pass through the Crystal Palace with Charlotte Brontë and witness the San Francisco earthquake with Jack London. In addition to the excitement of famous events, you'll also be immersed in evocative accounts of private experience, from Fanny Burney's astonishing 1811 narrative of her own mastectomy (undergone without anesthetic) to George Bernard Shaw's report of his mother's funeral. As Carey writes in his introduction, this is history deprived of generalizations: "The writers are strangers to omniscience." Yet they are a knowing lot regardless, and the source of a lifetime's reading pleasure.

What: History. *When:* 1987. *Edition:* Published in Britain as *The Faber Book of Reportage*. *Try: Eyewitness to America*, edited by David Colbert. *We Were There: An Eyewitness History of the Twentieth Century*, edited by Robert Fox.

True History of the Kelly Gang
Peter Carey (born 1943)

An Australian Outlaw Epic

Every country has its own outlaw mythology. In the folklore of the United States, famous bandits include Jesse James, Billy the Kid, and Bonnie and Clyde. But no American folk hero

has come to assume the massive stature that Ned Kelly (1855–1880) possesses in Australia. The son of an Irish convict father, Kelly stole horses as a child, murdered policemen, robbed banks, and took up as a "bushranger"—the Australian term for runaway convicts who evaded British authorities in the open continent. His notoriety grew until Kelly became a Robin Hood–like symbol of Irish-Australian opposition to the young country's Anglo elite. Today he's seen as an icon of the Australian psyche—untamed, independent, and a little crazy.

A tour de force of authorial invention and tonal control, Peter Carey's *True History of the Kelly Gang* tells the outlaw's story in his own voice, with the protagonist frantically scribbling down his story as he flees the police. Working from a long letter Kelly wrote in 1879, Carey invents an entire vocabulary and syntax of Kelly English: muscular, vernacular, and totally profane. True to the historical Kelly's style, there is not a comma anywhere in the nearly four hundred pages of his narration, which begins with an invocation to his (fictional) daughter:

19th-century illustration of Ned Kelly

Although the unforgettable voice of Kelly, which makes a century-old outlaw's tale breathtakingly immediate, may be the most memorable achievement of *True History of the Kelly Gang*, this book is also a rock 'em, sock 'em true crime tale of page-turning intensity. Carey—the most acclaimed Australian novelist since Christina Stead and Patrick White—had dug into his nation's colonial history before, in novels such as the award-winning *Oscar and Lucinda* (1988), which tells the story of a nineteenth-century romance between an English settler and an Australian heiress. But *True History of the Kelly Gang* goes further, taking great imaginative risks to embrace the past with a vengeance that turns it, for readers, into a living present.

What: Novel. *When:* 2000. *Awards:* Booker Prize and Commonwealth Writers Prize, both 2001. *Also By: Illywhacker* (1985). *Jack Maggs* (1997). *Parrot and Olivier in America* (2009). *Further Reading: Ned Kelly: A Short Life* by Ian Jones. *Try: The Collected Works of Billy the Kid* by Michael Ondaatje. *The Chant of Jimmie Blacksmith* by Thomas Keneally. *Daisy Bates in the Desert* by Julia Blackburn.

I lost my own father at 12 yr. of age and know what it is to be raised on lies and silences my dear daughter you are presently too young to understand a word I write but this history is for you and will contain no single lie may I burn in Hell if I speak false.

The Piano Shop on the Left Bank
Thad Carhart (born 1950)

A Parisian Tale of Music, Craft, and Friendship

Every morning, as he walked his children to school through his Paris neighborhood, American transplant Thad Carhart passed a modest storefront that intrigued him. "*Desforges Pianos: outillage, fournitures*" announced its stenciled sign, and the tools and components of piano repair displayed in its window—tightening wrenches, tuning pins, pieces of felt, small pieces of hardware—illustrated the work that went on behind the glass. Venturing inside on several occasions to express his interest in acquiring a used piano, Carhart was mysteriously rebuffed. The shop seemed as determined in its reserve as the most punctilious Parisian aristocrat. Carhart's cracking of the code of that reserve—he must, he learns, be recommended to the shop by one of its existing customers—is his first step into the "intricate world of mutual trust and obligation" that is the city's hidden community, "the complicated network of local relationships that it was extremely difficult for a foreigner to penetrate."

Admitted to its inner sanctum, Carhart discovers that the Desforges atelier is a wonderland of craft and culture, crammed with dismantled pianos of exquisite artistry, celebrated pedigree, and estimable provenance (had one indeed belonged to Beethoven?). Among its fascinating holdings he eventually comes upon a piano for himself, a Stingl baby grand (if Steinway is the only piano manufacturer you know, you are in for quite an education). As he describes the astonishing delivery of the imposing instrument to his apartment, recollects the allure and aggravations of his childhood piano lessons, and warmly recounts the rekindling of lost musical passion that the Stingl inspires, Carhart writes with an easygoing yet enthralling enthusiasm. Along the way, he effortlessly delivers an informative course in the history and construction of pianos and offers more insight into the French temperament than you might discover in a dozen weightier tomes. Best of all, he introduces us to an unforgettable cast of characters, including the tuner Jos, who sleeps in empty trains; Carhart's Hungarian teacher, Anna, who reacquaints the author with the pleasures of Bach and Bartók, Schumann and Schubert; and, most memorably, Luc, the master of the atelier, whose expertise and gift for friendship is portrayed with great affection.

The Piano Shop on the Left Bank is sheer delight.

What: Memoir. Music. Cities. *When:* 2000. *Also By: Finding Fontainebleau: An American Boy in France* (2016). *Further Reading: Pianoforte: A Social History of the Piano* by Dieter Hildebrandt. *88 Keys: The Making of a Steinway Piano* by Miles Chapin. *Try: A Corner in the Marais: Memoir of a Paris Neighborhood* by Alex Karmel. *The Secret Life of the Seine* by Mort Rosenblum. *The Countess of Stanlein Restored: A History of the Countess of Stanlein Ex Paganini Stradivarius Cello of 1707* by Nicholas Delbanco.

Papa, Please Get the Moon for Me
Eric Carle (born 1929)

A Merry Lunar Voyage for Parents and Toddlers

Any child born into a reading family after 1969 is no doubt familiar with Eric Carle's *The Very Hungry Caterpillar*, as well as several others by the artist who turned an eye for collage-based compositions into a new kind of picture book. Parents of those children, however, have a particularly warm spot in their hearts for *Papa, Please Get the Moon for Me*, a colorful mixture of illustration, imagination, and bookmaking ingenuity.

A little girl named Monica asks her father to bring her the moon to play with. Papa gets a very, very, very long ladder (one of the book's several fold-out pages is necessary to depict how very, very, very long it is) and climbs up into the sky to get it. But the moon is full—as another stunning fold-out spread reveals—and too big for Papa to carry. So Papa waits until it grows smaller, then carries the crescent back to Monica. The story is as simple and lovely as they come, and the pictures really do leap off the page. Kids will learn about the monthly lunar cycle, but what they—and their parents—will really remember is how much fun a book can be.

What: Children's. *When:* 1986. *Reading Note:* Ages three to five. *Also By: The Mixed-Up Chameleon* (1975). *The Grouchy Ladybug* (1977). *The Very Quiet Cricket* (1990). *Further Reading: The Art of Eric Carle. Try: The Rainbabies* by Laura Krauss Melmed and Jim LaMarche (see page 541). *Kitten's First Full Moon* by Kevin Henkes.

ROBERT A. CARO
(BORN 1935)

R obert Caro has won the highest acclaim as a biographer, his studies of first Robert Moses and then Lyndon Johnson (in four volumes to date, with a fifth and final installment still outstanding) being models of dogged reporting, diligent research, and narrative flair. His books observe, detail, and finally understand the theme of power—its effect upon the body politic in the shape of playgrounds and policy, housing and history—with uncommon awareness of its character and compromises. Caro's relish for the pragmatic realities of political practice is combined with a singular imaginative grasp of the drama of human potential politics ultimately enacts. And so, while they tell the stories of individual lives in exhaustive detail, Caro's volumes offer unparalleled scrutiny of the often hidden forces that shape public life in our democracy. *The Power Broker* is a five-act tragedy whose protagonist is as much twentieth-century New York City as it is Robert Moses. *The Years of Lyndon Johnson* uses the career of our thirty-sixth president to animate the larger saga of the ambitions, corruptions, and tortured virtues of our republic, told through the lens of its electoral and the legislative processes. As such, both works are compelling and necessary lessons in civics, historical verities, and human nature.

Robert A. Caro with research materials for his biography of Lyndon Johnson

The Power Broker
ROBERT MOSES AND THE FALL OF NEW YORK
Deconstructing a Master Builder

T he Power Broker—in its scope, energy, and achievement—possesses the monumental dimensions its subject deserves. That's saying a lot, for Robert Moses was for a good portion of the twentieth century the most powerful man in the economic capital of the world. From the 1930s to the 1970s, he shaped the physical destiny of New York City and its suburbs. He was the greatest builder America has ever known, constructing public works—bridges, dams, beaches, parks, roads, housing—on an unprecedented scale. Without the benefit of elective office, Moses built an empire whose reach and resources were longer and deeper than that of most legislative and governmental bodies, and he ruled it as an autocrat.

Caro tells this extraordinary human and political story with a special sensitivity to the ways and means of power, which Moses amassed, wielded, and corrupted in ways both brilliant and brutal. He was a singular combination of idealism, arrogance, inspiration, compromise, discipline, and ruthlessness, and the author brings these qualities vividly to the page as he chronicles Moses's genius for getting things done. To the reader's pleasure and reward, Caro's reportorial rigor is matched by a gift for

Robert Moses next to a model of lower Manhattan

shaping his mountains of research into compelling narratives; so deft is he at chronicling his subject's machinations that one races through this massive book with unstinting eagerness, engrossed in its larger-than-life drama of big dreams and bigger realities, extraordinary achievement and enduring failure.

What: Biography. Politics. Cities. *When:* 1974.
Award: Pulitzer Prize for Biography, 1975. *Further Reading: Robert Moses and the Modern City*, edited by Hilary Ballon and Kenneth T. Jackson, offers an impressive and generally admiring survey of Moses's accomplishments.

"Surely the greatest book ever written about a city."
—*David Halberstam on* The Power Broker

THE YEARS OF LYNDON JOHNSON

THE PATH TO POWER • MEANS OF ASCENT • MASTER OF THE SENATE • THE PASSAGE OF POWER

A Political Education

Embarking upon the reading of four long volumes about Lyndon Baines Johnson might not sound like a good idea, especially when you know the effort will only take you through the first seven weeks of his presidency, the rest of which will be treated in Caro's final volume, still a work in progress. But you'll be surprised to discover that the dimensions of the man—and his "years"—merit both the author's prodigious

labor and a reader's attention. While popular culture was quick to relegate LBJ to caricature in the wake of his fatal obtuseness with regard to our military debacle in Vietnam, Caro tells the tale of a larger-than-life force whose political genius was as formidable as his flaws, taking us from his childhood in the Texas Hill Country through his arrival on—and dominance of—first the Washington and then the national stage. Imagine tracing the development of a Shakespearean tragic hero through the formative stages of his life and you might have some idea of the resonating elements Caro finds in his subject's emerging character.

You might still need convincing, so start with the fourth volume, *The Passage of Power* (2012), which encompasses in its swift narrative the 1960 presidential election; LBJ's unsatisfying, often humiliating stint as John F. Kennedy's vice president; Kennedy's assassination and the subsequent national trauma; and, with incisive attention, the dramatic—one might aptly call them heroic—first seven weeks of Johnson's tenure in the White House, in which he showed himself to be a legislative genius, a courageous champion of civil rights, and, by no means least, a leader with enough probity and presence of mind to steer the country out of the crises of grief and government provoked by the assassination of JFK. It's a book nearly impossible to put down, and so stirring in its depiction of tragedy and triumph that one is compelled to go back to the beginning to uncover more about the man at the center of it. *The Path to Power* (1982) details Johnson's coming-of-age and the profound effect of the land that shaped him and the family misfortunes that tempered his will; *Means of Ascent* (1990) describes in detail his crooked, all-consuming path to the United States Senate; and *Master of the Senate* (2002) chronicles his virtuoso performance through the 1950s as Senate majority leader

New York's Daily News *announces Johnson's victory, 1964*

and cunning mastermind of a protracted campaign to pave the way for a landmark civil rights bill (as well as other, less noble initiatives).

Each book in the sequence has its own story to tell, with many digressions that illuminate political moments and contemporary issues and personalities; all are constructed in digestible episodes crafted to allow readers to dip easily back into these big books after days, weeks, or even months away. Together, they relate, with unsurpassed fascination, what happens when the American dream becomes entangled with the American realities of class, race, money, business, and influence—and, every once in a while, breaks free.

What: Biography. *When:* 1982–2012. *Awards: The Path to Power:* National Book Critics Circle Award, 1983. *Means of Ascent:* National Book Critics Circle Award, 1990. *Master of the Senate:* Pulitzer Prize for Biography, 2003; National Book Award, 2002. *The Passage of Power:* National Book Critics Circle Award, 2012. *Try: The Rise of Theodore Roosevelt* by Edmund Morris (see page 566). *Truman* by David McCullough (see page 537).

A Month in the Country
J. L. Carr (1912–1994)

Restoration in a Yorkshire Village

A Month in the Country may be as poised and perfect as fiction gets: Inspiration, atmosphere, and expression harmonize with an ease and expressiveness that leave a lovely, indelible image in the minds and hearts of its readers. The career of its author, J. L. Carr, was—as Michael Holroyd aptly puts it in his fine introduction to a recent reissue from New York Review of Books Classics—"relentlessly unconventional." When he was headmaster at

Kettering in Northamptonshire, his educational initiatives were ingenious and unorthodox, and the same may fairly be said of the several novels he composed after his retirement in 1967—with the glorious exception of this deeply charged, poetic novella.

At the outset of *A Month in the Country*, Tom Birkin, a World War I survivor and a veteran of a broken marriage, arrives in a remote Yorkshire village to restore a medieval mural in the local church. Setting up his summer abode in the bell tower, he is charmed by the blooming countryside even as he passes his days absorbed in resurrecting an anonymous artist's apocalyptic vision. It is, of course, Birkin's own restoration to faith in life that Carr tellingly portrays, through a season of consolation and renewal that's enduring despite its swift passage. Simple in outline and wonderfully well written, *A Month in the Country* is hauntingly beautiful in its effect.

What: Novel. *When:* 1980. *Also By: A Day in Summer* (1963). *The Harpole Report* (1972). *The Battle of Pollocks Crossing* (1985). *Try: The Go-Between* by L. P. Hartley. *Judgment Day* by Penelope Lively. *Adaptation:* A 1987 film version stars Colin Firth, Kenneth Branagh, and Natasha Richardson.

ALICE IN WONDERLAND
ALICE'S ADVENTURES IN WONDERLAND • THROUGH THE LOOKING-GLASS
Lewis Carroll (1832–1898)

A Perfect Confection of Whimsy, Wordplay, and Invention

When Oxford mathematics lecturer Charles Lutwidge Dodgson went picnicking one summer day with his dean's three daughters, he spun a little tale that he added to on subsequent occasions. The girls liked it so much that the middle child, Alice, who was Dodgson's favorite, asked him to write it down. And so he did, calling it "Alice's Adventures Underground." Later described accurately—and reverently—by Alexander Woollcott as "the most enchanting nonsense in the English language," it is the wildly inventive story of a young girl who, feeling bored one afternoon in a meadow, follows a talking rabbit (dressed in a waistcoat and consulting a pocket watch) into his rabbit-hole. Down she falls to a very strange place, where she is entangled in a string of "curiouser and curiouser" adventures, none of which makes any sense at all. Taking pills and drinking potions, she shrinks and grows and shrinks and grows, swims across a pool of her own tears, and meets one of the most fanciful and unforgettable casts of characters ever concocted: the Caterpillar and the Dodo, the Cheshire Cat, the Mad Hatter, and the Queen of Hearts. Free of moralizing or didacticism of any stripe, Dodgson's narrative floats freely on the intoxicating air of his whimsy and wordplay.

Three years after Alice Liddell asked him to write it down, Dodgson's book was published with the title changed to *Alice's Adventures in Wonderland* and the author's name disguised

as Lewis Carroll. That was 1865. *Through the Looking-Glass, and What Alice Found There*, a sequel in which Alice joins the game on a giant chessboard, discovers the poem "Jabberwocky," and encounters Tweedledum and Tweedledee and other nursery rhyme characters, appeared in 1872.

More than the sum of its parts, Carroll's Alice oeuvre has taken root in our collective imagination like few other literary creations. Despite—or perhaps because of—its nonsensical

Hand-colored illustration of Alice by John Tenniel, ca. 1865

pedigree, it has proved to be an addictive pleasure for analysts seduced by its dense mix of childish frivolities, hallucinatory happenings, logical puzzles, and keen adult observations. Carroll's imagery, phrases, and characters have not only been attached to myriad toys and games, but continue to enliven the language in everything from rock 'n' roll lyrics to ordinary conversation. Most remarkably, although the Alice books date from the nineteenth century and are as ingrained in our culture as any stories ever told, they remain as fresh as the day they were written, delighting new readers every day of every year.

What: Children's. Fantasy. *When: Alice's Adventures in Wonderland,* 1865. *Through the Looking Glass,* 1872.

Editions: In the very first paragraph of the story, Alice wonders "what is the use of a book without pictures or conversations?" Modern editions of Carroll's masterpieces generally include the famous (and indispensable) illustrations by John Tenniel. Martin Gardner provides an inspired form of "conversation" in his exhaustive, inexhaustible, and justifiably revered *The Annotated Alice. Reading Note:* Recommended for family reading aloud. *Also By: The Hunting of the Snark* (1876). *Sylvie and Bruno* (1889). *Sylvie and Bruno Concluded* (1893). *Try:* The nonsense verse of Edward Lear. *Adaptations:* Too abundant to detail, but three worth noting are the 1951 Disney animated film; classical composer David Del Tredici's *Child Alice* for soprano and orchestra (1977–81), which includes *In Memory of a Summer Day,* the 1980 winner of the Pulitzer Prize for Music; and Robert Sabuda's stunningly engineered 2003 pop-up book.

Silent Spring
Rachel Carson (1907–1964)

A Prophetic Work of Environmental Warning

More than four decades before Al Gore's Oscar-winning documentary, *An Inconvenient Truth,* Rachel Carson's *Silent Spring* issued a chilling—and groundbreaking—warning about humanity's careless contamination of our planet. Researched and written over four years, it examines the interdependence of species in nature and postulates a world in which chemical pesticides have not only upset that delicate balance, but wiped out entire species as well. "As crude a weapon as the cave man's club," she writes, "the chemical barrage has been hurled against the fabric of life—a fabric on the one hand delicate and destructible, on the other miraculously tough and resilient, and capable of striking back in unexpected ways."

Carson's particular focus, prompted by the rising use of the pesticide DDT, is the relationship between insects and birds; the title refers to an imagined future in which birds have been extinguished along with the insects targeted by DDT and other chemical agents. Lyrically written, scientifically astute, and passionately argued, *Silent Spring* informed opinion and changed policy across the nation; it led to a ban on DDT and became a catalyst to the global environmental movement.

Before Rachel Carson decided to become a scientist, she wanted to be a writer (at age ten, she saw her first story published in *St. Nicholas Magazine*—as had children named William Faulkner, E. B. White, and Edna St. Vincent Millay before her). The eloquence her early ambition nurtured did much to make her attention to the natural world compelling for a broad readership, contributing to the polemical power of *Silent Spring.* At the same time, Carson's polished and persuasive prose ensured this book, as all her other works, a literary life as enduring as her prophetic scientific concerns.

What: Nature. *When:* 1962. *Edition:* The 40th anniversary edition contains essays by Edward O. Wilson and biographer Linda Lear. *Also By: Under the Sea-Wind* (1941). *The Sea Around Us* (1951). *The Edge of the Sea* (1955). *Further Reading: The Gentle Subversive,* a biography by Mark Hamilton Lytle. *Try: The Immense Journey* by Loren Eiseley (see page 247). *The Rarest of the Rare: Vanishing Animals, Timeless Worlds* by Diane Ackerman. *Footnote:* Carson was posthumously awarded the Presidential Medal of Freedom in 1980.

The Horse's Mouth
Joyce Cary (1888–1957)

A Portrait of the Artist As an Outrageous Old Man

Impossible, irresponsible, unreliable, and entirely unforgettable, Gulley Jimson, the narrator of this exhilarating comic masterpiece, is one of the most original figures in modern fiction. For better or worse, and usually for worse, Gulley is an artist. Nearly seventy, he is a painter still possessed by the urge to realize his visions. He'll do absolutely anything—lie, cheat, scrounge, steal—if he thinks it'll help him paint another painting. As he prowls the streets of London in the years immediately before the outbreak of World War II, he causes chaos and catastrophe all around him, pursuing his own destruction with a combination of cunning, high spirits, low morals, and self-deception that

Alec Guinness in the 1958 film adaptation

only a truly creative spirit could muster. (Cary reputedly modeled his protagonist in part on the poet Dylan Thomas.)

From straightforward panhandling to higher-order scheming (such as the episode in which he makes his way into the home of vacationing art collectors and sets about pawning everything they own), Gulley's off-canvas adventures fuel the novel with a reckless energy that conveys the egomaniacal concentration and liberating impulses of the artistic temperament,

even when those qualities lead to dissipation rather than accomplishment. "In a sense," writes Brad Leithauser in his introduction to a recent edition, "it hardly matters whether he's a major artist or . . . a minor one. Gulley stands for process, rather than production; aspiration, rather than achievement. Whenever he's in the act of painting, we believe in him wholly . . . even as we suspect that this painting, too, will go unfinished." An astute and fiercely funny portrayal of inspiration under siege, imprisoned by implacable circumstances and inflexible character, Cary's tale of Gulley Jimson nevertheless offers an intoxicating draft of the highest human comedy.

What: Novel. **When:** 1944. **Edition:** The 1999 New York Review of Books Classics edition includes Brad Leithauser's introduction. **Reading Note:** Although *The Horse's Mouth* stands by itself as a most satisfying novel, it is the third book in Cary's first trilogy. The preceding volumes—*Herself Surprised* (1941), told in the voice of Sara Monday, lover of both Gulley and an elderly lawyer named Tom Wilcher, and *To Be a Pilgrim* (1942), narrated by Wilcher—make good reading, too. **Also By:** *Mister Johnson* (1939). Second trilogy: *A Prisoner of Grace* (1952); *Except the Lord* (1953); *Not Honour More* (1955). **Adaptation:** Alec Guinness wrote the screenplay for the 1958 film version of *The Horse's Mouth*, in which he plays Gulley Jimson.

History of My Life
Giacomo Casanova (1725–1798)

An Unparalleled Life of Love and Adventure

"I have never read a book—either autobiography or fiction—which seems to give you a life so completely," wrote Edmund Wilson of the memoirs of this legendary libertine. And what

a life it was: Ecclesiastic and secretary, soldier and spy, financier, gambler, historian, translator, alchemist, violinist, accomplished seducer, ardent (and surprisingly tender and attentive) lover, and, last but not least, remarkable storyteller, Casanova swept through bedrooms, courts, and cities with reckless charm, talking his way, as one commentator put it, "from Paris to Saint Petersburg and back again."

There is a palpable urgency to *History of My Life* that resembles nothing so much as the perpetual present tense of a movie. Both compelling and entertaining, Casanova's narrative is alive with action and headlong momentum. Each episode is dramatic, sensual, and pictorial. To accompany him on his adventures in these pages is to discover, again in Wilson's words, "the eighteenth-century as you get it in no other book; society from top to bottom; Europe from England to Russia, a more brilliant variety of characters than you can find in any eighteenth-century novel." In sum (four thousand pages) or in part (don't miss his marvelous account of his escape from the Leads, Venice's fabled prison, which concludes the fourth volume), these memoirs are a delightfully diverting treasure.

18th-century portrait of Casanova by Anton Raphael Mengs

of the complete original text was made by Willard R. Trask between 1966 and 1971. For those willing to forgo the full flavor of Casanova's feast, a one-volume edition of Trask's translation (containing about a third of the complete work) has been issued in Everyman's Library.

What: Autobiography. History. *When:* Written 1789–98. *Editions:* Casanova's *History* has had a complicated publishing history, originally appearing in various abridged and edited versions in German and French between 1822 and 1838. The first English translation

Further Reading: The chapters on Casanova's memoirs in Edmund Wilson's *The Wound and the Bow* and Paul Zweig's *The Adventurer* are enlightening. *Try: The Diary of Samuel Pepys* (see page 622). *The Journals of James Boswell: 1762-1795.*

....

Spartina
John Casey (born 1939)

The Middle-Aged Man and the Sea
....

Dick Pierce is at sea, even on land. He is not well off. All he has is a lithe but inadequate skiff, a supply of lobster pots, a growing temper, a mortgage, and an unsteady marriage. He has worked the big fishing boats off the Rhode Island coast—he has even helped build a couple of them. If he could just finish the fifty-foot boat he has half built in his backyard, he might make the most of his strained circumstances, like the marsh grass he admires:

Dick loved the salt marsh. Under the spartina there was black earth richer than any farmland, but useless

to farmers on account of the salt. Only the spartinas thrived in the salt flood, shut themselves against the salt but drank the water. Smart grass. If he ever got his big boat built he might just call her Spartina.

Winner of the 1989 National Book Award, *Spartina* has been described as a classic tale of a man, a boat, and a storm, but that description only partially evokes the texture of the novel and the tempests its protagonist rides out. Casey deftly conjures both the manual work and the metaphorical romance of taking to sea in language that swims easily in both practical and poetic waters, while the weather through which Pierce must pass on his journey toward self-discovery takes several shapes, confronting him in the form of the tourists taking over the Narragansett shore, the undercurrents of class and money that trail disappointment in their wake, the exhilaration and disruption of infidelity, and—last but not least— the physical terror of a hurricane.

The solitary hero fighting to hold fast to a dream in a disenchanted, changing world is a classic figure in American literature, and *Spartina* has earned comparison to Hemingway's *The Old Man and the Sea* (see page 366). Yet Casey's tale is especially notable for setting its protagonist's quest for private nobility within the confines of a perfectly ordinary life. One thing is certain, as a *Time* reviewer noted, "They do not make novels like this very much anymore."

What: Novel. *When:* 1989. *Award:* National Book Award for Fiction, 1989. *Also By: An American Romance* (1977). *Testimony and Demeanor* (1979). *Compass Rose* (2010). *Try: Nobody's Fool* and *Empire Falls* by Richard Russo.

The Book of the Courtier
Baldassare Castiglione (1478–1529)

That Fine Italian *Sprezzatura*

The *Book of the Courtier* depicts the world of its author, Baldassare Castiglione, a nobleman in the service of the Duke of Urbino, who led the most sophisticated court in Italy in the early sixteenth century. Castiglione's volume, which he worked on for more than a decade, is a "courtesy book," a genre of the High Renaissance that propounded etiquette lessons, rules for moral behavior, and advice for nobles in navigating the waters of politics and politesse that always surround royalty. Through a series of dialogues, modeled on the classical precedents of Plato and Cicero, Castiglione argues that a true gentleman needs both military training and education in the humanistic disciplines, such as music and history. You might think of *The Book of the Courtier* as a cross between a drama of manners and a self-help book.

For Castiglione, the ultimate mark of a talented courtier—and the seed from his book that has endured across the centuries—is *sprezzatura*. The word is difficult to translate, and while it's sometimes rendered as "nonchalance," it has something of the knowingness captured in the French *savoir faire* as well. In its broadest sweep, the English "style" suggests the dash that *sprezzatura* assumes: It's the art of making the difficult look simple, giving the impression of effortlessness to activities that actually take great skill. Having brains or brawn isn't enough, Castiglione's characters agree: The real goal of the courtier is to conceal all artistry and make whatever is done or said appear effortless.

Published in Italy in 1528, when publishing was still a young technology, *The Book of the Courtier* was a smash—it rocketed across the Continent and found an especially eager audience in England, where its principles of good living were especially influential (a translation came out just as Queen Elizabeth I was coming to the throne). We know Shakespeare read it: Beatrice and Benedick's arguments in *Much Ado About Nothing* closely resemble one of the *Courtier*'s dialogues, and in *Richard III* the humpbacked future king complains that he is "not shaped for sportive tricks" and has none of the qualities that Castiglione endorses. *The Book of the Courtier* is still very much worth reading five centuries on for its unrivaled depiction of the aristocratic virtues and values of the Renaissance, and for its celebration of the kind of worldly grace to which even the humblest among us at times aspire.

What: Culture. History. *When:* 1528. *Further Reading: The Fortunes of the Courtier* by Peter Burke. *Try: The Prince* by Niccolò Machiavelli (see page 510). *The Autobiography of Benvenuto Cellini* (see page 141). *The Civilization of the Renaissance in Italy* by Jacob Burckhardt (see page 108).

O Pioneers!

Willa Cather (1873–1947)

A Landmark in American Literature

In Hanover, Nebraska, a Swedish immigrant dies and leaves his farm not to his sons, but to his daughter. Despite drought, economic depression, and the demands of the land the family inhabits, Alexandra Bergson, one of American literature's most vivid heroines, is determined to make a success of the farm through ambitious expansion and diligent husbandry. Weathering the challenges posed by her brothers and by her loneliness as a frontierswoman, she navigates practical and emotional complexities by means of an inner compass that, if not unerring, is enduringly true, even when she loses sight of it. As Cather writes, "Her personal life, her own realization of herself, was almost a subconscious existence; like an underground river that came to the surface only here and there, at intervals months apart, and then sank again to flow on under her own fields."

Describing this 1913 novel, Willa Cather characterized it as "the first time I walked off on my own feet—everything before was half real and half an imitation of writers whom I admired." The previous work was a 1912 novel (*Alexander's Bridge*) and a raft of stories published in various magazines, all influenced by Henry James and the European literary conventions of the time. Cather's friend Sarah Orne Jewett (author of *The Country of the Pointed Firs*) encouraged her to draw more confidently on her own experience in her writing, and from *O Pioneers!* forward her assembled experience would be distilled into a writing voice distinctly her own. Having moved as a child from leafy Virginia to newly settled Red Cloud, Nebraska, Cather abandoned the Great Plains after college for a professional life in Pittsburgh and New York. The themes of her creative oeuvre would follow a similar path, encompassing the struggles of the denizens of the prairie and of small-town America as well as the striving of artistic souls to free themselves from the constraints such circumscribed settings imposed. Yet even in *O Pioneers!*, Cather is alert to the

Willa Cather, mid-1920s

double-edged nature of liberation from family and community ties: "Freedom," a character close to Alexandra warns her, "so often means that one isn't needed anywhere."

The first book in a trilogy of "prairie novels" that includes the equally rewarding *The Song of the Lark* (1915) and *My Ántonia* (1918), *O Pioneers!* is the story of a woman who must learn what it means to come into her inheritance, just as it reveals the artistry of a writer who is discovering hers.

What: Novel. *When:* 1913. *Also By:* One of Ours (1922). *A Lost Lady* (1923). *The Professor's House* (1925). *Death Comes for the Archbishop* (1927). *Further Reading: Willa Cather: A Literary Life* by James Woodress. *Try: Giants in the Earth* by Ole Edvart Rølvaag. *The Tie That Binds* by Kent Haruf. *The Living* by Annie Dillard. *Adaptations:* The 1992 Hallmark Hall of Fame television movie stars Jessica Lange. Barbara Harbach's opera premiered in 2009.

The Poems of Catullus
Gaius Valerius Catullus (ca. 84 BC–ca. 54 BC)

What Is This Thing Called Love?

A contemporary of Cicero and Julius Caesar, Catullus created a small body of work that has survived as long as—and more vividly than—the grand political passions of those two estimable men. The poet's more than one hundred *carmina* are a mixture of short lyrics, epigrammatic verses, and a handful of lengthier (and generally less interesting) poems. Catullus's primary subject is love, or more properly, the course of infatuation, negotiation, yearning, pleasure, disaffection, heartache, and despair that is love's life cycle.

Distinctive, acute, clever, and conversational, the voice that animates his best lines rings clear in modern ears:

I hate and love. If you ask me to explain
  The contradiction,
I can't, but I can feel it, and the pain
  Is crucifixion.

Catullus might be said to have invented the tone of self-lacerating desire and angry ardor that runs through centuries of literary lamentations (and can even be heard echoing in popular songs—think of Rodgers and Hart's "I Wish I Were in Love Again"). Whether ecstatic with erotic impulse or keen with invective, Catullus's bursts of feeling are always articulated with sophisticated intelligence. His poems' intricate construction and devilishly alert self-consciousness turn everything they express, whether ribald insult or tender grief, into indelible verse. As Anne Carson, writing of Catullus's elegy for his brother, put it, "No one (even in Latin) can approximate the Catullan diction, which at its most sorrowful has an air of deep festivity, like one of those trees that turns all its leaves over, silver, in the wind." Even in translation, though, the leaves retain their allure.

What: Poetry. Antiquity. *When:* First century BC.
Editions: Catullus's Latin is so compact and distinctive that comparing translations can be both intriguing and instructive. Peter Green's recent bilingual edition is excellent and well annotated, but James Michie's older, rhyming renderings of the poems (quoted above) are worth seeking out. *Further Reading: Poets in a Landscape* by Gilbert Highet. *Try: The Art of Love* by Ovid. *Elegies* by Sextus Propertius. The poems of Andrew Marvell. *Adaptation:* Carl Orff set Catullan texts to music in his cantata from the 1940s, *Catulli Carmina.*

Melbourne
David Cecil (1902–1986)

A Political Life in a Polished Literary Gem

David Cecil's biography of the British statesman William Lamb, 2nd Viscount Melbourne, is reputed to have been John F. Kennedy's favorite book. If that's true, the thirty-fifth president had extremely good taste.

Melbourne's role as mentor to Queen Victoria upon her ascension to the throne at the age of eighteen is of considerable historical interest, but his life has a compelling narrative beyond his role as prime minister and early counselor to the young woman who became such an enduring monarch. In fact, Melbourne's life fell rather neatly into two parts, as reflected in the two halves of Cecil's work—*The Young Melbourne and the Story of His Marriage with Caroline Lamb*, published in 1939, and *Lord M, or the Later Life of Lord Melbourne*, which appeared in 1954. Each half is galvanized by a woman whose presence enriches with drama and character the events of Melbourne's political career.

Of privileged family, Melbourne advanced his position with leisurely aplomb throughout his youth. His charms met their match in those of Lady Caroline Ponsonby, whom he married in 1805. Seven years later she brought herself and her husband notoriety through her scandalous affair with Lord Byron (it was she who attached to the poet the famous epithet "mad, bad, and dangerous to know"). The story of Melbourne's marriage, and of his steadfast attachment to his wayward wife, is the fulcrum of *The Young Melbourne*, just as his mentoring of Victoria in her first three years as queen is the keystone of *Lord M.*

What gives this biography its literary life, however, is Cecil's deft depiction of personal and social relations. Discussing Victoria's earliest impressions of his subject, for instance, Cecil notes, "In her diary she harps on his moral virtues; 'a most truly honest, straightforward and noble-minded man,' she notes, 'there are not many like him in this world of deceit.'" Yet, with polite but keen insight, he suggests the truth about her impressions of Melbourne:

In addition to being wise and benignant, he was also extremely handsome, an accomplished master in the art of pleasing women, and one of the most fascinating talkers in Europe. As a matter of fact the Queen does not seem to have wholly realized how much of his attraction for her was due to these less serious qualities.

Cecil's understanding of the powerful currents through which his protagonist's life passed extends the reach of his narrative beyond the strictly biographical. Born in 1779, Melbourne fell—pushed by Lady Caroline—from the certainties of the Regency era into the Byronic tumult of the Romantic age, only to emerge on the shore of the Victorian epoch leading its determining personality by the hand. Cecil's sensitivity to Melbourne's singular progress shapes a book that provides the reading pleasure of the great English novels, for it boasts not only the illuminating alertness of Austen but the expansive intelligence of George Eliot as well.

What: Biography. **When:** *The Young Melbourne and the Story of His Marriage with Caroline Lamb* (1939); *Lord M, or the Later Life of Lord Melbourne* (1954). *Edition:* Find a later edition that combines both parts in one volume. *Also By: The Stricken Deer or The Life of Cowper* (1929). *Sir Walter Scott: The Raven Miscellany* (1933). *The Fine Art of Reading and Other Literary Studies* (1957). *Further Reading: Lord Melbourne, 1779–1848* by L. G. Mitchell. *Melbourne* by Philip Ziegler. *Try: Queen Victoria: A Personal History* by Christopher Hibbert. *Disraeli* by Robert Blake. *Samuel Johnson* by W. Jackson Bate (see page 418).

....

Journey to the End of the Night
Louis-Ferdinand Céline (1894–1961)

The Dark Masterpiece at the Dawn of Black Humor

The American critic Alfred Kazin described Céline's style exactly: "He writes like a lunging live wire, crackling and wayward, full of danger." The dangerous nerve that runs through his first and best novel, *Journey to the End of the Night*, has enlivened modern literature through its pervasive influence on writers from Henry Miller to Philip Roth, Samuel Beckett to William S. Burroughs.

That nerve—characterized by an energy that is touchy, vitriolic, vicious, mocking, misanthropic, savagely sarcastic, and relentlessly mordant in its intelligence, but shot through with an astonishing eloquence nonetheless—is the voice of Bardamu, the autobiographical novel's first-person narrator. Like his creator, Bardamu has horrific experiences in the First World War, travels to the jungles of Africa, proceeds to New York and employment in an automobile factory in Detroit, then returns to France to become a doctor in the slums of suburban Paris. He ultimately seeks bitter refuge from the mad world in his work at a private insane asylum. Throughout Céline's detailing of the sordid misadventures of this nihilistic antihero, a furious black comedy infuses each episode; screwing reality to a hallucinatory pitch, Céline wrings a thrilling, terrifying music from life's misery, cruelty, and absurdity.

His breathless, savage prose, with its constant use of ellipses and its "hasty, panting tone" (as the author himself characterized it), is one of the seminal inventions of the modern imagination, and the book in which it was born remains shocking and strangely exhilarating today.

What: Novel. *When:* 1932. *Editions:* The first English translation of *Voyage au bout de la nuit* appeared in 1934. New Directions published Ralph Manheim's excellent new version in 1983. *Also By: Death on the Installment Plan* (1936). *Guignol's Band* (1941). *Castle to Castle* (1957). *North* (1960). *Rigodon* (1969). *Try: Tropic of Cancer* by Henry Miller. *Naked Lunch* by William S. Burroughs. *Footnote:* Céline's anti-Semitic writings prior to the outbreak of World War II led to his brief imprisonment in Denmark at the war's end, in response to a French warrant for his arrest as a Nazi collaborator. Although suspicions of collaboration were unfounded, his anti-Semitism is documented in works such as the polemic *Trifles for a Massacre* (1937).

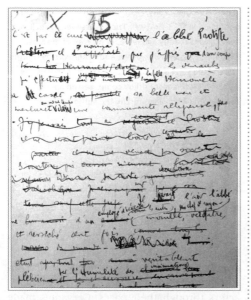

A page from the handwritten first draft of Journey to the End of the Night

The Autobiography of Benvenuto Cellini
Benvenuto Cellini (1500–1571)

A Golden—and Gilded—Renaissance Life

Many artists have had tumultuous personal lives, but few have as crazy a story to tell as the Renaissance sculptor and goldsmith Benvenuto Cellini. He survived prison and plague, befriended popes and princes, had affairs with too many people to count (women and men), made dozens of enemies who were bent on betrayal, and, not to be forgotten, even killed a couple of folks. His rollicking autobiography opens with a famous invocation: "All men of whatsoever quality they be, who have done anything of excellence, or which may properly resemble excellence, ought, if they are persons of truth and honesty, to describe their life with their own hands." Our hero has no doubt that excellence is his stock-in-trade: He's absurdly self-confident, and his memories are an amalgam of truth, exaggeration, and outright delusion. Indeed, mixed into his autobiography are some tall tales that are a little hard to measure today, such as claims that he once conjured up a brigade of devils in the middle of the Roman Coliseum, or that he changed the weather by firing his guns into a rain cloud.

But he is one hell of a storyteller, and these embellishments don't detract from the pleasure of his narrative. On the contrary, they burnish the brio of this vivacious, over-the-top tale of a man assured of his own greatness and in constant struggle with rivals and the law. And many of the details in Cellini's autobiography have been independently verified: his banishment from Florence, for example, and his murder of a rival goldsmith in Milan.

As an artist, Cellini is best known today for decorative works, and he doesn't

Cellini's Perseus with the Head of Medusa, *1554*

figure in the first rank of Italian sculptors of his time. His spectacularly racy autobiography, on the other hand, has no peers: It's the most important autobiography of the Italian Renaissance, and it's as thrilling, as fast paced, and as dangerous as a drag race.

What: Autobiography. *When:* Written in the 1560s; first published in 1728. *Edition:* There are several excellent translations readily available. *Try: Lives of the Most Excellent Painters, Sculptors, and Architects* by Giorgio Vasari (see page 820). *What Did I Do?* by Larry Rivers. *Adaptation:* Hector Berlioz composed an opera, *Benvenuto Cellini,* inspired by the author's life.

Don Quixote
Miguel de Cervantes (1547–1616)

The Invention of Fiction

Miguel de Cervantes sits in exalted company as one of the progenitors of modern literature, and therefore of the modern mind and the culture it inhabits. That Cervantes and two of his companions in eminence—Michel de Montaigne and William Shakespeare—were alive and writing at the same time is one of the wonders of history. Through essay, dramatic verse, and novel, this trio gave shape to what we have come to take for granted as the human mindscape. Indeed, one might argue that the literary revolution Montaigne, Shakespeare, and Cervantes fomented at the midpoint of the last millennium was every bit as influential in nourishing the historical courses of the Enlightenment and democracy as the scientific revolution. For all three, writing was an inquiry rather than a memorial. Even today their works retain a kind of provisionality that interacts with the personal perspective and experience readers bring to it: They are more like organisms made of words than immutable texts. (Reading Montaigne's *On Experience* at nineteen is substantively different from reading it at fifty-nine, and you can do your own math on *King Lear;* Don Quixote's delusions become more sympathetically poignant the older we get.)

While the singularities of Montaigne and Shakespeare are easy to see and wear

Cover of the first edition of Don Quixote, *1605*

a grandeur that is undeniable, Cervantes's achievement is disguised not only by its humble comic dress, but also by the amorphous being and volubility of the narrative form he created for it: the modern novel, in which a story interrogates itself even as it puts its characters through their paces. Cervantes made fiction itself a tool of inquiry, letting stories intersect, interrupt, and reimagine each other in the lives of his characters (much as they do in the course of our real lives). He uncovered a new world for literary endeavor as surely as the seagoing stalwarts of his time explored new continents. If Montaigne's legacy is represented by the essay and Shakespeare's by the soliloquy, Cervantes might be seen to have bestowed upon us, through his own work and that of every novelist who became his heir, the colloquy between the inside of our heads and the outside world that the novel embraces and that *Don Quixote* empowered fiction to undertake.

In the story of Don Quixote, a misguided hero besotted by popular romances of chivalry and steadied only by the hands of a capable and long-suffering companion, Sancho Panza, Cervantes managed to depict—in comedy high and low and in episodes alternately satiric, hilarious, and moving—the battle between idealism and realism that is the unresolved, and perhaps unresolvable, conflict of human existence. He also created two of the most

19th-century engraving of Don Quixote and the Windmills *by Héliodore Joseph Pisan*

memorable characters in all literature; that their renown was fast and far-traveling is evidenced by the fact that in 1607, just two years after publication of the novel's first part in Spain, top prize in a festival competition in a small mining town in the mountains of Peru was awarded to impersonations of the pair. Four centuries later, *Don Quixote* still has the power to educate and delight us, and those who've yet to read it should be prepared to be transported, astonished, amused, and vastly entertained by Quixote's follies, Sancho's instinctive resourcefulness, and—most of all—Cervantes's ingenuity.

Cervantes's personal experience gave him an education that makes Charles Dickens's school of hard knocks seem an almost cozy classroom. A professional soldier who received a crippling injury in the Battle of Lepanto, he was soon afterward captured by Barbary pirates and sold into slavery for several years before being ransomed by his family and returned to

Spain. Back home, he became a government agent who proved so lacking in business skills that he landed in prison as a result of irregularities in his financial accounts. The trauma of his life tempered his youthful conceptions of honor and bravery, and the military glory he once sought was shown to be illusory by the reality of his wounds and the lack of worldly recompense for his suffering; reconciling his early ideals with his career of disenchantment left him in a quandary that his imagining of *Don Quixote* transformed into a profound—and new—understanding of human nature. "When Don Quixote went out into the world," Milan Kundera would write hundreds of years after Cervantes's death (in *The Book of Laughter and Forgetting*; see page 455), "that world turned into a mystery before his eyes. That is the legacy of the first European novel to the entire subsequent history of the novel. The novel teaches us to comprehend the world as a question. There is wisdom and tolerance in that attitude."

The certainties Cervantes had carried with him into battle—the aforementioned ideals of honor and patriotism and the feudal hierarchies of service, duty, and reward that supported them—are, in the course of *Don Quixote*'s narrative, sportingly undone. The book's revelation of the primacy—and, often, tawdriness—of lived events is delivered in a series of episodes in which Quixote mistakes everyday items for emblems of the adventure tales he loves, encoding them with the kind of symbolic significance the chivalric romances championed. So, to the reader's delight, Quixote tilts at windmills he imagines to be dangerous giants, confuses a chamber pot for a cavalier's helmet and dons it accordingly, and spins a vision of a delicate lady love called Dulcinea from the sturdy musculature of a local girl who has no idea she is the source of such a fantasy. The discomfiting consequences of these escapades are lost on Quixote, and Sancho Panza must navigate the perils they provoke for both of them, a task he performs with loyalty, cleverness, and no little luck.

That Quixote is delusional is beyond argument; that his exploits entertain us is also beyond dispute—the laughter his quests prompt is one of literature's great joys. Yet Cervantes never mocks his protagonist, but rather portrays his errant knight-errant with a sympathy that bestows upon him an unabashed dignity, steeped in the character's stubborn desire to make meaning in a way that motivates mind, heart, and soul; that his passions remain heroic despite all the embarrassments of conduct and circumstance they generate is a tribute to Quixote's yearnings, to the wiles and wisdom of Sancho Panza, and to the sensibility of their creator, who, beleaguered in life, is, in the end, triumphant on the page.

As, from the beginning, was *Don Quixote*: So popular was its original publication that it spawned pirated continuations with enormous success, prompting Cervantes to compose and issue a sequel of his own a decade after the first appeared. In part two, Cervantes brilliantly treats Quixote and Sancho as figures whose adventures, as fictional characters who have infiltrated the real world of readers, have assumed the same kind of influence the chivalrous denizens of romance exerted on Quixote in part one. Alert not only to its own artifice but to its existence in the world as a book, *Don Quixote* is a story about stories and how they shape our lives—a brilliant feat of narrative magic that illustrates storytelling's unscientific but unshakable presence at the root of our humanity. On the one hand an elegy for idealism, it is also a celebration of the power of our fictive apprehensions of the world, and the empathy they foster, to make unidealized life more livable.

What: Novel. *When:* 1605 (part 1); 1615 (part 2). *Edition:* There are more than a score of English translations; contemporary readers will be well served by Edith Grossman's 2003 version. *Also By: La Galatea* (1585). *The Exemplary Novels* (1613). *Further Reading: The Man Who Invented Fiction* by William Egginton. *Try: Gargantua and Pantagruel* by François Rabelais (see page 656). *The Life and Opinions of Tristram Shandy, Gentleman* by Laurence Sterne (see page 756). *The History of Tom Jones, A Foundling* by Henry Fielding (see page 273). *Adaptations: Don Quixote* has been adapted many times for stage, screen, and television. The musical treatment, *Man of La Mancha*, achieved acclaim upon its 1965 premiere, winning five Tony Awards; it was made, less successfully, into a 1973 film starring Peter O'Toole, Sophia Loren, and James Coco. A fine unabridged audiobook of the Grossman translation is narrated by George Guidall.

The Amazing Adventures of Kavalier & Clay
Michael Chabon (born 1963)

Coming of Age in the Golden Age of Comics

Michael Chabon made a positive impression on readers and critics alike with his promising first novel, *The Mysteries of Pittsburgh* (1988), a coming-of-age story in which a college grad struggles with his sexuality and his father's shady profession. His second novel, *Wonder Boys* (1995)—depicting the misadventures of a novelist-professor who has written thousands of pages of an unfinished, and unfinishable, novel—reads like a terrific Hollywood romp, and was made into one, starring Michael Douglas. After each of these novels, Chabon published a well-received story collection, but none of this early success quite prepared readers for his ambitious and inventive third novel. With *The Amazing Adventures of Kavalier & Clay*, Chabon knocked one out of the park, and won a Pulitzer Prize to boot.

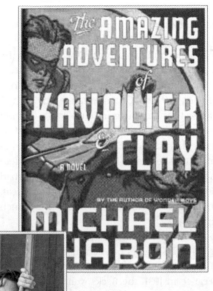

The titular heroes are Joe Kavalier and Sammy Klayman (who changes his name to Clay), teenage Jewish cousins who share a love of drawing and a fascination with Harry Houdini. As the book begins, it's 1939, and Joe has just managed a perilous escape from Nazi-occupied Prague to Brooklyn. He's eager to earn money to bring his family to America before any harm befalls them. Employed by the Empire Novelty Company, which advertises its wares in comic books, a relatively new phenomenon, Sammy has an idea: Why doesn't Empire publish its own comics? Soon Sammy and Joe are the masterminds behind successful creations such as the otherworldly Luna Moth, based on a girl they both love (albeit differently), and the Escapist, who uses super-Houdini techniques to fight fascism. As he narrates the cousins' rise to prominence, Chabon paints a wonderful portrait of the golden age of comics. At the same time, life outside the comics frame

Michael Chabon, 2002

intersects with Kavalier and Clay's fantastic world: There's the war, the young men's relationships, Joe's concern for his family, the burgeoning of pop culture, the role of Jews within that, and even a golem. From Prague to Brooklyn and back again, Chabon's imagination wraps us in the welcome embrace of a capacious and satisfying story. All of which means one needn't be a comics aficionado to appreciate Chabon's surprising, amusing, thought-provoking, language-rich, continent-spanning novel.

What: Novel. *When:* 2000. *Award:* Pulitzer Prize for Fiction, 2001. *Also By: A Model World: And Other Stories* (1990). *Werewolves in Their Youth: Stories* (1999). *The Final Solution* (2004). *The Yiddish Policeman's Union* (2007). *Telegraph Avenue* (2012). *Moonglow* (2016). *Further Reading:* Two volumes of *The Amazing Adventures of the Escapist* (2004), which purport to be the collected works of Chabon's fictional heroes, are actually coauthored by Chabon and friends. *Try: Men and Cartoons* by Jonathan Lethem. *The Brief Wondrous Life of Oscar Wao* by Junot Díaz (see page 211).

Clémentine in the Kitchen
Samuel Chamberlain (1895–1975)

An American Family's Education in French Home Cooking

This charming volume, which recounts the gastronomic education of Phineas Beck, his wife, and two children—pseudonymous stand-ins for the Chamberlains—during the decade that a Burgundian cook named Clémentine ruled their culinary roost first in France, then in New England, is an endearing treat. Published in 1943, Chamberlain's affectionate memoir of Americans eating well abroad and at home is both entertaining and practical, with a splendid assortment of traditional French recipes.

A "family of incorrigible epicures" settling into an eighteenth-century stone house in the "sleepy country town" of Senlis in the Ile-de-France in 1931, the Becks went through five cooks in eight weeks before the pink-cheeked Clémentine arrived on their doorstep. Not only was she smiling where others were dour, fastidious where others were slovenly, she was a Burgundian and a bona fide *Cordon Bleu*, with a firm command of classic French fare. She is in the kitchen cooking within an hour, and a member of the family in no time. She tutors them in the ways of market shopping, snail hunting, and wine making, and feeds them masterful, well-balanced meals. The warmth of her personality emanates from the kitchen to enhance every aspect of the family's home life, and Chamberlain depicts the spread of her influence with infectious good cheer. When the coming war forces the Becks to pack their bags and their new sensibilities and flee to safety in America, Clémentine returns with them to Massachusetts, where worry for family and friends caught in occupied France adds a poignant emotional undercurrent to this paean to a cook and her cooking.

What: Food & Drink. Memoir. *When:* 1943. *Edition:* The author was a well-known etcher and photographer. The 1988 edition, revised by his daughter Narcisse and published by David R. Godine, is illustrated with Chamberlain's images. *Also By: Bouquet de France* (1952). *Etched in Sunlight: Fifty Years in the Graphic Arts* (1968). *Try: The Auberge of the Flowering Hearth* by Roy Andries de Groot (see page 202). *The Art of Eating* by M. F. K. Fisher (see page 275).

Products of the Perfected Civilization
SELECTED WRITINGS OF CHAMFORT
Sébastien-Roch Nicolas Chamfort (1741–1794)
Translated and introduced by W. S. Merwin

Epigrams and Adages from Revolutionary France

"All of the passions lead to exaggeration. That is why they are passions." There's nothing so comforting as a well-turned thought, especially when, like this one, it allows us to view our own foolishness with a cool and sophisticated eye. That's why aphorisms wear so well: They claim a brief order for the mind that arrives like a moment of physical grace for the clumsy. Reading them, we feel poised for wisdom.

Sébastien-Roch Nicolas Chamfort (generally known by just the last of these several names), a French aphorist of the eighteenth century, was a master of the most delicate art of capturing crystalline thoughts in words:

In affairs of importance men show themselves at their best advantage; in small matters they are seen as they are.

Someone said that Providence was the Christian name of chance; a pious soul might say that chance is a familiar name for Providence.

An ultimately rueful revolutionary, Chamfort was a moralist whose irony was finely tuned to the turbulent temper of his times, the foibles of social behavior, and the practical virtues of venerable vices. In this endlessly browsable volume, American poet W. S. Merwin has selected, introduced, and artfully translated a feast of Chamfort's maxims, aphorisms, and anecdotes. His rich book provides a fascinating portrait of the age (and of such contemporaries as Voltaire, Laclos, de Sade, and Casanova) as well as a plethora of perfectly pitched *bon mots* that are a delight to ponder—and, at opportune moments, if you're quick enough, repeat.

What: Philosophy. Literature. *When:* Chamfort's *Pensées, maximes et anecdotes* were published posthumously in 1795. Merwin's 1969 volume was the first modern English translation. *Further Reading: Chamfort: A Biography* by Claude Arnaud. *Try: The Maxims of La Rochefoucauld,* translated by Louis Kronenberger. *The Notebooks of Joseph Joubert,* translated by Paul Auster.

The Big Sleep
Raymond Chandler (1888–1959)

Meet Philip Marlowe

It was about eleven o'clock in the morning, mid October, with the sun not shining and a look of hard wet rain in the clearness of the foothills. I was wearing my powder-blue suit, with dark blue shirt, tie and display handkerchief, black brogues, black wool socks with dark blue clocks on them. I was neat, clean, shaved and sober, and I didn't care who knew it. I was everything the well-dressed private detective ought to be. I was calling on four million dollars.

Dashiell Hammett may have invented the hardboiled detective story, but nobody wrote it better than Raymond Chandler. With his stylized prose and flair for similes, he gave his detective Philip Marlowe a voice that would become the hallmark of the genre, as demonstrated in the five sentences quoted here—the opening paragraph of Chandler's first novel, *The Big Sleep.* The millionaire Marlowe is calling on that mid-October morning is General Sternwood, father of two troublesome twentysomething daughters, one of whom is being blackmailed. In trying to sort out just what kind of fix Carmen Sternwood has gotten herself into, Marlowe quickly finds himself enmeshed in a tangled web of sex, lies, and naughty photographs. Not to mention murder.

Marlowe is the protagonist in all of Chandler's novels, and the movies drawn from these fictions proved to be a heavy influence on American film noir, just as the books influenced generations of detective novelists. One of Chandler's heirs, Robert B. Parker, author of the acclaimed Spenser mysteries, summed up his legacy this way: "Chandler seems to have created the culminating American hero: wised up, hopeful, thoughtful, adventurous, sentimental,

Poster for the 1946 film adaptation

cynical, and rebellious." His black brogues have been hard to fill.

What: Mystery & Suspense. **When:** 1939. **Also By:** Chandler published one story collection and seven novels, which include *Farewell, My Lovely* (1940), *The High Window* (1942), *The Lady in the Lake* (1943), and *The Long Goodbye* (1954). **Try:** *The Maltese Falcon* by Dashiell Hammett (see page 346). *L. A. Confidential* by James Ellroy. **Adaptations:** The 1946 Howard Hawks film stars Humphrey Bogart as Marlowe and Lauren Bacall as Vivian Sternwood (William Faulkner reputedly worked on the screenplay). The 1978 remake, set in England instead of California, stars Robert Mitchum as Marlowe and James Stewart as the general. **Footnote:** Chandler's last novel, *Poodle Springs*, left unfinished at the time of his death, was completed by Robert B. Parker and published in 1989.

Can't We Talk About Something More Pleasant?

A MEMOIR

Roz Chast (born 1954)

The Graphic Novel Comes of Age

Since her work as a cartoonist began appearing in *The Village Voice* and *The New Yorker* in the late 1970s, Roz Chast's distinctive combination of scraggly linework, schlumpy figures, and off-kilter frame of mind has made her a singular presence in American humor. Her single-panel cartoons often involve absurdist disjunctions between image and caption (a portrait of an utterly mundane family, for instance, on an utterly nondescript couch, is labeled "The Cradle of Mankind"), yet the laughter they provoke is frequently tinged with slight distress, for her artistry illustrates, albeit with comic nonchalance, how ill—or at least how oddly—equipped we are for the enormity of life.

Can't We Talk About Something More Pleasant? is Chast's first full-length book project, and it brings her peculiar gifts to bear on a theme particularly suited to them: the end days of her parents and her own shifting reactions to their senescence and mortality. Prompted by the unprecedented intimacy of the material, Chast imbues her graphic memoir with an astonishing honesty and emotional eloquence, extending her idiosyncratic perspective on everyday life to the most dumbfounding subject of all: everyday death.

In one finely encapsulated set piece after another, Chast tells the story of her quirky, prickly parents, Elizabeth and George, schoolteachers whose codependence alienated their daughter but sustained them till their final farewells. Along the way, she chronicles a lost era of Brooklyn life: "Not the Brooklyn," Chast writes, "of artists or hipsters or people who made—and bought—$8.00 chocolate bars. This was *deep* Brooklyn, the Brooklyn of people who have been left behind by everything and everyone." Simply seeing her depiction of a retail establishment labeled "Bruised Fruit Store" or a bank passbook with the legend "Flatbush Scrimpers" calls to mind poignant, and pregnant, realities of twentieth-century urban life. Her page layouts are alluringly varied, from traditional nine-panel matrices to full-page spreads (the cathartic image of her dad welcoming his wife home from the hospital is breathtaking), and everything in between. One radical move is to deploy large blocks of distinctively hand-lettered text alongside a single illustration, like some perverse version of a Beatrix Potter tale.

Chast's anecdotes about her daughterly duties as her mother and father age and their bodies fail are unsentimental—she is hard on both herself and her parents (for their less-than-optimal and stubborn choices)—yet tender, wry yet mournful. And powerfully resonant: The unique details of the Chast household assume a universal significance, especially for any reader who has shared similar experiences.

This book is a bold guidebook for a journey every child of aging parents has to undertake, leavened with courage and uncertainty, anger and angst, regrets and small victories.

What: Graphic Novel. *When:* 2014. *Also By: Unscientific Americans* (1982). *The Party, After You Left* (2004). *Theories of Everything: Selected, Collected, and Health-Inspected Cartoons, 1978–2006* (2006). *Try: Fierce Attachments* by Vivian Gornick. *Special Exits* by Joyce Farmer.

The Songlines
Bruce Chatwin (1940–1989)

Wandering to the Roots of Wonder

Dashing, prodigiously talented, with a mysterious knack for alighting upon alluring geographical and literary destinations, Bruce Chatwin passed through the crowded city of travel writing with a spectral, Keats-like splendor; he even died before his time, but left behind at least two masterpieces, *In Patagonia* and *The Songlines*. The latter is a travel book of a peculiar, and peculiarly rewarding, kind: Its landscape is the vast, and largely uninhabited, stretch of Central Australia, yet its landmarks are outcroppings of ideas—presented in pages labeled "From the Notebooks"—that reach from Bedouin proverbs to Baudelaire, Herodotus to Heidegger, all centering on the question of human restlessness.

The frame of Chatwin's fictionalized narrative is a journey undertaken with a companion named Arkady, an eccentric Australian of Russian heritage whose worldly possessions are limited to a harpsichord and a shelf of books. The path they embark on is a pursuit of the "Songlines" that give the book its title, "the labyrinth of invisible pathways which meander all over Australia and are known . . . to the Aboriginals as the 'Footprints of the Ancestors' or the 'Way of the Law.'" These elusive phenomena are not easily described, being part mythic (the itineraries of the Ancestral Beings who carved forms out of the formless world by "singing out the name of everything that crossed their path—birds, animals, plants, rocks, waterholes—and so singing the world into existence"), part spiritual (the sacred dimension of the present), and part geographical. You might best think of them as the "lay of the land" in two senses: both the contours of the terrain and a song that chronicles and celebrates all that the topography sustains. What Chatwin reveals about these "dreaming tracks" and the way they are marked, as well as the role they play in the lives of the native people, is fraught with fascination. Just as satisfying is Chatwin's relaxed yet watchful report of the personalities he encounters way out on the frontier of nothing—or is it everything?—in this engaging and wholly original exploration of the wisdom of wandering.

What: Travel. *When:* 1987. *Also By: In Patagonia* (1977). *The Viceroy of Ouidah* (1980). *On the Black Hill* (1982). *Further Reading: Bruce Chatwin* by Nicholas Shakespeare. *Try: The Traveller's Tree* by Patrick Leigh Fermor. *Shadow of the Silk Road* by Colin Thubron.

THE SONGLINES
Bruce Chatwin
author of In Patagonia

The Canterbury Tales
Geoffrey Chaucer (ca. 1343–1400)

English Literature Is Born—with Laughs

In England before the fourteenth century, serious literature was composed in one of two languages: Latin, the language of scholars, or French, the language of court. It took ages for English itself, the language of common folk, to be accepted as a legitimate literary tongue. The author who did most to effect the change was Geoffrey Chaucer: courtier, diplomat, part-time astronomer, and Britain's greatest poet of the Middle Ages.

The Canterbury Tales, Chaucer's most enduring work, began in the 1380s as a loose collection of stories, myths, and fantastical anecdotes—most in verse, though some in prose—that were all written in different voices. Only in the 1390s did Chaucer start to think of his baggy assemblage as a single narrative, conceiving a framing story, called the "General Prologue," in which the tales' various narrators are introduced as pilgrims on their way from London to Canterbury Cathedral, which houses the shrine of Saint Thomas à Becket:

15th-century engravings of a squire and cook from The Canterbury Tales

> And specially from every shires ende
> Of Engelond to Canterbury they wende,
> The holy blisful martyr for to seeke
> That hem hath holpen whan that they were seke.

The pilgrims, a mixed crew of squires and commoners, decide to partake in a story-telling competition, with the winner getting a free meal at a London tavern. Their tales range widely across styles and genres, from romance to sermon to *fabliau* (a type of bawdy comedy), and even include a scientific treatise. "The Knight's Tale," for example, is a long and elegant story of courtly love and romantic rivalry, but that's quickly followed by "The Miller's Tale," a dirty yarn about two students trying to bed a married woman, recounted by a drunkard (it's a good starting point for modern readers wanting to test the lasting entertainment value of the venerable work). Perhaps Chaucer's most famous creation is the Wife of Bath, a promiscuous widow who has outlasted—and outwitted—multiple husbands. Her tale relates the lessons learned by a lusty knight who must redeem himself from his sexual transgressions by discovering what women want and, in the end, submitting to it.

Censored, expurgated, or banned outright for centuries (one American school struck it from the syllabus as recently as the 1990s), *The Canterbury Tales* retains its power because it's a rollicking read, full of lavishly beautiful poetry spiced with hilarious comedy. The big question is this: Should you read the *Tales* in the original Middle English or in a modern translation? Our language has changed substantially in the six-hundred-plus years since Chaucer wrote, and many editions include either substantial footnotes to his text or side-by-side columns so that readers can follow the Middle English and the translation in parallel, which is perhaps the ideal option. However you decide to plunge into this unquestioned masterpiece, do try to read at least some of it in the original: You'll hear the sound of English literature coming into being.

What: Poetry. Literature. *When:* ca. 1390. *Edition:* Two Penguin Classics volumes—one retaining the original Middle English spelling and the second presenting Nevill Coghill's lucid and excellent modern versification—serve readers well. *Also By: The House of Fame* (ca. 1378–81). *The Parliament of Fowls* (ca. 1378–81). *Troilus and Criseyde* (ca. 1382–86). *Further Reading: The Life and Times of Chaucer* by John Gardner. *Try: The Decameron* by Giovanni Boccaccio (see page 85). *Don Quixote* by Miguel de Cervantes (see page 142). *Adaptation:* Michael Powell and Emeric Pressburger's 1944 film, *A Canterbury Tale,* evokes Chaucer's original to tell a wartime fable.

Dawn of Art: The Chauvet Cave

THE OLDEST KNOWN PAINTINGS IN THE WORLD

Jean-Marie Chauvet (born 1952), Eliette Brunel Deschamps (born 1947),
and Christian Hillaire (born 1952)

The First Picture Book

Whatever we may know, or suspect, about paleolithic cave paintings such as those found at Lascaux or Altamira, their very existence answers a sort of psychic need. The prehistoric art—majestic figures of animals spare in their outline, yet supple in their strength and beauty—speaks across millennia with an eerie yet emphatic human voice; it suggests that the first sparks of consciousness were sacred enough to be recognized and hoarded as secrets in underground chambers.

Dawn of Art chronicles—in text and scholarship, appreciation and analysis, and, most importantly, in astonishing, detailed color photographs—the discovery made in the Ardèche Valley of France in December 1994: a cave, untouched for thousands of years, filled with Stone Age bear skeletons, the remains of fires, and, staggeringly, more than three hundred paintings and engravings of animals. Radiocarbon dating has established these images to be more than thirty thousand years old; they are the oldest known paintings in the world, nearly twice as old as those found at Lascaux. With text by the three explorers who uncovered the Chauvet cave—Jean-Marie Chauvet, Eliette Brunel Deschamps, and Christian Hillaire—and with nearly one hundred large color photographs, Dawn of Art is a stunning volume, documenting a thrilling discovery as it provokes both thought and awe.

What: Art. Archaeology. *When:* 1996. *Further Reading: The Mind in the Cave: Consciousness and the Origins of Art* by David Lewis-Williams. *Try: The Cave of Lascaux: The Final Photographs* by Mario Ruspoli. *The Cave Beneath the Sea* by Jean Clottes. *Adaptation:* Werner Herzog's 2011 documentary, *Cave of Forgotten Dreams,* offers a fascinating look into the wonders of Chauvet.

Paintings on the walls of the Chauvet cave

The Stories of John Cheever
John Cheever (1912–1982)

Mythological Dreams in Suburbia

The sixty-one stories gathered here were written in the three decades after the end of World War II; most were originally published in *The New Yorker*, then collected in slim volumes that had been largely forgotten by the time this fat, retrospective tome was issued to popular success and critical acclaim in 1978. While the nearly seven-hundred-page *Stories of John Cheever* delivers much more than the sum of its parts, it must also be proclaimed—with pleasure and admiration—that those parts remain more gloriously particular than its author's enduring reputation as the "Chekhov of suburbia" implies.

As Paul Gray noted in a very astute profile in *Time* magazine at the time the book first appeared, "one of the surprises to be found in *The Stories of John Cheever* is that the stories are almost always better than people remember." Better because they're broader in their embrace of human nature and primal emotions—fear, love, shame, guilt—than their milieu of commuter ennui suggests. What Cheever calls in his preface the "sometimes dated paraphernalia" of the tales—the ever-present cigarettes, the constant stream of cocktails, the hats on every head—does not disguise the undomesticated need and deep nostalgia of characters "whose gods were as ancient as yours and mine, whoever you are."

John Cheever, 1964

The ancient gods are aptly invoked, for Cheever's tales are in their largest dimensions little myths—replete with Furies and Graces, implacable fates, torments and jealousies beyond the comprehension of the figures at their mercy. Ravaged by these forces, Cheever's feckless protagonists are left to fend for themselves by the faithless mores of modern life. The flaws of his characters are both embarrassing and perversely endearing. There's the venial weakness of Johnny Hake, who, in "The Housebreaker of Shady Hill," is driven by need and fear to sneak into a neighbor's home and steal a wallet. And the desperate desire of Francis Weed in "The Country Husband," who is driven to distraction by the presence of his children's babysitter, which "seemed to put him into a relationship to the world that was mysterious and enthralling." And the delusional heroics of Neddy Merrill, who decides to make his way home across Westchester County by navigating a chain of backyard pools in "The Swimmer."

These three characters, and their many counterparts throughout the Cheever canon, are seen through a lens of artifice in which corruption and innocence are as indistinguishable as overlapping clouds. Although Cheever's people seldom prove themselves up to the task of redemption, they seldom lose hope of its embrace; like nymphs pursued by insatiable divinities, these recognizable modern Americans survive—and perhaps even triumph—through their transformation by Cheever's hands into figures of warning, yearning, and human imperfection.

What: Short Stories. *When:* 1978. *Awards:* National Book Critics Circle Award, 1978. Pulitzer Prize for Fiction, 1979. National Book Award, 1979. *Also By: The Wapshot Chronicle* (1957). *Bullet Park* (1969). *Falconer* (1977). *Further Reading: The Journals of John Cheever* (1991). *Try: Eleven Kinds of Loneliness* by Richard Yates. *The Maples Stories* by John Updike (see page 817). *Adaptation:* "The Swimmer" was made into a 1968 film starring Burt Lancaster.

ANTON CHEKHOV
(1860–1904)

Following a generation of Russian novelists—Tolstoy and Dostoevsky chief among them—whose works confronted on the largest scale the purposes of existence, the mysteries of faith, and the meanings of history, Anton Chekhov in his stories and plays honored the small trials of the heart. With a tender but unbending care, he attended to the hopes and fears that define both our disease and our well-being (not for nothing was he a physician). His understanding of the dialogue between aspiration and disappointment that shapes our emotions informs his work, offering as telling an education in human feeling as can be found in literature, delivered in deceptively diminutive packages.

Stories
A Literary Revolution

According to a traveling companion, when Anton Chekhov visited Italy in 1891, he was more interested in observing everyday events, such as how porters handled luggage, than in seeing famous sites. This may not surprise readers of his stories. Indeed, Chekhov's tales—in their focus on seemingly inconsequential and often pointedly unresolved incidents rather than dramatic episodes that leave a tidy lesson in their wake—instigated a quiet but enduring revolution in the history of fiction. The Russian's influence, in English alone, reaches from Virginia Woolf to Ernest Hemingway, from Katherine Mansfield to William Trevor to Raymond Carver (whose story "Errand" is about Chekhov's death).

Even though his efforts never exceeded novella length, Chekhov was a prolific producer of prose fiction. The gallery of characters he created in his tales includes a wide range of Russian society—peasants and bureaucrats, students and soldiers, lovers and prisoners—and his exploration of stream-of-consciousness brought their inner lives to the page with a revelatory intimacy. Read "The Student," "Ward No. 6," "The Huntsman," "A Boring Story"— you'll soon be ready for more. And if the book you are reading now were gathering 1,000 *pages* to read before you die, the thirty-five that make

Anton Chekhov, 1900

up "The Lady with a Little Dog" would likely be among them.

What: Short Stories. *When:* 1880–1903. *Editions:* Constance Garnett's thirteen-volume *Tales of Chekhov* (ca. 1920) is the benchmark of English translations; countless single-volume selected stories offer alternative and more recent translations, including superb renderings by the team of Richard Pevear and

Larissa Volokhonsky. *Also By: A Journey to Sakhalin* (1895). *A Life in Letters* (translated by Rosamund Bartlett and Anthony Phillips; 2004). *Further Reading: Anton Chekhov: A Life* by Donald Rayfield. *Reading Chekhov: A Critical Journey* by Janet Malcolm. *Try: Dubliners* by James Joyce (see page 420). Stories of William Trevor (see page 804) and Alice Munro (see page 573).

PLAYS
THE SEAGULL • UNCLE VANYA • THREE SISTERS • THE CHERRY ORCHARD
Archetypal Dramas of Modern Life

"Why do you always wear black?" a schoolteacher asks a young woman at the start of *The Seagull*. "I'm in mourning for my life," she replies. It's true that Chekhov's plays are filled with unhappy people, and if you suffer through a bad production, you might think there is not much more to them than miserable Russians moping on country estates, moaning about failed affairs and thwarted ambitions. Then again, an inept production of *Oedipus the King* might make Greek tragedy seem like some sick combination of soap opera and horror movie. But just as Aeschylus and Sophocles treat the fundamental and enduring themes of human existence—fate, inheritance, savagery, pride, justice—so Chekhov treats the worries of our daily lives: loneliness, love, financial uncertainty, the persistent pangs of time's passing.

Chekhov wrote more than a dozen plays, but the last four are his most accomplished and most performed, and the quartet—because of their original realization by Konstantin Stanislavski under the auspices of the Moscow Art Theater—are seminal works in theatrical history. In *The Seagull* (1896), two generations of actors and playwrights struggle with unfulfilled love. In *Uncle Vanya* (1899–1900), the disappointments of aging and romance rub up against life-affirming moments of passion, learning, and labor. *Three Sisters* (1901) depicts sophisticated Muscovites struggling to adjust to life in the country. And *The Cherry Orchard* (1904), perhaps his most telling achievement, uses the auction of a family estate to contrast the fortunes of the fallen aristocracy with those of the rising bourgeoisie; yet the atmosphere the play creates transcends social and political circumstances to engage both the inexorability of time and the unappeasable misgivings of human nature.

In each of these works, subtext is as powerful as action: Characters often speak around their emotions, and a seemingly inconsequential line about the weather or plans for the day can have overwhelming emotional force. Deeply humanistic, Chekhov's four dramatic masterpieces are emblematic of our modern domestic lives in the same way Greek tragedies are emblematic of a more cosmic and radical vision of human agency. Distanced from the gods and their interventions, Chekhov's characters move through their modest calamities, losing the homes, habits, vocations, and loves that might provide fragile protection against the long loneliness that terrifies us all.

What: Drama. **When:** 1896–1904. *Edition:* Peter Carson's excellent translations of all four plays, plus the earlier *Ivanov*, are available in a single Penguin Classics volume. *Also By:* Plays: *Platonov* (1881); *Ivanov* (1887). *Further Reading: Dear Writer, Dear Actress: The Love Letters of Anton Chekhov and Olga Knipper*, edited and translated by Jean Benedetti. *Try: A Month in the Country* by Ivan Turgenev. *The Dead* by James Joyce. *The Glass Menagerie* by Tennessee Williams.

Costume designs for a staging of The Cherry Orchard *by David Lvovick Borovsky, 1995*

Alexander Hamilton
Ron Chernow (born 1949)

The Founding Father Who Broke the Mold

Early in his fascinating biography of perhaps "the foremost political figure in American history who never attained the presidency," Ron Chernow writes that Alexander Hamilton's "life was so tumultuous that only an audacious novelist could have dreamed it up." Or, as time would tell, an audacious musical theater impresario: Prompted by his reading of this deeply researched yet compelling tome, Lin-Manuel Miranda would turn its subject's life into a groundbreaking polyrhythmic spectacle that, in 2016, would garner a record-setting sixteen Tony nominations (it won eleven, including Best Musical). If Hamilton was not fated to become president, he would, as a consolation prize, become something of a rock star two centuries after his death.

Born out of wedlock in the Caribbean, orphaned at an early age, Hamilton was a precocious young man whose talent was recognized by local benefactors who sponsored his travel to New York in 1773, where he pursued an education at the institution that would later become Columbia University. He soon became embroiled in the struggle for independence that gripped the age, rising quickly to become George Washington's chief adjutant in the revolutionary army and going on to play a key role, in the aftermath of victory, in the Constitutional Convention. As primary author of the *Federalist Papers*, Hamilton was instrumental in the institutionalizing of American ideals in our nation's founding documents. In his tenure as first secretary of the Treasury, as Chernow lucidly relates, Hamilton created—not without opposition—a national bank and set policies that established the legal and moral basis for securities trading in the new country, and for federal investment in fledgling industries as well. His influence on our financial system has been unmatched, and enduring.

Portrait of Alexander Hamilton

But that's by no means all: "The magnitude of Hamilton's feats as treasury secretary," Chernow writes, "has overshadowed many other facets of his life: clerk, college student, youthful poet, essayist, artillery captain, . . . battlefield hero, congressman, abolitionist, Bank of New York founder, state assemblyman, . . . orator, lawyer, polemicist, educator, patron saint of the *New-York Evening Post*, foreign-policy theorist," and more. Chernow gives us the full sweep of his activities, including his marriage to the admirable Elizabeth Schuyler, member of one of the most prominent families in New York, with whom Hamilton had eight children, and his dalliance with Maria Reynolds, an affair that can claim pride of place as the first political sex scandal to shake the new republic. "No immigrant in American history has ever made a larger contribution than Alexander Hamilton," Chernow tells us—and he did it all before his death at forty-seven in a duel with Aaron Burr, our third vice president. He was too protean, too smart, too reckless and charismatic a figure for his full likeness to be caught in a statue, much less on the ten-dollar bill, so one is grateful to Chernow for capturing it in these pages, and for inspiring others to rejuvenate his legacy.

What: Biography. **When:** 2004. **Also By:** *The House of Morgan* (1990). *Titan: The Life of John D. Rockefeller, Sr.* (1998). *Washington: A Life* (2010). **Further Reading:** *The Federalist Papers* by Alexander Hamilton, James Madison, and John Jay. **Try:** *Founding Brothers* by Joseph J. Ellis (see page 250). **Adaptation:** Chernow's book was the inspiration for Lin-Manuel Miranda's phenomenally successful musical, which premiered off Broadway in 2015; Miranda's book, *Hamilton: The Revolution*, written with Jeremy McCarter, contains the full libretto accompanied by an intriguing account of the show's development.

The Worst Journey in the World

ANTARCTIC 1910–1913

Apsley Cherry-Garrard (1886–1959)

Worst Journey, Best Adventure Book

Given this book's dramatic title, it's no surprise that it has always had readers. Yet its stature has grown in the decades since its original publication, so much so that the critic A. Alvarez would make the following claim for it in the late 1990s: "*The Worst Journey in the World* is to travel writing what *War and Peace* is to the novel or Herzen's *Memoirs* are to autobiography: the book by which all the rest are measured." That is just what Apsley Cherry-Garrard's chronicle of polar exploration is: the greatest travel and adventure narrative ever written.

Its author accompanied Captain Robert Falcon Scott on the latter's ill-fated journey to Antarctica in 1910–12. At age twenty-four, "Cherry" (as he was familiarly known) was the youngest member of the expedition. He wasn't one of the four who went with Scott on the last leg of the actual trip to the South Pole, but Cherry did belong to the team that eventually discovered the bodies of Scott and the others in the frozen wasteland of the "Great Ice Barrier." That story is told here, but the "worst journey" itself was a different, albeit related, affair. A few months before Scott finally set out to reach "the last place on earth," Cherry and two companions embarked on what Scott himself was to call "the hardest journey ever made": a five-week march across sixty-seven miles of unrelenting, nearly unimaginable darkness and cold to the never-before-seen breeding grounds of the Emperor penguin. The goal: to bring back penguin eggs for scientific study. The limits of endurance have seldom been so sorely tested, and the author's account of this incredible trek is sure to amaze even the most well-traveled armchair explorer.

Gripping and poignant, Cherry's story is not without a bracing, bitter humor. He introduces it with a sardonic flourish ("Polar exploration is at once the cleanest and most isolated way of having a bad time which has been devised"), and his account of his reception at the British Museum when he attempts to deliver the hard-won eggs two years after his ordeal is one of the most blackly comic episodes you are ever likely to come upon.

What: Adventure. Travel. Exploration. *When:* 1922. *Further Reading: Cherry: A Life of Apsley Cherry-Garrard* by Sara Wheeler. *Try: Endurance* by Alfred Lansing (see page 463). *We Die Alone* by David Howarth (see page 391). *The Birthday Boys* by Beryl Bainbridge (see page 41). *Adaptation:* A BBC television film was broadcast in 2007.

The Man Who Was Thursday

A NIGHTMARE

G. K. Chesterton (1874–1936)

Anarchy, Orthodoxy, and a Roaring Good Read

To read the work of Gilbert Keith Chesterton is to have the exhilarating and sometimes disconcerting experience of watching a serious mind at play. This is true regardless of the strand of his voluminous output you explore: detective story or saint's life, theological rumination or political debate, literary criticism or speculative fiction. None of the descriptors that have attached themselves to him—theologian, Christian apologist, philosopher, mystery author—do justice to the range and reward of his writing. Chesterton wrote eighty-odd books and thousands of essays, newspaper columns, and radio talks; nearly every page he penned bears the hallmarks of his style—an invigorating blend of conviction, invention, and, most of all, spirited paradox.

His classic Father Brown stories are charming intellectual crossword puzzles posing as mysteries; his faithful yet vivid explorations of the lives of Thomas Aquinas, Francis of Assisi, and Charles Dickens, whose secular sainthood Chesterton did much to create, are as much about the reach of his subjects' imaginations as their biographical coordinates; his inquiries into his own religious thinking are the expression of a reactionary, magnanimous faith (it wouldn't take a subversive editor to suggest that a better title for the provocative, and profoundly edifying, 1908 book that Chesterton titled *Orthodoxy* might well be *Quirkiness*).

Although no single volume sums up the pleasures of reading Chesterton, the inquisitive reader might well begin with *The Man Who Was Thursday*, one of several works in a vein of speculative fiction that Chesterton plied with idiosyncratic ingenuity; other tales in a similar mode are *The Man Who Knew Too Much* (1922) and *The Napoleon of Notting Hill* (1904). A plot that begins with a discussion of freedom versus discipline in poetry is soon set spinning into a nightmarish realm in which anarchists bent on destroying the world and undercover agents allied against them infiltrate each other's plans,

purposes, and sense of reality. It's a surreal and ebullient fantasia on the mutability of evil and the focused, if hidden, power of good faith—and it's great fun.

Chesterton's influence has been extraordinary and lasting, on prelates and political figures no less than on admitted literary heirs such as Jorge Luis Borges and Neil Gaiman. His work is particularly fetching for young minds of an intellectual bent with a taste for big themes and eternal incongruities. He is, in fact, like the best high school teacher you could ever have—one who opens the gates to a castle of culture that was somehow hiding in the back of your mind. The kind of inspired instruction that Chesterton offers helps us, to borrow his own words, "contrive to be at once astonished at the world and yet at home in it."

What: Mystery & Suspense. *When:* 1908. *Also By:* Fiction: *The Club of Queer Trades* (1905); *The Innocence of Father Brown* (1911). Nonfiction: *St. Francis of Assisi* (1923); *The Everlasting Man* (1925); *Saint Thomas Aquinas* (1933). *Further Reading: Chesterton and the Romance of Orthodoxy: The Making of GKC, 1874–1908* by William Oddie. *Try: The Secret Agent* by Joseph Conrad.

The Riddle of the Sands
Erskine Childers (1870–1922)

A Sailing Classic—and the First Modern Spy Novel

" A yachting story, with a purpose," Erskine Childers wrote to a correspondent while he was composing *The Riddle of the Sands* at the beginning of the twentieth century. The purpose was political: to alert an unprepared England to the threat posed by German ambitions. It was by no means the only example of "invasion fiction" created by British writers at the time to stir their sleepy country to naval investment, but it was the most influential in promoting the

cause of military readiness, and—more important for later generations of readers—it has proven the most enduring, for the simple reason that it is a rip-roaring good yarn.

The story begins as the narrator, Carruthers, a member of the Foreign Office, is invited on a sailing trip by his friend Davies. Soon it becomes clear that the yachtsman has something more in mind than a pleasure cruise; in fact, Davies believes he has discovered a dangerous German conspiracy to invade England hatching in the sandy Frisian Islands in the North Sea. Through wild weather and heavy fog both literal and metaphorical, the two must chart their way to a clear understanding of the threat.

Based in large degree on the author's own cruising in the North Sea, *The Riddle of the Sands* is suffused with salty details large and small; the almost tactile sense of the sailors' exertions only adds to the larger arc of suspense Childers draws with emphatic precision. Although *The Riddle of the Sands* would be its author's only novel, it boasts many notable offspring, having inspired generations of thriller writers from John Buchan to Ken Follett. For readers of today, it remains a compelling adventure.

What: Mystery & Suspense. Adventure. Novel. *When:* 1903. *Further Reading: The Tragedy of Erskine Childers: Dangerous Waters* by Leonard Piper. *Try: The Thirty-Nine Steps* by John Buchan (see page 105). *Eye of the Needle* by Ken Follett. *Adaptation:* The 1979 film stars Michael York and Jenny Agutter. *Footnote:* Despite serving Britain in World War I, Childers was an ardent champion of Irish Home Rule; eventually joining the Irish Republican Army, he was executed by firing squad after being captured by Free State forces during the Irish Civil War.

The Awakening
Kate Chopin (1851–1904)

A Pioneering American Novel of the Frontiers of Desire

T he story is simple enough: Edna Pontellier, wife of a New Orleans businessman and mother of two, is aimlessly dissatisfied with her role as society wife. On a holiday on Grand Isle, something in her is swayed by the music of a pianist and the company of a young man. Experiencing a modicum of independence, she yearns for more. Upon her return home, she embarks upon a series of actions—social and sexual—that lead to fleeting moments of fulfillment and an unfortunate end. Although the modern reader is sympathetic to Edna's "awakening," and cheers the "new-born creature, opening its eyes in a familiar world that it had never known," Chopin's contemporaries were relentless in their disapproval of both heroine and author, greeting the book with scandalized indignation and condemning it as utterly immoral.

In the July 1899 issue of *Book News*, Chopin responded to the critical attacks:

Having a group of people at my disposal, I thought it might be entertaining (to myself) to throw them together and see what would happen. I never dreamed of Mrs. Pontellier making such a mess of things and working out her own damnation as she did. If I had had the slightest intimation of such a thing I would have excluded her from the company. But when I found out what she was up to, the play was half over and it was then too late.

Even if Chopin is speaking tongue in cheek, she nevertheless suggests the novel's real distinction; unlike Flaubert's Emma Bovary, say, with whom she is often compared, Edna Pontellier seems free to find a fate that has not been determined by the author at the outset. Chopin, no doubt drawing on her own experience as a woman constrained by the expectations of her time, is truer to life than to literary convention, and the forthright wonder with which Edna discovers her destiny pulses with growing confidence.

Beautifully written, Chopin's once scorned tale of liberation has become an acknowledged classic in the century since her death. It certainly deserves that status.

What: Novel. *When:* 1899. *Edition:* Most editions also contain a selection of Chopin's best stories. A Library of America volume contains her complete works. *Also By: At Fault* (1890). *Bayou Folk* (1894). *A Night in Acadie* (1897). *Further Reading: Unveiling Kate Chopin* by Emily Toth. *Adaptations:* The novel was adapted for the screen in 1982 as *The End of August*, then again in 1991 as *Grand Isle*.

The Murder of Roger Ackroyd
Agatha Christie (1890–1976)

The Queen of Crime

Agatha Christie may well have more books in print than any other writer in history—two billion is a figure regularly bandied about. Born in Devonshire in 1890, she discovered her gift for mystery fiction while working as a nurse during World War I. It was a talent she would exploit—to the delight of countless readers—for more than six decades in more than eighty volumes, nearly half of which featured Hercule Poirot, the punctilious and ingenious Belgian detective introduced in her debut novel, *The Mysterious Affair at Styles*. Another novel and a book of stories starring Poirot appeared before the success of *The Murder of Roger Ackroyd* in 1926 made Christie a bestselling author and, in her grandson's apt phrase, "a household name." So popular would Poirot himself prove that when he met his death in 1975, in the novel *Curtain*, he became the first fictional character to have an obituary on the front page of the *New York Times*.

But to the case at hand. Like many of Christie's best puzzles, *The Murder of Roger Ackroyd* takes us to an English village whose cozy society has been disrupted by death. In King's Abbot, where Poirot has retired to garden, the suicide of the widowed Mrs. Ferrars is surrounded by rumors that she had killed her husband a year earlier. When well-off Roger Ackroyd, with whom the widow had been dallying, is found murdered in his locked study, Poirot puts down his gardening tools and begins digging into the criminal intrigue. As always in Christie, there is an abundance of suspects, one seeming more likely than the next, as well as clues hidden in plain sight to all but Poirot, whose "little grey cells"—as he invokes his fabled brainpower—allow no assumptions to cloud his ratiocination. The book—and the case—comes to a stunning conclusion in a plot twist so unusual, it would reverberate throughout the golden age of mystery that Christie's intricately constructed tales heralded.

Agatha Christie, ca. 1926

Poirot, of course, isn't Christie's only famous detective: There's also Miss Marple, the gossip-loving amateur who features in a dozen novels of her own. In her autobiography, Christie reveals that this second beloved sleuth may well have been inspired by her favorite character in *The Murder of Roger Ackroyd*—Caroline Sheppard, sister of the doctor who narrates that mystery. Miss Sheppard is "an acidulated spinster, full of curiosity, knowing everything, hearing everything: the complete detective service in the home"—exactly like Jane Marple, who would make her debut in *The Murder at the Vicarage* (1930), four years after *Roger Ackroyd* was published.

What: Mystery & Suspense. **When:** 1926. *Also By: The Mysterious Affair at Styles* (1920). *Murder on the Orient Express* (1934). *And Then There Were None* (1939). **Further Reading:** *Agatha Christie: An English Mystery* by Laura Thompson. *Talking About Detective Fiction* by P. D. James. **Try:** *The Unpleasantness at the Bellona Club* by Dorothy L. Sayers. *A Man Lay Dead* by Ngaio Marsh. **Adaptations:** Adapted for the stage by Michael Morton as *Alibi* in 1928, it became the first sound film of a Christie work, under the same name, three years later. It was also the basis of an episode in the *Agatha Christie: Poirot* television series, starring David Suchet.

■ For Winston Churchill's *Their Finest Hour*, see page 202.

The Hunt for Red October
Tom Clancy (1947–2013)

CIA Adventure on the High Seas

N ow that Tom Clancy's debut novel can be seen in retrospect as the book that launched a thousand enterprises, from Clancy's several fiction series to a quintet of Jack Ryan films to numerous video game franchises, its unconventional entry into the publishing world is all the more remarkable. Published by the US Naval Institute Press in 1984, *The Hunt for Red October* became an unexpected but modest hit for the generally under-the-radar publisher, whose mission is to promote an understanding of sea power and other issues of national defense. But soon, abetted in no small part by President Ronald Reagan's praise for its page-turning excitement, Clancy's novel grew into an extraordinary commercial success.

The novel recounts the exploits of CIA analyst Jack Ryan and his associates as they conspire with a group of defecting Soviet officers to steal a technologically advanced nuclear submarine and cover their tracks from the Kremlin. Deploying complex knowledge of espionage and military science to both tether the book's flights of transporting suspense and direct its characters' passage—via cunning and courage—through rough seas of duty, loyalty, and honor, Clancy created what would prove to be a pioneering work in a new generation of techno-thrillers, paving the way for a legion of bestselling successors from the likes of Stephen Coonts, Vince Flynn, and Dale Brown.

What: Novel. *When:* 1984. *Also By: Patriot Games* (1987). *The Cardinal of the Kremlin* (1988). *The Sum of All Fears* (1991). *Try: Bomber* by Len Deighton. *Where Eagles Dare* by Alistair MacLean. *Adaptation:* The 1990 film stars Alec Baldwin and Sean Connery.

Rome and a Villa
Eleanor Clark (1913–1996)

A Timeless Sojourn in the Eternal City

" T he person never lived," writes Eleanor Clark, "whose apprehension was up to more than bits and moments of Rome, from Goethe and Stendhal on down." And yet those bits and moments, as many an imaginative tourist might attest, can inform the mind with a cultural legacy nourishing enough to last a lifetime. There are few better testaments to that legacy than this erudite, meditative, mesmerizing book. Surrendering her spirit to the genius of the place that she describes, Clark replicates in words, in a way one would likely bet impossible, the experience of finding oneself awake in Rome.

Rome and a Villa is the product of Clark's sojourn in Italy at the end of the 1940s. Her portrait of Rome eternal, and of the Holy City during the Holy Year of 1950 (with ancillary sketches devoted to the career of the Sicilian bandit Salvatore Giuliano and to the haunting magnificence of Hadrian's Villa), is clearly the distillation of intense personal and intellectual engagement. It surveys the continuous history of emperors and popes, saints and poets, architecture and aesthetics through a sensibility stylishly captured in Clark's watchful prose. She is a virtuoso of the semicolon, nurturing a mode of thinking—patient, elaborative, ruminative—too little fostered in language, much less in life. Her very sentences are essayistic, making sallies toward meanings that are palpable but too fluent to pin down; they posit the truth that Rome, despite its pomp and grandeur, is a place of whispers and secrets, "where you are always being reminded of something, you cannot tell what, but it is like the fear of falling down a deep well."

In both gaze and glance she stays alert to the beauty and wisdom about her, whether decorative—no one has written more brilliantly of the exhilaration of Rome's fountains—or essential: "those freakish squares and the narrow streets around them, most vividly in the old quarters, Trastevere and all the part between the Corso and the Tiber, do not constitute an *outside* in our sense, but a great rich withinness, an interior. . . . In Rome to go out is to go home."

What: Cities. Travel. *When:* First published in 1952, the book was reissued in 1974 with a substantial new preface and an additional essay. *Also By: The Oysters of Locmariaquer* (1964). *Baldur's Gate* (1970). *Eyes, Etc.* (1977). *Try: A Roman Journal* by Stendhal. *Roman Mornings* by James Lees-Milne.

Childhood's End
Arthur C. Clarke (1917–2008)

Prelude to a Space Odyssey

After Arthur C. Clarke collaborated with director Stanley Kubrick on the creation of the 1968 film *2001: A Space Odyssey*, the novelist found himself launched into the celebrity stratosphere. Not that he was without acclaim as an author previously, of course. Since the publication of the exceptional *Childhood's End* fifteen years earlier, Clarke's star as a writer of science fiction had been in the ascendant, fueled by his ability to plumb depths of emotion while at the same time exploring lofty philosophical ideas—to say nothing of his skill at telling a good story.

The decade of *Childhood's End*'s publication was rife with tales of alien invasions and "first contact," especially in lowbrow cinema, as films like *The Day the Earth Stood Still* (1951), *Invaders from Mars* (1953), and *This Island Earth* (1955) attest. Clarke's novel fits neatly into that subgenre, but uses the familiar tropes freshly and with maximum sophistication, yoking them to the then cutting-edge, and soon to be popular, mystical speculations of the French Jesuit Pierre Teilhard de Chardin about the ultimate fate of consciousness.

The book opens with the "invasion" of Earth a fait accompli. Spaceships of the Overlords hang over several major metropolises, their inhabitants unseen. The point of contact with the people of Earth is an invisible alien being named Karellen, whose perfect English and command of superior technologies are deployed in pursuit of an unbending mandate: The planet must function as a single unit, with all local rivalries subsumed.

Over the next fifty years, under the guidance of the aliens, the planet becomes a utopia, and the Overlords choose to reveal themselves at last (their resemblance to classical devils, or demons out of Albrecht Dürer, made them reluctant to show themselves until mankind had become accustomed to the benefits of their rule). While the alien elite now circulates freely, one edict remains strictly in force: Humans cannot travel among the stars. Irked by this forbidding fiat, a human named Jan Rodricks stows away aboard a spaceship returning to the Overlord homeworld. He will be gone for forty years of relativistic time. Upon his return to Earth, he finds Homo sapiens extinct, replaced by mutant children who are being groomed by the ineffable Overmind, the force whom even the Overlords obey. Jan, the last man on Earth, witnesses the final explosive transcendence of our heirs as they are absorbed into the cosmic consciousness.

Childhood's End—like Clarke's subsequent work, *The City and the Stars* (and *2001* as well)—exudes a rich and almost gnostic sense of loss at the same time as it conjures the breathtaking possibility of a new, if unfathomable, unfolding of reality. For a thinker who radiated an engineer's practicality (he forecasted orbital satellites and their uses before any such things existed), Clarke also harbored a poet's soul, giving him perhaps the perfect apparatus for crafting science fiction that reveled in a melancholy hope, both thrilling and perilous.

What: Novel. **When:** 1953. **Also By:** *Rendezvous with Rama* (1973). *Imperial Earth* (1976). *The Fountains of Paradise* (1979). **Further Reading:** *The Phenomenon of Man* by Pierre Teilhard de Chardin. *The Physics of Immortality* by Frank J. Tipler. **Try:** *The Dark Light Years* by Brian W. Aldiss. *The Ophiuchi Hotline* by John Varley. *Yesterday's Kin* by Nancy Kress.

Between the World and Me
Ta-Nehisi Coates (born 1975)

Matters of Life and Death

All our phrasing—race relations, racial chasm, racial justice, racial profiling, white privilege, even white supremacy—serves to obscure that racism is a visceral experience, that it dislodges brains, blocks airways, rips muscle, extracts organs, cracks bones, breaks teeth. You must never look away from this.

The "you" that Ta-Nehisi Coates is instructing is his fifteen-year-old son, to whom this unsettling book is addressed—just as James Baldwin, a half century earlier, began *The Fire Next Time* as a message to his fifteen-year-old nephew. Each book is a meditation on the reality of black experience in America, and they speak to each other across five decades of history in which inequality and violence, at least as far as the younger author sees it, stripped the hope of the Civil Rights era and left its dream naked and afraid.

Ta-Nehisi Coates, 2015

of a parent who knows he cannot protect his child from the embedded racism he has seen claim with impunity the lives of friends and relations brings a new dimension to a familiar fear, the one Coates felt as a constant companion of his own Baltimore childhood and coming-of-age:

Coates's book is prompted in part by his inability to offer any comfort to his son after the latter's disillusionment in the aftermath of the killing of Michael Brown in Ferguson, Missouri, and the exoneration of the police officers at whose hands he died: "I did not tell you that it would be okay, because I have never believed it would be okay." The paternal anguish

When I was about your age, each day, fully one-third of my brain was concerned with who I was walking to school with, our precise number, the manner of our walk, the number of times I smiled, who or what I smiled at, who offered a pound and who did not—all of which is to say that I practiced the culture of the streets, a culture concerned chiefly with securing the body.

But, as Coates fiercely argues, American institutions and policies past and present have conspired to deny black people "the right to secure and govern our own bodies." As he looks back on his own youth and, especially, as he reflects on the tragic death of his friend Prince Jones, his focus on the physicality of oppression in daily life—threatened or realized, it's always in the offing—gives the effects of racism, and the abstractions we often use to obscure them, a local habitation and a name that could not be closer to home for father and son. Unforgiving and unforgettable, *Between the World and Me* is a book to be reckoned with, its raw feeling as searing as its formidable eloquence; the questions it raises are weightier than any answers, one fears, can lift.

What: Essays. *When:* 2015. *Award:* National Book Award for Nonfiction, 2015. *Also By: The Beautiful Struggle: A Father, Two Sons, and an Unlikely Road to Manhood* (2008). *We Were Eight Years in Power: An American Tragedy* (2017). Graphic Novels: *Black Panther: A Nation Under Our Feet: Book 1* (2016); *Book 2* (2017). *Try: Collected Essays* by James Baldwin (see page 43). *The New Jim Crow: Mass Incarceration in the Age of Color Blindness* by Michelle Alexander. *Citizen* by Claudia Rankine (see page 659).

A Classical Education
Richard Cobb (1917–1996)

A Shocking Personal History from a Master Historian

"How would *you* wash an axe if it had traces of blood on it, and you wanted to remove the traces?"

In the spring of 1950, Richard Cobb was asked that question by his old schoolmate Edward Ball. Cobb, who had no firsthand experience with bloodstained axes, supposed that he would immerse the thing in boiling water. "He looked at me triumphantly (he always liked being in the right) and said: 'Well, that is exactly what I did; and Chief Inspector Mahoney told me that that was just where I went wrong: it got the blood encrusted in the pores of the metal. He said I should have washed it in *cold* water, which would have left no trace.'"

A Classical Education is a memoir, not a mystery, so there's no harm in pointing out that even if Edward *had* used cold water, he wouldn't have gotten away with the 1936 murder of his mother; it left quite an incriminating mess in the house. And, as Cobb describes it, the killing also leaves quite an impression on the reader—as does the crime's grotesquely comic aftermath, which at one point finds Edward running out of gas in downtown Dublin with his victim's body in a rug on the floor of his car's backseat. "It was," says Edward, "a bit embarrassing, don't you see?"

The strange, splenetic, and disturbed wife of a prominent Dublin surgeon, "Medea," as Edward called his mother (his name for his father was the similarly learned and caustic "Moloch"), met a terrible fate. And Cobb is of course horrified by his friend's "suburban butchery," both before and after the sensational crime. At the same time, he can't help liking awful Edward. *A Classical Education* tells the story of the friendship from their schoolboy days in England to their reconnection in Paris after Edward's thirteen-year imprisonment and beyond. Cobb deftly sketches the autobiographical background that gives context to his remarkable saga, keeping readers both riveted and delightfully, if at times appallingly, entertained.

One of the leading British historians of the French Revolution, Cobb brings to his memoir the same idiosyncratic focus and flair that animate his scholarly works. Throughout the book, the reader's fascination is held as much by the author as by his murderous friend; like some amiable but not entirely harmless relation of Patricia Highsmith's Tom Ripley, he narrates his gruesome tale with a confidence and concentration that is creepily seductive—a reaction, one suspects, that Cobb would relish. Long after Edward Ball had served his time for the murder of his mother, Cobb brought him to dinner at the high table of Balliol College,

Oxford. Seating his guest next to a retired law professor, Cobb announced, "My guest has a keen interest in the penal system." As one of Cobb's former students would remember him, "He was both an example of the scholarly life and a lord of misrule."

What: Memoir. *When:* 1985. *Also By: The People's Armies* (1961–63). *A Second Identity: Essays on France and French History* (1969). *Death in Paris 1795–1801* (1976). *Still Life: Sketches from a Tunbridge Wells Childhood* (1983). *The End of the Line: A Memoir* (1997). *Try: Hermit of Peking* by Hugh Trevor-Roper (see page 805). *Another Self* by James Lees-Milne (see page 471).

Life & Times of Michael K
J. M. Coetzee (born 1940)

A Nobel Laureate's Evocation of Elemental Freedom

In outline, the narrative of *Life & Times of Michael K* sounds relentlessly bleak. After losing his job as a civil service gardener, a disfigured man of limited mental capacity leads his impoverished, critically ill mother out of a war-torn city so that she might die in the place where she spent her girlhood, the only happy time in her memory. She dies along the way, and Michael K seeks refuge on a deserted farm in the country; there his life is pared down to essentials as he learns to live off the land. Even in his remote retreat, he cannot evade the nameless war: It sweeps down on him and finally relegates him to a work camp. Passive to the point of near-starvation, unable to live as either prisoner or parasite, he eludes even charity to reclaim his own poor existence, ennobled by being "neither locked up nor standing guard at the gate." At the end of the book, he imagines living by teaspoons of water, just as, as an infant unable to suckle because of his harelip, he was nourished by teaspoons of milk.

Relentlessly bleak, yes. And yet, on the strength of Coetzee's fierce vision and the declarative lucidity of his prose, extraordinarily life affirming as well. In his brief idyll working the soil on the abandoned farm, Michael K's fundamental solitude expands to embrace the fruits of the seeds he has discovered on his journey, and he begins to cultivate himself: "I am becoming a different kind of man," he thinks. Despite the fact that his sprouts of hope are soon blighted by the violence around him, this gardener's simplicity seems richer and more human than the abstractions and ideologies laying waste to the countryside. The cumulative force of *Life & Times of Michael K* is astonishing, and is aptly captured in Cynthia Ozick's praise of Coetzee's writing in this book: "The grain of his sentences is flat and austere, and so purifying to the senses that one comes away feeling that one's eye has been sharpened, one's hearing vivified, not only for the bright proliferations of nature, but for human unexpectedness." Despite its rich literary pedigree—there are strains of Kafka, Voltaire, and *Robinson Crusoe*—the novel has a footprint entirely its own.

What: Novel. *When:* 1983. *Awards:* Booker Prize, 1983. Coetzee was awarded the Nobel Prize in Literature in 2003. *Also By:* Fiction: *In the Heart of the Country* (1977); *Waiting for the Barbarians* (1980); *Disgrace* (1999); *Elizabeth Costello* (2003); *Diary of a Bad Year* (2007). Memoirs: *Boyhood: Scenes from Provincial Life* (1997); *Youth: Scenes from Provincial Life II* (2002). *Try: Nip the Buds, Shoot the Kids* by Kenzaburō Ōe. *The Conservationist* by Nadine Gordimer.

Earthly Paradise
Colette (1873–1954)
Edited by Robert Phelps

A Long Life of Love and Letters

One of France's greatest modern writers, Colette was larger than both life and literature. Born in a provincial backwater in 1873, she died in Paris eighty-one years later. In the intervening decades she shaped a legend grand enough to earn the distinction of a state funeral, like Victor Hugo before her (she was also the first woman to attain the rank of Grand Officer of the Legion of Honor). Although her first books—the sensationally popular and slightly scandalous Claudine novels—were written at the prodding of her first husband, a Parisian schemer and sophisticate several years her senior who had them published under his name, Colette soon became famous in her own right. In her youth a provocative music hall performer, throughout her life a voluptuary whose erotic affairs were legendary, she was also the author of more than six dozen volumes alive with her independent spirit and ingenious appetite for being.

Colette as Le Petit Faune in Le Désir, la Chimère et l'Amour at the Théâtre des Mathurins, Paris, 1906

Any page of Colette is a vivid translation of experience into a generous language of perception and embrace. The personal quality that animates her writing crosses genres with abandon to give the wide variety of prose she penned—fiction, memoir, essays, reportage—a unity of effect and a power of expression that transcend any individual work. Accordingly, this volume, an "autobiography" artfully drawn from her writings by Robert Phelps, offers the best introduction to her world and a splendid representation of her genius. It is also a great and fascinating joy to read. Phelps gathers extensive passages from Colette's books—such as Sido (1929), her fictionalized memoir of her mother; The Vagabond (1910), the novel based on her notorious music hall life; The Pure and the Impure (1932), an evocative exploration of love and desire; and her most famous tale, Gigi (1944)—as well as a marvelous assortment of excerpts from her memoirs, letters, and notebooks. He convincingly makes the case that, "like Montaigne or Thoreau or Whitman, Colette appears destined to become one of those writers whose literary achievement, however extraordinary, is itself caught up in something ampler: a personal myth, an emblematic image that merges the private life and the public art into a greater whole." Entering into this Earthly Paradise, the reader is met with the scent of those secrets that hold the substance of the heart, the human intimacies that are Colette's enduring subject.

What: Autobiography. Literature. *When:* 1966, gathering writings from throughout Colette's lifetime. *Also By: The Complete Claudine* (1900–03). *The Tendrils of the Vine* (1908). *Chéri* (1920). *My Mother's House* (1922). *The Last of Chéri* (1926). *My Apprenticeship* (1936). *Further Reading:* In addition to *Close to Colette,* a charming memoir by Maurice Goudeket, her third and last husband, there are two excellent biographies: *Secrets of the Flesh* by Judith Thurman and *Creating Colette* by Claude Francis and Fernande Gontier.

Sailing Alone Around the Room
NEW AND SELECTED POEMS
Billy Collins (born 1941)

An Invitation to Poetry

Billy Collins is a very funny guy, and there aren't too many former Poet Laureates of whom that can be said. Even though Collins's voice (to rip from its careful context one of his own lines) "sounds in places very casual, very blue jeans," it embraces a great range of reading, observation, and contemplation. Take the poem "Marginalia," in which we meet Duns Scotus and James Baldwin; an egg-salad-dripping, lovestruck devotee of *The Catcher in the Rye*; and, most memorably, Irish monks in their scriptoria, scribbling private notes in the margins of the Gospels:

> anonymous men catching a ride into the future
> on a vessel more lasting than themselves.

Be his subject poetry workshops or forgetfulness, saxophones or cows, canceling a vacation or nursing a hangover, Collins shapes his poems with a gentle but incisive humor that is ingratiating, intelligent, and, with delightful regularity, inspired. In his work the immediate genius of a stand-up comic is allied with the slow intelligence—the layering of life, learning, and lyrical intuition—of an accomplished poet, so that the reader is transported over the edge of understanding and, for a moment, suspended in the freedom of an imaginative leap.

What: Poetry. *When:* 2001. *Also By: Nine Horses* (2002). *The Trouble with Poetry and Other Poems* (2005). *Ballistics* (2008). *Try: Map: Collected and Last Poems* by Wislawa Szymborska (see page 769). *Delights and Shadows* by Ted Kooser. *Adaptation:* Collins is a marvelous reader of his own work. *Billy Collins Live: A Performance at the Peter Norton Symphony Space* captures the poet's voice in a 2005 public reading.

Carrying the Fire
AN ASTRONAUT'S JOURNEYS
Michael Collins (born 1930)

An Astronaut's Account of the First Trip to the Moon

An unrivaled account of the greatest adventure of our time—perhaps of all time—told by one of its protagonists, *Carrying the Fire* remains too little known. Collins was a member of the three-man crew of Apollo 11 on the first lunar landing mission, in July 1969; while his colleagues Neil Armstrong and Buzz Aldrin explored the moon's surface, Collins remained aboard the command module, circling in space and preparing for the critical re-docking maneuvers. Written with grace, insight, humor, and fine style, the book entertainingly relates the author's experiences as a test pilot and astronaut, providing a valuable firsthand chronicle of the Apollo program

Buzz Aldrin during the first moon walk

from the training of those who manned the spacecraft to the design and construction of its intricate machinery. In the words of Charles Lindbergh, Collins "combines a contemplative mind and poet's eye with the essentially practical approach of a participating astronaut." Alert to the anxieties and apprehensions of both astronauts and engineers, Collins tellingly communicates the human drama of the historic flight even as he commemorates the heroic dimensions of a feat of physical, technological, and personal daring that the vagaries of modern wonder still keep us from aptly honoring. A man on the moon—imagine that!

What: Adventure. Exploration. Technology. *When:* 1974. *Also By: Mission to Mars* (1990). For young readers: *Flying to the Moon: An Astronaut's Story* (1994). *Further Reading: Of a Fire on the Moon* by Norman Mailer. *The Right Stuff* by Tom Wolfe.

The Hunger Games
Suzanne Collins (born 1962)

A Newly Minted Fabled Hero

A story is a form of adventure, and as genres, science fiction and fantasy are more adventurous than most. Fictive forays into invented terrains stimulate us to construct a world in our heads, making the reading as inventive as the writing. This complicity can be compelling, for details that may be recognizable from our mundane activities take on new meaning when they are recast as pieces in a larger puzzle whose true contours are hidden in chapters yet to unfold. Like ancient myth, contemporary speculative fiction often strips life of naturalistic comforts, leading us into expansive lands where our hunger for our lives to have some greater cosmic meaning stands a chance of being fed—at least until the book is closed.

As story and as media phenomenon, Suzanne Collins's *The Hunger Games* is at the top of the pile of wildly popular dystopian teen fiction that has dominated twenty-first-century bestseller lists (in no small part by appealing to readers well beyond their teen years). In the nation of Panem, power and fortune are centralized in the Capitol, to which twelve outlying Districts must pay tribute each year in the form of one boy and one girl, aged between twelve and eighteen, who are chosen by lottery to participate in the games that give the book its title: a cruel tournament requiring them to fight to the death in televised battles for the entertainment of the Capitol audience.

Combining the stark fatalism of fairy tales, and all they intuit about human experience,

Katniss Everdeen wax figure at Madame Tussauds, London

with the desperate ethos of reality TV, and all *it* exhibits of human nature, Collins's gripping tale coheres around the resilient and resourceful Katniss Everdeen. She navigates a dangerous path through the fatal games and carries our hopes through the pages of this book and its two sequels. Themes from ancient mythology, Christian theology, and the social battlefield of the high school cafeteria have all been invoked in explaining the book's allure, which only indicates how rewarding a tale *The Hunger Games* proves to be. It stakes out imaginative territory people already inhabit, if not in their daily comings and goings, then in their closest encounters with themselves. And Katniss Everdeen earns, and holds, our hearts and minds, like Robin Hood and other brave outlaw heroes of yore.

What: Novel. *When:* 2008. *Also By: Catching Fire* (2009). *Mockingjay* (2010). *Try: Ender's Game* by Orson Scott Card (see page 126). *The Golden Compass* by Philip Pullman (see page 647). *Battle Royale* by Koushun Takami. *Adaptations:* Jennifer Lawrence plays Katniss in the film *The Hunger Games* (2012), directed by Gary Ross, and in three more films in the series: *The Hunger Games: Catching Fire* (2013), *The Hunger Games: Mockingjay, Part One* (2014), and *The Hunger Games: Mockingjay, Part Two* (2015), all directed by Francis Lawrence.

The Moonstone
Wilkie Collins (1824–1889)

"The first, longest, and the best of English detective novels."—T. S. Eliot

Those of you who may wonder what a highbrow modernist like the author of *The Waste Land* could possibly know about the pleasures of detective stories will be happy to learn that T. S. Eliot's esteem for Wilkie Collins's achievement was shared by no less a mystery master than Dorothy L. Sayers, creator of that most charming of sleuths, Lord Peter Wimsey. Collins was a contemporary, collaborator, and, until a late-life falling-out, confidant of Charles Dickens, and although his literary reputation may pale next to that of his colorful friend, Collins's influence on the course of fiction and the collective life of readers may be even greater. In his work—and in *The Moonstone* preeminently—he created an imaginative matrix for novels of detection and suspense so capacious it encompasses nearly the entire mystery/thriller genre that sprang up in his wake, flourished throughout the twentieth century, and still dominates bestseller lists today.

The Moonstone is certainly his masterpiece. The seed of its story is planted in a prologue that describes the theft of a sacred gem (the yellow diamond of the title) from an Indian palace during the English army's storming of Seringapatam in 1799. The mysterious Moonstone, and the curse that accompanies it, remains at the center of the intricate plot—replete with romance, duplicity, violence, secrets, villainy, and virtue—that the subsequent five hundred pages detail, most of it transpiring in England a half century after the initial scene, when Rachel Verinder comes into possession of the jewel upon her uncle's death. She has barely had the time to admire her inheritance before it is stolen from her dressing room.

In one of Collins's brilliant strokes, the complicated story that ensues is told by multiple narrators, including the wonderfully digressive Gabriel Betteredge, the house-steward of the Verinders (a man who charmingly and repeatedly invokes *Robinson Crusoe* with a devotion most mortals reserve for scripture); Miss Clack, a religiously fanatical poor relation (who cuts an unforgettably comic figure through the mounting tension); Mr. Bruff, the family's venerable lawyer and counselor; Franklin Blake, a young man smitten with Rachel yet cast under suspicion by events; and, most telling of all, Sergeant Cuff of Scotland Yard, who, in his mixture of professional expertise and personal idiosyncrasies (he is a keen fancier of roses), is the progenitor of a thousand and one fictional detectives.

While the plot of *The Moonstone* is compelling, it is the play of these distinctive voices upon our understanding of events that makes the book truly absorbing. Clues are laid out carefully and, in retrospect at least, quite tellingly, but their meaning is obscured as we read by the shifting perspectives and personalities of the narrators. In the same way, the exoticism of the diamond that is the story's catalyst disguises Collins's real invention in domesticating the melodrama of the Gothic tale and inviting its titillating energy into recognizable drawing rooms, thus laying the table for Agatha Christie and countless other novelists who would set murderous puzzles close to home.

Psychological acuity, formal virtuosity, the social and human amplitude of a Victorian novel, and the narrative pulse of a thriller add up to make *The Moonstone* the prototype of "the book you can't put down." T. S. Eliot was right.

What: Novel. Mystery & Suspense. *When:* 1868. *Also By: The Dead Secret* (1857). *The Woman in White* (1860). *No Name* (1862). *Armadale* (1866). *Further*

Reading: The Secret Life of Wilkie Collins by William M. Clarke. *Try: Bleak House* by Charles Dickens (see page 220). *The Complete Sherlock Holmes* by Arthur Conan Doyle (see page 171). *Drood* by Dan Simmons. *Adaptations:* Collins adapted *The Moonstone* as a play. A motion picture was made in 1934, and a BBC/ Masterpiece Theatre version aired in 1996. *Footnote:* The depiction of opium addiction in the novel is based on personal experience. Collins was addicted to laudanum and for years was convinced that a doppelgänger (to whom he referred as "Ghost Wilkie") was following him around. He also claimed to have no memory of writing some parts of *The Moonstone.*

The Worm Forgives the Plough
John Stewart Collis (1900–1984)

An Ode to the Sweat of the Brow and the Fruit of the Land

The Worm Forgives the Plough comprises two books, each originally published separately: *While Following the Plough* (1946) recounts the author's experience as a hired hand on a couple of farms in England in the early 1940s; *Down to Earth* (1947) begins with ruminations on his labors on the land, and continues with a chronicle of his efforts to clear and thin an ash wood in Dorset. The twinned narratives echo and amplify each other, the author's extraordinary sensibility—an amalgam of poetic, scientific, philosophic, and visionary impulses—blossoming in eloquent, carefully nurtured prose.

When I had made some big piles of branches, I was instructed to burn them, which I did. A pleasant task—for to reduce bulk to practically nothing, to make a hard thing soft, to cause substance to become insubstantial, is as interesting as making something out of nothing.

Collis is not to manual labor born, and his initial awkwardness as a laborer is charmingly depicted. We watch his mishaps, mistakes, and misalliances with tools, machinery, and animals, and eavesdrop on his misunderstandings of the shorthand instructions of his foremen and fellow workers. We feel his relief when, left alone in barn or field, he is able to master—through a mixture of trial and error, luck, and repetition—the rudiments of jobs both simple and arcane. As a result, we become personally engaged in his transformation from observer to participant; at the same time, we are informed and inspired by the observer's power to evoke the ancient and intricate significances of the tasks he undertakes. Respectfully precise, his descriptions of planting, pruning, plowing, and other daily chores are filled with a hard-won practical intelligence that is happily wed to wonder.

Both parts of *The Worm Forgives the Plough* are composed of sequences of short chapters, most no more than two or three pages in length. Although these genial, discursive essays seem composed, like exquisitely deliberated journal entries, for the author's own edification, they are often ripe with profound implications, working plots of fertile thought in which the reader can recognize the patterns man makes in nature, and nature makes in time. Out of all the closely observed details, and the hours of physical exertion, Collis hones earthbound meditations that transport us, on the back of his own labors, into inviting and inspiring realms of contemplation.

What: Nature. Memoir. *When:* 1973 (first edition combining *While Following the Plough* and *Down to Earth*). *Also By: The Triumph of the Tree* (1950).

The Moving Waters (1955). *Paths of Light* (1959). *Bound Upon a Course: An Autobiography* (1971). *Living with a Stranger: A Discourse on the Human Body* (1978). *Further Reading: John Stewart Collis: A Memoir* by Richard Ingrams. *Try: The Open Air* by Richard Jefferies. *The Outermost House* by Henry Beston (see page 74). *The Magic Apple Tree: A Country Year* by Susan Hill.

Memoirs of a Medieval Woman

THE LIFE AND TIMES OF MARGERY KEMPE
Louise Collis (born 1925)

The Adventures of an Apprentice Saint

The *Book of Margery Kempe* constitutes one of the first autobiographies in English, despite the fact that its author could neither read nor write. Dictated in the 1430s, it was not published in its entirety until a copy of the Middle English original was uncovered in a private British library five hundred years after its composition.

Born in Norfolk around 1373, Margery Kempe lived a long and extraordinary life. She managed a brewery, married, and gave birth to fourteen children before taking a vow of chastity (bringing a new resonance to Saint Augustine's famous prayer: "Lord give me chastity, but not yet") provoked by a mystical vision of Christ. Divine visitations—and conversations—would continue to haunt and guide her as she undertook arduous pilgrimages in expiation of an early sin. Her excursions included a journey to the Holy Land, a sojourn in Rome, a trip to the shrine of Santiago de Compostela, and a voyage to Norway. In addition to sharing the trials of medieval travel with her fellow pilgrims, she encountered several notable figures of the age, including the anchoress Julian of Norwich, author of *Revelations of Divine Love*, a classic of English mysticism.

In *Memoirs of a Medieval Woman*, Louise Collis transmutes *The Book of Margery Kempe* into a highly readable biographical narrative, enhancing her chronicle of her subject's earthly adventures and heavenly exaltations with material drawn from other contemporaneous sources. The result is an enlightening tour of the medieval world in the company of a woman at once ordinary and uncommon.

What: History. Religion & Spirituality. *When:* 1964 (published in England as *The Apprentice Saint*). *Further Reading: Margery Kempe and Her World* by Anthony Goodman. *Try: The Book of the City of Ladies* by Christine de Pizan (see page 257).

The Fringes of Power
DOWNING STREET DIARIES 1939–1955
John Colville (1915–1987)

Inside the War Cabinet:
The Diary of Churchill's Private Secretary

N ot only is this generally considered to be one of the truly indispensable books about World War II—"There is no better portrait of Churchill at the height of his powers," said one reviewer when *The Fringes of Power* was first published—but it is also one of the most dramatic and vivid diaries of the twentieth century.

In the late spring of 1940, eight months after the outbreak of war, Winston Churchill replaced Neville Chamberlain as prime minister of Great Britain. John Colville, who had joined Chamberlain's staff the previous October (and fortuitously begun his diary the month before that), stayed on as private secretary to the indefatigable new PM. Colville initially shared the widespread skepticism about his mercurial new boss ("I spent the day in a bright blue new suit from the Fifty-Shilling Tailors, cheap and sensational looking, which I felt was appropriate to the new Government"). But as the war's darkest days enshadowed Britain in the summer of 1940, when it looked as if a seemingly invincible Nazi war machine was preparing to cross the Channel from occupied France, Colville came to appreciate Churchill's dynamic, uncannily intuitive leadership and his unquenchable optimism: "It is refreshing to work with somebody who refuses to be depressed even by the most formidable danger that has ever threatened this country."

Serving thereafter at the PM's side for the rest of the war, as well as during Churchill's troubled postwar return to office, Colville was able to record a prismatic, day-by-day portrait of one of history's great leaders: "Few public figures in all history have assumed so many mantles, displayed such an unlikely mixture of talents, experienced over so wide a span of years such a variety of triumphs and disasters, and been successively so suspected and so trusted, so disliked and so admired by his fellow countrymen." Offering an invaluable firsthand perspective on Churchill the man and, especially, his conduct of the war, *The Fringes of Power* does indeed represent what Churchill biographer William Manchester called "a priceless legacy."

What: Biography. Diaries & Letters. History. War.
When: 1985. *Further Reading: Churchill: A Life* by Martin Gilbert. *Their Finest Hour* by Winston Churchill (see page 202). *The Last Lion* by William Manchester.

....

The Complete Sherlock Holmes
Sir Arthur Conan Doyle (1859–1930)

The Adventures of Fiction's Favorite Sleuth

There was only one student in the room, who was bending over a distant table absorbed in his work. At the sound of our steps he glanced round and sprang to his feet with a cry of pleasure. "I've found it! I've found it," he shouted to my companion, running towards us with a test-tube in his hand. "I have found a re-agent which is precipitated by haemoglobin, and by nothing else." Had he discovered a gold mine, greater delight could not have shone upon his features.

"Dr. Watson, Mr. Sherlock Holmes," said Stamford, introducing us.

"How are you?" he said cordially, gripping my hand with a strength for which I should hardly have given him credit. "You have been in Afghanistan, I perceive."

"How on earth did you know that?" I asked in astonishment.

"Never mind," said he, chuckling to himself. "The question now is about haemoglobin. No doubt you see the significance of this discovery of mine?"

Thus Sherlock Holmes was introduced to Dr. Watson, and to the world as well. The passage is from Arthur Conan Doyle's first Holmes story, "A Study in Scarlet," which appeared in *Beeton's Christmas Annual of 1887* and acquainted the public with a detective whose genius and eccentricity have held readers in thrall for more than a century. It would be hard to name another modern literary character who has achieved such international celebrity.

Even in the brief passage quoted above, several of Holmes's intriguing qualities are immediately apparent: the excitable intellect, the passion for scientific inquiry, the preternatural skill at quickly interpreting, in revelatory detail, evidence that is in plain sight but invisible to everyone else. Conan Doyle's conception of a scientific, rationally deductive detective was based in part upon Dr. Joseph Bell, a professor with whom the author had studied during his medical education at the University of Edinburgh. "He was a very skillful surgeon," Conan Doyle wrote in his autobiography, "but his strong point was diagnosis, not only of disease, but of occupation and character." Combining Bell's diagnostic gifts with elements drawn from the early detective tales of Edgar Allan Poe and Wilkie Collins, Conan Doyle imagined an investigator who would solve cases "on his own merits and not through the folly of the criminal"; as a result, perhaps for the first time in the genre, the detective himself becomes the focus of the reader's fascination.

Arthur Conan Doyle, ca. 1895

The fascination was quick to take hold. Having read "A Study in Scarlet," the editor of *Lippincott's Monthly Magazine* asked Dr. Conan Doyle to write another Holmes tale; the result was "The Sign of Four," published in 1890. The next year saw the launch of *The Strand Magazine*, and six shorter Sherlock Holmes adventures soon appeared in its pages. If the author had had his way, that might have been the end of the

sleuth and his sidekick, Dr. Watson (who, as the often amazed narrator, offers a perfectly ordinary foil to the entirely remarkable Holmes). For although Conan Doyle had abandoned his career as a doctor to live by his pen, his ambition was to make his literary reputation by writing historical novels rather than tales of detection. When *The Strand* asked for six more Holmes stories, Conan Doyle named an exorbitant price as a deterrent; to his surprise, they readily agreed to his terms. After this second set of cases had run, *The Strand* requested twelve more, and again the author named a price he was sure would be prohibitive. Once more the magazine happily agreed: Sherlock Holmes proved too popular to be put to rest. (Indeed, eager to be free of his creation, Conan Doyle completed this additional *Strand* commission with "The Final Problem," a story in which he seemed to kill Holmes off in an encounter with his archenemy, the evil genius Professor Moriarty. Fortunately, the outrage among readers was such that the author eventually reopened the Holmes casebook, producing a stream of new stories throughout the rest of his writing career.)

While the success of the Holmes tales can properly be seen as a catalyst for the boom in crime and detective literature that began in the early twentieth century and seems to grow larger every year, the pleasure of Conan Doyle's narratives rests only in part on the cleverly contrived and ingeniously unraveled mysteries that provide their plots. The real joy for readers is the atmosphere the author creates through the evocation of both Victorian London and the peculiarly seductive realm of No. 221B Baker Street, where Holmes abides. The fogbound allure of the former is almost as strong as the curious and compelling air—filled with pipe smoke, the residual scent of chemical experiments, the energy inspired by Holmes's various stimulants, and the strains of his violin—of the protagonist's rooms; both play major roles supporting the mesmerizing ratiocinations of our hero, whose bold confidence and bracing brainpower never fail to astonish us (and, of course, the faithful Watson).

What: Mystery & Suspense. *When:* The first tale was published in 1887, the last in 1926. *Editions:* There are nearly sixty stories and novels of Sherlock Holmes, collected into numerous and various volumes, with several complete editions in print. *The New Annotated Sherlock Holmes,* issued by W. W. Norton in 2004 (*The Novels*) and 2005 (*The Complete Short Stories*; two volumes), is a must-have for devoted Sherlockians. *Also By:* The historical novels for which Conan Doyle yearned to be known remained his favorite works; *The White Company* (1891) and *Sir Nigel* (1906) are the best. Also worth seeking out are his comic tales of a French soldier in the Napoleonic army, *The Exploits of Brigadier Gerard* (1896) and *The Adventures of Gerard* (1903), and the Professor Challenger adventures, including *The Lost World* (1912) and *The Poison Belt* (1913). *Further Reading: Arthur Conan Doyle: A Life in Letters* by Jon Lellenberg, Daniel Stashower, and Charles Foley. *The Man Who Created Sherlock Holmes* by Andrew Lycett. *Try: The Seven-Per-Cent Solution* by Nicholas Meyer, a 1974 novel in which the great sleuth joins forces with Sigmund Freud, is one of the better contributions to the character's afterlife. Also, *The Beekeeper's Apprentice* by Laurie R. King. *Adaptations:* Too many to name, in every form of media. *Footnote:* The first two Holmes tales were ineptly illustrated; part of what made the *Strand* series that followed them a success were the illustrations by Sidney Paget, who was responsible for the enduringly famous deerstalker cap and cape.

Son of the Morning Star
CUSTER AND THE LITTLE BIGHORN
Evan S. Connell (1924–2013)

A Riveting Witness to a Bloody Clash of Cultures

At the dawn of the 1980s, with more than two decades of fiction under his belt, Evan S. Connell published two volumes of historical essays—*A Long Desire* and *The White Lantern* (each highly recommended for their deft, erudite, and enchanting explorations of intriguing figures and events of the past)—and began work on a third. One of the new essays was to be focused on the battle of the Little Bighorn, in which Sioux warriors, led by Sitting Bull, vanquished American troops under the command of General George Armstrong Custer in 1876. But Connell's consideration of the incident familiarly known as "Custer's Last Stand" quickly grew into a book: *Son of the Morning Star.* Published in 1984, this unusual, minutiae-laden, deeply imagined work of history, military scrutiny, and anthropological investigation by a critically acclaimed but generally neglected novelist became a phenomenal bestseller.

The work of an idiosyncratic but engaging storyteller, *Son of the Morning Star* is discursive,

Chief Sitting Bull, 1885

elegant, and unflinching. *The Christian Science Monitor* called it "the story of Gen. George Armstrong Custer as Flaubert would have written it"; it's a nice compliment, but the book is better than that, because, for all his literary sophistication, Connell is more interested in insight than eloquence. He brings his subject—a thrilling narrative in itself, even when simply told—to life with complex, careful sympathies. In his words, "Our nineteenth-century campaign to suppress or exterminate Indian tribes, undertaken with the best of nineteenth-century intentions, was not altogether noble. We should understand this." By the end of this fierce, compulsively readable exploration of a legendary encounter, we do understand this truth—in all its fatal, fateful consequences.

What: History. *When:* 1984. *Also By:* Connell's pair of novels depicting the lives of a Middle-American couple, *Mrs. Bridge* (1959) and *Mr. Bridge* (1969), are deservedly renowned. *Further Reading: The Last Stand: Custer, Sitting Bull, and the Battle of the Little Bighorn* by Nathaniel Philbrick. *Try: Empire of the Summer Moon: Quanah Parker and the Rise and Fall of the Comanches, the Most Powerful Indian Tribe in American History* by S. C. Gwynne. *Adaptation: Son of the Morning Star* was adapted into a TV miniseries in 1991.

Enemies of Promise
Cyril Connolly (1903–1974)

A Peerless Appraisal of the Perils of the Literary Life

Cyril Connolly founded and edited a famous literary magazine (*Horizon*), wrote a novel (*The Rock Pool*; 1936) and several other books, and was for decades one of Britain's most influential literary journalists and book reviewers. In his own eyes, however, this eminent man of letters was a failure because he never wrote the masterpiece that he and others expected him to produce. It was a failure he dwelt on throughout his life, never more eloquently than in the pages of this book. Detailing the formation of his own sensibility, with engaging autobiographical essays on his schooling at St. Cyprian's (where his schoolmates included Cecil Beaton and George Orwell) and Eton, *Enemies of Promise* combines personal history, advice, and shrewd critical commentary into an unconventional how-not-to guide to a literary vocation.

"Those whom the Gods would destroy, they first call promising," Connolly writes, announcing his overriding theme with a demonstration of the aphoristic elegance of his own prose. In Connolly's view, the discipline required to write books of enduring value is subject to myriad distractions. One of them is domesticity: "There is no more sombre enemy of good art than the pram in the hall." Others are journalism, politics, and bohemian extravagance. Too much money is also a danger, as is too little. Working late in the day, working early—both are problematic. In fact, living is an enemy of promise, if a writer lets it be. (And for the record, Connolly, a legendary bon vivant, always let it be.)

"By turns funny, astute and elegiac"—to borrow the apt adjectives of Connolly's biographer Jeremy Lewis—*Enemies of Promise* offers a bracing education for aspiring writers; it's filled with expressive pleasures and intuitions about life and literature that will reward readers, too.

What: Writing. Literature. Autobiography. *When:* 1938; revised edition 1948. *Also By: The Unquiet Grave: A Word Cycle by "Palinurus"* (1944; a fascinating, original compendium of aphorisms and commentary). *The Selected Essays of Cyril Connolly* (1984). *Further Reading: Cyril Connolly: A Life* by Jeremy Lewis. *Try:* As an encouraging practical antidote to Connolly's pessimism, see *Becoming a Writer* by Dorothea Brande. *Footnote:* According to Jeremy Lewis, Connolly was told by his British editor that the American edition of *Enemies of Promise* "had sold a mere 325 copies, but both Warner Brothers and Twentieth Century Fox had expressed interest in the film rights. 'I hope they make a wonderful film of *Enemies of Promise* with Shirley Temple as Promise and Ginger Rogers and Fred Astaire as Eton boys,' Connolly replied."

JOSEPH CONRAD
(1857–1924)

Joseph Conrad, ca. 1904

Joseph Conrad is a writer of great allure and enormous influence. On the latter score, the shadows of style and subject his fiction cast have colored the work of an impressive roster of modern masters, including William Faulkner, André Malraux, Graham Greene, Gabriel García Márquez, V. S. Naipaul, John le Carré, Joan Didion, and J. M. Coetzee. On the other hand, his allure, in characteristically Conradian way, is something of a subterfuge, for his reputation as a spinner of seagoing tales in exotic locales might lead us to expect a different kind of reading experience than his books deliver. There is action, yes, but it's often hard to follow the details of what exactly is happening, to say nothing of what we're supposed to think about it; even the identity of the teller can be elusive.

Part of the slipperiness comes from the fact that, despite the trappings of ships and the accoutrements of adventure, the real events unfold in moral rather than physical realms. Conrad's stories are constructed to conjure an ethical and psychological climate, an authorial atmosphere that is more like a meteorological system than a plot; it's a weather that carries in its winds the worries of modern civilization, chief among them authenticity (*Lord Jim*), imperialism (*Under Western Eyes*), and terrorism (*The Secret Agent*). Because his narratives can be so knotty, the moods they summon so confusing and diffuse, it's best to start with a book in which Conrad engages us with direct address, such as his memoir *A Personal Record*, before entering the murkier territory of his signature novels, to which *Heart of Darkness* offers the most revealing portal.

A Personal Record
Recollections in a New Language

A few strokes brought us alongside, and it was then that, for the very first time in my life, I heard myself addressed in English—the speech of my secret choice, of my future, of long friendships,
of the deepest affections, of hours of toil and hours of ease, and of solitary hours, too, of books read, of thoughts pursued, of remembered emotions—of my very dreams! . . . As to the quality of the address itself I cannot say it was very striking. Too short for eloquence and devoid of all charm of tone, it consisted precisely of the three words "Look out there!" growled out huskily above my head.

So writes the great English novelist, the Polish-born Józef Teodor Konrad Korzeniowski, near the conclusion of this arresting memoir. Like all Conrad's writing, it forgoes direct statement for an amalgam of meditation, sensation, image, and revelation. In short, the author transports the turning points of his life—childhood in Poland and Ukraine, going to sea against the wishes of his inland people, the strange compulsion that inspired *Almayer's Folly*, his first novel—into the imaginative universe of the English language, a universe Conrad was not born into, but entered in adulthood with "a strange and overpowering feeling that it had always been an inherent part of myself." Although it has long been overshadowed by the achievement of his fictional masterworks, *A Personal Record* remains a most inviting expression of Conrad's furtive genius.

What: Memoir. *When:* 1912. *Also By: The Mirror of the Sea* (1906). *Notes on Life and Letters* (1921). *Try: Speak, Memory* by Vladimir Nabokov (see page 580). *Lost in Translation: A Life in a New Language* by Eva Hoffman.

Heart of Darkness
A Seminal and Unsettling Story Within a Story

In the course of roughly a hundred pages, *Heart of Darkness* will journey, with a strangely leisurely intensity, into realms of depravity best encoded in the dying cry of Kurtz, the delusional, despicable character at its enigmatic core: "The horror! The horror!" Yet Joseph Conrad's influential novella begins in a setting of utmost serenity. Five men are relaxing on a yacht anchored in the Thames, looking seaward at sunset. The vista inspires the narrator to muse on the adventures of "the great knight-errants of the sea" who had embarked upon their explorations on the very waters he surveys: "What greatness had not floated on the ebb of that river into the mystery of an unknown earth! . . . The dreams of men, the seed of commonwealths, the germs of empires."

But his reverie is interrupted, and its encomium to imperial nobility overturned, by one of his companions: "'And this also,' said Marlow suddenly, 'has been one of the dark places on the earth.'" He goes on to invoke the arrival of the Romans in Britain two thousand years earlier, and the incomprehensible reality they faced—"all that mysterious life of the wilderness that stirs in the forest, in the jungles, in the hearts of wild men"—in order to subvert the glory that accrues to colonizers: "The conquest of the earth, which mostly means the taking it away from those who have a different complexion or slightly flatter noses than ourselves, is not a pretty thing when you look into it too much." The unnamed narrator

1899 edition of Blackwood's Magazine, *in which* The Heart of Darkness *was serialized*

resumes command for a moment, only to set the stage for his almost complete surrender of the rest of the tale to his loquacious companion: "we knew we were fated, before the ebb began to run, to hear about one of Marlow's inconclusive experiences."

The fateful experience in question involves Marlow's stint as a riverboat captain in the ivory trade in the Belgian Congo. In the employ of an enterprise known simply as "the Company," Marlow leads an expedition upriver in search of Kurtz, a Company man who has not been heard from in a year, and who, it turns out, has established himself as a despot among the natives. The lurid shadow of Kurtz's madness looms over Marlow's telling—and the reader's memory of the tale—but it is merely a culmination of the creeping dread that infuses every mile of the river voyage. The tangled web of Company intrigue and corruption—the organization seems drunk on a cocktail of absurdity, suspense, and black comedy mixed of equal parts Franz Kafka, Eric Ambler, and Joseph Heller—suggests that bureaucracy breeds brutality, if only by establishing an etiquette that ignores it. The heart of darkness may not be a destination, it seems, but a companion.

Although this extraordinarily concentrated work has been hailed, denounced, and hailed all over again for its attitudes about race and colonialism, an exact interpretation of its themes remains unsettlingly elusive. Like a distillation of the longer fiction that Conrad would write in its wake—*Lord Jim* (1900), *Nostromo* (1904), *The Secret Agent* (1907)—this gripping and groundbreaking novella, despite its powerful dramatic arc, is profoundly, almost creepily unresolved. The peculiar fact, reinforced by the quotation marks in which nearly every paragraph is couched, that *Heart of Darkness* is a story being told within another story is the only sure thing about it. That narrative self-consciousness, and the pulsating stream of Marlow's expression, would make it one of the most crucial fictions of the modern era. "Inconclusive," yes, but unforgettable.

What: Novella. When: Serialized in Blackwood's Magazine in 1899; first published in a collection (Youth: A Narrative and Two Other Stories) in 1902. Also By: Chance (1913). Victory (1915). The Shadow Line (1917).

Further Reading: The Dawn Watch: Joseph Conrad in a Global World by Maya Jasanoff. Adam Hochschild's King Leopold's Ghost recounts the Belgian king's reign of terror in the Congo. Try: Lord of the Flies by William Golding (see page 322). The Poisonwood Bible by Barbara Kingsolver (see page 448). Adaptation: Heart of Darkness was the basis for Francis Ford Coppola's Apocalypse Now (1979), which relocated the story to war-torn Vietnam.

The Road from Coorain
Jill Ker Conway (1934–2018)

Finding a Way Out from Down Under

Jill Ker Conway's account of her coming-of-age in Australia in the middle of the twentieth century is a deft evocation of landscape and memory. Through those two dimensions a small girl grows, against cultural and familial odds, into a determined young woman on the verge of a voyage to America, where she will pursue her aspirations as a historian and, ultimately, achieve renown as the first female president of Smith College.

The book opens with an extended description—a tribute that is both affectionate and awestruck—of the western grasslands of New South Wales, the lonely red-dusted outback that is home to kangaroos, kookaburras, and a delicate web of life: "not the luxuriant design of a book of hours by any means, but a tapestry nonetheless, designed by a spare modern artist." Conway's parents raised the author and her two brothers on a sheep station there that was so remote that she was seven before she saw another female child. Yet her early years, as absorbingly depicted here, were filled with the interest and stimulation of nature, labor, and learning; they would come to an end in tragedy, with a period of intense drought and her father's death, in a cruel paradox, by drowning.

Conway's narrative moves to a larger canvas as it encompasses her teenage years in Sydney and her education at that city's university; her intelligence and ambition, however, are thwarted by the sexist constraints of higher education in 1950s Australia, as well as strained

relations with her increasingly demanding ("she went on and on like a fugue") and unreasonable mother. Breaking with the stoic inheritance that had been instilled in her from her earliest days, Conway opts out, accepting a fellowship at Harvard and leaving Australia for America:

My parents, each in his or her own way, had spent the good things in their lives prodigally and had not been careful about harvesting and cherishing the experiences that nourish hope. I was going to be different. I was going to be life-affirming from now on, grateful to have been born, not profligate in risking my life for the sake of the panache of it, not all-too-ready to embrace a hostile fate.

In the pages of this moving book, we witness a destiny discovering itself, as it would in a nineteenth-century novel. In fact, throughout Conway's narrative, a reader can't help but think of Dorothea Brooke, the heroine of George Eliot's Middlemarch (see page 248), and wonder if this is the sort of autobiography Dorothea might have penned if she had not had such an accomplished novelist to tell her tale.

What: Memoir. When: 1989. Also By: The Road from Coorain ends with Conway's departure for America; her subsequent life and career are depicted in two excellent sequels, True North (1995) and A Woman's Education (2001). Try: My Brilliant Career by Miles Franklin (see page 296). Under My Skin by Doris Lessing. Don't Let's Go to the Dogs Tonight by Alexandra Fuller. Adaptation: A Masterpiece Theatre production was released in 2002.

Memories of the Great and the Good
Alistair Cooke (1908–2004)

**Distinguished Profiles of Performers,
Politicians, and Personalities**

I f you are of a certain age, you may remember him as the man behind the microphone for the world's longest-running spoken-word radio program: His weekly *Letter from America* was heard on Britain's airwaves and around the world for fifty-eight years. Or you may remember him as the dapper host of PBS's Masterpiece Theatre from 1971 to 1992. But as this book clearly demonstrates, there was another side to Alistair Cooke: Curious readers should know that he was an accomplished print journalist with a real gift for the brief biographical sketch known as "the profile."

There's so much "personality" journalism around these days that it's easy to forget just how absorbing and memorable profiles can be when they're as well crafted and thoughtful as those found here. In these twenty-three shrewd and insightful exercises in "appreciative criticism" ("Most of these pieces tend to find, and rejoice in, what is best about their subjects"), Cooke celebrates "a variety of well-known people I have met, known, 'covered,' admired or liked throughout sixty-odd years of journalism." His subjects are wonderfully various, ranging from Duke Ellington to Erma Bombeck, Harold Ross to Winston Churchill ("The Last Victorian" is frequently cited as an especially acute portrait), George Bernard Shaw to Eleanor Roosevelt, Gary Cooper to Robert Frost, Barry Goldwater to P. G. Wodehouse. The last gets credit for the

Alistair Cooke in his library, ca. 1950

best sound bite in a book filled with great ones: "There was a ban on me in Hungary for a while, which is just as mysterious as their reading me at all." And although the names of some of Cooke's "well-known people" may no longer be instantly recognizable (John Nance Garner? George Aiken? Francis Chichester?), it is nonetheless a pleasure to make their acquaintance in the author's urbane company.

What: Biography. Journalism. *When:* 1999 (collecting pieces written from the 1950s through the 1990s). *Also By:* *Six Men* (1977). *Letter from America, 1946–2004* (2004). *Alistair Cooke's America* (1973). *Further Reading: Alistair Cooke: A Biography* by Nick Clarke. *Try: Life Stories: Profiles from* The New Yorker, edited by David Remnick.

Talleyrand
Duff Cooper (1890–1954)

**A Debonair Biography of the Man Who
Outmaneuvered Napoleon**

C harles Maurice de Talleyrand-Périgord (1754–1838) wielded political influence with unparalleled effectiveness throughout the most dramatic decades in the history of France. As the

nation passed quickly from *ancien régime* to revolution to Napoleonic Empire to restoration of the Bourbon monarchy, it seemed that Talleyrand alone was left standing in the wake of the tumultuous events. There is no better emblem of his instinct for survival than Duff Cooper's description of his escape from the looming Terror in

1793: "It was from Danton's own hand, in the Ministry of Justice, which stood then where it stands to-day in the Place Vendôme, that Talleyrand received his passport at one o'clock in the morning of the first of September. On the following day the massacres began."

That brief passage also gives some sense of the page-turning pleasures of the book at hand. Changing colors with the changing times, "supported," as Cooper writes, "by high ambition and unburdened by scruples," the noble-born Talleyrand parlayed his clerical training into a bishopric, his ecclesiastical power into a revolutionary profile, his political authority into an alliance with Napoleon, and his disaffection with the emperor into a leadership position in the provisional government that paved the way for the restoration. He played critical—and sometimes duplicitous—roles on the international stage as well, especially, as Cooper relates in one of his finest chapters, at the Congress of Vienna in 1814–15. "It is he, after all," Cooper quotes Napoleon as saying of Talleyrand, "who best understands this age and society, both the Governments and the peoples." At the same time, Talleyrand's duties under church and state did nothing to constrain his pursuit of romantic liaisons and personal enrichment. In short, Talleyrand was a character worthy of contemporary novelists such as Stendhal or Dumas.

Cooper, a British diplomat who served most notably as war secretary from 1935 to 1937 and as ambassador to France from 1944 to 1948, follows his chameleon protagonist through a forest of intrigues with perfect pace and style, distilling facts and incidents into polished prose that is a joy to read. His chronicle of an exciting epoch enriches our historical understanding, and his portraits of the men and women of the era are drawn with a wise and worldly eye. Most enjoyably, the author shows a decided affinity for his clever, amorous, and brilliant hero.

What: Biography. *When:* 1932. *Also By: Old Men Forget* (autobiography; 1953). *The Duff Cooper Diaries: 1915–1951* (2005). *Further Reading: The Lives of Talleyrand* by Crane Brinton. *The Ruin of Kasch*, by Roberto Calasso, is a virtuoso amalgam of literature, history, and philosophy that, according to Italo Calvino, takes up two subjects: "the first is Talleyrand, and the second is everything else." *Try: Melbourne* by David Cecil (see page 139).

The Last of the Mohicans
A TALE OF 1757
James Fenimore Cooper (1789–1851)

Into the Woods with America's First Frontier Hero

In the pages of this classic adventure tale you'll meet one of the greatest heroes in American literature, Nathaniel Bumppo, a rugged scout and woodsman who goes by any number of nicknames, among them Natty, Leatherstocking, Pathfinder, Deerslayer, and Hawkeye. *The Last of the Mohicans* is the second in the series of five Leatherstocking Tales that James Fenimore Cooper wrote about Natty; it followed *The Pioneers*, a portrait of frontier life at the end of the nineteenth century in which Bumppo appears as an old man. The character in the first novel proved so popular that Cooper brought him back, this time in the prime of life, in *The Last of the Mohicans*, which is set during the French and Indian Wars, more than three decades before the earlier book.

In the woods of what is now upstate New York, Natty and a pair of noble Mohicans, Chingachgook and his son Uncas, the last members of their once-great tribe, come to the aid of the beautiful Munro sisters, Alice and Cora. The young women have become pawns in the struggle between their father, the commander of Fort William Henry, a British outpost, and Magua, a renegade Huron brave who seeks revenge against Colonel Munro for past humiliations. As serial dangers beset the group, Natty and his companions struggle valiantly to keep the Munros and their other charges out of peril.

Cooper's exciting, action-packed yarns helped shaped the romantic notion of the pre-Revolutionary American wilderness as a stage for nobility of character and resourceful courage. Although not always historically accurate, they do imbue the uncorrupted forest with an imaginative promise that reflects the overwhelming power the unsettled continent had in shaping the fears and fortunes of the early colonists. That promise found no better embodiment than Natty Bumppo, and Natty had no better adventure than *The Last of the Mohicans*.

What: Novel. *When:* 1826. *Also By:* Leatherstocking Tales: Both *The Pioneers* (1823) and *The Prairie* (1827) treat Natty's life after the events recounted in *The Last of the Mohicans*, whereas *The Pathfinder* (1840) and *The Deerslayer* (1841) are concerned with his youth. Also of note is *The Leatherstocking Saga* (1954), a compilation edited by historian Allan Nevins, which collects the parts of all five novels that pertain to Natty and arranges them in a single chronological narrative. *Adaptation:* The most recent film of *The Last of the Mohicans* was released in 1992. It was directed by Michael Mann and stars Daniel Day-Lewis. *Footnote:* Don't miss "Fenimore Cooper's Literary Offences" (1895), a hilariously devastating critique in which Mark Twain pokes fun at the author's sometimes mannered style: "Cooper's art has some defects," Twain writes. "In one place in *Deerslayer*, and in the restricted space of

THE LAST OF THE MOHICANS.

His dark eye glanced swiftly and keenly on every side of him. His rifle lay untouched and apparently unnoticed within reach of his hand.

Illustration from an early 19th-century edition

two-thirds of a page, Cooper has scored 114 offenses against literary art out of a possible 115. It breaks the record."

Torregreca

LIFE, DEATH, AND MIRACLES IN A SOUTHERN ITALIAN VILLAGE

Ann Cornelisen (1926–2003)

An Outsider in an Insular World

*T*orregreca is an extraordinary social document, a candid account of a Protestant American woman's encounter with the Catholic, peasant culture of southern Italy as it endured through the late 1950s. Arriving in an impoverished village (here called Torregreca) in the region of Basilicata with the intention of establishing a nursery school for the benefit of its denizens, the author quickly becomes the subject of gossip as an independent woman in a society bound by ancient spells of tradition that have only slowly dissipated across the centuries. The clash of cultures is both comic and poignant, but Cornelisen's resourcefulness in the face of the medieval, almost metaphysical sense of futility that holds the villagers in thrall is unremitting: "No matter what the problem, my solutions were greeted with 'It can't be done'; but it could be, and it was."

From the nuns of the Convent of San Fortunato to the old shoemaker who lovingly recites Dante every night to men who gather in his shop, Cornelisen deftly portrays the complex humanity of a varied cast of characters, and, powerfully, lets some, such as her landlady-maid, Chichella Fascide, the widowed mother of three young children, speak for themselves. Despite her new neighbors' initial suspicion, Cornelisen soon becomes a fixture of the community and—successfully launching the nursery—eventually enters its folklore, as she discovers upon her return to Torregreca several years after the period the book describes.

For a stranger to penetrate a parochial world, as Cornelisen did during her time in the village, is itself a creative act of the first order: What ingenuity, compassion, and presence of mind it requires. All of these qualities animate the pages of her book, which takes the surprising measure of circumscribed lives with clarity and candor. But *Torregreca* is much more than a documentary: Imagine a Henry James heroine, escaping not only the conventions of America but also the strictures of the novelist's sentences to discover her own language of curiosity and soulfulness, and you'll have some sense of Ann Cornelisen's literary achievement. At its heart, *Torregreca* is the moving testament of a sensibility reshaped by its encounter with the obdurate truths of a foreign reality. It is a work of great humanity and nobility—of storytelling in the best, most fundamental sense.

What: Memoir. Sociology. Place. *When:* 1969. *Also By: Vendetta of Silence* (1971). *Women of the Shadows: Wives and Mothers of Southern Italy* (1976). *Strangers and Pilgrims: The Last Italian Migration* (1980). *Any Four Women Could Rob the Bank of Italy* (1983). *Try: Christ Stopped at Eboli* by Carlo Levi (see page 480). *Memorial* by Ferdinando Camon (see page 120).

Cronopios and Famas
Julio Cortázar (1914–1984)

A Sparkling Collection of Whimsical Fictions

Regardless of whether you yourself are a *cronopio*, a *fama*, or even an easygoing *esperanza*—more about each of them in a moment—you still need to read this collection of short fictions. Why? Because, as Nobel Laureate Pablo Neruda declared, "Anyone who doesn't read Cortázar is doomed. Not to read him is a serious invisible disease which in time can have terrible consequences. Something similar to a man who has never tasted peaches. He would be quietly getting sadder, noticeably paler, and, probably, little by little, he would lose his hair."

Neruda's fantastical warning sets just the right tone for a consideration of the highly imaginative work of Julio Cortázar, a leading light of the Latin American literary boom that exploded in the 1960s. Born in Brussels of

Julio Cortázar, 1969

Argentinian parents and residing for most of his adult life in Paris, Cortázar wrote "poems, fantasies, novels, anti-novels, stories, and written games, all kinds of adventures in language," as one of his translators, Alastair Reid, described them. At their most distinctive, these antic inventions mingle the realistic and the genially surreal in such a way that they open the reader's eyes afresh to the simple marvels of everyday life.

That's certainly the effect of reading *Cronopios and Famas*, Cortázar's whimsical, freewheeling 1962 *jeu d'esprit*. It begins with a section called "The Instruction Manual" that includes such bracingly unhackneyed texts as "Instructions on How to Sing," which opens with the startling directive "Begin by breaking all the mirrors in the house." The second and third sections consider "Unusual Occupations" and "Unstable Stuff," while the book's eponymous final section offers snapshot-like glimpses of Cortázar's personal mythological landscape. It's there you'll meet the creative and hopelessly impractical *cronopios* (a word invented by Cortázar), the type-A *famas* (literally, "fames"), and the easygoing *esperanzas* ("hopes")—recognizable human types rendered colorfully emblematic by the ingenuity of this singular author.

What: Short Stories. *When:* Originally published 1962 in Argentina; translation by Paul Blackburn, 1969. *Also By: Hopscotch* (1963; translation 1966). *All Fires the Fire and Other Stories* (1966; 1973). *62: A Model Kit* (1968; 1972). *A Manual for Manuel* (1973; 1978). *Try: Epitaph of a Small Winner* by Joaquim Maria Machado de Assis (see page 508). *Labyrinths* and *Ficciones* by Jorge Luis Borges (see page 87).

> **"I once called him the Simón Bolívar of the Latin American novel; he liberated us all with a new, airy, humorous, and mysterious language, both everyday and mythical."**
>
> —*Carlos Fuentes on Julio Cortázar*

Conversations with Glenn Gould
Jonathan Cott (born 1942)

You'll Never Listen to Music in the Same Way Again

Classical pianist Glenn Gould (1932–1982) made his recording debut in 1955 with a stunning version of Bach's *Goldberg Variations*. The disc caused a sensation on its initial release, and it remains one of the bestselling classical albums of all time. Though Gould went on to enjoy an outstanding career, he became as famous for his eccentricities as for his brilliant, if often controversial, musicianship. Among his oddities was his reclusiveness: He retired from public performing in 1964, lived alone for most of his life, and gave few interviews.

One journalist, however, to whom Gould did speak regularly was Jonathan Cott, whose *Conversations with Glenn Gould* consists, for the most part, of the transcript of an epic telephone conversation the two men had over the course of several days in 1974. From the opening words of Cott's introduction—"'The nut's a genius,' the conductor George Szell once remarked after

Cover of Glenn Gould's 1955 recording of Bach's Goldberg Variations

attending a performance in Cleveland by the Canadian pianist Glenn Gould"—it is impossible not to be fascinated by the idiosyncratic Gould and his brilliant talk. What impromptu riches we are privileged to share in these freewheeling, provocative soliloquies about the classical repertoire and favorite composers

(Orlando Gibbons), about pianists who influenced him (Rosalyn Turek), about music theory and the aesthetics of studio recording, about "the entire tactile kinetic commitment" involved in playing the piano, about Gould's need for solitude, his love of radio, his many legendary peculiarities, and, for good measure, why he thinks the records of Petula Clark are better than those of The Beatles.

Gould's conversation makes for refreshing, exhilarating, thought-stretching reading: You'll finish this book feeling amused and smarter—more alert to the playful and profound powers of both music and mind. If you already know a thing or two about classical music, you'll find it all deeply absorbing; if you're unfamiliar with the genre, you're likely to find yourself inspired to rectify that situation as soon as possible, with Gould's own

recordings of Bach leading the way. Cott is a wily, unobtrusive interviewer throughout, and his introduction is both an affectionate memoir of Gould and a superb brief statement of the pianist's achievements.

What: Music. *When:* 1984. *Reading Note:* Gould's two recordings of Bach's *Goldberg Variations* (1955 and 1980) make wonderful accompaniments to his conversation. *Also By: He Dreams What Is Going On Inside His Head* (1973). *Dinner with Lenny: The Last Long Interview with Leonard Bernstein* (2013). *Further Reading: The Glenn Gould Reader,* edited by Tim Page. *Wondrous Strange: The Life and Art of Glenn Gould* by Kevin Bazzana. *A Romance on Three Legs: Glenn Gould's Obsessive Quest for the Perfect Piano* by Katie Hafner. *Try:* In his 1991 novel *The Loser,* Austrian novelist Thomas Bernhard offers a fictive rumination on Gould and his genius.

Stravinsky
CHRONICLE OF A FRIENDSHIP, 1948–1971
Robert Craft (1923–2015)

The High Life of High Art

This is a remarkable memoir—a keenly observed, intensely intelligent, affectionately cast diary of the last twenty-three years in the life of Igor Stravinsky (1882–1971), kept by the great composer's factotum, colleague, and friend, the noted conductor and writer Robert Craft. Beginning in 1948, when Craft was twenty-five, he joined the Stravinsky household as a sort of musical acolyte to the maestro, but he soon became a confidant—indeed, a surrogate son—to the composer and his wife, Vera. In the diary entries that compose this book, Craft's erudition in matters of music and culture illuminates with insight, wit, and at times sardonic canniness the rarefied personalities and situations he was fortunate to witness firsthand. The cast of characters that animates his journal is extraordinary, and the conversations caught by Craft make us intimates of T. S. Eliot and Aldous Huxley, Evelyn Waugh and Ingmar Bergman, Balanchine and Giacometti and Schoenberg, Kennedy and Khrushchev, to name a few.

Robert Craft working with Igor Stravinsky on the score for The Flood, *1962*

W. H. Auden, the librettist for Stravinsky's 1951 opera, *The Rake's Progress*, saunters through these pages like the Muses' most enchanted minion, lighting up Craft's chronicle with both eccentricity and eloquence. Stravinsky himself appears as an emblem of creative energy; that the artistic achievements and other activities Craft chronicles belong to the composer's seventh, eighth, and ninth decades is astonishing. Vera Stravinsky is shown to be a woman of savvy and noble parts—not least, Craft's narrative portrays a moving and utterly surprising love story. Exhilarating in its range of reference and discernment, a pleasure to read and return to again and again, *Stravinsky: Chronicle of a Friendship* represents one of the primary cultural documents of the twentieth century.

What: Diaries & Letters. Music. *When:* 1972; revised 1994. *Edition:* Craft's 1994 revision extends the original text by more than a third, adding previously unpublished diary entries and newly composed postscripts to each year. *Also By: Places: A Travel Companion for Music and Art Lovers* (2000). *An Improbable Life: Memoirs* (2002). *Further Reading: Stravinsky in Pictures and Documents* by Vera Stravinsky and Robert Craft. *Try: Diaries 1907–1914: Prodigious Youth* and *Diaries 1915–1923: Behind the Mask* by Sergey Prokofiev.

The Red Badge of Courage
Stephen Crane (1871–1900)

A Novel of War Within and Without

The Red Badge of Courage is an American classic and a landmark in the literature of war. Yet it is a book that is very easy to understand too quickly. Although it is subtitled *An Episode of the American Civil War*, the novel offers little detail specific to the War Between the States other than the blue and the gray of the respective combatants' uniforms. There is an almost complete absence of place names, and no discussion at all of the motivating factors fomenting the bloody struggle or of the military strategies at work in the campaign at hand. Even the protagonist, Henry Fleming, is treated emblematically, being most often referred to as "the youth"; other important presences in the book are also distinguished by generic adjectives: the "tall soldier," the "loud soldier," the "tattered man." For all its naturalism and gritty engagement of the experience of battle, the book constantly reaches beyond its immediate realities to fulfill the author's intention, as expressed in a letter to a friend, of writing "a psychological portrait of fear."

The story begins with Union troops resting on the bank of a river. Word reaches the soldiers that they're soon to see action. The youth, a new recruit inspired to enlist by boyish imaginings of heroism on the battlefield, wonders how he'll perform under fire. Will he fight like a man or flee in terror? When he finally finds himself in harm's way, there's no question of flight—he's trapped in the midst of his fellow soldiers and the confusion of combat: "For some moments he could not flee, no more than a little finger can commit a revolution from a hand." But shortly after that, a surprise counterattack by Confederate forces catches Henry's regiment off guard, and flee he does. For several powerful chapters he wanders through the war-torn landscape, as Crane depicts the impressionistic reality of Henry's fright and alarm. The youth meets many wounded soldiers and quickly comes to envy them, believing that a wound is a "red badge of courage." Pursued by shame, haunted by the death about him, he stumbles into a retreating line of Union soldiers; in the frenzied chaos, he is slammed in the head with the butt of a rifle. Without valor or effort, he now wears a scar.

The next day, reunited with his regiment, Henry again winds up in battle, but this time he fights fiercely. He distinguishes himself in subsequent engagements as well, and the novel ends as he reflects upon his bravery: "He knew that he would no more quail before his guides wherever they should point. He had been to touch the great death, and found that, after all, it was but the great death. He was a man."

Yet to read the novel as the story of a callow youth tempered into manhood by the heat of

Depiction of the Civil War battle of Stones River

battle undermines the ironic power of Crane's tale, in which the hero's destiny is so clearly shaped by contingency, cowardice, and luck (for good or ill). Stripped from any context, the carnage Crane so tellingly describes is shadowed with futility. Even his ultimate assessment of his personal growth toward manhood is a projection that echoes the naïve visions of glory that impelled his enlistment. Although *The Red Badge of Courage* is deservedly praised for the groundbreaking realism of its depiction of a soldier's experience, what's most original about the book is its insistence on the primacy of what is going on in Henry's head: That's where the battle to become a man is fought, Crane's tale suggests, and that is a battle that is never really won.

What: Novel. *When:* 1895. *Also By: Maggie: A Girl of the Streets* (1893). *The Open Boat and Other Tales of Adventure* (1898). *Stephen Crane: Prose and Poetry* (The Library of America, 1984). *Further Reading: Stephen Crane: A Critical Biography* by John Berryman. *Try: In Our Time* by Ernest Hemingway (see page 364). *The Naked and the Dead* by Norman Mailer. *Adaptation:* John Huston directed the 1951 film version starring World War II hero Audie Murphy.

The Andromeda Strain
Michael Crichton (1942–2008)

Suspense Goes Viral

Although physician Michael Crichton previously published several pseudonymous novels, *The Andromeda Strain* was his first bestseller, and the storytelling élan it displayed would inform nearly four decades of inventive, often medically or scientifically minded thrillers. (*The Great Train Robbery*, an atmospheric tale of a gold heist in 1855 London published in 1975, is a thematic exception, but sheer delight nonetheless.) So fecund was his imagination, and so sure his touch, that his phenomenal success between covers was replicated in both television and the movies.

In *Andromeda*, a military satellite's return to Earth in Arizona has deadly consequences for the team sent to recover it—and, quite soon, for the population of a nearby town. Can the cause of the strange fatalities—the victims' blood clots in minutes—be diagnosed and neutralized before devastation spreads? Presented as fact, the book is a fast-paced adventure, with the focus on the mutations of the extraterrestrial microbe and the fast-evolving threat it poses. The substance of the plot reflects the formula Crichton would deploy with equal finesse in later works such as *The Terminal Man* (1972), *Jurassic Park* (1990),

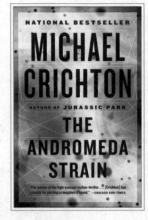

and *Prey* (2002): From a seed unearthed by some emergent field of research, suspense grows until a far-fetched peril seems not only plausible, but as real as tomorrow's headlines. The combination of cutting-edge science and sheer narrative bravado breeds a kind of terror of discovery that puts his best efforts firmly in the lineage of H. G. Wells's *The Time Machine* or Arthur Conan Doyle's *The Lost World* (a title Crichton would borrow for his prequel to *Jurassic Park*). In a word, they're unputdownable.

What: Mystery & Suspense. *When:* 1969. *Also By:* *Disclosure* (1994). *Timeline* (1999). *Try: Outbreak* by Robin Cook. *The Hot Zone* by Richard Preston. *Adaptation:* The 1971 film was directed by Robert Wise.

The Moving Toyshop
Edmund Crispin (1921–1978)

The Adventures of an Eccentric Oxford Don

If you can imagine a plot that has imbibed too much champagne, you'll have some idea of the giddy pleasures of this classic 1946 mystery, in which Oxford don Gervase Fen and poet Richard Cadogan unravel a murderous scheme so convoluted your head will be spinning even if you're drinking tea.

The plot is so tangled—and, frankly, so implausible—we can dispense with a description, and get straight to the heart of this book's pleasure: the eccentricities of Fen, professor of English language and literature and Fellow of St. Christopher's, a fictional college that Edmund Crispin locates in the vicinity of Oxford's very real St. John's (which the author attended with the poet Philip Larkin, to whom *The Moving Toyshop* is dedicated). Fen's immense erudition is a droll instrument with which he deliriously probes the circumstances at hand, strewing arcane references and obscure (but exact) quotations all about him. Even his pub games are high-spirited in

their high-mindedness (take the contest called Detestable Characters in Fiction, in the chapter titled "The Episode of the Indignant Janeite," by which Fen and Cadogan manage to offend a nearby devotee of *Pride and Prejudice*).

Fast, funny, and whimsically winning, *The Moving Toyshop* is a comic fantasia disguised as a donnish detective story. We follow Fen and Cadogan through scenes of madcap invention (the scene in which they pursue a witness through an orchestra and choir rehearsal is priceless) until the mystery of the disappearing toyshop is unraveled and we are rather drunk with a peculiar joy. There are ten more Crispin volumes to supply the hair of the dog.

What: Mystery. Humor. *When:* 1946. *Also By: Holy Disorders* (1945). *Swan Song* (1947). *Love Lies Bleeding* (1948). *Frequent Hearses* (1950). *Further Reading: Bruce Montgomery/Edmund Crispin: A Life in Music and Books* by David Whittle. *Try: The Third Policeman* by Flann O'Brien. *The Victoria Vanishes* by Christopher Fowler. *Footnote:* Edmund Crispin is the pseudonym of composer Bruce Montgomery.

Little, Big
John Crowley (born 1942)

A Magical, Mystical, Slightly Mad Masterpiece

In its purest form, storytelling is a means of enchanting experience. Under a story's spell, the ineffable emanations of life—the secrets we carry within us but that are never quite revealed to the world in the comings and goings of everyday reality—are summoned into an almost palpable existence. Rare is the novel that taps this clear spring of imagination, but John Crowley's 1981 fantasy, *Little, Big*, is one that does.

But calling it fantasy isn't quite right, for the book crosses boundaries at every turn, from fairy tale to bildungsroman, family saga to romance, myth to tale of political intrigue; it exists in its own charmed realm, much like the two literary precedents it often invokes and to which it has been compared, *A Midsummer Night's Dream* and *Alice's Adventures in Wonderland*. The sprawling multigenerational saga begins with a young man named Smoky Barnable "making his way on foot northward from the great City to a town or place called Edgewood," where he'll meet Daily Alice Drinkwater, marry into her strange and wonderful family, take up residence in their architectural kaleidoscope of a house, and attempt to sort out just what sort of tale he's wandered into. Smoky, like most of the characters in *Little, Big*, knows he's in a tale that connects him—and the Drinkwater clan—to a larger destiny, one that involves the faded fortunes of the fairy world that borders Edgewood, to say nothing of the politician Russell Eigenblick, formerly Holy Roman Emperor Frederick Barbarossa and recently elected president of the United States. Infatuations and transformations ensue in both city (an enhanced version of modern New York) and country (the magical world of Edgewood, suffused with the lore of fairyland), as Smoky, Daily Alice, and their progenitors and progeny (for the narrative moves backward and forward in time) attempt to trace their private lives and loves through the larger landscape of myth and metaphor. Even memories take on lives of their own, engaging in the eternal round of romance and metamorphosis that Crowley beautifully evokes.

All this may sound confusing, but a willing suspension of disbelief and the author's winsome gifts for words and wonder will soon have you spellbound. Playful and capacious, *Little, Big* is a fey and fateful fable of what it means for an individual to find a place in the larger world.

What: Novel. *When:* 1981. *Also By:* The Deep (1975), *Beasts* (1976), and *Engine Summer* (1979) are also published together as *Otherwise*. The *Ægypt* tetralogy comprises *Ægypt* (1987), *Love & Sleep* (1994), *Dæmonomania* (2000), and *Endless Things* (2007). Also: *The Translator* (2002); *Lord Byron's Novel: The Evening Land* (2005); and *Four Freedoms* (2009). *Try:* *The King of Elfland's Daughter* by Lord Dunsany. *Lud-in-the-Mist* by Hope Mirrlees. *The Land of Laughs* by Jonathan Carroll.

> **"This book is indescribable: a splendid madness, or a delightful sanity, or both. Persons who enter this book are advised that they will leave it a different size than when they came in."**—*Ursula K. Le Guin on* Little, Big

Complete Poems, 1904–1962
E. E. Cummings (1894–1962)

Liberating Verse

There is something inexplicably joyful about the poetry of E. E. Cummings—not happy, exactly, but vivid and exuberant. Simultaneously intimate and expansive, his poems achieve what the *Norton Anthology of Modern Poetry* labeled "a magnificent, subversive smallness." The smallness, of course, is the most striking feature of their appearance and effect: Beginning with his name on the title page, famously set without capital letters as "e. e. cummings," his verse still speaks with a lowercase insistence both tender and willful.

His orthographic idiosyncrasy is more than just a calling card, however. In a more conceptual sense, Cummings uses the page as a kind of mental landscape or field of play. His unorthodox experiments in syntax, punctuation, and enjambment make his work typographically distinct by giving it an almost topographical identity: Traversing his poetry requires a different kind of exercise than reading the work of other poets. Sometimes it looks like letters and lines are the remains of an explosion of sorts, or they present themselves as elements of a graphic doodle composed at random:

E. E. Cummings, ca. 1933

```
the
   sky
        was
can  dy lu
minous
       edible
spry . . .
```

At a time in literary history when the lyric was losing its shape, Cummings restored its physicality by, paradoxically, deconstructing traditional structures and stanzas, as if to demonstrate that their function was not just to measure sound, but also to help inspiration find a place in the world—a presence set in type, if not stone. The poet's disruption of expectations, his playful instigating of grammatical disorder, of verbal junction and disjunction, seem to liberate an energy in words that conventional usage constrains:

> my father moved through dooms of love
> through sames of am through haves of give,
> singing each morning out of each night
> my father moved through depths of height

Beneath their beguiling (and at times befuddling) façades, Cummings's poems do serious work, encouraging the language into new powers of expression. His many sonnets, eccentric though they be, are among the best of the twentieth century, combining rhymes and off-rhymes with a casual confidence; his love poems are equally distinguished, putting linguistic virtuosity at the service of erotic longing (and, as he might say, nearing) with an ingenuity reminiscent of seventeenth-century metaphysical master John Donne (see page 228). He alternates a wise guy's satiric revolt against "the Cambridge ladies who live in furnished souls" with an extraordinary gift for the evocation of wonder:

> the hours rise up putting off stars and it is
> dawn
> into the street of the sky light walks scattering poems

His poetry proves, again and again, that no familiarity—not dawn nor death nor laughter nor love—is quite as straightforward as it seems.

What: Poetry. *When:* 1904–62. *Edition:* There are many volumes that gather representative selections from the poet's work; a comprehensive edition of the *Complete Poems*, edited by George James Firmage, was published in 2016. *Also By: The Enormous Room* (1922), an autobiographical novel, is a classic of World War I literature. *Further Reading: e. e. cummings: a life* by Susan Cheever. *Try:* The poems of Marianne Moore.

Rebellion in the Backlands
Euclides da Cunha (1866–1909)

The National Epic of Brazil

A richly detailed blend of historical narrative and social treatise that documents a bloody civil war, *Rebellion in the Backlands* is something like the secular scripture of Brazil. Its literary value has been vouchsafed by the likes of Peruvian Nobel Laureate Mario Vargas Llosa, who found in it inspiration for a six-hundred-page novel, and American poet Robert Lowell, who considered Euclides da Cunha's book better than *War and Peace*.

Born in 1866, Cunha began his career as a military engineer, but he soon left the army and became a journalist. Embedded with the Brazilian army, he traveled to Bahia, in the northeast of the country, where he encountered the rebellious followers of Antônio Conselheiro, a charismatic figure who led a breakaway "empire" that considered itself independent of republican Brazil. The conflict between the central government and the rebels eventually escalated into the War of Canudos, Brazil's worst civil conflict, which raged between the army and Conselheiro's followers in 1896 and 1897, leaving twenty-five thousand people dead. *Rebellion in the Backlands* details this struggle in vivid terms, and although Cunha is clearly a supporter of the government troops, he's frequently overwhelmed by the bravery and ingenuity of the insurgents. Racial and cultural theories of the time held that the Bahian rebels must be inferior (*caveat lector*: *Rebellion in the Backlands* does contain some creepy sections about evolutionary theory and racial identity), and Cunha himself accuses them early on of "collective insanity." Yet ultimately the author finds himself in grudging admiration of the rebels, noting that "in spite of three centuries of underdevelopment, the sertanejos did not rival our troops in acts of barbarism."

On the flag of the Federative Republic of Brazil, draped over a blue disc of sky, is the motto *Ordem e Progresso*: order and progress. Yet in Cunha's hands we see how a government that believes it has these forces on its side can commit acts of true savagery. *Rebellion in the Backlands* doesn't just document one of the signal events of the history of our hemisphere. It calls into question the entire positivist orientation of the nineteenth century, the belief in an inevitable march of progress, which, as humanity would learn to its horror, was setting the stage for a darker era to come. The terrors of religious fundamentalism and crusading government retribution are as relevant in our day as they were in Cunha's, and in *Rebellion in the Backlands* we see the tragic consequences of these furious energies.

What: History. Literature. *When:* 1902. *Editions:* The standard English version is the one by Samuel Putnam. A new translation, by Elizabeth Lowe, was published as *Backlands* in 2010, and is quoted here. *Also By: The Amazon: Land Without History* (1906). *Further Reading: The War of the End of the World* by Mario Vargas Llosa. *Try: The Devil to Pay in the Backlands* by João Guimarães Rosa. *The Book of Lamentations* by Rosario Castellanos.

The 40th Infantry Battalion in Canudos, 1897

■ **For Michael Cunningham's *The Hours*, see page 870.**

. . . .

The Decline and Fall of Practically Everybody
Will Cuppy (1884–1949)

Hilarious History Lessons
. . . .

I n the annals of American humor, Will Cuppy deserves a chapter all his own, but, with characteristic caginess, he instead lurks among the annotations, now and then emerging to cast a jaundiced squint at the passing parades of history and nature. His parting shot—published posthumously in 1950 as a result of the editorial spadework of his friend Fred Feldkamp (and earning a place on the bestseller lists in no small part because of enthusiastic on-air readings by CBS broadcaster Edward R. Murrow)—was fittingly titled *The Decline and Fall of Practically Everybody*.

From the Egypt of the pharaohs to the Athens of Pericles, from Hannibal and his elephants to Attila and his Huns, from merrie olde England to the shores of America, Cuppy enters the lists of history and returns unimpressed. His

tour of the past is conducted without reverence, awe, or wonder, and his deadpan narrative cuts women (Lady Godiva, Lucrezia Borgia, and Madame du Barry) and men (Henry VIII, Philip II of Spain—"Philip the Sap" to our distinguished author—Columbus, Montezuma, and Miles Standish) down to size with equal comic zeal. Here he is on France's Louis XIV:

Some scholars explain Louis's dullness by his royal position, kings being more or less out of touch, but this would hardly account for the symptoms. Others say he was deliberately kept in a state of ignorance by his teachers when he was a boy. No professors, however, could have turned out so perfect a job unless the pupil showed a natural aptitude of no mean order.

The text is complemented by Cuppy's sardonic footnotes, which are not to be missed, and splendidly witty illustrations by William Steig.

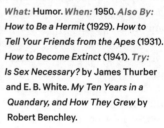

What: Humor. *When:* 1950. *Also By: How to Be a Hermit* (1929). *How to Tell Your Friends from the Apes* (1931). *How to Become Extinct* (1941). *Try: Is Sex Necessary?* by James Thurber and E. B. White. *My Ten Years in a Quandary, and How They Grew* by Robert Benchley.

D, E, F, G

Memoirs of Lorenzo Da Ponte
Lorenzo Da Ponte (1749–1838)

A Man of Culture on the Make

What a range of characters animates this remarkable book: the brilliant librettist of Mozart's greatest operas (*Le nozze di Figaro, Don Giovanni, Così fan tutte*), a priest and a professional gambler, a bordello proprietor and a political agitator, a court poet and a grocer, the first professor of Italian literature at Columbia University. That all those occupations are the resumé of one man—Lorenzo Da Ponte—gives some indication of the singularity of the author and his autobiography. From Venice to London to New York, in the company of the likes of Mozart, Casanova, and Clement Moore (author of "The Night Before Christmas"), Da Ponte leads us on a merry, artful, larger-than-life chase of reminiscence and entertainment. As pianist and music historian Charles Rosen rightly puts it, "His *Memoirs* are not an intimate exploration of his own identity and character but rather a picaresque adventure story."

Da Ponte's attention to operational details—guiding an opera past censors to performance, assembling an Italian library in early-nineteenth-century New York—offers a unique perspective on the pragmatic inspiration so often needed to fuel the flight of creative genius. And if the author's facts are sometimes suspect, and he seems more interested in settling scores than in describing how they came to be written, his brio never flags.

What: Memoir. *When:* Four volumes: 1823–27 in Italian; Elisabeth Abbott's English translation appeared in 1929. *Edition:* The New York Review Books edition features Charles Rosen's preface. *Further Reading: The Librettist of Venice: The Remarkable Life of Lorenzo Da Ponte* by Rodney Bolt. *Try: History of My Life* by Giacomo Casanova (see page 135).

Matilda
Roald Dahl (1916–1990)

Little Girl, Big Powers

Roald Dahl's roster of youth-delighting tales is as rich as that of any twentieth-century children's author. From *The Gremlins* (1943) to *The Minpins* (1991), Dahl created marvelous confections for young readers for nearly five decades. Standing out among his storytelling treats is *Matilda*, whose superheroine is heroic—and triumphant—first and foremost because she loves to read. "She travelled all over the world while sitting in her little room in an English village," Dahl tells us early on, once Matilda has escaped from the dreary confines of her unaffectionate family through the good graces of the local librarian.

Her mom and dad are, admittedly, a problem. "Matilda longed for her parents to be good and loving and understanding and honourable and intelligent," Dahl explains. "The fact that they were none of these things was something she had to put up with." And put up with it she does, with ingenuity and a sense of purposeful mischief designed to win the hearts of the author's intended audience. As she falls under the beneficial sway of her teacher, Miss Honey, Matilda also discovers unexpected telekinetic powers by which she upends the nasty regime of her school's tyrannical headmistress, Miss Trunchbull.

When a small girl vanquishes oppressive adults, what young reader won't experience a vicarious thrill? Indeed, a good portion of Dahl's popularity can be traced to the fact that he never underestimates young people, either as readers or as protagonists. A delicious conspiratorial tone—as if writer and reader know something the grown-ups don't—runs like a current through his narratives; he has a knack for making kids feel they are in on a great joke being told at the expense of their elders, especially the mean ones. It's an archness that, in his books for children, stops just short of wickedness, a line he gleefully crosses in his splendid stories for adults, such as those in *Tales of the Unexpected* (1979).

What Dahl brought to writing for kids was an irreverence that proved to be the raison d'être of his art—a verve that, because it strikes an incorrigible chord with even the best behaved of his readers, conjures a liberating energy all too seldom captured between covers.

What: Children's. *When:* 1988. *Also By: James and the Giant Peach* (1961). *Charlie and the Chocolate Factory* (1964). *Fantastic Mr. Fox* (1970). *The Twits* (1980). *The BFG* (1982). *Try: Mistress Masham's Repose* by T. H. White. *The Great Good Thing* by Roderick Townley (see page 802). *Adaptations:* The novel inspired a 1996 film directed by Danny DeVito, as well as two musical versions for the theater, the second of which, *Matilda the Musical* (2010), commissioned by the Royal Shakespeare Company and written by Dennis Kelly and Tim Minchin, has won audience acclaim and many awards in both Britain and America. There is also a splendid audiobook read by Kate Winslet.

In Xanadu
A QUEST
William Dalrymple (born 1965)

Following the Trail of Marco Polo to the Pleasure-Dome of Kubla Khan

How many readers, fascinated by the allure of Marco Polo's travels on the Silk Road, have daydreamed of following in the fabled Venetian's footsteps? About the very same number, you can safely bet, that has lacked the recklessness, resourcefulness, and antic energy such an adventure would require. Each one will welcome the acquaintance of William Dalrymple, who possesses all these qualities, as well as an imagination attuned to the living—if sometimes distant and dusty—legacies of history and literature that are the best companions for such a journey.

Dalrymple was a twenty-two-year-old Cambridge student when he made the trip,

backpacking across Asia along Polo's seven-hundred-year-old, twelve-thousand-mile route. Adventures large and small met him and his various companions at every stage of the trip, and the author's style is supple enough to engagingly capture both current realities and the spectral presences of the past. His intrepid erudition informs every page with lore and learning, and Dalrymple is always alert to wonder:

The Euphrates! Is there another river which carries with it so many associations? . . . The same river cleaned the men who built the Ziggurat of Ur, watered down the wine in the goblets at Nebuchadnezzar's feast, and irrigated the Hanging Gardens of Babylon.

From his point of departure, the Church of the Holy Sepulchre in Jerusalem, to his final destination, the ruins—immortalized in Coleridge's haunting poetic vision—of Kubla Khan's pleasure-dome in Xanadu (now Shangdu in Mongolia), Dalrymple is an eloquent, funny, entertaining guide. This is as fine a literary excursion as you could ever hope to, well, book.

What: Travel. History. *When:* 1990. *Also By: City of Djinns: A Year of Delhi* (1993). *From the Holy Mountain: A Journey Among the Christians of the Middle East* (1997). *The Last Mughal: The Fall of a Dynasty: Delhi, 1857* (2006). *Further Reading: The Travels of Marco Polo* (see page 635). *Try: Mani* by Patrick Leigh Fermor. *Shadow of the Silk Road* by Colin Thubron.

··

THE DIVINE COMEDY
INFERNO • PURGATORIO • PARADISO
Dante Alighieri (1265–1321)

An Epic of This World and the Next

From the dark wood of its beginning, down through the nine circles of hell, across the seven terraces of purgatory, and into the ten heavens of paradise, Dante's medieval tour de force gives us, in T. S. Eliot's estimation, the greatest altitude and the greatest depth of human passion any writer has ever delivered. Our mythic picture of the afterlife, which casts such long shadows on our here and now, owes much to the poet's magnificent imagining of sin and suffering, penance and hope, love and light. His poem is a repository of legend, romance, politics, learning, and belief no less exquisite for its all-encompassing scope. Not least, Dante's language exhibits a vivacity of form and expression that makes his masterpiece a school of eloquence. *The Divine Comedy* may be the most perfectly, purposefully proportioned piece of writing one will ever come across: one hundred cantos of one hundred lines each, apportioned into three-line stanzas (one extra line per canto for good luck) of precisely joined, interlocking rhymes. The language has a forward motion that imbues the formal choreography with a narrative energy that never lets up.

One is tempted to think the poem's shapeliness corresponds to the coherence of the religious vision it ultimately inscribes. But that would underestimate the author's art, for although *The Divine Comedy* is indeed the epic of Christian culture, expressing the metaphysics and theology that nourished and defined the medieval mind, it is also very much rooted in this world, and especially in the savage politics of fourteenth-century Florence, which had forced Dante into exile during the years of the *Comedy*'s composition. *Inferno* in particular, in addition to being an exciting tale filled with enough ingeniously envisioned horrors to furnish perils for a thousand video games, is by turns a gossip column gleefully unmasking the wickedness of the author's contemporaries, a social satire assembling a scabrous catalog of scandals and peccadilloes, a political polemic advancing one side of the fabled conflict between the rival Florentine factions of Guelphs and Ghibellines, and a sort of virtuoso tweet storm dedicated to the settling of dozens of personal scores. (Where better to immortalize your enemies, after all, than in their own private nooks in hell?)

All of which forces us to recognize that, whatever celestial realms it eventually reaches, *The Divine Comedy* is a poem that starts out with its hands in the dirt, so to speak, and *becomes* transcendental in its course, dropping the trappings of spite, envy, factionalism, and temporal concerns as it follows the poet-protagonist along his spiritual journey, from the punishments of the netherworld, through the expiations of purgatory, into the ethereal pleasures of paradise. A vision forged from fractious parts, it is a *created* unity, even though critics often assume its flawless structure reflects a larger cultural symmetry. As history makes plain, such a shared sense of society didn't really exist in medieval Italy; Dante imagined it, and fashioned from the demotic tongue, as opposed to the prevailing Latin, a new literary

The Comedy Illuminating Florence *by Domenico di Michelino, 1465*

language that marked the invention of modern Italian.

Best of all, *The Divine Comedy* is an adventure story that begins with a human quandary: A middle-aged man, in search of renewal, gets lost in a dark wood. That moment may be the most famous midlife crisis of all time; here's how Allen Mandelbaum renders the opening in English:

When I had journeyed half of our life's way,
I found myself within a shadowed forest,
for I had lost the path that does not stray.

The shade of Virgil appears to guide the narrator through the underworld and a panoply of sinners, monsters, and torments, the last described with an almost gleeful relish: The lustful are eternally blown back and forth by harsh winds, for instance, while heretics are entombed in flames and the profligate are chased and torn to pieces by dogs, over and over again, endlessly. The poet's infernal tour is also a catalog of unforgettable characters, such as the lovers Paolo and Francesca, lured into illicit passion by the seductions of a book, or the Homeric hero Odysseus, condemned by his cunning and curiosity to wander the world without a final destination.

Although the stories in hell are better than those in purgatory and heaven, sin being a sexier subject than penance or blessedness, the poetry never palls. Throughout, Dante infuses his trilogy with a current of feeling that humanizes the austere theological arc of his pilgrim's progress, encompassing the spectrum of earthly relations from envy and jealousy to love both sensual and chaste. The wealth of experience and emotion conveyed in his conception of life and afterlife is filled with enough learning and lessons to enlighten a thousand lifetimes; he makes out of eschatological speculations an epic as thrilling as those of Homer, as filled with human sensibility as Virgil's—one in which all the deadly sins, and all the longed-for virtues, are given speaking roles. In sum: Don't miss the sinful wonders of *Inferno*, then make your own judgment on atonement and salvation.

What: Poetry. Religion & Spirituality. *When:* Written 1308–21; first published in Italy in 1472. *Editions:* There are scores of complete English translations, including versions in verse by Henry Wadsworth Longfellow, Dorothy L. Sayers, John Ciardi, and Clive James; most recommendable, for its clarity and eloquence, is Allen Mandelbaum's (1982–86), although reading around in all of them can be instructive, enlightening, and fun. The prose translations of both John D. Sinclair (1948) and Charles S. Singleton (1970–75) are augmented by extensive notes and commentary, providing invaluable assistance to the reader. *Also By: La vita nuova (The*

New Life; ca. 1293). Il convivio (The Banquet; ca. 1304). Further Reading: Dante by R. W. B. Lewis. Reading Dante: From Here to Eternity by Prue Shaw. Dante's Inferno: Translations by Twenty Contemporary Poets edited by Daniel Halpern. Try: The Aeneid by Virgil (see page 823). Paradise Lost by John Milton (see page 553). Footnote: The author titled his work La commedia when it was published shortly before his death in 1321; it was Boccaccio (see page 85) who gave it the attribute "divine."

The Dew Breaker
Edwidge Danticat (born 1969)

The Secret History of Cruelty and Sorrow

The Dew Breaker is a story sequence that reveals the hidden past of a quiet Brooklynite—father, landlord, local businessman—and in so doing opens ethical and emotional wounds inflicted by the political brutality that savaged his native Haiti in the 1960s. Edwidge Danticat's pages are peopled by torturers, victims, accomplices, and innocent inheritors of the legacy of suffering engendered by the Duvalier regime, and they bear scars, and hopes, and consciences that will not heal. Terror is made all the more wrenching by the intimacy in which its repercussions are discovered: a father confessing his past to his daughter on a park bench; a married couple reuniting in a basement apartment shared with other tenants after seven years of separation; a family in a church pew attending Midnight Mass on Christmas Eve. The magic is that, despite their contribution to the larger narrative arc of the book, each of the nine stories can stand on its own as an emblem of the human costs of the Haitian diaspora.

Deceptively simple in outline and expression, these fleet tales are nonetheless fraught with profound experience; beneath the surface exposition of Danticat's prose runs an anguished awareness of how thin the constructs of home and civilization are, how susceptible to violence our social orders and personal identities can be. The last, longest, and title tale ("dew breaker," one who violates the tranquility of dawn, is a translation of the Creole slang for "torturer"), reaches back to the work's opening to connect the dots of people, incidents, and aftermaths that have been placed on the pages in between. A torturer is rescued from murderous cruelty—his own—by a woman's blind humanity, a tenderness intuited in the confusion of her own despair; their encounter sets in motion decades of fear, resignation, and timid renewal amidst memories that shape a hollow grief, "a penance procession that has yet to end."

The Dew Breaker is a book about Haiti, oppression, and the coercion of history; about the circumstances and coincidences that make a family; about the transgressions and transformations that make conundrums of the evil and the good among us; about the unassuageable severity of immigrant lives. It's about loss and longing and love, all three as present and unpredictable as weather: the atmosphere of our solace and sorrow, which the chambers of our days—bedrooms, workplaces, churches—can never quite contain, although that sorrow and that solace have nowhere else to go.

What: Short Stories. When: 2004. Also By: Breath, Eyes, Memory (1994). Krik? Krak! (1995). The Farming of Bones (1998). Brother, I'm Dying (2007). Claire of the Sea Light (2013). Try: Love, Anger, Madness by Marie Vieux-Chauvet. A Distant Shore by Caryl Phillips. A Mercy by Toni Morrison.

"What did they do to you?" she asked.

This was the most forgiving question he'd ever been asked. It suddenly opened a door, produced a small path which he could follow.

—from The Dew Breaker

The Voyage of the *Beagle*
Charles Darwin (1809–1882)

Field Notes for a Scientific Revolution

A travel journal as much as a scientific document, Charles Darwin's first book records
the observations of a British gentleman scholar
on a voyage to the Southern Hemisphere, an
expedition whose ultimate outcome would be
a revolution in our understanding of the natural world (and a disruption of our certainties
about the spiritual one as well).

When the HMS *Beagle* was preparing to
set sail from Plymouth Sound in 1831, Captain
Robert FitzRoy was persuaded that he would
need someone who shared his interests to
accompany him—and Darwin, then twenty-
two years old and a novice scientist, was proposed. The companionship was fortuitous,
for the journey, originally planned for two
years, lasted five. Throughout that time, while
the *Beagle* surveyed the coasts, Darwin frequently journeyed inland, and in his travels
in Australia, New Zealand, and the islands of
the Pacific and Indian Oceans he encountered
everything from political revolution to earthquakes. In Tierra del Fuego, at the extreme
point of South America, he noted the "odd mixture of surprise and imitation" that the "savages" exhibited when they met the British. He
traveled widely in Brazil, from Rio de Janeiro
north to Bahia, and was horrified by the realities of slavery: "It makes one's blood boil, yet
heart tremble, to think that we Englishmen and
our American descendants, with their boastful
cry of liberty, have been and are so guilty."

Darwin, born in Shropshire and a desultory student at Cambridge (he preferred riding
and shooting to spending time in the library),
did not seem on course to become one of the
most influential figures in history when he
embarked on his sea voyage in 1831. But the
geological formations he saw on his journey,
the wildlife he documented, and the fossils he
collected—especially in the primeval natural
wonderland of the Galápagos Archipelago—and
brought back to England eventually led him to
propound his world-shaking theory of natural selection by writing *On the Origin of Species*
(1859). That book, of course, is Darwin's seminal
work, and it is a model of lucid and painstaking
exposition, unfolding seismic ideas with a calm,
courteous conviction. Most of Darwin's writings, and particularly his modest *Autobiography*
(1887), are characterized by an inviting conge-
niality, born of the social milieu that shaped
him (which, just as much as its protagonist's
scientific achievements, is brilliantly captured
in Janet Browne's highly recommended biography). Yet none of Darwin's other books possess
the sense of adventure and emergent discovery inherent in *The Voyage of the* Beagle; these
qualities give its pages a lasting freshness and
fascination.

What: Nature. Science. Travel. *When:* 1839 (originally
published as *Journal and Remarks*). *Also By: The*
Descent of Man (1871). *The Expression of Emotions*
in Man and Animals (1872). *Further Reading: Darwin*
and the Beagle by Alan Moorehead. *Charles Darwin: A*
Biography (two volumes: *Voyaging* and *The Power of*
Place) by Janet Browne. *Try: The Journals of Captain*
Cook by Captain James Cook. *Joseph Banks: A Life*
by Patrick O'Brian. *The Beak of the Finch* by Jonathan
Weiner. *Adaptation:* A wonderful seven-part series,
The Voyage of Charles Darwin, aired on the BBC in 1978.

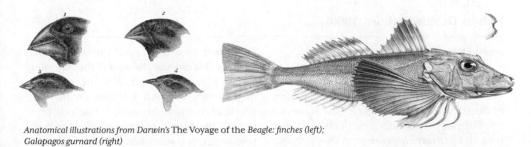

Anatomical illustrations from Darwin's The Voyage of the Beagle: *finches (left);
Galapagos gurnard (right)*

The Geography of the Imagination

FORTY ESSAYS

Guy Davenport (1927–2005)

A One-Man Renaissance

Long before the advent of the internet, Guy Davenport seemed to find hyperlinks in everything he read, allowing him to make connections between disparate ideas and far-flung subjects. His gifts for concentration and discovery were formed early, as we learn in "Findings," one of the last of the forty essays collected in *The Geography of the Imagination*; it's a charming evocation of childhood outings with his father to look for Native American arrowheads in Georgia and South Carolina in the upper Savannah valley. On these excursions, Davenport writes, "I learned that there are people who see nothing, who would not have noticed the splendidest of tomahawks if they had stepped on it, who could not tell a worked stone from a shard of flint or quartz, people who did not feel the excitement of the whoop we all let out when we found an arrowhead." The remarkable thing about this book is that, despite the often knotty material Davenport's intelligence surveys, it is filled with the alertness and excitement of a boy's eyes alighting on treasure. The riches include the work of philosophers Spinoza and Wittgenstein; of modernist poets Ezra Pound, Charles Olson, and Louis Zukofsky; of American originals such as Walt Whitman, Charles Ives, and Eudora Welty; of prehistoric cave artists, nineteenth-century natural historians, and twentieth-century surrealists; of Herman Melville and J. R. R. Tolkien.

Even when you are unfamiliar with the subject of Davenport's focus, you're likely to be enthralled by what he sees; his abiding theme is the making and meaning of culture, and he follows it through thickets and forests with unerring step, clearing unseen paths for his readers. "The imagination," he writes, "is like the drunk man who lost his watch, and must get drunk again to find it. It is as intimate as speech and custom, and to trace its ways we need to reeducate our eyes." Reeducating our eyes, metaphorically speaking, is Davenport's program precisely, as he wends his graceful way through the ideas of writers, thinkers, and artists in essays that are discursive, witty, learned, and bold, filled with enough ideas per page to keep one thinking for a week. *The Geography of the Imagination* is the kind of book that makes us better readers: more curious, more perceptive, and more likely to discover connections ourselves.

What: Essays. *When:* 1981. *Also By: Tatlin! Six Stories* (1974). *Every Force Evolves a Form: Twenty Essays* (1987). *7 Greeks* (translations; 1995). *The Hunter Gracchus and Other Papers on Literature and Art* (1996). *Try: The Pound Era* by Hugh Kenner (see page 441). *A Temple of Texts* by William H. Gass. *River of Shadows* by Rebecca Solnit (see page 735).

Tracks

Robyn Davidson (born 1950)

An Australian Odyssey, by Camel

"The lunatic idea," writes Robyn Davidson of the genesis of the trip that is the subject of *Tracks*, "was, basically, to get myself the requisite number of wild camels from the bush and train them to carry my gear, then walk into and about the central desert area." Unlike most lunatic ideas, this one saw the light of the sun—quite a lot of it, in fact. In April 1977, after two years of preparation (which included an intensive course in getting-to-know-your-humped-back-beasts), the twenty-seven-year-old Davidson—who by her own admission had "never changed a light-bulb, sewn a dress, mended a sock, changed a tyre, or used a screwdriver"—set out to cross the rugged outback of her native Australia accompanied by four camels and a dog (and, as things developed, the occasional photographer).

Tracks tells the story of her six-month, 1,700-mile journey through a timeless landscape inhabited by strange and sometimes threatening life forms. Given to passionate ruminations on the false reality a camera can capture, the Aboriginal way of life, and the pleasures and powers of solitude, Davidson is also stubborn, resourceful, and tough. She survives the onslaughts of both nature and civilization to tell her tale with a robust, wry humor that is vivid and engaging. A genuinely unforgettable trek.

What: Travel. Adventure. *When:* 1980. *Award:* Thomas Cook Travel Book Award, 1980. *Also By: Travelling Light* (1989). *Desert Places* (1996). *Further Reading:* Rick Smolan's *From Alice to Ocean* presents his photographs of Davidson's trip together with excerpts from *Tracks.* *Try: A Lady's Life in the Rocky Mountains* by Isabella L. Bird. *Outback* by Thomas Keneally. *Daisy Bates in the Desert* by Julia Blackburn. *Adaptation:* John Curran's 2013 feature film stars Mia Wasikowska.

THE DEPTFORD TRILOGY
FIFTH BUSINESS • THE MANTICORE • WORLD OF WONDERS
Robertson Davies (1913–1995)

Storytelling Magic from a Canadian Conjurer

A boy packs a rock into a snowball and throws it at a friend, who ducks out of the way; the missile hits a pregnant woman, provoking premature labor. The Deptford Trilogy follows the unforeseen and ever-widening effects of that misguided prank across decades and continents, through the lives of many characters and into realms of religion, psychology, and magic. From page one, the reader is lured into a high-spirited and often very funny chase—after passing facts, ultimate truths, and continuous entertainment—by a virtuoso storyteller.

The first novel, *Fifth Business* (1970), focuses on Dunstan Ramsay, the boy who ducked, tracing his life as a soldier, teacher, and scholar of saints in the enduring shadows of Percy "Boy" Staunton, young snowball thrower and eventual business titan, and Mary Dempster, the unfortunate—but perhaps holy—target of the errant projectile. The tale begins with the wintry incident and ends with Boy Staunton's death decades later in mysterious circumstances. It is a fast-paced narrative in which the author's gifts for observation and invention summon into being a reality that is both familiar and deliciously weird, peopled—like the tales of Dickens—with characters whose attributes are exaggerated to a degree that refines, rather than destroys, our recognition of their essential humanity.

Davies's flamboyant naturalism continues in the second part of the trilogy, *The Manticore* (1972), in which the journey of discovery belongs to David Staunton, Boy's son and Dunstan's student. The final installment, *World of Wonders* (1975), is the province of Mary Dempster's prematurely born child, Paul, who has been transformed by his life as circus performer, actor, and illusionist into the larger-than-life magician Magnus Eisengrim. The three novels—each of which, remarkably, stands on its own and can be read independently of the others—echo and amplify one another. Their shared concerns encompass the haunting power of the ghosts of the past, the spiritual emanations of mundane experience, the ancient and collective truths that animate our psychological adventures (a good part of *The Manticore* details David Staunton's Jungian analysis in Switzerland), and the liberating gift of wonder. Together, these themes provide an elaborate symbolic underpinning to works that never cease to bestow page-turning pleasure.

What: Novels. *When:* First omnibus edition, 1985. *Also By:* Fiction: The Salterton Trilogy (1951–58); The Cornish Trilogy (1982–88); *The Cunning Man* (1994). Nonfiction: *One Half of Robertson Davies* (1977). *Try: The Magus* by John Fowles. *The Sea, the Sea* by Iris Murdoch (see page 577).

The Selfish Gene
Richard Dawkins (born 1941)

A Meme Is Born

Richard Dawkins was only thirty-three in 1976 when he published *The Selfish Gene*, a landmark of popular science that summarized a genetic view of evolution then gaining currency among biologists. It was such a success that its title has entered the lexicon. But the title, as Dawkins has admitted, is a bit of a misnomer. He doesn't believe in a *selfishness* gene that helps certain organisms survive and propagate. Instead, he argues that Darwin's survival of the fittest takes place not at the level of the species or even the single organism, but at the much deeper level of genetic material. The gene is the unit that seeks to replicate itself, at whatever cost; organisms are merely "survival machines" that house genes and offer them the possibility of reproduction. So, in contrast to the organism-based view that the "strongest" animals or plants pass on their genetic material to the next generation, Dawkins's gene-based view proposes that evolutionarily advantageous traits are the effect, not the cause, of natural selection.

The Selfish Gene has another claim to fame: It's where Dawkins coined the word "meme," which he defined as an idea with "high survival value, or infective power" (and which has since been popularized to describe viral videos or goofy internet jokes, too). Although Dawkins is a proud Darwinian—indeed an obstreperous one, as his popular later books on atheism make clear—he bridles at the idea that genetics alone can explain the whole of human life. Other kinds of "replicators," not just genes, have evolutionary force, and to fully understand evolution, he writes, we need to understand not just biology but culture, not just genes but memes. And that makes *The Selfish Gene* an essential book not just for scientists, but for anyone evolving through our tumultuous intellectual age.

What: Science. *When:* 1976. *Also By: The Blind Watchmaker* (1986). *River Out of Eden* (1995). *The God Delusion* (2006). *An Appetite for Wonder: The Making of a Scientist* (2013). *Further Reading: Richard Dawkins: How a Scientist Changed the Way We Think,* edited by Alan Grafen and Mark Ridley. *Try: Darwin's Dangerous Idea* by Daniel C. Dennett. *Darwin's Ghost: "The Origin of Species" Updated* by Steve Jones.

■ For Dorothy Day's *The Long Loneliness*, see page 31.

How Proust Can Change Your Life
Alain de Botton (born 1969)

Invaluable Advice from a Reclusive Hypochondriac

Novels belong in Fiction, advice belongs in Self-Help, and never the twain shall meet. Or at least they didn't until Alain de Botton dared to explore the various ways in which

French novelist Marcel Proust (1871–1922) could teach readers to live richer, fuller, happier lives.

You might at first think that such an approach to the estimable Monsieur Proust has to be tongue in cheek, if not an outright joke. After all, despite his literary genius, the author of *In Search of Lost Time* (see page 644) was a reclusive hypochondriac who, according to de Botton, spent years of his own rather dreary life in a cork-lined room, "lying in a narrow bed under a pile of thinly woven woolen blankets writing an unusually long novel without an adequate bedside lamp." Furthermore, that "unusually long novel" was a *novel* after all, and although readers certainly do learn from fiction, the lessons don't normally consist of specific, concrete guidance about how best to conduct oneself. De Botton, however, while charmingly playful, is indeed serious about looking to the pages of Proust's great book, and even to Proust's eccentric life, for such guidance.

In Search of Lost Time, as de Botton reads it, is "a practical, universally applicable story about how to stop wasting time and start to appreciate life"—in other words, a how-to book.

As in "How to Take Your Time," "How to Suffer Successfully," "How to Express Your Emotions," "How to Be a Good Friend," "How to Be Happy in Love," and even "How to Put Books Down." These are all chapter titles in this smart and entertaining 1997 study, and they point to the kinds of life-changing lessons that de Botton derives—by eloquent and cunning literary ingenuity— from Proust's life and writing. His book is an unexpected, genre-bending delight.

What: Advice. Literary Criticism. *When:* 1997. *Also By: On Love* (1993). *The Consolations of Philosophy* (2000). *The Architecture of Happiness* (2006). *Further Reading: In Search of Lost Time* (see page 644). *Try: The Year of Reading Proust* by Phyllis Rose. *How to Live: Or A Life of Montaigne in One Question and Twenty Attempts at an Answer* by Sarah Bakewell.

The Complete War Memoirs of Charles de Gaulle
Charles de Gaulle (1890–1970)

One Man's War, One Nation's Destiny

Even before their actions are interred in the tomb of time, great leaders can become emblems of stolid, ineluctable purpose. In the annals of World War II, perhaps no figure has appeared more so than Charles de Gaulle, whose every image seemed to exude—in posture, pose, and attitude—an inflexible pride. The richness of the mind and the emotions of the

Winston Churchill and General Charles de Gaulle take part in the Armistice Day parade in Paris, November 11, 1944

soul behind that rigid posture, and the nobility and intransigence of the will that stiffened it, are revealed in this enormous book, which collects all three volumes of the author's wartime memoirs: *The Call to Honor 1940–1942*, *Unity 1942–1944*, and *Salvation 1944–1946*.

From its opening pages, with its sonorous invocation of the exalted idea of France's special destiny that was de Gaulle's treasured inheritance, this eloquent testament records the confluence of national and personal fortunes that determined his course through the years of Nazi occupation, as he fled to London in 1940 to organize the Free French forces and establish a government-in-exile. Throughout his chronicle, de Gaulle's military education brings a vivid practical dimension to his commentary and analysis, while his fierce loyalty to the sovereignty and heritage of France provokes innumerable confrontations with the Allied High Command (see, for instance, his fascinating account of his debate with Churchill and Eisenhower regarding the campaign in Alsace late in the conflict). The product of an overwhelming personality in all its ego and honor, self-justification and courage, stubbornness and vision, these memoirs evoke the military, political, and cultural themes of France's midcentury crisis with great eloquence and dignity. To read them is to discover that Churchill was not the only great writer among the Allied leadership.

What: War. Autobiography. History. *When:* Original volumes published in France 1955–59. One-volume American edition first published in 1964. *Editions:* Translated by Jonathan Griffin (*The Call to Honour*) and Richard Howard (*Unity* and *Salvation*). *Also By: Memoirs of Hope* (1970). *Try: The General: Charles de Gaulle and the France He Saved* by Jonathan Fenby.

||||||||||||||||||||||||||||||||||||||||| B O O K N O T E |||||||||||||||||||||||||||||||||||||||||

CIVILIZATION IN THE BALANCE

Their Finest Hour
Winston Churchill (1874–1965)

Winston Churchill's six-volume history, *The Second World War*, was the prime impetus for his being awarded the Nobel Prize in Literature in 1953; in the years immediately after its publication, it provided the outlines for the standard narrative of the conflict from the Allied point of view. (The story of Churchill's construction of the work with a team of researchers given, by special arrangement, unparalleled postwar access to government archives, is fascinating in itself, and well told in David Reynolds's *In Command of History*.) "I have followed," Churchill writes in describing his approach, ". . . the method of Defoe's *Memoirs of a Cavalier* . . . in which the author hangs the chronicle and discussion of great military and political events upon the thread of the personal experiences of an individual." The personal experiences are, of course, his own, and they add a unique immediacy to the sweeping columns of fact and fate he has marshaled as a historian, which, to the reader's delight, are orchestrated with the rhetorical skill that was Churchill's particular genius as a statesman. The second—and the best—book in the sextet, *Their Finest Hour*, covers the fall of France and the eight months of 1940 during which Britain stood alone against the Third Reich, with the author's noble oratory often its first line of defense. This is history in the grand manner: compelling, sobering, stirring.

The Auberge of the Flowering Hearth
Roy Andries de Groot (1910–1983)

Discovering a Paradise of Custom and Cuisine

Nearly two decades before Peter Mayle's *A Year in Provence* created what seems to be a permanent vogue for food-enriched, wine-soaked sojourns in off-the-beaten-path European villages, Roy Andries de Groot composed the genre's precursor and masterpiece.

His poised, cultivated chronicle of the delights he discovered at a modest inn in the high Alpine valley of La Grande Chartreuse in southeastern France is the book that many well-read gourmets treasure above all others—and recommend to the uninitiated with an enthusiasm generally reserved for an undiscovered restaurant or an inexpensively wondrous bottle of wine.

The book starts with a storyteller's flair, as the author reveals that he was drawn to his subject by the cryptic information he read on the labels of bottles of his favorite after-dinner drink, Green Chartreuse. "What did the rather mysterious words and phrases mean? Who were these 'Pères Chartreux' who distilled the liqueur at 'La Grande Chartreuse' by a 'secret process' known only to them?" In search of answers, de Groot soon found himself traveling on a road through a narrow cleft in a five-thousand-foot granite wall that led to his remote and mystifying destination.

But that's only the background to *The Auberge of the Flowering Hearth*. The real story begins when de Groot settles in at the inn that gives the book its name, a hostelry whose uncommon cuisine was the emblem of a graceful way of life in tune with nature and its seasons. Befriending the two proprietors, the Mademoiselles Yvette and Ray, de Groot is initiated into the simple rites that seem to bless

the meals cooked on the open, wood-burning hearth bedecked with wrought-iron chains and heavy cauldrons, grill bars and a turning spit. (In spring and summer, when the hearth is cool, antique copper pots hold the flowers and plants that give the inn its name.) On several lovingly chronicled return trips, de Groot was a willing student of the Mademoiselles' accumulated culinary wisdom, observing with pleasure the ins and outs of their livelihood—negotiating the local market, planning the seasonal menus, craftily building a discriminating wine cellar. While detailed recipes, perfectly amenable to American kitchens, make up the second portion of the book, it is de Groot's substantial opening narrative of his experiences in the company of the Mademoiselles as they go about their daily business that makes this book such a delicacy.

What: Food & Drink. Travel. *When:* 1973. *Edition:* Revised with new preface, 1983. *Also By: Feasts for All Seasons* (1966). *In Search of the Perfect Meal* (1986). *Try: The Tuscan Year* by Elisabeth Romer (see page 672). *Footnote:* Working for the British Ministry of Information in 1939, de Groot suffered eye injuries in the Blitz that resulted, twenty years later, in total blindness—a fact that readers may find surprising, considering the adventurousness and descriptive richness of his later food and travel writing.

Microbe Hunters
Paul de Kruif (1890–1971)

The Thrill of the Hunt—
Under a Microscope

Few books convey the romance of science—the intense excitement of close observation, the intuitive leaps that link phenomena, the disappointment of failed hypotheses, the triumphant clarity of successful experiment—better than this one. The enduring 1926 bestseller by bacteriologist-turned-writer Paul de Kruif is a colorful account of the careers and discoveries of the pioneers of the microscopic world. There's Anthony Leeuwenhoek, the seventeenth-century Dutch tradesman

whose remarkable hand-ground lenses led to the discovery of microorganisms and to the first steps in the development of microbiology; Louis Pasteur, the nineteenth-century French scientist whose experiments in bacteriology—in addition to creating a rabies vaccine and inventing the now ubiquitous process that bears his name—were instrumental in validating the germ theory of disease; and Paul Erhlich, whose "magic bullet" effectively treated syphilis and pointed the way to other twentieth-century research that proved crucial in the advancement of antibiotics. Presenting these scientific trailblazers as the "hunters," "explorers," and "fighters of death" that they truly were—including some "done to death by the immensely small assassins they were studying"—de Kruif infuses his profiles with an extra dose of drama that brings a page-turning pleasure to the real scientific history he imparts. That we are still racing against the spread of infectious diseases, with all the benefit of history and modern technology on our side, makes the stories of de Kruif's heroes that much more compelling.

What: Science. *When:* 1926. *Reading Note:* This book is an ideal inspiration to adolescents with an interest in science. Its dramatic enthusiasm—there are lots of exclamation points!—is, dare one say it, infectious. *Also By: Hunger Fighters* (1928). *Men Against Death* (1932). *The Sweeping Wind: A Memoir* (1962). *Try: The Medical Detectives* by Berton Roueché (see page 678). *Microbe Hunters: Then and Now*, a collection of pieces by modern scientists working in the field, edited by Hilary Koprowski and Michael B. A. Oldstone.

....

Giants and Heroes

A DAUGHTER'S MEMORIES OF Y. A. TITTLE

Dianne Tittle de Laet (born 1949)

A Football Legend and His Classicist Daughter

S tunned by a brutal tackle, reduced to his knees and intent on his breath, rivulets of blood running as freely as sweat down his brow, Y. A. Tittle was the subject, in his final season, of one of the most telling sports photographs ever published: a portrait of the athlete as noble warrior, the man of skill, strength, and cunning battered by the rough work of the world. That figure has been brought to vivid, complex life in his daughter's generous and wholly original book—as is the commanding Tittle who, as quarterback of the Baltimore Colts and San Francisco 49ers throughout the 1950s, and as field marshal of the New York Giants for three inspiring seasons in the early 1960s, earned his place in the Pro Football Hall of Fame. What else would you expect from a girl who, at six years of age, while watching her father ply his trade in San Francisco's Kezar Stadium, answered the query of a fan by saying no, she wasn't going to be a cheerleader: "I am going to write a book about Greek mythology and be buried under a cypress tree."

In this questing, good-humored, heartfelt memoir, Dianne Tittle de Laet weaves family history, football lore, and her own vocations as poet, harpist, and classicist into a curious and lifelike tapestry of biography and anecdote,

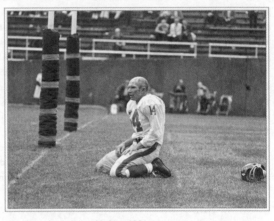

Y. A. Title after being tackled in a 1964 game

reminiscence and affection. The poetry of Pindar is juxtaposed with the effort of athletes such as Frank Gifford, Andy Robustelli, and Big Daddy Lipscomb, and the author uses all of her emotion and erudition to explore the dearest questions: Who is my father? What does it mean to be a family? How do we measure excellence? Why do we strive? Isn't life—and isn't love—mysterious, and grand?

What: Sports. Memoir. *When:* 1995. *Also By: Praise Songs: Poems* (1988). *Further Reading: The Million Dollar Backfield: The San Francisco 49ers in the 1950s* by Dave Newhouse. *Giants Among Men* by Jack Cavanaugh. *Try: Backseat Quarterback* by Perian Conerly. *The Bookmaker's Daughter* by Shirley Abbott.

1874 Currier and Ives lithograph of Robinson Crusoe and his man Friday

Robinson Crusoe
Daniel Defoe (1660–1731)

The Classic Adventure of Survival on a Desert Island

Inspired by the real-life experience of Alexander Selkirk (1676–1721), a Scottish sailor who was marooned for more than four years on a South Pacific island, *Robinson Crusoe* gave enduring form to fundamental themes of the Western imagination. With his parrot and parasol, the castaway Crusoe is an emblem of survival, self-sufficiency, resourcefulness, and the ingenuity that shapes civilization from the raw materials of nature. He is also the hero of what many literary historians call the first novel in English.

The story is simple, and compelling: Against the advice of his father, a young man eschews the timid certainties of a comfortable life and runs off to sea in search of adventure. Despite misfortune on his first voyage, he persists in pursuing the promise of travel, until at last he finds himself washed up on a desert island, the sole survivor of a shipwreck. Salvaging items—provisions, tools, guns, and powder—from the storm-tossed vessel, Crusoe overcomes his despair and applies himself to the task of making a home in his unfamiliar surroundings. For the next two decades, in solitude, he re-creates in his island wilderness as much as he can of the civilized world.

From the book's opening sentence, Crusoe addresses the reader in a voice—direct and declarative in the manner of casual speech—that was something new in literature. But it is only when Crusoe begins building his lonely habitat, narrating in matter-of-fact detail his projects and activities, that Defoe's fresh genius truly takes hold. As Nobel Laureate J. M. Coetzee has observed, "For page after page—for the first time in the history of fiction—we see a minute, ordered description of how things are done." What Coetzee terms Defoe's "pure writerly attentiveness" imbues what he describes with unexpected presence:

By being a great artist and forgoing this and daring that in order to give effect to his prime quality, a sense of reality—[Defoe] comes in the end to make common actions dignified and common objects beautiful. To dig, to bake, to plant, to build—how serious these simple occupations are; hatchets, scissors, logs, axes—how beautiful these simple objects become. Unimpeded by comment, the story marches on with magnificent downright simplicity.

And we march with it, until, like Crusoe, we are brought up short by a footprint on the beach: "It happened one day about noon," we read, "going towards my boat, I was exceedingly surprised with the print of a man's naked foot on the shore, which was very plain to be seen in the sand." With this startling discovery, Defoe's story opens out to welcome first "my man Friday," whom Crusoe saves from cannibals, and then the victims of another shipwreck. By the time he is rescued himself after twenty-eight years, Robinson Crusoe can embark for England from the midst of a small community that has taken root in the long-lonely precincts of his ordeal. But not before, alone on his island, he has cast a narrative spell that has enthralled readers for nearly three centuries.

What: Novel. *When:* 1719. *Edition:* The Scribner Classics edition contains N. C. Wyeth's stunning illustrations. *Reading Note:* Modern readers immersed in the tale may find themselves wriggling through Crusoe's reflections on the religious dimensions of his experience. *Also By: The Farther Adventures of Robinson Crusoe* (1719). *Moll Flanders* (1722). *A Journal of the Plague Year* (1722). *Roxana* (1724). *A Tour Through the Whole Island of Great Britain* (1724–27). *Further Reading: In Search of Robinson Crusoe* by Tim Severin. *Selkirk's Island: The True and Strange Adventures of the Real Robinson Crusoe* by Diana Souhami. *Try:* For three modern fictional reimaginings of the Crusoe story, see Muriel Spark's *Robinson*, Michel Tournier's *Friday*, and J. M. Coetzee's *Foe. Adaptations:* Notable cinematic adaptations include *The Adventures of Robinson Crusoe* (1954), directed by Luis Buñuel; Brian Haskins's *Robinson Crusoe on Mars* (1964); and Caleb Deschanel's *Crusoe* (1989).

Diary of a Provincial Lady
E. M. Delafield (1890–1943)

A Forebear of Bridget Jones and Her Diary

(Query, mainly rhetorical: Why are nonprofessional women, if married and with children, so frequently referred to as "leisured"? Answer comes there none.)

E. M. Delafield's Provincial Lady first appeared in 1930. Her first *Diary* would be followed by three more in the course of the next decade. These charming volumes proved immediately and enduringly popular, and Delafield's creation is today seen, in her deceptively casual chronicling of her domestic activities, as a style-setter for later writers who deployed aspects of her mode of self-address in both journalism and fiction.

In the first volume of the series, we are immediately swept up in the diarist's life with her husband, Robert, and their family in a very English village in the shires. The Provincial Lady's struggle to keep up proper appearances as she manages the household (including her cook and her children's slightly terrifying French governess) and holds her own in the orbit of the formidable Lady B., the sun of the village's social system, is depicted with amusing attention to detail. The protagonist's overburdened schedule is viewed through a poised intelligence that is observant, ironic, and often laugh-out-loud funny:

Final straw is added when Lady B. amiably observes that I, at least, have nothing to complain of, as she always thinks Robert such a safe, respectable husband for any woman. Give her briefly to understand that Robert is in reality a compound of Don Juan, the Marquis de Sade, and Dr. Crippen, but that we do not care to let it be known locally.

Readers seeking astute yet gentle social satire at its British best will be richly rewarded by acquaintance with Delafield's wonderful Provincial Lady.

What: Novel. *When:* 1930. *Also By: The Provincial Lady Goes Further* (1932; also published as *The Provincial Lady in London*). *The Provincial Lady in America* (1934). *The Provincial Lady in Wartime* (1940). *Straw Without Bricks: I Visit Soviet Russia* (1937), although later republished as *The Provincial Lady in Russia*, was not written as part of the series. *Further Reading:* For Delafield's influence on later writers, see Cynthia Zarin's excellent profile, "The Diarist," in *The New Yorker* of May 9, 2005. *Try: Henrietta's War* by Joyce Dennys. *Provincial Daughter* by R. M. Dashwood (Delafield's daughter). *Bridget Jones's Diary* by Helen Fielding.

Nova
Samuel R. Delany (born 1942)

An Audacious Invention, Still Burning Bright

A perfectly realized rehabilitation of the hoary space opera (which, pre–Star Wars, sorely needed rejuvenation; for more on Space Operas, see page 26), Samuel R. Delany's *Nova* is still as forward-looking and peerless today as at its birth, when it catapulted its twenty-five-year-old author to the top of the science fiction scene.

Our galaxy in the year 3172 is segmented among three political entities: the Draco group, the Pleiades Federation, and the Outer Colonies. The last—mainly a frontier source of commercially vital raw materials, including the all-important element Illyrion—is the smallest player. Dominant, older Draco, which includes Earth, wields its power mainly through its starship monopoly, helmed by the Red family, whose scions are Prince Red and his sister, Ruby. The most powerful clan in the Pleiades is that of the Von Rays, whose standard-bearer is young Lorq—a rebel out to break Draco by securing vast quantities of Illyrion and making that scarce energy substance common. Naturally, Prince Red and Ruby seek to stop him. Complicating the instinctive hatred among the three is Lorq's countervailing romantic fascination with Ruby.

So far, we could be describing the setup for your typical space opera; what distinguishes Delany's art is the sophisticated attention applied to this future's politics, culture, and economies, making his novel both an absorbing adventure in ideas and a clandestine commentary on the time of its composition, the turbulent year 1968. Certainly, the posse of outré characters he creates enlivens the telling, including Mouse, an untutored Earth gypsy and master of the sensory-syrynx, a "musical" instrument of astounding capabilities; the Tarot-reading Tyÿ; and Katin, an overeducated fellow with the oddest idea: to resurrect that extinct art form called "the novel."

Nova represents Delany's distillation and transmogrification of such influences as Ray Bradbury (see page 91), Theodore Sturgeon, Cordwainer Smith, and Alfred Bester (see page 73). The contending Shakespearean dynasties; the quirky, deeply inhabited characters; the poetic language (rococo, yet somehow still limpid); the portrait of a future radically estranged from ours, where our era is mythic to theirs, while they are myths-to-come for us; the layered symbolism—all these aspects are drawn from the past masters cited, yet are fused into an organic whole whose likes had never before been seen. Most novas burn out to cinders, but this one—vital, prescient, affecting, a genuine work of art—blazes as brightly as ever.

What: Science Fiction. Novel. *When:* 1968. *Also By: Empire Star* (1966). *Dhalgren* (1975). *Triton* (1976). *Stars in My Pocket Like Grains of Sand* (1984). *Try: Evolution's Darling* by Scott Westerfeld. *Light* by M. John Harrison. *The Praxis* by Walter John Williams.

Great Books

MY ADVENTURES WITH HOMER, ROUSSEAU, WOOLF,
AND OTHER INDESTRUCTIBLE WRITERS OF THE WESTERN WORLD

David Denby (born 1943)

Reading Homer Through the Midlife Crisis

I had forgotten. I had forgotten the extremity of its cruelty and tenderness, and, reading it now, turning the Iliad *open anywhere in its 15,693 lines, I was shocked. A dying word, "shocked." Few people have been able to use it well since Claude Rains so famously said, "I'm shocked,* shocked *to find that gambling is going on here," as he pocketed his winnings in* Casablanca. *But it's the only word for excitement and alarm of this intensity.*

Those are the opening sentences of *Great Books*, and you won't be more than a page beyond them before you are looking to dip into Homer's epic for yourself.

Denby, an acclaimed film critic, had initially encountered Homer three decades earlier, as a freshman at Columbia University. Now he was rereading the *Iliad* as part of a midlife adventure: going back to college with the specific purpose of reading his way through his alma mater's two core-curriculum (i.e., "great books") courses. In the company of students and professors, with his own family life (as son, husband, parent) and career providing both context and commentary, Denby considers the contours of our culture and the transmission of its traditions. He celebrates the "special character of solitude and rapture" the act of reading still engenders, despite the reverberating acoustics of the "media cave" in which we live. Major themes he confronts in the classics—identity as fate (*Oedipus Rex*; see page 740), education (Plato's *Republic*), parenthood and old age (*King Lear*; see page 716)—are related tellingly to his own life: The wisdom of the books reflect and illuminate his experience in ways that reveal their enlightening, equivocal truths. With a student's anxieties and an older man's urgencies, Denby leads us on an evocative journey through a treasure-laden library of literature and philosophy that stretches from Montaigne to Marx, Saint Augustine to Jane Austen, Virgil and Dante to Joseph Conrad and Virginia Woolf. The result is a volume of learning and of soulfulness, one in which the author—bless him—willingly commits "the unspeakable sin (in academic circles) of belletrism—the sin of writing the book for the reader's pleasure and my own."

What: Books. Memoir. When: 1996. Also By: American Sucker (2004). Lit Up: One Reporter. Three Schools. Twenty-Four Books That Can Change Lives (2016). Try: Why Read the Classics? by Italo Calvino. The Things That Matter: What Seven Classic Novels Have to Say About the Stages of Life by Edward Mendelson.

||||||||||||||||||||||||||||||||||||||| **MORE TO EXPLORE** |||||||||||||||||||||||||||||||||||||||

BOOKS ON BOOKS

For inveterate readers, the biggest bookstore in the world is never big enough, and 1,000 books will no doubt seem too few to last a lifetime, no matter how carefully they're chosen. Even when we're spoiled for choice, and the pile of volumes on the bedside table is tottering dangerously, books that add more volumes to our to-be-read stack are special treasures. They bring delight in themselves, whether or not we manage to work our way through all the neglected classics, forgotten gems, or personal enthusiasms we cull from their pages. Here are six indispensable examples, each, like David Denby's *Great Books*, a useful, entertaining, addictive companion to a reading life.

"Bequest of Wings"

Annis Duff (ca. 1904–1986)

An ex-librarian and bookseller at the time her first child was born (she would go on to a distinguished career as an editor of children's books for Viking Press), Annis Duff here tells how she used the thing she knew best—books—as "a sort of springboard into all the other things she knew her [children] must learn." Along the way, she and her husband discover much that they need to learn as well, making *"Bequest of Wings"* not only a marvelous account of one family's pleasures with books, but also a quiet, lovely, and quite wise primer on parenting. The common ground of shared reading—from nursery rhymes to little stories about trains that go, from fairy tales to poetry, from funny books to narratives of adventure—that grows as a family does is tenderly mapped, as are the pleasures of reading, and learning, aloud. Duff is especially good at translating what can be found between covers into a wider knowledge of life, sharing insight on how books are gateways not only to the meaning and use (and fun) of words, but to art, music, nature, and research as well. *"Bequest of Wings"* was published in 1944, and the surface of Duff's exposition of course reveals its age; yet beneath it, a timeless vein of generosity, intelligence, and love remains.

"I think of the lady who went into a bookshop to buy gifts for nephews and nieces; after she had been shown a great many books she said, 'But these are all old books.' Whereupon the bookseller remarked gently, 'Yes, Madam, but the children are always new.'"

The List of Books
Frederic Raphael (born 1931) and Kenneth McLeish (1940–1997)

In this stunningly smart and deceptively capacious little volume, we're given an annotated guide to key reading in more than forty subject areas. The authors' discrimination pinpoints the volumes and the writers and thinkers we need to know about—and even what we need to know about them. The latter is all the more remarkable since

Raphael and McLeish limit their commentaries generally to less than five short lines per book entry; their terse annotations display an epigrammatic erudition that is astonishing—and amusing. Of the author of *King, Queen, Knave* they write, "Nabokov stands alone in the modern canon, the idiosyncratic instance of an artist jealous of his own uniqueness . . . his variety, wit and teasing literary iconography make [him] both nightmare and addiction." They are as astute on sociology as they are on fiction, and they bring a bracing connoisseurship to topics as diverse as "Art and Design," "Economics," "Home and Garden," "Reference," "Religion," and "Sex and Love." Published in 1981 and consequently dated in some areas, *The List of Books* remains a multifaceted gem; go online and find a used copy now—you won't regret it.

Book Lust
Nancy Pearl (born 1945)

Librarian Nancy Pearl has a knack for tying parcels of good reading in ribbons colored by the occasions of our reading. This 2003 compendium of lists, annotated with conversational commentary, is witty, informative, and refreshingly rangy, covering everything from "Academic Mysteries" to "African Colonialism: Fiction," "Bicycling" to "Boys Coming of Age," "Chick Lit" to "China Voices," *"Romans-Fleuves"* to "Russian Heavies." Especially delightful are her knowing "Too Good to Miss" encomiums for writers as various as Hamilton Basso, George MacDonald Fraser, Ward Just, Iris Murdoch, Connie Willis, and Van Reid.

A Reader's Delight
Noel Perrin (1927–2004)

Most passionate readers have a small shelf of special treasures, those "favorite books that he or she keeps urging friends to read,"

as Noel Perrin puts it. "All the books have in common is that the owner thinks they are wonderful." In *A Reader's Delight* (1988), we are given the privilege of browsing Perrin's own collection of favorites. The cordial and elegant essays he penned in praise of books that, although perhaps falling "just short of classic status," have made their way into his heart and mind, are the best sort of recommendations, for his affectionate judgments are personal, intelligent, insightful, surprising, genuine, and, best of all, infectious. His interest is wide-ranging in terms of genre and provenance—"There are books here by Americans, by Englishmen and women, by an Italian diplomat and a Dutch resistance fighter (who both wrote in English), by a pair of Russian brothers, by a Japanese monk"—and his willingness to be pleased is wholly admirable (after all, it is the ignorant, as Dr. Johnson said, who imagine that refusing to be pleased is a mark of sophistication).

Bound to Please
Michael Dirda (born 1948)

"If Proust, while listening to late Beethoven string quartets, had written *I, Claudius* and set it in the future, the result might resemble this measured, autumnal masterpiece." So writes Michael Dirda of Gene Wolfe's *The Book of the New Sun*, a four-volume monument of science fiction inspiration. It's hard to imagine any other critic weaving such a web of references to conjure that particular description, or so artfully beckoning readers toward new territory. Scholar, enthusiast, and literary journalist extraordinaire, Dirda, whose long career as a stalwart of the *Washington Post Book World* led to a Pulitzer Prize for distinguished criticism in 1993, is as adept at illuminating the complexities of Proust, Pushkin, and Baudelaire as he is at championing the pleasures of ghost stories, thrillers, and comic novels. *Bound to Please* is a 2005 collection that illustrates, first and foremost, Dirda's joy in his profession and his affection for the books and authors it allows him to explore. "[Think] of these articles," he writes in his introduction, "as old-fashioned appreciations, a fan's notes, good talk." You'll scour shelves a long time before finding a more edifying and enjoyable expression of why we open books in the first place: to lose ourselves in story, to exercise our intellects, to dwell in states of mind and lands of adventure the houses we inhabit cannot hold.

Ten Years in the Tub
Nick Hornby (born 1957)

For the ten years between 2003 and 2013, with interruptions now and then, Nick Hornby, novelist (*About a Boy; High Fidelity*), screenwriter (*An Education*), and soccer-obsessed memoirist (*Fever Pitch*), contributed a column called "Stuff I've Been Reading" to *The Believer* magazine. If you happened upon them on their initial publication, you won't be surprised to discover that they seem no less entertaining and memorable on rereading them in *Ten Years in the Tub* (2013); in fact, the cumulative effect of their gathering only adds to our delight in Hornby's book foraging. Each column starts with two lists, "Books Bought" and "Books Read," and the frequent lack of balance between the two evokes the life of a book lover better than any detailed explication could. Hornby's tastes are catholic, and he ranges freely from contemporary fiction to classic literature, sports biographies to literary lives, books on music to whatever strikes his fancy. ("At my eldest son's school fair I bought *The Case of Mr. Crump*, yet another Penguin classic I'd never heard of, because on the cover it had a blurb from Sigmund Freud.") If you want to know how funny he can be, turn to June/July 2006 and read his parody of what he calls the post–Malcolm Gladwell school of essays, which he inserts into his musing on *Freakonomics* by Steven D. Levitt and Stephen J. Dubner. It begins, "On the face of it, World War II and Pamela Anderson's breasts would seem to have little in common. And yet on closer examination, the differences seem actually much less interesting than the similarities." Irreverent, impulsive, insightful, Hornby's reader's diary is pure pleasure.

Clear Light of Day
Anita Desai (born 1937)

Two Sisters in History's Long Shadow

The success of the Indian independence movement, which ended British rule in 1947, has always been tempered by a painful legacy: the partition of the British raj into two sovereign states, divided by religion. The creation of Hindu-majority India and Muslim-majority Pakistan bred years of violence and displacement that have matured into permanent unrest. And as Anita Desai shows in *Clear Light of Day*, a moving and atmospheric novel suffused with heat, sound, and heartache, the partition of India cleaved families apart as well.

The novel opens in modern India, specifically in Old Delhi, the once elegant Mughal city that now stands dilapidated next to the current

Anita Desai, 1991

capital, New Delhi. Tara Das, whose husband is a diplomat, is returning home from abroad. Bim, her older sister, still lives in the crumbling family home in Old Delhi, caring for their autistic brother. The sisters clearly love each other, but their relationship is strained—and as the novel flashes back to their childhood in independence-era India, we see why. In the Das family the parents are, to put it kindly, unconcerned about their children's welfare. As the country erupts in religious and political upheaval, the family comes apart as well; decades later the wounds remain fresh.

Filled with insight into the legacy of partition, *Clear Light of Day* is very much a family novel. It's a story of secrets, regrets, jealousy, commitment, forgiveness, and love, through which Desai evokes the easy-to-mask but impossible to disguise verity that one can never leave one's family. As one sister says to the other late in the novel, in a truth that colors family life as thoroughly as it saturates history, "It's never over. Nothing's *over*, ever."

What: Novel. **When:** 1980. **Also By:** *Fire on the Mountain* (1977). *The Village by the Sea* (1982). *In Custody* (1984). *Fasting, Feasting* (1999). **Try:** *Midnight's Children* by Salman Rushdie (see page 683). *Heat and Dust* by Ruth Prawer Jhabvala (see page 415). *Family Matters* by Rohinton Mistry.

The Brief Wondrous Life of Oscar Wao
Junot Díaz (born 1968)

A Quixote for Our Time?

The first thing that strikes you is the prose: It's fast and agile, unafraid to mix ingredients. English and Spanish and Spanglish combine to energize the sentences, which move easily between different modes of discourse—expository, conversational, professorial, confidential, ribald, tender, rambunctious—but never stray for long from speech rhythms. Now shouting, now murmuring, now explaining or exhorting, the voice of the narrator—a man named Yunior, as we will eventually discover—relates the life of his friend Oscar de Leon, an overweight, nerdy, sensitive boy possessed of—or more exactly by—what Díaz has called "outré interests." Yunior's narration also encompasses the times of Oscar's family (including his sister, Lola, Yunior's former love), immigrants to New Jersey from the Dominican Republic.

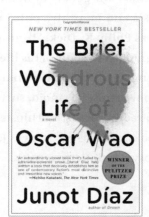

NEW YORK TIMES BESTSELLER
The Brief Wondrous Life of Oscar Wao
a novel
WINNER OF THE PULITZER PRIZE
Junot Díaz
author of Drown

Yunior's linguistic exuberance is fueled by a current of vast, eclectic erudition drawn from across the spectrum of culture, from vintage television shows to video games and role-playing universes, from science fiction and fantasy literature to comic books and the superhero sagas they've engendered, from the amorous travails of Cyrano de Bergerac to the portraiture of John Singer Sargent. (The range of the book's reference grazing is evidenced in the title; when Yunior teases Oscar about his physical resemblance to the ill-fated Oscar Wilde, another friend's accent transforms "Wilde" to "Wao," and the name sticks.)

Yunior's transporting, invigorating, often hilarious monologue is from time to time interrupted by other voices, including a series of lengthy and entertaining footnotes that elaborate historical and political contexts "for those of you who missed your mandatory two seconds of Dominican history."

The book's style is powerful, and it needs to be, because it must treat several spheres of action and dimensions of experience, diverse in register and implication. There are Oscar's adolescence and coming-of-age, marked by intellectual precociousness, social awkwardness, lust for but lack of luck with girls, and all the accoutrements of an urban American upbringing, from acne to bullying to loneliness to SAT prep classes; there's a familial tragedy played out across several generations, and eluding catharsis, in the lives of Lola and the siblings' mother, Hypatía Belicia Cabral; there's a vivid evocation of the Dominican diaspora, replete with immersion in the oppressively surreal and brutally physical force fields of the Trujillo dictatorship. Indeed, the shadows of the Dominican past are strong enough to make the Jersey landscape seem ill-equipped to live up to history; they loom over the story like clouds from the larger weather pattern called the *fukú americanus*, or, as Yunior tells us, "more colloquially, fukú—generally a curse or a doom of some kind; specifically the Curse and the Doom of the New World." Only a spell as ominous and irresistible as the fukú can explain the emotional dissonance between the characters' daily lives in Paterson and the suffering that seems to be their inheritance; it's an affliction Oscar comes to know by heart, even as he loses himself in Tolkien or *Watchmen* in the Garden State.

Like Don Quixote with his chivalric romances, Oscar goes into battle with the only weapons he knows—comic book plots and superheroic ambitions—tilting at windmills and more dangerous realities until his peculiar picaresque comes to an untimely end. Along the way, his story bounces back and forth between yearning and nostalgia, tenderness and violence, nerdiness and nobility, anguish and—not least, and almost inexplicably—joy.

What: Novel. *When:* 2007. *Awards:* National Book Critics Circle Award, 2007. Pulitzer Prize for Fiction, 2008. *Also By: Drown* (1996). *This Is How You Lose Her* (2012). *Try: The House on Mango Street* by Sandra Cisneros. *In the Time of Butterflies* by Julia Alvarez. *The Amazing Adventures of Kavalier & Clay* by Michael Chabon (see page 145).

PHILIP K. DICK
(1928–1982)

Perhaps no other author who got a start in the Grub Street of mass-market paperback originals and monthly "pulp" magazines has ever risen to such prominence as Philip K. Dick. His utterly unique fiction, allied to the quirky and quixotic biographical details of his life, have brought him a species of literary canonization along with pop culture name-branding via the critical adjective "phildickian." His powerfully paranoid, surreal, and gnostic tableaux are invoked by journalists, conspiracy theorists, and hipsters alike. Hollywood has made numerous films from his books, and writers such as Jonathan Lethem continue to find inspiration in PKD's idiosyncratic fictive acuity.

The fate of the little man against the large and uncaring forces that dominate our world; the eternal quest for mystical reassurances and glimpses of a higher plane of existence; the battle to preserve a tender and feeling soul in the midst of dehumanizing and deracinating conditions; the paranoia engendered by global events beyond all human comprehension; the role of humans in the great chain of being, downward to the beasts or upward to celestial aliens; the virtues and traps of self-knowledge: Such

Philip K. Dick, 1982

are the themes and concerns that are obsessively reshuffled in Dick's works, finding freshly bizarre and unforgettable representations with each outing. And against all expectations about the broader appeal of naturalism, the deep strangeness of Dick's novels speaks to the contemporary condition more resonantly than the books of many more conventional, and more determinedly "serious," writers.

A fellow with one foot in the pulp literature that he loved and the other in esoteric tracts from the great savants and seekers of Western and Eastern traditions, Dick was a man of brilliant, fruitful, fateful contradictions. Always on the edge of bankruptcy (at times reduced to shopping for his own dinner of horse meat at the Lucky Dog Pet Food store), he had to pump out novels fast for low advances, relying on amphetamines to stimulate his production. Like some combination of beatnik, alchemist, pirate, and philosopher, Dick invented worlds so weird and wonderful they seem to both reflect the zeitgeist and glimmer with deeper, more elusive truths.

The Man in the High Castle
The Axis of Alternative History

Picking up a Hugo Award in 1963, this was the book that marked Dick's transition, at least on the fan radar, from merely offbeat and amusing to brilliant and insightful. Oddly—or perhaps predictably, given its mass appeal—*The Man in the High Castle* features the lowest quotient of disturbing reality fractures of any tale in Dick's science fiction output.

Offering an alternate history that would become quite common as a fictional scenario but was exceedingly fresh at the time of its publication, the novel posits that the Axis powers have won World War II and come to subjugate the West. The United States is broken into a zone of Nazi domination in the east; a small, impotent, independent buffer state around the Rockies; and a Japanese-controlled zone in the west. His California upbringing and lifelong residency inclined Dick to set his book there, and we see a host of proletarian and middle-class characters going about their daily business, striving to endure the yoke of conquest. Central as an icon of rebellion is the character Hawthorne Abendsen, an author whose masterpiece, *The Grasshopper Lies Heavy*, dares to imagine a mirror image of his present, its timeline unfolding from an Allied victory. Abendsen's vision, we finally learn, stems not from mere imagination, but from the muse of a cosmos attempting to rescue itself from a failure of justice.

Despite the thriller-like political machinations and a few melodramatic set pieces,

the real allure of the book lies in its depiction of fully realized individuals striving with varying degrees of both hypocrisy and authenticity to live right lives in a wrong environment. By turning upside down the postwar structures and balances that the reader knows by heart, Dick illustrates the essential arbitrariness of the universe—and the need for empathy when victor becomes vanquished, and vice versa.

What: Novel. Science Fiction. *When:* 1962. *Award:* Hugo Award for Best Novel, 1963. *Also By: Eye in the Sky* (1957). *Time Out of Joint* (1959). *Dr. Bloodmoney, or How We Got Along After the Bomb* (1965). *Further Reading: Only Apparently Real: The World of Philip K. Dick* by Paul Williams. *Try: The Sound of His Horn* by Sarban. *The Iron Dream* by Norman Spinrad. *SS-GB* by Len Deighton. *Adaptation:* A television series produced by Amazon Studios premiered in 2015.

The Three Stigmata of Palmer Eldritch
A Phildickian Fantasia

If one were assigned the unenviable task of selecting a single book as a showcase for all of Dick's tropes, tactics, tricks, themes, and tics, *The Three Stigmata of Palmer Eldritch* might well be the best choice. In its pages, we see in incredibly effective form the majority of the imagery, incidents, characters, and themes the author became known for: consumerist brainwashing; peculiar drugs; simulacra; Manic Pixie Girlfriends Who Are Truly Other Than What They Seem; psychic powers, especially precognition; the universe as a hostile minefield; egomaniacal sociopaths who become both more and less than human; sassy cybernetic constructs; shifting internal monologues; the inanity of mass media and pop culture; shifting levels of reality. They're all here, wrapped around, underlying, and enclosing a captivating story line.

On harsh Mars the human settlers solace themselves with CAN-D, a drug that allows them to enter a consensual virtual reality. Crash-landing his spacecraft, the robber baron industrialist Palmer Eldritch returns from a visit to the enigmatic aliens of Proxima bearing a rival drug, Chew-Z, which has much more insidious effects than CAN-D. While others try to stymie the industrialist's designs, Eldritch begins to permeate the very fabric of the universe, manifesting out of nowhere as a cyborg with a robotic right hand, artificial eyes, and steel teeth—his three stigmata. Can anyone stop the universe from unraveling? Or will the face of Palmer Eldritch be forever emblazoned on the sky?

Dick juggles so many subsidiary plots and strata of existence that we're likely to experience a deliciously disorienting drug-like response just from the reading; the unsettling mind-bending effect is unlike that of any other book.

What: Novel. Science Fiction. *When:* 1965. *Also By: The Penultimate Truth* (1964). *Martian Time-Slip* (1964). *Ubik* (1969). *Further Reading: Divine Invasions: A Life of Philip K. Dick* by Lawrence Sutin. *Try: Philip K. Dick Is Dead, Alas* by Michael Bishop. *Gun, with Occasional Music* by Jonathan Lethem. *Humpty Dumpty: An Oval* by Damon Knight.

Do Androids Dream of Electric Sheep?
The Source Book for *Blade Runner*

Rutger Hauer as a replicant in the 1982 film Blade Runnner

As the basis for the first and best adaptation of a Dick novel to film (Ridley Scott's 1982 *Blade Runner*), this book occupies a central place in the PKD oeuvre. But its virtues and affect are different from the cinematic interpretation, more in line with Dick's core preoccupations.

The protagonist Rick Deckard, bounty hunter of androids, is less of an action hero than the movie's leading man, Harrison Ford (more schlubby might be a closer description). Deckard's relationship with his wife exhibits a kind of *Peyton Place* suburban angst, echoing PKD's more naturalistic fiction; it would be like something out of John Updike if Updike wrote while wearing 3-D glasses and saw through them visions of New Age self-improvement. A key theme is humankind's decimation of the animal kingdom and its subsequent resort to ownership of faux animals as status symbols and talismans. Related phildickian concepts—such as "kipple," the self-multiplying detritus of tchotchkes that plague modern life—are also brilliantly explored. Most importantly, the philosophical nucleus of the novel—the puzzle of whether androids are human, what rights they possess, and how one distinguishes them from natural humanity—is thrillingly imagined. All told, *Do Androids Dream of Electric Sheep?* is a vital excursion into imaginatively uncanny territory that seems more eerily prescient with each passing year.

What: Novel. Science Fiction. *When:* 1968. *Also By: Flow My Tears, the Policeman Said* (1974). *A Scanner Darkly* (1977). *VALIS* (1981). *Further Reading: I Am Alive and You Are Dead: A Journey into the Mind of Philip K. Dick* by Emmanuel Carrère. *Try: The Hacker and the Ants* by Rudy Rucker. *Love in the Age of Mechanical Reproduction* by Judd Trichter. *Adaptation:* The 2017 film *Blade Runner 2049* takes up the tale thirty years on, with Harrison Ford reprising his role as Rick Deckard.

CHARLES DICKENS
(1812–1870)

C harles Dickens may well be the most ingenious author in English literature. The energy of his inventiveness gave birth to a gallery of characters—from Oliver Twist to Ebenezer Scrooge—whose lives have overflowed the boundaries of his books to become permanent fixtures in the collective imagination. So strong is the shadow cast by his work—and by such monuments of storytelling as *Great Expectations* and *A Tale of Two Cities*—on our idea of the novel that it obscures how sui generis his writing is. A hundred years after the author's heyday, J. B. Priestley was insightful—and brave—enough to suggest that "this great novelist was not, strictly speaking, a novelist at all." Indeed, the gifts of observation and inspiration that Dickens possessed (or that possessed him) demanded their own creative venue, and his books seem not so much plotted by their author as traversed: If London had not existed to be his muse, he would have had to invent another city as teeming and multitudinous, as physically present and as psychologically unfathomable to engage his genius. Unlike Austen or Trollope, Flaubert or Henry James, Dickens does not manage the action of his tales within defined social or aesthetic borders; rather, he leads the reader down avenues and alleyways that are strange, vivid, filled with looming, often murky phenomena. At once familiar and ominous, the Dickensian world is a dreamscape in which states of heart and mind are rendered from an excess of palpable detail.

When we open one of his formidable tomes, we soon recognize a peculiar sense of dynamism: It's as if the author has not set out to write a novel, but has been dropped into a pulsing reality he has to write his way through, improvising a narrative out of the available material, much in the way we must construct a life. That may be why so many of his novels—the early, Dickensian-defining ones especially, such as *Oliver Twist* and *Nicholas Nickleby*, culminating in *David Copperfield*—begin with the birth of a protagonist and follow his adventures into adulthood, as if chronology provides the only possible organizing principle. No surprise, then, that the stories are ultimately about fate, which may seem to unfold around his heroes, but is more truly dependent upon their discovering, one step at a time, the destinations of their personal journeys.

This "biographical" approach suggests a reason his supporting characters, who contribute so much to our pleasure in reading Dickens, are so boldly drawn, their defining traits exaggerated to within an inch of caricature. Think of Wackford Squeers, the wicked schoolmaster in *Nickleby*, or the obsequious Uriah Heep in *Copperfield*, or the eternally disappointed bride, Miss Havisham, in *Great Expectations*. For all their vivid presence and comic (even when sinister) verve, these figures are described not as beings but as experiences. What we remember of people in our own pasts has a similar quality. Recall your favorite aunt and you'll see in miniature what Dickens does at scale: The qualities that define a person in recollection are those that are larger than life, markers for the whole being that serve as milestones in memory. Just so, his characters are both less naturalistic and *more real* than the creations of other novelists, the way a snapshot colored with reminiscences can coalesce our lived experience more tellingly than a return visit to its physical setting. It is the way our minds and our memories work, animating people and places whenever we turn our attention to them fully. Uniquely, Dickens does this not only with his characters, but also with streets and buildings, landscapes and weather, moral challenges and social conventions, even government offices: There has never been a more exact description of what bureaucratic processes feel like than that of the Circumlocution Office in *Little Dorrit*. Dickens discovered stories wherever he looked—in the shape of chimneys, in law courts, in fog—even before he peopled them with characters. He knew that we live in stories every minute, and found them for us everywhere; no other writer sweeps us up into the moment-by-moment storyness of life in quite the same way.

All of which can make his novels—to some literary scholars, at least—seem messy, rambunctious, and arbitrary in construction, imperfect equations when their parts are summed. The enduring popularity of his creations proves a more general truth: For readers, if not critics, the formal perfection of a book is not as important as its imaginative life.

David Copperfield

"Of all my books, I like this the best."
—*Charles Dickens*

Whether I shall turn out to be the hero of my own life, or whether that station will be held by anybody else, these pages must show.

S o begins this marvelous narrative, a novel so filled with character, invention, suspense, and inspired storytelling that one finishes it with an overwhelming regret: The turning of the last page closes the book on such a vivid world that one feels immediately impoverished.

Dickens famously called *Copperfield* the "favourite child" of his literary brood, and its autobiographical frame goes some way toward explaining why. The eighth of his novels to be written, it is the first one narrated in the first person, and, from the opening words, the direct address of the protagonist is captivating. The coming-of-age tale that David relates has many points of contact with Dickens's own experiences as the son of a debtor, as an adolescent employee in a factory, as a parliamentary reporter, and, lastly, as a successful novelist.

The book is peopled with enough memorable characters to sustain the careers of a half dozen storytellers. The cast includes—to mention only a few—David's imperious aunt, Betsey Trotwood, who comes to his rescue with an asperity as sharp as her magnanimity is deep; Aunt Betsey's simple-minded protégé and muse, Mr. Dick; the improvident, incorrigibly optimistic, and unabashedly grandiloquent Mr. Micawber; the charming, caddish seducer Steerforth; the unforgivable, unforgettably named Uriah Heep, whose unctuous servility cannot mask his evil intent; and David's childhood housekeeper and lifelong ally, the stalwart Peggotty, whose caring nature reflects the unaffected nobility of her family of Yarmouth fishermen. Through all the plotting and sub-plotting, the overriding sentiment of Dickensian fiction—that there is a goodness abroad in the world that courses beneath the surface complexion of beauty, the façades of wealth and privilege, and the social currency of fashion, even when we least expect it—carries the hero of this novel toward the satisfaction of a happy ending. You shouldn't read only one Dickens, but if you do, make it *David Copperfield*.

What: Novel. *When:* 1849–50. *Also By: The Posthumous Papers of the Pickwick Club* (1836–37). *Further Reading: Charles Dickens: His Tragedy and Triumph* by Edgar Johnson. *Dickens* by Peter Ackroyd. *Charles Dickens: A Life Defined by Writing* by Michael Slater. *Try: Vanity Fair* by William Makepeace Thackeray (see page 777). *Midnight's Children* by Salman Rushdie (see page 683). *Adaptations:* The story has been filmed on numerous occasions, with pride of place going to the 1935 MGM version, directed by George Cukor and starring Freddie Bartholomew as David, Edna Mae Oliver as Aunt Betsey, and W. C. Fields as Mr. Micawber. The audiobook performed by Martin Jarvis could not be better.

Oliver Twist
The Orphan as Hero

" Please, sir, I want some more" is among the most famous utterances in Dickens. It's spoken by a very small orphan named Oliver Twist to the man in charge of ladling out the meager meals Oliver shares with his fellow inmates in the workhouse established by society to house impoverished youngsters. In a single sentence, it conjures all the forces at the heart of Oliver's tale: innocence, want, mischief, hunger, boldness, desperation, misfortune. And, last but not least, institutionally sanctioned cruelty: "The master aimed a blow at Oliver's head with the ladle, pinioned him in his arms, and shrieked aloud for the beadle."

Oliver Twist was its author's second novel, telling a continuous story in a way his first, the delightful but episodic Pickwick Papers, did not. What's innovative in the book is not its shape, however, but its focus: Never before had a child been put so center stage in a novel; more importantly, while Wordsworth had evoked it in verse, never before had childhood been treated in a prolonged narrative as a state of being in its own right, with all the colors and contours of an emotional landscape as fully developed as an adult's.

As Oliver progresses from workhouse minion to undertaker's assistant to conscript in the thieving army of urchin pickpockets led by the Artful Dodger and in thrall to the seedy ringleader Fagin, the reader is treated to a searing social satire on the treatment of paupers and bereft children, a vivid portrait of the urban criminal underworld, and a suspenseful if murky plot that is a roller coaster of melodramatic hopes and fears, degradations and redemptions. It's an exhilarating chase, led by a young writer learning to harness his extraordinary creative energy.

What: Novel. *When:* 1838. *Also By: The Old Curiosity Shop* (1841). *Try: Treasure Island* by Robert Louis Stevenson (see page 758). *Smith* by Leon Garfield. *Dodger* by Terry Pratchett. *Adaptations:* The best of several film versions is David Lean's 1948 movie starring John Howard Davis as Oliver and Alec Guinness as Fagin. Lionel Bart's 1960 musical *Oliver!,* and the

"Please, sir, I want some more." James Mahoney illustration for Oliver Twist, *1871*

subsequent film based on it, which won the Academy Award for Best Picture in 1969, have amplified the story's place in the popular imagination. The audiobook performed by Martin Jarvis sets a high standard.

The Life and Adventures of Nicholas Nickleby
Pure Storytelling Bliss

The title given this novel for its serial publication (over nineteen months in 1837 through 1839) sums up its rambunctious plot: *The Life and Adventures of Nicholas Nickleby, Containing a Faithful Account of the Fortunes, Misfortunes, Uprisings, Downfallings and Complete Career of the Nickleby Family*. A descendant of the picaresque novels of Tobias Smollett (see page 733) and Henry Fielding (see page 273), *Nickleby* inherits from its literary forebears a penniless young hero who—equipped only with luck and native wit—must make his way in the world against forces of iniquity, depravity, and greed. Those evil attributes are embodied especially in Nicholas's dastardly uncle, Ralph, who is determined, out of sheer malice, to thwart his nephew's fortune, just as the Cheeryble brothers, Nicholas's eventual employers and perfect models of Dickensian benevolence, are determined to help him make it.

Before he gets to the Cheerybles, however, Nicholas is apprenticed by his uncle to Wackford Squeers, the very model of a modern wicked schoolmaster, whose educational establishment, Dotheboys (say it as three words: "Do-the-boys") Hall, provides ample opportunity for Dickens to attack the brutal conditions of contemporary boarding schools. Nicholas's subsequent adventures include a stint in a traveling theater company, depicted by the author with much relish and comic verve, and several encounters with the spiteful initiatives of his uncle, each designed to obstruct Nicholas's success or threaten the virtue and well-being of his sister and mother. With luck, stalwart friends, and a good heart, our hero, of course, triumphs, not without timely help from Newman Noggs, a failed gentleman impressed by poverty into the service of Ralph Nickleby—until he emerges from his own shadow to upset his employer's villainous designs.

What: Novel. *When:* 1837–39. *Also By: The Life and Adventures of Martin Chuzzlewit* (1842–44). *Try: The Expedition of Humphry Clinker* by Tobias Smollett (see page 733). *The History of Tom Jones, A Foundling* by Henry Fielding (see page 273). *Adaptations:* David Edgar's two-part, nine-hour theatrical presentation for the Royal Shakespeare Company brought new audiences to *Nickleby* in the 1980s in both England and America, and was filmed for television. Feature films from 1947 (directed by Alberto Cavalcanti) and 2002 (directed by Douglas McGrath) are also worth seeking out, as is the audiobook read by Simon Vance.

A Christmas Carol
From Humbug to the Happiest of Holidays

You know the story of this quintessential holiday tale, but have you ever read it? So many times has the tale been told—in numerous stage and screen adaptations—that we are apt to take the power of its invention for granted. Yet no retelling comes close to capturing the humor and human sympathy, the delicious spookiness and ultimate good cheer of Dickens's original narrative.

In less than a hundred pages, *A Christmas Carol* relates, with an imaginative richness that belies its brevity, how the crabbed soul of an uncaring old man, Ebenezer Scrooge, is summoned back to generous life by the visitations of four spirits: first the shade of his deceased business partner, Jacob Marley, and then the spirits of Christmas Past, Christmas Present, and Christmas Yet to Come. Through their hauntings, Scrooge is moved by fear and understanding to embrace the abandoned affections of his youth, confront the meanness of his current existence, and recognize the sordid end he'll meet if he does not change his ways.

All of the author's famous gifts are on display in this cheering fable of a miser's Christmas Eve metamorphosis from misanthrope to man of good will, including his talent for deft characterization (in the figure, for instance, of Scrooge's clerk, the put-upon but ever hopeful Bob Cratchit); for poignant sentiment (in the figure of Cratchit's lame son, Tiny Tim); and for ingenious monikers (was any curmudgeon ever more aptly named than Ebenezer Scrooge?). If the volume you are holding was nine hundred books shorter, *A Christmas Carol* would still be in it.

What: Novella. *When:* 1843. *Reading Note:* No story is better suited to a family read-aloud than *A Christmas Carol*. *Also By:* Dickens's other Christmas tales include *The Chimes* (1844) and *The Cricket on the Hearth* (1845). *Further Reading: The Man Who Invented Christmas* by Les Standiford. *Adaptations:* Beginning with Dickens's own spirited readings, dramatic presentations of the tale have been legion. On film, two especially worth watching are the versions from 1938 (starring Reginald Owen) and 1951 (starring Alastair Sim). Bill Murray played the lead in *Scrooged*, an enjoyable 1988 update. The animated television musical, *Mister Magoo's Christmas Carol* (1962) is something of a classic in its own right. For listening, the unabridged audiobook performance by Jim Dale is highly recommended.

19th-century illustration from A Christmas Carol

Dombey and Son
A Family's Fortune

The first novel that Dickens planned in detail before beginning composition, *Dombey and Son* marks a turning point in his development, ushering in the period of his mature works. Abandoning the pleasures of the picaresque and the improvisatory impulses of his earlier novels, it gains in their stead a surer sense of structure and thematic coherence, allowing Dickens to inform his story with a more focused social consciousness. As a result, in concert with telling the tale of a man of business and his family, the narrative of *Dombey and Son* illuminates the tumultuous changes wrought, in mid-nineteenth-century England, by the Industrial Revolution and the rise of mercantile culture.

In outline, the plot is simple: A successful shipping magnate, Paul Dombey, is desperate for a male heir to validate for the next generation the name of the family firm, Dombey and Son. His pride blinds him to the havoc his single-mindedness wreaks in the lives of his daughter, his ill-fated wife, and the sickly son she gives birth to, young Paul, who will die before he reaches adolescence. Around this frame are wrapped several comic, dramatic, and suspenseful sub-plots, as well as penetrating passages on the effects of new economic forces, which threaten—with the full support of Mr. Dombey—to transform human interaction to "a mere matter of bargain and sale, hiring and letting." The most powerful of these forces is the advent of the railroad, to which Dickens returns throughout the book, charting how its tracks disrupt the "law and custom" of every neighborhood they cleave, eventually pulling precincts and people into the magnetic influence of the economic development they speed. From the opening chapter, in which the word "house" is ominously informed by its dual meaning as both the family's home and the firm of Dombey and Son, to the last, in which Mr. Dombey reaches a level of self-knowledge that allows sentiment to temper strict calculation, the emotional strains of *Dombey and Son* echo those of *A Christmas Carol*—in a minor key, perhaps, but on a grander scale.

Throughout, Dickens writes with a confidence that makes this novel, although one of his lesser known, among his most satisfying.

What: Novel. *When:* 1846–48. *Also By: Hard Times* (1854). *Try: The Way We Live Now* by Anthony Trollope. *Buddenbrooks* by Thomas Mann. *Adaptation:* There is a compelling audiobook performance by Frederick Davidson. *Footnote:* Dickens's contemporary William Makepeace Thackeray, who was serializing his great novel *Vanity Fair* (see page 777) at the same time the publication of *Dombey and Son* was in progress, reportedly arrived at the office of the magazine *Punch* with his fellow writer's latest installment in hand, exclaiming, "There's no writing against such power as this—one has no chance! Read that chapter describing young Paul's death: it is unsurpassed—it is stupendous."

Bleak House

A Treasure House of Invention and Sentiment

Although it lacks the affectionate warmth of *David Copperfield* and the narrative unity of *Great Expectations*, *Bleak House* is considered by many critics to be its author's greatest achievement. Unlike those other two novels, which, of course, have their own ardent champions, *Bleak House* is not steeped in childhood or focused on the unfolding of a childhood's layers of hopes and sorrows in later life; it is a novel of adulthood, a nuanced exploration of social mores, economic and legal entanglement, romantic passion, mature love, and murderous envy.

Innovative in its structure, it is told in two distinct and alternating voices. The first—third-person, present tense, omniscient in perspective—ranges widely through the fashions and foibles of contemporary society, from the sclerotic and treacherous confusion of the Chancery courts to the dilettantish do-gooding of self-regarding philanthropy. Immediate and often satiric, this voice is contrasted with the first-person narration of Esther Summerson, an apparent orphan with a real heart of gold, whose modesty, capability, and emotional intelligence bring a reflective and generous cast to the storytelling.

Along with the dual narration, the complexity of the plot, which is fed by many tributaries, creates an atmosphere of obscure machination that is perfectly evoked by the novel's famous opening paragraphs, in which the actuality of all of London seems to be diffusing itself into a sodden, shadowy netherworld: "Fog everywhere. Fog up the river, where it flows among green aits and meadows; fog down the river, where it rolls defiled among the tiers of shipping." At the center of this netherworld, "at the very heart of the fog," Dickens writes, "sits the Lord High Chancellor in his High Court of Chancery." There, *Jarndyce v. Jarndyce*, the notoriously protracted case of a contested will that has consumed the best energies of several generations of litigants, spins its web of futility and disappointment—a web that, one way or another, ensnares the characters of *Bleak House*, from Esther to the young lovers, Ada Clare and Richard Capstone; from John Jarndyce, Esther's noble and gentle savior, to Sir Leicester and Lady Dedlock; from the homeless street sweeper, Jo, to the insidious attorney Tulkinghorn. As always in Dickens's best novels, the cast of ancillary personalities is rife with memorable actors, including the resolutely shiftless Howard Skimpole and the relentlessly observant Inspector Bucket, the first professional sleuth to play a central role in a major English novel.

This capacious book—it runs to nearly a thousand pages—seems to be a compendium of everything its author had learned about inventing characters and telling stories. It weaves several strands of popular (or soon to be popular) fiction—social satire, romance, sentimental education, the novel of sensation, and the detective story—into a single vast tapestry of reading that is surprising, intellectually compelling, and wholly satisfying.

What: Novel. *When:* 1852–53. *Also By: Little Dorrit* (1855–57). *Try: The Woman in White* by Wilkie Collins. *The Quincunx* by Charles Palliser. *Adaptations:* The BBC has produced three television versions of the novel, the award-winning, fifteen-episode

Dickens giving a public reading. Illustration by George C. Leighton, ca. 1870.

2005 miniseries being the most recent. Look for the audiobook read by Hugh Dickson.

A Tale of Two Cities
The Classic Novel of the French Revolution

It was the best of times, it was the worst of times, it was the age of wisdom, it was the age of foolishness, it was the epoch of belief, it was the epoch of incredulity, it was the season of Light, it was the season of Darkness, it was the spring of hope, it was the winter of despair . . .

A *Tale of Two Cities* may have the most famous opening of any novel ever written, the frequent application of its words outside the novel's specific context giving it an edge over the nearest competition, *Anna Karenina* (see page 799) and *Pride and Prejudice* (see page 33). Echoing the dichotomies invoked in its opening sentences, the work unfolds in a series of parallels and mirrorings, alternating between London and Paris in the years before and during the French Revolution. Indeed, the plot turns on the uncanny resemblance between two men, Charles Darnay and Sydney Carton, the first a progressive noble from an aristocratic, cruelly reactionary French family, the second a brilliant but dissolute English lawyer who both represents and resents Darnay, ultimately coming to his rescue when the Frenchman falls afoul of the Revolution's unforgiving fervor.

Despite being among its author's most widely read novels, A *Tale of Two Cities* is the least Dickensian. Swept along by the rapid movement of the complex plot, and the frantic history that propels it, the narrative reveals character through action and incident rather than through Dickens's more typical reliance on dialogue and personality quirks. Missing, too, is the sense of comedy that leavens and enlivens even the darkest of his other books. As a consequence, A *Tale of Two Cities* is the neatest storytelling contrivance in Dickens's oeuvre. Although it lacks the warmth and humor of his other tales, it has the alternately intimate and violent passions of the Revolution—both brilliantly embodied in the baleful figure of Madame Defarge, knitting and scheming with ruthless intensity—to meld its themes of vendetta, betrayal, regret, sacrifice, and resurrection into a headlong chronicle of historical drama and personal nobility. The pageant concludes with Carton's final thoughts, nearly as memorable in expression as the novel's first lines: "It is a far, far better thing that I do, than I have ever done; it is a far, far better rest that I go to than I have ever known."

What: Novel. *When:* 1859. *Also By: Barnaby Rudge* (1840–41). *Try: The French Revolution* by Thomas Carlyle. *History of the French Revolution* by Jules Michelet. *A Place of Greater Safety* by Hilary Mantel (see page 523). *Adaptations:* This is one of Dickens's most adapted tales, with many dramatizations for screen, stage, and radio. The most indelible is the 1935 MGM film starring Ronald Coleman as Sydney Carton. Richard Pasco's audiobook reading is superb.

Great Expectations
Destiny's Promises

L ike *David Copperfield*, *Great Expectations* is the story of a child's coming-of-age, told in the first person. Like *David Copperfield* as well, it is the story of a young man's coming to grips with his unassuming legacy and practical place in the world. More nuanced and darker in mood than the earlier novel, however, *Great Expectations* is its author's deepest working of the terrain of childhood and the fears and fates that spring from it. Anchored in a Kentish village, around which the years and events of the complicated plot will revolve, the book returns Dickens to his native ground in search not of autobiographical details, but of the familiar spirits and psychological tempers that nurtured his imagination: the injuries of class, the uncertainties of love, the snobberies of fashion, the limited purview of personal agency, the coincidence—or is it more?—that links crime and fortune, or goodness and inequity.

From the thrilling opening scene—in which the young Philip Pirrip (or simply Pip, as he introduces himself) is surprised on a visit to his parents' graveside by an escaped convict who presses the boy into his service—we are seized by the story and pulled into its embrace. As we follow Pip's progress—his thralldom to the alluring young Estella; his fascination with Miss Havisham (one of Dickens's greatest characters, a woman so traumatized by disappointment that she has sat for years, transfixed by loss, in the setting of her unconsummated wedding celebration); the arrival of his "great expectations" in the form of an inheritance whose source is mysterious; his estrangement from his good and noble brother-in-law, Joe Gargery—we are held rapt by the choreography of character, incident, and brilliantly paced suspense.

Dickens notoriously rewrote the final scene, mitigating the bleakness of his original ending to offer the promise of a fulfilling reconciliation between Pip and Estella. Whatever the particulars of the pair's destiny, the rich satisfactions of the novel remain. In the end, *Great Expectations* is not really about expectation at all, but about regret, and as powerfully so as any book in our language. Where Pip's literary sibling David Copperfield is discovering his future, making his way in the world, the protagonist of *Great Expectations* is uncovering his past, illuminating all the shadows of the self that remembrance can conjure. Moving with narrative verve between London and the countryside, the book depicts in vivid colors the humbling of youthful presumptions by the inscrutable and—for the lucky, at least—wisdom-inducing quandaries of life.

What: Novel. *When:* 1861. *Also By: Our Mutual Friend* (1864–65). *Try: Jack Maggs* by Peter Carey. *Mister Pip* by Lloyd Jones. *Adaptations:* David Lean's 1946 film, starring John Mills as Pip, is the best cinematic adaptation of any Dickens novel, and one of the most celebrated movies of all time. The audiobook read by Martin Jarvis is every bit as praiseworthy.

Poems
Emily Dickinson (1830–1886)

Literature's Most Famous Nobody

I'm Nobody! Who are you?
Are you—Nobody—Too?

Emily Dickinson has what may be the most distinctive voice in American poetry. Immediately recognizable, it is modest and intimate, often invoking an inviting sense of potentiality: "'Hope' is the thing with feathers— / That perches in the soul—" begins one poem, and here's the first stanza of another:

I dwell in Possibility—
A fairer House than Prose—
More numerous of Windows—
Superior—for Doors—

And yet there's a streak of wild darkness animating her verse as well, which, combined with an elliptical syntax, can bring the reader up short with mysterious evocations:

Daguerreotype of Emily Dickinson, ca. 1846

My Life had stood—a Loaded Gun—
In Corners—till a Day
The Owner passed—identified—
And carried Me away—

The myth of Emily Dickinson is that she lived her life shut away in a room in her father's house, dressed in white, churning out poems nobody knew about until they were found in a drawer after her death. And this legend is partly true. Dickinson was granddaughter to an Amherst College founder and daughter to a congressman who had reservations about educating women. "He buys me many Books," she once wrote, "but begs me not to read them—because he fears they joggle the Mind." Nonetheless, Dickinson was educated; she had suitors and romantic attachments, but rejected marriage proposals, choosing the life of a recluse over more typical paths for a middle-class woman in Civil War America. She did write poems endlessly, from the time she was a child until her death, and she occasionally sought the opinions of friends and advisers about the quality of the work. A handful of poems were published during her lifetime. She might have published more, but in the same way that she chose solitude over what she perceived as servitude, she seems to have preferred to keep her poetry to herself rather than have anyone edit it or try to influence the way she wrote.

Unlike the popular romantic poetry of the era, and much like herself, Dickinson's poetry is enigmatic.

Tell all the Truth but tell it slant—
Success in Circuit lies

But the enigmas of her imagery and expression sound notes with a bell-like beauty and precision; even at her most gnomic, as in the lines just quoted, she writes with an oracular confidence that echoes with deep resonance despite the fact that her exact meaning is hard to parse (in this quality, her most unexpected descendant in the family tree of American poetry may be Bob Dylan).

Although she must have been buffeted by the winds of her time—religious fervor, civil war—very little of their sway can be felt in her poetry. She counseled against mistaking the "I" in any poem for the poet. Although her tumultuous friendships and amorous affairs are no doubt reflected in her writing, their real-life coordinates are hard to plot. All of this has added to her peculiar stature as one of literature's great unsolved mysteries, and may also explain her poetry's nearly universal appeal. She wasn't writing about her *life* so much as she was writing about *life*. And death:

Because I could not stop for Death—
He kindly stopped for me—
The Carriage held but just Ourselves—
And Immortality.

What: Poetry. *When:* The first volume of Dickinson's poetry was published in 1890, but this and other early editions of her work were not always faithful to the author's intentions. The poems were properly edited and collected for the first time, in three volumes, in the 1955 Harvard University Press edition. *Further Reading: My Wars Are Laid Away in Books: The Life of Emily Dickinson* by Alfred Habegger. *Lives Like Loaded Guns: Emily Dickinson and Her Family's Feuds* by Lyndall Gordon. *Try:* The poems of E. E. Cummings (see page 188), Marianne Moore, and Louise Bogan.

The Year of Magical Thinking
Joan Didion (born 1934)

The Gravity of Grief

"We tell ourselves stories in order to live," begins the title piece in Joan Didion's famous 1979 collection of essays, *The White Album*. What exactly, an older Didion asks in *The Year of Magical Thinking*, do we tell ourselves when death sits down at our dinner table?

On December 30, 2003, Didion and her husband, the novelist John Gregory Dunne, went to a hospital to visit their daughter, Quintana, who was in an induced coma as part of a severe course of treatment for a mysterious illness and septic shock. Later that evening, they returned to their Manhattan apartment and sat down to dinner. They talked about their day. In the middle of their conversation, John slumped in his chair, raised his hand, and died.

"John was talking, then he wasn't," Didion writes in this spare and deeply affecting mourning diary, one of the most significant books of recent times to reckon with the weight and obligations imposed by death, and by the untethering from normalcy grief brings. "This is my attempt," Didion tells her readers, and herself, "to make sense of the period that followed, weeks and then months that cut loose any fixed idea I had ever had about death, about illness, about probability and luck, about good fortune and bad, about marriage and children and memory, about grief, about the ways in which people do and do not deal with the fact that life ends, about the shallowness of sanity, about life itself."

In the months after her husband's death (her year of "magical thinking," or imagining that circumstances can change if only she wishes hard enough), Didion falls prey to crippling bereavement, her grief a state of strange, unstinting siege. She turns to science in search of impossible answers, and speaks to friends only to discover that their friendship provides no succor. All she can do—slowly, uncertainly—is start to make sentences, erecting, to steal her own words from another context, "a barricade against some deep apprehension of meaninglessness." The author's keen discernment, with which she had previously illuminated America's cultural anxieties and political fictions through four decades of essays and novels, must now describe the most elusive of phenomena: absence.

What is most moving in Didion's anatomy of grief is that it offers no false comfort. In the wake of tragedy, we may hope to find in books some testament that the worst will pass if only we "work through" our pain. Nothing doing. Coming to terms with death, Didion shows us, means coming to the only terms it allows, which are the same as life's, but lonelier: "We tell ourselves stories in order to live." And there's something so true and nourishing in the telling here that *The Year of Magical Thinking* seems—paradoxically—a necessary, life-enhancing miracle, and a boon to those whose grief is boundless.

What: Memoir. *When:* 2005. *Award:* National Book Award for Nonfiction, 2005. *Also By: Slouching Towards Bethlehem* (1968). *The White Album* (1979). *After Henry* (1992). *Blue Nights* (2011). *Try: A Grief*

Joan Didion with husband John Gregory Dunne, 1976

Observed by C. S. Lewis (see page 486). *A Widow's Story* by Joyce Carol Oates. *Say Her Name* by Francisco Goldman. *The Iceberg: A Memoir* by Marion Coutts. *Adaptation:* Didion's stage adaptation of the book premiered on Broadway in 2007, starring Vanessa Redgrave. *Footnote:* In the course of Didion's mourning, her daughter's health worsened. Quintana died before *The Year of Magical Thinking* was published, but Didion did not revise her manuscript in the face of this new loss; instead, she published a second volume, *Blue Nights* (2011), which tackles the altogether different sorrow of a mother outliving her child.

Pilgrim at Tinker Creek
Annie Dillard (born 1945)

Stalking Wonder

"Never lose a holy curiosity," Einstein said. That's one of the dozens of valuable quotations a reader gleans from *Pilgrim at Tinker Creek*, a book suffused with the very quality the great physicist urges us not to surrender. Part naturalist, part metaphysician, a self-described "wanderer with a background in theology and a penchant for quirky facts," Dillard is a visionary in the exact sense; although her sight is fixed firmly on the physical world of muskrats and monarch butterflies, snakeskins and pond water, it is powerful enough to discern that science, at its most profound, is first and last a form of contemplation.

"I am not a scientist," Dillard insists. "I explore the neighborhood." The neighborhood is a valley in Virginia's Blue Ridge, and it boasts a creek that flows with water, life, and wonder; luckily for the reader, the explorations of the author are fed just as steadily by a river of reading that nourishes the ruminations the native flora and fauna inspire. In the fifteen essays gathered here, Dillard bears witness to the passing glories of the seasons and nature's enduring beauty and violence. The personal narrative she unhurriedly unravels through her descriptions of her outings, her study of grasshoppers and praying mantises, her observation of newts and herons—to say nothing of her engagement with the thoughts of sages as diverse as Werner Heisenberg and Julian of Norwich—is vivid and intimate. As a result, her prose excursions are ideal invitations to contemplation; they're like walks in the woods between covers.

What: Nature. Essays. Memoir. *When:* 1974. *Award:* Pulitzer Prize for General Nonfiction, 1975. *Also By:* Essays and Memoir: *Holy the Firm* (1977); *Living by Fiction* (1982); *Teaching a Stone to Talk* (1982); *An American Childhood* (1987); *The Writing Life* (1989); *For the Time Being* (1999). Fiction: *The Living* (1992); *The Maytrees* (2007). *Further Reading:* Marius von Senden's *Space and Sight*, collecting accounts of people, blinded by cataracts since birth, whose vision was surgically restored, is a book you will want to seek out after reading Dillard's essay "Seeing." *Try: Walden* by Henry David Thoreau (see page 786). *The Primal Place* by Robert Finch. *A Natural History of the Senses* by Diane Ackerman.

Winter's Tales
Isak Dinesen (1885–1962)

A Twentieth-Century Scheherazade

The author of these unforgettable tales is hidden in two layers of disguise. The first is a pen name that might lead the unsuspecting to think this modern Danish master— "Never heard of him"—was a man. The second is a life on the big screen that has obscured her achievement as one of the most enchanting writers of the twentieth century.

Her real name was Karen (Dinesen) Blixen, and she wrote two loose versions of her life story, first in *Out of Africa* (1937) and again in *Shadows on the Grass* (1960). The 1985 film of the former introduced millions of moviegoers to Blixen—played by Meryl Streep—as a baroness in colonial Kenya, a woman who fell in love with aloof men and told exotic tales over long, quiet dinners at her farm "at the foot of the Ngong Hills." That she grew coffee and had a penchant for unfortunate liaisons was quite clear; that she was an artist of extravagant gifts was not.

Although she wrote poetry and a treatise *On Modern Marriage* while in Africa, her literary career began in earnest upon her return to Denmark in the early 1930s. Curiously enough, her first literary success was in America, where *Seven Gothic Tales* became a sensation as a Book-of-the-Month Club selection in 1934. In that book, and in the even more haunting *Winter's Tales*, Dinesen carved out a distinctive niche in modern letters. Writing in a stately, distinctive English (she translated her works back into her native tongue for their Danish publication), Dinesen created an atmosphere that blended the abiding steadiness of the fairy tale with the heightened psychic sensitivities of Gothic themes. The apprehension that her style creates is complemented by what might be called the intrinsically foreign, at times even otherworldly, nature of her settings. Like the lord in "Sorrow-Acre," one of the eleven pieces collected in *Winter's Tales*, the reader of Dinesen always seems "to be walking, and standing, in a kind of eternity"—a timelessness we recognize as the realm of the storyteller.

One of the author's very best tales, "Sorrow-Acre" has at its core a brutal bargain the lord makes with a woman whose son is being held on suspicion of having committed a crime. To win her boy's liberty, the old woman must, with her own hands, mow a large field in a single day. From this simple premise, and in less than forty pages, Dinesen weaves a tale that is breathtakingly wise in its illumination of innocence and experience and in its understanding of the "salvation and beatification" that tragedy supplies to human lives. From a small, circumscribed plot of land, and from the eternal human plots of necessity, desire, and fate, Dinesen harvests a vision of existence that is unflinching and revelatory in its truth and beauty.

Other stories in *Winter's Tales* relate, with similar magical effect, the progress of an author's despair, the masquerade of an ardent lover, the dreams of a child, and the longing of a king. Suffused with both the ominous darkness and the glad promise of folktales, they are polished to a gem-like brilliance by this modern master's singular finesse.

What: Short Stories. *When:* 1942. *Also By:* Fiction: *Last Tales* (1957); *Anecdotes of Destiny* (1958; containing what may be Dinesen's most famous story, "Babette's Feast"); *Ehrengard* (1963). *Further Reading:* Judith Thurman's biography, *Isak Dinesen: The Life of a Storyteller*, is fascinating and first-rate. *Try: Stories of Three Decades* by Thomas Mann. *Kingdoms of Elfin* by Sylvia Townsend Warner.

■ For Michael Dirda's *Bound to Please*, see page 209.

Ragtime
E. L. Doctorow (1931–2015)

A Dazzling Tale of the Turn of the Twentieth Century

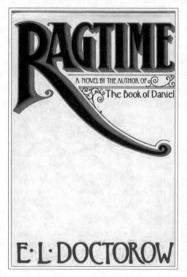

E. L. Doctorow's shelf of twelve novels is well worth reading end to end—not in a binge-reading rush, but at a measured pace, say one every year or two. For the reader doing so, the true dimensions of the author's imagination will take on a proper sense of majesty. From *The Book of Daniel* (1971), his immersive fictional foray into the public and private aftershocks of the trial and execution of Julius and Ethel Rosenberg, to his powerful portrayal of the hypnotic force and violent trauma of battle in *The March* (2005), his novel about General William Tecumseh Sherman and the end of the Civil War, each individual work has its own distinctive artifice and literary poise. Together, they reveal a nuanced, profound apprehension of history, memory, and mortality, and of the lives we live in their midst and at their mercies.

The most famous work on that shelf, of course, is *Ragtime*, which won enormous popularity and critical acclaim well before the success of the film and Broadway adaptations. The book is first and foremost a good read, animated with complex characters, real and invented, and several absorbing plotlines that intersect in the narrative's ingenious design. The overarching story is about a well-to-do family in New

Rochelle, a suburban satellite of Manhattan, as the twentieth century begins. A second family, immigrant and Jewish, enters the action from Manhattan's Lower East Side, where the father, a street vendor of his own artful paper-and-scissor creations, and his young daughter (especially) catch the eye of the notorious Evelyn Nesbit, one of America's first cover girls. Nesbit's husband, Harry K. Thaw, is on trial for murdering Nesbit's seducer, the architect Stanford White. In addition to the triangle of lovers, whose escapades are lifted more or less directly from the tabloids of the time, many other historical figures occupy places on Doctorow's pages (albeit often engaged in nonhistorical acts), from the anarchist Emma Goldman and the reformer Jacob Riis to the escape artist Harry Houdini, the financier J. P. Morgan, the industrialist Henry Ford, and, lest we make an unintended slip, Sigmund Freud, who amusingly visits Niagara Falls. A third family is introduced in the shape of a newborn infant abandoned in the garden of the first family's house in New Rochelle. The baby is the child of a black maid and a ragtime pianist, Coalhouse Walker, whose forays into radical politics—or, depending on your point of view,

quest for social justice—will drive the story to its explosive conclusion.

The layering of fiction and fact, ephemera and history, headline news and private heartache is alluring, giving the book a surface glamour that is at once entertaining and compelling. Equally captivating are the juxtapositions of poverty and wealth, leisure and labor, sex and politics, idea and emotion. And although it is lucidly declarative, it is peculiarly told: There is a matter-of-factness to Doctorow's prose, no matter how outlandish its content, that keeps the telling—appropriately enough given the book's title—a little offbeat. The narrative itself is syncopated, playing off our expectations of history to present an entirely new music, one that holds us in thrall and creates no little sense of wonder.

What: Novel. *When:* 1975. *Awards:* National Book Critics Circle Award, 1975. *Also By: Loon Lake* (1980). *Billy Bathgate* (1989). *The Waterworks* (1994). *Try: Michael Kohlhaas* by Heinrich von Kleist. *Legs* by William Kennedy. *The Alienist* by Caleb Carr. *Adaptations:* The 1981 film was directed by Milos Forman; the musical, with book by Terrence McNally, lyrics by Lynn Ahrens, and music by Stephen Flaherty, had its original Broadway production in 1998.

This House of Sky
LANDSCAPES OF A WESTERN MIND
Ivan Doig (1939–2015)

Memoirs of a Montana Childhood

"In the last year of the 1960s," the author wrote about the genesis of this book, "when this country was going through convulsive self-questioning, I was as usual out of step. It was getting clearer and clearer to me what I was in life. I was a relic." In this, Ivan Doig was like his father, Charlie, and his maternal grandmother, Bessie Ringer, who together had raised him. *This House of Sky* is the story of these three survivors, and of the environment—the hardscrabble world of Montana sheep ranching—that shaped them all, and which they each outlasted.

The book begins with the death of the six-year-old Ivan's mother, and follows the

boy through summers of sheep and winters of sheep and snow—through weeks, months, and years in which Charlie's resourceful toil on farms and ranches remains, always, at the mercy of the intractable weather. Even the communities that welcome the Doigs are seasonal, coming and going like the snows. Short on luck, they are long on love, especially when ranch cook Bessie joins Charlie and his father to form an uneasy but inseparable trio.

All this gives you no idea that *This House of Sky* is one of the most beautiful books you will ever read. Doig was blessed—as his choice of "relic" above indicates—with a gift for refreshing common experience and everyday struggle with the benediction of the right words.

In powerful writing about the landscape of Montana and the influence it has exerted on the spirit and culture of its inhabitants; about ranching and its associated works and days; about memory, family, and all the ramifications of kinship, Doig poignantly charts the translation of experience from labor to language across the generations.

What: Memoir. *When:* 1978. *Also By:* Memoir: *Heart Earth* (1993). Other nonfiction: *Winter Brothers: A Season at the Edge of America* (1980). Novels: *English Creek* (1984); *Dancing at the Rascal Fair* (1987); *The Whistling Season* (2006); *The Bartender's Tale* (2012). *Try: The Big Rock Candy Mountain* by Wallace Stegner.

Poems and Sermons
John Donne (1572–1631)

Setting Body and Soul to Words

No *man is an island. For whom the bell tolls. Death be not proud.* John Donne's most famous phrases come down to us as if from a pulpit, wearing the solemn dress of the meditations and devotions from which they spring. And although he was indeed a brilliant religious writer in both verse and prose, his reputation as the greatest of the seventeenth-century English Metaphysical poets rests as much on poems of a more earthly nature. The descriptor "metaphysical" was coined by Samuel Johnson and applied, in a not especially laudatory way, to the penchant for Donne and others of his poetic ilk (notably Andrew Marvell and George Herbert) to embed their intellectual embrace of experience in extended conceits, such as the one in which Donne compares his lover's body to the New World:

> Licence my roving hands, and let them go
> Before, behind, between, above, below.
> O my America, my new found land,
> My kingdom, safeliest when with one man
>   manned,
> My mine of precious stones, my empery,
> How blessed am I in this discovering thee!

In this and other gorgeously frisky love poems, Donne conjures an amorous playfulness that is as physical as it is metaphysical, and sexy even today.

Erotic ingenuity is not the only way the physicality of Donne's writing strikes us: No poet in English before him, and few if any after, have exhibited with such relish and authority a grasp of the weight, force, and material substance of individual words, as in this beginning of the most famous of his *Holy Sonnets* (spirituality, apparently, stripped no vehemence from his poetic impulse):

> Batter my heart, three-personed God; for, you
> As yet but knock, breathe, shine, and seek to
>   mend;
> That I may rise, and stand, o'erthrow me, and
>   bend
> Your force, to break, blow, burn, and make
>   me new.

The sequence of single-syllable words, the collision of their sound-shapes, the headlong impetuosity—violence, even—of his importuning of the Lord is stunning, yet wrought with as much care as his intricate similes. Donne's art, in the prose of his sermons on mortality and salvation as well as in his poetry, is one of construction as much as thought: He chooses his materials and fits them together in the same way a joiner builds a cabinet, creating objects that are strong, useful, enduring, beautiful. Unexpected speech rhythms give his lines a tension between relaxation and constraint that moves across the two extremes of his sensibility—sensual and religious—and defines a style wholly his own (a few lines of Donne are as surely identifiable as a few bars of Stravinsky). Fit for both pleasure and contemplation, his words provide an absorbing consolation, be their intended enchantment in this world or the next.

What: Poetry. Religion & Spirituality. **When:** 1612–33. **Edition:** *The Complete Poetry and Selected Prose of John Donne*, edited by Charles M. Coffin and issued by the Modern Library, is an excellent collection of the essential works. **Try:** The poetry of Andrew Marvell and George Herbert. Prose works by Sir Thomas Browne (see page 102). **Adaptation:** *The Holy Sonnets of John Donne* is a 1945 song cycle composed by Benjamin Britten.

U.S.A.

THE 42ND PARALLEL • 1919 • THE BIG MONEY
John Dos Passos (1896–1970)

E Pluribus Unum

John Dos Passos's trilogy U.S.A.—comprising *The 42nd Parallel* (1930), *1919* (1932), and *The Big Money* (1936)—stands today like an unvisited historical monument in the annals of American literature, a Grant's Tomb of the bookshelf. Despite its acceptance as a classic, and its being ranked twenty-third on the Modern Library list of the 100 best English-language novels of the twentieth century, it seems to be little read today. Yet Dos Passos's innovative, panoramic documentary of America's emergence from its nineteenth-century cocoon onto the world stage during and after World War I is as timely a piece of fiction as one could imagine encountering in the echo chamber of our contemporary political discourse.

Dos Passos's works are not conventional novels, but rather collages of "newsreels," stream of consciousness descriptions, set pieces offering capsule biographies of inventors and thinkers such as Thomas Edison, the Wright Brothers, Thorstein Veblen, and Charles Steinmetz, and running narratives following the development of a handful of characters. They were bold at the time of writing and remain striking today. As Alfred Kazin astutely writes of the first book in the series, "We soon recognize that Dos Passos's contraption, his new kind of novel, is in fact . . . the greatest character in the book itself."

U.S.A. is like a vast history painting, a montage of carefully constructed panels juxtaposed to create a composite "voice" more vivid, more resourceful, more impersonal, and more capacious than that heard in ordinary literary composition. Dos Passos wanted to find a wavelength strong enough to broadcast the speech of the people entire, with all its messy and often anguished noise. In the end, the variegated prose of these books brings into sharp focus the faults at the core of our national identity, then and now. Immigrants of different nationalities are greeted with an all-too-familiar fear and aggression ("those damn lousy furreners"), and the realization of the gulf between the haves and the have-nots—be it having economic power, political means, or constabulary force—is similarly recognizable: "all right we are two nations," we read as *The Big Money* approaches its conclusion in the turmoil surrounding the trial and execution of Sacco and Vanzetti.

Through it all, we revel in the author's keen eye for the headlines, news flashes, and song lyrics that shaped the public mind in the first flush of mass media (how prescient Dos Passos was in his understanding of both its stimulating and stupefying effects). So although the trilogy may be at times dated in expression, it is also alive with a kind of scriptural foreshadowing, intuitive in its understanding of our enduring national character and the conflicts at the core of it—between capitalism and the commonweal, finance and labor, the individual and the community, the familiar and the strange, the little guy and the big guy, us and them. Indeed, if U.S.A. has been out of fashion, it may be time for it to come back in: It's like a reading of the entrails of American modernity, a prophecy that is wise to the collective nature of the democratic enterprise and therefore alert to the disillusion that can threaten it when our sense of all-being-in-this-together is more real as phantom than as fact.

What: Novels. *When:* 1930–36. *Also By: Three Soldiers* (1921). *Manhattan Transfer* (1925). District of Columbia Trilogy: *Adventures of a Young Man* (1939); *Number One* (1943); *The Grand Design* (1949). *Try: Berlin Alexanderplatz* by Alfred Döblin. *The Grapes of Wrath* by John Steinbeck (see page 752). *History* by Elsa Morante (see page 565).

FYODOR DOSTOEVSKY
(1821–1881)

I ntensity is the currency of Dostoevsky's literary legacy: No one before him had used the novel so violently, unleashing in fiction the darkest urgencies of human psychology well before analysts annotated and therapists thought to tame them. Whereas his contemporary Tolstoy tried to write the world, charting a path toward unearthly empathy along itineraries that embraced life's matter-of-factness at every step, Dostoevsky probed the interior lives of sinners and searchers and gave them a terrifying imaginative reality that would hold readers rapt. All of his books, even his own notebooks, are expeditions into the

Statue of Dostoevsky at the Russian State Library

terra incognita of the self, exploring psychological states as if they were organisms with their own pathologies. In this, he was both ahead of his time and behind it, for just as he foretold Freud's scrutiny of the unconscious, so he reconfigured a universe of religious impulses, of demons and dread and despair, in naturalistic rather than supernatural terms. Without the certitudes of dogma to steady belief, faith itself became more essential and more ominous. His radical skepticism about positivist views of political progress or human nature seemed, to generations of writers who followed him, more true to life than Tolstoy's ultimate magnanimity, and much of modern literature, from psychological thrillers to existential dramas, springs from Dostoevsky's fertile, fevered brain.

Crime and Punishment
The Original Psychological Thriller—
Still Thrillingly Original

Is life unfair? Is circumstance fate? Can we ever take the law into our own hands to change it? Fyodor Dostoevsky's first major novel poses these questions in the tale of a man who enacts brutal crimes in order to break the strictures of his social destiny. For Rodion Romanovich Raskolnikov, the handsome but penniless "ex-student" at the center of *Crime and Punishment*, the Saint Petersburg of the 1860s is a cesspit of nepotists and shysters. He convinces himself it would be no worse off without a certain greedy pawnbroker; it might even be a better place if she were eliminated. Surely, he thinks, he'd use her money more productively than she does. Killing her would not only be a demonstration of his moral superiority, but an act of altruism for society at large.

Not surprisingly, Raskolnikov's actions have consequences he does not anticipate, and in the aftermath of his murders of the moneylender and her sister, the reader is plunged into the roiling psychological weather that shadows a man so arrogant and deluded that he believes himself a sort of Napoleon, above the laws of state and God. The ensuing storm engulfs his harried family, friends, and acquaintances, driving the plot through a landscape of cruelty, guilt, nihilism, love, poverty, and compassion that is as gripping as it is harrowing.

When he wrote this bleak tale of immorality and desperate (and uncertain) redemption, Dostoevsky himself was teetering on the edge of financial ruin; he had recently returned from exile in Siberia, his magazine had folded, and he was under such tight deadlines that he had to write both this novel and *The Gambler* at the same time. But those pressures helped Dostoevsky forge, in *Crime and Punishment*, a story that retains its searing presence a century and a half later. Of all the big, fat Russian novels of the nineteenth century, this one may be the most accessible—and the questions it poses about our desires and responsibilities remain as fresh as ever.

What: Novel. **When:** 1866. **Edition:** The 1992 translation by Richard Pevear and Larissa Volokhonsky is the recommended contemporary version. **Also By:** *The Double* (1846). **Further Reading:** "Dostoevsky's Unabomber" by Cynthia Ozick, collected in *Quarrel and Quandary*. **Try:** *Brighton Rock* by Graham Greene. *The Fall* by Albert Camus. *An American Dream* by Norman Mailer.

Notes from Underground
The Outsider Steps In

A tour de force of authorial concentration and psychological acuity, Dostoevsky's groundbreaking novella invites us into the bowels of mid-nineteenth-century Saint Petersburg, even as it charts a stylistic and thematic course for a great deal of modern fiction to be written beyond Russian borders. A very unreliable narrator—he's never named, though critics refer to him as the Underground Man—can't wait to show us how miserable life can be. "I am a sick man . . . ," his testament begins.

"I am a wicked man. An unattractive man. I think my liver hurts."

Spiteful, angry, self-obsessed, and neurotic in the extreme, the Underground Man has quit his job as a midlevel government functionary and lives, at forty, in a wretched room. Addressing his story to an audience of educated Russians he both envies and despises, he launches into a heated rant about free will and fantasies of progress, mocking new philosophical ideas and lambasting the endless potential of our species for self-delusion. Stopping and starting, apologizing for his vehemence and then lashing out anew, the Underground Man is clearly unbalanced, teetering on the edge of an abyss he can't help staring into.

In the book's second half, as he reminisces on his former life, we find his behavior in society as perverse as his meditations at home. A piddling slight by an officer at a tavern leads to pages and pages of resentment, culminating in an absurd attempt at vengeance that the officer doesn't even notice. A dinner party, at which he hates everyone in attendance, ends in social disgrace. And a brief infatuation with a prostitute, whom he attempts to save and then abandons, marks his final descent to his underground misery.

Although the narrator is always on the brink of collapse, the author is in total control, skewering the utilitarian and positivist ideals gaining currency in Russia at the time of writing. Indeed, Dostoevsky's lack of faith in human progress infuriated many of the novella's contemporary readers, not least socialists who were horrified by his portrait of humanity as irrational and impulsive. Today, however, *Notes from Underground* endures less as a political text than as a bold, brilliant character study, an indelible portrait of a man at the margins. It doesn't just pave the way for Dostoevsky's later, grander novels of alienation: In its rambling form and philosophical complexity, *Notes from Underground* paves the way for the entirety of modernism.

What: Novella. **When:** 1864. **Edition:** Of the many available translations, that of Richard Pevear and Larissa Volokhonsky stands out. **Also By:** *The House of the Dead* (1862). **Try:** *Journey to the End of the Night* by Louis-Ferdinand Céline (see page 140). *Invisible Man* by Ralph Ellison (see page 252).

The Brothers Karamazov
"The most magnificent novel ever written."
—Sigmund Freud

Dostoevsky's final novel is one of the supreme achievements in all fiction. It creates "an impression of controlled and measured grandeur," according to Joseph Frank, the author's biographer, "a grandeur that spontaneously evokes comparison with the greatest creations of Western literature. *The Divine Comedy, Paradise Lost, King Lear, Faust*—these are the titles that naturally come to mind as one tries to measure the stature of *The Brothers Karamazov.*"

At the heart of Dostoevsky's story is a crime—the murder of the loathsome Fyodor Karamazov. Each of his sons seems to be implicated. The prime suspect is the eldest, Dmitri, a spendthrift playboy whose hatred of his father boils over when they become rivals for a woman named Grushenka. Ivan and Alyosha are Fyodor's sons from his second marriage. An intellectual, Ivan subscribes to all the fashionable -isms: rationalism, atheism, nihilism. Alyosha, by contrast, is a man of faith and a novice in the local monastery. Completing the dysfunctional family circle is the repellent Pavel Smerdyakov. He's Fyodor's flunky but is rumored to be his illegitimate son as well. Simply put, these brothers are not only larger-than-life, but bigger than practically any other figures in literature, especially in the dimensions of their interior lives. Dostoevsky gives extraordinary expressive energy to each of them; like many of his novels, this one proceeds by dramatic argument in page upon page of intense, often philosophical dialogue. And the moral stakes could not be higher, for *The Brothers Karamazov* dramatizes with unmatched vigor the conflict between reason and faith, exploring questions about free will, human suffering, and whether "everything is permitted" if there is no God (questions perhaps most famously encapsulated in Ivan's unforgettable tale of The Grand Inquisitor).

"Perhaps no novel of [Dostoevsky's] was so slowly and deliberately written," critic Ernest J. Simmons once mused about *The Brothers Karamazov*, "as though he felt that his immortality would rest upon this work alone." It doesn't— but it could.

What: Novel. *When:* 1880. *Edition:* Published in 1990, Richard Pevear's and Larissa Volokhonsky's revelatory translation won the PEN/Book-of-the-Month Club Translation Prize. *Also By: The Idiot* (1868). *The Possessed* (1872). *Further Reading: Dostoevsky,* Joseph Frank's five-volume biography. *Dostoevsky: The Making of a Novelist* by Ernest J. Simmons. *Try: The Greek Passion* by Nikos Kazantzakis (see page 432). *Adaptation:* The 1958 film stars Yul Brenner, William Shatner, and Richard Basehart as the brothers.

Narrative of the Life of Frederick Douglass, an American Slave

Frederick Douglass (1818–1895)

An Unparalleled Testament of Suffering, Liberty, and Eloquence

In the 1840s, Frederick Douglass was touring the country as an orator with the Anti-Slavery Society, describing to rapt audiences the horrors of America's institutionalized bondage and persecution. His eloquence and passion won him renown, but also stoked rumors that he had never been a slave at all, for how could any former field hand speak like Cicero? Dismayed and hungry for justice, Douglass sat down to write this first version of his autobiography; its success didn't just silence his detractors, it brought new power to the growing chorus of citizens raising their voices in support of abolition.

As Douglass relates on the opening page of his narrative, his father was a white man, perhaps the master of the plantation on which he was born. While still in infancy, he was separated from his mother, Harriet Bailey: "I never saw my mother, to know her as such, more than four or five times in my life; and each of these times was very short in duration, and at night." Growing up enslaved, the young Frederick witnessed awful brutality, including the savage whipping of his aunt, and felt the fear that held slaves in its grip. As he approached adolescence, he was sent to serve a family in Baltimore, where his new master's wife began to teach him the alphabet. The master angrily stopped the lessons, since teaching a slave to

Daguerreotype of Frederick Douglass, 1848

read was both dangerous and illegal. But the interruption proved to be a turning point for Douglass, as he relates:

Though conscious of the difficulty of learning without a teacher, I set out with high hope, and a fixed purpose, at whatever cost of trouble, to learn how to read. The very decided manner with which he spoke, and strove to impress his wife with the evil consequences of giving me instruction, served to convince me that he was deeply sensible of the truths he was uttering. It gave me the best assurance that I might rely with the utmost confidence on the results which, he said, would flow from teaching me to read. What he most dreaded, that I most desired.

Later Douglass worked at the home of a cruel young master, where he had to beg and steal to have enough to eat, and was lent to the horrific Edward Covey, on whose farm Douglass was "made to drink the bitterest dregs of slavery." Worked to the bone, beaten without cause, Douglass soon rose up against Covey and eventually escaped to the north—although in this book he doesn't disclose how, since he refuses to risk shutting "the slightest avenue by which a brother slave might clear himself of the chains and fetters of slavery."

Douglass's *Narrative* was not the first account by a former American slave of life in bondage, but it was undoubtedly the most influential. It was such a success, in fact, that Douglass briefly fled to Britain amid fears he could be recaptured. While in Britain he was able to raise funds—$710.96—to purchase his emancipation. He wrote further autobiographical installments, covering his experiences during and after the Civil War, but the original *Narrative* remains his enduring literary achievement, bearing compelling witness to America's racial injustice and to the character and courage of those who struggled to abolish it.

What: Autobiography. *When:* 1845. *Also By: My Bondage and My Freedom* (1855). *Life and Times of Frederick Douglass* (1881). *Further Reading: Frederick Douglass* by William S. McFeely. *Try: Incidents in the Life of a Slave Girl* by Harriet Jacobs. *Up from Slavery* by Booker T. Washington (see page 836). *The Autobiography of Malcolm X* (see page 876). *To Be a Slave* by Julius Lester.

"Dreiser's great first novel, Sister Carrie, which he dared to publish thirty long years ago and which I read twenty-five years ago, came to housebound and airless America like a great free Western wind, and to our stuffy domesticity gave us the first fresh air since Mark Twain and Whitman." —*Sinclair Lewis, Nobel Prize Lecture, 1930*

Sister Carrie
Theodore Dreiser (1871–1945)

The Price of Success

In the opening scene of Theodore Dreiser's first novel, *Sister Carrie*, Caroline Meeber, eighteen years old, wearing a plain blue dress and worn shoes, is on a train bound for Chicago. "Dreaming wild dreams of some vague, far-off supremacy," she has four dollars in her bag and an equally vague plan to live with her sister until . . . what? Soon enough disillusioned by the reality of her meager new life, she will scrape and scheme and love and fall on hard times—use and be used—before ultimately finding the material success she seeks, as an actress in New York City.

Grudgingly published in 1900, and only after expurgations at the behest of Dreiser's publishers, the book was not promoted and found limited distribution, although it still managed to shock the establishment attention that fell upon it, as Kate Chopin's *The Awakening* (see page 158) had the previous year. As with Chopin's novel, what disturbed readers even more than Carrie's disreputable choices was the fact that Dreiser didn't make her pay for them: She comes out on top, whereas the opposite is true for George Hurstwood, the married man she runs away with, who descends from worldly success to destitution and despair.

The utter commercial failure of *Sister Carrie* would keep Dreiser from writing another book for some time, but he eventually regained his creative footing in a series of works, culminating in *An American Tragedy* in 1925, in which all the contradictions of the nation's expanding energies—especially those rooted in money, sex, commerce, social conventions, and status—were portrayed as baleful and dangerous influences. These forces, as Dreiser relentlessly dramatized, shaped the lives of individuals with a logic, and a luck, of their own. Writing with an earnestness that granted society more agency and potency than any novelist before him, save perhaps Balzac, had allowed, Dreiser pioneered an American naturalism that left a path for Sherwood Anderson, Sinclair Lewis, Saul Bellow, and several generations of other accomplished novelists to follow. With little investment in style (which would mark him as a big target for less talented but cleverer successors, who took pleasure in assaulting his "plodding" prose), and with no irony, Dreiser created fictions so immersed in obdurate reality that absorption in them is compelling, unsentimental, and true to life in its unfathomable play of fortunes and misfortunes.

What: Novel. *When:* 1900. *Also By:* Jennie Gerhardt (1911). *The Financier* (1912). *The "Genius"* (1915). *Try:* Eugénie Grandet by Honoré de Balzac. *Jude*

the Obscure by Thomas Hardy (see page 352). *The Awakening* by Kate Chopin (see page 158). *The House of Mirth* by Edith Wharton. *Adaptation:* William Wyler's 1952 film adaptation, starring Jennifer Jones and Laurence Olivier, is titled *Carrie*.

The Souls of Black Folk
W. E. B. Du Bois (1868–1963)

Seminal Evocations of Culture, Spirit, and Sorrow

"I sit with Shakespeare and he winces not," writes the author of *The Souls of Black Folk*, embracing the Bard's iambic pentameter to claim learning and culture as rights akin to life, liberty, and the pursuit of happiness. Indeed, the biography of William Edward Burghardt Du Bois might merit a Shakespearean drama of its own, for it began during the era of Civil War Reconstruction and ended at the height of the civil rights movement—Du Bois died, in Ghana, on the eve of the March on Washington that would culminate in the "I have a dream" oratory of Martin Luther King Jr. In the decades in between, Du Bois studied with William James, became the first African American to receive a PhD from Harvard, publicly advocated for integration and equality in opposition to the more gradualist programs of Booker T. Washington, cofounded the NAACP, and was a pioneer in the field of social science.

His powerful mind found its most memorable expression in this collection published in 1903. Comprising fourteen essays that blend history, philosophy, sociological observation, human interest, and personal experience with extraordinary eloquence, *The Souls of Black Folk* asks trenchant questions ("How does it feel to be a problem?" "Would

Portrait of W. E. B. Du Bois, ca. 1904

America have been America without her Negro people?") and answers them with a compassionate consideration of the brutal realities that shape African American lives and a sophisticated understanding of the complicated legacies of slavery. The book's final essay defines and celebrates "the spiritual heritage of the nation" memorialized in the "Sorrow Songs" in which slaves encompassed experience as tragic and as deeply lived as any ever addressed in a soliloquy. "Through all the sorrow of the Sorrow Songs," Du Bois writes, "there breathes a hope—a faith in the ultimate justice of things [. . .] that sometime, somewhere, men will judge men by their souls and not by their skins." That hope and that faith animate this book's witness to hard truths and exacting aspirations.

What: Culture. Essays. *When:* 1903. *Also By:* Du Bois published dozens of books, almost all about issues of race and history, including *John Brown: A Biography* (1909), *Black Reconstruction in America* (1935), and *The Autobiography of W. E. B. Du Bois* (1968). *Further Reading:* A two-volume biography, *W. E. B. Du Bois: Biography of a Race, 1868–1919* and *W. E. B. Du Bois: The Fight for Equality and the American Century, 1919–1963* by David Levering Lewis. *Reconsidering "The Souls of Black Folk"* by Stanley Crouch and Playthell Benjamin. *Try: Up from Slavery* by Booker T. Washington (see page 836).

■ For Annis Duff's *"Bequest of Wings,"* see page 208.

Rebecca
Daphne du Maurier (1907–1989)

The Pinnacle of Romantic Suspense

"Last night I dreamt I went to Manderley again."

That's the famous opening sentence of *Rebecca*, a suspenseful romantic tale that has cast its irresistible spell over millions of readers since it was published in 1938. The "I" is the novel's unnamed narrator. She is a timid and inexperienced young woman who, after a whirlwind romance, becomes the wife of the handsome and sophisticated widower Maxim de Winter. Manderley is de Winter's isolated estate on the Cornish coast of England. When the couple takes up residence there, the new Mrs. de Winter discovers that although her predecessor, the beautiful Rebecca, is dead, her memory lives on. Indeed, the first Mrs. de Winter is much more than just a memory— she is an eerily insistent, troubling presence in the life of her successor. For example, Rebecca's servant, the sinister Mrs. Danvers, remains ferociously loyal to her late mistress, seeing to it that Rebecca's private rooms are maintained as she left them and that her clothes are kept ready to be worn. It slowly begins to dawn on the second Mrs. de Winter that only by solving the mystery of her predecessor's fate can she herself become the true mistress of Manderley.

Rebecca unfolds with what one reviewer called "the relentlessness of a vivid nightmare." The same can be said about most of Daphne du Maurier's unputdownable tales: Her special gift was for crafting literate, gripping stories that are better written and show greater psychological insight than run-of-the-mill page-turners. As the *New York Times* put it, "du Maurier is in a class by herself"—and *Rebecca* is her finest achievement.

What: Novel. *When:* 1938. *Also By: Jamaica Inn* (1936). *My Cousin Rachel* (1951). *The Birds, and Other Stories* (1952). *The House on the Strand* (1969). *Don't Look Now* (1971). *Further Reading: The Rebecca Notebook and Other Memories* by du Maurier (1980). *Daphne du Maurier* by Margaret Forster. *Try:* Susan Hill's *Mrs. de Winter* and Sally Beauman's *Rebecca's Tale* are "sequels" to *Rebecca*. *Adaptation:* Alfred Hitchcock's first American feature film was his 1940 adaptation of *Rebecca*, starring Laurence Olivier and Joan Fontaine. It won the Academy Award for Best Picture.

The World As I Found It
Bruce Duffy (born 1951)

A Brilliant Novel of War, Thought, and Philosophers in Love

The World As I Found It is a sprawling novel ripe with personal drama, family struggles, romantic entanglements, and philosophy— yes, philosophy, for at the center of the tale is the enigmatic real-life philosopher Ludwig Wittgenstein, along with his not-always-so-collegial (but just as real-life) University of Cambridge colleagues Bertrand Russell and G. E. Moore. Celebrated retrospectively for both his private eccentricities and his knotty and intense investigations into the workings of the mind, Wittgenstein published only one book in his lifetime, the seductively forbidding *Tractatus Logico-Philosophicus* (1922), which comprises a series of economical statements beginning with the assertion (in the translation by D. F. Pears and B. F. McGuinness), "The world is all that is the case," and concluding seventy-odd pages later with a mysterious acknowledgement of the limits of logic and language: "What we cannot speak about we must pass over in silence."

A gripping tale about the tortured Wittgenstein may sound improbable, even oxymoronic, but Duffy magically pulls it off, assisted, of course, by the presence of Russell, an intellectual—and sexual—swashbuckler of the first order. Leading the reader from the colleges of Cambridge to fin-de-siècle Vienna, from the amorous hothouses of Bloomsbury to world-war battlefields, *The World As I Found It* mixes gossip, history, research, invention, and plenty of ideas into a compulsively readable novel. The result is fiction that engages experience from the hot pursuit of love to the analytical quest for life's determinedly ineffable meaning.

What: Novel. *When:* 1987. *Also By: Last Comes the Egg* (1997). *Disaster Was My God: A Novel of the Outlaw Life of Arthur Rimbaud* (2011). *Try: Under the Net* by Iris Murdoch. *Wittgenstein's Mistress* by David Markson. *Wittgenstein's Poker: The Story of a Ten-Minute Argument Between Two Great Philosophers* by David Edmonds and John Eidinow.

ALEXANDRE DUMAS
(1802–1870)

A lexandre Dumas first made a name for himself as an innovative playwright in Paris in the early nineteenth century. In 1838, aware of the new market for serializations, he tried his hand at fiction, refashioning one of his theatrical works as a prose narrative. The success of that venture led him to form something of a story mill; employing other writers and researchers to provide him with material, the flamboyantly gifted Dumas would add his own inspiration—refining and embellishing the particulars in action-packed installments published under his own name (his partner in planning *The Three Musketeers* and its sequels, as well as *The Count of Monte Cristo*, was one Auguste Maquet). Although Dumas's collaborative creative process has at times prompted critical dismissal of his work, the popularity and influence of his tales are undeniable. Of more importance to the common reader, the compelling force of Dumas's storytelling—his unrivaled command of a tale's movement across a large historical canvas—marks every page of his novels as his own, whatever its inception.

1867 caricature of Alexander Dumas on the front page of La Lune, *a 19th-century French magazine*

The Three Musketeers
The Original Action Heroes

S et in the seventeenth-century reign of Louis XIII and peopled with historical personages such as Cardinal Richelieu and the Duke of Buckingham, *The Three Musketeers* recounts the swashbuckling adventures of an impetuous young swordsman named d'Artagnan and the trio of soldiers in the king's service who give the book its title: Athos, Porthos, and Aramis. Aspiring to join their ranks as a musketeer, d'Artagnan follows his temper and his taste for amorous entanglement into perilous situations from which his new friends must extricate him. Duels, romantic liaisons, and court intrigue come fast and furious as the dialogue-driven chapters fly by. The heroes' primary antagonist, the scintillatingly seductive Milady, is one of the most vivid and alluring villains in all literature, and nearly a match for d'Artagnan and his fellows. Literary entertainment gets no better than this: You'll lose hours and hours of valuable time, and relish every moment.

What: Novel. *When:* First serialized in *Le Siècle* in 1844. *Edition:* Richard Pevear's fresh 2006 translation is the new standard in English. *Also By:* Dumas wrote two sequels to *The Three Musketeers: Twenty Years After* (1845) and *The Vicomte de Bragelonne* (1848–50); this huge work contains the tales sometimes published separately in English as *Louise de la Vallière* and *The Man in the Iron Mask*). *Try: The Scarlet Pimpernel* by Baroness Orczy. *Scaramouche* by Rafael Sabatini. *Adaptations: The Three Musketeers* has inspired countless adaptations, and d'Artagnan has been played on-screen by Douglas Fairbanks, Gene Kelly, Michael York, and Chris O'Donnell.

The Count of Monte Cristo
The Fastest 1,200 Pages You Will Ever Read

When it comes to page-turners, *The Count of Monte Cristo* is the great granddaddy of them all. Despite the novel's gargantuan dimensions—it runs to more than twelve hundred pages in most editions—each of its chapters is like an exhibit in a compendium of narrative suspense; it's hard to imagine any thriller plot on page or screen that isn't foretold in the fantastic adventures of Edmond Dantès.

Dantès is an earnest, responsible young sailor who, as the novel begins, has returned to Marseilles to marry his beloved Mercédès. Yet on the eve of their wedding, he is nefariously accused of being a traitor, wrongfully convicted, and sentenced to life imprisonment in an impregnable château. So begins Dumas's sprawling tale of vengeance, cunning, patience, and hope. As Dantès is transformed into the unforgettable figure who gives the book its title, he comes to combine the

---

A FORMULA FOR SUSPENSE

Kiss the Girls
James Patterson (born 1947)

Although anticipatory tension has been an element of tale spinning since the first story was spun, the edge of fictional suspense grew sharper as novelistic techniques evolved, from the cliff-hanging chapter endings of serial novels, to the predictable-with-a-twist plots of classic detective stories, to the fast-paced formula franchises—pumped with the adrenaline of cinematic pacing—that dominate today's bestseller lists. Indeed, in recent decades, the thriller has come into its own, with story lines as purposefully efficient as cardio training and as chiseled in form as six-pack abs. And James Patterson might be seen as the genre's personal trainer.

Spinning tales in multiple series and with multiple writing partners, as well as producing stand-alone novels by the dozen, James Patterson is an heir to Alexandre Dumas in industry, success, and manufacturing efficiency, to say nothing of disgruntled critical carping. But, with his books having sold well over three hundred million copies, Patterson has certainly earned the contemporary crown as King of the Page-Turners. The fecundity of his plotting is harvested with a control of pacing that gives his books the kind of consistency once produced in the songs of Tin Pan Alley. The second book to feature his recurring hero, psychologist and policeman Alex Cross, *Kiss the Girls* (1995) is a catchy, compelling, and—it is about tracking a serial killer, after all—undeniably suspenseful tune.

attributes of Odysseus, Robin Hood, a Western gunslinger, and James Bond, meting out his artful and implacable justice with equal doses of vindictiveness and generosity.

What: Novel. *When:* 1844–45. *Also By: Queen Margot* (1845). *The Black Tulip* (1850). *Try: Les Misérables* by Victor Hugo (see page 394). *The Scarlet Pimpernel* by Baroness Orczy. *Adaptations:* Alfred Bester's science fiction novel, *The Stars My Destination* (see page 73) is an inspired riff on the Dumas classic. Countless film and television adaptations have been produced, not only in France, America, and England, but in Mexico, Egypt, Spain, India, Italy, Japan, Portugal, Brazil, Argentina, and Turkey as well.

The Adventures of Ibn Battuta
A MUSLIM TRAVELER OF THE FOURTEENTH CENTURY
Ross E. Dunn (born 1941)

On the Trail of a Peerless Medieval Wanderer

Illustration of Ibn Battuta and a map of his journey by Hanna Balicka-Fribes

In June 1325, twenty-one-year-old Abu 'Abdallah Muhammad Ibn Battuta left his home in Tangier and set out on a pilgrimage to Mecca. Although that not inconsiderable journey would take a year, it proved to be only the first step in Ibn Battuta's life of unparalleled peregrination. Over the next three decades, he traveled more than seventy-five-thousand miles almost entirely by land, visiting Egypt and Persia, Samarkand and Constantinople, Sumatra and modern Tanzania, the Crimea and the southern steppes of Russia, Granada and Mali, even India, Ceylon, and China. His epic adventure, as Evan Connell once memorably put it, "makes the journey of Marco Polo look like a stroll around the block. Nobody else, with the single exception of Magellan—who was aboard ship—traveled such a distance until the nineteenth century."

More than six hundred years after Ibn Battuta's ultimate return to Morocco, historian Ross E. Dunn provided modern readers with a fascinating book about the medieval traveler's remarkable career. Using Ibn Battuta's own account of his journeys (the *Rihlah*, or *Travels*, dictated upon his return in 1353) as his primary source, Dunn chronicles his insatiably curious subject's exploits as scholar, diplomat, companion of royalty, even as a victim of pirates. But he also draws on history outside of the *Rihlah* to place its protagonist in a rich cultural context, creating a complex history of the vibrant and sophisticated Muslim world Ibn Battuta traversed. By illustrating the international scope of medieval Islamic civilization, with its cosmopolitan society of princes, merchants, scholarship, and sacred learning, Dunn's study of Ibn Battuta's traveling life takes readers on an eye-opening historical journey.

What: History. Travel. *When:* 1986; revised edition, 2004. *Further Reading:* British travel writer Tim Mackintosh-Smith has followed Ibn Battuta's footsteps in two entertaining volumes, *Travels with a Tangerine* and *The Hall of a Thousand Columns.* James Rumford's *Traveling Man* is a stunningly illustrated account, for readers ages 8 to 12, of Ibn Battuta's travels.

The Game of Kings
Dorothy Dunnett (1923–2001)

A Rich Tapestry of Historical Fiction

Kids who are readers love to fall under the spell of a series of books, and why should adults be any different? Any saga is enhanced by the knowledge that our pleasure in its unfolding will continue beyond the bounds of the volume in hand, that the world in which we've invested our imagination will pay interest for hundreds and hundreds of pages to come. That's but one of the pleasures promised and delivered by Dorothy Dunnett's captivating, erudite, and addictive historical novels. The Lymond Chronicles, set in Scotland, England, Europe, and the Middle East in the middle of the sixteenth century—between the Scottish border wars of the late 1540s and the coronation of Elizabeth I at the start of 1559—tell the tale of Francis Crawford, an outlaw Scottish nobleman endowed with both a hero's bearing and a maverick's recalcitrance. Learned in languages, literature, and philosophy, accomplished in the martial arts as well as the more refined domains of music and theater, he possesses both intellect and wit to match the undeniable élan of his courage, daring, and troublemaking—the last quality a product of the pride he is unable to compromise, much less conquer.

Intricately plotted and carefully researched, Dunnett's novels are imbued with romance and irony in equal measure. The author's mastery of suspense complements the vigor of her invention as she follows her protagonist across a large historical canvas peopled with many historical figures; his exciting endeavors take him to France, Malta, the Ottoman court of Suleiman the Magnificent in Constantinople, and the Moscow of Ivan the Terrible. For readers of The Game of Kings, the first book in the series, however, all those travels remain in the future, as they keep company with Francis Crawford on his return to Scotland, after half a decade in exile, to clear his name from a charge of treason. What ensues upon his arrival in his homeland is told with the tensely unfolding logic of a compelling mystery, albeit one enriched with the historical milieu that Dunnett so deftly animates, setting the stage for the five additional novels that complete Crawford's adventures.

What: Novel. *When:* 1961. *Also By:* The five other novels in the Lymond series are *Queens' Play* (1964); *The Disorderly Knights* (1966); *Pawn in Frankincense* (1969); *The Ringed Castle* (1971); *Checkmate* (1975). Dunnett's House of Niccolò sequence, a prequel to the Lymond saga rendered in eight novels published between 1986 and 2000, offers a more luxuriantly historical but equally captivating reading experience. *Further Reading: The Dorothy Dunnett Companion* and *The Dorothy Dunnett Companion Volume II*, both by Elspeth Morrison. *Try: The Brothers of Gwynedd Quartet* by Edith Pargeter. *The Founding* by Cynthia Harrod-Eagles. *The Sunne in Splendour* by Sharon Kay Penman.

My Family and Other Animals
Gerald Durrell (1925–1995)

The Idyllic—and Amusing—Childhood of a Naturalist in the Making

It's a cliché that an unhappy childhood gives a writer ideal material. In the case of Gerald Durrell, however, just the opposite occurred: A blissfully happy childhood not only supplied him with wonderful matter for several bestselling books, but also started him on his life's path to a career as a famous naturalist, zoologist, and conservationist. As he once remarked, "If I had the craft of Merlin, I would give every child the gift of my childhood."

The saga begins in England in the early 1930s. The unconventional Durrell family, having had its fill of the lousy English summer weather, packs up and heads to the sunny Greek island of Corfu. Teeming with exotic birds and beasts—from toads, tortoises, scorpions, and geckos to porpoises and a pigeon named Quasimodo—Corfu is heaven for an animal-loving ten-year-old like Gerry. (On the other hand, his mother, sister, and brothers —including budding novelist Lawrence—are less than thrilled when Gerry starts filling the fridge with his zoological specimens.)

In the "Speech for the Defence" that prefaces this witty and beguiling volume of reminiscences, the author reveals that he'd intended to write a straightforward natural history of Corfu. "But," he confesses, "I made a grave mistake by introducing my family into the book in the first few pages." Readers will be glad for his error. Warmly humorous, replete with intriguing natural history, and delighting in the merry eccentricities of the Durrell household, *My Family and Other Animals* is a splendid trip in very good company.

What: Nature. Memoir. *When:* 1956. *Also By:* My Family and Other Animals is the first volume of the Corfu Trilogy,

Statue of Gerald Durrell on the Channel Island Jersey

which continues in *Birds, Beasts and Relatives* (1969) and *The Garden of the Gods* (1978). Other books: *A Zoo in My Luggage* (1960) and *Menagerie Manor* (1964). *Try: All Creatures Great and Small* by James Herriot (see page 371). *Ring of Bright Water* by Gavin Maxwell (see page 533). *Adaptations:* The BBC has twice adapted *My Family and Other Animals* for television— in 1987 as a series, and in 2005 as a single program.

THE ALEXANDRIA QUARTET
JUSTINE • BALTHAZAR • MOUNTOLIVE • CLEA
Lawrence Durrell (1912–1990)

"When you are in love with one of its inhabitants, a city can become a world."
—Lawrence Durrell

At one point in The Alexandria Quartet, a character warns another that in life, "each fact can have a thousand motivations, all equally valid, and each fact a thousand faces," thus revealing the underlying tenet of Lawrence Durrell's absorbing and brilliantly slippery tetralogy, which presents four views of the same series of events. Set in the sensual city of Alexandria just before (and eventually during) World War II, Durrell's tale of love, duplicity, and the vagaries of desire begins as an exiled Irish schoolteacher named Darley seeks to unravel his obsessions with two women, both now lost to him. Each volume revisits the events that haunt Darley's memory,

approaching them from a different perspective while adding new characters and incidents that turn the story inside out. For instance, what the reader learns in the intensely romantic *Justine* (1957), in which Darley attempts to comprehend his passion for the title character, is in many ways contradicted in *Balthazar* (1958), in which a different narrator exposes unsuspected political dimensions to what Darley has narrated in the first book; the third and fourth volumes, *Mountolive* (1958) and *Clea* (1960), do not so much clarify as elaborate upon the first two. Along the way, the story and the storytelling get richer and more complicated, and the motives, actions, and destinies of the extensive cast of lovers are entangled and unwound in an intricately choreographed passage through time. Durrell's ravishing prose, and the palpable presence of Alexandria itself, give the fictional mélange of romance, espionage, eroticism, and melodrama—there are enough twists and turns of plot to fuel a decade of daily soap operas—an organic intensity that is riveting and beautiful. Written by Durrell at a breakneck pace, the four novels are best read with the same fevered energy.

What: Novels. *When:* 1957–60. *Editions:* Changes and corrections were made, and new prefaces added, once the tetralogy was complete, but most current editions rely on the unrevised originals. *Also By:* Fiction: *The Black Book* (1938); The Avignon Quintet (1974–85). Durrell's travel books have also won wide acclaim: try *Prospero's Cell* (1945) or *Reflections on a Marine Venus* (1953). *Further Reading:* Durrell's correspondence with Henry Miller, *The Durrell-Miller Letters, 1935–1980*, makes terrific reading. *Try:* The works of Henry Miller and Vladimir Nabokov. The Cairo Trilogy by Naguib Mahfouz. *Adaptation:* The 1969 George Cukor film of the first volume, *Justine*, stars Michael York as Darley and Anouk Aimée as Justine.

Darwin Among the Machines
THE EVOLUTION OF GLOBAL INTELLIGENCE
George Dyson (born 1953)

An Electrifying Treatise on Nature and Technology

E xhilaratingly interdisciplinary, historically erudite, speculatively visionary, *Darwin Among the Machines* leads us from the seventeenth-century ideas of Thomas Hobbes to the net-worked capacities of today's digital reality. Along the way, George Dyson introduces his readers to an extraordinary cast of scientists, philoso-phers, mathematicians, novelists, and computer pioneers, creating—by way of scholarship, fable, conjecture, and an astonishing ability to synthe-size disparate modes of thought—an open-ended exploration of the development of collective mechanical intelligence, in theory and practice. It is an enlightening journey.

Dyson's wide-ranging intellectual history begins with Hobbes's vision of society as its own life form, a "Leviathan" possessed of "a diffuse intelligence that was neither the supreme intel-ligence of God nor the individual intelligence of the human mind." Giving intelligence a mind of its own, so to speak, Hobbes advanced ideas of reasoning that would lead, eventually, to binary computing machines. As Dyson traces thinking about "thinking machines" across the centuries, he erodes easy distinctions between biological and mechanical life, suggesting that intelligence is an evolutionary process that transcends the differences between nature and technology.

Dyson's explication of myriad themes, although intricate, is both inviting and con-tinually rewarding. The energy of his creative connections sparks the best kind of intellectual exercise, leaving us with a fresh perspective on the digital realm we all reconnoiter daily via the World Wide Web. Not unlike Hobbes's *Leviathan*, this digital "organism" is greater than the sum of its parts. Can Dyson be right that its evolution "may embody a collective wisdom greater than our own"? No matter how you are disposed to answer that question, you're unlikely to find a more stimulating guide to the roots and ramifications of the information age and our still developing networked world.

What: Technology. Science. *When:* 1997. *Also By:* *Baidarka: The Kayak* (1986). *Project Orion: The True Story of the Atomic Spaceship* (2002). *Turing's Cathedral* (2012). *Further Reading:* Samuel Butler's 1863 essay, "Darwin Among the Machines" provided a kernel of inspiration for the book. Kenneth Brower's *The Starship and the Canoe* is a double biography of the (very young) author and his father, physicist Freeman Dyson. *Try: Gödel, Escher, Bach* by Douglas Hofstadter (see page 380). *The Soul of a New Machine* by Tracy Kidder. *The Age of Spiritual Machines: When Computers Exceed Human Intelligence* by Ray Kurzweil.

E

The Name of the Rose
Umberto Eco (1932–2016)

A Medieval Sherlock—and More

The year is 1327, a time of political intrigue and theological wrangling between the furtive powers of the papacy and the earthly forces of the Holy Roman Empire. At an unnamed Franciscan abbey— housing a labyrinth in which is hidden the greatest library in Christendom, including forbidden works of uncanny and encoded knowledge—monks are suspected of heresy, and Brother William of Baskerville, a master logician, is dispatched to investigate. Demonstrating uncommon deductive skills upon his arrival, William is soon asked to apply his keen mind to an unexpected matter. A manuscript illuminator from the abbey's scriptorium has fallen to his death outside the monastery walls: Is it suicide or murder?

Umberto Eco, 1983

So begins *The Name of the Rose*, the most unlikely of modern international bestsellers (there are more than a few passages in Latin!). The first novel by Umberto Eco, an Italian professor, newspaper columnist, and book editor, it combines its author's academic interest in semiotics (the study of how cultures communicate via signs) with the allure of esoteric erudition to create a seductive variation on the most comfortable of reading pleasures: the classic English mystery. After all, what better setting could there be for a ratiocinative sleuth to probe a murderous puzzle than a cloister? And what is Brother William if not a playfully embellished precursor of the great deductionist Sherlock Holmes? Eco even endows him with a Dr. Watson of his own in the figure of Adso of Melk, the trusty sidekick and scribe who recounts the events.

Yet by locating his detective story in the historical, political, religious, and philosophical milieu of a medieval monastery, Eco is also free to lead readers well beyond the genre while amplifying his plot's intricate suspense. He imagines a series of monastic killings that seem to foretell the apocalypse even as they dramatize the clash of worldviews that pits pope against emperor, material rewards against spiritual purity, idea against action, and words against things. Catnip for semioticians, *The Name of the Rose* is a real treat for the common reader, too.

What: Novel. **When:** 1980 in Italian; English translation by William Weaver, 1983. **Edition:** Most paperback editions now include Eco's enlightening *Postscript to "The Name of the Rose,"* originally published as a separate volume. **Also By:** Fiction: *Foucault's Pendulum* (1988); *The Island of the Day Before* (1994); *The Prague Cemetery* (2010). Nonfiction: *Six Walks in the Fictional Woods* (1994). **Further Reading:** *The Key to "The Name of the Rose"* by Adele J. Haft, Jane G. White, and Robert J. White. **Try:** *Ficciones* by Jorge Luis Borges (see page 87). *Invisible Cities* by Italo Calvino (see page 120). *Quicksilver* by Neal Stephenson (see page 755). **Adaptation:** A Hollywood film starring Sean Connery was released in 1986.

■ For E. R. Eddison's *The Worm Ouroboros*, see page 795.

Bright Air, Brilliant Fire
ON THE MATTER OF MIND
Gerald M. Edelman (1929–2014)

The Biology of Mind

After winning the 1972 Nobel Prize in Physiology or Medicine for his work in immunology, Dr. Gerald M. Edelman set out to discover how the phenomenon of mind emerges from the brain's bundle of tissue. In pursuing his investigations, Edelman applied the theory of natural selection to the problem of consciousness, painting a picture—rich with physiological detail and neurological complexity—of the adaptation of the nervous system as it reflects the life experience of each human being. As Oliver Sacks, a champion of Edelman's ideas, once suggested, such an approach to consciousness seems true to life—to the "continual revision and reorganization of perception and memory" that are characteristic of our experience; it incarnates (and scientifically, to boot) the specter of individuality—of sensibility, will, identity—that always haunts us.

Bright Air, Brilliant Fire summarizes for a general audience Edelman's researches and speculations, which have met with some controversy and criticism, especially from advocates of a computational, rather than a strictly biological, view of the brain's functioning. Nonetheless, Edelman's ideas, combining elements of physiology, psychology, and philosophy, are provocative and invigorating. His book is dense with reports on the dance of neurons, their connections, and their patterns; it is vivid with opinion and experiment, and animated by Edelman's erudition in the arts as well as the sciences; it is often witty, at times difficult; it is, finally, exhilarating in its sweeping vision of how we, quite literally, make up our minds as we go along.

What: Science. *When:* 1992. *Also By: A Universe of Consciousness* (with Giulio Tononi; 2000). *Wider than the Sky* (2004). *Second Nature: Brain Science and Human Knowledge* (2006). *Try: Essays in Radical Empiricism* by William James. *The Enchanted Loom: Chapters in the History of Neuroscience*, edited by Pietro Corsi. *Consciousness and the Brain* by Stanislas Dehaene.

The Book of Ebenezer Le Page
G. B. Edwards (1899–1976)

An Old Man of the Channel Islands, in Love with Life

"There may have been stranger recent literary events than the book you are about to read, but I rather doubt it," wrote John Fowles, author of *The French Lieutenant's Woman* (see page 294), in his introduction to the original 1981 edition of this compelling novel. The only work of G. B. Edwards, who began writing it in the last decade of his life and who died in 1976 at the age of seventy-seven, its posthumous publication was greeted with astonishment and delight by a broad audience of readers.

The singularity of *The Book of Ebenezer Le Page*—"its voice and method are so unusual that it belongs nowhere on our conventional literary maps," Fowles continued—is partly explained by its distance, in setting, subject, and style, from the familiar neighborhoods of our literary capitals. Chronicling in his cranky, funny, and vivid voice his life on the English Channel island of Guernsey, fisherman and tomato grower Ebenezer Le Page bears witness to a twentieth century that has seen the island's traditions overwhelmed by war, tourism, and modernity. Along the way, he delivers a long, rich, intricate story filled with friendship, kinship, feuds, sorrow, love, humor, tragedy, and joy—in other words, with real life passionately experienced and fervently embraced. Brimming with incident and anecdote, the island-bound novel is peopled with a vivid array of characters, from Ebenezer's childhood chum Jim Jahy, killed in World War I, to Liza Quéripel, the love of Ebenezer's life and the object of his enduring yet unsettled affection, from his quarryman father to a catalog of bickering aunts, uncles, and cousins. The book also knows, in the shape of occupying Nazis, the darkening influence of offshore history.

Edwards created a style that is vibrant and beautiful, wholly original and yet never obscure. In it he renders a world complete, with, in Nobel Prize winner William Golding's words, "such inbuilt authenticity you hardly seem to be reading at all, but living."

What: Novel. *When:* 1981. *Try:* Edwards's book is hard to connect to others one-to-one, as the following summation from astute critic Michael Dirda suggests: "Imagine a novel that blends Thomas Hardy, Stella Gibbons's *Cold Comfort Farm*, and Proust—an improbable combination, no doubt, yet one that hints at the salt and humor and pathos and richness of *The Book of Ebenezer Le Page.*"

Animating his fictional alter ego's narrative with Guernsey accents and French patois,

> **"A masterpiece . . . One of the best novels of our time. . . . I know of no description of happiness in modern literature equal to the one that ends this novel."**
> —*Guy Davenport,* New York Times

....

A Visit from the Goon Squad
Jennifer Egan (born 1962)

In Search of Lost Tunes

What kind of novel would Marcel Proust have written if he'd listened to the Rolling Stones instead of Beethoven's late quartets? The answer might well be something very much like *A Visit from the Goon Squad*, Jennifer Egan's virtuosic and open-hearted tale of music and mortality. Like *In Search of Lost Time* (see page 644), Egan's novel—or maybe it's a book of short stories, though the distinction isn't that important—takes as its focus the passage of time, imperceptible in itself but undeniable in its effects. Children's fantasies and teenagers' dreams are placed in juxtaposition to the tempered

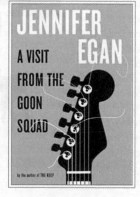

realities of adulthood and the ravages of old age. All of us, Egan suggests, get mugged by the "goon squad" of time. And none of us really sees it coming.

Like the music it evokes, *Goon Squad* is catchy, inviting in both form and duration: It moves with the tempo and tunefulness of rock 'n' roll. In fact, like a vintage pop LP, it's divided into two "sides," A and B. Each chapter is a kind of musical track as well, a freestanding "song" that slots into the larger concept album; each takes place in a different time period, from the late 1960s into some year in the near future; each focuses on a different character; and each is written in a distinct narrative style (one chapter,

Jennifer Egan, 2013

figures such as Bennie Salazar, a bassist in an undistinguished San Francisco punk band who later succeeds—or sells out—as a record executive. Bennie's career tracks the massive upheavals of the music industry, and throughout *Goon Squad* popular songs, heard first on records and eight-track tapes and then on fraying cassettes and scratched CDs, are verities in the emotional lives of its characters, which Egan captures with wit, grace, and no little wisdom.

What: Novel. *When:* 2010. *Awards:* National Book Critics Circle Award for Fiction, 2010. Pulitzer Prize for Fiction, 2011. *Also By: The Invisible Circus* (1995). *Look at Me* (2001). *The Keep* (2006). *Manhattan Beach* (2017). *Try: V.* by Thomas Pynchon. *The Ground Beneath Her Feet* by Salman Rushdie. *The Sense of an Ending* by Julian Barnes.

devoted to "Great Rock & Roll Pauses," is composed in PowerPoint slides). What links the separate pieces is a constellation of overlapping

---

Travels with Lizbeth

THREE YEARS ON THE ROAD AND ON THE STREET

Lars Eighner (born 1948)

A Man and His Dog, Homeless

L ars Eighner became homeless in 1988. He took to scavenging food and other necessities for himself and his dog Lizbeth from the big trash containers called Dumpsters. What he found in some of them, he reveals, horrified him. But don't jump to conclusions: It's not what you think.

The Dumpsters in question were the ones used by students at the University of Texas. And it was as he waded through heaps of discarded student essays that Eighner found himself "horrified to discover the kind of paper that now merits an A in an undergraduate course." (He adds that, on the other hand, he was "grateful for the number of good books and magazines the students throw out.") Eighner's observation about what qualified as first-rate college work in the late 1980s is startling and hilarious. It could have come only from a person who somehow managed, in the midst of stupefying misfortunes, to remain alert to the world around him and to keep an unpitying eye on himself, which is indeed what Eighner managed to do

during the three years of homelessness that are the subject of *Travels with Lizbeth*.

Lars Eighner with his constant companion Lizbeth, 1993

The book sometimes reads—quite wonderfully—as if written by an eighteenth-century man of letters who, under some bookish spell, has ventured out of his well-appointed literary home and wandered onto the perilous social realism shelf of the library. Eighner's quirky and sophisticated style makes his attention to the immediate anxieties of his circumstance more arresting. And his attachment to his canine companion supplies a patient tenderness that transcends the hard realities the two confront. It doesn't feel quite right to call a memoir of homelessness "charming," but Eighner's forthright and often funny account of the torments and challenges that he and Lizbeth faced while roughing it in Texas, California, and points in between is exactly—and unforgettably—that.

What: Memoir. *When:* 1993. *Also By: Elements of Arousal: How to Write and Sell Gay Men's Erotica* (1994). *Pawn to Queen Four* (1995). *Try: The Autobiography of a Super-Tramp* by W. H. Davies. *Down and Out in Paris and London* by George Orwell. *Grand Central Winter: Stories from the Street* by Lee Stringer.

The Immense Journey

AN IMAGINATIVE NATURALIST EXPLORES THE MYSTERIES OF MAN AND NATURE

Loren Eiseley (1907–1977)

A Scientist's Meditative and Inspiring Speculations

Loren Eiseley was born in Lincoln, Nebraska. He received a diagnosis of tuberculosis in 1933, spent time riding the rails like a hobo, then settled down to become an anthropologist. He received his PhD in 1937 and became the chairman of the anthropology department at the University of Pennsylvania in 1947. A decade later, *The Immense Journey*, a collection of thirteen poetic, ruminative essays on our evolutionary history and relationship to the natural world, became a popular and critical success. Eiseley brought an imaginative personal perspective to science writing, garnering comparisons to other literary figures— he's been called both "a twentieth-century Thoreau" and "a Proust miraculously turned into an evolutionary anthropologist." But the best brief characterization of Loren Eiseley came from the admirer who described him as a writer who "never decided whether he was a scientist or a poet, and whose work demonstrates the irrelevance of the distinction."

The catalysts for the speculations gathered in *The Immense*

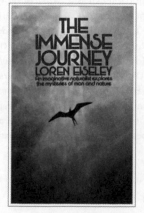

Journey range from a crack in a sandstone wall to the magic of flowing water, from the mysteries of the ocean's bottom to how the emergence of flowering plants changed the face of the planet. Indeed, emergence both grand and particular—of life forms in time, of the snout of an unseen creature from a fetid pool—is an emblematic theme in Eiseley's thinking. He wears his scientific learning lightly, and often uses it to amplify the meanings of an observation we might well have made ourselves. Best of all, he enlarges his scientist's perspective with the capacity of a gifted writer's words; these are essays that—in the beauty and measure of their language—inspire in the reader the kind of serene, profound engagement with existence that is both exhilarating and, in the deepest sense, restorative.

What: Science. Nature. Essays. *When:* 1957. *Also By: Darwin's Century* (1958). *The Unexpected Universe* (1969). *The Night Country: Reflections of a Bone-Hunting Man* (1971). *All the Strange Hours: The Excavation of a Life* (1975). *Try: The Lives of a Cell* by Lewis Thomas (see page 781). *Pilgrim at Tinker Creek* by Annie Dillard (see page 224).

Middlemarch
George Eliot (1819–1880)

The Wisest Novel in English Literature

At the center of George Eliot's vast portrait of the provincial city of Middlemarch, its society and inhabitants, is the story of Dorothea Brooke, a "home epic" of a bright, brave young woman learning how to live and what to live for. Dorothea's passage from high-minded youthful ideals to the humbling truths of adulthood and love begins with her misguided marriage to the dour scholar Edward Casaubon, many years her senior, who is engaged in work on an ever-unfinished "Key to All Mythologies." As Dorothea's

Portrait of George Eliot, pen name of Mary Anne Evans

romantic visions of intellectual fulfillment and collaboration are clouded by Casaubon's dull actuality, Eliot brilliantly charts her protagonist's awkward development through stages of disappointment and regret to an unexpectedly empowering embrace of life's inescapable limits.

Around her heroine's drama of growth through constriction, Eliot choreographs an expansive dance of characters and subplots: There are the honorable surgeon, Mr. Lydgate, distracted from his instincts by the fetching, flighty Rosamond Vincy; Rosamond's feckless brother, Fred, and his forthright yet forgiving sweetheart, Mary Garth; the local banker Bulstrode and the blackmailing Raffles, whose mutual secrets complicate the plot with coincidences and conflicts worthy of Dickens; and, not least, Will Ladislaw, the charismatic art student and second cousin to Casaubon whose hidden love for Dorothea provides the enormous tale with a sustained heartbeat.

Most memorable of *Middlemarch*'s characters, however, is no character at all, but the imaginative, intuitive, profoundly discerning narrative voice that meditates upon the events and personalities it describes with sympathy and magnanimity. The passions of the plot and reflections on their meaning are delivered seamlessly, with a blend of philosophy and storytelling few novelists have risked, and fewer still have mastered. Readers are apt to find themselves asking, "What happens next?" and "What shape is my own life taking?" in one and the same breath as Eliot illuminates the truth of our existence: As Time has its way with us, our dreams, if not forgotten, are focused by force of circumstance on smaller and smaller ground. The determining acts of our lives are seldom propelled for long by the force of young and noble impulse, but rather are formed by the ways and wayward means of the wider world. "For there is no creature whose inward being is so strong," Eliot writes, "that it is not greatly determined by what lies outside it." That's the fruit of this book's wisdom; the tree on which it grows is strong, vigorous, and beautiful, life enhancing in every way.

What: Novel. *When:* Originally published in serial form, 1871–72; first one-volume edition, 1874. *Also By: Adam Bede* (1859). *The Mill on the Floss* (1860). *Silas Marner* (1861). *Daniel Deronda* (1876). *Further Reading: George Eliot* by Jenny Uglow. *Try: Wives and Daughters* by Elizabeth Gaskell. *The Portrait of a Lady* by Henry James (see page 409). *Adaptation:* No film can capture the narrative voice that animates Eliot's masterpiece. Nonetheless, a credible television miniseries was made for Masterpiece Theatre in 1994.

"One of the few English novels written for grown-up people."
—*Virginia Woolf on* Middlemarch

Four Quartets
T. S. Eliot (1888–1965)

A Modernist's Book of Uncommon Prayer

> Time present and time past
> Are both perhaps present in time future,
> And time future contained in time past.
> If all time is eternally present
> All time is unredeemable.

These are the opening lines of *Four Quartets*, and they evoke the presence of an austere yet inviting cleric, speaking earnestly as he summons from a modest pulpit the themes a church is built to house: eternity, redemption, roads taken or untrod.

> Footfalls echo in the memory
> Down the passage which we did not take
> Towards the door we never opened
> Into the rose-garden.

Despite its seriousness, the voice's quest for meaning is congenial and not without empathic concern; it knows that "human kind / Cannot bear very much reality."

Because the imagined pastor speaking to us is T. S. Eliot, high priest of literary modernism, the voice that holds our attention passes through a tensile web of allusions—encompassing the Bhagavad Gita (see page 75) and *The Divine Comedy* (see page 194), the ancient Greek philosophy of Heraclitus and the Christian mysticism of Julian of Norwich, historical incidents from the English Civil War to the London Blitz—as it explores a realm of poetic imagery and profound rumination. We may not know how we got into a church, but, as at weddings and funerals, it feels like the right place for the reverent pursuit of matters of life and death.

Beginning with the publication of "The Love Song of J. Alfred Prufrock" in 1915, Eliot built a once unassailable reputation of cultural eminence through a small but astonishing series of masterpieces, most notably "Gerontion" (1920), *The Waste Land* (1922), "The Hollow Men" (1925), and "Ash Wednesday" (1930). Each left in its wake a series of indelible

T. S. Eliot, 1948

phrases that with their slightly off-foot, rhythmically charged prosody seemed to heighten and refresh both common speech and the language of The Book of Common Prayer (see page 87) with the same immersive intuition that Bob Dylan would bring to the reinvention of the folk song tradition several decades later. (It's not hard to chart a course from *The Waste Land* to Dylan's "Desolation Row," once one sets upon the path.) As Dylan would after him, Eliot exhibits a gift for recombinant imitation that makes his verse both steeped in tradition and incontestably unique, imbued with an almost oracular magic that makes gnomic imagery resonate with strange significance: "Garlic and sapphires in the mud / Clot the bedded axle-tree." Like all of Eliot's verse, *Four Quartets* is filled with what he calls, in an homage to poet Walter de la Mare, "the inexplicable mystery of sound." And prayer:

> The dove descending breaks the air
> With flame of incandescent terror
> Of which the tongues declare
> The one discharge from sin and error.

Written in the years before and during World War II, the *Quartets* consist of four long poems, each cohering around a season, one of the four natural elements (earth, air, water, fire), and a place: "Burnt Norton," an English manor house and garden; "East Coker," a village in Somerset, home to Eliot's ancestors (and, ultimately, resting place of the poet's ashes); "The Dry Salvages," a group of rocks off Cape Ann, Massachusetts; and "Little Gidding," seventeenth-century home to the Christian familial community of Nicholas Ferrar, which lived under the guidance of the Book of Common Prayer. Now formal and now free, Eliot's verse wends its way through these locations like the river he invokes at the outset of "The Dry Salvages": strong, flowing, impersonal and inspiring, animated with currents of consolation and desire that cannot measure the meaning of existence, but merely, and truly, carry it along. There is no other book of poetry quite like *Four Quartets*.

What: Poetry. **When:** 1943. **Award:** Nobel Prize in Literature, 1948. **Also By:** *Murder in the Cathedral* (1935). *Collected Poems 1909–1962* (1963). *Selected Prose of T. S. Eliot*, edited by Frank Kermode (1975). **Try:** *Revelations of Divine Love* by Julian of Norwich. *A Gilded Lapse of Time* by Gjertud Schnackenberg. **Footnote:** The type for the first British edition of Eliot's seminal poem *The Waste Land* was hand-set by Virginia Woolf for the Hogarth Press, which she ran with her husband, Leonard.

Founding Brothers
THE REVOLUTIONARY GENERATION
Joseph J. Ellis (born 1943)

The Sibling Rivalries That Shaped Our Nation

We've become accustomed to casting Washington, Jefferson, Franklin, Hamilton, and other figures who were instrumental in the formation of our republic in a fatherly role, bestowing upon them a dispassionate and collective paternal wisdom that supports the enduring popular assumption that "Founding Fathers Know Best." But this view makes it easy to overlook the extent to which they argued long and hard with one another. As Joseph J. Ellis reminds us about the 1790s in the fledgling United States, "the political dialogue within the highest echelon of the revolutionary generation was a decade-long shouting match." The Founders, in other words, were more like competing siblings than the conventional view allows; familiarity bred contention, and these hot-headed brothers often brawled—intellectually, politically, and sometimes even physically.

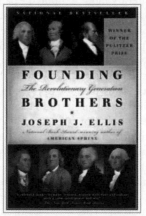

What were they fighting about? Individual rights. Slavery. The extent of federal powers. These and other crucial issues faced America in the uncertain decade after the Constitution was ratified in 1788. Calling those years the most decisive in America's history, Ellis here focuses on six specific incidents that illustrate the founders' wrangling, ranging from widely known events to clandestine encounters. Among the former would be the duel between Aaron Burr and Alexander Hamilton, as well as George Washington's Farewell Address to Congress upon his retirement from public life; among the latter, the secret dinner between Hamilton, Jefferson, and James Madison, during which some major wheeling and dealing (on the assumption of state debts by the federal government and the future location of the national capital on the banks of the Potomac) was done.

In fluent prose enlivened by his splendid eye for the physical characteristics of his protagonists, Ellis renders each episode with an inviting dramatic flair and keen insight into the characters of the players. He puts his close knowledge of the historical context in the service of the reader, illuminating the issues of the day with insight and erudition. It's hard to imagine a better introduction

Depiction of the duel between Aaron Burr and Alexander Hamilton

to the period—or to the small library of bestselling books on the revolutionary generation—than *Founding Brothers*.

What: History. **When:** 2001. **Award:** Pulitzer Prize for History, 2001. **Also By:** *Passionate Sage: The Character and Legacy of John Adams* (1993). *American Sphinx: The Character of Thomas Jefferson* (1998). *His Excellency: George Washington* (2004). *American Creation: Triumphs and Tragedies at the Founding of the Republic* (2007). **Try:** *John Adams* and *1776* by David McCullough. *Alexander Hamilton* by Ron Chernow (see page 155). *Revolutionary Characters: What Made the Founders Different* by Gordon S. Wood.

|||||||||||||||||||||||||||||||||||||||||| **MORE TO EXPLORE** ||||||||||||||||||||||||||||||||||||||||||

FOUNDING MOTHERS

Over the past few decades, America's Founding Fathers have become permanently enshrined not only in our history books, but also, it sometimes seems, at the top of the bestseller lists. Because of the efforts of writers such as Joseph J. Ellis (opposite page), Ron Chernow (whose *Alexander Hamilton* inspired Lin-Manuel Miranda's phenomenal Broadway hit, *Hamilton: The Musical*), and David McCullough (*John Adams; 1776*), biographical works about leaders of the revolutionary era have enjoyed an extraordinary popular vogue. Slowly and with less fanfare, the women behind the men have come into their own as subjects for gifted biographers and historians, as the three books recommended here attest.

Dearest Friend: A Life of Abigail Adams
Lynne Withey (born 1948)

Dearest Friend (1981) is an authoritative biography of the resourceful person who would become our second First Lady when her husband, John, succeeded George Washington as president. Before she assumed that role, she stayed at home to manage the family farm and raise four children while John was off fomenting revolution and imagining independence for the new nation. The letters that make up her half of their remarkable correspondence during this period express the hopes and anxieties she shared with other ordinary citizens, revealing Abigail to be a figure of forceful character and quick wit—qualities Withey's book brings to memorable life.

Book of Ages:
The Life and Opinions
of Jane Franklin
Jill Lepore (born 1966)

Jill Lepore's 2013 book is both a portrait of Benjamin Franklin's sister Jane and a provocative exploration of the status of ordinary women in the revolutionary era. The youngest daughter of the seventeen Franklin children (Benjamin, six years her senior, was the youngest son), Jane married at fifteen and bore twelve children, only one of whom would survive her. Her circumscribed life—as homebound and obscurely domestic as her brother's was expansive and renowned—is illuminated by Lepore's vivid reading of her subject's opinionated and

Portrait of Louisa Johnson Adams by Gilbert Stuart

perceptive—if less than polished—correspondence and private writings. The author's probing consideration of the different fortunes of brother and sister is haunting and revelatory.

Mrs. Adams in Winter:
A Journey in the Last
Days of Napoleon
Michael O'Brien
(1948–2015)

In *Mrs. Adams in Winter* (2010), Michael O'Brien takes as his subject another Mrs. Adams, the wife of Abigail's son John Quincy, who would serve as the sixth president of the United States from 1825 to 1829. O'Brien's marvelous biography of Louisa Johnson Adams chronicles this intrepid future First Lady's journey across Europe with her young son in 1815, as an escaped Napoleon makes a renewed bid for power; among other things, it's a terrific adventure story.

Invisible Man
Ralph Ellison (1914–1994)

The Evidence of Things Unseen

Vivid, unpredictable, insinuating, uncomfortably intimate, the voice that tells *Invisible Man* is one of the most supple and powerful instruments ever fashioned in American prose. From the book's opening sentences, its unnamed narrator stakes out the novel's unconventional territory: "I am an invisible man. No, I am not a spook like those who haunted Edgar Allan Poe; nor am I one of your Hollywood-movie ectoplasms. I am a man of substance, of flesh and bone, fiber and liquids—and I might even be said to possess a mind. I am invisible, understand, simply because people refuse to see me." Across nearly six hundred pages, this voice whispers, shouts, sings, keens, and ruminates as the narrator relates the events that have led him to the current home in which he hibernates, a "hole" in a basement that he has wired with 1,369 lights to illuminate the inner life the outside world refuses to see. His skin is black, his soul is blue, his mind is lit with both desperation and deep thought.

Naturalistic and surreal, fantastic and fatally true to the African American experience, *Invisible Man* follows its hero from his early days in the Deep South to a college campus, from employment at Liberty Paints in New York City to engagement with a progressive political organization known as the Brotherhood. In whatever sphere he moves, and no matter the color of the people around him, no one credits his identity: "When they approach me they see only my surroundings, themselves, or figments of their imagination—indeed, everything and anything except me." If race is the obvious reason many refuse to see him, the anonymity of individuals in mass society is another. Ellison's dramatization of his protagonist's plight, in scenes of conversation and confrontation that range from subway rides to job interviews, political rallies to urban riots, is stunning in its visceral impact; a surge of imminent yet reluctant violence is channeled through a voice that is filled in equal parts with defiance, fear, pain, and longing. Through its urgency and irony, the voice of Ellison's unseen man implicates the reader in realities as complex as those any American novel has contained, in prose that commands the resources of both vernacular and literary language with startling virtuosity.

What: Novel. *When:* 1952. *Edition:* Recent editions include Ellison's 1981 essay about the novel's composition. *Award:* National Book Award, 1953. *Also By:* Essays: *Shadow and Act* (1964); *Going to the Territory* (1986). Fiction: *Flying Home and Other Stories* (1996); *Three Days Before the Shooting . . .* (2010; unfinished second novel, published posthumously). *Further Reading: Ralph Ellison: A Biography* by Arnold Rampersad. *Trading Twelves: The Selected Letters of Ralph Ellison and Albert Murray* edited by John Callahan. *Try: Notes from Underground* by Fyodor Dostoevsky (see page 231). *Native Son* by Richard Wright (see page 872). *The Stranger* by Albert Camus. *Footnote:* In his novel *The Magic Keys*, Albert Murray draws a fictionalized portrait of Ralph Ellison, his longtime friend.

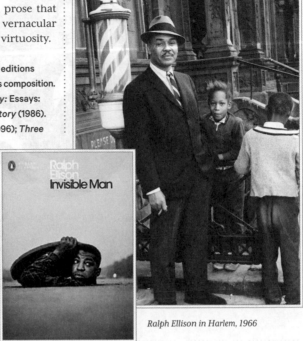

Ralph Ellison in Harlem, 1966

Essays and Lectures
Ralph Waldo Emerson (1803–1882)

The Unparalleled Eloquence of a 19th-Century Nonconformist

Revered in his own day and in the decades after his death, the Sage of Concord is comparatively neglected today. Yet it takes only a few pages of his prose to see how valuable his words remain.

Emerson was a philosopher, poet, and essayist. Though he's credited with being one of the fathers of Transcendentalism, the New England movement that privileged idealism over empiricism and found a natural divinity in all things, he valued independent thought above adherence to any creed or system. Intuiting, and perhaps inspiring, an essential element of the American spirit, he championed self-reliance, individualism, and—in one of his most indelible phrases—enjoying "an original relation to the universe." He "lived for ideas," according to his biographer Robert D. Richardson, "but he did

so with the reckless, headlong ardor of a lover." That palpable passion, married to a preternatural eloquence, makes his essays exhilarating reading.

Indeed, Emerson's prose transcends the modesty of the forms he worked in. "After Shakespeare," in Harold Bloom's estimation, "it matches anything else in the language." It is seeded with arresting epigrams that strike sparks in a reader's mind: "Perception makes." "Common sense is genius dressed in its working clothes." "Earth laughs in flowers." "Language is fossil poetry." "In skating over thin ice, our safety is in our speed." "The years teach much which the days never know." As we read Emerson, sentences such as these scratch the surface of our own experience to reveal the depths it hides. "There is creative reading as well as creative writing," Emerson also wrote, and his style encourages us to engage in it.

Since the best of Emerson is the phrase, the sentence, the paragraph—call it the majestic sound bite (he was, after all, a riveting public speaker)—the best way to approach his work may be to just open it anywhere and start reading. A representative collection—there are many—will include key pieces such as *Nature*, "The American Scholar," "Self-Reliance," and "Experience." Then, once you've begun, follow this bit of Emersonian advice: "Somewhere the author has hidden his message. Find it, and skip the paragraphs that do not talk to you."

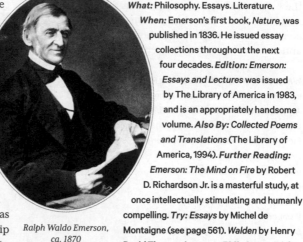

Ralph Waldo Emerson, ca. 1870

What: Philosophy. Essays. Literature. *When:* Emerson's first book, *Nature*, was published in 1836. He issued essay collections throughout the next four decades. *Edition: Emerson: Essays and Lectures* was issued by The Library of America in 1983, and is an appropriately handsome volume. *Also By: Collected Poems and Translations* (The Library of America, 1994). *Further Reading: Emerson: The Mind on Fire* by Robert D. Richardson Jr. is a masterful study, at once intellectually stimulating and humanly compelling. *Try: Essays* by Michel de Montaigne (see page 561). *Walden* by Henry David Thoreau (see page 786). *Ceremonials of Common Days* by Abbie Graham.

" 'Tis the good reader makes the good book."

—Ralph Waldo Emerson

....

Crazy Salad
SOME THINGS ABOUT WOMEN
Nora Ephron (1941–2012)

Wit, Wisecracks, and Worldly Wisdom

In the country of good reading, personal journalism might seem like a neglected city that has lost its industry, a once-thriving town that time has passed by, its urbane aspect dulled by outdated references and unfashionable ideas. Yet it can also be a fascinating destination for the intrepid reader with a taste for discerning writers, for in few other modes of writing is discernment itself both method and matter; it's not the subjects of the pieces per se that hold our interest, but the dynamic engagement of the author's mind.

Such is the case with Nora Ephron's *Crazy Salad*, a collection of magazine pieces from the 1970s. Like all the best journalism, it is opportunistic from start to finish: "I began writing a column about women in *Esquire* magazine in 1972," Ephron writes in the preface to a later edition. "Self-indulgent specifics first: I needed an excuse to go to my tenth reunion at Wellesley

College, and I was looking for someone to pay my way to the Pillsbury Bake-Off. Beyond that, and in general, it seemed clear that American women were going through some changes; I wanted to write about them and about myself." Which she proceeds to do, with sharp wit and large intelligence. The first piece, "A Few Words About Breasts," reveals her approach, mixing reflection, finely tuned social antennae, and a self-awareness both shrewd and funny, all the while evincing the disorienting self-assessment that is central to the wider context of American womanhood. She writes about the growing pains of the women's movement with both insight and impatience, and about figures of contemporary notoriety, from porn star Linda Lovelace to presidential secretary Rose Mary Woods, with a nose for both news and the deeper scents of cultural meaning. (Her review of transgender travel writer Jan Morris's brave memoir, *Conundrum*, interestingly, is uncharacteristically nearsighted.)

Ephron would go on to become famous as a screenwriter and film director, but she found a tone in these columns that would shape her creative identity through the big screen dreams of *Sleepless in Seattle* and *You've Got Mail*. This distinctive voice was eventually given deeper resonance in a spate of personal essays written later in life, collected in *I Feel Bad About My Neck* (2006) and *I Remember Nothing* (2010), in which youthful insecurities had matured into older, sometimes wiser, but no less recognizable unease. Her gift for making the clichés of our lives entertaining, enlightening, and, from time to time, revelatory, never left her.

What: Essays. Journalism. *When:* 1975. *Also By: Wallflower at the Orgy* (1970). *Scribble Scribble* (1978). *Try: Metropolitan Life* by Fran Lebowitz. *If You Can't Live Without Me, Why Aren't You Dead Yet?!* by Cynthia Heimel.

The Epic of Gilgamesh

The Oldest Story in the World

He saw what was secret, discovered what was hidden,
    he brought back a tale of before the Deluge.
He came a far road, was weary, found peace,
    and set all his labors on a tablet of stone.

At least a thousand years older than *The Iliad* or the Hebrew Bible, *The Epic of Gilgamesh* has claim to being literature's most ancient tale. Its title character was a historical king who ruled the Mesopotamian city of Uruk in the first half of the third millennium BC. The earliest surviving texts detailing his exploits are written in Sumerian and date from around 2100 BC. A subsequent poem, written in Akkadian (Old Babylonian) several centuries later, gave the epic its enduring outline (an edited and amplified version of this work, prepared by the priest Sîn-lēqi-unninni in the first millennium BC, is the basis for all modern translations).

Lost for more than two thousand years, *Gilgamesh* was rescued from oblivion in the middle of the nineteenth century, when a horde of clay tablets inscribed with wedge-shaped characters was unearthed in the excavations of the ruins of Ninevah, the ancient Assyrian capital in what is now Iraq. The eventual decipherment of the cuneiform script led to the initial translation of fragments of the story by a British Museum curator named George Smith; subsequent archaeology and scholarship pieced together the rest of what we now recognize as the world's first literary masterpiece, for encoded on the broken tablets is a tale that echoes with all the themes that still define the essence of our existence: life and death, love and fear, courage and duty, desire.

The tale centers on the friendship between Gilgamesh, an arrogant and grasping ruler, and Enkidu, a wild creature who, once humanized by the arts of eros embodied by the priestess Shamhat, becomes the king's friend and inseparable companion, but only after he and Gilgamesh engage in a fierce fight. Their adventures on a series of quests eventually lead to Enkidu's death. Inconsolable in his grief for is friend, Gilgamesh embarks upon a heroic journey to the ends of the earth in search of his ancestor Utnapishtim, who has been given

Illustration of an ancient Assyrian statue of Gilgamesh

eternal life. This ancient being relates the tale of the great flood (clearly a prototype of the biblical tale of Noah), but fails to pass on to Gilgamesh the secret of immortality.

As the narrative unfolds from the initial hubris to the ultimate humbling of its hero, Gilgamesh is ennobled by his discovery of friendship, his experience of grief, and his acceptance of the human condition. For our part as readers, we are filled with wonder at witnessing the contours and powers of the human imagination invoked with primal urgency and eloquence.

What: Antiquity. Mythology. Literature. *When:* First extant fragments, 2100 BC. *Editions:* The Penguin edition, featuring the scholarship and translation of Andrew George (quoted here), is superb. Stephen Mitchell's translation is also beautifully rendered, and his long introductory essay is a fascinating survey of the epic's origins and history. *Further Reading: The Buried Book: The Loss and Rediscovery of the Great Epic of Gilgamesh* by David Damrosch. *Try: Poems of Heaven and Hell from Ancient Mesopotamia*, edited by N. K. Sandars. *Beowulf* (see page 68).

> **"Approach what lies ahead not as you might the poems of Homer but as a book part-eaten by termites or a scroll half-consumed by fire."** —*Andrew George on* The Epic of Gilgamesh

Praise of Folly
Desiderius Erasmus (ca. 1466–1536)

Life Lessons from the Patron Saint of Humanists

Waspish, subversive, bitingly ironic, and endlessly entertaining, *Praise of Folly* has endured for five hundred years as a masterpiece of humanistic inquiry and opposition to dogmatism. The book begins as a straight satire. Folly, in the guise of a jester, speaks for herself in a parodic declamation, insisting she is the world's greatest benefactor—desire, flattery, youth, and vitality all follow her lead, and Jupiter himself has to fall in behind her when he wants to father a child. When someone observes that no humans have ever built a house of worship for her, Folly first responds with a droll observation: "I cannot but wonder at the ingratitude." But what need does Folly have for a temple? "The whole world is my temple," Folly suggests. "Nor will there ever be a lack of worshipers, as long as there is no lack of men."

Yet *Praise of Folly* soon pivots from this cheeky beginning, and the goddess becomes a mouthpiece through which the author propounds more serious themes. He argues for religious tolerance, peace across Europe, rights for women (including, shockingly for the time, access to university education), and the coexistence of pleasure and scholarship. You can see the dogmas of the Middle Ages taking cover as you read *Praise of Folly*, which puts doubt, skepticism, critical thinking, and even delight not in opposition to religion, but in a more complementary pose. As Erasmus writes in one typically aphoristic passage, "the summit of happiness is reached when a person is ready to be what he is."

The greatest of all the Renaissance humanists, Desiderius Erasmus of Rotterdam was an independent scholar whose extraordinary contemporary influence was both personal and intellectual; his vast correspondence and his grasp of the promise of the nascent publishing and book industries in Europe placed him at the center of what might be called a pioneering cultural network. He wrote in a highly polished Latin that attested to his admiration for classical antecedents, whose works he promulgated in superb new editions. Over an uncommonly long career (he lived to be sixty-nine), he also prepared rigorous—and revelatory—revised versions of the New Testament in both Latin and Greek, and he wrote prodigiously on ecclesiastical subjects and on topics of general interest. He even put together a book of proverbs (*Adagia*) whose contents—for example, "In the country of the blind, the one-eyed man is king"—have become part of our common language. His name has become shorthand for erudition but also worldliness—indeed, the European Union's cross-border student exchange program is named Erasmus, a tribute to his pan-European identity.

With its rejection of dogmas and insistence on skepticism and inquiry, *Praise of Folly* played a major role in the Protestant Reformation, although Erasmus himself did not; he strongly advocated for reform, but disdained Martin Luther's absolutist stances and remained a member of the Catholic church his whole life. Half a millennium on, the power of Erasmus's masterpiece has not waned; in fact, it's both disturbingly and providentially relevant in our contemporary moment, when religious belief and humanistic scrutiny are often violently opposed.

1523 portrait of Erasmus by Hans Holbein the Younger

What: Philosophy. *When:* 1509. *Edition:* Betty Radice's translation for Penguin Classics is graceful and well annotated. *Also By: Adages* (1500). *Handbook of the Christian Soldier* (1503). *Education of a Christian Prince* (1515). *Colloquies* (1518). *The Freedom of the Will* (1524).

Further Reading: Erasmus and the Age of Reformation by Johan Huizinga. *Erasmus of Christendom* by Roland H. Bainton. *Try: The Consolation of Philosophy* by Boethius. *Utopia* by Thomas More. *Philosophical Dictionary* by Voltaire.

||||||||||||||||||||||||||||||||||||||||||||||||| B O O K N O T E |||||||||||||||||||||||||||||||||||||||||||||||||

The Book of the City of Ladies
Christine de Pizan (1364–ca. 1430)

Preceding Erasmus's *Praise of Folly* by more than a century, Christine de Pizan's *Book of the City of Ladies* is another medieval allegory whose message has not lost its force. The first laywoman in Europe to make her living solely by her writing, Pizan used her gifts to refute the misogyny of philosophers, poets, orators, and churchmen, who, the author asserts at the outset, were unanimous in their view that "female nature is wholly given up to vice." Drawing upon classical mythology, ancient history,

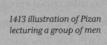

scripture, and the lives of the martyrs, Pizan cites examples of female virtue and achievement, honoring women who were warriors, inventors, scholars, oracles, artists, saints. An anthology of entertaining stories, her book is also an important intellectual document and a fierce argument for women's education: "If it were customary to send little girls to school and teach them the same subjects as are taught to boys," Pizan wrote at the turn of the fifteenth century, "they would learn just as fully and would understand the subtleties of all arts and sciences."

1413 illustration of Pizan lecturing a group of men

The Virgin Suicides
Jeffrey Eugenides (born 1960)

The Haunting Voices of Adolescence

You might think that a novel centered on the suicides of five teenage sisters would merit adjectives such as "grotesque," "gruesome," "Gothic." But those are not the words that first come to mind upon finishing this luminous, curious, lyrical, compelling, funny, eerie, and entirely original debut novel. That Jeffrey Eugenides has made something magical and rare out of subject matter on the one hand so sensational—a quintet of suicides all in the same family, all in the same year—and so banal—coming of age in a suburb of Detroit in the 1970s (complete with soundtrack by Jim Croce, Bread, Carole King, and their contemporaries)—is a source of lasting wonder.

The story is told by a collective narrator, a "we" who speaks for a group of boys who, as adolescents, are besotted with the mystifying Lisbon sisters, and, as adults, have remained transfixed by memories of the girls' mysterious lives and unfortunate ends. As the story is told through ruminative evocations of suburban life—school hallways and locker rooms, lawns and summer insects, the sneaky imminence of cigarettes and sexual allure—Eugenides conjures the mythologizing innocence of childhood and adolescence through the boys' curatorial, obsessive, and bewildered summoning of their past. The suicides punctuated their idyllic youth with such unreal finality that they seem to have invented death: "There had never been a funeral in our town before, at least not during our lifetimes."

As it probes the years for clues to the puzzle of the Lisbon girls, the narrative ranges through several modes: nostalgic, confessional, documentary, philosophical, sentimental, investigatory, droll, bemused, sagacious—yet never loses its freshness and immediacy. It sustains a personal connection to a time and place that you might more likely find in a memoir than a novel, while managing to invest the familiar tropes of suburban life with the inscrutable aura of an oracular destiny. Summoning a voice that embodies with expressive exactitude a quality of growing up that has slipped through the sentences of most novels concerned with it, Eugenides captures its nature as a communal experience with breathtaking, heartbreaking sympathy.

What: Novel. *When:* 1993. *Also By: Middlesex* (2002). *The Marriage Plot* (2011). *Try: During the Reign of the Queen of Persia* by Joan Chase. *The Corrections* by Jonathan Franzen. *Never Let Me Go* by Kazuo Ishiguro. *Adaptations:* Kirsten Dunst stars in Sophia Coppola's 2000 film adaptation. There is also an excellent unabridged audiobook read by Nick Landrum.

EURIPIDES
(ca. 480 BC–406 BC)

Greek tragedy casts a long shadow across the Western mind. From Aristotle to Freud, Seneca to Racine to Stravinsky, Shakespeare to *The Sopranos*, its intuitions about human existence have remained relevant, enduring long after its illuminations of fate, morality, and mortality first enlightened ancient audiences. What's especially astonishing is the smallness of the body of extant work—some thirty-odd relatively short plays—that has supplied us with such a large legacy of wisdom; more astonishing still is that roughly 60 percent of that dramatic estate is the endowment of one author: Euripides.

Bust of Euripides, ca. 330 BC

Out of the ninety plays that scholars agree Euripides composed, less than a score have come down to us. Nonetheless, these works, written over the course of three decades, suggest a complete oeuvre as rich as Shakespeare's; it has the same kind of sweep and surprise—the same messy but meaningful energy—as the infinite variety of Shakespearean invention. Indeed, the ancient tragedian's rhetorical ingenuity in exploring his characters' inner lives through linguistically intricate speeches makes it natural for us to see these "arias" (as they are sometimes called by writers on his work) as ancestors of the soliloquies of Hamlet, Lear, and Macbeth.

Again as in Shakespeare, and as opposed to what we find in Aeschylus and Sophocles, there is something bracingly provisional in the tragedies of Euripides, as if the dramas themselves are attempts to figure things out rather than to explain a preexisting philosophy. To the reader, the plays feel like emergent creations rather than settled classics; they dramatize life by every available theatrical means, combining the tragic and the comic, the romantic and the political, in uncanny and unnerving ways. Exalted figures, pulled from the heroic contexts of the mythological past, enter Euripides's dramatic present to be brought low by exigencies of circumstance and passion they cannot escape; they are noble one moment and ridiculous the next—then, often enough, noble once more.

Compared with Aeschylus and Sophocles, the other Greek tragedians whose work survives, Euripides had no public stature as soldier or public figure; in fact, he was made fun of by the comic playwright Aristophanes, who portrayed him mercilessly as a foggy-headed intellectual disconnected from the real world (indeed, legend has it that Euripides retreated to an island cave to write). Although he was blamed by some of his contemporaries for destroying tragedy, we might today characterize his innovations as creative destruction. Reading Aeschylus or Sophocles, we know where we stand, no matter how spooky the surroundings; their works are austere cathedrals that evoke awe at the grandeur of the savage urgencies and moral hazards of human nature. Not so when we read Euripides: Wonder is replaced by worry and wariness as we—like his characters—are surprised by life.

Alcestis
Ancient Post-Modernism

A king—Admetus—is offered a "Get Out of Death" card, but it doesn't come free: He must find someone to take his place. Selflessly, his wife—Alcestis—volunteers to pay the price for him. Her expressions of love and farewell to Admetus and their children on her deathbed are filled with dignity and imposing grief, but what ensues after her passing, on the plot's way to rescuing her from the underworld, turns from the tragic toward the comic (though many of the characters' speeches seem suspended somewhere between the two).

So is *Alcestis* a comedy or a tragedy? The answer is both, and that ambiguity is what makes it the most beguiling of Euripides's surviving plays. Its tragicomic pose has appealed to many poets, most recently Ted Hughes and Anne Carson; their translations are quite different—Hughes's is august and severe, whereas Carson's is more informal, even droll—but each offers an excellent path into the most mysterious play of the ancient Greek canon.

What: Drama. *When:* 438 BC. *Editions:* There are many translations of Euripides; a good bet is to start with those in *The Complete Greek Tragedies*, edited by

Engraving of Medea helping Jason
seize the Golden Fleece

David Grene and Richmond Lattimore. For *Alcestis*, modern translations by poets Ted Hughes and Anne Carson are worth seeking out. *Further Reading: Euripides Our Contemporary* by J. Michael Walton. *Try: The Cocktail Party* by T. S. Eliot.

Medea
Vengeance Is Hers

First, the backstory: Jason and the Golden Fleece is one of the grandest adventures in Greek mythology, in which a man who should be king, dispossessed at birth, regains his rightful place in the world by running a gauntlet of endeavor that is fabulous in every sense of the word. Abetted by the Argonauts, a band of thrill seekers named after the vessel that conveys them to the ends of the earth, and rescued time and again by an enchantress as resourceful as he is brave, Jason returns in glory from his quest to capture the Golden Fleece.

And now the tragedy: The woman whose magic makes Jason a hero is Medea, with whom he fathers a family after their exploits on the *Argo*. When Jason abandons her to pursue a more politically advantageous match, Medea's desire for revenge engulfs even her love for her children, who become pawns of her

passion—and of Jason's opportunism. Medea's story, as rendered by Euripides in this fierce and unforgettable play, is nothing like the fairy tale of the fleece: It's a tale of psychological terror with few equals in the annals of storytelling.

What: Drama. *When:* 431 BC. *Also By: Hippolytus* (428 BC). *The Suppliants* (ca. 423 BC). *Electra* (ca. 422–416 BC). *Iphigenia at Aulis* (ca. 414–413 BC). *Try: Medea* by Seneca. *Medea: A Modern Retelling* by Christa Wolf. *Jason and Medeia* by John Gardner. *Adaptation:* Pier Paolo Pasolini's 1969 film stars Maria Callas.

The Trojan Women
After *The Iliad*

At the very end of Homer's *Iliad*, four women in turn mourn over the body of the fallen Trojan hero, Hector: his sister, Cassandra; his wife, Andromache; his mother, Hecuba; and his sister-in-law Helen, whose beauty sparked the war that led the fallen warrior to a death that is a portent of the destruction of Troy itself. These four are *The Trojan Women* of Euripides's play, which begins after the events of *The Iliad*, in the days—hours, actually—after their city's fall to the Aegean forces.

Engraving of Pentheus being torn apart by Bacchae

But *The Trojan Women* is more than a mere repetition of what, at the time of the play's writing, was an already ancient tale of Troy's burning and the slaughter of its men and subjugation of its women and children by a savage enemy. Only a few months before this tragedy was first staged, Athenian forces had imposed the same brutal terms of massacre and enslavement on the citizenry of Melos in retribution for that island city's refusal to join the alliance against Athens's rival, Sparta. By telescoping for his audience the foregone grief of the Trojan women with the fresh suffering of their counterparts on Melos, Euripides created a work that has endured as one of the most powerful expressions of the human costs of militarism and war, a play both artful and authentic in equal measure.

What: Drama. *When:* 415 BC. *Try: The Trojan Women* by Jean-Paul Sartre. *Adaptation:* The 1971 film version stars Katharine Hepburn, Vanessa Redgrave, Geneviève Bujold, and Irene Papas.

The Bacchae
Take a Walk on the Wild Side

Euripides's last play opens with a figure in a smiling mask announcing himself to the audience as a god incognito, returned to Thebes to reveal his divinity and demand reverence. He is Dionysius, and the rites he intends to establish among the Thebans are celebrations of instinct over reason, impulse over order, subversion over convention—to say nothing of the wild music, frenzied dancing, drunken orgies, and human sacrifice that are either referenced or enacted in the ensuing scenes.

Even Quentin Tarantino might pale at the violence inherent in the action of this ancient play, and it is fair to say that few dramas weirder than this one have been conceived and staged since its premiere. Fewer still have intimated so well the conflicting compulsions that contend in our psyches, from cruelty to compassion. It takes a vengeful god, perhaps—and a dramatist of genius, certainly—to force us to see so deeply into the mystery of what it means to be human.

What: Drama. *When:* 405 BC. *Further Reading: The Birth of Tragedy* by Friedrich Nietzsche (see page 588). *Try: The Oresteia* by Aeschylus (see page 9). The plays of Sophocles (page 739). *Adaptation:* Hans Werner Henze's 1966 opera, *The Bassarids*, with libretto by W. H. Auden and Chester Kallman, is based on *The Bacchae*.

A Fan's Notes
Frederick Exley (1929–1992)

A Loser's Literary Triumph

In this desperately honest and savagely funny "fictional memoir," Frederick Exley portrays himself as one of life's real losers; by all accounts, it's an unflinching self-portrait. Drifting, during his twenties and thirties, in and out of work and through several stints in a mental hospital, "Ex" is a heavy-drinking would-be writer who never actually manages to put down on paper the Big Book that would make him famous. Yet it is fame, "undying fame," that inspires this self-pitying failure's elaborate daydreams. From his late father, who had been a locally idolized high school athlete, Ex has received a dangerous legacy: "Other men might inherit from their fathers a head for figures, a gold pocket watch all encrusted with the oxidized green of age, or an eternally astonished expression; from mine I acquired this need to have my name whispered in reverential tones."

As fate would have it, though, it's Ex who does the whispering, and the name most often—and most tellingly—on his lips is that of Frank Gifford, the real-life football hero who had been Exley's collegiate contemporary at the University of Southern California in the 1950s, a "golden boy" glimpsed from afar. In the decade since, as Ex's life has unraveled, Gifford has become a champion on the New York Giants, Ex's favorite team. Thus does Ex, the fan, enjoy a vicarious taste of fame by rooting for Gifford and the Giants with the kind of unrestrained enthusiasm that serves as a reminder that "fan" is short for "fanatic."

Imagine Gatsby without the gumption, the dedication, or a pinnacle of hope from which to plummet, and you have some idea of the passionate ne'er-do-well who drinks, dreams, and repeatedly self-destructs through these pages of paradoxically stately prose—the stateliness itself one long and resonant exercise in self-deprecating candor. For all the misbehavior and bizarre characters Exley embraces with abandon, the sentences he composes in the shadow of "that long malaise, my life" are filled with an energy and rueful humor that are infectious and unforgettable. They fully earn him the roar of the reading crowd.

What: Novel. Memoir. *When:* 1968. *Also By:* Pages from a Cold Island (1975). Last Notes from Home (1988). *Try:* The Crack-Up by F. Scott Fitzgerald. The Horse's Mouth by Joyce Cary (see page 135). The Sportswriter by Richard Ford. Exley: A Novel by Brock Clarke. *Adaptation:* A little-seen film, starring Jerry Orbach, was made in 1972.

"Strong, beautiful, American, one of a kind."
—*Kurt Vonnegut on* A Fan's Notes

The Spirit Catches You and You Fall Down

A HMONG CHILD, HER AMERICAN DOCTORS,
AND THE COLLISION OF TWO CULTURES

Anne Fadiman (born 1953)

A Tragedy of Body and Soul

While the terrain of human life is material, its climate is cultural, its borders metaphysical. Disease inhabits all three of these domains with real and often anxious consequences, despite the fact that we—in the West, at least—are accustomed to appealing primarily to science and its worldview when confronted with sickness, disregarding the other outlooks that shape the nature of our lived experience. We assume the efficacy of a strictly scientific approach to disease and place our bets accordingly, often rightly so. But as Anne Fadiman puts it toward the end of this book, articulating the beliefs of the psychiatrist and medical anthropologist Arthur Kleinman, "every illness is not a set of pathologies but a personal story"—a tale that has a significance beyond the data and clinical descriptions a medical record can capture. What is lost when these other dimensions—cultural, philosophical, spiritual, each a purveyor of meaning, after all—are not brought to bear on our understanding of suffering or invoked to illuminate our existence when it is in the shadow of mortality?

Such questions have seldom been so powerfully posed for readers as they are in Fadiman's carefully researched, sympathetically wrought 1997 book about a Hmong girl named Lia Lee, the child of Laotian refugees, who is afflicted with severe epilepsy and whose treatment is thwarted by misdiagnosis, the language barrier between her parents and the staff at California's Merced County Medical Center, and the cultural chasm between Western empiricism and Hmong animism. Where the former sees an electrochemical storm at the root of Lia's neurological disorder, the latter sees "soul loss," the title of the book being a translation of the Hmong description of epileptic symptoms as the effect of a soul-thieving spirit. Over the years of her early childhood, Lia's chart grew to more than 400,000 words, Fadiman tells us: "Every one of those words reflected its author's intelligence, training, and good intentions, but not a single one dealt with the Lees' perception of their daughter's illness." What's telling in this account of Lia's tragedy, however, is not the medical missteps it details, or the animal sacrifices conducted in parking lots by the Lees and their Hmong community to assuage the effects of unseen but imminent spirits, but rather the dedication of doctors even when the tools at their command prove therapeutically ineffective as well as humanly futile, and the unshakeable love and bewildered but unrelenting endurance of the Lee family.

So although *The Spirit Catches You and You Fall Down* is written about a specific case of neurological crisis affecting one baby and her family in a particular time and place, it expands from those circumscribed actualities into an extraordinarily rich portrait of frailty, expertise, faith, endeavor, and fate, which is, of course, how the best stories work. This one, by exploring both personal catastrophe and public health, reveals, in a way that is oddly but unmistakably inspiring, how tender and tenuous any grasp on experience can be.

What: Medicine. Anthropology. *When:* 1997. *Edition:* The 2012 edition contains a new afterword by the author. *Award:* National Book Critics Circle Award

for General Nonfiction, 1997. *Also By: Ex Libris: Confessions of a Common Reader* (1998). *At Large and At Small: Familiar Essays* (2007). *Try: Illness as Metaphor* by Susan Sontag. *Hmong Means Free: Life in Laos and America*, edited by Sucheng Chan. *Mountains Beyond Mountains* by Tracy Kidder.

The Chemical History of a Candle
Michael Faraday (1791–1867)

Science Illuminated by Candlelight

Michael Faraday, ca. 1861

This captivating little book collects six demonstration lectures originally addressed to a group of young people at London's Royal Institution in 1860 by the eminent British experimental scientist best known for his contributions to our understanding of electricity. Elucidating the chemical and physical properties and processes that conspire in a burning candle, Faraday delivers a splendid course in what was called, in his epoch, "natural philosophy." One of the most treasured and widely disseminated works of popular science ever written, it has been fondly recalled as a formative inspiration by many scientists, including Oliver Sacks.

Beginning with the structure, mobility, and brightness of a flame, Faraday proceeds to explore the nature of water, hydrogen, and oxygen, and the function and weight of the atmosphere. He explains capillary attraction and discusses the carbon content of living things, the production of carbon dioxide, and the properties of carbonic acid, as well as respiration and its analogy to the burning of a candle. Throughout his presentations, his lucid descriptions and clear thinking encourage the reader's delight in the unsuspected intricacies of a familiar happening. "There is not a law under which this universe is governed," Faraday explains at the outset, "which does not come into play and is not touched upon in these phenomena." Illuminating by candlelight the pleasures of

Illustration of one of Faraday's candle experiments

scientific learning, Faraday amply supports this assertion, sparking wondering minds of all ages with the thrill of observation, experiment, and deduction.

What: Science. *When:* 1860. *Further Reading:* Alan Hirshfeld's *The Electric Life of Michael Faraday* offers the general reader a splendid introduction to its subject's fascinating life and discoveries. *Try: Uncle Tungsten,* Oliver Sacks's delightful "memories of a chemical boyhood." *Footnote:* Apprenticed to a bookbinder at the age of fourteen, Faraday took the opportunity to read the materials that came across his worktable, including the article on electricity in the third edition of the *Encyclopedia Britannica,* which would inspire his scientific career.

WILLIAM FAULKNER
(1897–1962)

R eading William Faulkner is like hiking into a lost world where, as he famously wrote, "The past is never dead. It's not even past." The past as a presence is palpable in his sentences, which weave back and forth in time and space, especially the time and space of the South's failing history, which has dimensions all its own—it is in fact a history that isn't history, but some human form of atmosphere. Faulkner's language—framed in formal experiments, filigreed with a variety of voices, of dictions and dialects and syntactical idiosyncrasies—creates a world less physical

William Faulkner, early 1940s

than Hemingway's, and certainly less social (even if more communal) than Fitzgerald's, to mention the two contemporaries with whom he is often grouped.

The reality Faulkner demands that we engage in his fiction is not so much described by the words on the page as invoked by them. While *A Farewell to Arms* and *The Great Gatsby* are powerful because they are compactly conceived and executed as familiar novels, the sentences of *The Sound and the Fury*, *As I Lay Dying*, and the dozen other novels set by Faulkner in Yoknapatawpha, the fictional avatar of his native Lafayette County in Mississippi, spill out of their covers and blend with one another to form a rich delta of fertile invention. In that soil he found a way to grow stories that weren't about individuals, or about society, but about enduring nature—human and other—and the culture it engenders. By doing so, he expanded the possibilities of the novel in ways that inspired writers beyond the United States, most notably in Latin America, where, following the lead of Jorge Luis Borges (see page 87), who made the first Spanish translation of Faulkner's *The Wild Palms*, Gabriel García Márquez (see page 308), Mario Vargas Llosa, and Carlos Fuentes would claim Faulkner as an empowering influence.

Faulkner's vision of life is less dreadful than Hemingway's, less wistful than

Fitzgerald's, and more melodramatic and mythic than both. He writes as if he were luring some wild life-form out of a dense fog and unpacking the meaning carried on its back. Or not: Sometimes it's just fog. But for all the difficulty, there is a sense of noble sufferance in Faulkner—"They endured" are the last words of his masterpiece, *The Sound and the Fury*—that is akin to beauty, and often awful in both the modern and the archaic senses. What he conjures out of the morbid historical tensions of the South are fictions that proffer a human counterweight to time, imbuing humanity with the same unfathomable capacity as the weather. Hemingway said of him, "How beautifully he can write and as simple and as complicated as autumn or as spring." And, somehow, as inscrutable as both.

The Sound and the Fury
A Modernist Milestone

T he Sound and the Fury was Faulkner's fourth novel. In it, he bravely indulged the experimental impulse that, under the guidance of his editors, he had kept in check in his previously published work, creating one of the landmarks of modern—and modernist—fiction. The book comprises four sections, three set on the days of Easter weekend in 1928, and one (the second as ordered in the novel) set eighteen years earlier. Together, they brood on thirty years of sorrow in the life of the Compson family, aristocratic Southerners whose fortunes have fallen far and messily, and whose members cannot come to grips with their loss of financial stature, local prestige, moral compass, and meaningful relation to their land, their history, and each other.

The novel is not easy reading, for the four parts have distinct styles, none of which is straightforward. The first, second, and third are each narrated by a different Compson brother, often through a stream of consciousness that makes for a vivid but disjointed parsing of events; the final segment assumes a third-person perspective, although, on first reading, this does little to make its pages more lucid than what's come before.

At the start, *The Sound and the Fury* takes literally the tale-telling metaphor from *Macbeth* that gives the novel its name: "Life's but a walking shadow, / . . . a tale / Told by an idiot, full of sound and fury, / Signifying nothing." The idiot doing the telling is Benjy Compson, the youngest sibling, a thirty-three-year-old of deficient mental capacity who can express himself to others only through grunts and moans. Yet he has a preternatural intuition of things gone wrong, and Faulkner's ingenious portrayal of his ominous apprehensions offers a cryptic but telling portrayal of the family's decline and fall. All that the reader comes to piece together by the end of the novel—the family's financial dissipation; the promiscuous disgrace of their sister, Caddy; the suicide of Quentin, the gifted oldest child, during his freshman year at Harvard; the stress of current degradations on the embittered middle brother, Jason, who is left as head of the family—is portended in Benjy's uncanny monologue, a disturbed mix of memories and real-time impressions that is disorienting,

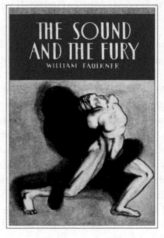

puzzling, maddening, and gripping. The novel's three subsequent sections flesh out Benjy's impressionistic ramblings with exposition, character, and various flavors of desperation. They're told in turn by Quentin, as he plunges toward self-destruction in Cambridge; by Jason, as he schemes through his bitterness to wring some payoff from the vexations of his inheritance; and by an omniscience assuming, to some degree, the point of view of the black domestic help that both sustains the family and acts as a kind of Greek chorus for the Compson tragedy.

Remarkably, our disorientation coalesces into a rich reality as we progress through the book. Reading it is like being lost in a wood, our anxiety and growing fear making us close observers of every leaf, tree, and shaft of sunlight, our acute perception not clarifying, but threatening. We come to feel the nature of the forest in a way we never would if we were following a clearly marked path. The brilliance of the novel's final section is the way it makes us feel that we've emerged from danger through the grace of some guiding hand, albeit one that is extended without any assurance or explanation. In the end, the author imbues the experience of this clan of afflicted, misguided, depressive, impetuous, cruel, and shortsighted people with a tragic sense of life that transcends their sad circumstances, and is beyond their ken as well.

What: Novel. *When:* 1929. *Award:* Nobel Prize in Literature, 1949. *Also By: Flags in the Dust* (1973; unabridged version of *Sartoris*, which was first published in 1929). *The Wild Palms* (1939). *The Hamlet* (1940). *Intruder in the Dust* (1948). *Collected Stories of William Faulkner* (1950). *A Fable* (1954). *The Town* (1957). *The Mansion* (1959). *The Reivers* (1962). *Further Reading: Becoming Faulkner: The Art and Life of William Faulkner* by Philip Weinstein. *Try: To the Lighthouse* by Virginia Woolf (see page 869). *All the King's Men* by Robert Penn Warren (see page 834). *Lie Down in Darkness* by William Styron. *Beloved* by Toni Morrison (see page 569).

As I Lay Dying
More Than Words Can Say

" My mother is a fish," says Vardaman, the youngest child of Addie Bundren, the dying matriarch of Faulkner's bold novel of 1930. Addie's health is deteriorating rapidly, and her eldest son, Cash, is hewing the most beautiful coffin he can manage right outside her bedroom window. Wretchedly poor, the Bundrens watch Addie die, then make their way with her corpse, its coffin in a mule-drawn wagon, across the fictional Yoknapatawpha County to fulfill her wish to be buried in her hometown of Jefferson. Along the way, they curse and fight and scream and hallucinate over the loss of the woman who held their lives together, enduring flood, fire, and all sorts of other calamities. It's so blackly comic that laughter is eclipsed by a state of fretful, threatened animation that is part Gothic grotesquerie, part ramshackle picaresque, and part Old Testament. There's no other book quite like it.

In fact, in the estimation of the critic Harold Bloom, *As I Lay Dying* "may be the most original novel ever written by an American." But originality has its price. It can be tough going for the reader, even if, in comparison to his earlier novel *The Sound and the Fury*—which Faulkner himself described to his agent as "a real son of a bitch"—*As I Lay Dying* is a slightly easier read. You'll need some time to get used to the novel's polyvocal structure (a radical and influential literary innovation), which features fifteen different narrators in the course of its 250-odd pages. For instead of offering different perspectives on a common reality, Faulkner's multivoiced construction fractures the very idea of a single, perceptible truth (the section that details Addie's death, for example, is narrated by a character who isn't even there).

Addie herself, from beyond the grave, narrates her own chapter, a tour de force of stream-of-consciousness prose in which she laments that her life had been circumscribed by the very language she used to describe it (an intuition that many feminist thinkers would echo and elaborate in scholarly works half a century later):

That was when I learned that words are no good; that words dont ever fit even what they are trying to say at. When he was born I knew that motherhood was invented by someone who had to have a word for it because the ones that had the children didn't care whether there was a word for it or not. . . .

And so when Cora Tull would tell me I was not a true mother, I would think how words go straight up in a thin line, quick and harmless, and how terribly doing goes along the earth, clinging to it, so that after a while the two lines are too far apart for the same person to straddle from one to the other . . .

Faulkner's intent as a writer was to bridge the gap between words and life that Addie so astutely senses—to set down lines of words that would somehow connect us to the terrible doing human lives are entangled in. He wanted to make "sin" and "love" and "fear" more than just sounds, more than what Addie called them: "a shape to fill a lack." No wonder his novels are so abstruse, and so worth the effort to fathom.

What: Novel. **When:** 1930. **Try:** *Wise Blood* by Flannery O'Connor. *Getting Mother's Body* by Suzan-Lori Parks. *Salvage the Bones* by Jesmyn Ward.

Light in August
Life Without Parole

Two strangers come to town; only one will leave alive. Lena Grove is a pregnant, unmarried young woman looking for the father of her child; Joe Christmas, who arrived three years earlier, is a drifter whose orphanhood haunts his every relation and whose appetites are mired in flesh and blood. The pair heads a *dramatis personae* that reads like the character checklist handed out on the first day of a Southern Gothic writing course: There's a disgraced former minister, a bootlegger, a vindictive orphanage employee, a zealous suitor of the sullied heroine, a righteous adoptive father, and a grandmother whose maternal instincts override circumstantial evidence. All are caught in the violence of a present so remote from any alternative future that their inner lives have no direction. Their identities are in thrall to poverty, racism, ignorance, and intolerance, and the sociopathy all four engender when there is no way to escape their grip.

If the present is violent, the past is oppressive, exerting its force by a strange sort of osmosis. Fevers of the blood course invisibly and unabated until they break in fear, sex, rage, murder, castration—one might even say that the catalog of stock plot points matches the character list in brutal predictability. Yet even though all these familiar pieces are laid out on the page, they are put together in a way so inventive and unexpected that melodrama is turned into something not only meaningful, but almost majestic, transcending its material to create an imaginative space more like a film than a conventional novel. Faulkner's prose is like a camera that shapes our experience of character and incident by controlling the pace and angle of our discovery. He's not telling a preexisting story, but revealing it in sentence after sentence—as a movie is revealed shot by shot—until the emergent reality bears witness to some higher truths than verisimilitude can ever approach. It's remarkable, unsettling, and unforgettable.

ABSALOM, ABSALOM!

WILLIAM FAULKNER

A MODERN LIBRARY BOOK

What: Novel. **When:** 1932. **Try:** *Their Eyes Were Watching God* by Zora Neale Hurston (see page 397). *The Heart Is a Lonely Hunter* by Carson McCullers (see page 536). *A Heart So White* by Javier Marías.

Absalom, Absalom!
The Best-Laid Plans

Faulkner's polyphonic narratives make his novels more than the sum of their parts and their plots more reverberant than the events they describe. His best works create worlds that are pulled out of hurtling time only by the telling, as if they must be lured from history and memory by the author's spell to take any shape at all before our eyes. How else could he do justice to his abiding apprehensions of both Southern culture and human nature?

There is no truer way, as novelist Richard Ford would write in reference to *Absalom, Absalom!* some seven decades after its publication, "to register and imagine life" in all its "swarming, confusing, simultaneous, mistake-ridden, obsessive, occasionally hilarious, pathetic, violent" gravity.

The novel forms, disperses, then coalesces again and again around the story of Thomas Sutpen, who arrives in Yoknapatawpha County in 1833 with slaves, a French architect, and a "design": to work his will on a large parcel of land, planting cotton and erecting an extravagant estate house, to establish himself as a pillar of the precinct's aristocracy. He summons his own grandeur out of thin air and polishes it with the sweat of slaves.

The decline and fall of the Sutpen design over the next century is like the degeneration of the Compson family in *The Sound and the Fury* imagined on a larger stage (Quentin Compson also has a central role in *Absalom, Absalom!*). Indeed, if *Light in August* is something like film noir, *Absalom, Absalom!* is a grand opera. Again, several narrators rehearse the same story, one whose melodramatic outlines are sketched for us in early chapters. The repetitions and amplifications of characters and events are passed from one voice to another like musical themes and leitmotifs being passed from soloist to chorus to ensemble to orchestra as Faulkner's language swirls and swells and subsides, only to swell again, culminating in Quentin's closing aria in response to a questioning of his feelings for the South: *"I dont. I dont! I dont hate it! I dont hate it!"*

The saga of Thomas Sutpen and his heirs is a story of people who, as one character puts it, outlive themselves by years and years and years, just as Sutpen's design will dissipate across the decades. The same fate will be met by the specter of Southern "nobility"—the ideals of honor, chivalry, and purity that drive Quentin mad and Sutpen's heirs into a strange penury of circumstance and spirit. No matter the certainties of the present, Faulkner tells us again and again, the past always in large part determines the future, just as the untamed grace of the natural order outlasts the will of any human one, for the violence necessary to impose the latter will eventually consume it. That, of course, is the lesson of all tragedy, from the Greeks to the Elizabethans and beyond, a line of literary wisdom in which *Absalom, Absalom!* takes a place as a wild yet worthy American descendant.

What: Novel. **When:** 1936. *Try: The Oresteia* by Aeschylus (see page 9). *The Keepers of the House* by Shirley Ann Grau. *The Known World* by Edward P. Jones.

A Time of Gifts
Patrick Leigh Fermor (1915–2011)

A Travel Writer in a Class by Himself

With a borrowed knapsack and a small weekly allowance (a single British pound), Patrick Leigh Fermor set out from London in 1933 on a journey that might today seem unthinkable. After arriving by boat in Holland, the eighteen-year-old walked—*walked!*—from Amsterdam all the way across Central Europe to Constantinople in Turkey. It took him a year and a half, during which he assumed different perspectives: He was a high-spirited young adventurer with a talent for making friends; he was a knowledgeable and insatiably curious student of history and culture; and he was a sharply observant eyewitness of the moods and circumstances that were leading Europe inexorably toward World War II.

It wasn't until more than forty years later that Fermor reconstructed his travels from old notebooks and memory, publishing two opulent narratives that recount his trek. *A Time of Gifts*, which covers the initial stage of the journey—"from the Hook of Holland to the Middle Danube"—was the first installment; *Between the Woods and the Water* (1986), which follows him from Prague to the Balkans, was the second. (A third and final volume, awaited by the author's admirers as eagerly as Harry Potter fans anticipated the boy wizard's last adventure, was at last published posthumously in 2013 as *The Broken Road*; incomplete and not fully polished by Fermor, it is nonetheless a substantial and welcome work.) Together, the two books published during Fermor's lifetime rank among the best autobiographical travelogues in English. The older Fermor's descriptions of his younger self's exploits on barges and in beer halls, of his nights passed in barns and in castles, of his encounters with laborers, scholars, and aristocrats—all are suffused with both the innocence of youthful adventure and the sophistication of age's experience, erudition, and reflection. It is an uncommonly rich combination.

The inherent interest of Fermor's tale is enriched by the beauty of his prose. His books can be opened at random with pleasure: So captivating is his voice, so exhilarating his language, that one is beguiled wherever one begins. His exactitude of description and mastery of archaic vocabulary make a dictionary a recommended companion. As travel writer Jan Morris notes in her introduction to a recent edition of *A Time of Gifts*, "Envy is the writer's sin, as everyone knows, but there can be few writers in the English-speaking world who resent Patrick Leigh Fermor's pre-eminence as one of the great prose stylists of our time. He has no rivals, and so stands beyond envy."

What: Travel. Autobiography. **When:** 1977. **Also By:** *The Traveller's Tree: A Journey Through the Caribbean Islands* (1950). *The Violins of Saint-Jacques* (1953). *A Time to Keep Silence* (1957). *Mani: Travels in the Southern Peloponnese* (1958). *Roumeli: Travels in Northern Greece* (1966). *Three Letters from the Andes* (1991). *Try: Prospero's Cell* by Lawrence Durrell. **Footnote:** During World War II, Patrick Leigh Fermor participated in a daring commando raid on the island of Crete, described in W. Stanley Moss's *Ill Met by Moonlight* (see page 570).

THE NEAPOLITAN NOVELS

MY BRILLIANT FRIEND • THE STORY OF A NEW NAME • THOSE WHO LEAVE AND
THOSE WHO STAY • THE STORY OF THE LOST CHILD

Elena Ferrante (born 1943)

The Lives of Girls and Women

"We climbed slowly toward the greatest of our terrors of that time, we went to expose ourselves to fear and interrogate it." So Elena Greco, called Lenù by those who know her, describes the adventure that cements her friendship with Raffaella Cerullo, known familiarly as Lina or Lila, a friendship that Lenù will narrate across six decades in the novels of Elena Ferrante's Neapolitan Quartet. It's a description that might well serve as an epigraph to the work as a whole—or, come to think of it, as a motto for anyone hoping to muster some kind of nobility in the midst of life's relentless testing of our resourcefulness.

The four books follow the two girls from first grade through adolescence, young adulthood, marriage, motherhood, the confusions of middle age, the demanding uncertainties of working lives, all the way into the unavoidable diminishments of old age. Ferrante's sweeping portrait of the private dramas and public contexts of the lives of Lenù and Lila, as well as those of the broad cast of characters who accompany them through the years, is the story of relationships forged by the stresses of a specific time and place—a hardscrabble urban neighborhood in Naples from the 1950s through the turn of the millennium—whose hold on its inhabitants remains unbending even after animation has been drained from its streets. Characterizing with fidelity the envies and jealousies that color, and sometimes corrupt, our lasting affections, Ferrante's quartet portrays the inherent conspiracy of two women aligned by consent and contingency against the powers that be.

For Lenù, whose voice addresses us across nearly seventeen hundred pages, and Lila, her brilliant—as well as ruthless and inscrutable—friend, those powers inhabit their native precincts with obscure yet ominous presence, starting with the figure of Don Achille, the menacing black market entrepreneur who looms as large in the girls' imaginations as he does in their impoverished community's economy. (It is his apartment they are climbing toward in the sentence quoted above.) As the neighborhood, like the narrative, moves across generations, Don Achille's shadowy authority will be usurped by the flashier malevolence and more visible energies of the Solara brothers, contemporaries of Lenù and Lila; yet while local power changes hands, and faces, the stubborn violence of its oppressions haunts the fortunes of those within its reach.

The first novel in the set, *My Brilliant Friend*, is devoted to the girls' school days and teenage years; it begins with them playing with their dolls and ends—in cliff-hanging form—in the middle of Lila's tumultuous wedding. The apprehensiveness of childhood—the uncanny allure of dark cellars, the liberating mischief of stone throwing or shouting in a tunnel—is perfectly drawn, as are the classroom rivalries of girls and boys that foreshadow relationships between them that will develop and transform as elementary learning is outweighed by the lure and luck of circumstance. The fatalism in which their lives are steeped, the sense that life is a collusion of blunt, featureless forces, is captured in scene after scene, but never more tellingly than in a single sentence describing the demise of a neighbor's husband: "One night he came out of the house as usual and died, perhaps murdered, perhaps of weariness." Indeed, the fatalistic privation—intellectual as well as economic—of the neighborhood's constant and constricted present is what Lenù desires to escape, although even she is conflicted about the costs, and what Lila, at the end of *My Brilliant Friend*, will marry into—and marry well, as far as such surrender goes, for the time being.

Lenù's love of learning, of books and writing, sets her apart from the neighborhood; dutiful, studious, ultimately vocational, she is contrasted with Lila, whose intuitive intellect is fueled by a surreptitious course of cavalier study. Lenù needs Lila's intrepid mind to help expand her own, and Lila needs Lenù to scout the wider world she lacks the confidence to explore, especially after their educational paths fork and Lenù goes on to secondary school, university, and literary life. The titles of the subsequent novels—*The Story of a New Name, Those Who Leave and Those Who Stay*, and *The Story of the Lost Child*—outline what transpires as the two women grow, go their separate ways, then reconvene their collaborative destiny. The saga—filled with melodramatic changes of fortune, amorous and political engagements and retrenchments, the humblings and humiliations of yearnings unfulfilled, conveniences yielded to—has been hailed as a singularly intense and encompassing story of friendship between women.

It is surely that, and more, for Ferrante's story turns on how her protagonists must confront not just the defining realities of gender but also summon the unscripted responses to family and community, to culture and society, to making a living and forging an identity that all of us are called upon to make, and from which many of us shrink. How, Ferrante asks, do human beings create, and keep, meaning when the means afforded us are limited, often merciless, and always mortal? In a context that gives them little agency without struggle, little money without venality, little opportunity without guile, little education without sacrifice, not even any viable religion, there is no future—and, as the precocious Lila realizes at an early age, no purchase on the past either. There are only the demands of the ever-present now, which become more pressing and oppressive day by day, month by month, year by year.

As Ferrante knows and as Lenù learns in the course of the lifetime she chronicles, being born in that neighborhood was a life sentence, unless you could learn to compose another to lead you out of its endless getting and wanting, the stultifying solace and demand of love, family, fate. So these books are about friendship, yes, but they are also about the never-solved riddle of how one can rescue a self from the primacies of raw experience, especially experience as vehement and violent as that which Lenù and Lila were born into. If Lenù, looking back, can compose her way out of that world, she can never leave it behind. Ferrante's portrait of a writer as a young, middle-aged, and old woman is imbued with the knowledge that the syntax of women's lives is more complicated than that of men—by convention surely, but by nature as well. Such knowledge honors the fact that the demands of the quotidian world and its social relations are more stubborn and creative than we can ever be. Women live with this in ways men, generally speaking, do not, and in ways that literature seldom reveals.

There is nothing heroic in Ferrante's heroines: They are two women trying to make lives out of the time and material afforded them. We witness their struggle to do so in a fiction whose nerve and scope and sympathy make most novels of equal ambition seem somehow quaint.

What: Novels. *When: My Brilliant Friend* (2011). *The Story of a New Name* (2012). *Those Who Leave and Those Who Stay* (2013). *The Story of the Lost Child* (2014). *Editions:* English translations by Ann Goldstein. *Also By: Troubling Love* (1992). *The Days of Abandonment* (2002). *Frantumaglia: A Writer's Journey* (2003). *The Lost Daughter* (2006). *Try: Cat's Eye* by Margaret Atwood (see page 28). *Swing Time* by Zadie Smith. *Footnote:* "Elena Ferrante" is a pseudonym; despite much investigative probing and some credible theories about her identity, the author remains officially unnamed.

Coming of Age in the Milky Way
Timothy Ferris (born 1944)

A Stellar History of Cosmology

The skies of our ancestors hung low overhead. When the ancient Sumerian, Chinese, and Korean astronomers trudged up the steps of their squat stone ziggurats to study the stars, they had reason to assume that they obtained a better view that way, not, as we would say today, because they had surmounted a little dust and turbulent air, but because they had got themselves appreciably closer to the stars.

S o begins Timothy Ferris's exciting—there's no more appropriate word—history of man's apprehension of space and time, from Babylon's astronomers to Berkeley's astrophysicists. Across the millennia, he distills a great deal of science into a narrative enlivened by deft portraits of a remarkable cast of characters including Eudoxus, the fourth-century BC astronomer who was a student of Plato; Aristarchus of Samos, who saw the sun at the center of the universe seventeen hundred years before Copernicus; the wily and opportunistic Galileo; the socially awkward, intellectually sophisticated Johannes Kepler; the peerless mathematician (and obsessive alchemist) Isaac Newton; and many less notorious thinkers, inventors, and explorers, right up through the modern age of relativity, quarks, and quantum mechanics.

Combining consummate storytelling with expert explication of complex ideas, Ferris's study of the evolution of our understanding of the cosmos—an evolution in which the cosmos itself seems to be transformed by each new flicker of human intuition or discovery—is the kind of book that will have you regaling your most curious friends with the learning you pick up in its pages. Einstein once said, "The most incomprehensible thing about the universe is that it is comprehensible"; this scientific history conveys the true wonder of that paradox while teaching us an enormous amount about the ever-expanding nature of the world that we inhabit.

What: Science. *When:* 1988. *Also By: The Whole Shebang: A State-of-the-Universe(s) Report* (1997). *Seeing in the Dark: How Backyard Stargazers Are Probing Deep Space and Guarding Earth from Interplanetary Peril* (2002). *The Science of Liberty: Democracy, Reason, and the Laws of Nature* (2010). *Further Reading: The Book of the Cosmos: Imagining the Universe from Heraclitus to Hawking,* edited by Dennis Richard Danielson. *Try: A Brief History of Time: From the Big Bang to Black Holes* by Stephen Hawking. *The Age of Wonder* by Richard Holmes.

QED

THE STRANGE THEORY OF LIGHT AND MATTER

Richard P. Feynman (1918–1988)

Science as Discovery—and Delight

A lthough Richard Feynman spent five decades on the leading edge of theoretical physics, he never lost his gift for applied explanation of the often abstruse ideas that were his métier. During the Rogers Commission hearings on the 1986 space shuttle *Challenger* disaster, Feynman famously made clear the flaw that caused the craft's disintegration seventy-three seconds after take-off with a simple exhibit: He immersed gasket material in a glass of ice water to illustrate how cold temperatures on launch day led to critical seal failures. And although his career

Richard Feynman, 1959

achievements included participation in the Manhattan Project, which developed the atomic bomb during World War II; pioneering work in quantum electrodynamics, for which he shared a Nobel Prize in 1965; and the planting of the conceptual seeds that have since grown into nanotechnology, he was distinguished from other physicists of his stature by his passion for sharing what he knew. A onetime collaborator, inventor Danny Hillis, put it this way after Feynman's death: "I suspect his motivation was not so much to understand the world as it was to find new ideas to explain. The act of discovery was not complete for him until he had taught it to someone else."

In this brilliant, breezy explanation of quantum electrodynamics (QED), Feynman treats the layperson to a tour of the curious world of light and matter. His learning is leavened with a fine sense of the absurd. Explaining the methods of QED theorists like himself, he says, "You will have to brace yourselves for this—not because it is difficult to understand, but because it is absolutely ridiculous: All we do is draw little arrows on a piece of paper—that's all!" It's an ideal introduction to ideas that have taken science far beyond the realm of common sense into new regions of natural wonder. Like all of Feynman's books, it is enlivened by the incisive, irreverent, and

frequently very funny voice of a legendary scientist happy to entertain his readers at the same time as he is stretching their minds.

What: Science. *When:* 1985. *Also By:* "*Surely You're Joking, Mr. Feynman!*": Adventures of a Curious Character (1985). "What Do You Care What Other People Think?": Further Adventures of a Curious Character (1988). Six Easy Pieces: Essentials of Physics Explained by Its Most Brilliant Teacher (1994). The Pleasure of Finding Things Out (1999). *Further Reading:* Genius: The Life and Science of Richard Feynman by James Gleick. *Try:* The Trouble with Physics by Lee Smolin.

Engraving of the discovery of "foundling" Tom Jones in Squire Allworthy's bed, ca. 1756

The History of Tom Jones, A Foundling
Henry Fielding (1707–1754)

An 18th-Century Comic Romp—and a Groundbreaking English Novel

One of the first great comic novels in English, and still one of the most entertaining in any language, *Tom Jones* is a gloriously robust and bawdy adventure boasting what Samuel Taylor Coleridge called "one of the most perfect plots ever planned." Its author

had begun his literary career by parodying the most popular novel of his day, the sanctimonious *Pamela: Or Virtue Rewarded*, in two works, *Joseph Andrews* and *Shamela* (the title says it all). Having upended *Pamela*, so to speak, Fielding set out to write a novel that was truer to real life, with a hero who, though undeniably good at heart, is also a high-spirited young man with lusty appetites.

Tom Jones is just such a fellow. He starts life as a "foundling"—an abandoned baby of unknown parentage. Raised in the country by Squire Allworthy, Tom tries his best to behave. His true love is Sophia Western, the beautiful daughter of a neighboring squire. Sophia returns Tom's love, but marriage is impossible because of his lowly birth. Meanwhile, Tom's misdeeds (including dalliances with other local lasses), as well as various misunderstandings, result in his banishment from the Allworthy estate. He heads to London to make his fortune. Sophia, in an effort to avoid an arranged marriage, follows. Colorful characters and amusing escapades keep things moving briskly along.

Throughout, a delightful running commentary is provided by the author ("I intend to digress," he warns the reader early on, "as often as I see occasion"). Fielding stays close by the reader's side, as it were, chatting constantly about what's going on. He is especially fond of commenting upon his role as writer, embracing the liberating playfulness the novel form allows.

In the end, Tom discovers his true identity, and his inherent goodness is fully acknowledged—and rewarded. Everyone gets his or her just desserts as the whole rollicking romp draws to a happy close, making *Tom Jones* one of the most satisfying entertainments in the annals of the "Republic of Letters," a term coined within the covers of Fielding's masterwork.

What: Novel. *When:* 1749. *Also By: Shamela* (1741). *Joseph Andrews* (1742). *Jonathan Wild* (1743). *Amelia* (1751). *Journal of a Voyage to Lisbon* (1755). *Try: The Expedition of Humphry Clinker* by Tobias Smollett (see page 733). *The Life and Adventures of Nicholas Nickleby* by Charles Dickens (see page 218). *The Sot-Weed Factor* by John Barth (see page 54). *Adaptation:* In 1963, Tony Richardson's screen adaptation of *Tom Jones* won four Academy Awards, including those for Best Picture and Best Director. *Footnote:* Although it was an immediate bestselling success, *Tom Jones* was condemned as "lewd" by its eighteenth-century critics—and blamed for earthquakes that rocked London the year after it was published!

Time and Again
Jack Finney (1911–1995)

The Fundamental Things Apply

Jack Finney's immersive time-travel novel, in which assiduously researched details of life in late-nineteenth-century Manhattan are choreographed with imaginative élan into a fleet but intricate narrative, is treasured by legions of readers. The author spices his suspenseful plot with a beguiling, factual nostalgia that incorporates historical curiosities and actual events: Pieces of the torch-bearing arm of the Statue of Liberty are seen displayed in Madison Square Park, awaiting the icon's assembly; a massive fire consumes the offices of the *New*

York World. The effect is amplified with vintage photographs as well as drawings by the book's protagonist, a twentieth-century advertising illustrator named Simon Morley.

What gives Si's drawings their charm, and the story its charge, is that he has found a way to travel back in time to do his sketching of 1880s New York on-site, so to speak. Under the aegis of a secret government project unfolding in late 1970, Si is immured in the famous Dakota apartment building overlooking Central Park; the furnishings are a replica of a Victorian domestic setting from a century earlier, providing a congenial environment for the self-hypnosis that will transport him into the past. What ensues is a tale of international espionage in the present, blackmail and murder in the past, and romance across temporal dimensions, one that carries the reader along for a heady, time-defying ride.

What: Novel. *When:* 1970. *Also By: The Body Snatchers* (1955; revised edition published as *Invasion of the Body Snatchers,* 1973). *About Time: 12 Short Stories* (1986). *From Time to Time* (1995; sequel to *Time and Again). Try: Bid Time Return* by Richard Matheson (also issued as *Somewhere in Time). Winter's Tale* by Mark Helprin. *The Time Traveler's Wife* by Audrey Niffenegger.

The Art of Eating
M. F. K. Fisher (1908–1992)

Poet of the Appetites, Master of Prose

Mary Frances Kennedy Fisher was author of more than two dozen books, each one an exercise in seductive and generous literary taste. Although food was often her ostensible subject, Fisher's real theme was human hunger, and through her long career she played elegant variations on our essential wants and their various satisfactions. "It seems to me," she explained, "that our three basic needs, for food and security and love, are so mixed and mingled and entwined that we cannot straightly think of one without the others."

In an unconventional and passionate life, Fisher lived in France, Switzerland, and California, consorting with three husbands, assorted lovers, and a vibrant network of family, friends, and correspondents. She savored the fried egg sandwiches of her childhood as intensely as the fine wines of her Parisian honeymoon. Despite the countless writers who've followed in her footsteps, she remains unmatched in her ability to put into words the sensuous power of food and the imaginative sway of musing appetites. No one has written with more relish of the simple yet sophisticated pleasures to be found in dining alone, or of the peculiar tastes and traditions of a family kitchen.

The Art of Eating is an omnibus that collects Fisher's first five gastronomical books, written between 1937 and 1949. The singularity of Fisher's early work is evidenced by the fact that the *New York Times* called her debut—a book about food with no pretense of being a cookbook—"unique," "different," "shocking," and "odd." That book, *Serve It Forth* (1937), was followed by *Consider the Oyster* (1941), an enchanting tribute to the enigmatic bivalve, and *How to Cook a Wolf* (1942), which considers the gustatory dilemmas posed by a tight budget. *The Gastronomical Me* (1943), a memoir that may just be Fisher's finest work, and *An Alphabet for Gourmets* (1948–49), twenty-six essays originally published in *Gourmet* magazine, complete the satisfying menu of *The Art of Eating*. All told, it's a compendium that documents the triumph of what the once-doubting *Times* eventually came to recognize as M. F. K. Fisher's "one-woman revolution in the field of literary cookery."

What: Food & Drink. Memoir. Essays. *When:* The collection *The Art of Eating* was first published in 1954. *Also By:* Almost all of Fisher is worth seeking out, particularly *A Cordiall Water* (1961), *With Bold Knife and Fork* (1968), *Among Friends* (1970), *Two Towns in Provence* (1983), *Sister Age* (1983), and *A Life in Letters: Correspondence 1929–1991* (1997). *Try: The Auberge of the Flowering Hearth* by Roy Andries de Groot (see page 202). *Between Meals: An Appetite for Paris* by A. J. Liebling (see page 491). *Blue Trout and Black Truffles* by Joseph Wechsberg.

|||||||||||||||||||||||||||||||||||||||||||||||| B O O K N O T E |||||||||||||||||||||||||||||||||||||||||||||||||

A PHILOSOPHER AT TABLE

The Physiology of Taste
MEDITATIONS ON TRANSCENDENTAL
GASTRONOMY

Jean Anthelme Brillat-Savarin
(1755–1826)
Translated and annotated by
M. F. K. Fisher (1908–1992)

Brillat-Savarin's 1825 collection of profound and playful musings on gastronomy opens with twenty aphorisms that stake out his territory. The first four are worth quoting, because they exude the flavor of all that follows:

I. The Universe is nothing without the things that live in it, and everything that lives, eats.

II. Animals feed themselves; men eat; but only wise men know the art of eating.

III. The destiny of nations depends on how they nourish themselves.

IV. Tell me what you eat, and I shall tell you what you are.

Composed in aphorisms, anecdotes, and brief topical essays, the book can be picked up at any time and opened to any page; it is a browser's delight, best sampled serendipitously. The thirty "meditations" that make up the meat of the book cover a wide range of gustatory subjects, from underlying matters such as taste, the senses, and the pleasures of the table to overriding concerns such as the end of the world, sleep, dreams, death, and digestion. Brillat-Savarin's appetite is catholic; he tackles turkeys, truffles, chocolate, and coffee with equal gusto. His penchant for theorizing is as French as his fondness for food, and he applies it to subjects as diverse as frying, gourmandism, obesity, and restaurants. Imagine a postprandial conversation, fueled by fine wine and cognac, with a worldly and loquacious uncle whose store of anecdote and eloquence seems endless, and you'll approach the pleasures that await you in this quirky masterpiece. It is unrivaled to this day as a compendium of food lore, culinary observations, and philosophical ruminations on the art of eating and the art of living.

Fortunately, because of the labors and inspirations of M. F. K. Fisher, Anglophone readers lose nothing in translation, for Fisher's version of Brillat-Savarin's chef d'oeuvre is not only exquisitely translated, but made immeasurably richer by her amplification of the text in her own notes and glosses. It is guaranteed to bring hours of diversion and delight—and perhaps even a few minutes of the promised transcendence—to any food-loving reader.

F. SCOTT FITZGERALD
(1896–1940)

In 1936, F. Scott Fitzgerald, past his prime though only forty, wrote a sequence of brief personal reflections for *Esquire* that were shocking in their candor, self-deprecation, and despair. They would be assembled later into a single essay, under the heading "The Crack-Up," by the author's friend and literary executor, Edmund Wilson, who used the piece to give the title to a volume of scattered prose, correspondence, and tributes to Fitzgerald published five years after the novelist's death in 1940 at the age of forty-four.

F. Scott Fitzgerald and his wife, Zelda, 1923

When *The Crack-Up* appeared, Fitzgerald's enduring reputation was anything but assured. But in the decades since, his own saga (and that of his wife, Zelda) of youthful glamour declining into dissipation has given a seductive afterglow to his first two novels, *This Side of Paradise* (1920) and *The Beautiful and Damned* (1922), while his last two, *The Great Gatsby* and *Tender Is the Night*, have shone brighter and brighter by the light of their own elegiac resonance.

While his erstwhile friend (and fellow prisoner on high school reading lists) Ernest Hemingway attended to the physical world, stripping experience of past and future, Fitzgerald assessed the social whirl, where position and relations, rather than mere presence, supply significance—a significance that, by definition, is always ephemeral, no matter how sweet. For youth and beauty are always fleeting, desire never outruns its longing, and any good party is always over too soon. Not surprisingly, then, Fitzgerald's greatest fiction is reflective—of surfaces, social graces, morning-after regrets—and reflecting, brooding upon the same process of breaking down—of love, vitality, purpose—that he ultimately reads in his own face in the mirror of "The Crack-Up."

The Great Gatsby
The End of the Future

F. Scott Fitzgerald went through a half-dozen titles for his novel about love and death in the Jazz Age; they all sound faintly ridiculous today: *Among Ash-Heaps and Millionaires*; *Trimalchio in West Egg*; *Under the Red, White, and Blue*; *The High-Bouncing Lover*. We all know the one that finally stuck, and why: Its title character, the desperately rich Jay Gatsby, embodies both the promise and the peril of the American dream like few other characters in literature.

We don't meet Gatsby until nearly a third of the way into the novel that bears his name. Instead Fitzgerald lets Nick Carraway, a young Midwesterner fresh out of Yale, lead us into a universe of glittering parties, tawdry drinking spells, and fierce social rivalries. Nick has rented a house on Long Island and becomes friends with Tom Buchanan, a fellow Yalie, and his wife, Daisy; he also falls for Daisy's friend Jordan Baker, a professional golfer who cheated to win her first tournament. All of them have heard about Nick's mysterious neighbor Gatsby: Although hundreds of New Yorkers show up to his lavish parties, almost no one knows who he is or where he's from. He's rumored to be a bootlegger, or perhaps a more sinister criminal, but the liquor and the fun are flowing at his expense, and the people who might otherwise question his past are mystified by its enigmatic shape. For it turns out that Gatsby, with his bright yellow car and shirts so beautiful they make women burst into tears, is different from what anyone supposed—and that despite his life of excess and vivid notoriety, it is the pursuit of love that will prove his undoing.

On one level, *The Great Gatsby* is a remarkably trenchant, and enduringly relevant, examination of how money talks (not for nothing does Gatsby respond to Nick's remark about Daisy's vocal flirtations with the words: "Her voice is full of money"). Then as now, establishment wealth meets the newly minted variety with a privileged prejudice that keeps the outsider not only outside, but off guard, no matter how impressive his riches. In an attempt to find his footing, Gatsby pretends that he

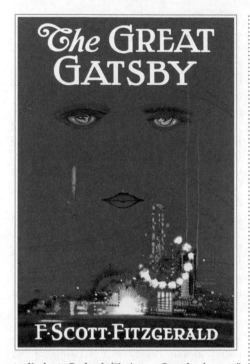

past or future, and thereby catches the mood of our national life—and the contradictions of our national character, for which the American Dream never quite fulfills its promise—with poignant fidelity.

Gatsby believed in the green light, the orgiastic future that year by year recedes before us. It eluded us then, but that's no matter—tomorrow we will run faster, stretch out our arms farther. . . . And one fine morning—

So we beat on, boats against the current, borne back ceaselessly into the past.

What: Novel. When: 1925. Further Reading: *The Far Side of Paradise* by Arthur Mizener. *Max Perkins: Editor of Genius* by A. Scott Berg. Try: *The Green Hat* by Michael Arlen. *On the Road* by Jack Kerouac (see page 442). *A Fan's Notes* by Frederick Exley (see page 262). Tom Carson's inventive novel *Daisy Buchanan's Daughter* takes its seed from Fitzgerald's novel and expands it through the twentieth century. Adaptations: *Gatsby* has been adapted into five films (and counting), an opera, a play, a comic book, and even a video game in which you earn points by swilling martinis.

studied at Oxford ("he's an Oggsford man," his fixer Wolfsheim likes to say) not because of any European pretensions, but to disguise his true roots from the Ivy League crowd he's infiltrated. For all his savvy, he misses relevant social signals, most notably at a painful lunch with some East Egg WASPs. And yet, while Gatsby's colorful suits and car—and the ingenuity with which he makes himself up as he goes along—may shock and bewilder the old-money types who party at his house, Fitzgerald paints him as a far more sympathetic character than his heedlessly entitled counterparts, whose unthinking cruelty reaches monstrous heights by the novel's end.

A book of shimmering social surfaces and hauntingly evanescent private depths, *The Great Gatsby* imbues its fleet narrative with a formal elegance that has been readily apparent even to the generations of high school students to whom it has been assigned—generally long before they might understand the novel's grasp of how the intensity of life slips ineluctably away. But it is in its realization of that theme that the work's true genius lies: Gatsby's ultimately futile attempt to recapture his youthful passion for Daisy Buchanan makes almost palpable the present's inability to live up to either

Tender Is the Night
The Far Side of Paradise

T he Great Gatsby is so formally elegant, so tightly plotted, and yet so profligate with charms that the reader is under its sway from start to finish. In contrast, *Tender Is the Night*—the last of F. Scott Fitzgerald's four completed novels, and the author's favorite—sprawls among dozens of characters and settings across Western Europe before and after World War I. Although its messy, heartbreaking story of mental illness, alcoholism, and the disintegration of a marriage is somehow unsatisfying compared with *Gatsby*'s perfectly balanced narrative, *Tender Is the Night* is for many readers more powerful in its enduring pull: As Fitzgerald unfolds the tale of Dick and Nicole Diver, we pass through infatuation, seduction, and ardor only to end in a kind of strange regret. Few other fictions evoke as well as this one the emotional weather of real life, the currents and temptations that envelop us without ever quite finding rest in an embrace.

The couple at the heart of the book (modeled partly on Fitzgerald's friends, the glamorous American expatriates Gerald and Sara Murphy, and partly on the author and his wife, Zelda), are the nexus of a fashionable social set on the French Riviera. Rosemary Hoyt, a teenage movie star vacationing with her mother, is taken with both of them—with Dick especially. Dick, a noted psychotherapist, is tempted by Rosemary, but checks himself. He knows that Nicole will be devastated if he strays, and in a long flashback to a Swiss clinic we learn why: Nicole has a history of mental illness, and Dick is not just her husband, but her doctor as well. Marrying her, despite their therapeutic relationship, Dick gained access to a world beyond his means, for Nicole's family possesses one of the largest fortunes in Chicago. Yet as the years unfold, both Nicole's mental state and Dick's career start to unravel, and the romance of their good fortune gives way to despair and dissipation.

Fitzgerald needed seventeen drafts to complete *Tender Is the Night*, and even then he wasn't happy with it; after poor reviews and worse sales, he made notes for a planned revision. In the years after the author's death, a friend—editor Malcolm Cowley—tried to follow his intentions, and in 1951 a second version of the novel was published; both versions remain in print today. Fitzgerald's 1934 edition features a zigzagging timeline and frequent flashbacks, whereas the posthumous one exhibits less experimental chronology. Today most critics hail the original *Tender Is the Night* as Fitzgerald's crowning glory (after *Gatsby*, of course), but whichever you read, you'll feel the force of Fitzgerald's prose and the almost unbearably intense emotion of its depictions. For one moment, Dick and Nicole Diver seem to have it all: love, money, friends, social standing. But all too soon their perfect lives, like Gatsby's dream of Daisy, are revealed to be fragile and uncertain. Underpinning their tale is the author's brutal grief for his own wasted talent and dissolute existence in the years after his early success. His desire for a sense of poise he cannot maintain seems to amplify the strains of sorrow that render the Divers' story so hard to forget, no matter how flawed its form.

What: Novel. *When:* 1934. *Edition:* Malcolm Cowley's revised 1951 version of the novel also remains in print. *Also By:* The Last Tycoon (1941). *Further Reading: Living Well Is the Best Revenge* by Calvin Tomkins. *Everybody Was So Young* by Amanda Vaill. *Try: The Good Soldier* by Ford Madox Ford (see page 288). *Light Years* by James Salter (see page 696). *Z: A Novel of Zelda Fitzgerald* by Therese Anne Fowler. *Adaptations:* The 1962 film stars Jason Robards and Jennifer Jones. The 1985 BBC miniseries, starring Mary Steenburgen and Peter Strauss, is superior, but difficult to find.

Offshore
Penelope Fitzgerald (1916–2000)

Afloat on the Thames with an Heir to Jane Austen

This beguiling novel—for which Penelope Fitzgerald won the Booker Prize—concerns a colorful bunch of misfits living on houseboats and barges along the Battersea reach of the Thames River in London. From the start, we're charmed by the author's keen wit and poised expression:

The barge-dwellers, creatures neither of firm land nor water, would have liked to be more respectable than they were. They aspired toward the Chelsea shore, where, in the early 1960's, many thousands lived with sensible occupations and adequate amounts of money. But a certain failure, distressing to themselves, to be like other people, caused them to sink back, with so much else that drifted or was washed up, into the mud moorings of the great tideway.

Biologically they could be said, as most tideline creatures are, to be 'successful.' They were not easily dislodged.

The vessels Fitzgerald's characters inhabit range from the shipshape to the slowly sinking. When *Dreadnought*, a craft in the latter category, is put up for sale, it sets in motion a plot that soon reveals every leak and hazard in these unsettled lives, several of which have loosed their moorings and begun to drift into chaos. The quite respectable couple on *Lord Jim*, for example, seem headed for a breakup; the male prostitute who calls the eponymous *Maurice* home is having difficulties with the chap who uses the hold as a storehouse for stolen goods; the two young waifs on *Grace* despair of their feckless mother's ever managing to reunite with their sulking father (who won't live on a boat). With a comic choreography worthy of Jane Austen, and an affectionate perspicacity regarding human nature that is reminiscent of the same, Fitzgerald leads the motley crew through a dance of confusions and emotions that is suffused with a droll, delightful grace.

The author had one of the most remarkable careers in contemporary literature. Born in England and educated at Oxford University's Somerville College, she published her first book at age fifty-nine and her first novel two years later. Over the next two decades she became one of Britain's most admired writers, and toward the end of the 1990s her fiction enjoyed great popular success in America as well. Fellow novelist Sebastian Faulks once said that reading one of her tales "is like being taken for a ride in a peculiar kind of car. Everything is of top quality—the engine, the coachwork and the interior all fill you with confidence. Then, after a mile or so, someone throws the steering-wheel out of the window." Nicely put, and a fine description of how it feels to take the *Offshore* plunge.

What: Novel. **When:** 1979. **Award:** Booker Prize, 1979. **Also By:** *The Bookshop* (1978). *Human Voices* (1980). *Innocence* (1986). *The Beginning of Spring* (1988). *The Gate of Angels* (1990). *The Blue Flower* (1995). **Try:** *The Girls of Slender Means* by Muriel Spark. *Hotel du Lac* by Anita Brookner.

Harriet the Spy
Louise Fitzhugh (1928–1974)

Adolescent Espionage

I n the opening pages of Louise Fitzhugh's *Harriet the Spy*, our protagonist—eleven-year-old Harriet M. Welsch—is trying to coax her best friend, Sport, to join her in her favorite game: Town.

See, first you make up the name of the town. Then you write down the names of all the people who live in it. You can't have too many or it gets too hard. I usually have twenty-five.

She proceeds to detail—with considerable elaboration—how she sets her imaginary world in motion, but Sport isn't convinced. "Don'tcha wanta play football?" is Sport's first, and pretty much lasting, response.

Harriet does not want to play football; she aspires to be a writer, and devotes most of her waking life to pursuit of that ambition, within the possibilities allowed by her childhood routines on the Upper East Side of Manhattan. The focus of her days, in fact, is the "spy route" she travels every afternoon after school, observing from a distance the kids, residents, and shopkeepers in the neighborhood and recording her thoughts about them in her ever-present notebook. She is precocious, perspicacious, inquisitive, and not always kind, which comes back to haunt her when her notebook falls into the hands of her classmates. Having to fight the taunts and retributions of the "Spy Catcher Club"

assembled against her is almost more than our fledgling author can bear. Almost, but not quite: She is resilient and resourceful, our Harriet, and with advice from her former nanny, Ole Golly, and help from a teacher or two, she regains her footing on the slippery slopes of adolescence.

Like an outsider Nancy Drew, Fitzhugh's Harriet has won the esteem—"allegiance" is probably a better word—of countless young girls who've mimicked her notetaking (as well as her unwavering love for tomato sandwiches). She is, in a word, beloved, most likely because her stance apart—as writer, as spy, or just as a keen but innocent intelligence trying to find a place for itself in the world—resonates with even the most articulate young readers in ways they can't quite explain.

What: Children's. *When:* 1964. *Also By: The Long Secret* (1965). *Nobody's Family Is Going to Change* (1974). *Sport* (1979). *Try: From the Mixed-Up Files of Mrs. Basil E. Frankweiler* by E. L. Konigsburg (see page 452). *Absolutely Normal Chaos* by Sharon Creech. *Beezus and Ramona* by Beverly Cleary. *The Golden Compass* by Philip Pullman (see page 647). *Adaptations:* Bronwen Hughes directed the 1996 movie starring Michelle Trachtenberg and Rosie O'Donnell. A further television adaptation, *Harriet the Spy: Blog Wars* appeared in 2010.

GUSTAVE FLAUBERT
(1821–1880)

While other authors of his time, such as Alexandre Dumas (see page 237), produced pages by the bucket-load, Gustave Flaubert, as his correspondence reveals, could agonize for hours over a single sentence, and his celebrated search for *le mot juste* (the right word) has made him a heroic guide for novelists ever since. It's fair to say that what we now call "literary fiction" was born of Flaubert's punctilious composition of *Madame Bovary*, and the ultimate influence of its approach on all realist narration is so pervasive that it has by now become invisible. As critic James Wood has written, Flaubert "is the originator of the modern novel; indeed, you could say that he is the originator of modern narrative—that the war reporter and the thriller writer owe as much to him as the avant-garde fictionist."

1935 sketch of Gustave Flaubert

Seamless as Flaubert's method may be, in the pages of *Madame Bovary* you can, with a little application, take apart scenes and chart precisely how—phrase by phrase, image by image—the sentences construct the book's indelible reality with a meticulousness that the sweep and dash of Dumas would never allow. To say that the progression from Dumas to Flaubert is simply "out with story, in with style" would belie the power of the tale *Madame Bovary* tells, or the more diffuse but cumulatively devastating effect of *Sentimental Education*, or the emotional force of the tale "A Simple Heart." In other words, there are rewards to reading Flaubert that reach beyond perfection.

Madame Bovary
A Touchstone in Fiction's History

The story *Madame Bovary* tells is simple in its outline. Charles Bovary is a country doctor. Emma Rouault is the lovely young daughter of a gentleman farmer. They marry. Emma quickly grows restless. Life with Charles—"his settled calm, his serene dullness"—doesn't satisfy Emma's romantic yearnings. She dreams of bliss, passion, rapture. She longs to experience love, *true* love, the kind she's read about in books. Eventually Emma has an affair. It ends in heartbreak. She has another affair. It, too, brings her only unhappiness. And deeper unhappiness soon follows.

Shallow, impetuous, dishonest, and short-sighted, Emma Bovary is not exactly a likeable heroine. She lies constantly, spends other people's money without reservation, and has little to no affection even for her own child. Yet by the novel's end she has become so real

Illustration of Madame Bovary commissioned for the first edition of the novel, 1857

that we can almost feel her presence, and her brutal end is not just tragic but heart-rending. How does Flaubert do it? Through an unprecedented act of close observation, one that has mesmerized generations of readers even as it revolutionized the novel as an art form. Before Flaubert, novelists were moralists or entertainers. The creator of *Madame Bovary*, by contrast, was an examiner, one with the objectivity and detachment of a forensic scientist; *le mot juste* is "scrutiny."

Flaubert was prosecuted for obscenity in 1857, after *Madame Bovary* appeared in serialized form. The government of the time wanted to suppress the novel for its depiction of adultery and its skewering of bourgeois morality. But of course the opposite happened: Flaubert was acquitted, and the novel became a bestseller not just in France but internationally. (Leo Tolstoy, whose *Anna Karenina* has often been read as a reaction to Flaubert's work, had his copy of *Madame Bovary* bound together with an edition of *Othello*.) Its power to scandalize has long since receded; in a *Fifty Shades of Grey* world, the novel's sex scenes seem positively tame. Yet *Madame Bovary* remains captivating for a different reason: Its distillation of lived and observed experience somehow gives the reader more imaginative substance than the most far-flung adventure, turning an unlikely and all-too-familiar protagonist ("Madame Bovary, c'est moi," the author famously declaimed) into an unforgettable heroine.

What: Novel. *When:* 1857. *Editions:* Francis Steegmuller's 1957 translation of *Madame Bovary* is available in a Modern Library edition. Lydia Davis's excellent 2010 translation is in Penguin Classics. *Also By: Three Tales* (1877). *Further Reading: Flaubert and Madame Bovary: A Double Portrait* by Francis Steegmuller. *Try: Anna Karenina* by Leo Tolstoy (see page 799). *Tess of the d'Urbervilles* by Thomas Hardy. *The Awakening* by Kate Chopin (see page 158). *The House of Mirth* by Edith Wharton. *Adaptations:* Vincente Minnelli directed the 1949 film starring Jennifer Jones, James Mason, Van Heflin, and Louis Jourdan. A 1991 remake, directed and with a screenplay by Claude Chabrol, stars Isabelle Huppert as Emma Bovary.

Sentimental Education
The End of a Love Affair

Flaubert's *Sentimental Education* is one of the great novels of Paris, its story of a young man's love for an older woman unfolding against the backdrop of the revolution of 1848, which ended with the abdication of King Louis-Philippe and the establishment of the Second Republic. Yet the headlines that description may suggest—*Passion! Ambition! Insurrection!*—might lead one to expect a book very different from the one Flaubert composed. For the author's genius ultimately delivers a tale in which the Romantic imagination itself comes to its end—not with a bang but a whimper. Flaubert's biting view of bourgeois enervation, polished by painstaking research and observation, is a lens of such power that it transforms a history of a historical epoch into an anatomy of social and psychological truths. Never has irony proved so nuanced, or so revelatory.

Not for nothing does the novel open with its protagonist, Frédéric Moreau, leaving Paris to return to his family home in the provinces. He'll travel back and forth several times in the pages that follow as Flaubert follows the young law student through his roller-coaster infatuation with an older married woman, Madame Arnoux. Frédéric is intelligent and charming, but he's also a bit of a dilettante, and he's neither wiser nor more mature after his romantic adventures than he was before them. "Women's hearts," he reflects late in the novel, "were like those desks full of secret drawers that fit one inside another; you struggle with them, you break your fingernails, and at the bottom you find a withered flower, a little dust, or nothing at all!" As it is with women, so with politics. Frédéric, who's scored a handsome but not enormous inheritance from an uncle, is fairly unaffected by the ongoing revolution of 1848. While his acquaintances call for an end to social hierarchy, Frédéric just goes along for the ride; he half-heartedly tries to get a seat in the new National Assembly, with no success. In sum, Frédéric doesn't make much of his life—not because of some tragic fatal flaw, but for the very normal reasons (fear, laziness, bad luck) that so many of us come up short; Flaubert's deceptive masterpiece is look-ing glass as well as lens.

Reviled by critics when it was first published in 1869, *Sentimental Education* has grown more relevant and even more attractive in the century and a half since. Its detached posture, not to mention its pessimism about both love and politics, shocked the French establishment, but today Flaubert's ironic incisiveness feels bracingly—perhaps even timelessly—contemporary.

What: Novel. *When:* 1869. *Also By: Bouvard and Pécuchet* (1881). *The Dictionary of Received Ideas* (1911). *Further Reading: Flaubert: A Biography* by Frederick Brown. *Try: The Red and the Black* by Stendhal (see page 754). *Lost Illusions* by Honoré de Balzac (see page 47). *The Line of Beauty* by Alan Hollinghurst.

From Russia, with Love
Ian Fleming (1908–1964)

Bond. James Bond.

In James Bond, who made his first appearance in 1953's *Casino Royale*, Ian Fleming created a fictional character who would—courtesy of the fabulous global success of the Bond film franchise in the 1960s and beyond—outgrow his modest literary origins to become an icon of modern masculinity. But even before his various movie incarnations (beginning with *Dr. No*, starring Sean Connery, in 1962) outfitted him with an over-the-top supply of gadgets, girls, and explosions, the Bond of the novels—cool, slightly cruel, sexually alert, expert with weaponry—captured the imaginations of common readers and cold warriors.

From Russia, with Love, the fifth of Fleming's Bond adventures, perfectly conveys the panache of his hero, who is blunt enough to blunder into danger but always sharp enough to find a way out. Taking place largely in Istanbul and on the Orient Express, it details a plot by SMERSH (the Soviet counterintelligence agency) to kill Bond as the first gambit in an elaborate scheme to discredit the British Secret Service at large. Fleming leads us through the thrills, spills, entanglements, and escapes of high make-believe with aplomb, leaving Agent 007 in Paris, and in peril, at the end—poised no doubt for further adventures (to say nothing of his coming film career).

What: Novel. *When:* 1957. *Also By: Casino Royale* (1953). *Goldfinger* (1959). *Further Reading: Ian Fleming: The Man Behind James Bond* by Andrew Lycett. *Try: The Great Impersonation* by E. Phillips Oppenheim. *The Secret Servant* by Gavin Lyall. *Adaptation:* Sean Connery played Bond in the 1963 movie. *Footnote:* Just as Tom Clancy's *The Hunt for Red October* (see page 160) benefited from a plug by Ronald Reagan in the 1980s, so, more than two decades earlier, did *From Russia, with Love* get a boost in sales when President John F. Kennedy listed it among his ten favorite books in an interview with *Life* magazine in 1961.

Sean Connery as James Bond in the 1963 film adaptation

Brazilian Adventure
Peter Fleming (1907–1971)

A Pioneering British (Mis)Adventurer

"It all began with an advertisement in the Agony Column of *The Times*," writes Peter Fleming of the April 1932 morning on which his perusal of the personals in the London paper launched his career as an author. You must admit that an ad saying "ROOM TWO MORE GUNS" does catch the eye. Offering himself as one of the "guns" sought to fill out a party of explorers headed to South America, Fleming, then an assistant editor at a magazine, would end up discovering a new kind of travel book.

Peter Fleming, 1936

Brazilian Adventure is a very funny account of a frankly ludicrous expedition for which, Fleming notes, "Rider Haggard might have written the plot and Conrad designed the scenery." Fleming and his companions march, fight, and canoe through three thousand miles of savage country in search of an English explorer, Colonel P. H. Fawcett, believed to be missing in the jungles of Central Brazil. But, as might be expected of a story whose initial section is titled "Through the Looking Glass," everything here is somehow out of whack, and made even whackier by the portentous jungle setting.

Published in 1933, Fleming's stylish and refreshingly original first book was distinguished by a self-deprecating sense of humor that was new to travel writing. The author, a rather unlikely explorer, delighted in his own improbableness and in the comic inconsequentiality of the poorly planned excursion. As Fleming's biographer, Duff Hart-Davis, put it, "Until he came on the scene, travel and travel books had been treated with excessive reverence and solemnity; but then, with a single, sustained burst of self-mockery, *Brazilian Adventure* blew the whole genre sky-high."

Peter Fleming went on to write many other books, but they may have less to do with his lasting fame than the thrillers written by his brother—for Ian Fleming, creator of James Bond, acknowledged that he modeled the immortal 007 on his intrepid, debonair older sibling.

What: Adventure. Travel. *When:* 1933. *Also By:* One's Company: A Journey to China (1934). News from Tartary (1936). Invasion 1940 (1957). The Siege at Peking (1959). *Try: A Short Walk in the Hindu Kush* by Eric Newby (see page 585).

Gone Girl
Gillian Flynn (born 1971)

You Don't Know What You've Got Till It's Gone

In his memoir, *Pack My Bag*, the vitally original British novelist Henry Green wrote, "Prose should be a long intimacy between strangers with no direct appeal to what both may have known." He wasn't thinking of tales of suspense, and his own idiosyncratic work has little in common with this Gillian Flynn bestseller, the story of a marriage's unraveling and the suspicion that falls on the husband in the wake of his wife's disappearance. But it is Flynn's knowing exploitation of the intimate pact between writer and reader, her head-turning violation of it, that tightens *Gone Girl*'s grip on our attention. The workings of Flynn's chilling novel turn on issues of faithfulness and trust, not only between husband and wife, but between author and audience. This last intimacy Flynn violates with such deviousness that she turns a standard thriller of love gone sour into a stunning psychological puzzle that seduces us in the way it's told, and then is deepened by keen insight into the disappointments, duplicities, and distortions that derail speeding plots from the track toward happy endings.

What: Novel. *When:* 2012. *Also By: Sharp Objects* (2006). *Dark Places* (2009). *Try: The Postman Always Rings Twice* by James M. Cain. *Shadow Tag* by Louise Erdrich. *Notes on a Scandal* by Zoë Heller. *Adaptation:* The 2014 movie, starring Ben Affleck and Rosamund Pike, was directed by David Fincher.

The Civil War
A NARRATIVE
Shelby Foote (1916–2005)

"The American *Iliad*"

There are thousands—make that tens of thousands—of books on the Civil War: memoirs and biographies of generals; accounts of common soldiers; hour-by-hour chronicles of campaigns and individual battles; studies of slavery and emancipation; analyses of the social and cultural circumstances of both sides; examinations of military tactics and leadership qualities; considerations of political and moral rhetoric as well as of carnage and suffering—in short, it's hard to imagine that any aspect of the conflict has been unexamined at length in print, as either history or fiction, or both. So it is a mark of true distinction to call Shelby Foote's *The Civil War* essential reading on the War Between the States.

Foote set out in the early 1950s to write a short, single-volume history of the struggle; two decades and three thousand pages later, he completed his monumental trilogy, which details the combat from beginning to end in meticulous detail. The genius of the work is suggested by its subtitle—*A Narrative*—for Foote calls upon his considerable skill as a novelist to portray the war not only as a series of discrete martial events, but also as a larger story destined to follow its own dramatic trajectory

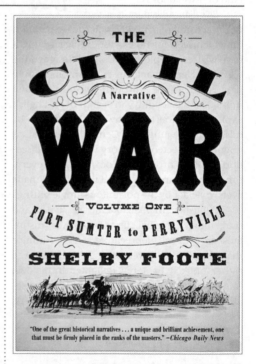

— THE —

CIVIL

A Narrative

WAR

— VOLUME ONE —

FORT SUMTER to PERRYVILLE

SHELBY FOOTE

"One of the great historical narratives . . . a unique and brilliant achievement, one that must be firmly placed in the ranks of the masters." *–Chicago Daily News*

as it makes its bloody way from Fort Sumter to Perryville, Fredericksburg to Meridian, Red River to Appomattox. Although other writers may better illuminate the economic and political underpinnings of the war, Foote evokes its heroic and tragic dimensions on a scale no one else has approached. As a result, *The Civil War* is more than just a historical record; it earns a place alongside the most significant works of American literature. In the words of historian Robert Massie, it is "the American *Iliad*."

What: History. War. *When:* Volume 1: *Fort Sumter to Perryville* (1958); Volume 2: *Fredericksburg to Meridian* (1963); Volume 3: *Red River to Appomattox* (1974). *Also By:* Fiction: *Love in a Dry Season* (1951); *Shiloh*

(1952). Nonfiction: *The Novelist's View of History* (1981); *Stars in Their Courses: The Gettysburg Campaign, June–July 1863* (1994). *Further Reading: Battle Cry of Freedom* by James M. McPherson. *Try: A Stillness at Appomattox* by Bruce Catton. *Andersonville* by MacKinlay Kantor (see page 429). *The Killer Angels* by Michael Shaara (see page 704). *Footnote:* Foote's on-camera commentary in Ken Burns's epic PBS documentary *The Civil War* sparked renewed interest in this trilogy when the television series aired in 1990.

Johnny Tremain
Esther Forbes (1891–1967)

A Boy's-Eye View of Revolutionary Boston

No books are ever as good as those that capture our fancy in the first blush of our love of reading. Enlivening already thrilling historical events with vivid characters and page-turning drama, Esther Forbes's novel of the American Revolution—and of Johnny Tremain's personal and political adventures in the shadow of the looming rebellion—has remained a favorite of young readers for decades. Few preteens will fail to see themselves in Forbes's protagonist, and the identification is strong enough to last a lifetime, compelling revisits to the tale and, when the time comes, reading it aloud to the next generation.

When the novel begins, Johnny is a gifted apprentice in the shop of silversmith Ephraim Lapham. His talents have made him indispensable to his aging master's business, fostering an unattractive arrogance. But Johnny is humbled when an accident during the crafting of a silver basin for John Hancock, for which the young artisan has sought instruction from Paul Revere, cripples his hand, rendering him unable to continue in the trade. After sulking and struggling to resign himself to his diminished abilities,

he finds work delivering a patriot newspaper, thereby entering the orbit of the Sons of Liberty, who are determined to gain American independence from Britain. Joining his new friends in the Boston Tea Party and other intrigues, Johnny discovers a purpose larger than himself, embracing ideals that temper his youthful callowness with a keen awareness of integrity and honor. As he matures, so does the revolutionary movement, until the excitements of Forbes's plot culminate in the Battles of Lexington and Concord.

Peopled with a vivid cast of characters and portraying emotions familiar to adolescents as well as adults, *Johnny Tremain* transforms the facts of history into a story readers can't put down, and won't easily forget.

What: Children's. *When:* 1943. *Award:* Newbery Medal, 1944. *Also By: A Mirror for Witches* (1928). *Paul Revere and the World He Lived In* (1942). *Try: My Brother Sam Is Dead* by James Lincoln Collier and Christopher Collier. *Carry On, Mr. Bowditch* by Jean Lee Latham. *Adaptation:* There is a 1957 Disney film. *Footnote:* Fans of *The Simpsons* may remember that even not-so-eager reader Bart finds himself captivated by Johnny's tale.

The Good Soldier
Ford Madox Ford (1873–1939)

"The finest French novel in the English language." —John Rodker

"This is the saddest story I have ever heard." Arrestingly melodramatic, the famous opening sentence of *The Good Soldier* immediately puts readers on notice: Do not take at face value everything you're told by John Dowell, the narrator of this "saddest story." And teasing out the truth from the unreliable Dowell's blinkered and often self-deluding version of events is one of the chief pleasures of this exquisite 1915 novel by the prolific man of letters Ford Madox Ford.

Ford's tale, which he described as his attempt to incorporate into a novel "all that I knew about writing," principally charts the tangled relationships between two "leisured" couples: the American Dowell and his wife, Florence, and the philandering Edward Ashburnham (English gentleman and the "soldier" of the title) and his wife, Leonora. Florence's affair with Edward; its unhappy consequences; the hypocrisy, deceit, and viciousness of the affluent idle: How, the reader wonders, can Dowell, that exasperating milquetoast, have remained oblivious to it

all? Now, in retrospect, after having been told the truth by Leonora, he alternates between self-pitying bewilderment and unconvincing outrage as he tries to put the past back together again.

Ford's artistry shows itself in the black comedy of Dowell's narration, which appears at first to be meanderingly conversational and digressive but turns out to be as lethally well constructed as a ticking time bomb. Frequently cited as a "novelist's novel" and as one of the great modernist works of the early part of the twentieth century, *The Good Soldier* was once described by a friend of Ford's as "the finest French novel in the English language." That wonderfully apposite quip points unforgettably to the book's most distinctive characteristics: the intricate craftsmanship of its construction, and the emotional and psychological sophistication of its storytelling.

What: Novel. When: 1915. Also By: The Fifth Queen (trilogy; 1906–08). Parade's End (tetralogy; 1924–28). Further Reading: Ford Madox Ford by Alan Judd. Try: The Golden Bowl by Henry James. Howards End by E. M. Forster. Adaptation: Filmed for British television in 1981.

"There is no novelist of this century more likely to live than Ford Madox Ford."
—Graham Greene

Independence Day
Richard Ford (born 1944)

The Continuing Adventures of Life, Liberty, and the Pursuit of Happiness

From earliest childhood, our very own once upon a time, we tell ourselves a story that seeks to establish our place in the world. The drama of growing up commences when we begin to realize that our story is not the same

as the one told about us, that the imagined self who is the soul's protagonist is not an exact replica of the apparent self others address. By adulthood, we're forced to side in the rush of circumstance with one self more often than the other, and thus, inadvertently, as we settle into middle age, we decide which story, the world's or our own, will dictate our works and days. As Frank Bascombe, the narrator of this novel, puts it when he overhears his son being addressed by a doctor, "Here is the voice of the outer world become primary. . . . While mine—the silenced voice of worry, love, patience, impatience, comradeship, thoughtlessness, understanding and genial acquiescence—is the small voice of the old small life losing ground." Bascombe's small voice, also channeled by Ford in *The Sportswriter* (1986), *The Lay of the Land* (2006), and *Let Me Be Frank with You* (2014), is one of the most remarkable creations in recent American fiction.

Bascombe is a realtor in New Jersey, a divorced father of two, a reader of Emerson, a former sportswriter, and the author of a book of short stories. In the course of a July Fourth weekend, Frank tries to sell a house to an intransigent couple, has a date, checks in on the residents of his rental properties, and drives to Connecticut to pick up his troubled adolescent son for an unfortunate jaunt to the Baseball Hall of Fame. Along the way, Frank divulges—in a voice at once compelling, easygoing, funny, and astute—his continuing struggle to weave his own story into the world's with a minimum of contradiction. It is a rich, discursive narrative, breezily engaging and filled with places and movement and keen observations of everything from real estate values and suburban traffic to progress and permanence and the bottomless loves and losses parenthood harbors. Possessed of an anxious self-assurance, Frank's perceptions and emotions are genuine enough to shine searching

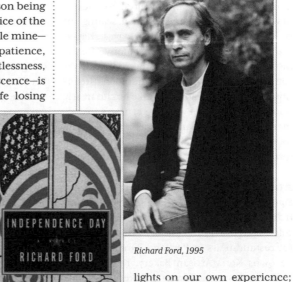

Richard Ford, 1995

lights on our own experience; we've heard his voice before, inside our own heads. Depicting Frank's hopeful fumblings toward his son, his ex-wife, his girlfriend, and—most of all—himself, Ford offers a heartrending but exhilarating anatomy of human feeling. This is a wise and welcome book, revealing life, and teaching us something about how to live it.

What: Novel. *When:* 1995. *Edition:* Ford contributed an introduction to the 2009 Everyman omnibus edition of the three Bascombe novels. *Awards:* In 1996, *Independence Day* was awarded both the Pulitzer Prize and the PEN/Faulkner Award for Fiction, the first book so honored in a single year. *Also By: Rock Springs* (1987). *Women with Men* (1997). *A Multitude of Sins* (2002). *Canada* (2012). *Try:* The Rabbit novels of John Updike. *Larry's Party* by Carol Shields. *American Pastoral* by Philip Roth (see page 677).

Flour Water Salt Yeast

THE FUNDAMENTALS OF ARTISAN BREAD AND PIZZA

Ken Forkish (born 1958)

"Human hands, time, and fire"

A successful technology professional for twenty years, Ken Forkish chucked suit, tie, commute, and all the other accoutrements of the corporate grind for a new career that would soon have him arriving at work at 3:30 AM each day. That's when he would begin his baker's round of daily tasks: hauling fifty-pound bags of flour and twenty-kilo buckets of water around the empty kitchen, scaling out yeasts, mixing doughs, baking loaves shaped the afternoon before. This ceremony of early morning chores, imminently practical yet somehow sacramental, was ordered in fifteen-minute intervals that would take him to nearly noon as he worked—with the artisan's instruments of "human hands, time, and fire"—the four elements that make up the title of his book into miracles of taste and nourishment.

Beginning with his discovery, in 1995, of an article about Paris's legendary Poilâne bakery in *Smithsonian* magazine, Forkish's transformation from IBM salesman to one of America's most celebrated bakers and one of the most successful restaurateurs in Portland, Oregon (where he owns Ken's Artisan Bakery, Ken's Artisan Pizza, and Trifecta Tavern & Bakery), is a tale of inspiration, perspiration, and the demanding austerity of simple pleasures. His story—engaging, well told, alive with his keen attention—is braided through the rich curriculum of techniques and processes that have made this an enlightening textbook for aspiring artisan bakers great and small. Each of the many recipes is replete with clear instructions in and accessible guidance to the principles and science behind ingredient ratios, the autolyse method of mixing flour and water, fermentation, and the like, putting a variety of delicious doughs and loaves within a home baker's reach. Yet the techniques and recipes are only the surface of a deep well of wisdom even a non-baker will find profoundly meaningful, for what really distinguishes Forkish's book is its generous transmission of the restorative power that comes from immersive understanding of any subject, craft, or skill. Such power relies as much on pleasure and wonder as on mastery, and is oddly inexhaustible. *Flour Water Salt Yeast* is definitive proof that cookbooks, like novels or symphonies, can introduce us to compelling characters and even transporting sentiments; its author's passion is infectious, enduring, and worth savoring.

What: Food & Drink. *When:* 2012. *Award:* James Beard Foundation Book Award, 2013. *Also By: The Elements of Pizza* (2016). *Try: The French Laundry Cookbook* by Thomas Keller. *Tartine Bread* by Chad Robertson. *52 Loaves: One Man's Relentless Pursuit of Truth, Meaning, and a Perfect Crust* by William Alexander.

....

A Passage to India
E. M. Forster (1879–1970)

A Novel of Consummate Artistry

Edward Morgan Forster's career as a novelist had a strange, almost mystifying shape. Between 1905 and 1910, he wrote four novels that met with some acclaim. Yet his fifth novel, *A Passage to India*, would not appear until 1924, fourteen years after *Howards End*, the last of his early quartet. More curious still, *A Passage to India* would be the last novel Forster published in his lifetime, despite the fact that he would live for nearly another half century, dying in 1970 at the age of ninety-one. A sixth novel, *Maurice*, largely written in 1913 and 1914, was issued posthumously, having been withheld by the author because of its portrayal of homosexual characters. Although it has been speculated, most recently by Wendy Moffat in her fine biography, *A Great Unrecorded History*, that the author's long novelistic silence had its roots in his inability, in the face of societal convention, to explore homosexuality more freely in his work, the idea might also be advanced that Forster's muse, having inspired him to the height of perfection in *A Passage to India*, was daunted by the prospect of navigating a return trip. That's how consummately telling this marvelous novel is.

There's nothing extraordinary about the plot; in its outline, the tale is a simple mapping of cultural collision and misapprehension. A charming but mercurial Indian surgeon, Dr. Aziz, strikes up a relationship with an elderly English lady, Mrs. Moore, in a mosque. Mrs. Moore has traveled to Chandrapore to visit her son, Ronny Heaslop, the city magistrate,

*Visiting the Malabar Caves—
still from the 1984 film adaptation*

in the company of Ronny's intended, Adela
Quested. "One touch of regret—not the canny
substitute but the true regret from the heart—
would have made him a different man, and the
British Empire a different institution," writes
Forster of Heaslop, a dutiful civil servant who
knows his place—and everyone else's—in the
social order the Raj engenders. The misalli-
ance between East and West is deftly drawn by
Forster as he overlays one comedy of manners

(whose center is the English Club) upon
another (revolving around Aziz and his Indian
friends). A simple traffic accident, for example,
becomes in the author's witty and observant
description a perfect embodiment of the ever-
converging, never-reconciled cultural—even
cosmic—differences that separate the book's
two worlds.

The destructive rather than comic consequences of those differences suffuse the

novel's central event, an expedition to the local marvel, the Marabar Caves, organized by Dr. Aziz for the benefit of Mrs. Moore and Miss Quested. The outing ends in calamity, with Miss Quested racing from the scene to accuse Aziz of assaulting her in one of the caverns.

It is easy to see the book as a depiction of irreconcilable differences between East and West, or as a definitive answer to the subject Aziz and his confidants debate early on: "whether or no it is possible to be friends with an Englishman." And yet the book's exploration of the ways people fail to connect transcends sectarian boundaries. Nor is the novel "about" colonialism: Colonialism is the glass through which human nature, and its befuddling intersection with custom and convention, are observed. The bewildering tenuousness of *all* personal relationships is Forster's great subject; the urgency of the need expressed in the epigraph to *Howards End*—"Only connect"—runs through the varied scenes of *A Passage to India* like the current of a slow but unstoppable river. Despite the muddle Forster's characters make of relationships, each one is given an individuality—and through that individuality a dignity—that seems

to echo in every sentence he or she speaks. Like Miss Quested, each of the major figures becomes a "real person"—"no longer examining life, but being examined by it"—with a gravity and solidity few fictional creations can match.

Philosophical profundities and everyday realities, petty jealousies and pregnant poetry are conjured one after the other with subtle intelligence and art. Forster's masterful absorption of the colors, tones, and shadows of life and language provides an almost symphonic literary score that lifts the details of his characters and their actions into some new dimension that sets this book apart—in manner, mood, and mystery —from any other you have ever read.

What: Novel. *When:* 1924. *Also By:* Fiction: *Where Angels Fear to Tread* (1905); *The Longest Journey* (1907); *A Room with a View* (1908). Nonfiction: *Aspects of the Novel* (1927); *The Hill of Devi* (1953). *Further Reading: Concerning E. M. Forster* by Frank Kermode. *Try: Middlemarch* by George Eliot (see page 248). *The Good Soldier* by Ford Madox Ford (see page 288). *Chef* by Jaspreet Singh. *Adaptation:* David Lean's acclaimed 1984 film features an ending controversially different from that of the book.

....

The Day of the Jackal
Frederick Forsyth (born 1938)

Step-by-Step Suspense

T he meticulous plotting of meticulous plots: That's Frederick Forsyth's trademark, indelibly apparent in his very first novel, *The Day of the Jackal*. This taut narrative of a 1963 assassination attempt on French president Charles de Gaulle proves that drama, like the devil, is in the details; throughout his intricate chronicle of the techniques and activities of a professional assassin, hired by a homegrown terrorist group incensed by de Gaulle's decision to grant independence to Algeria, Forsyth exhibits a peerless gift for spinning facts into suspense.

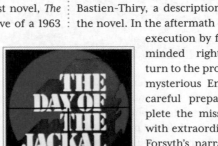

The intrigue Forsyth describes is fictional, but takes its inspiration from a number of real attacks on de Gaulle, including one planned by French air force officer Jean-Marie Bastien-Thiry, a description of which opens the novel. In the aftermath of Bastien-Thiry's execution by firing squad, likeminded right-wing militants turn to the professional killer—a mysterious Englishman—whose careful preparations to complete the mission are detailed with extraordinary precision in Forsyth's narrative. From theft of passports to the forging of identity papers, from the careful concoction of several disguises to the manufacture of a slim and portable sniper's rifle, the reader is given a methodical tour of a murderous underworld, all the more fascinating because its violence is realized through the artisanal, punctilious labors of forgers and gunsmiths. The preparations of the Jackal—the killer's code name—are enthralling in their relentless ruthlessness, and the investigative research and desperate energies of the detectives on his trail are equally absorbing. Forsyth's work has spawned a tribe of imitators that is now in its second generation, but the original article has lost none of its appeal:

The Day of the Jackal is the epitome of a page-turner.

What: Mystery & Suspense. **When:** 1971. **Award:** Edgar Award for Best Novel, 1972. **Also By:** *The Odessa File* (1972). *The Dogs of War* (1974). *The Fourth Protocol* (1984). **Try:** *A Coffin for Dimitrios* by Eric Ambler (see page 17). *Eye of the Needle* by Ken Follett. *The Bourne Identity* by Robert Ludlum (see page 500). **Adaptations:** The superb 1973 film is directed by Fred Zinnemann and stars Edward Fox as the Jackal. There is also an excellent audiobook read by Simon Prebble.

A Dictionary of Modern English Usage
H. W. Fowler (1858–1933)

Alarms and Diversions for Word Geeks

A lexicographer, per Samuel Johnson, the granddaddy of the breed, is a "harmless drudge," but Henry Watson Fowler may be the exception that proves the rule. It is one of the pleasures of his peerless *Dictionary of Modern English Usage* that, as astonishing as it may seem, its entries—an A-to-Z of questions of grammar, syntax, style, and the choice, formation, and pronunciation of words—reveal their author to be a man of good humor and good cheer.

Fowler's first venture into the quagmire of English prose was *The King's English*, a conventionally organized but unconventionally witty grammar composed with his brother Francis and issued in 1906. Five years later, the siblings published a second collaboration, *The Concise Oxford Dictionary of Current English*, which met with great acclaim and won them both lexicographical laurels. Yet it is the 1926 *Dictionary of Modern English Usage*, which Henry planned with Francis yet composed alone after his brother's untimely death in 1918, that has earned the volume known as "Fowler's" an uncommon reverence from generations of authors. "You must *own* a copy," Evelyn Waugh exhorted young writers in the *New York Herald Tribune*, and that advice remains sound today.

How can a volume devoted to such a dry subject elicit such enthusiasm? And why should we pay any attention to Fowler today? Are not his instructions a bit fusty, unfit to survive in the flurry of change the relentless dynamism of language unceasingly provokes? Perhaps—well, *yes*. And yet Fowler's encyclopedic pondering—replete with examples—of hundreds of matters of grammar and usage, as well as scores of individual words, is delivered with such grace and wit that his book is a joy to consult. Prescriptive without being pedantic, Fowler lays down rules with the worldliness of a connoisseur who can recommend wines because he knows both their vintages and their intoxications; sharing a glass with him is an education even if we find his precepts confining and his palate outdated. Animated throughout with brief humorous essays (try "Elegant Variation," "Fused Participle," "Novelty-Hunting," or "Unequal Yokefellows"), his seven-hundred-odd pages are filled with delights, and his defanging of such beastly problems as *Preposition at end* and *Split infinitive* are not to be missed.

In short, this most elegant, most essential of all English usage books will not only help you refine your writing, think more clearly, and bring you generally closer to heaven, but provide you with hours of entertaining reading as well. It is a treasury of fine expression, which, in the words of the *Times Literary Supplement*, will "delight everybody who ever had a thought for language."

What: Writing. Language. **When:** 1926. **Editions:** Look for the original 1926 text, most recently available in an edition from Oxford University Press with an introduction by linguist David Crystal. The 1965 revision by Sir Ernest Gowers is a passable alternative, but at all costs avoid R. W. Burchfield's third edition of 1996, which, by giving primacy to a descriptive rather than a prescriptive approach to matters of usage, updated Fowler's by removing most traces of Fowler. *Further Reading:* *The Warden of English: The Life of H. W. Fowler* by Jenny McMorris. *Try: Johnson's Dictionary: A Modern Selection* by E. L. McAdam Jr. and George Milne. *Garner's Modern American Usage* by Bryan A. Garner.

The French Lieutenant's Woman
John Fowles (1926–2005)

A Victorian Novel with a Modern Twist

The story John Fowles tells in his third novel begins on the English seaside at Lyme Regis, Dorset, in 1867. Yet it is told by a wry, erudite narrator who lets readers know he is writing exactly one hundred years later. In a tour de force of storytelling that is transporting, intriguing, and breathtaking in its shifting perspectives, Fowles combines suspense, romance, and invention into an emotionally satisfying and intellectually engaging whole.

As the novel opens, Charles Smithson is walking along the sea with his paramour, Miss Ernestina Freeman. He spies a mysterious woman standing on a breakwater, gazing intently out at the horizon. In response to his query, Ernestina informs Charles that the woman is Sarah Woodruff, spurned lover of a French lieutenant whose return she futilely awaits. Thus begins Charles's obsession with the beautiful Sarah—the obsession that screws the plot of *The French Lieutenant's Woman* tighter and tighter, despite the novelist's diverting digressions regarding the differences between the Victorian and the modern world, between the nineteenth-century novel and its late-twentieth-century counterpart.

A master of a storytelling resourcefulness that always has us asking, "What happens next?," Fowles here recasts the pleasures of the Victorian novel into modern literary dress in a way that only enhances their allure. To cap it off, he offers two endings, challenging the reader's own ideas of romance, of the rights and wrongs of society's whims, even of the nature of fiction itself. As Christopher Lehmann-Haupt wrote in his 1969 *New York Times* review of this enthralling work, "set an alarm clock . . . it's not good for the circulation to sit in one position" for too long.

Meryl Streep played Sarah in the 1981 film

What: Novel. *When:* 1969. *Reading Note:* The epigraphs that announce every chapter—from the likes of Darwin, Tennyson, Austen, Arnold, Cardinal Newman, and Karl Marx—compose a stimulating commonplace book all by themselves. *Also By: The Collector* (1963). *The Magus* (1966; revised edition, 1977). *The Ebony Tower* (1974). *Daniel Martin* (1977). *Mantissa* (1982). *A Maggot* (1985). *Try: Possession* by A. S. Byatt (see page 118). *Adaptation:* An acclaimed film was made in 1981, with Meryl Streep and Jeremy Irons in the lead roles; director Karel Reisz and screenwriter Harold Pinter worked out a film-within-a-film device that got them over the twin hurdles of the modern-day narrator and the double ending.

The Diary of a Young Girl
Anne Frank (1929–1945)

Coming of Age in an Age of Horror

Anne Frank's intimate two-year record of her family's hiding from the Nazis in an Amsterdam attic is one of the most famous, powerful, and beloved books of the twentieth century. Encapsulating the terror of the Holocaust in the domestic drama of the Franks' anxious existence and the private yearnings of the author's adolescence, *The Diary of a Young Girl* puts a tender human face on the suffering of countless victims of Hitler's regime.

Otto Frank led his wife and two daughters from Germany to Amsterdam in 1933, after Hitler's rise to power. But in the ensuing years Nazi influence spread to Holland, and in July 1942 the Franks went into hiding in what Anne would call the "Secret Annex," a concealed, narrow, three-story space at the back of a warehouse, where they were soon joined by the Van Daans and their son, Peter, and later, an elderly dentist named Mr. Dussel. A few weeks earlier, Anne had been given a blank journal for her thirteenth birthday; addressing this coveted diary as "Dear Kitty," she would use its pages to set down her experiences, ruminations, and emotions until August 1944, when the Franks were betrayed and arrested.

Although often referred to as "The Diary of Anne Frank" (the title used by the stage and screen adaptations), the book's correct title, *The Diary of a Young Girl*, suggests one of the reasons for the book's extraordinary effect on generations of readers: In the midst of terrifying circumstances, the author's words are always alive with a recognizable teenager's awkward mix of independence and vulnerability, silliness and

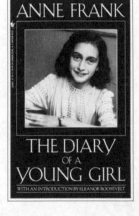

soulfulness, honesty and wishful thinking, resentment and rebellion, guilt and responsibility. At the same time, Anne Frank's astonishing gifts of observation and expression, her precocious intuition and sagacity, allow this young girl to speak to us as only the most exceptional writers can.

Anne and her sister, Margot, died at Bergen-Belsen in March 1945; their mother died at Auschwitz. Otto alone survived the camps. After the war, he discovered that Miep Gies, the woman who'd helped hide the family, had rescued Anne's diary. He prepared it for publication in 1947. As a result, despite the fact that her life was cut short, Anne Frank's words and her memory will outlive us all.

What: Autobiography. History. *When:* 1947; first US publication 1952. *Edition: The Diary of Anne Frank: The Definitive Edition* (1995; edited by Otto Frank and Mirjam Pressler and translated by Susan Massotty) contains about a third more material than the first publication, restoring passages—concerning Anne's budding sexuality, her parents' marriage, and her feelings toward her mother—that Otto Frank had omitted. *Also By: Anne Frank's Tales from the Secret Annex* (reminiscences and stories; revised edition in English, 1983). *Further Reading: Anne Frank: A Portrait in Courage* by Ernst Schnabel. *Anne Frank Remembered: The Story of the Woman Who Helped to Hide the Frank Family* by Miep Gies with Alison Leslie Gold. *Inside Anne Frank's House: An Illustrated Journey Through Anne's World* by Hans Westra. *Adaptations:* The 1955 play, adapted by Frances Goodrich and Albert Hackett, won the Pulitzer Prize for Drama. The film version, directed by George Stevens, was released in 1959, and television versions have been made in both America and Britain.

"Because the diary was not written in retrospect, it contains the trembling life of every moment—Anne Frank's voice becomes the voice of six million vanished Jewish souls."—*Meyer Levin*

My Brilliant Career
Miles Franklin (1879–1954)

A Writer Grows Up Down Under

My *Brilliant Career* is a little like *Jane Eyre*: the story of a girl charting a course through adversity and uncertainty toward a life of agency and fulfillment. But just as the demeanor of Miles Franklin's protagonist, Sybylla Melvyn, does not exhibit the demure discretion of Charlotte Brontë's Jane, so her progress toward adulthood lacks the romantic resolution (in both senses of both words) that characterizes the story of her Victorian predecessor. On the one hand, Sybylla's awkward, urgent energy as she battles the impoverishments of the Australian bush in her quest to discover a brilliant literary career are worlds away from Jane Eyre's quiet determination as she crosses the borders of class and service; on the other, "Reader, I didn't marry him," might well serve as epigraph for Franklin's book, so perfectly does it encapsulate the author's overturning of the audience's expectations—to say nothing of the hopes of Sybylla's worthy but hapless suitor, Harold Beecham.

Miles Franklin

If Franklin's teenage masterpiece (she wrote it when she was seventeen or so, and saw it published when she was twenty-one) is something like *Jane Eyre*, it's something more like Laura Ingalls Wilder's Little House books (see page 435) rewritten by Saul Bellow's Augie March (see page 66). Alive with the labor and everyday calamity of pioneer life, Sybylla's voice is riveting: innocent, canny, uncouth, vigorous, unforgettable.

If the souls of lives were voiced in music, there are some that none but a great organ could express, others the clash of a full orchestra, a few to which nought but the refined and exquisite sadness of a violin could do justice. Many might be likened unto common pianos, jangling and out of tune, and some to the feeble piping of a penny whistle, and mine could be told with a couple of nails in a rusty tin-pot.

Narrating her attempts to find a way out of her ramshackle existence, Sybylla pens sketches of family near and extended, and of misadventures both comic and disillusioning, that are drawn on a field of ambition colored with acute understanding of the limited roles available to women in her world:

It came home to me as a great blow that it was only men who could take the world by its ears and conquer their fate, while women, metaphorically speaking, were forced to sit with tied hands and patiently suffer as the waves of fate tossed them hither and thither, battering and bruising without mercy.

"The word wife finished me up," Sybylla tells us, and her narration relates her fierce if fumbling attempts to fashion a future free from the drudgery and suffering that claimed the years of her mother, her aunt, and other female relatives and acquaintances. Setting her sights on a "brilliant career" in the literary world, she aspires to write herself out of, or into, her fortune.

Miles Franklin's own commitment to composing a different life for herself, from a starting point very much like Sybylla's, would lead to a career—several careers, in fact—of extraordinary adventurousness and accomplishment in America, England, and back again, ultimately, in Australia; her purposeful picaresque makes Jack Kerouac seem like a stay-at-home. Throughout her peregrinations, she kept writing, with increasing success and esteem. In the 1946 preface she wrote for *My Career Goes Bung*, her sequel to *My Brilliant Career* (written soon after the first book, but unpublished for decades), Franklin writes, "I have kept faith with that girl who once was I." Indeed she had.

What: Novel. *When:* 1901. *Also By: Old Blastus of Bandicoot* (1931). *All That Swagger* (1936). Writing as Brent of Bin Bin: *Up the Country* (1928). *Further Reading: Her Brilliant Career: The Life of Stella Miles Franklin* by Jill Roe. *Try: The Getting of Wisdom* by Henry Handel Richardson. *I Capture the Castle* by Dodie Smith (see page 730). *Adaptation:* Gillian Armstrong's acclaimed 1979 film stars Judy Davis.

Flashman
George MacDonald Fraser (1925–2008)

Adventures of an Entertaining Historical Rogue

Flashman is the name of a bully who is expelled for drunkenness from Rugby School in the 1857 novel *Tom Brown's School Days* by Thomas Hughes. A century after Hughes's book, George MacDonald Fraser had the inspired idea of resurrecting "Flashy" and inventing for him a post-expulsion career. And what a gloriously deplorable career it has turned out to be! In a series of twelve hugely entertaining historical novels, Sir Harry Paget Flashman shows himself to be a cowardly soldier, a lecherous rogue, an unmitigated scoundrel—and, to the delight of countless readers, one of the great comic characters of modern fiction.

Flashman is the first book in the romping series. It is narrated, as are all the installments, by the dastardly blackguard himself; novelist Fraser professes to act merely as the editor of "the Flashman papers"—bawdy, action-packed memoirs in which Flashy recounts his globe-trotting life from the late 1830s to the early years of the twentieth century. One of the unique pleasures of the Flashman saga is the way its disgraceful hero turns up in the thick of so many famous episodes of the Victorian era, ranging from the Charge of the Light Brigade and the Battle of Little Big Horn to the Indian Mutiny, the Anglo-Zulu War, and the Taiping Rebellion. In *Flashman*, it's the First Anglo-Afghan War of 1839–42 that keeps Flashy busy (when, that is, he isn't involved in one of his innumerable amorous escapades). Although meticulously accurate in his rendering of historical events, Fraser employs a judiciously skeptical perspective on the past—a perspective, it has to be said, that is robustly politically incorrect.

In addition to the Flashman yarns, Fraser has applied his splendid storytelling skills to many other excellent books in various genres.

What: Novel. *When:* 1969. *Also By:* Flashman series: *Royal Flash* (1970); *Flash for Freedom!* (1971); *Flashman at the Charge* (1973); *Flashman in the Great Game* (1975); and seven more. Other fiction: *The General Danced at Dawn* (1970); *McAuslan in the Rough* (1974); *The Candlemass Road* (1993). Nonfiction: *The Steel Bonnets: The Story of the Anglo-Scottish Border Reivers* (1971); *Quartered Safe Out Here* (1994). *Try: Sharpe's Tiger* by Bernard Cornwell. *Adaptation:* Richard Lester's film *Royal Flash* (1975) stars Malcolm McDowell.

> **"If there was a time when I felt that watcher-of-the-skies-when-a-new-planet stuff, it was when I read the first Flashman."**
> —*P. G. Wodehouse*

My Father's Fortune

A LIFE

Michael Frayn (born 1933)

Between the Lines of a Happy Life

There is a hushed but resonant moment toward the end of Michael Frayn's generally merry memoir of his father. It occurs when the author recalls a letter, uncharacteristic in its emotional directness, that his father sent after returning home from a hospital stay for a serious procedure. Recalling the moment as he writes, decades after the event, Frayn says,

I'm so moved by what he says . . . that I find it difficult even to copy it here: "There were many times in hospital when your visits seemed the mainstay of my existence."

And here's what I find even more difficult to say: I didn't reply.

That the father, Tom Frayn, a hearing-impaired asbestos salesman with a buoyant personality (and a persistent comic regret at his son's failure to become an accomplished cricketer) was prompted by the specter of mortality to overcome his native reticence is almost as moving as the fact that the son, whose literary facility has been on display for some 250 pages, can summon no response. Happy families may be all alike, as Tolstoy said, but even they are rife with mysteries.

To illuminate his family's own, Frayn, an internationally acclaimed dramatist and novelist, recounts his parents' courtship; the scenes of his unexceptional upbringing, including the drama of the London Blitz and the domestic tragedy of his mother's untimely death just after the war's end; and his father's genial advance through otherwise ordinary years. The book, like the characters who people it, is high-spirited and funny, alive with Tom Frayn's exuberant embrace of life, even in adversity, and with the extended eccentricities that are the through-line of any family's narrative. It is

poignant as well as humorous, filled with surprises engendered by the younger Frayn's scrutiny of a past he's never really set his mind to.

That the writer's mind is fertile and original is evidenced by the shelf of volumes that bear his name (and the shelf of awards that accompany them), from the comic intricacies of his theatrical farce *Noises Off* to the scientific and moral quandaries of *Copenhagen*, his Tony Award–winning play about the nuclear physicists Niels Bohr and Werner Heisenberg; from his marvelous translations of five Chekhov plays to his sinuously plotted psychological novel of the home front during World War II, *Spies*. And yet, in this straightforward chronicle of his father's unremarkable days, he discovers a truth best expressed by the literary critic Hugh Kenner: "What you're taking for granted is always more important than whatever you have your mind fixed on."

As his warmhearted reminiscences approach their conclusion, Frayn realizes the homeliest of truths: We're not—most of us, at least—heroes of literature or history, but merely figures going around on the repetitive and lulling carousel of day-to-day living. And maybe our relationships of love and fidelity are, when all is said and done, simpler than we think, less psychologically fraught than we are taught to fear, but present and sustaining nonetheless, even if difficult to find words for, as Michael Frayn so lovingly does in *My Father's Fortune*.

What: Memoir. *When:* 2010. *Also By:* Plays: *Benefactors* (1984); *Democracy* (2003). Fiction: *Towards the End of the Morning* (1967); *A Landing on the Sun* (1991). *Try: A Mass for the Dead* by William Gibson (see page 314). *Untold Stories* by Alan Bennett. *Basil Street Blues: A Memoir* by Michael Holroyd. *Adaptation:* The absolutely marvelous audiobook is read by Martin Jarvis.

"The same strange thought recurs, and it's one that it's taken me all these years to think: the realization that he loved my sister and me and that we brought him happiness. Perhaps that's why he would detour halfway across South London to drop in. And when he put the hat and the smile round my door and saw me sitting there, it could be that he felt something of what I feel when I catch sight of *my* children."

—*from* My Father's Fortune

The Interpretation of Dreams
Sigmund Freud (1856–1939)

Journey to the Interior

Any wanderer through the land of modern thought walks in the shadow of Sigmund Freud's looming monument; yet, pervasive as the influence of his thought has been, it still stands—at least for those not directly implicated in psychoanalytic therapy—somehow remote from the traffic of our lives. And increasingly so: In our age of neurobiology, cognitive science, and pharmaceutical remedies, it's fashionable to dismiss Freud as irrelevant and to view his ideas as benighted or passé. Yet this contemporary minimization of Freud's insight ignores a larger fact: His most profound discoveries are now axiomatic truths, and we neither credit nor attack them because they've become so completely internalized. Freud himself would no doubt enjoy the irony.

Take the idea, elaborated in *The Interpretation of Dreams*, that dreams express a person's deep-seated desires. This is not an eternal proposition; it had to be discovered, and it was Freud, really, who brought it to light in this relatively early work. Detailing his consideration of the dreams of his patients as well as his own reveries, Freud develops his hugely influential theory of the unconscious, which gives primary importance to the libido, or the animalistic sexual energy that drives our inner lives.

(Freud's division of the psychic apparatus into id, ego, and superego comes later, in *Beyond the Pleasure Principle*.) The dream is a means of "wish fulfillment," Freud argues, in which our secret and often unsuspected desires can finally be conveyed.

The Interpretation of Dreams also introduces the idea of the Oedipus complex. Drawing on both clinical observations of children and

Sigmund Freud, ca. 1921

literary sources—not just Sophocles's tragedy but also *Hamlet*, a great favorite of Freud, who was a gifted, even revelatory, reader—the psychoanalyst proposes that every boy experiences a latent sexual desire for his mother, which causes him shame and places him into mortal competition with his father. (A parallel desire among girls interested Freud later in his career.)

It's unfortunate that Freud, whose books are among the most influential ever written, is so seldom read nowadays. Whatever the scientific merits of his psychoanalytic models —and they are hardly flawless—Freud largely invented the modern notion of the mind, and Western art and literature of the last century are almost unintelligible without him. He is also, unlike many major figures of German-language thought, a clear and accessible writer, and *The Interpretation of Dreams* is a pleasure to read. All of his writings, to the uninitiated, are surprisingly vivid and literary, filled with the exhilarating struggle of putting the most intimate secrets into words. The critic Harold Bloom once wrote that Freud has to be seen as a prose version of Shakespeare. That may be an exaggeration, but it's less far off the mark the more one thinks about it: Like the Bard, the father of psychoanalysis found previously hidden means to express what it means to be human.

What: Psychology. *When:* 1900. *Edition:* James Strachey's 1955 version remains the standard in English. *Also By: The Psychopathology of Everyday Life* (1904). *Leonardo da Vinci and the Memory of His Childhood* (1910). *Totem and Taboo* (1913). *Beyond the Pleasure Principle* (1920). *The Future of an Illusion* (1927). *Civilization and Its Discontents* (1930). *Further Reading: Freud: A Life for Our Times* by Peter Gay. *Freud: Biologist of the Mind* by Frank J. Sulloway. *Try: In the Freud Archives* by Janet Malcolm (see page 516). *The Beast in the Nursery: On Curiosity and Other Appetites* by Adam Phillips (see page 625).

The Feminine Mystique
Betty Friedan (1921–2006)

One of the Most Influential Books of the 20th Century

"We can no longer ignore that voice within women that says, 'I want something more than my husband and my children and my home,'" Betty Friedan concluded in the first chapter of her landmark 1963 study of her contemporaries. Friedan discovered her theme when she was asked, in 1957, to conduct a survey of her Smith College classmates on the fifteenth anniversary of their graduation, and noted in their responses the recurrent dissatisfaction with where they found themselves. Why, Friedan set out to investigate, were so many American women of her time and class unhappy?

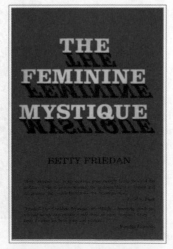

Many other sociologists, psychologists, and, if truth be told, fiction writers of the postwar era had uncovered significant streams of culturally induced malaise in the population at large, from David Riesman's *The Lonely Crowd* to Norman Mailer's "The Man Who Studied Yoga." By the 1950s and early 1960s, the urgent, dangerous, and even heroic contexts of the Great Depression and World War II, each with its own sense of larger peril and purpose, had been replaced by the comforts of consumerism and conformity, which, for many, were easy enough, but increasingly empty. What was different and brilliant in Friedan's book— controversial and caustic to some, inspiring and empowering to others—was its focus on women and its scrutiny of the unease underlying the accepted notions of domestic bliss. Most powerful was Friedan's insight into the manufactured nature of the narratives available to women to shape an idea of happiness that was personal and organic rather than rooted like a potted plant in mass-produced notions of marriage and motherhood. How, Friedan asks, could women become protagonists in the stories of their own lives?

Friedan is especially good in her analysis of the controlling forces of the ideals of femininity and domesticity she sees as dispiriting to women of her own generation: the advertising gurus glorifying the virtues of housework and housewifery; the unnatural psychosexual patrimony of Sigmund Freud; the male editors of "women's" magazines; the quiet conspiracy of educators bent on keeping female students cordoned off from the more liberating and egalitarian precincts of learning and professional advancement. Bearing personal as well as historical witness to the struggle to claim equal rights and opportunities, *The Feminine Mystique* was a catalyst for the women's movement of the 1960s and beyond, and remains—despite its now remote frames of reference and citation—a striking, noble, and relevant call to attention.

What: Feminism. Sociology. *When:* 1963. *Also By: The Second Stage* (1981). *The Fountain of Age* (1993). *Try: A Room of One's Own* by Virginia Woolf. *The Second Sex* by Simone de Beauvoir (see page 59). *The Female Eunuch* by Germaine Greer. *Backlash: The Undeclared War Against American Women* by Susan Faludi.

....

The Poetry of Robert Frost
Robert Frost (1874–1963)

A Favorite Poet and His Disguises

M any, if not most, of the best-known modern American poems were written by Robert Frost: "Stopping by Woods on a Snowy Evening," "The Road Not Taken," "Fire and Ice," "Dust of Snow," "'Out, Out—,'" "Birches," to name a few. Indeed, it is fair to say that, for a good part of the twentieth century, Frost was our unofficial national poet—and, with John F. Kennedy's invitation to compose a poem for the 1961 presidential inauguration, he became, toward the end of his life, something like an official one, too.

In the popular imagination he was a crotchety, weathered New Englander, but Robert Frost was actually born in San Francisco, and his first book was issued by a British publisher. Conventional ideas of his verse are similarly upended by the facts of the poems themselves. Although it may seem benignly old-fashioned in form and content—in form, because it rhymes; in content, because it deals with homespun themes such as the natural world and rural living—Frost's work grows out of a deep, dark strain of thought that adds

Robert Frost speaking with students

substance and a resonating majesty to his invitingly familiar imagery. Take a poem like "Acquainted with the Night":

I have stood still and stopped the sound of feet
When far away an interrupted cry
Came over houses from another street,

But not to call me back or say good-by;
And further still at an unearthly height,
One luminary clock against the sky

Proclaimed the time was neither wrong nor right.
I have been one acquainted with the night.

Here the poet, using the plainest of diction and setting the simplest of scenes, wraps himself—and the reader—in the cloak of loneliness with which darkness subsumes the light of every day. Such ominous emotional reality is never far from the natures—human and earthly—that Frost explores with his probing instruments of sound and sense. The pleasures of poetry, with its uncanny ability to plumb the well of experience (and sometimes even fathom its depths), has had few greater champions than this quiet, cunning American bard whose work, much like life itself, combines a welcoming directness with unexpected and sometimes treacherous turnings in its search for beauty, and for usable truths.

What: Poetry. *When:* 1916–63. *Edition:* The Library of America edition of Frost's *Collected Poems, Prose, and Plays* is highly recommended. *Awards:* Pulitzer Prizes for Poetry in 1924, 1931, 1937, and 1943. *Further Reading: Robert Frost: A Life* by Jay Parini. *The Cambridge Companion to Robert Frost,* edited by Robert Faggen. *Try:* The poems of Thomas Hardy, Richard Wilbur (see page 853), and Seamus Heaney. *Adaptation:* The knottiest of American composers, Elliott Carter, produced what may be his simplest and most beautiful work in his 1943 setting of Frost's "The Rose Family."

Critical Path
R. Buckminster Fuller (1895–1983)

Applying Unlimited Genius to Limited Resources

A mental giant in a five-foot-two frame, R. Buckminster ("Bucky") Fuller died with forty-seven honorary degrees, twenty-eight patents, twenty-nine books, a Presidential Medal of Freedom, and a Nobel Peace Prize nomination to his name. Yet despite his long career as an industrial designer, architect, engineer, mathematician, philosopher, cartographer, poet, teacher, and protoenvironmentalist, many people have never heard of him. Descended from a long line of New England nonconformists (the Transcendentalist woman of letters Margaret Fuller was his great-aunt), Fuller was a classic case of genius ahead of its time. Twice expelled from Harvard and a failed businessman in his early adulthood, he was dismissed as a crackpot at least as often as he was hailed as a visionary. But imaginative he certainly was, and his enduring creativity manifested itself in memorable coinages ("synergetics" and "Spaceship Earth," to mention just two). His most famous creation, the geodesic dome—a structure of interlocking polygons that becomes proportionally lighter and stronger the larger it is—provides, in both its resourceful practicality and its lack of limiting dimensions, a perfect metaphor for Fuller's thought.

Published two years before Fuller's death, *Critical Path* is the record of a lifetime's intellectual passion, idiosyncratically tracing humanity's progress from prehistory through the development of modern political and corporate structures. Both speculative and quirky in its approach, it is laced with Fuller's personal experiences and his economic, environmental, technological, and ethical concerns, as well as his pioneering attention to issues of survival and sustainability. His commitment to the mission of making shelter, transportation, and other basic life supports more efficient and more affordable, while being mindful of the Earth's limited resources—of doing more with less—animates every page.

Fuller spent a good part of his later life traveling the globe, delivering manic lectures on his ideas and ideals to rapt students. The culmination and summation of his life's work and thought, *Critical Path* is the book for those who missed out on the live show.

What: Philosophy. Technology. Environment. *When:* 1981. *Reading Note:* Fuller's mind didn't work quite like anyone else's, as is clear from page one. If you find his style a struggle, try skipping right to chapter 4, "Self-Disciplines of Buckminster Fuller," which offers an orienting overview of his life and thought. *Also By: Nine Chains to the Moon* (1938). *Ideas and Integrities* (1963). *Further Reading:* For more on Fuller's life and thought, see Hugh Kenner's *Bucky: A Guided Tour of Buckminster Fuller*. *Footnote:* On July 12, 2004, the United States Post Office released a commemorative stamp honoring Buckminster Fuller on the fiftieth anniversary of his patent for the geodesic dome—and his 109th birthday.

R. Buckminster Fuller with geodesic dome models

The Recognitions
William Gaddis (1922–1998)

A Labyrinthine Masterpiece

In 1975, William Gaddis published *JR*, which runs to more than seven hundred pages. Receiving admiring reviews and winning a National Book Award, *JR* revived interest in *The Recognitions*, Gaddis's only previous book, a thousand-page behemoth that had been published twenty years earlier. Although a devoted band of readers had championed Gaddis's initial effort all along, it took the second book to prompt a reassessment of the first's merits and position it among the widely acknowledged modern classics. More importantly, its influence nourished a rich vein of subsequent American fiction by the likes of Robert Coover, Thomas Pynchon, and David Foster Wallace.

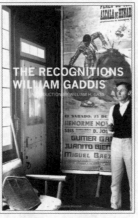

The theme of *The Recognitions* is forgery. The main character is Wyatt Gwyon (although in this slippery narrative, he will appear under other names as well), whose talent as a painter deflects him from following his father's path into the ministry. Forsaking New England for Europe, he discovers a gift for making copies of Renaissance masterpieces—as well as "new" originals from the same period. As the book's intricate plot unfolds, Gwyon's skills as a forger are exploited by shady art world figures around the globe. Questions of faith and fraudulence, pretense and the search for authenticity shadow the moral progress (or more often failings) of several protagonists as the setting moves from Spain to Paris, Rome to New York City to Latin America.

Throughout, the author's allusive prose and elliptical narration seduce the reader through a slow flirtation. Once Gaddis's peculiar music gets into your head, it starts to spirit you along like an eccentric lover urging you to unfamiliar indulgences—and unexpected laughter, too. For Gaddis has an unerring eye for the foibles and fatuities of both art and life, and his satirical invention is vivid, ebullient, and vastly entertaining, once you've come to recognize it.

What: Novel. *When:* 1955. *Also By: JR* (1975). *Carpenter's Gothic* (1985). *A Frolic of His Own* (1994). *Further Reading:* Jack Green's *Fire the Bastards!* is a broadside excoriating the initial, uncomprehending reviewers of *The Recognitions*. Steven Moore's extraordinary *Reader's Guide*, explaining the novel's myriad references and illuminating its sometimes obscure action and expression, is available online at williamgaddis.org. *Try: The Public Burning* by Robert Coover. *Underworld* by Don DeLillo. *Infinite Jest* by David Foster Wallace.

"The ur-text of postwar fiction."
—*Jonathan Franzen on* The Recognitions

A Lesson Before Dying
Ernest J. Gaines (born 1933)

The Dignity of Resistance

I t is 1940s Louisiana, and the innocent black man named Jefferson who had the bad luck to be in a store when a white shopkeeper was killed has been falsely charged with robbery and murder, convicted, and sentenced to death. We know how events will turn out, just as the characters do, because inevitability is the central reality of the all-too-real fictional world Ernest J. Gaines creates in this spare and moving novel. But it's not the central truth.

Ernest J. Gaines in a Louisiana bayou

Set in a time and place where racial segregation, Jim Crow injustice, political oppression, and poverty promise no future and guarantee little enough present to the black men and women brought to life in its pages, *A Lesson Before Dying* is told by Grant Wiggins, who has returned to Louisiana to teach at the poor church school on the plantation where he was raised. He has grown unhappy with his decision to come back to this small, familiar world after having left it to attend college, and he dreams of leaving once again, for good. Holding himself aloof from those around him, Wiggins is reluctant to interfere when his aunt and her friend Miss Emma, godmother of the wrongly condemned man, ask him to visit the slow-witted Jefferson as he awaits electrocution. They want him to help Jefferson rediscover some dignity after having been compared to a hog in court by his own attorney during the closing arguments at his trial. "I want the teacher make him know he's not a hog, he's a man," says Miss Emma. "I want him know that 'fore he go to that chair."

Neither man embraces the idea, and for several visits, Jefferson won't talk. But, under pressure from the two elderly women and from his girlfriend, Wiggins sticks with it, slowly bridging the gap between himself and Jefferson so that the doomed man learns to confront his inhuman fate by embracing his human one, thereby connecting both men to the wider community in unexpected ways. What's inevitable proves to be filled with profound surprises, not the least of which is the legacy of wisdom the student leaves his teacher.

What: Novel. *When:* 1993. *Award:* National Book Critics Circle Award, 1993. *Also By: Catherine Carmier* (1964). *The Autobiography of Miss Jane Pittman* (1971). *A Gathering of Old Men* (1983). *Try: To Kill a Mockingbird* by Harper Lee (see page 469). *Dead Man Walking* by Sister Helen Prejean. *Adaptation:* The 1999 made-for-television movie, which stars Don Cheadle, Mekhi Phifer, and Cicely Tyson, won two Emmy awards.

The Great Crash, 1929
John Kenneth Galbraith (1908–2006)

An Enlightening Explanation of Economic Catastrophe

W all Street roared good and loud during the last years of the Roaring Twenties. Americans were gripped by a stock-buying mania that sent share prices bounding upward. In turn, the rising prices led more and more people to borrow money to buy more and more shares, creating a stock market "bubble" leavened by rampant speculation. On October 24, 1929 ("Black Thursday"), the bubble burst, and the Great Crash ensued. Over the next few days, the market collapsed, and through the next couple of years the value of shares continued to erode. From a high of 381.17 in September 1929, the Dow Jones Industrial Average declined to a low of 41.22 in July 1932. (The 1929 high wouldn't be reached again for twenty-five years.)

The crash of 1929 is the most dramatic event in American economic history, and it is nowhere more tellingly explained than in the pages of this classic book. Galbraith was a revered economist, respected diplomat and government adviser, longtime Harvard professor, and, most important to readers, superb writer and good old-fashioned storyteller. *The Great Crash* is a work of both sprightly narrative and astute analysis, as entertaining as it is enlightening. Detailing the "vision and boundless hope and optimism" that encouraged the boom, as well as the economic policies,

John Kenneth Galbraith in his library, 1965

investment strategies, and lack of safeguards that dangerously inflated it, Galbraith explains just what happened, and why. Along the way he reveals a good deal about the psychological perils and financial pitfalls of an irrationally exuberant economy, providing insight that has remained relevant throughout the intervening decades (as investors caught up in the more recent bubbles would have profited to learn).

His book gives the lie to the common definition of economics as "the dismal science."

What: History. Economics. Business. *When:* 1954. *Also By: The Affluent Society* (1958). *The New Industrial State* (1967). *Money: Whence It Came, Where It Went* (1975). *A Life in Our Times: Memoirs* (1981). *A Short History of Financial Euphoria: A Hymn of Caution* (1993). *Further Reading: Extraordinary Popular Delusions and the Madness of Crowds* by Charles Mackay. *I.O.U.: Why Everyone Owes Everyone and No One Can Pay* by John Lanchester.

Street sale after the 1929 financial crash

THE FINANCIAL GOLIATH OF THE GILDED AGE

Morgan: American Financier
Jean Strouse (born 1945)

Larger-than-life figures are often the hardest to see clearly, for the light of their influence and the shadow of their reputation both work to obscure the vision of anyone trying to assess their characters and achievements. In the Gilded Age and the formative years of American financial hegemony, no figure loomed larger than J. P. Morgan (1837–1913). By dint of an extraordinary organizational intelligence, Morgan created financial and industrial structures that made him the most powerful banker in the world. He supplied the capital and creative energy that engendered vast railroad systems and corporate trusts, and was instrumental in the development of General Electric and U.S. Steel. As we read in *Morgan: American Financier* (1999), he "presided over a massive transfer of wealth from Europe to the United States, and, at a time when America had no central bank, acted as monitor of its capital markets and lender of last resort." For his actions and impact, his memory has been blessed and cursed; praised by the founder of *Forbes* magazine as "the financial Moses of the New World," he has been more often pilloried in the public imagination as the most baronial of the robber barons and— as John Dos Passos put it— "boss croupier of Wall Street."

Jean Strouse brings a subtle intelligence to bear on the life of the great man, humanizing him through his peculiarities and sensitivities: He was one of the most ambitious art collectors the world has ever known; rhinophyma turned his nose into a "hideous purple bulb," as if in a cartoonist's vision of a plutocrat; he pursued foreign travel to evade regular depressions and nervous collapses ("He could, he said, do a year's work in nine months but not in twelve"). More tellingly, she reveals his character through the nitty-gritty of his financial maneuverings and his faith, not in money, but in trust. "Is not commercial credit based primarily upon money or property?" he

East Room at The Morgan Library & Museum, New York City

was once asked at a federal hearing. "No sir," he replied, "the first thing is character."

Morgan's own character was complex, enigmatic, and mysterious enough to support a novel by Edith Wharton or Henry James, and Strouse does it justice, following it through real-life economic dramas with exceptional narrative flair. Her account of the suspense of the 1907 financial panic, detailing Morgan's perspicacity and his ability to pressure other bankers into seeing the national interest as their own, is nothing short of thrilling. Absorbing across its seven hundred pages, *Morgan* offers a captivating education in American history and politics, in the world of capital markets and financial engineering, in the impulses and intuitions of a singular collector of art and antiquities, and, not least, in the joys of getting lost in a book.

One Hundred Years of Solitude
Gabriel García Márquez (1927–2014)

A Magically Ancient Modern Masterpiece

One Hundred Years of Solitude is a novel so strange, so rich, so perfect in its singularity and timeless in its tenor, one can scarcely believe it was written as recently as 1967. At its start we are treated to an inkling of the author's narrative conjuring: "Many years later, as he faced the firing squad, Colonel Aureliano Buendía was to remember that distant afternoon when his father took him to discover ice." Past, present, and future are entwined in what seems at first a simple opening sentence, and the book's persistent themes of memory, prophecy, and wonder are introduced in a manner so intriguing that we barely stop to notice because we're eager to discover what's to come.

Gabriel García Márquez, 1972

Gabriel García Márquez's chronicle of the mythical town of Macondo, and of the bizarre, impossible, beautiful, and desolate history, through seven generations of the family of its founders, José Arcadio Buendía and his wife, Úrsula Iguarán, is one of the marvels of modern literature. It is peopled with extraordinary characters: from José Arcadio and Úrsula's descendants (a plethora of José Arcadios and Aurelianos among them) to the heart-stoppingly striking Remedios the Beauty, the dirt-eating Rebeca, Mauricio Babilonia, an ill-starred mechanic constantly accompanied by a swarm of yellow butterflies, and Melquíades, the gypsy who seems to orchestrate the Buendías' passage through time. It is equally replete with remarkable events: an insomnia plague that threatens the memory of the entire town, a five-year rainstorm that follows the massacre of three thousand striking banana workers by government troops, an unsuspected facility in Latin that springs to the lips of the patriarch when his senility leads to his being tethered to a tree in the yard for his sunset years.

The author's vaunted magical realism imbues mundane events with a majesty commensurate with their emotional resonance, as in this description of the aftermath of the second José Arcadio's mysterious death by gunshot:

A trickle of blood came out under the door, crossed the living room, went out into the street, continued on in a straight line across the uneven terraces, went down steps and climbed over curbs, passed along the Street of the Turks, turned a corner to the right and another to the left, made a right angle at the Buendía house, went in under the closed door, crossed through the parlor, hugging the walls so as not to stain the rugs, went on to the other living room, made a wide curve to avoid the dining-room table, went along the porch with the begonias, and passed without being seen under Amaranta's chair as she gave an arithmetic lesson to Aureliano José, and went through the pantry and came out in the kitchen, where Úrsula was getting ready to crack thirty-six eggs to make bread.

Economic, political, and historical forces—the colonialism represented by the banana company, the never-ending revolutionary campaigns of Colonel Aureliano Buendía and his insurgents, the arrival of the railroad—make incursions into Macondo, but they sweep through the life of the family like weather patterns, leaving devastation in their wake. So although one can read the novel as a metaphorical history of Colombia, the author's homeland, or as a more far-reaching fable of the forces of inexorable decay that fuel nature and overcome civilizations—and it is, decidedly, both—the more fundamental spirit of the book engages the perplexities of time and memory on a human scale. From that initial sentence, the author leads us into a different dimension, in which temporal reality is not a line, but a Möbius strip, turning in on itself in one continuous and endless loop. García Márquez once said he found the key to writing the book in the stories told him over and over again by his grandparents, and the character of such recountings indeed infuses the book with its peculiar atmosphere. The past and its personalities have been polished by use and repetition into legends, ennobled by the nostalgia and emotion of the teller, as if the pages themselves have evolved their own memory, and—to quote the manuscript of Melquíades decrypted in the book's final pages—"concentrated a century of daily episodes in such a way that they coexisted in one instant," or, let us say, in a single seductive, mesmerizing novel.

What: Novel. *When:* 1967. *Edition:* Gregory Rabassa's magnificent English translation from the Spanish was published in 1970. *Award:* Nobel Prize in Literature, 1982. *Also By: Leaf Storm* (1955). *No One Writes to the Colonel* (1961). *The Autumn of the Patriarch* (1975). *Chronicle of a Death Foretold* (1981). *Love in the Time of Cholera* (1985). *Try: Men of Maize* by Miguel Ángel Asturias. *The Lost Steps* by Alejo Carpentier. *The Death of Artemio Cruz* by Carlos Fuentes.

The Spare Room
Helen Garner (born 1942)

At the Limits of Life and Friendship

Some writers are instruments rather than artificers. It's not story they are after, or shapely forms, not beauty or *le mot juste*, but rather an assaying of life's raw materials. The best of these writers, and Helen Garner is one, create bodies of work that are hard to classify; their books often walk an uneasy border between fact and imagination, questioning our accepted notions of fiction and nonfiction, which we too often, too easily conflate with our ideas of truth and falsehood.

For some critics, there is something unseemly—somehow compromised—about such literary enterprise, and the authors instigating it find themselves magnets for controversy, as Garner has been in her native Australia, starting with pockets of dismissive reaction to the *cinema verité* aesthetic of her first novel, *Monkey Grip* (1977), and continuing with shock in some quarters at the bracing political incorrectness of

The First Stone (1995), her inquiry into allegations of sexual harassment at an Australian university, and distaste for the sensationalistic aspects of later books about actual murder cases. For an American example of the phenomenon, one might think of Norman Mailer (minus the impulsive celebrity and penchant for grand theorizing), and there is something telling in the fact that Garner, like Mailer, began as a novelist but discovered her most compelling authorial voice in nonfiction, as if the stories she could conjure were not complex and contradictory enough to occupy her talents fully.

The Spare Room chronicles the experience of a novelist named Helen whose Melbourne life is upended when Nicola, an old friend in the final stages of terminal cancer, arrives for an extended visit. Although the book is labeled a novel, the connection between the characters and situations the book describes mirrors real events in Garner's life, calling into question the nature of its fiction (to the consternation of several critics when *The Spare Room* was published). Regardless, the frankness of the telling is revelatory: Helen's impatience with Nicola's faith in the quack course of treatment that has brought her from Sydney, Nicola's indulgence of her own desperation, and the harsh realities of disease, friendship, and looming mortality are rendered with striking candor, whether the emotion of the moment be anger or tenderness. "A wave of sickening rage swept through me," Garner writes at one point. "I wanted to smash the car into a post, but for only her to die—I would leave the keys in the ignition, grab my shoulder bag, and run for my life." And at another:

For this too would be required of me: like her other carers, whom I came to love in the intimacy of our labour, I would have to help carry her to the lavatory, where I learned to wash her arse as gently as I had washed my sister's and my mother's, and as some day someone will have to wash mine.

Keenly observed and fiercely expressed, *The Spare Room* is clinical in its attention to how we cope, or fail to, with the frailty of bodies and emotions, with the ineluctable shortcomings of our hearts and lives. We're alternately frustrated with Nicola and appalled at Helen, and we read on, expecting a resolution that never comes, except when we realize we've just finished a book that makes us uncomfortable, not with the tale we've been told, but with the limits of life itself—a book that forces us to scrutinize our inadequacies in the face of love and death. Like all Garner's writing, *The Spare Room* explores the unproven ways in which people learn to live with themselves by committing, or not committing, private parts of themselves to others. In such exchanges, Garner tells us, honor is always at stake, even though we can't help but handle it clumsily and attempt to grasp it as it falls from reach.

What: Novel. **When:** 2008. **Also By:** *Honour & Other People's Children* (1980). *The Children's Bach* (1984). *Joe Cinque's Consolation* (2004). *This House of Grief: The Story of a Murder Trial* (2014). **Try:** *Fierce Attachments* by Vivian Gornick.

Cranford
Elizabeth Gaskell (1810–1865)

Mrs. Gaskell's Wisdom

"In the first place," begins Elizabeth Gaskell's episodic novel, "Cranford is in possession of the Amazons; all the holders of houses above a certain rent are women." If a married couple moves into the village, the narrator, Mary Smith, explains, the husband soon goes missing: "he is either fairly frightened to death by being the only man in the Cranford evening parties, or he is accounted for by being with his regiment, his ship, or closely engaged in business all the week" in a neighboring commercial town. "In short," she sums up, "whatever does become of the gentlemen, they are not at Cranford. What could they do if they were there?"

While town and tale are dominated by widows and single ladies—notably the spinster Jenkyns sisters, Deborah and Matty—the social roles that animate the interactions between characters are dependent, ultimately, on the legacies of fathers and husbands, and the tension between independence and reliance this creates is quietly dramatized by the author. She is astutely sensitive to the way economic demands, although unspoken as a matter of politeness, define relations even in such a small society as Cranford's.

Gaskell's alertness to the ramifications of station and advantage, or their lack, does nothing to dim the bright charms of the community she depicts. Her narrative of visits, card games, snobberies, and mutual support in times of need makes Cranford a pleasant literary destination. As convention gives way to generosity when Matty's livelihood is threatened after her sister's death, the real women Gaskell has created on the page assume a distinction in our imaginations that their stature in an obscure village might never earn them in life.

Although they have never won as wide a readership as those of Jane Austen or George Eliot, the books of Mrs. Gaskell (for so, in mid-nineteenth-century fashion, she signed them) possess similar qualities of intelligence, perception, and insight. What's most winning, and most reminiscent of Austen and Eliot, is the author's compassionately ironic voice, which surveys the women of Cranford with a mixture of amusement and affection that exudes real wisdom.

What: Novel. *When:* Serialized 1851–53; first book publication, 1853. *Also By: Mary Barton* (1848). *North and South* (1854–55). *Wives and Daughters* (1864–66). *The Life of Charlotte Brontë* (1857). *Further Reading: Elizabeth Gaskell: A Habit of Stories* by Jenny Uglow. *Try: Middlemarch* by George Eliot (see page 248). *Lark Rise to Candleford* by Flora Thompson (see page 783). *Adaptation:* A superb television miniseries, starring Judi Dench, was produced by the BBC in 2007.

The Glass Palace
Amitav Ghosh (born 1956)

A Newly Minted Old-Fashioned Novel Spanning a Century of Burmese Days

"You see," says a character near the very end of this enormous novel, "in classical writing, everything happens outside—on streets, in public squares and battlefields, in palaces and gardens—in places that everyone can imagine." Modern fiction habituates readers to much smaller rooms, restricting the breadth of its storytelling to privileged privacies. One of the most refreshing of the many pleasures that Amitav Ghosh's absorbing book delivers is its sweeping, serious, transporting public dimension. Beginning in Mandalay in 1885, *The Glass Palace* traces several generations through more than a century in the history of Burma (now Myanmar), from the cannon fire that signals the British invasion through the Indian exile of the last Burmese king, the degradations of empire, the drama of World War II, and the uncertain decades leading up to the nation's current political turmoil.

The complex tale is wrapped in the fortunes of the eleven-year-old orphan, Rajkumar, whom we meet on the first page and accompany through his long journey from poverty to wealth via the teak and rubber industries, and in the fate of his descendants. Replete with richly drawn characters and thoroughly imagined incidents, the novel encompasses courtly intrigue, colonial violence, economic

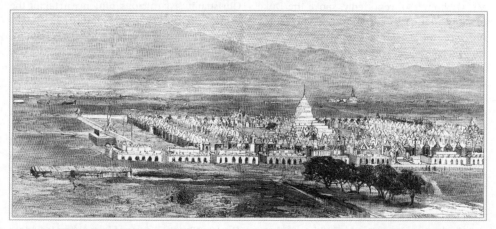

Royal pagoda at Mandalay, 1885

adventurism and transformation, and questions of social and national identity, yet remains at its heart a saga of love at first sight—a love strong enough to cross years and borders. Best of all, Ghosh's creative intelligence suffuses every paragraph, making *The Glass Palace* a riveting and unforgettable exhibition of the storyteller's art.

What: Novel. *When:* 2000. *Also By:* Nonfiction: *In an Antique Land* (1992). Fiction: The Ibis Trilogy: *Sea of Poppies* (2008); *River of Smoke* (2011); *Flood of Fire* (2015). *Further Reading: The River of Lost Footsteps: A Personal History of Burma* by Thant Myint-U. *Try: Red Earth and Pouring Rain* by Vikram Chandra. *The Piano Tuner* by Daniel Mason. *The Map of Love* by Ahdaf Soueif.

....

"Each night from 10.30 to 12 I read Gibbon out loud. I read slowly, richly, not to say juicily; and like Prospero's isle the room is full of noises— little, dry, gentle noises. Some matter-of-fact man of blunt or gross perceptions might say it was the ashes cooling in the grate, but I know better. It is the little creatures of the night, moths and crickets and spiderlings, a mouse or two perhaps and small gnats in a wailful choir, come out to listen to the Gibbonian music."
—*George Lyttelton,* The Lyttelton Hart-Davis Letters *(see page 503)*

The History of the Decline and Fall of the Roman Empire
Edward Gibbon (1737–1794)

A Historical Monument of Resounding Prose
....

"Another damned, thick, square book! Always scribble, scribble, scribble! Eh! Mr. Gibbon?" So, reportedly, spoke the Duke of Gloucester when Edward Gibbon presented him with the second volume of his enormous *History of the Decline and Fall of the Roman Empire.* Thick and square defines all six of the history's eventual volumes, each of which is filled with the scholarship, intelligence, and fine style that characterizes this most majestic of English-language scribblers.

Gibbon's reach, in detailing the empire's decline from AD 180 to the fall of Constantinople in 1453, is ambitious; yet his grasp of the vast sweep of events and culture is so sure, his prose so glorious, his store of primary sources so rich, that we are treated to the satisfactions of a deeply pleasurable read. Indeed, although there is much compelling intelligence in Gibbon's argument that the degradation of civic virtue sealed Rome's slow but sure fate (to say nothing of his somewhat scandalous judgment of Christianity's pernicious influence in taking the Roman eye off the incentive of the here-and-now and directing its gaze toward the hereafter), it is the author's literary facility that continually rewards and astonishes the reader. Take his description of the emperor Gordian: "Twenty-two acknowledged concubines, and a library of sixty-two thousand volumes, attested the variety of his inclinations, and from the productions which he left behind him, it appears that the former as well as the latter were designed for use rather than ostentation." Or this: "Of the various forms of government which have prevailed in the world, an hereditary monarchy seems to present the fairest scope for ridicule." Or this: "But the power of instruction is seldom of much efficacy, except in those happy disposi- tions where it is almost superfluous." Gibbon's own power of instruction is prodigious, for his *History* advances a vision of conduct and a philosophy of life both useful and inspiring, informing our understanding of the influence of laws and manners on civil society and of the conflicting principles of pleasure and action in the lives and legacies of both individuals and states. From the moderation of Augustus to the immodesties of Nero, from the advent of the saints to the invasions of Attila, from the foun- dation of Constantinople to the conquests of Genghis Khan and Tamerlane, Gibbon covers an extraordinary expanse of human experience in this exacting work, which remains unmatched in both extent and eloquence.

What: History. *When:* 1776–88. *Edition:* J. B. Bury's multivolume complete edition, with useful commentaries, is standard. The well-executed Penguin abridgement is an excellent one-volume alternative. *Also By: Memoirs of My Life and Writings* (published posthumously in various editions). *Further Reading: The Fall of the Roman Empire: A New History of Rome and the Barbarians* by Peter Heather. *Try: The Histories* and *The Annals* by Tacitus (see page 770). *Reflections on the Revolution in France* by Edmund Burke (see page 110). *The History of England* by Thomas Babington Macaulay.

Cold Comfort Farm
Stella Gibbons (1902–1989)

High Comedy—with Something Nasty in the Woodshed

Imagine a Jane Austen heroine stumbling into an episode of *The Beverly Hillbillies*, with the hillbillies portrayed by method actors. That will give you something of the flavor of this giddy tale, which presents a picture of country life that is roaringly bizarre—and hilarious.

Flora Poste is a sophisticated Londoner whose education has been "expensive, ath- letic and prolonged." When she is orphaned at nineteen, she heads off to stay with the Starkadders, her distant cousins on her late mother's side. They have a dilapidated farm in the village of Howling—a place that turns out to be perfectly named, for what Flora discovers at Cold Comfort Farm is enough to make anyone scream. Amos Starkadder, the head of the fam- ily, is a fire-and-brimstone preacher: "There'll be no butter in hell," is the kind of thing he likes to say. Amos's wife, Judith, is obsessed with her lunk of a son, Seth, a rather sullen sop to the misery in which she wallows. Adam Lambsbreath, the elderly farmhand, preserves such ancient rural traditions as "clettering" (washing dishes with a twig). He also looks after the cows, the aptly named Graceless, Pointless, Feckless, and Aimless. And finally there's the imposing Aunt Ada Doom, who never misses a chance to remind everyone that when she was young, she "saw something nasty in the woodshed." Can Flora fend for herself among this strange crew and the other unforget- table cranks Stella Gibbons has created (Mrs. Smiling! Mr. Mybug!!)? She can, and does, ris- ing to each and every ridiculous challenge they present as she attempts to "tidy up affairs."

Cold Comfort Farm is a brilliant parody, skewering literary models from the novels of Thomas Hardy and D. H. Lawrence to the pop- ular regional country fiction of the 1930s. But erudition is not required to enjoy Gibbons's riotous comedy, a novel the London *Sunday Times* once called "very probably the funniest book ever written."

What: Novel. Humor. *When:* 1932. *Also By: The Bachelor* (1944). *Westwood* (1946). *Here Be Dragons* (1956). Gibbons also penned two volumes of stories that are sequels of a sort: *Christmas at Cold Comfort Farm* (1940) and *Conference at Cold Comfort Farm* (1949). *Further Reading: Out of the Woodshed: The Life of Stella Gibbons* by her nephew Reggie Oliver. *Adaptation:* The excellent 1995 film was directed by John Schlesinger from a script by Malcolm Bradbury and stars Kate Beckinsale, Eileen Atkins, and Stephen Fry.

A Mass for the Dead
William Gibson (1914–2008)

A Luminous Memoir of Unexceptional Lives

In this eloquent volume, Gibson, a celebrated playwright (author, most notably, of *The Miracle Worker*), relates, with affection, anguish, wonder, and extraordinary sympathy, the story of his father and mother: their families and their courtship, their determined yet unspectacular search for economic security and domestic comfort in and around New York City in the first two-thirds of the twentieth century, their dedicated parenthood, their illnesses and deaths. It is the story as well of the author's own growth from boy to man, from happy child to disaffected youth to fledgling writer to father and—as his parents reached the end of their lives—once again blessed and reverent son.

Beginning with a meditation on a missal he finds among his late mother's effects, Gibson shapes his chronicle to the outline of a requiem mass, interspersing his continuous narrative with passages of evocative contemplation. In doing so, he fashions a language lofty enough to honor the generosity of life's generations, yet supple enough to capture all the commonplaces—of parents and children, affection and argument, birth, marriage, death—that those generations inhabit. As he describes his father's undistinguished but steadfast working life in a Manhattan office, his own youthful alienation—by means of politics, education, and art—from his upbringing, and his mother's hardworking and determined widowhood, Gibson illuminates familiar circumstances in a way that infuses particular events with larger meanings. By the end of the book, the lessons of family have come full circle, as the author marvels at his own nascent fatherhood and embraces the legacy of his parents' simple, struggling benevolence.

Happy families may be all alike, as Tolstoy asserted, but true and good books about them are rare. This is one of the very best, vivid with candor, sentiment, and faithfulness, and graced with a magnanimity that has made it fiercely loved by a small circle of knowing readers.

What: Memoir. *When:* 1968. *Reading Notes:* Gibson's elevated language at the outset requires a little patience; once you're past page fifty or so, his narrative builds its own contemplative momentum. His several knotty poems, interspersed with his chapters, are best engaged once one has read the whole book. *Also By:* Plays: *The Miracle Worker* (1956); *Two for the Seesaw* (1958); *Golden Boy* (with Clifford Odets; 1964). Prose: *The Seesaw Log* (1959); *A Season in Heaven* (1974). *Try: Hunger of Memory* by Richard Rodriguez (see page 671). *This House of Sky* by Ivan Doig (see page 227).

Pattern Recognition
William Gibson (born 1948)

Cyberspace Seer

Seven years of relative obscurity for Canadian writer William Gibson would pass between his first fiction sale—the short story "Fragments of a Hologram Rose" in 1977—and the appearance of his debut novel, *Neuromancer*, as a mass-market paperback original. This was a breakthrough book for more than the author, for *Neuromancer* crystallized several emergent trends in science fiction while announcing the advent of a new dimension of human (and machine) experience, to which Gibson applied the name "cyberspace." Gibson's role as herald of cyberpunk has made him one of the most admired and influential writers of our age.

Even as his books continue to display his trademark mix of fleet action, idiosyncratic characters tossing off sharp dialogue, pithy social commentary, techno-exegesis galore, and no little world-weariness, Gibson's vision has continued to evolve: "Science fiction's best use today," he has asserted, "is the exploration of contemporary reality rather than any attempt to predict where we are going. Earth is the alien planet now."

Pattern Recognition brilliantly maps this alien landscape. The novel's main character is Cayce Pollard. She's a marketing whiz, a high-flying "cool hunter." (Gibson's ear for contemporary talk, from multinational branding jive to the hacker poetry of cyberspeak, is pitch-perfect.) She is also obsessed with "the footage," snippets of mysterious video being released periodically on the internet. When Cayce is hired to find out who makes the clips, she discovers that web links can form an old-fashioned web of intrigue, including a 9/11 subplot. Ultimately, what's most memorable about Pattern Recognition is its detailed rendering of the profound disorientations of today's connected culture: In the vast placelessness of an urgently mobile universe, everyone can reach everyone else instantly, but nobody really knows where anybody is. Fortunately, that's not the case for us as Gibson's readers. In Pattern Recognition we know exactly where we are: in the hands of a writer with unusual insight into the way we live now.

What: Science Fiction. When: 2003. Also By: The Sprawl Trilogy: Neuromancer (1984); Count Zero (1986); Mona Lisa Overdrive (1988). The Bridge Trilogy: Virtual Light (1993); Idoru (1996); All Tomorrow's Parties (1999). The Blue Ant Trilogy begins with Pattern Recognition and continues with Spook Country (2007) and Zero History (2010). Try: The Zenith Angle by Bruce Sterling. Snow Crash by Neal Stephenson. The Quantum Thief by Hannu Rajaniemi.

Howl and Other Poems
Allen Ginsberg (1926–1997)

A Beat Generation Rhapsody

I n addition to being presences in our minds, books are objects in the world. Occasionally, the physical manifestation of a particular volume can become an emblem of an era, amplifying, if not transcending, its contents as an icon of a cultural moment. Such was the case with Allen Ginsberg's Howl and Other Poems, Number Four in the Pocket Poets series issued by San Francisco's City Lights Books. The small, squarish Pocket Poets, with their stark cover design—a black-bordered white field displaying, in distinctive typography, title and author—were emanations of a new wave in literary engagement in the mid-1950s, with Howl its most representative recognizable icon. Over the next decade, the Pocket Poets edition of Howl would serve as a kind of calling card for the counterculture that bubbled beneath the surface of fifties conformity, then burst into mainstream consciousness as the fantasia of the 1960s began to sound.

Allen Ginsberg, 1958

Issued in 1956, and the subject of an obscenity prosecution almost immediately, the book achieved a notoriety that sensationalized its subject matter but did not obscure its poetic originality and invention. Dedicated, and in large part addressed, to the writer Carl Solomon, whom Ginsberg had met in a psychiatric hospital, *Howl* is an incantatory elegy for the frenzied, foolish, ecstatic, diffuse, and beatific vitality of a band of outsiders Ginsberg identifies with, and celebrates. It begins with a burst of verbal energy that never lets up:

I saw the best minds of my generation destroyed by
    madness, starving hysterical naked,
dragging themselves through the negro streets at dawn
    looking for an angry fix,
angelheaded hipsters burning for the ancient heavenly
    connection to the starry dynamo in the machinery
    of night . . .

Ginsberg's prosody explodes the formal conventions of contemporary verse with lines measured in breaths rather than metric feet, each flight of words taking off from a fixed base note that serves as a kind of aural punctuation. His liberation of the line, and the tumbling juxtaposition of images and ideas it enables, would have a profound influence on works as diverse as the autobiographical X-rays of Robert Lowell's *Life Studies* and the oracular phantasms of Bob Dylan's *Highway 61 Revisited*.

Documenting and mythologizing the dreams and delinquencies of his Beat Generation comrades—Jack Kerouac, Neal Cassady, William S. Burroughs, Herbert Huncke, and a posse of unnamed others—"Howl" sets their quixotic wanderings in fervid pursuit of stimulation, sex, enlightenment, and intoxication against the staid but ominous landscape of industrialized capitalism ("Moloch whose love is endless oil and stone! Moloch whose soul is electricity and banks!"). It's a howl indeed, a scream into the dark night of the soul that is haunted by ghosts of William Blake and Walt Whitman, and alive with inspiration, memory, humor, sorrow, and no little bravery.

What: Poetry. When: 1956. Also By: Kaddish and Other Poems (1961). Reality Sandwiches (1963). Planet News (1968). The Fall of America: Poems of These States (1973). Further Reading: Allen Ginsberg: A Biography by Barry Miles. Try: America: A Prophecy by William Blake. Leaves of Grass by Walt Whitman (see page 850). Gasoline by Gregory Corso. A Coney Island of the Mind by Lawrence Ferlinghetti.

....

The Little Virtues
Natalia Ginzburg (1916–1991)

A Syntax for Wisdom

Day by day, our standards slip: What in our youth we took for granted is slowly but surely overwhelmed by the unrelenting business of living. Soon, too soon, the light under our bushel can barely be glimpsed beneath the dust of circumstance. Reading can help restore our sense of our best selves, and few books do it as tellingly as *The Little Virtues*, a slim volume of autobiographical essays by Natalia Ginzburg, one of Italy's finest twentieth-century writers. Through quiet scrutiny of her own experience, Ginzburg invokes personal resources that are larger if less calculable than material comforts —even if largely, and always, aspirational. The title essay is a touchstone of wisdom. It begins with this:

As far as the education of children is concerned I think they should be taught not the little virtues but the great ones. Not thrift but generosity and an indifference to money; not caution but courage and a contempt for danger; not shrewdness but frankness and a love of truth; not tact but love for one's neighbour and self-denial; not a desire for success but a desire to be and to know.

What's bracing about Ginzburg's guidance is the subtle movement of her focus, as the essay unfolds, from the education of children to the conduct of their parents. As she persuades us of the importance of allowing our children the space and silence to develop a sense of purpose—an ardor for some aspect of being outside the parameters of material reward— and then to nourish a privacy big enough to amplify it, she directs our gaze to our own lives. In doing so, she forces us to consider whether we have first formed, and then kept, faith with anything larger than the immediate demands of our day-to-day existence.

Her essay "Human Relationships" abstracts one person's sense of being in the world from infancy through childhood, adolescence, young adulthood, and maturity until it earns—in twenty pages, no less!—the kind of magnanimous, humane conclusion Tolstoy might deliver at the end of one of his enormous novels. Her reductions in scope are a concentration of the flavors of life rather than a diminishment; she does to emotions what Hemingway did to sentences, stripping them of gesture and flourish to expose, declaratively, their building blocks of sense and feeling and expression.

Fortune's blows certainly sharpened Ginzburg's unflinching yet compassionate gaze; the first piece in *The Little Virtues*, "Winter in the Abruzzi," recounts her family's internal exile in a poor province during World War II because of her husband's anti-Fascist activities (his resistance would eventually lead to his torture and death in prison in Rome in 1944). In the decades that followed, Ginzburg would create a shelf of novels and works of narrative nonfiction that were often original, sometimes eccentric, always eloquent, and widely acclaimed, but her essays give her canny, caring stoicism its most singular and lasting form.

What: Essays. *When:* 1962. *Edition:* English translation by Dick Davis, 1986. *Also By: All Our Yesterdays* (1952). *Voices in the Evening* (1961). *Family Lexicon* (1963). *The Manzoni Family* (1983). *A Place to Live and Other Selected Essays* (2002), chosen and translated by novelist Lynne Sharon Schwartz, is a superb alternative selection that duplicates some of the content of *The Little Virtues*. *Try: Independent Spirit* by Hubert Butler (see page 115). *Everywhere I Look* by Helen Garner.

Passing the Time in Ballymenone
Henry Glassie (born 1941)

The Lore of the Irish

No trip is more telling than one that uncovers the hidden dimensions of local truths. Wrapped in the blankets of custom and story, worry and work, such truths may appear to sleep while the wider world hurries about its shouting business, but they often possess the persistence and the profundity of the deepest dreams. In this rich, remarkable study of the common lore and labor of Ballymenone, a rural community in Northern Ireland, eminent folklorist Henry Glassie presents "a community's history by its own historians," weaving a web of talk and story, text and context that is leavened by the residents' native wit and weighted with life and death's natural gravity.

Glassie came to Ballymenone in 1972, the most violent year of the Ulster "troubles." Largely Catholic in Protestant Ulster, isolated in part for political reasons, Ballymenone at the time the book describes lacked electricity and running water, yet was steeped in the enduring present of its own traditions. In a few years the customs Glassie first met would be rapidly quarantined into a distant past by economic and technological advances, and the shared culture he articulates would lose some of its common currency. So his record is as poignant as it is vivid; his expertise in ethnographic observation is enhanced by the telling alertness of his eyes, ears, and heart. Throughout his book's many pages, which are alive with voices, music, laughter, and—always—stories, the author happily proves himself "at war with academic conventions, at peace with the gentle wisdom of old men," suffusing his scholarship with eloquent human sympathy.

What: Place. Anthropology. *When:* 1982. *Also By: Art and Life in Bangladesh* (1997). *The Stars of Ballymenone* (2006). *Further Reading: Irish Folktales*, edited by Henry Glassie. *Try: Akenfield* by Ronald Blythe (see page 84).

1787 portrait of Goethe by Johann Heinrich Tischbein

JOHANN WOLFGANG VON GOETHE
(1749–1832)

N o author—not even Shakespeare—has had the sweeping influence over English literature that Johann Wolfgang von Goethe exerted over German writing. He was the definitive figure of the Germanic Enlightenment. His genius was felt not only in one or two genres, but across the entire breadth of letters, from novel and short story to epic and lyric verse, from drama to memoir to philosophical and even scientific treatises. His collected works run to more than a hundred volumes and seem to brood over non-Germanic European culture like a marble bust, impressive but remote; as W. H. Auden and Elizabeth Mayer write in the introduction to their Penguin Classics translation of the author's *Italian Journey*, to most English-speaking readers Goethe is merely a name, a figure of enormous reputation lacking any particular animation. Even his most famous works—*The Sorrows of Young Werther*, *Wilhelm Meister's Apprenticeship*, *Faust*—have an affective strangeness that makes them difficult to embrace for those reared on more naturalistic fiction. Their invention seems to hail not just from a foreign land, but from an altogether different planet, on which metaphorical ideas frame recognizable human aspirations in nightmarish or exaggerated circumstances, as in Faust's compact with the devil. In this sense, and somewhat weirdly, his most complementary modern analogue may be Franz Kafka: We read of Werther's lovesickness and Faust's soul-peril with the same rapt attention we bring to Gregor Samsa's transformation into an insect in the later writer's *The Metamorphosis* (see page 426).

The Sorrows of Young Werther

Desperate Love—
and an 18th-Century Sensation

What: Novel. *When:* 1774. *Edition:* There are several excellent English translations; among the more recent, Stanley Corngold's (published as *The Sufferings of Young Werther*) stands out. *Also By: Wilhelm Meister's Apprenticeship* (1796). *Try: The Red and the Black* by Stendhal (see page 754). *Sentimental Education* by Gustave Flaubert (see page 283). *Adaptation: Werther,* an 1892 opera by Jules Massenet.

E very young person who's written despair-ing romantic poems or a melodramatic diary, or even wallowed in the sadness of songs of unrequited love, has an ancestor in Werther, Goethe's first consequential literary creation. The book in which he appears is for the most part an epistolary novel, consisting of letters from the lovesick title character to a friend who never appears. As a result, reading it is a kind of eavesdropping, as Werther shares his activities, conversations, and reflections with an intimacy of tone and an effusion of feeling that are peculiarly engaging despite the extent of his self-absorption. Traveling from the city to a small town to take care of a family inheri-tance, Werther grows to like the simplicity and quaintness of country life. But he falls madly in love with a local girl, Charlotte, who admires him but is already engaged. Both Charlotte and her fiancé (later husband) treat Werther with the greatest kindness, but Werther cannot contain his feelings, and spirals into suicidal depression. The end isn't pretty.

A massive bestseller upon its release in 1774, *Werther* made Goethe, aged just twenty-four, into a continental celebrity with a cult following. Newspapers of the time describe "Werther fever" sweeping the continent, with youthful readers dressing like their lovelorn, idealistic hero—yellow trousers, blue jacket, open necked shirt. More than a few of these readers followed Werther to his extreme end: The book led to a wave of suicides, and worried officials in Germany and elsewhere banned the book in an attempt to halt the epidemic.

Werther is an icon of the German liter-ary movement known as Sturm und Drang ("storm and stress"), a pre-Romantic style that orchestrated emotional extremes. Although Goethe's later work—the novel *Elective Affinities*, the poetry, and especially *Faust*—may be more elegant, *Werther* retains across the centuries all the passion and sentiment that made it so explosive in the Age of Enlightenment.

Faust

The Immortal Telling of an
Enduring Legend

A mong the scores of marvelous works Goethe penned, one towers over the rest: the two-part tragedy *Faust*. This enormous drama is the ultimate realization of the abiding legend of a man of ambition who sells his soul to the devil in exchange for secret power and worldly gratification.

Dr. Heinrich Faust is an academic lumi-nary bedecked with degrees, acclaim, and cultural respect; yet, when the reader is intro-duced to him, Faust is writhing in despair at his desk, unnerved by the vanity and futility of his intellectual pride. For all his learning, he feels he knows nothing at all; his first words are a famous lament (here in Randall Jarrell's unrhymed translation):

> Law, medicine, philosophy,
> And even—worse luck—theology
> I've studied with passionate resolution,
> I've learned, alas! from top to bottom;
> And stand here now, poor fool that I am,
> No wiser than I was before.
> I am called Master, Doctor even;
> For ten years, up and down and back
>   and forth,
> I've led my students by the nose—
> And I see there's nothing we can know!

As Faust is contemplating suicide, the devil enters the scholar's studio in the guise of a poodle. Unlike the monstrous devil of the tra-ditional Faust legend, Goethe's Mephistopheles is an inveterate charmer: witty, philosophical, and with a marked taste for wine and women. He promises to serve Faust on earth—delivering not only knowledge but earthly pleasures—if

Scene from Charles Gounod's opera
Faust

Faust will serve him afterward in hell. The desperate Faust agrees, although he adds an important clause to their deal: The devil gets possession of his soul only if Faust finds satisfaction in one moment of his life—enough satisfaction to wish that instant of his life could last forever.

In part one, Faust and Mephistopheles remain in Germany, where the twosome wreak havoc at a bar and party with abandon on Walpurgis Night, a festival of revelry akin to Halloween. Faust enters into a passionate, disastrous love affair with the innocent maiden Gretchen, whose tragic fate is a by-product of Faust's inordinate desires. Part two, by contrast, takes place in a more expansive, mythical world: Faust is transported on a cloud, sleeps with Helen of Troy, founds a city, and—in a scene that had special piquancy during the later days of Weimar hyperinflation—prints paper money to counteract the Holy Roman Emperor's shortage of gold. As Goethe engages themes of history, human nature, politics, and metaphysics, the overreaching professor of part one is transformed into an Everyman.

Faust consumed Goethe for most of his life. He started on it when he was still a student, and would go on to publish fragments and revise the texts for the next half century. Its reputation, not to mention its length, may be off-putting, but don't be discouraged from at least tackling part one, the more accessible

and exciting portion, which stands on its own as a complete play (many English-language editions contain only the first half). You might think of part two as a bonus for the afterlife.

What: Drama. *When:* Part one, 1808; part two, 1832.
Editions: There are many translations into English. Randall Jarrell's poetic version (part one only) is a stunning literary work in its own right. David Luke's superb translation of the complete work in the Oxford World Classics series is also highly recommended. *Try: The Tragical History of Doctor Faustus* by Christopher Marlowe. *The Master and Margarita* by Mikhail Bulgakov (see page 107). *Doctor Faustus* by Thomas Mann. *Adaptations:* Scenes from *Faust* have been set to music or evoked by an extraordinary roster of musicians, from Franz Schubert to Hector Berlioz, Charles Gounod, Arrigo Boito, and Randy Newman. There have also been several movie adaptations, most famously F. W. Murnau's silent film of 1926.

Italian Journey
An Ideal Travel Chronicle

In the pages of Goethe's memoirs, and especially in this wonderfully evocative travel journal, the image of remote intellect his reputation conjures is in retreat, replaced by a fully human figure whose voice is as engaging as his intellect is compelling. Indeed, *Italian Journey* may be the most personable and immediately engaging of all his works, and is the perfect place for a reader to make his acquaintance. In its pages, we accompany Goethe as he escapes the habits and demands of his official responsibilities and public renown in Germany, where, in addition to his literary fame, he was prominent as a member of the inner circle and administrative government of the Duke of Saxe-Weimer, Karl August. As if to prove his escape was more than metaphorical, Goethe set out on his Italian sojourn in a coach at three o'clock in the morning, under cover of both darkness and an assumed name; why shouldn't a great poet, after all, apply the trappings of imagination to his own itinerary?

He was thirty-seven years old, and his translators W. H. Auden and Elizabeth Mayer describe the book that came of his trip—to Verona and then Venice, from Naples to Rome and Sicily and back again—as a psychological document "dealing with a life crisis which, in various degrees of intensity, we all experience somewhere between the ages of thirty-five and forty-five." Although there is insight in that characterization, Goethe did not compose *Italian Journey* until nearly three decades after the events it describes, and even though he relied on contemporaneous notebooks and letters to supply much of the detail, there is a fictive shape to his narration that has as much to do with permanent aspiration as with midlife crisis. Even an intellect as fine and as fertile as Goethe's requires distance from its own conventions to refresh its longing, and the gradual, casual invigoration of his alertness and attention as he relives his earlier journey upon the page proves restorative to the reader as well, a kind of idealized rehearsal of what our own travels might be like if we had world enough and time to savor them with similar imagination.

What: Travel. *When:* 1817. *Edition:* The translation by Auden and Mayer is superb. *Also By: From My Life: Poetry and Truth* (autobiography in four volumes, 1811–33). *Further Reading: Conversations with Goethe* by Johann Peter Eckermann. *Try: A Roman Journal* by Stendhal. *Rome and a Villa* by Eleanor Clark (see page 160).

Dead Souls
Nikolai Gogol (1809–1852)

A Swindler's Progress Through Provincial Russia

In the library of great nineteenth-century Russian novels, *Dead Souls* stands out as the most bizarre, eclipsing in its strangeness even the tortured subjectivity of Dostoevsky's most fervid pages. Proceeding from an outrageous comic premise, *Dead Souls* hastens through the Russian landscape with demoniacal energy, its author probing provincial life with keen observations of character and custom even as he explodes the boundaries of realism with fantastical impressions and inventions. Imagine Charles Dickens writing a travelogue about a country

Portrait of Nikolai Gogol

imagined by Edgar Allan Poe and you'll have some sense of the literary flavor—and pleasure—of Gogol's tale.

Gogol's protagonist is Pavel Ivanovich Chichikov, a swindler who moves through the countryside working an ingenious scam. Landowners of the time could buy and sell the serfs who worked their estates; these peasants were known as "souls," and the landowners paid a government tax on each of them. When a peasant died, however, the tax still had to be paid until the next census—the soul remained on the books. Chichikov's ghoulish scheme is to buy these "dead souls" and, while they remained in bookkeeping limbo, mortgage them as if they were live chattel. We follow Chichikov in and out of trouble as he visits various unsavory estate owners and tries to strike deals for the purchase of their deceased peasantry. Each wild episode is narrated with a manic attention to detail that gives the narrative a modern immediacy, while Gogol's epic similes and lyrical bursts supply a mocking commentary throughout.

Through it all, Gogol's eye for human folly never fails, and it is that alertness that gives the book its outsize animation. Playwright Clifford Odets best captured the novel's vivid effect on the reader: "Where else," Odets asked, "has one met such a group of brawling men, all of them straining, pleading, expostulating —bellowing to be released from the printed page? In Homer, in Shakespeare, in Rabelais, but not in many other places. Here are characters who veritably fly at the reader's throat."

What: Novel. *When:* 1842. *Edition:* The Modern Library edition uses B. G. Guerney's translation, which Vladimir Nabokov called an "extraordinarily fine piece of work." *Also By: Taras Bulba* (1835; short novel). *The Inspector General* (1836; play). The author's short story masterpieces "Nevsky Prospect" (1835), "The Nose" (1836), and "The Overcoat" (1842) can be found in *The Collected Tales of Nikolai Gogol,* translated by Richard Pevear and Larissa Volokhonsky (1998). *Further Reading: Nikolai Gogol* by Vladimir Nabokov. *Try: Oblomov* by Ivan Goncharov (see page 323). *Footnote:* Gripped by a religious mania, Gogol burned the manuscript of a proposed second part of *Dead Souls* a few weeks before he died.

Lord of the Flies
William Golding (1911–1993)

Boys Will Be Boys

William Golding wrote more than a dozen books, won the 1980 Booker Prize for *Rites of Passage,* and was awarded the Nobel Prize in Literature in 1983. Yet despite his considerable achievement, his reputation largely rests on the frightening tale that readers found in his first novel, *Lord of the Flies.* Assigned at least once to nearly every student in the English-speaking world, Golding's chilling depiction of the descent into savagery of schoolboys stranded on a deserted island stirs to menacing life as we turn the pages; terror coils behind the words like a patient predator stalking its prey.

It is a tribute to the author's narrative gifts that we take his storytelling prowess for granted, falling into the story's grip as we discover the boys' predicament. With them we explore the island on which their plane—meant to ferry them from war to safety—has crashed. Realizing they are without adult supervision, they embrace the promise of adventure familiar to them from books such as *Swallows and Amazons* (see page 660) and *The Coral Island*: "Until the grown-ups come to fetch us we'll have fun." Yet their attempts to organize themselves, elect a leader, and hunt for food soon go awry; rivalries, fears, and cruelties undermine, then overwhelm, their civilizing games with devastating consequences.

Written in the wake of World War II and under the shadow of nuclear threat, *Lord of the Flies* focuses a sunstruck magnifying glass on large themes: the innateness of good and evil, the presumption of youth's innocence, the fragility of any social contract. Much of the book's timeless appeal dwells in its endless analyzability (to the delight of English teachers everywhere). But

Scene from the 1963 film adaptation

more than six decades of term papers have done little to weaken its hold on our collective imagination—witness the fact that not one but two of the most popular television shows of the twenty-first century, *Survivor* and *Lost*, have Golding's horrific fable at their roots. *Lord of the Flies* exudes the ominous resonance that emanates from myth rather than fiction, echoing with fears that summon both adrenaline and apprehension.

What: Novel. *When:* 1954. *Award:* Nobel Prize in Literature, 1983. *Also By: Pincher Martin* (1955). *The Spire* (1964). *Darkness Visible* (1979). *Further Reading: William Golding: The Man Who Wrote "Lord of the Flies"* by John Carey. *Try: A High Wind in Jamaica* by Richard Hughes (see page 392). *High-Rise* by J. G. Ballard. *Adaptations:* Two films have been made. Peter Brook's 1963 version is far more memorable than Harry Hook's 1990 remake.

Darwin's Dreampond
DRAMA IN LAKE VICTORIA
Tijs Goldschmidt (born 1953)

A Scientific Sojourn in Tanzania

Part scientific record and part literary travelogue, biologist Tijs Goldschmidt's book combines a report on some years spent in Tanzania in the 1980s, classifying Lake Victoria's numberless variety of cichlid (a perch-like fish) species, with a winning, wide-ranging account of a cultured mind transplanted from Holland to an exotic locale to contemplate the wonders of evolution, ecology, extinction, and, now and then, existence. The reader is intrigued by the easy alliance of erudition and informal charm from the start, when we come upon the author, in a leaky boat on the great lake (actually, we learn, Victoria is "a freshwater sea. A shallow saucer filled with water, about the size of Switzerland"), conversing in Swahili with his native colleagues ("'Look,' I said. '*Mawingu kama picha ya mbwana Salomoni Ruysdael, m'Holanzi,* a sky like one in a painting by the Dutchman Mr. Salomon van Ruysdael'").

The evolutionary wonder of the objects of Goldschmidt's attention is juxtaposed with the scientists' relentless designation of one new species after another: Goldschmidt and his fellow taxonomists identified species "enthusiastically during the first years, almost reluctantly later on, as nothing is more stultifying than discovering something unique every week." The author's alternation of scientific and narrative passages is justly measured, and his wit and his writing—its energy delivered fresh and direct in Sherry Marx-Macdonald's translation—a joy.

What: Science. *When:* 1994; first edition in English, 1996. *Further Reading: The Cichlid Fishes: Nature's Grand Experiment in Evolution* by George Barlow. *Try: The Beak of the Finch* by Jonathan Weiner. *Chasing Kangaroos* by Tim Flannery. *Your Inner Fish* by Neil Shubin.

Oblomov
Ivan Goncharov (1812–1891)

Hamlet Without Tragedy

If you think the "couch potato" belongs exclusively to modern America, you haven't met Oblomov. As far as torpor is concerned, one might say that the hero of this Russian classic was ahead of his time, doing nothing so well that he would become a nineteenth-century emblem of inertness.

How did he do it? To start, the title character of Ivan Goncharov's biting treatment of the Russian nobility spends the first third of the novel in his dust-covered room; in fact, he can barely make it off the sofa. Despite a loving childhood and a first-rate education, Oblomov cannot make a decision or bring himself to act on even the smallest questions. As news drifts in from outside his room—about the declining fortunes of his country estate, especially—Oblomov fantasizes about grand reforms and substantial changes, but imagining them is as far as he can go. When his friend Stolz comes to harass him into action, Oblomov dismisses any exertion as a waste of time. As it is with his career, so it is with romance: A proposal to the beautiful Olga ends up collapsing as Oblomov envisions servants gossiping and soon sacrifices even love to idleness.

Goncharov's novel, originally published serially, had such an effect in its time that it inspired a new Russian word: *oblomovshchina*, or "Oblomov-itis," a fake clinical diagnosis of the paralysis of privilege. Although the book's satire of Russian nobility is trenchant and funny, the author knows that his protagonist suffers from something more insidious than mere laziness, for Oblomov isn't empty or corrupt: He's intelligent, perceptive, and capable of deep friendship and passionate attachments. Indeed, the psychological inertia that Goncharov depicts, which seems to be strangely fostered by the very talents and advantages Oblomov possesses, retains its relevance today, and not just in terms of "couch potatoes."

He was . . . painfully aware that entombed within himself there was this precious radiant essence, moribund perhaps by now, like a gold deposit lying buried deep in the rock that should long ago have been minted into coin and put into circulation.

This treasure was, however, buried deep under a great heap of sludge and silt. It was as if someone had stolen the gifts that life had handed to him on a plate and locked them away in his inmost recesses.

That the someone may well be himself does nothing, of course, to diminish his dilemma: "Something was preventing him from throwing himself wholeheartedly and uninhibitedly into life's race and from letting the wind fill his sails." Despite his distance from us in time and place, Oblomov's quandary quite often remains our own.

What: Novel. *When:* 1859. *Edition:* There are several good English translations, Stephen Pearl's, quoted here, among them. *Also By: A Common Story* (1847). *The Precipice* (1869). *Try: Bartleby the Scrivener* by Herman Melville. *Something Happened* by Joseph Heller (see page 363). *A Confederacy of Dunces* by John Kennedy Toole. *Adaptation:* The acclaimed 1980 Russian film adaptation was directed by Nikita Mikhalkov.

The Goncourt Journal
Edmond de Goncourt (1822–1896) and Jules de Goncourt (1830–1870)

Literary Dispatches from the Capital of the 19th Century

Much of the pleasure of reading is found not in our ultimate assessment of a book as a whole—its placement on a scale of perfection—but rather *in medias res*—in the moment-by-moment engagement a paragraph or a passage can offer. Indeed, there is a literature of pages that is every bit as rewarding as the literature of volumes; connoisseurs of the former often find themselves turning to journals, diaries, and letters to indulge their preference for leisurely appreciation over the headlong rush toward the destination of a final plot twist. And when it comes to such reading, few works provide as rich a field for mental sauntering as the journals of the brothers Goncourt.

One might say that Edmond and Jules de Goncourt shaped the model of the modern man of letters: By dint of informed taste and obsessively self-studied sensibilities, they—by their own lights, at least—rose above the trivialities of the bourgeois world to dwell in a state of intermittent inspiration and perpetual ennui. Their high-minded artistic ambition as determined, if unsuccessful, novelists was matched to a worldly predilection for decadent pursuits, and their *Journal* is a kind of conversational companion to the highly wrought

Edmond and Jules de Goncourt, 1861

soliloquies of Charles Baudelaire (see page 55). As Geoff Dyer notes in his introduction to a recent reissue of Robert Baldick's superb selection from the brothers' voluminous diaries, the Goncourts were "self-styled 'John-the-Baptists of modern neurosis.'" Yet for all the brothers' self-absorption—perhaps because of it—*Pages from the Goncourt Journal* is a joy to read.

Beginning in 1851 and continuing almost to the end of the century (after Jules's death in 1870, Edmond maintained the chronicle alone), the daily record of incidents, reflections, gossip, and indiscretions is spiced not only with insights into literature, art, and fashion, but also with witness to historical events such as the 1870–71 Siege of Paris and the subsequent uprising that gave birth to the Commune: "The

sufferings of Paris during the siege? A joke for two months. In the third month the joke went sour." The loneliness of authorship—"I keep hearing people say that nobody is capable of self-abnegation and self-sacrifice any longer. Yet I have sacrificed to literature, if not a grand passion, a very serious and tender affection"—is balanced with its conviviality: "Dinner at the Café Riche with Flaubert, Zola, Turgenev, and Alphonse Daudet." There are discoveries all the more striking for the offhandedness of their narration: "Yesterday I spent the whole day in the studio of a strange painter called Degas. After a great many essays and experiments and trial shots in all directions, he has fallen in love with modern life, and out of all the subjects in modern life he has chosen washerwomen and ballet-dancers. When you come to think of it, it is not a bad choice."

As addictive to readers as they clearly were to their writers, the journal entries attempt to capture what Jules described as "all the interesting things which are lost in conversation." To an astonishing degree, they succeed; if Paris was the capital of the nineteenth century, the Goncourts were its devilish recording angels.

What: Diaries & Letters. *When:* Written 1851–96; Edmond began issuing excerpts publicly in the last decade of his life. The complete *Journal* was eventually published in many volumes between 1956 and 1959. *Edition: Pages from the Goncourt Journal*, edited and translated by Robert Baldick, is an ideal selection. *Try:* The journals of André Gide. The diaries of Virginia Woolf. The diaries of James Lees-Milne. *Footnote:* The Prix Goncourt, France's most prestigious award for imaginative prose, was established by Edmond's bequest; the first Prix Goncourt was awarded in 1903.

....

There Is a World Elsewhere
AUTOBIOGRAPHICAL PAGES
F. González-Crussi (born 1936)

Memoirs of a Pathologist
....

D r. Frank González-Crussi is a pathologist who has composed several volumes of urbane and animated essays, including *Notes of an Anatomist* (1985) and *Suspended Animation: Six*

Essays on the Preservation of Bodily Parts (1995), that do graceful justice to the lessons of mortality his medical work engages. While the morbid—in the exact sense—concerns of his profession lead him to explore such uncommon subjects as cadavers, coroners, and graveyards, his civilized perspective makes his writing, in the words of novelist John Banville, "a love letter to life, in all its strangeness, beauty and mystery."

There Is a World Elsewhere is a single long narrative that depicts González-Crussi's journey from the mythological realms of early childhood through the realities of his youth in a Mexico City barrio, from his apprenticeship in his family's pharmacy through his studies at university and the completion of his medical training in the United States (where he has made his career, largely at the Northwestern University Medical Center). González-Crussi's language is courtly and mannered, intricate and original, colored with nuance nourished by both clinical precision and the sometimes giddy exactitude of a wide vocabulary (*nimiety* and *swank*, *murine* and *eclosion*, *muniment* and *vespertine*). The doctor's erudition and experience inhabit a larger range of reference and a richer cultural context than we are accustomed to in contemporary writing, and his

sensibility—profoundly philosophical, witty and shrewd, compassionate—is built right into the sinews of his sentences; his use of prose as an instrument of ruminative inquiry evokes ancestral masters of English (Sir Thomas Browne, for one), and it turns his exercise in recollection into a singularly absorbing volume. Prophesying the literary judgments of posterity is a fool's game, but F. González-Crussi's cultivated and idiosyncratic approach to exploring the substance of both life and death makes it easy to imagine future generations, ages hence, discovering his writing with welcome and wonder.

What: Autobiography. *When:* 1998. *Also By: The Five Senses* (1989). *The Day of the Dead* (1993). *On Being Born and Other Difficulties* (2004). *Try: The Lives of a Cell* by Lewis Thomas (see page 781). *Mortal Lessons: Notes on the Art of Surgery* by Richard Selzer. *Body of Work: Meditations on Mortality from the Human Anatomy Lab* by Christine Montross.

···

The Panda's Thumb
MORE REFLECTIONS IN NATURAL HISTORY
Stephen Jay Gould (1941–2002)

A Compendium of Scientific Curiosity

The *Panda's Thumb* is one of several books of essays assembled from biologist Stephen Jay Gould's popular and long-running column in *Natural History* magazine. Like others in the series (including *Ever Since Darwin*, *Hen's Teeth and Horse's Toes*, and *The Flamingo's Smile*), it collects small marvels of thinking, writing, and inquiry. Take the title essay of the book at hand, which offers a model of the essayist's leisurely pursuit of scientific purpose. It begins with an invocation of one of Charles Darwin's more obscure works, *On the Various Contrivances by Which British and Foreign Orchids Are Fertilised by Insects*, cuts to observation of newly arrived pandas at the Washington Zoo, then proceeds to a consideration of the panda's "thumb," ostensibly a sixth finger essential to the animal's dexterous stripping of its beloved staple, bamboo. But as Gould reveals, this

thumb is not a digit at all, but rather an adaptive accommodation of a small component of the wrist. In a few pages of graceful prose, he presents a short and fascinating course in the often inelegant but always workable ways of evolution: "Odd arrangements and funny solutions are the proof of evolution—paths that a sensible God would never tread but that a natural process, constrained by history, follows perforce."

In the thirty other essays the book comprises, Gould writes with wit and insight about sea turtles and sponges, magnetic bacteria and matricidal mites, the Piltdown Man fraud, and, unforgettably, the unfortunate maturation of Mickey Mouse. His interest in a specific curiosity never fails to illuminate some abiding principle of evolutionary theory. "Nature's oddities are more than good stories," he proves again and again. "They are material for probing the limits of interesting theories about life's history and meaning." And, in these inviting essays, material for very good reading, too.

What: Science. Essays. *When:* 1980. *Award:* National Book Award, 1981. *Also By: The Mismeasure of Man*

(1981). *Wonderful Life: The Burgess Shale and the Nature of History* (1989). *The Structure of Evolutionary Theory* (2002). *Try: The Lives of a Cell* by Lewis Thomas (see page 781). *River Out of Eden: A Darwinian View of Life* by Richard Dawkins.

Personal History
Katharine Graham (1917–2001)

A Woman of Influence

As its title implies—with a matter-of-factness characteristic of its author—this is a book in which public and private meet. Katharine Graham was publisher of the *Washington Post* in its exciting and dangerous glory years, from the 1960s through the 1980s; she approved the publication of the Pentagon Papers and backed her reporters and editors as they investigated and broke the Watergate stories that would lead, ultimately, to the resignation of President Nixon in 1974. She became the first female CEO of a *Fortune* 500 company, and remained for decades a pillar of Washington's insular but powerful social and political elite.

Katharine Graham at The Washington Post

How she came to be the steward of her family's publishing enterprise and, as it would turn out, for a critical time in our nation's history something of a steward for the republic itself, is a tale that grows increasingly surprising as it unfolds. Her privileged upbringing culminated in her marriage to Philip Graham, to whom her father handed the reins of the *Post*; Katharine lived in the shadow of her husband's brilliance, infidelity, and mental imbalance until his suicide in 1963. The author's description of the dark period surrounding the failure of her marriage and Philip's tragic end is remarkable for the sense of her own weakness and pain it conveys while also portraying the slow, almost simmering emergence of the will and probity that would see her through. She is gracious about the encouragement she received from friends and confidantes as she was considering assuming control of the newspaper, and some of these conversations read like vivid details in the vast canvas of a nineteenth-century novel.

I was talking about hanging on to the paper until the children, especially the boys—since in those days that's how I thought—were old enough to run it. I recall Luvie firmly and distinctly saying, "Don't be silly, dear. You can do it."

"Me?" I exclaimed. "That's impossible. I couldn't possibly do it. You don't know how hard and complicated it is. There's no way I could do it."

"Of course you can do it," she maintained.... "You've just been pushed down so far you don't recognize what you can do."

What's striking is not the emotional or confessional nature of any of her narrative—except for the number of occasions she admits to being unready for some crisis or responsibility thrust upon her, Graham is a straightforward rather than a reflective storyteller—but rather the quietly subversive way she must overturn her own assumption that she lacks the agency to choose the right path forward. Yet choose it she nearly invariably does, coaxing herself onto a wider stage and steeling herself to circumstances, like the heroine of a novel confronted with things she thinks beyond her ken but decides she must face up to nonetheless.

Reading this engrossing book is like watching as the protagonist of a tale told in the third person takes the pen away from the remote and omniscient author and determines to write the next chapters of her life herself. One imagines Graham overcoming some great reserve in writing this book, then employing all the habits of an orderly and businesslike mind to their best advantage in doing so. If it's a little flatly told, the tale it relates is round enough to occupy a reader's imagination fully:

A woman comes into her own when her private self becomes a public one, and goes on to command attention and respect in the service, by and large, of the world's greater good. She's a heroine worthy of George Eliot, and suggests what might have happened to Dorothea Brooke if history had given her a wider stage than the precincts of Middlemarch. Although *Personal History* is not as well written as *Middlemarch*, one might say that, in the strange illumination books cast on life, it is as well lived.

What: Autobiography. *When:* 1997. *Awards:* Pulitzer Prize for Biography or Autobiography, 1998. *Also By: Katharine Graham's Washington* (anthology curated by Graham; 2002). *Try: The Powers That Be* by David Halberstam. *A Good Life: Newspapering and Other Adventures* by Ben Bradlee. *Footnote:* Meryl Streep portrays Graham in Steven Spielberg's 2017 film, *The Post.*

The Wind in the Willows
Kenneth Grahame (1859–1932)

From Private Bedtime Story to Universal Classic

Despite the fact that he spent his working life as an official of the Bank of England, Kenneth Grahame remained a child at heart. His first two books, *The Golden Age* and *Dream Days*, written in the last decade of the nineteenth century while the author was still a bachelor, collect tales and reminiscences that lovingly evoke the imaginative camaraderie of a family of youngsters. Depicting their secrets, games, and adventures, Grahame's nostalgic vignettes are wistful celebrations of the innocence and ingenuity of childhood.

Although both books met with acclaim, it was not until late fatherhood introduced Grahame to a new form—the bedtime story—that the author's genius fully flowered. In fact, the genesis of *The Wind in the Willows* can be traced to the evening of his only child's fourth birthday, when Grahame was called upon to soothe the boy's crying fit with tales of moles and water rats. Over the next three years, in bedside tales and letters to young Alastair, Grahame invented the characters and episodes he would weave together to make his masterpiece.

From its first pages, in which the amiable Mole and the resourceful Water Rat inaugurate their friendship with a waterborne picnic, *The Wind in the Willows* transports us to a genial and welcoming world. The story of life on the riverbank is peopled with a cast of players—Rat and Mole, the formidable Badger, the ebullient, alluringly incorrigible (and apparently, quite Alastair-like) Toad—who move right into the family room of one's imagination and take up residence as old friends. While Toad's antic escapades with caravan and motorcar provide comedy and excitement, the quirks and qualities of his fellow characters prove to be every bit as charming and memorable.

No childhood should pass without a trip down Grahame's river, or a walk through his Wild Wood. As for adults, they should never stray from these haunts for very long, for *The Wind in the Willows* is one of the archetypal works of English literature: In no other book

Ernest H. Shepard sketch of Rat and Mole for 1931 edition

are the quiet motives of the soul—comfort and friendship, wonder, the grace of nature and the ideal of home—so magically realized.

What: Children's. *When:* 1907. *Edition:* Over the years, *The Wind in the Willows* has drawn the talents of many illustrators, but no artist has so perfectly captured the spirit of Grahame's characters as Ernest H. Shepard, who took the author's direction ("I love these little people, be kind to them") to heart. *Further Reading:*

My Dearest Mouse collects, in facsimile, Grahame's letters to Alastair—a "first draft" of *The Wind in the Willows. Try: The Mouse and His Child* by Russell Hoban (see page 378). *Watership Down* by Richard Adams (see page 7). *Footnote:* Grahame's working title for the book was *Mr. Mole and His Mates.* At the urging of his British publisher, he changed it to *The Wind in the Reeds,* by which title it was announced in both England and America before—at last—being changed to *The Wind in the Willows.*

Personal Memoirs of U. S. Grant

Ulysses S. Grant (1822–1885)

The Vivid and Disarming Memoirs of a Civil War Hero

The esteemed military historian John Keegan has called Ulysses S. Grant's memoirs of his career as a soldier and his Civil War generalship "perhaps the most revelatory autobiography of high command to exist in any language." Mark Twain, who published it, thought Grant's book was the most remarkable work of its kind since the *Commentaries* of Julius Caesar (and the more critically distanced Edmund Wilson, in his own *Patriotic Gore*, concurred). Writing with vigor and clarity, with a directness that captures the narrative sweep of events, and with hands-on intelligence of the strategies and tactics described, Grant unexpectedly penned one of the most remarkable and compelling volumes in American history.

He was born in frontier Ohio, attended West Point, and served with distinction in the Mexican-American War. Once that conflict ended in 1848, Grant served without any special distinction in the peacetime military until 1854, when he ventured into civilian life and proved an utter failure as a businessman. In 1861 the Civil War came to his rescue, and he, ultimately, came to the nation's. As a low-level commander he enjoyed great success, and in late 1863 President Lincoln put him in charge of the Union armies. His military triumphs opened the door to two terms in the White House, beginning in 1869. However, after leaving office in 1877 he again ran into business difficulties. This time they brought him and his family to the brink of destitution.

It was then that he set about writing his memoirs in a desperate attempt to raise some money. Completed less than a week before Grant died of throat cancer, *Personal Memoirs* did turn out to be a huge bestseller. What is even more amazing, however, is that Grant managed, under the trying physical and financial circumstances, to produce a masterpiece. Focusing almost entirely on his military life, *Personal Memoirs* is an honest, insightful account of the campaigns Grant survived in both the

Mexican-American War and in the brutal struggle between the Union and Confederate armies. His remarkable ability to visualize landscapes— what historian James M. McPherson has called his "topographical memory"—allows him to lucidly describe the movements of past engagements, such as those at Shiloh, Vicksburg, and Chattanooga, just as it had enabled him to resolve the confusion of troops and terrain into effective orders on the battlefield. Throughout, the acuity of his military intelligence is matched with a personal humility and a magnanimity toward his opponents—witness his description of Lee's surrender at Appomattox—that attest to the author's hard-won nobility of spirit.

What: War. History. Memoir. *When:* 1885. *Edition: The Personal Memoirs of Ulysses S. Grant: The Complete Annotated Edition*, edited by John F. Marszalek with David S. Nolen and Louie P. Gallo. *Further Reading: Grant: A Biography* by William S. McFeely. *Grant* by Ron Chernow. *Grant: A Novel* by Max Byrd is an excellent fictional treatment. *Try: Recollections and Letters* by Robert E. Lee. *Memoirs* by William Tecumseh Sherman. *From Manassas to Appomattox* by James Longstreet. *The Passing of the Armies* by Joshua Chamberlain.

Ulysses S. Grant, 1864

The Tin Drum
Günter Grass (1927–2015)

Once Upon the Worst of Times

I t was 1940 when Günter Grass attempted his first novel; he was thirteen years old. As he grew to maturity after World War II, in which he briefly served as a teenaged tank gunner in Hitler's Waffen-SS—a fact he would keep secret for more than six decades—he struggled to compose poetry and plays, but was daunted by critic Theodor Adorno's dictum that it was "barbaric to write a poem after Auschwitz." Like other young, politically active writers of his generation, Grass thought that the German language itself had been corrupted by Nazism, and that writing in the shadow of its horrors might be redeemed only "by becoming memory and preventing the past from coming to an end," as he would explain in the lecture he delivered upon being awarded the Nobel Prize in 1999.

Published in 1959, Grass's first novel, *The Tin Drum*, assumed this responsibility in a curious way, to brilliant and controversial effect, enlisting gritty fantasy and wild invention to prove that remembrance is an insidious organism both familiar and monstrous, and far more slippery than the hard facts of history might suggest. Narrated from an insane asylum by Oskar Matzerath, a thirty-year-old who has not grown an inch since the age of three, when—in possession of a tin drum his mother had given him and all the faculties of an adult, or so he claims—he determined not to grow beyond the three feet he then stood. Anything but innocent, this childlike figure who can, and frequently does, shatter glass with his voice, is the most unreliable of narrators, rendering the experience of Germans before, during, and after the war as a kind of Brothers Grimm story in which both "once upon a time" and "happily ever after" have disappeared; what's left is an intimate pageant of primal emotions, grotesque characters, and bizarre incidents that enchant the reader's imagination with a kind of wicked glee. Satire and tragedy, thwarted love stories and a stunted Bildungsroman, cruelties visited upon the little drummer and evils

instigated by him, fables of the familial past and the brutal realities of the war's nightmarish present—all combine in *The Tin Drum* to make a resonating world only the most capacious fiction could contain. Like the most indelible fairy tale, Grass's masterpiece leaves images rooting around in our minds that are ominous and enduring, fraught with a meaning we can neither evade nor explain.

What: Novel. *When:* 1959. *Editions:* The first English version, by Ralph Manheim, issued in 1962, has been superseded by the 2009 translation by Breon Mitchell. *Award:* Nobel Prize in Literature, 1999. *Also By: The Tin Drum* is the first volume of Grass's Danzig Trilogy, completed with the novella *Cat and Mouse* (1961) and the novel *Dog Years* (1963). Also of note are the novel *Crabwalk* (2002) and the memoir *Peeling the Onion* (2006). *Try: The Dwarf* by Pär Lagerkvist (see page 460). *The Master and Margarita* by Mikhail Bulgakov (see page 107). *The Clown* by Heinrich Böll. *Adaptation:* Volker Schlöndorff's 1979 film adaptation won the Golden Palm at Cannes and the Oscar for Best Foreign Language Film.

Good-bye to All That

AN AUTOBIOGRAPHY

Robert Graves (1895–1985)

An Unforgettable Farewell to Arms— and to a Way of Life

I n *The Great War and Modern Memory*, his clas- sic study of the literature of World War I, Paul Fussell calls *Good-bye to All That* the best mem- oir of that conflict. No argument here, for its depiction of a soldier's experience of "the war to end all wars" is unforgettable in its bitter sardonicism and fierce attention to the bru- tal actualities of violence. Yet this early auto- biography, published in 1929, when Robert Graves was still in his early thirties, bids a mor- dant farewell to more than just the horrors of combat.

The title has long since entered the lan- guage as a phrase used to refer to a traumatic experience which renders a return to former habits impossible ("my sole contribution to Bartlett's *Familiar Quotations*," the author, an admired poet and accomplished novelist, joked later in his career). Such was certainly the case for Graves, who at twenty-one enlisted as a captain in the Royal Welsh Fusiliers within days of England's declaring war on Germany in 1914, and it was also the case for many of his Edwardian peers. For all of them, the savagery of combat, the terrors of the trenches, and the absurdities of military bureaucracy meant "good-bye" to youth, innocence, idealism, even patriotism—good-bye, in short, to their seem- ingly immutable prewar way of life.

Graves's backward glance is by no means tinged with nostalgia. Indeed, the chapters treating his coming-of-age before the war began to exhibit no fondness at all for the elite schools and class-ridden culture in which he was bred. When war does come, it arrives as the final, fatal nail in the coffin of the past Graves wishes to put behind him. His brilliant matter- of-fact descriptions of the bloody devastation he saw and his relentless witness to the indi- vidual courage and collective powerlessness of soldiers caught in a vicious circle of mean- ingless death leaves the reader shell-shocked and disbelieving. His clear-eyed exposure of

bureaucratic bungling—exhibited in docu- ments such as a letter from a colonel to Graves's mother, in which the death of her son is mis- takenly announced—injects a cruel and bracing humor into his litany of atrocities.

As might be expected of the co-author of a highly regarded handbook on writing well (*The Reader Over Your Shoulder*), Graves recounts his life, both in uniform and out, in a supple, vigorous prose that is a model of how English should be written. He is also a supremely gifted storyteller who can blend tragedy and comedy in ways poignant, rueful, and hauntingly true to life:

Samson lay groaning about twenty yards beyond the front trench. Several attempts were made to rescue him. He had been very badly hit. Three men got killed in these attempts; two officers and one man, wounded. In the end his own orderly managed to crawl out to him. Samson sent him back, saying that he was riddled through and not worth rescuing; he sent his apologies to the Company for making such a noise.

Filled with vignettes as powerful and moving as this one, *Good-bye to All That* remains one of the most telling memoirs in the literature of war, and one of the most striking autobiographies of the twentieth century.

What: War. Memoir. *When:* 1929. *Editions:* The readily available Anchor paperback contains Graves's 1957 revision of the original text; this later version is less acerbic and severe than the 1929 original, which is worth seeking out. *Also By: I, Claudius* (1934). *Claudius the God* (1935). *The White Goddess: A Historical Grammar of Poetic Myth* (1948). *Watch the North Wind Rise* (1949). *The Greek Myths* (1955). *Collected Poems* (various editions, 1948 through 1975). *Further Reading: The Great War and Modern Memory* by Paul Fussell. *Try: The Complete Memoirs of George Sherston* by Siegfried Sassoon (see page 699). *Storm of Steel* by Ernst Jünger. *All Quiet on the Western Front* by Erich Maria Remarque (see page 664).

Autobiography of a Face
Lucy Grealy (1963–2002)

The Pain of Feeling Ugly

Lucy Grealy was nine years old when it was discovered she had cancer. Years of grueling treatment followed, including nearly thirty operations and the partial removal of her jaw. The resulting facial disfigurement left the young girl prey to the taunts of peers ("The cruelty of children is immense, almost startling in its precision"), as well as to the conviction that "I *was* my face, I *was* ugliness." Looking back, Grealy summed up her childhood and young adulthood this way: "It was the pain from that, from feeling ugly, that I always viewed as the great tragedy in my life. The fact that I had cancer seemed minor in comparison."

Autobiography of a Face is Grealy's powerful, riveting account of growing up during those two decades in a society whose true religion often seems to be the worship of physical perfection. The normal details of a childhood—schoolrooms and playgrounds, family relations, the solace pets provide, the desire to be special in one's own and in others' eyes—are in Grealy's memoir given deepened significance by the shadow of her fate. Given the wrenching subject matter and the intensity of feeling involved, it is astonishing that her writing should be so polished, her language so lyrically arresting, her authorial voice so poised and un-self-pitying.

What's more, Grealy's memoir is a work of profound reflection, most notably in its meditations on how one constructs an identity in accordance with, or in defiance of, one's "looks." Writing with wit and vigor, she transforms pain into a brave and often dancing light that reaches far beyond her own circumstances to illuminate our common ideas of beauty and truth, self-consciousness and doubt. Her humbling story has the strength to fundamentally alter the way we think about ourselves and the world.

What: Memoir. *When:* 1994. *Further Reading:* Novelist Ann Patchett describes her intimate friendship with Grealy in *Truth & Beauty*, written after Grealy's death, from an apparent heroin overdose, in December 2002. *Try: Poster Child* by Emily Rapp.

The Dead of the House
Hannah Green (1927–1996)

A Singular Legacy, and an Exquisite Novel

A novel that at times seems not very far removed from memoir, Hannah Green's lyrical evocation of the history of an Ohio family is a book of precious strength, as beautifully composed as any American novel written in the second half of the twentieth century.

Covering a period that runs roughly from the 1930s through the 1950s, *The Dead of the House* is narrated by a woman of the author's age and background. Through the three parts of her tale, in which she progresses from childhood through adolescence into adulthood, Vanessa climbs a family tree as enchanted as a forest, its deep roots entwining the present in all the entanglements of the past. "I thought that if I did go into your woods," she says as a child to her grandfather, "I would go back into the past and I'd never be able to come out again." Which is an apt description of what Vanessa does in this book, ruminating on the fate of her family—an old American breed of pioneers and preachers, businessmen and distant women—at the same time as she steps into her self through the familiar crises of coming-of-age: first boyfriend, sibling rivalry, encounter with death. But *The Dead of the House* is by no means a conventional family saga; it's more like a book of poems in which meanings are glimpsed rather than grasped, and in which recollection is recast as reverie.

As Vanessa comes into her own present out of the embrace of her family's past, Green captures our common passage from the almost mythic realm of our childhoods into the realities of our adult lives. Her unforgettable book is a telling evocation of how we are shaped by our inheritance, bound to our dead by those qualities bestowed on us "by the strange accidents of time, of blood, of love."

What: Novel. *When:* 1972. *Also By: Little Saint: The Hours of Saint Foy*, published posthumously in 2000. *Try: The Catherine Wheel* by Jean Stafford.

"And whenever I want to remind myself of how it felt to be young, I am going back to read the section entitled 'Summer Afternoon, Summer Afternoon.' This is evocation at the level of magic." —*Wallace Stegner on* The Dead of the House

---

GRAHAM GREENE
(1904–1991)

I n 2012, the acclaimed travel writer Pico Iyer published a book-length essay about his long intimacy as a reader with Graham Greene, capturing in his title—*The Man Within My Head*—the fascination Greene has held for many. It's something of a mystery how Greene's oeuvre, consisting mostly of books that take the unassuming dimensions of commercial fiction, can so haunt the mind, insinuating profound questions of imposture and authenticity into our ruminations and—Greene being Greene—our prayers.

For much of his career, Graham Greene divided his output into "novels" and "entertainments"—the former comprising his explorations of religious themes (as in *The Power and the Glory* and *The End of the Affair*, discussed on pages 335 and 336) or the moral complications of international politics (*The Quiet American* [1955], *The Comedians* [1966]), the latter encompassing stories of suspense whose plots he spun with an almost malicious relish that generations of book lovers have found addictive (*The Ministry of Fear* [1943], *The Third Man* [1949]).

In his best novels, Greene's talents combine to transform page-turning into a kind of pilgrimage, amplifying the what-happens-next of the narrative at hand with the more mysterious what-happens-next in which our lives unfold. The distinguishing landmarks

Graham Greene at his desk

of the alluring literary landscape known as "Greeneland" are the questions of virtue and desire, rectitude and compromise, shame and salvation that we'd ask ourselves if we had the time and courage to ponder the meaning of our own motives and activities. Engaging us as readers first and as seekers second but more lastingly, his novels remind us of something we already suspect but seldom articulate—a conviction that life must have higher stakes than we are wont to play it for. What gives his work its enduring hold on our imaginations is his uncanny ability to capture between covers the suspense in which our souls exist. Really.

Alida Valli and Joseph Cotten in the 1949 film The Third Man

The Power and the Glory
Sinner's Progress

Set in Mexico in the 1930s, when the Catholic Church has been outlawed by the revolutionary government, *The Power and the Glory* portrays a corrupted and courageous cleric's devotion to his calling, despite his alcoholism (Greene gives him no name other than "the whisky priest"), his licentiousness (his fatherhood is emblem of his forsaken chastity), and his tortured alertness to his unworthiness. Knowing he risks execution by carrying the sacraments from village to village and nourishing as best he can the spiritual needs of the poor, he struggles to uphold the vision of a God who both eludes and exhilarates him. He is stalked in his travels by a young police lieutenant whose fervent belief in political realities poses a philosophical as well as a physical threat to his prey, deepening the stakes of the chase. Damned if he does and damned if he doesn't, the whisky priest is a hero who, in his very unfitness for the role, reveals the imaginative nobility of faith, hope, and love even in—especially in—the most unexalted settings. That he is not a good priest, and maybe even not a very good man, defines the human quandary that gives Greene's narrative its profound resonance.

What: Novel. *When:* 1940. *Also By: The Heart of the Matter* (1948). *A Burnt-Out Case* (1960). Greene's 1939 Mexican travel book, *The Lawless Roads*, is an illuminating complement to the novel he set in the same landscape. *Further Reading: The Life of Graham Greene* by Norman Sherry (three volumes). *Try: The Diary of a Country Priest* by Georges Bernanos (see page 72). *The Greek Passion* by Nikos Kazantzakis (see page 432). *Under the Volcano* by Malcolm Lowry (see page 498).

The Third Man
The Classic Thriller of Post–World War II Vienna

Of Greene's many self-described entertainments, perhaps none is more compactly satisfying than the novella he penned before composing the screenplay for *The Third Man*, which starred Orson Welles in one of his most memorable screen incarnations: the charming and sinister Harry Lime.

Spare, fast-paced, and utterly gripping, *The Third Man* concerns the adventures of Rollo Martins, a comic, earnest figure summoned to Vienna in the aftermath of World War II by his boyhood chum Lime. Arriving to discover that his friend has apparently been killed in a traffic accident, Martins is troubled by police allegations of Lime's sordid criminality and by his own growing suspicion that the "accident" may have really been murder. Cleverly upsetting one expectation after another for both Martins and the reader, Greene fashions a roaring good tale set in the shadowy underworld of Vienna's postwar political intrigue—and in the equally murky precincts of his own devilish morality.

The cinematic version of this tale is one of the great movies of all time, its imagery indelible; it is a tribute to Greene's gifts that remembering the film while reading only enhances the pleasure of his cunning narrative.

What: Mystery & Suspense. Novella. *When:* 1950. *Also By: A Gun for Sale* (1936). *The Confidential Agent* (1939). *Further Reading: Graham Greene: A Life in Letters,* edited by Richard Greene. *Try: A Coffin for Dimitrios* by Eric Ambler (see page 17). *Rogue Male* by Geoffrey Household (see page 390). *The Spy Who Came In from the Cold* by John le Carré (see page 467). *Adaptations:* In addition to Welles, Carol Reed's 1949 film stars Joseph Cotten, Alida Valli, and Trevor Howard. There is a superb audiobook read by Martin Jarvis.

The End of the Affair
A Poignant and Startling Love Story

A compelling tapestry of brooding desire, obsessive jealousy, and religious belief,

The End of the Affair tells the story of Maurice Bendrix, who, stung by the abrupt end of an affair with a friend's wife, has hired a private investigator to follow the woman who walked out of his embrace nearly two years before. What he ultimately discovers calls everything he has previously believed into question. It's a haunting exploration of love, both human and divine, and of the force of faith in a faithless age. Of all Greene's novels, *The End of the Affair* may best embody, if not explain, his mysterious imaginative power.

What: Novel. *When:* 1951. *Also By:* Greene's travel and autobiographical writings offer fascinating glimpses into his imagination. Try *Journey Without Maps* (1936), *A Sort of Life* (19710), and *Ways of Escape* (1980). *Further Reading: The Love-charm of Bombs: Restless Lives in the Second World War* by Lara Feigel. *Try: The Heat of the Day* by Elizabeth Bowen. *The Child in Time* by Ian McEwan. *Adaptation:* The 1999 film, directed by Neil Jordan, stars Ralph Fiennes and Julianne Moore.

Grimms' Tales for Young and Old
THE COMPLETE STORIES
Jacob Grimm (1785–1863) and Wilhelm Grimm (1786–1859)
Translated by Ralph Manheim

Once Upon a Time and Forever Frightening

Stories are humanity's greatest tools; with them, men and women manipulate those essential elements of experience—fears and hopes, faiths and terrors, worry, grace, wonderment—that otherwise are so intangible. Generations of storytellers have used these implements to widely differing purpose and effect, yet few have been such worthy craftsmen as the brothers Jacob and Wilhelm Grimm: Their tales hew hidden forests of psychology into cupboards of compact narrative, each one a

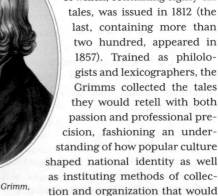
Jacob and Wilhelm Grimm, 1843

Pandora's box of fateful apprehensions. Except for the Bible, it's hard to imagine a book so rooted in our collective subconscious as the Grimms' *Children's and Household Tales*, the first edition of which, containing eighty-six tales, was issued in 1812 (the last, containing more than two hundred, appeared in 1857). Trained as philologists and lexicographers, the Grimms collected the tales they would retell with both passion and professional precision, fashioning an understanding of how popular culture shaped national identity as well as instituting methods of collection and organization that would

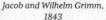

Little Red Riding Hood and the wolf from a 1865 edition of Grimms' Fairy Tales

"Rapunzel," "Rumpelstiltskin," "The Frog Prince," and "Hansel and Gretel." Be warned that in the Disneyfied versions through which most of us first became acquainted with these stories, the protagonists and their persecutors behave in much more civilized fashion than their Grimm originals. Any unexpurgated edition of the tales, like the one beautifully translated by Ralph Manheim, surprises readers with the full flavor of these menacing stories, ripe as they are with cruelty, violence, sex, cannibalism, and an endless inventory of inventive evil determined to threaten innocent good. There is a darkness at the core of these beloved tales that can still set our hearts beating faster. Reading them is eye-opening, gut-wrenching, and eerily, creepily compelling; the Grimms' cabinet of wonders is a storehouse of venomous and inescapable dreams.

What: Culture. Short Stories. *When:* 1812–57. *Editions:* Manheim's is the most accomplished contemporary English translation. Jack Zipes's *Complete Fairy Tales of the Brothers Grimm* is a good alternative that includes a few additional tales culled from manuscripts and letters. *Further Reading: The Uses of Enchantment* by Bruno Bettelheim. *The Hard Facts of the Grimms' Fairy Tales* by Maria Tatar. *The Brothers Grimm: From Enchanted Forests to the Modern World* by Jack Zipes. *Try: Fairy Tales* by Hans Christian Andersen (see page 19). *Adaptations:* Too numerous to count!

provide the foundation for the future field of folklore studies.

Among the tales they gathered, edited, polished, and published are, of course, many favorites, such as "Cinderella," "Snow White," "Sleeping Beauty," "Little Red Riding Hood,"

■ For John Grisham's *The Firm*, see page 809.

Life and Fate
Vasily Grossman (1905–1964)

What Comes After *War and Peace*

In 1962, Vasily Grossman wrote a letter to Nikita Khrushchev, pleading for the publication of his book, *Life and Fate*: "There is no sense, no truth, in the present situation, whereby I am physically free, but my book, to which I have given my life, remains in jail," he protested. "I ask you to release my book." Grossman was hoping that the thaw in Russia's repressive intellectual climate, ushered in by the new premier's slow divergence from Stalinist orthodoxy, might allow the author's panoramic portrait of Soviet experience, in all its human color and totalitarian bleakness, a public life. His persistent demands for its release would meet no approval before his death in 1964. He was told by the authorities that his novel could not be issued for two or three centuries; one imagines he took cold comfort in that

Vasily Grossman, 1945

clandestine acknowledgment that his fiction's truth was likely to be enduring.

Grossman was the country's most famous war correspondent. His dispatches from the front during World War II had made him a legend; he learned of the massacre of tens of thousands of Jews at Babi Yar in the Ukraine, and he was the first journalist to offer a firsthand report, in "The Hell of Treblinka," from a Nazi death camp. His brave acquaintance with atrocity fueled his bold equation of Stalinism with Nazism in *Life and Fate*, identifying in each the repellent logic of "the mechanics of probabilities and of human aggregates" that is Fascism's soulless protocol. But that's just one strand of the novel's magnificent fabric of struggle, sympathy, horror, and hope.

Life and Fate begins in the fall of 1942 with the launch of the German siege of Stalingrad and proceeds to fold the entire history of that two-year battle into a narrative puzzle that pieces together nearly every strata of Soviet society as its scenes move from battlefield to scientific institute to labor camp. As in *War and Peace* (see page 798), not just the life of the nation but the life of larger, border-crossing historical cataclysms are reflected through the experience of one family—the Shaposhnikovs—and its extended circle of friends, relations,

lovers, colleagues. Dozens of characters enact tales of love and conflict, fidelity and infidelity, courage and cowardice, brutality and tenderness. The sweep of the whole is Tolstoyan, but the spectrum of human feeling Grossman traverses is mapped in a series of small-scale encounters as searing and as sensitive as a set of Chekhov tales. And although the closely observed rendering of the violence at Stalingrad is riveting, it is Grossman's evocation of the aftermath of the Russian victory—when the ruins of the city are no longer symbols of resistance but merely ruins—that is truly devastating. The gallery of griefs he characterizes throughout the novel echoes with abiding sorrow: "A soul can live in torment for years and years, even decades, as it slowly, stone by stone, builds a mound over a grave; as it moves towards the apprehension of eternal loss and bows down before reality."

The great theme of the book, surprising in such an enormously imagined work, is the particularity of individual experience and the difficulty of possessing it in both a totalitarian state and in the individual-erasing shadows of history. But, for Grossman, those shadows never erase the responsibility of each of us to try to find a spark of goodness to guide us. "Human history is not the battle of good struggling to overcome evil," one of Grossman's characters writes. "It is a battle fought by a great evil struggling to crush a small kernel of human kindness." *Life and Fate* memorializes the heroes of that battle, on stages great and small, as tellingly as any fiction ever has.

What: Novel. *When:* Completed 1959; first published in Switzerland in 1980, and in Russia in 1988. *Edition:* English translation by Robert Chandler, 1985. *Also By:* *Everything Flows* (Russian publication, 1989; English translation by Chandler, 2009). *A Writer at War: A Soviet Journalist with the Red Army, 1941–1945* (2005 in Russian and in English). *The Road: Stories, Journalism, and Essays* (2010). *Further Reading: The Bones of Berdichev: The Life and Fate of Vassily Grossman* by John Garrard and Carol Garrard. *Try: War and Peace* by Leo Tolstoy (see page 798). *The War: 1941–1945* by Ilya Ehrenburg. *Stalingrad: The Fateful Siege: 1942–1943* by Antony Beevor.

Time and the Art of Living
Robert Grudin (born 1938)

Savoring the Past, the Present, and the Future

I t's a rare book that brings more meaning to one's daily life; this is one. An amalgam of philosophy, advice, speculation, aphorism, and anecdote, Robert Grudin's text is posed in numbered paragraphs, each one self-contained, each turning the idea of time—which, as Grudin shows, comprehends, contradicts, and can comfort us as well—to a particular angle for examination and reflection. Whether discussing alarm clock time or eternity, a game of Scrabble or letter writing, *Romeo and Juliet* or an idyllic autumn spent in the Tuscan hills, Grudin has an easy way of exposing kernels of insight. Like all good teachers (until 1998 he was a professor of English at the University of Oregon), he develops one theme into many, revealing how time informs our understanding of freedom, science, nature, literature, history, art, morality, politics, identity, growth, and aging—and how our attention to time can enhance such simple pleasures as sitting around talking, too.

Time and the Art of Living lends itself to slow, bit-by-bit, never-ending reading. Open it to any page for even a moment and its wisdom will sharpen your awareness: You'll see into the meanings of your past, present, and future in surprising, useful, and sometimes exhilarating ways. This playful, profound book on the medium and measure of our lives may prove to be one of the most practical *and* philosophically rewarding books you'll ever read. Make time for it.

What: Philosophy. Advice. *When:* 1982. *Reading Note:* An excellent bedside book or early morning companion. *Also By: Time and the Art of Living* is the first volume of a loose trilogy that continues with *The Grace of Great Things: Creativity and Innovation* (1990) and *On Dialogue: An Essay in Free Thought* (1996). *Try: How Proust Can Change Your Life* by Alain de Botton (see page 200).

"A book to savor, treasure, linger over: the rare and amazing spectacle of man thinking, of mind at work."
—*Edward Abbey on* Time and the Art of Living

The Little World of Don Camillo
Giovanni Guareschi (1908–1968)

Divinely Human Comedies Set in an Italian Village

I n a word, this book is lovable. Its comic short stories portray life in a remote Italian village in the aftermath of World War II, where local incidents and trivial disputes—a crack in the church wall, an errant firecracker, the looming shadow of the town's first "skyscraper" (two stories!)—are disguised as great calamities. This is largely because most of the episodes assume the form of fervent skirmishes between the title character, who is an unconventional priest, and his rival Peppone, the Communist mayor of their town in the Po Valley. Don Camillo and his foil are constantly arguing, fomenting the passions of their respective loyalists (who prove to be as fickle as the day is long). And yet the priest and the mayor always end up, begrudgingly and often secretly, in cahoots. Their theological and political differences are tempered by the respect that has grown from their reliance upon each other in navigating the squalls that threaten their little world, and their personal stores of pride and pigheadedness prove no match for the shared sympathy they bring to their collusion in keeping the peace. "To Men of Goodwill," the volume's concluding tale, in which the two trade news while painting the figures of a Nativity scene, is one of the loveliest Christmas tales you'll ever read.

An international bestseller in the 1950s, Guareschi's fiction—illustrated with his own charming drawings—captures human nature at its most petty, most generous, most stubborn, and most tender. His stories are wise in the ways of man and God (who, speaking directly from the crucifix in Don Camillo's church,

Statue of Don Camillo in Brescello, Italy

plays a major role, cajoling the often obstinate priest not only to step lively along the straight and narrow, but to bend to the commands of tolerance and forgiveness as well).

What: Short Stories. *When:* 1948; translated into English by U. V. Troubridge, 1950. *Also By:* Guareschi wrote a total of 347 Don Camillo stories. Other collections in English include *Don Camillo and His Flock* (1952), *Don Camillo's Dilemma* (1954), and *Don Camillo Takes the Devil by the Tail* (1957). *Try: Tortilla Flat* by John Steinbeck. *Monsignor Quixote* by Graham Greene. *Adaptations:* Five films starring the comedian Fernandel as Don Camillo appeared in the 1950s and 1960s. *The World of Don Camillo*, directed by and starring Terence Hill, was released in the early 1980s.

H, I, J, K

H

Hiroshima Diary

THE JOURNAL OF A JAPANESE PHYSICIAN AUGUST 6–SEPTEMBER 30, 1945

Michihiko Hachiya, MD (1903–1980)

An Eyewitness Account of the Dawn of Nuclear War

On August 6, 1955, ten years to the day after the atomic bomb was dropped on Hiroshima, Michihiko Hachiya's *Hiroshima Diary* was published in America. Unparalleled as an eyewitness account of the explosion and its aftermath, Hachiya's *Diary* is something more than that, too, for it was composed by a doctor as well as a victim. Its author's medical training and position as director of the Hiroshima Communications Hospital (within a mile of the epicenter of the explosion) imbue his chronicle with a broad and deep perspective on the distress of the city and its inhabitants.

From the opening pages, Dr. Hachiya offers an intimate portrayal of the suffering of Hiroshima and its citizens; he describes the incomprehensible shock and preternatural effects of the blast, and goes on to chronicle the immediate terror and overwhelming logistical nightmare of the ensuing weeks. Initially confined to a bed by his own wounds, he nevertheless attends to the injuries and pain of his fellow patients and doctors, recording with unrelenting clarity the fear and fatigue, the bravery and grief, the desperate need and even the petty grievances that gather in every corner of the shattered, overcrowded hospital. He gives individual faces and voices to the indiscriminate misery the bomb delivered.

Hiroshima in the aftermath of the US atomic bomb, 1945

At first unaware of the nature of the weapon that could have caused such vast destruction, Dr. Hachiya and his colleagues are puzzled by the symptoms that present themselves in the days after the detonation. There is poignant drama in his growing understanding of the extent of the tragedy and in the juxtaposition of the excitement of intellectual discovery with the horror engendered by the realization of the inexorable effects of radiation sickness.

A half century later, Dr. Hachiya's chronicle retains its historical interest and documentary power: No other work rivals its searing representation of the actual experience of the consequences of nuclear warfare. It retains as well the inspiring force of its indelible depiction of resourcefulness and fortitude in the face of devastation and uncertainty.

What: History. War. Memoir. *When:* 1945; first American publication, 1955. *Further Reading: Hiroshima* by John Hersey. *Letters from the End of the World: A Firsthand Account of the Bombing of Hiroshima* by Toyofumi Ogura. *Try: Voices from Chernobyl* by Svetlana Alexievich (see page 15).

I Was a Stranger
Sir John Winthrop Hackett (1910–1997)

A World War II Catastrophe— and a Great Escape

One of the most dramatic encounters of World War II, the Battle of Arnhem took place over the course of nine days in September 1944 as part of Operation Market Garden. This bold plan involved the dropping of some thirty thousand Allied paratroopers behind enemy lines in hopes of capturing the eight bridges that crossed the rivers and canals on the Dutch-German border. The final bridge was on the Rhine at Arnhem, and for the Allies it proved "a bridge too far"; suffering nearly twice as many casualties as they'd endured during the D-Day landings, they failed to secure their objective.

GENERAL SIR JOHN HACKETT

I WAS A STRANGER

His famous wartime memoir

www.AviationAutographs.com

I Was a Stranger plunges readers into the thick of Arnhem's unfolding catastrophe. Brigadier John Hackett is in command of the Fourth Parachute Brigade, which will be practically wiped out in the course of the fighting. He suffers nearly fatal wounds and then finds himself in a hospital being abandoned to the Germans by the retreating English and American forces. After his life is saved by what, under the circumstances, is miraculously expert surgery, Hackett is spirited out of the sick bay by the Dutch resistance movement, which is valiantly helping scores of trapped Allied soldiers elude the Nazis. The months that Hackett spends in hiding, and his own eventual getaway (on a ramshackle old bicycle, no less), give his memoir a page-turning suspense, and his laconic fortitude ("There seemed to be a good deal of blood about, apparently coming from somewhere above my left knee") imbues his storytelling with an irresistible, stiff-upper-lip distinction. This last quality, together with his deep appreciation of others' bravery, makes his memoir one of the most stylish examples of the literature of escape.

What: War. Memoir. *When:* 1977. *Also By: The Profession of Arms* (1963). *The Third World War: August 1985* (1979; a bestselling—and, it turned out, utterly inaccurate—Cold War prognostication). *The Third World War: The Untold Story* (1982). *Further Reading: The Battle of Arnhem* by Christopher Hibbert. *A Bridge Too Far* by Cornelius Ryan. *Try: The Walls Came Tumbling Down* by Henriette Roosenburg (see page 673). *Footnote:* After retiring from the military, Hackett became a visiting classics professor at King's College, London. He told *Contemporary Authors,* "I have been described as an academic who in a prolonged fit of absence of mind became a four-star general."

The All of It
Jeannette Haien (1921–2008)

Fathoming Love's Deep Currents in Rural Ireland

A priest stands fishing in a salmon stream, pondering the dark secret that the death of a parishioner has revealed, and the astonishing tale the woman who survives the deceased has told him. In this stunning, rapid, beautiful novel set in a village in the west of Ireland, mortality and morality, sin and sympathy, compromise and commitment are joined in an emotional embrace that is magical, consoling, memorable. It's hard to say anything more without spoiling the delicate surprise of this spare novel. Poet Mark Strand put it precisely right: "The only book I know in which innocence follows experience. A truly amazing thing."

What: Novel. *When:* 1986. *Also By: Matters of Chance* (1998). *Try: Collected Stories* by Frank O'Connor (see page 598). *Amy and Isabelle* by Elizabeth Strout. *Round Rock* by Michelle Huneven.

The Best and the Brightest
David Halberstam (1934–2007)

In the Corridors of Power That Led to Vietnam

When he returned home from his Pulitzer Prize–winning stint as a wartime correspondent in Vietnam for the *New York Times*, David Halberstam turned his attention to the question of how America had gotten so hopelessly entangled in Southeast Asia. *The Best and the Brightest*, an absorbing chronicle of our policy makers' confused—but seemingly always confident—progress into the military quagmire, reveals what he discovered.

The book opens with a fascinating report on the construction of John F. Kennedy's foreign policy team, an Ivy-pedigreed, dauntingly credentialed group that included McGeorge Bundy, Walt Rostow, and Robert McNamara. (Vice President Lyndon Johnson expressed his awe at their assembled brilliance to his mentor, Speaker of the House Sam Rayburn, who replied with sage reserve, "They may be every bit as intelligent as you say, but I'd feel a whole lot better about them if just one of them had

David Halberstam, 1978

run for sheriff once.") As Halberstam's narrative unfolds, it offers valuable lessons in the brokerage of power; in American party politics and foreign affairs from World War II through the 1960s; in the features, grand and petty, of the often conveniently faceless American establishment; in the arrogance accompanying the dizzying, debilitating elevation of expertise.

Charting the way the government pushed deeper and deeper into a war it refused to understand (often despite its own intelligence), the author focuses on the "best and the brightest" who came to Washington in the heady days of the early 1960s and ended up orchestrating a foreign policy disaster that would turn the body politic on its head. As Halberstam himself puts it, his "is not a book about Vietnam, but a book about America, and in particular about power and success in America, what the country was, who the leadership was, how they got ahead, what their perceptions were about themselves, about the country and about their mission." As such, it is ever timely.

What: History. Politics. *When:* 1972. *Also By: The Powers That Be* (1979). *The Reckoning* (1986). *The Children* (1998). *War in a Time of Peace: Bush, Clinton, and the Generals* (2001). *The Coldest Winter: America and the Korean War* (2007). *Try: A Bright Shining Lie: John Paul Vann and America in Vietnam* by Neil Sheehan.

In Retrospect: The Tragedy and Lessons of Vietnam by Robert S. McNamara. *Footnote:* In addition to his political journalism, Halberstam wrote splendid books on sports, including basketball (*The Breaks of the Game,* 1981), rowing (*The Amateurs,* 1985), baseball (*Summer of '49,* 1989), and football (*The Education of a Coach,* 2005).

String Too Short to Be Saved
Donald Hall (born 1928)

Harvesting Memories from a New England Farm

I n this affectionate and moving volume, poet Donald Hall recalls—in stories and vignettes that are deftly rendered and deeply felt—the summers he spent as a boy on his grandparents' New England farm. In chapters filled with work and weather, horses and hired hands, Hall shares his youthful engagement with the chores and adventures the days delivered: haying, blueberry picking, rounding up heifers escaped from their pasture. Characters who impressed him indelibly in his boyhood—such as the eccentric loner Washington Woodward, whose false but fierce economy left a legacy of thousands of scavenged and straightened nails—are recalled with both candor and tenderness, the small dramas of their lives drawn with rueful understanding.

As Hall grows up, his attentions to farm life are shadowed by his grandparents' mortality, and by the slow but sure vanishing of the customs and the culture that sustained them. And yet his own inheritance is never diminished by nostalgia, but rather enriched by the voices the act of recollection summons. He writes of the "long anthology" of stories his grandfather told him during the days they worked the farm together: "He was giving his life to me, handing me a baton in a race, and I took his anecdotes as a loving entertainment, when all of them, even the silliest, were matters of life and death." Animating his book with amusing characters and incidents, Hall slowly brings into a single focus the overlapping remembrances of childhood and age to which we all, sooner or later, bear witness. By doing so, he allows us to honor the figures from our own past who hover like angels over our shoulders, and who we, running as fast as we can through our days, months, and years, seldom fix in our gaze. What a beautiful book this is.

What: Memoir. *When:* 1961. *Edition:* For the 1979 edition, Hall contributed an epilogue describing his return to the farm to live in 1975. *Award:* Hall was named the fourteenth US Poet Laureate in 2006. *Also By:* Poetry: *White Apples and the Taste of Stone: Selected Poems 1946–2006* (2006). Prose: *Fathers Playing Catch with Sons* (1985); *Seasons at Eagle Pond* (1987); *Life Work* (1993). *Try: Cider with Rosie* by Laurie Lee (see page 470). *First Person Rural* by Noel Perrin.

A Drinking Life
A MEMOIR
Pete Hamill (born 1935)

Back Where He Came From

T his book builds from the author's first memory—a four-year-old's view of an apartment in Brooklyn in the winter of 1939—to a scene a little more than three decades later: It is New Year's Eve in 1972, and Pete Hamill, now a famous newspaperman, is celebrating at a crowded Manhattan bar. But his mind is wandering, and in his heart he's wondering about the cost of the drinking life he's led. Staring into his vodka and tonic, he tells himself, "*I'm never going to do this again.*"

"I finished my drink," he writes. "It was the last one I ever had."

In the 250-odd pages between those two moments, Hamill details, with energy, affection, and honesty, his upbringing as the child of Irish immigrants, his boyhood, youth, and early career, his loves and struggles and regrets—all of it colored by the culture of drinking that both nurtured and hobbled his growth toward manhood. Funny and candid, he captures working-class urban life in the 1940s and 1950s with a reporter's keen attention and a novelist's insight into the faiths and failures of human nature (that latter quality would develop into the fine works of fiction he would write subsequent to putting period to *A Drinking Life*).

Although his memoir takes its shape from Hamill's decision to stop drinking, calling it the story of his battle with alcohol doesn't really do it justice. There have been a lot of books that wallow in the havoc drinking wreaks, but you'll never read another so alert to how the communion that takes place in bars consoles drinkers for the destinies they've been dealt, and may lack the gifts or gumption to alter. "Maybe everybody was right, from my father to Brother Jan," Hamill writes of the advice he received about finding steady work in the Navy Yard instead of

finishing high school and pursuing his dream of becoming a cartoonist:

It was arrogant, a sin of pride, to conceive of a life beyond the certainties, rhythms, and traditions of the Neighborhood. . . . Who did I think I was? Who the fuck did I think I was? Forget these kid's dreams, I told myself, give 'em up. Do what everybody else does: drop out of high school, go to work, join the army or navy, get married, settle down, have children. . . . I'd drink on the way home from work and spend most weekends with my friends in the saloons. I'd get old. I'd die and my friends would see me off in Mike Smith's funeral parlor across the street from Holy Name. That was the end of every story in the Neighborhood. Come on: let's have a fucking drink.

Pete Hamill at the Daily News

This, then, is not a book about drinking, but about growing up—about braving the clash between the camaraderie and comfort of the neighborhood and the exhilarating, terrifying loneliness of a wider world. That Hamill was strong enough to do so, without forgetting where he came from, makes this ultimately both a happy and a heartfelt testament.

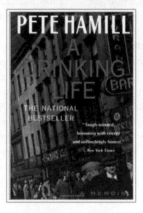

What: Memoir. *When:* 1994. *Also By: Nonfiction: Piecework* (1996); *Diego Rivera* (1999). Fiction: *Snow in August* (1998); *Forever* (2003); *North River* (2007). *Try: Stop-Time* by Frank Conroy. *Those Drinking Days* by Donald Newlove. *The Tender Bar* by J. R. Moehringer.

The Maltese Falcon
Dashiell Hammett (1894–1961)

Introducing Sam Spade

Dashiell Hammett dropped out of school at the age of fourteen and worked an assortment of odd jobs before gaining employment

as an operative for the Pinkerton detective agency from 1915 to 1921. Taking his Pinkerton experience as inspiration, he started writing fiction in the early 1920s. Although his productive years as an author were few—his literary career, for all intents and purposes, ended with the publication of *The Thin Man* in 1934—his stories and novels would be lastingly influential. In fact, Hammett is largely credited with the invention of the modern hard-boiled detective novel, wherein a crime is a crime, rather than a peripheral plot device, and a private detective is a tough-talking guy who solves it for cash. As Raymond Chandler said, "Hammett gave murder back to the kind of people who do it for a reason, not just to provide a corpse; and with means at hand, not with handwrought dueling pistols, curare, and tropical fish."

The Maltese Falcon is Hammett's best work, not least because its protagonist is the now-archetypal private eye, Sam Spade. Hired by a

femme fatale under false pretenses—Brigid O'Shaughnessy initially claims to be a Miss Wonderly, searching for her missing sister—Spade eventually learns that what she's really after is a precious statuette of a falcon, said to be gold and jewel encrusted under its nondescript surface. By the time he discovers this, however, his partner, Archer, and the man Archer was tailing at Miss Wonderly's behest are both dead, and Spade is suspected of killing them. As he and Brigid race other dangerous stalkers in pursuit of the black bird, Spade gets further embroiled with the beautiful dame, until he finds himself in a mess from which only a difficult decision will save him. Spade may look like "a blond satan" and operate according to his own moral code, but the book's denouement makes clear where he draws his lines. Private eyes in books and on film have been following his lead ever since, holding readers and audiences rapt.

What: Mystery & Suspense. *When:* 1930 (originally serialized in *Black Mask* the previous year). *Also By:* *Red Harvest* (1929). *The Dain Curse* (1929). *The Glass Key* (1931). Hammett also wrote short stories, the best of which feature the detective known as the Continental Op. *Further Reading: Dashiell Hammett: A Life* by Diane Johnson. *Try: The Big Sleep* by Raymond Chandler (see page 147). *The Drowning Pool* by Ross Macdonald. *The Deep Blue Good-By* by John D. MacDonald. *Adaptation:* John Huston's 1941 film, starring Humphrey Bogart as Sam Spade and featuring Mary Astor, Sydney Greenstreet, and Peter Lorre, is one of Hollywood's shining achievements.

A Romantic Education
Patricia Hampl (born 1946)

From St. Paul to Prague, on Wings of Meditative Prose

This is the story—thoughtful, generous, lyrical—of a young woman's Minnesota childhood; of her coming-of-age in the 1960s; of a journey to the Prague of her family's past. That simple description gives no hint of the passionate gift this book gives its reader: a telling

glimpse at how our hearts and minds make homes for themselves in this homesick world.

The book begins when the author is five, seated before the only bookcase in her grandmother's St. Paul home, which, tellingly ("ours wasn't a reading family"), isn't in the house itself, but in the vestibule hallway. She is poring over an album of sepia photographs of the "Golden" Prague of the nineteenth century, and her grandmother is drawn to sit down with her, inspired to reverie by the images of the city of her own youth.

"So beautiful," she was crying melodramatically over the album. "So beautiful." I had never seen an adult cry before. I was relieved, in some odd way, that there was crying in adulthood, that crying would not be taken away.

The child observes the deep hollows eyeglasses have made on the sides of her grandmother's nose, and the adult author ponders them for a passage into the mysteries of memory that is so profound that one could linger for a day in the first few pages of this book. Soon enough, however, we find ourselves among the rooms and hamburgers and relatives of Hampl's childhood, each recollection provoking an affectionate and pensive meditation on the family life that nurtured her.

"I come from people who have always been polite enough to feel that nothing has ever happened to them," Hampl writes, but she learns—and teaches us—to grasp the unsung substance of ordinary and modest lives, and to abide in the buried imagination that sustains them. She is not in quest of her inheritance, really, but in search of something beyond her known world to give that inheritance a deeper resonance. No surprise, then, that her education leads her to an exploration of her Czech heritage as she journeys to Prague in the 1970s, no longer golden but "pewter-gray" beneath the dull sky of Soviet domination. Her evocation of life under socialism in the days before the Velvet Revolution is as vivid as her probing of her formative years in Minnesota, and in curious, compelling counterpoint to it: "In the act of remembering, the personal environment expands, resonates beyond itself, beyond its 'subject,' into the endless and tragic recollection that is history."

By turns poetic, reflective, narrative, and journalistic, Hampl's pursuit of private destiny finds in Prague a liberating dimension that most memoirs lack. The voice that conveys it, while always talking intimately to us, echoes with experience larger and deeper than its own, and thereby achieves a beauty and eloquence as rare as the understanding it communicates. This is a book to dwell in.

What: Memoir. Travel. **When:** 1981. **Edition:** For the 1999 reissue, on the tenth anniversary of the Velvet Revolution, Hampl composed a substantial afterword based on her annual return trips to Prague. **Also By:** *Virgin Time: In Search of the Contemplative Life* (1992). *Blue Arabesque: A Search for the Sublime* (2006). *The Florist's Daughter: A Memoir* (2007). *The Art of the Wasted Day* (2018). **Further Reading: Prague in Black and Gold** by Peter Demetz. **Try:** *Italian Days* by Barbara Grizzuti Harrison. *The Three Golden Keys* by Peter Sís (see page 726).

Hunger
Knut Hamsun (1859–1952)

Down and Out and Deep Inside

Oslo, the Norwegian capital, is situated on the edge of a fjord and is one of the most beautiful cities in Europe. But you wouldn't know that from *Hunger*, Knut Hamsun's intense, groundbreaking, partly autobiographical short novel about a struggling young writer trying to maintain his dignity in an uncaring world. The novel's unnamed narrator introduces Oslo— or Kristiania, as it was called before Norway won its independence from Sweden—as "that strange city no one escapes from until it has left its mark on him." For him, it's a place of neither natural beauty nor cultural sophistication: It's a capital of alienation, where an artist can starve while thousands of city dwellers shuffle past.

Hamsun's narrator has nowhere to live and can barely afford to eat, and the hunger that gnaws at his body also starts to have its way with his mind. Swinging between moments of profound optimism and utter misery, pride and despair, he spools out an unsparingly intimate monologue, tipped with half-crazed visions and hallucinations. There's not much action: He struggles to write; he sits on park benches; he

broach political and social questions, Hamsun directs his gaze inward—to the mind of one man in intolerable conditions and to the effects of urban life on the human soul.

Hunger, published in 1890, rocketed the unknown Hamsun to national and international fame; he went on to win the Nobel Prize, although his sympathy for the Third Reich in his last years tarnished his reputation and has made him the object of intense debate in contemporary Norway. This first novel, though, with its bold interiority, fed the streams of consciousness that would irrigate the work of James Joyce, Virginia Woolf, and other modern masters, and Hamsun's influence has been substantial ("Hamsun taught me to write," Ernest Hemingway once said). By focusing almost entirely on the inner world of his troubled narrator, Hamsun produced a work that remains strikingly fresh more than a hundred years since its publication.

lucks into a bit of food or money one day, wants for both the next; and so it goes. Tiny frustrations are elevated into catastrophes, whereas the real disasters of hunger and poverty are merely ordinary life. Unlike his compatriot Henrik Ibsen, whose dramas look outward to

What: Novel. *When:* 1890. *Award:* Hamsun was awarded the Nobel Prize in Literature in 1920. *Also By: Mysteries* (1892). *Pan* (1894). *Growth of the Soil* (1917). *Further Reading: Enigma: The Life of Knut Hamsun* by Robert Ferguson. *Try: Tropic of Cancer* by Henry Miller. *My Struggle* by Karl Ove Knausgaard.

A Sorrow Beyond Dreams
Peter Handke (born 1942)

Elegy on a Mother's Suicide

Peter Handke is an acclaimed and controversial Austrian author best known as an avant-garde playwright and novelist; he also cowrote the screenplay for Wim Wenders's magnificent film *Wings of Desire*. But one of his best works is the small and anguished elegy he wrote soon after his mother's suicide in the 1970s, *A Sorrow Beyond Dreams*. The writing itself—constricted in its focus, matter-of-fact in its depiction of the author's emotional uncertainty and his inability to elevate the unfulfilling facts of his mother's existence—seems grief stricken, as if the words must be pulled by force of will and duty through the wearying weight of sorrow.

As Handke unfolds his mother's personal history in short bursts of narrative and epigrammatic commentaries, we learn of the penury of war and the confines of village life, of fleeting youthful gaiety and enduring everyday humiliations, of a constant effort to keep up appearances in a burgeoning era of consumerism, of debilitating illness and eventual despair—in other words, the yearnings and desperations of an ordinary life unredeemed by joy. Reaching for the familiar companionship of words, the writer is at a loss: "intensely as I sometimes feel the need to write about my mother, this need is so vague that if I didn't work at it I would, in my present state of mind, just sit at my typewriter pounding out the same letters over and over again." His doleful-ness and restraint result in a remarkable "act of piety," as critic Michael Wood has perfectly described it, "an expression of respect: this woman's bleak life is not to be made into 'litera-ture.'" What it is made into, for all of Handke's reticence, is a probing, poignant expression of sympathy, desolation, and the limits of both words and love.

What: Memoir. *When:* 1972; first English edition, translated by Ralph Manheim, 1974. *Edition:* The New York Review Books Classics edition has an introduction by Jeffrey Eugenides. *Also By:* Handke has published many books in a variety of genres; his prose works include *The Goalie's Anxiety at the Penalty Kick* (1970), *Short Letter, Long Farewell* (1972), *The Weight of the World* (1977), and *Slow Homecoming* (1983). *Try: A Very Easy Death* by Simone de Beauvoir. *The Year of Magical Thinking* by Joan Didion (see page 223).

84, Charing Cross Road
Helene Hanff (1916–1997)

Single White Bibliophile Seeks Out-of-Print Companions

No sense beating about the bush: No volume conveys the enduring and serendipitous charm of books as happily as this one. It begins in October 1949, with an inquiry that Helene Hanff, a freelance writer in New York, posts to Marks & Co., a bookshop at 84, Charing Cross Road, London. The reply, noting that the vol-umes Hanff has requested have been shipped under separate cover, is politely British, addressed "Dear Madam" and signed with the initials FPD. "I hope 'madam' doesn't mean over there what is does over here," Hanff writes when she pays her bill, and one of the funniest and most moving correspondences in print is launched.

It takes a few months for Frank P. Doel to disclose his name, more than two years for him to venture "Dear Helene," and five more to begin matching her sarcasm. But long before that, friendship has blossomed. Soon real-izing that the British are still on war rations, Hanff begins sending care packages for Doel's coworkers and family. As a thank-you, Doel's wife sends a tablecloth hand-embroidered by their elderly neighbor. Before she knows it, Hanff is corresponding with all of them—the neighbor included.

Although Hanff's love for books informs the entire twenty-year correspondence, it's her outrageous humor, especially when contrasted with Doel's proper manner, that makes the

exchange priceless. At the mercy of his ability to fill her requests, Hanff is never funnier than when she's taunting Doel for taking too long or for sending something substandard. At such times, even her typing gets excited:

WHAT KIND OF PEPYS' DIARY DO YOU CALL THIS? this is not pepys' diary, this is some busybody editor's miserable collection of EXCERPTS from pepys' diary may he rot.

i could just spit.

where is jan. 12, 1668, where his wife chased him out of bed and round the bedroom with a red-hot poker?

As one book leads to another, we follow an autodidact's idiosyncratic path through English literature. Along the way, our enjoyment is deepened by the rich human story these letters tell.

What: Diaries & Letters. Books. *When:* 1970. *Also By: Underfoot in Show Business* (1961). *The Duchess of*

Bloomsbury Street (1973). *Q's Legacy* (1985). *Try: The Lyttelton Hart-Davis Letters* by George Lyttelton and Rupert Hart-Davis (see page 503). *Books: A Memoir* by Larry McMurtry. *Adaptations:* A stage adaptation was performed off Broadway and in London's West End. The 1987 feature film stars Anne Bancroft and Anthony Hopkins.

Sleepless Nights
Elizabeth Hardwick (1916–2007)

The Makeup of Memory

Elizabeth Hardwick, 1978

Early in the twentieth century, Marcel Proust imagined a map of memory that, literally and figuratively, has dwarfed all others ever since. The French novelist's researches into lost time promised a revelation of a past recalled entire, each of its intimate sensations resonating in an intricate web of remembrance. Several decades later, the esteemed American woman of letters Elizabeth Hardwick wrote a book that feels slim enough to fit into the folds of one of Proust's elaborate sentences, yet—in the brilliance of its reminiscences, inventions, and impressions—captures the reality of recollection in a way less fabulous but in some ways more telling than Proust's.

Calling itself a novel, yet narrated by a woman named Elizabeth who shares many of the author's biographical details, *Sleepless Nights* is a retrospective fashioning of fragments, anecdotes, observations, regrets, and affections that has the uncertain shape but powerful presence of memory as it actually haunts us: not the past recaptured, but the past as a continuous, inconstant companion. Memories of girlhood in Lexington, Kentucky—of high school and horse culture, of dancing at Joyland Park and slipping into the tents of evangelical prayer meetings—segue into scenes set on the stage of Manhattan sophistication, as a young woman of heart and mind makes her way into the wider world where she waits for Billie Holiday in the bar of the Hotel Braddock in Harlem. Observation meets understanding at every turn, and the shifting perspectives of Hardwick's intelligence are thrilling; a

paragraph that begins with the "woeful, watery macaroni" of the Automat can end with a perfect evocation of the allure of the metropolis for restless youths: "Every great city is a Lourdes where you hope to throw off your crutches but meanwhile most stumble along on them, hobbling under the protection of the shrine."

Reportorial vignettes, letters home, journal entries, character portraits, ruminations, and aphorisms follow upon one another across concentrated paragraphs that give Hardwick's two hundred pages the feel of a much longer book. As Geoffrey O'Brien noted in his introduction to a recent reissue of the book, "embedded in *Sleepless Nights* are a hundred potential novels, swarming milieus compacted into gists." Embedded here as well is the distillation of one woman's sensibility, a consummately composed scrapbook of love, loss, and recognition that captures memory in its truest form: the pillow book of our sleepless nights.

What: Novel. Memoir. *When:* 1979. *Edition:* The New York Review Books Classics edition features Geoffrey O'Brien's introduction. *Reading Note:* Hardwick's prose here is lapidary, the narrative's progress episodic and at first disorienting. But read it as you would listen to a friend's confidences—don't interrupt!—and soon the book's intimacy will exert its spell. *Also By:* Fiction: *The Ghostly Lover* (1945); *The Simple Truth* (1955). Essays and Criticism: *A View of My Own* (1962); *Seduction and Betrayal: Women and Literature* (1974); *Bartleby in Manhattan and Other Essays* (1983). *Try: The Dead of the House* by Hannah Green (page 333). *Where I Was From* by Joan Didion.

Jude the Obscure
Thomas Hardy (1840–1928)

Hearts Insurgent

Thomas Hardy was the son of a stonemason. Like Jude Fawley, the protagonist of this, his last novel, Hardy lacked the means to pursue the university education he desired. When his formal schooling came to an end at age sixteen, he was apprenticed to a church architect, but continued study of the Greek and Latin classics on his own time, began writing poetry and fiction, and, with the publication of *Far from the Madding Crowd* in 1874, achieved fame as a novelist.

His major novels are set in a region Hardy calls Wessex, an amalgam of the characteristics of modern English districts including Dorset, Wilshire, and Devon. This gives the novels a unity of place and provides an imaginative landscape that nourishes the thematic concerns connecting them: the pervasive indignities of social inequity and class division, the dehumanizing effects of industrialization, the power of the repressive sexual mores and double standards that institutionalize the subjugation of women, the unsettling truth that intellect as much as passion is thwarted by want of privilege. The Wessex scenery grounds the novels in a reality that offers an oddly consoling counterweight to the flights of violence and melodrama that drive their plots and give Hardy's fiction its distinctive color. This color, as Virginia Woolf astutely observed, belongs to a "wild spirit of poetry which saw with intense irony and grimness that no reading of life can possibly outdo the strangeness of life itself, no symbol of caprice and unreason be too extreme to represent the astonishing circumstances of our existence."

Jude the Obscure is the story of an orphaned, intellectually ambitious young man who works as a stonemason at Christminster (a Wessex version of Oxford) rather than attending its classes, as he yearns to do. He is tricked into marrying a girl who claims to be carrying his child and who then deserts him. The heart of the book is Jude's relationship with an independent-minded cousin, Sue Bridehead, with whom he makes a home and has children

Paying respects at Hardy's grave in Poets' Corner, Westminster Abbey

despite the fact that both are married to other people. Tragic consequences ensue, as if their love, like Jude's hunger for learning, is fated to be met with punishment, no matter the nobility of spirit that impels it. Sue and Jude are rebels without a cause, revolutionaries without a program, renegades with no weapons but their underprivileged, socially impoverished hearts. Not for nothing was Hardy's working title for their tale *Hearts Insurgent*.

Like *Tess of the d'Urbervilles* before it, *Jude the Obscure* was charged by contemporary critics with immorality and derided for its views on marriage and religion (in fact, wags were quick to dub it "Jude the Obscene"). So heated was the controversy it provoked that Hardy forsook fiction completely and devoted himself to poetry for the remaining three decades of his life, composing works that would secure him a reputation as one of the masters of early modern English verse.

What: Novel. *When:* 1894–95. *Editions:* The novel was first published serially; volume publication, with significant emendations, followed; a third and definitive edition appeared in 1912. *Also By: Far from the Madding Crowd* (1874). *The Return of the Native* (1878). *The Mayor of Casterbridge* (1886). *Tess of the d'Urbervilles* (1891). *Collected Poems* (1919). *Further Reading: Thomas Hardy: The Guarded Life* by Ralph Pite. *Thomas Hardy: The Time-Torn Man* by Claire Tomalin. *Try: Adam Bede* by George Eliot. *Precious Bane* by Mary Webb. *Wolf Solent* by John Cowper Powys. *Adaptations:* The BBC adapted the novel for a 1971 television miniseries. The 1996 film version features Christopher Eccleston and Kate Winslet. *Footnote:* Although Hardy's ashes are interred in Westminster Abbey's Poet's Corner, his heart is buried separately, in his native Dorset.

The Silence of the Lambs
Thomas Harris (born 1940)

A Chilling Taste of Terror

"We've developed a questionnaire," FBI Section Chief and Special Agent Jack Crawford tells trainee Clarice Starling. "It applies to all the known serial murders in modern times. The blue is for the killer to answer if he will, and the pink is a series of questions an examiner asks the killer, getting his reactions as well as his answers. It's a lot of paperwork." Armed with this questionnaire and the protection of a file folder, Agent Starling comes face-to-face with the cannibalistic murderer Dr. Hannibal Lecter, who is serving nine consecutive life sentences in a mental institution. So the forces of social order meet the urges of the sociopath; one side of that equation, as the reader soon recognizes, is seriously underprepared.

Hannibal Lecter is one of the most chillingly drawn villains in the annals of modern fiction. In addition to being a serial killer with a developed taste for his victims—"A census taker tried to quantify me once," he tells Starling as she reveals her paperwork. "I ate his liver with some fava beans and a big Amarone"—he is also a preternaturally gifted psychologist with a diabolically empathic alertness to what makes people, be they good or evil, tick. He is perverse, polite, charming, brilliant, and brutal, and the FBI would like to lure him into helping with an ongoing investigation of a string of savage killings of young women that have left them baffled. Instead, he ensnares Agent Starling into his own web, intuiting her secrets and fashioning his escape even as he provides a trail of enigmatic but illuminating clues that lead her to a solution of the case. Twisted minds, tortured bodies, and a straight line of perfectly pitched suspense add real horror to Thomas Harris's novel, yet it is the riveting allure of Hannibal Lecter, the singular character at its core, that puts it in a class of its own as a modern thriller.

What: Novel. *When:* 1988. *Also By: Red Dragon* (1981). *Hannibal* (1999). *Try: The Killer Inside Me* by Jim Thompson. *Adaptation:* The 1991 motion picture, directed by Jonathan Demme and starring Anthony Hopkins and Jodie Foster, swept all the major Academy Awards.

Forests

THE SHADOW OF CIVILIZATION

Robert Pogue Harrison (born 1954)

A Cultural Expedition into the Woods

In sources ranging from the *Epic of Gilgamesh* (see page 255) to Samuel Beckett's *Endgame*, through invented landscapes stretching from the giant-inhabited prehistoric precincts described in Giambattista Vico's eighteenth-century *New Science* to the menacing thickets of the Brothers Grimm and the inspirational woods of *Walden*, Robert Pogue Harrison explores the role that forests have played in the cultural life of the West. "A sylvan fringe of darkness" defining the limits of civilization but also encompassing the extravagance of our imagination, forests, Harrison argues, have cast a formative shadow on the construction of our customs and our conception of ourselves. Into the woods we've gone, from earliest antiquity, to seek enchantment, terror, or our gods, to lose and find our way; out of the woods we've come to make homes, villages, cities, and institutions.

Knotty with ideas but gracefully composed, *Forests* is strewn with wonders, for even at its most arcane, Harrison's learning is always revealing unexpected yet recognizable truths (you'll never consider a wall, for instance, in quite the same way again). Through his own dense grove of allusion, reference, and intuition, Harrison illuminates this natural influence that has informed our inner lives, shaping our psyches at the same time as it has helped determine our understanding of religion, law, family, and more. Tying modern ecological concerns to the most ancient faiths and fears, he has composed a work of scholarship that is at root about what it means to be human.

What: Culture. Literary Criticism. *When:* 1992. *Also By: The Dominion of the Dead* (2003). *Gardens: An Essay on the Human Condition* (2008). *Juvenescence: A Cultural History of Our Age* (2014). *Try: Landscape and Memory* by Simon Schama (see page 700).

Act One

AN AUTOBIOGRAPHY

Moss Hart (1904–1961)

There's No Business Like Show Business, and No Book About It Like This One

Despite the exceptional scope of his accomplishments as playwright (including *You Can't Take It with You*, with George S. Kaufman, which won the Pulitzer Prize for Drama in 1937), screenwriter (including *Gentleman's Agreement*, an Oscar winner for Best Picture in 1947), and theater director (including the legendary original production of *My Fair Lady* in 1956), Moss Hart was only fifty-seven years old when he died in 1961. And although this autobiography, published two years before his death, covers less than half of his short and thrilling life, it is as rich and satisfying as any reader could wish.

Act One begins with the future impresario's first glimpse of Broadway, at age twelve, as he is running an errand for the owner of the Bronx music store that employed him. It ends fourteen years later with his first triumph on the Great White Way: the 1930 opening of *Once in a Lifetime*, his initial collaboration with Kaufman. The four-hundred-odd intervening pages provide ample evidence of Hart's unerring knack for holding an audience spellbound. Its chapters are populated with vivid characters and poignant scenes. You won't forget Aunt Kate, who brightened the bleak poverty of his childhood by sharing her extravagant passion for the theater. Your heart will ache when you read the Christmas Eve episode in which Hart's impoverished father, with only a few coins in his pocket, futilely tries to buy his son a holiday present along a row of Bronx pushcarts. And, as the author pursues his theatrical

Moss Hart in Times Square, 1959

apprenticeship, you'll be carried away by his infatuation with every aspect of backstage life. From the exuberant abandon of creativity to the intricate exigency of mounting a production, from the thrill of performance to the intoxication of acclaim, the reader experiences the joyful allure of the theater in the context of one young man's coming-of-age.

What: Autobiography. *When:* 1959. *Also By:* Three of Hart's collaborations with Kaufman, *Once in a Lifetime, You Can't Take It with You,* and *The Man Who Came to Dinner,* are published in the Library of America volume *Kaufman & Co.: Broadway Comedies. Further Reading: Dazzler: The Life and Times of Moss Hart* by Steven Bach. *Try: The Street Where I Live* by Alan Jay Lerner. *Ghost Light* by Frank Rich.

The Essential Haiku
VERSIONS OF BASHŌ, BUSON & ISSA
Edited by Robert Hass

A Gallery of Poetic Snapshots

In ways more sophisticated than a photograph, a poem can memorialize the meeting of self and world, layering in the apprehensions of time, mood, and perception that both ground our insights in sensible reality and set them flying through the ether of consciousness. No poetic form is better suited to the purpose of mental snapshots than haiku, the rigorous, deceptively simple seventeen-syllable Japanese form whose trio of masters are celebrated in this book, compiled with intelligence and affection by former US Poet Laureate Robert Hass. The three poets are Matsuo Bashō (1644–1694), Yosa Buson (1716–1783), and Kobayashi Issa (1763–1828), characterized by Hass as "Bashō the ascetic and seeker, Buson the artist, Issa the humanist." Hass's commentary on the life and work of each poet is informed and astute, and his "versions" of one hundred or so poems by each master are deeply pleasing, their concentrated spirits potently distilled (they're "versions" because Hass is too sensitive to the differences between English and Japanese prosody and technique to dub them "translations"). Here's a favorite from Issa:

New Year's Day—
everything is in blossom!
I feel about average.

Hass's attention to haiku's fundamental elements, including seasonality and quick pivots of thought, allow him to succeed in his attempt to give "some sense of the variety and intensity of experience this small form can sustain." He has also gathered selections from each poet's intriguing prose writings, enlarging his portraits of the virtuoso miniaturists, of whom he aptly writes: "About the things of the world, and the mind looking at the things of the world, and the moments and the language in which we try to express them, they have unusual wakefulness and clarity."

What: Poetry. *When:* 1994. *Also By:* Hass's own excellent poetry includes: *Field Guide* (1973), *Praise* (1979), and *Time and Materials* (2007). *A Little Book on Form: An Exploration into the Formal Imagination of Poetry* (2017). *Further Reading: A History of Haiku* by R. H. Blyth. *The Haiku Handbook* by William J. Higginson. *Try: The Narrow Road to the Deep North* by Matsuo Bashō (see next page). *A Zen Wave: Bashō's Haiku and Zen* by Robert Aitken.

POET IN MOTION FROM THE EPHEMERAL TO THE ETERNAL

The Narrow Road to the Deep North
Matsuo Bashō (1644–1694)

Written late in the seventeenth century, the travel writings of Matsuo Bashō, the most revered of haiku masters, are the culmination of an eight-century Japanese literary tradition. Just as Bashō elevated the customarily lighthearted haiku into a supple and profound poetic form despite the strictness of its seventeen-syllable constraints, so he transfigured the casual record of a journey into an embodiment of contemplative expression and cultural sensibility, combining both prose and poetry in a single narrative.

In his youth, the author chose to abandon the samurai milieu into which he had been born in order to devote himself to poetry. In his maturity, he took up the study of Zen, and, in search of both enlightenment and imagery, ultimately embarked on a life of wandering, making pilgrimages to locations long celebrated by earlier Japanese poets. These holy places, already illuminated by his literary forebears, formed a collective cultural landscape that Bashō explored with an eloquent combination of reverence, wit, and inspiration. His handling of familiar themes, as translator Donald Keene has written, was not unlike a pianist offering a fresh interpretation of Beethoven's well-known sonatas. *The Narrow Road to the Deep North*, the last of the several journeying narratives he composed, is the most memorable.

That this short work of only fifty pages or so is a literary rather than a documentary composition is apparent not only in its ruminative tone and in the many haiku that appear throughout its text, but also in the fact that the author revised it for more than five years after completing the 1,500-mile walking trip on which it is based. (Indeed, the diary of one of the poet's companions on his journey, which remained unpublished until 1943, presents contradictory accounts of some of the incidents Bashō describes.) While it begins by invoking the everlasting (in Nobuyuki Yuasa's translation: "Days and months are travellers of eternity. So are the years that pass by"), it embodies in its own careful composition the truth that words can capture the beauty of natural phenomena and the poignancy of human experience. Even the deeds of the most glorious warriors, forgotten by time, rely on the power of poetry for their memorials, as in this haiku composed at the site of a ruined castle (and beautifully rendered by Keene):

> The summer grasses—
> For many brave warriors
> The aftermath of dreams.

Spare, contemplative, evocative, and richer than its economy of scale suggests, Bashō's *Narrow Road* collects in one exquisite work the ephemeral sights of a samurai-era traveler, the mystical visions of a Zen devotee, and the timeless intuitions of a poetic luminary.

NATHANIEL HAWTHORNE
(1804–1864)

Even among the generation of American originals to which he belonged, Nathaniel Hawthorne stands out as, frankly, a little weird. He was different in kind from his contemporaries of similar literary stature, each of whom was rooted in a real world, no matter how far the reach of their language and imagination took them. Emerson's essays extended the culture and cadences of lecture hall and pulpit to encompass new realms of moral and intellectual discovery, Melville's novels infused the hardtack of maritime life with the rich and elemental flavors of elusive meanings, and Thoreau's sauntering around Walden Pond charted the organic wanderings of a mind inspired by the exactitude and quiet ecstasy of nature.

One can imagine these authors ensconced in their respective realities, however far their work might journey from them; yet Hawthorne, regardless of how much biographical detail we seek, always remains otherworldly, inhabiting a peculiar dominion of fancy and fateful destinies that unfold like ghostly reflections of the lives we lead. His best tales and novels, especially *The Scarlet Letter* and *The House of the Seven Gables*, cast strange spells when they're first encountered, and have a haunting and lasting power. When we return to their pages after years away, adulthood uncovers new meanings. The strange and contemplative patience of Hawthorne's style, exhibiting less concern for plot than for the psychological states that spiritualize time, casts an aura of moonlight that, to invoke his words from the prologue to *The Scarlet Letter*, lures his imaginings from quotidian settings into a "neutral territory, somewhere between the real world and fairy-land, where the Actual and the Imaginary may meet, and each imbue itself with the nature of the other."

19th-century engraving of Nathaniel Hawthorne

This, of course, is where—in our daydreams and aspirations, reminiscences and regrets, hopes and fears—we all live for more of our hours than we might care to admit, and it's the domain that Hawthorne's works evoke with such uncanny power.

Tales and Sketches
Warning Labels for Existence

No matter how dulled by circumstance our inmost eye, it never stops seeking meaning. The ever-present sense of allegory this creates deep in our consciousness is like a wild wood of tangled significance through which we move, often unable to see the trees for the forest. The strictures of received morality may offer clearly defined paths through the ominous growth that envelops us, but they are useful mostly because they speed us—on a blinkered straight and narrow—past the wilds of uncertainty the wood contains. Take one step astray and we may be lost in a jungle of fear, guilt, and sin with no direction home.

Such a metaphorical conceit might well serve as an abstract for Hawthorne's stories and sketches, collected throughout his career in books such as *Twice-Told Tales* (1837), *Mosses from an Old Manse* (1846), and *Tanglewood Tales* (1853). At their best, as in "My Kinsman, Major Molineux," "The Minister's Black Veil," "Young Goodman Brown," "The Birth-Mark," "Rappaccini's Daughter," and "Feathertop," they combine the impersonality and inevitability of Greek tragedy with the enigmatic wisdom and sportive cruelty of fables. Through these creations, which feel quite often like devices enlivened with uncanny animation, the author gazes into the embodied psychology of human emotions to reveal an immensity that his protagonists can recognize but never quite comprehend. The effect of reading a Hawthorne story is akin to the feeling we sometimes get when standing on the ocean shore: How tenuous our sense of time and self becomes in the face of the immense, imperturbable power of the sea.

Let the simple and unsettling domestic horror story called "Wakefield" serve as an emblem for the rest. The plot couldn't be simpler: A man walks out of his house one day and never returns, only to take up residence around the corner, where he resides for twenty years on the periphery of his previous existence. He offers no word of explanation—indeed, extends no communication at all—to his wife, whose haunted days the reader observes, as it were, through her parlor window. No motive or sympathy is extended to Wakefield by the author, either: The reader observes his bizarre actions as the most mundane of familiar neighborhoods is slowly enveloped in a portentous metaphysical cloud arriving from just the other side of regular weather. At the end of his "adventure," and just as inexplicably, he returns home, entering "the door one evening, quietly, as from a day's absence."

Amid the seeming confusion of our mysterious world, individuals are so nicely adjusted to a system, and systems to one another, and to a whole, that, by stepping aside for a moment, a man exposes himself to a fearful risk of losing his place forever. Like Wakefield, he may become, as it were, the Outcast of the Universe.

It is like an episode, a century in advance, from *The Twilight Zone*, a sort of philosophical proof whose outcome is not certainty but a heightened sense of apprehension. Like so many of Hawthorne's imaginings, it brings us up short with the recognition that, however unfathomable the universe may be, something out there is not fooling; our consequent trepidation is matched with a peculiar awareness of blessing. *There but for the grace of God, go I*, the reader thinks: *I'd better watch my step, even if I'm not sure what I am looking out for.*

What: Short Stories. **When:** Most of Hawthorne's short fiction was composed between 1830 and 1852. **Edition:** There are countless editions, the most comprehensive being the Library of America volume, *Tales and Sketches*, issued in 1982; this includes the contents of the volumes mentioned in the text above as well as additional material. **Further Reading:** *Hawthorne* by Henry James. **Try:** *The Piazza Tales* by Herman Melville (see page 544). The stories and novellas of Henry James (see page 408).

The Scarlet Letter
A Woman in the World

The story, at least in outline, is probably familiar. Its setting is seventeenth-century Boston, during the Puritan era. Hester Prynne wears the scarlet "A" that marks her as an adulteress. While she thus pays openly for her sin, the "godly" Reverend Arthur Dimmesdale endures the torments of a guilty conscience: His identity as Hester's lover and the father of her child, Pearl, remains secret. Meanwhile, Roger Chillingworth, Hester's estranged husband, looks to avenge himself on Dimmesdale, befriending him in order "to burrow into the clergyman's intimacy, and plot against his

Poster for the 1926 film adaptation

soul." One can certainly understand the judgment rendered by Henry James in his famous 1879 study of Nathaniel Hawthorne's life and work: "no story of love was surely ever less of a 'love story'. . . . [It] will probably long remain the most consistently gloomy of English novels of the first order." Even Hawthorne himself, in "The Custom-House," the long and curious prologue to the novel proper, regrets the tale's "stern and sombre aspect; too much ungladdened by genial sunshine."

But neither plot summary nor verdict of gloominess does justice to the book's imaginative resonance and singularity, beginning with that playful prologue, a framing tale about the discovery by the book's putative author—who bears many points of resemblance to Nathaniel Hawthorne—of documents that inspired his retelling of Hester Prynne's ordeal. Describing his own experience as a government-appointed surveyor in the Salem custom-house, the narrator offhandedly establishes the thematic context for the tale he will ultimately tell about a woman ostracized by her community:

But it is a strange experience, to a man of pride and sensibility, to know that his interests are within the control of individuals who neither love nor understand him, and by whom, since one or the other must needs happen, he would rather be injured than obliged.

Hester's own sensibility, streaked with independence, nourishes an inner life that grows strong enough to lift the veil of guilt others have imposed upon it. She embodies a presence and purpose that make her one of the most vivid heroines in American literature (and a fitting counterpart to her fictional contemporaries Catherine Earnshaw of *Wuthering Heights* and Jane Eyre, who startled English fiction about the same time as Hester appeared in print). The rich and evolving psychology with which Hawthorne imbues her exposes the Puritan dichotomy of good and evil as too simple to engage the real equations of human feeling that add up to a life. Stripped of the comforts, constraints, and contradictions of conventional morality by being placed outside its bounds, Hester must teach herself how to infuse self and sentiment into her days in a way that provides a kind of confidential consolation. She transmutes her shame, and translates her longing and her loneliness, into a wisdom that abides in this world rather than the next, a wisdom that her daughter will assume as her inheritance, and that every reader would do well to see as the gift redeeming this novel's apparent gloom:

Pearl kissed his lips. A spell was broken. The great scene of grief, in which the wild infant bore a part, had developed all her sympathies; and as her tears fell upon her father's cheek, they were the pledge that she would grow up amid human joy and sorrow, nor forever do battle with the world, but be a woman in it.

What: Novel. *When:* 1850. *Also By:* The Blithedale Romance (1852). The Marble Faun (1860). *Try:* The Awakening by Kate Chopin (see page 158). *Adaptations:* Film adaptations of The Scarlet Letter include a 1917 black-and-white silent version and a "freely adapted" 1995 version starring Demi Moore, Gary Oldman, and Robert Duvall. *Footnote:* The Scarlet Letter was one of the earliest mass-produced books in America, with a first printing of 2,500 copies; it was an immediate bestseller.

Adam's Task
CALLING ANIMALS BY NAME
Vicki Hearne (1946–2001)

Dogs, Cats, Horses—and Moral Philosophy

"Dog trainers and philosophers can't make much sense of each other," writes Vicki Hearne. Perhaps that's not surprising. What *is* surprising, and what this book reveals, is just how rich their talk might be if they took the time to try.

Working with animals in stables and kennels, yet drawn by temperament to university libraries, Hearne was frustrated that the different worlds of discourse her interests occupied were so far apart. She knew that the conversation that takes place between animals and effective trainers demands sensitivity and imagination on both sides, but that its true character goes against the grain of the prevalent behaviorist theories, which reduce animal lives to a calculus of rewards and punishments. For the way trainers really communicate relies on the notion that "animals are capable not only of activities requiring 'IQ' . . . but also of a complex and delicate (though not infallible) moral understanding." Enlivened with the practical knowledge her experience as a trainer of dogs and horses has brought her, and illuminated by her wide reading in philosophy and literature, Hearne's pages are alive with an exhilarating intellectual energy. They bring T. S. Eliot, Wittgenstein, and Dickens together with an Airedale named Salty, a "crazy" horse named Drummer Girl, and a bull terrier named Belle to enhance our understanding of morality, authority, responsibility, orthodoxy, dignity, courage, and, not least, language itself. You'll be astonished at how much learning is involved in "teaching a dog what 'Sit' means."

What: Animals. Nature. Philosophy. *When:* 1986. *Reading Note:* Cat lovers note chapter 10, "What It Is About Cats." *Also By: Bandit: Dossier of a Dangerous Dog* (1991). *Try: Man Meets Dog* by Konrad Lorenz (see page 498). *Footnote:* When the Audubon Society marked its centennial in 1998 by compiling for its signature magazine an "Audubon canon" of enduringly significant books that "enrich or refine our awareness of nature," *Adam's Task* was one of the thirteen works chosen.

Blue Highways
A JOURNEY INTO AMERICA
William Least Heat-Moon (born 1939)

Delight and Misdirection on the Back Roads of the United States

One wintry day in 1978, thirty-eight-year-old English professor William Least Heat-Moon learned that neither his employer nor his wife would be needing him anymore. Lying awake that night, he was struck by an idea, and a quintessentially American idea it was: "A man who couldn't make things go right could at least go." A month later, off he went, embarking upon a journey along the back roads of the United States, the two-lane highways marked in blue on old road maps. Deciding to travel in a circle instead of a straight line (to provide himself the promise of coming round again), Heat-Moon left his native Missouri for a three-month, thirteen-thousand-mile journey "in search of places where change did not mean ruin."

Heat-Moon traveled alone, yet hardly a page passes in which he does not meet a character who enhances the conversations struck up by circumstance or curiosity. Buying a piece of pie in a coffee shop or following a road to a half-built steel boat he spies along a riverbank, the author has "a genius," as Robert Penn Warren put it, "for finding people who have not even found themselves, exploring their lives,

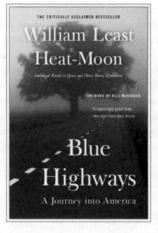

capturing their language, and recreating little (or big) lost worlds." That makes for good company for the reader, and Heat-Moon's evocative, expressive prose is a fine companion all by itself, delivering easygoing yet pensive pleasure as it describes landscape and weather, flora and fauna, men and women from all walks of life. Woven into the itinerary are many careful, colorful strands of local history that are both informative and entertaining.

Pick up *Blue Highways* when you have the urge to read and nothing particular on the top of your list: Before Heat-Moon hits Kentucky, you'll be hooked and eager to relish his wanderings from Nameless, Tennessee, to Remote, Oregon, from Why, Arizona, to Whynot, Mississippi.

What: Travel. **When:** 1982. **Also By:** *PrairyErth, a Deep Map* (1991) is an in-depth portrait of Chase County, Kansas. *River Horse* (1999) is the account of a cross-country trip made by waterways. **Try:** *Travels with Charley* by John Steinbeck (see page 753). **Footnote:** Born William Trogdon, the author derived his pen name from his father's homage to his Native American Osage descent: "My father calls himself Heat-Moon, my elder brother Little Heat-Moon. I, coming last, am therefore Least." (The hyphen did not appear in the first edition of *Blue Highways*. The author resorted to it after being addressed too many times as "Mr. Moon.")

Stranger in a Strange Land
Robert A. Heinlein (1907–1988)

A Martian Named Smith

A corn-fed Midwesterner, Robert Heinlein was a no-nonsense ex-military man who, somewhat surprisingly, worked for most of his life in the dicey realm of the pulps and the

abstract sphere of the sciences. His view of his role as a writer was decidedly down-to-earth: "I must always bear in mind that my prospective reader could spend his recreation money on beer rather than on my stories; I have to be aware every minute that I am competing for beer money—and that the customer does not have to buy." Despite his keen eye on the marketplace, Heinlein created fiction characterized by imaginative flights and conceptual flourishes that are both out of this world and intensely relevant to the lives of his readers.

His most famous and influential work, albeit not his most brilliantly speculative, is surely *Stranger in a Strange Land*, a book whose questioning of social mores and religious certitude have made it as congenial to some readers as it has been controversial to others. Astonishingly entertaining, yet full of meaty philosophical and quotidian barbs, rife with pathos and laughs, this novel—whether in its original form or the expanded author's cut—remains as poignant and provocative as the day it was issued. A quarter century after the first human voyage to Mars ends in a haze of mystery with the vanishing of its crew of four married couples, a second expedition discovers a human survivor, Valentine Michael Smith, born on the spaceship of the original journey and raised by the indigenous Martians, who are as different from our species as they are more technologically advanced. He journeys to Earth—not willingly, for he deems it exile from his true family, but at the behest of his spooky Martian elders, who wish to use him as a conduit to gather knowledge about humankind in the service of their own interstellar intrigues.

Back "home," Mike is initially incarcerated in a hospital by the world government that regards him as the hottest potato ever dropped in its lap. Rescued by a loving nurse named Jill, he ends up in the care of Jubal Harshaw, a bestselling, curmudgeonly author (whom many critics have seen as Heinlein's alter ego: Think Norman Mailer crossed with Stephen King). Jubal gets Mike his freedom, but he also sets in motion the alien's ultimate martyrdom. With his telekinetic powers, his mastery of mind reading and astral projection, Mike is a superman bound to earn the distrust of normal folks. Yet his worst offenses, in a society bound by strictures of organized religion, prove to be his attitudes toward sex, money, love, equality, and death. His heretical ideas spark a new belief system—the Church of All Worlds—that at first unleashes a liberating energy but ultimately provokes a violent response from the threatened powers-that-be.

Heinlein packs this book with a lifetime of pithy aperçus (for example, "the slickest way to lie is to tell the right amount of truth—then shut up"); Mark Twain–like rueful satire and cantankerousness; poignant human desires and dreams; and political shenanigans of various stripes. The plot moves with purpose, yet allows for entertaining detours (Mike as a carnival performer, for instance) and lengthy disquisitions from Jubal on every topic imaginable. From one angle the book looks to be as tragic as the story of Christ, an obvious template for Mike's ascent and demise, but it also manages to evoke, delightfully, the screwball afterlife comedy of Thorne Smith (see *Topper*, page 634).

Unique in the genre when it appeared, *Stranger in a Strange Land* compels immersive reading with its suspense and grace, and had immense cultural fallout during the 1960s. It continues to absorb, entertain, and jostle readers today.

What: Science Fiction. *When:* 1961. *Award:* Hugo Award for Best Novel, 1962. *Also By: Beyond This Horizon* (1948). *Double Star* (1956). *Starship Troopers* (1959). *The Moon Is a Harsh Mistress* (1966). *Friday* (1982). *Further Reading: Robert A. Heinlein: In Dialogue with His Century* by William H. Patterson: vol. 1, *Learning Curve, 1907–1948*; vol. 2, *The Man Who Learned Better, 1948–1988. Try: The Man Who Fell to Earth* by Walter Tevis. *Cat's Cradle* by Kurt Vonnegut. *Godbody* by Theodore Sturgeon. *Footnote:* "Grok"—a coinage in Heinlein's invented Martian tongue—has migrated into common usage (and most dictionaries), with the meaning of "to grasp" or "to comprehend intuitively."

JOSEPH HELLER
(1923–1999)

Despite an initial burst of mixed reviews, Joseph Heller's first novel, *Catch-22*, the product of eight years' labor, would go on to become a seminal book of the 1960s and, by eventual consensus, be recognized as one of the pinnacles of modern literature (it took the number seven spot on the Modern Library's list of the best one hundred novels of the twentieth century). His debut ultimately earned Heller a career's worth of acclaim, yet a small group of connoisseurs believes its reputation continues to unjustly overshadow his even better second novel, *Something Happened*—a judgment that was shared by Heller himself. In both cases, a genius for unflinching comic exposure of the shibboleths America holds dear, at war and at work, is on bracing, brilliant, rueful, and—sadly—still timely display.

Joseph Heller, 1974

Catch-22
From Here to Absurdity:
An Irreverent World War II Classic

The title of Joseph Heller's first novel has become—aptly enough—a catchphrase, common parlance for the kind of double bind that bureaucracies breed with astonishing fecundity.

There was only one catch and that was Catch-22, which specified that a concern for one's own safety in the face of dangers that were real and immediate was the process of a rational mind. [A pilot] was crazy and could be grounded. All he had to do was ask; and as soon as he did, he would no longer be crazy and would have to fly more missions. . . . If he flew them he was crazy and didn't have to; but if he didn't want to he was sane and had to.

Captain John Yossarian, the protagonist of Heller's pioneering and influential satire, is "moved very deeply by the absolute simplicity" of the "spinning reasonableness" that Catch-22 expressed: "There was an elliptical precision about its perfect pairs of parts that was graceful and shocking, like good modern art."

From those parts Heller spins a novel of mordant originality, exposing the obscenity of war via a blackly comic machinery that is fueled by Yossarian's attempts to escape its horror. Himself a veteran of sixty World War II missions as a B-25 wing bombardier, Heller devoted several years in the aftermath of that service (after a brief stint in academia and concurrent with a career as an advertising writer) to capturing on the page the mind-bending absurdities military authorities could spawn. Like *Candide* (see page 824), the novel presents its action in a recurring pattern in which the protagonist applies his energies to the task, it turns out, of learning the same lesson over and over again. Stationed on an island in the Mediterranean in the waning days of the war, Yossarian feels acutely that he is under siege, not only from the German enemy but also from the friendly fire of ridiculous regulations, circular logic, and red tape that the US Army Air Force trains on him. He'd like to complete his tour of duty, but his commander keeps raising the number of missions required to do so; he thinks going crazy will provide a way out, but finds he is not crazy enough to outwit Catch-22. So he bides his time, finding numerous ways to avoid flying while hoping to summon the inspiration for some other way out. Heller peoples Yossarian's dead-end path with vivid types and zany characters, the most unforgettable being the mercenary mess officer Milo Minderbinder, who embraces private war profiteering with such stunning resourcefulness and bottomless venality that he soon directs an international syndicate that gleefully transcends the conflict between Allies and Axis in the interest of turning a buck.

Appearing in 1961, *Catch-22* was unlike any other novel the Second World War had inspired. As Eliot Fremont-Smith later wrote, it "came when we still cherished nice notions about WWII. Demolishing these, it released an irreverence that had, until then, dared not speak its name." As Yossarian put it, "That's some catch, that Catch-22."

What: Novel. War. *When:* 1961. *Also By:* A sequel, *Closing Time*, appeared in 1994. *Try: Kaputt* by Curzio Malaparte (see page 515). *Johnny Got His Gun* by Dalton Trumbo. *Slaughterhouse-Five* by Kurt Vonnegut (see page 827). *Adaptation:* A film version directed by Mike Nichols and starring Alan Arkin appeared in 1970. *Footnote:* For the near-decade he spent composing the book, Heller's working title was "Catch-18" (the first chapter was published in a magazine under this title); as publication approached, the novel was renamed *Catch-22* to avoid confusion with Leon Uris's bestseller *Mila 18*.

Something Happened
A Life of Quiet Desperation

The product of thirteen years' gestation, *Something Happened* is an anatomy of middle-aged disenchantments that is both wildly funny and suffused with a desperate sorrow. Its narrator, Bob Slocum, is an office worker on the wearying escalator of a senseless though sometimes vicious corporate track; a husband whose marriage resides in a different dimension from his heart; a father terrified by the opacity, vulnerability, and willfulness of his children; an individual whose once eager innocence has been tarnished by the indefinable something that so surely happened to set him in his hopeless ways. Although Slocum's narration embodies his banal life, Heller's almost surreal focus on its very banality transforms it, by an astonishing act of literary sleight of hand, into something mesmerizing. The speech-based composition (usually simple phrases or sentences: "I get the willies when I see closed doors"; "In the office in which I work there are five people of whom I am afraid") gives Slocum a familiar voice at the same time as it provides the novelist with exhibits in his carefully, caustically curated museum of social and psychological worry in late-twentieth-century America. Heller keeps turning Slocum's simple observations around—"Each of these five people is afraid of four people (excluding overlaps), for a total of twenty, and each of these twenty people is afraid of six people, making a total of one hundred and twenty people who are feared by at least one person. Each of these one hundred and twenty people is afraid of the other one hundred and nineteen")—until the beam of his invention strikes every available facet. Not much happens in *Something Happened*, but not much has to: The story Heller is telling is unfolding in our own house, or right next door.

What makes the book truly remarkable is the depth its humorous surface eventually

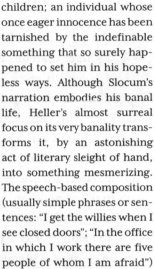

reveals. For, though the circumspect adventures of Bob Slocum will provoke unrelenting laughter from a reader of twenty-two, they will not seem so amusing to a reader twice that age, who will trace the sadness and rueful unease the author has carefully woven between the lines. With increasing tension, that older reader will be praying for release from self-recognition as the pages are turned.

As darkly comic as *Catch-22*, but more deeply felt, *Something Happened* plumbs the private terrors of a nearby life with haunting acuity.

What: Novel. **When:** 1974. *Also By: Good as Gold* (1979). *God Knows* (1984). *Portrait of an Artist, as an Old Man* (2000). *Try: Independence Day* by Richard Ford (see page 288). *Then We Came to the End* by Joshua Ferris. *Personal Days* by Ed Park.

ERNEST HEMINGWAY
(1899–1961)

L arger than life at the height of his fame, Hemingway and his reputation seem to grow smaller each year. His carefully tended celebrity and the boorish machismo that came to overtake his fine-grained early fascination with violence and death have obscured for many the delicate artistry and fierce attention that made him one of the most original English-language writers of the twentieth century. His influence on the course of modern literature is incalculable, and his best voice remains fresh and mysteriously vivifying; it has much to tell us about growing up, about solitude and resourcefulness, about the peculiarity of men's regard of women (if not vice versa), about fear and the stories we tell to surmount it. His experiences as a young man in the First World War colored everything he knew, turning his apprehensions of both war and peace into Romantic intimations of mortality. The truths he has to tell are profoundly poetic, and they are diminished by the attempt to paraphrase them.

In Our Time
True at First Light

Ernest Hemingway, 1953

Following upon the appearance of two small volumes in Paris, *In Our Time* was Hemingway's first full-length book, and his first published in the United States. It is composed of sixteen stories, each followed by a brief prose interlude—often a paragraph, never longer than a single page—labeled as a numbered "chapter." The chapters—scenes of peril and desperation drawn from the battlefield, the bull ring, and the annals of American urban violence—act as a kind of visceral punctuation to the stories, giving an ominous historical context. The conscious, almost precious ordering of *In Our Time* marks the earnest literary ambitions of its young author. This is the work of an aesthete, albeit one who has had his nose rubbed in real life during his wounding experiences of war.

Norman Mailer once advanced the idea that "style comes to young authors about the time they recognize that life is out there ready to kill them, kill them quickly or slowly, but something out there is not fooling." The disciplined directness of Hemingway's expression—the way each word seems chosen and set with care, the modulation of cadence, the telling use of quiet—informs a style of stunning alertness as he explores youth's conversion from innocence to experience. Although the character of Nick Adams is not central to every tale, the course of his coming-of-age shapes the book's development. We share his youth and his admiration for his doctor father ("Indian Camp"), the confusions of his first romance ("The End of Something"), his friendships ("The Three-Day Blow"), the aftermath of his wartime ordeal and his fragile determination to make a home for himself in a homeless world ("Big Two-Hearted River"—a tale of trout fishing that plumbs deep waters without straying very far from the camp Nick carefully pitches between two trees). All the while, the something out there that's not fooling infiltrates the space between the lines to intensify the hues of Hemingway's attention to life, love, and death. Despite—or perhaps because of—its often miniaturist scale, *In Our Time* may well be the truest expression of its author's prodigious gifts.

What: Short Stories. *When:* 1925; revised, with added introductory story, 1930. *Also By:* The story remained Hemingway's most authentic métier, and the Finca Vigia edition of *The Complete Short Stories* is bright with masterpieces. *Further Reading: Hemingway: A Life Without Consequences* by James R. Mellow. *Try: Winesburg, Ohio* by Sherwood Anderson.

A Farewell to Arms
Casualties of Love and War

A*Farewell to Arms* was Hemingway's second novel, appearing in 1929, three years after *The Sun Also Rises*. Mining autobiographical terrain, it draws upon the author's experience

as an ambulance driver during World War I. Although it authentically evokes the fraught tedium of military work and the drama of battle and its aftermath (the section depicting the Italian army's ragged retreat from Caporetto is one of the most memorable chapters in the literature of war), the book's beating heart is the love story between its narrator, American volunteer Frederic Henry, and Catherine Barkley, an English nurse.

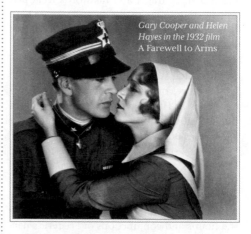

Gary Cooper and Helen Hayes in the 1932 film A Farewell to Arms

The novel begins with a paragraph of austere and measured beauty: "four deceptively simple sentences, one hundred and twenty-six words," per Joan Didion's admiring audit. "Only one of the words has three syllables. Twenty-two have two. The other hundred and three have one. Twenty-four of the words are 'the,' fifteen are 'and.'" The passage describes rocks and water and trees and leaves and marching soldiers with careful concentration, as if the writer is struggling to get a purchase on reality through means of clear description (the tenor of the style reflects the prose experiments of Gertrude Stein, the young Hemingway's mentor). One would be mistaken to read the declarative lucidity of this paragraph—or the rest of the book—as an expression of confidence or strength. For all its reticent solidity, it is imbued with a fragility the stoic voice struggles to mask: The small words are not so much facts as they are handholds to aid Frederic's halting progress through the welter of memory and emotion the narrative he is embarking upon must encompass.

"Abstract words such as glory, honor, courage, or hallow," Frederic will write much later in the novel, "were obscene beside the concrete names of villages, the numbers of roads, the names of rivers, the numbers of regiments and the dates."

This sentence is often taken as an emblem of Hemingway's own philosophy, yet the empirical rigor of his style at its best does not embody a code of conduct, but a caution. The hero of *A Farewell to Arms*, like Nick Adams before him, traffics in fear and failure more than courage, and his words treat private wounds. (One might do well to note here that the "Hemingway hero" of public lore would come to wear the face of Robert Jordan, protagonist of the author's 1940 novel of the Spanish Civil War, *For Whom the Bell Tolls*, who is a far more conventional figure than his predecessors in Hemingway's oeuvre—a scion in the line of romantic heroes that produced the Humphrey Bogart of *Casablanca* and his heirs.)

Even the tenor of Frederic's and Catherine's infatuation is anxious and fretful. Indeed, readers may find the initial stages of their affair a little too quick, their cooing a little too kittenish. But their words of love, like the nouns and conjunctions of Frederic's narration, are awkward attempts to grasp hold of some meaning in the midst of the war's destruction. The romantic passion they will cling to begins as a tissue of emotional invention, needy and nearly transparent from each side. And yet the ultimate force of their conspiracy of wishing will provoke Frederic's desertion and disavowal of the war—"it was not my show anymore"—and their escape to Switzerland, where Catherine and their baby will die in childbirth. Their desperate attempt to redeem a lost world with something sacred of their own creation—a great love, a child, a separate peace—expires in disillusion and grief. Still, the couple's—indeed, the author's—longing for a destination beyond loneliness, beyond courage, beyond the frailties of self and the futilities of history, is fraught with noble yearning.

What: Novel. *When:* 1929. *Also By: The Sun Also Rises* (1926). *For Whom the Bell Tolls* (1940). *Further Reading: The Only Thing That Counts: The Ernest Hemingway/Maxwell Perkins Correspondence, 1925–1947.* "Last Words" by Joan Didion, *The New Yorker*, November 9, 1998, quoted on page 365, is the

best tribute to Hemingway's style you'll ever read. *Try: The English Patient* by Michael Ondaatje. *Adaptations:* The 1932 film stars Gary Cooper and Helen Hayes. A 1957 remake features Rock Hudson and Jennifer Jones.

The Old Man and the Sea
A Tall Tale and a Late Masterpiece

Published in 1952, this novella was greeted with wide popular acclaim; it won the Pulitzer Prize in 1953 and was the catalyst for the Swedish Academy's bestowal of the Nobel Prize a year later. For all its knowing description of the tools and techniques of fishing, it is a tall tale of sorts, chronicling an elderly Cuban fisherman's epic contest—"communion" might be a more accurate word—with an enormous marlin. Across several days and nights, the weary but determined Santiago tracks the hooked creature, until he at last claims his catch, which is so big that it must be strapped to the side of his skiff, where it is inexorably attacked and eaten by sharks before the old man can get back to port.

Santiago meets his disappointment with great dignity. The sentiment he expresses as he helplessly watches the sharks destroy his hard-won prize—"A man can be destroyed but not defeated"—has been widely heralded as the author's own, the book celebrated for its allegedly uplifting message of perseverance. Yet the novella's simplicity and fleet forward motion, its fable-like arc of struggle and symbolism, only mask its ineluctable expression of what Gabriel García Márquez rightly called Hemingway's one essential theme: "the uselessness of victory." The book's sturdy, stalwart, almost ancient eloquence is haunted with echoes of the sure but ineffable truths of tragedy: We sense some profound meaning, but we can't quite put words to it. The tale outlasts its interpretation, as only the strongest stories can.

What: Novella. *When:* 1952. *Awards:* Pulitzer Prize for Fiction, 1953. Hemingway was awarded the Nobel Prize in Literature in 1954. *Also By: Green Hills of Africa* (1935). *Islands in the Stream* (1970). *Further Reading: Notes from a Sea Diary: Hemingway All the Way* by Nelson Algren. *Try: The Pearl* by John Steinbeck. *A Whole Life* by Robert Seethaler. *Adaptation:* A film version, starring Spencer Tracy, was released in 1958.

Dune
Frank Herbert (1920–1986)

Spice Is the Variety of Life

Before the publication of *Dune*, Frank Herbert was seen as a journeyman author, competent but undistinguished. But after the arrival of *Dune* (heralded in the smaller fandom of the era by its raw publication as installments in *Analog* magazine), and its quick capture of two major awards (including the inaugural Nebula Award for Best Novel), Herbert was lionized as a science fiction master and even something of a prophet, someone with an intuitive grasp of the nascent 1960s zeitgeist (eco-awareness, mysticism, multiculturalism, rebellion). Ironically, however, by becoming "the man who wrote *Dune*," he lost the ability to really interest readers in his subsequent projects not connected with that franchise; nevertheless, his achievement in *Dune* and its sequels remains both seminal and enduring.

The book had a long gestation. Inspired by a visit to the famed sand dunes of Oregon, Herbert delved into research on environmental science and related matters as he began to chart the long, complex backstory of his epic, which ultimately came to span some twenty-one thousand years of future history. Through canny and judicious textual references throughout his saga, he would use the imaginative foundation his investigations provided to convince readers that they were entering a milieu as gloriously irreducible as the world outside their windows.

Herbert's interstellar empire is dominated by what amount to feuding royal households and a variety of guilds (space pilots, cerebral Mentats, Sardaukar warriors, the Bene Gesserit sisterhood of mind witches) under an overarching Emperor. (If this setup sounds familiar, attribute the resonance to the fact that perhaps no fictional work influenced George Lucas more in the creation of Star Wars than *Dune*.)

The hero, Paul, belongs to House Atreides, whose main rival is House Harkonnen, guided by the obese and malign Duke Vladimir. When House Atreides is given control of the planet Arrakis—whence flows the invaluable product called "spice" that underpins interstellar travel—battle is joined.

Forced by deadly attacks to seek refuge with the "primitive" Arrakis desert dwellers known as the Fremen, who control the giant sandworms that produce the spice, Paul and his mother, Lady Jessica, get a valuable education in proletarian strengths. The young lad and his guiding Bene Gesserit mother begin to travel—partly consciously, partly serendipitously—down the path of Paul's destiny, which is to become nothing less than the superhuman ruler of the entire galaxy. The novel's depiction of the hero's transformation, and the price his spice-induced prescience exacts, is pitiless yet still fosters pathos.

From its fairy-tale opening—"In the week before their departure to Arrakis, when all the final scurrying about had reached a nearly unbearable frenzy, an old crone came to visit the mother of the boy, Paul"—to its bodice-ripper closing line—"While we, Chani, we who carry the name of concubine—history will call us wives"—the book blends the swashbuckling excitement of Dumas with the esoteric inner-space journeys of Saint Theresa and the fevered practical exploits of Lawrence of Arabia. So although Herbert's fusing of adventure, realpolitik, and dropout soul-searching perfectly caught the spirit of the mid-1960s, it did so by invoking long-standing cultural myths whose resonance transcends that era. As thickly textured as any purely historical fiction by Hilary Mantel (see page 523), the book also obeys the science fiction imperatives of estrangement, perceptual breakthrough, and societal speculation.

In conjunction with Kevin J. Anderson, Frank Herbert's son Brian has now produced more books relating to the *Dune* mythos than his father did. These competent prequels satisfy the desire of readers to see the legendary characters from the epic's backstory in action and to examine the logistical underpinnings of *Dune*'s "present." They even contain rare flashes of the awe and majesty and baroque weirdness of the originals. But the essential arc of the messianic life of Paul Atreides is contained within *Dune* and its first two sequels, *Dune Messiah* (1969) and *Children of Dune* (1976), which together form a mind-expanding saga of justice, power, abnegation, and exaltation unparalleled within the realm of science fiction—and seldom matched beyond it.

What: Science Fiction. *When:* 1965. *Awards:* Nebula Award for Best Novel, 1965; Hugo Award for Best Novel (shared), 1966. *Also By: God Emperor of Dune* (1981). *Further Reading: Dreamer of Dune: The Biography of Frank Herbert* by Brian Herbert. *Try: A Door into Ocean* by Joan Slonczewski. *Grass* by Sheri Tepper. *Hidden Empire* by Kevin J. Anderson. *Adaptations:* The 1984 film by David Lynch betrays the text in favor of the director's signature concerns. The television miniseries from 2000, directed by John Harrison, delivers a more authentic version. *Footnote: Dune* in manuscript endured more than twenty rejections, until it was finally accepted by the firm of Chilton—best known at the time for its car-repair manuals.

Histories
Herodotus (ca. 485 BC–ca. 425 BC)

Father of History, Father of Prose

Generally regarded as the earliest example of historical writing in the literature of the West, the *Histories* of Herodotus tell the story of the war between the mighty Persian empire of Darius and Xerxes and the small band of independent Greek city-states that repelled their invasion in the first half of the fifth century BC. At the same time, informed by its author's observant travels through Greece, Egypt, North Africa, Mesopotamia, and even southern Russia, it presents an astonishingly wide-ranging survey of the geography, customs, and culture of the then-known world.

Herodotus's account of the Persian Wars would alone justify his book's classic status: It is through his narrative that generations upon generations have learned of the battles of Marathon (where the Greeks turned back Darius), Thermopylae (where Leonidas and a squadron of three hundred Spartans, knowing they would die, led the tiny force that deterred the advance of many thousand Persian troops),

Engraving of Herodotus

and Salamis (the naval battle in which the Greek fleet routed the invaders). Not to be missed is book 7's description of the bridge of boats that Xerxes had constructed to span the Hellespont; impressive as it is, the project's logistical achievement is not nearly as memorable as the hubris of the Persian leader, who ordered the sea whipped and shackled when its violent storms upset his plans.

Yet in addition to its military concerns, the *Histories* is filled with material of great ethnographic interest (as a result, Herodotus's fatherhood has often been expanded to cover anthroplogy as well as history). His digressive narrative is fueled by an insatiable curiosity into the manners and mores of societies other than his own; book 2 of the *Histories*, for example, is something like an ancient antecedent to a modern tourist guide to Egypt. Embedded in his method is the insight that human institutions influence events as much as the wisdom or whimsy of the Olympians, and the idea that inquiry into the matter and meaning of these human constructs will instruct as well as delight. (It is worth noting that the Greek word *historie*, which Herodotus applies to his text, means "research" or "inquiry" rather than what we understand as "history.")

As important as his other achievements are, his most significant is often the most overlooked: The mind of Herodotus was just about the first to wander the world in prose, and in his rambling, engagingly inquisitive narrative he discovers and refines this literary tool as one of literature's essential instruments of invention and investigation. From the headwaters of his *Histories* flow not only long rivers of historical writing, but, ultimately, the deep waters of the novel, essay, and memoir as well.

What: History. Antiquity. *When:* ca. 400 BC. *Editions:* Although other translations of the text (notably Robin Waterfield's for Oxford World Classics) are more engaging, the extensive annotation, commentary, and maps that accompany Andrea Purvis's version in *The Landmark Herodotus* make that volume invaluable. *Further Reading: The World of Herodotus* by Aubrey de Selincourt. *The Way of Herodotus: Travels with the Man Who Invented History* by Justin Marozzi. *Travels with Herodotus* by Ryszard Kapuscinski. *Try: The History of the Peloponnesian War* by Thucydides (see page 787). *Guide to Greece* by Pausanius. *The History of Rome from Its Foundations* by Livy.

Dispatches
Michael Herr (1940–2016)

"The best book to have been written about the Vietnam War." —C. D. B. Bryan, New York Times Book Review

Between 1967 and 1969, journalist Michael Herr was in Vietnam, reporting on the war for *Esquire* magazine. *Dispatches* is his episodic personal account of that experience. The conflict Herr covered has sometimes been referred to as America's "first rock 'n' roll war," and there's certainly a head-banging, heavy-metal swagger to the author's juiced-up prose. Listen, for instance, to this description of coming under fire:

Under Fire would take you out of your head and your body too, the space you'd seen a second ago between subject and object wasn't there anymore, it banged shut in a fast wash of adrenaline. Amazing, unbelievable, guys who'd played a lot of hard sports said they'd never felt anything like it, the sudden drop and rocket rush of the hit, the reserves of adrenaline you could make available to yourself, pumping it up and putting it out until you were lost floating in it, not afraid, almost open to clear orgasmic death-by-drowning in it, actually relaxed. Unless of course you'd shit your pants or were screaming or praying or giving anything at all to the hundred-channel panic that blew word salad all around you and sometimes clean through you.

Herr's harrowing narrative unfolds in cinematic jump cuts, each incident appearing as if caught in the sudden lurid glow of a flare bursting over a jungle landscape at night, illuminating bodies and death, fear and chaos. Through each stunning sequence, Herr remains alert to the trauma, terror, language, and longing of the soldiers he is watching kill and die. An electric pulse of desperation sears their humanity, and the author bears witness to the pain of the burns.

Herr spent three or four years after the war struggling with despair himself, unable to finish his book, and the passage of time adds a reflective power to his account:

After enough time passed and memory receded and settled, the name itself became a prayer, coded like all prayer to go past the extremes of petition and gratitude: Vietnam Vietnam Vietnam, say again, until the word lost all its old loads of pain, pleasure, horror, guilt, nostalgia. Then and there, everyone was just trying to get through it, existential crunch, no atheists in foxholes like you wouldn't believe.

When *Dispatches* was published in 1977, novelists John le Carré and Robert Stone offered telling but not uncommon praise: The former called it "the best book I have ever read on men and war in our time," and the latter said that "it may be the best personal journal about war, any war, that any writer has ever accomplished." More than four decades later, Herr's chronicle remains unsurpassed as a portrait of a war whose every face wore an exaggerated grimace.

What: War. *When:* 1977. *Also By: The Big Room* (1987). *Walter Winchell: A Novel* (1990). *Kubrick* (2001). *Further Reading: Nam: The Vietnam War in the Words of the*

Men and Women Who Fought There by Mark Baker. *Try: A Rumor of War* by Philip Caputo. *If I Die in a Combat Zone, Box Me Up and Ship Me Home* by Tim O'Brien. *Fear and Loathing in Las Vegas* by Hunter S. Thompson (see page 783). *Adaptation:* Elizabeth Swados mounted a musical adaptation in 1979. *Footnote:* Herr wrote the narration for Francis Ford Coppola's 1979 movie, *Apocalypse Now;* he also contributed to the screenplay of Stanley Kubrick's 1987 Vietnam film, *Full Metal Jacket.*

Zen in the Art of Archery
Eugen Herrigel (1884–1955)

Target Practice for the Soul

Anyone who has ever swung a golf club or sewn a quilt knows that such activities, if they're to be done well, require a special kind of contemplative attention. You need to know technique, of course, but the more you are conscious of it as you pursue your goal—be it putting the ball in the hole or producing a lovely coverlet—the less likely you are to achieve the desired result. In fact, the best way to attain the success you seek is to reach a level of focus at which you forget technique entirely. Now,

imagine that your goal is not a lower handicap or a better bedspread, but rather the focus of mind that gets you there—the transcendent discipline of sustained concentration; then you'll have some idea of both the inspiration and the lessons of this ultra-slim 1953 book.

When Eugen Herrigel, a German professor of philosophy, went to Tokyo in the 1940s, he studied ikebana (the Japanese art of flower arranging), apprenticed to a master of archery, and spent six years studying Zen Buddhism through those activities. *Zen in the Art of Archery* is his distillation of that experience, an attempt to make the purpose of Zen practice understandable to those outside of its native culture. Despite the wide dissemination of Zen ideas in the ensuing years, Herrigel's book remains an illuminating, graceful, and inspiriting introduction, through Western eyes, to the meditative insight of Eastern philosophy.

What: Religion & Spirituality. Philosophy. *When:* 1948; first English edition, 1953. *Edition:* The Vintage paperback, translated by R. F. C. Hull, contains an introduction by D. T. Suzuki. *Also By: The Method of Zen* (1960), a posthumous work compiled from Herrigel's copious notes. *Further Reading: Zen Mind, Beginner's Mind* by Shunryu Suzuki. *Zen Bow, Zen Arrow: The Life and Teachings of Awa Kenzo, the Archery Master from "Zen in the Art of Archery"* by John Stevens. *Try:* For a more direct introduction to Zen by a Westerner, try *The Way of Zen* by Alan Watts. For a colorful treatise on Eastern and Western aesthetics, try Kakuzo Okakura's *The Book of Tea* (see page 601).

All Creatures Great and Small
James Herriot (1916–1995)

A Veterinarian's Storied Life

All Creatures Great and Small begins with a scene that, in another writer's hands, might be gruesome: The narrator, a rather newly minted veterinary doctor, describes himself as facedown on a cobbled floor in a pool of nameless muck, arm deep inside a straining cow, as he attempts to adjust the position of an unborn calf to ensure its safe passage from its mother's womb. "I was stripped to the waist and the snow mingled with the dirt and the dried blood on my body," explains James Herriot (the pen name of James Alfred Wight) at the opening of this beloved book, a semi-autobiographical account of a Yorkshire veterinarian, the animals he treated, and, most tellingly of all, the farmers, families, and neighbors of the town of Darrowby and the surrounding countryside. Herriot's professional attention to the calves, horses, dogs, cats, and other creatures he treats is matched by an unassuming sensitivity to the quirks and charms of the people—by turns cranky, crusty, amiable, and tender—who bring the animals to him.

Indeed, it is the human, community story that lifts Herriot's episodic narratives into a special class that, despite its constant engagement with life, death, and other elemental matters, is among the most joyful and delightful volumes you will ever open. Even the precarious and painful drama of the opening pages resolves itself into the "little miracle" of a healthy birth, "something," Herriot relates, "that would never grow stale no matter how often I saw it." The reader is bound to feel the same way about the tales collected in this book and its sequels.

What: Animals. *When:* 1972. *Edition: All Creatures Great and Small* was the title given the first American edition, which incorporated two works published previously in Britain: *If Only They Could Talk* (1970) and *It Shouldn't Happen to a Vet* (1972). *Also By: All Things Bright and Beautiful* (1974). *All Things Wise and Wonderful* (1977). *The Lord God Made Them All* (1981). *Further Reading: The Real James Herriot: A Memoir of My Father* by his son, Jim Wight. *Try: Tarka the Otter* by Henry Williamson (see page 858). *Now Then Lad...: Tales of a Country Bobby* by Mike Pannett. *Adaptations: All Creatures Great and Small* inspired a 1975 television film as well as a popular BBC series that ran, intermittently, from 1978 through 1990. The audiobook, read by Christopher Timothy, is a delight.

My Past and Thoughts
Alexander Herzen (1812–1870)

The 19th-Century Russian Masterpiece You Haven't Read

Born the illegitimate son of a wealthy Russian landowner in 1812, Alexander Herzen would play a significant role in fanning the flames of revolutionary thinking that spread throughout Europe in the nineteenth century. Despite his illegitimacy, he led a privileged childhood and was the beneficiary of both a fine education and a generous inheritance; nevertheless, he grew up preoccupied not with wealth and the nobility, but with poverty and the disparities of class. As a result of his political outspokenness, he lived much of his life in exile, although that did little to diminish his influence in his homeland, for his Free Russian Press, based in London, issued periodicals (most notably *The Bell*) that were smuggled past the czar's censors and welcomed by a sizable readership. Nourishing a wide and vibrant circle of associates and correspondents, Herzen was a catalyzing force in the evolution of socialist ideas in Russia and throughout Europe.

All of which might lead one to worry that Herzen's autobiography might be a dreary slog through polemical prose. But nothing could be further from the truth: *My Past and Thoughts* is one of the most eloquent, humane, and compelling memoirs ever written. Each episode is animated by the author's profound sensitivity to people and place, and the whole is imbued with a Tolstoyan magnanimity. The heading of the opening pages—"My Nurse and the *Grand Armée*"—exhibits the shifting perspectives that characterize the many chapters to follow, and Herzen's portrayal of his father's encounter with Napoleon gives an early example of his ability to deftly evoke the personalities of players upon the historical stage. As the narrative progresses through his coming-of-age and education, his relationships with family, servants, and tutors, his political awakening and his internal exile within Russia before his departure from Moscow in 1847 (he would never return to his homeland), the reader is swept up in a fascinating current of memory and meditation that flows into the years of his maturity in Paris and London. Through these decades abroad, his ideological engagement and attendant activities supply just one strand in a vast tapestry of fierce friendships, domestic tragedy, marital humiliation, financial setback, and hard-won wisdom. Indeed, for a writer impelled by political ideals,

19th-century engraving of Alexander Herzen

Herzen is remarkably attuned to the fatefulness of life's uncertainties and to the emotional texture of human relations and experience. Like the greatest novels, Herzen's autobiography seems to know more about life than its plot alone reveals. As the esteemed philosopher Isaiah Berlin wrote, *My Past and Thoughts* is "a literary masterpiece to be placed by the side of the novels of Herzen's contemporaries and countrymen, Tolstoy, Turgenev, Dostoevsky." Don't miss it.

What: Autobiography. History. **When:** 1867. *Editions:* Most readily available is a 1973 one-volume abridgement of Herzen's massive original, translated by Constance Garnett, edited by Dwight Macdonald, and introduced by Isaiah Berlin. Earlier four- and six-volume editions in English are worth seeking out to savor the full scope of Herzen's masterpiece. *Also By: Who Is to Blame?* (1847). *From the Other Shore* (1850). *Try: The Romantic Exiles* by E. H. Carr. *Russian Thinkers* by Isaiah Berlin. *Footnote:* Although there's no adaptation of the memoirs per se, Berlin's essays on Herzen and his circle were the inspiration for Tom Stoppard's theatrical trilogy, The Coast of Utopia (2002).

The Glass Bead Game
Hermann Hesse (1877–1962)

A Masterwork Both Playful and Profound

Imagine a game in which the player is called upon to use all the insights, noble thoughts, works of art, and products of scientific and scholarly inquiry that have shaped civilization. In his last novel, Hermann Hesse conceived of just such a pastime, an elaborative imaginative enterprise whose rules "constitute a kind of highly developed secret language" that allows a Magister Ludi (Master of the Game) to manipulate "the total contents and values of our culture." On the immense body of intellectual values the past has handed down, "the Glass Bead Game player plays like the organist on an organ."

The game's masters are the revered elite of Castalia, "a small Province dedicated to things of the mind," primarily the Glass Bead Game itself. Hesse's novel, set a few centuries into the future, purports to be the biography of the great Magister Ludi Joseph Knecht. Knecht's story—as well as the history of Castalia and its famous game—is related by a narrator whose solemn pedantry is at humorous odds with the high spirits of Hesse's invention of a land that is the ultimate ivory tower. The tale of Knecht's escape from that tower to engage in the rough work of the wider world is a complex and moving culmination of the author's lifelong exploration of themes of nature, culture, and identity; convention and rebellion; spirituality and the pursuit of higher ideals; and, especially, the need for communion between action and contemplation. Largely to honor this book's achievement and ideas, the Nobel Prize in Literature was awarded to Hesse in 1946.

What: Novel. Philosophy. *When:* 1943. *Edition:* Also published as *Magister Ludi.* The translation by Richard and Clara Winston, with an insightful foreword by Theodore Ziolkowski, is highly recommended. *Award:* Nobel Prize in Literature, 1946. *Reading Notes:* The book, unbeknownst to the earnest narrator, is filled with jokes and artifice. Astute readers will note the portraits of influential figures Hesse has embedded in the tale, including Thomas Mann (in the character named Thomas von der Trave), the philosopher Friedrich Nietzsche (Fritz Tegularius), and the historian Jacob Burckhardt (Father Jacobus). *Also By: Siddhartha* (1922), a novel set in India and shaped by Hesse's interest in Oriental mysticism, and *Steppenwolf* (1927), a surrealistic portrait of the artist as outsider, were both embraced by the 1960s counterculture and remain Hesse's most famous works. Other novels include *Peter Camenzind* (1904), *Demian* (1919), and *Narcissus and Goldmund* (1930). *Try: Doctor Faustus* by Thomas Mann.

An Infamous Army
Georgette Heyer (1902–1974)

The Queen of Regency Romance—and More

Georgette Heyer may fairly be said to have found, nurtured, and raised to adulthood that flourishing foster child of Jane Austen, the Regency romance. Through dozens of novels, beginning with *The Black Moth* (1921), composed when the author was seventeen to amuse her sickly brother, Heyer deployed wit, invention, research, and an astute sense of human nature (and the way desire shifts and shapes it) to construct confections of plot and character distinguished by both satisfying storytelling and authentic historical flavor. The world she created—of rakish male leads and eccentrically honest women whose confidence in their own agency unsettled convention—would enthrall millions of readers and influence, both directly and by literary osmosis, thousands of romance authors for whom she scouted new territory in popular fiction.

An Infamous Army shows how, as in the novels of Patrick O'Brian and Bernard Cornwell, a gift for narrative entertainment can be enriched by the tang as well as the trappings of history. Beginning in Brussels in the weeks leading up to Waterloo, the story is choreographed—with a willful and flirtatious widow and an adjutant of the Duke of Wellington at the center—as a swirl of affections, scandalous behaviors, and secret assignations. The dance continues with increasing energy until the shadow of Napoleon comes into view; then Heyer deftly turns her hand to an astonishingly vivid and engrossing account of the Battle of Waterloo, which must run its bloody course before heroic events give way again to the unhistoric but ever hopeful beating of private hearts (and a happy ending). A perfect combination of romantic allure and historical absorption, *An Infamous Army* is a marvelous introduction to the joy of reading Georgette Heyer.

What: Novel. *When:* 1937. *Also By: Regency Buck* (1935). *The Spanish Bride* (1940). *The Foundling* (1948). *The Grand Sophy* (1950). *Cotillion* (1953). *Sprig Muslin* (1956). *Frederica* (1965). *Further Reading: Georgette Heyer: A Critical Retrospective*, edited by Mary Fahnestock-Thomas. *Try: A Wild Pursuit* by Eloisa James. *Lord of Scoundrels* by Loretta Chase.

Kon-Tiki

ACROSS THE PACIFIC BY RAFT
Thor Heyerdahl (1914–2002)

A Masterpiece of Modern Exploration

Originally published in Norwegian in 1948 and issued in an English translation by F. H. Lyon two years later, *Kon-Tiki* has earned a place as one of the classic true-life adventure stories of modern times. At last count, Thor Heyerdahl's unforgettable narrative had been translated into sixty-seven languages and had sold more than thirty million copies internationally.

Who could have foreseen such wild success for a book about six men crossing more than four thousand miles of the Pacific on a primitive balsa-log raft, a voyage undertaken to test an obscure theory concerning transoceanic contact between the prehistoric civilizations of South America and Polynesia? Part of the book's immediate and enduring appeal, no doubt, can be traced to its romantic portrayal of scientific investigation: A maverick thinker conceives a theory at odds with accepted wisdom and sets out on a task demanding enormous courage to prove it. Was Polynesia in fact settled by voyagers from the east, as Heyerdahl contended? Heyerdahl himself was always careful to claim no proof for his larger theory in the wake of the *Kon-Tiki* expedition; what his journey across the Pacific sought to establish, rather, was the *possibility* that balsa rafts constructed by Stone Age seafarers could have weathered the trip. In dramatizing that possibility through 101 days of difficult, dangerous, and exhilarating journeying, the author and his colleagues won the hearts and minds of countless readers.

The book itself is a swift and satisfying chronicle. Heyerdahl quickly sketches the genesis of the expedition, then relates the search for balsa logs in the mountains of Ecuador and the actual construction of the raft in Peru (the logs lashed together with three hundred lengths of hemp rope). Once the raft sets out to sea, the reader, no less than the crew, is swept up in the rigor and revelations of the voyage. After more than three months on the open ocean, buffeted by the elements and astonished by the marine life they encounter, the sailors at last sight land—the remote coral atoll Puka-Puka.

Although experts today, relying largely on language studies, still dismiss the wider applications of Heyerdahl's thesis, they cannot dispute the hold *Kon-Tiki* has had—and no doubt will continue to have—on generations of

Thor Heyerdahl and crew member aboard Kon-Tiki

armchair adventurers. To read it is to experience the thrill of endeavor as well as the harsh and serene beauties of the natural world.

What: Adventure. Exploration. *When:* 1948 in Norwegian; first American edition, 1950. *Also By: Aku-Aku: The Secret of Easter Island* (1957). *The Ra Expeditions* (1970). *Fatu-Hiva: Back to Nature* (1974). *Early Man and the Ocean* (1978). *Adaptation:* Heyerdahl's film documenting the voyage was awarded the 1951 Academy Award for Best Documentary Feature. *Try: The Worst Journey*

in the World by Apsley Cherry-Garrard (see page 156). *The Brendan Voyage* by Tim Severin. *Footnote:* Well before he had tasted his own literary success, William Styron, working as a junior editor at McGraw-Hill, failed to recognize the merit of *Kon-Tiki* when the manuscript came across his desk. As he relates with rueful amusement in the closely autobiographical early pages of his 1979 novel *Sophie's Choice*, he dismissed it in these words: "a long, solemn and tedious Pacific voyage best suited, I would think, to some kind of drastic abridgement in a journal like the *National Geographic.*"

The Destruction of Lord Raglan
Christopher Hibbert (1924–2008)

From Bad to Worse in the Crimea

I n the spring of 1854, what the *Times* of London proudly called "the finest army that has ever left these shores" set out from England to wage war against Russia. Within a comparative blink of an eye, that splendid army was in shambles, mired in the horrific campaign now known as the Crimean War and "violently awakened from a dream of past glory into a modern world where heroism was not enough."

As recounted movingly by Christopher Hibbert, the stages of the British army's disintegration in the Crimea make painful, riveting reading. Disease scythes through the ranks before a shot is even fired. A nightmarishly inefficient supply system leaves the troops unsheltered, unfed, and fighting in bloodied rags. Overtaxed medical facilities become mere charnel houses. The aristocratic officer corps bickers endlessly, sulks in luxury, or springs into wrongheaded action. And action, when it comes, is vast slaughter, the carnage crowned by the war's most famous, most futile, most

heartbreaking incident, the Charge of the Light Brigade at the Battle of Balaclava.

At the center of all this chaos presided the British commander in chief, Lord Raglan, who had survived the loss of his right arm at the Battle of Waterloo. Hibbert shapes his spellbinding narrative around the tragic fate of Raglan, who, though vilified by many as an aloof ditherer, is in Hibbert's view a grossly maligned figure. With the shattering story of the charge as its emotional focal point, *The Destruction of Lord Raglan* stands out as one of the most intensely affecting military histories of recent times. It is also one of the most mesmerizingly readable, and helps explain why its author was considered among the finest popular historians of his generation.

What: History. War. *When:* 1961. *Award:* Heinemann Award for Literature, 1962. *Also By: Wolfe at Quebec* (1960). *Agincourt* (1964). *London: The Biography of a City* (1970). *The Story of England* (1992). *Try: The Reason Why* by Cecil Woodham-Smith. *Waterloo: A Near Run Thing* by David Howarth.

The Talented Mr. Ripley
Patricia Highsmith (1921–1995)

A Deadly Game of Double Identity

T he genre of crime fiction—hatched by Edgar Allan Poe and Wilkie Collins in the late

nineteenth century, nurtured by Conan Doyle and Christie, Hammett and Stout, and a host of other writers through the first half of the twentieth—was by the 1950s sustaining itself on a fairly predictable diet of tropes. A reader could begin a book not knowing whodunit, yet be secure in the knowledge that whoever did was bound, by book's end, to get what he deserved.

Then along came Patricia Highsmith. Her addictively readable novels offered neither the cozy comforts of ratiocinative sleuthing nor the satisfying conclusions of justice triumphant. Her protagonists were more likely to be villains than detectives, and, whatever their crime, the author might well let them get away with it. Her elegant and terrifying mysteries are like long walks in the shadowy wood of one's own ineffable anxieties. Her most brilliant creation, the suave, repellent, fascinating, and psychopathic Tom Ripley, made his first appearance in this perversely appealing tale. He would go on to grace, in his dark way, four subsequent novels in the series known to Highsmith aficionados as the "Ripliad."

Ripley's debut is quite simply one of the most engrossing novels you'll ever find in any genre. The twenty-five-year-old Mr. Ripley is an antihero awaiting his cue when fate arrives

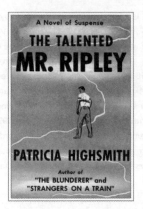

A Novel of Suspense

THE TALENTED MR. RIPLEY

PATRICIA HIGHSMITH

Author of "THE BLUNDERER" and "STRANGERS ON A TRAIN"

in the form of the wealthy father of Ripley's college acquaintance, Dickie Greenleaf. Dickie has gone to Italy and—seduced by beauty of several kinds—won't come home; the elder Greenleaf hires Ripley to persuade him. Introduced into a world of style, wealth, and sophistication, Ripley finds himself right at home in Dickie Greenleaf's European life, and will stop at nothing to stay there.

What: Mystery & Suspense. **When:** 1955. **Also By:** The Ripley sequels are *Ripley Under Ground* (1970), *Ripley's Game* (1974), *The Boy Who Followed Ripley* (1980), and *Ripley Under Water* (1991). Highsmith's first novel, *Strangers on a Train* (1950), caught the attention of Alfred Hitchcock; later works include *A Game for the Living* (1958), *A Suspension of Mercy* (1965), and *The Tremor of Forgery* (1969). *Try: A Judgement in Stone* by Ruth Rendell (see page 666). **Adaptations:** The 1960 French film *Plein Soleil* (starring Alain Delon, released in the United States as *Purple Noon*) and the 1999 Hollywood adaptation (starring Matt Damon, Jude Law, and Gwyneth Paltrow) both depart from Highsmith's novel in ways that make the story far more conventional.

Goodbye, Mr. Chips
James Hilton (1900–1954)

Terms of Endearment

James Hilton's touching story of an English schoolmaster is simple, sweet, and unforgettable. Arthur Chipping—nicknamed Mr. Chips—has taught for most of his long life at a boarding school called Brookfield, ripening, as we learn in gently unfolding flashbacks, from an uncertain and undistinguished youthful instructor into a steady, benevolent presence in the lives of three generations of students. The narrative sketches his early career, his unexpected, happy, and sadly short-lived marriage, his slow but steady—inevitable, it seems—assumption of the role of beloved embodiment of Brookfield's traditions, his retirement at sixty-five, and his quietly triumphant return a

few years later to take command of the institution when its staff is depleted by the demands of World War I. Mildly eccentric, thoroughly kind-hearted, a strict but not insensitive disciplinarian, he is a man of rectitude and decency who seeks to instill those values in his students. By maintaining calm in every storm and inspiring maturity and loyalty in his pupils, Mr. Chips wins the devotion of term after term of students. He has likewise won over generations of readers.

You can read it in the time it would take to drink a pot of tea, yet the warm sentiments in which it steeps you will linger long after you've closed its covers. *Goodbye, Mr. Chips* will certainly make you think fondly of the good teachers you've had, but there is more to the book's sentimental pull. For the aged Chipping's lot—here is the secret of this small tale's disproportionate poignancy—might well resonate with anyone gazing down the long corridor of the past: "Did any emotion really matter when the last trace of it had vanished from human memory; and if that were so, what a crowd of emotions clung to him as to their last home before annihilation! He must be kind to them, must treasure them in his mind before their long sleep."

What: Novel. *When:* 1934. *Also By: Lost Horizon* (1933). *Random Harvest* (1941). *Try: Stoner* by John Williams (see page 856). *To Serve Them All My Days* by R. F. Delderfield. *Adaptations:* There have been two movies and two miniseries. Best is the 1939 version, which won Robert Donat an Oscar for Best Actor. Oddest is the 1969 musical film starring Peter O'Toole and Petula

James Hilton at a 1934 book signing

Clark. *Footnote:* Hilton won a screenwriting Oscar in 1942, for *Mrs. Miniver.*

A Rage in Harlem
Chester Himes (1909–1984)

Noir in Broad Daylight, and All Through the Night

A *Rage in Harlem* is the first in Chester Himes's cycle of eight Harlem detective novels (nine if you count *Plan B*, unfinished at the time of his death), and it introduces the two cops—Grave Digger Jones and Coffin Ed Johnson—whose presence ties the books together, even if the duo plays a somewhat peripheral role here. The action of *A Rage in Harlem* centers on counterfeiting, theft, and confidence games, with all three types of deception applied equally to both love and money by characters hapless and savvy, seductive and scheming, helpless and swindling.

Like all of the books in the series, *A Rage in Harlem* blares an urban tune that is scary, funny, and exhilarating. As Grave Digger and Coffin Ed move center stage in the next book (*The Real Cool Killers*; 1959) and beyond, their pragmatic and knowing tolerance of misbehavior of many stripes is matched by an easy way with violence and intimidation when it suits their needs. Their attempts to recognize and protect innocence in the midst of so much brutality, including their own, is the human puzzle at the core of these books; the two protagonists might have been invented to illustrate the difficulties informing F. Scott Fitzgerald's famous dictum: "The test of a first-rate intelligence is the ability to hold two opposed ideas in the mind at the same time, and still retain the ability to function." For Jones and Johnson, such cognitive dissonance is all in a day's work, and it goes some way toward illuminating Himes's innovative blend of close description and exuberant invention: "Realism and absurdity are so similar in the lives of American blacks one cannot tell the difference," he would write in his autobiography, *The Quality of Hurt* (1972).

Himes's tales of flimflams, drug deals, murders, ribaldry, and black-and-blue city living are remarkable creations, revealing through their fierce hilarity a lot about the racial realities of twentieth-century America. The style Himes deploys—streetwise in its alertness, cinematic in its intense focus and rapid scene-shifting, literary in its linguistic élan—is a wonder, pushing the sensibility of Hammett and other hard-boiled mystery writers into feverish new imaginative territory.

What: Mystery & Suspense. *When:* 1957. (Originally published under the title *For Love of Imabelle*, it has also appeared as *The Five-Cornered Square*.) *Award:* Grand Prix de Littérature Policière, 1958. *Also By: The Crazy Kill* (1959). *Cotton Comes to Harlem* (1965). *Blind Man with a Pistol* (1969). *Further Reading: Chester Himes: A Life* by James Sallis. *Try: The Conjure-Man Dies* by Rudolph Fisher. *Mumbo Jumbo* by Ishmael Reed (see page 663). *LaBrava* by Elmore Leonard (see page 474). *Adaptations:* Filmed in 1991, starring Forest Whitaker and Gregory Hines. Other movies drawn from Himes's Harlem cycle are *Cotton Comes to Harlem* (1970) and *Come Back, Charleston Blue* (1972).

The Mouse and His Child
Russell Hoban (1925–2011)

A Tale Told of a Wind-Up Toy, Full of Sound and Fury, Signifying Everything

Russell Hoban has blessed readers with a stunning variety of imaginative pleasures: From the classic toddler's picture book *Bedtime for Frances* (1960), about a young badger putting off sleep, thereby trying the patience of her exasperated parents, to the brilliant novel *Riddley Walker* (1980), an exploration of a post–nuclear holocaust that comes complete with a reinvention of English. It's a fairly safe bet that the work of few other authors covers the range—in audience, mood, invention, and substance—traversed by his creations.

The Mouse and His Child is a third masterwork standing between the poles of the Frances books and *Riddley Walker*. The mice in question are toys: "a large one and a small one, who stood upright with outstretched arms and joined hands. They wore blue velveteen trousers and patent leather shoes, and they had glass-bead eyes, white thread whiskers, and black rubber tails." When a key is wound in the father's back, he dances in a little circle, swinging his child up off the ground and down again.

They start out in a toy shop, where they live happily with stuffed and clockwork friends in a beautiful dollhouse.

Hoban's haunting, imaginative tale details their dangerous, often desperate exploits after they are sold and venture out into the cruel world and the treacherous, fearful territory of the resourceful Manny Rat. Through suffering, disappointment, inspiration, and tenacity, the mouse and his child defeat their wind-up fate, reaching a happy haven against all odds. Although the book is not without humor, their journey is a tense, dark, and sometimes unsettling passage. Rightly, the author defended his tale against those who suggested that it may be too bleak for young readers: "Its heroes and heroines found out what they were and it wasn't enough, so they found out how to be more." As he concluded, "That's not a bad thought to be going on with."

And there's more to be said to readers both young and old: *The Mouse and His Child* is an eloquent, breathtaking exploration of what it means to be alive on this earth. No kidding. It's as powerful, as heartrending, and as memorable as any novel you'll ever encounter.

What: Children's. When: 1967. Editions: The author's then-wife Lillian Hoban provided the pen-and-ink drawings for the original edition; a sumptuous 2001 reissue was illustrated by David Small. Reading Note: Recommended for sophisticated readers of 12 and up, and for younger ears in a family read-aloud. Also By: For children: Bread and Jam for Frances (1964); A Baby Sister for Frances (1964); Best Friends for Frances

(1969). For adults: Turtle Diary (1975); Pilgermann (1983). A Russell Hoban Omnibus is a rich anthology published in 1999. Try: Mrs. Frisby and the Rats of NIMH by Robert C. O'Brien. The Tale of Despereaux by Kate DiCamillo. Adaptation: The 1977 animated film features the voices of Peter Ustinov, Cloris Leachman, and Sally Kellerman.

Alan Turing: The Enigma
Andrew Hodges (born 1949)

The Father of the Computer Age

The life of Alan Turing offers proof, if proof be needed, that mathematics, as surely as literature, can lead readers into realms of imagination, drama, suspense, glory, and horror. It is a tale of abstract genius, practical heroism, persecution for private acts, and posthumous public honor, and, in Andrew Hodges's informed and illuminating biography, it is very well told.

To detail the extent of Turing's genius requires a considerable grasp of mathematical logic, which Hodges possesses and admirably deploys in the service of the reader, clearly explicating abstruse ideas. Suffice it to say here that Turing's representations of algorithmic and computational ideas in formal and hypothetical constructs, such as "Turing machines" and the "Turing test," are the headlines over an extensive body of work that has won him renown as the father of both modern computer science and the field of artificial intelligence.

During World War II, Turing's work for Britain's Government Code and Cypher School at Bletchley Park was instrumental in breaking Germany's Enigma code and contributed significantly to the ultimate Allied victory over the Nazis. Awarded the Order of the British Empire by King George VI for his secret wartime service, Turing would nonetheless be victimized in the security-obsessed postwar public arena; prosecuted for acts of homosexuality, he agreed to undergo hormone therapy rather than serve a prison sentence. He died of cyanide poisoning in 1954, an apparent suicide. He was not yet forty-two years old.

Hodges explores Turing's thought in depth, placing his subject's mathematical and historical achievements in context; he also tells Turing's personal story with sensitivity and appropriate indignation. Altogether, this is a biography of extraordinary dimensions.

An Enigma encryption machine owned by Alan Turing

What: Biography. Mathematics. When: 1983. Edition: The 2012 edition features a new preface by the author. Also By: One to Nine: The Inner Life of Numbers (2007). Further Reading: The Annotated Turing: A Guided Tour Through Alan Turing's Historic Paper on Computability and the Turing Machine by Charles Petzold. Try: Enigma: The Battle for the Code by Hugh Sebag-Montefiore. Turing's Cathedral by George Dyson. Adaptation: The 2014 film The Imitation Game, starring Benedict Cumberbatch as Turing, is based in large part on Hodges's book. Footnote: Turing received an official apology from British Prime Minister Gordon Brown in September 2009 and, four years later, a formal pardon from Queen Elizabeth II.

Mr. Blandings Builds His Dream House
Eric Hodgins (1899–1971)

A Renovation Comedy

"I must say," said Mrs. Blandings... "I must say it all seems rather terribly ramshackle."

The real-estate man smiled. "You've got to be able to visualize," he said.

Anyone possessed by the fantasy of finding the perfect house in the country, or by the urge to restore a somewhat-less-than-perfect one, or by the inspiration to construct a dream dwelling from scratch, would do well to read this savagely funny novel as a cautionary fable before going any further. First published in 1946, this tale of the ill-fated house hunters Mr. and Mrs. J. H. Blandings is perfectly apt today (all that's needed is a sizable multiplier to adjust the costs for inflation).

Beginning with their search for their "ideal" house outside the city, the story follows the couple's fortune on its long slide downhill. First, they're swindled into buying an overpriced old farmhouse, only to find they must tear it down. That's the good news; building its replacement is a purgatory of annoyances, surprises, and cost overruns so detailed, it makes the cramped apartment they're abandoning look like paradise. Eric Hodgins's chronicle of the couple's passage from domestic innocence to architectural experience is a sardonic pleasure. Those of you who have seen the delightful and wildly popular movie starring Cary Grant and Myrna Loy will be glad to know that the book is even more gleefully sarcastic. And what comic novel wouldn't be enhanced by imagining those two as the tale's protagonists? The story is wittily complemented by the illustrations of William Steig.

What: Novel. Humor. *When:* 1946. *Also By: Blandings' Way* (1950). *Episode: Report on the Accident Inside My Skull* (1964). *Try: The Egg and I* by Betty MacDonald. *The Walls Around Us* by David Owen. *Adaptations:* The Grant/Loy film dates from 1948. A 2007 remake, under the title *Are We Done Yet?*, stars Ice Cube.

Gödel, Escher, Bach
AN ETERNAL GOLDEN BRAID
Douglas R. Hofstadter (born 1945)

The Exhilarating Intellectual Pursuit of the Mind's I

"I still remember," wrote George Johnson in *Scientific American* more than a quarter century after the publication of this book, "standing in the aisle of a bookstore in Washington, D.C., where I had just finished graduate school, devouring the pages. *GEB*, as the author calls it, is not so much a 'read' as an experience, a total immersion into Hofstadter's mind. It is a great place to be."

Johnson's pleasure in *Gödel, Escher, Bach* is one that many readers have been surprised to share—surprised because *GEB* represents nearly eight hundred pages of elaborate argument, replete with philosophical dialogues, diagrams and illustrations, parts of musical scores, logic formulas, and other diversions, all speculating on the theme of how consciousness emerges from matter. The range of "motley topics" (the phrase is the author's) the book encompasses is mind-boggling, and covers categories mathematical, scientific, musical, artistic, philosophical, epistemological, and cognitive: "fugues and canons, logic and truth, geometry, recursion, syntactic structures, the nature of meaning, Zen Buddhism, paradoxes, brain and mind, . . . ant colonies, . . . translations, computers and their languages, DNA, proteins, the genetic code, artificial intelligence, creativity, consciousness and free will." Together these ideas illuminate Hofstadter's core focus on formal patterns in

Gödel, passes through the infinite visual loops of M. C. Escher's drawings, and stops to listen to the baroque sound machines of J. S. Bach—but those are only three touch points in what one reviewer has called "an entire humanistic education between the covers of a single book." Best of all, for all its intricacy and erudition, *GEB* is compelling, entertaining, and vital reading—a joyful book of boundless inspiration.

What: Philosophy. Science. Mathematics. Language. *When:* 1979. *Edition:* The 20th-Anniversary Edition has an excellent new preface by the author. *Awards:* Pulitzer Prize for General Nonfiction and National Book Award for Science, 1980. *Reading Note:* Just dive in, and keep swimming till you meet the current. *Also By: The Mind's I: Fantasies and Reflections on Self and Soul* (with Daniel C. Dennett; 1981). *Metamagical Themas: Questing for the Essence of Mind and Pattern* (1985). *Le Ton Beau de Marot: In Praise of the Music of Language* (1997). *Eugene Onegin: A Novel in Verse* (a translation of Pushkin's masterpiece; 1999, see page 648). *Try:* The novels of Richard Powers, particularly *Galatea 2.2* and *The Gold Bug Variations.*

nature and in art that allow meaningless symbols to "acquire meaning despite themselves." In just such patterns Hofstadter believes we can discover "how it is that animate beings can come out of inanimate matter."

His search for nothing less than the roots of self and soul begins with the incompleteness theorem of mathematical logician Kurt

The Private Memoirs and Confessions of a Justified Sinner
James Hogg (1770–1835)

Did the Devil Make Him Do It?

Just what is a "justified" sinner? According to the Calvinist doctrine of "unconditional election," God chooses certain people to be saved—and because of their election, their actions are justified as the will of God. "To think that a justified person can do no wrong," says the mother of Robert Wringhim, the justified sinner of James Hogg's novel. "Who would not envy the liberty wherewith we are made free?"

Imagine the narrative possibilities the idea affords. Hogg, a Scottish poet famous in his lifetime as the Ettrick Shepherd, certainly did. His strange and compelling 1824 book, combining elements of mystery thriller and Gothic horror story, psychological study and religious allegory, is a masterpiece of Scottish literature. In its satire of faith-based extremism and its

playful narrative games, his book is simultaneously scary and comic; its portrayal of the corrupting influence of fanaticism on moral feeling has surprising relevance for our own day and age.

The book begins with an account, purportedly written a century after the events it describes, of the circumstances leading up to Wringhim's murder of his half brother, George Colwan. This is followed by Wringhim's own memoir, related at a heightened pitch, with special attention to the wiles of a certain Gil-Martin, whose influence tempts Robert toward his crime. Is Gil-Martin real or imaginary, an alter ego or the devil incarnate? That's part of the drama of good and evil, doubt and conviction that Hogg enfolds in his mysterious tale. The twin narration—to say nothing of the postscript, in which Hogg himself appears as a character rather than the author of the book we are reading—gives the whole an uncertainty that keeps the reader tantalized and off balance, and is wholly appropriate to Hogg's themes of spiritual anxiety and moral quandary. The result is a gripping, surprising, and singular reading experience.

What: Novel. When: 1824. Also By: A Shepherd's Delight: A James Hogg Anthology (1985). Further Reading: Electric Shepherd: A Likeness of James Hogg by Karl Miller. Try: The Strange Case of Dr. Jekyll and Mr. Hyde by Robert Louis Stevenson (see page 759). An American Dream by Norman Mailer.

One Hundred Views of Mount Fuji
Katsushika Hokusai (1760–1849)

Old Man Mad About Drawing

An exercise in contemplative engagement, *One Hundred Views of Mount Fuji* is a picture book of profound eloquence, earning a perhaps unexpected place amid the text-drenched volumes that surround it here. Most famous as the creator of the image *Under the Wave off Kanagawa*, also known as *The Great Wave*, Katsushika Hokusai lived a long life fueled with protean energy, opportunistic alertness, and boundless artistry. These qualities were matched by a fund of eccentricity he drew upon to promote his talent across a career that spanned seven productive decades, engendering tens of thousands of sketches, paintings, and woodblock prints, including contributions to illustrated board games, instruction manuals, and cutout dioramas. His capacity for constant reinvention is evidenced by the fact that he relocated often—more than ninety times by most accounts—and changed his name with regularity.

When he began *One Hundred Views of Mount Fuji* in 1832, at the age of seventy-three, he had taken to signing his works "Old Man Mad About Drawing." Conceived as a book, and in fact issued in three volumes in 1834 and 1835, *One Hundred Views* should not be confused with the earlier (1826–33) monumental series of colored woodblock prints, *Thirty-Six Views of Mount Fuji*, which includes *The Great Wave* and is generally considered Hokusai's masterpiece. In contrast, the later work is executed entirely in black and gray, with evocative shading providing visual nuance and subtly expressive moods. Its images celebrate the holy mountain in radically various perspectives, aspects, and

guises: We see it behind hanging strips of cloth outside a dyer's premises, beyond an umbrella set out to dry in a yard, through the close stems of swaying bamboo. Hokusai's study of Fuji's enduring and implacable presence through the ephemeral activity of everyday living is a form of prayer, a book-bound pilgrimage across the expanses of time, space, and human busyness that the venerated volcano watches over and somehow blesses. The book is a strange, mysterious story as well; turning the pages from one image to the next, we are treated to a visionary, detailed, and often witty visual monologue on life, death, man, and nature by a wise, irreverent old genius whose extraordinary attention is a source of both inspiration and solace.

What: Art. **When:** 1834–35. **Edition:** The 1988 edition prepared by Henry D. Smith and published by George Braziller is recommended for its commentary and its printing, but may be hard to find; keep looking.

Also By: Hokusai's Mount Fuji: The Complete Views in Color by Jocelyn Bouquillard. *Further Reading: Hokusai* by Gian Carlo Calza. *Try: Hiroshige: One Hundred Famous Views of Edo* by Melanie Trede. *Adaptation:* Roger Zelazny's Hugo Award–winning story "24 Views of Mount Fuji, by Hokusai" is an intriguing literary footnote to the artist's work.

"From the age of six I had a mania for drawing the shapes of things. When I was fifty I had published a universe of designs. But all I have done before the age of seventy is not worth bothering with. . . . When I am eighty you will see real progress. . . . At a hundred I shall be a marvelous artist."
—*From Hokusai's postscript to* One Hundred Views of Mount Fuji

■ For Oliver Wendell Holmes Jr. and Harold J. Laski's *Holmes-Laski Letters,* see page 504.

Footsteps
ADVENTURES OF A ROMANTIC BIOGRAPHER
Richard Holmes (born 1945)

On the Trail of His Own and Others' Lives

Richard Holmes is an acclaimed biographer with a special affinity for the writers and thinkers of the Romantic era. His peerless, award-winning volumes on Percy Bysshe Shelley and Samuel Taylor Coleridge combine scholarly acumen with imaginative insight in a way that makes for riveting as well as informative reading. Holmes seems to have a natural respect for a reader's curiosity, and his narrative gifts engage it every step of the way; it doesn't hurt that his chosen subjects weren't always well behaved, leading lives of notorious and fascinating variety.

Footsteps is a different sort of work, a "mongrel book," in the author's characterization, "being part pure-bred biography, part travel, part autobiography, together with a bad dash of Baskerville Hound." The whole is more than the sum of its parts, and entirely delightful. It begins with footsteps that are quite real, as the eighteen-year-old Holmes tracks Robert Louis Stevenson's travels with a donkey through the Cévennes, and then turn more scholarly as the budding biographer becomes absorbed in the lives of Mary Wollstonecraft, William Wordsworth, Percy Bysshe Shelley, and Gérard de Nerval while living in Paris and Italy. His researches into Romanticism resonate with his own experiences in the turmoil of the late 1960s—the countercultural rhetoric of Paris in 1968 echoing down streets still haunted by earlier revolutionary fevers—and his efforts to master rendering the lives of others mirror his struggle to shape a life of his own. The result is a tale that enlivens learning with adventure and reveals how scholarly exertions can lead to emotional as well as intellectual truths. It would be too much to claim that the personality of the author is a match for the charisma of his subjects, yet it is Holmes's own developing character—and his preternatural gift for weaving an engrossing tale from threads of information and intuition—that make this account of the making of a biographer an unforgettable literary excursion.

What: Biography. Memoir. Travel. When: 1985. Also By: Shelley: The Pursuit (1974). Coleridge: Early Visions (1989). Dr. Johnson and Mr. Savage (1993). Coleridge:

Darker Reflections (1999). The Age of Wonder: How the Romantic Generation Discovered the Beauty and Terror of Science (2008). Further Reading: Travels with a Donkey in the Cévennes by Robert Louis Stevenson. Try: A Second Identity and Paris and Elsewhere by Richard Cobb.

■ For Richard Holmes's *Dr. Johnson and Mr. Savage*, see page 418.

HOMER
(ca. 800 BC)

A s a stock through slow simmering of vegetables, bones, and meat is reduced to the essence of its constituent flavors to become both a rich source of nourishment and a base for all manner of culinary elaboration, so Homer's ancient poems captured human experience so powerfully that they have not only stood on their own, but, through repeated readings across the generations, have also come to form the foundation of nearly all the literature that has been imagined in the West. Three thousand years after their composition, *The Iliad* and *The Odyssey* continue to pass on the most concentrated lessons of human inheritance.

Although different in the nature of their telling and the substance of their tales, each epic emanates from the body of history and legend known as the Trojan War, a conflict that, whatever the exact dimensions of its factual reality, informed Greek culture in seminal ways, engendering vibrant traditions of mythological and literary lore. Most scholarship suggests that invading Greek forces did indeed lay siege to Troy, a city in what is now northwest Turkey, sometime in the thirteenth or twelfth century BC, culminating in its destruction after ten years of fighting. As the most familiar version of the saga has it, the war was provoked when Paris, son of Priam, the Trojan king, abducted Helen, the wife of Menelaus, king of Sparta. The Greeks amassed an army to pursue her, under the generalship of Agamemnon, the Mycenaen king (thus did the beautiful Helen earn immortality as "the face that launched a thousand ships"). Since Troy, as revealed by the archaeological discoveries of

Heinrich Schliemann and others, had strategic prominence over the trade routes that passed through the Dardanelles, realpolitik offers a less romantic explanation of the events Homer would mine in his unforgettable poems.

But just who was the poet who proved equal to such a grand legacy? What do we know about him? (If, indeed, Homer was a he at all: The writer Samuel Butler, best known for his novel *The Way of All Flesh* [see page 116], advanced the idea that the bard was a woman in *The Authoress of the Odyssey*, published in 1897.) Both *The Odyssey* and *The Iliad* come down to us from texts that can be traced to Athens in the sixth century BC, and expert consensus dates their composition two or three hundred years earlier. From antiquity, Homer was believed to be a blind bard who, it is generally accepted today, selected, arranged, polished, and set down in writing the fruits of an enduring oral tradition.

Even if one concedes a collective and incremental compositional history for the poems,

HOMERI
OPERUM
OMNIUM
quæ exstant
TOMUS PRIOR
five
ILIAS
GRAECE ET LATINE.
Juxta Editionem emendatiſſimam
& accuratiſſimam
SAMUELIS CLARKE.

96457

AMSTELAEDAMI,
Apud J. WETSTENIUM.
MDCCXLIII.

Frontispiece and cover of 1743 edition of The Iliad

their structural unity and compelling pulse suggest the application of the powers and attentions of a single poet at some point in the evolution of the works. For beyond doubt, the reader senses in the artistry of the Homeric lines—from the poetic magic of the famous similes of *The Iliad* to the "And-what-happened-next?" enchantments of the stories within stories that propel the narrative of *The Odyssey*—the presence of a mind articulating experience by catching it in a web of carefully woven words. Ancient, at times austere, the poet of *The Iliad* and *The Odyssey* speaks in a human voice not heard in Gilgamesh's epic (see page 255) or in the first books of the Bible (see page 76). Of all the wonders found in Homer, then, this may be the most wondrous of all: the invention of authorship.

The Iliad
An Unmatched Epic of Gods, Heroes, and Mortal Truths

The Iliad is a narrative of divine stratagems and military exploits, of fierce courage and heroic endeavor—a tale, clearly, of epic imagination. Yet the sense of pageantry the poem evokes obscures what may be its most telling characteristic: the peculiar angle from which Homer chooses to view antiquity's most fabled war, focusing on only a few weeks in a decade-long struggle. Even though the events the poem narrates transpire in the conflict's final year, they encompass neither the war's climax nor the ultimate Greek victory (readers of epics would have to wait for Virgil's *Aeneid* to hear the story of the horse that tricked Troy into defeat).

As *The Iliad* begins, ten years of inconclusive warfare have clouded the landscape with an air of futility, and men of action are left to brood upon their fates. Foremost among them is Achilles, most famous of the Greek warriors, who has nursed a grievance against his general, Agamemnon, into petulant rage, refusing to take up arms. The quarrel of the two great men over a captive woman brings out the worst in each of them: As Achilles sulks in his tent, the commander of the Greek forces parades about, revealing himself to be a jealous bully, drunk on his own arrogance. Their behavior belongs not to heroes, but to pampered celebrities.

Homer rises above them both, imbuing his simple plot with a visceral yet panoramic intelligence that measures brutal hand-to-hand duels and the machinations of divinities with the same poetic equanimity. What happens? The Greeks, lacking their most effective weapon and distracted by Achilles's fit of temper, suffer reverses, provoking Patroclus, the sulking hero's dearest companion, to don his friend's fearsome armor and enter the fray in hopes of striking terror into the Trojan ranks. When Achilles learns that Patroclus has been killed by Hector, son of King Priam and Troy's noble champion, his sorrow is inconsolable; at last he returns to the field to avenge his friend. With savage resolve, he vanquishes Hector and drags the slain man's body three times around the walls of Troy, refusing to surrender the corpse to Hector's family.

Throughout, *The Iliad* is filled with astonishing passages of martial valor (see the feats of the Greek warrior Great Ajax, and his engagements with Hector, in books 7, 14, and 15), divine invention (the fashioning of Achilles's shield by Hephaestus in book 18), and magical inspiration (the scene, in book 19, in which Achilles's horse foresees his destiny), but what are most stunning in the end are the scenes that unfold on a human scale. Unforgettable among these are Hector's farewell to his wife and child, and the communion of grief shared by Priam and Achilles in the epic's final pages, when the aged king surreptitiously enters the Greek encampment to beg for the return of Hector's remains so that he may give his son the dignity of a proper burial.

The mercy that suffuses the poem's conclusion is hard-won. All the might expended in its earlier episodes—the insensate force that, as Simone Weil has noted in a brilliant essay on *The Iliad*, turns human beings into things—has been rendered from the spirits of these proud and powerful men. What is left is the suffering that is the only real spoil of war, the fateful wound of our fragile, common humanity.

What: Poetry. Antiquity. War. *When:* ca. 800 BC. *Editions:* There have been many superb translations into English. Richmond Lattimore's 1951 version does especial justice to the sonorous measures of the original Greek, whereas the more recent interpretation by Robert Fagles (1990) is more supple and compellingly readable. Contemporary readers will be well served by either one, although the Fagles includes a valuable essay and notes by Bernard Knox. *Further Reading: War and the Iliad* by Simone Weil and Rachel Bespaloff. *The War That Killed Achilles* by Caroline Alexander. Readers looking for insight into the transmission of oral narrative poetry should turn to Albert Lord's fascinating study, *The Singer of Tales*, which illuminates what may well have been Homer's method through an examination of twentieth-century Yugoslav practitioners of the ancient art. *Try: The Oresteia* by Aeschylus (see page 9). *The Aeneid* by Virgil (see page 823). *Ransom* by David Malouf. *Adaptation:* Derek Jacobi's audiobook of the Fagles translation is magnificent. *Footnote:* The poem takes its name from the Greek word for Troy, *Ilion*.

The Odyssey
An Unsurpassed Itinerary of Invention and Adventure

What can one say about a story that has been entertaining, enchanting, and educating the human race from the very border of recorded history until today? Homer's epic poem of the wandering and homecoming of Odysseus (aka Ulysses) is a grand adventure, where fact, myth, gods, and people meet, settle, then set off again, transformed by one another. It is one of the very few books, classic or not, that no one should miss and that every reader can enjoy.

If *The Iliad*, like its sturdy hero, is something of a hedgehog, *The Odyssey*, like its wily and resourceful protagonist, is a fox. ("The fox knows many things, but the hedgehog knows one big thing," wrote the ancient poet Archilochus, as famously quoted by the philosopher Isaiah Berlin.) *The Iliad* is a constellation of brilliant tableaux—capturing feats and fears, angers and griefs—while *The Odyssey* is a voyage of narration; where the former honors intensity, the latter celebrates duration—it is a tale that unfolds not moment by moment but backward and forward across the years, every episode connecting far-flung dots of present and past, youth and age, foreign lands and native ground. Because it culminates in its hero's triumphant homecoming, *The Odyssey* reveals how the passage of time accrues personal meaning, making the arc of a life more significant than the points that plot its individual days.

The tale begins two decades after Odysseus left his kingdom in Ithaca to join the Greek forces in their assault on Troy. In his absence, his son, Telemachus, just one month old at the time of Odysseus's departure, has grown to manhood, and is restless for his father's return: It has been ten years since the end of the Trojan War, and still Odysseus has not come home. His faithful wife, Penelope, is beset by suitors who think the absent hero dead; they have overrun the household, and Penelope has promised to marry one upon completion of a burial shroud she is weaving for Odysseus's aged father, Laertes. As cunning as her husband, Penelope each night unweaves what she has woven by day, forestalling an unhappy fate.

Encouraged by the goddess Athena (disguised divinities propel the action throughout with heavenly impulsiveness and ingenuity), Telemachus sets out in search of news of Odysseus. He sails to visit Nestor, his father's former comrade in arms, and the court at Sparta of Menelaus and Helen, now reconciled after Troy's defeat, where he learns of Odysseus's captivity on the island of the sea nymph Calypso. The scene then shifts, at the beginning of the fifth of the poem's twenty-four books, to Mount Olympus, where Zeus orders Calypso to set Odysseus free. Homer's hero flees by raft to the land of the Phaeacians, where he repays the hospitality of King Alcinous and his daughter, Nausicaa, by relating what has

Athena telling Penelope of the return of Telemachus

befallen him on his seemingly endless quest for home. His account of his exploits is a catalog of fabulous and unforgettable adventures, including landing on the narcotic island of the Lotus-Eaters; victorious battle with the Cyclops; encounters with the man-eating Laestrygonians and the enchantress Circe, who turned men to swine; a visit to the land of the dead; hearing but not succumbing to the seductive song of the Sirens (Odysseus has his crew plug their ears with wax and tie him to the mast); navigating past the twin sea monsters of Scylla and Charybdis; and more. If there is a genetic code for storytelling, it surely can be mapped in Odysseus's wanderings.

Narrative itself is the currency of the book, and a reader's encounter with *The Odyssey* crackles with the energy of "What happens next?" Once Odysseus departs Phaeacia and he and Telemachus return to Ithaca, events accelerate through scenes of recognition, revenge, and reconciliation that are thrilling, poignant, and suffused with the kind of transporting satisfaction that can make stories more reliable than life, but only when they are inspired by the rarest blessing of the Muses.

What: Poetry. Adventure. *When:* ca. 800 BC. *Editions:* As with *The Iliad*, there are many excellent translations. Lattimore, Fagles, and Allen Mandelbaum have superb versions, but especially recommendable is the 2017 translation by Emily Wilson, which is both startling in its freshness and eminently readable. *Further Reading: The World of Odysseus* by M. I. Finley. *Homeric Moments* by Eva Brann. *Try: Omeros* by Derek Walcott. *The Penelopeia* by Jane Rawlings. *The Lost Books of the Odyssey* by Zachary Mason. *Adaptation:* The audiobook performance of the Fagles translation, by Ian McKellan, makes splendid listening.

The Poetry of Gerard Manley Hopkins
Gerard Manley Hopkins (1844–1889)

The "Inscape" Artist

The music of Hopkins's poetry is like no other: It has a wild beauty all the more impetuous for the intricate lacings of rhyme and rhythm that constrain it. Very little of this peculiar Victorian's verse was published, or even read, in his lifetime, for his literary vocation was secondary to a religious one. After his conversion to Catholicism at the age of twenty-two, he entered the Society of Jesus; he would eventually be ordained a Jesuit priest. "The world is charged with the grandeur of God," begins a beloved Hopkins sonnet, and in his best work his two callings come together to create a sense that the *word* as well as the world is charged with divine majesty. His evocation—in poems such as "God's Grandeur," "Pied Beauty," and "The Windhover"—of the holy spirit that animated his belief are astonishing flights of language and prosody; the very sound of his daring lines describes a breathtaking leap of faith across the chasm of silence all prayer must cross.

For Hopkins, sanctity was invested in individuation; his intensely mystical invocations of natural phenomena and spiritual intuitions are thus attached to particularities of color and movement.

Glory be to God for dappled things—
  For skies of couple-colour as a brinded cow;
    For rose-moles all in stipple upon trout that swim;
Fresh-firecoal chestnut-falls; finches' wings;
  Landscape plotted and pieced—fold, fallow, and plough;
    And all trades, their gear and tackle and trim.

His songs of soulful searching and exuberant praise are vivid with design and pattern. They generate what he memorably calls an "inscape," a spiritual terrain in which he can mine the melody and meaning he finds infused in the realm of the senses. The poetry that he unearths from this inner landscape will enchant any reader willing to be carried away by its ravishing onslaught of passionate belief and poetic ingenuity.

What: Poetry. *When:* 1918. *Edition: The Major Works*, in the Oxford World Classics series, contains all Hopkins's poetry and a rich collection of his prose. *Reading Note:* Read Hopkins aloud, and let the sound lead the sense. *Also By:* Hopkins's prose, collected in various volumes of journals and letters, also makes absorbing reading. *Further Reading: Gerard Manley Hopkins: A Life* by Paul Mariani. *Exiles: A Novel* by Ron Hansen. *Try:* The poetry of Hart Crane and Robert Bridges.

The Odes of Horace
Horace (65 BC–8 BC)

The Birth of Poetry as We Know It

If reading the literature of antiquity teaches us one thing, it is that life's big problems—how to reconcile oneself to the vagaries of love and fortune, or to the certainties of time; how to acknowledge mortality yet step lightly and with purpose in its shadow; how to express and conduct oneself; how to weigh and weather the human and political follies that surround us—don't change all that much.

Two thousand years ago the Roman poet Horace had wisdom to dispense on each of these themes, and his sophisticated, elegant poems remain well worth pondering today. In fact, his verses have shaped some of our most enduring and useful answers to such perpetual concerns: "*Carpe diem, quam minimum credula postero*" ("Seize the day, have no faith in the future"), he famously exhorts, and "*Aequam memento retus in arduis / Servare mentem*" ("Remember to face adversities with an even temper"). Equanimity is the poet's abiding theme, and he extols the pursuit of a golden mean—a measured life free from extravagance and the anxious futility of worldly ambition.

Although his artistry is amply evident in his satires and verse epistles, his ironic intelligence and knowing embrace of passing pleasures are on their best display in his four books of odes. In these short poems, whose subjects are drawn from the poet's reflections on the news of the day and his ordinary encounters, Horace brings his philosophical bent to bear on the older Greek models his poetic forms imitate and reinvent. In their combination of conversational address, verbal and aural intricacy, and profound thoughtfulness, the Horatian *Odes* represent the archetypal inspiration from which our tradition of lyric poetry descends. Even in translation, the power of their influence and the pleasure of their eloquence are readily apparent.

What: Poetry. Antiquity. *When:* The first three books of odes were published in 23 BC, the fourth about ten years later. *Editions:* There is a rich tradition of Horace translation in English, beginning with John Dryden in the seventeenth century. James Michie's complete modern translation is superb (the beautifully designed original 1963 Orion edition is worth seeking out). J. D. McClatchy's superlative 2002 anthology of new translations by thirty-five contemporary poets testifies to Horace's enduring relevance. *Also By: Satires* (35 BC–30 BC). *Epistles* (20 BC–14 BC). *The Art of Poetry* (18 BC). *Further Reading: Poets in a Landscape* by Gilbert Highet. *Try:* Poems of *Sappho* (see page 697). Richard Wilbur's *Collected Poems, 1943–2004* (see page 853).

Great River

THE RIO GRANDE IN NORTH AMERICAN HISTORY
Paul Horgan (1903–1995)

The Epic History of a River and the Four Civilizations It Watered

Paul Horgan's monumental study of the Rio Grande and its many confluences—natural and elemental, human and societal, religious and political, national and military—is an epic distinguished by the author's scholarly rigor and literary style. A wealth of research and detail is marshaled across nearly a thousand pages, but it is ordered with such formal elegance, and imparted in sentences and paragraphs shaped by such a musical measuring of language, that reading Horgan's massive tome is spellbinding in an expansive, leisurely way: It's as if we are being carried along on the tide of a capacious, vibrant, and event-filled historical symphony.

Horgan's appreciation of the overlapping cultures (Native American, Spanish, Mexican, and Anglo-American) and the historical sovereignties (Spain, Mexico, Texas, and the United States) the river has nourished is animated by his attention to human character in action. "While respecting the responsibilities of scholarship," he writes, "I took every opportunity, when the factual record supported me, to stage

a scene." As a result, in addition to being given thorough investigations of the river's ancient geological and geographical character and rich anthropological insights into customs from Pueblo weaving to preparations for Catholic

Mass on the frontier, the reader is treated to an endless stream of vividly drawn incidents. These involve farmers and ranchers, missionaries and generals, statesmen and rebels, and they range in time from primeval epochs through the Spanish conquest and the war with Texas to the era of Woodrow Wilson.

Great River is an extraordinary accomplishment, spanning centuries with intelligence, grace, and, quite often, real beauty in its evocation of the grandeur of the physical and imaginative landscapes it traverses. Its narrative rewards either close concentration or browsing with instruction and delight.

What: History. *When:* 1954. *Edition:* The original hardcover edition, published in two volumes and still readily available secondhand, presents the text more spaciously than the single-volume paperback, affording much more pleasant reading. *Awards:* Pulitzer Prize for History and Bancroft Prize, 1955. *Also By:* Nonfiction: *Lamy of Santa Fe: His Life and Times* (1975). Fiction: *The Fault of Angels* (1933); *A Distant Trumpet* (1960); *The Peach Stone: Stories from Four Decades* (1967). *Try: The Year of Decision 1846* by Bernard DeVoto. *Beyond the Hundredth Meridian: John Wesley Powell and the Second Opening of the West* by Wallace Stegner.

■ For Nick Hornby's *Ten Years in the Tub*, see page 210.

Rogue Male
Geoffrey Household (1900–1988)

The Essential Thriller

*R*ogue Male is a classic of elemental suspense, the story of a man on the run with nothing to rely on but his own courage, endurance, and ingenuity. Through his voice, we chart the coordinates of his predicament: Captured with his hunting rifle trained on a Central European dictator, our hero has been tortured and left for dead by the forces of the vicious leader. Escaping by the skin of his teeth, he nurses himself back to health as he wends his wary way across the continent and back to his native England, where he finds no safety; the government can offer no protection, and the dictator's henchmen are in relentless pursuit. Severed from society, the hunted man heads for the countryside to plot survival in the wild. Even the sanctuary he finds proves perilous.

Household's first-person narrative is lean and headlong, offering just enough detail to keep the plot spinning in a wide but ever-tightening circle. Was our hero really trying to assassinate a head of state? Was it Hitler he had in his rifle's sight when he was captured? What intrigue was he engaged in before his ill-fated adventure? Despite our uncertainty about the exact nature of his activities, we are nonetheless natural allies of this gentleman-turned-prey, and instinctive enemies of the shadowy international evil embodied by his pursuers. The unnamed protagonist's terror and alertness provide all we know of his identity, and they are, marvelously, a personality in full. His apprehensiveness is screwed so tight that every aspect of town or country observed in his stealthy transit seems to be throbbing with threatening attention to his presence. Stripped of any connection that would provide an identity, he is thrown upon the severe mercy of the natural world, in which he is nothing more or less than a creature fiercely focused on keeping himself alive.

Fleet and engrossing, *Rogue Male* is a seminal thriller, a precursor to the novels of Frederick Forsyth, Ken Follett, and countless others. It retains its page-turning excitement today.

What: Mystery & Suspense. *When:* 1939. *Also By:* *Rogue Justice* (1982), a sequel of sorts published four decades later, lacks the snap and eerie mystery of the original. Household wrote two other books nearly as good as *Rogue Male*: *Watcher in the Shadows* (1960) and *Dance of the Dwarfs* (1968). Other novels: *Fellow Passenger* (1955) and *The Three Sentinels* (1972). *Try:* *The Thirty-Nine Steps* by John Buchan (see page 105). *The Day of the Jackal* by Frederick Forsyth (see page 292). *Adaptation:* Filmed as *Man Hunt* in 1941, directed by Fritz Lang and starring Walter Pidgeon.

We Die Alone
David Howarth (1912–1991)

A Thrilling Adventure Chronicle of World War II

An epic tale of survival against staggering odds, *We Die Alone* is one of the most astonishing and enthralling true adventure stories ever written. It is set in Nazi-occupied Norway in March 1943, and begins with a four-man commando raid that goes spectacularly wrong and leaves all but one of the expatriate Norwegian resistance fighters dead or captured. The lone survivor is twenty-six-year-old Jan Baalsrud, and though he too has been seriously wounded, he manages to escape the ambush and takes off on an incredible trek into the wilds of the Lyngen Alps. The Nazis pursue him relentlessly; he suffers frostbite, snow-blindness, and a terrible fall in an avalanche. Then, delirious and near death, he finally chances on a cabin where the first of a series of remarkably brave and clever men and women come to his aid. These "ordinary heroes" will eventually get the crippled Baalsrud across the Swedish border to safety and freedom. The amazing story of how they do it—and of how Baalsrud survives the doing—will leave readers agog at the strength and courage the human spirit can summon when pushed to the limits of hope and endurance. Fittingly, David Howarth's 1955 narrative is as singular as its modest hero—who, it should be noted, in later life always downplayed his own part in the story of his escape by asserting that "All I did was run away."

What: Adventure. War. *When:* 1955. *Edition:* The Lyons Press paperback edition of *We Die Alone* features an introduction by historian Stephen E. Ambrose. *Also By:* *Waterloo: Day of Battle* (1968). *Trafalgar: The Nelson Touch* (1969). *Pursued by a Bear: An Autobiography* (1986). *Try: The Long Walk* by Slavomir Rawicz (see page 662). *The Walls Came Tumbling Down* by Henriette Roosenburg (see page 673).

World of Our Fathers
THE JOURNEY OF THE EAST EUROPEAN JEWS TO AMERICA AND THE LIFE THEY FOUND AND MADE
Irving Howe (1920–1993)

From Eastern Europe to the Lower East Side

From the outset, Irving Howe stakes large claims for the story he will tell: "The year 1881 marks a turning point in the history of the Jews as decisive as that of 70 AD, when Titus's legions burned the Temple at Jerusalem, or 1492, when Ferdinand and Isabella decreed the expulsion from Spain." That's because the assassination of Czar Alexander II on May 1, 1881, led to government-inspired attacks on Jews throughout Russia; those attacks in turn led the Jews, whose hopes had been encouraged by Alexander's "modest liberalism," to ask what turned out to be a momentous question: Should they "continue to regard themselves as

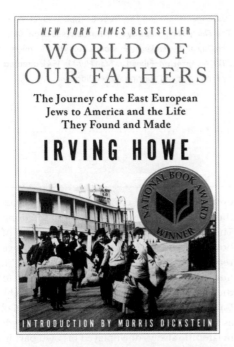

NEW YORK TIMES BESTSELLER

WORLD OF OUR FATHERS

The Journey of the East European Jews to America and the Life They Found and Made

IRVING HOWE

NATIONAL BOOK AWARD WINNER

INTRODUCTION BY MORRIS DICKSTEIN

their first steps out of the Old World, through the ordeal of an Atlantic crossing in steerage, to arrival at Ellis Island and entrance into the teeming life of the Lower East Side of Manhattan. It then chronicles in rich detail the immigrant generation's attempt to maintain its Yiddish culture while forging a uniquely Jewish-American way in the new society. Howe's sweeping narrative ranges widely, evoking through both anecdote and analysis the many vivid realms of immigrant life—from Yiddish literature and theater to socialist politics, from settlement houses to synagogues, sweatshops to Hebrew schools. His enormous erudition and keen intelligence are matched throughout by an obvious affection for the aspirations and experiences that shaped the culture that had nourished him, and to which his book is such an invaluable tribute.

What: History. *When:* 1976. *Award:* National Book Award for History, 1977. *Also By: Politics and the Novel* (1957). *The Critical Point* (1973). *A Margin of Hope: An Intellectual Autobiography* (1982). *Socialism and America* (1985). *A Critic's Notebook* (1994). *Further Reading: A Living Lens: Photographs of Jewish Life from the Pages of the "Forward"* edited by Alana Newhouse. *Try: Call It Sleep* by Henry Roth (see page 675). *The Rise of David Levinsky* by Abraham Cahan. *At the Edge of a Dream* by Lawrence J. Epstein. *Footnote:* Irving Howe was one of the first recipients of a MacArthur Foundation "genius" award.

permanent residents of the Russian empire or should they seriously consider the possibility of a new exodus?" Many chose the latter course, and over the next four decades some two million Eastern European Jews fled their homelands and came to America, a large proportion of them settling in New York City.

World of Our Fathers is a monumental history of that great migration. A panoramic survey, it traces the migrants' journey from

A High Wind in Jamaica
Richard Hughes (1900–1976)

On the High Seas with Pirates— and a Band of Ruthless Children

An adventure story—for adults—about children kidnapped by pirates on their way to England from Jamaica, this singular work of fiction is enthralling. Strange, funny, and fantastic, it's also beautiful and terrifying; it trails themes of innocence and betrayal through dark waters of violence, humor, primal emotion, and suspense.

The tale begins in the lush environs of the Caribbean island on which the five

Bas-Thornton children, ranging in age from three to twelve, frolic almost ferally on the fringes of their English parents' attention. When their home is destroyed by the high winds of a hurricane, the Bas-Thornton progeny—along with two offspring of another family—are packed up and sent for safety back to Britain. Yet the protective measure backfires: The merchant ship on which the children embark is soon overtaken by a group of pirates, even though, as the ever helpful, reflective, and merrily intrusive narrator explains, "Piracy had long since ceased to pay, and should have been scrapped years ago: but a vocational tradition will last on a long time after it has ceased to be economic, in a decadent form."

If the pirates are decadent, the children occupy a moral condition both furtive and fearless, a state of sensuous secrecy that is drawn with astonishing vividness as Hughes deftly leaps the psychological divide that separates youth from adulthood. Occupying the minds of his fictional charges, the author reveals that the difference between these two dimensions of life is not one of age, but of essence. As the provocative narrator posits at one point, "Possibly a case might be made out that children are not human either: but I should not accept it. Agreed that their minds are not just more ignorant and stupider than ours, but differ in kind of thinking (are *mad*, in fact)." Hughes's children embody the existential tremors and confidences of childhood with uncanny verisimilitude; as a result, they are far more intriguing—and often more dangerous—than his pirates.

A High Wind in Jamaica transports both its characters and its readers into a timeless storytelling realm that might have been summoned into being by the imaginative

collaboration of Sigmund Freud, Gabriel García Márquez, and the Brothers Grimm. The artfully offbeat style creates a peculiar eloquence, and the setting and the preposterous incidents suggest a children's book gone wild (think *The Secret Garden* gone fertilely to seed). The result creates in the reader the eerie anxiety one feels tossing sleeplessly in the middle of a warm, stirring summer night; the world outside the windows is alive with heat, the threat of storms, and dark mysteries, and every breeze is ominous, tantalizing, ingenious, both a threat and a promise. What an unsettling, alluring, mesmerizing book!

What: Novel. *When:* 1929. *Edition:* Originally published in the United States under the title *The Innocent Voyage. Also By: In Hazard* (1938). *The Fox in the Attic* (1961), *The Wooden Shepherdess* (1973). *Further Reading: Richard Hughes: A Biography* by Richard Perceval Graves. *Try: The Turn of the Screw* by Henry James. *Peter and Wendy* by J. M. Barrie (see page 53). *Lord of the Flies* by William Golding (see page 322). *Adaptation:* Alexander Mackendrick directed the 1965 film, which stars Anthony Quinn and James Coburn (and also features future novelist Martin Amis among its cast of child actors).

....

The Fatal Shore
THE EPIC OF AUSTRALIA'S FOUNDING
Robert Hughes (1938–2012)

The Astonishing Story of the Birth of Australia

....

History contains few moments more dramatic than the arrival in Australia of her earliest British colonizers. The year is 1788, almost two decades after Captain James Cook became the first European to make landfall on the continent. Since his brief stopover no others have followed him—till now. Robert Hughes sets the scene in *The Fatal Shore*,

his monumental and enthralling account of Australia's founding:

European history had left no mark at all. Until the swollen sails and curvetting bows of the British fleet came round South Head, there were no dates. The Aborigines and the fauna around them had possessed the landscape since time immemorial, and no other human eye had seen them. Now the protective glass of distance broke, in an instant, never to be restored.

The shattering moment is stunningly drawn, but there's a twist to the story Hughes is quick to relate: The eleven arriving ships carried just over a thousand people, among whom were more than seven hundred convicts—548 male and 188 female. For the incredible truth is that the British government had conceived the idea of turning the unexplored continent into a jail, a "thief colony." This unprecedented system of "convict transportation" was to last for some eighty years, during which time more than 160,000 men, women, and children were shipped in bondage to Australia; it was "the largest forced exile of citizens at the behest of a European government in pre-modern history."

No surprise then that Australia's creation is a one-of-a-kind historical epic—and, in this truly monumental book, a one-of-a-kind historian has done it justice. The Australian-born Robert Hughes is best known for his work as an art critic for *Time* magazine and the television series that accompanied his groundbreaking book on modern art, *The Shock of the New*, but in these compulsively readable pages he proves to be an insightful, incisive chronicler of historical events, sociological imperatives, and cultural development. Astutely attentive to the harsh realities of Australian transportation for prisoners and captors, Hughes is also alert to its profound effects on the Aboriginal population. His superb prose is equal parts eloquence, erudition, and stylistic electricity, and its powerful effects are amplified by the words of the convicts themselves, culled from letters, diaries, and other sources. Indeed, the book, as Hughes declares, "is largely about what they tell us of their suffering and survival, their aspiration and resistance, their fear of exile and their reconciliation to the

Robert Hughes, 1971

once-unimagined land they and their children would claim as their own." It's an engrossing, surprising tale that here has found its ideal teller.

What: History. *When:* 1987. *Awards:* In 1988, *The Fatal Shore* won two prestigious British awards: the W. H. Smith Literary Prize and the Duff Cooper Prize. *Also By: The Shock of the New* (1980). *Nothing If Not Critical: Selected Essays on Art and Artists* (1990). *Culture of Complaint: The Fraying of America* (1993). *American Visions* (1997). *Goya* (2003). *Things I Didn't Know* (2006). *Try: For the Term of His Natural Life* by Marcus Clarke. *The Birth of Sydney* by Tim Flannery. *A Commonwealth of Thieves* by Thomas Keneally. *Adaptation:* In 2000, Robert Hughes presented a six-part television series, *Australia: Beyond the Fatal Shore*, produced for the BBC and PBS.

Les Misérables
Victor Hugo (1802–1885)

An Epic Tale of Injustice and Adversity, Love and Hope

In his long life, Victor Hugo amassed glory on a scale we can scarcely imagine today. Upon his death in 1885 at the age of eighty-three, his body was laid in state in Paris beneath the Arc de Triomphe, and tens of thousands paid their respects to the revered poet, dramatist, and novelist before he was buried (in a pauper's coffin, as his will stipulated) in the Panthéon. Hugo's epic funeral dwarfs the earthly farewell

cl. Jean Valjean. · Jacquin. · Une Femme. · (2 T.) Mme Magloire. · Melle Baptistine. · Un Brigadier. · Mr. Miriel

T.) _ Javert. · Fantine. · (4^eT.) _ La Tenardier. · Fantine. · Tenardier. · (3^eT.) _ Petit Gervais.

T.) Fauchelevent. · Un Ouvrier. · (6^eT.) Jean Valjean. · (8^eT.) Sœur Simplice. · Fantine. · (9e T.) _ Cosette.

e T.) Claquesous. · Tenardier. · Montparnasse · Eponine. · (11e T.) _ Cosette. · (12^eT.) Fauchelevent.

Illustration from an 1878 edition of Les Misérables

of other writers the way *Les Misérables*—in its length, scope, and magnanimity—towers over all but a handful of novels.

The product of two decades of literary labor, *Les Misérables* was begun while the author enjoyed political favor in Paris, and finished during Hugo's nineteen-year political exile in the Channel Islands. At the core of its vast narrative is Jean Valjean, a peasant imprisoned for stealing a loaf of bread to feed his sister's starving children. This rash act will haunt him through all the events that follow, for even though the noble Valjean can escape prison, he cannot escape his past, which relentlessly pursues him in the body of the implacable Inspector Javert. Hugo's fierce advocacy for the poor and oppressed (the book's title might be translated as "The Wretched" or "The Outcasts") runs like an electric current through the intricate plot that leads readers from the countryside to the urban underworld, from the Battle of Waterloo to the Parisian sewers through which Valjean flees in one of the most famous episodes in all of fiction. Teeming with unforgettable characters—including the saintly bishop known as Monseigneur Bienvenu, the young and unfortunate seamstress Fantine, her orphaned daughter Cosette, the street urchin Gavroche, the villainous Thénardier, and the fiery revolutionary Marius—*Les Misérables* encompasses historical events, societal injustice, personal suffering and sacrifice, and love in all its hopes and heartaches. As the author leads the reader down what seems to be every alleyway in Paris,

he wears on his billowing sleeve the human sympathy that animates the most unforgettable novels.

What: Novel. *When:* 1862. *Editions:* The standard English translation was made by Hugo's friend Charles Edwin Wilbour; astonishingly, Wilbour translated the fifteen-hundred-page novel in time for it to be published in New York in 1862, the same year it appeared in France. It is a mark of Hugo's popularity that translators working in several other tongues matched Wilbour's achievement. A superb translation by Julie Rose, the most complete and textually reliable to date, appeared in 2008, and supersedes all previous versions. *Reading Note:* Hugo intersperses his massive tale with interesting but often lengthy digressions on history, slang, the Parisian sewer system, and much more. Abridged versions omit many of these passages, making the narrative fleeter but less rich. Stick to an unabridged version, and if you find yourself bogged down in unwanted detail, skip ahead to pick up the thread of the action. *Also By:* Hugo's other famous novel is *Notre-Dame de Paris* (1831, translated as *The Hunchback of Notre Dame*), but in his day he was known first and foremost as a poet and playwright. *Further Reading: The Novel of the Century: The Extraordinary Adventure of "Les Misérables"* by David Bellos. Graham Robb's 1997 biography, *Victor Hugo*, is magnificent. *Try: A Tale of Two Cities* by Charles Dickens (see page 225). *Adaptations:* Many film, television, and radio adaptations exist, but most famous is the award-winning Cameron Mackintosh/Royal Shakespeare Company musical that premiered in London in 1985 and on Broadway in 1987.

The Autumn of the Middle Ages
Johan Huizinga (1872–1945)

Tapping the Historical Imagination

Dutch historian Johan Huizinga's seminal 1919 work, *Hersttij der Middeleeuwen*—a cultural history of France and the Netherlands in the fourteenth and fifteenth centuries—was first translated into English in 1924 as *The Waning of the Middle Ages*. The book had been only moderately successful in Huizinga's homeland, but was a big hit in the English-speaking

world. Viewing the age through the trifocal lens of art, literature, and chivalry, Huizinga argued that the Renaissance was less the birth of the modern age than it was the death of the medieval. More importantly, his focus on the imagination of the era to reveal the emotions, ambitions, and collective psychology of the past offered a revolutionary perspective on the human significance embedded in cultural evidence, as when he asserted that the paintings of Van Eyck and Memling, for instance, might reveal more than documents about human experience in the Middle Ages. A work of deep humanism and literary sensibility, *The Waning of the Middle Ages* remained popular with academic and lay readers alike for almost three quarters of a century.

As it happens, though, the translator of that 1924 edition, Frederik Jan Hopman, had taken liberties with Huizinga's text—omitting almost a third of the work and rearranging or mistranslating certain parts, including the title. In 1996, a new translation was published, this one by Rodney Payton and Ulrich Mammitzsch, as *The Autumn of the Middle Ages*. The new complete version is faithful to Huizinga's original in tone and substance, and also includes a broader range of illustrations of works under discussion, allowing readers to enjoy—in the words of Francis Haskell—"one of the greatest, as well as one of the most enthralling, historical classics of the twentieth century . . . in the form that was obviously intended by the author, even if their views of the book will not, I think, be fundamentally altered."

What: History. *When:* 1919. (1924 translation, *The Waning of the Middle Ages*, by Frederik Jan Hopman; definitive 1996 translation by Rodney Payton and Ulrich Mammitzsch.) *Also By:* Erasmus (1924). *Homo Ludens* (1938). *Try: The Civilization of the Renaissance in Italy* by Jacob Burckhardt (see page 108). *The Making of the Middle Ages* by R. W. Southern. *The Embarrassment of Riches* by Simon Schama.

Their Eyes Were Watching God
Zora Neale Hurston (1891–1960)

A Woman of Substance

A llying her literary gifts with her academic training, Zora Neale Hurston published examinations of folklore, story collections, plays, novels, and a memoir. She studied at Barnard and Columbia with pioneering anthropologist Franz Boas and was the recipient of two Guggenheim fellowships. Hurston became a prominent figure in the Harlem Renaissance of the 1930s, although her work, especially her fiction, was controversial among her fellow authors. Her refusal to write political novels about black people defined by the white world, together with her practice of rendering speech in black southern dialect—particularly in *Their Eyes Were Watching God*—inspired intense criticism from Richard Wright (see page 872) and other prominent contemporaries.

Yet dialect is only one of the literary registers Hurston employs in *Their Eyes Were Watching God*. A second tonality,

Zora Neale Hurston, ca. 1940

suffused with a quality akin to the calm confidence of scripture, is sounded in the book's first sentence—"Ships at a distance have every man's wish on

board"—and resonates with wisdom throughout the subsequent pages. The novel tells the
story of Janie Crawford, a woman born in unfavorable circumstances whose grandmother
wants her to have the chance at happiness she
never did and that Janie's mother also missed.
Searching for love and fulfillment, Janie runs
away from the husband her grandmother finds
her, marries another man and then a third,
named Tea Cake, with whom she at last discovers a satisfying relationship—until tragic and
violent events destroy their peace.

Told to her friend Pheoby upon Janie's
return to her hometown after Tea Cake's death,
Their Eyes Were Watching God is a powerful novel
girded by the author's ideals. Janie's instinc-
tual sense of the self she inhabits—an identity
that extends beyond the descriptive categories
that might otherwise define her as an African
American, a woman, or a wife—is vividly conveyed, imbuing the book with a spirit of affirmation that its heroine embodies throughout
her tribulations.

Despite the accomplishment of *Their Eyes
Were Watching God* and her other writing (including the superb *Tell My Horse: Voodoo and Life in
Haiti and Jamaica*, published one year later),
Hurston's books quickly fell out of print.
Retreating into obscurity, she died in a welfare
home and was buried in an unmarked grave.
The revival of her work, which began with
novelist Alice Walker's March 1975 essay in *Ms.*
magazine, "In Search of Zora Neale Hurston,"
culminated two decades later in the publication of two Hurston volumes in the Library of
America.

What: Novel. **When:** 1937. **Also By:** *Jonah's Gourd
Vine* (1934). *Mules and Men* (1935). *Moses, Man of the
Mountain* (1939). *Dust Tracks on a Road* (1942). *Seraph
on the Suwanee* (1948). **Further Reading:** *Zora Neale
Hurston: A Literary Biography* by Robert E. Hemenway.
Wrapped in Rainbows: The Life of Zora Neale Hurston
by Valerie Boyd. **Try:** *Cane* by Jean Toomer. *The Healing*
by Gayl Jones. **Adaptation:** The 2005 television movie,
produced by Oprah Winfrey, stars Halle Berry.

Brave New World
Aldous Huxley (1894–1963)

A Savage Satire of a Future of Perfect Stability

"Because our world is not the same as
Othello's world," says Mustapha
Mond, Resident World Controller
of Western Europe, to John the
Savage, an outsider weaned on
the words of Shakespeare, who
questions Mond's contention
that no residents of the World
State under his control could
understand the Bard's great
work. "You can't make flivvers
without steel—and you can't
make tragedies without social
instability," Mond continues. "The
world's stable now. People are
happy; they get what they want,
and they never want what they can't
get."

What people can't get in the technologically determined society of Aldous Huxley's
imagined future are family, religion, literature, art, individuality, love, or a genuinely human relationship of any sort.
In this brave new world, poverty,
conflict, and unhappiness have all
been eliminated by way of controlled breeding and the anti-
depressant influence of the
ubiquitous tranquilizer *soma*.
Everyone is promiscuous but
nonreproductive; babies are
all fabricated in labs according to quotas, courtesy of
Bokanovsky's Process, which
mass produces identical twins
who are channeled into five established castes, Alpha to Epsilon.
London is populated with functionaries such as the Assistant

*Portrait of
Aldous Huxley, 1927*

passionless liaisons, perfect conformity, and complete state control—until John arrives from the New Mexico Savage Reservation to disturb the thoughtless peace.

Reminiscent of *Gulliver's Travels*, Huxley's fiercely funny portrait of a civilization gone mad with manufactured happiness is ingeniously satiric, hilariously imaginative, and eerily prescient. Its unbridled invention makes it a most entertaining cautionary tale.

What: Novel. *When:* 1932. *Also By:* Novels: *Crome Yellow* (1921); *Antic Hay* (1923); *Point Counter Point* (1928); *Time Must Have a Stop* (1944). *Ape and Essence* (1948) is another venture into dystopian fiction, whereas his last novel, *Island* (1962), paints a happier future. Nonfiction: *The Devils of Loudon* (1952); *The Doors of Perception* (1954). *Further Reading:* In 1958, Huxley published *Brave New World Revisited*, an extended essay considering developments of society in light of his novel (compared with which it is rather lifeless). *Try: Gulliver's Travels* by Jonathan Swift (see page 767). *Fahrenheit 451* by Ray Bradbury (see page 91). *The Handmaid's Tale* by Margaret Atwood. *Adaptations: Brave New World* has been adapted several times for both movies and television, without real success. *Footnote:* Inveterate readers will appreciate the amusing essay on packing books for a vacation that appears in Huxley's *Along the Road* (1925).

Predestinator and the Arch-Community-Songster. Henry Ford has been deified (as in "Year of Our Ford"), hypnopaedia (sleep-teaching) controls learning, naked children play sexual games such as "Centrifugal Bumble-puppy," and "feelies" have taken the pleasure of movies to a whole new level. It is a world of

In the Vineyard of the Text

A COMMENTARY TO HUGH'S *DIDASCALICON*

Ivan Illich (1926–2002)

When Books Were the New Technology

"The book has now ceased to be the root-metaphor of the age," writes Ivan Illich, "the screen has taken its place." But just as there was a time before screens, Illich makes clear in this enlightening volume, there was a cultural age before books as well. The centrality of books to our idea of culture, the author asserts, was an epochal phenomenon, the beginning of which can be traced to "a technical breakthrough which took place around 1150, three hundred years before movable type came into use."

To illustrate his point, Illich, an Austrian philosopher and Catholic priest, tells the story of reading during that long-ago period of transition, and in so doing turns a profoundly scholarly work on an obscure medieval manuscript into an enlightening essay in ideas. As a medium for his research and speculation, Illich examines a treatise written by the French theologian Hugh of Saint-Victor (1096–1141). Hugh's *Didascalicon*, an early encyclopedia and a guide to the art of reading, anticipates the leap from monastic texts, designed for oral, collective recitation, to scholastic works, which were texts organized for silent, contemplative, individual study. The springboard for the leap, Illich explains, was a series of innovations—improved punctuation, indentation, titles and headings, chapters, indices—that enabled a new mode of treating words on a page. (Illich highlights the twelfth-century invention of the alphabetical index, pointing out the astonishing fact that it had not occurred to eighty-five previous generations of alphabet users—nearly three millennia worth!—to organize things alphabetically.) As a result of these features, the author was changed from the teller of a story to the creator of a text, and the audience was transformed from listeners into silent readers. All that we know and love of the bookish life followed, including notions that have shaped our understanding of self and society: "That which we mean today when, in ordinary conversation, we speak of the 'self' or the 'individual,'" Illich writes, "is one of the great discoveries of the twelfth century. Neither in the Greek nor in the Roman conceptual constellation was there a place into which it could have fitted." The book would become that place.

If the book, as Illich posits in this stimulating work, revealed the self, who knows what revelations the screen will ultimately engender? For anyone interested in such questions, or in the history of reading and the evolution and influence of letters, sentences, paragraphs, and the objects in which they've flourished for the past eight hundred years, *In the Vineyard of the Text* is an exhilarating intellectual adventure.

What: Books. Culture. *When:* 1993. *Reading Note:* The text is dense, but the argument is lucid. *Also By: Deschooling Society* (1971). *Tools for Conviviality* (1973). *Medical Nemesis* (1975). *Further Reading: ABC: The Alphabetization of the Popular Mind* by Illich and Barry Sanders. *Try: Avatars of the Word: From Papyrus to Cyberspace* by James J. O'Donnell.

The World According to Garp
John Irving (born 1942)

Sublime and Ridiculous, Ridiculous and Sublime

" In the world according to Garp, an evening could be hilarious and the next morning could be murderous," we read at the end of the penultimate chapter of this teeming, tumultuous book. It's an apt summary of what has come before. The story of the novelist T. S. Garp and his mother, Jenny Fields, of Garp's wife and their sons, of the transsexual former football player who becomes something of a bodyguard to Jenny when her autobiography thrusts her into the feminist limelight, and of sundry individuals and families who cross the paths and hearts of those just mentioned, *The World According to Garp* starts out hard to believe, quickly becomes hard to put down, and remains forever hard to forget.

John Irving, 1978

At one point in the narrative, Garp describes life as an X-rated soap opera, and Irving's plot would merit no more than that description if he were not such a terrific writer. His litany of crises and violent calamities—rape, mutilation, adultery, assassination, a fatal automobile accident, and countless other horrible occurrences—would be repellent, even revolting, in other hands, but his storytelling is infused with such a transporting inventive impulse that his characters transcend their woes, tapping an emotional vitality that is both poignant and powerful.

Energy is the currency of Garp's world; the book starts quick and just gets quicker:

Garp's mother, Jenny Fields, was arrested in Boston in 1942 for wounding a man in a movie theater. This was shortly after the Japanese had bombed Pearl Harbor and people were being tolerant of soldiers, because suddenly everyone was a soldier, but Jenny Fields was quite firm in her intolerance of the behavior of men in general and soldiers in particular.

From twenty-two-year-old nurse Jenny's self-defensive slashing of this soldier on page one, Irving takes us on a roller-coaster ride through the jaw-dropping circumstances of Garp's conception, his education, his adulthood, his burgeoning then blocked career as a writer, his marriage and fatherhood, and, always, his changing relationship with his wildly eccentric mother. Themes of lust, gender, creativity, and the unfathomable reality of unforeseen tragedies nourish the novel's passage through decades, and the years themselves are part of the tale: Like a nineteenth-century novelist, Irving gives his creations enough time, and a broad enough social canvas, to become not just characters, but *lives*. As Dickens did before him, he approaches emotional truths by means of exaggerations built upon exactitudes of observation, and, when he is on his game, the reader follows him breathlessly. As uproariously funny as it is imaginative, *The World According to Garp* is Irving's talent at its freshest and most invigorating.

What: Novel. **When:** 1978. **Award:** National Book Award, 1980. **Also By:** *The Water-Method Man* (1972). *The Hotel New Hampshire* (1981). *The Cider House Rules* (1985). *A Prayer for Owen Meany* (1989). *A Widow for One Year* (1998). **Try:** *The Life and Adventures of Nicholas Nickleby* by Charles Dickens (see page 218). *World's End* by T. C. Boyle. **Adaptation:** The 1982 movie stars Robin Williams as Garp, Glenn Close as his mother, and John Lithgow as the transsexual Roberta Muldoon.

The Berlin Stories
Christopher Isherwood (1904–1986)

He Was a Camera in 1930s Berlin

"Even in style, in form, [Christopher Isherwood's] work was strikingly appropriate. He had found the way around falsity and exaggeration by simplicity and directness. One had the feeling, often, that this was not fiction at all. The stories seemed entirely natural and easy: they were simply strokes of good luck, seized upon by a clever author. The luck to have been in Berlin, the luck to meet Sally Bowles." That's Elizabeth Hardwick writing in the *New York Review of Books* in 1964, referring to Isherwood's legendary *Berlin Stories*, a combination of his two best books, *The Last of Mr. Norris* (1935) and *Goodbye to Berlin* (1939). The impression Hardwick describes was fueled by Isherwood's basing the stories on his own experiences and acquaintances, going so far as to include a narrator named Christopher Isherwood in *Goodbye to Berlin*.

"I am a camera with its shutter open, quite passive, recording, not thinking," the author famously wrote in that volume, and although Isherwood's skills as an observer are indisputable, they are enhanced by their alliance to his extraordinary, though never ostentatiously deployed, literary gifts. As one early reviewer wrote, "Every detail seems true because each is the result of a sharp verbal focus in his mind." That's one reason why, despite the fact that they have been nearly subsumed by now in the stage and film adaptations drawn from them (*I Am a Camera* and the musical *Cabaret*), Isherwood's originals retain their startling power on the page. Set in Berlin in the early 1930s, the stories depict a desperately carefree world of decadence and fatalism in the shadow of looming Nazi violence. The first set of stories revolves around the friendship of the narrator (here called William Bradshaw, employing the author's middle names) with the sinister con man Arthur Norris, and the second is dominated by the figure of Sally Bowles, an aspiring cabaret performer. Populated by offbeat characters—mainly expatriates drawn to the shabbily chic cafés of the city—*The Berlin Stories* vivifies a bawdy world of vice and debauchery that is drunk on gossip, rumor, and a burgeoning terror. Adept at capturing the awful loneliness of licentiousness, Isherwood portrays a demimonde so intent on the pursuit of hedonism that it frantically evades any heroic impulses in the face of political brutality; but in this, of course, his characters were not alone.

What: Novels. *When: The Last of Mr. Norris,* 1935 (also published as *Mr. Norris Changes Trains*)*; Goodbye to Berlin,* 1939; reissued jointly as *The Berlin Stories* in 1946. *Also By:* Fiction: *Prater Violet* (1945); *Down There on a Visit* (1962); *A Single Man* (1964). Autobiography: *Lions and Shadows* (1938); *Kathleen and Frank* (1971); *Christopher and His Kind* (1976); *My Guru and His Disciple* (1980). *Further Reading: Berlin in Lights: The Diaries of Count Harry Kessler (1918–1937). Try: Berlin Cabaret* by Peter Jelavich. *The Emperor Waltz* by Philip Hensher. *Adaptations: The Berlin Stories* are the basis for John Van Druten's 1951 play, *I Am a Camera,* and the 1966 Broadway musical, *Cabaret,* both of which became movies of the same names.

The Remains of the Day
Kazuo Ishiguro (born 1954)

A Novel of Manners Turned Outside In

Long recognized as one of the most accomplished novelists of his generation, Kazuo Ishiguro was awarded the Nobel Prize in Literature in 2017. Born in Japan in 1954, he arrived in England when he was five, and—although his parents, who had every intention of returning to their homeland, kept up his Japanese education—there he and his family remained. The cultural duality of his upbringing has informed his work, notably in his first two books, *A Pale View of Hills* (1982) and *An Artist of the Floating World* (1986), but his third and best-known novel is steeped entirely in the English milieu.

The Remains of the Day tells, in the first person, the story of Stevens, a proper British butler who has spent three decades in service at Darlington Hall. Stevens has been devoted to his career, playing a reliably unobtrusive role in polishing the etiquette of the upper class while pursuing—in action and, increasingly, in reflection—the goal of greatness in his profession. His dedication to duty is such that he has relegated his private emotions so far below stairs that he seems unable to retrieve any feelings at all. Nothing—not even his father's dying—is allowed to interfere with his focus on his appointed rounds.

As the book opens in July 1956, Stevens is setting off on a motoring trip, courtesy of Darlington Hall's new American owner. With characteristic single-mindedness, he plans to use his holiday to visit Miss Kenton, once Darlington's housekeeper, in hope of luring her back to her former position. Over six days—marked, comically, by one automotive mishap after another—Stevens reveals to the reader, and more slowly and less certainly to himself, the disorder beneath the hood of his meticulously maintained life. As he ponders his past in the unfamiliar leisure of his journey, the gradual realization of all that decorum has kept at bay infuses his memory with regret and sorrow. "All those years I served him," he thinks of Lord Darlington, who ended his days in public shame because of

Kazuo Ishiguro, 2011

his Nazi sympathies, "I trusted I was doing something worthwhile. I can't even say I made my own mistakes. Really—one has to ask oneself—what dignity is there in that?"

No matter the character he is speaking through, Ishiguro possesses what Robert McCrum has called "a voice with tremendous authority." That authority allows him, almost magically, to engage us entertainingly at the same time as he wrenches our hearts—to say nothing of Stevens's, which breaks beneath the weight of the unreliable life story he has fashioned for himself with such consummate and misguided care. *The Remains of the Day* is a masterpiece of exquisite irony, embroidered around an understanding of human frailty that the author insinuates onto every page, even while it eludes the grasp of the butler who tells the tale.

What: Novel. **When:** 1989.
Awards: Booker Prize, 1989.
Nobel Prize in Literature, 2017.
Also By: *The Unconsoled* (1995).
When We Were Orphans (2000).
Never Let Me Go (2005). *The Buried Giant* (2015). **Try:** *Howards End* by E. M. Forster. **Adaptation:** The 1993 Merchant Ivory film, starring Anthony Hopkins and Emma Thompson, was nominated for eight Oscars, including Best Picture.

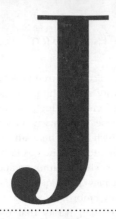

Life Among the Savages
Shirley Jackson (1916–1965)

A Savagely Funny Journey into the Family Room

As one grows older, keeps house, and has children, a fact of life emerges to cloud the previously clear, far vistas of fine young minds: Everyone is fighting off a creeping state of chaos that relentlessly threatens to overrun home, hearth, and mental health. Day-to-day living seems to be an obstacle-strewn survival course that resets itself each morning. In this slightly fictionalized account of her own family's life, Shirley Jackson (author of the horrifying story "The Lottery," which you may remember from a school anthology) plumbs the depths of domestic bliss, recounting her life with husband and four children under ten, in one of the funniest, most enjoyable books you'll ever read—and a precursor to the work of Jean Kerr, Erma Bombeck, and other chroniclers of the relentless comedy of motherhood's emergencies. Jackson's portraits of her children are rich with humor and understanding, and the whole family comedy is unbearably believable. To top it off, she's a terrific writer: You'll want to quote entire paragraphs to friends. Like this one:

Our house is old, and noisy, and full. When we moved into it we had two children and about five thousand books; I expect that when we finally overflow and move out again we will have perhaps twenty children and easily half a million books; we also own assorted beds and tables and chairs and rocking horses and lamps and doll dresses and ship models and paint brushes and literally thousands of socks. This is the way of life my husband and I have fallen into, inadvertently, as though we had fallen into a well and decided that since there was no way out we might as well stay there and set up a chair and a desk and a light of some kind; even though this is our way of life, and the only one we know, it is occasionally bewildering, and perhaps even inexplicable to the sort of person who does not have that swift, accurate conviction that he is going to step on a broken celluloid doll in the dark.

What: Novel. Memoir. **When:** 1953. **Also By:** A sequel: *Raising Demons* (1957). Fiction: *The Lottery and Other Stories* (1949); *The Haunting of Hill House* (1959); *We Have Always Lived in the Castle* (1962); *Just an Ordinary Day* (previously uncollected stories; 1996). *Further Reading: Shirley Jackson: A Rather Haunted Life* by Ruth Franklin. *Try: Please Don't Eat the Daisies* and *Penny Candy* by Jean Kerr.

■ For Shirley Jackson's *The Haunting of Hill House*, see page 633.

The Death and Life of Great American Cities
Jane Jacobs (1916–2006)

On the Streets Where We Live

Published in 1961, *The Death and Life of Great American Cities* would prove to be one of the most influential books on urban planning and policy ever written. Just as important for readers, its author's powers of perception are allied to considerable literary gifts, and so its pages are animated with descriptions of city life as vivid as any ever penned. Moreover, the book's influence has extended far beyond the strictly urban beat, for Jacobs's insights into the way cities work—from the uses of sidewalks to the nature and nurture of neighborhoods—have much to tell us about the way we live networked lives.

Her method is simple. Using New York as her laboratory, she finds a street she likes and studies what about it contributes to its health and that of its denizens; or she finds a space whose failure is apparent—the always-empty inner mall of a housing project, say—and discovers why it is shunned by the neighborhood despite the careful designs of urban planners. She wears her sociology lightly, and she is biting in her critique of those who survey the complex knottiness of urban experience as something to be disentangled in the interests of an abstract, sterile neatness. "There is a quality even meaner than outright ugliness and disorder," she explains, "and this meaner quality is the dishonest mask of pretended order, achieved by ignoring or suppressing the real order that is struggling to exist and to be served." Her eyes may be fixed on streets and parks, traffic and zoning, walkers and shopkeepers, but her vision bears witness to a coherent philosophy that provides a fresh perspective on how we should live. Jacobs writes about our need to dwell in meaningful surroundings with an epigrammatic incisiveness that makes her intelligence not only lucid, but portable to a wide variety of experience, whether city bound or beyond.

What: Cities. *When:* 1961. *Also By: The Economy of Cities (1969). Cities and the Wealth of Nations (1984). Systems of Survival (1992). Further Reading: The Power Broker: Robert Moses and the Fall of New York* by Robert A. Caro (see page 130). *Eyes on the Street: The Life of Jane Jacobs* by Robert Kanigel. *Try: Soft City* by Jonathan Raban. *The Image of the City* by Kevin Lynch.

Jane Jacobs, 1968

Beyond a Boundary
C. L. R. James (1901–1989)

On the Playing Fields of Trinidad

This is one of the best and most surprising sports books a reader can discover. Best, because it evokes, with wit and great style, the spell of awe, action, facts, and figures a game can cast over a boyhood, thereby informing a fan's spirit for a lifetime; surprising because its subject is cricket *and* its author was a Marxist revolutionary of enormous intellectual sophistication and ardent political convictions, a pioneer of the modern African liberation movement.

C. L. R. James was born in Trinidad and grew up in a house that faced a cricket ground. By standing on a chair and looking out the window, "a small boy . . . could watch practice every afternoon and matches on Saturday." Which is just what the young James did whenever he wasn't outside playing cricket and running around himself— or inside reading *Vanity Fair* (which he did obsessively, beginning at the age of eight, to the point where he knew pages of Thackeray's famous novel by heart—surprising indeed). Although his fascination with cricket lore and his intense extracurricular reading diverted his attention from his studies at the Queen's Royal College, the government secondary school in which he was enrolled at the age of ten, all three focuses of his formative years—cricket, literature, and Oxbridge-inflected education—infused his mind with the English public school code. Fundamental to this was a sense of sportsmanship and fair play epitomized in the competitive etiquette of the sport he loved. One of the revelations of this book is the way James persuasively suggests that certain elements of the British imperial legacy are the seeds from which his later commitment to social justice grew.

"Cricket is a game of high and difficult technique," James writes. "If it were not it could not carry the load of social response and implications which it carries." James deftly traces those implications, engaging serious questions about race, class, and colonialism, and about the political, psychological, and sociological significance of sports in general; yet the book never loses its autobiographical emotion or the transporting charm of James's lifelong reverence for the game and the lessons it has to teach. He brilliantly illuminates the dramatic and aesthetic pleasures spectators find upon a playing field, as well as the abilities and inspirations of particular players, from the legendary Victorian W. G. Grace ("the best-known Englishman of his time") to the members of the triumphant West Indian side, led by Frank Worrell, the first black captain, that bested Australia in the famous Test matches of 1961.

Considering those contests, and Worrell's teammate Garfield Sobers, James offers a description an American sportswriter might once have applied to Ted Williams or Joe DiMaggio: "Never was such ease and certainty of stroke, such early seeing of the ball and such late, leisured play, such command by a batsman not only of the bowling but of himself. He seemed to be expressing a personal vision." That's just what James does in this memorable, singular book, and the force of his vision—alert with political insights and sociological analyses—is all the more powerful because it never precludes a fan's joy, nor the sharing of it.

What: Sports. Memoir. *When:* 1963. *Reading Note:* Familiarity with cricket's sometimes baffling terminology is not necessary to enjoy James's book. *Also By: The Black Jacobins: Toussaint L'Ouverture and the San Domingo Revolution* (1938). *Mariners, Renegades, and Castaways: The Story of Herman Melville and the World We Live In* (1953). *The C. L. R. James Reader* (1992). *Further Reading: C. L. R. James: Cricket's Philosopher King* by Dave Renton. *Try: Cardus on Cricket* by Neville Cardus.

Cultural Amnesia

NECESSARY MEMORIES FROM HISTORY AND THE ARTS

Clive James (born 1939)

An Uncommon Commonplace Book

"Clive James is a brilliant bunch of guys," a New Yorker wag once aptly wrote. Across several decades, all of them have kept very busy producing a body of work—essays, television reviews, memoir, poetry, fiction, songs, wisecracks—that is broad, deep, and smart, exhibiting an unmatched combination of brio and brilliance. James may be the most entertaining intellectual you'll ever read. If you want the most satisfying cover-to-cover encounter with his intelligence, pick up the first volume of his autobiography, Unreliable Memoirs, a hilariously funny narrative of his coming-of-age in Australia before setting off to Cambridge. Or try As of This Writing: The Essential Essays 1968–2002, where you will be treated to illuminating encapsulations of disparate writers and subjects you always wanted to know more about, even if they're completely new to you: One of James's talents is a gift for offhand instruction that makes a love of learning infectious.

Cultural Amnesia, on the other hand, is admittedly a bit of a mess. "In the forty years it took me to write this book," James discloses at the outset, "I only gradually realized that the finished work, if it were going to be true to the pattern of my experience, would have no pattern. It would be organized like the top of my desk, from which the last assistant I hired to sort it out has yet to appear." The resulting volume is a collection of forty-odd brief essays, each prompted by a sentence, epigram, or passage James has highlighted in the course of his wide reading. To use a coinage from another age, it is at heart a "commonplace book," a personal journal preserving passages of particular interest; what makes Cultural Amnesia uncommon is the way each quotation James collects leads to a consideration of its import, as well

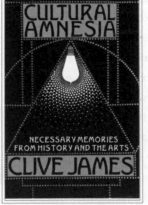

as the circumstances, character, and fate of the person who said or wrote it. Piecing together and embellishing the strands of his reading life, James reveals how they've informed both an intellectual consciousness and a moral conscience. "I wanted to write about philosophy, history, politics and the arts all at once, and about what had happened to those things during the course of the multiple catastrophes into whose second principal outburst (World War I was the first) I had been born in 1939," James explains. His gallery is large enough to include the jazz giant Louis Armstrong and the French political philosopher Raymond Aron, the Roman historian Tacitus, the British miniaturist Beatrix Potter, and such emblems of mid-twentieth-century courage and suffering as Egon Friedell and Heda Margolius Kovály (whose stories are unforgettable). In a perfect example of James's cultural catholicity, the actor Tony Curtis stands next to Ernst Robert Curtius, scholar of medieval Latin literature.

The whole enterprise is an impassioned and—by dint of James's glorious style—engaging defense of the reading life: "somewhere within the total field of human knowledge," he writes, "humanism still beckons to us as our best reason for having minds at all." This massive, sprawling, quirky exploration of one man's humanistic vocation leaves us not only with a remarkable reading list, but with a thinking list as well. In its idiosyncratic way, it's a book you can't put down, and will never exhaust.

What: Essays. *When:* 2007. *Reading Note:* Dip in anywhere and let serendipity be your guide. *Also By: May Week Was in June* (1990). *Try: Cannibals and Christians* by Norman Mailer. *The Collected Essays, Journalism, and Letters* by George Orwell (see page 608). *What Are Intellectuals Good For?* by George Scialabba.

HENRY JAMES
(1843–1916)

H enry James seems ripe for parody: the meandering sentences, with their intricate choreography of subordinate clauses; the insistent emphasis on the ineffability of what the characters are trying to express; the minute-by-minute attention to the minutiae of social exchange and evasion; the rarefied experience of Americans abroad, as their awkward energies collide with the elegance and etiquette of European sophistication; the endless patience with which the author pursues nuances of sensation, like a naturalist stalking elusive butterflies—it can all be a little maddening. And yet: What James knew, and what he translated into the art of fiction, was just how much of life is in fact felt rather than acted out. He was keenly aware of how much more of our time is spent in worry, or regret, or anticipation, than in sureness or endeavor, and of how much more closely we live to our feelings than to our ideas (unless, of course, we're fooling ourselves, and maybe others, with the kind of unknowing self-deception often on display in James's pages). Which is to say that what James explored in his ruminating prose, with a scrutiny no previous novelist had applied, was the character of our interior life: the privacy in which so much of our existence is passed and in which, ultimately, we find, or lose, our way. James intuited that our weightiest moments are internal and often

Henry James, ca. 1863

unresolved, and it's his arresting skill in measuring those moments that gives his work its special aura. His calibrations of consciousness were captured in fictions short and long, each offering his readers distinctive pleasures, but both embodying the seductive charms of a storytelling suffused with an eloquent sympathy.

The Aspern Papers
A Haunting Tale of Venice and Obsession

It's no surprise that the name Henry James will conjure, for many readers, visions of enormous novels complicated by intricate sentences. But James was prolific in shorter form, too, writing more than a hundred tales, a good number of which are longer than conventional short stories. Mesmerizing intellectual entertainments in their own right, the best of these novellas also offer enticing invitations to the rigors, and ultimate rewards, of his more ambitious fictions. In these works, the parenthetical probing that characterizes his novels' narration—embodied so often in the clausal hesitations and qualifications that can make the sense of his sentences hard to hold fast—gives way to more direct dramatization of James's explorations of heart and mind. Although the brilliant and chilling *Turn of the Screw* (1898) and the alluring *Daisy Miller* (1879) are more famous among James's smaller gems, *The Aspern Papers*—with its Venetian setting, literary preoccupations, psychological tension, and moody suspense—may be the most perfect distillation of the author's storytelling gifts.

All of James's tales are ghost stories of a sort, the characters haunted by some absent person, unattainable ideal, or elusive memory that exerts an uncanny influence on their conduct, evoking a sense of menace that is distinctively his. In *The Aspern Papers* the ghost is the famous (and invented) poet Jeffrey Aspern and the ghost-hunter is the tale's unnamed narrator, the devoted co-editor of Aspern's work who has never had occasion to speak to a person who actually knew the poet. When he discovers that an old lover lives on, sequestered in a decrepit Venetian palace with her spinster niece, he suspects she has some of Aspern's papers—and there's nothing he won't do to get them: "Hypocrisy, duplicity are my only chance. I'm sorry for it, but there's no baseness I wouldn't commit for Jeffrey Aspern's sake." Presenting himself on the doorstep of the Misses Bordereau as a would-be lodger, he worms his way closer to his literary treasure, and, heartlessly, into the niece's heart.

Felicities of style abound; describing the Bordereaus' abode, James writes, "It was not particularly old, only two or three centuries; and it had an air not so much of decay as of quiet discouragement, as if it had rather missed its career." And the evocations of Venice are as good as any lovers of that city will ever come across:

... with its little winding ways where people crowd together, where voices sound as in the corridors of a house, where the human step circulates as if it skirted the angles of furniture and shoes never wear out, the place has the character of an immense collective apartment, in which Piazza San Marco is the most ornamented corner and palaces and churches, for the rest, play the part of great divans of repose, tables of entertainment, expanses of decoration.

It's a perfect setting indeed for a tale of obsession, heartbreak, and civilized horror.

What: Novella. *When:* Serialized in *The Atlantic Monthly*, March, April, and May 1888; revised and republished in the New York Edition of James's works (1907–09). *Also By:* Novellas and stories of note: *The Lesson of the Master* (1892); "The Real Thing" (1893); "The Middle Years" (1895); *The Figure in the Carpet* (1896); *In the Cage* (1898); *The Beast in the Jungle* (1903). *Try: Territorial Rights* by Muriel Spark. *Don't Look Now: Selected Stories of Daphne du Maurier. Footnote:* In his notebooks, James recorded the anecdote that inspired *The Aspern Papers*. An acquaintance told him of a "Shelley-worshipper" who rented a room in the home of an elderly former lover of Byron, hoping she would die while he was in residence, allowing him to get his hands on letters of Shelley's she allegedly possessed. Relocating the scene from Florence to Venice, the author put the tale to his own imaginative use.

The Portrait of a Lady
A Woman of Independent Means

James's novels grew in sophistication and expressive sensitivity throughout his long career, culminating in a trio of late-period revelations: *The Wings of the Dove* (1902), *The Ambassadors* (1903), and *The Golden Bowl* (1904). Yet his masterpiece in the form remains *The Portrait of a Lady*, published in 1881. We can even witness his fictional artistry mature in one of that book's key scenes, in which his protagonist, Isabel Archer, sits alone in her drawing room through a quiet night, meditating on the ruins of her marriage to the supercilious aesthete Gilbert Osmond. For page upon page, no action unfolds other than the gradual dawning of both the morning and her self-awareness. She ponders how she—who once seemed so original a young woman in possessing "intentions of her own" rather than expecting a man to furnish her with a destiny—has come to the grim reality of her present unhappiness, shaped with perverse connoisseurship by her husband: "She had effaced herself when he first knew her; she had made herself small, pretending there was less of her than there really was."

In the seclusion of that room, Isabel remembers how capacious her character is, and might be again. On the surface, *The Portrait of a Lady* is about an American ingenue who charts a singular path into the wider world only to find her singularity no match for that world's designs and duplicities; at its depth, it's about how intrepid solitude must become to help an individual maintain her identity under the onslaught of society's charms and expectations. The novel hurtles toward a close in which Isabel is surprised by a predictable death, an unforeseen passion, and the impulsive purpose of both duty and identity. Her departure from England for Italy on the book's final page has left generations of readers disappointed in her seeming acquiescence to an unhappy fate: Is she headed back to Osmond? But James makes no declaration about her motives or intent. All we know is that she has started toward Rome and some undetermined future. The irresolution of this massive novel is the author's deference to the vitality of his protagonist, and to the diffidence she must turn to action if she is to take to heart the admonition of an undaunted suitor before her departure: "You must save what you can of your life." In

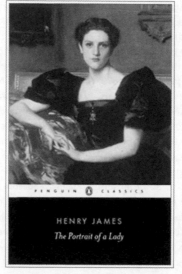

HENRY JAMES
The Portrait of a Lady

not imagining Isabel's fate to completion, James grants her a reality few fictional characters ever earn, giving her story a secrecy so profound, a privacy so telling, that it may help readers save what they can of their own.

What: Novel. *When:* 1881. *Edition:* James's revised version, for the New York Edition of his work (1908), is more polished and somewhat less adventurous than the original, which many readers prefer. *Also By: The Europeans* (1878). *Washington Square* (1880). *The Tragic Muse* (1890). *What Maisie Knew* (1897). *Further Reading: Portrait of a Novel: Henry James and the Making of an American Masterpiece* by Michael Gorra. *Henry James: The Conquest of London, 1870–1881* by Leon Edel. *Try: Middlemarch* by George Eliot (see page 248). *The Age of Innocence* by Edith Wharton (see page 844). *Adaptations:* There is a superb audiobook read by Juliet Stevenson. Jane Campion's 1996 film stars Nicole Kidman as Isabel. *Footnote:* Max Beerbohm's 1912 send-up of the high-Jamesian style, "The Mote in the Middle Distance," may be the most deft literary parody in English. If you find James insufferable, you'll find Beerbohm's imitation of him hilarious; if you love James, you'll find it even funnier.

The Collected Ghost Stories of M. R. James
M. R. James (1862–1936)

Warnings to the Curious

"For many aficionados of the genre, these are the finest spooky tales in the English language," asserts critic Michael Dirda, one of the ghost story's most devoted acolytes. An accomplished medievalist, Montague Rhodes James was a Cambridge don and provost at Eton, and his tales often center on a sedate scholar's inadvertent encounter with the eerie.

A mere three dozen stories constitute nearly all of James's literary output, which he composed in his off-hours and often shared in Christmas readings to his students. No surprise, then, that a James story is just the thing for a winter's evening read-aloud by a fireside, when the comfort of domestic security is challenged by the cozy threat of supernatural specters. No surprise, either, that the storytelling is invitingly uncomplicated, addressing the reader directly as it accumulates small, colorful digressions to establish a field of ordinariness that will be quietly transformed by the creeping sense of unexplained phenomena.

Famously, the protagonists of James's stories are often antiquarians, men given to rummaging in realities they assume to be safely ensconced in the distant past but that turn out to be filled with amulets, inscriptions, volumes, objects, and artifacts better left untouched. Their meticulous piecing together of paper trails can lead to uncanny places, where fear is not so much embodied as suggested by the shadows of imposing sensations or the palpable presence of ominous creatures. A reticent understatement is the seductive hallmark of James's wooing of terror in the reading: No gruesome, bloody shocks break his evocative spells. Just one small step down a seemingly prosaic, predictable path and James's characters can find

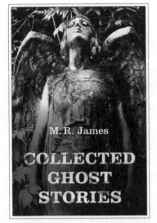

themselves over the edge of the familiar world in an environment of enigma, uncertainty, and evil portent, like the poor fellow who purchases a mezzotint that—well, better not to spoil it. "The Mezzotint" is one of the author's best tales, and—like "Oh, Whistle, and I'll Come to You, My Lad," "Casting the Runes," "Canon Alberic's Scrap-Book," "Count Magnus," and "A Warning to the Curious"—should not be missed.

What: Short Stories. *When:* 1931. *Further Reading: Warnings to the Curious: A Sheaf of Criticism on M. R. James,* edited by S. T. Joshi and Rosemary Pardoe. *Try: Madam Crowl's Ghost and Other Tales of Mystery* by Sheridan Le Fanu, edited by M. R. James. *Meddling with Ghosts: Stories in the Tradition of M. R. James,* edited by Ramsey Campbell. *Cold Hand in Mine: Strange Stories* by Robert Aickman. *Adaptation: Curse of the Demon,* Jacques Tourneur's 1957 film, effectively captures the eerie qualities of James's "Casting the Runes."

A Taste for Death
P. D. James (1920–2014)

A Mystery of Faith

P. D. James's last novel was *Death Comes to Pemberley* (2011), a sequel of sorts to *Pride and Prejudice,* continuing Jane Austen's story of Elizabeth Bennet and Fitzwilliam Darcy. Published in the author's ninety-first year, it was clearly a labor of love, smartly integrating characters from other Austen novels as well as the one providing its central inspiration. Both the aesthetic and the atmosphere of the original are deftly evoked, although, as the title suggests, James brings her own area of literary expertise to

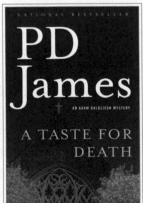

bear by introducing murder into the domain of the Darcys' privileged happiness. That she succeeds in creating a satisfying and accomplished novel in the shadow of such a revered work is a tribute to James's skill and good taste—qualities in ample evidence in every volume on the impressive shelf of acclaimed detective fiction that preceded her final work.

Long before *Death Comes to Pemberley,* it would have been fair to characterize James's thoughtful and meticulously plotted mysteries as having an air of Austen about them, if one could imagine Austen writing about homicide and police investigations with the same acuity she brought to social conventions. Despite the different etiquette prompted by crime scenes and gruesome violence (James's mysteries are by no means of the "cozy" variety), the reader is engaged by a similar conversation between intelligence and experience, manners and meaning. For like her literary forebear, James developed a knack for infusing her storytelling with larger themes. This was never more apparent than in *A Taste for Death*, the seventh of her set of fourteen novels featuring Scotland Yard detective Adam Dalgliesh, a man of parts whose complex personality—he's a poet as well as a Jaguar-driving inspector—imbues his cases with both gravitas and grace.

The book begins with a precision of time, place, and other coordinates—a police procedural, after all, being in essence a fatal novel of manners. An old woman and a young boy discover two dead bodies in a church. In life, the two men lying in the vestry, both with their throats slit, could hardly have been more different: One was a local vagrant, the other a baronet and a rising star in politics. In one of the most puzzling investigations of his long career, Commander Dalgliesh must unravel the twisted threads that yoked them together in death. As James details his investigations, the plot resonates with themes of faith and doubt that give unexpected dimensions to the question "What happens next?" Fellow crime novelist H. R. F. Keating, creator of the delightful Inspector Ghote, summed up James's achievement in this book best when he wrote, "By entering the worlds and minds of all her main characters—suspects, investigators, bystanders—she has been able to say more about life than has hitherto been attempted in the crime form."

What: Mystery & Suspense. *When:* 1985. *Also By: Cover Her Face* (1962). *An Unsuitable Job for a Woman* (1972). *The Children of Men* (1992). *The Private Patient* (2008). *Try: Payment in Blood* by Elizabeth George. *Last Seen Wearing* by Colin Dexter. *The Vault* by Ruth Rendell.

WILLIAM JAMES
(1842–1910)

I n the museum of American genius, no luminary shines with as much liveliness as the doctor, philosopher, and psychologist William James. Even in its exploration of the most profound themes, and despite the shadows of melancholy from which his brilliance clearly emerges, his work sparkles with a wit one can only describe as playful. Although never unserious, his writing is animated by a dynamism that seems somehow commensurate with life's own uncontainable energy. As a professor at Harvard, he must have been a marvelous teacher; that suspicion is confirmed by the testimony of two quite different students who came under his sway: the future sociologist and historian W. E. B. Du Bois (see *The Souls of Black Folk*, page 235), and the budding literary experimentalist Gertrude Stein (see *The Autobiography of Alice B. Toklas*, page 751). Du Bois called James "my friend and guide to clear thinking," while Stein honored him as "my big influence when I was at college." It will take only a few pages of his prose to convince any reader of James's gift for inspiration, as the two books singled out here attest.

The Selected Letters of William James

Edited by Elizabeth Hardwick

A Correspondence Course in Wisdom

What: Diaries & Letters. *When:* 1961. *Further Reading: The Thought and Character of William James* by Ralph Barton Perry. *A Stroll with William James* by Jacques Barzun. *Try:* The letters of Oliver Wendell Holmes Jr., including *Holmes-Laski Letters* (see page 504). *Footnote:* For the record, the complete correspondence of William James runs to twelve volumes.

Whether encapsulating a truth experience has taught us but we've never before articulated—"Nothing so fatiguing as the eternal hanging on of an uncompleted task"—or skewering society's received ideas on the point of his pen—"the moral flabbiness born of the exclusive worship of the bitch-goddess SUCCESS"—James offers insight, and, quite often, trenchant advice about how to live without ever resorting to bromides.

His cast of correspondents is both familiar and illustrious, beginning with his brother Henry (see page 408) and his sister Alice (see page 764) and including Oliver Wendell Holmes Jr. (see page 504), Henry Adams (see page 6), John Dewey, and George Santayana. James's struggles with youthful irresolution and with bouts of disquiet and despair make his brilliance approachable and lend an enduring power to his encouragements:

William James, ca. 1895

Remember when old December's darkness is everywhere about you, that the world is really in every minutest point as full of life as in the most joyous morning you ever lived through; that the sun is whanging down, and the waves dancing, and the gulls skimming down at the mouth of the Amazon, for instance, as freshly as in the first morning of creation; and the hour is just as fit as any hour that ever was for a new gospel of cheer to be preached.

It's hard to imagine a more uplifting bedside book than a volume of James's correspondence, and this selection edited and introduced by Elizabeth Hardwick—perfect but for its lack of the "SUCCESS" letter to H. G. Wells quoted above—is the best one to start with.

The Varieties of Religious Experience

In the Stream of Consciousness

James brings the poise of a sage and the instincts of an experimental psychologist to this cogent and gripping book, an intensely curious study of "the feelings, acts, and experiences of individual men in their solitude." Although it may seem odd that the thinker responsible or the clearest articulation of the principles of Pragmatism should so ambitiously and carefully address religious experience as well, the two themes are, in James's practice, closely allied as attempts to find a workable grasp on the flux of life. No other philosophical thinker offers the reader such a palpable sense that his words on the page are grappling with the very tangles we must unravel to make the smallest meaning for ourselves: "The philosophy which is so important in each of us is not a technical matter; it is our more or less dumb sense of what life honestly and deeply means," he writes in *Pragmatism* (1907). "It is only partly got from books; it is our individual way of just seeing and feeling the total push and pressure of the cosmos."

How we bend and sway, straighten up and take strength from that push and pressure is the subject of *The Varieties of Religious Experience,* which collects the talks James delivered as the Gifford Lecturer in Natural Religion at the University of Edinburgh in 1900–1902. In characteristically Jamesian fashion, the book avoids theoretical constructs to enter the chambers of confusion—and sometimes consolation—in which we live. Discussion of theology, institutional dogma, and ecclesiasticism is eschewed to focus on the experiential consequences of the religious impulse, which James defines as "the belief that there is an unseen order, and that our supreme good lies in harmoniously adjusting ourselves thereto." ("All our scientific and philosophic ideals are altars to unknown gods," he had written some years before.)

Seeing this belief in an unseen order as a psychological need to make a music of meaning more resonant than the simple scales of rationalism, James explores the soul's struggle to adapt to the "buzzing blooming confusion" of the universe it dwells in so uncertainly. He illuminates his pages with anecdotes, reflections on his wide literary, scientific, and religious reading, and a preternatural gift for indelible images. In his leisurely, learned, insightful ruminations on "the sick soul" and "the divided self," on states of grace and states of despair, on conversion, saintliness, mysticism, and more, he furthers his lifelong exploration of the "stream of consciousness"—a phrase he coined—that is the medium of our existence. His acknowledgment of the reality of personal forces tempers the scientific perspective he brings to bear in a way that makes us listen harder to this incomparable educator, who knows so much, and nothing by rote.

What: Religion & Spirituality. *When:* 1902. *Also By: The Will to Believe* (1897). *A Pluralistic Universe* (1909). *Further Reading: William James: In the Maelstrom of American Modernism* by Robert D. Richardson. *Try: The Idea of the Holy* by Rudolf Otto. *Mysticism* by Evelyn Underhill.

The Origin of Consciousness in the Breakdown of the Bicameral Mind
Julian Jaynes (1920–1997)

An Exhilarating Theory of the Genesis of Thought

On any list of intellectually provocative volumes, this brilliant exploration of the nature, origin, and history of consciousness earns a place near the top. Jaynes posits that human consciousness was not inherent in animal evolution, but rather is a learned process, based on metaphorical language, that emerged roughly three thousand years ago in response to historical stresses and increasing social complexity. Consciousness, Jaynes asserts, grew out of an earlier mentality he calls the "bicameral" (two-chambered) mind, in which human beings experienced what were essentially auditory or verbal hallucinations that they interpreted as the voices of gods and that directed their actions.

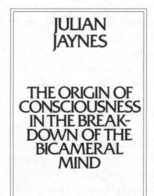

His thesis, baldly stated, sounds a bit bonkers, and his imagery is certainly sensational. But following the development of his ideas through his compelling text, which is strewn with historical, archaeological, neuroscientific, psychological, and literary corroborative evidence, one discovers a wonderland of startling perceptions where things seem to shimmer with new meaning. (He offers particularly fascinating discussions of *The Iliad* and *The Odyssey*.) Jaynes's ideas remain controversial; although they are engaged by some contemporary thinkers and scientists, such as Daniel Dennett, they are dismissed by others. Whether or not you are convinced by the author's arguments, his speculations are guaranteed to invigorate your thinking about thought, language, antiquity, and human nature.

What: Psychology. Antiquity. *When:* 1977. *Further Reading:* "Julian Jaynes's Software Archeology" by Daniel C. Dennett (collected in *Brainchildren*). *Reflections on the Dawn of Consciousness: Julian Jaynes's Bicameral Mind Theory Revisited*, edited by Marcel Kuijsten. *Try: Consciousness Explained*, also by Dennett. *Phantoms in the Brain: Probing the Mysteries of the Human Mind* by V. S. Ramachandran and Sandra Blakeslee.

Heat and Dust
Ruth Prawer Jhabvala (1927–2013)

A Descendant of Austen in the Footsteps of Forster

A novel of manners is a comedy when conventions are shared, small confusions multiply into big ones, and misunderstandings are resolved in marriage. The fiction of Jane Austen is, of course, both the mother and the perfect exemplar of the form. Not much more than a century after Austen, E. M. Forster explored what happens when established customs can no longer encompass—or repress—the urges, emotions, and advances of an age; thus Austen's comedy matured into an ironic

Ruth Prawer Jhabvala with director James Ivory and producer Ismail Merchant, 1981

ruefulness that, in Forster's last novel, *A Passage to India*, crosses the border into more fateful terrain. Ruth Prawer Jhabvala's *Heat and Dust* continues the journey.

Imagine a novel of manners adrift from the moorings of English country society and tenuously contained within "the Civil Lines" of a British colonial enclave in Satipur, India, in 1923. Having joined her husband, Douglas, there, Olivia Rivers finds herself unable to adapt to the provincial isolation of her compatriots. Drawn outside the stultifying social circle of her fellow British wives, Olivia falls in love with the rogue Nawab, a minor Indian prince, and secretly spends her days with him—until circumstances and a scandal threaten both her secret and her life. Tellingly, Olivia's story is revealed years after the fact, as it is discovered by a descendant who has traveled to India in the 1970s to find out exactly what happened to her infamous forebear. The younger woman

becomes entangled in a new Indian life of her own, one that echoes and expands the meaning of Olivia's experience, and the stories of both lives are rendered by Jhabvala in a resonating counterpoint that extends, in a cross-cultural setting, the illuminating novelistic visions of Austen and Forster before her.

Jhabvala was born in Germany to Jewish parents who fled to England in 1939. Raised in Britain, she married an Indian architect in 1951 and spent two decades in India before making New York her primary residence in 1975. Not surprisingly, her many books draw on her knowledge of disparate cultures and the often tangled traffic between them, none more rewardingly than *Heat and Dust*. In addition to the acclaim she has earned for her fiction, Jhabvala is one of the most celebrated screenwriters of our time, having won Oscars for her adaptations of two of E. M. Forster's novels, *A Room with a View* and *Howards End*.

What: Novel. *When:* 1975. *Award:* Booker Prize, 1975. *Also By: The Householder* (1960). *In Search of Love and Beauty* (1983). *East Into Upper East: Plain Tales from New York and New Delhi* (1998). *My Nine Lives: Chapters of a Possible Past* (2004). *Try: A Passage to India* by E. M. Forster (see page 290). *The Raj Quartet* by Paul Scott. *Adaptation:* Film adaptation by Ismail Merchant and James Ivory, 1983. *Footnote:* Jhabvala received a third Oscar nomination, in 1994, for *The Remains of the Day.* Her screenplay *Jane Austen in Manhattan* was filmed in 1980.

Harold and the Purple Crayon
Crockett Johnson (1906–1975)

The Intrepid Toddler Who Could

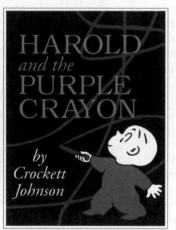

With the aid of a magic purple crayon, a small but very resourceful boy named Harold draws himself into an assortment of delightful adventures. Deciding to go for a walk in the moonlight, he draws a moon and a long straight path, then sets off. The products of his purple crayon—a tree, a dragon, a picnic, a sailboat, a mountain, a hot air balloon—contribute to his adventures, until he grows tired enough to head home. Even then, his crayon points the way, "making" his bed and "drawing" up his covers. It's hard to imagine a more ingenious concept for a picture book, or a more delightful celebration of the powers of the imagination.

Harold is the most winning of protagonists, and his adventures delight readers from the earliest age. His initial adventure was followed by several sequels: *Harold's Fairy Tale* (1956), *Harold's Trip to the Sky* (1957), *Harold at the North Pole* (1958), *Harold's Circus* (1959), *A Picture for Harold's Room* (1960), and *Harold's ABC* (1963). You'd be hard pressed to find a youngster who wouldn't love these clever, immensely likable books (or an adult who wouldn't delight in sharing them).

What: Children's. *When:* 1955. *Also By: Barnaby* (1943). *Who's Upside Down?* (1952). *Barkis* (1956). *Ellen's Lion* (1959). *Try: The Zoom Trilogy* by Tim Wynne-Jones (see page 875). *Adaptations:* Harold has been a star of short films and an Emmy Award–winning television series. *Footnote:* Johnson was married to the prolific children's book author Ruth Krauss; he illustrated several of her classic works, including *The Carrot Seed* (1945).

A Johnson Reader
Samuel Johnson (1709–1784)
Edited by E. L. McAdam Jr. and George Milne

The Uncommon Reader

Samuel Johnson looms over the conventional history of English literature like a presiding judge, the man of letters par excellence. Poet, essayist, and editor, commentator and conversationalist, lexicographer and sage, Dr. Johnson lived by his pen and his wits, setting standards that both comprehended the qualities of our language and expanded its literary and expressive possibilities. Johnson's *A Dictionary of the English Language*, published in 1755, is one of the most singular (and entertaining) works of scholarship ever composed, shaping both the past and the future of its subject. The prefaces and annotations of his edition of Shakespeare, published a decade after the *Dictionary*, gave the dramatist's works a living and a lasting presence as incarnations of real life rather than as Elizabethan monuments. His *Lives of the Most Eminent English Poets* (1779–81) surveyed the poetical tradition with a sensibility attentive enough to hear in even provincial versifiers a universal voice. His essays, published under the rubrics *The Rambler* (1750–52) and *The Idler* (1758–60) were—and still remain—secular sermons remarkable for their intuitions and moral eloquence. His poems, such as *The Vanity of Human Wishes* (1749), along with *Rasselas* (1759), his narrative exploration of the subject of happiness, and his travelogue, *A Journey to the Western Islands of Scotland* (1775), only add to the scope and standing of his bibliography.

And yet: No one work really comes close to carrying his stature, and modern readers might find themselves at a loss as to how to read him. It's best to follow the lead of Johnson himself, who left school at the age of sixteen and, unable to afford university, spent the next few years in his father's bookshop, plunging into dozens of books with a cursory but apprehensive eye, in vigorous pursuit of what Edmund Wilson once called "the miscellaneous learning of the bookstore, unorganized by any larger purpose, the undisciplined undirected curiosity of the indolent lover of reading." In other words, pick up a sampler of Johnson's work, and dip into it as the spirit moves you; McAdam and Milne's *A Johnson Reader* is an excellent resource for this, containing several of his best essays, the prefaces to Shakespeare and the *Dictionary* (with selections therefrom), biographical writings, poetry, and letters. Your estimation of Johnson's achievement—and your wonder at the relevance of his insights into life as well as literature—will grow with every paragraph you read.

Engraving of Samuel Johnson, ca. 1750

Nearly all Johnson's work was done on deadline ("No man but a blockhead ever wrote, except for money," he once said) and it was often late; yet for all the hurry and opportunistic impulses that drove him, he managed to become, by virtue of the architectural strength and intellectual poise of his sentences, from epigram to period, something like the master builder of our literary language.

What: Literature. Literary Criticism. *When:* The McAdam-Milne anthology, published in 1964, collects works written between 1744 and 1784. *Try:* Henry Darcy Curwen's *A Johnson Sampler*, a perceptive and valuable thematic sorting of emblematic passages from Johnson's work, is also recommended.

||||||||||||||||||||||||||||||||||||| **MORE TO EXPLORE** |||||||||||||||||||||||||||||||||||||

THE BIOGRAPHICAL JOHNSON

"Johnson the man," one anthologizer of his work has written, "was greater than Johnson the writer," and at least three marvelous biographical works provide ample evidence in support of this assertion. As impressive as his strictly literary achievement remains, Johnson's enduring reputation rests on the personal attributes so deftly rendered by three of his biographers. James Boswell captured the fluency and expressiveness of his friend's fabled conversation in an enormous, contemporary life that became a classic as soon as it was published. Some two centuries on, W. Jackson Bate revealed the quality of his subject's character in overcoming physical and mental affliction. And Richard Holmes, writing most recently, has animated as never before Johnson's gift for friendship and the human truths—"poised," as Holmes attests, "between fact and fiction"—that any life story turns on.

The Life of Samuel Johnson
James Boswell (1740–1795)

In a recent book about Boswell's masterpiece, Adam Sisman declared that it "stands next to other biographies as Shakespeare stands beside other playwrights: towering above them all." In no small part that is because its subject possessed a personality and a way with words that might have been fashioned by the Bard himself.

Johnson's celebrated *Lives of the Poets* led Boswell to acknowledge at the outset

Engraving of Samuel Johnson by E. Finden, ca. 1760

that "To write the Life of him who excelled all mankind in writing the lives of others [. . .] may be reckoned in me a presumptuous task." A hard-drinking ne'er-do-well, Boswell ended up taking seven years to accomplish it. Having met Johnson in 1763, he focused his biography on his subject's life from that point on. Thus Johnson's first fifty-three years take up less than one-fifth of Boswell's *Life of Samuel Johnson* (1791), whereas the rest is animated with Boswell's day-to-day proximity to the esteemed man, producing a sociability, rare in lives of the great. The narrative is further enlivened by the contrast between the two men: Their differences in age, temperament, politics, and religion might have ended their relationship if they hadn't been so congenial in other respects—especially in their mutual appetite for conversation. Thanks to Boswell's service as an early oral historian, Johnson's incomparable talk fills the *Life*'s thousand-plus pages; just as he commanded the attention of his contemporaries, so Johnson still commands ours, speaking to us "in a clear and forcible manner," as Boswell writes, "so that knowledge, which we often see to be no better than lumber in men of dull understanding, was, in him, true, evident, and actual wisdom."

Samuel Johnson
W. Jackson Bate (1918–1999)

With focus on the early years and the working life of letters that is outside Boswell's purview, W. Jackson Bate presents a character study as enlightening about the vagaries of human nature—and as reassuring in its depiction of how such wandering energies might nonetheless find a meaningful destiny—as any you are likely to read. Tracing Johnson's coming-of-age and cobbling together of a career as he faces financial obstacles,

debilitating bouts of melancholia and guilt, and a range of bodily ailments, Bate writes with sympathy and insight of how this brilliant misfit overcame his inner demons to make a majestic way in the outer world by means of his powers of observation and expression:

> *. . . the almost desperate clutch outward to fact and objective reality of any sort in order to cleanse and free the dark subjective self—with all its frantic fears, and all its blind and destructive treacheries, including self-treachery—and to pull it, in self-preservation, up from the serpent pit of subjective isolation into sanity, light, and stability.*

Infused with the riches of intellectual clarity and moral acuity displayed in Johnson's writing, Bate's 1977 book is unexpectedly moving, a tale of genius, consolation, and wisdom that will shore up a reader's defenses against the sorrows and surprises of life. Truly.

Dr. Johnson and Mr. Savage
Richard Holmes (born 1945)

About a dozen years older than Johnson, Richard Savage was a minor poet and a major rogue, notorious for his misbehavior. Somewhat inexplicably, given the younger man's evident probity, the two struck a bond of friendship, and spent many impoverished evenings together on long walks through London. Johnson seemed to invest their relationship with considerable private resonance, and was clearly under Savage's spell, so much so that six months after the latter's death, and some five years after their separation, he penned *The Life of Mr. Richard Savage* (1744). This composition, the author's first significant work of prose, represented, as Holmes convincingly argues, a new form of life-writing, shaped by their intimate night walks: "It was to be like an extended conversation in the dark, taking ordinary facts and anecdotes, and pursuing them towards the shadowy and mysterious regions of a life, at the edge of the unknown or unknowable."

Reconstructing Savage's story by his own research, Holmes investigates how Johnson informed it with his emerging knowledge of human nature and emotion, revolutionizing biography and the romantic notion of the poet as well. If Boswell's *Life* unfolds as a period miniseries deploying a rambunctious cast in a comedy of conversational manners, and Bate's biography is a darker chronicle of tragic personal dimensions transformed by toil into an inspirational dramatic arc, then Holmes's 1993 *Dr. Johnson and Mr. Savage* might be seen as a dazzling independent film that takes elements of the same story and fashions them into a brilliant meditation on the biographical enterprise itself—and therefore on the subject of how we take the measure, and find the meaning, of any life at all, including, Johnson might propose, our own.

A False Spring
Pat Jordan (born 1941)

The Breaks of the Game

"I see myself daily as I was then, framed in a photograph on the desk in my attic room. The picture was taken on June 27, 1959, at County Stadium in Milwaukee, Wisconsin, a few minutes before the Milwaukee Braves were to take the field against the Chicago Cubs." The Pat Jordan in the picture, eighteen years old and recently signed to his first professional baseball contract, is wearing a Braves uniform and engaged in small talk with future Hall-of-Famer Warren Spahn, then the ace in Milwaukee's rotation. The image, as the older Jordan who ponders it well knows, captures a moment lit with the promise of a golden future: big-league success, cheering crowds, World Series rings.

That future never unfolded. Jordan pitched three years in the minor leagues—"at towns like McCook, Davenport, Waycross, Eau Claire, and Palatka"—watching his dreams shrink as his control, and his career, floundered: "I never did pitch a game in Milwaukee County Stadium, nor did I ever again speak to Warren Spahn." Nonetheless, having moved on to marriage, fatherhood, college, teaching, and writing, Jordan remained defined by baseball, and a decade after he left the mound—still thinking of himself "not as a writer who once pitched, but as a pitcher who happens to be writing just now"—he composed a memoir that is filled with the lore of the game, the heat of competition, the camaraderie of the locker room, nostalgia and regret, bewilderment at time's unhittable slow curves. Following his fortunes from backyard catches with his father to his stellar high school career, the heady days of his wooing by pro scouts to the heartache of his eventual failure, Jordan composed one of the best-written, truest memoirs you'll ever read—not just about baseball, but about growing up as well.

What: Sports. Memoir. *When:* 1975. *Also By: The Suitors of Spring* (1973). *A Nice Tuesday* (1999). *The Best Sports Writing of Pat Jordan* (2008). *Try: Ball Four* by Jim Bouton. *A Season in the Sun* by Roger Kahn.

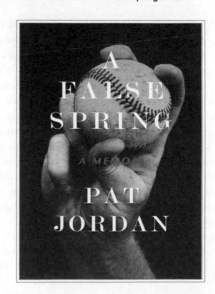

JAMES JOYCE
(1882–1941)

For the better part of the twentieth century, James Joyce haunted modern literature like a mythological figure, ensconced at the center of a labyrinth of difficulty. The encrypted majesty of his masterpiece, *Ulysses*, cast the alternately recondite and playful genius of Joyce's writing in a forbidding light (to say nothing of the maniacal experimentation of its successor, *Finnegans Wake*, one of the oddest and most impenetrable books ever penned). And yet, as a reader's progress through the three works discussed below reveals, the high-mindedness of the author's literary vocation was allied to a preternatural alertness to the tenor and texture of everyday life. As a result, Joyce's calling to pursue the ambitions of ever-reaching young artists like his alter ego, Stephen Dedalus, was tempered by a painstaking sympathy for the illusions and emotions of ordinary people.

James Joyce, 1928

Dubliners
An Invitation to an Irish Master

Dubliners is one of the most admired collections of short stories in world literature. Published in 1914, it was Joyce's first book of prose. Although the fifteen stories follow different characters through disparate situations, the collection's overarching unity of theme and imagery shapes an experiential itinerary through childhood, young adulthood, maturity, and public life. Many of the stories hinge on an "epiphany," a telltale moment of illumination that Joyce defined as "a sudden spiritual manifestation, whether in the vulgarity of speech or of gesture or in a memorable phase of the mind itself."

Born in Dublin, Joyce exiled himself from the city beginning in 1904, when he was twenty-two. In his writing, however, he never left—his imagination stayed firmly grounded in his native soil. The emphatically autobiographical

Dubliners collectively relates events that take place in the city between 1894 and 1905. While Joyce's attitude toward Ireland was harshly critical, he considered it part of his artistic mission to initiate "the spiritual liberation of my country." (This adversarial stance, as manifested in the certain bleakness and alleged sordidness of some of the stories, led to a decade-long delay in the book's publication.) Yet his severe regard is balanced by an intimate, almost secret empathy toward the undistinguished characters he dwells upon: the child viewing the corpse of Father Flynn in "The Sisters," the boy in first pursuit of romantic disenchantment in "Araby," the conflicted young woman too diffident to elope in "Eveline," the political functionaries going about their business in "Ivy Day in the Committee Room."

Although several of Joyce's stories are recognized as masterpieces of the genre, "The Dead," the book's longest and its final tale, must be singled out as one of the finest works of fiction in English; its concluding sentences concentrate the music and magic of our language into a breathtaking—and heartbreaking—spell. If you never read anything else by James Joyce, do not forsake "The Dead."

What: Short Stories. *When:* 1914. *Edition: James Joyce's Dubliners: An Illustrated Edition, with Annotations* by John Wyse Jackson and Bernard McGinley. *Further Reading: Dublin's Joyce* by Hugh Kenner. *Try:* The stories of Chekhov (see page 153) and Frank O'Connor (see page 598). *Adaptations:* John Huston's film *The Dead* was released in 1987. The 2000 audiobook read by Frank McCourt and others is splendid.

A Portrait of the Artist as a Young Man
The Story of a Vocation

Once upon a time and a very good time it was there was a moocow coming down along the road...

Joyce's first novel begins with an evocation of the sensations of infancy. Snatches of story and song and smell (for even the highest flights of this author's aesthetic fancy are rooted in common realities) are summoned to the page. In this elemental welter of sound and sense, Joyce suggests, a writer's education begins.

Stephen Dedalus is the writer in question, and the early portions of Joyce's fiercely autobiographical coming-of-age novel show him growing up and then rebelling against his family, his country, and his religion, while never quite escaping his conflicted affection for each. The narrative proceeds in richly textured yet sometimes enigmatically unfolded episodes: a family Christmas dinner in which the spirit of the season is overthrown by political argument; Stephen's first sexual experience and subsequent bouts of adolescent debauchery; a religious retreat that prompts a fervent but short-lived embrace of piety. Each episode represents

a measure of Stephen's emotional, educational, and cultural inheritance, a strand, if you will, of his imagination's DNA. As he is on the verge of entering university, a liberating epiphany sets him firmly on the course of artistic aspiration, and a clutch of pages of enlightening theorizing on aesthetics and intellection follow; never has the thrill of cerebral exertion been so viscerally conveyed.

Although Stephen is a compelling figure, any reader past the prime of youth will recognize the egotism of his earnestness; emphasizing his hero's self-involvement, Joyce subtly reminds us that this uncompromising young artist has not yet really set pen to paper. The author's verbal magic, on the other hand, is everywhere apparent; the melodies he conjures in this mesmerizing and indelibly original portrait are transporting, from the simple observation of a bird—"He watched their flight; bird after bird: a dark flash, a swerve, a flash again, a dart aside, a curve, a flutter of wings"—to the expression of Stephen's most eloquent temerity: "to try slowly and humbly and constantly to express, to press out again, from the gross earth or what it brings forth, from sound and shape and colour which are the prison gates of our soul, an image of the beauty we have come to understand—that is art." Although those words may be presumptuous on the part of Stephen Dedalus, they capture with exactitude what his creator would achieve, triumphantly if often obscurely, in his next book.

A PORTRAIT OF THE ARTIST AS A YOUNG MAN

What: Novel. *When:* Written between 1904 and 1914, *Portrait* was published in 1916. *Further Reading: James Joyce* by Richard Ellmann. *Try: The Prelude* by William Wordsworth (see page 871). *The Magic Mountain* by Thomas Mann (see page 521). *The Letters of Samuel Beckett, Volume 1: 1929–1940. Adaptations:* Bosco Hogan, T. P. McKenna, and John Gielgud star in the 1977 film directed by Joseph Strick. The Naxos audiobook, read by Jim Norton, is a fine complement to a reading of the text. *Footnote:* The fragmentary *Stephen Hero*, published posthumously in 1944, is an early version of *Portrait*.

Ulysses
A City in a Book

··

Picking up Stephen Dedalus's trail a few years on—his wings clipped, the fledgling artist has returned to Dublin from Paris no further along in the pursuit of his promise—*Ulysses* is perhaps the most famously difficult of all modern novels. Its difficulty, however, doesn't lie in the story it tells, which, in its essentials, is quite simple: The book recounts certain events, most of them not in the least extraordinary, that occur in Dublin on June 16, 1904. The narrative focuses primarily on two men whose paths cross at various points during the day: Stephen, now twenty-two and a teacher, and Leopold Bloom, a middle-aged husband and father who makes his living selling advertising for a Dublin paper. Bloom's wife, Molly, is the principal female character; the book ends with her celebrated soliloquy—and, despite the seven-hundred-odd pages of literary virtuosity that precede it, one can fairly say her concluding rhapsody steals the show.

What does make *Ulysses* more difficult than most novels is the manner of its telling. There are three major reasons for this. First, Joyce often uses a "stream of consciousness" technique that allows a character's thoughts to speak directly, without the conventional mediation of the author, as when Bloom enters a restaurant: "Stink gripped his trembling breath: pungent meatjuice, slop of greens. See the animals feed." Readers who initially find the technique disorienting quickly grow accustomed to this type of eavesdropping. Second, as is suggested by the book's title, the episodes in *Ulysses* correspond at many points to those in *The Odyssey* (see page 386), Homer's tale of the Greek hero's long and winding journey home from the Trojan War. Not only did Joyce intend these parallels—he explained that he meant them to demonstrate the "epic" or "heroic" nature of everyday life—but he himself supplied them to the novel's first commentators to aid their explications of its intricacy.

Third, there's the challenge presented by Joyce's sentences themselves. In few other books is the prose itself so much a character, changing in style from one chapter to the next,

enacting what it describes rather than merely describing it. The stylistic richness and bravura of *Ulysses* are both daunting and exhilarating, often in the same line. The concentration of Joyce's powers makes each passage a treasure to be excavated, each page its own Troy. (Sample Bloom window-shopping at a silk merchant—four short sentences in which the author later revealed he had invested a full day's labor: "A warm human plumpness settled down on his brain. His brain yielded. Perfume of embraces all him assailed. With hungered flesh obscurely, he mutely craved to adore.") Joyce's embrace of sound and sense is all-encompassing, subsuming within his narrative a startling variety of tone: Newspaper headlines, barroom slang, the languages of the law and of civil authority, catechism—all are given their turn on the stage.

Beneath all the complexity, Dublin remains the Muse, if not the real hero, of Joyce's epic. No other work of literature had ever set out to replicate—and celebrate—the noise of urban life with such alertness, art, spite, and glee. Capturing the city he loved and despaired of in all its hunks and colors, grime and glory, grievances and yearnings, Joyce created a literary metropolis that hums, moans, shouts, and sings with the collective music of the human comedy. There is no other book like it.

What: Novel. *When:* 1922. *Edition:* In recent years, there has been much controversy surrounding "corrected" editions of *Ulysses*, but the readily available 1960 version of the text (1961 in the United States) is your best choice. *Reading Note: Ulysses* is best tackled with a guide to orient you, episode by episode. An especially helpful one is *The New Bloomsday Book* by Harry Blamires. *Also By: Finnegans Wake* (1939). *Further Reading: Myselves When Young* by Frank Budgen. *The Pound Era* by Hugh Kenner (see page 441). *Try: Life: A User's Manual* by Georges Perec (see page 623). *Adaptations: Ulysses in Nighttown*, a 1958 stage adaptation, featured Zero Mostel as Bloom. Joseph Strick's film of *Ulysses* was released in 1967. *Bloom*, a film starring Stephen Rea, appeared in 2004. The Naxos audiobook, read by Jim Norton and Marcella Riordan, offers a surprisingly vivid companion to the printed text. *Footnote:* June 16th is now celebrated as "Bloomsday" in literary precincts around the world.

Memories, Dreams, Reflections

C. G. Jung (1875–1961)

An Influential Mind Reader

A long with Sigmund Freud, Carl Gustav Jung is one of the architects of the museum of the psyche erected in the early decades of the twentieth century to put our dreams, desires, and anxieties on display for examination. Whereas Freud's approach mined what might be called a "personal" unconscious through strata of repressed sexuality, Jung espoused a more expansive view of personality and its subliminal veins. He discovered that, as far as our unconscious lives are concerned, there is even more that doesn't meet the eye than Freud imagined.

Compared with his older colleague, Jung is a wilder and more difficult figure. Indeed, as far as the character of modern psychology is concerned, he is something of the id to Freud's ego. As the founder of analytical psychology, Jung made major contributions to the modern understanding of the mind; his concept of the "collective unconscious"—in which certain dispositions and beliefs are common across humankind—has entered the intellectual lexicon (as, it must be noted, have other Jungian coinages, such as the "archetype," the "complex," "introversion" and "extroversion," and "synchronicity"). Yet Jung was also prone to mysticism, with side interests in alchemy and astrology. In midlife he was afflicted with debilitating visions and hallucinations, which he documented in the strange volume known as *The Red Book*, a handwritten manuscript illustrated with swirling occult-inflected paintings that was not published until 2009, nearly fifty years after his death.

His most broadly influential work, *Memories, Dreams, Reflections*, also published posthumously, is an autobiography of sorts, grafting his work and life together in a single story. In this book we can look behind Jung's psychological writings to see the man who struggled so fiercely to conceive them. Early in his career he was a devoted disciple of Freud; when their conceptions of the unconscious began to diverge, they broke their relationship, at severe personal cost. Jung found his writing became more difficult, and he was

Carl Jung, ca. 1940

anxious about the relevance of his work. "My whole being," he writes at one point, "was seeking for something still unknown which might confer meaning upon the banality of life."

Jung is constantly gripped by fears of the world's vacuity, so much so that at times he falls into despair. Striving to describe significance in time's tantalizing void forms the central thread of his career, and it helps to explain why a scientist such as Jung would also find mystical topics so seductive. *Memories, Dreams, Reflections* is a valuable introduction to the fundamentals of his psychological principles, but more than that, it is a portrait of the search for meaning in the modern world, a task no less pressing in this century than it was in the previous one—or, it must be said, in all the collective ones before that.

What: Psychology. Autobiography. When: 1963. Also By: Psychology of the Unconscious (1912). Man and His Symbols (1964). The Red Book (2009). Further Reading: Carl Jung by Paul Bishop. Jung and the Making of Modern Psychology: The Dream of a Science by Sonu Shamdasani. Try: The Interpretation of Dreams by Sigmund Freud (see page 299). The Origins and History of Consciousness by Erich Neumann. The Hero with a Thousand Faces by Joseph Campbell.

The Phantom Tollbooth
Norton Juster (born 1929)

Boredom Banished

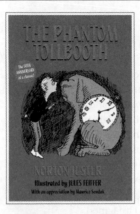

Like many kids, Milo, the protagonist of Norton Juster's quick-witted fantasy, is chronically bored. Until the day, that is, when a mysterious package appears in his room without explanation. He unwraps it to discover a small replica of a turnpike tollbooth complete with assembly instructions, notices on placards ("SLOW DOWN APPROACHING TOLLBOOTH," "PLEASE HAVE YOUR FARE READY," and "HAVE YOUR DESTINATION IN MIND"), and a map to places with strange names. Who'd ever heard of a city called Dictionopolis?! Naturally enough, having put the tollbooth together, there is nothing for Milo to do but climb into his toy car and drive it through his unexpected gift.

What follows is one of the most exuberant, clever, silly, mind-bending, and joyous expeditions in children's literature—a festival of puns, homonyms (including such figures as the Whether Man and the Senses Taker), logical conundrums, and topsy-turvy adventures in which Milo meets unforgettable characters, has his assumptions upended, and tries his hand at such things as conducting the colors of a sunrise.

At the outset of his journey into the Lands Beyond, a wrong turn leads him into the Doldrums, a region bereft of thought and laughter. Fortunately, Milo is confronted by a ticking watchdog named Tock, who becomes his companion as he moves on to explore an exotic realm of dichotomies, where letters and numbers vie for prominence, and the competing claims of their respective capitals, Dictionopolis and Digitopolis, can't be reconciled unless Milo and Tock rescue the two princesses—Rhyme and Reason—who have been banished to the Castle in the Air. Our heroes' pursuit of this objective leads them through an amusement park of whimsical rides and intellectual roller coasters that unfailingly leave young readers happily reeling.

The Phantom Tollbooth was composed by architect Juster to distract himself from another book he was contracted to write—a volume for young readers on urban aesthetics. The fun he was having as he played hooky is palpable on every page. Juster's neighbor, the cartoonist Jules Feiffer, drew pictures to accompany the text, and the complete work was then delivered to Random House, whose editors had the good sense to publish it even though just about everyone believed it would be over kids' heads. Some of it may well be, but that just means ten-year-olds love it even more at fifteen, and more than that at forty. If you didn't read it as a kid, count yourself lucky. What a treat you have in store!

What: Children's. *When:* 1961. *Also By:* Juster's other beloved classic is *The Dot and the Line: A Romance in Lower Mathematics* (1963). More recent books include *The Hello, Goodbye Window* (2005) and *Sourpuss and Sweetie Pie* (2008), both illustrated by Chris Raschka, and *The Odious Ogre* (2010), also illustrated by Jules Feiffer. *Further Reading: The Annotated Phantom Tollbooth*, annotations by Leonard S. Marcus. *Try: Alice's Adventures in Wonderland* by Lewis Carroll (see page 133). *The Chess Set in the Mirror* by Massimo Bontempelli. *Adaptations: The Phantom Tollbooth* was made into an animated film by Chuck Jones in 1970. Among the stage adaptations is a musical with music by Arnold Black and lyrics by Sheldon Harnick.

"I read it first when I was ten. I still have the book report I wrote, which began, 'This is the best book ever.'"

—*Anna Quindlen on* The Phantom Tollbooth

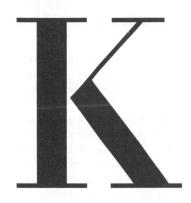

FRANZ KAFKA
(1883–1924)

Franz Kafka can be a forbidding writer, but his idiosyncratic blend of fable-like clarity and horror-tale trepidation has always proved perversely alluring. So much so that, in the decades after his death, modern literary culture became addicted to the uncanny thrill of his enervating, blackly—even obscurely—comic, dread-heightening narration. His gifts as a writer are visible across all genres: in his seminal novels *The Trial* and *The Castle*; in his nonfiction, such as the paradox-filled *Zürau Aphorisms*; in his celebrated letters and diaries, which oscillate between deep passion and utter gloominess; and, perhaps most tellingly, in his stories, which offer a potent distillation of his imaginative world.

The Trial
A Scripture for the Age of Anxiety

It's certainly not the way Josef K, an ambitious chief clerk of a large bank, thought he'd be celebrating his thirtieth birthday: with two unnamed "agents" bursting into his apartment. K is arrested—but the agents won't say of what crime he's accused. He is ordered to court—but they won't tell him what time his case starts, the judges are inaccessible, and the court itself seems to occupy the airless rooms of a dingy tenement building. He tries to get a lawyer—but there's no point proclaiming his innocence, K is informed, because no one has ever been acquitted. As his perverse persecution wears on, K succumbs to paranoia and, ultimately, guilt. He *must* be guilty, K starts to think. Why else would he be here?

The undisputed master of twentieth-century alienation, Franz Kafka spins in *The Trial* a tale as terrifying as it is mysterious. The

Franz Kafka, 1923

novel so captured the contemporary mind that the word "Kafkaesque" was coined—and gained currency far beyond the author's readership—to describe situations that echo Josef K's: hopeless struggles against obdurate or surreal bureaucracies, with no opportunity afforded the victim to escape the system. Kafka's bleakness often rides an edge of comic apprehension, but the comedy is so black that even the humor is alarming. When K complains to his warders that he doesn't know any law that accounts for the arrest of an innocent man, they merely laugh: "He admits that he doesn't know the law and yet he claims he's innocent!"

Kafka wrote most of *The Trial* in 1914 and 1915, while he was working at the Workers' Accident Insurance Institute of the Kingdom of Bohemia, where he processed compensation claims for injured industrial workers. But he never completed *The Trial* (fittingly, the lack of conclusion seems wholly appropriate to everything that has come before), and upon his death from tuberculosis at just forty-one, he expected it to be burned—per his instructions—with the rest of his unpublished work. Thank goodness his friend Max Brod refused Kafka's order, for a great deal of modern literature would be unimaginable without this dark, absurdist masterpiece. Kafka's literary influence remains pervasive, and can be seen in authors as disparate as Haruki Murakami (who named one of his novels *Kafka on the Shore*) and J. M. Coetzee (who adapted part of *The Trial* in his book *Elizabeth Costello*). More importantly, in *The Trial* and his other works, he evokes the kind of fear that is familiar enough for us to recognize, but—like the Old Testament deity—too strange and terrifying for us to name.

What: Novel. *When:* 1925. *Edition:* The first English translation, by Willa and Edwin Muir, appeared in 1937. Several others have recently appeared, none fundamentally altering a reader's experience of the work. *Also By: The Castle* (1926). *Amerika, or The Man Who Disappeared* (1927). *Further Reading: The Nightmare of Reason: A Life of Franz Kafka* by Ernst Pawel. *Try: Sanitorium Under the Sign of the Hourglass* by Bruno Schulz. *The Cave* by José Saramago. *Kafkaesque: Stories Inspired by Franz Kafka*, edited by John Kessel and James Patrick Kelly. *Adaptations:* Orson Welles

filmed *The Trial* in 1962. A second movie version, with a screenplay by Harold Pinter and performances by Kyle MacLachlan and Anthony Hopkins, was released in 1993.

The Complete Stories
Fairy Tales of Fear and Trembling

Anatomizing the absurdity of modern life through ever more bizarre situations and ironies, Kafka's tales have a force out of all proportion to their small scale (one, the cat-and-mouse story "A Little Fable," is just three sentences long). Yet within their deceptive dimensions, they seem to move elemental psychological states—guilt, fear, unknowing—around a symbolic chessboard in a game whose rules we don't quite understand, but whose stakes are clearly high.

Although the stories can be read as a unit, several have gained fame on their own. In "A Hunger Artist," a man in a cage starves himself in forty-day-long performances of fasting, for audiences that are at first enthralled but grow increasingly unimpressed. "In the Penal Colony," which resembles *The Trial* in some ways, is set on an unnamed island settlement where the condemned are tortured with an elaborate contraption. "The Judgment" depicts, with an autobiographical sensitivity, a rivalry between father and son that escalates from trivialities to murderous extremes.

The most famous of the stories, surely, is "The Metamorphosis," an early effort; written in 1912, it's among the few works Kafka saw published during his lifetime. It opens with one of the most bizarre first sentences in literature: "As Gregor Samsa awoke one morning from uneasy dreams he found himself transformed in his bed into a gigantic insect." From that strange beginning Kafka leads us through the remainder of his protagonist's life. At first, Gregor tries to keep his job as a traveling salesman, but eventually he retreats to the prison of his bedroom, where he crawls along the walls and is desperate for the affection of his sister, Grete. Kafka never explains how or why Gregor has changed from human to insect, and the other characters—quite unsettlingly for the reader—seem only mildly perturbed by the bug's presence among them. As in all of Kafka's work, the incomprehensible and the absurd are taken at face value—as if to remind us that his bizarre inventions are not escapes from the world we live in, but cracked mirrors that reflect the fathomless depths that lurk behind the surfaces of everyday experience.

What: Short Stories. *When:* 1904–24. *Edition:* Published in English in one volume in 1971; translated by Willa and Edwin Muir, Tania and James Stern, and Eithne Wilkins and Ernst Kaiser. *Also By: Diaries 1910–1923* (1948–49). *Letter to His Father* (1953). *Letters to Felice* (1967). *Try: Selected Stories* by Robert Walser. *Ficciones* by Jorge Luis Borges (see page 87). *Kafka Americana* by Jonathan Lethem and Carter Scholz. *Kafka's Soup* by Mark Crick.

The Boys of Summer
Roger Kahn (born 1927)

A Grand Slam of a Baseball Book

"You may glory in a team triumphant, but you fall in love with a team in defeat," Roger Kahn observes, reflecting on his own passionate attachment to the Brooklyn Dodgers. Kahn covered "dem Bums" as a sportswriter for the *New York Herald Tribune* during the summers of 1952 and 1953, in the middle of the team's run of "Wait till next year" World Series defeats at the hands of the hated Yankees, their intracity rivals.

The Bums of the early fifties were based at legendary Ebbets Field. The star of the team was second baseman Jackie Robinson, who only a few years earlier had become the first African American player in the major leagues. Other future Hall-of-Famers on the club were Pee Wee Reese, Roy Campanella, and Duke Snider. The roster also included such Brooklyn paragons as Gil Hodges, Andy Pafko, Carl Furillo, Clem Labine, Carl Erskine, and cunning spitballer Preacher Roe. Kahn got to know them all, both on and off the field, in their playing days, then decided—to the good fortune of readers—to renew his acquaintance with them a couple of decades later. *The Boys of Summer* is a series of poignant and pleasurable encounters with middle-aged men battling, generally with grace and good humor, "the implacable enemy, time." Kahn's conversations with the former stars are illuminated

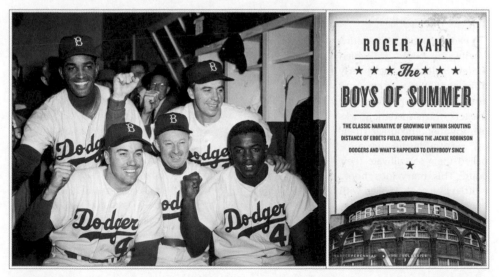

Jackie Robinson (far right) and teammates after game one of the 1952 World Series

throughout with powerful memories of clutch hits, key pitches, and crushing disappointments: "There was a bench where we sat in the bullpen," recalls Labine of the afternoon New York Giant Bobby Thomson's stunning ninth-inning home run robbed the Dodgers of the National League title. "If you can find it, you'll see a chunk of wood is missing. That's where I took a bite."

The brutal day-to-day realities of Robinson's historic, heroic entry into the major leagues is viewed from several perspectives, casting the ball field dramas into a deeper light. Most telling of all, Kahn's sensitivity to the players' new roles—Erskine's devotion to his Down syndrome child, the embittered Furillo's laboring days on the construction site of the World Trade Center, Roy Campanella's wheelchair-using

dignity, Robinson's grief over his troubled son—makes *The Boys of Summer* about much more than baseball. As Peter Prescott wrote on its first publication, it's also "a book about pain and defeat and endurance, about how men anywhere must live."

What: Sports. *When:* 1972. *Also By: A Season in the Sun* (1977). *Good Enough to Dream* (1985) is an especially engaging book that details Kahn's one-year ownership of a minor-league team, the Utica Blue Sox. *The Era: 1947–1957, When the Yankees, the New York Giants, and the Brooklyn Dodgers Ruled the World* (1993). *Try: Wait Till Next Year* by Doris Kearns Goodwin. *What I Learned from Jackie Robinson* by Carl Erskine. *A Day of Light and Shadows* by Jonathan Schwartz.

When French Women Cook
Madeleine Kamman (1930–2018)

Remembrance of Meals Past

Where are you, my France, where women cooked, where the stars in cooking did not go to men anxious for publicity but to women with worn hands stained by vegetables peeled, parched by work in house, garden or fields, wrinkled by age and experience. Where are you?

R eaders have a natural affinity for books in which writers celebrate their early influences: the relatives and acquaintances, mentors and masters who fanned the sparks of inspiration, encouraged their early enthusiasms, or compelled them to cultivate their craft. This marvelous book, written by a cook, is filled with the same sort of affection, nostalgia, and gratitude. In eight chapters, Madeleine Kamman celebrates the women (from her great-grandmother Marie-Charlotte to Magaly Fabre, matriarch of a wine domaine) from whom

she received, and with whom she has shared, the blessings of her vocation.

Happily for the reader, each of the eight women profiled represents a different area of France, allowing Kamman to survey her native cuisine from Normandy to Provence. Although it is packed with recipes as rich with recollection and as fond of time and place as the photographs in a family album, Kamman's personal testament is not only about food, but also about one woman's respect for the culture that nurtured her: "a civilization that was human, tender, enjoyable and lovable."

What: Food & Drink. Memoir. *When:* 1977. *Also By: The Making of a Cook* (1971). *Dinner Against the Clock* (1973). *In Madeleine's Kitchen* (1984). *Try: The Auberge of the Flowering Hearth* by Roy Andries de Groot (see page 202). *Simca's Cuisine* by Simone Beck. *Lulu's Provençal Table* by Richard Olney.

Andersonville
MacKinlay Kantor (1904–1977)

A Searing Novel of the American Civil War

MacKinlay Kantor, 1956

Andersonville, Georgia: As many Union soldiers lost their lives there as at Antietam, Bull Run, Shiloh, Fredericksburg, Chancellorsville, Chickamauga, and Gettysburg combined. But it was not the site of a battle; no, Andersonville—officially Camp Sumter—was a Confederate prison camp in southern Georgia, where between February 1864 and May 1865 nearly 13,000 Union prisoners died from disease, malnutrition, and acts of violence committed by both guards and fellow inmates. After the war, the camp's warden, Henry Wirz, would become the only Confederate officer to hang for war crimes.

By making a prison the focal point of his mammoth Civil War novel, MacKinlay Kantor sets his compassionate but unflinching appraisal of a bloody historical burden not in fields of glory, but in a morass of suffering that envelops soldiers of North and South alike. Andersonville festers with physical pain and emotional exhaustion: The torments of wounds, weather, and incarceration overwhelm inspirations of martial courage or even duty. Within the confines of the prison, the broader conflict—indeed, the divided nation—seems held in fearful, anguished captivity. Stories of myriad individuals are told, evoking every corner of the country and every walk of life, yet there is no overarching plot, just the plot of ravaged earth the prison represents. Peacetime distinctions have been slaughtered and homogenized by combat; no larger narrative coheres, even as the book's relentless momentum builds from page to page. What Stendhal does to the Battle of Waterloo in *The Charterhouse of Parma*, and what Tolstoy does to the Battle of Borodino in *War and Peace*, Kantor does to an entire war, stripping it of grand themes of passion and purpose to render a common welter of desperate experience. Soldiers and civilians are sharply drawn, but their pasts and futures are held hostage by the present.

Andersonville reduced them to a single pattern: they were stamped out of that pattern by the enormous heavy die of confinement, like a row of . . . toy tin wretches holding hands.

There are vignettes of redemption within the violence, and figures of decency and nobility, but the light they cast only reveals how deep the shadows that surround them are. This idiosyncratic epic is historical fiction on both a grand and a human scale; historian Bruce Catton called it "the best Civil War novel I have ever read," and the superlative takes proper measure of Kantor's achievement.

What: Novel. *When:* 1955. *Award:* Pulitzer Prize for Fiction, 1956. *Also By: Long Remember* (1934). *Spirit Lake* (1961). *If the South Had Won the Civil War* (1961). *Further Reading: This Was Andersonville* by John McElroy. *Try: Gone With the Wind* by Margaret Mitchell (see page 557). *Life and Fate* by Vasily Grossman (see page 337). *The Killer Angels* by Michael Shaara (see page 704). *Adaptation:* The 1996 television film was directed by John Frankenheimer. *Footnote:* Kantor's book-length narrative poem, *Glory for Me* (1945), was the basis for the classic film of American soldiers returning from World War II, *The Best Years of Our Lives.*

The Liars' Club

A MEMOIR

Mary Karr (born 1955)

An Electrifying Account of an East Texas Childhood

Mary Karr begins her gritty narrative on the violent night in 1961 when her mother, Charlie Marie Moore Karr, was carted away because she was "nervous" (read "crazy"). In the hardscrabble East Texas oil refinery town of Leechfield, Charlie had always stood out. She had "artist's airs" about her, a hangover no doubt from her abortive escape to New York. She drank too much. She went through husbands like Zsa Zsa Gabor and had a tongue that was sharp and quick: "You could see evil in the crotch of a tree, you old fart," she snaps at the nosy neighbor who criticizes her for breastfeeding her baby on her own porch.

In other words, Charlie Karr was a real handful, and her daughter's portrait of her is unflinching. But Charlie isn't the only eccentric in the family, nor the only one possessed of a ferocious flair for the vernacular—a flair Karr is particularly adept at capturing on the pages of this justly praised memoir. Focusing on her seventh and eighth years, Karr creates a world of child-eyed views that are deepened and colored by the before and after, by anecdotes of grandparents, and by her own adult musings on the barren, sometimes cruel precincts of her upbringing.

The stark hues of her depiction of her mother are balanced by the gentler tones of the author's memories of P. J., her more reliable (when present) father. Karr catches the soft-spoken rhythms of the extravagant, intricately imagined tales P. J. would tell in the company of his cronies, the pals who formed the "Liars' Club" that regularly gathered in the American Legion bar. "Just being out of the house with Daddy . . . ," Karr writes, evoking the power of her father's presence, "lights me up enough for somebody to read by me."

Mary Karr didn't have a storybook childhood. As *The Liars' Club* brings home, it was filled with unreliable adults and unpredictable but ever present furies. Nonetheless, and quite remarkably, it is truly and harshly beautiful, an exceptionally intense, honest, and quite funny coming-of-age tale, written in language that sings with indelible poetry.

What: Memoir. *When:* 1995. *Also By: Cherry: A Memoir* (2000). *Lit: A Memoir* (2009). *The Art of Memoir* (2015). *Try: Stop-Time: A Memoir* by Frank Conroy. *Autobiography of a Face* by Lucy Grealy (see page 333).

The Perfect Stranger

P. J. Kavanagh (1931–2015)

False Starts and Fateful Endings

People spend a lot of time looking for *The Perfect Stranger*. Not people who haven't read it yet (although, admittedly, they might have a bit of trouble finding it), but rather readers who have already discovered its pleasures. They hunt through their shelves for a copy to share with a congenial soul they've just described it to, only to come up empty-handed, because—now they remember—they've already lent it out to someone else. It's the kind of book one can't help passing on to friends.

Poet P. J. Kavanagh's incandescent memoir, written while he was still in his midthirties, charmingly follows his stumblings through youth's starting gates, until he's pulled fully into life's race by a sudden, certain, powerful attraction. His sketches of his early youth amid the "commonplace brutalities" of boarding school, his wandering search for inspiration in postwar Paris, and his service in the Korean War are suffused with a fine attention to realities at hand and an amused alertness to the "vague, over-wrought longing of youth." But what distinguishes this account of one young literary man's coming-of-age is the appearance of the perfect stranger who gives the book its title, and who, as his wife-to-be, gives the author's aimless yearning a sense of destination. The headlong disorientation of falling in love has seldom been so charmingly rendered. The author's evolving understanding of the "unclenchings of the heart" that open it to happiness blesses his book with a special grace, and makes his tale the more poignant for its unexpected ending.

What: Memoir. *When:* 1966. *Also By: A Song and Dance* (1968). *Collected Poems* (1992). *Further Reading: The Swan in the Evening,* a memoir by novelist Rosamond Lehmann, mother of Sally Phillips, Kavanagh's wife and the "perfect stranger" of the title. *Try: Instead of a Letter* by Diana Athill (see page 27). *Say Her Name* by Francisco Goldman.

....

Palm-of-the-Hand Stories
Yasunari Kawabata (1899–1972)

Essential Fictions
....

In 1968, the Nobel Prize in Literature was awarded to a Japanese writer for the first time. That writer was Yasunari Kawabata, who was honored for his "narrative mastery, which with great sensibility expresses the essence of the Japanese mind." Kawabata had made a name for himself with his spare, sensual, and impressionistic novels, most notably *Snow Country* (1948), *Thousand Cranes* (1949), and *The Old Capital* (1962). Yet the author felt that the essence of his art was contained in his short works, which he called *tanagokoro no shousetsu,* or "stories that fit into the palm of one's hand." In 1988, seventy of those stories were collected and translated by Lane Dunlop and J. Martin Holman. They are what today might be called flash fiction, most just two or three pages long. Written between 1924 and 1972 (and presented chronologically), they are varied in both style and subject matter, but share a common aesthetic and emotional palate.

The poet Mary Jo Salter characterized *The Old Capital* as "less a narrative than a prose poem of images meeting and mating over time." That's an apt description as well of the cumulative effect of these palm-of-the-hand stories; imbued with a melancholic eroticism, the tales distill beauty and sadness into their purest states as the lingering imprints of experience. Filled with promise unfulfilled and

Yasunari Kawabata, 1970

nostalgia undirected, the stories often condense convoluted plots into oblique narratives. In "God's Bones," a waitress suffers a miscarriage and delivers her grief and uncertainty to four men, each of whom may have been the father of the unborn baby. In "Glass," a husband has the revelatory and confusing experience of encountering his wife as a young girl in the pages of a story. Throughout the book, Kawabata's gift for capturing the lights and colors of the physical world illuminates every vignette. The final tale, "Gleanings from Snow Country," was the author's last literary effort before his suicide in 1972. It reduces his first novel to palm size, tracing its lines of passion and fate as only the most gifted palmist can.

What: Short Stories. *When:* Written from 1924 to 1972; collected in English, 1988. *Award:* Nobel Prize in Literature, 1968. *Also By: The Master of Go* (1951). *The Sound of the Mountain* (1952). *Beauty and Sadness* (1965). *Try: Kokoro* by Natsume Soseki. *The Paper Door and Other Stories* by Shiga Naoya. *The Old Man at the Railroad Crossing and Other Tales* by William Maxwell.

The Greek Passion
Nikos Kazantzakis (1883–1957)

Christ Recrucified

For many years, Nikos Kazantzakis was a European traveler, occupied in various capacities in the fields of law, philosophy, and politics, all the while pursuing his literary vocation by translating significant works (*The Divine Comedy*, for example) into Greek and composing his own plays, prose, and poetry. Especially notable is his 1938 epic, *The Odyssey: A Modern Sequel*, which picks up where Homer left off and follows its wily hero on a boundless spiritual quest—one that includes encounters with the Buddha, Christ, and Don Quixote. In later years, Kazantzakis's focus turned to fiction, and he is best known today for two novels whose fame has been enhanced by the movies they inspired: *Zorba the Greek* (Anthony Quinn was nominated for an Oscar in the title role in 1964) and *The Last Temptation of Christ* (controversially filmed by Martin Scorsese in 1988). Less well known than either of these, but unforgettable once discovered, is *The Greek Passion*, which embraces all of the author's enduring concerns—faith and doubt, good and evil, political oppression, human weakness, divine mysteries—in a deceptively simple tale.

The story unfolds in the 1920s in a Greece under the thumb, and at the mercy, of its Turkish rulers. The residents of Lycovrissi, a relatively stable, even affluent village, are embarking on preparations for their Passion Play, a reenactment of the trial, suffering, and death of Jesus performed once every seven years. Roles are assigned, and the casting of the apostles, Mary Magdalen, and Judas as well as Jesus is spot on: The villagers fall naturally into their parts long before they take the stage.

As the narrative progresses, events conspire to make a symbolic dramatization harrowingly real. Christian refugees arrive seeking food and shelter, their homes having been leveled by the Turks, but they are turned away by Lycovrissi's religious elders. In turn, a shepherd named Manolios, who has thoroughly and emphatically embraced his character as the village's chosen Christ, challenges the elders' decision and determines to help those in need, setting off a moral and political struggle that pulls the eternal meditations of the Passion into a murderous here and now. In its incarnation of transcendental themes, *The Greek Passion* entwines the power of gospel parable, the terror of ancient tragedy, and the social fidelity of the modern novel in a searing, singular way.

What: Novel. *When:* 1948 in Greek; 1954 in English, translation by Jonathan Griffin. British editions bear the title *Christ Recrucified. Also By: Zorba the Greek* (1946). *The Last Temptation of Christ* (1951). *Report*

to Greco, an autobiographical amalgam of fact and fiction (1961). *Try: The Brothers Karamazov* by Fyodor Dostoevsky (see page 232). *The Work of Betrayal* by Mario Brelich. *Adaptations:* The novel inspired Bohuslav Martinů's 1957 opera of the same name. Jules Dassin's film from the same year, *He Who Must Die,* is also based on the book.

■ For John Keats's *Letters of John Keats,* see page 504.

The Face of Battle
John Keats (1934–2012)

John Keegan is printed as "John Keegan (1934–2012)"

War Through the Eyes of Ordinary Soldiers

" What is it like to be in a battle?" When this book was first published in 1976, it amazed readers by answering that question in a revelatory way. For as John Keegan, who was at the time senior lecturer in War Studies at Britain's Royal Military Academy at Sandhurst, explained, most accounts of battles gave hardly any real insight into "the predicament of the individual on the battlefield." Traditional "battle pieces," for example, with their stylized imagery and highly selective, discontinuous treatment of the fighting, described battles as if from above the fray, treating soldiers as mere pawns; similarly, the "decisive battle" school of military history was less interested in the personal ordeal of combat than in the big-picture mechanics and implications of victory or defeat.

Keegan, by contrast, set out to look at three famous battles—Agincourt (1415), Waterloo (1815), and the Somme (1916)—through the eyes of the ordinary soldiers who fought in them. Combining sensitive reading of anecdotal and official histories with research into contemporary weaponry and analyses of strategic decisions, Keegan creates a vibrant and thoughtful portrait of men at war. How did they "control

their fears, staunch their wounds, go to their deaths"? Although the battles' social contexts and weaponry (the "arrow cloud" at Agincourt, rifle fire at Waterloo, the Somme's "steel rain") differed, Keegan powerfully demonstrates that certain fundamental aspects of battle remained the same. Notable among these similarities were the "wildly unstable physical and emotional environment" of the battlefield and "the universality of fear," which, although kept in partial check by coercion or "inducements," was most effectively overcome by a soldier's desire to acquit himself with honor in the eyes of his immediate comrades.

Readers unfamiliar with but curious about the literature of war would be smart to take Keegan's masterpiece as their entrée to this compelling genre. But if you're only ever going to read one volume of military history, make it this one.

What: History. War. *When:* 1976. *Edition:* An illustrated edition was published in 1989. *Also By: Six Armies in Normandy* (1982). *The Mask of Command* (1987). *A History of Warfare* (1993). *The Iraq War* (2004). *Try: Agincourt* by Christopher Hibbert. *Waterloo: A Near Run Thing* by David Howarth. *The First Day on the Somme* by Martin Middlebrook (see page 548).

"In this book, which is so creative, so original, one learns as much about the nature of man as of battle."
—*J. H. Plumb on* The Face of Battle

The Secret of the Old Clock
Carolyn Keene

Where There's a Will, There's a Way

The first three women to sit on the Supreme Court of the United States, Sandra Day O'Connor, Ruth Bader Ginsburg, and Sonia Sotomayor, have something in common besides mastery of the law: their childhood love for the Nancy Drew mysteries. No doubt this youthful infatuation had something to do with finding a crime-solving role model, but one suspects there is more to it than that. As Sandra Tsing Loh put it in a review of *Girl Sleuth*, Melanie Rehak's excellent book about Nancy Drew's creators, "The real allure of Nancy Drew is that, almost uniquely among classic or modern heroines, she can follow—is allowed to follow—a train of thought."

A word about those creators: "Carolyn Keene" is the pseudonym for a group of ghostwriters who, over several decades, have composed and revised the Nancy Drew tales. Mildred Wirt Benson (1905–2002) wrote the original text for *The Secret of the Old Clock*, the first Nancy Drew, and is also credited with writing books two through seven and eleven through twenty-five of the original Nancy Drew series; the 1959 version of *The Secret of the Old Clock*, which softens Nancy's character somewhat, was a revision by Harriet Stratemeyer Adams (1892–1982), the daughter of Edward Stratemeyer, the serial mastermind who founded the publishing syndicate that produced not only the Drew books, but those featuring the Hardy Boys, Tom Swift, the Bobbsey Twins, and the Happy Hollisters as well.

The Stratemeyer books combined a few key elements to hook young readers: Their protagonists were kids with agency, smart and plucky enough to take matters into their own hands; plots revolved around mysteries to be solved or hidden truths to be revealed; the

action spoke louder than any larger message; and the tale never talked down to the audience. Continuity, of course, was part of the appeal: Immersion in a familiar world is the seduction and consolation of any series, and that's as true of Rex Stout's Nero Wolfe (see page 763) as it is of Nancy Drew. (J. K. Rowling's celebrated Harry Potter sequence relies on the same core components to capture readers' attentions, with the addition of stupendous special effects and a richer architecture of good and evil.)

Yes, the books are formulaic, so there's no need to rehearse the details of Nancy Drew's debut: Suffice it to say there's a missing will, and various parties with different motives are invested in the revelation—or concealment—of the inheritance it holds. Nancy asserts herself, gets in and out of danger, and triumphs in the end, with some broader benefit to the community as well as her ego. She's tough, with a bit of guile to boot, and readers root for her with the same kind of fervor and identification a fan affords a favorite athlete, or, for that matter, a budding historian might lavish on the young Napoleon or Marie Antoinette. Stories drive vocations as much as study does, giving developing minds a reach that can culminate, hundreds of books and years of learning later, in scholarly or—in the case of our trio of Supreme Court luminaries—judicial grasp.

Lest one think the readerly inspiration attested to by Justices O'Connor, Ginsburg, and Sotomayor is a "girl thing," one need only note that Barack Obama, asked for his favorite childhood books in 2015, put the Hardy Boys second on the list; and Silicon Valley titan Marc Andreessen has traced his fascination with technology to his early reading about a teenaged inventor hero: "I have the complete series of *Tom Swift* from the 1910s to 1950s in my office," he told the *Financial Times*. "That was probably the single most important thing I read." As Emerson said, it's the good reader that makes the good book.

What: Children's. **When:** 1930; revised 1959. *Reading Notes:* The original Nancy Drew books (as with the Hardy Boys) are richer in the telling; the revised versions, however, have the considerable benefit of stripping racial and ethnic stereotypes from the tales. *Also In Series: The Hidden Staircase* (1930), *The Bungalow Mystery* (1930), and dozens more. *Further Reading: Girl Sleuth: Nancy Drew and the Women Who Created Her* by Melanie Rehak. *Try: The Hardy Boys: The Tower Treasure* by Franklin W. Dixon. *Trixie Belden and the Secret of the Mansion* by Julie Campbell. *Harry Potter and the Sorcerer's Stone* by J. K. Rowling (see page 680).

|||||||||||||||||||||||||||||||||||||| **MORE TO EXPLORE** ||||||||||||||||||||||||||||||||||||||||

BEST FRIENDS FOREVER: THE JOY OF SERIES

In the library of childhood reading, there's no nook quite as comfortable as the one that holds the series books: Traveling time after time to Oz (see page 56), or solving repeated mysteries in the company of Nancy Drew (see opposite page), or battling the dark arts with Harry and Hermione (see page 680), young readers— and parents, too, if they're lucky— develop an attachment to an involved and evolving imaginative world that is nourishing and sustaining. To discover a new series is akin to moving into a new neighborhood: Initial trepidation is soon overcome as characters and setting conspire in elaborating a cozy familiarity. And there's no better way to encourage an eager early reader than to let him or her make friends with congenial characters who are easy to visit again and again. Such friends are made for a lifetime, broadening a child's understanding of the wider world from first acquaintance to fond reminiscence. Here are the initial installments in a trio of notable sequences that stand as representatives of the many others—from Mary Pope Osborne's Magic Treehouse books to Rick Riordan's Percy Jackson series, from Lucy Maud Montgomery's *Anne of Green Gables* (see page 564) to Arthur Ransome's *Swallows and Amazons* (see page 660)—an eager younger reader has in store.

The Boxcar Children
Gertrude Chandler Warner (1890–1979)

....

In these simple yet suspenseful tales, Jessie, Benny, Violet, and Henry Alden—the Boxcar Children—roam the American countryside finding mysteries to solve, crimes to unravel, and many new people to meet. The orphaned siblings live an idealized life under the sole guidance of a grandfather who trusts them enough to let them wander freely through their safe yet adventurous world. Gertrude Chandler Warner wrote the first nineteen books between 1924 and 1976, and nearly 150 titles by other authors have since filled out the series. The tales are filled with explorations and discoveries, and fine attention to the sort of domestic practicalities—building fires, gathering food, washing up, making camp—that seem magical outside the familiar walls of home. Ideal for family read-alouds for ages five and up.

Little House in the Big Woods
Laura Ingalls Wilder (1867–1957)

....

In 1917, Laura Ingalls Wilder, a newspaper columnist of local renown for the *Missouri Ruralist*, wrote, "I am beginning to learn that it is the sweet, simple things of life which are the real ones after all." She was fifty years old; a decade or so later, she wrote a memoir of her upbringing, called *Pioneer Girl*, for which she couldn't find a publisher. With some advice and guidance from her daughter, Rose Wilder Lane, Wilder recast her memories as a book for young readers, *Little House in the Big Woods*. A celebration of the resourcefulness and resilience of a settler family, it set the template for seven books to follow, which, together, have earned Wilder and her books enduring popularity— so much so that when *Pioneer Girl* was finally published in 2014, by the South Dakota State Historical Society, it became a surprise bestseller. That original manuscript depicts a harsh, hardscrabble life—darker, more dangerous, more makeshift and impoverished, and less innocently "can-do" than that depicted in the Little House stories. Reading the original memoir makes it clear how much Wilder invested in reshaping her raw material into a golden age glowing with the virtues of individual agency and self-sufficiency, and a nostalgia for the "sweet, simple things of life" that were never all that sweet and simple—which is to say she sheltered her recollections, like her parents sheltered her, from the violence and vagaries of the frontier. The result is, collectively, a transporting narrative of do-it-yourself survival, filled with detailed descriptions of everything from digging a well and framing a house to drying plums and making a rag doll. It's a handmade, homemade world that beguiles young readers with its code of capability, and envelops in a sentimental embrace what is, as Wilder wrote to her daughter, "only the struggle to live, through the winter, until spring comes again."

Betsy-Tacy
Maud Hart Lovelace
(1892–1980)

Maud Hart Lovelace's 1940s series, which chronicles the lifelong friendship of Betsy, a resourceful storyteller, and Tacy, the very bashful girl who moves in next door the summer before they enter the first grade, is set in friendly Minnesota. As they follow Betsy and Tacy and

their friend Tib up and down hills, real and figurative, from elementary school through *Betsy's Wedding* (1955), readers can share the shape and substance, the romance and circumstance, of growing up. "Betsy's mother," the author writes, "was a great believer in people having private corners," and Lovelace's lovely books allow children an inviting alcove of their own in which to measure their experience.

A Dresser of Sycamore Trees

THE FINDING OF A MINISTRY

Garret Keizer (born 1953)

The Daily Life of Grace

Garret Keizer is a man of several parts: husband and father, high school teacher of English, Episcopal minister and part-time parish priest, writer of courage and struggling wisdom. This last not least, by any means. Sentence by sentence, his work engages the enduring dilemmas of human existence and the circumstantial trials of contemporary life. Indeed, one of his singular gifts is for illustrating how closely the two are entwined.

His subjects, like his mind, are curious in every sense of the word. In one of his books, *The Enigma of Anger* (2002), he ponders an all-too-familiar emotion in ways that illuminate the dim, deep corners of our psyches. In another, *Help: The Original Human Dilemma* (2004), he considers the idea—and the ideal—of helping others, from the story of the Good Samaritan to the reality of a contemporary New York City street corner, examining the core of our nature with an intelligence both playful and profound. In a third, *The Unwanted Sound of Everything We Want* (2010), he has written a pensive and surprising book about noise.

A Dresser of Sycamore Trees is an account of how he "came to be the lay minister of a small Episcopal parish in an old railroad junction town in the northeast corner of Vermont." A book about the life of the spirit in a world necessarily caught up in getting and spending,

Keizer's memoir is very much of that material world as well, parsing the family, work, and community conversations that shape us with fine attention to the demands and desires they convey. His hands-on sense of holiness grapples with epiphanies and aggravations with equal eloquence. His writing honors his readers' experience as much as his own, and that's no small achievement for a preacher: "All I can hope to do," he writes of his congregation, "is to remind them of what they know, to enliven what they know—that is, to make it more accessible to their imaginations, and thus to their faith." Such empathetic engagement makes his reflections as useful as they are probing. They are also quite often very funny, as when he describes a visit to an Anglican monastery, aptly capturing the push-and-pull of the spiritual urge: "The impulse to fall to one's knees coexisted in a visitor like me with the impulse to head for the parking lot screaming." *A Dresser of Sycamore Trees* is an inspiriting book, its alertness to what one reader calls "the extraordinary dailiness of grace" both uncanny and true-to-life.

What: Memoir. Religion & Spirituality. **When:** 1991. *Also By: Privacy* (2012). *Getting Schooled: The Reeducation of an American Teacher* (2014). *Try: A Measure of My Days: The Journal of a Country Doctor* by David Loxterkamp. *Word from Wormingford: A Parish Year* by Ronald Blythe.

The Story of My Life

Helen Keller (1880–1968)

An Awe-Inspiring Autobiography

A miracle and a miracle worker: That's how Mark Twain characterized the author of this book and the woman who made its writing possible. The former, Helen Keller, lost her sight and hearing a few months before her second birthday; a few years later, the latter, Anne Mansfield Sullivan, an inexperienced teacher, twenty years old and half blind herself, traveled from Boston to Helen's home in Tuscumbia, Alabama, to try to educate her. Keller was seven when Sullivan arrived, an unmanageable, incommunicative child, prone to tantrums and violent outbursts. Bestowing upon her charge via resolute discipline and relentless instruction the ability to interpret her sensory experience and, via imagination and analogy, translate it into language, Sullivan unlocked the mind and heart of a woman Winston Churchill would call "the greatest woman of our age."

Sullivan worked her miracle by hand, quite literally, describing the world's phenomena in a manual alphabet she delivered to Helen's palm. "*I spell in her hand everything we do all day long, although she has no idea as yet what the spelling means,*" Sullivan wrote (emphasis hers) in one of the letters that are a valuable appendage to any edition of Keller's narrative. But soon—and suddenly—Sullivan's fingers connected to Helen's understanding, as Keller relates:

Some one was drawing water and my teacher placed my hand under the spout. As the cool stream gushed over one hand she spelled into the other the word water, first slowly, then rapidly. I stood still, my whole attention fixed upon the motions of her fingers. Suddenly I felt a misty consciousness as of something forgotten—a thrill of returning thought; and somehow the mystery of language was revealed to me. I knew then that "w-a-t-e-r" meant the wonderful cool something that was flowing over my

Helen Keller (left) with teacher Anne Sullivan, ca. 1900

hand. *That living word awakened my soul, gave it light, hope, joy, set it free!*

The Story of My Life, written and published just before Keller graduated from Radcliffe College, is a testament to the miracle Sullivan effected. It is an astonishing document, earnest and celebratory in a way that silences—humbles, really—any sense of either irony or pity. It also served as the inspiration for William Gibson's play *The Miracle Worker*, which, on stage in 1959 and on screen three years later, concentrated the two women's experience into an intellectually and emotionally exhilarating drama. But beyond the thrilling, dramatic elements, Keller's story evokes deep and provocative themes of mind and matter, nature and intellect, forcing us to think about how—exactly—we make sense of things by abstracting language from experience. Is every word a spell, a sixth sense that conjures meaning from what reality delivers, however we receive it? That Keller was alert to such perplexing questions, and had much to say in answer to them, is made abundantly apparent in the pages of *The World I Live*

In (1908), in which she asserts, "The bulk of the world's knowledge is an imaginary construction." But such knowledge, as her own life and learning demonstrated, is nonetheless real and nonetheless miraculous for that.

Keller's life beyond the compass of this autobiography—her decades of labor as a humanitarian, political activist, and as advocate for the blind and deaf—was large, but her legacy is largest, in Cynthia Ozick's eloquent description, as "an epistemological marker of sorts: proof of the real existence of the mind's eye."

What: Autobiography. **When:** 1903. **Edition:** The 2003 restored edition edited by Roger Shattuck and Dorothy Herrmann offers the most complete version of the text, with valuable supplementary materials. **Also By:** *Midstream: My Later Life* (1929). *Teacher: Anne Sullivan Macy* (1955). **Try:** *Helen and Teacher: The Story of Helen Keller and Anne Sullivan Macy* by Joseph P. Lash. *Helen Keller: A Life* by Dorothy Herrmann. **Adaptations:** William Gibson's 1959 play *The Miracle Worker* was adapted for film and stars Anne Bancroft as Sullivan and Patty Duke as Keller; both actresses won Academy Awards.

Part of Our Time

SOME RUINS AND MONUMENTS OF THE THIRTIES

Murray Kempton (1917–1997)

"Murray Kempton is the best we have, and better than we deserve." —*Joan Didion*

Murray Kempton was widely acknowledged to be one of the great journalists of his time, although such an appreciation seems too modest by half. In his long career as a columnist, Kempton proved that the facts that are a reporter's hard cash were for him merely the currency that vivified a much broader economy of life. For Kempton, value was measured not just by the immediate dimensions of events and headlines, but by the less exact but more penetrating measures of Greek tragedy and the New Testament.

His style embraces such subtle complexity —social, moral, political, personal—that it reads like that of no other newspaperman, often

astonishing the reader with its combination of intricacy and aphoristic intelligence. Take the opening of the chapter in the book devoted to the strange affair of Alger Hiss and Whittaker Chambers, in which radical politics, loyalty, class, espionage, and fear combined to make not only controversial history but unresolvable drama as well: "The world of shabby gentility is like no other; its sacrifices have less logic, its standards are harsher, its relation to reality is dimmer than comfortable property or plain poverty can understand." From this unexpected beginning, Kempton proceeds to illuminate with extraordinary acumen the mysterious personalities whose "partnership," to use Kempton's word, seemed to hold so much of America's Cold War ideological ferment in its elusive and enigmatic embrace.

Murray Kempton, 1968

The joint portrait of Hiss and Chambers is one of the ten pieces that make up *Part of Our Time*, which the author describes as "a series of novellas that happen to be about real persons." The linking theme of the chapters is the "myth of the nineteen thirties"—a social myth of revolution in which the forces of labor and the allure of Communist ideals combined to wring life-changing obligations from Kempton's subjects.

Names that may be familiar—Sacco and Vanzetti, John L. Lewis, Walter Reuther, Paul Robeson, A. Philip Randolph, James T. Farrell, Clifford Odets—pass through these pages, but the focus is often on figures consigned to history's dustbin. Writing two decades after the events he describes, while the nation was in the grip of a different fever, flamed by Joseph McCarthy and as flawed as the one it sought to eradicate once and for all, Kempton brings the commitments and contradictions of his reformers and revolutionaries to life with uncommon perspicacity. A reader's interest in the era and its issues may be nil at the start, but *Part of Our Time* mines the past to explore not historical truths but human verities. It does so with such startling sagacity that you'll close the book with an enlarged understanding of the guilt and glory that abide—whatever the politics of the moment—in what the author calls "the pilgrim soul of man."

What: History. Politics. *When:* 1955. *Edition:* The New York Review Books Classics edition contains an excellent introduction by David Remnick. *Also By: America Comes of Middle Age* (1963). *The Briar Patch* (1973). *Rebellions, Perversities, and Main Events* (1994). *Further Reading: The American Earthquake* by Edmund Wilson. *Alger Hiss, Whittaker Chambers, and the Schism in the American Soul,* edited by Patrick A. Swan. *Try: Independent Spirit* by Hubert Butler (see page 115).

A Boy at the Hogarth Press
Richard Kennedy (1910–1989)

Coming of Age Among Woolfs

Who knows what transformations the digital revolution will ultimately deliver to the shelves that constitute a reader's autobiography—that private collection of volumes that can be symbols of a book lover's journey through life as well as literature. But one can hope that the pleasure of books as objects will never entirely disappear, for some volumes are just lovely in their very bookishness, and *A Boy at the Hogarth Press* is one.

Square in shape and short in length, its type arranged with a rambling grace across pages and around the author's evocative pen-and-ink drawings, this small, singular book relates Kennedy's experience as an awkward sixteen-year-old apprentice at Leonard and Virginia Woolf's Hogarth Press. The press was at the heart of the cultural coterie of Bloomsbury in the 1920s, and Kennedy's episodic memories are filled with glimpses of the personalities of the Woolfs and their celebrated friends and familial and artistic relations. The book also details the hands-on nature of the Hogarth operation, from typesetting to press work, book sales to packing parcels. Whether setting type in the printing room or composing her own novels behind doors, Mrs. Woolf is a fascinating if enigmatic presence, often quite funny; when Kennedy, having seen a review that called her the "English Proust," asks her opinion of the French novelist, "she laughed and said she couldn't do French cooking, but it was very delicious."

The well-meaning young man's attempts at industriousness sometimes go awry, to the consternation of Mr. Woolf and the restrained delight of his older office mates, and his apprenticeship will end in catastrophe when he orders the wrong size paper cut for the uniform edition of Mrs. Woolf's work. But, like many calamities that befall the young, those remembered

here by the author—along with the skating parties, cricket matches, and intellectual pursuits that enlivened his Bloomsbury experience—are imbued with the fond amusement maturity affords the ungainly youth it has left behind. Artful, observant, affectionate, and wry, *A Boy at the Hogarth Press* is perfectly charming.

What: Memoir. **When:** 1972. **Edition:** Fittingly, the original edition was the first book published by the now-fabled Whittington Press; it was printed on a handpress by John and Rosalind Randle over a year of weekends and holidays. Several trade editions followed. *Also By: A Parcel of Time* (1977). *Further Reading: Downhill All the Way: An Autobiography of the Years 1919–1939* by Leonard Woolf. *Thrown to the Woolfs: Leonard and Virginia Woolf and the Hogarth Press* by John Lehmann. *Try: Period Piece* by Gwen Raverat (see page 661).

Talking Like the Rain
A READ-TO-ME BOOK OF POEMS
Edited by X. J. Kennedy (born 1929) and Dorothy M. Kennedy (1931–2018)
Illustrated by Jane Dyer (born 1949)

Poems to Read Aloud—and Remember

From the earliest age, children recognize that words are spells, and need little encouragement to find enchantment in their arrangement. Which is a good thing, for poetry teaches the mind to compose itself, and the earlier lessons begin, the more resonant they prove. It's natural, then, that every nursery needs an anthology of poems, and you'll find none better than this marvelous volume, which, thanks to the acumen of editors Dorothy and X. J. Kennedy and the exquisite artwork of Jane Dyer, entrances both eye and ear. The selection of poems encompasses the silly and the serious, the familiar and the fresh, the lilting and the lulling, the funny and the fabulous, the tender and the touching, the classic and the contemporary. The poets represented include Langston Hughes, Christina Rossetti, Robert Louis Stevenson, Wallace Stevens, May Swenson, Maxine Kumin, and Robert Frost, and the more than one hundred selections are arranged into sections such as "Play," "Families," and "Birds, Bugs, and Beasts." The imaginative reach of the verse is extended and enhanced by the careful inspiration of their visual presentation across the large pages; Dyer's work deserves the highest praise. This is a book any poetry lover will love, and love to share with the littlest readers. (And odds are your kids will come home in search of it when their own children are born.)

The Pound Era

Hugh Kenner (1923–2003)

A Museum in a Book

Even when it first came out in 1971, Hugh Kenner's monumental key to the titanic age of literary modernism in the first half of the twentieth century had an air of elegy about it. Each page seemed to reassemble for the reader a portion of an elaborate mosaic that revealed the brilliance of an almost mythological constellation of writers. Kenner's most striking revelations are about Ezra Pound, the figure he puts at the center of the creative generation that included James Joyce and T. S. Eliot, Wyndham Lewis and William Carlos Williams, among many other contemporaries, not to mention (poetic time being the most figurative of media) Sappho and Homer, Dante and Li Po. Pound's gifts were scattered through a long career across famously incomprehensible pages, and condemned to a justly infamous legacy by his reprehensible conduct in support of Fascism during the Second World War; nevertheless, Kenner argues convincingly, the poet's influence on aesthetic ambitions and linguistic renewal are both arresting and enduring.

Ezra Pound in Venice, 1964

Kenner's subjects were steeped in bookish culture across epochs and even continents, and his chapters reveal layers of lost learning beneath the surface of modernism's maze. He turns each work that represents it, from Eliot's *The Waste Land* to Joyce's *Ulysses* (see page 422) to Pound's *Cantos*—into a city to be excavated, a kind of Troy, several strata deep, packed with treasures of insight and imagination. The finds of his vast and delicate archaeological excavation are collected into a cabinet of wonders, concentrating both the disciplined energies and the wild enthusiasms of disparate, disruptive works into a coherent exposition that is erudite in the extreme and exhilarating in every chapter. Blending biography, history, linguistics, and close criticism into a narrative that conducts the reader down each alley the artists explored, Kenner has constructed both a museum of their collaborative mind and a kind of Rosetta Stone to their works.

A difficult book, but a seductive one, it presumes an interest in its protagonists, and even some knowledge of their achievements; yet, since its themes—the evolution of language, the engendering of images, the life of story—are seminal to the making of meaning, the reach of *The Pound Era* is wide and its resonance deep. With diligence and elegance, Kenner turns the modernist construct of camouflage and obfuscation inside out, connecting all the dots and drawing lines between them in a way that awakens our intelligence to new perspectives. The author's own stylistic genius transmutes all the complexities (and sometimes confusions) of Joyce, Pound, and their confreres into sentences as taut and spring-loaded as any his masters made. Composed with a sense of calibration that is unique, *The Pound Era* reaches far beyond its ostensible purview—and the figure at its center—to instruct us in how to read, how to muse, and how to mine the ore of invention cultural history has passed along to us. Kenner's masterpiece is a work of art in its own right, and may well be the greatest—most eloquent, most mind-expanding, even most beautiful—work spawned by the period it celebrates.

What: Culture. Literary Criticism. *When:* 1971. *Also By: Dublin's Joyce* (1956). *The Stoic Comedians: Flaubert, Joyce, Beckett* (1962). *The Counterfeiters: An Historical Comedy* (1968). *A Homemade World: The American Modernist Writers* (1975). *Try: The Geography of the Imagination* by Guy Davenport (see page 198).

> **"Whoever can give his people better stories than the ones they live in is like the priest in whose hands common bread and wine become capable of feeding the very soul, and he may think of forging in some invisible smithy the uncreated conscience of his race."**
> —*Hugh Kenner,* The Pound Era

On the Road
Jack Kerouac (1922–1969)

Cultural Milestone and Gospel of the Beat Generation

Within the catalog of books to read before you die, there is a very short list of books to read between the ages of fifteen and twenty, and *On the Road* is certainly near its top. Jack Kerouac's novel has qualities that transcend its youthful appeal, but none measures up to the intoxication it can deliver to a teenaged reader with a taste for the heady brew of romanticism, adventure, and unfettered selfhood an improvised road trip promises.

Legend has it that *On the Road* was written in a single burst of creative energy over three weeks in 1951, typed out single-spaced and without paragraph breaks onto a 120-foot scroll that the author had taped together for the purpose of continuous and spontaneous composition. ("That's not writing, that's typing," sniffed Truman Capote dismissively.) In large degree the legend is true: The scroll has survived, and was purchased by a collector in 2001 for $2.4 million. But the myth masks the truth that Kerouac had been plotting the novel in his mind for some time, and relied in his frenetic scrollwork on material already conceived and set down in notebooks over the previous several years. And, as the version of the scroll's contents published in book form in 2007 reveals, there was much revision to the text before the novel was published in 1957. That said, there is no denying the fact that the directness and incantatory vitality of the book's prose owes much to the author's artistic impulsiveness. There is a sort of ecstasy of expression in its pages that is Kerouac's enduring hallmark, and that beguiles readers in the first chapter:

They rushed down the street together, digging everything in the early way they had, which later became so much sadder and perceptive and blank. But then they danced down the streets like dingledodies, and I shambled after as I've been doing all my life after people who interest me, because the only people for me are the mad ones, the ones who are mad to live, mad to talk, mad to be saved, desirous of everything at the same time, the ones who never yawn or say a commonplace thing, but burn, burn, burn like fabulous yellow roman candles exploding like spiders across the stars and in the middle you see the blue centerlight pop and everybody goes "Awww!"

Indeed, the transitory enchantment of fireworks is an apt emblem of the story the book tells. The "Roman candle" that lights up the story is the figure of Dean Moriarty, "the holy con-man with the shining mind," with whom the narrator, Sal Paradise, becomes infatuated. Searching for his father, collecting and abandoning wives and lovers, talking of poetry and philosophy through drunken nights, Dean shoots back and forth across the country on the trail of kicks and revelations. Sal—a bookish, curious adventurer evading the sober comforts of his own more conventional dreams—is in thrall to Dean's life force throughout most of the book, and joins him on the road in frantic pursuit of epiphanies: "Somewhere along the line," Sal writes, "I knew there'd be girls, visions, everything; somewhere along the line the pearl would be handed to me."

Not quite; or "Yes, but. . . ." The beatific inspiration of Dean, the "HOLY GOOF," as Sal calls him, soon dissipates in the desperation of its own rootlessness, and the novel ends with Sal on a pier in New York City, staring across the river toward the immensity of the continent the mighty, metaphoric road traverses. Like Gatsby praying to the green light on Daisy's dock at the end of an earlier American masterpiece, Sal senses what both Fitzgerald and Kerouac came to know: Promise has no surer destination than nostalgia and regret.

Jack Kerouac in Tangier, 1957, with notes by Allen Ginsberg

Kerouac's achievement in *On the Road* has been obscured by the book's role as the gospel of the Beat Generation, and devotees of that literary and cultural moment will be pleased to find most of its heroes—Allen Ginsberg, William S. Burroughs, Gregory Corso, Neal Cassady (the model for Moriarty)—moving through its pages, wearing only the thinnest disguises. But the book's real genius is this: It captures the numinous, liberating, strangely dangerous joy that overcomes you the first time you stay out all night—and that, with all due respect to Mr. Capote, is more than just typing. It is to Kerouac's everlasting credit that he rendered

with equal exactitude the curious ruefulness that comes with the dawn.

What: Novel. *When:* 1957. *Edition:* A bound edition of the 1951 scroll version of the novel was published as *On the Road: The Original Scroll* in 2007. *Also By: The Dharma Bums* (1958). *The Subterraneans* (1958). *Lonesome Traveler* (1960). *Big Sur* (1962). *Visions of Cody* (1972). *Further Reading: Kerouac: A Biography* by Ann Charters. *Try: Go: A Novel* by John Clellon Holmes. *The Savage Detectives* by Roberto Bolaño. *Adaptation:* The 2012 film directed by Walter Salles stars Sam Riley, Kristen Stewart, and Amy Adams.

The Living Thoughts of Kierkegaard
Søren Kierkegaard (1813–1855)
Edited by W. H. Auden

An Introduction to a Profound Philosopher

Søren Kierkegaard was a Danish philosopher and a maverick Christian theologian. In the opinion of Ludwig Wittgenstein, whom many consider the leading figure in twentieth-century philosophy, Kierkegaard was "by far the most profound thinker of the [nineteenth] century." He is universally acknowledged as one of the originators of existentialism, a philosophy that stresses the subjectivity of existence and the need for man to give meaning to life in an indifferent and absurd universe through self-defining action and choice. Via the work of Jean-Paul Sartre, Albert Camus, and many others, existentialism has exerted a powerful influence on modern literature.

Søren Kierkegaard, ca. 1840

Besides being among the key figures in the history of thought, Kierkegaard was an extraordinarily original and inventive writer—so much so, that finding one's way into his work can be daunting. For example, some of Kierkegaard's most important books consist of several substantial parts that are each written under a different pen name. Does Kierkegaard reveal his own beliefs through any of these masks? Apparently not: "In the pseudonymous works,"

he once claimed, "there is not a single word which is mine." At the same time, Kierkegaard and his multiple authorial personalities make brilliant use of such techniques and styles as satire, sermon, polemic, aphorism, and fiction. What ultimately unites this compelling and remarkably various body of work, however, is Kierkegaard's abiding concern with the meaning of existence.

A good way to start reading Kierkegaard is with this thematically arranged anthology, drawn from the full range of his writings, put together in 1952 by the English poet W. H. Auden. From the subjectivity of truth to faith's umbilical connection to despair, *The Living Thoughts of Kierkegaard* is a splendid presentation of the philosopher/theologian's dominant themes; it is also a powerful invitation to ponder, as Kierkegaard so fiercely did, what it means to be a human being.

What: Philosophy. *When:* 1952. *Also By: Either/Or: A Fragment of Life* (1843). *Fear and Trembling* (1843). *Concluding Unscientific Postscript* (1846). *The Sickness Unto Death* (1849). *Try: A Short Life of Kierkegaard* by Walter Lowrie. *Irrational Man: A Study in Existential Philosophy* by William Barrett.

Kilvert's Diary
Francis Kilvert (1840–1879)

Vicarage Life in Wiltshire and Wales in the Victorian Era

Covering the years 1870 to 1879, the diary of the Reverend Francis Kilvert is an addictive pleasure, offering an unparalleled portrait of life in the English countryside in the mid-Victorian era. Few diaries are as enjoyable to read.

A vicar's son who spent most of his short life (he died at age thirty-nine, within a month of his marriage) in Wiltshire and Wales, Kilvert was a man of modesty and good cheer. His diary entries are filled with the simple pleasures and everyday encounters of a clergyman's quiet life, although they frequently blush with his infatuation with a comely young woman. Attentive to natural phenomena and the whims of the weather, he is a pleasure to follow on his long walks from one village to another through the rolling landscape of the Welsh borders. He is pleasantly unselfconscious in documenting his daily rounds among his often doting parishioners, and his easy acquaintance with both gentry and laborers introduces readers to a variety of Victorian experience. Over the course of the decade his diary covers, Kilvert fashions an intimate portrait of an age and a way of life that in our hurried era seems unfamiliar: Time is so expansive, small distances are so great, conversation is so fruitful, and nature is so close that one feels truly transported to another world—a world it is a long delight to visit.

What: Diaries & Letters. *When:* Selections from the diaries, edited by William Plomer, were first published in three volumes in 1938–40. *Edition:* Plomer also edited a one-volume abridged edition in 1944. *Further Reading: Francis Kilvert and His World* by Frederick Grice. *Try: The Diary of a Country Parson* by James Woodforde. *Chronicles of a Curate* by Fred Secombe.

"Sunday, 14 April 1872. The beauty of the view, the first view of the village, coming down by the Brooms this evening was indescribable. The brilliant golden poplar spires shone in the evening light like flames against the dark hill side of the Old Forest and the blossoming fruit trees, the torch trees of Paradise blazed with a transparent green and white lustre up the dingle in the setting sunlight. The village is in a blaze of fruit blossom. Clyro is at its loveliest. What more can be said?"
—*from* Klivert's Diary

Why We Can't Wait
Martin Luther King Jr. (1929–1968)

A Seminal Work of the Civil Rights Movement

Never before have I written so long a letter. I'm afraid it is much too long to take your precious time. I can assure you that it would have been much shorter if I had been writing from a comfortable desk, but what else can one do when he is alone in a narrow jail cell other than write long letters, think long thoughts and pray long prayers?

That's from the close of "Letter from Birmingham Jail," the centerpiece of *Why We Can't Wait*, and the book's thematic fulcrum. The audience Martin Luther King Jr. is addressing is a group of eight white clergymen who had published an opinion piece in the *Birmingham News* describing the nonviolent campaign of protests against segregation led by King and others as the "unwise and untimely" acts of impatient extremists. King read the newspaper article in the city jail, to which he had been consigned on Good Friday, 1963, for violating a new municipal injunction issued to thwart the demonstrations.

King began to compose his response in the margins of the newspaper in which the clergy's statement appeared, contin-ued writing on scraps of paper provided by a fellow inmate, and finally concluded his epis-tle on a pad his attorneys were allowed to leave him. The letter ultimately made its way, first by mimeographed copies and later by magazine and news-paper publication, to a wide national audience and into the *Congressional Record*. Marshaling arguments moral, religious, and political, King expounded on the ethical imperatives that connect those three realms. "Injustice anywhere is a threat to justice everywhere," he declared, and he censured the moderation of fellow clergy in the face of ineq-uity: "All too many others have been more cau-tious than courageous and have remained silent behind the anesthetizing security of stained-glass windows." His erudition and eloquence are powerfully invoked to justify the urgency moti-vating the protesters in Birmingham:

Just as Socrates felt that it was necessary to create a tension in the mind so that individuals could rise from the bondage of myths and half-truths to the unfettered realm of creative analysis and objective appraisal, so must we see the need for nonviolent gadflies to create the kind of tension in society that will help men rise from the dark depths of prejudice and racism to the majestic heights of understanding and brotherhood.

Like Lincoln before him, King could match rhetorical cadences to topical events, inflecting them with enduring values, and "Letter from Birmingham Jail" echoes with the resonance of other signal documents in American history. The rest of *Why We Can't Wait* augments its intensity with a more program-matic agenda for a civil rights revolution, an agenda that would bear fruit in landmark legisla-tion in the mid-1960s. Although dated, even this portion of the book seems ever relevant, sadly enough, to our national discourse.

What: History. *When:* 1964. *Also By: A Testament of Hope: The Essential Writings of Martin Luther King, Jr.* edited by James Melvin Washington (1986). *Further Reading: Gospel of Freedom: Martin Luther King, Jr.'s Letter from Birmingham Jail and the Struggle That Changed a Nation* by Jonathan Rieder. *Try: Collected Essays* by James Baldwin (see page 43). *America in the King Years* by Taylor Branch (see page 93).

STEPHEN KING
(BORN 1947)

W hen readers are deeply entranced by a story," Stephen King once said, "they forget the storyteller completely. The book is all they care about." Yet King's own imagination is so fecund and powerful that his presence looms large in the minds of countless devoted readers (and sometimes seems to shadow the sleep of his detractors, too). King's appetite for the grotesque and his gift for plotting mesmerizing tales are tied to an extraordinary sensitivity to the tensions and textures of everyday life. It is this combination of the everyday with the unimaginable that makes his horror fiction so compelling and so frightening.

Stephen King, 1975

As with any author of King's output and popularity, fans can—and do—argue endlessly about which constitutes his "best book." Best known are those that have been adapted by Hollywood and integrated into our vernacular: *Carrie* (1974), *The Shining* (1977), and *Misery* (1987) are all sources of oft-referenced imagery, and both the novella *Rita Hayworth and Shawshank Redemption*, from the collection *Different Seasons* (1982), and *The Green Mile* (1996) have pools of passionate admirers swelled by the very successful cinematic adaptations of each. The author himself is partial to the emotionally resonant *Lisey's Story* (2006) and to the multi-volume Dark Tower series.

Perhaps most interesting in the long run are the novels in which King's alertness to the American ordinary supplies the springboard for fantastical premises that seem to have evolved in some laboratory of fictional experiment, such as *The Stand* (1978; revised and expanded edition, 1990), *It* (1986), and *11/22/63* (2011). In these ambitious works, King's fascination with the bubbles in which we live—psychological, historical, economic, cultural—gives his tales a Dickensian relish and exuberance. Where Dickens wrote to discover on the page the dominant social force of his

time—the city—King deploys equal authorial energy to explore the less palpable but no less powerful social force of ours: the pervasive virtual reality we inhabit thanks to the homogenizing saturation of mass media and communication. As Dickens used sentiment and a gift for revealing caricature to create a portrait of Victorian England and a singular catalog of human nature, so King has used horror and his preternatural antennae for the shared shorthand of popular culture to capture not only the anxieties of our epoch, but the primal terrors they reflect.

Carrie
A Prom Night to Remember

*C*arrie was King's first published novel (at one point during its composition, he has said, it was rescued from the wastebasket by his wife). It reveals the nature of his inspiration in its most elemental form, embodying the raw force of his narrative method. "I'll try to terrify you first, and if that doesn't work, I'll try to horrify you, and if I can't make it there, I'll try to gross you out," he once explained. In *Carrie*, he does all three with relentless energy, beginning with a bloody flourish a long career of tapping readers' fears "at the subconscious level where savage things grow."

Sixteen-year-old Carietta White is a social misfit tormented by her fanatically religious mother and ridiculed by her peers. Unable to fit in, too unknowing to avoid the vicious taunts of her classmates, Carrie takes what comfort she can in her peculiar telekinetic ability: By concentrating on objects, she can make them move. Yet even this distinction is sinful in her mother's eyes, and her psychic faculties are suppressed—until an unexpected act of kindness leads Carrie, with unfamiliar hopefulness, to her senior prom. On that fateful night, the doomed girl's persecution is taken to a new level by a malicious conspiracy, and the force of her clandestine power is finally released in a frenzy of revenge on a gymful of teens. Never has the cruelty and furious emotion that lurks beneath the surface of adolescent social life been so horrifyingly and gleefully imagined.

What: Novel. Horror. *When:* 1974. *Also By:* King's many other works include *'Salem's Lot* (1975), *The Dead Zone* (1979), and *Pet Sematary* (1983), as well as books written as Richard Bachman and with Peter Straub. *Try: The Haunting of Hill House* by Shirley Jackson (see page 633). *The Exorcist* by William Peter Blatty. *Adaptations:* The 1976 film, starring Sissy Spacek as Carrie, was the first horror movie to receive Academy Award nominations. In 2002, the story was remade as a TV movie. A 1988 Broadway musical closed after five performances.

11/22/63
Time Travel to a National Nightmare

Although its ramifications are intricate, the seed of *11/22/63* is quite simple: A man named Jake Epping, living in Maine in 2011, finds a portal into the past (to September 9, 1958, at 11:58 AM, to be exact) and decides to travel back in time to prevent the assassination of President John F. Kennedy by Lee Harvey Oswald. As Epping navigates the five years between his arrival at the end of the 1950s and the fateful day in Dallas that gives this novel its name, King applies his usual attention to detail to vividly portray the vanished world his protagonist has entered, playfully using Epping's foreknowledge of events to enliven the narrative.

King reportedly had the idea for this novel before *Carrie* was published, and kept it percolating for nearly four decades before tackling it. In the interim, he developed structural skills that serve him—and the reader—well as the plot moves back and forth between alternative chronologies. The seductive mysteries that still surround the assassination complicate Epping's preparation for intervention (if Oswald acted alone, for instance, foiling him is a focused task; but if he didn't?), and the outcome of potential success may be as dangerous as failure—and perilously unimaginable.

Although it required considerable research and a keener eye on the historical record than much of the rest of King's work, *11/22/63* is less of a departure than it may seem. It might even be seen as a kind of thematic prequel to his earlier novels set in subsequent decades, a glimpse into a less frenetic America in which citizens have not yet been transmuted into consumers and swallowed by a faceless economic maw. The very title of the book memorializes a national trauma as deep as almost any in our history, and its story encompasses other instances of factual horror—the Cuban Missile Crisis, the war in Vietnam—that trigger the same terrors as King's invented ones. Filled with vivid details and fascinating implications regarding the dependencies of time and the rippling effects of any attempt to intervene in its flow, *11/22/63* is both spine-tingling and thought-provoking, a page-turning thriller and an exhilarating attempt to fathom what fiction can grasp.

What: Novel. *When:* 2011. *Award:* Los Angeles Times Book Prize, 2012. *Also By: Under the Dome* (2009). *Mr. Mercedes* (2014). *Finders Keepers* (2015). *End of Watch* (2016). *On Writing: A Memoir of the Craft* (2000) is a useful and especially appealing volume. *Try: Replay* by Ken Grimwood. *American Tabloid* by James Ellroy. *Adaptation:* James Franco plays Jake Epping in the 2016 television series based on the book.

The Poisonwood Bible
Barbara Kingsolver (born 1955)

Into Africa

Barbara Kingsolver's novels seem to expand our sense of life and our capacity to tackle it. Before she published *The Poisonwood Bible* in 1998, she had won wide readership for novels and stories that charted the struggles of women to find—or make—homes in the contemporary world, often in the face of trying circumstances. Leavened by humor and an alertness to the public and private echoes of clashing cultures, the drama of these books—*The Bean Trees* (1988), *Animal Dreams* (1990), and *Pigs in Heaven* (1993)—have a domestic core, enlarged by the author's expansive imagination. They're wonderfully readable and strangely—remarkably—encouraging.

Although *The Poisonwood Bible* is in some ways just as intimate as the earlier books in its depiction of a family's life, its scope and setting are anything but domestic. At the start of the story, the family in question belongs to Nathan Price, an American fundamentalist missionary who has brought his wife and four daughters into the Congo to convert the Africans to his brand of evangelical Christianity. Yet as the narrative unfolds from 1959 through the 1980s—it is told alternately in the voices of the five Price women—the family slips from Nathan's grasp, each of its members declaring her independence from his patriarchal and increasingly fanatical rule. One might even say they enact in miniature the turmoil of rebellion, confusion, corruption, growth, and loss that the Congo itself suffers in its battle for independence from Belgian colonial rule and American interference.

Kingsolver is brilliant at delineating the peculiar estrangements that infiltrate families.

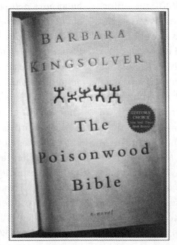

The girls weather cultural displacement ("We came from Bethlehem, Georgia, bearing Betty Crocker cake mixes into the jungle," says one), physical discomfort, and emotional and political awakening. As they do so, each embraces or evades the historical moment with fateful consequences; tragedies of close-order and large-scale oppression transpire in tandem. The author's huge ambition is matched by her fidelity to the tenor of each major character's soul, giving her novel an extraordinary, compelling power.

At the end of the book, looking back on their African experience many years later, one of the sisters says, "History holds all things in the balance, including large hopes and short lives." So do novels—at least the best of them, of which *The Poisonwood Bible* is certainly one.

What: Novel. *When:* 1998. *Also By:* Fiction: *Prodigal Summer* (2000); *The Lacuna* (2009). Nonfiction: *High Tide in Tucson* (1995); *Animal, Vegetable, Miracle* (2007). *Try: The Grass Is Singing* by Doris Lessing. *Burger's Daughter* by Nadine Gordimer. *At Play in the Fields of the Lord* by Peter Matthiessen.

***

Just So Stories for Little Children
Rudyard Kipling (1865–1936)

How the Leopard Got His Spots—and More

What a strange case is that of Rudyard Kipling. Born in Bombay in 1865, he was educated in England before returning to India to work as an editor on a newspaper in Lahore. By the age of thirty-two, he'd written scores of popular stories, collected in volumes such as *Plain Tales from the Hills*, *Soldiers Three*, and *Wee Willie Winkie* (all first published in 1888); the novel *The Light That Failed* (1891); an astonishing assortment of poems, collected in *Barrack-Room Ballads* (1882) and other volumes;

and such children's classics as *The Jungle Book* (1894) and *Captains Courageous* (1896). By the age of forty-two, he had won the Nobel Prize in Literature—the first English language writer to do so—yet from that point on, Kipling's literary career began what one biographer has called a "long recessional" until his death in 1936.

Because of the colonialist, even jingoist stance of a significant portion of his work—the poem "The White Man's Burden" being just one example—it is easy to see the decline in his reputation as a reflection of the fortunes of the Empire to which it was closely allied. It is even easier, in critic V. S. Pritchett's words, "to tie his politics around his neck and sink him." But, by virtue of the extra-political reaches of his imagination, Kipling keeps afloat in readers' affections through such cherished works as the inspirational poem "If—" (1910); the unforgettable adventure story "The Man Who Would Be King" (1888), the marvelous novel of India and espionage, *Kim* (1901); and a host of other poems, sketches, and stories. This is in no small part because it is impossible to read a page of Kipling without being startled by a phrase or sentence that is animated with the spring of speech rhythms but starched with a unique confidence and poetic poise. The dynamism of his verbal gift is palpable, and the force of his ingenuity transporting: Sound, sense, and narrative invention combine to paint pictures of a sensually rich world that resembles the real one but is really—delightfully—a conjuring.

There is no better place to meet Kipling and his gifts than in his *Just So Stories*, written for, and no doubt first spoken to, his young daughter. The twelve tales it collects provide wildly satisfying answers to questions worthy of a child's imagination: how the camel got his hump, for instance, how the alphabet was made, and how the elephant got his trunk. Each tale is addressed to the narrator's "Best Beloved," with whom any listening child will certainly identify:

In the High and Far-Off Times the Elephant, O Best Beloved, had no trunk. He had only a blackish, bulgy nose, as big as a boot, that he could wriggle about from side to side; but he couldn't pick up things with it. But there was one Elephant—a new Elephant—an Elephant's Child—who was full of 'satiable curiosity, and that means he asked ever so many questions.

The spinning of the tales is so entwined in Kipling's prose that any parent reading the *Just So Stories* aloud is transformed into a master storyteller, and every Best Beloved will be happy to listen again and again. Which is a good thing, since it maps a path to a land of language, lore, and wonder that no reader should miss.

What: Children's. *When:* 1902. *Award:* Nobel Prize in Literature, 1907. *Also By: Stalky & Co.* (1899). *Traffics and Discoveries* (1904). *Puck of Pook's Hill* (1906). *Debits and Credits* (1926). *Something of Myself for Friends Known and Unknown* (1937). *Further Reading: The Long Recessional: The Imperial Life of Rudyard Kipling* by David Gilmour. *Try: The Aesop for Children*, illustrated by Milo Winter. *How the Whale Became and Other Stories* by Ted Hughes.

Rudyard Kipling, ca. 1892

One of Kipling's illustrations for the Just So Stories

■ For Russell Kirk's *Old House of Fear*, see page 634.

Death of My Aunt
C. H. B. Kitchin (1895–1967)

A Neglected Gem from the Golden Age of British Mystery

I n *Death of My Aunt*, the young London stockbroker Malcolm Warren is hurriedly called to visit his rich aunt Catherine at her country estate. Before the weekend is over, Catherine is dead, and her shy nephew is transformed into an unlikely, but ultimately successful, sleuth. Nevertheless, it's not the sleuthing that makes this novel so memorably enjoyable; it's the wry intelligence of the inconvenienced, slightly out-of-sorts Warren, whose offhand characterizations of the people and circumstances he encounters are just what one often looks for when seeking literary entertainment: good and diverting company. *Death of My Aunt* is the kind of book that, discovered unexpectedly on the shelf in a friend's guest room during an overnight visit, will make you happily late for dinner, and eager to turn in early after the meal is done.

What: Mystery & Suspense. *When:* 1929. *Also By:* Mysteries: *Crime at Christmas* (1934); *Death of His Uncle* (1939). Other fiction: *The Book of Life* (1960). *Try: Murder at the Vicarage* by Agatha Christie. *The Documents in the Case* by Dorothy L. Sayers. *Tragedy at Law* by Cyril Hare.

The Oldest Dead White European Males
AND OTHER REFLECTIONS ON THE CLASSICS
Bernard Knox (1914–2010)

In Defense of a Classical Education

W hy read the works of Sappho or Sophocles, or assess the characters of Achilles and Antigone? Why examine the whims of Aphrodite or Apollo, the adventures of Odysseus, or the anger of Medea? Why consider the virtues and failings of Athenian democracy? Why take the measure of mythology or tragedy? What is in the few dozen battered books that have come down to us from ancient Greece to warrant their exhumation so many ages hence?

These are the questions classicist Bernard Knox addresses in this splendid book. His cogent reflections touch upon many answers: that the Greeks have provided the foundation for the edifice of Western culture, and so familiarity with their works provides insight into our society's present strengths and stresses; that we have much to learn in the pages of the ancients about eloquence, argument, inquiry, and conduct; that the longer our human perspective, the more meaningful will be its focus on civilization's failures and successes. The best evidence he offers in defense of a classical education, however, is never stated, but is obvious throughout: It is that it might allow one to think with the lucidity of Mr. Knox, and to traverse, as he does so agilely herein, vast terrains of learning with perspicacity and poise.

What: Antiquity. *When:* 1993. *Also By: The Heroic Temper: Studies in Sophoclean Tragedy* (1964). *Essays Ancient and Modern* (1989). *Backing into the Future* (1994). And don't miss Knox's invaluable introductions to Robert Fagles's acclaimed translations of *The Iliad, The Odyssey,* and *The Aeneid. Further Reading: The Norton Book of Classical Literature,* edited by Knox. *Try: Classical Bearings* by Peter Green.

From the Mixed-Up Files of Mrs. Basil E. Frankweiler

E. L. Konigsburg (1930–2013)

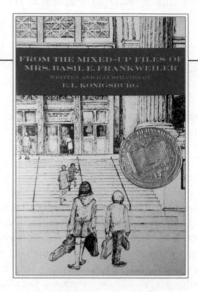

Hiding Out in the Metropolitan Museum

After earning a college degree in chemistry, getting married, pursuing graduate studies, teaching science, and bringing three children into the world and seeing them off to school, E. L. Konigsburg embarked upon a career writing and illustrating children's books. She published her first two in 1967, the elaborately titled *Jennifer, Hecate, Macbeth, William McKinley, and Me, Elizabeth*, and *From the Mixed-Up Files of Mrs. Basil E. Frankweiler*. The former was named a Newbery Honor Book; the latter won the prestigious Newbery Medal as the year's most distinguished contribution to American literature for children, and remains one of the best-loved books of our time. (Konigsburg was the first—and is still the only—author to have two titles on the Newbery list in the same season.)

The heroine of *From the Mixed-Up Files* is Claudia Kincaid, a straight-A student one month shy of her twelfth birthday. The eldest of four children and the only girl, Claudia feels taken for granted by her Greenwich, Connecticut, parents. Tired of doing all the chores, getting the smallest allowance in her class, and always doing the right thing, she decides she'll run away just long enough to teach her mother and father a lesson in "Claudia appreciation." Not being one for hardship, however, she concocts an elaborate plan to hide out in the Metropolitan Museum of Art in Manhattan. Since she knows she'll need more than just round-trip train fare ("Living in the suburbs had taught her that everything costs"), Claudia decides to take along her thrifty nine-year-old brother, Jamie, who not only has savings but also has a radio. Blending into groups of field-trip students during the day, hiding in bathroom stalls at closing time (their feet on the seats), the kids succeed in their plan, and their first days at the Met—they sleep in antique beds and bathe in fountains—are the stuff of perfect and playful fantasy. But the book really takes off when

Claudia determines to solve the mystery of the museum's latest acquisition, a beautifully sculpted marble angel. Dogged pursuit of clues leads Claudia and Jamie to Farmington, Connecticut, and into the curious world of Mrs. Basil E. Frankweiler, the statue's eccentric former owner.

The whole story, which is told in the form of a letter from Mrs. Frankweiler to her lawyer, is as delightful and unforgettable as Claudia herself, who has proved to be one of the most influential characters in modern children's literature.

What: Children's. *When:* 1967. *Award:* Newbery Medal, 1968. *Also By:* Konigsburg won her second Newbery Medal for *The View from Saturday* (1996). Her many other excellent books include *A Proud Taste for Scarlet and Miniver* (1973), *The Second Mrs. Gioconda* (1975), and *The Outcasts of 19 Schuyler Place* (2004). *Further Reading:* Konigsburg's *TalkTalk: A Children's Book Author Speaks to Grown-Ups. Try: A Wrinkle in Time* by Madeleine L'Engle (see page 473). *Mrs. Frisby and the Rats of NIMH* by Robert C. O'Brien. *Adaptations:* The 1973 film stars Ingrid Bergman as the titular museum donor; that role was reprised by Lauren Bacall for the 1995 TV movie. An excellent audiobook, narrated by Jan Miner, offers a splendid way for a family to share the pleasures of the tale. *Footnote: From the Mixed-Up Files* has earned its own subsection in "FAQ for Kids" on the Metropolitan Museum's website.

Into Thin Air
A PERSONAL ACCOUNT OF THE MT. EVEREST DISASTER
Jon Krakauer (born 1954)

Disaster at the Top of the World

"But boyhood dreams die hard, I discovered, and good sense be damned." So writes Jon Krakauer early in *Into Thin Air*, explaining how he found himself about to embark on an expedition to the top of Mount Everest in 1996. Commissioned by *Outside* magazine to deliver an article on the rise of Everest as an expensive theme park—once a trip for only the most experienced adventurers, an ascent to the peak was increasingly being marketed as an invigorating holiday for any amateur with $65,000 to spare—Krakauer, a seasoned climber, had been given the opportunity to fulfill a youthful ambition. And on the morning of May 10, after fifty-seven hours without sleep, he indeed reached the summit. Yet, freezing and hypoxic, his mental capacity as weakened as his physical strength, he was unable to appreciate his achievement—and he had no idea of the catastrophe that was about to unfold.

As he began the difficult descent, an unexpected storm struck. Although Krakauer struggled safely back to his camp, more than two dozen climbers, from his own and other parties, were still on the mountain. Eight, stranded by the fierce weather, would lose their lives, including two of Everest's most famous guides, Rob Hall and Scott Fischer. Krakauer's gripping account of the events of that tragic day, from the rigors of his own experience to the deadly horrors the fatal storm delivered, is one of the most riveting and harrowing adventure stories ever told, set down, as the author puts it, in "the calamity's immediate aftermath, in the roil and torment of the moment."

What: Adventure. *When:* 1997. *Also By: Eiger Dreams: Ventures Among Men and Mountains* (1990). *Into the Wild* (1996). And, in another vein entirely, *Under the Banner of Heaven: A Story of Violent Faith* (2003). *Further Reading: The Climb* by Anatoli Boukreev and G. Weston DeWalt and *Left for Dead* by Beck Weathers offer two different survivor perspectives on the same events. *Try: Touching the Void* by Joe Simpson. *Starlight and Storm* by Gaston Rébuffat. *Annapurna* by Maurice Herzog. *Adaptations:* An IMAX film crew was on the mountain at the time of the storm; their documentary, *Everest*, was released in 1998. A TV movie, *Into Thin Air: Death on Everest*, aired in 1997.

Mount Everest, site of the disaster detailed in Into Thin Air

A Hole Is to Dig
Ruth Krauss (1901–1993)
Illustrated by Maurice Sendak (1928–2012)

A Little Dictionary of Delights

Ruth Krauss's ingenious inventory of first definitions—compiled with the inspired assistance of many children—is a delight in every way, revealing how the world shapes words, and words return the favor. From "A hole is to dig" to "Hands are to hold," from "Toes are to dance on" to "Eyebrows are to go over the eyes," from "Mashed potatoes are to give everybody enough" to "The sun is so it can be a great day," Krauss's words, engaging in themselves, are enhanced and animated by the marvelous drawings of an illustrator at the very beginning of his career: Maurice Sendak (see page 703). By turns hilarious, endearing, and uncannily profound, Krauss's tiny masterpiece is catnip for kids, and strangely—almost blissfully—satisfying for adults.

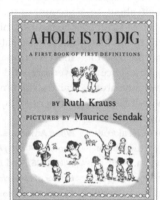

What: Children's. *When:* 1952.
Reading Note: For sharing with readers age 2 and up. *Also By Krauss and Sendak: A Very Special House* (1953). *Open House for Butterflies* (1960). *By Krauss with Other Illustrators: The Carrot Seed* (1945). *The Happy Day* (1945). *The Backward Day* (1950). *I Can Fly* (1950). *Try: The Nutshell Library* by Maurice Sendak. *Handmade Secret Hiding Places* by Nonny Hogrogian.

The Structure of Scientific Revolutions
Thomas S. Kuhn (1922–1996)

When the Paradigms Start to Shift

The conventional view of discovery long held that scientific knowledge was cumulative. Through experiment scientists described the contours of hard truths, and through further experiment they confirmed and refined those descriptions without reference to nonexperimental influences. As a graduate student, Thomas Kuhn, who would go on to teach both the history and philosophy of science at Harvard, Berkeley, and MIT, observed that this model had little in common with science in practice. In 1962, he published a book that would change the way the scientific enterprise is viewed both in and beyond the laboratory, becoming along the way, in the words of Lawrence Van Gelder in his *New York Times* obituary for Kuhn, "a profoundly influential landmark of 20th-century intellectual history." Dense and deeply erudite, *The Structure of Scientific Revolutions* is not an easy read, yet the provocative themes it articulates repay a reader's pondering.

Kuhn argues that science is not a gradually and logically advancing discipline, but rather a "series of peaceful interludes punctuated by intellectually violent revolutions"—that scientists are generally not innovators who question everything, but conservative figures who most often work within established methodologies and patterns of thought, even going so far as to resist developments that would seem to shed doubt on current wisdom. Only when the prevailing view of nature undergoes a "paradigm shift"—because of some "new sort of fact" that existing frameworks cannot assimilate—do scientific revolutions occur; they are fomented not by added knowledge so much as by anomaly. (The cross-discipline popularity of the phrase "paradigm shift" in public discourse today is one of the legacies of Kuhn's book.) Science does not advance, Kuhn says; it turns itself upside down whenever an idea existing outside the proverbial box meets its thinker (Copernicus, say, or Einstein), effectively rewriting scientific history up to that moment—at which point the process starts all over again.

By asserting that science is not progress toward a fixed goal but an evolutionary unfolding of understanding, Kuhn incited controversy; his book about the nature of revolutionary thinking was, in itself, revolutionary.

And in its nuanced way, his deep dive into the nature of knowledge endowed the unknown with renewed majesty.

What: Science. *When:* 1962. *Also By: The Copernican Revolution* (1957). *The Essential Tension: Selected Studies in Scientific Tradition and Change* (1977). *The Road Since Structure: Philosophical Essays, 1970–1993* (2000). *Try: The Double Helix* by James D. Watson (see page 837). *The Age of Wonder* by Richard Holmes.

The Book of Laughter and Forgetting
Milan Kundera (born 1929)

A Playful Novel of Freedom and Its Discontents

A leading literary figure in the celebration of cultural freedom that characterized the Prague Spring of 1968, Milan Kundera saw his books banned upon the Soviet invasion in August of that year. A little over a decade later, four years after relocating to France, his Czech citizenship was revoked upon publication of *The Book of Laughter and Forgetting*, a work that won him international acclaim.

The novel is constructed of seven interwoven (and often interrupted) tales that are meant to illuminate one another. The stories, sparely told, are playfully digressive, animated by the yearnings and aspirations of a swirling cast of poets, waitresses, lovers, dissidents, angels, and nudists. These inhabit a fictive space that transcends—but paradoxically is not beyond the reach of—political reality. The interruptions come in the form of dancing bits of commentary by the author, encompassing history and autobiography, philosophy and music theory, as well as flights of fancy and metaphor. All are choreographed in both tight and loose circles around the themes of laughter and forgetting. Why? Because humor and memory, along with erotic intimacy, provide the individual's last, best hope against the inhumanity of power.

THE BOOK OF LAUGHTER AND FORGETTING

So, you may be wondering, what exactly happens in the book? Nothing to whet an appetite for action: People go about ordinary lives, looking for lovers, lost letters, fading memories, the meaning of Eugène Ionesco's play *Rhinocéros*. They succeed or fail, their exertions providing welcome pretexts for the diversions of the supple and surprising narrative voice, which is the book's true glory. Tolerant, probing, and ruefully good humored, it celebrates the secret (and not always momentous) lives of memory and meaning that totalitarian authority strips from its subjects, and which Kundera, through his exhilarating art, seeks to restore.

What: Novel. *When:* 1979. *Editions:* The first edition in English, translated by Michael Henry Heim, was published in 1980. A new translation, commissioned and supervised by the author, was made by Aaron Asher in 1996. *Also By: Laughable Loves* (1970). *Life Is Elsewhere* (1973). *The Farewell Party* (1976). *The Unbearable Lightness of Being* (1984). *Immortality* (1990). *Slowness* (1995). Kundera's trio of essays on the history and uses of the novel—*The Art of the Novel* (1986), *Testaments Betrayed* (1993), and *The Curtain* (2005)—are marvelous appraisals of the form. *Try: The Bass Saxophone* and *The Engineer of Human Souls* by Josef Skvorecky. *The Feast of Love* by Charles Baxter (see page 58).

Angels in America

A GAY FANTASIA ON NATIONAL THEMES

Tony Kushner (born 1956)

A Theatrical Communion of Saints, Sinners, and Citizens

To consider the list of characters in Tony Kushner's *Angels in America* is to envision a television skit of scattershot satirical energies: a gay couple whose lives combine the family inheritances of Jewish guilt and WASP prerogative; a young Mormon husband and wife, he closeted and career minded, a clerk to a federal appeals court judge, she agoraphobic and navigating her apartment-bound metropolitan life with Valium and hallucinatory visions; an Orthodox rabbi; a Reagan administration Department of Justice public relations flak; a doctor; a drag queen; the "World's Oldest Bolshevik"; mannequins from the Diorama Room in the Mormon Visitors Center; Ethel Rosenberg; and, finally, a chorus of angels.

That Kushner manages to make of these figures not a mash-up of cultural attitudes but an engrossing human drama of breathtaking sentiment and intelligence is remarkable enough, but that he does so by making his drama cohere around the person of Roy M. Cohn is astonishing. Historically, Cohn was prosecutor of the espionage case that culminated in the execution of the Rosenbergs in 1953, the chief counsel to Communist-chasing Senator Joseph McCarthy during the Army-McCarthy hearings later that decade, and subsequently a demonic Manhattan power broker who brought a kind of sordid genius to his representation of clients that included Mafia bosses, Roman Catholic cardinals, socialites, and real estate developers. Cohn died from symptoms of AIDs in 1986, protesting the diagnosis, and his homosexuality, until the last.

The AIDs epidemic in Reagan-era America provides the context for Kushner's surreal and emotionally evocative portrayal of the currents of desire, repression, grief, and empathy that course through both the body politic and the heart romantic. The dialogue is sharply etched, ingeniously angled, often funny; Kushner's virtuoso scripting of Cohn manning the telephone while addressing a protégé in his office is a case in point:

ROY (To Joe): *Oh sit.* (To Harry) *You hold. I pay you to hold fuck you Harry you jerk. Half-wit dickbrain.* (Hold button, then he looks at Joe. A beat, then:)

I see the universe, Joe, as a kind of sandstorm in outer space with winds of mega-hurricane velocity, but instead of grains of sand it's shards and splinters of glass. You ever feel that way? Ever have one of those days?

The angels come and go as ethereal corroboration of the dream reality—the psychic weather—that colors our days and nights in both public and private realms. By combining magical realism with melodrama, satire, and naturalism, Kushner moves his audience across dimensions of experience—sexual, historical, biological, political, interpersonal, religious—that are usually more contiguous in life than in art. The result, both in performance and on the page, is an experience as disconcerting as it is rewarding, a play both unflinching and magnanimous.

What: Drama. *When:* Part one, *Millennium Approaches*, premiered in 1991; part two, *Perestroika*, in 1992. The entire two-part play premiered on Broadway in 1993. *Edition:* Kushner's Revised and Complete Edition was published in 2013, incorporating revisions made in the course of the work's performance history. *Awards: Millennium Approaches* won the Pulitzer Prize for Drama and the Tony Award for Best Play in 1993; *Perestroika* won the Tony for Best Play the following year. *Also By: A Bright Room Called Day* (1985). *Death & Taxes: Hydriotaphia and Other Plays* (2000). *Homebody/Kabul* (2001). *Caroline, or Change* (2002). *Try: Long Day's Journey into Night* by Eugene O'Neill (see page 604). *The Normal Heart* by Larry Kramer. *The Laramie Project* by Moisés Kaufman. *Adaptation:* Kushner adapted his play for the 2002 HBO miniseries directed by Mike Nichols and starring Al Pacino and Meryl Streep.

L, M, N, O

L

Dangerous Liaisons
Pierre Choderlos de Laclos (1741–1803)

Evil Geniuses of Desire

Witty, wealthy, vengeful, and bored, the glamorous antiheroes of Pierre Choderlos de Laclos's 1782 novel, *Dangerous Liaisons* (*Les Liaisons Dangereuses*), are connoisseurs of sex as pastime, game, and weapon. The sinisterly charming Vicomte de Valmont has his eye on a beautiful but married visitor, Madame de Tourvel, and determines to have her. But his co-conspirator, the Marquise de Merteuil, asks if he won't concentrate on despoiling the teenage Cécile de Volanges instead, so as to exact some revenge for the Marquise. Cécile is

1796 illustration of a scene from Dangerous Liaisons

fresh from the convent and, though promised in marriage to another, is infatuated with an unsuitable chevalier named Danceny. Valmont and the Marquise pretend to want to help the young lovers, when in fact it's Valmont's intention to get Cécile into his bed, and the Marquise's to get Danceny into hers. To compound matters, Cécile's mother sends a letter to Madame de Tourvel, warning her away from the rogue Valmont, unaware of his designs on her own daughter. And running like an electric charge through all these other currents of desire is a promise from the Marquise to sleep with Valmont if he's able to seduce Madame de Tourvel, with whom he's actually falling in love. But as their brilliantly tangled and cynically woven web begins to unravel, Valmont and the Marquise will find themselves seeking revenge on each other.

Entirely epistolary in form, the novel unfolds in the characters' own words, lending a fraught intimacy to the narrative: Each voice echoes thrillingly in the cruel emptiness that Valmont and the Marquise have made the context of the collective correspondence. The fact that any one of the letters could easily land in the wrong hands only heightens the aura of danger and intrigue that surrounds the complex sexual diplomacy. And what could be more enticing than the allure of an envelope housing a steamy missive inside?

Through his scandalous invention, author Choderlos de Laclos made his book a commentary on the corruption and libertinism of the ancien régime less than a decade before its collapse beneath the passionate energies of the Revolution. With its vivid depiction of the depraved impulses of its aristocratic protagonists and the cunning immorality of empowered desire, it's no wonder *Dangerous Liaisons* is still seducing readers more than two hundred years hence.

What: Novel. *When:* 1782. *Also By: On the Education of Women* (1785). *Try: The Nun* by Denis Diderot. *No Tomorrow* by Dominique-Vivant Denon. *The Good Soldier* by Ford Madox Ford (see page 288).

Adaptations: The book has been staged and filmed many times. Milos Forman's film *Valmont* (1989) stars Colin Firth, and *Cruel Intentions* (1999) recasts the plot among Manhattan teenagers. A 2004 French production starring Catherine Deneuve and Rupert Everett is also notable, but best of all is Stephen Frears's award-winning 1988 movie, *Dangerous Liaisons*, which stars Glenn Close, John Malkovich, Michelle Pfeiffer, Uma Thurman, and Keanu Reeves.

The Princess of Clèves
Madame de Lafayette (1634–1693)

Turning the Heart Inside Out

" The last years of Henry II's reign saw a display of opulence and gallantry such as has never been equalled in France," begins this pioneering novel, written a century after the period it describes and populated with historical figures, a notable exception being its fictive heroine. She is an heiress of marriageable age—sixteen years old—who, because of intrigues beyond her control, finds her nuptial prospects limited to a proposal from the Prince de Clèves, an unexceptionable figure whom she does not love. With characteristic candor, she declares this fact to him even as she accepts his hand. Soon after the wedding, the princess meets the gallant Duc de Nemours and finds his charms almost irresistible. Almost, because despite the strength of their mutual attraction, the princess will not betray her vows to her husband, even as she confesses to him her ardor for the other man.

The princess's firm grasp on ideals of virtue despite the cavalier decadence of prevailing convention causes her increasing anguish. Gossip and circumstantial evidence provoke confusion all around, and it does not end well for anyone concerned—except, that is, the reader. For in this slim book Madame de Lafayette, astutely recognizing deep and shifting emotional realities beneath the social and political currents of the court, composed an innovative kind of fiction that had few

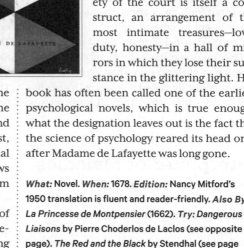

antecedents. Forgoing external action—the traditional matter of narrative fiction at the time she wrote—for interior states of thought and feeling, Lafayette confers both resonance and relevance upon the inner life. Her puzzle-like revelation of motive and event, with several characters delivering portions of what the reader wants to know, compels us to piece together the world she is describing. More tellingly, it suggests that the society of the court is itself a construct, an arrangement of the most intimate treasures—love, duty, honesty—in a hall of mirrors in which they lose their substance in the glittering light. Her book has often been called one of the earliest psychological novels, which is true enough; what the designation leaves out is the fact that the science of psychology reared its head only after Madame de Lafayette was long gone.

What: Novel. *When:* 1678. *Edition:* Nancy Mitford's 1950 translation is fluent and reader-friendly. *Also By: La Princesse de Montpensier* (1662). *Try: Dangerous Liaisons* by Pierre Choderlos de Laclos (see opposite page). *The Red and the Black* by Stendhal (see page 754). *Adaptations:* The novel has inspired several films, notably Jean Delannoy's 1961 version, adapted for the screen by Jean Cocteau, starring Marina Vlady and Jean Marais. *Footnote:* In 2009, French readers adopted Madame de Lafayette's masterpiece as a symbol of dissent against President Nicolas Sarkozy, who had repeatedly disparaged the book and ridiculed its enduring place on required reading lists.

The Dwarf
Pär Lagerkvist (1891–1974)

Taking the Measure of Human Nature

A philosophical novel invested with drama and intrigue by the insidious intimacy of its narrator, an embittered retainer at the court of a Renaissance Italian prince, *The Dwarf* views human nature through the window of a misanthropy as keenly observant as it is unreliable. Imagine a book-length interior monologue by a character as insinuating as *Othello's* Iago, and you'll have some idea of the alluring confidences of the dwarf, Piccoline, and of the Shakespearean intuitions into human nature that Pär Lagerkvist evokes.

"I am twenty-six inches tall," Piccoline begins, "shapely and well proportioned, my head perhaps a trifle too large." As his diary unfolds, we meet his patron, a prince clearly modeled on Machiavelli's ("the only one I have ever known whom I do not despise"), and become acquainted with the romantic and political intrigues of the city-state they inhabit. The arrival of the wizardly Bernardo—a paragon who, in his work on a mural of the Last Supper, a portrait with an enigmatic smile, and various military inventions, reflects the figure of Leonardo da Vinci—adds aesthetic dimensions to Piccoline's commentary. A familiar at court who is nonetheless never unaware of his status as an outsider, the dwarf is possessed by an envy that leeches the virtue from all he perceives.

All the pastimes and profundities of life—love, religion, poetry, politics, astrology, court etiquette and pretension, children, play, art—are withered by his scrutiny, and yet his alertness is such that we recognize the perspicacity of his gaze: "Human beings need flattery; otherwise they do not fulfill their purpose, not even in their own eyes."

Seduced by the fierce passions of Piccoline, the reader is led in his company through the heat of battle and the horrors of plague—and ultimately into a prison cell—without ever leaving the claustrophobic orbit of the dwarf's jealousy and discontent. Along the way, Lagerkvist's novel, written during the twentieth-century agony of World War II, expands into an enigmatically eloquent questioning of the inspiration at the heart of Renaissance humanism: Can man, *The Dwarf* unforgettably asks, really be the measure of all things?

What: Novel. *When:* 1944. *Edition:* English translation by Alexandra Dick, 1945. *Award:* Lagerkvist was awarded the Nobel Prize in Literature in 1951. *Also By: Barabbas* (1950). *The Marriage Feast* (stories written over three decades; English edition 1954). *The Sibyl* (1956). *Further Reading: The Prince* by Niccolò Machiavelli (see page 510). *Try: Notes from Underground* by Fyodor Dostoevsky (see page 231). *The Fall* by Albert Camus. *The Tin Drum* by Günter Grass (see page 331).

Interpreter of Maladies
Jhumpa Lahiri (born 1967)

Indian Immigrants, Indelible Stories, Universal Truths

Jhumpa Lahiri—just thirty-two when this, her first book, was published—is a rare writer who has combined literary sophistication with commercial success. *Interpreter of Maladies* not only won the Pulitzer Prize for Fiction, but also spent weeks atop the bestseller charts; *Unaccustomed Earth* (2008), a subsequent collection, shot straight to number one when it was released nine years later—an almost unheard of feat for an author of short stories. Part of Lahiri's appeal comes from her deft layering of substance and style: While she reckons with some of the most profound themes of contemporary global life, she does so in an unadorned voice whose effect recalls that of another great short story writer, Alice Munro. And just as Munro uses what may seem at first a small canvas of Canadian life to intuit the distant longings of the human heart, so—in *Interpreter of Maladies*, especially—Lahiri uses the displacements and transformations of America's diverse population of Indian immigrants to illuminate the home truths of an increasingly unbounded world.

Her debut collection opens with "A Temporary Matter," a quiet but haunting tale in which a young couple accustoms itself to hourlong nightly electricity cuts in their Boston neighborhood as they try to navigate the spaces that loss and heartbreak have insinuated between them. The title tale is a tour de force of fraught and comic culture clashes, revolving around an Indian American family and the local guide they ask to inform their sightseeing—and, as it turns out, something more than that—on a vacation in India. In "This Blessed House," newlyweds who've moved into a new home in Hartford discover the many religious tchotchkes the previous owners have left behind. Although the bride wants to keep and display this diverting collection of Christian figurines, the husband believes they have no place in the pious Hindu household he envisions; the tension between new and old, the lightness of the moment and the weight of tradition, fuels a sort of screwball

Jhumpa Lahiri, 2003

comedy that hurtles into unexpected emotional depths. And in "Mrs. Sen," perhaps the most memorable story in *Interpreter of Maladies*, the wife of a math professor babysits a friend's son and regales him with stories of her life in Calcutta, where she purchased her impressive collection of saris and regularly bought fresh fish at the markets that dot the city. In America, she longs for halibut and mackerel, but she cannot drive to the fishmonger, an emblem of the gulf that immigration has put between herself and her native habits.

Interpreter of Maladies is distinguished throughout by Lahiri's sympathetic recognition of desires that are not quite up to their own fulfillment, of loves that are dislodged but nevertheless accommodated to new surroundings, of goodness that must make do with the indifferent destinies life has in store for it. Like uncanny and lasting benedictions, her haunting evocations of human frailty leave readers strangely heartened.

What: Short Stories. *When:* 1999. *Award:* Pulitzer Prize for Fiction, 2000. *Also By: The Namesake* (2003). *The Lowland* (2013). *Try: Selected Stories, 1968–1994* by Alice Munro (see page 573). *The Inheritance of Loss* by Kiran Desai. *Arranged Marriage* by Chitra Banerjee Divakaruni.

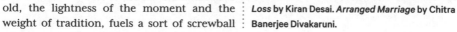

Notes on a Cowardly Lion
THE BIOGRAPHY OF BERT LAHR
John Lahr (born 1941)

A Comic Genius in Close-Up

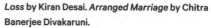

Bert Lahr (1895–1967) will always be remembered as the Cowardly Lion in *The Wizard of Oz*. When that film came out in 1939, the comic actor's long and glorious career was just past its midpoint. Starting out in burlesque in 1910, Lahr would find success in every aspect of the entertainment business over the next

fifty-seven years: vaudeville, Broadway musicals and comedies, television, advertising (he was featured in the popular "Betcha can't eat just one" campaign for Lay's Potato Chips), and many other movies in addition to *Oz*. Perhaps his most brilliant triumph, and certainly his most surprising, came as Estragon in the 1956 American premiere of Samuel Beckett's *Waiting for Godot*, a play Lahr claimed not to understand. The director, Herbert Berghof, disagreed: "I think he understands it better than any critic I've ever read, better than anybody who has ever read about it, and I think he understands it better than Beckett." Kenneth Tynan called Lahr's acting in *Godot* "one of the noblest performances I have ever seen."

John Lahr is an acclaimed theater critic—and Bert Lahr's son. *Notes on a Cowardly Lion* was his first book, and it remains one of the most eloquent and rewarding volumes about show business ever written. The author's fascination with his own father is allied to an incisive theatrical intelligence. He sensitively plumbs the grief surrounding Lahr's relations with his vaudeville partner and early love Mercedes, whose mental illness haunted the actor throughout his life ("You understand, John, I was very ambitious," the older man tells his son, "and I just didn't see anything but my plans"). He is equally adept at delineating the intricate choreography of comedy routines, deciphering backstage logistics, and portraying the psychological demands of both onstage artistry and offstage uncertainty. Imbued with both critical acumen and filial affection (the latter all the more moving for being candid and clear-eyed), John Lahr's book is an absorbing and poignant testament.

What: Biography. Theater. Film. *When:* 1969. *Also By:* *Prick Up Your Ears: The Biography of Joe Orton* (1978).

Coward: The Playwright (1983). *Automatic Vaudeville: Essays on Star Turns* (1984). *Light Fantastic: Adventures in Theatre* (1996). *Show and Tell:* New Yorker *Profiles* (2000). *Honky Tonk Parade:* New Yorker *Profiles of Show People* (2005). *Tennessee Williams: Mad Pilgrimage of the Flesh* (2013). *Try: Act One* by Moss Hart (see page 354). *Buster Keaton Remembered* by Eleanor Keaton and Jeffrey Vance.

The Leopard
Giuseppe Tomasi di Lampedusa (1896–1957)

The Passing of a Sicilian Prince

"It is not only species of animal that die out, but whole species of feeling," says Conchis in John Fowles's novel *The Magus*. That sentence might well stand as epigraph to *The Leopard*, Giuseppe Tomasi di Lampedusa's eloquent lament for the passing of the Sicilian aristocracy and the way of life it cultivated. Set largely in the three decades after 1860, when the unification of Italy and the energy of a new, bourgeois merchant class threatened the ancient feudal order of the island, Lampedusa's novel dramatizes the changing of the guard through the experience of Don Fabrizio, prince of the house of Salina. The wealth of his estates affords him the leisure to passively observe the tumultuous events around him even as he, an amateur astronomer, ponders the unfolding of celestial time. His tragic sense of life infuses the incidents of the novel—the invasion of Sicily by Garibaldi, assignations and liturgies, property inspections and consultations with clergy, the marriage of a favored nephew to the daughter of a vulgar parvenu, a grand ball—with regret and fateful melancholy. He knows that just as history, in the form of Berbers, Bourbons, and church, has nourished the traditions he treasures, so it now has created forces that will soon forget that fruitful legacy—without, he is certain, improving the lot of most Sicilians.

Like a house grave with the weight of years, its rooms decadent with heavy furniture and fabric, *The Leopard* exudes confidences. The secrets encompass love and death, privilege and corruption, and they suffuse the book with tidal forces that Don Fabrizio can acknowledge only with something akin to resigned admiration. The aristocrats, insurgents, peasants, and relatives that people his world are drawn with skepticism and sympathy in equal measure; the grand novel they inhabit—rich, tender, engrossing, intoxicating—is not easily put down.

What: Novel. *When:* 1958; English translation by Archibald Colquhoun, 1960. *Also By: Two Stories and a Memory* (1962). *Letters from London and Europe* (2010). *Further Reading: The Last Leopard: A Life of Giuseppe Tomasi di Lampedusa* by David Gilmour. *Try: The Charterhouse of Parma* by Stendhal. *War and Peace* by Leo Tolstoy (see page 798). *Gone With the Wind* by Margaret Mitchell (see page 557). *Adaptation:* The 1963 film, directed by Luchino Visconti and starring Burt Lancaster and Claudia Cardinale, won the Palme d'Or at the 1963 Cannes Film Festival. *Footnote:* The author, a gentleman scholar and the last hereditary prince of Lampedusa, published next to nothing in his lifetime. He died before *The Leopard* was published to immediate acclaim.

Endurance

SHACKLETON'S INCREDIBLE VOYAGE

Alfred Lansing (1921–1975)

The Man to Call When There Is No Way Out

Despite the fact that it never reached its destination, HMS *Endurance* has earned a noble berth in history. And while there have been numerous accounts of its now famous voyage, no one tells the story better than Alfred Lansing. Written four decades after the events it describes, it is based on extensive interviews with surviving members of Shackleton's crew and upon the original diaries they kept despite the desperate circumstances of their Antarctic ordeal. The result is the rarest sort of book—a real-life adventure that outshines the most excited praise a publisher can put on its cover: *thrilling! gripping! suspenseful! intense! a classic rousing tale!* True, true, true—and then some.

In August 1914, just as World War I was about to engulf Europe, Sir Ernest Shackleton and his men set out to cross the last uncharted continent. Their ambitious plan was to traverse Antarctica via the South Pole, from a starting point on the Weddell Sea to a terminus at McMurdo Sound. But before they could arrive at their intended base, the *Endurance* was trapped by the ice. "What the ice gets," Shackleton said, "the ice keeps," and his ship drifted for nearly a year before being crushed by the icepacks. For the next five months Shackleton and his crew of twenty-seven drifted on floes, castaways in one of the most savage regions of the world. Eventually they made their way to Elephant Island. From there, Shackleton and five companions set out to find help.

Nearly a month later, they arrived at a small whaling station—but only after a nine-hundred-mile journey in an open boat through some of the world's heaviest seas, and then an overland trek through glaciers and mountains across the island of South Georgia—an unprecedented feat all by itself. Organizing a relief party, Shackleton led four expeditions before he finally succeeded in returning to Elephant Island to rescue the rest of his men. Miraculously, not a single life was lost in the expedition's two years of tribulation.

Lansing's vivid narrative illustrates why the brutal, dramatic, courageous history of the *Endurance* and her crew has earned an unparalleled place in the annals of exploration. On nearly every page it displays the singular character of a man unrivaled in his ability to motivate, inspire, and lead a company to light through the bleakest, most frightening darkness. And to know that it actually happened—*incredible!*

What: Adventure. Exploration. *When:* 1959. *Further Reading: South: A Memoir of the* Endurance *Voyage* is Shackleton's own account of the expedition. Published in 1998, Caroline Alexander's *The* Endurance: Shackleton's Legendary Antarctic Expedition *combines meticulous research with 170 of Frank Hurley's original—and unforgettable—expedition photographs. Roland Huntford's *Shackleton* is an excellent biography. *Try: Scott's Last Expedition: The Journals of Robert Falcon Scott. The Worst Journey in the World* by Apsley Cherry-Garrard (see page 156). *Adaptations:* Among many television treatments, two stand out: *Shackleton*, a dramatic film starring Kenneth Branagh, and *The Endurance,* a documentary narrated by Liam Neeson, based on Caroline Alexander's book.

"For scientific leadership, give me Scott; for swift and efficient travel, Amundsen; but when you are in a hopeless situation, when there seems to be no way out, get on your knees and pray for Shackleton."

—*Sir Raymond Priestley*

Sons and Lovers
D. H. Lawrence (1885–1930)

A Novelist and His Hero Come of Age

David Herbert Lawrence was one of the most influential and controversial British writers of the twentieth century, and *Sons and Lovers* is his most autobiographical novel. In its pages, he came of age as a novelist by re-creating—through the story of Paul Morel, an artistic boy with a fierce attachment to his mother—his own formative years in an English coal-mining village.

Gertrude Morel's maternal possessiveness and Paul's filial affection are both extreme. Lawrence charted the development of this nearly incestuous bond in a letter he wrote the year before the book was published. "It follows this idea: a woman of character and refinement goes into the lower class, and has no satisfaction in her own life. She has had a passion for her husband, so her children are born of passion, and have heaps of vitality. But as her sons grow up she selects them as lovers—first the eldest, then [Paul]. These sons are urged into life by their reciprocal love of their mother—urged on and on. But when they come to manhood, they can't love, because their mother is the strongest power in their lives, and holds them." There you have the gist of the Oedipal drama of *Sons and Lovers*: Eventually Paul, a promising painter, finds himself torn between his love for his overbearing mother and his desire for the two beautiful young women—Miriam Leivers and Clara Dawes—he is unable to choose between.

Although the key to *Sons and Lovers* is the relationship between Paul and his mother, Paul's father, Walter, a coal miner whose working-class vitality hardens with age into a brutish alienation from the cultural aspirations of his wife and son, casts a long shadow over the novel. Lawrence's evocations of the simple pleasures of the mining village's residents, and his tender yet unsentimental alertness to landscape and to the pulses of the natural world, are imbued with a selfless attention that belongs to Walter's blunt reality rather than to Gertrude's world of romantic and self-absorbed attachments. The novel's language moves between these two poles with captivating prowess, from passages of watchful description to paragraphs that chart the swell, curl, break, and undertow of passionate yet never fixable emotions. Indeed, part of the book's singularity is the way its expressiveness conveys so much more than any schematic outline of Paul's dilemma can describe.

Frank O'Connor once said that *Sons and Lovers* starts out as a nineteenth-century novel and ends up as a twentieth-century one; as a result, readers are treated in its pages to both the rich setting and narrative rootedness of the former and the exhilaratingly

D. H. Lawrence, 1929

uneasy explorations of psychological and sexual dynamics that characterize the latter. Stamped with Lawrence's fierce authority, the whole is more than the sum of its parts. Although *Women in Love* and *Lady Chatterley's Lover* are no doubt Lawrence's most famous novels, *Sons and Lovers*, in Kate Millett's words, "is a great novel because it has the ring of something written from deeply felt experience. The past remembered, it conveys more of Lawrence's own knowledge of life than anything else he wrote. His other novels appear somehow artificial beside it."

What: Novel. *When:* 1913. *Also By: The Rainbow* (1915). *Women in Love* (1920). *Twilight in Italy* (1916). *Studies in Classic American Literature* (1923). *The Plumed Serpent* (1926). *Lady Chatterley's Lover* (1928). *The Complete Poems of D. H. Lawrence* (1964). *Further Reading: Flame into Being: The Life and Work of D. H. Lawrence* by Anthony Burgess. *Out of Sheer Rage: Wrestling with D. H. Lawrence* by Geoff Dyer. *D. H. Lawrence: A Personal Record* by Jessie Chambers (real-life model of the novel's Miriam). *Try: Jude the Obscure* by Thomas Hardy (see page 352). *Adaptations:* The 1960 film adaptation, starring Dean Stockwell as Paul Morel and Trevor Howard as Paul's father, received several Academy Award nominations, including one for Howard. The 2003 British television film stars Rupert Evans.

Gardening for Love
THE MARKET BULLETINS
Elizabeth Lawrence (1904–1985)

A Green-Thumbed Storyteller Works a Communal Plot

Elizabeth Lawrence has been called "the Jane Austen of the gardening literary world," but her amiable graciousness and respect for native soil is a bit too surely planted in the American South for the description to do her justice. Perhaps a better comparison is to her own friend Eudora Welty, who in fact introduced Lawrence to the world of agricultural market bulletins so lovingly celebrated in this book. Published by Departments of Agriculture in numerous states and privately in several others, market bulletins, Lawrence explains, are circulars in which "farmers advertise their crops . . . and their wives list the seeds and bulbs and plants that they sell for pin money." These gardeners who sell their flowers through the mail, Lawrence writes, "are amateurs in the true sense of the word: they garden for love." In addition to the yard plants, houseplants, and window plants they send off with friendly letters, these gardeners also share their stories:

Like Eudora's novels, the market bulletins are a social history of the Deep South. Through them I know the farmers and their dogs, their horses and mules, and the pedigrees of their cattle. I wonder whether the widow with no family ties found a home with an elderly couple needing someone to take care of them; whether the family of cotton pickers found work and a house near school and church. . . . And I wonder who bought the little farm with the pecan trees and good clear well water.

Gardening for Love was published posthumously, seamlessly edited by Allen Lacy from Lawrence's unfinished manuscripts and notes. It chronicles the author's decades of correspondence with a remarkable array of gardeners in the South and beyond—from Mrs. U. B. Evans, who grew seventeen different kinds of crinum (a flowering bulb) on a plantation near Ferriday, Louisiana, to Joe Smith, of Lamoni, Iowa, who published his own monthly bulletin for almost fifty years—for whom the market bulletins provided sociable sources of income, news, expertise, and comfort. The book welcomes readers into a world of flowers and friendship as rich and restorative as a spell in the garden on a fine day. Even better, it introduces the uninitiated to the works of a writer of rare delicacy, strength, and substance.

What: House & Garden. *When:* 1987. *Also By: A Southern Garden* (1942). *The Little Bulbs* (1957). *Through the Garden Gate* (1990, collecting essays written between 1957 and 1971). *Further Reading: Two Gardeners: A Friendship in Letters* collects Lawrence's correspondence with Katharine S. White; its editor, Emily Herring Wilson, wrote *No One Gardens Alone: A Life of Elizabeth Lawrence. Try: Losing Battles* by Eudora Welty. *The Essential Earthman: Henry Mitchell on Gardening. Footnote:* As an online search for "agricultural market bulletins" reveals, the world Lawrence describes is still thriving, in both print and electronic versions.

Independent People
Halldór Laxness (1902–1998)

An Icelandic Masterpiece

Who wants to read five hundred pages about a sheep farmer in Iceland? You do. And once you've done so, you'll want to tell every book-loving friend you have about it, too.

As we learn in the poet Brad Leithauser's introduction to a recent American edition of *Independent People*, an American on a layover in an Icelandic airport once took a 120-mile cab ride just to shake the hand of the man who had written it. That's the kind of devotion that this novel inspires. Set in the early twentieth century yet suffused with the ghosts of medieval Icelandic sagas and even older narratives, it's the magnum opus of Halldór Laxness, Iceland's most revered author. Recounting a sheep farmer's fierce struggle to achieve a small measure of economic independence, it embraces themes of love, duty, poetry, and mortality with an intensity of imagination both absorbing and exhilarating.

All this despite the bleak circumstances *Independent People* details: It's filled with the care and feeding and herding of sheep, with families consigned to one-room hovels perched above stables, with dampness and cold and hunger, with brutal births and deaths, with betrayals, misalliances, and mistakes that remain vivid for years. On the one hand, a closed but carefully described fist, the novel is steeped in a fierce naturalism that shows how the characters' experience is stunted by the determining power of the conditions they struggle futilely to rise above. On the other, an open palm crossed with the longest lines of love and fate, Laxness's tale of Bjartur of Summerhouses and his wives, daughters, sons, and, yes, sheep, reaches through impoverishment to connect with the enchanted, if malign, world of spirits and curses that bears witness to ancient realities too large for realism.

Stubborn and foolish and often uncaring, Laxness's protagonist works his way to prosperity before careening back to the poverty in which he began. As he moves through the decades, Bjartur performs feats of fortitude that seem lifted from the annals of legend—see the stirring storm scene—while his relations endure ordeals that belong to some dark fairy tale. He survives the storm, for instance, only to find that his wife has died in childbirth, alone on their croft, while the baby—fathered not by Bjartur, but by another—has weathered the winter cold by the beastly grace of a dog curled up around her. This child, whom he names Asta Sollilja (Beloved Sun-lily), will prove as flinty and resourceful as her adoptive father, and the bond that forms between them, though not resilient enough to hold them close constantly, is deep enough to outlast their tempers.

Bjartur and Asta Sollilja are just two of a cast of compelling figures with whom Laxness peoples the book. The social and the private landscapes of the novel are illuminated by an authorial intelligence that hovers over all, changing the colors of the days depicted with the unassuming prowess of a cloud. Like the stories embedded in the Hebrew Bible, that of Bjartur and his family embodies the eternal drama by which physical privation and primitive intuitions are transmuted into the embattled nobility of human being. Dwelling among the riches of this book, one feels part of an engendering process by which the simplest raw materials of life are mined, smelted, polished, and otherwise transformed into gems of hard truth and tender wonder.

What: Novel. *When:* Published in Icelandic in two parts, 1934–35. English translation by J. A. Thompson, 1946. *Edition:* The Vintage paperback contains Leithauser's eloquent introduction. *Award:* Nobel Prize in Literature, 1955. *Also By: World Light* (1937–40). *Iceland's Bell* (1943–46). *Further Reading: The Islander: A Biography of Halldór Laxness* by Halldór Guðmundsson. *Try: One Hundred Years of Solitude* by Gabriel García Márquez (see page 308). *The Book of Ebenezer Le Page* by G. B. Edwards (see page 244).

"I can't imagine any greater delight than coming to *Independent People* for the first time."
—*Jane Smiley*

The Spy Who Came In from the Cold
John le Carré (born 1931)

The Best Espionage Novel of All Time?

A British intelligence agent throughout the 1950s and into the 1960s, David Cornwell, under the pseudonym John le Carré, went on to use his personal experience of the ethically destitute climate of Cold War espionage to create a fictional world more unglamorous, chilling, and dispirited than any previously ventured by a writer of spy thrillers—and more gripping and compelling in just about every way. In thrall to "the expediency of temporary alliances" that makes them pawns in an amoral but mortal calculus, his always compromised characters move through an alienated existence wearing the masks of their assumed identities. The price of their disguises is le Carré's recurring theme, and it is nowhere more powerfully explored than in *The Spy Who Came In from the Cold*.

In this, le Carré's third novel and the one that made his reputation, we meet Alec Leamas:

"Aware of the overwhelming temptations which assail a man permanently isolated in his deceit, Leamas resorted to the course which armed him best. Even when he was alone, he compelled himself to live with the personality he had assumed." It's Berlin in the early 1960s, and the agents in Leamas's command are being killed. When the last of them dies, Leamas carries his failure back to London, relieved to finally be "coming in from the cold." But his spymaster, Control, has a different idea, deploying Leamas in the all-too-congenial role of disgraced former agent in order to initiate a complicated game of cat and mouse designed to protect a British double agent operating in the upper echelons of East German intelligence. The intricately plotted puzzle is rivetingly plausible, especially because the spies are being strung along by their superiors as cunningly as the readers are being strung along by le Carré. A love story

wends its way through the tale as well, adding its sad weight to the several other kinds of heartbreak the author so tellingly exposes.

More than a thriller (but very much that), *The Spy Who Came In from the Cold* is a novel in which one man's weariness, confusion, and pervasive doubt cross the border of his peculiar occupation to resonate with broader, if less dramatic, human truths. It is very hard to forget.

What: Mystery & Suspense. *When:* 1963. *Award:* Edgar Award from the Mystery Writers of America for Best Mystery Novel, 1965. *Also By: Tinker, Tailor, Soldier, Spy* (1974). *The Honourable Schoolboy* (1977). *Smiley's People* (1979). *The Night Manager* (1993). *The Constant Gardener* (2001). *A Legacy of Spies* (2017). *Further Reading: My Silent War: The Autobiography of a Spy* by Kim Philby. *Try: The Human Factor* by Graham Greene. *Adaptation:* The 1965 film of *The Spy Who Came In from the Cold* stars Richard Burton.

A Wizard of Earthsea
Ursula K. Le Guin (1929–2018)

A Primal Work of Modern Fantasy

At the outset, the novel orients us on Gont, a single mountain in a storm-racked ocean, one of the dozens of islands that, we will come to discover, make up the Earthsea archipelago. Gont, we are told, is a land famous for wizards, and what we are about to read is the tale of how the greatest of these, known as Ged, came of age and tempered his improvidence to become—after suffering through trials that tested both his mettle and his magical powers—dragonlord and Archmage.

Ged begins his adventures as a wild and untended rural boy whose facility with the word-based magic of his island leads to his adoption by a mage and his arrival at a school for wizards. A prodigal student, Ged dares too much out of vain motives, inadvertently

unleashing an ancient shadow upon the world, an evil that he must find the cunning and courage—and, hardest of all, the humility—to master. Although destined for greatness, Ged is neither saintly nor privileged; his proclivity for making the kinds of mistakes any reader might make in his shoes endears him to us, rendering both his failures and his triumphs all the more meaningful.

Since its publication in 1968, *A Wizard of Earthsea* has cast a spell on readers and exerted enormous influence on writers as diverse as Neil Gaiman, Junot Díaz, and Margaret Atwood (the latter has called Le Guin's novel one of the "wellsprings" of fantasy literature). The richness of the tale, and that of the five Earthsea sequels that followed it, relies in large part on the deep mythic backstory Le Guin layers into her fascinating maritime geography; this resonant network is augmented by an organic system of magic that eschews glibness for the arduousness of any true craft.

If *A Wizard of Earthsea* is often characterized as a young adult novel, it may be because it engages, with probity and a sense of reverence, themes often underplayed in books for grown-ups: ethics, empathy, and understanding of the vital ecological balance in which both nature and culture are implicated and entwined. Why these thematic concerns are less prominent in books for adults is puzzling, since they provide the coordinates

for the moral compass we require to actually be grown up. Which is to say that adults will profit from this novel, and from the cycle it spawned, as much as their children.

What: Fantasy. *When:* 1968. *Also By:* In the Earthsea Cycle: *The Tombs of Atuan* (1971); *The Farthest Shore* (1972); *Tehanu* (1990); *Tales from Earthsea* (2001); *The Other Wind* (2001). Other books: *The Left Hand of Darkness* (1969); *The Lathe of Heaven* (1971); *The Dispossessed* (1974); *Always Coming Home* (1985). *Try: The Riddle-Master of Hed* by Patricia A. McKillip. *The Ice Is Coming* by Patricia Wrightson.

To Kill a Mockingbird
Harper Lee (1926–2016)

Innocence and Injustice in an Alabama Town

Harper Lee's *To Kill a Mockingbird* is near the top of the list of most-beloved American novels. Set in Depression-era Alabama, it is the story of six-year-old Jean Louise Finch, better known as Scout; her older brother, Jeremy, nicknamed Jem; and their father, Atticus Finch, a middle-aged lawyer whose brave defense of Tom Robinson, a black man accused of raping a white woman, provides the fulcrum of the plot. Told through Scout's eyes, the narrative renders small-town experience through the hues of wonder and worry that color childhood, and through the lenses of illusions large and small: ideals of justice, idealization of a father, confidence that the wheels of the world might well turn things right in the end, whatever obstacles are strewn in their path.

Although the famous film starring Gregory Peck as Atticus is largely faithful to the book, especially in following the dramatic arc supplied by Tom Robinson's trial, it doesn't entirely capture the warmth and humor that pervades Scout's telling, which is enlivened with a streak of satire that belies her age (as, from time to

time, does her precocious way with words). The people of the town, and especially the Finches' neighbors, among them the mysterious Boo Radley, are vivid presences; their personalities provide a largely friendly context for Scout's upbringing, even as she comes to realize the

Harper Lee, 2007

racial prejudice and violence that shadow the community she inhabits. This widening sense of context enables her—and the reader—to recognize Atticus's nobility and courage.

The novel was both a popular and critical success when it was first published, becoming an immediate bestseller and winning the 1961 Pulitzer Prize for Fiction. The Oscar-winning movie, released the following year, only burnished its reputation as a contemporary American classic. Yet, in the decades after publication of her phenomenal debut, Lee lived almost defiantly out of the public eye, at least until the controversial 2015 publication of *Go Set a Watchman*. This first draft of *To Kill a Mockingbird* is set twenty years later, when Scout is not so innocent nor Atticus so admirable—rendering their earlier incarnations, and the drama of conscience and compassion they enact in *Mockingbird*, all the more cherishable.

What: Novel. *When:* 1960. *Award:* Pulitzer Prize for Fiction, 1961. *Further Reading: Scout, Atticus, and Boo: A Celebration of Fifty Years of "To Kill a Mockingbird,"* edited by Mary McDonagh Murphy. *Try: The Heart Is a Lonely Hunter* by Carson McCullers (see page 536). *Other Voices, Other Rooms* by Truman Capote.

Adaptation: The 1962 film adaptation, starring Gregory Peck as Atticus Finch, looms as large in filmdom as the book does in publishing. *Footnote:* Upon completion of *Mockingbird*, Lee traveled to Holcomb, Kansas, with her childhood friend Truman Capote (said to be a model for the character of Dill in *Mockingbird*) to assist in the early stages of his research for *In Cold Blood* (see page 125), which Capote dedicated to her.

Cider with Rosie
Laurie Lee (1914–1997)

A Cotswold Boyhood Recalled with Eloquence and Wonder

Childhood is much larger than any adult can ever remember. For a child, time dawdles without minutes, experience expands without the markings of names or categories, emotions arrive and depart like natural disasters. In this remarkable memoir of a Cotswold boyhood just after the First World War, Laurie Lee manages to convey the size of early consciousness with a power that is charming, magnificent, and rare. "I was set down from the carrier's cart at the age of three; and there with a sense of bewilderment and terror my life in the village began," he begins, and he goes on to describe his feelings as he stood momentarily in a patch of grass—"I had never been so close to grass before"—that was taller than he was:

For the first time in my life I was out of the sight of humans. For the first time in my life I was alone in a world whose behaviour I could neither predict nor fathom: a world of birds that squealed, of plants that stank, of insects that sprang about without warning. I was lost and did not expect to be found again. I put back my head and howled, and the sun hit me smartly on the face, like a bully.

Lee recounts his coming-of-age in prose that is vivid in its casual majesty. Home life with a brood of siblings, school life with an assortment of fellow students, imaginative life in its wonder, perplexity, and desperate innocence—

all pass before us, not just recalled but quick-ened with a youthful eye and enthusiasm. Carrying the common tune of family and vil-lage life, Lee embellishes it with lyrical evoca-tions of the fitful energies of adolescence—so fierce and tender, awkward and arrogant, "valiant and easy." The author animates as well the last days of his village, portraying the sea-soned existence that would soon vanish from his Cotswold valley as the twentieth century overtook the countryside's well-tempered time: "I belonged to that generation which saw, by chance, the end of a thousand years' life." In its language and its yearnings, this is among the most beautiful books you'll ever read.

What: Memoir. *When:* 1959. *Also By: A Rose for Winter: Travels in Andalusia* (1955). *As I Walked Out One Midsummer Morning* (1969). *A Moment of War: A Memoir of the Spanish Civil War* (1991). *Further Reading: Laurie Lee: The Well-Loved Stranger* by Valerie Grove. *Try: Lark Rise to Candleford* by Flora Thompson (see page 783). *Akenfield* by Ronald Blythe (see page 84). *This House of Sky* by Ivan Doig (see page 227). *Adaptations:* Thrice filmed for television: in 1971 for the BBC, in 1999 for Masterpiece Theatre, and in 2015 again for the BBC.

Another Self
James Lees-Milne (1908–1997)

The Radiantly Comic Autobiography of a British National Treasure

James Lees-Milne is among the most cel-ebrated of modern diarists; his published journals, which span the years 1942 through 1993, offer a witty, personalized social and cul-tural portrait of contemporary and—because of his many years in the service of the National Trust—landmark Britain. An unabashed aesthete, Lees-Milne found his vocation in the preservation of the "infi-nitely fragile and precious" heri-tage of the great country houses and the "man-fashioned land-scape" that surrounds them.

Although his diaries make fascinating reading, Lees-Milne's most memorable book is *Another Self*, a fictionalized autobiogra-phy that narrates the author's early years in a sequence of delightfully self-deprecating—and very funny—vignettes. The episodes encompass his child-hood in Worcestershire under the mismatched wings of a flighty mother and an obdurate father; his studies at Eton and Oxford; his first employment as secretary to Lord Lloyd and Sir Roderick Jones, chairman of Reuters; hilari-ous holidays in Portugal and bandit-ridden

Corsica; and army service at the start of the Second World War (from which point his dia-ries take up his life story).

Freed from the diary's daily measure, Lees-Milne shapes his memories into perfectly poised comic episodes that proceed inexora-bly from demure setup to farcical conclusion. The aesthete's hand is revealed in every chap-ter, each one a set piece filled with deft characterization, out-rageous anecdote, implausible occurrence, and climactic sur-prise. Some of the scenes are so ridiculously amusing (take the account of how the author shortsightedly marched a pla-toon of Irish Guards over the cliffs of Dover) that the reader can't help but picture the pro-tagonist of these pages—so bum-bling and yet so charmed—as the young Alec Guinness. Quite sim-ply, *Another Self* is a joy to read.

What: Autobiography. *When:* 1970. *Also By:* Diaries 1942–1993 (published in twelve volumes, 1975–2005; three-volume abridgement by Michael Bloch published 2006–2008). *Roman Mornings* (1956). *People and Places* (1992). *Try: Some People* by Harold Nicolson. *Playing for Time* by Jeremy Lewis. *Untold Stories* by Alan Bennett.

■ For Fritz Leiber's *Two Sought Adventure*, see page 795.

....

The Cyberiad
FABLES FOR THE CYBERNETIC AGE
Stanislaw Lem (1921–2006)

A Mind-Expanding Master of Science Fiction

....

S adly, the Polish writer Stanislaw Lem does not enjoy the kind of popularity in English-speaking realms that his brilliant, funny, and philosophical inventions deserve. Intellectually daring and as mordant as the speculations of Jonathan Swift, Lem's novels and stories exhibit a sprightly fabulism that leaves the reader invigorated and eager for more. Time and again, he takes the conventional apparatus of science fiction and playfully leads the reader into the far reaches of time, space, and imagination. Rockets and—especially—robots have a big role in his prodigious output, but his technological fascination wanders through networks of ideas and existential dilemmas that vibrate with human significance.

Stanislaw Lem, 1973

This is certainly true of the wacky fables and allegories found in *The Cyberiad*, which offers an appealing introduction to the author's universe through its chronicle of the interstellar doings of a pair of robots, Trurl and Klapaucius. These two chums, nearly omnipotent "constructors" (they can literally shift the position of stars in the heavens, but, in a typical Lem touch, do so only for the purpose of spelling out an advertisement), are generally benevolent. They also, for all their powers, possess a highly entertaining, bumbling quality reminiscent of Laurel and Hardy. Their adventures across a galaxy inhabited by similar non-fleshy beings (the rare biological humans, all primitives, are dubbed "palefaces") involve chivalric quests and dictator-toppling acts of charity. Central to the volume is the robots' search for the civilization that possesses "the Highest Possible Level of Development." Lem uses this improbable pursuit of an ideal society as an itinerary along which he displays both his erudition and his amusement at the foibles of all thinking beings. Readers seduced by the attractions of his mind can explore it further in the dozens of scintillating works that constitute his oeuvre.

What: Science Fiction. Short Stories. *When:* 1965 in Polish; English translation by Michael Kandel, 1974. *Also By: The Star Diaries* (1957). *Solaris* (1961). *Memoirs Found in a Bathtub* (1961). *Mortal Engines* (1971–76). *The Chain of Chance* (1976). *Try: More than Human* by Theodore Sturgeon. *Cosmicomics* by Italo Calvino. *The Complete Roderick* by John Sladek. *Adaptation:* Lem's collection was the inspiration for Krzysztof Meyer's opera *Cyberiada*, which was composed in 1970 and saw its premiere in Germany in 1986.

A Wrinkle in Time
Madeleine L'Engle (1918–2007)

Across the Universe with Family and Friends

Despite its rocky road to publication—twenty-six rejections were logged by the author before the book found a home at Farrar, Straus and Giroux—Madeleine L'Engle's *A Wrinkle in Time* met with immediate success, winning wide readership as well as the 1963 Newbery Medal as the most distinguished contribution to American literature for children. It has remained continuously in print for more than a half century and, more importantly, has remained alive in the imaginations of the several generations of readers who have fallen in love with it.

There are many reasons for that affection, but the most obvious is apparent on the book's first page, which starts with an arch invocation of melodramatic novelistic atmosphere—"It was a dark and stormy night"—but quickly comes to a pitch-perfect evocation of its teenage emotional equivalent:

The house shook.

Wrapped in her quilt, Meg shook.

She wasn't usually afraid of weather.—It's not just the weather, she thought.—It's the weather on top of everything else. On top of me. On top of Meg Murry doing everything wrong.

Troubled, feisty, and, as we shall discover, remarkably resourceful, thirteen-year-old Meg is one of the most unforgettable heroines in twentieth-century young adult fiction. Her family is rather memorable, too. There are her sympathetic parents, both of whom are scientists and one of whom, her father, has gone missing in the course of his research into the space-time continuum. Despite their brilliance, the adult Murrys nonetheless—thrillingly for the adolescent reader—rely on their children for aid and solace. There are also twin siblings, Sandy and Dennys; her little brother, Charles Wallace, an eccentric genius in the form of a five-year-old; and a romantic interest for Meg in the person of her neighbor and schoolmate, Calvin O'Keefe. The highly naturalistic dynamics of this group are alluring in themselves, but take on richer and surprising new dimensions with the appearance of three beneficent yet scatterbrained, and entirely awesome, aliens—Mrs. Whatsit, Mrs. Who, and Mrs. Which—who are the catalysts and companions for Meg and company's interstellar adventures in search of the missing parent.

Along the way, L'Engle depicts societies utopian, dystopian, and in between, augmenting the action with the enigmas of quantum physics and grounding its resolution in the verities of Christian virtue: humility, hope, love. Readers won't want to put the book down, and will be happy to have four subsequent volumes in the Time Quintet to pick up when they do.

What: Fantasy. *When:* 1962. *Award:* Newbery Medal, 1963. *Also By:* In the Time Quintet: *A Wind in the Door* (1973); *A Swiftly Tilting Planet* (1978); *Many Waters* (1986); *An Acceptable Time* (1989). Other fiction: *Meet the Austins* (1960); *A Ring of Endless Light* (1980). *Try:* *The Mystery of Mont Saint-Michel* by Michel Rouzé. *The Wolves of Willoughby Chase* by Joan Aiken. *When You Reach Me* by Rebecca Stead. *Adaptations:* As befits its popularity, L'Engle's book has been adapted many times, including several stage versions, a television film, a graphic novel, and even an opera (composed by Libby Larsen). Ava DuVernay directed the 2018 feature film starring Reese Witherspoon, Oprah Winfrey, and Mindy Kaling. *Footnote:* "It was a dark and stormy night" is, infamously, the opening sentence of Edward Bulwer-Lytton's 1830 novel *Paul Clifford*, and has become an enduring emblem of bad writing.

Friends in High Places
Donna Leon (born 1942)

Mysteries of Venice

The key to a successful mystery series may be the habits of the detective: They must be distinctive enough to support an identity, regular enough to become familiar, idiosyncratic enough to be intriguing over many volumes, congenial enough to lure us back for more. Think Rex Stout's Nero Wolfe (see page 763) with his beer and orchids.

Donna Leon's protagonist, Commissario Guido Brunetti of the Venetian Questura, is not as outsize in form, nor in his predilections, as Stout's sedentary sleuth, but the modesty of his private passions—reading ancient history; a devotion to his wife, Paola, a feisty professor of literature, and his children, Raffi and Chiara; a practical connoisseurship of food and wine—perfectly describes his character. Ruminative and a touch melancholic, he is a good and compassionate man whom Leon makes deeply interesting. (Is there anything harder for a writer to do?)

A fine cast of supporting players adds to the appeal of Brunetti's cases. In addition to the commissario's immediate family, there's his father-in-law, Count Orazio Falier, one of the richest and most well-connected men in Venice. At work, there's the fatuous top cop, Vice-Questore Patta, and Brunetti's arsenal of devoted,

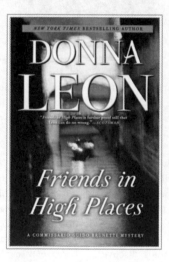

if not always effectual, lieutenants. And, from the third book in the series on, there's the alluring Signorina Elettra, Patta's secretary, a stylish, resourceful, and cunning woman who seems able, to Brunetti's constant amazement, to tap a global network of allegedly secure and private information. Last but not least, there is Venice itself, brooding, beautiful, and deadly. Leon, an American expatriate, draws her adopted home with casual yet knowing precision.

Friends in High Places is the ninth book in the series and a splendid representative of its mature pleasures. It features Leon's fully developed cast of characters, a rich serving of Venetian atmosphere, and an especially intricate plot, in which the murder of a bureaucrat puts Brunetti on a trail of intrigue that leads him surprisingly close to home. As always, his navigation of the tide of municipal corruption leaves him on the shore of a lagoon of moral quandaries as old and inscrutable as the city itself.

What: Mystery & Suspense. *When:* 2000. *Also By: Death at La Fenice,* the first in the series, was published in 1992; Leon's twenty-seventh Commissario Brunetti novel, *The Temptation of Forgiveness,* was published in 2018. *Further Reading: Brunetti's Venice: Walks with the City's Best-Loved Detective* by Toni Sepeda. *Try: Death of an Englishman* by Magdalen Nabb. *Lucifer's Shadow* by David Hewson.

LaBrava
Elmore Leonard (1925–2013)

King of the Capers

Elmore Leonard's Edgar Award–winning novel is the story of Joe LaBrava, an ex–Secret Service agent who gets involved with a

former movie star he first became infatuated with as an adolescent, when he was wowed by her big-screen allure. Decades later, in real life, Jean Shaw is still a stunner, and she's being harried by a couple of menacing—albeit colorful—thugs. Set in Florida's South Beach before its recent glitzy renaissance, this 1983 thriller evokes the atmosphere of the films noirs that Shaw once starred in as well as the bygone glamour of an older, celebrity-studded Miami. But what it delivers best of all is its author's trademark blend of hardboiled suspense, high-spirited invention, and outrageous characters; it's both funny and frightening at the same time.

Leonard is often praised by writers and critics for his "pitch-perfect dialogue," but that isn't quite right, and it sells his real achievement short. Nobody talks like people talk in Leonard's books (as he is the first to admit). What is true is that few writers have his knack for bringing humanity to life through speech, and speech alone. That this is the result of energetic literary artifice rather than accurate recording is the real key to the pleasure his novels provide. The seemingly improvisatory ingenuity of his dialogue gives his books an aliveness from page to page that is compelling, exhilarating, and exceedingly rare. Really addictive, too.

Elmore Leonard, 1980

(1985). *Killshot* (1989). *Get Shorty* (1990). *Try: The Dreadful Lemon Sky* by John D. MacDonald. *One for the Money* by Janet Evanovich. *Native Tongue* by Carl Hiaasen. *Footnote:* In addition to his capers, Leonard has penned plenty of excellent Westerns; try *Hombre* (1961).

What: Mystery & Suspense. *When:* 1983. *Award:* Edgar Award for Best Novel, 1984. *Also By:* *Swag* (1976). *Glitz*

Zibaldone
Giacomo Leopardi (1798–1837)

A One-Volume Library of Learning, Culture, and Melancholy

Although Giacomo Leopardi is generally regarded as Italy's finest poet after Dante, his prose writing has a genius all its own, especially his *Operette Morali* ("Moral Essays"). These pieces, often composed in dialogue form, are witty, philosophical, and strangely invigorating elaborations of the theme that happiness is impossible anywhere in the universe. His early life was enriched but largely circumscribed by his father's ten-thousand-volume library, and his cloistered coming-of-age, combined with persistent illness, contributed to a disillusioned maturity. Yet despite his pervasive melancholy, encounters with Leopardi's work prove both tonic and reviving to restive souls; reading it can be like talking to one's best self, finding solace in the life lessons only solitude has the savvy to admit.

Although editions of his *canti* ("poems") or his essays might well earn a place on any reader's list of necessary books, his *Zibaldone* (literally, "hodgepodge") is in a class by itself, for this monumental volume of Leopardi's notebooks is one of the most singular cultural works not only of the nineteenth century, but of all time. Encompassing an extraordinary range of subjects—antiquity, language, history, metaphysics, science, the evolution of human society and institutions, aesthetics, poetry, the passions, theology, and, most tellingly, human nature as reflected in all of these—*Zibaldone* is like an intellectual scripture filled with learning, rumination, revelation, stories, invocations, ancient wisdom, emerging scientific discoveries, and imaginative epiphanies. It is also characterized, from time to time, with the longueurs of a scriptural testament as well. It grapples with the substance of living and dying and thinking and feeling with a mental facility, analytic precision, and literary felicity that are startling and overwhelming but never stray too far from this remarkable author's experience and memory. The more than two thousand closely set pages of the complete English translation are not easy reading by any means, nor do they reward end-to-end concentration. Just open this book anywhere, and prepare for wonders.

What: Philosophy. Diaries & Letters. *When:* Leopardi's notebooks were composed in the years 1817–32; they were published in Italy between 1898 and 1900 in seven volumes. *Edition:* The first complete translation in English, edited by Michael Caesar and Franco D'Intino, appeared in 2013. *Also By:* Leopardi's rich but complicated bibliography is best represented to readers in three volumes in English, encompassing his poetry (1819–37), essays (1823–28), and correspondence (1817–37): *Canti: Poems* (bilingual edition), translated by Jonathan Galassi (2010); *The Moral Essays*, translated by Patrick Creagh (1983); *The Letters of Giacomo Leopardi*, translated by Prue Shaw (1998). *Further Reading: Leopardi: A Study in Solitude* by Iris Origo. *Try: Essays* by Michel de Montaigne (see page 561). *The Waste Books* by Georg Christoph Lichtenberg.

■ For Jill Lepore's *Book of Ages*, see page 252.

DORIS LESSING
(1919–2013)

Publishing books over a span of nearly sixty years, Doris Lessing created fictional worlds both naturalistic and visionary. From her first book, *The Grass Is Singing* (1950), through the autobiographical Martha Quest novels (known collectively as the Children of Violence series), to her most famous single volume, the formally inventive *The Golden Notebook* (1962) and beyond, Lessing's fiction is characterized by its scrutiny of political conditions and its alertness to psychological and sexual quandaries that are very much

Doris Lessing, 1990

of this world. Her decision to set off, in the late 1970s, for an extended voyage into outer space—in the five novels that compose *Canopus in Argos: Archives*—was unexpected to say the least, and produced work unlike anything she had previously published. To consider her work entire, as the Swedish Academy did in honoring her with the Nobel Prize in Literature in 2007, is to contemplate a vast, variegated oeuvre that encompasses the colonial oppression of the African veld, the idealized romance of communism and the skepticism it leaves in its wake, feminism and the complications it breeds for women and men both, and the mysteries of the spirit that can shape individual lives as well as the fate of imagined intergalactic empires. Throughout her career, Lessing exercised an earnest ethical judgment rare in modern letters, embodying in story after story the urgent energy of a truth-seeker unbowed before life's violence and grief. We might as well call that urgency faith, for it reflects the resolve expressed in her most famous maxim: "Whatever you are meant to do, do it now. The conditions are always impossible."

The Grass Is Singing
Murder on the Veld

The Grass Is Singing opens with a newspaper announcement that Mary Turner has been found dead on the porch of her ramshackle farmhouse. Her husband, Dick, is wandering mad in the bush, and her Bantu servant, having confessed to the murder, has been arrested. What follows is the story of how Mary went from being a contented urban career woman, unencumbered in every way, to a deranged farm wife, suffering the constrained economic and psychological circumstances of life as a "poor white" on the veld, taking out her unhappiness on her failure of a husband and a string of native houseboys. It is the story of how the expectations of her time and place—the 1940s in Rhodesia—led her to forsake her freedom for marriage at thirty and, ultimately, for a loneliness and isolation that distill into misery the potent malevolence of rural colonialism, in which the suspicions and resentments of "us against them" overtake sympathy for both self and others. Unlikeable but complex, she evokes pity and horror even as the reader comes to "understand the country" she inhabits: a land of racial and class distinctions that formalize cruelty into a terrifying etiquette of oppression and brutality. The Grass Is Singing is a brilliant portrait of a time and place that, while steeped in remote particulars, reflects essential human fears and failings that are never all that far from home, no matter where we live.

What: Novel. When: 1950. Also By: The Children of Violence Novels: Martha Quest (1952); A Proper Marriage (1954); A Ripple from the Storm (1958); Landlocked (1965); The Four-Gated City (1969). Nonfiction: African Laughter: Four Visits to Zimbabwe (1992). Try: Don't Let's Go to the Dogs Tonight by Alexandra Fuller. Adaptation: A 1981 British film, starring Karen Black, was released in the United States in 1984 as Killing Heat.

The Golden Notebook
A Novel Like No Other

"After all," says Molly Jacobs to her friend Anna Wulf, the novelist who is the protagonist of Lessing's 1962 masterpiece, "you aren't someone who writes little novels about the emotions. You write about what's real." At more than six hundred pages, The Golden Notebook itself is certainly not little, and the reality it portrays, as well as the manner of that portrayal, make it a landmark work. As to what Anna Wulf does or doesn't write, both are central to the book's unfolding. Having published one successful novel, an autobiographical work of her coming-of-age in Southern Rhodesia, Anna, now living in London, suffers from writer's block, at least in terms of marketable fiction. There is, however, no shortage of words put on paper—specifically, entries into the several notebooks that Anna keeps. Each is a distinct color, partitioning her experiences and imaginings into slices of life, and self: The black notebook revisits her youth and early adulthood in Africa, the red scrutinizes her involvement in politics and the Communist Party, the yellow volume captures passages from a stalled novel about a failed love affair, and the blue notebook is a journal detailing her daily activities as well as her reveries and reflections. The segmentation of her life into separate notebooks reflects Anna's ongoing struggle to hold the pieces of her subjective being together in a world in which disparate demands—psychological, sexual, political, maternal—threaten to pull it apart, just as public expressions of kindred pressures are propelling the fragmentation of the society around her.

Structurally innovative, *The Golden Notebook* interweaves long passages from Anna's notebooks with episodes of a conventionally narrated tale of Molly and Anna's friendship in 1950s London, disrupting chronology and continuity in the process. The various sections of the framing narrative of the women's relationship might make up a short novel of their own; told mostly through extended conversations in which Anna and Molly speak to each other with vivid frankness, these portions of *The Golden Notebook*, to which Lessing ironically gives the title *Free Women*, are stunning in their expression of the hopes and uncertainties captured in the friends' engagements with—and estrangements from—work, love, children, husbands, causes. Their ostensible liberation from contemporary expectations of women finds them nonetheless locked in embraces too tight, and perhaps too dear, to entirely escape.

Taken together, the *Free Women* chapters tell a bracing story of the aging of ideals and the struggle to bring them to a livable maturity; yet beneath that story's tidy fictional progression, another narrative—that of Anna's notebooks—pulls us into an adventure of deeper and more dangerous energies, one so real and variegated that only an imaginative act of extraordinary reach could contain it. *The Golden Notebook* is such an act, a chronicle of breakdown that creates a mysterious healing order of its own. Although its depictions of radical politics and the gestation of mid-twentieth-century feminism supply the "headlines" that have won *The Golden Notebook* a prominent place in the history of the modern novel, the full story it reports is more nuanced, intimate, human, and, in the way of all true and lasting fiction, more useful for our understanding of the worries and wonders of our own lives.

What: Novel. **When:** 1962. **Also By: Novels:** *Briefing for a Descent into Hell* (1971); *The Memoirs of a Survivor* (1975); *The Good Terrorist* (1985). **Nonfiction:** *Under My Skin: Volume One of My Autobiography, to 1949* (1994); *Walking in the Shade: Volume Two of My Autobiography, 1949 to 1962* (1997). **Try:** *The Waves* by Virginia Woolf. *The Mandarins* by Simone de Beauvoir. *Burger's Daughter* by Nadine Gordimer.

Re: Colonised Planet 5, Shikasta
Out of This World

From 1979 to 1983, Doris Lessing published a series of science fiction novels that shocked readers of her previous books, which had firmly established her literary reputation for social and psychological realism. Her extraterrestrial journey began with *Shikasta*—the full title, indicating the pretense of its documentary form, is *Re: Colonised Planet 5, Shikasta: Personal, Psychological, Historical Documents Related to Visit by Johor (George Sherban), Emissary (Grade 9) 87th of the Period of the Last Days*—and continues through four additional volumes. The series was ultimately collected under the omnibus title *Canopus in Argos: Archives*.

Detailing the history of an intergalactic empire, Lessing's space fiction, informed by the author's fascination with Sufism, posits a universe evolving toward a higher spiritual consciousness across a complex cosmology of planets and alternate dimensions of being known as "zones." Planet 5, Shikasta, is an Earth-like realm bent on its own destruction;

the novel details its history, its spiritual degeneration, and the imperial powers' attempts to reconnect its denizens to higher truths. Lessing's complex and at times obscure visionary architecture looms over but never overwhelms her storytelling gifts, and from page to page we follow a powerful and resilient thread of human feeling through a labyrinth of foreboding and catastrophe. The figurative landscape and the reading experience it engenders recall the early books of the Bible, with their tribes and prophets and cowering individuals trying to make sense of the great, unsettled tracks of time, nature, and unknowingness in which they find themselves. Indeed, Lessing herself has written that *Shikasta* takes the Old Testament as its starting point. "It is our habit to dismiss the Old Testament altogether," she continues, "because Jehovah, or Jahve, does not think or behave like a social worker." She is of another opinion, clearly, and turns to the Hebrew Bible for inspiration in order to imagine a canvas large enough to portray themes of fate, knowledge, time, determinism, consciousness, politics, and teleology in ways contemporary novels seldom do. In *Shikasta* and its subsequent elaborations, Lessing presents an apocalyptic, alarming, and hauntingly meaningful testament of her own.

What: Science Fiction. *When:* 1979. *Edition:* Available in a single volume, or together with its sequels in an omnibus edition, *Canopus in Argos: Archives* (1992). *Also By:* The other Canopus novels are *The Marriages Between Zones Three, Four, and Five* (1980); *The Sirian Experiments* (1981); *The Making of the Representative for Planet 8* (1982); and *Documents Relating to the Sentimental Agents in the Volyen Empire* (1983). *Further Reading: The Sufis* by Idries Shah. *Try: Anathem* by Neal Stephenson. *Adaptations:* Philip Glass has written operas, with libretti by Lessing, based on *The Making of the Representative for Planet 8* and *The Marriages Between Zones Three, Four, and Five.*

The Gentleman in Trollope
INDIVIDUALITY AND MORAL CONDUCT
Shirley Robin Letwin (1924–1993)

How to Live Decently

Although steeped in the world of Anthony Trollope, Shirley Robin Letwin's curious and uncategorizable book is not a study of the work of that novelist per se. Rather, the vast canvas of Trollope's novels provides Letwin with the raw material for what is in actuality a philosophical study, one that blessedly exhibits in abundance a quality absent from most such works: a resonance that rings true with our experience of the world. There is no need to be conversant with Trollope's fiction to follow Letwin's thought (although, having followed it, you're unlikely not to want to sample at least a volume or two). And there is no need to be put off by her subject on grounds of gender: "The most perfect gentleman in Trollope's novels," writes Letwin, "is Madame Max Goesler."

Just as Letwin's concept of the gentleman includes both women and men, so does

Caricature of Anthony Trollope by Frederick Waddy

it include a wide variety of social and economic stations. Despite the circumscribed subject its title suggests, her book is about the largest themes: how to live decently, how to understand and conduct oneself. Letwin finds embodied in the figure of the gentleman "a radically unfamiliar attitude to our mortal condition and in particular to the nature and significance of individuality." The morality that results from this attitude, Letwin explains, is "unusually complicated"; it responds flexibly to changing circumstance and is alert to the limits of both knowledge and convention without adopting cynical or relativist beliefs. "For a gentleman, individuality has nothing to do with rejecting all constraints or pursuing 'self-realization,'" Letwin argues. "In the arts, disciplines, skills, manners, habits, institutions, conventions, traditions, and rules that constitute civilization, men find the limits that can shape their experience. They learn to make distinctions and connexions in what is presented to them and so to make their world meaningful."

Throughout her book, using examples from Trollope and other novels, Letwin explores themes of character, conduct, integrity, manners, love, virtue, and ambition with a rich concentration of thought and expression (if you take notes, you'll reach its conclusion with a valuable anthology of epigrams). Side by side with her philosophy, she offers obliquely a brilliant assessment of the genius of the English "society novelists"—Austen, Fielding, Thackeray, Dickens, and Eliot, as well as Trollope—who, as Henry James put it, "know their way about the conscience," and teach us how to navigate its deepest waters. Her surprising book earns a spot on a shelf just below Montaigne; one might spend a lifetime absorbing its lessons in hopes of inhabiting the "gentleman's world" that she describes, a world full of nuances "that does not require a choice between rebellion and submission, violence and reason, alienation and unity, struggle and apathy, certainty and nihilism."

What: Philosophy. Literary Criticism. *When:* 1982. *Reading Note:* Letwin's scholarly tone can at times be daunting, but her eloquence is such that readers will not go far without finding a useful comment on how to live. Read with confidence, and you'll find even random browsing of *The Gentleman in Trollope* rewarding. *Also By: The Pursuit of Certainty* (1965). *The Anatomy of Thatcherism* (1993). *On the History of the Idea of Law* (2005). *Further Reading: The Warden* by Anthony Trollope (see page 806). *Try:* Michel de Montaigne's *Essays* (see page 561). Samuel Johnson's "Rambler" essays (see page 416). *Love, Life, Goethe* by John Armstrong.

Christ Stopped at Eboli
THE STORY OF A YEAR
Carlo Levi (1902–1975)

"It remains as hard to classify as every beautiful book." —Paolo Milano

It's possible to misread the title of this book and fall under the misapprehension that its theme is tied to the appearance—real or metaphorical—of Christ in a small town. In fact, Levi's title represents an entirely different idea, namely that Christ—and all the history, spiritual and temporal, that followed in his wake—never made it to the tiny village of Gagliano in southern Italy, where the author was confined as a political prisoner in 1935 because of his opposition to Fascism. "We're not Christians," the people he meets there tell him. "Christ stopped short of here, at Eboli."

An amalgam of human interest, psychological intuition, sociological observation, and political attention, Levi's account of his year in Gagliano is a singular book about "a world apart, . . . hedged in by custom and sorrow, cut off from History and the State, eternally patient, . . . [a] land without comfort or solace, where the peasant lives out his motionless civilization on barren ground in remote poverty, and in the presence of death." And yet the desolate place soon comes to exert a pull on readers as strong and as affecting as the grip in which it holds the author. His training as a doctor allows Levi a privileged position, which in turn leads to intimate insights into the personalities of his neighbors, from the local witch to the lonely old priest. Although Christ and History may be absent from Gagliano, superstitions and mortality are vivid presences, and Levi conveys their influence in the character sketches, conversations, stories, and sensitive political ruminations that make up his chronicle. The "hedged-in" world of the peasants he honors in these pages reveals, paradoxically, that the defining human values may be more elemental than we are accustomed to suspect, and life's mysteries more fundamental than the sophistication of civilization pretends. The unsentimental, austere eloquence of the author's expression is unforgettable, and imbues *Christ Stopped at Eboli* with a rare and telling beauty.

What: Memoir. *When:* 1945; English translation by Frances Frenaye, 1947. *Also By: The Watch* (1948). *Words Are Stones: Impressions of Sicily* (1956). *Try: Torregreca: Life, Death, and Miracles in a Southern Italian Village* (see page 180) and *Women of the Shadows* by Ann Cornelisen. *Memorial* by Ferdinando Camon (see page 120). *Adaptation:* Adapted for the screen by Francesco Rosi in 1979.

If This Is a Man
Primo Levi (1919–1987)

Survival in Auschwitz

In 1946, with his internment in Auschwitz still fresh in his mind, the Italian scientist Primo Levi started writing down his memories of the death camp on the back of train tickets and pieces of scrap paper. He wasn't planning to write a book, he later explained; all he wanted to do was unburden himself, writing down his thoughts as an act of therapy. Yet soon the random recollections started to cohere into a larger testimony, one of the first autobiographical texts from a survivor of the Holocaust and one of the most powerful works of nonfiction published in the twentieth century: *If This Is a Man*. (Although the book was issued in the United States as *Survival in Auschwitz*, the British title more accurately reflects the Italian original and the author's intent.)

Levi, a member of the Italian resistance, was arrested by Fascist Blackshirts in late 1943; eventually handed over to the Nazis, he was transported to Auschwitz in a cattle car in the winter of 1944. He arrived with

Primo Levi, 1940

650 other Jews; when the Red Army liberated the camp, he was one of only twenty survivors of that group. In *If This Is a Man*, Levi doesn't ascribe any religious or philosophical meaning to his time in the camp, nor does he try to understand how a civilized European country could suddenly transform itself into a factory of death. He does not interpret; he only bears witness, revealing the everyday horrors of life at Auschwitz, from its grim economy with a currency of morsels of bread to the brutal manner in which the Nazis stripped away humanity:

We became aware that our language lacks words to express this offense, the demolition of a man. . . . Nothing belongs to us any more; they have taken away our clothes, our shoes, even our hair; if we speak, they will not listen to us, and if they listen, they will not understand. They will even take away our name.

Our moral obligation to remember the Holocaust, a responsibility that grows stronger as the number of survivors declines, has made Levi's book a document of world-historical importance. The sensitivity and eloquence of its author, drawn from such bitter experience, would find expression in many other books, including memoirs, fiction, poetry, and essays. Most notable among these is *The Periodic Table* (1975), Levi's autobiographical collection of short pieces—each tied to one of the chemical elements—that combines his training as a chemist with his literary vocation and that his contemporary Italo Calvino called "the best introduction to the psychological world of one of the most important and gifted writers of our time."

What: Autobiography. History. *When:* 1947; revised edition, 1958. *Edition:* Translated from the Italian by Stuart Woolf, 1962. *Also By:* The Reawakening (1958). Moments of Reprieve: A Memoir of Auschwitz (1981). If Not Now, When? (1982). Other People's Trades (1985). The Drowned and the Saved (1986). *Further Reading: The Double Bond: Primo Levi, A Biography* by Carole Angier. *Primo Levi: A Life* by Ian Thomson. *Try: One Day in the Life of Ivan Denisovich* by Alexander Solzhenitsyn (see page 737). *This Way for the Gas, Ladies and Gentlemen* by Tadeusz Borowski. *Fatelessness* by Imre Kertész.

Tristes Tropiques
Claude Lévi-Strauss (1908–2009)

Transcending the Travelogue

" I hate travelling and explorers." An odd sentence, one might think, for a Frenchman to use at the outset of an account of his expeditions in the jungles of Brazil. But just so does anthropologist Claude Lévi-Strauss embark upon this narrative of his progress across the ocean, then up the Amazon to observe the lives of indigenous tribes: the Caduveo, Bororo, Nambikwara, and Tupi-Kawahib. The reader expecting a picturesque travelogue will find the author true to his first words, for the exotic itinerary that leads Lévi-Strauss to such remote destinations—and to an illuminating portrayal of "human society reduced to its most basic expression"—is not the primary journey *Tristes Tropiques* describes. That distinction belongs to the voyage that begins and ends in the mind of the protagonist: a bold and exacting intellectual adventure that transports us, page by page, to unexpected outposts of thought, imagery, and intellection.

Lévi-Strauss's structuralist approach to anthropology made him one of the most influential thinkers of the twentieth century, and although *Tristes Tropiques* certainly contains a formative application of his ideas in its close attention to the customs of the Amazonian tribes, it is the book's personal voice—literary, ruminative, probing, reflexive—that truly distinguishes this account of his 1930s experience in Brazil, written two decades after the events it chronicles. "Beyond the rational," he writes when describing his education, "there exists a more important and valid category—that of

Claude Lévi-Strauss on the Amazon, ca. 1936

the meaningful," and it is to that category that Lévi-Strauss deftly assigns all he perceives. As Susan Sontag recognized in her essay "The Anthropologist as Hero," "the greatness of *Tristes Tropiques* lies not simply in [its] sensitive reportage, but in the way Lévi-Strauss uses his experience—to reflect on the nature of landscape, on the meaning of physical hardship, on the city in Old World and the New, on the idea of travel, on sunsets, on modernity, on the connection between literacy and power." His stunning extended meditation on the difference between sunrise and sunset, scientifically the same event yet experientially so distinct, is just one example of his genius for conveying the sensations evoked by events yet inaccessible to expertise. The intellect he trains on his anthropological subjects complements the intuition he applies to himself—most powerfully in the chapter titled "The Making of an Anthropologist"—throughout this amalgam of memoir, inquiry, storytelling, and philosophy. The result is a work that, as Sontag suggests in comparing it to Montaigne's *Essays* (see page

561) and Freud's *Interpretation of Dreams* (see page 299), not only elaborates a comprehensive vision of the human condition, but also provides new tools for exploring it.

What: Autobiography. Anthropology. *When:* 1955; revised edition, 1968. *Edition:* John and Doreen Weightman's translation of the 1968 edition is recommended. *Also By:* Among Lévi-Strauss's best-known books are *The Elementary Structures of Kinship* (1949), *Structural Anthropology* (volume 1, 1958; volume 2, 1973), *The Savage Mind* (1962), *The Raw and the Cooked* (1964), *The Origin of Table Manners* (1968), and *Myth and Meaning* (1978). *Further Reading:* "The Anthropologist as Hero" by Susan Sontag, in *Against Interpretation. Try: Argonauts of the Western Pacific* by Bronislaw Malinowski. *Footnote:* Regarding the title, the translators write, "The possible English versions, such as 'Sad Tropics,' 'The Sadness of the Tropics,' 'Tragic Tropics,' etc., do not quite correspond either in meaning or in implication to 'Tristes Tropiques,' which is at once ironical and poetic, because of the alliteration, the taut rhythm ... and the suggestion of 'Alas for the Tropics!'"

Rosemary's Baby
Ira Levin (1929–2007)

A Pioneering Work of Paranormal Horror

S tephen King once described Ira Levin as "the Swiss watchmaker of suspense novels: he makes what the rest of us do look like cheap watches in drugstores." *Rosemary's Baby*, Levin's second novel, appeared fourteen years after his debut, the classic murder mystery *A Kiss Before Dying* (1953), the tale of an ambitious young man who will stop at nothing to achieve his goal of marrying into the upper class. The gripping storytelling, with its combination of suspense and social climbing—imagine a crossbreeding of John O'Hara and Patricia Highsmith—won Levin an Edgar Award for Best First Novel and revealed his penchant for ingenious plotting. This skill would remain on display in all his novels, including *The Stepford Wives* (1972), *The Boys from Brazil* (1976), and, perhaps most famously, *Rosemary's Baby*, whose position as the bestselling horror novel of the 1960s was magnified by Roman Polanski's sensational 1968 film adaptation.

Mia Farrow in the 1968 film

The book begins with the most innocent of premises: A young Manhattan couple moves into a larger apartment as they get ready to start a family. Rosemary becomes pregnant just as her husband, a struggling actor, finally lands a Broadway role while becoming devoted to the eccentric elderly couple next door, who take Rosemary under their wing. Initial uneasiness at their ministrations turns into a growing suspicion of their motives, and Rosemary begins to imagine all sorts of dark doings. Or *is* she imagining them? The suspense ratchets up as what she expects while she's expecting takes a diabolical turn—proving, of course, that just because you're paranoid doesn't mean they aren't out to get you. The devil is in the details.

What: Mystery & Suspense. **When:** 1967. **Also By:** *This Perfect Day* (1970). *Deathtrap* (1978). *Son of Rosemary* (1997). **Try:** *The Other* by Thomas Tryon. *The Exorcist* by William Peter Blatty. **Adaptations:** Polanski's film, starring Mia Farrow, won popular and critical acclaim. Farrow also reads a superb audiobook version.

C. S. LEWIS
(1898–1963)

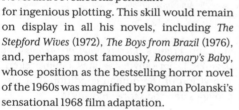

C. S. Lewis was the twentieth century's foremost Christian apologist, an Oxbridge don and Renaissance scholar of uncommon erudition, a good friend of J. R. R. Tolkien and with him an anchor of the literary society known as the Inklings, and the celebrated fabulist who penned both an epic space trilogy—*Out of the Silent Planet* (1938), *Perelandra* (1943), and *That Hideous Strength* (1945)—and the magical *Chronicles of Narnia*. "If wit and wisdom, style and scholarship are requisites for passage through the pearly gates," *The New Yorker* once opined, "Mr. Lewis will be among the angels." Legions of devoted readers, young and old, would certainly agree.

C. S. Lewis, 1947

The Lion, the Witch and the Wardrobe

A Fantasy for Children of Every Age

"I never appreciated children till the war brought them to me," C. S. Lewis once wrote. Like many others, he'd taken in air-raid refugees during the Second World War. One of them was fascinated with an old wardrobe in Lewis's house, and that planted a seed that the author would nurture into one of the classic works of children's literature.

"Once there were four children whose names were Peter, Susan, Edmund, and Lucy," the book begins. Sent away from London during the war, they are taken in by a professor who lives in a very large house in the country: "It was the sort of house that you never seem to come to the end of, and it was full of unexpected places." On the first day of exploring their new abode, little Lucy discovers a mirror-fronted wardrobe in an otherwise bare room; creeping into it, she crosses an unmarked threshold to find herself in an unexpected place indeed—a snow-covered wood. Curiosity lures her forward toward a lamppost and a strange figure, half man, half goat, holding an umbrella. As she soon discovers, she has wandered into Narnia, a fantastical realm corrupted by the influence of an evil White Witch who has usurped the power of a mighty lion

king, Aslan, and cast the land into permanent winter, "without any Christmas."

Lewis held the view that "a children's story which is enjoyed only by children is a bad children's story." Wanting his book to offer something to older readers as well, he shaped the Pevensie children's Narnian escapade into a religious allegory of betrayal, forgiveness, and resurrection. And although the children's efforts, in league with the lion, to battle the forces of the witch can certainly be read that way, it is the imaginative elements of the storytelling, rather than its allegorical underpinnings, that continue to entrance readers of all ages and faiths: the close-to-home possibility of magic, the icy allure of the Narnian landscape, the talking animals, the names like charms (Mr. Tumnus, Aslan, the castle called Cair Paravel), the satisfying drama of good versus evil. And, for a man unfamiliar with raising kids, Lewis is remarkably adept at capturing the motives of sibling rivalry, such as Edmund's envy of Lucy's discovery, and using them to fuel the engines of his marvelous adventure.

The seed that grew into *The Lion, the Witch and the Wardrobe* also sprouted six additional Narnia tales. All of these are worth reading, but none is as thrilling, magical, and memorable as the first. It is an ideal tale for a family to read aloud together.

What: Children's. Fantasy. *When:* 1950. *Also By:* Young fans graduating from the Narnia books might turn next to Lewis's space trilogy, mentioned on page 485. Older readers seeking deeper immersion in Lewis's Christian imagination will find it in *The Screwtape Letters* (1942). His scholarly work *The Allegory of Love: A Study of Medieval Tradition* (1936) is a masterpiece of literary criticism. *Further Reading: The Magician's Book: A Skeptic's Adventures in Narnia* by Laura Miller. *C. S. Lewis: A Biography* by A. N. Wilson. *Try: The Children of Green Knowe* by L. M. Boston. *Tom's Midnight Garden* by Philippa Pearce. *The Golden Compass* by Philip Pullman (see page 647). *Adaptations:* In addition to the big-budget film of *The Lion, the Witch and the Wardrobe* released in 2005, there have been excellent animated (1979) and live-action (1988) television versions.

A Grief Observed
A Solace for Sorrow

Although not as widely popular as *The Chronicles of Narnia*, C. S. Lewis's many works of Christian reflection, such as *The Problem of Pain* (1940) and *Mere Christianity* (1952) have proven enduringly valuable to people of faith (and even to those possessed by doubt). Yet no book Lewis wrote in any vein has likely provided as much practical and spiritual consolation as *A Grief Observed*, his searching meditation on the anguish he suffered upon the death of his wife after a brief, intensely happy marriage.

"No one ever told me that grief felt so like fear," he begins, and it is a fitting initiation to the strange education he undergoes.

I look up at the night sky. Is anything more certain than that in all those vast times and spaces, if I were allowed to search them, I should nowhere find her face, her voice, her touch? She died. She is dead. Is the word so difficult to learn?

As he turns over and over through the memory of his love, his religious faith—heretofore so sure—seems frail in the face of his disconsolateness:

You never know how much you really believe anything until its truth or falsehood becomes a matter of life and death to you. It is easy to say you believe a rope to be strong and sound as long as you are merely using it to cord a box. But suppose you had to hang by that rope over a precipice. Wouldn't you then first discover how much you really trusted it?

Yet it is the strength of his faith that, ultimately, returns Lewis to the land of the living. *A Grief Observed* is a moving testament to one man's Christianity, and an eloquent witness to the depth of emotion that surrounds our ends.

What: Memoir. *When:* 1961. *Also By: The Case for Christianity* (1942). *Miracles* (1947). *Surprised by Joy* (1955). *Try: The Perfect Stranger* by P. J. Kavanagh (see page 430). *The Year of Magical Thinking* by Joan Didion (see page 223). *Adaptation: Shadowlands*, a 1993 film starring Anthony Hopkins and Debra Winger, dramatizes the story of Lewis's marriage. *Footnote:* The book was originally published under the pseudonym N. W. Clerk.

CHRONOLOGICAL NARNIA

Although *The Lion, the Witch and the Wardrobe* was the first tale written in the series, *The Magician's Nephew*, published five years later, is a prequel that answers many questions about Narnia and its denizens. In fact, in terms of Narnian chronology, the sequence of books is different from the order of their composition, and runs like this:

The Magician's Nephew (published 1955)

The Lion, the Witch and the Wardrobe (1950)

The Horse and His Boy (1954)

Prince Caspian (1951)

The Voyage of the Dawn Treader (1952)

The Silver Chair (1953)

The Last Battle (1956)

Charles Wilson Peale's portraits of Lewis (left, ca. 1807) and Clark (right, 1810)

The Journals of Lewis and Clark

Meriwether Lewis (1774–1809) and William Clark (1770–1838)
Edited by Bernard DeVoto

How the West Was Mapped

In the first month of 1803, President Thomas Jefferson sent a secret message to Congress requesting funds for an expedition to explore the Missouri River and seek the Northwest Passage to the Pacific, make contact with the land's native peoples, and expand the potential of the fur trade and other commercial ventures. In May, the United States concluded the Louisiana Purchase, thus taking possession of a good portion of the land such an expedition would cross. One year later, on May 14, 1804, under the leadership of Meriwether Lewis and William Clark, the aptly named Corps of Discovery—a band of thirty-odd people, including the interpreters Toussaint Charbonneau, a French Canadian, and his Shoshone wife, Sacajawea—set out from Saint Louis on what would be a twenty-eight-month, eight-thousand-mile journey to the mouth of the Columbia River on the Oregon coast and back again.

At the behest of President Jefferson, Lewis and Clark kept extensive journals of their mission across country upon which, Lewis writes, "the foot of civilized man had never trodden." Meticulously recording their routes and progress; the weather they witness; their discipline and invention in assembling, fabricating, and husbanding provisions; their hunger, cold, and other discomforts; and their often friendly, sometimes anxious encounters and negotiations with Native American tribes, the explorers document their adventures in extraordinary empirical—if less than grammatically and orthographically elegant—detail. The grandeur and surprises of the magnificent landscape they traverse are palpable to the reader. Although one might take issue with Lewis's assertion of the primacy of his party's "civilized" presence on the already-peopled land, there can be no doubt of the freshness of the wonder they experienced. Uncertainty was the only fixed point in their unmapped advance: Every hill ascending before them, every fork in a river, was an invitation into the unknown. The maps they drew, and the strange flora and fauna they observed (the Corps added scores of plants and animals to the catalogs of naturalists, including the grizzly bear and the prairie dog) added not only to the young nation's store of knowledge, but also to its westering sense of manifest destiny.

There are numerous editions of the journals in print. The one edited and issued by Bernard DeVoto in 1953 is, in the words of Stephen E. Ambrose, "the ideal selection for the citizen-reader," delivering "the heart of the story, without sacrificing the narrative or much of the natural history." In any edition, however, the Lewis and Clark journals remain an enduring national treasure.

What: History. Exploration. *When:* The first edition was published in 1814. *Try:* Once you've read the firsthand account, try Stephen E. Ambrose's blockbuster, *Undaunted Courage: Meriwether Lewis, Thomas Jefferson, and the Opening of the American West.* Two good novels based on the expedition are Brian Hall's literary *I Should Be Extremely Happy in Your Company* and Howard Frank Mosher's comical *The True Account.*

Liar's Poker
RISING THROUGH THE WRECKAGE ON WALL STREET
Michael Lewis (born 1960)

A Comedy of Capitalism Gone Wild

Liar's Poker is the deliciously comic story of how an art history major from Princeton parlayed a master's degree from the London School of Economics—and an advantageous seating arrangement at a dinner for the Queen Mother—into a position as a bond trader on Wall Street in the high-flying 1980s. It offers an irreverent inside look at the world of investment banking as it flourished before the crash that came before the crash that came before the most recent crash. Which is to say that, although the details of life on the Street may have undergone some transformations in the intervening years, the general tenor of Lewis's tale of outsized egos and preposterous sums of money retains its ring of truth.

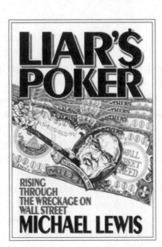

"Never before," Lewis tells us, with the good humor that makes his narrative so enjoyable, "have so many unskilled twenty-four-year-olds made so much money in so little time as we did this decade in New York and London." From interviews to training program to humiliation and success on the trading floor, Lewis's account of his two-year apprenticeship at the chest-beating, soon-to-be-scandal-ridden firm of Salomon Brothers entertains the reader with an engaging parade of ambition, greed, pomposity, deception, and collective shortsightedness masquerading as business savvy. Despite targets as big as barns, including Salomon's CEO John Gutfreund (dubbed the "King of Wall Street" by a business publication in 1985, the monarch would resign in some disgrace in 1991) and the risk shaman John Meriwether (whose genius was so inscrutable it would nearly scuttle the entire global economy in 1998), Lewis is never mean-spirited; his behind-the-scenes chronicle of the workings of Wall Street is enlightening, acutely observed, and very, very funny.

What: Business. Memoir. *When:* 1989. *Also By: The New New Thing: A Silicon Valley Story* (2000). *Moneyball: The Art of Winning an Unfair Game* (2003). *The Big Short: Inside the Doomsday Machine* (2010). *Flash Boys: A Wall Street Revolt* (2014). *Further Reading: When Genius Failed: The Rise and Fall of Long-Term Capital Management* by Roger Lowenstein. *Try: The Bonfire of the Vanities* by Tom Wolfe (see page 866). *F.I.A.S.C.O.: Blood in the Water on Wall Street* by Frank Partnoy.

Voices of the Old Sea
Norman Lewis (1908–2003)

Travels with a Writer's Writer

When Norman Lewis died at age ninety-five in 2003, one of his obituaries noted that the prolific writer "had never crossed the mysterious barrier separating the admired from the famous." Five years later, Julian Evans would give his biography of Lewis the title *Semi-Invisible Man*. But, although he may never have achieved fame, Lewis did garner the admiration of discriminating readers, including many fellow authors. For example, P. D. James, Anthony Burgess, and Eric Newby counted him among the finest travel writers of the age, and Graham Greene and Will Self dropped the adjective to champion Lewis as one of the finest twentieth-century British writers period. In short, Norman Lewis earned the distinction of being, as one critic put it, "the supreme writer's writer," whose more than thirty books include several masterpieces of the travel genre.

One of those classic works is *Voices of the Old Sea*, which vividly recounts the three summers Lewis spent, immediately after the end of World War II, in the remote Spanish fishing village of Farol on what is now the Costa Brava. At the time Lewis first arrived in the community, Farol still bore traces of the medieval heritage that shaped it; life revolved around seasonal sardine catches and ancient feuds—feuds between individuals, feuds between families, feuds with the neighboring village. As Lewis would later remark in his autobiography, in Farol he had chanced upon "the remnants of an archaic Mediterranean society of Chaucerian scenes and pilgrimages, village enchanters, fishermen who spoke in blank-verse, pre-Christian credences and taboos, and none of us would ever see its like again."

From the book's opening pages, in which Lewis is given a cat by an imperious grandmother ("everything she said carried instant conviction, and the villagers said that she was inclined to make God's mind up for him"), an alien milieu is brought to familiar life with great immediacy. And although the author indeed remains "semi-invisible" throughout, everything he sees is made palpable to our mind's eye. Summer by summer, Lewis witnessed the old order's passing, as postwar tourism began to change Farol utterly. In the limpid, elegant prose that was his trademark, he chronicled the various changes—some of them terribly sad, others absurdly funny—in this eloquent elegy to the old sea's influence.

VOICES OF THE OLD SEA

What: Travel. *When:* 1984. *Also By:* Spanish Adventure (1935). A Dragon Apparent: Travels in Indo-China (1951). Golden Earth: Travels in Burma (1952). The Honoured Society: The Sicilian Mafia Observed (1964). Naples '44: An Intelligence Officer in the Italian Labyrinth (1978). Jackdaw Cake: An Autobiography (1985; expanded edition, I Came, I Saw, 1994). Further Reading: Semi-Invisible Man: The Life of Norman Lewis by Julian Evans. Try: Old Calabria by Norman Douglas. The Face of Spain by Gerald Brenan.

"The best travel writer of our age, if not since Marco Polo."
—Auberon Waugh on Norman Lewis

Main Street
Sinclair Lewis (1885–1951)

A Love-Hate Affair with Small-Town Life

M*ain Street* was the first significant success of the first American writer to win the Nobel Prize in Literature. A scathing anatomy of small-town narrow-mindedness in the early years of the twentieth century, *Main Street* tells the story of Carol Milford, an idealistic young woman who works at a library in Saint Paul. After marrying Dr. Will Kennicott, Carol agrees to settle down in Gopher Prairie, Will's hometown (which Lewis modeled after his own Minnesota hometown of Sauk Centre). Although Carol hopes to lead Gopher Prairie out of what she considers its dull and complacent ordinariness, her eager attempts at transforming the town into a place of beauty and culture are thwarted by the entrenched snobbery, hypocrisy, and provincialism that define it. What's frustrating to Carol is often quite funny to the reader, as when she attempts to foist George Bernard Shaw's "Androcles and the Lion" on a drama club bent on mounting "The Girl from Kankakee." In search of a more fulfilling life, Carol eventually deserts the smug confines of the town for Washington, D.C., only to return to Gopher Prairie and her family in the end, chastened but not entirely defeated by her retreat: "I've never excused my failures by sneering at my aspirations. I do not admit that Main Street is as beautiful as it should be! I do not admit that Gopher Prairie is greater or more generous than Europe! I do not admit that dishwashing is enough to satisfy all women!" Dr. Kennicott, for his part, mutters "Yes, dear," and asks if she's seen the screwdriver.

Sinclair Lewis, 1923

Though *Main Street* was a huge success (it went through eleven printings in the months immediately after publication), it scandalized the American public: Lewis claimed that the book was read "with the same masochistic pleasure that one has in sucking an aching tooth." More than eighty years on, Lewis's satire remains brisk and keenly observed, his targets not as far from our experience as we might hope. And tellingly, his acerbic vision is not without a veiled affection for the comforts of conformity that shaped his own youth; indeed, that affection sharpens the focus of his portraits of the people of Gopher Prairie. As *Time* magazine noted in its 1951 obituary of Lewis, "His great merit was that he gave the US and the world a sense of the enduring strength (ugly or not) of Main Street; and that he made Americans on all main streets [. . .] stop hustling long enough to wonder uneasily where they were going."

What: Novel. *When:* 1920. *Award:* Nobel Prize in Literature, 1930. *Also By: Babbitt* (1922). *Arrowsmith* (1925). *Elmer Gantry* (1927). *Dodsworth* (1929). *It Can't Happen Here* (1935). *Cass Timberlane* (1945). *Try: Winesburg, Ohio* by Sherwood Anderson. *Sister Carrie* by Theodore Dreiser (see page 234). *Footnote:* The Pulitzer Prize jury of readers recommended unanimously that *Main Street* receive the fiction award for 1921, but the prize committee gave it to Edith Wharton's *The Age of Innocence* instead. Still smarting from this slight, Lewis refused the Pulitzer for *Arrowsmith* in 1926, objecting in public to the stated qualification that the winning work be representative of "the wholesome atmosphere of American life."

Between Meals
AN APPETITE FOR PARIS
A. J. Liebling (1904–1963)

An Ode to Eating and the Charms of Paris

A legendary reporter, Abbott Joseph Liebling wrote with speed and grace on a dizzying array of subjects, from politics, boxing, and New York eccentrics to such key events of the Second World War as the D-Day landings at Normandy and the liberation of Paris, both of which he witnessed firsthand. He covered the ups and (mostly) downs of journalism itself in his long-running Wayward Press column in The New Yorker, the magazine that was home to most of his work for nearly three decades. Besides being a terrific writer, he was an inspired eater, and in the autobiographical Between Meals he created his literary pièce de résistance by celebrating his culinary muse.

That muse abided in Paris, and she began seducing Liebling in his boyhood, as he describes in an amusing chapter devoted to a 1911 family visit to the city, when the author was seven years old. His early infatuation blossomed into a giddy and determined passion when the twenty-two-year-old Liebling persuaded his father to underwrite a year of study at the Sorbonne. Making the most of this paternal generosity, Liebling applied himself wholeheartedly to his education in the pleasures of the French table, informing his appetite and refining his taste for the food and wine purveyed by a paradise of restaurants he explored with an acolyte's devotion. He dedicated special attention to the unsung dishes (tripe in many guises, for instance) and unheralded vintages that kept costs down without constraining delight.

While Liebling's gourmandizing apprenticeship in the shadow of the Sorbonne is the heart of the book, its lessons are deepened in flavor by his tributes to later mentors such as Yves Mirande, a musical comedy writer of astonishing appetite, able to match Liebling course for course (the book is dedicated to Mirande). Also celebrated are the formidable proprietors of restaurants as sophisticated in their cooking as they were modest in their appearance. Herculean meals are savored with a delicious specificity, intoxicating the reader with the vividly evoked aromas of a pot-au-feu or the bouquet of a Tavel supérieur.

Moving back and forth in time, Liebling follows his love affair with Paris from naive ardor to nostalgic afterglow, ultimately shadowing his youthful enthusiasms with the awareness of age and loss that return trips reveal. How satisfying it is to share the hunger, intoxication, and joie de vivre of his recollection.

What: Memoir. Food & Drink. Place. When: 1962. Also By: Back Where I Came From (1938). The Road Back to Paris (1944). The Honest Rainmaker (1953). The Earl of Louisiana (1961). Further Reading: The Food of France by Waverly Root. Try: Two Towns in Provence by M. F. K. Fisher. The Auberge of the Flowering Hearth by Roy Andries de Groot (see page 202).

Einstein's Dreams
Alan Lightman (born 1948)

Brief Mysteries of Time

Suppose that time is not a quantity but a quality, like the luminescence of the night above the trees just when a rising moon has touched the treeline.

It's easy to race through Alan Lightman's enchanting fictional exploration of time. In thirty brief chapters, Lightman—an astrophysicist who became the first professor at MIT to receive a joint appointment in the sciences and the humanities—presents a series of speculative worlds purportedly dreamed by the young patent clerk Albert Einstein over two and a half months in 1905, the year in which work on his theory of special relativity came to fruition.

Elegantly imagined and fetchingly, often lyrically, composed, Lightman's variations on his protean theme liberate time from our usual conception of it. In his imaginative explorations, time can be circular, or flow backward, or repeat itself ceaselessly, slow down at higher altitudes, become visible, or take the form of a nightingale, darting and flying beyond the reach of pursuers bent on catching it to hold it fast.

The little tales, incidents, and situations Lightman invents to quicken Einstein's slumbers are both intellectually provocative and spiritually stimulating evocations of the most pervasive and mysterious element of existence. Which is to say that, although racing through these dreams is delightful, lingering over them is more rewarding still.

What: Novel. *When:* 1993. *Also By: Time Travel and Papa Joe's Pipe* (1984). *A Sense of the Mysterious* (2005). *Mr g* (2012). *Further Reading: Subtle Is the Lord: The Science and the Life of Albert Einstein* by Abraham Pais. *Try: Cosmicomics* and *Invisible Cities* (see page 120) by Italo Calvino.

■ For Abraham Lincoln's *Abraham Lincoln: Speeches and Writings,* see page 861.

Venice for Pleasure
J. G. Links (1904–1997)

The Best Guide to a City Ever Written

There aren't many guidebooks one might consider essential to a reading life, but J. G. Links's *Venice for Pleasure* is the exception that proves the rule. Inspiring devotion from the countless travelers who, since the book's first publication in 1966, have used it to gain a nuanced introduction to the fabled city, its cultured charms exceed its utilitarian purposes.

As Links describes his jewel of a book, "this is for the most part a book about the outsides of buildings, seldom about their contents. It is about Venice, the city, not about its possessions, and very little about its people." In fact, in one of the book's most winning passages, Links takes the reader by the elbow and steers him away from the Scuola San Rocco, home to a celebrated brood of Tintorettos: "We may well be asked on our return what we thought of these Tintorettos and it would be unthinkable to visit Venice without seeing them. Never let it be said that I suggested such a thing. I only point out that the stairs are steep, the pictures, though wonderful, profuse and that they will

still be there tomorrow, and, indeed, on our next visit to Venice." The conspiratorial "we" is a key to the volume's appeal as Links conducts the visitor on a number of walks that lead, by labyrinthine and digressive routes, straight into the heart of Venice's enigmatic genius. Each itinerary is a course in secrets taught by a cultivated and leisurely master who cheerfully dispenses knowledge from a vast store of learning, observations, curiosities, exotica, and sophistication. Along the way, Links weaves a spell that evokes the joy of urban wanderings, the enduring fascination of beauty, the ambience of time, and the pleasure of coming upon a welcome café at just the moment one's feet need a rest, and one's mind a respite.

What: Cities. Travel. *When:* 1966. *Edition:* Ninth revised edition, 2015. *Reading Note:* Links is an unparalleled guide to the character of Venice; for practical advice

on hotels, restaurants, and shopping, look elsewhere. *Also By: Canaletto* (1976). *Travellers in Europe* (1980). *Further Reading: The Stones of Venice* by John Ruskin (see page 684). *The World of Venice* by Jan Morris. *Try: Venice Observed* by Mary McCarthy. *John Kent's Venice.*

Complete Stories
Clarice Lispector (1920–1977)

"One of the hidden geniuses of the twentieth century."—*Colm Tóibín*

Some writers occupy chairs, some rooms, some houses—some whole neighborhoods of affect and action. Others of singular inspiration, such as James Joyce, compose entire cities with their words, or, like Kafka, create strange dominions entirely their own; still others of capacious imagination—think Proust or Virginia Woolf—conjure from psychology and social relations a superreality as shifting and encompassing as the weather, thereby describing with revelatory attention the climate of our lives. While the work of Clarice Lispector puts her in the same league as such extraordinary literary magicians, what's most remarkable about it is the way it moves, with grace and no little glamour, from humdrum domestic scenes to ominous visionary realms to streams of feeling as stealthy, dangerous, and exhilarating as the wind. (No kidding: Commenting on a new translation of Lispector's novel *Hour of the Star* for the *Financial Times*, Katherine Boo wrote, "I felt physically jolted by genius." Exactly.)

Take Lispector's story "Love," first published in 1952. It starts out as a woman named Ana, carrying groceries she just purchased, boards a tram in Rio de Janeiro to take her home, where she is expecting to prepare dinner for her family and some company. We are made privy to her thoughts, which revolve around her daily life with a kind of desperate sensitivity to what its normality encloses:

The only thing she worried about was being careful during that dangerous hour of the afternoon, when the house was empty and needed nothing more from

Statue of Clarice Lispector by Edgar Duvivier, unveiled in Rio de Janeiro in 2016

her, the sun high, the family members scattered to their duties. As she looked at the clean furniture, her heart would contract slightly in astonishment. But there was no room in her life for feeling tender toward her astonishment—she'd smother it with the same skill the household chores had given her.

And then, provoked by her observation of a fellow passenger—a blind man chewing gum—her consciousness grows dizzy with uneasiness, compassion, fear, and benevolence as she navigates her bus ride, her arrival home, her preparation of dinner, and her cleaning up afterward with her husband. The tale is a marvel of concentration and expression, not so much terrifying as it is alert to the wonder and its furtive uncertainty (which is what, after all, makes it wonderful); it is like an episode from the lives of the saints, grounded in mundane reality yet filled with danger and grace and the palpable evidence of things unseen.

Born in Ukraine in 1920, Lispector came to Brazil as an infant and moved to Rio de Janeiro as a teenager. At the age of twenty-three, she published her first novel, *Near to the Wild Heart* (1943), to sensational acclaim. Soon after, she married a diplomat and spent the next period of her life in Europe and the United States, returning to Brazil in 1959. All the while, she was writing, as she would until her death in 1977, creating a body of fiction that is singular, mysterious, and worth reading in its entirety. If her *Complete Stories* stands out above her novels, it is because, as Benjamin Moser suggests in the introduction to this volume, the book is "a record of woman's entire life"—from adolescence to adulthood, from solitude to marriage and back again, from motherhood to loneliness, from beauty and youthful vigor to the blemishes and physical frailty of age—"written over a woman's entire life." Before Lispector, Moser continues,

"a woman who wrote throughout her life— *about* that life—was so rare as to be previously unheard-of. The claim seems extravagant, but I have not identified any predecessors."

"In painting as in music and literature," Lispector once argued, "what is called abstract so often seems to me the figurative of a more delicate and difficult reality, less visible to the naked eye." It is that more delicate and difficult reality that Lispector captures in these stories, a reality not hung on a plotline or conforming to a conventional narrative, but following the inspirations and intuitions, the rhythms and hesitancies, the anxieties and epiphanies of unfolding experience. They are as truthful and electrifying as any an inner life has ever spun.

What: Short Stories. *When:* 1950–79. *Edition:* The American edition of *Complete Stories*, translated by Katrina Dodson and published by New Directions in 2015, was the first to collect all the author's short fiction. *Also By: The Passion According to G. H.* (1964). *Água Viva* (1973). *The Hour of the Star* (1977). *A Breath of Life* (1978). *Further Reading: Why This World: A Biography of Clarice Lispector* by Benjamin Moser. *Try: Thus Were Their Faces* by Silvina Ocampo. *Ninety-Nine Stories of God* by Joy Williams. *Footnote:* A Twitter account posting quotations from Lispector's writing— @RecitoClarice—has more than a million followers.

The Voyages of Doctor Dolittle
Hugh Lofting (1886–1947)

Cruising the World in Conversation with Animals

The *Voyages of Doctor Dolittle* is the second book in Hugh Lofting's beloved series about a very kind doctor who can talk to animals, and the one that most happily conveys the richness of the author's invention. If the good doctor's linguistic wizardry weren't entertaining enough, he also has a habit of falling into fanciful adventures in the company of his trusty (and loquacious) sidekicks Polynesia the Parrot, Jip the dog, Chee-Chee the monkey, and Dub-Dub the duck (to mention a few of the more prominent creatures in Dolittle's household). Also on hand is the boy Tommy Stubbins, the local cobbler's son who is pulled into Dolittle's curious orbit.

It is young Stubbins, in fact, who narrates this account of an epic journey from their home base in the English village of Puddleby-on-the-Marsh to the floating atoll called Spidermonkey Island, where they hope to examine the rare Jabizri beetle. In the course of their travels, Dolittle and company brave a shipwreck, encounter the Great Glass Sea Snail, and solve the mystery of the disappearance of the great naturalist known as Long Arrow. Throughout, Lofting's wit and warmth, and the beautifully realized characters (both human and animal), provide a happy counterpoint to the compelling melody of their perilous escapades, making *The Voyages of Doctor Dolittle* a perfect vehicle in which to explore the pleasure and promise of storytelling.

What: Children's. *When:* 1922. *Edition:* For the 2001 Books of Wonder edition, Patricia and Frederick McKissack gently and smartly edited the original text to eliminate instances of racially and culturally insensitive language, as they did for their similarly fine 1997 Books of Wonder edition of *The Story of Doctor Dolittle*. Both Books of Wonder volumes are spectacularly illustrated by Michael Hague. *Award:* Newbery Medal, 1923. *Also By:* Additional books in the series include *Doctor Dolittle's Post Office* (1923), *Doctor Dolittle's Circus* (1924), and *Doctor Dolittle's Zoo* (1925). *Try: Charlotte's Web* by E. B. White (see page 845). *Mrs. Frisby and the Rats of NIMH* by Robert C. O'Brien. *Adaptations:* Required listening: the BBC Radio audiobook, read by playwright Alan Bennett in an unforgettable performance. Two feature films centered on Lofting's character—a 1967 musical starring Rex Harrison, and a 1998 comedy starring Eddie Murphy—lack the audiobook's distinction.

The Call of the Wild
Jack London (1876–1916)

"The greatest dog story ever written."
—Carl Sandburg

L ike Buck, the big dog that is this book's protagonist, the reader of *The Call of the Wild* is swiftly and irrevocably swept from the "sunkissed" world of its opening pages into a realm of elemental and unsparing experience. A favorite of his owner, Buck has known a placid, even pampered life in California's Santa Clara Valley—until the day this "sated aristocrat" is dog-napped and finds himself "jerked from the heart of civilization and flung into the heart of things primordial." Sold first to a man supplying sled dogs to those caught up in the Klondike gold rush of the late 1890s, and then to a pair of Canadian government couriers, Buck soon learns that, in order to survive in the harsh Northland, he must submit to "the law of club and fang." Instincts long dormant begin to reawaken in him, and London thrillingly depicts the process of Buck's "decivilization" as he acclimates himself to his alluring, impulsive new life.

Even as he develops bonds of loyalty and love with one master, John Thornton, Buck is remade by the wild into a fierce and merciless creature, eventually abandoning the world of men altogether. Answering nature's irresistible call, he joins his wolfish brethren and is last seen running with them through the wilderness, sounding "a song of the younger world, which is the song of the pack."

That, in brief, is the story of *The Call of the Wild*, a book that—despite the way its subject and style contrasted with the gentility of contemporary popular fiction—was an immediate sensation, earning Jack London's place in the public eye as the most celebrated author of his

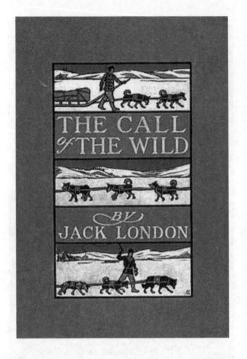

A young Jack London and his dog Rollo, 1885

day. A hundred years later, readers are still falling under its spell.

What: Children's. *When:* 1903. *Also By:* London was a prolific writer. His other classic dog novel, *White Fang* (1906), inverts the plot of *The Call of the Wild*, describing a dog's progression from savagery to civilization. Don't miss it, or his stunning story, "To Build a Fire" (1908).

Further Reading: Irving Stone's *Sailor on Horseback: The Biography of Jack London* is an aptly romantic treatment of London's extraordinary life. *Try: Never Cry Wolf* by Farley Mowat. *Ordinary Wolves* by Seth Kantner. *Adaptations:* There have been several film and television adaptations of *The Call of the Wild*, most notably one directed by D. W. Griffith (1908) and another, starring Clark Gable, directed by William Wellman (1935).

The Art of the Personal Essay

AN ANTHOLOGY FROM THE CLASSICAL ERA TO THE PRESENT

Edited by Phillip Lopate (born 1943)

The Pleasures of the Personal

This wonderful volume, admirably assembled and introduced by Phillip Lopate, reveals how eloquent a private voice can be when its secrets are revealed on a public page. From Seneca in first-century Rome ("On Noise" and "Asthma") and Sei Shōnagon in tenth-century Japan ("Hateful Things") to *New Yorker* laureates James Thurber and E. B. White and Nigerian Nobel Laureate Wole Soyinka, Lopate

has put together a nearly ideal reader in the most intimate of genres: the informal essay.

Progenitors of the modern form are here—Montaigne and Samuel Johnson, Joseph Addison and Richard Steele (founders of the eighteenth-century *Spectator*), the magnificent William Hazlitt, Charles Lamb—as well as a rich sampling of their most celebrated heirs: Robert Louis Stevenson and George Orwell and Virginia Woolf, Thoreau and Mencken, Borges and Barthes and James Baldwin. But there are many serendipities, too: Maria Edgeworth's "An Essay on the Noble Science of Self-Justification," Max Beerbohm's "Going Out for a Walk," Junichiro Tanizaki's "In Praise of Shadows," Joan Didion's "In Bed," Natalia Ginzburg's "He and I." Each piece is alive with the confidences and consolations of an ideal of imaginary friendship, the kind in which another's predilections and perceptions illuminate and expand upon our own.

So many favorites find a place between Lopate's covers: Walter Benjamin's "Unpacking My Library," Woolf's "Street Haunting," Annie Dillard's "Seeing," Hubert Butler's "Beside the Nore" and "Aunt Harriet," Robert Benchley's "My Face," F. Scott Fitzgerald's "The Crack-Up," Scott Russell Sanders's "Under the Influence," M. F. K. Fisher's "Once a Tramp, Always," Richard Rodriguez's "Late Victorians." It's hard to imagine a more perfect bedside book.

What: Essays. Literature. *When:* 1994. *Reading Note:* Dip in anywhere. *Also By: Against Joie de Vivre* (1989). *Portrait of My Body* (1996). *Further Reading: The Norton Book of Personal Essays,* edited by Joseph Epstein. *Try:* Michel de Montaigne's *Essays* (see page 561). *United States* by Gore Vidal. *Independent Spirit* by Hubert Butler (see page 115).

Arctic Dreams
IMAGINATION AND DESIRE IN A NORTHERN LANDSCAPE
Barry Lopez (born 1945)

Intimate Attention in a Vast Wilderness

Like its sibling at the southern end of the globe, the Far North exerts a magnetic pull on the imagination of many readers, as the plethora of books about Arctic and Antarctic explorers attest. The sheer adventure of the harrowing expeditions of Scott, Shackleton, and others certainly accounts in no small degree for the popularity of such works, yet there is undoubtedly something more. The elemental purity of the extreme landscapes presents a field for action—indeed, for existence itself—that is wondrous and terrifying, stripped of life's familiar props and comforts.

No book captures this quality with more concentration than *Arctic Dreams.* "It is precisely because the regimes of light and time in the Arctic are so different," Lopez writes, "that the landscape is able to expose in startling ways the complacency of our thought about land in general." And not just about land, but about creation in all its vast scale and intimate detail. The product of nearly five years' travel as a field biologist in the Arctic, from the Bering Strait in the west to the Davis Strait in the east, Lopez's narrative invites us to observe—and celebrate—the glorious particularities of nature and culture that distinguish what at first appear to be nothing more than "great, unrelieved stretches of snow and ice." From plovers' eggs that glow "with a soft, pure light, like the window light in a Vermeer painting" to a snowy owl with its "aura of primitive alertness," from ancient Eskimo traditions to modern scientific discoveries, from the travels of Saint Brendan in the sixth century to those of Rockwell Kent in the twentieth, Lopez moves seamlessly between observation and reflection, chronicle and natural history. He approaches every aspect of his subject with appreciation, exactitude, and reverence. Reviewing this book for the *New York Times,* the esteemed nature writer Edward Abbey rightly called it "jubilant," and aptly described Lopez as a man "who can't wait to get up in the morning. What is prodigious about him is not so much his travels, which are impressive, but how happy he is in the course of them."

What: Nature. Travel. *When:* 1986. *Award:* National Book Award, 1986. *Also By:* Lopez has published a number of nonfiction books, most notably *Of Wolves and Men* (1978), as well as several story collections, including the trio *Desert Notes* (1976), *River Notes* (1979), and *Field Notes* (1994). *Try: Desert Solitaire: A Season in the Wilderness* by Edward Abbey (see page 2). *The Snow Leopard* by Peter Matthiessen. *Coming into the Country* by John McPhee.

Man Meets Dog
Konrad Lorenz (1903–1989)

A Landmark Exploration of Our Best Friendship

"**A**n epoch-making episode, a stroke of genius whose meaning in world history is greater than that of the fall of Troy or the discovery of gunpowder." What is Konrad Lorenz, the Nobel Prize–winning ethologist and one of the most influential naturalists of the twentieth century, talking about? The moment when our forerunners first tempted wild jackals to keep close to a human encampment at night and, by means of their presence, gained a kind of watch against nocturnal predators: "the clamor [the jackals] set up on the approach of a beast of prey announced from afar the appearance of the marauder."

In the years since 1954, when Lorenz's landmark *Man Meets Dog* was first published in the United States, other scenarios have been developed to account for the origin of the miraculously close partnership between canines and humans. But few if any of them

have been more influential or more inspired by such undisguised love for "man's best friend." Thanks to long and affectionate observation of the dogs in his own life, Lorenz's writing brims with striking details and pleasing anecdotes as he addresses both practical and theoretical questions familiar to any dog owner. *Man Meets Dog* is not primarily a training manual, and yet, through its brilliant hypotheses and its thoughtful, humane advice, any curious human can arrive at a deeper understanding of the canine worldview and how it defines relations both among dogs and between dogs and humans. In these civilizing pages, a wise and kindly mentor teaches readers a lot about dogs—and about themselves, too.

What: Animals. Nature. *When:* 1950, in Germany. Published in the United States in 1954; translation by Marjorie Kerr Wilson. *Also By: King Solomon's Ring* (1949). *On Aggression* (1963). *Try: Adam's Task* by Vicki Hearne (see page 359).

■ For H. P. Lovecraft's *The Case of Charles Dexter Ward*, see page 633.

■ For Maud Hart Lovelace's *Betsy-Tacy*, see page 436.

Under the Volcano
Malcolm Lowry (1909–1957)

An Infernal Evocation of Dissolution

"**H**ell," Jean-Paul Sartre famously wrote, "is other people." Geoffrey Firmin, the figure at the center of Malcolm Lowry's swirling novel, would disagree; for the dissipated former British diplomat known as "the Consul," hell is himself, and he cannot escape the suffocation of his own fevered embrace.

Under the Volcano details—in streams of consciousness, flights of lyricism, and luxuriant jungles of symbol and phantasm—the last day of the Consul's life. It is 1938, and the forty-one-year-old Firmin is drowning in drink. The day, as it happens, is the Day of the Dead, and the Mexican town in which the book is set is vivid with ominous festivities. Firmin's ex-wife, Yvonne, has just rejoined him after a year's absence. Also on hand is his younger half-brother, Hugh, who also happens to be Yvonne's former lover. Both Yvonne and Hugh want to rescue Geoffrey from his descent into dissolution, and they follow him hour by hour from bar to bar as the Consul turns through the circles of his own inferno, his existence reduced to nothing more than "his rejection of life." Even that perverted sense of purpose will be gone before this Day of the Dead runs its course, for Firmin will be murdered—by mistake—at the book's close. The novel's final sentence rings out like a verdict: "Somebody threw a dead dog after him down the ravine."

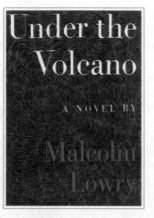

There isn't much plot to *Under the Volcano*, and what there is is bleak in both outline and incident. Nevertheless, Lowry's muscular, incantatory, allusive, and intoxicating prose makes his creation one of the most powerful novels you will ever read. Like a transfixing musical composition, it sweeps us into another world that's animated with resonances we can't quite explain. As Lowry wrote in a letter to a potential publisher, it "can be regarded as a kind of symphony"; indeed, the literary music it makes is seductive and spellbinding, reverberating with the impassioned futility of one man's terror, guilt, and remorse.

What: Novel. *When:* 1947. *Reading Note:* Episodic, allusive, and idiosyncratic, Lowry's style can be disorienting; concentration is required. *Also By: Ultramarine* (1933) was the only other book Lowry published in his lifetime. *The Voyage That Never Ends* (2007) is an anthology of Lowry's letters, poems, and selections from his posthumously published manuscripts. *Further Reading: Malcolm Lowry: A Biography* by Douglas Day. *Inside the Volcano: My Life with Malcolm Lowry* by Jan Gabrial (Lowry's first wife and a real-life counterpart to the novel's Yvonne). *Malcolm Lowry's Volcano: Myth, Symbol, Meaning* by David Markson. *Try: The Power and the Glory* by Graham Greene (see page 335). *Omensetter's Luck* by William H. Gass. *Adaptation:* John Huston directed the 1984 film version of *Under the Volcano*, which stars Albert Finney and Jacqueline Bisset. *Footnote:* The author's thirty-one-page letter in defense of *Under the Volcano*, penned to publisher Jonathan Cape, persuaded the London house to reverse its original decision to reject the novel.

The Way Things Are

THE *DE RERUM NATURA* OF TITUS LUCRETIUS CARUS

Lucretius (ca. 99 BC–ca. 55 BC)
Translated by Rolfe Humphries

Lessons from a 2,000-Year-Old Man

Rolfe Humphries's lucid, graceful translation of the expansive philosophical poem *De Rerum Natura*, written by Titus Lucretius Carus in the first century BC, allows modern readers to enjoy one of the more unusual and rewarding products of Latin literature. In 7,500 hexameter lines that convey a wealth of natural imagery, scientific inquiry, and meditation both metaphorical and metaphysical, Lucretius charts the workings of the universe on an ambitious intellectual journey informed by the teachings of the Greek philosopher Epicurus, who lived some three centuries before the Roman poet.

Using the Epicurean idea of the atomic basis of matter as a springboard, *De Rerum Natura* launches a vision of a cosmos that, in its origins and operations, is material rather than divine. Arguing against superstition and religion, Lucretius limns a coherent system of natural history, physics, psychology, and ethics that strives to liberate the human spirit from fear of death and bondage to the overwhelming gods. With equal insight, he treats the essential qualities of the five senses and the less palpable practicalities of cosmology, the mechanics of sex and the ravages of disease (the poem concludes with an unforgettable evocation of plague-ridden Athens), the emergence of civilization and the timeless reality of "our terrors and our darknesses of mind." The poet's attention is finely tuned, his voice—and this is the genius of Humphries's rendering— agile and immediate. Lucretius's powerfully imagined vision of "the way things are" is an epic of *thinking*, of figuring out where we live (in the broadest possible sense) and what we live for (in an equally expansive imagining of personal responsibility for one's own destiny). By treating the two-thousand-year-old poem not as a scholarly text but as a living document of a man's search for meaning, Humphries connects ancient wisdom to humanity's enduring awareness of spiritual restlessness:

> Men seem to feel some burden on their souls,
> Some heavy weariness; could they but know
> Its origin, its cause, they'd never live
> The way we see most of them do, each one
> Ignorant of what he wants, except a change,
> Some other place to lay his burden down.
> One leaves his house to take a stroll outdoors
> Because the household's such a deadly bore,
> And then comes back, in six or seven minutes—
> The street is every bit as bad. Now what?
> He has his horses hitched up for him, drives,
> Like a man going to a fire, full-speed,
> Off to his country-place, and when he gets there
> Is scarcely on the driveway, when he yawns,
> Falls heavily asleep, oblivious
> To everything, or promptly turns around,
> Whips back to town again. So each man flees
> Himself, or tries to, but of course that pest
> Clings to him all the more ungraciously.

Title page of 1768 French edition of Lucretius's work

A surprising precursor to the later ruminations of Wordsworth, Yeats, and the T. S. Eliot of *Four Quartets*, *The Way Things Are* is one of the most neglected treasures of classical culture.

What: Philosophy. Poetry. Science. *When:* First century BC; the Humphries translation, 1968. *Editions:* Anthony M. Esolen's eloquent, eminently readable 1995 version, *On the Nature of Things*, is also superb, and features an especially informative introduction. Other translators have used the title *On the Nature of the Universe*. *Further Reading: Three Philosophical Poets* by George Santayana. *Try: The Botanic Garden* by Erasmus Darwin. *Four Quartets* by T. S. Eliot. *Before It Vanishes: A Packet for Professor Pagels* by Robert Pack.

The Bourne Identity
Robert Ludlum (1927–2001)

An Agent Secret Even to Himself

Espionage is by definition a web of secrets, codes, nuances, duplicities. To set an amnesiac loose in such a nexus of determinedly shifting identities adds an extra shot to the conventional spy novel cocktail. This is what Robert Ludlum famously did in *The Bourne Identity*, the seed from which would grow not only two more volumes in his own trilogy—*The Bourne*

Supremacy (1986) and *The Bourne Ultimatum* (1990)—but also a posthumous extension of the brand in a shelf of novels by Eric Van Lustbader, to say nothing of the Bourne film franchise.

Relying more on suspense than detonations, Ludlum's original is highly charged storytelling nonetheless, the story of a man on the run who must decide the direction and purpose of his flight without the benefit of knowing his past. Framed by an international terrorist, suspected by his CIA superiors, abetted by a woman who at first tries to turn him in, Jason Bourne makes his way across Europe, fleeing assassins each step of the way and bumping into his forgotten backstory every other. It's unclear to him, and to the reader, which is more dangerous, but it is great fun finding out.

In several wildly popular blockbusters published in the 1970s, Ludlum lifted spy fiction out of the melancholy and reflective shadows John le Carré (see page 467) had so richly painted through his careful attention to the unheroic inner lives of intelligence agents. Bringing dramatic action back into the foreground, Ludlum pitted his underdog protagonists against vast and nefarious conspiracies of corporate, military, and political interests. In doing so, he created a transporting realm of fantasy that wore all the trappings of worldly insight into what really happens behind the headlines—and nowhere more thrillingly than in *The Bourne Identity*.

What: Mystery & Suspense. *When:* 1980. *Also By: The Scarlatti Inheritance* (1971). *The Matarese Circle* (1979). *The Parsifal Mosaic* (1982). *Try: The Day of the Jackal* by Frederick Forsyth (see page 292). *The Unlikely Spy* by Daniel Silva. *Adaptations:* The 1988 television movie stars Richard Chamberlain. The 2002 film version, which differs significantly from the book, features Matt Damon in the title role.

■ For Valeria Luiselli's *The Story of My Teeth*, see page 509.

Five Days in London
MAY 1940

John Lukacs (born 1924)

When Hitler Stood on the Brink of Victory

It is John Lukacs's opinion that Adolf Hitler "came closest to winning the Second World War" during the period from the 24th to the 28th of May 1940. Why those five days? Because, as this concise and gripping history reveals, that was when the inner circles of the British government nearly decided to negotiate a peace treaty with the Nazi leader.

The reason for seeking a deal was obvious: German troops, having swept through Europe for more than a year, had finally arrived at Britain's doorstep. On the night of May 23, with a quarter-million British soldiers apparently trapped across the English Channel in Dunkirk, England seemed Hitler's for the taking.

Despite the dire outlook, Britain ultimately refused to seek a negotiated peace. As Lukacs convincingly demonstrates, this was chiefly because of Winston Churchill, who had become prime minister only two weeks earlier. Although the new leader was viewed with distrust by many in the government, Churchill managed—during the Friday-to-Tuesday period that is the focus of Lukacs's vivid narrative—to convince his Cabinet colleagues to rally behind him, establishing as official British policy the unswerving resolve to fight on no matter what. "Then and there," Lukacs writes, Churchill "saved Britain, and Europe, and Western civilization."

Since Hitler lost the war, it can appear in retrospect as if his defeat was inevitable.

Lukacs's compelling study is a powerful reminder that this was far from the case. By chronicling the behind-the-scenes drama of those fraught days in May, Lukacs reveals just how valiant was Britain's determination to, in Churchill's famous words, "fight on the beaches, [. . .] fight on the landing grounds, [. . .] fight in the fields and in the streets," and to "never surrender." *Five Days in London* stands as an eloquent testament to the significance of the memorial set in the floor just inside the ceremonial doors of Westminster Abbey, a dark stone inscribed with these three words: "Remember Winston Churchill."

What: War. History. *When:* 1999. *Also By: Confessions of an Original Sinner* (1990). *The Duel: 10 May–31 July 1940: The Eighty-Day Struggle Between Churchill and Hitler* (1991). *The Hitler of History* (1997). *A Thread of Years* (1998). *Further Reading: Their Finest Hour* by Winston Churchill (see page 202). *Try: Invasion 1940* by Peter Fleming.

Adventures on the Wine Route
A WINE BUYER'S TOUR OF FRANCE
Kermit Lynch (born 1941)

Days of Wine and Noses

In 1972, a young man named Kermit Lynch opened a little wine shop in Berkeley, California, hoping to introduce neighborhood customers to the sort of artisanal wines he was passionate about. A year later, invited to accompany an importer on a buying trip to France, he discovered his true calling. In the decades between then and now, Lynch has sniffed, swirled, and tasted his way to prominence as one of America's most renowned importers of wines of character made the old-fashioned way—especially those that won't break the bank. Both a merchant and a critic of sorts, he managed to educate and entertain at the same time, mostly in the pages of his beloved newsletter, always replete with colorful tales of how he discovered his new offerings, who made them, what the makers fed him, and the various serendipities and calamities of his researches. Subscribers looked forward to reading his impassioned write-ups as much as they did to tasting the wines.

Adventures on the Wine Route exhibits all the characteristics that made his communications

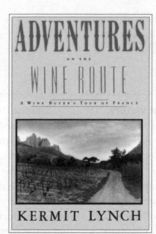

to customers so satisfying. Part memoir and part travelogue, it is also a manifesto about the wine business and the ways in which conglomeration, trends, and market demands can threaten the very things that make the fruit of the vine worth savoring. Peppered with gorgeous (and often amusing) black-and-white photos by Gail Skoff, it is suffused with the qualities the author seeks in casks and bottles—nuance, surprise, subtlety, expression, authenticity. By turns wise and very funny, Lynch—to say nothing of the many quirky vignerons he introduces us to—is good company indeed on this delightfully readable tour of the wine regions of France.

What: Food & Drink. Travel. *When:* 1988. *Also By: Inspiring Thirst: Vintage Selections from The Kermit Lynch Wine Brochure* (2004) is a beautifully produced and endlessly browsable book. *Further Reading:* Richard Olney's *Lulu's Provençal Table*, a celebration of the food and wine of Domaine Tempier, Lynch's favorite vineyard. *Try: The Auberge of the Flowering Hearth* by Roy Andries de Groot (see page 202). *Puligny-Montrachet* by Simon Loftus. *A Life Uncorked* by Hugh Johnson.

The Undertaking
LIFE STUDIES FROM THE DISMAL TRADE
Thomas Lynch (born 1948)

Vital Essays on Death

In addition to being a widely published poet, Thomas Lynch is a mortician, the proprietor of Lynch & Sons, the only funeral parlor in the small town of Milford, Michigan. ("Every year I bury a couple hundred of my townspeople. [. . .] I have a corner on the market.") Lynch's several decades in "the dismal trade" have made him particularly aware of the ways in which the living weather death—how we find ourselves "looking up while digging down, trying to make some sense of all of it, disposing of our dead with sufficient pause to say they'd lived in ways different from rocks and rhododendrons and even orangutans and that those lives were worth mentioning and remembering."

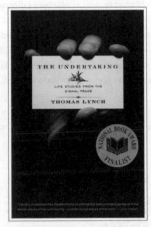

Lynch's intimate familiarity with death as a presence in our lives, plus his poet's feel for rich, down-to-earth language, distinguish the twelve essays in *The Undertaking*. Poignant, lamenting, and good-humoredly morbid, Lynch's meditations on our mortality explore such themes as the bonds between the living and dead, the ties of family and community, and, especially, the customs and ceremonies by means of which we humans create meaning: "Just as we declare the living alive through baptisms, lovers in love by nuptials," Lynch observes, "funerals are the way we close the gap between the death that happens and the death that matters. It's how we assign meaning to our little remarkable histories."

Whether ruminating on his embalming of his own father or on the afterimages of the dead that accompany him down a familiar street, Lynch's essays offer a perspective on common experience that is singular and profound. Greeted with praise and prizes by the literary world, it has also had a notable effect on popular culture: Alan Ball, the creator of the hit HBO series *Six Feet Under*, has credited *The Undertaking* as the primary inspiration for that offbeat show, which focused on a family-run funeral home in Los Angeles.

What: Essays. Memoir. *When:* 1997. *Also By: Bodies in Motion and At Rest: On Metaphor and Mortality* (2000). *Booking Passage: We Irish and Americans* (2005). *Try: Day of the Dead and Other Mortal Reflections* by F. González-Crussi. *How We Die* by Sherwin B. Nuland.

The Lyttelton Hart-Davis Letters
George Lyttelton (1883–1962) and Rupert Hart-Davis (1907–1999)

A Bookish and British Friendship in Letters

The six volumes of correspondence between George Lyttelton, a retired Eton schoolmaster, and Rupert Hart-Davis, Lyttelton's former student and one of Britain's most prominent men of letters, are the books to turn to when you want to let your mind relax in the company of erudite, stylish, congenial conversation. The talk—which unfolds in the weekly epistles the gentlemen exchanged from 1955 until Lyttelton's death in 1962—bustles with Hart-Davis's incessant activity (including editing the letters of Oscar Wilde, publishing a celebrated array of authors, and occupying the center of London's literary culture) and brims with his elder's wide reading, rich store of experience, and pure delight in having an audience for the comings and goings of his fertile mind. Crammed with marvelous bons mots (try this one, quoted early on by Lyttelton: "that state of resentful coma which scholars attempt to dignify by calling research"), arcane yet curiously pleasing cricket metaphors, and civilized chitchat of the highest order, these letters make up an ideal and ever-inviting course of reading. A book-loving insomniac could ask for no better bedside companions.

What: Diaries & Letters. Books. *When:* Published in six volumes, 1978–84. *Editions:* In addition to the six original individual volumes, the letters have been issued in three paperback double volumes. A representative single-volume sampling of the correspondence was published in 2001. *Reading Note:* The exchanges are filled with references to friends, British politics, and cricket lore, some annotated, some not. Unfamiliarity with them does nothing to diminish the reader's enjoyment; let the rhythm of the weekly conversation carry you along. *Also By:* Lyttelton: *George Lyttelton's Commonplace Book* (2002). Hart-Davis: *Hugh Walpole: A Biography* (1952). *The Letters of Oscar Wilde* (1962; editor). *The Arms of Time: A Memoir* (1979). *The Power of Chance: A Table of Memory* (1991). *Halfway to Heaven: Concluding Memoirs of a Literary Life* (1998). *Further Reading:* Craig Brown's *The Marsh Marlowe Letters* is a clever parody of Lyttelton and Hart-Davis's exchanges. *Try: Holmes-Laski Letters: The Correspondence of Mr. Justice Holmes and Harold J. Laski, 1916–1935* (see below). *The Element of Lavishness: Letters of Sylvia Townsend Warner and William Maxwell, 1938–1978* (see page 833).

|||||||||||||||||||||||||||||||||||| MORE TO EXPLORE ||||||||||||||||||||||||||||||||||||

MAIL CALL

Sometimes, and especially when we pick up a book before bed, the pleasure we seek in reading is independent of plot or chapter or extended argument—we just want to get lost for a few moments in the intimacy that good writing can hide between its lines. Delving into other people's correspondence is a wonderful way to find such satisfaction in segmented, episodic doses. Ranging page by page from the casual to the businesslike, the conversational to the profound, letters offer a distinctive kind of engagement for readers as they eavesdrop on the thoughts of others. Here's a list of not-to-be-missed collections.

Letters of John Keats
John Keats (1795–1821)

Keats's poems are altars of sound, sense, and shape; no reader's life is complete without some reverent acknowledgment of at least the great odes ("On a Grecian Urn," "To Indolence," "On Melancholy," "To a Nightingale"). And yet, as marvelous as Keats's verse is, his most lasting and necessary contribution to a reader's life list is his letters, which constitute a kind of scripture for the life of the imagination. Their mix of passing detail with flights of inspiration, even revelation, gives them a visionary energy few other texts can rival. A letter composed between February 14 and May 3, 1819, and addressed to his brother and his sister-in-law, who had emigrated to Louisville, Kentucky, suggests the scope of the poet's epistolary enthusiasms. Encompassing everything from the black eye Keats received during a game of cricket (courtesy of an errant ball) to drafts of verses from "La Belle Dame sans Merci" and the "Ode to Psyche," to commentary on his current reading (Voltaire), this family packet of news and musings also finds time for an incisive disquisition on human nature. This last culminates in an extended description of our world of pains and troubles as not a vale of tears, but rather a "vale of Soul-making"—a passage inspired enough to bring one's entire life into new focus. Written over a period of only four years, often in obvious haste, yet frequently imbued nonetheless with the deepest colors of insight and wisdom, Keats's letters are a treasure. The 1970 selection by Keats biographer Robert Gittings is the best of many editions that have been issued.

Holmes-Laski Letters
THE CORRESPONDENCE OF MR. JUSTICE HOLMES AND HAROLD J. LASKI, 1916–1935

Oliver Wendell Holmes Jr. (1841–1935) and Harold J. Laski (1893–1950)

That one of the most prolific and intriguing of American letter-writers was also a Supreme Court justice is something of a surprise—and a complete delight. This enormous correspondence between Oliver Wendell Holmes and the British economist and political theorist Harold J. Laski is something like the Everest of epistolary friendships, with two fertile, searching minds nourishing each other over the course of nineteen years, from 1916 to 1935. Commencing when Justice Holmes was seventy-five and Laski only twenty-three, it continued until the older man's death. There's a great deal on law and politics, but lots of literary and philosophical import as well (Laski was an inveterate book hound, and reports on his browsing abound). That the younger correspondent appears to have a penchant for exaggerating—at times even fabricating—the extent of his activities and influence, and that this tendency was not entirely lost on Holmes, adds spice to the rich feast. The presence of both sides of the exchange—not always a given in volumes of letters—enhances the enjoyment of our postal eavesdropping. The 1953 two-volume set was edited by Mark DeWolfe Howe.

Bernard Shaw: Collected Letters, 1874–1950

George Bernard Shaw (1856–1950)

On the BBC, there has for decades been a popular program in which public figures reveal the recorded music they would wish to have at hand if they were stranded alone on a desert island. If there was a reader's equivalent, it might well be called *The Insomniac's Bookshelf*, and anyone familiar with George Bernard Shaw's *Collected Letters* would hope to find them on it in the wee small hours of the night.

The great dramatist (see page 718), music critic, and all-purpose provocateur is good company by virtue of his wit, his ideas, and his relentlessly contrarian nature. He exhibits remarkable facility in turning the details of business dealings with agents, linguistic entanglements with translators, production problems with directors, and even simple refusals of social invitations into vivid set pieces. In short, he is funny as hell, and more resoundingly eloquent than a chorus of angels in heaven. Whether narrating, in markedly high spirits, his mother's funeral ("she would have enjoyed it enormously," he asserts as he describes the scene in which his mother's ashes are sifted after her cremation), complaining to the management of Covent Garden about a lady's reckless millinery, or conducting playful—and extended—paper courtships of actresses such as Ellen Terry and Mrs. Patrick Campbell, he is unfailingly entertaining. His range of correspondents is impressive—from Henry James to heavyweight boxer Gene Tunney—but it is the sentence-by-sentence pleasure his letters offer that makes them so amusing, so riveting, and so valuable. Written between 1874 and 1950 and published in four volumes, edited by Dan H. Laurence, between 1965 and 1988.

The Habit of Being
LETTERS OF FLANNERY O'CONNOR

Flannery O'Connor (1925–1964)

This book is the source of two enormous pleasures: First, it

Flannery O'Connor, 1952

allows us to enjoy one of American literature's most curious and penetrating voices, one equally at home discussing the behavior of chickens or the philosophy of Saint Thomas Aquinas. Second (more selfish and more fun), it lets us pretend, for days on end, that we, too, regularly receive—and are worthy of—such literate, droll, and considered discourses on books, writing, religion, peacocks, and what editor Sally Fitzgerald felicitously calls "the habit of being," as distinct from "the habit of art." O'Connor's artistic imagination—so strange, severe, and fiercely haunting in her revelatory short fiction (see page 597) and novels—is softened but no less forceful in her discursive epistles. We're given an inspiring acquaintance with a woman of steely wit and steely faith, the former alert to the absurdities about her, the latter attuned to first and last things. Published in 1979, collecting letters written between 1948 and 1964.

M

Leo Africanus
Amin Maalouf (born 1949)

Adventures of a 16th-Century Mediterranean Traveler

This transporting novel, a fictional autobiography of the celebrated geographer, adventurer, and scholar al-Hasan ibn Muhammad al-Wazzān al-Zayyātī, magically leads readers across the borders of their own parochialism—whether physical, historical, or imaginative. Born in Moorish Granada in 1488, Hasan fled Spain with his family to Fez to escape the Inquisition, journeyed extensively through Africa and the Middle East, was captured by Sicilian oceangoing brigands and taken to Rome and presented to Pope Leo X, who baptized him as Johannes Leo. While in Italy he wrote a trilingual medical dictionary (in Latin, Arabic, and Hebrew) as well as his famous *Description of Africa*, for which he is remembered as Leo Africanus.

From this remarkable life, the Lebanese writer Amin Maalouf has fashioned a marvelous narrative in which the civilizations of Islam and Christendom engage each other in the experience of a single person. Beginning with an account of the expulsion of Arabs and Jews from Spain by Ferdinand and Isabella, the story follows its protagonist's family to Fez, then traces his peregrinations through cosmopolitan Cairo, across the Sahara to Timbuktu, to the Constantinople of Suleiman and the Rome of Raphael and the High Renaissance. Hasan's exploits as merchant and diplomat give him, and the reader, an enlightening view of the flux of the sixteenth-century Mediterranean world.

Organized into forty chapters corresponding to the first forty years of Hasan's life, the book is part history, part travelogue, and, delightfully, part picaresque, replete with pirates and princesses; it places its hero within view of many of the prominent events and personalities of his politically and culturally dynamic time. Satisfying in the many tales it weaves and in the fabled settings it evokes, *Leo Africanus* is a novel of intellectual discovery and storytelling enchantment.

What: Novel. *When:* 1986 in French; English translation by Peter Sluglett, 1989. *Also By:* Fiction: *The Rock of Tanios* (1993); *Balthasar's Odyssey* (2000). Nonfiction: *The Crusades Through Arab Eyes* (1984); *Origins: A Memoir* (2004). *Further Reading: Trickster Travels: A Sixteenth-Century Muslim Between Worlds* by Natalie Zemon Davis. *The Adventures of Ibn Battuta* by Ross E. Dunn (see page 239). *Try: Creation* by Gore Vidal.

The Towers of Trebizond
Rose Macaulay (1881–1958)

From High Comedy to High Mass— And Many Places in Between

Tell me you're not intrigued by a novel that begins, "'Take my camel, dear,' said my aunt Dot, as she climbed down from this animal on her return from High Mass."

Over a long career, Rose Macaulay's grandly individual talent expressed itself in clever comedies of manners (*Keeping Up Appearances*, 1928), thoughtful forays into idiosyncratic scholarship (*Pleasure of Ruins*, 1953), and profound inquiries into the elusive nature—and stuttering nurture—of religious faith (tellingly captured in two posthumously published volumes of letters to an Anglican priest in America, *Letters to a Friend 1950–1952* and *Last Letters to a Friend 1952–1958*). All three strands of her literary intelligence are interwoven with élan in her final novel, her masterpiece *The Towers of Trebizond*.

A wonder of eccentricity, absurdity, adventure, wit, learning, and style, the novel is narrated by an Englishwoman named Laurie, who is accompanying her aunt and that free-spirited missionary's consort, the Rev. the Hon. Hugh Chantry-Pigg, on a trek from Istanbul to the fabled Trebizond. Exploiting the appeal of the ancient terrain to modern pilgrims of various stripes ("I wonder who else is rambling about Turkey this spring," says Aunt Dot. "Seventh-Day Adventists, Billy Grahamites, writers, diggers, photographers, spies, us, and now the B.B.C."), the first part of *The Towers of Trebizond* is leavened with comic questions. Will Father Chantry-Pigg be able to establish a High Anglican mission in Turkey? Will Dot emancipate Turkish women by coaxing them to wear hats?

As the book progresses and Laurie is left to her own devices, her grapplings with loves both sacred and profane push the book's high spirits onto a loftier plane of inquiry. There the tantalizing uncertainties of belief are revealed to be as eerily evocative as the most legend-laden ruin. Must faith's reach always exceed its grasp? Traveling with Rose Macaulay and her characters, the answer remains in doubt, but the trip, at least, is heavenly.

What: Novel. *When:* 1956. *Also By:* Fiction: *Keeping Up Appearances* (1928). *Staying with Relations* (1930). *The World My Wilderness* (1950). Nonfiction: *Personal Pleasures* (1935). *Fabled Shore* (1949). *Further Reading:* *Rose Macaulay: A Writer's Life* by Jane Emery. *Try:* *Travels with My Aunt* by Graham Greene.

Anybody Can Do Anything
Betty MacDonald (1908–1958)

A Happy Family Fends Off the Great Depression

In the late 1920s, after having enjoyed a girlhood of piano lessons, ballet, and the like, young Betty MacDonald moved with her new husband onto a chicken farm. The dilapidated forty-acre property was buried deep in the wilds of Washington State's Olympic Peninsula, where the towering peaks of the Olympic Mountains were, to Betty at least, like disagreeable guests who would never, ever leave. Once the newlyweds had settled down on their farm, which had neither running water nor electricity, they set about raising chickens—and, before long, children—in an environment that demanded that they work, work, and work some more, all day and every day, year in and year out. The book MacDonald wrote detailing their labors—*The Egg and I* (1945)—belied the backbreaking effort it described by being as lighthearted and humorous as any reader could hope for. (If her first book didn't prove the author's talent for turning hardship into comic gold, its sequel, *The Plague and I* [1948], her account of nine months in a tuberculosis sanitarium, certainly did.) The success of *The Egg and I* was extraordinary: It sold more than a million copies in the year after its publication, and was made into a 1947 film starring Claudette Colbert and Fred MacMurray.

Although that debut made MacDonald's name as a writer, the liveliest and most satisfying of her four excellent memoirs is *Anybody Can Do Anything*, a high-spirited celebration of family love and laughter. The story opens in 1931, when MacDonald, whose maiden name was Bard, returns with her two daughters to the happily chaotic, close-knit Bard household after four years on the aforementioned chicken farm (marriage being less tractable, it seems, than memoir). The Depression is darkening the country at the time, but it doesn't depress the Bards any, least of all Betty's sister Mary, who looks upon the national crisis as a personal challenge, a time to put to the test her belief that "anybody can do anything, especially Betty." The latter isn't at all convinced that this is the case, believing it the more prudent course to look for a job "with a salary, and duties

Betty MacDonald, 1946

mediocre enough to be congruent with my mediocre ability. I had in mind sort of a combination janitress, slow typist and file clerk." But Mary's spunky attitude carries the day and leads Betty into one crazy job after another, including a memorable brief stint as secretary to a gangster. MacDonald has a lot of fun at the expense of the offices she finds herself in and the bosses and coworkers she encounters (for example, "One of the first things I learned and loved about the Government was that I wasn't the only bonehead working for it"). But it's the affectionate portrait of her zany family that brings out the down-to-earth best in MacDonald the writer, and that remains delightful even today.

What: Memoir. **When:** 1950. **Also By:** *Onions in the Stew* (1955). In addition to her memoirs, MacDonald wrote a popular series of books for children featuring Mrs. Piggle-Wiggle, a sort of American Mary Poppins. **Try:** *My Sister Eileen* by Ruth McKenney. *Life Among the Savages* by Shirley Jackson (see page 404). *The Prize Winner of Defiance, Ohio* by Terry Ryan.

Epitaph of a Small Winner
Joaquim María Machado de Assis (1839–1908)

A Brazilian Comic Novel Far Ahead of Its Time

At the outset, the protagonist of this fictional autobiography, Braz Cubas, announces that he is dead, then proceeds to narrate the tremors and trials of his undistinguished life in Rio de Janeiro from his cheerful position beyond the grave, detailing the suspicions, envies, and failed romantic quests that filled his days. The episodes, etched in irony, add up to a paean to pessimism that is as startling as it is amiable. Taking account, in the last chapter, of the pluses and minuses of his earthly existence, Cubas decides that they balance each

other out. Yet the reader who concludes that our hero died "quits with life" would be mistaken, "for," he writes in farewell, "upon arriving on this other side of the mystery, I found that I had a small surplus, which provides the final negative of this chapter of negatives: I had no progeny, I transmitted to no one the legacy of our misery."

Sound bleak? It's not. Machado de Assis animates his tale with such ebullient energy that the tone of *Epitaph of a Small Winner* is positively jaunty. Cubas's interjections, asides, and nonstop commentary on the narrative are filled with all sorts of antic invention, from a chapter consisting of a conversation rendered entirely in ellipses and punctuation—no words at all—to another devoted to praising his legs, which have carried him to his destination despite the fact that his mind has been preoccupied with Virgilia, the object of his affections:

Blessed legs! And yet some people treat you with indifference. Even I, until then, had a low opinion of you, and I got angry when you became tired, when you could not go beyond a certain point and left me as eager to fly and as unable to do so as a chicken with its legs tied.

On this occasion, however, you were a ray of sunshine . . . in appreciation of which kindness I have now immortalized you.

First published in Brazil more than a hundred years ago, Machado de Assis's masterpiece of iconoclasm is fueled with an irreverence, both literary and philosophical, that seems decades

ahead of its time. It is one of the funniest and most original novels you'll ever read.

What: Novel. *When:* 1881. *Editions:* Translated as *Epitaph of a Small Winner* by William Grossman, 1952. Translated as *The Posthumous Memoirs of Brás Cubas* (a more exact rendering of the Portuguese title) by Gregory Rabassa, 1997. The Grossman version is preferred. *Also By:* Quincas Borba (1891; avoid the translation titled *Philosopher or Dog?*). Dom Casmurro (1899). Esau and Jacob (1904). Counselor Ayres' Memorial (1908). *The Psychiatrist and Other Stories* (collection published in English, 1963). *Further Reading: Machado de Assis: The Brazilian Master and His Novels* by Helen Caldwell. *Try: The Life and Opinions of Tristram Shandy, Gentleman* by Laurence Sterne (see page 756). *Zeno's Conscience* by Italo Svevo (see page 766). *The Invention of Morel* by Adolfo Bioy Casares.

Try: The Life and Opinions of Tristram Shandy, Gentleman by Laurence Sterne (see page 756). Zeno's Conscience by Italo Svevo (see page 766).

||||||||||||||||||||||||||||||||||||||||| B O O K N O T E |||||||||||||||||||||||||||||||||||||||||

A GLEAMINGLY ORIGINAL INVENTION

The Story of My Teeth
Valeria Luiselli (born 1983)

E*pitaph of a Small Winner* is a singular book, but those looking for a novel that delivers a similar sense of comic extravagance can turn to Valeria Luiselli's equally remarkable *The Story of My Teeth*, published in Mexico in 2013 and issued in America, in a splendid translation by Christina MacSweeney, two years later. In its pages, the narrator, with a jauntiness and erudite insouciance worthy of Braz Cubas, looks back on his life as a traveler, legendary auctioneer, and collector of teeth—including those of Plato, Petrarch, Chesterton, and Virginia Woolf. Most wonderfully, he has replaced his own unfortunate molars, incisors, and so on with those that once belonged to Marilyn Monroe.

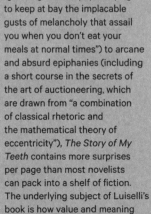

From revelations of mundane experience ("I started leafing through a newspaper, trying to keep at bay the implacable gusts of melancholy that assail you when you don't eat your meals at normal times") to arcane and absurd epiphanies (including a short course in the secrets of the art of auctioneering, which are drawn from "a combination of classical rhetoric and the mathematical theory of eccentricity"), *The Story of My Teeth* contains more surprises per page than most novelists can pack into a shelf of fiction. The underlying subject of Luiselli's book is how value and meaning attach themselves to art and literature—in other words, how stories shape significance—and its overriding spirit is one of invention, exhilaration, and delight.

The Prince
Niccolò Machiavelli (1469–1527)

An Unrivaled Guide to the Practice of Power

" Machiavellian": The adjective resounds with a kind of insidious music, a melody built on chords of cunning, duplicity, and bad faith. And yet the mind the term immortalizes—as represented in this book, one of the most astute and influential works of political science ever penned—might better be described as canny, forthright in pursuing the "truth about human things," and possessed of a fierce and unprecedented fidelity to the way the world really works. "Many have imagined republics and principalities which have never been seen or known to exist in reality," Machiavelli writes in this legendary volume, "for how we live is so far removed from how we ought to live, that he who abandons what is done for what ought to be done, will rather bring about his own ruin than his preservation."

Published five years after its author's death, *The Prince* advanced a revolutionary theory of statecraft. The traditional view of governance held that a ruler earned the respect and obedience of his subjects by ruling virtuously. But the principle at the heart of *The Prince* is that virtue as such has no place in politics. Moral strictures and ethical commandments, Machiavelli argues, must never tie a prince's hands; his only concern is to get and keep power. "It must be understood that a prince . . . cannot observe all of those virtues for which men are reputed good, because it is often necessary to act against mercy, against faith, against humanity, against frankness, against religion, in order to preserve the state." In other words, when it comes to governing, the end justifies the means. It is a notion for which Machiavelli was condemned for centuries (some contemporaries called him an agent of the devil), but seldom by those in a position to understand his perception's utility. Today we call Machiavelli's devilish pragmatism "realpolitik."

Born in Florence, Niccolò Machiavelli served the city-state as a diplomat for many years after the ruling Medici family was driven from power in 1494. When the Medicis returned, however, he was imprisoned, tortured, and exiled. By combining his firsthand experience of cutthroat political turbulence with extensive research into historical precedents and a keen sense of how self-interest shapes human behavior, he composed a Renaissance textbook on power that has never gone out of date, and that remains both readable and stylish in its urbane attention to political imperatives.

What: Politics. History. *When:* Written ca. 1513; published posthumously in 1532. *Also By: Discourses on Livy* (1531). *Florentine Histories* (1532). *Further Reading: Machiavelli in Hell* by Sebastian de Grazia. *Machiavelli and His Friends: Their Personal Correspondence*, edited by James B. Atkinson and David Sices. *Machiavelli: A Biography* by Miles J. Unger. *Try: The Art of War* by Sun Tzu. *Footnote:* As his correspondence and his theater works prove, Machiavelli was a thinker of wit and sensitivity; this lighter side of the man often styled a dark genius is captured by Salman Rushdie in his rollicking novel *The Enchantress of Florence.*

Engraved portrait of Niccolò Machiavelli

Whisky Galore
Compton Mackenzie (1883–1972)

Saved by Shipwrecked Scotch in the Hebrides

When Sergeant-Major Alfred Ernest Odd, on leave from the army in February 1943, returns to the Hebridean islands of Little and Great Todday, he discovers that wartime rationing has brought about the unthinkable: The islanders are running out of whisky! Now, on the Toddays the daily dram is truly *uisge beatha*, the "water of life." So it's no surprise that "the drought" begins to put everyone on edge, disrupting the smooth course of island affairs to the point of jeopardizing the marriage plans of Sergeant Odd himself.

Fortune, however, eventually smiles on the islanders. The SS *Cabinet Minister*, bound for New York, runs aground a few hundred yards from Little Todday with a cargo of liquid gold: thousands and thousands of bottles of first-class whisky. "It may be doubted if such a representative collection of various whiskies has ever been assembled before." The roll call of the shipwrecked brands is itself very nearly intoxicating: "There were Highland Gold and Highland Heart, Tartan Milk and Tartan Perfection, Bluebell, Northern Light, Preston Pans," and so on through Queen of the Glens, Bonnie Doon, Auld Stuart's, and Fingal's Cave. Before you can say *slàinte mhath, slàinte*

mhor ("good health, great health"), a parched band of industrious Toddaymen, working in their boats under cover of darkness, have relieved the stranded *Minister*'s packed hold of *uisge beatha gu leòir*—"whisky galore!" Life on the Toddays is soon back to normal, or maybe it's even better than ever. And the sergeant-major is finally able to call Peggy Joseph his wife.

Based on events surrounding the 1941 shipwreck of the SS *Politician* off the island of Eriskay, Compton Mackenzie's spirited novel is a tidily constructed comic yarn that unwinds with the irresistible narrative momentum of a tall tale.

What: Novel. **When:** 1947. **Edition:** *Whisky Galore* is available as part of *The Highland Omnibus* (Penguin, 1983), which also includes Mackenzie's *The Monarch of the Glen* (1941) and *The Rival Monster* (1952). **Also By:** *The Four Winds of Love* (six volumes, 1937–45). *Thin Ice* (1956). *My Life and Times* (1963–71). **Further Reading:** The facts underlying Mackenzie's fiction are explored in Roger Hutchinson's *Polly: The True Story Behind "Whisky Galore."* **Try:** *The Secret of Santa Vittoria* by Robert Crichton. **Adaptation:** Alexander Mackendrick's 1949 film *Whisky Galore!* is considered one of the best of the classic comedies from Britain's Ealing Studios. In the United States, because of a ban on using the names of alcoholic beverages in movie titles, *Whisky Galore!* became *Tight Little Island*.

Eastern Approaches
Fitzroy Maclean (1911–1996)

An Incredible 20th-Century Man of Action

A superlatively well-written account of momentous doings and stirring times, *Eastern Approaches* has long claimed a spot on the shelf of adventure masterpieces. Anyone interested in twentieth-century history or

susceptible to the romance of undercover intrigue will be enthralled by Fitzroy Maclean's ripping memoir. First published in 1949, it relates the exploits that occupied the young Eton- and Cambridge-educated author during the years immediately before and after the outbreak of World War II. With the shrewd and rakish fearlessness of a true man of action, Maclean intrepidly snooped around Stalin's off-limits Russia in the late 1930s. Then he helped found Britain's legendary SAS (Special Air Service) and spearheaded daring raids behind Rommel's Afrika Korps lines in the Western Desert. In 1943, he parachuted into German-occupied Yugoslavia as Prime Minister Churchill's personal representative; for two years he commanded the British mission that was supporting Marshal Tito's partisans. Maclean, in short, dashed from one hot spot to the next, with scarcely a lull.

Best of all for the reader, these astonishing, courageous, history-making exploits are narrated in prose that's so fluid, muscular, and rattlingly paced that Maclean could probably have made walking the dog sound gripping, had he ever stooped to anything quite so mundane.

Fitzroy Maclean, ca. 1965

What: Adventure. History. Memoir. **When:** 1949. **Edition:** The first American edition was titled *Escape to Adventure. Also By: Disputed Barricade: The Life and Times of Josip Broz-Tito, Marshal of Yugoslavia* (1957). *Highlanders: A History of the Scottish Clans* (1995). *Further Reading: Fitzroy Maclean* by Frank McLynn. *Past Forgetting: A Memoir of Heroes, Adventure, Love* and *Life with Fitzroy Maclean* by Veronica Maclean. *Try: A Man Called Intrepid* by William Stevenson. *Footnote:* Was Fitzroy Maclean a model for Ian Fleming's James Bond? It was often said—though not by him—that he was. For another writer also said to have inspired 007, see *Brazilian Adventure* (page 285).

Confessions of a Philosopher

A JOURNEY THROUGH WESTERN PHILOSOPHY

Bryan Magee (born 1930)

An Invitation to Explore the Life of the Mind

Until I was five I shared a bed with my sister, three and a half years older than me. After our parents had switched out the light we would chatter away in the darkness until we fell asleep. But I could never afterwards remember falling asleep. It was always the same: one moment I was talking to my sister in the dark, and the next I was waking up in a sunlit room having been asleep all night.

So begins this remarkable memoir, with a vignette that has the emblematic assurance of a Dutch painting, one no doubt labeled "The Philosopher Is Called to His Vocation." "That going to sleep was something I did every night yet never experienced was for years a source of active mystification to me," the author continues, inviting us to recognize—with an easily familiar example—just how much life gives us to think about.

Bryan Magee has spent a lifetime pursuing the study of philosophy, both as writer and as teacher (at Oxford as well as at several universities in the United States), and his *Confessions* offers the most engaging introduction to the flavor and relevance of philosophical pursuit that any contemporary reader is likely to discover. He roots the fundamentals of philosophy in the wonder provoked by everyday experience, pondering the nature of reality and the limitations of knowing with the same freshness of mind that characterized the inquiry and surprise of that young boy awakening into new light. More broadly, his colorfully composed account of his own education and career provides readers a lucid and inviting medium through which to contemplate philosophical ideas and their historical development. From Plato to Schopenhauer to Karl Popper, from the pre-Socratics to the logical positivists to the existentialists, Magee plots the progress of humanity's search for meaning while narrating his own, doing both with expressive eloquence and invigorating intellectual rigor.

What: Philosophy. Autobiography. *When:* 1999. *Also By:* On Blindness: Letters Between Bryan Magee and Martin Milligan (1995). The Philosophy of Schopenhauer (1997). The Story of Philosophy (1999). The Great Philosophers (2001). *Try: What Does It All Mean?* by Thomas Nagel. *Sophie's World: A Novel About the History of Philosophy* by Jostein Gaarder. *Think: A Compelling Introduction to Philosophy* by Simon Blackburn.

NORMAN MAILER
(1923–2007)

Two photos vie for the reader's attention on the back cover of the original edition of Norman Mailer's 1967 novel, *Why Are We in Vietnam?* One, in black and white, is a close-up of the author's face in earnest pose. The other, a color snapshot that looms over the first, presents a portrait of the artist with a ripe black eye; it exudes an aura of wary and none-too-sober belligerence. The contrast between the two pictures is summed up by the caption that accompanies them, invoking a question engendered by the writer's personal history of public antics, exhibitionism, and troubling fascination with violence: "Will the real Norman Mailer please stand up?" Like Orson Welles, who despite no end of creative scuttling could never pass out of the shadows thrown by *Citizen Kane*, Mailer—in the wake of his own stunning debut, the critically and popularly acclaimed World War II novel *The Naked and the Dead*—went on to diffuse his enormous talent into alternately (and sometimes simultaneously) brilliant and benighted projects that too often were less than the sum of their dazzling parts. And yet, as with Welles's distinctive imagery, Mailer's vivid intelligence illuminated a portion of any page he wrote, no matter his subject.

Norman Mailer, 1969

Which is a way of saying that Mailer's genius may not be best served by the need to choose specific volumes to represent it (the same is true of his contemporary and occasional combatant, Gore Vidal, see page 822). Still, in two books, *The Armies of the Night* and *The Executioner's Song*, his inspiration held true from first page to last, and these works—the former antic and ebullient, the latter unadorned, somber, and impersonal—offer a fitting introduction to his outsize ambitions and his idiosyncratic yet influential expansion of the possibilities of imaginative prose.

The Armies of the Night
HISTORY AS A NOVEL, THE NOVEL AS HISTORY
A Political Picaresque

It was not until he composed the autobiographical interludes that knit together his unwieldy 1959 anthology, *Advertisements for Myself*, that Mailer found a style fit for the peculiarities of his perception. The quarrelsome, insightful, digressive, metaphorical, freewheeling voice revealed in those passages would go on to shape the extraordinary journalistic essays that distinguished his work in the early 1960s (especially worth seeking out are "Superman Comes to the Supermarket," his report on the 1960 Democratic convention, which nominated John F. Kennedy for president, and "Ten Thousand Words a Minute," an account of the first heavyweight title bout between Sonny Liston and Floyd Patterson and a dynamic meditation on journalism, boxing, and death).

Mailer's forays into nonfiction reached their most satisfying destination in *The Armies of the Night*, a third-person account of his adventures during the 1967 March on the Pentagon to protest the war in Vietnam. Chronicling his drunken performance before an audience at Washington's Ambassador Theater the night before the march, then his own arrest and brief incarceration the following day, Mailer minutely observes the assembled forces of the

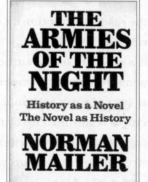

THE ARMIES OF THE NIGHT

History as a Novel
The Novel as History

NORMAN MAILER

demonstrators (including literary colleagues such as Robert Lowell and Dwight Macdonald), the police who confront them, and the passing passions of the zeitgeist these opposing forces embody. As acutely aware of the limitations of the Left's assumptions as he is of the dangers of the Right's violent sanctimony, he nonetheless casts the keenest eye on the intuitions and pretensions of his protagonist, "Norman Mailer." By injecting this ambiguous comic hero into the center of his narrative of a historical event, Mailer etches a penetrating and very funny portrait of a nation in the throes of a soul-searing political fever. The book's baroque style and picaresque mode is both a send-up of the earnest New Journalism of its era and its most idiosyncratic and memorable product.

What: Journalism. History. Memoir. *When:* 1968. *Awards:* Pulitzer Prize for General Nonfiction, and National Book Award for Arts and Letters, both in 1969. *Also By:* In the aftermath of *Armies*, Mailer would produce a number of journalistic works in the same rich vein, notably *Miami and the Siege of Chicago* (1968) and *Of a Fire on the Moon* (1970). The latter, a report on the Apollo moon landing, contains detailed descriptions of the technology of space flight that are trenchant and telling. *Try: Fear and Loathing: On the Campaign Trail '72* by Hunter S. Thompson. *The Briar Patch: The People of the State of New York v. Lumumba Shakur et al.* by Murray Kempton. *Political Fictions* by Joan Didion.

The Executioner's Song
An American Epic of Crime and Punishment

Brenda was six when she fell out of the apple tree. She climbed to the top and the limb with the good apples broke off. Gary caught her as the branch came scraping down. They were scared. The apple trees were their grandmother's best crop and it was forbidden to climb in the orchard. . . .

She was six and he was seven and she thought he was swell.

After the imaginative and verbal fecundity of Mailer's work throughout the 1960s and 1970s, in which the ornate sentences seemed to be feasting on some literary Miracle-Gro, the stripped-down prose of his massive book about the murderer Gary Gilmore is shocking. Its declarative simplicity pulls the reader urgently through a landscape of violence, emptiness, and everyday family bewilderment that is as profound and dramatic a depiction of American life as Mailer would draw; in its secret modulations of cadence and image, the writing is as artful as any he ever composed. Despite its journalistic pedigree, Mailer subtitled the book "A True Life Novel," and it was awarded the Pulitzer Prize for Fiction.

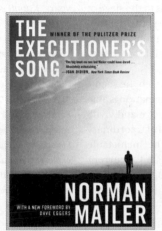

"This book," the author writes in his afterword, "does its best to be a factual account of the activities of Gary Gilmore and the men and women associated with him in the period from April 9, 1976, when he was released from the United States Penitentiary at Marion, Illinois, until his execution a little more than nine months later in Utah State Prison." The first half of the narrative, "Western Voices," tracks Gilmore's uneasy reentry into society after more than a decade of incarceration for various crimes, detailing his relations with his family, his romance with Nicole Barrett, and the vicious murders that would lead to a death sentence—a sentence he refused to appeal.

The second half, "Eastern Voices," records the legal wrangles and journalistic opportunism that turned Gilmore's atrocities—and the tragedies of his victims—into a media frenzy. Mailer based his chronicle in large part on interviews conducted by Lawrence Schiller, who secured media rights to Gilmore's story and thus became both a character in *The Executioner's Song* and a partner of sorts in its creation.

Violence, crime, misdirected courage, perilous love, dreams of reincarnation, institutional insularity, the senseless and insatiable hunger of mass media—the themes that haunt the one thousand pages of *The Executioner's Song* are a catalog of the author's enduring preoccupations. Yet, only in this book—in which Mailer refrains from engaging them directly and offers little embellishment to the simple narration of incident, event, and emotion—did he create a work of literature in which characters brought these themes to life, and death.

What: Novel. Journalism. *When:* 1979. *Award:* Pulitzer Prize for Fiction, 1980. *Also By: Harlot's Ghost* (1991). *Oswald's Tale: An American Mystery* (1995). *Further Reading: Shot in the Heart* by Mikal Gilmore is a superbly written family memoir by Gary's younger brother. *Try: In Cold Blood* by Truman Capote (see page 125). *Adaptation:* Mailer scripted the 1982 television film, which stars Tommy Lee Jones.

Kaputt
Curzio Malaparte (1898–1957)

A War Novel Like No Other

Nothing can convey better than this hard, mysterious German word Kaputt—which literally means, "broken, finished, gone to pieces, gone to ruin," the sense of what we are, of what Europe is—a pile of rubble.

Originally published in Naples in 1943, this novel—which might be more accurately described as a personal narrative in which the inspirations of fiction try to keep pace with the horrors of reality—was inspired by Malaparte's time as a correspondent on the Eastern Front during the two previous years. In the opening scene, a cultivated conversation with Prince Eugene of Sweden (brother of King Gustav V) and Axel Munthe (the internationally celebrated doctor and famous author of *The Story of San Michele*) sets the stage sardonically for the savagery to come, as the narrator will soon embark upon a journey through surreal landscapes of atrocity to bear witness to the siege of Leningrad, the massacre of Jews, the depravity of Nazi leaders and their minions, and the comprehensive, incomprehensible obscenity of humanity itself.

The narrator has seen so much, he seems possessed by his visions: His imagination is able to engage all the horrors of the age and vivify them in episode upon episode of extraordinary power, each contributing to the ineluctable verdict that is this novel's title and recurrent theme. The reader is led through a museum of destruction by a guide with the sensitivity

of Proust—sounds and smells waft their way across pages, borders, years—and the battered instincts of a front-line correspondent. There is not one scene or setting that is reminiscent of any other novel of World War II, and there are several—the desperate horses frozen in the ice of Lake Ladoga is one—that will haunt you for years. *Kaputt* is one of the great neglected books of our time.

What: War. Novel. *When:* 1943; English translation by Cesare Foligno, 1949. *Also By: The Volga Rises in Europe* (1943). *The Skin* (1949). *Those Cursed Tuscans* (1956). *Try: Every Man Dies Alone* by Hans Fallada. *Life and Fate* by Vasily Grossman (see page 337). *Catch-22* by Joseph Heller (see page 362). *Footnote:* The book *Malaparte: A House Like Me*, by Michael McDonough, explores the extraordinary house—the setting for Jean-Luc Godard's 1963 film, *Contempt*—that Malaparte built on the island of Capri.

In the Freud Archives
Janet Malcolm (born 1934)

Extraordinary Drama Behind the Psychoanalytic Curtain

Founded in 1951, the Sigmund Freud Archives were established to collect, conserve, and make available to scholars materials related to the life and work of the father of psychoanalysis. The name evokes the image of august chambers paneled in solemnity. But in Janet Malcolm's penetrating profile of one turbulent period in the history of the Archives (the late 1970s and early 1980s), another picture emerges, one colored with the fireworks set off by the clash of petty egos and unbridled ids. It is a compelling, intelligent, and even amusing tale of personalities and ideas wrangling in the shadow of Freud's influence.

There are three figures at the center of Malcolm's chronicle, each one brilliant in his own way. First is Kurt Eissler, an eminent

analyst and author "of profound erudition and prodigious industry" who, in its first three decades, was the guiding hand behind the Archives. Second is Jeffrey Moussaieff Masson, a professor of Sanskrit who came late to psychoanalysis yet managed to quickly enter its inner sanctum. Through a combination of charm, deference, scholarship, temerity, and cunning, he soon found himself, by Eissler's good graces, appointed the Archives' project director for a new edition of Freud's complete correspondence. Older scholars who had tried for years to gain access to the trove of unpublished sources Masson now had control over were filled with venomous envy toward this upstart, and things only got worse when Masson began to question not only the master's theories, but his fundamental honesty. Freud's daughter and Masson's mentor were not pleased: "Anna Freud and Eissler dropped me," Masson tells Malcolm. "Analysts won't speak to me. They avoid me on the street. They are afraid to be seen with me." The third of the book's protagonists, and perhaps the most intriguing, is an independent scholar named Peter Swales. A former assistant to the Rolling Stones and a self-taught Freud expert, Swales has a knack for research that helps him uncover undiscovered primary sources that generations of historians of psychoanalysis have overlooked.

In the Freud Archives is an engrossing account of what happened between these three men during Masson's stormy tenure as project director. It is a smart, swift narrative enlivened by Swales's renegade energy and Malcolm's devastating profile of Masson, whose insufferable personality—drawn largely in his own words—is dumbfounding, to say the least. Although there is no murder, Malcolm's nonfiction tale delivers all the pleasures—eccentric personalities, gripping questions of motive and evidence, conflict in a clubby setting—of a topflight mystery.

What: Psychology. Journalism. *When:* 1984. *Edition:* The New York Review Books Classics edition includes a 1997 afterword by the author. *Also By: Psychoanalysis: The Impossible Profession* (1981). *The Journalist and the Murderer* (1990). *The Silent Woman: Sylvia Plath and Ted Hughes* (1994). *Reading Chekhov: A Critical Journey* (2001). *Further Reading: The Assault on Truth: Freud's Suppression of the Seduction Theory* by Jeffrey Moussaieff Masson. *Try: Revolution in Mind* by George Makari. *Footnote:* In 1984, Masson sued Malcolm for libel, alleging the *New Yorker* journalist had maliciously fabricated quotations that were presented as his exact words. Protracted litigation followed, with aspects of the case being adjudicated by the Supreme Court (*Masson v. The New Yorker Magazine, Inc. et al,* 501 US 496 [1991]), before a jury ruled against Masson in 1994.

A Book of One's Own
PEOPLE AND THEIR DIARIES
Thomas Mallon (born 1951)

The Pleasures of Literary Eavesdropping

Keep: diaries are the only kind of writing to take that verb. One doesn't "keep" a poem or a letter or a novel, not as one actually writes it. But diaries are so much about the preservation and protection of the self that they demand the word right from the moment they're being composed.

Connoisseurs of reading reserve a special shelf for volumes of diaries and letters: There's something special about the immediacy and provisional nature of the invention that enlivens the pleasures of their prose. "In diaries, as in life," suggests Thomas Mallon, "people are much more changeable than they are in novels." Diaries in particular offer a kind of communion with the writer—a participation, almost, in the writing—that neither memoir nor fiction can.

In this singular, curious, deeply satisfying book, Mallon surveys the land of diaries, traversing centuries and continents to consider the works and days, the thoughts and passions, the doubts and delights of scores of diarists. He is a sensitive reader, inquisitive and informative, with a fine attention to the quirks and qualities of the material under his inspection. And he's a wonderful, amusing stylist in his own right, as his comments on the youthful entries of the novelist Evelyn Waugh—"[he] is so often drunk in the twenties that one doesn't so much read his diaries as marinate in them"— and the psychoanalyst Karen Horney—"One can hear the girl turning into the doctor right at the comma"—make clear.

Mallon has organized his subject by grouping his scribblers together as Chroniclers, Travelers, Pilgrims, Creators, Apologists, Confessors, and Prisoners, and the people met under each rubric—from Samuel Pepys to Virginia Woolf, Francis Kilvert to Clara Milburn, George Templeton Strong to Thomas Merton, Trotsky to Lindbergh, Anne Frank to

Albert Speer—are an engrossing lot. His capsule portraits of each diarist and his or her methods and milieus cohere into a compelling gallery of human experience, one that illustrates the fascinating opacity of private lives and the surprises of self and circumstance that every day delivers to even the most reflective individuals. An excellent, enticing bibliography supplements Mallon's text.

What: Diaries & Letters. Literary Criticism. *When:* 1984; reissued with new introduction by the author, 1995. *Also By: Stolen Words: Forays into the Origins and Ravages of Plagiarism* (1989). *Yours Ever: People and Their Letters* (2009). *Further Reading: The Pleasures of Diaries: Four Centuries of Private Writing,* edited by Ronald Blythe. *Try: The Diary of Samuel Pepys* (see page 622). *Kilvert's Diary* by Francis Kilvert (see page 445). *A Moment's Liberty* by Virginia Woolf (see page 868).

The Voices of Silence
André Malraux (1901–1976)

A Testament to Human Creativity

This is a wonder book of a curious kind, a magician's explication of the spells that artists—from the cave painters of antiquity to the masters of the Renaissance to Rembrandt and Cézanne—have cast over both time and eternity. Art, André Malraux argues, has a life of its own, and in *The Voices of Silence* he attempts to catch its profound and protean essence.

The specific spells in question are represented by the more than six hundred reproductions of works from all epochs and nations that he presents in illustration of his idea that modern printing technology allows us to make of our cultural inheritance a "museum without walls." (Note: He was writing decades before the internet would make his metaphor more vivid than he could ever imagine.) Beginning with a discussion of the way the museum has changed our understanding of art, he sets out on an expedition to investigate the evolution of the creative act and apprehend what it reveals about human nature (and about human intuitions of the divine as well). His traversal of artistic legacies and living traditions from ancient India to Picasso's Paris is probing and ruminative, alternately exact, as in his many astute examinations of individual artists, and speculative, as in his frequent reliance on his considerable eloquence to connect the dots of his inquiries into, in Edmund Wilson's phrase, "mankind's passion and purpose."

Malraux was a man of action (his early adventures in Indochina fueled several works of

André Malraux at home, ca. 1953

fiction), letters (his 1933 novel *Man's Fate* is widely regarded as a twentieth-century masterpiece), and politics (he served as France's first minister of cultural affairs under Charles de Gaulle). How he managed to sit still long enough to compose this massive book—itself a distillation of his even more extensive, three-volume *Psychology of Art* (1947–49)—is something of a marvel, to some degree explained by the energy and liveliness of the mind that animates its pages. What a thrill it is to follow Malraux's thoughts as he spins them into intimations, theories, and majestic perspectives. He is learned rather than scholarly, and as a result his big book is something like a museum itself, one we can tour at our leisure, all the while listening to the most cultivated voice in our ear. Rich and wise, a bottomless well of absorption, *The Voices of Silence* is a volume for the permanent library, one to be revisited at will and opened at random again and again. It's a lifelong talisman for any curious reader.

What: Art. When: 1951; English translation by Stuart Gilbert, 1953. Also By: Nonfiction: The Metamorphosis of the Gods (1957); Anti-Memoirs (1967); Picasso's Mask (1974). Fiction: Man's Hope (1938). Try: The Roots of Civilization by Alexander Marshack (see page 527). The Geography of the Imagination by Guy Davenport (see page 198).

Goodbye, Darkness
A MEMOIR OF THE PACIFIC WAR
William Manchester (1922–2004)

The Costs of Combat

In the incredibly powerful opening pages of *Goodbye, Darkness*, William Manchester describes the first time he killed a Japanese soldier. It happened during combat on the island of Okinawa in 1945, and it left the young marine utterly shattered—sobbing and trembling and soiled by his own piss and vomit. It illustrates the memorable point that he makes later on: "War is never understated. Combat as I saw it was exorbitant, outrageous, excruciating, and above all tasteless."

Manchester fought at Okinawa, Guadalcanal, and in other famous Pacific island battles during the furious struggle with Japan at the close of the war. Three decades later, he found himself troubled by nightmares arising from repressed memories of those experiences. "It was ironic. For years I had been trying to write about the war, always in vain. It lay too deep; I couldn't reach it." Now his recollections were surfacing unbidden. So in 1978 the renowned historian and biographer revisited the Pacific. "The chief reason for going," he reflects, "was to try to find what I had lost out there and retrieve

"The most moving memoir of combat in World War II that I have read."
—*William L. Shirer on* Goodbye, Darkness

Marine charging during the Battle of Okinawa, 1945

it. Not only would I go back to my islands; I would visit all the major battlefields to discover, if possible, what we had done there and why we had done it, the ultimate secrets of time and place and dimension and being."

The result of Manchester's pilgrimage is a visceral, devastating, emotional, and deeply moving book, a multifaceted portrait of the war in the Pacific theater that is distinguished by its fidelity to the fate of soldiers.

What: War. History. Memoir. *When:* 1980. *Also By: The Death of a President: November 20–November 25, 1963* (1967). *American Caesar: Douglas MacArthur, 1880–1964* (1978). *The Last Lion: Winston Spencer Churchill,* volume 1: *Visions of Glory 1874–1932* (1983); volume 2: *Alone, 1932–1940* (1988). *Try: With the Old Breed: At Peleliu and Okinawa* by E. B. Sledge. *Guadalcanal Diary* by Richard Tregaskis. *Utmost Savagery: The Three Days of Tarawa* by Col. Joseph H. Alexander.

Hope Against Hope
Nadezhda Mandelstam (1899–1980)

Bold Poetry, Bitter Truths, Brave Witness

Osip Mandelstam (1891–1938) was the foremost Russian poet of the twentieth century. Late in the year 1933, he wrote a poem mocking Josef Stalin, the leader of the Soviet Union. When the scathing verses came to the attention of the authorities, Mandelstam was arrested and sent into exile; arrested again in 1938, he died in a labor camp later that year.

Nadezhda Mandelstam shared the life of the poet from 1919 until his disappearance into the gulag; their marriage, while unconventional, weathered the most turbulent years in Russian history. In their nearly two decades together, the couple was constantly on the move, and Nadezhda made great personal sacrifices in support of her husband's creativity; she accompanied him into exile and worked as a translator to earn their keep. For decades after his death she preserved his work, often in her own memory, until it no longer had to be kept secret.

In 1964, Nadezhda began writing this powerful chronicle of the years between Osip's first arrest and his death. The resulting memoir is one of the most formidable books of the twentieth century, a towering achievement that was hailed in the *New York Times Book Review* as "the most luminous account we have—or are

likely to get—of life in the Soviet Union during the purges of the 1930s." In addition to being a fierce and detailed testament to the hellishness of life under Stalin's terror, *Hope Against Hope* is a moving love story, one that happens to offer considerable insight into the poetic process. And although Osip and other writers, especially poet Anna Akhmatova, are Nadezhda's primary focus, her impassioned narrative also gives readers a vivid impression of the indomitable author herself, whom Clarence Brown, in his introduction, describes as "a vinegary, Brechtian, steel-hard woman of great intelligence, limitless courage, no illusions, permanent convictions and a wild sense of the absurdity of life." Once met in these pages, Nadezhda Mandelstam is impossible to forget.

What: Memoir. Literature. *When:* 1970, in Max Hayward's English translation. *Also By:* In *Hope Abandoned,* published in 1972, the author tells the story of her life before and after the years described in *Hope Against Hope. Further Reading:* By Osip Mandelstam: *Selected Poems,* translated by Clarence Brown and W. S. Merwin, and *The Noise of Time: Selected Prose,* translated by Clarence Brown. *Try: Moscow Memoirs* by Emma Gerstein. *The Whisperers: Private Life in Stalin's Russia* by Orlando Figes. *Footnote: Hope Against Hope* is a play on words: In Russian, *nadezhda* means "hope."

Ongoingness
THE END OF A DIARY
Sarah Manguso (born 1974)

The Continuous Life

This is a very small book: fewer than a hundred pages, many of them covered with text for only half of their expanse. It collects thoughts and observations in concise, discrete segments of prose, often just a single sentence, as if the author were assembling a kind of secular devotional to document and amplify her contemplation of her days.

Composed as a kind of pendant to the massive diary that poet and memoirist Manguso kept for a quarter century, which runs to 800,000 words (that diary being, she writes in an afterword, "the writing that stands in for my entire life"), *Ongoingness* is a series of reflections on her obsessive impulse to record life, her urge to memorialize it in words, in the shadow of her growing recognition of how effortlessly time evades capture. Alert enough to temper its certainties with the erosive force of time's indifferent hand, Manguso's museum of aperçus tells us so much about writing, love,

marriage, motherhood, and mortality, with such poignant realism, that one ponders her words with gratitude and wonder. Every page seems to carry an epiphany: "Today was very full, but the problem isn't today. It's tomorrow. I'd be able to recover from today if it weren't for tomorrow. There should be extra days, buffer days, between the real days." And: "I used to exist against the continuity of time. Then I became the baby's continuity, a background of ongoing time for him to live against."

In short, *Ongoingness* is a volume to treasure: a rendering of time that is both usefully wise and entirely exhilarating.

What: Autobiography. Diaries & Letters. *When:* 2015. *Also By: The Two Kinds of Decay* (2008). *The Guardians: An Elegy for a Friend* (2012). *300 Arguments: Essays* (2017). *Try: Within the Context of No Context* by George W. S. Trow (see page 807). *Artful* by Ali Smith (see page 728). *Dept. of Speculation* by Jenny Offill.

> **"I tried to record each moment, but time isn't made of moments; it contains moments. There is more to it than moments."** —*Sarah Manguso, from* Ongoingness

The Magic Mountain
Thomas Mann (1875–1955)

A Fairy Tale of Cultural Disease

Critics have consecrated three enormous novels of the first decades of the twentieth century as the holy trinity of European modernist fiction, and two of them are especially forbidding. James Joyce's *Ulysses* (see page 422), dense with wordplay, opaque Irish jokes, and intricacies of architecture and allusion, is not

for beginners. Marcel Proust's *In Search of Lost Time* (see page 644), three thousand pages long, with sentences that snake through unbroken paragraphs in tireless exposition of emotional states that take many pages to resolve, can feel like a protracted course in applied patience. But *The Magic Mountain*, Thomas Mann's sly, satirical novel of illness and civilization in the years before World War I, is supremely readable;

more than any other modern novel of its caliber, it's a book you can take to bed with you, for its slow unwinding of individual destinies within a communal setting evokes something akin to the feelings you might have watching the most high-minded miniseries ever filmed. Which is not to say it isn't profound, and funny, too, filled with human foibles of every kind and replete with sexual as well as intellectual passions. All told, its unprecedented fusion of realism and symbolism appeals to the heart as much as the brain.

Thomas Mann, ca. 1916

Set almost entirely at a sanatorium in the Swiss Alps, where well-to-do patients from across Europe are recovering from tuberculosis, *The Magic Mountain* tells the story of Hans Castorp, a young man from Hamburg, who arrives to pay a short visit to his ailing cousin Joachim. But his stay at the International Sanatorium Berghof (Dr. Behrens, supervising physician) ends up lasting much longer than he'd planned: Seven years later, he's still there breathing the mountain air, unable to return to the world below. (Not for nothing does Mann assert, in his very short foreword to this enormous narrative, that the story we are about to read has a number of things in common with fairy tales.) Up on the mountain "uniformity reigns, movement from point to point is no longer movement; and where movement is no longer movement, there is no time."

In the timeless and sickly idyll that Castorp embraces more than suffers, he meets a rotating cast of invalids who debate all the political and philosophical questions of the day, with pages left over for gossiping about one another's predilections. The disease of Castorp and his fellow patients is Europe's illness, Mann implies, and, for all its liveliness of character and incident, the novel is an elegy for a culture that the author inferred was approaching its demise. When Castorp finally comes down from the mountain at the very end of the book, he falls in the violence of the continent's total war. The profound, caustic irony of Mann's

masterpiece is that it begins disguised as a classic bildungsroman, a "novel of education" in which a young protagonist goes through trials that prepare him for life, and slowly reveals itself to be something else entirely: an elaborate fable of arrested development, a depiction of the futile energies that surround but never assuage our apprehension of mortality.

The elegiac tone pervades Mann's work from *Buddenbrooks* (1901) through *Death in Venice* (1925) and *Doctor Faustus* (1947), infusing his imagined worlds with the sense of an unavoidable ending—and of an unconsummated, unconsummatable desire. Paradoxically, it's matched with a furtive streak of urbane amusement that underlines how the creations of human culture—mercantile, aesthetic, ideological—are in the end no match for the biological imperatives and historical entropies that conspire against them. In his stories and novels, especially *The Magic Mountain*, Mann managed nonetheless to find a perfection of form to honor the imperfections of our lives.

What: Novel. *When:* 1924. *Editions:* The 1996 translation by John E. Woods has supplanted the original English version by H. T. Lowe-Porter. *Award:* Nobel Prize in Literature, 1929. *Also By: Disorder and Early Sorrow* (1925). *Mario and the Magician* (1930). *Joseph and His Brothers* (comprising four novels published individually between 1933 and 1943). *Try: The Man Without Qualities* by Robert Musil (see page 578).

A Place of Greater Safety
Hilary Mantel (born 1952)

The Best of Times and the Worst of Times

Hilary Mantel is one of the most admired and decorated novelists in Britain today, as the popular and critical acclaim of her two Man Booker Prize–winning novels on the life of Thomas Cromwell—*Wolf Hall* and *Bring Up the Bodies*—have proved. Yet her success was not predestined, a fact illustrated by the slow fate of her first novel, *A Place of Greater Safety*. Although she finished writing it in 1979, it found its way into print only in 1992, after years of rejections from publishers who thought that historical fiction was lightweight by definition, a once pervasive attitude that Mantel's own work has done much to change. In each of her novels, historical or contemporary, she displays the same exacting command, telling stories with an unfussy directness that is both precise and intense.

In *A Place of Greater Safety*, we meet three ambitious young men whose lives will be forged in the crucible of revolution—provincials who've arrived in Paris just in time for the storming of the Bastille. They are the fiery journalist Camille Desmoulins, the pragmatic and hideously ugly orator Georges Danton, and the "incorruptible" lawyer Maximilien de Robespierre. These three friends luxuriate in the upheaval of 1789, and as the old order collapses, they establish themselves at the heart of the emergent government. But soon revolutionary fervor gives way to the violence of the Reign of Terror, and Robespierre's uncompromising virtue places him at odds with the more moderate and more libertine Danton. "It's you idealists who make the best tyrants," Danton tells Robespierre. To which l'Incorruptible responds—in the modern speech that is a hallmark of Mantel's historical novels—"It seems a bit late to be having this conversation. I've had to take up violence now, and so much else. We should have discussed it last year."

Mantel does much more here than narrate the story of the French Revolution. She brings it to life, fleshing out the dreams and the desires of men and women who changed the world, intertwining personal upheavals with political

Illustration of the storming of the Bastille, July 14, 1789

ones to render history as a living thing. On Mantel's pages, the past becomes as vibrant—and as anxious—as the present.

What: Novel. *When:* 1992. *Also By: Fludd* (1989). *A Change of Climate* (1994). *An Experiment in Love* (1995).

Beyond Black (2005). *Further Reading: Citizens: A Chronicle of the French Revolution* by Simon Schama. *Try: The Year of the French* by Thomas Flanagan. *The Siege of Krishnapur* by J. G. Farrell. *The Many Lives & Secret Sorrows of Josephine B.* by Sandra Gulland.

Mystery Train
IMAGES OF AMERICA IN ROCK 'N' ROLL MUSIC
Greil Marcus (born 1945)

"Probably the best book ever written about rock." —Rolling Stone

When *Mystery Train* was published in 1975, it was unanimously hailed as the best "rock book" ever. Not that it had a lot of competition. Relatively few serious books, good or bad, had been written about the music. That *Mystery Train* remains in the running for the distinction, however, is a tribute to Greil Marcus's early and still unrivaled discernment. Seeing rock as more than the music of the moment, he was able to trace its roots back to the cultural resources that nourished it, discovering as he did so what the music revealed about the "visions and versions of America" that inform our national imagination.

Marcus describes *Mystery Train* as "an attempt to broaden the context in which the music is heard; to deal with rock 'n' roll not as youth culture, or counterculture, but simply as American culture." He does this by analyzing the work of six artists. Two of them he calls "Ancestors": Harmonica Frank Floyd (1908–1984), an obscure "vocal contortionist" who developed "a music of staggering weirdness"; and Robert Johnson (1911–1938), the legendary Mississippi blues singer and guitarist. The other four Marcus labels "Inheritors." Of these, one—the songwriter and film composer Randy Newman—is still active today, while the rest are not: the group called The Band, best remembered for their work with Bob Dylan and their song "The Night They Drove Old Dixie Down"; Sly Stone, whose records with Sly and the Family Stone were characterized by a high-energy soul/rock sound; and Elvis Presley, who looms over the whole story like the gifted but doomed hero he was. Through close listening and a bold grasp of popular music's broader, deeper contexts, Marcus illuminates the character of "Ancestors" and "Inheritors" alike, revealing how their common intuitions and individual inspirations "dramatize a sense of what it is to be an American; what it means, what it's worth, what the stakes of life in America might be."

What: Music. Lifestyle & Pop Culture. *When:* 1975; sixth revised edition, 2015. *Also By: Lipstick Traces: A Secret History of the Twentieth Century* (1989). *Dead Elvis* (1991). *Invisible Republic: Bob Dylan's Basement Tapes* (1997; alternate title: *The Old Weird America*). *Like a Rolling Stone: Bob Dylan at the Crossroads* (2005). *The Shape of Things to Come: Prophecy and the American Voice* (2006). *Further Reading: Searching for Robert Johnson* by Peter Guralnick. *This Wheel's on Fire: Levon Helm and the Story of The Band* by Levon Helm with Stephen Davis. *Try: Chronicles, Volume One* by Bob Dylan.

Robert Johnson

The Infatuations
Javier Marías (born 1951)

A Meditative Masterwork Disguised as a Murder Mystery

In a Madrid café, María Dolz, the narrator of this novel, is attracted by the happiness of a married couple she observes there every morning. That happiness, so certain and unthreatened at first blush, will be short-lived; *The Infatuations* begins with an invocation of the last time María saw the husband, which was also, she relates, "the last time his wife, Luisa, saw him," before he was fatally stabbed in the street in an act of random violence.

Apparently random, that is. As María slowly becomes entangled—both speculatively and amorously—in the posthumous world of the victim's widow and associates, disturbing clues connect the brutal homicide to an unexpected web of deceit and passion. But readers opening *The Infatuations* expecting a thriller will be disappointed, for Javier Marías's novel, despite possessing the armature of a mystery, finds its energy not in its plot but rather in the metaphysical coils of its telling. In sinuous, exploratory sentences, María slowly unravels not only the evidence she uncovers about the couple that has infatuated her, but also the tenuous threads of coincidence, love, chance, time, and obsession that have connected her life to theirs.

Widely considered a major figure in contemporary Spanish literature, Marías is the prolific author of several novels in addition to his remarkable, twelve-hundred-page trilogy, *Your Face Tomorrow* (2002). His early labors as a translator—of Shakespeare, Sir Thomas Browne, Robert Louis Stevenson, Henry James, Joseph Conrad, and William Faulkner—inform his own prose with a singular combination of music and meaning. If it is a developed taste, it is a lasting one, for his style—digressive, allusive, pondering—brings a kind of psychological and aesthetic acuity to his work that invites readers (much as Proust does) into a new dimension. The mental intricacies of emotions, and the pulsing engagement of the present while past and future remain both looming and oblivious, are illuminated via a meandering inquiry that is both seductive and hypnotic. Reading Marías has the ruminative intensity and meditative calm of smoking a cigarette, without the carcinogenic consequences.

"What I love most," Marías has said of his own reading, "is something that leaves some trace, that leaves some echo, that once the book is closed, once you finish reading the book, it's still echoing in your mind—and not just for a couple of days, but for a long, long time." That is a fine description of the allure of *The Infatuations*.

What: Novel. *When:* 2011; English translation by Margaret Jull Costa, 2013. *Also By: The Man of Feeling* (1986). *All Souls* (1989). *Written Lives* (1992). *Tomorrow in the Battle Think on Me* (1994). *Dance and Dream* (2004). *Poison, Shadow, and Farewell* (2007). *Try: The Rings of Saturn* by W. G. Sebald. *The Speed of Light* by Javier Cercas.

West with the Night
Beryl Markham (1902–1986)

A Good Woman in Africa

When pioneer aviator Beryl Markham completed the first east-to-west solo flight across the Atlantic in 1936, her achievement was greeted with great fanfare. In 1942, she published *West with the Night*, the first-person account of her life and accomplishments in British East Africa—hunting with natives as a girl, training racing horses as a young woman, becoming a bush pilot and carrying mail, passengers, and supplies to the remote corners of the Sudan, Tanganyika, and Kenya—which culminates in her description of that historic transatlantic trip. The book, too, was greeted with acclaim, notably from Ernest Hemingway, who wrote, in a letter to his editor, Maxwell Perkins, "she has written so . . . marvelously well, that I was completely ashamed of myself as a writer." Yet somehow *West with the Night* fell off readers' radar.

It remained forgotten until the 1980s, when a new edition appeared (with Hemingway's praise gracing the back cover). Thus, in the year of her death, Markham became a celebrity and bestselling author all over again, the reading public embracing what Hemingway called her "bloody wonderful book." In the end, his envy may have been misplaced. Since Markham's death, there has been some speculation that the book was penned by her lover, and later husband, screenwriter Raoul Schumacher. With the manuscript missing, Markham's authorship is not likely to be proved or disproved, but *West with the Night* is a stunningly written story of a remarkable life, regardless of who wrote it—as passages like this one surely prove:

WEST WITH THE NIGHT

BERYL MARKHAM

Like all oceans, the Indian Ocean seems never to end, and the ships that sail on it are small and slow. They have no speed, nor any sense of urgency; they do not cross the water, they live on it until the land comes home.

What: Autobiography. **When:** 1942. **Also By:** Markham's eight short stories, some of which are believed to have been cowritten with Schumacher, are published as *The Splendid Outcast* (1987). *Further Reading:* Two biographies: *The Lives of Beryl Markham* by Errol Trzebinski and *Straight on Till Morning* by Mary S. Lovell. *Try:* The African memoirs of Markham's friend Karen Blixen (who wrote as Isak Dinesen; see page 225), *Out of Africa* and *Shadows on the Grass*. Also, *The Flame Trees of Thika: Memories of an African Childhood* by Elspeth Huxley. *Adaptations:* There are no direct adaptations of the book, but Markham's life was the subject of a 1986 PBS documentary, *A World Without Walls*, and the 1988 TV movie *Beryl Markham: A Shadow on the Sun*.

---

the lives and times of archy and mehitabel
Don Marquis (1878–1937)

The Greatest Cockroach Poet of All Time

As E. B. White put it in his introduction to a 1950 reissue of this volume, "Among books of humor by American authors, there are only a handful that rest solidly on the shelf. This . . . is one of those books. It is funny, it is wise, it is tender, and it is tough." And it is written by a cockroach.

The remarkable archy first appeared in 1916, in Don Marquis's newspaper column for the *New York Sun*. A cockroach who had a former existence as a *vers libre* bard, archy composed his comic commentaries on the world at large late at night, by hurling himself headfirst onto each key of the sleeping Marquis's typewriter (the logistics of holding down the shift key are too much for an insect to manage, which accounts for his trademark lowercase). His poetic compositions recount his adventures, often with his companion mehitabel, a cat in her ninth life who claims to be a reincarnation of Cleopatra and who occasionally commandeers the keys. His reflections on current events (such as Prohibition), human history, fellow denizens of the natural world, beer, literary labors, and enduring existential questions mix the world-weariness of a newsman, the wisecracking embitterment of a barfly, and the melancholic self-absorption of a Hamlet (see "Why Not Commit Suicide") into a voice that is antic, addictive, and unforgettable. To wit:

what is your favorite dish
said mars and do you believe
in the immortality of the soul
stew i said and yes
at least mine is immortal
but i could name several others
that i have my doubts about
        —from "archy hears from mars"

What: Humor. Poetry. *When:* 1940. *Editions:* The 1950 reissue includes E. B. White's memorable tribute to Don

Marquis (also available in *Essays of E. B. White*) and retains the illustrations by George Herriman (of Krazy Kat fame). The most complete edition is *Annotated Archy and Mehitabel*, edited by Michael Sims (2006), which contains many poems previously not reprinted and presents all the works in their original order of publication, with expert notes. *Try: Krazy & Ignatz 1925–1926: "There Is a Heppy Lend Fur, Fur Awa-a-ay"* by George Herriman. *Old Possum's Book of Practical Cats* by T. S. Eliot.

....

The Roots of Civilization
THE COGNITIVE BEGINNINGS OF MAN'S FIRST ART, SYMBOL AND NOTATION
Alexander Marshack (1918–2004)

How Marking Time Planted the Seeds of Culture

I magine when *Homo sapiens* started thinking. What might those first thoughts have been like? A clue to the answer came to Alexander Marshack thanks to "a bit of bone."

It was the early 1960s. At work on a book about the dawning of the space age, and trying to explain to his readers the origins of science and civilization, Marshack became intrigued by the markings on the quartz-tipped handle of an African bone tool that was several thousand years old. Other scholars interpreted such markings as decoration or prehistoric doodling; Marshack thought otherwise. He wondered if the incisions might instead be a kind of notation—marking, for instance, the phases of the moon. His speculation that the ancient artifact "contained some storied meaning" raised the possibility that the cognitive capacities of primeval humans tens of thousands of years ago were more richly developed than had previously been imagined.

Marshack's hunch about that ancient bit of notched bone started him off on a scholarly treasure hunt that led, a decade later, to the publication of this book, an exhilaratingly original work of archaeological and anthropological research. Analyzing myriad relics of the Ice Age, the book advances a revolutionary theory about the seeds of what would ultimately

blossom into art, culture, and civilization. In essence, Marshack posits that our prehistoric ancestors had begun to structure their mental universe in terms of the seasons and other temporal yardsticks, and that it was this "time-factored" mental activity—"the cognitive ability to think sequentially in terms of process within time and space"—that developed into symbolic thinking.

As revealed in this remarkable (and profusely illustrated) volume, Marshack's story of discovery—he was, after all, an amateur in these realms of study at the start—is as exciting as his findings would prove to be provocative. His theory of time-factoring reshaped our image of prehistory and of essential human traits in radical ways. "It was a whole new interpretation and a whole new perspective," said Ian Tattersall of the American Museum of Natural History, at the time of the author's death in December 2004. Tattersall added that Marshack was "one of the giants on whose shoulders the current generation of researchers stands." But this book's intellectual thrills aren't reserved for specialists. Any reader who has ever been fascinated by the evolution of consciousness, for example, or the cave paintings at Lascaux, will find in Marshack's pages endless material for rumination about our earliest ancestors and their profoundly thought-provoking first thoughts.

What: Anthropology. Antiquity. Archaeology. History. *When:* 1972. *Edition:* In 1991 Moyer Bell Ltd. issued a revised and expanded edition, including a new foreword and a new concluding chapter titled "Two Decades Later." *Further Reading:* Calvin Tomkins's April 22, 1974, *New Yorker* profile of Marshack and his work, "Thinking in Time," makes fascinating reading, as does "Prehistoric Eyes," an essay by Guy Davenport collected in *Geography of the Imagination* (see page 198). *Try: The Mind in the Cave* by David Lewis-Williams. *The Dragons of Eden* by Carl Sagan (see page 691).

"One of the seminal books of our time."

—Howard Gardner on The Roots of Civilization

Life of Pi
Yann Martel (born 1963)

One Man in a Boat—with a Tiger

Imagine a cross between Rudyard Kipling's *Just So Stories* (see page 449) and Gabriel García Márquez's *One Hundred Years of Solitude* (see page 308), and you'll get some idea of the playful originality, exuberant invention, and sheer reading pleasure to be found in the pages of *Life of Pi*.

The "Pi" of the title is Piscine Molitor Patel, an Indian boy named after a swimming pool. As we learn in the first of the novel's three parts, he passes his early youth in Pondicherry, where his father runs a zoo. The young Pi exhibits a penchant for spiritual exploration, and undergoes a religious expansion—rather than a conversion—by adding elements of Christianity and Islam to his native Hindu beliefs.

The second part of the novel details what happens when his family decides to immigrate to Canada. Traveling on a vessel that carries many of the zoo's animals, they meet with calamity in the form of shipwreck, and Pi finds himself in a lifeboat shared with a hyena, a zebra, an orangutan, and, most importantly,

a 450-pound tiger named Richard Parker. Nature takes its hungry course, and soon enough it is just Pi and Parker in the boat on a 227-day voyage across the Pacific, replete with ruminations and adventures (the most memorable being a sojourn on an island stocked with meercats and carnivorous algae). They finally land safely in Mexico, and the final section narrates Pi's hilarious debriefing there by two incredulous representatives of the Japanese Ministry of Transport, who are investigating the capsizing of the original ship.

Whimsical and amusing, *Life of Pi* encompasses a great deal of human experience—from theology to zoology, desperation to wonder—in its drifting current of story. It's marvelous, in the exact sense of the word.

What: Novel. *When:* 2001. *Award:* Man Booker Prize for Fiction, 2002. *Also By: The Facts Behind the Helsinki Roccamatios* (1993; revised 2004). *Self* (1996). *Beatrice and Virgil* (2010). *Try: The Famished Road* by Ben Okri (see page 602). *The Curious Incident of the Dog in the Night-Time* by Mark Haddon.

■ For George R. R. Martin's *A Game of Thrones*, see page 796.

The Eighteenth Brumaire of Louis Bonaparte
Karl Marx (1818–1883)

Tragedy, Farce, and the Philosophy of History

Karl Marx's most influential work, *The Communist Manifesto*, written with Friedrich Engels in 1847 in response to a commission from the Communist League, begins with what has become one of the most famous sentences ever penned: "A spectre is haunting Europe—the spectre of Communism." More than a century and a half later, one is tempted to make reference to it with a revision: "A spectre is haunting capitalism—the spectre of Karl Marx." For, despite the dissolution of the USSR in 1991 amid the apparent triumph of democracy and the dominance of market economies, history, wily as ever, may be taking another turn. Rampant and rising inequality; the perversion of wealth creation through increasingly abstract modes of exchange; the prospect, through artificial intelligence and robotics, of the alienation of workers not just from their work but from the idea of labor itself—these factors have made aspects of Marx's thought apropos again. (Thomas Piketty's 2013 international bestseller, *Capital in the Twenty-First Century*, applied a version of Marx's method of research into long-term economic data to illuminate the shaky conceptual assumptions of free market and meritocratic thinking, albeit drawing very different conclusions than a traditional Marxist analysis might.)

In any case, and whatever one's estimation of the insurgencies that have waved his name as a banner, Marx remains worth reading for his philosophical and historical insight, and never more so than in *The Eighteenth Brumaire of Louis Bonaparte*, a social and political consideration of events in France between 1848 and 1851 that culminated in a coup d'état in December of the latter year. The title alludes to the date on the revolutionary calendar (Eighteen *Brumaire*, or November 9, 1799) on which the first Napoleon (uncle of Louis Bonaparte) seized supreme power in France, and sets up Marx's memorable opening: "Hegel remarks somewhere that all great, world-historical facts and personages occur, as it were, twice. He has forgotten to add:

Early 20th-century portrait of Karl Marx

the first time as tragedy, the second as farce." Although *The Communist Manifesto* is a polemic first and last, and Marx's magnum opus, *Das Kapital* (first volume, 1867), unfinished by the author and by and large unfinishable by the common reader, is often as hard to read as it was to write, *The Eighteenth Brumaire* is dense but stylish, witty even, in its view of particular events through the lens of historical ideas:

Men make their own history, but they do not make it just as they please; they do not make it under circumstances chosen by themselves, but under circumstances directly found, given and transmitted from the past. The tradition of all the dead generations weighs like a nightmare on the brain of the living.

Regardless of what one makes of Marx's ultimate interpretation of his subject, his act of engaging it is exhilarating, leading one to think about the role that history plays in contemporary events, and therefore what influence a complete detachment from historical context—as our relentlessly scrolling internet version of reality seems to demand—might have. By prompting us to look at political and economic phenomena from a fresh angle, the exercise of reading Marx leads not necessarily to answers but certainly to questions of enduring relevance.

What: History. Philosophy. *When:* 1852. *Edition: The Marx-Engels Reader,* edited by Robert C. Tucker, contains the text in its entirety, smartly annotated and in the company of other relevant works. *Also By: Economic and Philosophic Manuscripts of 1844* (1844). *The Class Struggles in France* (1850). *Grundrisse* (1857). "The Civil War in France" (1871). *Further Reading: Karl Marx: His Life and Environment* by Isaiah Berlin. *Karl Marx: A Life* by Francis Wheen. *Try: The European Revolutions, 1848–1851* by Jonathan Sperber.

Nicholas and Alexandra
Robert K. Massie (born 1929)

The Epic History and Family Drama of Imperial Russia's Fall

Robert Massie's 1967 account of the fall of Imperial Russia paints a vast and fascinating historical canvas that is vividly illuminated by the family drama the author sees as its focal point: the hemophilia of Tsarevich Alexis, only son and heir of Nicholas II, last czar of all the Russians. The illness had particular significance for the author, as he reveals in his introduction, because it was shared by his own son. In another book, Massie has described how *Nicholas and Alexandra* sprang from a bit of research left over from a story on hemophilia he had written for the *Saturday Evening Post.* "For years," Massie explained, "I had heard the story of Rasputin and the Tsarevich. But it was only in outline—brief, remote, indistinct, blurred. Historians passed over it quickly, usually in no more than a sentence or two. Somehow to me, both as the father of a hemophiliac and as a product of the rigorous historical discipline I was trained in at Oxford, this treatment seemed inadequate." Massie began learning as much as he could about "the most famous hemophiliac" and the mysterious holy man who, because he seemed able to control the boy's bleeding, was entrusted by the czar with greater and

Tsar Nicholas II and Tsarina Alexandra Fyodorovna, 1894

greater power—with disastrous effects for the Romanovs and their rule.

Yet it is not just Massie's personal connection to his subject, or his sensitive attention to the Romanovs' intimate concerns, or even his rich portrayal of Rasputin's sinister influence that makes *Nicholas and Alexandra* such a memorable and enduring volume. The material the author marshals is rich enough in politics, personalities, and intrigue to provide the plots of any number of Russian novels, a shelf of studies of royal dynasties and military alliances, and at least one storybook romance (that between the title characters). Massie's mastery in ordering this enormous trove—the astuteness of his historical emphases, his deft characterizations, the felicity of his prose—all combine to shape a single massive and absorbing narrative. As it unfolds, the familial dilemma becomes the kernel of an astonishing chronicle of history, religion, and revolution, one that encompasses both the twilight of Imperial Russia and the martyrdom of Nicholas, Alexandra, and their five children. Still, despite the scale and spectacle of the book's subject, it is the human qualities of this doomed family—faith and love, courage and dignity in the face of a horrific fate—that in the end move readers most.

What: History. *When:* 1967. *Also By: Journey* (1975; with Suzanne Massie). *Peter the Great* (1980). *Dreadnought: Britain, Germany, and the Coming of the Great War* (1991). *Castles of Steel: Britain, Germany, and the Winning of the Great War at Sea* (2003). *Catherine the Great: Portrait of a Woman* (2011). Relying on records that came to light after the breakup of the Soviet Union, *The Romanovs:* *The Final Chapter* (1995) expands Massie's research into the family's fate. *Try: Tsar: The Lost World of Nicholas and Alexandra* by Peter Kurth, a stunningly illustrated volume. *Adaptation:* Filmed in 1971 by Franklin J. Shaffner, *Nicholas and Alexandra* won two Academy Awards and was nominated for several more, including Best Picture.

Tales of the City
Armistead Maupin (born 1944)

Bet You Can't Read Just One

A young, conservative Southerner, Associated Press journalist Armistead Maupin was transferred to San Francisco in the early 1970s. There he had an awakening both sexual and professional, and began writing a weekly serial for a local paper, penning fictional vignettes about young denizens of a Russian Hill apartment building and their unforgettable landlady. Only five installments in, the paper folded, but Maupin knew he was on to something. In 1976, he pitched his "Tales of the City" to the *San Francisco Chronicle*—this time as a daily. The paper said yes, Maupin got busy, and the city by the bay soon grew attached to its daily dose of his funny, touching, flamboyant stories. Four years later, Maupin's tales would be collected in book form. That was just the beginning.

Though it took a little while, Maupin's first book found a devoted national following. He kept writing the serial, which would quickly fill five more books: *More Tales of the City* (1980), *Further Tales of the City* (1982), *Babycakes* (1984), *Significant Others* (1987), and finally *Sure of You* (1989), the only one of the original sequence not first serialized. Three other novels featuring the same set of characters would follow after a hiatus of nearly two decades: *Michael Tolliver Lives* (2007), *Mary Ann in Autumn* (2010), and *The Days of Anna Madrigal* (2014). Although the focus at the start of the series is on Mary Ann Singleton, a naïve, newly arrived Cleveland transplant, and her friendship with Michael Tolliver, a gay man called "Mouse," Maupin's *Tales* encompass a rich array of people—gay and

Armistead Maupin, 1989

straight, male and female, financially struggling and well-off—who reside at (or pass in and out of) 28 Barbary Lane. The immediacy of the serial telling allows the author to indulge his gift for social satire at the same time as he is accumulating an alert social history; his artistic hand is light, yet the entertainment it weaves exhibits a recognition of the weighty search for affection and security that grounds the unbearable lightness of our lives. His characters fall in and out of love, deceive each other and reveal themselves, and, most characteristically, accept and forgive one another. Because of the episodic nature of the *Tales*, their cultural currency, and their ties to the city in which they are set, Maupin has often been compared to Dickens; he earns the distinction as well by his remarkable capacity for respecting—indeed, honoring—the particularity of every point on the spectrum of human nature.

The first volume introduces us to twenty-somethings of various backgrounds and pro-clivities, and is satisfying all by itself. As the years and tales wear on, as AIDS strikes the gay community, and as Maupin himself ages, the tenor naturally shifts to a somewhat darker register. But even those who love the later books a little less than the first—and even high-brow readers who assure themselves that all are no more than "guilty pleasures"—can't help

but read straight through all six. Rare is the reader who wouldn't happily read more, for these tales, like the lives they gather into a witty and compassionate narrative, are much more than the sum of their parts.

What: Short Stories. *When:* 1978–89. *Editions:* In addition to uniform paperbacks, the tales have been published in a variety of omnibus volumes. *Also By: Maybe the Moon* (1992). *The Night Listener* (2000). *Try: Auntie Mame* by Patrick Dennis. *Dancer from the Dance* by Andrew Holleran. *Adaptations:* The Peabody Award–winning 1993 PBS miniseries of volume one sparked enough controversy that the next two volumes were adapted by Showtime instead, airing in 1998 and 2001. All three miniseries star Laura Linney and Olympia Dukakis.

A Genius in the Family
Hiram Percy Maxim (1869–1936)

A High-Spirited Memoir of an Unconventional Father

"I suspect I had one of the most unusual fathers anybody ever had. I was his firstborn. He knew considerably less than nothing about children and he had to learn how to be a father. He learned on me. He did not learn easily."

The author thus introduces his mem-oir of the lunacy of childhood in the orbit of a brilliant paternal moon, Hiram Stevens Maxim, one of the most renowned engineers and inventors of his day. Maxim senior, a resourceful Maine Yankee who, during the period this book chronicles, had set up a shop in Manhattan and a home in Brooklyn, made his fame and fortune with the Maxim machine gun, the first efficient automatic fire-arm (its benefits to the British military in the Sudan would eventually lead to Maxim's being knighted by Queen Victoria). In addition to developing numerous other useful industrial devices, he also made a fundamental contribu-tion to the development of the incandescent lamp, and narrowly missed being acknowl-edged as its inventor (in a patent suit Edison proved priority by only a matter of days).

Yet this distinguished inventor was also a man who, in dignified top hat and Prince Albert coat, would daily vault over the gate of his Brooklyn property or sprint full tilt—"for exercise"—down the middle of Court Street. Such events are nothing compared with the more elaborate antics related in these pages, such as the day Hiram Stevens tied a bushel of peaches to a tree one by one to "prove" to his child the fertilizing prowess of the dead cat the boy had been instructed to plant near its trunk. Or the incident in which father and son blew beans through a brass tube at a building across the street to disrupt the flirtations of a police-man and a housemaid. Or the pains the elder Maxim took to manufacture a two-headed coin with which his four-year-old son could call a local shopkeeper's bluff: "Sure, kid, I'll give you the dog. Just bring me a penny with two heads."

Completely unselfconscious in his pater-nal responsibilities, the elder Maxim treated the younger as an equal in his remarkable adventures, no matter how outrageous the situation his ingenuity might concoct. Writing from the perspective of his own middle-aged fatherhood, the author looks back with an affectionate, clear-eyed bewilderment at the child rearing he underwent, providing readers with a singular and entirely delightful reminiscence.

What: Memoir. *When:* 1936. *Also By: Horseless Carriage Days* (1937). *Try: Surely You're Joking, Mr. Feynman!*

and *What Do You Care What Other People Think?,* both by Richard P. Feynman. *Footnote:* The author was an inventor in his own right—a pioneer in the development of both gasoline and electric vehicles. His work on a muffler for automobile exhaust led to the invention of the silencer for firearms.

Ring of Bright Water
Gavin Maxwell (1914–1969)

A Man and His Otters

" I sit in a pitch-pine panelled kitchen–living room, with an otter asleep upon its back among the cushions on the sofa, forepaws in the air, and with the expression of tightly shut concentration that very small babies wear in sleep." So begins this classic of nature writing, a book about a lapsed Scottish aristocrat who returns to the Western Highlands to embrace nature and solitude, keeping house with an otter or two. But that quick description, charming as it may be, doesn't quite do it justice.

The well-born Maxwell took a circuitous route to that remote kitchen–living room in Sandaig (called Camusfeàrna in the book), having passed through preparatory schools and Oxford, served in World War II, and purchased the Isle of Soay in the Hebrides, where he proved a business failure in his attempt to establish a basking shark fishery. In 1956, he ventured through the unexplored marshlands of Iraq and returned to Scotland with an otter named Mijbil, who would take up residence

with him at Camusfeàrna. All of this is detailed in *Ring of Bright Water,* as is the companionship they shared in a remarkable landscape, carefully observed by Maxwell and eloquently enriched by his strong, supple language. Suffused with a quirky intelligence and a fascinatingly variegated psychological texture rare in nature writing, *Ring of Bright Water* is a moving record of one man's fierce attachments—to sea and soil, solitude and independence, and, last but not least, two marvelous otters named Mijbil and Edal.

What: Nature. *When:* 1960. *Edition:* A 2011 paperback from David R. Godine combines Maxwell's masterpiece with its excellent but lesser-known sequels, *The Rocks Remain* (1963) and *Raven Seek Thy Brother* (1968). *Also By: A Reed Shaken by the Wind* (1957). *Lords of the Atlas* (1966). *Further Reading: The Saga of "Ring of Bright Water": The Enigma of Gavin Maxwell* by Douglas Botting. *Try: My Family and Other Animals* by Gerald Durrell (see page 240). *Born Free* by Joy Adamson. *All Creatures Great and Small* by James Herriot (see page 371). *Adaptation:* The 1969 movie stars Bill Travers.

A Year in Provence
Peter Mayle (1939–2018)

A Restorative Sojourn in the South of France

This charming narrative, in which former advertising executive Peter Mayle chronicles his inaugural year as a British expatriate in Provence, offers a refreshing respite from

one's own routine. In pursuit of a long-savored dream of the sweet life in the South of France, Mayle and his wife purchased a two-hundred-year-old stone farmhouse between the medieval hill villages of Ménerbes and Bonnieux in the Luberon, set to work on its restoration, and settled—sometimes with élan, sometimes with awkward Englishness—into the rhythms and rituals of Provençal life.

Their encounters with neighbors nosy and nice, obdurate bureaucrats, and talented if persnickety tradesmen are described with easy comedy, and Mayle's sketches of villages, markets, vineyards, and restaurants—of the customs of the country and the pleasures and vexations of making an old house habitable—merrily transport us to a sunnier clime. There we linger over meals and enjoy long, lazy evenings in the company of a good writer and a curious yet comfortable assortment of characters. It's hard to imagine a happier armchair trip.

What: Travel. *When:* 1989. *Also By: Toujours Provence* (1991). *Encore Provence* (1999). *French Lessons* (2001). *Try: The Auberge of the Flowering Hearth* by Roy Andries de Groot (see page 202). *Under the Tuscan Sun* by Frances Mayes. *Adaptation:* A 1993 BBC miniseries stars John Thaw and Lindsay Duncan.

The Road
Cormac McCarthy (born 1933)

Two Good Guys vs. Apocalypse

It starts simply enough: A father and son, waking after a night camping in the wilderness, prepare to journey onward. But we're soon aware that the simplicity belongs to no pastoral idyll—the sky is endlessly gray, the rivers are the color of oil, and ash drips from above. Nearly all plants and wildlife have gone extinct. The nights, Cormac McCarthy writes, are "blinding cold and casket black." Millions—billions—of people have died, and those unlucky enough to have survived exist on the sharp edge of starvation, either prey or predator in the cannibalistic food chain that catastrophe has unleashed. Apocalypse has come to America.

Father and son, unnamed and emaciated by hunger, are trying to reach the sea, where they hope they'll have a better chance of survival. As they cross the devastated terrain, they must fend off marauders who target their sparse supplies and will likely try to eat them. But the two do not give up; the father insists that they are still "the good guys" in this no-good landscape, no country for old—or even young—men. McCarthy never reveals what disaster has befallen the planet, but that it's irreversible is clear. Although the pair clings to a hope that they are "carrying the fire" of some future happiness, the humanity they cherish is recognizable mostly by its evolving absence:

He'd had this feeling before, beyond the numbness and the dull despair. The world shrinking down about a raw core of parsible entities. The names of things slowly following those things into oblivion. Colors. The names of birds. Things to eat. Finally the names of things one believed to be true. More fragile than he would have thought. How much was gone already?

The Road adds a fierce elegiac note to Cormac McCarthy's career-long exploration of violence, alienation, and brutality among men. He began as an acclaimed author of Southern Gothic novels with religious overtones (*The Orchard Keeper*, 1965; *Child of God*, 1973) before relocating—in a hail of bullets and bloodshed—to the American West in his pivotal fifth novel, *Blood Meridian* (1985), a hellish fever dream that Joyce Carol Oates described as an "epic accumulation of horrors" and Harold Bloom called "the ultimate Western, not to be surpassed." McCarthy's subsequent Border Trilogy continued his exploration of the themes and landscapes of the West, without the nightmarish carnage—and feral imaginative energy—of *Blood Meridian*.

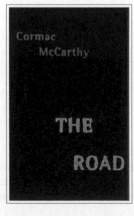

While *The Road* offers a potent distillation of many of McCarthy's fictional concerns, the ecological imperative that underlies it maps fresh territory; there is a new tenderness as well in the aching filial affection that abides in the father-son bond as it is threatened by an unrelentingly terrifying reality. It is a moving, riveting tale, an indelible vision of a future Wild West whose arrival—given the spate of climate-soaked catastrophes that dominate our news—seems more possible every day.

What: Novel. *When:* 2006. *Award:* Pulitzer Prize for Fiction, 2007. *Also By:* The Border Trilogy: *All the Pretty Horses* (1992); *The Crossing* (1994); *Cities of the Plain* (1998). *No Country for Old Men* (2005). *Try: I Am Legend* by Richard Matheson. *Blindness* by José Saramago. *Adaptation:* The 2009 film stars Viggo Mortensen.

Make Way for Ducklings
Robert McCloskey (1914–2003)

A Picture-Perfect Family Tale

In baseball, there's a statistic called slugging percentage that students of the game use to determine a player's productivity at the plate. If one were to devise a similar measure for books, it's hard to imagine any author would have a higher slugging percentage than children's book maestro Robert McCloskey, whose eight volumes might be characterized as four triples (see *Also By* below) and four home runs: *Blueberries for Sal* (1948), *One Morning in Maine* (1952), *Time of Wonder* (1957), and, most memorable of all, *Make Way for Ducklings*, published in 1941.

Beautifully drawn and visually composed with great but unobtrusive care (text and images are arranged so that even the turning of pages is part of the book's storytelling charm), *Make Way for Ducklings* relates the adventures of a newlywed mallard couple searching for a place to start their family. They fly over Boston looking for a suitable spot, surveying the city's famous landmarks before alighting on an island in the Charles River. Eight ducklings are born—the delightfully named Jack, Kack, Lack, Mack, Nack, Ouack, Pack, and Quack. The book reaches its high point when Mrs. Mallard decides to lead her progeny ashore and into the city to meet Mr. Mallard in the Public Garden. Their passage through the busy streets is aided by a helpful consort of policemen, led by the friendly Michael, who stop traffic along their route to allow them passage to a happy ending.

Make Way for Ducklings is as charming a picture book as you're likely to discover, and no

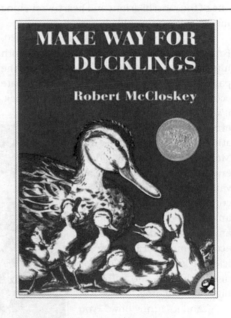

reading life is complete without it. If and when you are blessed with children and grandchildren or nieces and nephews, make sure they read it, too—with you.

What: Children's. *When:* 1941. *Award:* Caldecott Medal, 1942. *Also By: Lentil* (1940). *Homer Price* (1943). *Centerburg Tales* (1951). *Burt Dow, Deep-Water Man* (1963). *Try: Paddle-to-the-Sea* by Holling C. Holling. *Katy and the Big Snow* by Virginia Lee Burton. *Footnote:* McCloskey's toddler's tale has been named the official children's book of Massachusetts, and the ducklings' journey along Charles Street is now memorialized in the Boston Public Garden by bronze statues of Mrs. Mallard and her brood.

Angela's Ashes
A MEMOIR
Frank McCourt (1930–2009)

Funny and Forgiving Stories of an Irish Catholic Childhood

"It was, of course, a miserable childhood: the happy childhood is hardly worth your while," writes Frank McCourt at the outset. "Worse than the ordinary miserable childhood is the miserable Irish childhood, and worse yet is the miserable Irish Catholic childhood." So he introduces the story of his own upbringing, one of the most hilarious and heart-wrenching memoirs you're ever likely to read.

McCourt was born in Brooklyn in 1930. Four years later, his parents returned with him to their native Ireland. *Angela's Ashes* is the painful reminiscence of the family's desperate economic slide back to the slums of Limerick; it's about incapacitating poverty and the countless humiliations and deprivations the McCourts suffer as they daily endure life on the brink of starvation. It is filled with the close comforts and closer conflicts of an extended family, with pints and priests and all the other accoutrements of Irish chronicles. It is, in short, a catalog of loss, distress, and faith both blind and blinding.

"And it's funny how?" you might ask. The answer lies in the joy of McCourt's marvelous creation. For, despite its litanies of dolor and grief, what one remembers about this book are

the stories woven into the pattern of its protagonist's youth, stories so rich in character and humor that we are prone to forget (and the author, it seems, to forgive) the extreme circumstances that engulf Frankie and his brothers. The storyteller's words, animated with wit and mimicry, convey with equal skill the drunkard father's charm, the saintly mother's resilience, the mischievous escapades of boys, the diagnostic skill of grandmothers, and the intricate disorder of Catholic schools (don't miss Frank's classroom recitation of his composition, "Jesus and the Weather"). Miraculously, McCourt makes laughter ring through every step of his remembered purgatory, lifting the world's weight and weariness with nothing more than the lilt of his voice.

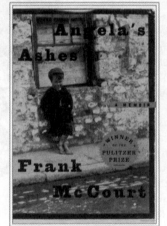

What: Memoir. *When:* 1996. *Awards:* National Book Critics Circle Award, 1996. Pulitzer Prize for Biography or Autobiography, 1997. *Also By:* 'Tis: A Memoir (1999). *Teacher Man: A Memoir* (2005). *Try: An Only Child* and *My Father's Son* by Frank O'Connor. *Home Before Night* by Hugh Leonard. *A Drinking Life* by Pete Hamill (see page 345). *Adaptation:* Emily Watson and Robert Carlyle star in the 1999 film version of *Angela's Ashes. Footnote:* Before becoming a memoirist in his sixties, McCourt had spent his working life in education, much of it as a writing teacher in New York City's Stuyvesant High School.

The Heart Is a Lonely Hunter
Carson McCullers (1917–1967)

A Tender Tale of Lives of Quiet Desperation

It is preternaturally fitting that two of America's most penetrating mediums of loneliness, the

artist Edward Hopper and the novelist Carson McCullers, are buried in the same cemetery in Nyack, New York. Alone together for eternity, do the painter of *Nighthawks* and the author of

The Heart Is a Lonely Hunter compare notes on the solitudes they channeled into such memorable works?

Published when its author was only twenty-three, *The Heart Is a Lonely Hunter* still stands as one of the most acclaimed debuts in the history of American fiction. Set in the 1930s, in a southern town much like the one in which McCullers was raised, it revolves around the enigmatic figure of John Singer, a thirty-two-year-old deaf-mute who finds himself on his own after ten years of sharing a silent routine with his only friend and fellow mute, Spiros Antonapoulos. When Antonapoulos, after a stretch of increasingly erratic behavior, is committed to an asylum, Singer finds himself more isolated than ever, until he comes to board in the house of the Kelly family and becomes the confidant of four of the town's loneliest souls: the café owner Biff Brannon, the heavy-drinking political radical Jake Blount, the black doctor Benedict Copeland, and the curious twelve-year-old girl with unattainable dreams of a musical future, Mick Kelly.

These four uneasy characters, estranged from family, friends, and community by the remoteness of their longings, find consolation in the hushed politeness of Singer's company. All the while, McCullers dignifies their wants and disappointments with the unblinking alertness of her gaze. Her novel encompasses themes of alienation, race, politics, and impoverished promise, yet its genius is in the kindness with which it tends the small and wild garden of the heart.

Her friend and contemporary Tennessee Williams wrote that McCullers "owned the heart and the deep understanding of it, but in

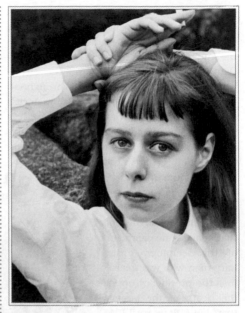

Carson McCullers, 1955

addition she had that 'tongue of angels' that gave her power to sing of it, to make of it an anthem." That anthem sounds throughout the desolate precincts of *The Heart Is a Lonely Hunter* with an eerie, indelible loveliness that—like the misfits who inhabit this book—a reader is unlikely to forget.

What: Novel. **When:** 1940. **Also By:** *Reflections in a Golden Eye* (1941). *The Member of the Wedding* (1946). *The Ballad of the Sad Café* (1951). **Further Reading:** *The Lonely Hunter: A Biography of Carson McCullers* by Virginia Spencer Carr. **Try:** *The Glass Menagerie* by Tennessee Williams. *The Giant's House* by Elizabeth McCracken. **Adaptation:** The 1968 film stars Alan Arkin.

Truman
David McCullough (born 1933)

Fanfare for the Common Man

" We can never tell what is in store for us," Harry Truman once said, and David McCullough has wisely chosen those words as the epigraph to the monumental life of our thirty-third president. Reflecting America's own best image of itself as a land of opportunity, hardworking pragmatism, and no-nonsense nobility, McCullough tells Truman's surprising story in revelatory detail, following "the man from Missouri" from the obscurity of a family farm to the unexpected destiny that awaited him in the White House and on the world stage.

Along the way we pass through the battlefields of the Great War, "the shirt store" in which the young Truman plied his trade as haberdasher, the smoke-filled back rooms of the Kansas City Democratic Party machine, and the chambers of the United States Senate. Throughout, McCullough's mastery of archival materials and his extensive interviews with the subject's friends, family, and Washington associates allow him to vividly portray both Truman and the twentieth-century history in which he would loom so large.

It's an astonishing tale, really, and McCullough tells it with a relish for all the facts that shaped the character of the seemingly ordinary man who was thrust into the presidency upon the death of the larger-than-life FDR in April 1945. Scarcely four months later, the new chief executive made the momentous decision to drop atomic bombs on Japan, thus ending the Second World War. Although that decision remains Truman's defining historical moment, McCullough's understanding of the man and the values and politics that shaped him illuminates Truman's many achievements, from the initiation of the Marshall Plan and NATO to the desegregation of the armed forces

and the firing of General Douglas MacArthur To say nothing of his 1948 "whistle-stop" campaign, which culminated in the biggest upset in the history of presidential elections—and the famous photograph of the beaming victor displaying a *Chicago Daily Tribune* with the erroneous headline "Dewey Defeats Truman."

Both meticulous historian and consummate storyteller, McCullough writes with unfailing clarity and unflagging narrative zest. Happily, his huge book—the text runs to nearly a thousand pages—is compelling from first page to last.

Election badge, 1948

What: Biography. History. When: 1992. Award: Pulitzer Prize for Biography, 1993. Also By: The Great Bridge: The Epic Story of the Building of the Brooklyn Bridge (1972). The Path Between the Seas: The Creation of the Panama Canal 1870–1914 (1977). Mornings on Horseback: The Story of an Extraordinary Family, a Vanished Way of Life, and the Unique Child Who Became Theodore Roosevelt (1981). John Adams (2001). 1776 (2005). Further Reading: Plain Speaking: An Oral Biography of Harry S. Truman by Merle Miller. Try: The Rise of Theodore Roosevelt by Edmund Morris (see page 566). The Years of Lyndon Johnson by Robert A. Caro (see page 131).

Lonesome Dove
Larry McMurtry (born 1936)

An Epic Saga of the American West

Men of action require a field to work, and few fields have proven as fertile in this regard—in life and in the imagination—as the American West. Larry McMurtry's 1985 epic, *Lonesome Dove*, may be its richest literary harvest. Set in the late 1870s, it tells the story of a cattle drive from the Rio Grande to Montana, led by two former Texas Rangers, Augustus (Gus) McCrae and Woodrow F. Call, who have been friends for three decades.

Along the way, McMurtry enlists all the familiar elements of Western lore: a hero capable and wise, yet easygoing (Gus), and another stoic, reticent, and duty-driven (Call); a whore with a heart, if not of gold, then glittering with allure; rogues disguised as friends; hostile Indians and bands of renegades; sheriffs in relentless pursuit and women both passionate and profoundly pragmatic; and a young cowboy who will inherit the dusty dreams of his elders. There are gunfights and campfires and natural wonders, storms and kidnappings, rapes and killings, loves lost and found and sacrificed, torches carried across years and miles. The sweep of drama and incident—and of history—is matched by the moment-by-moment intimacy of character and feeling that McMurtry masterfully portrays. Colored by savage, tragic consequences, his book is also leavened with great good humor and generous understanding, capturing the landscape of human nature with such nuance and magnanimity that 850 pages hardly seems enough to contain its lives. (To readers' delight, McMurtry must have shared the sentiment, for he expanded the tale forward and backward in time in three subsequent novels published between 1993 and 1997: *Streets of Laredo, Dead Man's Walk,* and *Comanche Moon.*)

For all its cowboy grit and glory, *Lonesome Dove* is more than just a celebration of the Western ethos. As Gus and Call set out on their journey, they are seeking not just fresh grazing land for their herd, but something meaningful for themselves as well—not a future so much as a present filled with necessities: tasks, obstacles, dangers, exploits. They chase the engagement of exertion to keep the uncertainties and diminishments of age at bay. ("You should have died in the line of duty, Woodrow," Gus tells his pal at one point. "You'd know how to do that fine. The problem is you don't know how to live.") Unlike Clara Allen, Gus's old flame and the one person who has learned to make a home in the West's unsettled world, they never learn how to dwell, but must keep moving on even as they more and more regret their passing. Clara knows the cost of their restlessness, and so, of course, does McMurtry: It's a knowledge that gives the page-turning pleasure of his book a profound, expressive afterglow.

What: Novel. *When:* 1985. *Award:* Pulitzer Prize for Fiction, 1986. *Also By: The Last Picture Show* (1966). *Terms of Endearment* (1975). *Sacagawea's Nickname: Essays on the American West* (2001). *Try: Monte Walsh* by Jack Schaefer. *The Good Old Boys* by Elmer Kelton. *Adaptation:* The 1989 television miniseries *Lonesome Dove* has an all-star cast headed by Robert Duvall, Tommy Lee Jones, and Danny Glover. *Footnote:* In addition to his career as a novelist and screenwriter (he shared an Academy Award for the script for *Brokeback Mountain*), McMurtry has been one of America's most prominent booksellers and rare-book scouts, a career he celebrates in *Books: A Memoir* (2008).

Robert Duvall and Tommy Lee Jones in the television film of Lonesome Dove *(1988)*

Plagues and Peoples
William H. McNeill (1917–2016)

Charting the Epidemic Proportions of History

Starting out with fewer than six hundred men, Hernando Cortez managed to conquer the Aztec empire. The ease and speed with which the Spanish invaders subjugated a population that numbered in the millions is puzzling, to say the least. In his attempt to fathom the Aztec catastrophe, William McNeill stumbled upon an interesting clue: On the night the Aztecs first drove Cortez from Tenochtitlan, an epidemic of smallpox, a disease another Spanish cohort had introduced into the region, was raging in the city. The enormous physical and psychological effects of the disease, McNeill surmised, had to have played a large part in the Aztecs' failure to dispose of the Spanish threat. Such speculation, McNeill writes, "began to uncover a dimension of the past that historians have not hitherto recognized: the history of humanity's encounters with infectious diseases, and the far-reaching consequences that ensued whenever contacts across disease boundaries allowed a new infection to invade a population that lacked any acquired immunity to its ravages." It is this dimension that McNeill explores in this fascinating book, which details the pervasive ways in which disease has determined the shape of history.

Although the parallel paths of plagues and peoples are fascinating in themselves, McNeill is not content simply to chart chronology. Exploring how human behaviors and developments—agricultural innovation, fluctuations in population density, migration, invasion, and predation—have played a role in the complex pattern of disease since the dawn of man, as well as the counterinfluences of stabilization and immunization, McNeill mapped new territory, much of it necessarily speculative but nonetheless fascinating and enlightening. From the ancient epidemic that left Athens outmanned by Sparta to the Black Plague of the Middle Ages, from the effects of the horse messengers and trading caravans of the Mongol empires on the spread of infectious illnesses to the ecological impact of medical science after 1700, McNeill outlines a sweeping historical drama in this eminently readable and thought-provoking book.

What: History. Medicine. *When:* 1976. *Edition:* In 1998 a new chapter and preface were added, addressing the outbreak of AIDS in the 1980s. *Also By:* McNeill's many titles include *The Rise of the West* (1963); *The Human Condition: An Ecological and Historical View* (1980); *The Pursuit of Power: Technology, Armed Force and Society Since AD 1000* (1982); and *The Human Web: A Bird's-Eye View of History* (2003; with J. R. McNeill). *Try: Microbe Hunters* by Paul de Kruif (see page 203). *Guns, Germs, and Steel* by Jared Diamond.

Oranges
John McPhee (born 1931)

The Fruit of One Writer's Inspired Curiosity

The first word about oranges came in 500 BC, in the second book of the Confucian *Five Classics*. The last word, or pretty close to it, is found in John McPhee's surprising book-length report on the botany, history, and business of oranges. Whether discussing the orangeries of European monarchs or the orange barons of Frostproof, Florida—in fact for the length of a whole book devoted solely to *Citrus sinensis*—McPhee is entertaining, informative, and entirely captivating. A reviewer in *Harper's* magazine summed up the book's appeal: "It's a delicious book, in a word, and more absorbing than many a novel."

In just under 150 pages, McPhee tells us where, why, and how oranges grow, who grew them first and who grows them now, and how market pressures—particularly shoppers' misguided notion that an orange must be orange—affect all of the above. He also tells us about oranges in Renaissance art and entertains us with several centuries' worth of orange history and lore. As with all of McPhee's work, *Oranges* is at heart a human interest story—we not only meet the people who work the modern orchards, but are left with an entirely different feeling about our own breakfast fare. Delightful in itself, *Oranges* is also an ideal introduction to one of the most rewarding bodies of contemporary writing you're likely to come across.

Through several decades and more than two dozen books, McPhee—staff writer for *The New Yorker* since 1965 and renowned Princeton writing teacher—has blazed an idiosyncratic trail through diverse places (from the Pine Barrens of New Jersey to Alaska's wilderness) and subjects (basketball, birchbark canoes, atomic energy, geology, food, fish, trucking). Whether writing about Frank Boyden, the animating spirit of Deerfield Academy (*The Headmaster*), environmentalist David Brower (*Encounters with the Archdruid*), or the various "orange men" who lead him through their world, he has an uncanny instinct for following intriguing people into thickets of anecdote and information. His curiosity is matched to a clarity of style and a flair for narrative that lure readers into the happy state we can only call "McPheeishness," where we are always on the verge of discovering the most fascinating stuff we never knew we wanted to know.

What: Nature. Journalism. *When:* 1967. *Also By:* Highlights among McPhee's many superb works include his book on Alaska, *Coming into the Country* (1977) and his four volumes on geology: *Basin and Range* (1981); *In Suspect Terrain* (1983); *Rising from the Plains* (1986); and *Assembling California* (1993). This quartet was collected into one volume with additional material as *Annals of the Former World* (1998), which was awarded a Pulitzer Prize for General Nonfiction in 1999. *Try: The Botany of Desire* by Michael Pollan. *The Orchid Thief* by Susan Orlean. *Salt: A World History* by Mark Kurlansky.

The Rainbabies
Laura Krauss Melmed (born 1950)
Illustrated by Jim LaMarche (born 1952)

A Picture Book to Love for Parents and Toddlers

A picture book is often a shared family treasure, and few contemporary illustrated stories have been more shareable—or more treasurable—than this magical volume, in which a childless couple discovers twelve tiny babies in the raindrops of a spring moonshower. They nurture and protect them with love, luck, and courage. Strange dangers rear their heads, but the man and woman remain steadfast in their devotion to their accidental infants. When Mother Moonshower comes to reclaim her dozen progeny, she bears a remarkable gift for the wife and her husband. Laura Krauss Melmed has told her beautiful story so well—in the imagery, rhythms, and resonance of a true fairy tale—that one turns the pages both awed and overjoyed. Jim LaMarche's paintings are perfectly matched to the tenor of the tale. *The Rainbabies* is the kind of book that stays in a family across the generations.

What: Children's. *When:* 1992. *Reading Notes:* Age 4 and up for shared reading. *Also By:* Melmed and LaMarche also collaborated on *Little Oh* (1997). By Melmed, illustrated by Henri Sorensen: *I Love You As Much . . .* (2001). Written and illustrated by LaMarche: *The Raft* (2000). *Try: Bub, or The Very Best Thing*, written and illustrated by Natalie Babbitt. *The Tub People* by Pam Conrad, illustrated by Richard Egielski.

BY THE BESTSELLING AUTHOR OF *I LOVE YOU AS MUCH...*
LAURA KRAUSS MELMED

The Rainbabies

ILLUSTRATED BY JIM LAMARCHE

HERMAN MELVILLE
(1819–1891)

H erman Melville's career started off well enough. After years on the seas, his early autobiographical novels detailing adventures in exotic climes sold brilliantly, and he was on course to become one of the leading writers of the age. But when his immense novel *Moby-Dick* appeared in 1851, the reviews were scathing—"so much trash belonging to the worst school of Bedlam literature," said one—and sales were worse. Melville's reputation never recovered. *Pierre: or, The Ambiguities*, which he published the next year, bombed completely. Publishers rejected later novels, and he ended up working as a customs inspector at the Port of New York, channeling his literary energy into rather impenetrable poetry, including the epic *Clarel: A Poem and Pilgrimage in the Holy Land* (1876). He was so forgotten that his last masterpiece, the novella *Billy Budd*, went undiscovered for nearly three decades after his death, and was published only in 1924. In retrospect, of course, his great novel of the white whale takes up most of Melville's legacy, but even though *Moby-Dick* remains in a class by itself, readers should not let its long shadow obscure the startling originality of his other work, which comprises one of the quirkiest and most surprising authorial shelves in all literature.

Etching of Herman Melville after a portrait by Joseph O. Eaton

Moby-Dick
An Unparalleled Literary Voyage

P erhaps it was the scale of *Moby-Dick*—the most ambitious novel ever written in America to that point, a rollicking ocean of maritime adventure, Christian allegory, metaphysical disquisition, natural history, literary escapade, and social criticism—that scared off readers of the time, because no modern reader of *Moby-Dick* can fail to be impressed by its astounding intensity. On board the *Pequod*, a ship that sets off from Nantucket, our narrator Ishmael and his fellow crewmen think they are in the business of hunting whales for oil. But Captain Ahab, the ship's grim, peg-legged skipper, has other ideas: He is out for revenge on the white whale who bit off his limb. His obsessive hunt for Moby-Dick will occupy him and the rest of the crew until the novel's end—but not before Melville takes us on an imaginative voyage that is at once a seafaring thriller, a workplace comedy (complete with scenes of

Illustration of Moby-Dick

grizzled sailors harvesting whale sperm), and an almost Shakespearean dramatization of man's fate.

Today *Moby-Dick* appears both in its complete version and in abridged forms that elide whole chapters on the economics of whaling or the biology of sea mammals. But if you're going to tackle this monumental work, embrace the whole conception. For, despite the fact that critics chase the specter of the Great American Novel with the single-mindedness with which Ahab pursues the whale across these pages, Melville's masterpiece long ago delivered the goods. From bustling seaport to shipboard society, from the isolated ocean wilderness to expanses of ideas as forbidding as nature itself, *Moby-Dick* is a literary voyage unlike any other you'll undertake, a strange and compelling secular Bible that has all the character and incident, lamentations and longueurs of the original—and more than a little of its sense of revelation, too.

What: Novel. *When:* 1851. *Edition:* The University of California Press issue of the Arion Press edition, as designed by Andrew Hoyem with illustrations by Barry Moser, is both majestic and eminently readable. *Also By: Typee* (1846). *Omoo* (1847). *Mardi* (1849). *White-Jacket* (1850). *Further Reading: Melville: His World and Work* by Andrew Delbanco. *Why Read Moby-Dick?* by Nathaniel Philbrick. *Try: Typhoon* by Joseph Conrad. *Leviathan, or the Whale* by Philip Hoare. *Adaptations:* John Huston directed the 1956 film in which Gregory Peck stars as Captain Ahab and Orson Welles plays Father Mapple; Ray Bradbury wrote the screenplay. Frank Muller's audiobook is a masterpiece in itself—an astonishingly vivid reading.

The Piazza Tales
A Cabinet of Curiosities

I f *Moby-Dick* is a heaping chest of treasure, the volume known as *The Piazza Tales*, six stories gathered for book publication in 1856, is a necklace of faceted gems. Three are cut with special ingenuity and polished to high brilliance: "Bartleby, the Scrivener: A Tale of Wall Street," "Benito Cereno," and "The Encantadas, or Enchanted Isles." The first is a strange tale—out of Hawthorne by way of Edgar Allan Poe, with a few digressions down alleys of Dickens, in the direction of the as-yet-undiscovered dominion of Kafka—about a law clerk named Bartleby who starts off his new job with great industry. But he soon begins to refuse to take up his pen, or to tackle any of the tasks demanded of him, responding to every request with the phrase "I would prefer not to." To say any more about a tale in which, pointedly, nothing gets done, would be a spoiler.

Based on an account of an actual mutiny on a slaving ship off the coast of Chile, "Benito Cereno" artfully angles the mirrors of unreliable narration to illuminate, in a suspenseful tale, the desperate eddies of race and power. "The Encantadas," a series of prose sketches that combine to form an imaginative travelogue of the Galápagos Islands, encompasses natural history, geological wonders, dramatic incidents, and meditations on isolation and cruelty; the writing might have come from the pen of Charles Darwin if he had brought the works of Samuel Beckett, rather than those of Alexander von Humboldt, to read while voyaging on the *Beagle*. Combining a fanciful breadth with a kind of spiritual austerity, Melville conveys that nature is strange, and human life stranger still, in ways that only some new kind of narrative might convey; as a result, the episodes of "The Encantadas" seem enchanted indeed.

All together, the stories of *The Piazza Tales* are so peculiar in atmosphere and expression—not difficult or obscure, but seductively offbeat, like an exploratory new music filled with oddly familiar resonance—that they are among the most remarkable prose works of the nineteenth century, experiments in perception that are quite, and quite wonderfully, weird.

What: Short Stories. *When:* 1856. *Also By: Israel Potter: His Fifty Years of Exile* (1855). *The Confidence-Man: His Masquerade* (1857). *Try: Tales and Sketches* by Nathaniel Hawthorne (see page 357). *Selected Stories* by Robert Walser. *Adaptations:* "Benito Cereno" was dramatized by poet Robert Lowell in *The Old Glory*. "The Encantadas" was given a musical setting by Tobias Picker in 1983; for the 1991 recording by the Houston Symphony Orchestra, Sir John Gielgud provided the narration.

The Metaphysical Club
A STORY OF IDEAS IN AMERICA
Louis Menand (born 1952)

How Four Thinkers Discovered Pragmatism

O f course you know about the profound cultural influences of the American Civil War and of Darwin's theory of natural selection; a few of you may be aware of the epistemological consequences of the mathematical law of errors. And most readers will recognize the names of the jurist Oliver Wendell Holmes Jr., the philosopher William James, the educator John Dewey, and—maybe—the logician Charles Sanders Peirce. But what you might never imagine is how these disparate events, notions, and personalities could be woven into a penetrating, sagacious, compelling *story*, which is just what Louis Menand has done in his vivid account of the development of the philosophical school of pragmatism, an "idea about ideas" that would define America's empirically minded encounter with modernity by insisting that the meaning of a proposition or action was not preexisting, but was defined by its observable consequences. ("Truth happens to an idea," as William James succinctly put it.)

Menand's collective biography of the quartet of thinkers named above, three of whom formed, in Cambridge, Massachusetts, in 1872, the club that supplies the book's title, is engaging and erudite, astonishing in its grace of conception and expression. It's an intellectual adventure of the first order, fun to read and filled with sparks of wisdom that will illuminate your thinking for a long, long time.

What: Philosophy. History. Biography. *When:* 2001. *Award:* Pulitzer Prize for History, 2002. *Also By: American Studies* (2002). *The Marketplace of Ideas* (2010). *Further Reading: Pragmatism* by William James. *The Common Law* by Oliver Wendell Holmes Jr. *Try: To the Finland Station* by Edmund Wilson.

A Mencken Chrestomathy
H. L. Mencken (1880–1956)

The Best of the "Bad Boy of Baltimore"

H. L. Mencken was a newspaperman—the greatest America has ever produced. Born in Baltimore and a lifelong resident of the city, he hammered out millions of words for its various dailies over the course of half a century. His voracious intelligence and boundless energy also made *The Smart Set* (1914–23) and *The American Mercury* (1924–33) the most vigorous and influential periodicals of their day. His virtuoso prose was robust and jauntily venomous; no journalist has ever stirred up more controversy more consistently than Mencken. He delighted in casting himself as the "great offender," an inexhaustible scourge of conventional wisdom and of the middle-class philistines he lampooned as the "booboisie." People adored him or they despised him—but they never ignored him.

Suffice it to say there is never a dull moment in Mencken, as this book, a 1949 bestseller, abundantly proves. The author's own selection of his best work from the previous four decades, the *Chrestomathy* (from the Greek, the word means "a collection of choice passages from an author or authors," and reveals Mencken's mastery of arcane as well as popular lingo) affords us the opportunity to engage his bracing genius in scores of columns, reviews, and essays. The range of subjects is astonishing: political conventions, crime and punishment, morals, government, democracy, music, literature, history, and the South, with keen comment on leaders from Lincoln to FDR, writers from Poe to Dreiser to Conrad, personalities from Walt Whitman to Rudolph Valentino, and composers from Beethoven to Wagner to both Johann and Richard Strauss.

Throughout the book's more than six hundred pages, Mencken's distinctive style is matched by his singular wit. It's fair to say that humor predominates here, and its ubiquity reveals Mencken to be one of the foremost

H. L. Mencken, 1930

of abounding quackeries," he writes in his preface, "and if we do not learn how to laugh we succumb to the melancholy disease which afflicts the race of viewers-with-alarm." On this score, as on many others, Mencken is a splendid teacher.

What: Culture. Humor. Journalism. Essays. *When:* 1949 (collecting pieces written from 1916 to 1942). *Reading Notes:* Dip in anywhere: This is an ideal bedside book. *Also By: The American Language* (1918; fourth edition, 1936; supplements, 1945 and 1948). Autobiography in three volumes: *Happy Days: 1880–1892* (1940); *Newspaper Days: 1899–1906* (1941); *Heathen Days: 1890–1936* (1943). *A Carnival of Buncombe: Writings on Politics* (1956). *A Second Mencken Chrestomathy* (edited by Terry Teachout, 1995). *Further Reading: The Skeptic: A Life of H. L. Mencken* by Terry Teachout. *Mencken: The American Iconoclast* by Marion Elizabeth Rodgers. *Try: Part of Our Time* by Murray Kempton (see page 438). *Footnote:* Mencken's *A New Dictionary of Quotations on Historical Principles from Ancient and Modern Sources* (1942) is a reference book that delivers hours of instruction and delight.

humorists in American literature, second, perhaps, only to Mark Twain. "We live in a land

---

On the Shoulders of Giants

A SHANDEAN POSTSCRIPT

Robert K. Merton (1910–2003)

Extravagantly Eccentric Erudition

" I f I have seen further," wrote Isaac Newton to fellow natural philosopher Robert Hooke, "it is by standing on the shoulders of giants." It is a graphic and memorable epigram, but what is its provenance? Was the figure minted by the great physicist, or was he merely borrowing another's coinage? And what, precisely, did Newton mean by it? In the pages of this exuberant intellectual adventure, the distinguished sociologist Robert K. Merton charts "the travels and adventures of the Newtonian aphorism," applying a method culled from the extravagant imagination of Laurence Sterne's comic masterpiece, *The Life and Times of Tristram Shandy* (see page 756). Writing in the Shandean mood, as Merton dubs it, "a mood continually reinforced by what one was serendipitously finding en

route," the author takes us through all sorts of scholarly research, digression, speculation, and good humor while tracking his subject.

Disguised as a letter to Harvard historian and Merton friend Bernard Bailyn—("Dear Bud" it modestly begins), *On the Shoulders of Giants*—or *OTSOG*, as it is known to its coterie of devotees—is filled with learning and play. Floating on an undercurrent of footnotes as amusing as they are abundant, Merton's discourse rushes ahead, doubles back, takes off in a dozen directions in history, literature, science, and sociology. It is abstruse and whimsical, parodic and pedantic; it is replete with insight into creativity, tradition, the transmission of knowledge, and the social context of discovery. *OTSOG* is sui generis, a stupendous roller coaster of a book, vertiginous in its passage, secure on its track. As Michael Dirda has perfectly put it, "Once people used to ask if such and such was 'funny ha-ha' or 'funny peculiar.' *On the Shoulders of Giants* is all the more wondrous for being, deliciously, delightfully, both."

What: Culture. History. *When:* 1965. *Also By:* The author of such esteemed (and straight-faced) works of sociology as *Social Theory and Social Structure* (1949), Merton composed, with Elinor Barber, one other book in a somewhat Shandean mood: *The Travels and Adventures of Serendipity* (2004). *Try: The Anatomy of Melancholy* by Robert Burton (see page 113). *The Road to Xanadu: A Study in the Ways of the Imagination* by John Livingston Lowes.

....

The Seven Storey Mountain
Thomas Merton (1915–1968)

A Revered 20th-Century Spiritual Autobiography

Thomas Merton is one of the most intriguing spiritual figures of the twentieth century. An enormously talented writer possessed of a bohemian temperament, a prodigious literary energy, and a searching mind, he retreated from the world in his early twenties, giving his spiritual restlessness a forbidding and yet ultimately freeing destination: a Trappist monastery in Kentucky. From the solitude of the Abbey of Gethsemani, he paradoxically attracted worldwide celebrity, becoming through the 1950s and 1960s an influential, esteemed, and at times controversial advocate of peace and social justice.

His fame was initially spread by the power and popularity of *The Seven Storey Mountain*, the bestselling autobiography he published in 1948, seven years after his arrival at Gethsemani (the title invokes the mountain of Purgatory in Dante's *The Divine Comedy*; see page 194). In chronicling the life that led up to his conversion to Catholicism and his retreat into the cloister, the narrative shadows the author's soul through the history and intellectual ferment of his times. Laced with wry humor, informed with an erudition that stretches from Duns Scotus's proof of the existence of God to the novels of D. H. Lawrence, Merton's narrative of his peripatetic life in this world—in France, England, and Rome, at Cambridge's Clare College and Columbia University, in upstate New York and other locales—is sustained with qualities of intelligence, struggle, and devotion that enhance the wonder of its earnestness. His discovery of his vocation as a priest, and its ultimate unexpected destination, is described with a freshness that continues to open a window for readers on the alluring and mysteriously rewarding austerities of the contemplative life.

What: Autobiography. Religion & Spirituality. *When:* 1948. *Also By:* Merton was astonishingly prolific. Highlights include *Seeds of Contemplation* (1949); *The Sign of Jonas* (1953); *No Man Is an Island* (1955); *Thoughts in Solitude* (1958); *Conjectures of a Guilty Bystander* (1966); and *The Journals of Thomas Merton* (in seven volumes, 1995–98). *Further Reading: The Man in the Sycamore Tree* by Edward Rice. *The Seven Mountains of Thomas Merton* by Michael Mott. *The Life You Save May Be Your Own: An American Pilgrimage* by Paul Elie. *Try: Confessions* by Saint Augustine (see page 29).

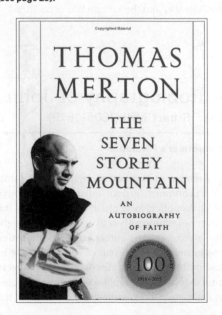

The First Day on the Somme
1 JULY 1916
Martin Middlebrook (born 1932)

The Worst Day of the Great War

The first day of the Battle of the Somme is one of history's most appalling military horror stories. The date was July 1, 1916. At precisely 7:30 that Saturday morning, tens of thousands of British troops began going "over the top," climbing from their trenches and setting out across the no-man's-land that separated them from their German opponents. British and French artillery had pounded the German front lines for days, and it was therefore expected that the methodically advancing soldiers would encounter little resistance from the enemy. This turned out to be a catastrophically incorrect assumption, and as German machine guns mowed down wave after wave of the unprotected, heavily encumbered attackers, July 1 turned into the British army's "blackest day of slaughter." Indeed, as Martin Middlebrook notes, the absolutely unimaginable casualties sustained in a matter of hours by the British—*nearly sixty thousand dead or wounded*—"stand comparison, not only with other battles, but with complete wars. The British army's loss on that one day easily exceeds its battle casualties in the Crimean War, the Boer War and the Korean War combined."

How could it have happened? Was it all the fault of the British commanders, such as the much-vilified generals Douglas Haig and Henry Rawlinson? Were the soldiers themselves at least in part to blame, since so many persisted in what had quickly revealed itself to be a suicide mission? For answers to these and the many other questions raised by the events of that July day beside the Somme River in northern France, the place to turn is this riveting, meticulously detailed, and deeply affecting account of the staggering tragedy. Drawing on sources ranging from official reports to interviews with hundreds of survivors, Martin Middlebrook not only explains, hour by hour, how the debacle unfolded, but also puts the battle into perspective in terms of the entire First World War.

What: History. War. *When:* 1971. *Also By: The Nuremberg Raid* (1973). *Convoy* (1976). *The Kaiser's Battle: 21 March 1918* (1978). *The Battle of Hamburg* (1980). *The Somme Battlefields* (with Mary Middlebrook; 1994). *Arnhem 1944* (1994). *Further Reading: Somme* by Lyn Macdonald. *The Somme: Heroism and Horror in the First World War* by Martin Gilbert. *Try: The Price of Glory: Verdun 1916* by Alistair Horne. *They Called It Passchendaele* by Lyn Macdonald.

Autobiography of John Stuart Mill
John Stuart Mill (1806–1873)

A Reformer's Formation

Member of parliament, civil administrator, economist, ardent feminist, and above all philosopher, John Stuart Mill bestrides the history of nineteenth-century English thought like a colossus. His autobiography, published posthumously in the year of his death, begins fascinatingly with a discussion of his very unorthodox education; he was homeschooled in Latin and Greek, and where students of the day often learned mathematics and logic by rote, Mill's father insisted the boy figure out every principle for himself, even at the age of eight. By his own admission, Mill was no wunderkind, insisting that when it came to natural gifts, he was "rather below than above par." But his exemplary, albeit eccentric, education, and his father's insistence on rational thought and personal discovery, gave the young Mill "an advantage of a quarter of a century over my contemporaries."

John Stuart Mill, ca. 1858

In 1821, after reading the work of the political philosopher Jeremy Bentham, the fifteen-year-old Mill decides to devote himself to becoming "a reformer of the world." He almost never gets started, however, for—his years of hard study having taken their toll—he becomes mired in depression: "the whole foundation on which my life was constructed fell down." It takes years before Mill recovers from his breakdown and feels ready to face life again. He eventually composes the masterpieces of political and philosophical thought *On Liberty* (1859)and *Utilitarianism*. As the influence of his ideas grows, the *Autobiography* shifts from personal reminiscences to a larger intellectual history of his era. His entry into politics is contextualized by the passage of the landmark Reform Act, and his advocacy against capital punishment and for women's suffrage are set, perhaps too modestly, in the media and political landscape of the day.

Any autobiography of a thinker as important as Mill would be worth reading. But Mill's autobiography is an especially critical volume, because almost all of his philosophical writing is tied to the political and moral agenda that would come to dominate the Victorian age. To understand his arguments on the limits of power in *On Liberty*, or his theories on the equality of the sexes in *The Subjection of Women* (1869), it's necessary to understand the man so keenly revealed in this extraordinary self-portrait.

What: Autobiography. When: 1873. Also By: Utilitarianism (1863). Further Reading: John Stuart Mill: Victorian Firebrand by Richard Reeves. Try: The Autobiography of Charles Darwin. The Education of Henry Adams by Henry Adams (see page 6). The Proper Study of Mankind by Isaiah Berlin.

Death of a Salesman
Arthur Miller (1915–2005)

Interpretation of Dreams

Arthur Miller's seminal drama begins with its hero, Willy Loman, returning home from a sales trip in a state of utter exhaustion; it's downhill from there—for Willy, at least. It's a tribute to the power of the playwright's conception and execution that the audience is held in a state of suspended trepidation—a kind of reverent state of recognition—as it watches a familiar life unravel before it.

Exposing the emptiness of simple-minded faith in material success and personal agency (the can-do confidence that rides, as one character admiringly puts it, "on a smile and a shoeshine"), Miller's story of a washed-up salesman lost in delusions of control over his circumstances is as shattering a view of the American Dream as has ever been penned. As the past and present of Willy's life, and the lives of his loyal wife, Linda, and his aimless sons, Biff and Happy, occupy the stage simultaneously, motivations and ambitions pass like clouds that shadow any hoped-for future with the cataclysmic weather on the horizon. When Linda implores her children to honor their father—"attention must be paid. He's not to be allowed to fall into his grave like an old dog. Attention, attention must be finally paid to such a person"—she describes the task Arthur Miller set himself, and performed with almost savage purpose, turning the attention of generations of readers and theater-goers to the tragedy next door.

What: Drama. *When:* 1949. *Awards:* Pulitzer Prize for Drama and Tony Award for Best Play, both in 1949. *Also By: All My Sons* (1947). *The Crucible* (1953). *A View from the Bridge* (1955). *The Price* (1968). *Further Reading:* Miller's *Salesman in Beijing* (1984) chronicles his experiences mounting the play in China in 1983. *Try: The Iceman Cometh* by Eugene O'Neill. *Glengarry Glen Ross* by David Mamet. *Adaptations:* The original Broadway production starred Lee J. Cobb as Willy and was directed by Elia

DEATH OF A SALESMAN

BY ARTHUR MILLER

Arthur Miller, 1956

Kazan. A 1985 television film directed by Volker Schlöndorff features Dustin Hoffman in the lead role.

Black Spring
Henry Miller (1891–1980)

Autobiographical Sketches from an American Original

Henry Miller, ca. 1960

"I too am not a bit tamed [. . .] I sound my barbaric yawp over the roofs of the world." That memorable declaration of artistic independence from Walt Whitman's *Leaves of Grass* comes to mind when reading Henry Miller's own untamed, barbaric yawp of a book, *Black Spring*. Like Whitman's poetry, Miller's prose is a song of the self, freewheeling and unashamedly egoistic. It is resolutely unliterary writing, arising from and celebrating the life of the street—"What is not in the open street is false, derived, that is to say, *literature*." The streets of Paris, the streets of Brooklyn, the streets of midtown Manhattan: Miller prowls them all in the course of *Black Spring*'s ten episodes, autobiographical fictions that read like free-associative monologues, dazzlingly exuberant riffs. The two high points are "The Angel Is My Watermark" and "The Tailor Shop." The former is Miller's celebrated account of painting a picture—no, not just a picture, a masterpiece, "my masterpiece!" And the latter—a novel's worth of material packed into a longish short story—is an especially vivid slice of autobiography drawn from Miller's experiences working in his father's shop in the heart of New York City. "The Tailor Shop" is also notable for including the line that became a sort of Millerian credo, the motto of his life and art: *"Always merry and bright!"*

Miller wrote *Black Spring* in between *Tropic of Cancer* (1934) and *Tropic of Capricorn* (1939). The books are a trilogy, but the *Tropics* are much more famous because their sexual explicitness has earned them notoriety and a place in the history of America's sexual revolution. (*Tropic of Cancer* was banned in the United States for decades until cleared of obscenity charges by the Supreme Court in 1964.) Yet *Black Spring*, which is far less explicit, may well be Miller's best book.

What: Novel. *When:* 1936. *Also By: The Colossus of Maroussi* (1941). *Sunday After the War* (1944). *The Air-Conditioned Nightmare* (1945). *Big Sur and the Oranges of Hieronymus Bosch* (1957). *Further Reading:* Don't miss George Orwell's valuable essay on Miller, "Inside the Whale." See also *Genius and Lust: A Journey Through the Major Writings of Henry Miller* by Norman Mailer. *Try: Leaves of Grass* by Walt Whitman (see page 850). *The Horse's Mouth* by Joyce Cary (see page 135).

> **"Get hold of *Black Spring* and read especially the first hundred pages. They give you an idea of what can still be done, even at this late date, with English prose."**
>
> —George Orwell

A Canticle for Leibowitz
Walter M. Miller Jr. (1923–1996)

Apocalypse Again and Again, Amen

The history of the novel is dotted with "one-hit wonders," writers who managed to turn out a single stunning book but who then receded into silence, failure, or futile attempts to recapture their former success. Yet, in literature at least, one book can be enough to ensure lasting glory, and that is the case with Walter Miller Jr., whose place in the science fiction pantheon seems assured by *A Canticle for Leibowitz*.

Miller had previously turned out many fine short stories for the magazines of his era, but the magnificent, unprecedented book that he fashioned from three standout novellas and issued in 1960 both elevated his stature and somehow simultaneously ended his career. He would never publish another novel in his lifetime; although he worked obsessively on a sequel (eventually completed by Terry Bisson and published as *Saint Leibowitz and the Wild Horse Woman* in 1997), he fell prey to the depression that eventually ended in his suicide.

His hardheaded yet incantatory novel, full of desert sunlight, dust, and spartan, censer-plumed chambers, opens more than half a millennium after a nuclear holocaust has plunged mankind back into the Dark Ages. In the American Southwest, the monks of the Abbey of the Blessed Leibowitz struggle to preserve the rare and incomprehensible documents that have survived the scathing Simplification, a period in which not just learning but literacy itself has been disdained and persecuted. The abbey is named for its founder, a Jewish electrical engineer in the American military who converted to Roman Catholicism and, in the wake of that now distant nuclear catastrophe, established a monastic order dedicated to hiding books and protecting scientific knowledge. Six hundred years later, the novice Brother Francis stumbles upon a cache of ancient documents and relics from the holy Leibowitz, and eventually travels to New Rome to be present for Leibowitz's elevation to sainthood.

Part two jumps forward another six hundred years. There is no real technology, but the passage of time has brought an increased historical awareness and a rejuvenation of scientific inquiry. Once again the monastery of Saint Leibowitz is the center of action, as a scholar comes to investigate its library holdings and is startled by the first electric light in a millennium or more. In part three, yet another six centuries onward, the world has returned to the *status quo ante*, if not to a higher plateau of understanding. Nuclear war has also returned, and the preservation of knowledge under threat of destruction is a renewed imperative.

Miller's tone throughout his recursively calamitous chronicle is alternately coolly ironic, despairing, affirmative, and resigned. The eternal parade of human folly—man as God made him, mitigated only by faith and education—gets the full scrutiny of his gimlet eye. Still, Miller's vision of cloistered savants struggling to maintain and transmit civilization amidst ineluctable chaos speaks to the most noble and altruistic impulses of the human soul. The book's enduring influence can be seen in postapocalyptic fiction as varied as Fred Saberhagen's Empire of the East series, Vernor Vinge's *Tatja Grimm's World*, and Neal Stephenson's *Anathem*.

What: Science Fiction. *When:* 1960. *Award:* Hugo Award for Best Novel, 1961. *Also By: Conditionally Human* (1962). *The View from the Stars* (1965). *Saint Leibowitz and the Wild Horse Woman* (1997; with Terry Bisson). *Further Reading:* "Rediscovering *A Canticle for Leibowitz*" by Walker Percy, in his *Signposts in a Strange Land: Essays. Try: Earth Abides* by George R. Stewart. *Engine Summer* by John Crowley. *Always Coming Home* by Ursula K. Le Guin. *Adaptations:* Curiously enough, although the book has never been filmed, three radio productions have appeared, the most complete being a fifteen-part 1981 version from NPR.

THE WORLD OF WINNIE-THE-POOH

WINNIE-THE-POOH • THE HOUSE AT POOH CORNER

A. A. Milne (1882–1956)
Illustrations by Ernest H. Shepard (1879–1976)

Growing Affection

What generous quantities of imagination, creativity, and emotion young children pour into the vessels of their stuffed animals, inventing personalities through which they explore the mysteries of human nature that are unfolding on a grander and less huggable scale all about them. It was the genius of A. A. Milne, observing his own son, Christopher, playing with his teddy bear, to immortalize such childhood inspiration in affectionate tales that are among the most endearing in all children's literature. The boy (Christopher Robin) imbues his bear (Winnie-the-Pooh) with indelible characteristics that have stood the test of both time and Disneyfication: Pooh is stalwart, friendly, and fanciful, possessed by a love of "HUNNY," a penchant for humming "hums" to himself, and a quintessential goodness. Toddlers find congenial his absorption in simple pleasures, such as the game of Poohsticks, a pastime of the bear's own invention in which players drop sticks into a stream off one side of a bridge and rush to the other to see which one the current carries faster. Although the bear's naïveté is funny, his unexpected ability to conjure clever solutions for troubling predicaments is even more delightful, as when he rides in Christopher Robin's upturned umbrella to rescue a friend from a flood. Winnie and his pals Piglet, Kanga and Baby Roo, Owl, Rabbit, Eeyore, and the bouncing Tigger are a most merry crew—merry, that is, except for Eeyore, an unforgettable gray donkey who leaves a gloomy trail wherever he goes.

It's hard to imagine better bedside reading for parents and tots than these celebrations of companionship and fanciful but nevertheless unconditional love. If they're lucky, young listeners will live to discover—when the time has come for them to read to their own little ones—that days spent in the Hundred Acre Wood with Winnie and Christopher Robin can return after decades with all their tenderness and wonder intact.

What: Children's. *When: Winnie-the-Pooh*, 1926, and *The House at Pooh Corner*, 1928. *Also By:* Two books of verse in which Christopher Robin and his bear also appear: *When We Were Very Young* (1924) and *Now We Are Six* (1927). *Further Reading: The Enchanted Places,* a memoir of childhood by Milne's son, Christopher. *Try: A Bear Called Paddington* by Michael Bond. *Little Bear* by Else Holmelund Minarik (see page 555). *Adaptations:* Winnie was a pioneer in the field of licensed merchandising, even before Disney took possession of the characters in 1961; since then, adaptations for film and television have been plentiful. *Footnotes:* In 1960, Alexander Lenard's Latin translation, *Winnie Ille Pu*, became the first book in that language ever to land on the *New York Times* bestseller list (where it remained for twenty weeks). The World Poohsticks Championships have been held annually in Oxfordshire since 1984.

Christopher Robin Milne and his bear, 1928

·····

Paradise Lost
John Milton (1608–1674)

Of Fallen Angels and the Fall of Man

A tale of forbidden fruit, *Paradise Lost* can be a forbidding poem, for it advances dense theological arguments about temptation, sin, predestination, and punishment in language that is radically unlike modern English: Milton's unrhymed pentameter lines, populated with an esoteric, Latinate vocabulary that can make even Shakespeare seem conversational, defy casual reading. Even Samuel Johnson, who greatly admired Milton's epic, believed that the poet "had formed his style by a perverse and pedantic principle." And yet, daunting as this monumental masterpiece appears, its narrative is nothing short of thrilling, its poetry sublime. Once a reader has learned to taste its delights and savor its language, no other writing seems as wildly nourishing.

Let's start with the story, which itself starts, as epics always do, *in medias res*: Satan and his band of fallen angels, having been cast out of heaven for their revolt against God, find themselves exiled in hell:

The dismal situation waste and wild,
A dungeon horrible, on all sides round
As one great furnace flamed, yet from those flames
No light, but rather darkness visible
Served only to discover sights of woe,
Regions of sorrow, doleful shades, where peace
And rest can never dwell, hope never comes . . .

From the outset, even though the task the poet sets himself is to "justify the ways of God to men," *Paradise Lost* is a tale of devils, and Satan is its most compelling protagonist. Although his pursuit of vengeance through the corruption of Adam and Eve soon unfolds as the poem's plot, all the other characters, even the Almighty, have supporting roles, despite theological and moral imperatives that might suggest otherwise. Think of a 1930s gangster film, with Pat O'Brien as a noble priest representing goodness and authority, and a young couple roughed up by life sent on their amorous and hopeful way in the final reel; the character who rivets the audience's attention—and wins their affection—is Jimmy Cagney as the criminal. Something very similar happens in *Paradise Lost*.

In its early episodes, as it makes its serpentine way to the Garden of Eden to recount Eve and Adam's fall from grace, the poem passes through an imaginative terrain that invests ideas of rebellion, fate, and free will with brilliant colors. In fact, Milton's artistic engagement with these themes overwhelms the certainties of any dogma, until the reader feels their metaphysical force as an almost physical presence. One might even characterize *Paradise Lost* as a book of spells, summoning from the air by the magic of its words a landscape majestic enough for the soul to inhabit, just as, in one of the poem's most stunning passages, the Lord summons animals from the earth on the sixth day of creation:

> ... when God said,
> Let the earth bring forth soul living in her kind,
> Cattle and creeping things, and beast of the earth,
> Each in their kind. The earth obeyed, and straight
> Opening her fertile womb teemed at a birth
> Innumerous living creatures, perfect forms,
> Limbed and full grown ...
> The grassy clods now calved, now half appeared
> The tawny lion, pawing to get free
> His hinder parts, then springs as broke from bonds,
> And rampant shakes his brinded mane ...

Milton's epic resounds with a majesty no other work in the language approaches; to feel its power one must speak it aloud, letting the sounds orchestrate the intricate sense into a melody beyond explanation, a kind of swelling reality that transports us from heaven and hell

to the human world, just as Adam and Eve, at the poem's close, set out toward history from the realms of myth:

> The world was all before them, where to choose
> Their place of rest, and providence their guide:
> They hand in hand with wandering steps and slow,
> Through Eden took their solitary way.

What: Poetry. *When:* 1667. *Edition:* A reader-friendly and very handsome edition, with a splendid introduction by novelist Philip Pullman, was issued by Oxford in 2005. *Reading Note:* Read a page aloud whenever you can, and don't fuss with explication; such short immersion paves the way for absorption. *Also By:* *Poems* (1645; including "On the Morning of Christ's Nativity," "L'Allegro," "Il Penseroso," and "Lycidas"). *Paradise Regained* (1671). *Samson Agonistes* (1671). *Further Reading: A Preface to "Paradise Lost"* by C. S. Lewis. *The Life of John Milton* by A. N. Wilson. *Try: The Aeneid* by Virgil (see page 823). *The Divine Comedy* by Dante Alighieri (see page 194). *Footnote:* Having gone blind many years before beginning *Paradise Lost*, John Milton composed the poem in dictation.

Hell as depicted in the first illustrated edition of Paradise Lost, *1688*

Little Bear
Else Holmelund Minarik (1920–2012)
Illustrations by Maurice Sendak (1926–2012)

A Book to Curl Up With

....

" I have always imagined that Paradise will be a kind of library," Jorge Luis Borges famously said, invoking the predigital dreams of generations of high-minded lovers of literature. At least some portion of more earthbound readers, one may suspect, would locate their bookish heaven not in a library but in a lap—on which they as a toddler sat, or on which they as a parent perched their progeny, to share a printed tale. No books are better suited to this readerly throne than Else Holmelund Minarik's heartwarming Little Bear stories, illustrated with fond wit by Maurice Sendak.

The first in Minarik's set of five Little Bear volumes was published in 1957 as the initial entry in Harper & Row's terrific I Can Read series, designed to employ simple stories and limited vocabulary to encourage fledgling readers. As far as *Little Bear* is concerned, utility in this regard does nothing to diminish its charm. Whether deciding what to wear, worrying that his mother has forgotten his birthday, or pretending to fly to the moon, Little Bear is uninterruptedly lovable, his mother unstintingly loving.

The family magic is continued in *Father Bear Comes Home* (1959), *Little Bear's Friend* (1960), *Little Bear's Visit* (1961), and *A Kiss for Little Bear* (1968). A set of these books is just about the best gift you could give your kids (to say nothing of yourself) in those fleeting months when their entire lives seem to rest in your lap; you can start sharing them as soon as your toddler's ready for books (and a first grader will be able to read them on his or her own).

What: Children's. *When:* 1957. *Also By: No Fighting, No Biting!* (1958). *Try: The Tale of Peter Rabbit* by Beatrix Potter (see page 637). *Goodnight, Moon* (see page 101) and *Little Fur Family* (see page 102) by Margaret Wise Brown. *Adaptation:* Little Bear has become a television franchise; stick to the original books.

A Fine Balance
Rohinton Mistry (born 1952)

A Sprawling Novel of Modern India

....

B orn and raised in Bombay but a longtime resident of Canada, a Parsi rather than a Hindu, a realist in an age of magic realists, Rohinton Mistry has never neatly fit expectations. The tightly focused artistry of his first two works of fiction, *Tales from Firozsha Baag* (1987) and *Such a Long Journey* (1991), gave no hint of the capacious creative vision his third book, *A Fine Balance*, would exhibit, earning him comparison to Dickens (see page 215), Tolstoy (see page 797), and—by one astute critic, at least—the Victor Hugo of *Les Misérables* (see page 394). The character-centric plot is enlivened by the author's ability to imbue his realism with close observation of suffering and attentive celebration of the infinite variety of facts and faces that populate the world. Mistry's alertness to forces of history and the legacy of social and political oppression, his compassion for the downtrodden and unlucky, and, most importantly, his fidelity to human truths that transcend caste and circumstance to inform the most circumscribed lives with joy, sorrow, grief, and love—all testify to the justness of the invocation of past masters when discussing *A Fine Balance*. They translate into a reading experience that is filled with the transporting wonder only the greatest novels inspire.

A Fine Balance is set in Mistry's native land, in an unnamed city by the sea. Although the novel takes numerous excursions into the past to relate the backstories of the main characters and their families, the book's present is 1975, and its action unfolds against the backdrop of the state of emergency imposed by Prime Minister Indira Gandhi; it is a time of tremendous social and political upheaval. At the center of the book is the forty-ish Dina Dalal, a Parsi widow determined to support herself and maintain her independence from her domineering older brother by making a go of her seamstress business. She takes in as a boarder a college student named Maneck, the son of Parsi acquaintances outside the city. On his way to introduce himself to Dina, Maneck meets an uncle and a nephew, Hindus born into the lowly leather-workers' caste who have broken with convention by training to be tailors. Before long, this pair is working for Dina and also living—secretly and illegally—under

her roof. Transcending their mutual distrust, they come together to form a family, one that will be happy and unhappy in its own consoling way.

What the four have in common is nothing more than a desire to improve their lot, however modestly, but that does not keep them out of trouble in Indira Gandhi's India. As Mistry's enormous tale progresses through its six hundred pages, we share their tribulations and their relations with an astonishing cast of characters (including the unforgettable Beggarmaster), and are carried through their trials on a current of humor that survives every hardship. We long for a happy ending for Dina and the rest, but on that score Mistry is too much of a realist not to disappoint us. Nevertheless, he leaves readers with a rare satisfaction, as critic Brooke Allen has aptly noted: "Occasionally a book does come along that rekindles our affection for the human race, and *A Fine Balance* is one of them."

What: Novel. *When:* 1996. *Also By: Tales from Firozsha Baag* (1987; US title: *Swimming Lessons and Other Stories from Firozsha Baag*). *Family Matters* (2001). *Try: A Suitable Boy* by Vikram Seth. *The Northern Clemency* by Philip Hensher.

Up in the Old Hotel
Joseph Mitchell (1908–1996)

The Connoisseur of Curious Characters

Of all the legendary scribes whose prose graced the columns of *The New Yorker* in its heyday, Joseph Mitchell is in a class by himself. His profiles of his preferred subjects—in his own description, "visionaries, obsessives, imposters, fanatics, lost souls, the-end-is-near street preachers, old Gypsy kings and old Gypsy queens, and out-and-out freak-show freaks"—offered an unparalleled portrait of Manhattan's

human comedy, penned by an offbeat Balzac whose eyes and ears missed no trick.

Mitchell's encounters with eccentrics and hardworking joes in and around the metropolis are a joy to read, and a lesson in the arts of observation and composition. Whether writing about the Fulton Fish Market or McSorley's Ale House on East Seventh Street, the author has a knack for knowing where to look, whom to engage in conversation, and how to listen; few writers short of Joyce have ever evoked

a Harvard-educated scion of a blue-blood Boston clan, through prodigious effort ("industry" is not the appropriate word), established a remarkable career as a bohemian panhandler in Greenwich Village from the 1920s to the 1940s. His meal ticket among the artistic and literary circles of the day (in addition to his noisy claim to be an adept in the language of seagulls) was the reputation he invented for himself as the author of a work in progress of such stupendous proportions—nothing less than "An Oral History of Our Time"—that it inspired the altruism of scores of fashionable, accomplished Villagers. Mitchell's acquaintance with Gould, and his research into the character's career, resulted in two *New Yorker* profiles: "Professor Sea Gull," published in 1942, and "Joe Gould's Secret," published twenty-two years later, both collected here. Together they form a curious, compelling tale, which ultimately reveals—to Mitchell's feigned or real surprise—the entirely unwritten fate of Gould's long-touted "Oral History."

Mysteriously, "Joe Gould's Secret" would prove to be the last piece of any consequence to issue from Joseph Mitchell, despite the fact that he reported to his office at *The New Yorker* on a daily basis for the next three decades. It would require a writer of Mitchell's own gifts to do justice to *that* story.

the undercurrents of a city's dynamism with Mitchell's sense of scope and scrutiny. Although the labeling of his work as bona fide nonfiction has been questioned—he was not shy about creating composite characters or ordering facts more artfully than reality supplied them—the power of his stories to deliver human truths and literary delights in equal measure remains unassailable.

Up in the Old Hotel collects much of his life's work, including that originally published in the volumes *McSorley's Wonderful Saloon, Old Mr. Flood, The Bottom of the Harbor,* and *Joe Gould's Secret.* The eponymous Mr. Gould,

What: Essays. Journalism. *When:* 1992, collecting work published over the previous fifty years. *Also By: My Ears Are Bent* (1938). *Further Reading: Man in Profile: Joseph Mitchell of* The New Yorker by Thomas Kunkel. *Try: The Telephone Booth Indian* by A. J. Liebling. *Friends Talking in the Night* by Philip Hamburger. *Adaptation:* Stanley Tucci plays Mitchell in his 2000 film adaptation of *Joe Gould's Secret.*

Gone With the Wind
Margaret Mitchell (1900–1949)

Still Bigger Than the Big Screen

It's easy to assume that this book's outsize reputation has been inflated by the monumental 1939 movie it inspired, so indelibly imprinted on our collective imagination are Vivien Leigh's Scarlett O'Hara and Clark Gable's Rhett Butler (to say nothing of the film's soaring theme music or the cinematic spectacle of the burning of Atlanta). Yet how many fictional worlds are vital enough to animate such larger-than-life screen incarnations?

The book's origins were serendipitous enough to suggest their own movie plot, in which an unknown talent is singled out by fate for fame and fortune. Laid up with an ankle injury in 1926, Margaret Mitchell began writing a Civil War story as a way to amuse herself, inspired by her own avid reading of historical novels. Mitchell had been born into a prominent Atlanta family and raised on stories of the War Between the States (though she was ten before anyone told her who won!). In crafting a tale of a Southern heroine as stubborn and shrewd as she was alluring, Mitchell drew on her encyclopedic knowledge of the period and on events from her own life, most notably her mother's death during the flu epidemic of 1918. Writing voluminously and haphazardly—last chapter first—she showed the book to nobody but her husband, who had suggested the diversion. When her ankle was healed, she put it away. Thanks to a fortuitous meeting with a visiting publisher a decade later, Gone With the Wind was eventually dusted off, completed, and published—to tremendous praise, unprecedented sales (despite the Depression), and the Pulitzer Prize.

History may be written by the winners, but fiction often finds its truths in the experience of the losers. Such is certainly the case with Gone With the Wind, which brings America's bloodiest war—and the Southern privileges it vanquished—to life with irresistible power (albeit with a blinkered sense of moral responsibility and historical reality when it comes to the unprivileged and enslaved). Although it is filled with dozens of characters—from the noble but timid Ashley Wilkes to the blustering but stalwart maid Mammy—it is Scarlett's book, and the combination of scheming, seduction, and sheer will by which she survives the collapse of her way of life makes her a heroine with few peers in American literature.

"The novel Gone With the Wind shaped the South I grew up in more than any other book," wrote the novelist Pat Conroy in 1996. Big enough for Hollywood, it was big enough to cast its own influence on history, too. Yet Mitchell's thousand-page opus earns its reputation on the most intimate of levels, enthralling individual readers into passionate engagement. Conroy again: "The novel allows you to lose yourself in the glorious pleasures of reading itself, when all five senses ignite in the sheer happiness of narrative." Although Mitchell never wrote another book—she spent the rest of her life responding personally to the thousands upon thousands of fan letters she received—generations have found this one impossible to put down.

Margaret Mitchell, 1938

What: Novel. *When:* 1936. *Award:* Pulitzer Prize for Fiction, 1937. *Also By:* Forty-five years after Mitchell's death another manuscript was discovered—a novella she'd written when she was sixteen; it was published in 1996 as *Lost Laysen. Further Reading: Margaret Mitchell's "Gone With the Wind": A Bestseller's Odyssey from Atlanta to Hollywood* by Ellen F. Brown and John Wiley Jr. *Frankly, My Dear: "Gone With the Wind" Revisited* by Molly Haskell. *Try: Vanity Fair* by William Makepeace Thackeray (see page 777). *Forever Amber* by Kathleen Winsor. *Lonesome Dove* by Larry McMurtry (see page 538). *Adaptation:* The 1939 David O. Selznick film is among the most famous, profitable, and award-winning films in Hollywood history. *Footnote:* Sequels, authorized and not, have been penned by Alice Randall, Alexandra Ripley, and Donald McCaig.

Hons and Rebels
Jessica Mitford (1917–1996)

Growing Up in the First Family of English Eccentricity

In their heyday, which was the 1930s and 1940s, the aristocratic Mitford sisters were regulars in British gossip columns and tabloids. As their mother wearily confessed, "Whenever I read the words 'Peer's Daughter' in a headline, I know it's going to be something about one of you children." She wasn't far wrong: The lives of the six daughters of Lord and Lady Redesdale were a collective miniseries of scandal and rebellion. The most notorious of the siblings were Unity and Diana. The former was an ardent fascist and Nazi sympathizer who became pals with Hitler and attempted suicide when war broke out between Britain and Germany; the latter married the heir to the Guinness Brewery fortune, only to divorce him and become the mistress of the leader of the British Union of Fascists. As for the other sisters, there was Nancy, who wrote popular novels (see *The Pursuit of Love*, below) and biographies; Deborah, who married the Duke of Devonshire and turned their estate, called Chatsworth, into one of England's stateliest homes; Pamela, who, in this company at least, kept a low profile; and Jessica, nicknamed "Decca," a passionate communist and muckraking journalist

whose books include *The American Way of Death*, a classic exposé of the funeral industry in the United States.

Hons and Rebels was Jessica Mitford's first book. ("Hons" is short for "Honourables"—that is, titled individuals, such as Lords and Ladies.) A forthright, poignant, and highly amusing memoir, it reveals what a "rich vein of lunacy" ran in the Mitford family and what an isolated and eccentric upbringing the children had before embarking on their respective headline-grabbing misadventures. From the whirl of the London social season (Unity, by the way, was known to bring her pet rat to fancy dances) to Miami's Bar Roma, which Jessica and her first husband ran for a time, *Hons and Rebels* reads—as one British reviewer aptly put it—"like extravagantly mannered fiction, except that it is all fabulously true." It offers a lively look at the wild side of the English upper crust.

What: Memoir. *When:* 1960. *Also By:* Poison Penmanship: The Gentle Art of Muckraking (1979). The American Way of Death Revisited (1998). Decca: The Letters of Jessica Mitford (2006). *Further Reading:* The Sisters: The Saga of the Mitford Family by Mary S. Lovell. The Mitfords: Letters Between Six Sisters, edited by Charlotte Mosley. *Try:* Sisters by a River by Barbara Comyns. Great Granny Webster by Caroline Blackwood.

The Pursuit of Love
Nancy Mitford (1904–1973)

Upper-Crust Comedy

For pure reading pleasure it's hard to beat Nancy Mitford's fast-paced and quick-witted comic novels of the English upper class in the 1930s and 1940s. Whether sending up life in the country or skewering high society in town, Mitford is unfailingly funny. Her plots are rollicking combinations of romance, misapprehension, and the constant battle between Bright Young Things and Dull Old Things. And her character portraits keep just this side of

caricature, while leaning well over the edge of hilarity.

The Pursuit of Love is particularly wicked for its thinly veiled portrait of Mitford's own extravagantly eccentric family, disguised here as the Radletts, who live at Alconleigh, an estate deep in the English countryside. The blustering father and the vague but doting mother keep ineffectual watch over their seven children as well as their niece Fanny, who narrates the story. For the record, Fanny is being raised by her aunt and uncle because her own stylish parents are just too glamorous for child rearing. Indeed, Fanny tells us that her mother, "having felt herself too beautiful and too gay to be burdened with a child at the age of nineteen [. . .] left my father when I was a month old, and subsequently ran away so often, and with so many people, that she became known to her family and friends as the Bolter." The novel's plot concerns itself primarily with the romantic misadventures of Fanny's cousin Linda, a wayward beauty who makes do with stand-ins for Mr. Right until, at last, he comes along—though not, alas, *for* long.

Displaying Mitford's addictively readable prose and her genius for satirizing aristocratic life as it was lived in the years between the world wars, *The Pursuit of Love* is sparkling entertainment.

What: Novel. *When:* 1945. *Also By:* Two sequels: *Love in a Cold Climate* (1949) and *Don't Tell Alfred* (1960). Other fiction: *Highland Fling* (1931); *Christmas Pudding* (1932); *Pigeon Pie* (1940); *The Blessing* (1951). Nonfiction: *Madame de Pompadour* (1954); *Noblesse Oblige* (1956); *Voltaire in Love* (1957); *The Sun King* (1966); *Frederick the Great* (1970). *Further Reading: The House of Mitford* by Jonathan Guinness, with Catherine Guinness. *Try: Vile Bodies* by Evelyn Waugh.

· ·

House Made of Dawn
N. Scott Momaday (born 1934)

An Award-Winning Novel of Disillusion and Reenchantment

Despite the fact that it was the first novel by an American Indian to win a Pulitzer Prize, and that it sparked what has come to be known as the Native American Renaissance, *House Made of Dawn*, in its outline, at least, relates a tale of alienation and discontent that is not uncommon in the annals of modern fiction. What distinguishes N. Scott Momaday's debut work is the manner of its telling, which intertwines the plight of its young American Indian protagonist with his culture's traditions, myths, and modes of apprehending both natural and spiritual experience. The author exhibits a reverence for language that invokes both the sacred power of prayers and spells and the composed inspirations of literary prose. He especially employs the laconic, rhythmic simplicity of Hemingway's style to fresh and telling purpose.

Told in shifting time frames, *House Made of Dawn* is the story of a Tano Indian

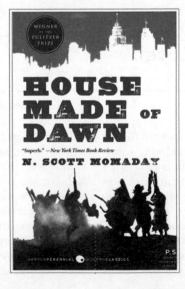

named Abel. Returning home from his World War II army service, Abel finds himself torn between the world he grew up in—his grandfather's world—and the sparkling promise of postwar America. The former, defined by the limits of the reservation and the limitless legacy of ancient wisdom, is spiritually rich but materially poor, while the latter is filled with the allure of seductive freedoms. Drawn to urban life, divorced from the communion with the land and the traditions of his heritage, Abel pursues an aimless life that leads to prison, dissipation, and despair. Momaday depicts Abel's downward spiral through a number of different perspectives, making us piece together the fragments of his shattered life in a way that makes its shattering more sorrowful. With the final illness and death of his grandfather, Abel embraces the rituals that have long connected the Tano living to their dead. As he struggles toward consolation and new hope, the author raises his language to an incantatory, elegiac pitch that is transporting.

What: Novel. *When:* 1968. *Award:* Pulitzer Prize for Fiction, 1969. *Also By: The Way to Rainy Mountain* (1969). *The Names: A Memoir* (1976). *In the Presence of the Sun: Stories and Poems, 1961–1991* (1992). *The Man Made of Words: Essays, Stories, Passages* (1997). *Further Reading: Growing Up Native American: An Anthology,* edited by Patricia Riley. *Try: Winter in the Blood* by James Welch. *Ceremony* by Leslie Marmon

Silko. *Love Medicine* by Louise Erdrich. *Adaptation:* The author collaborated on the 1987 film. *Footnote:* Momaday was born in Oklahoma during the Depression, to parents of Kiowa and Cherokee descent. He grew up on reservations and pueblos, often among American Indians whose language he didn't speak. In addition to his success as novelist, poet, and painter, he has pursued an academic career at several esteemed universities.

Essays
Michel de Montaigne (1533–1592)

Cartographer of the Inner Life

We all have a book inside us, or so the saying goes. The truly fortunate among us come to realize, at some point in our reading lives, that it was already written by Montaigne.

Four hundred years after the death of the author of the *Essays,* the discerning British journalist Bernard Levin captured the work's abiding power: "I defy any reader not to put down the book at some point and say with incredulity, 'How did he know all that about me?'" Levin's sentiment echoes a recognition made by many other luminaries across the centuries, from Voltaire to Virginia Woolf; that countless common readers continue to discover similar rewards in the pages of this Renaissance humanist can be verified in the comments section of nearly any book-centric website.

As the table of contents for any edition of the *Essays* attests, the objects of Montaigne's investigations range from small to large, everyday to erudite: "Of idleness"; "Of the education of children"; "Of solitude"; "A consideration upon Cicero"; "How our mind hinders itself"; "Against do-nothingness"; "Of thumbs"; "Of repentance." Importantly, he treats not only ideas, but familiar feelings—fear, friendship, impatience, laziness—that anchor his musings in our own experience. His famous skepticism springs from a sense of measure that strips vanity from both himself and the mighty: "on the loftiest throne in the world," he writes in the penultimate paragraph of "Apology for Raymond Sebond," the longest of his essays, "we are still sitting only on our own rump."

Invitingly, his entire enterprise is graced with a self-deprecatory wit that makes him a charming companion.

Michel Eyquem de Montaigne was a member of the French nobility who, in addition to managing his family estate, served as a courtier, a magistrate, and, like his father before him, mayor of Bordeaux. Although he could not entirely escape the turbulence of his time, including religious civil war and an outbreak of the plague, he did his best to view it philosophically. At the age of thirty-eight, he retreated from public life to the sanctuary of his château in the Dordogne, whose southern tower housed his library and the small study in which he worked. Over the next twenty years, surrounded by his books (his library purportedly contained fifteen hundred) and the thoughts they engendered, he would draft, revise, and refine the more than one hundred pieces that make up the complete *Essays.*

Aptly, the French word that Montaigne used to describe his efforts, *essai,* means "trial" or "attempt." These prose experiments began as something new, and, over the two decades of their creation, grew into something newer still. Starting out as brief considerations of a thought or theme in which Montaigne deployed his wide reading to chart the course of his ruminations with quotations from classical authors, they evolved into longer, more discursive, more personal tapestries of substance and subjectivity.

The originality of his project at its inception cannot be overestimated. "I myself am the matter of my book," he announces in his

Title page of the 1657 edition of Montaigne's Essays

prefatory note to the reader, knowing how unorthodox this is: "you would be unreasonable to spend your leisure on so frivolous and vain a subject." But while Montaigne does portray himself, as he warns, "entirely and wholly naked," his book is by no means an autobiography, and it is the manner in which the "matter of myself" is handled that constitutes its true genius. His famous skepticism stems from his intuition that neither knowledge nor self is a fixed entity; rather both—and especially the latter—are evolving, malleable states that contain within themselves their own arguments and contradictions. Montaigne was first to capture that on the page. In doing so, he may not have invented the inner life, but he did provide a pioneering way of apprehending it. If you imagine our existence as a continent and literature as its map, Montaigne planted his pen like a flag on a vast territory previously labeled "terra incognita."

His method is an active interrogation of moods, events, ideas, observations, texts, and emotions that has no predetermined outcome, or even direction: He frequently enough contradicts himself from essay to essay, and sometimes from one page to the next. The meaning we make of things, he knew, is always slippery, and the energy we expend in grappling with it was seldom recognized in the coherent stories humanity had always liked to listen to, and tell. Our moment-to-moment, season-to-season ruminations, worries, and engagements don't play on the wider stages of history, or epic poetry, or even tragic drama, for none of our lives live up to the sorts of story arc those forms support. Where there is supposed to be thematic development, we get a helter-skelter hurrying from no place in particular to no place special; where there is supposed to be consistency of conduct and identity, we get a strange alteration of fickleness and obstinacy; where there is supposed to be a grand finale, we get a denouement without a climax: If we're lucky, we pass away in peace and quiet, and if we're not, we wither away in disease and deterioration. What Montaigne found was that the available forms of writing, and so of contemplation, had no room for what is in fact the stuff of our lives—our habits and occupations, from clothing ourselves to associating with

others, from arguing with spouses and neighbors to cherishing our friends and playing with our pets. The *Essays* made room for it all, embodying the truth that what holds our days together is not time but the personal narrative of our attention.

Despite its daunting heft and its status as a classic, the *Essays* makes forgiving reading; you really can open it anywhere and find reward. Whether you read it with discipline or by the light of serendipity, you're bound to discover some private value in Montaigne's meditations. His learning was prodigious—indeed, a reader can get a near-complete education in classical culture through the quotations from Greek and Roman authors that provide the ligature of so many of the essays—yet he frequently disparages erudition as an end in itself. In "Of pedantry," he imagines a student returning home after years of schooling: "He should have brought back his soul full; he brings it back only swollen; he has only inflated it instead of enlarging it." Students of any age willing to devote fifteen minutes a day to traversing Montaigne's great map of the shifting contours of his own intelligence would no doubt present quite a different figure by the end of their journeys, for there are few volumes in which one can more fruitfully cultivate not only soulfulness but magnanimity.

"To compose our character is our duty, not to compose books, and to win, not battles and provinces, but order and tranquillity in our conduct," writes Montaigne in the final essay of this thousand-page book, whose existence seems—quite characteristically—to contradict the sentiment expressed. But then Montaigne's innovation was to illustrate how one might compose a character *by* composing a book, thereby helping those of us without his gifts to learn how to live appropriately—"without miracle and without eccentricity"—through our own works and days.

What: Essays. Philosophy. *When:* 1580–95. *Editions:* The first English translation, by John Florio in 1603, remains one of the glories of Elizabethan English, and an almost certain influence on William Shakespeare, Florio's contemporary. Donald M. Frame's 1957 translation, quoted here, is eloquent and highly recommended. M. A. Screech's 1991 version is more direct than Frame's, and a fine alternative. *Reading Note:* Start with two essays—one early ("Of idleness") and one late (the last, "Of experience")—and chart your course from there. *Also By: Montaigne: The Complete Works* (1957), edited by Donald Frame, includes the author's 1580–81 journal of his travels to Italy and other destinations (issued separately as *Montaigne's Travel Journal*, with an especially good introduction by Guy Davenport, in 1983), as well as assorted letters. *Further Reading: How to Live, or A Life of Montaigne*

in One Question and Twenty Attempts at an Answer by Sarah Bakewell is a superb and friendly guide to Montaigne's thought and method. *Try: The Journals of André Gide. Adaptation: The Autobiography of Michel de Montaigne*, assembled by Marvin Lowenthal and published in 1935, takes scissors and paste to the *Essays* to create a chronological autobiographical narrative out of Montaigne's own words; it is a perversely anachronistic—and fascinating—book.

Anne of Green Gables
L. M. Montgomery (1874–1942)

An Irrepressible, Irresistible Heroine

It's hard to imagine a young heroine more appealing than Anne Shirley, the joyful, smart, happily indefatigable orphan who supplies both the name and the heart of this perennially popular 1908 novel. Like Tom Sawyer, the red-haired, freckle-faced Anne lingers in readers' imaginations as an embodiment of childhood's anticipations and adventures. Her life beyond the pages of this book—and the seven sequels that Lucy Maud Montgomery penned in its wake—has inspired not only many film, stage, and television adaptations, but also a booming Green Gables tourism industry on Canada's Prince Edward Island, the setting for her tale.

Green Gables house on Prince Edward Island, Canada

The story is simple: Aging siblings Matthew and Marilla Cuthbert, who together live in Avonlea on Prince Edward Island, seek to adopt an orphan to help them with the endless chores on their farm, Green Gables. But the child who arrives from the orphanage in Nova Scotia is not a boy, as they expected, but a spirited and imaginative eleven-year-old girl. Once the shock wears off, Matthew and Marilla adapt to the surprise—which proves good practice, since Anne will continue to deliver surprises to their doorstep on an almost daily basis (as in the famous episode in which Anne dyes her hair green). Strong bonds soon develop between the three as Anne embraces life in Avonlea, and as the staid community, a bit more cautiously but ultimately with great affection, embraces her. Covering a period of five years filled with much laughter (and some tears, too), *Anne of Green Gables* charts its protagonist's school days, friendships, and budding romance with Gilbert Blythe, unraveling threads of plot that Montgomery will follow in subsequent books that detail Anne's later life, education, marriage, and motherhood.

From its first long, intricately constructed sentence, which combines a storytelling intimacy with sophisticated attention to character and setting (and leaves you eager to hear what happens next), *Anne of Green Gables* balances its innocent cheerfulness with an appraising intelligence that has a lot to tell readers young and old about human nature—and about the sympathy and generosity good books can breed.

What: Children's. *When:* 1908. *Also By:* Seven sequels, including *Anne of Avonlea* (1909) and *Anne of the Island* (1915). A second series by Montgomery, *Emily of New Moon* (1923–27) is also bound to please. *Further Reading: Before Green Gables*, a prequel by Budge Wilson, was published in 2008. *Try:* The Betsy-Tacy series by Maud Hart Lovelace (see page 436). *Adaptations:* The best of the many adaptations are the three films made in the 1980s starring Megan Follows as Anne. Of the several unabridged audiobook editions, the one performed by Shelly Frasier is especially good.

■ For Michael Moorcock's *Stormbringer*, see page 796.

■ For C. L. Moore's *Judgment Night*, see page 26.

History: A Novel
Elsa Morante (1912–1985)

A Novel of Rome During the Second World War

History may indeed be written by the victors, but, as the Italian novelist Elsa Morante illustrates in this sprawling saga of World War II–era Rome, its plot can remain impenetrable, especially to those who must navigate small lives through its looming shadows. Unaware of the import of battles and ignorant of politics, economics, and ideology, Ida Mancuso Ramundo, *History*'s ill-starred heroine, is a destitute, widowed schoolteacher who lives alone with her son until she is raped and impregnated by a Nazi soldier. After the birth of her second child, her two boys are what keep her putting one foot in front of another as she struggles to make her way through an increasingly bewildering world. Great events are happening all around her—one of the novel's most powerful scenes is Ida's witnessing of the exportation of Rome's Jews from the Tiburtina railroad station—but their meaning is beyond her comprehension.

Tellingly, Morante opens each chapter of her massive story with a timeline detailing the momentous historical events that run parallel with the humbler and more human tale of Ida and her family. Afraid, impoverished, gripped with paranoia in the face of physical affliction and the uncertain but relentless threats of Italy's racial laws, she leads a hand-to-mouth existence while her older son fights with the Resistance and her younger one engages the ravaged world with a joyful innocence both enchanting and precocious.

Informed by influences including surrealism, the fiction of her husband, Alberto Moravia, and the work of Katherine Mansfield, which Morante had translated while hiding out in the mountains south of Rome with Moravia during the Nazi occupation of the city, *History* is a sprawling narrative infused with moral outrage. By making one woman's harrowing fate both gripping and indelible, Elsa Morante composed what Alfred Kazin rightly called "one of the few novels in any language that renders the full horror of Hitler's war, the war that never gets in the books."

What: Novel. *When:* 1974; English translation by William Weaver, 1977. *Also By: House of Liars* (1948). *Arturo's Island* (1957). *Aracoeli* (1982). *Further Reading: Woman of Rome: A Life of Elsa Morante* by Lily Tuck. *Try:* The Abruzzo Trilogy by Ignazio Silone (see *Bread and Wine*, page 722). *The Woman of Rome* by Alberto Moravia.

THE BOOKSHOP NOVELS
PARNASSUS ON WHEELS • THE HAUNTED BOOKSHOP
Christopher Morley (1890–1957)

Two Charming Novels That Celebrate the Company of Books

These two lighthearted novels detailing the adventures of bookseller Roger Mifflin are delightful celebrations of the romance books promise inveterate readers. When we meet him at the beginning of *Parnassus on Wheels*, Mifflin is navigating his horse-drawn wagon (called "Travelling Parnassus") through the gate of the McGill farm: "a queer wagon," the narrator, Helen McGill, informs us, "shaped like a van," and sporting a sign advertising "Good Books for Sale: Shakespeare, Charles Lamb, R.L.S., and Hazlitt, and All Others." Inside are rows and rows of volumes old and new. Mifflin has, he explains to Miss McGill, spent the best part of seven years cruising the east coast of America dispensing literature with a missionary zeal. "Lord!," he will soon tell Helen, "when you sell a man a book you don't sell him just twelve ounces of paper and ink and glue—you sell him a whole new life." And a "whole new life" is just what Travelling Parnassus delivers to Helen McGill in this captivating comedy, as Mifflin—a self-described "bald-headed fool over forty selling books on a country road"— inspires in her a happy revolt from her normal routine.

Originally published in 1917, Christopher Morley's first love letter to the traffic in books remains a transporting entertainment, laced with literary lore and the names of enticing volumes. Its sequel, *The Haunted Bookshop*, which appeared two years later, finds Mifflin and McGill, married and ensconced in Brooklyn, having settled their volumes in a shop called Parnassus at Home. The rollicking plot, in which an ambitious young advertising man woos a comely young heiress by doggedly uncovering the designs of foreign agents operating down the block from Mifflin's den of serenity, provides amusing diversion while allowing more room for Mifflin (and Morley) to expound on the intrigue and intricacy of the bookseller's art.

Together, this pair of tales perfectly captures the mysterious allure of dusty old bookshops, which, despite the efficiencies of superstores and the internet, all book lovers are likely to treasure still.

What: Books. Novel. *When:* 1917 and 1919. *Also By:* *Shandygaff* (1918). *Modern Essays* (1921 and 1924). *Thunder on the Left* (1925). *Kitty Foyle* (1939). *Try:* *A Gentle Madness: Bibliophiles, Bibliomanes, and the Eternal Passion for Books* by Nicholas A. Basbanes. *Old Books, Rare Friends* by Leona Rostenberg and Madeleine B. Stern. *Sixpence House: Lost in a Town of Books* by Paul Collins. *Footnote:* In 1934, Christopher Morley founded the Baker Street Irregulars, a band of Sherlock Holmes aficionados. Over the years, members have included Franklin Roosevelt, Harry Truman, Rex Stout, and Isaac Asimov.

The Rise of Theodore Roosevelt
Edmund Morris (born 1940)

The Exciting Life of the Pre-Presidential T. R.

Theodore Roosevelt (1858–1919) was the twenty-sixth president of the United States. He remains our youngest chief executive (he was forty-two when he assumed the office upon the assassination of President McKinley), and he is certainly one of the most fascinating. Naturalist John Burroughs once said of his friend "T. R." that he was a "many-sided man, and every side was like an electric battery." In the Pulitzer Prize–winning *The Rise of Theodore Roosevelt*, acclaimed biographer Edmund Morris covers the unflaggingly energetic pre-presidential years of this dynamo.

It's quite a story. At various times in the course of Morris's nine-hundred-plus pages, Roosevelt reveals his remarkable talents as writer, rancher, soldier, and politician—to say nothing of his claim to the title of "fastest hand-shaker in history." Consider these highlights:

• While studying at Columbia Law School, T. R. wrote the still authoritative *Naval War of 1812*, which was published in 1882.

• Sickly and asthmatic as a boy, Roosevelt later devoted himself to what he called the "strenuous life." As a hunter and outdoorsman, he spent some time as a rancher in the Badlands of Montana, to which he moved to escape his grief after the tragically early death of his first wife in 1884.

Future president Theodore Roosevelt, 1883

• In 1898, T. R. resigned as assistant secretary of the navy to form, and eventually lead, the Rough Riders cavalry regiment. Their famous charges up Cuba's Kettle and San Juan Hills during the Spanish-American War made T. R. a national hero.

• Elected governor of New York in 1898, Roosevelt became William McKinley's vice-presidential running mate in the 1900 election, assuming the position of chief executive himself in September 1901 after McKinley's death. (It was that same month, incidentally, that Roosevelt apparently first used his famous slogan "Speak softly and carry a big stick.")

Morris makes the most of his rich material, orchestrating vast stores of incident and information into an engaging narrative that is a joy to read. He makes the force of T. R.'s larger-than-life presence felt in each of the varied contexts Roosevelt so vigorously dominated, illuminating as well the complicated character behind the trademark caricature—pince-nez, heavy mustache, dazzlingly big teeth—that history has handed down as his enduring image. Along the way, Morris also draws a detailed portrait of the age.

This enormous yet briskly compelling book is the first volume of Morris's T. R. trilogy. *Theodore Rex*, covering Roosevelt's presidency, appeared in 2001; it was followed nine years later by *Colonel Roosevelt*, which details its subject's post–White House career. Each is written with the same verve and intelligence that make *The Rise of Theodore Roosevelt* such a delight.

What: Biography. History. *When:* 1979. *Awards:* Pulitzer Prize for Biography and National Book Award, both 1980. *Also By: Dutch: A Memoir of Ronald Reagan* (1999). *Beethoven: The Universal Composer* (2005). *Further Reading:* Three books—*Hunting Trips of a Ranchman, The Wilderness Hunter,* and *The Rough Riders*—all by T. R. himself. *Try: The River of Doubt: Theodore Roosevelt's Darkest Journey* by Candice Millard. *Mornings on Horseback: The Story of an Extraordinary Family, a Vanished Way of Life, and the Unique Child Who Became Theodore Roosevelt* by David McCullough.

An 1886 map of the British Empire

Pax Britannica

THE CLIMAX OF AN EMPIRE

Jan Morris (born 1926)

The Zenith of Imperial Britain

"The sun never sets on the British Empire." There was a time the prideful assertion was true, as old maps—with British possessions, traditionally marked in pink, coloring the continents—confirm. "It was the largest Empire in the history of the world," according to Jan Morris, "comprising nearly a quarter of the land mass of the earth, and a quarter of its population." It reached its peak, in Morris's view, in June 1897, when Queen Victoria celebrated her sixtieth year on the throne. Soon the imperial sun would begin its slow descent, until hardly any "pink bits" tinted the globe, but to both the Queen and her subjects during the summer of Victoria's Diamond Jubilee, "the fabric of her great Empire must have seemed almost indestructible."

In *Pax Britannica*, Morris tries "to recall what the Empire was, how it worked, what it looked like, and how the British themselves then saw it." She does this through an imaginative historical "tour" that leads from Ireland to India, Canada to Rhodesia, highlighting events, themes, and ideas—Victoria's reign, shipping routes, the dissemination of seed and stock, economic imperatives, caste, law, art and architecture, military matters, the idea of fair play—that are reflective of both the adjective and the noun in "British imperialism." The gifts that have made her travel books some of the finest of her era are everywhere apparent, revealing this traveler in time to be especially adept at portraying the sensuous and social ambience of the far-flung objects of her attention. Alert to details of climate and geography, natural setting and urban culture, she imbues her narrative with a vividness often lacking in historical texts, and trenchantly portrays the people she meets along the way, including soldiers, sportsmen, administrators, and adventurers.

Although Morris is not blind to the dark side of imperialism, her primary focus is to capture Victoria's realm "at the height of its vigour, in an outburst of creativity, pride, greed and command." Her cadenced prose is pure pleasure to read—her inspirations can capture a panorama in a sentence she will then unpack through a dozen informative and entertaining pages. ("Throughout the length and breadth of the Empire," she begins one chapter, "a well-spoken, reasonably well-connected young man, with a few introductions in the right places, and a sufficiently entertaining line in small talk, could travel by himself without feeling the need for an hotel.")

Pax Britannica is actually the middle volume of Morris's trilogy on the rise (1837–1897) and decline (1897–1965) of the British Empire. But since the other books—*Heaven's Command* (1973) and *Farewell the Trumpets* (1978)—were published after *Pax Britannica*, this is one instance where you won't go wrong by plunging boldly into the middle of a vast, and vastly absorbing, narrative.

What: History. *When:* 1968. *Also By: The World of Venice* (1960). *Among the Cities* (1985). *Hong Kong: Epilogue to an Empire* (1997). *Trieste and the Meaning of Nowhere* (2001). *Try: The Scramble for Africa* by Thomas Pakenham. *Raj: The Making and Unmaking of British India* by Lawrence James. *Footnote: Pax Britannica* was originally published under the name James Morris; in 1972, the author took the name Jan upon completion of an eight-year process of sex change that began with hormonal therapy and concluded with surgery. Morris writes about the transformation in *Conundrum* (1974).

Beloved
Toni Morrison (born 1931)

Dearly Departed

" The past is never dead. It's not even past," says a character in William Faulkner's *Requiem for a Nun*, and novelist Toni Morrison, who devoted part of her master's thesis at Cornell to a study of Faulkner's work, seems to animate every intuition those words contain in the pages of her fifth novel, *Beloved*.

Set in post–Civil War Ohio, but crisscrossing time and space in an intricate series of flashbacks and shifting perspectives, *Beloved* tells the story of Sethe, a runaway slave raising the children she led out of Kentucky. She is tormented by what she has escaped and haunted by what she cannot: the memory of the infant daughter for whom Sethe chose doom rather than slavery. A ghost story in which the author reveals the spirit at the heart of her tale in her first sentences, the book's suspense is built not on surprise as much as upon the particularity of the unfolding grief that drives Sethe and her extended circle of family and old friends to the brink of madness. Infusing her realistic narrative with supernatural power and presence in the apparition who gives the book its

Toni Morrison, 1997

name, Morrison conjures emotional truths more powerful than a strict naturalism ever has access to. This is a novel about love, loss, regret, horror, the high price of freedom and the illusions it buys, and, perhaps most of all, the eternal human need, despite the sorrowful and unfulfilled promises of past and present, for "some kind of tomorrow."

Upon its publication, the critic John Leonard wrote that, without *Beloved*, "our imagination of the nation's self has a hole in it big enough to die from." Yet it does not diminish the novel's native eloquence to suggest that in its pages Morrison ponders, and makes palpable in an American way, themes that reach all the way back to Greek tragedy. "This is not a story to pass on," we read on the last page of *Beloved*. But such stories can't help themselves from being told eventually: That, in fact, is the most human truth of all, and readers far into the future will be grateful that Morrison, writing those words as she drew Sethe's tale to a close, had proved them wrong.

What: Novel. *When:* 1987. *Awards:* Pulitzer Prize for Fiction, 1988. Morrison was awarded the Nobel Prize in Literature, 1993. *Also By: The Bluest Eye* (1969). *Sula* (1973). *Song of Solomon* (1977). *A Mercy* (2008). *Try: Sanctuary* by William Faulkner. *The Women of Brewster Place* by Gloria Naylor (see page 584). *The Known World* by Edward P. Jones. *Adaptation:* The 1998 film stars Oprah Winfrey and Danny Glover.

Ill Met by Moonlight
W. Stanley Moss (1921–1965)

The True Account of the Kidnapping of a Nazi General

In this swashbuckling true story from the annals of World War II, two British Special Operations officers arrive surreptitiously in Nazi-occupied Crete armed only with a plan to kidnap the German general Karl Kreipe, commander of the Twenty-Second Panzer Grenadier Division. Abetted by a handful of crafty and colorful local partisans, the author and his comrade succeed in executing their mission, seizing Kreipe at gunpoint, then escaping through the Cretan foothills and across the Mediterranean to British-occupied Egypt, their German captive in tow. Moss's firsthand account of his 1944 adventure is a vivid diary of a remarkable feat of daring. That his colleague in the plot is one of the masters of modern English prose, Patrick Leigh Fermor (see page 269), adds literary interest to his gripping tale; Fermor's own account of aspects of the adventure, *Abducting a General*, appeared in 2014.

What: War. Adventure. *When:* 1950. *Edition:* The handsome 2001 Folio Society edition features an afterword by Patrick Leigh Fermor. *Also By: A War of Shadows* (1952). *Gold Is Where You Find It* (1956). *Try: The Cretan Runner* by George Psychoundakis. *Hide and Seek: The Story of a Wartime Agent* by Xan Fielding. *Adaptation:* A 1957 film was made by Michael Powell and Emeric Pressburger.

My First Summer in the Sierra
John Muir (1838–1914)

A Rapturous Celebration of Wilderness

"John Muir, Earth-planet, Universe."

That is the self-description with which, in 1867, John Muir inscribed the journal that would be published, posthumously, nearly fifty years later as *A Thousand-Mile Walk to the Gulf*. From the outset of his career as a naturalist, Muir was possessed by a sense of vocation that would not only inspire his own passionate appreciation of America's wilderness, but also, long after his own passing, ensure the preservation of its wonders for future generations.

John Muir in Yosemite, ca. 1902

Born in Scotland, Muir came to America as a boy when his family moved to a Midwestern farm. After studying at the University of Wisconsin and working as an industrial engineer, he devoted his life to the wildernesses of the West, particularly California's Yosemite Valley and the Sierra Nevada mountain range. In 1869, a sheep owner named Delaney offered Muir a job that gave him the opportunity of spending the summer in "the high, cool, green pastures of the Sierra." The job consisted of keeping an eye on 2,500 sheep—and one shepherd. It was the latter who really needed watching, as Muir explains: "The main thing, [Delaney] said, was to have a man about the camp whom he could trust to see that the shepherd did his duty." Muir eagerly accepted Delaney's offer, and the diary he kept during the three and a half months he spent in the mountains forms the bulk of *My First Summer in the Sierra*, an early reflection of Muir's awestruck reverence for the glories of the Earth that belongs among the classics of nature writing.

But even though they are often cast in an ecstatic vein, Muir's reflections are anchored by his emergent field knowledge of botany, geology, and glaciology. It is just this colloquy between lyrical enthusiasm and keen attention that makes Muir's writings such an eloquent emblem of his abiding legacy. Celebrated today as the "Father of the National Parks" for his work in petitioning Congress to establish the Yosemite and Sequoia preserves, he was also the founder, and for twenty-two years, the first president of, the Sierra Club. More broadly, his combination of scientific observation and visionary embrace of nature's harmonies mark him as a prophet of both the environmental movement and the study of ecology: "When we try to pick out anything by itself, we find it hitched to everything else in the universe."

What: Nature. Autobiography *When:* 1911. *Also By: The Mountains of California* (1894). *Our National Parks* (1901). *The Yosemite* (1912). *The Story of My Boyhood and Youth* (1913). *A Thousand-Mile Walk to the Gulf* (1916). *Further Reading: The Life and Letters of John Muir* by William Frederic Badè. *Rediscovering America: John Muir in His Time and Ours* by Frederick Turner. *Try: Walden* by Henry David Thoreau (see page 786). *Desert Solitaire* by Edward Abbey (see page 2). *The Wild Places* by Robert Macfarlane.

The Emperor of All Maladies
A BIOGRAPHY OF CANCER
Siddhartha Mukherjee (born 1970)

A Doctor's Brilliant Life of a Deadly Disease

A nearly five-hundred-page tome about the most fearsome of diseases may sound like a gloomy prospect, but Siddhartha Mukherjee's "biography" of cancer is a marvel of medical erudition, emotional gravity, and literary elegance: Our scientific learning and human understanding are so enhanced by its narrative that we're sorry to come to its end. The book's vast canvas encompasses medical and scientific history from ancient Egypt to modern America as Mukherjee details the trials and triumphs of experimental investigation from Percivall Pott's eighteenth-century discovery of environmental carcinogens in his work with London chimney sweeps to Sidney Farber's invention of the chemical treatment of leukemia in twentieth-century Boston. Throughout, Mukherjee's compelling ruminations on the extraordinary biological qualities of cancer, and the cells it both animates and destroys, are informed by his training as a hematologist and oncologist and his ongoing career as a cancer researcher and physician.

Through stories of patients, pathologists, and crusaders, *The Emperor of All Maladies* charts the evolution of our comprehension of the disease and new developments in its treatment, illuminating the effect of each on cancer's cultural and political resonance. Ingenuity and serendipity alike are celebrated, and blind alleys in the laboratory and bad judgments in public policy are explained with insight and valuable interpretation. Mukherjee's extra-scientific training—"I read pathologically," he has said—is apparent in both the grace of his writing and the breadth and relevance of the epigraphs that herald each chapter, drawn from such unexpected sources as Italo Calvino's *Invisible Cities* and the poetry of Anna Akhmatova, W. H. Auden, and Louise Glück. The sureness of his authorial voice allows him to deftly portray the dialogue between research and care that gives this work its haunting power, evoking again and again the complex ways in which medicine moves from abstraction to reality, from a diagram in a book to a patient standing before a doctor. Because of Mukherjee's rare combination of clinical intelligence, intellectual curiosity, and imaginative intuition, *The Emperor of All Maladies* does justice to the true life-and-death dimensions of its subject.

What: Medicine. Science. *When:* 2010. *Award:* Pulitzer Prize for General Nonfiction, 2011. *Also By: The Laws of Medicine: Field Notes from an Uncertain Science* (2015). *The Gene: An Intimate History* (2016). *Try: The Lives of a Cell* by Lewis Thomas (see page 781). *Doctors: The Biography of Medicine* by Sherwin B. Nuland. *The Secret History of the War on Cancer* by Devra Davis. *The Immortal Life of Henrietta Lacks* by Rebecca Skloot (see page 727). *Adaptation:* Ken Burns produced a film, directed by Barak Goodman, that aired in three parts on PBS in 2015.

The Hunger Angel
Herta Müller (born 1953)

A Haunting Novel from the 2009 Nobel Laureate

Herta Müller, a member of the German-speaking minority in Romania, spent her formative years under the thumb of one of the most brutal dictatorships in Europe. During the regime of Nicolae Ceaușescu, she worked as a translator at a factory but was forced out by the Securitate, the feared Romanian secret police, after she refused to become an informant. The Securitate harassed her for years, and Müller faced frequent death threats. Finally permitted to emigrate to Germany in 1987, Müller has published more than a dozen books—essays and poetry as well as novels—that chronicle the pressures of life in a police state.

The Hunger Angel, her lyrical and uncompromising masterpiece from 2009—the year she was awarded the Nobel Prize in Literature—is something different. A novel set at the end of World War II, it details a forgotten chapter of twentieth-century history: the deportation of Germans living in Eastern Europe to work in Soviet forced-labor camps. Leo, the book's young narrator, is at first almost excited to be expelled from his "thimble of a town, where every stone had eyes." But the labor camp, where he is required to shovel coal and compelled to scrounge for anything to eat, is far more brutal than he could have imagined. Leo is gay and knows he'll be killed if his secret is found out, but in truth he has barely any sexual desires at all. His feelings are reduced to exhaustion and desperate hunger, personified by the "hunger angel" that follows him everywhere:

The hunger angel climbs to the roof of my mouth and hangs his scales. He puts on my eyes and the heart-shovel goes dizzy, the coal starts to blur. He wears my cheeks over his chin. . . . I look up, the sky is filled with summer cotton wool, embroidered clouds, very still.

My brain twitches, pinned to the sky with a needle, at the only fixed point it has left, where it fantasizes about food.

Müller's narrative of the realities of the camps has power in itself, but what makes *The Hunger Angel* unforgettable is the gravity and uncanny grace of its expressionistic, beautifully knotty prose—"a kind of Habsburg German," as the author herself describes it, infused with Romanian elements and studded with invented words. (The book's German title is *Atemschaukel*, a Müller coinage meaning "breath-swing.") Utterly distinctive, so laden with emotion that it is almost unbearable at times, Müller's writing sets off relays of memories that span decades and cross borders. While the setting of her book is bleak, the prose is unremittingly vibrant: a haunting, mysterious soulfulness in the midst of so much material suffering.

What: Novel. *When:* 2009; English translation by Philip Boehm, 2012. *Award:* Nobel Prize in Literature, 2009. *Also By:* The Passport (1986). Traveling on One Leg (1989). The Land of Green Plums (1994). The Appointment (1997). *Try:* Poems of Paul Celan. One Day in the Life of Ivan Denisovich by Aleksandr Solzhenitsyn (see page 737). Fatelessness by Imre Kertész.

Selected Stories, 1968–1994
Alice Munro (born 1931)

A Nobel Laureate's Astonishing Gallery of Life

In "Miles City, Montana," a story appearing in Alice Munro's 1986 collection, *The Progress of Love*, a woman indelibly describes her domestic restlessness: "In my own house, I seemed to be often looking for a place to hide—sometimes from the children but more often from the jobs to be done and the phone ringing and the sociability of the neighborhood. I wanted to hide so that I could get busy at my real work, which was a sort of wooing of distant parts of myself." It is, of course, an injustice to the author's talent and achievement to point to just two sentences as emblematic of her work, yet this passage does suggest the resonant sympathy with which Munro depicts both the surface quiet and the eloquent, if often unspoken, undercurrents of undramatic lives. *Selected Stories, 1968–1994* gathers tales from her first eight books; six more collections of equal merit have followed to date.

Dear Life is the title of one of those later volumes (it was published in 2012), and few writers of her time have made every aspect of life's dearness so telling on the page.

Just as William Faulkner did with his fictional Yoknapatawpha County, Munro has spent most of her career writing about a single place, her native western Ontario. It was, in Munro's youth, at least, a place of small towns, religious probity, and strict standards of behavior— the sort of place that may have little fun for a child but proved to be fertile imaginative terrain for a budding writer. And just like Faulkner, if without the formal pyrotechnics and Southern Gothic intoxication, Munro discovers, through the close and empathetic observation of ordinary and deeply fallible people, more profundity than most authors could find in a teeming metropolis.

To reduce Munro's writing to plots is to miss the richness it creates. People grow up, marry, work, die—or do all of those things, as in the marvelous "The Bear Goes Over the Mountain" (the closing story in her splendidly titled 2001 book, *Hateship, Friendship, Courtship, Loveship,*

Alice Munro, 1986

Marriage). Events that sound minor or commonplace in summary are stunning as they unfold through unassuming paragraphs. Her stories shuttle through time without warning; they often begin in the middle, then jump to the past before hurtling forward and back again. They can span decades, or focus on a single day. They exhibit abrupt, almost violent shifts in tone, sometimes in a single paragraph. What elevates them to such extraordinary heights is Munro's acuity as an observer and a stylist, so subtle in each case that you may not grasp her art at first glance. That's why her work rewards rereading: It is short fiction for the long term, as the Swedish Academy recognized in awarding her the Nobel Prize in Literature in 2013.

What: Short Stories. When: 1996. Award: Nobel Prize in Literature, 2013. Also By: Lives of Girls and Women (1971). Runaway (2004). The View from Castle Rock (2006). Family Furnishings: Selected Stories, 1995–2014 (2014). Further Reading: Lives of Mothers and Daughters: Growing Up with Alice Munro by Sheila Munro. Try: Stories by Anton Chekhov (see page 153). The Collected Stories by William Trevor (see page 804). Birds of America by Lorrie Moore.

The Wind-Up Bird Chronicle
Haruki Murakami (born 1949)

Under the Spell of an Idiosyncratic Imagination

When the phone rang I was in the kitchen, boiling a potful of spaghetti and whistling along with an FM broadcast of the overture to Rossini's The Thieving Magpie, which has to be the perfect music for cooking pasta.

I wanted to ignore the phone, not only because the spaghetti was nearly done, but because Claudio Abbado was bringing the London Symphony to its musical climax. Finally, though, I had to give in. It could have been somebody with news of a job opening.

It's 10:30 in the morning, Toru Okada's cat is missing, and soon his wife will be, too. He'll conduct a long, spellbound search for both with the help of his sixteen-year-old neighbor and a pair of psychic sisters (one of whom dresses like Jackie Kennedy) while trying to fend off his wife's soulless but mediagenic brother, a popular but quite possibly seriously evil politician. But first Toru has to answer that phone call. What greets him isn't news of a job, but the voice of a strange woman who seems to know him and insists they'll need only ten minutes "to understand each other."

If Toru Okada is falling under a spell of sorts, so is the reader: that of a Haruki Murakami novel, in which an imaginative landscape littered with the products of contemporary commerce and culture is steeped in the intemperate weather of alienation, dreams, and loneliness. The narrative path through this distinctive world will look familiar to readers of both the hardboiled detective stories of Mickey Spillane and the metaphysically edged science fiction of Philip K. Dick, and there's more than a little Kafka in the air. Yet none of these analogs suggests the seamless weirdness that is Murakami's alone; he creates a field of fantasy that is simultaneously familiar and eerily otherworldly, quick with humor and eroticism, alive with a literary static electricity whose shocks are peculiarly addictive.

This energy pulses through Toru Okada's bewildering odyssey in *The Wind-Up Bird Chronicle*, a quest that brings him into unexpected proximity to historical horrors (specifically those surrounding Japan's brutal campaigns in Manchuria in the 1930s) and finds him spending a remarkable amount of rewarding time in the bottom of an empty well (you'll be surprised at how intriguing you may find it, too). What the critic Donald Morrison wrote of one of Murakami's books is true of them all, especially this one: "it defies both description and the urge to stop reading."

What: Novel. *When:* 1994 in Japanese; English translation by Jay Rubin, 1997. *Also By:* Novels: *A Wild Sheep Chase* (1982); *Norwegian Wood* (1987); *Kafka on the Shore* (2002); *1Q84* (2009). Nonfiction: *Underground* (1997); *What I Talk About When I Talk About Running* (2007). *Further Reading: A Wild Haruki Chase: Reading Murakami Around the World,* compiled by the Japan Foundation. *Try: Slaughterhouse-Five* by Kurt Vonnegut (see page 827). *Cloud Atlas* by David Mitchell. *The Last Samurai* by Helen DeWitt.

The Tale of Genji
Lady Murasaki Shikibu (ca. AD 978–1031)

A Japanese Classic That Maps the Landscape of the Novel

Written by a lady-in-waiting in Japan's eleventh-century imperial court, *The Tale of Genji* is sometimes referred to as the first novel ever written, although that is a matter of moderate dispute. What can't be denied, however, is something even more astonishing: The book seems to encompass in its one thousand pages a history of the form as it would unfold in the future. Beginning in a fairy-tale realm, its storytelling passes through uninhabited countries on the continent of fiction that will not be settled for several centuries; it ventures through the romance and the picaresque to discover the domestic, social, and psychological novel before any of these would be imagined by another writer.

The massive *Tale* contains two distinct parts: The first, more than twice as long as the second, concerns the life and many loves of a handsome prince named Genji. Child of the emperor and a courtesan who dies when Genji is very young, the prince is much favored by his father but will never assume the throne. His shifting fortunes and his numerous affairs of the heart provide the leisurely narrative structure, which is embellished with vibrant court detail—costume, architecture, politics, and ritual—and a multitude of characters, including a young girl, taken in and raised by Genji, who will become Lady Murasaki. (It's after this heroine that the author was subsequently named—her real identity, like much about her, remains unknown; what we do know is that she was more educated than the average girl in the Heian era, and that she wrote to entertain other ladies of the court.) The second part of the enormous pageant is focused on two young men—Kaoru, born to one of Genji's wives (although he is not the prince's son), and Niou, Genji's grandson—and traces the dramatic twists in their ill-starred infatuations with three sisters.

In his 1968 Nobel lecture, Yasunari Kawabata called *The Tale of Genji* and *The Pillow Book of Sei Shōnagon* (see page 721) "the supreme masterpieces of classical Japanese prose." He went on to say, "*The Tale of Genji* in particular is the highest pinnacle of Japanese literature.

Even down to our day there has not been a piece of fiction to compare with it. That such a modern work should have been written in the eleventh century is a miracle, and as a miracle the work is widely known abroad."

What: Novel. **When:** Between 1000 and 1031. *Editions:* Of the several translations in print, those by Edward G. Seidensticker (1976) and Royall Tyler (2001) each have considerable merit. *Also By: Diary of Lady Murasaki,* edited by Richard Bowring. *Further Reading:* Liza Dalby's *The Tale of Murasaki* is a fictionalized biography of the author. *Try: The Story of the Stone* by Cao Xueqin. *Adaptations:* Genji's story has been performed for centuries in a variety of styles and settings, from Japanese Kabuki to western opera. Several film animations and adaptations have been made in Japan.

Depiction of Lady Murasaki writing The Tale of Genji

The Sea, the Sea
Iris Murdoch (1919–1999)

Good Fun from a Philosopher-Novelist

"Yes, yes, I am Charles Arrowby and, as I write this, I am, shall we say, over sixty years of age. I am wifeless, childless, brotherless, sisterless, I am my well-known self, made glittering and brittle by fame."

Charles Arrowby, star of the fictional autobiography that is Iris Murdoch's 1978 novel, *The Sea, the Sea,* is an illustrious star of the London stage. Although he'd always said he would retire once he was past sixty, his friends, colleagues, and sundry lovers are surprised when he says goodbye to the bright lights and settles himself into a little house on an ugly stretch of coast (the better to keep tourists away). Vowing to be a better man than he has been and bent on reflection to that end, it is his intent to write a memoir. But it's delightfully clear from the moment he puts pen to page that he's too charmed by his every thought and action to see beyond the vanity each moment allows, and his document immediately turns from memoir to diary, recording the visitors, sea monsters, and obsessions that descend upon his seaside retreat.

Soon enough, however, fortune delivers the past to his present in the form of Hartley, the lost adolescent sweetheart who has matured into a stout old woman who hasn't given Arrowby a thought in decades. Undeterred by reality, Arrowby conjures romance and recaptured youth, kidnapping Hartley and casting her into a supporting role in his star vehicle. The story careers from naturalism to supernaturalism, from comedy to melodrama and back again, as Murdoch shepherds a large cast of players across Arrowby's stage in a fleetly amusing literary performance.

The author's richness of imagination—she exhibits a Dickensian ebullience in both her plotting and her characterizations—is allied, with exhilarating effect, to a palpable philosophical and moral vision. After all, Dame Iris Murdoch was an Oxbridge scholar of classics, ancient history, and philosophy, and her twenty-six novels are a thinker's legacy—crackling with ideas, filled with allusions, deftly blending insight with entertainment. *The Sea, the Sea,* which won the coveted Booker Prize, is no exception. Arrowby's flights may be fanciful, but the fiction that encompasses them never loses sight of the genuine spiritual impulses they trace. As Anatole Broyard wrote in the *New York Times* in 1986, "Miss Murdoch, who is a most intellectual writer, seems to find it fun to be so smart." And what could be more welcome to a reader than good, smart fun?

What: Novel. *When:* 1978. *Award:* Booker Prize, 1978. *Also By:* Murdoch was a prolific novelist; among her best known are *Under the Net* (1954), *A Severed Head* (1961), *The Black Prince* (1973), and *The Sacred and Profane Love Machine* (1974). She also wrote plays, poetry, and several volumes of philosophy and criticism, including *Existentialists and Mystics* (1997). *Further Reading:* Murdoch was married to the literary critic John Bayley, whose poignant book, *Iris: A Memoir of Iris Murdoch,* recounts their marriage and her descent into Alzheimer's. *Try:* The novels of A. S. Byatt (see page 118) and Muriel Spark (see page 743). *Footnote:* Kate Winslet and Judi Dench portray Murdoch in the 2001 film *Iris,* based on Bayley's memoir.

Iris Murdoch, 1963

The Man Without Qualities
Robert Musil (1880–1942)

A Masterpiece of Modernism Set in 1913 Vienna

Robert Musil's vast, unfinished novel is one of the twentieth century's most esteemed works of fiction. From its opening paragraph, Musil's distinctive style alerts us to the playful and peculiar attributes of his intelligence. In a tone simultaneously learned and lampooning, Musil describes the weather in intricate scientific detail (with reference to barometric pressure, isotherms and isotheres, the movements of the planets, and more), only to conclude with the simple experiential reality: "It was a fine day in August 1913." Such counterpoint runs throughout the scores of chapters that make up Musil's masterpiece. In fact, the gulf between the human truths of experience and the intellections the mind makes of them is the crux of its sprawling tale—although "tale" doesn't quite do justice to Musil's singular and often extremely funny anatomy of what critic George Steiner called the author's arch-theme: "the psychological, sexual, and social disorder in the doomed culture of Central Europe" in the years preceding World War I.

Robert Musil, 1930

The central figure of the book is Ulrich, a disaffected thirty-two-year-old mathematician who is devoting a year of his life to finding "an appropriate application for his abilities." His want of purpose is magnified by an acute and paralyzing sensitivity to all the possibilities before him ("a man without qualities," another character asserts, "does not say No to life, he says Not yet!"). His circle of friends and lovers is expanded when he joins the committee established by the Austrian aristocracy to celebrate the anniversary of the accession of Emperor Franz Joseph (the descriptions of this group's fatuous activities bring a gleefully satiric point to Musil's pen). As the sprawling novel progresses in essayistic chapters that afford the author the opportunity to range far and wide in his brilliant observations on being and behavior, psychology and art, self and society, Ulrich encounters alluring women, business moguls and men of letters, government officials, disenchanted artists, the homicidal rapist Moosbrugger, and dozens of other characters, including Agathe, the sister with whom he begins to explore dangerous new territories of passion and feeling.

So ambitious in its scope that its ultimate incompletion seems a foregone conclusion, *The Man Without Qualities* has often been hailed as the equal of Joyce's *Ulysses* (see page 422) and Proust's *In Search of Lost Time* (see page 644). But, lacking the formal rigor of the first and the aesthetic coherence of the second, its richness is of a different order. An intellectual engine that never comes to rest, Musil's masterpiece is alive with a play of erudition, insight, and acuity that, paragraph by paragraph, is its own unparalleled reward.

What: Novel. *When:* Published in German in three parts: volumes one and two, 1930–33; volume three, 1943. The first complete German edition appeared in 1978. *Edition:* In 1995, a two-volume edition of the entire work, including material left unpublished at the time of Musil's death, was issued in English by Knopf. Translated from the German by Sophie Wilkins and Burton Pike, it runs more than 1,700 pages. *Reading Note:* Although filled with brilliant writing throughout, the energy of Musil's larger inspiration grows less focused as the novel progresses. As the author himself wrote, "Volume One closes approximately at the high point of the arch; on the other side it has no support." *Also By: The Confusions of Young Törless* (1906). *Five Women* (1911–24). *Posthumous Papers of a Living Author* (1936). *Diaries 1899–1942* (published in English, 1998). *Try: Zeno's Conscience* (see page 766) and *As a Man Grows Older* by Italo Svevo.

VLADIMIR NABOKOV
(1899–1977)

"The cradle rocks above an abyss, and common sense tells us that our existence is but a brief crack of light between two eternities of darkness. Although the two are identical twins, man, as a rule, views the prenatal abyss with more calm than the one he is heading for at some forty-five hundred heartbeats an hour."

T hese two sentences—the opening chords of his autobiography, *Speak, Memory*—are quintessential Vladimir Nabokov. In them we witness his penchant for striking figures of speech, his unsentimental delineation of life's limits, his congenital attachment to twins (see *Ada, or Ardor*, his monumental novel of 1969), his urbane invocation of black comedy, and his pedantic exactitude in matters of nature and art (not for nothing was he an accomplished lepidopterist).

Born in 1899 in Saint Petersburg, Russia, he grew up in a liberal, cultured, aristocratic family, which was forced into exile when the Bolshevik Revolution broke out in 1917. He entered Cambridge University in 1919 and later lived in Paris and Berlin, where he began writing his first novels. After immigrating to the United States with his wife and child in 1940, Nabokov began composing his works in English. The sophistication and erudition of his fiction ally with an almost clinical sense of life's absurdity, which imbues his imagination with a captivating, albeit sometimes cruel, wit. A master in both his native and adopted tongues, he towers over modern letters from a perch entirely his own.

Vladimir Nabokov, 1974

Lolita
An Appalling and Astonishing
20th-Century Literary Landmark

In April 1947, Nabokov wrote to a friend that he was at work on "a short novel about a man who liked little girls." Eight years later, after several American publishers had turned it down, that no-longer-short novel was published in Paris to international acclaim—and outrage. For *Lolita* isn't about a man who just "liked" young girls: It is, in fact, about a thirty-seven-year-old named Humbert Humbert who has an extended sexual relationship with a twelve-year-old named Dolores Haze. ("She was Dolores on the dotted line. But in my arms she was always Lolita.") Put like this, the story sounds repellent. And yet *Lolita* has not only survived the outrage and sold many millions of copies but has also established itself as one of the most lavishly praised literary works of the twentieth century.

It is narrated by Humbert himself, now in jail for having killed the man he thinks was once his rival for Lolita's affections. Ostensibly addressing the jury that would try him for murder, Humbert recounts his doomed obsession with the girl he celebrates in the book's famous opening paragraph as the "light of my life, fire of my loins. My sin, my soul. Lo-lee-ta." A European scholar—at least by his own account—transplanted in the United States, Humbert masks his compulsion in prose that is refined, lyrical, and lovingly wrought, no doubt reflecting his creator's rejoicing in the resources of a new language (despite its virtuosity, *Lolita* was only Nabokov's third novel in English). As Humbert first schemes for proximity to his nymphet, then takes her on a car journey that crisscrosses America, the reader is treated to a comical tour of a vibrantly crass country—a travelogue vividly enough observed almost to distract attention from the perverse passion of the maniac at the wheel.

The writing is a wonder throughout. As John Updike once wrote of Nabokov's prose,

"a sorcerer's scintillant dignity made of every sentence a potentially magic occasion." That wizardry is what has earned *Lolita* its triumphant literary status, despite the wicked tale it tells.

What: Novel. *When:* 1955. *Also By:* Novels composed in Russian: *The Defense* (1930); *Laughter in the Dark* (1932); *Invitation to a Beheading* (1938). Novels composed in English: *The Real Life of Sebastian Knight* (1941); *Bend Sinister* (1947); *Pnin* (1957); *Pale Fire* (1962). *Further Reading: Vera (Mrs. Vladimir Nabokov)* by Stacy Schiff. *Reading "Lolita" in Tehran: A Memoir in Books* by Azar Nafisi (see opposite page). *Try: The Lover* by Marguerite Duras. *Memories of My Melancholy Whores* by Gabriel García Márquez. *Adaptations: Lolita* was filmed by Stanley Kubrick in 1962 and by Adrian Lyne in 1998. In the latter movie, Humbert Humbert is played by Jeremy Irons, whose 1997 audiobook recording of the complete novel is not to be missed.

Speak, Memory
AN AUTOBIOGRAPHY REVISITED
Remembrance of Things Past

Although Nabokov is best known as a novelist, the most exquisite of his books is this work of nonfiction, acclaimed as one of the finest autobiographies of our time.

Speak, Memory covers the thirty-seven years between Nabokov's earliest glimmerings of self-awareness—"the inner knowledge that I was I and that my parents were my parents"—and his departure for America. The same sumptuous prose, barbed wit, and uncannily keen perceptions that distinguish Nabokov's great novels characterize this memoir, which is at its most moving when he recalls the vanished world of prerevolutionary Russia. As he explains, it is his enchanted childhood that he mourns, not the loss of the material prosperity of his upbringing: "My old quarrel with the Soviet dictatorship is wholly unrelated to any question of property. The nostalgia I have cherished all these years is a hypertrophied sense of lost childhood, not sorrow for lost banknotes." Exploring the mysteries of time, memory, love, and loss, this dazzling, achingly lovely book is filled with tender affection exactingly portrayed.

What: Autobiography. Literature. *When:* Originally published under the title *Conclusive Evidence* in 1951; revised and retitled, the final edition was published in 1966. *Edition:* The Everyman Library edition of *Speak, Memory* includes an extra chapter, in which Nabokov poses as a reviewer of his own book. *Further Reading: Vladimir Nabokov: The Russian Years* and *Vladimir Nabokov: The American Years* by Brian Boyd. *Try: My Past and Thoughts* by Alexander Herzen (see page 371). *The Italics Are Mine* by Nina Berberova.

Reading *Lolita* in Tehran
Azar Nafisi (born 1955)

The Secret Lives of Literature

When the civil and religious strictures of Iran's Islamic Republic forced her from her position as a professor of literature at the University of Tehran, Azar Nafisi convened in her own home a salon for seven of her best women students. They would arrive each Thursday morning, remove the black chadors required by the government for women in public, and explore the precincts of *Lolita*, *Pride and Prejudice*, and other Western novels. Written after she had left Iran for the United States in 1997, Nafisi's memoir of these gatherings, as well as of her years as a student and a teacher in her native land, is both a telling personal testament and a moving group portrait of women trapped in the emotional and political conundrums provoked by the prescriptions of the Islamic Revolution.

In the pages of Nabokov, Austen, and Henry James that she and her students pore over and discuss, Nafisi discovers a democracy of voices that speaks to the real world these

Azar Nafisi, 2015

women inhabit, a world of political dilemmas, family demands, and romantic desires. Whether putting *The Great Gatsby* on trial in her classroom to defend the honor of the imagination—a marvelous episode—or revealing how the marriage-minded plotting and counterplotting of Austen's novels retains an enduring relevance, Nafisi sees in fiction not an escape from life, but rather an engagement with it at the most profound levels. Her "memoir in books" is a human story, peopled with characters whose hearts and minds we come to care about; it is, in the end, an altogether astonishing account of how literature can illuminate a private path to meaning even in the most benighted circumstances.

What: Memoir. Literary Criticism. *When:* 2003. *Also By: Things I've Been Silent About* (2008). *The Republic of Imagination: America in Three Books* (2014). *Further Reading: Lolita* (see page 579) and *Invitation to a Beheading* by Vladimir Nabokov. *The Great Gatsby* by F. Scott Fitzgerald (see page 277). *Washington Square* by Henry James. *Pride and Prejudice* by Jane Austen (see page 33). *Try: Ruined by Reading: A Life in Books* by Lynne Sharon Schwartz. *Iran Awakening* by Shirin Ebadi.

|||||||||||||||||||||||||||||||||||||||||||||||||| B O O K N O T E ||||||||||||||||||||||||||||||||||||||||||||||||||

REVOLUTION AND INDEPENDENCE, IN WORDS AND PICTURES

The Complete Persepolis
Marjane Satrapi (born 1969)

" We articulated all that happened to us in our own words," Azar Nafisi writes of the clandestine reading group her work describes, "and saw ourselves, for once, in our image." As *Reading "Lolita" in Tehran* is a memoir in and of words, so Marjane Satrapi's *Persepolis*, originally published in two volumes, is a memoir in pictures, a comic book that details its author's coming-of-age during the Islamic Revolution. Beginning in 1980, when Marjane is ten years old, the narrative reflects— in the developing sophistication of its language and sensibility— its protagonist's passage from simple family loyalties and cultural allegiance through the uncertainties of adolescence, when she is sent to study in Vienna,

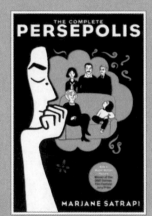

to her return to Tehran for university, marriage, and ultimate emigration to France. Her flat and deceptively simple art parses her experience panel by panel with enriching perspectives; her visual compositions are as adept at representing millennia of despotic history in a single frame as they are at illustrating her flirtation with conformity and rebellion in the face of political upheaval, fundamentalist oppression, and shatteringly violent war with Iraq.

Chronicling both the personal and the sociopolitical, Satrapi blends the two realms in a way both artful and true to the continuity of an individual's lived experience. As in the novels of Naguib Mahfouz and Gabriel García Márquez, the luck and loss of people moving from day to day are shown by Satrapi to embody a venerable culture and the soul of a nation.

A House for Mr. Biswas
V. S. Naipaul (born 1932)

A Nobel Laureate's Masterpiece

As any reader of V. S. Naipaul's mature work—or of Patrick French's startlingly candid 2008 biography—knows, Naipaul does not suffer fools gladly. Although he began his career with charmingly comic novels set in his native Trinidad, Naipaul went on to report— in both brilliant fiction and incisive travel books—on the world's grim political realities and the perplexities of its religious and colonial legacies. His work grew increasingly dour, yet it remained illuminated by his fierce intelligence and his acute perception of physical

V. S. Naipaul, 1978

dignity out of all proportion to his achievement. Born "the wrong way" and at the inauspicious hour of midnight, possessed of six fingers and an "unlucky sneeze" that (correctly) foretells bad fortune, Mr. Biswas lives a short life under the thumbs of fate, family (especially his in-laws), economic pressure, and professional disappointment, all the while harboring the dream of owning his own house. Naipaul relates Biswas's wayward pursuit of autonomy with such vivid and unsentimental attention to the cares and comedy of human relations that the novel transcends its West Indian milieu, delivering truths that are funny, poignant, painful, and universal. Infused with a simple man's wish to make a home for himself in this homeless world, *A House for Mr. Biswas* teems with complicated life. It is V. S. Naipaul's most loved, as well as one of his most lauded, books; the word "masterpiece" is often—rightly—used to describe it.

What: Novel. *When:* 1961. *Award:* Nobel Prize in Literature, 2001. *Also By: Miguel Street* (1959). *In a Free State* (1971). *Guerrillas* (1975). *A Bend in the River* (1979). *The Enigma of Arrival* (1987). *Further Reading: Sir Vidia's Shadow* by Paul Theroux. *The World Is What It Is: The Authorized Biography of V. S. Naipaul* by Patrick French. *Try: Midnight's Children* by Salman Rushdie (see page 683). *A Fine Balance* by Rohinton Mistry (see page 555). *Footnote:* Naipaul has written that the character of Mohun Biswas is partly based upon his father, whose correspondence with the author is collected in *Between Father and Son: Family Letters* (1999).

environments and social phenomena. The stylistic poise and narrative penetration of his prose have been lasting virtues.

Mohun Biswas, the protagonist of this early novel, is, as far as fools go, the exception that proves the Naipaul rule, for his foolishness is portrayed with such fidelity to ordinary experience and such fondness for the persistence of private aspirations that he assumes in the end a

A Beautiful Mind

A BIOGRAPHY OF JOHN FORBES NASH JR.

Sylvia Nasar (born 1947)

The Strange Journey of a Mathematical Genius

"This is the story of John Forbes Nash Jr. It is a story about the mystery of the human mind, in three acts: genius, madness, and reawakening."

So writes Sylvia Nasar in the prologue to her gripping biography of a man of genius whose mathematical intuition was so powerful that one colleague called him the most remarkable mathematician of his time. Before he was thirty years old, Nash had proposed an influential theory of rational behavior and promoted visionary computing concepts. His work was original and varied: He was a pioneer of game theory and differential geometry, and his ideas have proved relevant to subjects that range from artificial intelligence to markets and money to military decision-making.

Yet one winter morning in 1959, Nash walked into the common room at MIT and remarked that a story on the front page of the *New York Times* contained an encrypted message from inhabitants of another galaxy, a message that he alone could decipher. When a Harvard professor visiting him soon afterward in a hospital asked him how he could believe such nonsense, Nash replied, "Because the ideas I had about supernatural beings came to me the same way that my mathematical ideas did. So I took them seriously."

John Forbes Nash Jr., 2010

Paranoid schizophrenia crippled Nash's "beautiful mind" for decades, wreaking havoc with his public and private life in ways that Nasar describes with intelligence and sympathy. This dramatic life story includes a stunning final act: Inexplicably, in about 1989, Nash began to show signs of recovery and started doing significant mathematics again. After the inexplicable came the miraculous—in 1994, Nash shared the Nobel Memorial Prize in Economic Sciences (albeit for his early work in game theory). *A Beautiful Mind* is an extraordinary study of the fragile nature of genius.

What: Biography. Mathematics. *When:* 1998. *Award:* National Book Critics Circle Award for Biography, 1998. *Further Reading: The Essential John Nash* edited by Harold W. Kuhn and Sylvia Nasar. *A Beautiful Math: John Nash, Game Theory, and the Modern Quest for a Code of Nature* by Tom Siegfried. *Try: American Prometheus: The Triumph and Tragedy of J. Robert Oppenheimer* by Kai Bird and Martin J. Sherwin (see page 79). *Adaptation:* Ron Howard's loose film adaptation, starring Russell Crowe, won the 2001 Academy Award for Best Picture.

The Women of Brewster Place
Gloria Naylor (1950–2016)

Inner Lives in the Inner City

"No one cries when a street dies," writes Gloria Naylor in the epilogue to this searing novel, encapsulating the material and emotional emptiness that is often the legacy of complex dilemmas—political, economic, ethical, personal—too often simplified by the impoverishment of inner cities. Seven interlocking stories detail how several African American women come to find themselves on Brewster Place, revealing the loves and losses—of children, husbands, partners, futures, pasts—that hold them there. Together, the episodes explore the realms of emotion that transcend their urban environs, even as they

animate, then come to haunt, Naylor's dying street.

Whether writing of Mattie Michael, ruined by devotion to her criminal son, or Kiswana Browne, whose idealism brings her to the neighborhood over the objections of her family, or Cora Lee, who aspires to aspiration but can never submit to its discipline, the author evokes everyday tragedies of hope glimpsed, hope grasped, hope gone. Alert to both harrowing violence and simple pleasure—such as the joy of realizing as you return home late at night that someone is waiting up for you—the book can move in a page from the humdrum to the horrific, yet remains throughout illuminated by the dignity Naylor finds in lives that long for it and feel its lack. *The Women of Brewster Place* is like *The Grapes of Wrath* on a dead-end street: It has the same visceral power, and is just as wrenching in its clear-eyed imagination.

What: Novel. *When:* 1982. *Also By: Linden Hills* (1985). *Mama Day* (1988). *Bailey's Café* (1992). *The Men of Brewster Place* (1998). *Try: The Street* by Ann Petry. *The Bluest Eye* by Toni Morrison. *Adaptation:* The 1989 movie stars Oprah Winfrey.

A Short Walk in the Hindu Kush
Eric Newby (1919–2006)

Transporting Amusement from an Expert Amateur

This very funny book is an irresistible example of a characteristically English genre: You might call it the "Wacky but Intrepid School of Travel Writing." Books belonging to this happy group feature improbable travelers who embark, usually with little or no planning, on arduous journeys through remote and perilous regions. Newby's jolly narrative begins in a London fitting room, where he is at work as a not-very-successful salesman for a women's fashion designer. Nurturing a secret longing to explore "unknown territory" (and escape the Fashion Industry in general and the Spring Collection in particular), he fires off a telegram to a friend at the British embassy in Rio de Janeiro. One thing quickly leads to another, and soon Newby and his pal find themselves—after four days of "climbing lessons," if that's what you can call ambling over gentle slopes in Wales—in a remote and perilous region indeed: the Hindu Kush of northeastern Afghanistan. There, the fearsome peaks of the Nuristan range dare them to ascend. The narrative fares better than the travelers, building a steady comic momentum that is all the more entertaining for its detailed tabulation of their mishaps and mistakes. (The "short walk" of the title, by the way, on which they are invited by an Afghan elder, turns out to be seven hours long.)

As Evelyn Waugh pointed out in his introduction to the first American edition, *A Short Walk* "exemplifies the essential traditional (some, not I, will say deplorable) amateurism of the English . . . [their] wandering about the world for their amusement, suspect everywhere as government agents, to the great embarrassment of their officials." Fortunately, when it's the cheerful Newby inspiring the embarrassment, the armchair traveler is promised a very enjoyable journey.

What: Travel. *When:* 1958. *Also By: The Last Grain Race* (1956). *Something Wholesale: My Life and Times in the Rag Trade* (1962). *Slowly Down the Ganges* (1966). *Love and War in the Apennines* (1971). *The Big Red Train Ride* (1978). *A Traveller's Life* (1982). *Round Ireland in Low Gear* (1987). *Try: Brazilian Adventure* (see page 285) and *One's Company* by Peter Fleming. *Full Tilt: Ireland to India with a Bicycle* by Dervla Murphy. *Yemen: Travels in Dictionary Land* by Tim Mackintosh-Smith. *Into the Heart of Borneo* by Redmond O'Hanlon (see page 600). *A Walk in the Woods* by Bill Bryson (see page 104).

The Reckoning
THE MURDER OF CHRISTOPHER MARLOWE
Charles Nicholl (born 1950)

Reopening the Cold Case of an Elizabethan Playwright's Murder

On the morning of May 30, 1593, a businessman named Ingram Frizer met with three other men at a lodging house in Deptford, England. They spent the day quietly, but in the evening an argument broke out and Frizer stabbed one of his companions several times, killing him. The dead man was playwright

Christopher Marlowe, author of *Tamburlaine the Great*, *Dr. Faustus*, and *The Jew of Malta*. Born in 1563 (one year before Shakespeare), Marlowe was brilliant but dissolute, a quick-witted, atheistic rake who, for a time, may well have been the most popular dramatist in England. The official inquest into his death found that Frizer had acted in self-defense during a skirmish over the bill—the "recknynge," or "reckoning"—for some food and drink. Case closed—at least until Charles Nicholl came along four centuries later.

In *The Reckoning*, his ingenious literary-historical detective story, Nicholl demonstrates that once you start looking into the "great reckoning in a little room" (Shakespeare's sly allusion, in *As You Like It*, to his fellow writer's bloody fate), you find yourself drawn into the complicated treacheries of the Elizabethan underworld, "a world immediately familiar to readers of Deighton and le Carré," as a British reviewer of this book rightly put it. Examined in the context of this twilit world of intrigue and betrayal, plots and counterplots, Marlowe's death begins to look suspiciously like a political assassination. Nicholl is peerless at breathing vibrant life into exhaustive research, and in this Elizabethan thriller he has pieced together an exceptionally satisfying narrative, rich in its detailed evocation of sixteenth-century England and filled with a colorful gallery of writers, wits, spies, government ministers, "intelligencers," and "conny catchers." Crime solving never gets more literate than this, nor does literary history ever get more gripping.

1585 portrait of Christopher Marlowe

What: History. Mystery & Suspense. **When:** 1992. **Edition:** A revised and updated edition of *The Reckoning* was published in 2002. **Also By:** *The Chemical Theatre* (1980). *A Cup of News: The Life of Thomas Nashe* (1984). *The Fruit Palace* (1986). *Somebody Else: Arthur Rimbaud in Africa, 1880–91* (1997). *Leonardo da Vinci: Flights of the Mind* (2004). *The Lodger Shakespeare* (2007). **Further Reading:** *The World of Christopher Marlowe* by David Riggs. **Try:** The inspired last novel of Anthony Burgess, *A Dead Man in Deptford*, splendidly animates Nicholl's thesis.

Merry Hall
Beverley Nichols (1898–1983)

Garden of Delight

Some fall in love with women; some fall in love with art; some fall in love with death.

I fall in love with gardens, which is much the same as falling in love with all three at once.

So begins this amusing and surprising record of one man's garden—a season of digging, planting, weeding, and watching flowers bloom or go bust in the company of the waspiest of wits. Add a dash or two of P. G. Wodehouse, a good dose of E. F. Benson's Mapp and Lucia books, and a soupçon of Evelyn Waugh (including the attendant snobbery) to that description and you will get some idea of how droll and delightful Beverley Nichols's book is.

Although he is now remembered chiefly for a shelf's worth of engaging gardening books, Nichols—one of the dandiest of the Bright Young

Things who sparkled across England's social and cultural scene between the world wars—also composed novels, plays, mysteries, and travel books. His penchant for stylish notoriety is best embodied by two books from late in his career: *A Case of Human Bondage* (1966), which offers a scabrous portrait of Somerset Maugham in an account of that writer's marriage to—and divorce from—a friend of Nichols's, and *Father Figure* (1972), in which Nichols confesses the murderous impulses provoked by his abusive father.

But *Merry Hall* is as diverting, sophisticated, and graceful as a 1930s film musical. First published in 1951, his memoir of cultivating his garden in a cottage in the British countryside has lost none of its appeal.

What: House & Garden. Memoir. *When:* 1951. *Edition:* The lovely Timber Press facsimile edition reproduces William McLaren's original drawings. *Also By: Laughter on the Stairs* (1953) and *Sunlight on the Lawn* (1956) complete the trilogy *Merry Hall* began. *Down the Garden Path* (1932). *Garden Open Today* (1963). *Further Reading: Beverley Nichols: A Life* by Bryan Connon. *Try: In Your Garden* by Vita Sackville-West. *Old Herbaceous* by Reginald Arkell (see page 24).

"The most amusing garden writer of all times."

—The New York Times *on Beverly Nichols*

Portrait of a Marriage
VITA SACKVILLE-WEST AND HAROLD NICOLSON
Nigel Nicolson (1917–2004)

To Have and to Hold

In 1962, Nigel Nicolson, fulfilling his duty as executor of his mother's estate, was going through her personal papers when he discovered a locked Gladstone bag in her sitting room at Sissinghurst Castle, the family home. From the very beginning of this book, we know—from sitting room, tower, and leather portmanteau—that we are in the province of the English upper classes. Lovers of literature will recognize Nicolson's mother, Vita Sackville-West, as an author who was peripheral to the artistic and intellectual set known as Bloomsbury, and dear to the heart of its central figure, Virginia Woolf; their liaison gave birth to Woolf's marvelous novel *Orlando* (see page 870). Lovers of flora will know Sackville-West for the plots she cultivated within Sissinghurst's glorious gardens, now in the care of the National Trust. What readers are unlikely to suspect, however, are the truths

Vita Sackville-West, 1920

and consequences of her unusual fifty-year marriage to politician, diplomat, and author Harold Nicolson, which this book probingly but affectionately portrays.

The bag contained a substantial piece of autobiographical writing, penned when Sackville-West was twenty-eight, describing—perhaps attempting to fathom is a better way to put it—her desperate passion for another woman, Violet Trefusis. Sackville-West's own account makes up parts 1 and 3 of *Portrait of a Marriage*, and it bears witness to her gifts as one of the finest prose writers of her generation. Parts 2 and 4 contain her son's commentary on the affair and its repercussions, drawing on the letters of his mother and father as well as on the recollections of those who knew them; his skill as a biographer is put to judicious and compelling use. The final section of the book deals with the remaining years of their marriage, showing, in the younger Nicolson's words, "how my parents' love for each other survived all further threats to it."

And threats there were, and considerable ones, too. Harold Nicholson also pursued relations with people of his own sex, and long absences from each other marked most of Harold and Vita's shared decades. Yet their reciprocal devotion transcended both sexual incompatibility and the borders of conventional marital concord, even while each led a life in many ways defined—indeed, nourished—by the conventions of their culture and their class. Their love, their son reflects in his own middle age, "deepened with every passing year," ultimately engendering, in this candid and surprising volume, an irreducible testament to their hearts' confidence.

What: Biography. *When:* 1973. *Also By:* Nigel Nicolson also edited his father's diaries and letters and the letters of Virginia Woolf. He is the author of an excellent short biography of Woolf for the Penguin Lives series (2000), a volume of memoirs (*Long Life*, 1998), and several other books. *Further Reading: Vita and Harold: The Letters of Vita Sackville-West and Harold Nicolson*, edited by Nigel Nicolson. *Violet to Vita: The Letters of Violet Trefusis to Vita Sackville-West*, edited by Mitchell A. Leaska and John Phillips. *Try: All Passion Spent* by Vita Sackville-West (see page 690). *Adaptation:* A British television miniseries aired in 1990.

....

The Birth of Tragedy
Friedrich Nietzsche (1844–1900)

A Seminal Philosopher's Debut

What makes for an exhilarating read? Usually a gripping plot, magnificent writing, and well-drawn characters. There are, however, a few special books that are exhilarating because the author captures brilliant ideas and unprecedented insights with such vividness and immediacy that the reader is equally inspired. This is one of them.

At the precocious age of twenty-five, Friedrich Nietzsche was appointed Extraordinary Professor of Classical Philology at the University of Basel in

Friedrich Nietzsche, ca. 1880

Switzerland. His first book, originally titled *The Birth of Tragedy from the Spirit of Music*, was published three years later, in 1872. Nietzsche's radical reinterpretation of ancient Greek tragedy's origins was so controversial that instead of enhancing his reputation, the book short-circuited his academic career. The prevailing view was that a play such as Sophocles's *Oedipus Rex* demonstrated the serene rationalism of the "noble Greeks." Nietzsche argued, on the contrary, that the great tragedies reflected a powerful tension running throughout Greek culture: namely, the creative conflict between chaos and order, irrationality and reason, intoxication and lucidity. Nietzsche named these warring impulses after the Greek gods Dionysus and Apollo, and his analysis of the fierce struggle between "Dionysian" and "Apollonian" tendencies has been profoundly influential ever since.

The Birth of Tragedy is thus an important contribution to the history of ideas. It is also crucial to understanding the development of Nietzsche's thought. Yet the main reason it remains a thrilling experience for general readers is that Nietzsche's live-wire prose conveys the excitement of intellectual discovery, affording them an electrifying sense of what it's like to contemplate a subject from a

revolutionary angle, to grasp its complexities in a way no one previously has.

A curious feature of The Birth of Tragedy is that for the second edition, in 1886, Nietzsche wrote "An Attempt at Self-Criticism." This singular critique of the book's strengths and weaknesses prefaces modern editions of The Birth and provides a telling juxtaposition of Nietzsche's early and later styles.

What: Philosophy. **When:** 1872. **Also By:** Thus Spoke Zarathustra (1883–85). Beyond Good and Evil (1887). **Try:** The Greeks and the Irrational by E. R. Dodds. The Death of Tragedy by George Steiner.

The 9/11 Commission Report

Investigating the Facts and Lessons of September 11, 2001

"Imagination is not a gift usually associated with bureaucracies," asserts the National Commission on Terrorist Attacks Upon the United States late in its report, noting the failure of vision that had prevented America from foreseeing the threat that precipitated the horrible events of September 11, 2001. One might say with equal certainty that literary quality is not a characteristic usually associated with government documents, yet not the least of the astonishments this book contains is what Publishers Weekly aptly called its "absolutely compelling narrative intelligence." Despite the weight of its research and investigative findings, despite the detail of its assemblage of policy and intelligence data, The 9/11 Commission Report has a suspenseful, relentless forward motion that makes it nearly impossible to put down.

Beginning with a meticulous description of the movements of the hijackers and reconstruction of what took place on board the four

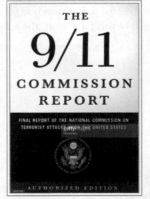

diverted flights, the report goes on to assess our preparedness and bewildered immediate response, to examine the history of the new terrorism of Osama bin Laden and al-Qaeda, and to consider counterterrorism programs and alternatives before proposing new strategies. Throughout the report's more than five hundred pages, the lucid exposition of both the facts and the wider contexts of our national loss, shock, and suffering rivet the reader. Although further information has already broadened our understanding of the threat of terrorism, it is unlikely that such knowledge—or revelations still to come—will alter the compelling interest of this remarkable historical document.

What: History. **When:** Created by Congress and the president in late November 2002, the 9/11 Commission issued its final report on July 22, 2004. **Edition:** W. W. Norton published the authorized edition. **Try:** The Looming Tower: Al-Qaeda and the Road to 9/11 by Lawrence Wright. 102 Minutes, by Jim Dwyer and Kevin Flynn, offers an unforgettable account of the fight to survive inside the Twin Towers from the time the first plane hit to the moment the second tower collapsed.

■ For Larry Niven's *Ringworld*, see page 27.

....

Mutiny on the *Bounty*
Charles Nordhoff (1887–1947) and James Norman Hall (1887–1951)

A Classic Tale of Treachery at Sea

....

In 1787, the HMS *Bounty* and her crew set sail for Tahiti. With fewer officers than usual and no marines, the ship was outfitted as a greenhouse for transporting breadfruit plants. These were to be harvested on the island and delivered to the West Indies to provide cheap food for slaves. After ten months at sea, the crew arrived in Tahiti, where they spent six months in the thrall of the island and its exotic charms—especially its women. When the work on the island was complete and the ship set out again (three men having been punished for desertion in the interim), a band of mutineers led by officer Fletcher Christian set the ship's commander William Bligh and eighteen of his loyal men adrift in the ship's launch. Thirteen more were kept on board by the mutineers to help run the ship. The motives for the mutiny have never been established beyond a reasonable doubt, but the mutineers' travels on the hijacked *Bounty*, the daunting open sea voyage of Bligh and his men, and the ultimate disposition of the case in the British courts have captivated writers, filmmakers, and audiences for generations.

Of the numerous accounts—documentary, historical, speculative, and fictional—that have been written, the best and most popular is the novelization by Charles Nordhoff and James Norman Hall. Published in 1932, *Mutiny on the Bounty* imagines the voyage out, the months in Tahiti, and the eventual uprising. (It's actually the first of a trilogy—the two subsequent books take up the *Bounty* after the crew's uprising, as the men return to Tahiti before they rediscover the lost Pitcairn Islands, dodge their navy pursuers, and ultimately destroy the ship.) Because the history is murky and Nordhoff and Hall are novelists, there's a lot of necessary supposition; the authors even go so far as to fill in the

Captain Bligh's mutineers set adrift, April 28, 1789

motives and characters of the men involved. Although this telling may not be the most historically accurate, it is the perfect introduction to an endless shelf of reading about a historical event. One of the great seafaring tales of all time, the story, like Shackleton's *Endurance* voyage, has assumed the aura of a modern myth.

What: Novel. Adventure. *When:* 1932. *Also By:* The second and third books of the trilogy are *Men Against the Sea* (1933) and *Pitcairn's Island* (1934). *Further Reading:* Among countless books about the mutiny is a collection of first- and secondhand narratives and historical documents—including accounts and testimony by William Bligh and Edward Christian, brother of Fletcher—published by Penguin Classics as *The Bounty Mutiny.* Also: *Mr. Bligh's Bad Language: Passion, Power and Theatre on the Bounty* by Greg Dening and *The Bounty: The True Story of the Mutiny on the Bounty* by Caroline Alexander. *Try: The Unknown Shore* by Patrick O'Brian. *Adaptations:* The 1935 and 1962 films, starring Clark Gable and Marlon Brando respectively, were based on Nordhoff and Hall's novel; the former won the Oscar for Best Picture. More historically accurate is the 1984 film *The Bounty,* which stars Mel Gibson.

Dakota

A SPIRITUAL GEOGRAPHY

Kathleen Norris (born 1947)

Taking Life by the Soul on the High Plains

After her grandmother's death, the poet Kathleen Norris returned from New York—where her days had been spent within the heady literary and artistic circles of the early 1970s—to the house built by her grandparents in an isolated town on the border between North and South Dakota. "It's hard to say why we stayed," she relates of herself and her husband, a fellow poet; but stay they did, and this book, written two decades later, reveals the roots that grew to entwine them. "I want to make it clear," Norris tells the reader early on, "that my move did not take me 'back to the land' in the conventional sense. . . . My move was one that took me deep into the meaning of inheritance, as I had to try to fit myself into a complex network of long-established relationships."

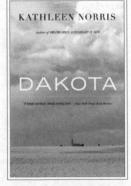

As her subtitle announces, the move was spiritual as much as physical, and *Dakota* encompasses both small-town life and large-souled yearnings as it weaves local history and the gossip of her neighbors into deeper meditations on doubt and faith. In Norris's evocative prose, we meet farmers, schoolkids, and other members of the community, and we consider the contemporary fates of descendants of European immigrants and Native Americans. We're asked to consider both "the real meaning of Jell-O in Dakota" and the lives of the Christian hermits known as the Desert Fathers. With intense respect, Norris describes her contact with a congregation of Benedictine monks whose patience and asceticism she finds congenial and nourishing. In the "Weather Reports" she places between her chapters, we see again and again nature's elemental face, like the palpable presence of an unfathomable deity. As Robert Coles has written of Norris, "Her writing is personal, epigrammatic—a series of short takes that ironically addresses the biggest subject matter possible: how one ought live a life."

What: Religion & Spirituality. Memoir. *When:* 1993. *Also By:* Three subsequent books explore Norris's engagement with Christian spirituality: *The Cloister Walk* (1996), *Amazing Grace: A Vocabulary of Faith* (1998), and *The Quotidian Mysteries: Laundry, Liturgy, and "Women's Work"* (1998). *The Virgin of Bennington* (2001) is a memoir of the very different life she led before her relocation to South Dakota. *Try: Pilgrim at Tinker Creek* by Annie Dillard (see page 224).

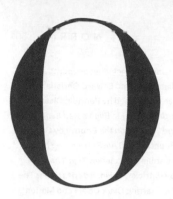

Dreams from My Father

A STORY OF RACE AND INHERITANCE

Barack Obama (born 1961)

The Child Is Father to the Man

Every American president writes a memoir after leaving office, and as a rule it's pretty dull—a perfunctory draft of history that minimizes failures, oversells accomplishments, and avoids controversy. And the few books presidents have published before taking office, from John F. Kennedy's (allegedly ghostwritten) *Profiles in Courage* to Richard Nixon's (allegedly ghostwritten) *Six Crises*, are primarily documents penned to burnish a political career. So it's fair to say that in the annals of presidential literature, *Dreams from My Father*, written by Barack Obama in his early thirties, is something very different. An emotional and at times disarmingly candid memoir "of race and inheritance," chronicling his life from childhood in Hawaii to Harvard Law School, the book was written before Obama was even a US senator from Illinois, let alone president of the United States. That makes it an uncommon and especially valuable memoir: unguarded, direct, and eminently readable.

The future president barely knew his father, a Kenyan academic—also called Barack Obama—who divorced the author's mother, Stanley Ann Dunham, a white anthropology student born in Kansas, when their child was three. Thereafter Dunham married an Indonesian man, and young Barack lived in Jakarta from 1967 to 1971; he later moved to

Barack Obama ca. 2004 (left); at Harvard Law School (right), 1990

Honolulu to live with his maternal grandparents. In his teenage years in Hawaii, a state with a unique racial makeup, Obama began to sense the significance of his heritage, which he writes about in language far franker than you'd expect from someone planning to pursue a political career:

When people who don't know me well, black or white, discover my background (and it is usually a discovery, for I ceased to advertise my mother's race at the age of twelve or thirteen, when I began to suspect that by doing so I was ingratiating myself to whites), I see the split-second adjustments they have to make, the searching of my eyes for some telltale sign. They no longer know who I am. Privately, they guess at my troubled heart, I suppose—the mixed blood, the divided soul, the ghostly image of the tragic mulatto trapped between two worlds.

In his university years, Obama's deepening self-identification as an African American comes into conflict not only with his love for his white mother and grandparents, but with his status as the child of a black African, divorced from the history of slavery and segregation. Things change, however, when he moves to Chicago. Galvanized by the election of Harold Washington as the city's first black mayor, Obama becomes a community organizer and also finds solace in a church led by the Reverend Jeremiah Wright (who would later marry him and his wife, Michelle, and cause him serious grief during his first presidential campaign). But even though Obama's racial identity seems to solidify as he grows older, his personal identity remains hazy—and only after a long visit to Kenya, where he meets his extended family and discovers truths about his father's life, does he comprehend the complex contours of his legacy.

There is little in *Dreams from My Father* to suggest that, just thirteen years after its publication, its author would be standing on the steps of the Capitol and taking the oath of office as the first black president of the United States. Nevertheless, the book stands on its own as one of the finest memoirs by any American writer on the resonance of racial differences and the journey of self-discovery these differences can shape. And the future of Obama's public presence can't help but add substance to this memoir's exploration of a private past.

What: Memoir. *When:* 1995. *Also By: The Audacity of Hope* (2006). *Of Thee I Sing: A Letter to My Daughters* (2010). *Further Reading: Barack Obama: The Story* by David Maraniss. *Try: Hunger of Memory* by Richard Rodriguez (see page 671). *The Color of Water* by James McBride. *My Life* by Bill Clinton. *Adaptation:* The author reads the superb audiobook version.

Master and Commander
Patrick O'Brian (1914–2000)

First Voyage on Alluring Seas

Master and Commander, which introduces readers to Captain Jack Aubrey and his friend, ship's surgeon and intelligence officer Stephen Maturin, is the thrilling first volume in an unparalleled series of novels that British-born Patrick O'Brian wrote about the Royal Navy—or "Nelson's Navy," as it's also called, in honor of Vice Admiral Horatio Nelson, hero of the Battle of Trafalgar. The series, acclaimed by Richard Snow in the *New York Times Book Review* as "the best historical novels ever written," unfolds across a score of books set during the late eighteenth and early nineteenth centuries, when Britain was battling with Napoleon's France.

The characters of both protagonists are well drawn: Aubrey is cheerful, outgoing, enamored of seaboard life and the exhilaration of battle, while Maturin is reserved and erudite, disliking violence but remarkably resourceful in advancing the British cause. *Master and Commander* opens with their first meeting, at a string quartet performance that, to Maturin's aggravation, Aubrey punctuates by ostentatiously marking the time. Maturin elbows him hard in the ribs, and one of modern literature's most enduring friendships begins.

That a series steeped in naval adventure begins with chamber music is a telling indication of the wit and sophistication of the Aubrey/Maturin novels. The contrast between the men's characters and interests (encompassing music, food, poetry, science, and natural history) provides a substantial foundation upon which O'Brian erects exciting plots of dangerous action. In *Master and Commander* and all the books that follow, authentic details of life aboard a man-of-war in Commodore Nelson's navy are admirably rendered, and the author's narrative skills deftly convey the excitement of ships closing in battle. As a bonus, O'Brian's mastery of history and geography supplies an engaging education in the midst of the page-turning pleasure. All in all, the vivid storytelling that distinguishes this book and its sequels leads the reader around the world in the best of company.

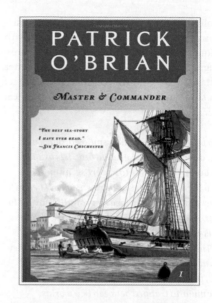

What: Novel. **When:** 1970. **Reading Note:** O'Brian's easy way with maritime lore and language can leave readers momentarily mystified. Keep help at hand with *A Sea of Words: A Lexicon and Companion to the Complete Seafaring Tales of Patrick O'Brian*, edited by Dean King. **Also By:** Nineteen other Aubrey/Maturin novels, plus one left incomplete at the time of O'Brian's death (see below). Other fiction: *The Golden Ocean* (1956); *The Unknown Shore* (1959). Nonfiction: *Men-of-War: Life in* *Nelson's Navy* (1974); *Picasso: A Biography* (1976); *Joseph Banks: A Life* (1987). **Further Reading:** *Patrick O'Brian: Critical Essays and a Bibliography*, edited by Arthur Cunningham. *Seamanship in the Age of Sail* by John Harland. **Try:** Novels by C. S. Forester, Alexander Kent, C. Northcote Parkinson, Dudley Pope, and John Biggins. **Adaptation:** *Master and Commander: The Far Side of the World*, a film starring Russell Crowe, was released in 2003. **Footnote:** Born Richard Patrick Russ in Buckinghamshire, the future author worked in British intelligence during World War II, then changed his name and invented a new identity for himself. Dean King's *Patrick O'Brian: A Life Revealed* tells the whole story.

THE AUBREY/MATURIN NOVELS

Master and Commander (1970)

Post Captain (1972)

H.M.S. Surprise (1973)

The Mauritius Command (1977)

Desolation Island (1978)

The Fortune of War (1979)

The Surgeon's Mate (1980)

The Ionian Mission (1981)

Treason's Harbour (1983)

The Far Side of the World (1984)

The Reverse of the Medal (1986)

The Letter of Marque (1988)

The Thirteen-Gun Salute (1989)

The Nutmeg of Consolation (1991)

The Truelove (1992) (UK title: *Clarissa Oakes*)

The Wine-Dark Sea (1993)

The Commodore (1994)

The Yellow Admiral (1996)

The Hundred Days (1998)

Blue at the Mizzen (1999)

21 (2004) (Unfinished at time of author's death; UK title *The Final Unfinished Voyage of Jack Aubrey*)

The Little Red Chairs
Edna O'Brien (born 1930)

Home and Away

In addition to being one of the most accomplished fiction writers in English in the past hundred years, Edna O'Brien possesses an intensity of purpose and a force of personality—one might more simply call this bravery—that make her seem a heroine worthy of Madame de Staël or George Eliot. O'Brien's rebellion against the repressive strictures of the Ireland in which she was raised is well documented. Her first novel, *The Country Girls* (1960), engaged sexual and social themes previously off-limits in the suffocating sanctimony of her mid-twentieth-century homeland. Indeed, her debut and its sequels (*The Lonely Girl*, 1962; *Girls in Their Married Bliss*, 1964) were condemned in churches, banned, and even, on occasion, burned. The acclaimed literary career that followed this incendiary beginning produced more than a dozen novels, several volumes of short stories, biographies of James Joyce (an early inspiration) and Lord Byron, plays, and a memoir.

Published in her eighty-fifth year, *The Little Red Chairs* is a fitting and, frankly, astonishing culmination of her literary gifts and creative courage. The novel moves with startling speed and surety from the lovely lanes of Irish provincial life into the bloodstained terrain of the Balkan War, spinning a web of fear, violence, and displacement as human decency is driven from domestic certainty and transformed into something lost and wandering. The central figure is Fidelma, a local beauty whose longing leads her unknowingly into the embrace of a brutal war criminal. Riven by guilt and recrimination, she must extricate herself to define a new sense of both self and home. O'Brien's fictive invention encompasses omniscient narration, Fidelma's interior monologues, and the voices of many other tellers of private tales within the larger one. The range of emotion realized in character and incident has a resonance that is both chilling and breathtaking, Shakespearean in its eloquence and intuition.

The book's title invokes the 11,541 red chairs that, in April 2012, were actually laid out in rows along the half mile of the main street in Sarajevo, one empty chair for every Sarajevan killed during the 1,425 days of the 1992–96 siege of the city. O'Brien's novel evolves from fairy tale to parable to historical tragedy as it marks the way stations of the refugees, real and metaphorical, whom the author honors with vivid elegy: "Nobodies, mere numbers on paper or computer, the hunted, the haunted, the raped, the defeated, the mutilated, the banished, the flotsam of the world, unable to go home, wherever home is." Reaching for beauty from roots of terror, *The Little Red Chairs* reads like a sacrament, with all the uncanny truths and consequences a sacrament invokes.

What: Novel. *When:* 2015. *Also By: Casualties of Peace* (1966). *A Pagan Place* (1970). *A Fanatic Heart* (1984). *House of Splendid Isolation* (1994). *Saints and Sinners* (2011). *Try: The Blind Man's Garden* by Nadeem Aslam. *Homegoing* by Yaa Gyasi. *Adaptation:* A superb audiobook version is performed by Juliet Stevenson.

At Swim-Two-Birds
Flann O'Brien (1911–1966)

A Comic Extravaganza from an Antic Irish Bard

This 1939 novel has never lacked for champions. It was recommended for publication by Graham Greene, who called it "one of the best books of our century." James Joyce, having received a copy from Samuel Beckett, thought it "a really funny book." And when it was left off a recent list of the hundred best novels in English in the past hundred years, the *New York Times* was moved to object to the slight:

"Where, oh where," asked the paper of record, "is Flann O'Brien?" But it was Dylan Thomas who best captured the earthy, Guinness-soaked, anarchic humor of *At Swim-Two-Birds* when he called it "just the book to give your sister if she's a loud, dirty, boozy girl!"

Steeped in the hilarious bawdry of Dublin college life, *At Swim-Two-Birds* is an inventive romp consisting of a story within a story within a story within a story, each being told by a writer whose characters seem bent on asserting their independence. Digressions meet themselves coming and going. The novel's labyrinthine narrative has been summed up best by Thomas C. Foster, as "the story of a young novelist playing with all his toys." The cleverest of O'Brien's juxtaposed plots involves characters who revolt against the author of their tale and put him on trial. Other strands of O'Brien's freewheeling creation consist of merry parodies of Irish myth and scenes of cowboys pursuing cattle rustlers (in greater Dublin, no less).

A "metafiction" long before the word came into literary fashion (the ancient and roughly equivalent Irish term would probably be "blarney"), O'Brien's book is fueled by a whimsy that is unique and unforgettable.

Incidentally, just as story nests within story here, so too was the author a kind of "nested" writer: "Flann O'Brien" was one of several pseudonyms of Irish civil servant Brian Ó Nualláin, who achieved additional renown under the pen name "Myles na gCopaleen," the legendary humorist whose column brightened pages of the *Irish Times* from 1940 to 1966.

What: Novel. Humor. *When:* 1939. *Also By:* The Third Policeman (written 1939–40; published 1967). *The Poor Mouth* (published in Irish, 1941; in English, 1973). *The Dalkey Archive* (1964). *The Best of Myles* (1968). *Further Reading: No Laughing Matter: The Life and Times of Flann O'Brien* by Anthony Cronin. *Try: Murphy* by Samuel Beckett. *Lanark* by Alasdair Gray.

■ For Michael O'Brien's *Mrs. Adams in Winter*, see page 252.

The Things They Carried
Tim O'Brien (born 1946)

War and Remembrance

The men of Alpha Company carry many things: gear, talismans, rations, cigarettes, candy, steel helmets, fear. One member of the platoon carries dope, one a hatchet, another a photo of a girl he loves who doesn't love him back (along with her cheerful letters). The things the soldiers battle are just as sundry, from enemies to injuries, loneliness to cowardice. Those who survive their tour in Vietnam will fight the memories they carry home with them. They are the boys-becoming-men who populate

Tim O'Brien's evocation of an ever-inchoate conflict, a war experienced not as a progression of campaigns and historical events but as an ominous, enveloping medium in which the lives of combatants were steeped until their very sense of reality assumed a different hue.

Before publishing *The Things They Carried*, twenty-two interwoven stories that tell of the lives of Alpha Company's members in and after Vietnam, O'Brien had written a memoir of his service in Southeast Asia, *If I Die in a Combat Zone, Box Me Up and Send Me Home* (1973), as well as an award-winning novel informed by the same experience, *Going After Cacciato* (1978), widely considered one of the most compelling fictional accounts of the war. *The Things They Carried* straddles the approaches of the earlier volumes, and in so doing amplifies their power. Narrated by a character named Tim, but with the words "a work of fiction" on the title page, the book intentionally and directly addresses its own veracity (see the chapter "How to Tell a True War Story").

Yet the author is not merely engaged in a literary argument about the distinctions between memoirs and novels. The individual episodes are absorbing in their own right, at the same time as each contributes to a larger picture of men at war: Tim's recollection of his failure to escape to Canada to avoid the draft ("I would go to the war—I would kill and maybe die—because I was embarrassed not to"); two soldiers' brawl over a missing jackknife; deaths by accident, killings with intent; patrols through a jungle whose presence is palpable enough to be surreal; the

American infantry near Phu Bai, South Vietnam, 1972

unforeseen distress of homecoming. Linking them is the recognition that even the horrible drama of combat can be grasped, to say nothing of communicated, only by following its realities beyond the battlefield into memory and imagination. There they must ultimately abide, O'Brien tells us. His narratives are both searing and fleeting, faithful to the urgency with which all of us, not only soldiers, struggle to hold on to whatever we carry in the only way we really can, trying to save our lives with stories.

What: Short Stories. *When:* 1990. *Also By:* O'Brien's subsequent (non-Vietnam) novels are *In the Lake of the Woods* (1994), *Tomcat in Love* (1998), and *July, July* (2002). *Try: Dispatches* by Michael Herr (see page 369). *Meditations in Green* by Stephen Wright. *Matterhorn* by Karl Marlantes. *Adaptation:* The 1998 film *A Soldier's Sweetheart*, starring Kiefer Sutherland, is based on the chapter, "Sweetheart of the Song Tra Bong."

The Complete Stories
Flannery O'Connor (1925–1964)

This Side of Paradise

Even in the hothouse of the literature of the American South, Flannery O'Connor appears as an exotic. Perhaps it's because she raised peacocks at her home in Milledgeville, Georgia, or because of the somehow defiantly settled life she led there with her mother. Perhaps it is the crippling effects of the lupus she endured throughout her writing life, until her death at age thirty-nine. Perhaps it is her fierce Catholicism, through which she viewed human existence with a lack of sentiment that might have scared both Hemingway and Mickey Spillane, to say nothing of priests or even popes.

More likely, though, it is her fiction itself: grotesque, violent, blackly comic, altogether startling. Take the title story of her first collection, "A Good Man Is Hard to Find": A squabbling family on a vacation trip from Georgia to Florida drives off the road into a ditch, where they are discovered by an escaped convict and his two acolytes, who casually murder them all. Not only does its title belie its content, but, as Elizabeth Hardwick once pointed out, you could even call it a *funny* story, despite the fact that six people are killed in it. In another tale, an old woman marries off her mentally deficient daughter to a one-armed drifter named Shiftlet, who behaves with ineluctable cruelty to his new relations, abandoning his wife and stealing his mother-in-law's car.

That one is called "The Life You Save May Be Your Own," again prompting the reflection that many of O'Connor's titles (for example, "Human Development," "Good Country People," "Revelation") have a savagely ironic relationship to the calamities their stories describe. In this, they are much like the "good news" of official religion, in which the brutalities of life are masked in bromides. Not for nothing did O'Connor write of Catholics who mistake a kind of false certainty for faith, "the Church for them is not the body of Christ but the poor man's insurance system." Replete with assault, arson, and other assorted threats, O'Connor's stories are like car crashes you just can't look away from, in which the vehicles end up too damaged to be recognizable and the people in them are subjected to graphic but hidden injury. You watch the collision with a kind of awful horror. A world charged with God is more dangerous than benign, O'Connor tells us, more like a strange book of prophecy than a list of beatitudes. This no doubt makes her fiction sound gruesome, perverse, and freakish, all of which it is; it is also haunting well beyond the borders of any particular dogma, because it speaks to enigmas that

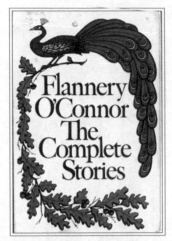

Flannery O'Connor The Complete Stories

human beings—human *being*—can never solve.

These stories are not parables, though they are often labeled as such. They are more like savage rites, their significance in some ways closer to Greek tragedy than Southern Gothic. Although the larger-than-life heroes of the former have been replaced by the flesh-and-blood figures of the latter, dispossessed and often desperate, the characters are still called to account by inscrutable forces of fate and suffering—which, O'Connor might say, are emblems of God's mysterious ways.

What: Short Stories. *When:* 1971. *Award:* National Book Award for Fiction, 1972. *Also By: Wise Blood* (1952). *The Violent Bear It Away* (1960). *Mystery and Manners: Occasional Prose* (1969). *The Habit of Being: Letters of Flannery O'Connor* (1979; see page 505). *Further Reading: The Life You Save May Be Your Own: An American Pilgrimage* by Paul Elie. *Flannery: A Life of Flannery O'Connor* by Brad Gooch. *Try: Collected Stories of Carson McCullers. Selected Stories* by Andre Dubus. *Footnote:* In an online poll conducted in 2009 by the National Book Foundation, O'Connor's *Complete Stories* was voted the best of all the books that had won the National Book Award for Fiction in the award's sixty-year history.

■ For Flannery O'Connor's *The Habit of Being*, see page 505.

Collected Stories
Frank O'Connor (1903–1966)

An Irish Master of the Short Story

Born in Cork, Ireland, Michael Francis O'Donovan was still in his teens when he became involved with the Irish republican opposition to British rule. He fought against the Anglo-Irish Treaty, which in 1921 laid the groundwork for the partition of Ireland into the Irish Free State and Northern Ireland, and was imprisoned by Free State forces during the Irish Civil War of 1922–23. After the war he became a teacher and librarian and pursued a career as a writer, adopting the pen name "Frank O'Connor" and producing a varied body of work in fiction, biography, history, travel, drama, memoir, and literary criticism; he also made many English translations of Gaelic poetry. But as American novelist Anne Tyler has noted, it is O'Connor's short stories "that guarantee his immortality." Sixty-seven of them are gathered in his *Collected Stories*.

As Richard Ellmann observes in his introduction to this volume, O'Connor's short stories "preserve in ink like amber his perceptive, amused, and sometimes tender observations of the fabric of Irish customs, pieties, superstitions, loves, and hates." They are especially attuned to the stubbornnesses that can define, ruin, or redeem a life, as when a father's pride forbids his acceptance of his brother's hand ("The Luceys") or the deceased make demands on the living ("The Long Road to Ummera" and "The Mass Island"). And yet O'Connor's local attention to priests and rebels, or to the repressive mores of church and small town, is merely an invitation to the author's powerful sensitivity to universal truths of conscience and character.

Across a wide spectrum of incident—from the book's first story, "Guests of the Nation," in which two Irish Republican Army soldiers befriend the Englishmen they have captured and will soon execute, to "Christmas Morning," in which a youngster discovers there is no Santa Claus at the same time as his mother's fears and cares become clear to him—O'Connor dramatizes the human condition with that rarest of writerly gifts, the common touch. He sought to convey "the tone of a man's voice,

speaking," and he caught that quality again and again. Although his tales are of the highest literary distinction, each one is remarkable for the ease of its telling (the author's correspondence with William Maxwell reveals O'Connor's endless and unstinting revision—even post-publication). They have the intimate, lived-in, and conspiratorial air that envelops any close exchange between speaker and listener, and they are animated with the energies—and frequently the humor—of living speech. As Ellmann expertly notes, O'Connor's stories "pass into our experience like incidents we have ourselves known or almost known," broadening our understanding of fate and family, life, love, and death. The power of their magnanimous scrutiny of mundane affairs is old-fashioned in its way, and timeless.

What: Short Stories. *When:* 1981, collecting stories published as early as 1931. *Also By: The Big Fellow: Michael Collins and the Irish Revolution* (1937). *The Mirror in the Roadway* (1956). *An Only Child* (1961). *The Lonely Voice: A Study of the Short Story* (1963). *My Father's Son* (1969). *Further Reading: The Happiness of Getting It Down Right: Letters of Frank O'Connor and William Maxwell* is a delightful literary correspondence. *Voices: A Life of Frank O'Connor* by James H. Matthews. *Try:* The stories of Anton Chekhov (see page 135). *Dubliners* by James Joyce (see page 420). *A Fanatic Heart* by Edna O'Brien. *The Collected Stories* by William Trevor (see page 804). *Footnote:* In the 1930s, O'Connor was director, with W. B. Yeats, of the famous Abbey Theatre in Dublin.

Are You Somebody?
THE ACCIDENTAL MEMOIR OF A DUBLIN WOMAN
Nuala O'Faolain (1940–2008)

Late-Blooming Self-Sufficiency

The self is shaped by sentences: Some are handed down to us by the court of circumstance, others by the verdict of our peers, others still by the overarching judgments of culture, church, family. Is it too far a reach, or too precious a wordplay, to say that to shape

our individual destinies we must shape our own sentences, recasting our experience into images and memories that enlighten the blindness of day-to-day struggles? Such is the truth that emanates from this compassionate memoir of an Irish journalist and television producer who restored her self in its writing, recovering all the lives that crossed hers on her way to her encounters with "the challenges of middle age and the challenges of loneliness."

The memoir begins with O'Faolain in her early thirties, living in London and working as a television producer with the BBC, at the end of a decade-long affair and, in her words, "entering a bad period in my life." A psychiatrist she consults in her depression tells her, "You are going to great trouble and flying in the face of the facts of your life, to re-create your mother's life." Circling back in an attempt to understand her upbringing and where it has brought her, the book traces the author's passage from a harrowing childhood as the second of nine siblings through a rebellious youth, distinction at school and university, and an unsettled adulthood of professional achievement, drinking and writing, longing and lingering regret.

Unsentimental and immediate in its explorations of the past, candid in its depictions of the coercive power of tradition and religion in shaping even the most liberated souls, *Are You Somebody?* is a self-interrogation in which every answer remains provisional, and every question endures to honor the uncertainty in which life unfolds.

What: Memoir. *When:* 1996. *Also By: My Dream of You* (2001). *Almost There: The Onward Journey of a Dublin Woman* (2003). *The Story of Chicago May* (2005). *Try: Angela's Ashes* by Frank McCourt (see page 536). *Whoredom in Kimmage* by Rosemary Mahoney. *Lit* by Mary Karr.

Into the Heart of Borneo
Redmond O'Hanlon (born 1947)

Laughter Among the Killer Insects

Redmond O'Hanlon is a British naturalist. He has a pleasant house in Oxford and a very pleasant job: For the past two decades he has been on the staff of the *Times Literary Supplement*. Perhaps because of his normally pleasant circumstances, he finds himself from time to time with an itch to explore places that are as exaggeratedly unpleasant as any on the planet. O'Hanlon began his career as a traveler-adventurer in 1983. With poet James Fenton and three native guides, he ventured, on foot and by boat, into the center of Borneo on an ultimately futile search for a rare two-horned rhinoceros.

The third-largest island in the world, Borneo lies southeast of Vietnam across the South China Sea. Its central jungle had gone unexplored for more than half a century. That the place has been given a wide berth isn't terribly surprising: The temperature runs to 120 degrees and the humidity is often 98 percent. It's the flora and fauna, however, that really earn the jungle its Keep Out sign. The creepy-crawlies that are native to Borneo sound like nightmare's brood. There are, for starters,

Redmond O'Hanlon at home, 2004

assassin bugs, joined by about 1,700 species of parasitic worm. There's also the toothpick fish, which can enter into a man's—no, it's too horrible to talk about. Then there are amoebic and bacillary dysenteries, yellow and blackwater and dengue fevers, cholera, typhoid—you get the idea.

Here, though, is the most remarkable thing about O'Hanlon's account of the two-month journey: It's as hilarious as it is scarifying. Knockabout farce enlivens practically every grueling step. When, for instance, the worn-out, beat-up expedition finally reaches its destination, the party celebrates by teaching a tricky disco move to friendly Ukit tribesmen.

No wonder the legendary traveler Eric Newby called *Into the Heart of Borneo* "certainly the funniest travel book I have ever read."

What: Travel. Nature. Humor. *When:* 1984. *Also By: In Trouble Again: A Journey Between the Orinoco and the Amazon* (1988). *No Mercy: A Journey to the Heart of the Congo* (1996). *Trawler: A Journey Through the North Atlantic* (2005). *Try: Pass the Butterworms* by Tim Cahill. *A Zoo in My Luggage* by Gerald Durrell. *The Sea and the Jungle* by H. M. Tomlinson (see page 801).

The Book of Tea
Kakuzo Okakura (1863–1913)

A Treatise Steeped in Asian Aestheticism

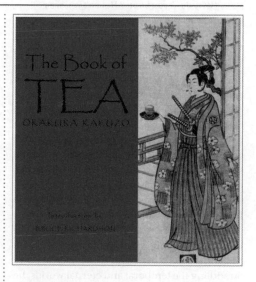

In the latter part of the nineteenth century, Japan determined to aggressively modernize itself. Ancient ways and objects were banned or derided. Students were sent abroad for Western educations, and English-language schools were established within Japan. One such institute was Tokyo Imperial University, where Kakuzo Okakura, son of a samurai-turned-merchant, met Harvard-educated professor Ernest Fenollosa, who had gone to Japan to teach philosophy and political science but had fallen under the spell of the nation's time-honored customs. Under Fenollosa's influence, Okakura became a walking paradox: a modern scholar dedicated to preserving the traditional culture of his homeland.

After traveling to Boston in 1904, Okakura stayed on to work for the Museum of Fine Arts, where he built a collection of Asian art unrivaled even in Asia. He befriended Isabella Stewart Gardner, doyenne of the city's cultural elite, who introduced him into her social circle.

Written in English and read aloud in Mrs. Gardner's salon, his essay *The Book of Tea* is an explication of the Japanese tea ceremony and the "religion of aestheticism" it represents, "a cult founded on the adoration of the beautiful among the sordid facts of everyday existence." Although Okakura's celebration of "Teaism" covers the history of tea, the religious

impulse that animates the ceremony, aspects of art appreciation, and flower arranging, it is no how-to. His treatise is to the tea ceremony as the ceremony itself is to Japanese life: an encapsulation of aesthetic, philosophic, and even moral ideals, "a tender attempt to accomplish something possible in this impossible thing we know as life."

Filled with quotable sentences, *The Book of Tea* is as much about East versus West and old versus new as it is about tea. Though a mere sixty-five pages, it is brewed with enough intellect and wisdom to inform a lifetime's meditation.

What: Philosophy. Culture. *When:* 1906. *Try: The Poetics of Space* by Gaston Bachelard (see page 39). *Thousand Cranes* by Yasunari Kawabata. *Footnote:* Okakura's book has influenced countless Western writers, thinkers, artists, and architects, including Frank Lloyd Wright, who credited it as the inspiration for his "architecture of the within."

The Famished Road
Ben Okri (born 1959)

The Story of an African Spirit-Child

"What are you doing here?" one of them would ask.

"Living," I would reply.

"Living for what?"

"I don't know."

"Why don't you know? Haven't you seen what lies ahead of you?"

The young boy being interrogated is Azaro, narrator of *The Famished Road.* What lies ahead of him is a long road of poverty, flood, earthquake, preternatural apparitions, political brutality, separation from his parents, reunion, desperation and mystery, communion with the dead, love and hope—all manner of life in its quotidian and mythical dimensions. That road runs through the center of Ben Okri's novel, a work of eerie beauty and, despite the book's supernatural compass, extraordinary fidelity to fundamental human emotions.

Denizen of an impoverished African village, Azaro is a child who has not lost touch with the spirit realm other children abandon at birth. Straddling the temporal and eternal worlds, he chooses a life in time (to the incredulity of his spirit interrogator in the passage quoted above), and his story is animated with both magical wonders and the everyday life of his family and their neighbors. While his parents struggle to keep Azaro among the living, the boy seeks to assume a solid identity in the shifting landscape of vision and actuality he describes.

The family's intimate milieu is suffused with myth, folktale, and belief, but grotesque political realities (echoing those of the author's native Nigeria) are never far away, and Azaro's father—a figure whose exertions as a laborer and heroics as a boxer are rendered with uncanny intensity—is determined to engage them, however futilely. Teeming incidents—his mother's cagey battles with the landlord, the drunken and dangerous revelry that spills from Madame Koto's bar, the oppressive presence of factional thugs—are filtered through Azaro's consciousness and woven by Okri into a mesmerizing narrative both mystifying and curiously true to life. Although the boy's tale is phantasmagorical, it aches with real human sentiment—imagine García Márquez crossed with Dickens and you'll approach something of the book's flavor.

Be warned: If you don't let the book carry you along, you'll soon be exhausted by your resistance to its rushing, unfettered imagination. But give in to the current of the author's musical prose and otherworldly visions and you are in for a transformative reading experience. Okri's book is bigger than life in just the way that, deep in our hearts, we know our lives are bigger than circumstantial evidence suggests.

Ben Okri, 1994

What: Novel. *When:* 1991. *Award:* Booker Prize, 1991. *Also By: Songs of Enchantment* (1993). *Astonishing the Gods* (1995). *In Arcadia* (2002). *Try: The Radiance of the King* by Camara Laye. *One Hundred Years of Solitude* by Gabriel García Márquez (see page 308). *Aké: The Years of Childhood* by Wole Soyinka (see page 742).

Tell Me a Riddle
Tillie Olsen (1912–2007)

Breaking the Silence of Broken Hearts

Of all the griefs the world can hold, regret can be the most corrosive. The heart's inventiveness in turning such anguish inward, allowing it to infiltrate conscience as well as consciousness, seems limitless, even though words are seldom a match for its true character. A slim collection of four stories, Tillie Olsen's *Tell Me a Riddle* is animated by speech rhythms, its narratives carried along on fits and starts of thoughts and ellipses of memory and emotion. Its genius is the way its prose conveys the abiding argument we have with our own failings and feelings and with the needs, demands, and affections of those closest to us.

The first tale begins like this: "I stand here ironing, and what you asked me moves tormented back and forth with the iron." (The first four words provide the story's title.) What follows reveals a woman's retrospective remorse for neglect of her firstborn, a daughter of some talent who is now nineteen years of age and into whose personality a teacher or counselor is seeking the mother's insight. Confronted by the external request—"'I'm sure you can help me understand her'"—the mother's interior voice broods upon the shortcomings of her motherhood, deficiencies compelled by personal and economic circumstance and by the sheer exhaustion of making ends meet, and weighs its effect on her daughter's character. The result is a searing dramatization of life—and love—stunted by class, and labor, and lack of leisure, of fate more earthbound than providential, but nonetheless determining. By the time we reach the end of this quietly shattering tale—only twelve pages since we began—we are staring at a sorrow so deep, we feel dizzy.

The title story, five times as long as "I Stand Here Ironing," depicts the bickerings of a married couple when the kids are gone and mortality comes to call. The wife and husband have nearly lost their lives in inarticulacy because they've lacked the solitude expression requires. In unpacking what this means to them, Olsen unflinchingly evokes profound emotions in a way that leaves the reader disturbed and humbled by something like the catharsis a tragic drama can deliver. The two stories in the middle of the volume—"Hey, Sailor, What Ship?" and "O Yes"—are marked by a similar empathy and originality. *Tell Me a Riddle* is an unforgettable book.

What: Short Stories. *When:* 1961. *Award:* The title tale won the O. Henry Award for Best Short Story of 1961. *Also By: Yonnondio: From the Thirties* (1974). *Silences* (1978). *Try: Enormous Changes at the Last Minute* by Grace Paley. *Portrait of My Mother, Who Posed Nude in Wartime* by Marjorie Sandor.

Long Day's Journey into Night
Eugene O'Neill (1888–1953)

A Broken Family—and a Masterpiece of American Drama

When Eugene O'Neill completed *Long Day's Journey into Night* in 1942, he was already the most acclaimed playwright in American history, with a string of hits and a Nobel Prize to boot. But O'Neill decided to lock *Long Day's Journey* in a vault, with instructions that it not be published until after his death. When it finally appeared in 1956, the reason for his reticence was clear: The play is an unflinching autobiographical drama, a searing exposé of parents and children who, for all their love for one another, have been devastated by addiction and loneliness.

The four-act play takes place on one day in a house in Connecticut, where the Tyrones—the successful actor James; his wife, Mary; and their sons, Jamie and Edmund—are spending the summer. All of them have substance abuse problems: The three men drink nonstop, while Mary has a history with morphine. Edmund (for which read "Eugene") is suffering from tuberculosis, and his parsimonious father won't pay for the medical treatment he needs—infuriating Mary, who slips back into narcotic use. The family's anguish comes as much from emotional brutality as from drugs and drink. Jamie has always been jealous of his younger brother, and their father has never had the career he thinks he deserved. And in its haunting final scene, in which the high-out-of-her-mind Mary proclaims she "was so happy for a time," O'Neill gives us an indelible image of the promise of our dreams running up against the shoals of reality.

Like his counterpart Edmund, O'Neill was the son of an actor, spent summers in Connecticut, suffered from tuberculosis, and had a marked fondness for drink. But *Long Day's Journey* is no mere autobiographical drama; despite its extreme emotional colors, it is experienced—through O'Neill's dramatic genius—as a portrait of every American family, of our guilt and shame as well as our capacity for love and forgiveness. The greatest American play ever? Perhaps. But this much is for sure: *Long Day's Journey into Night* is the play that established once and for all that American drama deserved a celebrated role on the stage of world literature.

What: Drama. *When:* Written 1941–42; published 1956. *Award:* Pulitzer Prize for Drama, 1957. *Also By: The Emperor Jones* (1920). *Anna Christie* (1922). *Mourning Becomes Electra* (1931). *Ah, Wilderness!* (1933). *The Iceman Cometh* (1939). *A Moon for the Misbegotten* (written 1941–43; first performed 1957) is O'Neill's sequel to *Long Day's Journey. Further Reading: O'Neill: Life with Monte Cristo* by Arthur and Barbara Gelb. *Eugene O'Neill: Beyond Mourning and Tragedy* by Stephen A. Black. *Try: Death of a Salesman* by Arthur Miller (see page 549). *A Delicate Balance* by Edward Albee. *Adaptation:* Sidney Lumet's 1962 film features Katharine Hepburn, Ralph Richardson, Jason Robards, and Dean Stockwell.

Eugene O'Neill on Cape Cod with his family, 1922

■ For R. B. Onian's *The Origins of European Thought About the Body, the Mind, the Soul, the World, Time, and Fate*, see page 628.

War in Val d'Orcia
Iris Origo (1902–1988)

Daily Life in Time of War: Tuscany, 1943–1944

June 12, 1944: Awakened by her husband at five AM with news that German soldiers are in the vicinity, Iris Origo spends an anxious morning with the refugee children housed at her farm in southern Tuscany. "In the afternoon," she writes,

while I am with the children in the garden rehearsing the "Sleeping Beauty," I hear a lorry drive up, and some of these same German troops come tramping, fully armed, into the garden. They do not look attractive. I go up to them, not without some inner apprehension, and ask them what they want. But the answer is unexpected: "Please— wouldn't the children sing for us?" The children sing O Tannenbaum *and* Stille Nacht *(which they learned last Christmas)—and tears come into the men's eyes. . . . So they climb into their lorry and drive away.*

Such surprising and poignant incidents are recounted again and again in this remarkable diary, which documents, with immediacy and no little eloquence, life in a remote area of the Tuscan countryside during eighteen months of the Second World War, from January 1943 through July 1944.

Its author was the child of Lady Sybil Cuffe of Desart Court in Ireland and the American diplomat William Bayard Cutting. She grew up at the Villa Medici in Fiesole, and came to Val d'Orcia upon her marriage to an Italian marquis. At their manor, La Foce, the Origos created a world of learning (she authored several splendid scholarly biographies), labor, and compassion, improving the land and the life of its natives. But neither their privilege nor their location spared them from the fears, perils, and uncertainties of wartime life, as this personal record proves. The ordinary tasks of living get harder by the day as the conflict closes in, while Iris's concern for the safety of the young refugees from Genoa and Turin who are in her charge grows greater. Rumors of the war's progress fill the air; cataclysmic events are occurring nearby, but no one is sure what they are or what they mean. Occupying German forces and advancing Allied soldiers pursue each other as Italian partisans and escaped POWs of every stripe roam the countryside. With shells exploding about them, the couple leads a beleaguered band— including sixty children—eight miles on foot to Montepulciano in the hope of escaping the violence of the retreating Wehrmacht.

One of the most remarkable records of the experience of noncombatants during World War II, *War in Val d'Orcia* is a testament to the nobility of "the shared, simple acts of everyday life," even—especially—in the face of destruction and death.

What: Diaries & Letters. War. **When:** 1947. **Also By:** *Leopardi: A Study in Solitude* (1935; revised 1953). *The Last Attachment: The Story of Byron and Teresa Guiccioli* (1949). *The Merchant of Prato* (1956). *The World of San Bernardino* (1962). *Images and Shadows: Part of a Life* (1970). **Further Reading:** *Iris Origo: Marchesa of Val d'Orcia* by Caroline Moorehead. **Try:** *Love and War in the Apennines* by Eric Newby.

GEORGE ORWELL
(1903–1950)

I n an irony that would be ruefully relished by the author himself, "Orwellian" has come to signify the opposite of the values George Orwell espoused. Informed by his anti-Stalinist allegory, *Animal Farm*, and his powerful imagining of a totalitarian future in *1984*, the adjective has come to stand for oppressive surveillance, the corruption of language for political purposes, and the ruthless redefinition of civic norms and historical facts in service of authoritarian ends. Orwell's enduring influence as a figure of conscience, of course, rests on his eloquent resistance to all the dangers "Orwellian" now calls to mind. Importantly, his own stances were neither rigid nor unequivocal, for he understood that the power of conscience was based not on conclusions but rather on constant questioning; he knew a moral compass is not a set of step-by-step directions, but a tool to judge direction relative to present context and, yes, permanent coordinates. As a result, he is that rare writer whose working journalism remains as edifying as his most celebrated masterpieces.

George Orwell, 1941

1984
Big Brother Is Still Watching Us

" I t was a bright cold day in April, and the clocks were striking thirteen."

From the outset, the time is out of joint in George Orwell's *1984*, but still easily—if ominously—within reach of our imaginations. The proximity of the future that Orwell's dystopian masterpiece depicts has always been a part of this novel's eerie power. Even now, six decades after it was written and more than a quarter century after its titular year has come and gone, *1984* continues to haunt us with its

aura of pernicious possibility. Orwell's warning of a spiritless, totalitarian time to come has lost none of its relevance.

There is no denying that there is a somewhat frightening family resemblance between the world he envisaged, in which independent thought is forbidden and privacy itself taboo, and our own world of media saturation and online omnivoraciousness. (Just wondering what the author's powerful imagination would make of the ubiquity of the internet and the rampant neo-realities of the social network is enough to give a thoughtful reader the creeps.) Although the real 1984 turned out to be not quite as threatening as the one Orwell posited, the specific oppressions he portrays are memorable because they are so nearly recognizable. Who can read about the phenomena Orwell invokes in his description of Oceania (a state that seems descended from England and America, engaged in "continuous war" with uncertain but unrelenting purpose) without admitting the existence of real-life parallels today: "doublethink," "Newspeak," "Thought Police"? From the posters with moving eyes captioned "Big Brother Is Watching You" to the telescreens that monitor every room and spew propaganda with perverse glee, we recognize a potential "later" that remains within reach of our actual "now." It would be hard to name another twentieth-century novel whose coinages have so successfully infiltrated our language and, therefore, our grasp of the reality we inhabit.

If you haven't read the book in a while, or if you've never read it but think you know what it's about, you may be surprised at the extent to which it is unwaveringly focused on a single individual. Winston Smith is a minor Party functionary in the totalitarian realm in which the Party's three paradoxical verities shout down all others:

WAR IS PEACE

FREEDOM IS SLAVERY

IGNORANCE IS STRENGTH.

Winston works in the duplicitously named Ministry of Truth, where he helps systematically rewrite the past so that it conforms to the current needs of those in power. ("'Who controls the past,' ran the Party slogan, 'controls the future: who controls the present controls the past.'") The trouble is that Winston retains traces of the ability to think for himself, which makes him, in Oceania's homogenized political climate, a "thought-criminal." Fearfully but doggedly embracing this doomed status, Orwell's protagonist engages in activities that lead to his arrest, torture, and "reintegration." His unlawful impulses include such simple activities as buying a journal and recording his thoughts, and as natural an inclination as forming a romantic attachment in the grimmest of circumstances, adding to the poignance of the loss of human freedom that Orwell describes with hopeless precision.

Orwell presents Oceania in sufficient detail to make it a convincing place; even for a reader experiencing it vicariously, it's hard to get the taste of the vile food or the oily Victory Gin out of one's mouth. Yet the most dreadful qualities of Oceanic rule are revealed in Orwell's illustration of how the totalitarian regime gets and keeps control of individual minds. A significant part of the novel is devoted to the unnerving physical and psychological degradation to which Winston is subjected in the Party's attempt to extinguish his flickering inner life. What is finally most chilling about *1984* is not its prescience about the dangers of totalitarianism, but rather its insight into the fragile qualities of mind, heart, and culture that we treasure as the surest manifestations of human nature. Tellingly, when Orwell finished the work in manuscript, he hesitated between the title he finally gave it and *The Last Man in Europe*.

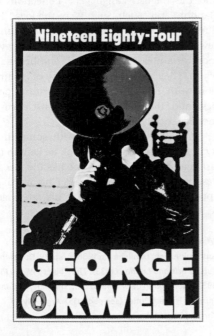

What: Novel. *When:* 1949. *Edition:* The Plume Centennial Edition of *1984* includes a foreword by Thomas Pynchon. *Also By: Burmese Days* (1934).

Keep the Aspidistra Flying (1936). Animal Farm (1945). Further Reading: Why Orwell Matters by Christopher Hitchens. Try: We by Yevgeny Zamyatin. Brave New World by Aldous Huxley (see page 398). Fahrenheit 451 by Ray Bradbury (see page 91). Adaptations: In addition to film and television versions of 1984, there is a 2005 opera based on the book, with music by Lorin Maazel and libretto by J. D. McClatchy and Thomas Meehan.

THE COLLECTED ESSAYS, JOURNALISM, AND LETTERS

AN AGE LIKE THIS, 1920–1940 • MY COUNTRY RIGHT OR LEFT, 1940–1943 • AS I PLEASE, 1943–1945 • IN FRONT OF YOUR NOSE, 1945–1950

Annals of a Working Writer

"From a very early age, perhaps the age of five or six, I knew that when I grew up I should be a writer." That's the opening of George Orwell's famous essay "Why I Write," and it is also the first sentence to appear in this four-volume set. Written in 1946, "Why I Write" is a perfect preface to this otherwise chronological presentation of collected essays, journalism, and letters, prepared after the author's

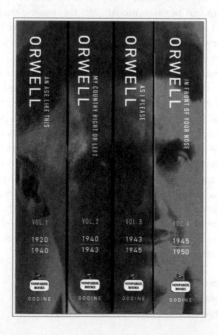

death by his wife, Sonia Orwell, and Ian Angus. In her introduction, Sonia Orwell writes that in these pages, which mix political and literary matters, "what we really hear is the sound of a personal voice, an individual talking at random of the things that concern him on many different levels." He argued out his ideas as he went along, she continues, as if he were "examining his thoughts in conversation."

The result for readers, as we move from letter to review to essay to weekly newspaper column, is one of the most fascinating engagements with a working writer we're likely to discover. Among the correspondence with publishers and commissioning editors (replete with bracing alertness to the need to pay the bills) there are marvelous musings on coffee and cigarettes, the vagaries of book reviewing, and how to make a proper cup of tea. There are also expositions of political realities, advocacy of (largely left-wing) causes, and reflections on crises from the Spanish Civil War to the Battle of Britain. On literary themes, we find analyses ephemeral and enduring on subjects as diverse as Dickens, Kipling, Henry Miller, and P. G. Wodehouse. Last, but by no means least, these volumes contain some of the finest essays in English literature, including "Shooting an Elephant," "My Country Right or Left," "Politics and the English Language," "Reflections on Gandhi," and "Such, Such Were the Joys." The different forms of prose make these volumes rewarding to read straight through and even more of a pleasure to pick up and browse at whim. They are a lifetime's library of rumination, with much to say about writing, politics, and the quandaries of conscience in modern society.

"At 50," Orwell wrote with some finality in the manuscript notebook he kept in the last year of his life, "everyone has the face he deserves." These are the last of his words to appear in this noble legacy to his career as a writer; he died at forty-six.

What: Essays. Journalism. Diaries & Letters. *When:* Four-volume set published in 1968. *Also By: Down and Out in Paris and London* (1933). *The Road to Wigan Pier* (1937). *Homage to Catalonia* (1938). *Try: Independent Spirit* by Hubert Butler (see page 115). *Arguably* by Christopher Hitchens.

16th-century engraving of Pyramus and Thisbe

Metamorphoses
Ovid (43 BC–AD 17)

An Epic Treasury of Tales of Wonder

Echo and Narcissus, Pentheus and Bacchus, Pyramus and Thisbe, Perseus, Tiresias, Jason and Medea, Pygmalion, Adonis, Midas, to say nothing of the familiar gods and goddesses—no book has a grander cast than this fabulous poem, which marks humankind's long graduation from myth to history. Ovid is the most magical of the Latin poets; his *Metamorphoses* is a pagan holy book in which Jove and his fellow divinities consort with natural elements to inspire, confuse, and intoxicate human beings with the ever-changing forms of spirit.

The rapid, loosely linked narratives collect a catalog of wonders. There's Arachne, the gifted weaver changed into a spider by a jealous Minerva; Baucis and Philemon, the loving married couple transformed upon their deaths into intertwining trees by a Jove grateful for their uncommon hospitality; and, at the beginning of the tenth of this epic's fifteen books, the story of Orpheus's ill-fated journey to the underworld to rescue his beloved Eurydice, as touching a tale as one will find in the Western mythological tradition—and a perfect passport into the precincts of Ovid's imagination.

A great many of the tales Ovid relates are enchanting, and many have served as inspiration for artists from Chaucer and Shakespeare to Benjamin Britten and Jean Cocteau. Others are disconcerting in their sexual assumptions; love conquers all in Ovid, even the gods, and its conquests are often violent. Still, to read the *Metamorphoses*, even at random, is to enter an enduring landscape fed by waters of tragedy and comedy that, for all the poet's fertile invention, seem drawn from the deepest, most unfathomable wells of human experience.

What: Mythology. Antiquity. *When:* Completed ca. AD 8. *Editions:* The Elizabethan translation of Arthur Golding, the first into English, was imaginatively plundered by Shakespeare; Ezra Pound called it "the most beautiful book in the language." Most modern readers will be better served by the translations of Rolfe Humphries (1955) and Allen Mandelbaum (1993). *Also By: Amores* (ca. 20 BC). *The Art of Love* (AD 1). *Fasti* (AD 8). *Tristia* (AD 9). *Further Reading:* David Malouf's absorbing novel of Ovid's exile, *An Imaginary Life*, makes rewarding reading. *After Ovid*, edited by Michael Hofmann and James Lasdun, is a fascinating recent anthology of work by more than forty poets invited to take the *Metamorphoses* as inspiration. *Try: Bulfinch's Mythology* by Thomas Bulfinch (see page 106). *The Marriage of Cadmus and Harmony* by Robert Calasso (see page 119).

P, Q, R

The Village of Waiting
George Packer (born 1960)

A Good Man in Africa

In 1982, George Packer, a fresh Peace Corps recruit, arrived in the tiny West African nation of Togo. "I was very young when I went, not just in years," he would write nearly twenty years later, in an afterword to the second edition of his book on his eighteen months in the peasant village of Lavié. What he discovered there was "not the newspaper Africa of lunatic presidents and gimcrack armies and relief camps peopled by ghosts, nor the picture-book Africa of voodoo and looped earlobes and lion hunts," but a reality so distant from anything he had known or imagined that its urgencies were disorienting. "The struggle to stay afloat took on endless variations in Togo," writes Packer. "And the white foreigner who'd come on an enlightened mission, and once there managed to keep his eyes open, quickly lost his bearings in the face of it."

Assigned to teach English in the local school, the author receives an education that dwarfs the one he delivers to his Togolese students. Engaging Lavié's inhabitants as he copes, or fails to, with his loneliness, anger, boredom, and fear, Packer portrays each encounter with a deft eye for the current moment but no illusion about the future that seems destined not to come. In local parlance, the village's name means "Wait a Little More," and the Africans Packer meets wait for rain, for the farming season to arrive, for toilets, dignitaries, power—all the elusive fruits of the economic development promised in the two decades since Togo's liberation from French colonial rule. Futility imbues everything from education to political resistance, whether the Togolese speak their native tongue, or French, or English: "*Etso*, the Ewé word for 'tomorrow,' also means 'yesterday'; schoolkids always mixed up *demain* and *hier*. To them, I suppose they meant the same thing—'not today.'"

The book is both a chronological narrative and a collection of exploratory topical essays: A chapter about a pair of family feuds in which Packer becomes entangled also reveals the chasm between his ideas about marriage and those of the men in Togo; a chapter on his visit to the hospital (where he receives a diagnosis of the onset of a nervous breakdown) also reflects on the nation's rampant illness, the intersection of Western medicine and traditional fetish priests, and burial rituals.

The author barely makes it through; in fact, he doesn't last out his two-year Peace Corps commitment, and disappointment haunts him. Yet the eloquence of his witness redeems Packer in the reader's eyes, if not his own. His embrace of the villagers' experience, despite his realization that his intentions are, in the end, both inadequate and irrelevant to their fate, is poignantly true to the inscrutable present in which they live.

What: Place. Memoir. *When:* 1988. *Also By:* Fiction: *The Half Man* (1991); *Central Square* (1998). Nonfiction: *Blood of the Liberals* (2000); *The Assassins' Gate: America in Iraq* (2005); *The Unwinding: An Inner History of the New America* (2013). *Further Reading:*

The Gnostic Gospels
Elaine Pagels (born 1943)

A Startling Scholarly Evocation of Early Christianity

The phenomenal popularity of *The Da Vinci Code* illustrated readers' fascination with the hidden history of Christianity—its alternative or dissident traditions, its suppressed or abandoned beliefs. And although the secrets revealed by the *Code* are fiction, the fact is that Christianity didn't become defined by a single, canonical set of tenets until centuries after Jesus died. Before that, there was a fascinating variety to Christian doctrine and a vigorous pluralism to the church.

The Gnostic Gospels, Professor Elaine Pagels's award-winning 1979 bestseller, is a landmark study of early Christianity's doctrinal and institutional diversity. The title refers to fifty-two manuscripts that were discovered in Egypt in 1945. These texts, known collectively as the Nag Hammadi Library, turned out to be the sacred writings of the Gnostics, an early Christian sect whose beliefs came in time to be judged as heretical by church authorities. Pagels shows that the writings of the Gnostics offer insights into the complexity of the fledgling Christian movement and its theological and political development. The Gnostics seem to have differed from other Christians on fundamental points, such as whether Jesus literally rose from the dead and whether God could be both male and female; the sect envisioned a role for women in the Christian church that was radically different from the one that eventually won official backing. By bringing Gnostic doctrines to light, and presenting her scholarly findings with clarity and literary grace, Pagels provides an eye-opening reassessment of the origins of Christianity and the evolution of the church.

What: Religion & Spirituality. *When:* 1979. *Awards:* National Book Critics Circle Award in Criticism, 1979. National Book Award in Religion, 1980. *Also By: Adam, Eve, and the Serpent* (1987). *The Origin of Satan* (1995). *Beyond Belief: The Secret Gospel of Thomas* (2003). *Reading Judas: The Gospel of Judas and the Shaping of Christianity* (with Karen L. King; 2007). *Further Reading: The Nag Hammadi Scriptures: The International Edition,* edited by Marvin Meyer. *Israel and the Dead Sea Scrolls* by Edmund Wilson (see page 862). *Try: The First Urban Christians* by Wayne A. Meeks.

The Cosmic Code
QUANTUM PHYSICS AS THE LANGUAGE OF NATURE
Heinz R. Pagels (1939–1988)

A Conversion Experience on a Road Paved with Quarks and Leptons

Asked to explain what motivated his dedication to his art, the cellist Yo-Yo Ma once responded that it was, more than anything else, the desire to get others to hear music he loved—to grab an audience's attention and say, in essence, "You've got to hear this." In writing *The Cosmic Code*, physicist Heinz Pagels was inspired by a similar need to share his wonder at the beauties and curiosities of his own field. The generous impulse of his invitation to explore "a new picture of reality requiring a conversion of our imaginations" still distinguishes his introduction to the strange world of quantum physics from the many other books on the subject that have been published since.

Quantum theory explores "the invisible organization of energy" that, according to the explanations of modern physicists, informs the universe. Although it can be perceived intellectually, quantum reality cannot be seen, felt, and observed in the same way the world of classical physics could. It is a realm of subatomic particles whose odd names—"quarks" and "leptons," "muons" and "hadrons"—suggest its strangeness. Eschewing mathematics and leavening his learning with personal reflections, anecdotes, and thoughtful reference to his own broad culture, Pagels traces the historical development of quantum theory from Einstein's relativity through Heisenberg's uncertainty and beyond (stopping, of course, to pet Schrödinger's cat), then leads us deep into the "rational but not visualizable" intricacies of matter that quantum theory seeks to explain. The new picture of the material world he shares with us is both lucid and mind-bending,

revealing an order in the behavior of the smallest particles that may indeed outline the architecture of the universe and provide a "unified field" for our conception of its progress from its first moments to its imagined end.

"If there are those who claim a conversion experience through reading scripture," Pagels writes, "I would point out that the book of nature also has its converts. They may be less evangelical than religious converts, but they share a deep conviction that the order of the universe exists and can be known."

What: Science. Nature. *When:* 1982. *Reading Note:* Modern physics is a fast-paced discipline; although some of the particularities of Pagels's book may have been superseded by new findings, his inviting overview retains its value and considerable charm, especially for the nonscientist. *Also By: Perfect Symmetry: The Search for the Beginning of Time* (1985). *The Dreams of Reason: The Computer and the Rise of the Sciences of Complexity* (1988). *Try: QED* by Richard Feynman (see page 272). *The Dancing Wu Li Masters* by Gary Zukav. *Seven Brief Lessons on Physics* by Carlo Rovelli. *Footnote: Before It Vanishes: A Packet for Professor Pagels* by Robert Pack is an intriguing cycle of poems inspired by Pagels's scientific writings.

MEMOIRS OF A PROVENÇAL CHILDHOOD
MY FATHER'S GLORY • MY MOTHER'S CASTLE
Marcel Pagnol (1895–1974)

A Magical Upbringing

The memory of childhood is a landscape, marked with human monuments—parents, relatives, first friends—and with enchanted objects and locales—houses, furniture, books, toys, fields, forests, backyards—that are each imbued with the colors of our earliest, most intimate, most innocent intelligence. You're unlikely to find any books that convey the imaginative terrain of early years as vividly

as these two lightly fictionalized memoirs of youth in Marseilles and, especially, summers in a Provençal village, written by the great French filmmaker Marcel Pagnol. Another Frenchman, Marcel Proust, may probe a child's mind more deeply, but even in its overture, *In Search of Lost Time* (see page 644) requires readers to venture forth upon an ocean, while Pagnol's recollections offer an easy day at the beach. Touching, generous, and gently comic in their portrayal of boyhood mischief, playful adventures, familial affections, and parental stresses and tenderness, *My Father's Glory* and *My Mother's Castle* are warm reminiscences in which Pagnol invites us to possess again the senses of welcome and of wonder that are childhood's happiest promises. Although the books follow, more or less, a single chronological narrative, the dramatic focus shifts from one parent to the other just as the titles suggest. You'll be sorry to surrender both—and the author's good company—as you turn the last page. Fortunately, the story continues in *The Time of Secrets* (1960) and *The Time of Love* (1977).

Marcel Pagnol in ceremonial dress, 1946

What: Memoir. **When:** *My Father's Glory* (1957) and *My Mother's Castle* (1958). **Edition:** The North Point Press edition includes both books in a translation by Rita Barisse. **Also By:** *Jean de Florette* (1962). *Manon of the Springs* (1963). **Try:** *Village in the Vaucluse* by Laurence Wylie. *Two Towns in Provence* by M. F. K. Fisher. *A Year in Provence* by Peter Mayle (see page 533). **Adaptations:** *My Father's Glory* and *My Mother's Castle* were lovingly, and individually, adapted for the screen by Yves Robert in 1990. **Footnote:** Don't miss any opportunity to view Pagnol's cinematic masterpieces, which include *Marius* (1931), *Fanny* (1933), *Harvest* (1937), and *The Baker's Wife* (1938).

The Portable Dorothy Parker
Dorothy Parker (1893–1967)

The Slings and Arrows of Outrageous Wit

If you're hedging your bets against a protracted airport delay, you might want to tuck a copy of *The Portable Dorothy Parker* into your knapsack. Few books have a higher entertainment-per-page ratio. Mrs. Parker, as she liked to be called, became one of the most quoted writers of her time because of her singular gift for sharpening truths into well-honed words; her barbed ability was unparalleled in her day and hasn't been equaled since.

Parker began her career writing captions for *Vogue* magazine (where she came up with such treasures as "brevity is the soul of lingerie") and went on to help establish the voice and tenor of *The New Yorker* before heading to Hollywood to write screenplays. She was a charter member of the legendary Algonquin Round Table, marched for Sacco and Vanzetti,

Dorothy Parker, ca. 1935

reported on the Spanish Civil War, helped found the Screen Writers Guild, and went through plenty of cigarettes and liquor while composing plays and several collections of poetry and stories (published with such memorable titles as *Enough Rope*, *Laments for the Living*, and *Death and Taxes*). In all her work, her eye is as keen as her words are clever; when her sense of humor seems savage, it's usually because her observation is so acute. As she put it in a *Paris Review* interview, "Wit has truth in it; wisecracking is simply calisthenics with words."

In 1944, she selected and arranged this collection of her stories and poems for presentation in a single volume. It has since been expanded to include some of her later stories, as well as theater reviews and essays, and the complete archive of her terrific Constant Reader book column from *The New Yorker*. Spanning her career and containing the bulk of her work, this is truly a treasure trove.

What: Humor. Poetry. Short Stories. *When:* 1973. *Further Reading: Dorothy Parker: What Fresh Hell Is This?,* a biography by Marion Meade. *Try: A Girl Like I* by Anita Loos. *Adaptations:* The O. Henry Prize–winning story "Big Blonde" was adapted for television in 1980. See also Alan Rudolph's 1994 film, *Mrs. Parker and the Vicious Circle.*

France and England in North America
Francis Parkman (1823–1893)

Empires in the Wilderness

Conceived in 1841, when its author was a sophomore at Harvard College, this monumental work would occupy Francis Parkman for the five decades that followed. Its first installment was published in 1865, its last in 1892, a year before his death. Together the seven volumes of *France and England in North America* constitute what Parkman called "the history of the American forest"—a magnificent panorama of exploration, settlement, politics, and religion in which the wilderness itself is a forceful presence, something like the orchestra in a late Verdi opera—a brooding environment that shapes and subsumes the thrilling voices of the individual characters, a captivating cast of explorers, warriors, martyrs, and diplomats.

La Salle and his New World claims

Beginning in the sixteenth century with the landing of a Huguenot party in Florida, Parkman's nearly three-thousand-page chronicle follows the fortunes of France in the New World for more than two hundred years, concluding with the defeat by the English of Louis XVI's continental ambitions on Quebec's Plains of Abraham in 1759 (the treaty of surrender was signed four years later). The author's historical sensibility commandingly encompasses the epic story of empires competing in unexplored terrain, and his literary prowess allows him to paint a vast canvas that captures the reader's imagination. In our encounter with Parkman's new world, it is as if nations and religions (and even history itself) have been transported to another planet, both primeval and futuristic, to unfold their destinies. The narrative of religious, commercial, and military forces in conflict is enlivened by tales of remarkable personages such as Samuel de Champlain, the mapper of the Saint Lawrence and the Great Lakes, and Isaac Jogues and his fellow Jesuit missionaries, later canonized as the North American Martyrs, who suffered extraordinary pains at the hands of the Native Americans whose own martyrdom Parkman was not so quick to honor. An entire volume is devoted to the exploits of René-Robert Cavelier, sieur de La Salle, who discovered the Mississippi River and claimed its vast basin—the Louisiana Territory—for France, and another to the struggle between Louis-Joseph de Montcalm and James Wolfe, the commanding French and English generals whose fatal confrontation determined the French and Indian Wars. (Parkman even introduces us to George Washington, assuming the historical stage for the first time—as a young commander of Virginia forces—in the decades preceding the Revolution that would ennoble him.)

Parkman's facts and judgments have been questioned by later scholars, who have taken particular umbrage at his stark painting of the colonization of North America as a battle between savagery and civilization. His epic's authority in the reading of history may be called into question, but its place in the history of reading—as one of the most transporting explorations of our past ever penned—remains unchallenged.

What: History. *When:* The work comprises seven books originally published separately: *Pioneers of France in the* New World (1865); *The Jesuits in North America in the Seventeenth Century* (1867); *La Salle and the Discovery of the Great West* (1869); *The Old Régime in Canada* (1874); *Count Frontenac and New France Under Louis XIV* (1877); *Montcalm and Wolfe* (1884); *A Half-Century of Conflict* (1892). *Edition:* The Library of America has issued a handsome two-volume set containing all seven books. *Also By: The Oregon Trail* (1847). *The Conspiracy of Pontiac* (1851). *Further Reading: Crucible of War* by Fred Anderson. *The Name of War* by Jill Lepore. *Try: History of the Conquest of Mexico* by William H. Prescott (see page 641). *Dead Certainties: Unwarranted Speculations* by Simon Schama.

···

Pensées
Blaise Pascal (1623–1662)

The Last Testament of a Mathematician and Philosopher

A child prodigy with a genius for mathematics and science, Blaise Pascal invented one of the earliest mechanical calculators. He also made influential contributions to projective geometry, probability theory, and the study of hydraulics and vacuums (he is credited with the invention of both the hydraulic press and the syringe). After a life-changing mystical religious experience in his early thirties, he devoted himself to theology and philosophy and produced two of the major works of seventeenth-century French literary prose. One is the *Provincial Letters* (1656–57), and the other is the *Pensées*, or *Thoughts*, a collection of notes for a project that was left unfinished at his death. The project was an apology for Christianity—an explanation and defense of the faith. Although the hundreds of brief texts that make up the *Pensées* are powerful as religious writings, they are also invaluable for their profound insight into the human condition—a condition, according to Pascal, defined by "inconstancy, boredom, unrest."

The idea that man suffers from existential restlessness inspired one of the most famous observations in the *Pensées*: "I have discovered that all the trouble in the world stems from one fact, man's inability to sit still in a room." His apology for Christianity is an apology for

Blaise Pascal

consciousness as well: "Man is but a reed," he writes in an often quoted passage, "the weakest thing in nature; but a thinking reed. . . . A vapor, a drop of water, is enough to kill him. But, though the universe might crush him, man would still be nobler than his destroyer, because he knows that he is dying, knows that the universe has got the better of him; the universe knows nothing of this." And yet, notwithstanding his avowal that "All our dignity consists in thought," he recognizes the limits of logic in controlling human nature: "The heart has its reasons, which reason does not know."

Despite his religious turning, the author never entirely abandons his mathematical bent. One of the most telling passages in the book describes "Pascal's Wager," which posits that, although we cannot prove God's existence, we should place a bet on the deity, since the upside is so much grander than the downside; here Christian apologetics advances the theory of probability, or vice versa. Throughout the *Pensées*, a twenty-first-century reader is likely to be struck by just how *modern* Pascal's thinking seems, but on reflection, perhaps "timeless" is a better word. After all, the philosopher's ruminations are nourished by the same anxiety the earliest humans might have experienced upon gazing into the night sky: "The eternal silence of these infinite spaces frightens me."

What: Philosophy. Religion & Spirituality. **When:** Incomplete at the author's death in 1662. **Edition:** The Penguin Classics translation by A. J. Krailsheimer is excellent, and recommended for the general reader. **Reading Note:** Best savored thought by thought: There is much to think about in each brief entry. **Further Reading:** *Pascal's Wager: The Man Who Played Dice with God* by James A. Connor. **Try:** *Confessions* by Saint Augustine (see page 29). *The Concept of Anxiety* by Søren Kierkegaard.

Doctor Zhivago
Boris Pasternak (1890–1960)

Art, Love, and Revolution

Even though its artistic achievement was hailed upon its original publication in Italy in 1957, and its author was awarded the Nobel Prize in Literature in the subsequent year, the true grandeur of *Doctor Zhivago* remains hidden for many by two factors: the shadow of Cold War politics surrounding its publication and the glamorous glow that still emanates from David Lean's 1965 film. But you should make no mistake about the rare reading experience Pasternak's novel offers: To get lost in its pages is to go beyond politics and glamour and encounter life itself in all its chaos and commotion, love and sorrow.

Not that a book about the turmoil of revolutionary Russia can escape history. Nor can a love story as passionate as that of Zhivago and Lara eschew romance. Yet both of these strands of the novel are swept up in the larger forces of fate that Pasternak marshals. In

Boris Pasternak, 1958

outline, *Doctor Zhivago* takes us from its hero's childhood before the Revolution into a manhood troubled by the far-reaching consequences of that event, from the terror of Bolshevik Moscow to the Ural Mountains, where Zhivago leads his family in a futile attempt to escape the suffering and strife of the historical tragedy. The plot adheres to no shapely design, but rather progresses through a welter of comings and goings, coincidences, chance encounters, and abrupt partings. It contains the sudden reversals of fortune of a fairy tale and the cataclysmic violence of an epic. Through it all, Zhivago's loves—for literature and the poetry he composes, for nature and the landscapes it orders, for Lara and the beauty she embodies—sustain him in the face of terror and cruelty. On every page, *Doctor Zhivago* embraces the heedless rush of existence with an abandon at odds with the carefully calibrated artifice and ironic detachment of most modern fiction.

"Zhivago" in Russian echoes the adjective meaning "living," and the doctor who bears that name, like the book that bears his, embraces "life, the thing itself"—in John Bayley's words—"and not the abstract vision of how it ought to be for which the tyrants of ideology drench the world in blood." Stirring and satisfying, it is as Edmund Wilson described it: "a great act of faith in art and in the human spirit."

What: Novel. *When:* Smuggled out of Russia, where Pasternak had spent decades writing it, *Doctor Zhivago* was first published in Italy in 1957. An English translation appeared the subsequent year. It was finally published in the author's homeland in 1988. *Award:* Nobel Prize in Literature, 1958. *Reading Note:* Two dozen "Poems of Yuri Zhivago" form an epilogue to the novel, and are well worth attention. *Also By:* Poetry: *My Sister—Life* (1917). Memoir: *Safe Conduct* (1931). *Further Reading: Letters: Summer 1926* collects a selection of correspondence between Pasternak and fellow poets Marina Tsvetayeva and Rainer Maria Rilke. *Try: Eugene Onegin* by Alexander Pushkin (see page 648). *Anna Karenina* by Leo Tolstoy (see page 799). *Possession* by A. S. Byatt (see page 118). *Adaptations:* David Lean's classic 1965 film stars Omar Sharif and Julie Christie. A Masterpiece Theatre miniseries aired in 2002.

Cry, the Beloved Country
Alan Paton (1903–1988)

Fiction with Its Hand on History

A novelist, educator, and political activist, Alan Paton was one of the first South African writers to gain an international reputation, mostly on the strength of this novel about the fate of two families, one black and one white, in the pre-apartheid era. Stephen Kumalo, a black Anglican pastor in a small village in the hills of what's now called KwaZulu-Natal, is summoned by a friend to the boomtown of Johannesburg, where he discovers that his sister has fallen into prostitution and his son has been arrested for murder. The victim turns out to be the son of James Jarvis, a white landowner who lives not far from Kumalo in the country. Paton intertwines the families' fates to expose the violence and the injustice of South African segregation. The narration frequently addresses the terror of the times, and its fearful effects, with almost biblical invocations:

Cry, the beloved country, for the unborn child that is the inheritor of our fear. Let him not love the earth too deeply.... Let him not be too moved when the birds of his land are singing, nor give too much of his heart to a mountain or a valley. For fear will rob him of all if he gives too much.

Paton's novel, his first and his most successful, was published just a few months before South Africa's government instituted apartheid, legitimizing racial segregation in all national institutions. A few years later, Paton was instrumental in founding a political party in opposition to the horrific policy, but the party was soon shut down by the government on the grounds that it—illegally—had both black and white members. Although Paton continued to fight for social justice, *Cry, the Beloved Country*, with its trenchant exposure of South Africa's mistrustful history, would prove to have more enduring influence than his political activity, reaching a worldwide audience of millions of readers and dramatizing the injustice and brutality that would ultimately become an international outrage.

What: Novel. *When:* 1948. *Also By: Too Late the Phalarope* (1953). *Tales from a Troubled Land* (1961). *Ah, but Your Land Is Beautiful* (1981). *Try: The Conservationist* by Nadine Gordimer. *A Dry White Season* by André Brink. *Adaptations: Cry, the Beloved Country* has been filmed twice, in 1951 and 1995. Notably, a year after its publication, the novel was adapted for the stage as *Lost in the Stars*, with music by Kurt Weill and book by Maxwell Anderson.

■ For James Patterson's *Kiss the Girls*, see page 238.

Medieval in LA: A Fiction
Jim Paul (born 1950)

An Exuberant Time Traveler

Jim Paul writes quirky, compelling narratives that exude a rare happiness—there's no other word for the feeling one gets from the colorful weave of learning, luck, insight, and invention that distinguishes his singular literary costume. His first book, *Catapult: Harry and I Build a Siege Weapon* (1991), is a funny, captivating tale of how the author and a friend are roped—by their own whimsy— into building a medieval siege weapon to fling rocks into the Pacific Ocean. His second, *What's Called Love: A Real Romance* (1993), is a comic account of the agonies, ecstasies, and other mood swings of new love; it illustrates the arduous path of ardor, even when it's traveling through the most romantic settings (in this case, France).

Paul's third book, *Medieval in LA*, however, is his true marvel. It begins with an in-flight spill of tomato juice on both white cotton pants and an open copy of a book about the rise of the modern mind in the West. From there it proceeds, via an offhand chronicle of a weekend sojourn among friends in Los Angeles, to chart a deft, delightful course through thickets of thinking on chance and fate, science and sensibility, faith and philosophy, randomness and the making of meaning. Despite the incessant lessons of modernity, Paul discovers, we still live in a medieval world, at least inside our heads.

We have all this information about the actual world, centuries of it since the scientific idea had taken hold, yet we still live mostly in the old realm, at the center of our own universe, finding our significance, manifesting our intentions.

In other words, outside the plane of our lives, "frigid, howling death" whooshes by, while inside the cabin we inhabit "the steady, adequately lighted reality we [have] constructed to enable our plans, a purely human place, not the actual world."

After he touches down in Los Angeles, Paul's hours unfold in brunches, shopping excursions, and other forms of genial socializing, while the flight of intellectual fancy inspired by the spilled tomato juice stops to pick up ideas and passengers—including William of Ockham and David Hume, John Cage and the Beverly Hillbillies—that illuminate his passage through time, space, and a day at the beach. Filled with dancing thoughts, provocative juxtapositions, and breathtaking leaps from everyday verities to eternal quandaries, *Medieval in LA* is light on its metaphorical feet, and a joy to ponder. It keeps you laughing, too.

What: Philosophy. Essays. *When:* 1996. *Also By: Elsewhere in the Land of Parrots: A Novel* (2003). *Further Reading: The Passion of the Western Mind* by Richard Tarnas. *Try: Mr. Wilson's Cabinet of Wonder* by Lawrence Weschler. *The Size of Thoughts* by Nicholson Baker.

THE GORMENGHAST TRILOGY
TITUS GROAN • GORMENGHAST • TITUS ALONE
Mervyn Peake (1911–1968)

The Other Side of Tolkien

Mervyn Peake lurks in the shadows of literature like a forgotten enchanter obscured by the main action of a fantasy sequence. In the royalty of the genre, one might even see him as J. R. R. Tolkien's dispossessed brother, ruling a realm wilder than the one the creator of *The Lord of the Rings* (see page 793) commanded. The difference is evident in their prose: Tolkien's writing is sturdy and occasionally poetic, but it pales next to Peake's idiosyncratic, virtuosic style. And where the former's heart lay with salt-of-the-earth types like Bilbo Baggins, the latter's allegiance was to eccentrics, artists, and rebels. Tolkien endorsed systems, hierarchies, and loyalties within both, while Peake railed against not only duties but against governance itself. But anyone of an expressive temperament or taste—admiring, say, the caricatural genius of Dickens and the inherent fatedness of Melville, or possessing a fondness for the Gothic or the baroque—will wander into Peake's imaginative realm with wonder, and likely return to it again and again.

A distant domain in the keeping of a noble family named Groan, Gormenghast is dominated by a vast and crumbling castle, a presence as unforgettable as any of the characters. Castle Gormenghast is an immemorial warren of chambers and turrets, basements and halls, kitchens and bedrooms, stables and courtyards, overlooked by the enormous Tower of Flints.

"This tower," Peake writes at the outset, "patched unevenly with black ivy, arose like a mutilated finger from among the fists of knuckled masonry and pointed blasphemously at heaven."

Into this stony, tapestried, haunted demesne—self-sufficient and self-perpetuating, xenophobically tradition bound, its days marked with pointless rituals—is born Titus Groan, a star-crossed heir to the ancestral line. But the infant is relegated to the background for a while as we are introduced to others: the villainous, sociopathic, uncontainable ambitious kitchen boy Steerpike; the loyal factotum Flay; Doctor Prunesquallor and his flighty sisters; Lady Fuchsia, Titus's big sister; and the boy's strangely self-absorbed parents, owl-mad Lord Sepulchrave and cat-besotted Countess Gertrude. By the time we reach the end of the volume that bears his name, Titus is barely a toddler, but we have become fully enmeshed in the alliances and rivalries of Gormenghast, and seen Steerpike evolve from an innocuous lackey into a power behind the throne, fueled with malice Shakespearean in its vivid characterization.

Book two, *Gormenghast*, follows Titus's maturation and inevitable conflict with Steerpike. There is change and challenge, death and destruction, fire and flood and madness—leading ultimately to Titus's revolt at the prospect of an eternity of "dead repetitions [and] moribund ceremonies." Choosing to leave the all-encompassing certitude of the ancient keep, he encounters, as the reader discovers in *Titus Alone*, a surprising outer world of advanced industry and sophisticated technology that is a daring disruption of the familiarities of the first two books.

A highly accomplished illustrator as well as writer, Peake provided stunning visual interpretations of his fictional visions. His sui generis trilogy, by turns silly and somber, heartening and dismaying, antique and modern, beams like some moonlit lighthouse summoning a certain breed of wanderers to its brilliant and peculiar beacon.

What: Fantasy. *When:* 1946–59. *Also By: Captain Slaughterboard Drops Anchor* (1939). *Mr. Pye* (1953). *Further Reading: Mervyn Peake* by John Watney. *Try: Gloriana* by Michael Moorcock. *Pile* by Brian W. Aldiss. *The High House* by James Stoddard. *Observatory Mansions* by Edward Carey. *Adaptation:* The excellent BBC miniseries from 2000, *Gormenghast*, adapts the first two books. *Footnote:* In 2011, Overlook Press published *Titus Awakes: The Lost Book of Gormenghast*, a fourth installment in the series worked up by Peake's widow, Maeve Gilmore, from her husband's sparse notes.

■ For Nancy Pearl's *Book Lust*, see page 209.

The Diary of Samuel Pepys
Samuel Pepys (1633–1703)

The Greatest Diary in the English Language

S amuel Pepys (pronounced "peeps") was an ambitious, hardworking civil servant who had a highly successful career as an official in the Royal Navy. He loved music, good food, women, and books (he possessed one of the most extensive libraries of his time). For almost a decade—from January 1660 to May 1669—he kept what is beyond question the greatest diary in the English language. Written in shorthand, and abandoned only because Pepys feared, mistakenly, that he was going blind, the *Diary* is a remarkably candid self-portrait, replete with revelations of habits such as his frequent book buying, his short-lived New Year's resolutions, and his constant pursuit of amorous dalliance, with consequent marital friction. It also offers a fascinating day-by-day picture of life in England's capital during an era that included the Restoration of King Charles II and the Great Plague of 1665, as in this entry from June 7 of that year:

This day, much against my will, I did in Drury Lane see two or three houses marked with a red cross upon the doors, and "Lord have mercy upon us" writ there; which was a sad sight to me, being the first of the kind that, to my remembrance, I ever saw. It put me into an ill conception of myself and my smell, so that I was forced to buy some roll-tobacco to smell to and chaw, which took away the apprehension.

What's best and most absorbing about the *Diary* is its vivid personal scale: For example, Pepys's unforgettable eyewitness account of the 1666 Great Fire of London—perhaps the most famous set piece in the entire chronicle—includes the detail that the diarist took time from his civic duties in the crisis to dig a pit to protect his papers, wine, and parmesan cheese from the rampaging flames.

The definitive edition of *The Diary of Samuel Pepys* runs to nine volumes, containing roughly three thousand pages (an *Index* and *Companion* occupy separate additional volumes). Readers who shy from committing themselves to Pepys in his million-and-a-quarter-word entirety will be well served by the excellent abridgment by Richard Le Gallienne, who justifiably asserts that his selection contains "all the extraordinary happenings, with sufficient of the ordinary happenings of Pepys' life . . . to justify [the reader] in feeling that he knows Samuel Pepys and the world he lived in." An additional attraction of this abridgment, which is available as a Modern Library edition, is the introduction by Robert Louis Stevenson. Claire Tomalin, Pepys's biographer, calls Stevenson's 1881 piece "the most perceptive essay ever written on the Diary." Another possibility is to read Pepys as he wrote—in daily installments. A website makes this approach easy and fun: pepysdiary.com posts annotated diary entries for every day of the year.

What: Diaries & Letters. *When:* Written 1660–69; first published in 1825. *Editions: The Complete Diary of Samuel Pepys, Vols. 1–11,* edited by Robert Latham and William Matthews (1971). The Le Gallienne abridgment is a superb single-volume version, available in the Modern Library Classics series. *Further Reading: Samuel Pepys: The Unequalled Self* by Claire Tomalin. *Try: The Journals of James Boswell: 1762–1795,* selected by John Wain. The diaries of James Lees-Milne 1942–1997 (in twelve volumes). *A Diary of the Century* by Edward Robb Ellis.

Life: A User's Manual
Georges Perec (1936–1982)

A Puzzle of Stories, Playful and Profound

Georges Perec was one of the leading members of Oulipo ("Ouvroir de littérature potentielle," or "Workshop of potential literature"), a group of avant-garde European writers who, starting in the early 1960s, used rules, games, and mathematical analogies to generate verse and prose. The constraints Perec applied to his own imagination could be daunting; for instance, he published in 1969 an entire novel without using the letter "E" (*La Disparition*, amazingly translated into English—still sans the letter "E" throughout—by Gilbert Adair, as *A Void*), and another novella where "E" is the only vowel that appears. Both, it must be said, are eminently readable, as is Perec's magnum opus, *Life: A User's Manual.*

The whole of Perec's novel is set in a single apartment building in Paris's seventeenth arrondissement, with ten floors and ten rooms on each floor (a helpful diagram is included). Perec's passion for chess influenced the intricate structure of the novel. He imagined the apartment block as an oversized ten-by-ten chessboard, on which he charts a chess puzzle known as the "Knight's Tour": Each chapter is two squares over and one square to the side from the previous one—mimicking

the moves of a knight on a chessboard—and no square is ever used twice. That is not the only formal principle at work here: Each chapter also has elements determined by an algorithm Perec devised to determine everything from the number of characters to the style of the writing and the colors of the walls. It's said that Perec spent three years formulating the protocols that govern *Life: A User's Manual.* But what's amazing is that, in the final novel, those controls are nearly invisible: All the formal games cohere into a single, seamless product, generated through sophisticated rules but never diminished by them.

Over the course of ninety-nine short chapters we visit every room—actually every room but one: It's a typical Perec joke to construct a meticulous system and then leave it slightly broken—and meet the oddball inhabitants of the building, ranging from a painter who erases his paintings to a radical Polish émigré to an archaeologist, a home-improvement tycoon, and an artisan of jigsaw puzzles. You can think of *Life: A User's Manual* as a modern version of *The Arabian Nights*, compressing countless tales into a single volume. At the same time, it's an ingenious homage to the realist novels of nineteenth-century France, using 11 Rue Simon-Crubellier as a microcosm for Parisian society. It does for the worldview of the realist novel what Dante's *Divine Comedy* does for the doctrine of Christian theology, and through a similar means: by embedding a wealth of detail into a formal discipline that achieves its own exuberant and timeless artistry.

Although its compositional gymnastics might make you think that reading *Life: A User's Manual* will be a pleasureless exertion, Perec's singular accomplishment is to have created a huge and complex experimental novel that's also a page-turner. Bursting with engaging characters and absorbing stories, this modern masterpiece allows us to see the infinite in the everyday, and the everyday in the infinite, too.

What: Novel. *When:* 1978. English translation by David Bellos, 1987; revised 2008. *Also By: Things: A Story of the Sixties* (1965). *A Man Asleep* (1967). *A Void* (1969). *W, or the Memory of Childhood* (1975). *Thoughts of Sorts* (1985). *Further Reading: Georges Perec: A Life in Words* by David Bellos. *Try: Exercises in Style* by Raymond Queneau. *Hopscotch* by Julio Cortázar. *The Castle of Crossed Destinies* by Italo Calvino.

Most of the Most of S. J. Perelman
S. J. Perelman (1904–1979)

A Humorist in a Class by Himself

Slangily sesquipedalian, as he might have put it himself, Sidney Joseph Perelman wrote like nobody else. In his work the anarchic clowning of the Marx Brothers (for whom Perelman cowrote two screenplays) was filtered through a literary sensibility that appears to have been shaped by such disparate influences as Fowler's *A Dictionary of Modern English Usage* (see page 293) and the stories in *Spicy Detective* magazine. Sentence by sentence, no other American writer has been as ingenious in turning the natural resources of our native tongue into burnished comic gold. Perelman himself inclined to a more jaundiced view of his accomplishments: "What Flaubert did to the French bourgeois in *Bouvard and Pecuchet*, what Pizarro did to the Incas, what Jack Dempsey did to Paolino Uzcudun, S. J. Perelman has done to American belles-lettres."

In addition to his stints in Hollywood (in 1956, he shared an Oscar for the screenplay for *Around the World in Eighty Days*), Perelman was a regular *New Yorker* contributor from the 1930s on. His short essays for it and other magazines displayed his brilliant skills as a parodist, incorporating hilariously self-deprecatory accounts of his misadventures as a world traveler (see the 1948 volume *Westward, Ha!*) and would-be country squire (see *Acres and Pains*, 1947).

Most of the Most of S. J. Perelman is where a reader will find many of Perelman's best comic sketches. The typically arresting titles— "Is There an Osteosynchrondroitrician in the House?" "Methinks He Doth Protein Too Much," "De Gustibus Ain't What Dey Used to Be"—demonstrate the author's unique mix of street-corner patter, recherché vocabulary, and deliriously punning wordplay.

S. J. Perelman, ca. 1961

What: Humor. *When:* 2000 (collecting works from 1930 on). *Edition:* An earlier anthology, *The Most of S. J. Perelman* (1958), featured somewhat different contents. *Reading Note:* Perelman is best savored in small doses; his style is too rich to be enjoyed in massive portions. *Also By: The Swiss Family Perelman* (1950). *The Ill-Tempered Clavichord* (1952). *The Road to Miltown, or, Under the Spreading Atrophy* (1957). *The Rising Gorge* (1961). *Baby, It's Cold Inside* (1970). *Don't Tread on Me: The Selected Letters of S. J. Perelman* (1987). *Try: The Benchley Roundup* by Robert Benchley.

Giving Up the Gun
Noel Perrin (1927–2004)

The Surprising History of Japan's Reversion to the Sword

I n 1543, a Chinese cargo ship arrived in Japan. On board were three Portuguese adventurers. Two of them bore primitive firearms. As Noel Perrin tells it, at the moment when the feudal master Lord Tokitaka saw one of the Portuguese take aim and shoot a duck, "the gun enters Japanese history." Within a month Tokitaka had acquired both weapons and ordered his chief swordsmith to learn how to make more. Soon the Japanese had mastered their manufacture and were using them with abandon; by the end of the century, they were fighting battles with more guns than any European nation possessed.

But three hundred years later, guns were almost unknown, and certainly unused, among the island's populace. For reasons peculiar to their culture, the Japanese had reverted to the sword and bow. Perrin's intriguing historical essay, covering the years 1543–1879 (a period coinciding, more or less, with Japan's self-imposed isolation from the rest of the world), tells the story of this reversion—a surprising, rare instance of a nation successfully resisting technological advance for the sake of larger cultural concerns: symbolism, aesthetics, ideas of bravery and the dignity and skill of warriors. Good scholarship gives substance to Perrin's fascinating tale, and his graceful, lucid writing makes reading *Giving Up the Gun* pure pleasure.

Noel Perrin

Giving Up the Gun
Japan's Reversion to the Sword, 1543–1879

What: History. War. Technology. *When:* 1979. *Reading Note:* At 120-odd pages, Perrin's monograph is as concise as it is compelling. *Also By: Giving Up the Gun* is something of an anomaly in Perrin's work. He is best known for his quartet of volumes describing life on his Vermont farm: *First Person Rural* (1978), *Second Person Rural* (1980), *Third Person Rural* (1983), and *Last Person Rural* (1991). Readers are urged to seek out his two volumes celebrating unjustly neglected books: *A Reader's Delight* (1988; see page 209) and *A Child's Delight* (1997). *Try: Japanese Inn* by Oliver Statler (see page 746).

■ For Noel Perrin's *A Reader's Delight*, see page 209.

The Beast in the Nursery
ON CURIOSITY AND OTHER APPETITES
Adam Phillips (born 1954)

Hamlet's Psychotherapist

A dam Phillips is intellectually seductive. A glance at the titles of his books—largely collections of incisive, knotty, highly literate essays—attests to their provocative allure: *On Kissing, Tickling, and Being Bored* (1993); *On Flirtation* (1994); *Darwin's Worms: On Life Stories and Death Stories* (1999); *Going Sane: Maps of Happiness* (2005); *Missing Out: In Praise of the Unlived Life* (2012). But it's not all flash; there's intense engagement, too. The intrepid reader is bound to mark the pages of Phillips's books with a plethora of exclamation points and underlinings, comments and agreements, question marks—with, in other words, the pleasure and surprise of learning. Few writers have Phillips's knack for startling into words the deep concerns of life: desire, disappointment, commitment, grief, rage, transience, mortality, and, most and best of all, happiness.

A practicing psychotherapist (and general editor of the Penguin Modern Classics translations of the works of Sigmund Freud), he seems determinedly at odds with the conventional earnestness of his profession. Sparkling with aphoristic elegance (for example, "After the death of God it is transience that takes up our time"), Phillips's writing is rigorous and profound without seeming to pursue either rigor or profundity as a destination. His essayistic path is agile rather than ponderous, an emergent process that allows the reader to share the energy and inspiration of his discoveries. Intensely literary, his work—in a wordplay he might find congenial—is *scriptural*, in the sense that writing and reading are fundamental to his endeavor. "Psychoanalysis," he writes, "does not need any more abstruse or sentimental abstractions—any new paradigms or radical revisions—it just needs more good sentences." Phillips can spot good sentences in others, too; one of the rewards of reading him is the delight of sharing his insights into not just Freud and other psychoanalytic writers, but also Shakespeare, Keats, Darwin, Henry James, and a seemingly endless shelf of classic and contemporary authors.

Nowhere are his gifts on better display than in *The Beast in the Nursery*, a book that presents an enlightening argument against the determinisms of science, and of religion, and of psychoanalysis, too, and in favor of the liberating reality of uncertain expectations. The author's goal is to restore what Nietzsche called "the innocence of becoming," which Phillips describes as "the haphazard, unaccountable, intent project of a life." He explores this project of becoming with something of the mental vitality, the exhilarating and perplexing linguistic scrutiny, and the mysteriously probing power of Hamlet's soliloquies. He'll leave you convinced you've seen the suffering and struggle of life more clearly, and maybe even feeling better able to face them. It's therapeutic surely, and thrilling.

What: Psychology. *When:* 1998. *Also By:* Promises, Promises (2000). On Balance (2010). Becoming Freud: The Making of a Psychoanalyst (2014). In Writing (2017). *Further Reading:* The Paris Review interview with Phillips ("The Art of Nonfiction No. 7") is well worth seeking out. *Try:* Straw Dogs: Thoughts on Humans and Other Animals by John Gray. Artful by Ali Smith (see page 728).

Zen and the Art of Motorcycle Maintenance

AN INQUIRY INTO VALUES

Robert M. Pirsig (1928–2017)

A Philosophical Inquiry on Two Wheels

Some books resonate deeply with the tenor of their times. Robert Pirsig's 1974 "inquiry into values" is a case in point. Rejected, according to the author, by dozens of editors before it finally found a publisher, it became an enduring publishing phenomenon, selling millions of copies.

A discursive narrative, *Zen and the Art of Motorcycle Maintenance* offers neither guidance to the practice of Buddhist discipline nor expert tips on motorcycle upkeep (although a good deal of attention is paid to the mechanical realities of keeping a bike humming—and the spiritual solace such tuning can furnish). The book has a skeletal plot: A man, his young son, and two friends are on vacation, riding motorcycles in the American West. But in the course of their trip, Pirsig ruminates on fundamental philosophical matters in an effort "to see if in that strange separation of what man is from what man does we may have some clues as to what the hell has gone wrong in this twentieth century." And what has gone wrong in his own life: A former college teacher of writing with a history of mental illness, he is in pursuit of truths that will illuminate the matter of Quality—what it is and how to achieve it in thought, expression, and life, not least in his troubled relations with his son.

Writing in *The New Yorker* at the time of its publication, George Steiner said that *Zen and the Art of Motorcycle Maintenance* invites comparison with *Moby-Dick*; it contains, he wrote, "a largesse of symbols, allusions, archetypes so spendthrift, so palpable, that only a great imaginer, shaping his material out of integral need, could afford it." Conversational in its account of the journey, focused and dense in its consideration of Greek thought, of classicism

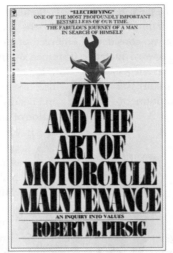

and Romanticism, of reason and feeling, *Zen and the Art* makes up in richness what it lacks in rigor. Pirsig's questing reach exceeds his grasp in the same way our own awkward questions about life's meaning outpace the capacity of our answers. His book is a renewing and exhilarating ride.

What: Philosophy. *When:* 1974. *Reading Note:* Like any long trip, *Zen and the Art* contains longueurs; drive fast through them and you'll soon find yourself on a more engaging road. *Also By: Lila: An Inquiry into Morals* (1991). *Further Reading: Guidebook to "Zen and the Art of Motorcycle Maintenance"* by Ronald L. DiSanto and Thomas J. Steele. *Try: Zen in the Art of Archery* by Eugen Herrigel (see page 370). *Shop Class as Soulcraft* by Matthew Crawford.

■ For Christine de Pizan's *The Book of the City of Ladies*, see page 257.

Collected Dialogues
Plato (ca. 428 BC–ca. 348 BC)

The Examined Life

I n Plato's *Phaedrus*, Socrates tells the story of the invention of writing, invoking the legend that the new art had first been presented to an Egyptian king, who questioned its value to humankind:

If men learn this, it will implant forgetfulness in their souls; they will cease to exercise memory because they rely on that which is written, calling things to remembrance no longer from within themselves, but by means of external marks. What you have discovered is a recipe not for memory, but for reminder. And it is no true wisdom that you offer your disciples, but only its semblance, for by telling them of many things without teaching them you will make them seem to know much, while for the most part they know nothing, and as men filled, not with

wisdom, but with the conceit of wisdom, they will be a burden to their fellows.

Writing, though, is not, in its truest form, about remembering, but about articulation, and through articulation, discovery; not about reminding, really, but about *minding*—and there is no better example of this than the works of Plato himself. His prose is a conveyance and shaper of ideas, and in his dialogues, he created a medium of colloquy that is supple, nuanced, flexible in its expressiveness, and often humorous. To read Plato is to encounter not only one of humanity's seminal philosophers, but one of its most resourceful writers as well, one who mastered in his sentences an astonishing range of tone, image, and emotion. His dialogues lead us into an imaginative landscape of enormous dimensions; it is nearly impossible to peruse his work without coming upon a passage that can set a mind spinning in rumination through midnight hours: the provocative consideration of the genesis of the written word quoted above, for instance, or the famous allegory of the cave in *The Republic*, which still casts profound shadows on our conceptions of the real and the ideal.

His dialogues have engaged readers and scholars for thousands of years because his cast of conversing Athenians debate questions of beauty, justice, love, knowledge, and being that are at the heart of human experience. The legendary figure of Plato's teacher, Socrates, is the star of the intellectual show, and it's fair to say that, although based on a historical personage, his role has been shaped and polished to allow the author to pose—and examine—his own enduring themes (Plato, in fact, never really speaks for himself in the dialogues). The most famous works are the *Apology*, which details the trial of Socrates and his noble embrace of philosophy in the face of death (summed up in the dictum "the unexamined life is not worth living"); the *Symposium*, a discourse in several voices on desire, love, and beauty; and the *Republic*, an investigation of justice that is a foundational work in Western political theory.

But Plato's thought and—just as important—his elegant writing make nearly all of his twenty-odd dialogues rewarding reading. His work embodies the transition in human expression from the recited to the composed, and in human discourse from the oracular to the rational, getting thought, and all that thought might entail, onto a page where it could be assessed, reassembled, argued with, and then reconfigured into

An 18th-century engraving of Plato

|||||||||||||||||||||||||||||||||||||||| B O O K N O T E ||||||||||||||||||||||||||||||||||||||||||||||

A QUIRKY AND FASCINATING SOURCEBOOK

The Origins of European Thought About the Body, the Mind, the Soul, the World, Time, and Fate
R. B. Onians (1899–1986)

Exploring the roots of a number of humanity's most developed, bountiful, and overarching branches of thought, this rich 1951 book by R. B. Onians provides fodder for hours, days, and months of speculation and reflection. It would be a fine companion for a castaway. In fact, one might even say that *The Origins of European Thought* itself describes its own desert island game, played by our species from our earliest consciousness. Adrift on our planet, alone with their thoughts, the imaginative among our forebears would pass the eons trying to comprehend the most enticing and endlessly unknowable—the most obvious and the most mysterious—themes of our existence: life, death, mind, body, soul, time, fate. What Onians does, in this unique, learned, stimulating, odd, and absorbing exploration, is report on the first few rounds of this pastime, plumbing depths of linguistic, literary, and archaeological evidence (predominantly, but not entirely, from Greece and Rome) to illuminate the early shape of humanity's answers to eternal questions—answers that continue to cast powerful shadows on all our wanderings and wonderings. You'll learn about everything from ancient explanations of hearing and sight to Homeric, Hindu, and Kabbalistic ideas about the prophetic power of sneezing but, more importantly, you'll be filled with awe at how much there is to figure out about our existence—and how brave and ingenious (and occasionally nutty) our ancestors were in applying themselves to that task.

wisdom. His speculation in ideas is a kind of fiction in which the world is represented as a series of definitions; these definitions can then be constructed into conversations, and thereby into significance spun from reflection, communication, and the search for meaning. Watching his mind at work through the window of his prose, we can almost see reason itself taking shape as a tool for making the world intelligible. What we absorb in the process still has relevance to our lives as citizens, as friends and lovers, and as seekers of fulfillment.

What: Philosophy. Antiquity. *When:* Fourth century BC. *Edition:* Many of the dialogues are available as individual volumes or in small anthologies, but the comprehensive *Collected Dialogues*, edited by Edith Hamilton and Huntington Cairns (and quoted here), gathers the best translations in English and is highly recommended. *Further Reading: The Music of the Republic: Essays on Socrates' Conversations and Plato's Writings* by Eva Brann. *The Trial of Socrates* by I. F. Stone. *Try: The Moral Essays* by Giacomo Leopardi. *Plato at the Googleplex* by Rebecca Goldstein.

The Bogey Man
A MONTH ON THE PGA TOUR
George Plimpton (1927–2003)

A Literary Lion Tees Off on the Tour

In 1968, *Paris Review* editor and weekend duffer George Plimpton joined the professional golf tour for a month. He played in three California tournaments, mingling with Arnold Palmer, Jack Nicklaus, and such memorable journeymen as the quick-tempered Bob Bruno, whose overreaction to a missed putt led to his disappearance on the way to the next tee. Alerted by a violent sound, an observer spotted Bruno deep in the woods: "My God, he's in there beating his driver against a stump!"

Plimpton had already survived several risky adventures in "participatory journalism," including sparring

George Plimpton on the links, 1966

with onetime light heavyweight boxing champ Archie Moore and playing quarterback in a preseason game for the Detroit Lions, an experience chronicled in the bestselling *Paper Lion* (1966). This time, at least, he was less likely to get hurt. However, it turned out that on the links the gentleman amateur was up against a tough opponent—namely, himself. "My woes in golf," declares the lanky 18-handicapper, "have been largely psychological." Indeed, fellow hackers will be particularly intrigued by Plimpton's bemused and detailed firsthand exploration of the game's innumerable psychological sand traps, from those within reach of the rankest amateur, such as golfing rage, to more arcane occupational hazards, such as the "yips"—"a nervous affliction that settled in the wrist and hands" and "ultimately drove the pros out of the game to teaching jobs at the country clubs."

But this book is too funny to be consigned to golfers alone. The game's rich lore and the entertaining company of players and caddies on the course and in the clubhouse afford Plimpton splendid opportunities to demonstrate that, although he may have been a hopelessly inelegant golfer, he was nearly flawless as a sporting raconteur.

What: Sports. Humor. *When:* 1968. *Also By: Out of My League* (1961). *Shadow Box: An Amateur in the Ring* (1977). *George Plimpton on Sports* (2005). *Try: A Good Walk Spoiled* by John Feinstein.

Letters of Pliny the Younger
Gaius Plinius Caecilius Secundus (AD 61–AD 113)

The Latest News from the Ancient World

Gaius Plinius Caecilius Secundus was dubbed Pliny the Younger to distinguish him from the uncle who adopted and raised him, the natural historian known to posterity as Pliny the Elder. As a lawyer and imperial official, the younger Pliny was conversant in the political, administrative, and literary topics of his age, and a good number of the letters that would win him lasting fame as an author are addressed to such notable contemporaries as the historians Suetonius (see page 765) and Tacitus (see page 770), as well as the emperor Trajan himself. Pliny's corpus of *litterae curiosius scriptae* ("letters written with special care") may well be the first letters composed with an eye to their collection and publication, which the author himself arranged during his own lifetime.

He is without a doubt a wonderful correspondent, with a pleasing, polished style and a keenly observant mind. Packed with attention to domestic customs, social manners, religious rituals, and governmental routine and intrigue, his reports are the richest source we have for reconstructing Roman life in the first century AD. Of more importance for the general reader, Pliny is a writer both relaxed and erudite, possessed of a discursive genius that is seductive. A narrative ease informs his many character sketches and depictions of nature, as is apparent in his account of a boy cavorting with—and eventually riding—a friendly dolphin off the coast of North Africa, and in the ghost story he tells about a haunted house in Athens, to name just two examples. Most interesting of all are the two letters that describe in detail the eruption of Mount Vesuvius in the year AD 79, the volcanic event that buried Pompeii and claimed the life of the elder Pliny, whose vocation as a naturalist compelled him to venture into the heat of the catastrophe:

By now ashes were falling on the ships, whiter and thicker the nearer they approached. Then pumice stones also descended, and stones which were black, charred, and split by the fires. Suddenly they were in shallow water and the shore-line barred their way with debris from the mountain. My uncle hesitated momentarily, wondering whether to turn back, but then, as the steersman advised that course, he said to him: "Fortune favours the brave. Head for the villa of Pomponianus."

A cultivated, compellingly readable companion, Pliny the Younger was best characterized by Frederic Raphael and Kenneth McLeish in a succinct note in their admirable volume, *The List of Books* (see page 209): "Urbane; ironic; cool—a Renaissance humanist before his time."

What: Diaries & Letters. Antiquity. *When:* AD 100–AD 109. *Editions:* P. G. Walsh's translation of the *Complete Letters* for Oxford World's Classics is recommended. *Ashen Sky: The Letters of Pliny the Younger on the Eruption of Vesuvius*, illustrated by Barry Moser, is an especially handsome volume. *Try: The Histories* and *The Annals* of Tacitus (see page 770). *The Diary of Samuel Pepys* (see page 622).

Plutarch's Lives
Plutarch (ca. AD 46–ca. AD 120)

A Compendium of Classical Role Models

Plutarch's "parallel lives" of Greek and Roman political and military leaders—in which Theseus is compared with Romulus, Alcibiades with Coriolanus, Alexander the Great with Julius Caesar, Demosthenes with Cicero, and so on—has been a storehouse of wisdom for twenty centuries. The author's pointed sense of drama and characterization made him a frequent source for Shakespeare, whose *Julius Caesar*, *Coriolanus*, and *Antony*

Plutarch in a 17th-century Bulgarian fresco

It must be borne in mind that my design is not to write histories, but lives. And the most glorious exploits do not always furnish us with the clearest discoveries of virtue or vice in men; sometimes a matter of less moment, an expression or a jest, informs us better of their characters and inclinations, than the most famous sieges, the greatest armaments, or the bloodiest battles whatsoever.

His considerable skills as a social historian are always in the service of his mission as a moralist, for his real concern is the fate of virtue and vice as his protagonists find themselves confronting the trials of private and public battles. Each life follows a similar pattern, with Plutarch focusing on upbringing and education first (his account of Alexander's relationship with his teacher, Aristotle, is especially memorable), then charting his subject's entry into the public sphere and the actions or decisions—the defining moments—that shaped his nature and reputation. The author's delight in anecdote and the revelation of personality is evident on every page, rewarding one's attention to antiquity with vivid and dramatic reading.

and *Cleopatra* were all based upon these *Lives*. Montaigne, Rousseau, and Emerson—among countless other celebrated thinkers—often mined his abundant illustrative lessons as well. By his direct effect on readers and through the reach of those writers in his debt, Plutarch can fairly be called one of the most influential writers who ever lived.

He makes his purpose clear at the beginning of his life of Alexander, in which he asserts that he pays "particular attention to the marks and indications of the souls of men":

What: Antiquity. History. Biography. *When:* AD 105–115. *Editions:* Sir Thomas North's influential English translation was published in 1579 (North's version was drawn not from the original Greek, but from the 1559 French translation of Jacques Amyot). Arthur Hugh Clough's nineteenth-century revision of the translation supervised by John Dryden, a century after North's work, offers the best text for modern readers, and is available in a Modern Library edition. *Also By: Moralia* (ca. AD 100). *Try: The Twelve Caesars* by Suetonius (see page 765).

Poetry and Tales
Edgar Allan Poe (1809–1849)

Macabre Masterpieces—and More

Edgar Allan Poe was the creator, in prose and poetry, of an eerie, highly wrought chamber music, different in both sound and sense from the compositions of his nineteenth-century literary contemporaries. Poe's writings orchestrate effects with such cunning that they hold readers in a singularly sensational spell: We remember what Poe's work feels like, just as we might remember the substance of other writers. There is nothing else quite like it.

Take "The Tell-Tale Heart," one of his most haunting tales. It opens with the narrator's

Edgar Allan Poe, ca. 1848

the patron saint of horror movies—his compact narratives employ an over-the-top evocation of terror to expose deep-seated yet familiar fears of guilt and exposure, as if the author were, a half century early, reinventing the fairy tale for the Freudian era: "If you only knew," he seems to say, "the dark secrets our telltale hearts contain."

Nonetheless, to focus only on his mastery of the macabre, or on his notorious biographical legend of alcoholism and degradation, is to sell Poe short. His only novel, *The Narrative of Arthur Gordon Pym of Nantucket*, is a visionary exploration of the themes the tales of horror distill, and his last work, *Eureka: A Prose Poem*, presages some of the findings of twentieth-century quantum physics. Perhaps most tellingly for readers of future generations, Poe more or less invented the detective story in three tales of ratiocination featuring the brilliant and eccentric C. Auguste Dupin: "The Murders in the Rue Morgue," "The Mystery of Marie Rogêt," and "The Purloined Letter." No less a luminary than Sir Arthur Conan Doyle would credit Poe's peculiar genius with imparting "the breath of life" to the form that Conan Doyle's own creation, Sherlock Holmes, would come to command.

invocation of his own sensitivity: "TRUE!—nervous—very, very dreadfully nervous I had been and am; but why will you say that I am mad? The disease had sharpened my senses—not destroyed—not dulled them."

Arthur Rackham illustration for "The Masque of the Red Death"

As the story unfolds, his acute susceptibility is transferred to the reader through a heightened pitch of language and a preternatural attention to sensory details; it's like a campfire ghost story caught in the telling, moonlight and leaf-rustling wind included. Seldom has creepiness been given such palpable aesthetic shape.

Poe's most famous stories—"The Fall of the House of Usher," "The Masque of the Red Death," "The Pit and the Pendulum," "The Black Cat," "The Cask of Amontillado"—exhibit a similar single-minded fascination of effect, and it is upon these tales that the author's enduring appeal is built. (His poems take his method to extremes, their ominous sonorities accumulating until they seem to be sounding lullabies for wicked children, with the consequence that they can be impossible to forget, as in the cases of "The Raven" and "The Bells.") Embracing popular forms of melodrama—Poe would become

What: Short Stories. Poetry. **When:** 1827–49. **Editions:** There have been countless editions of Poe's tales and poems. The authoritative *Poetry and Tales* from the Library of America (1984) offers a full selection, and also includes his novel, *The Narrative of Arthur Gordon Pym of Nantucket* (1838) and *Eureka: A Prose Poem* (1848). *The Portable Edgar Allan Poe*, in Penguin Classics, contains the essential works. **Also By:** *Edgar Allan Poe: Essays and Reviews* (Library of America, 1984). **Further Reading:** *Poe Poe Poe Poe Poe Poe Poe* by Daniel Hoffman. *Edgar A. Poe: Mournful and Never-Ending Remembrance* by Kenneth Silverman. **Try:** *The Strange Case of Dr. Jekyll and Mr. Hyde* by Robert Louis Stevenson (see page 759). *The Collected Ghost Stories of M. R. James* (see page 410). *H. P. Lovecraft: Tales*. **Adaptations:** Many of Poe's stories have been made into films. Among the best is Roger Corman's 1964 version of *The Masque of the Red Death*, starring Vincent Price.

MORE TO EXPLORE

A GATHERING OF GHOSTS

While Poe's virtuosity lifted horror to new literary heights, it played upon our oldest fears, ringing variations on an ancient form of narrative: the ghost story. One suspects that, along with boasts of bravery and hunting prowess, such tales may well have been a staple around our earliest firesides. With death as the perpetual mystery looming over all existence, and memory of the lost lingering on after their departure, how could ghostly specters not lurk in the wavering shadows?

One thing's for sure: Ghost stories have never lost their power to frighten, enchant, and entertain—witness pop culture, in which, in one form or another, the walking dead keep coming back. No matter how spooky or diverting, such tales hide behind their otherworldly aspects a strange element of reassurance in their positing of some kind of existence beyond the one we know. Here is a short list of ghostly tales, offering great variety in manner and mood, to satisfy a reader's urge for engaging the afterlife from a favorite chair.

The Case of Charles Dexter Ward
H. P. Lovecraft (1890–1937)

Inspired by the fusty, antiquarian glories of his hometown of Providence, Rhode Island, Lovecraft composed this short novel—which did not see publication until 1943, six years after his death—around the legend of a haunted mansion just a couple of blocks from his own dwelling place at the time of writing. It's set in the year 1918, when an impetuous and self-serving fellow named Charles Dexter Ward gets curious about his colonial-era

ancestor Joseph Curwen. Curwen's reputation for eternal youth, grave robbing, and experiments with monsters provokes his descendant to unwisely proceed with a resurrection of his wizardly forebear. As the reader might surmise, this is not a Good Idea.

As was his preference in so many tales, Lovecraft does not tell this story unadorned. He loved delivering mysteries, cosmic and quotidian, that had to be unraveled in scholarly fashion, by following a paper trail, with some dangerous physical investigations thrown in as well. (This Lovecraftian model informs much conspiracy fiction that came after him, from lowbrow to high; Thomas Pynchon's *The Crying of Lot 49* is one example of the latter.) The investigator here is one Marinus Bicknell Willett, family doctor to the Wards. As the reader follows the doctor's heroic exploits, Lovecraft's genius in evoking the abominable unearthly specters that can cluster in the imagination is on full display, allowing the reader to revel in, in the master's own words, "that half-tangible miasma of murk and foulness and anguished frenzy." Sound like fun? It is.

The Haunting of Hill House
Shirley Jackson (1916–1965)

From its very first sentence— "No live organism can continue for long to exist sanely under conditions of absolute reality; even larks and katydids are supposed, by some, to dream"—to its closing clause—". . . silence lay steadily against the wood and stone of Hill House, and whatever walked there, walked alone"—Shirley Jackson's penultimate novel constitutes a masterpiece of psychosexual anxiety. Her wickedly disturbing passion play, enacted by the four

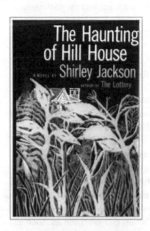

(later, six) individuals gathered at the cursed mansion known as Hill House, perfectly equates the interior state of the spinsterish protagonist, Eleanor Vance, with the confusing, calamitous rooms and the surrounding acreage of the titular dwelling. Both the chambers of the spooky domicile and those of Eleanor's cobwebbed mind are simultaneously overstuffed (with furniture and with phobias, respectively) and empty (of sane inhabitance, in each case). When at last Eleanor refuses to leave the place that has almost killed her, saying, "I was—happy . . . I don't want to go away from here," we realize we have witnessed the sad end of her struggle to defeat her own worst enemy: her stifled, cramped self, bound by the unbreakable chains of circumstance and character.

Besides serving as a quietly horrifying testament to one woman's disintegration, Jackson's mordant 1959 book also brings a fresh sophistication to the horror genre through its characters' recognition of what the plot will demand of them. By their conversation when they first meet, they make clear that they know they're enacting clichéd roles from myriad films and novels. But their ultra-modern awareness fails to forestall the actual terror, and this is perhaps Jackson's scariest assertion: The intellect is no real bulwark against the darkness. For Jackson's *Life Among the Savages*, see page 404.

Old House of Fear
Russell Kirk (1918–1994)

Most remembered today as the author of *The Conservative Mind* (1953) and one of the founders of the modern conservative movement, Russell Kirk also had a more playful side, revealed in his creation of three novels and a passel of deftly done short stories. Aficionados of supernatural fiction cherish these as much as like-minded politicos have admired Kirk's ideas.

In *Old House of Fear* (1961), Hugh Logan, agent for a rich American who wishes to purchase a Hebridean island, is summoned to the lonely isle of Carnglass. He finds his journey impeded by a series of obstacles and assaults that suggest some strange plot is brewing (as, of course, it is). When Logan finally arrives at Carnglass, he finds two women being held hostage: Lady MacAskival and her adopted heir, young Mary, who possesses a preternatural—or is it supernatural?—innocence. Their captor is a satanic figure who manifests a barely concealed perpetual wound in his forehead, which he dubs his "Third Eye." The ghost of Lady MacAskival's husband hovers about, as well as a Pan-like figure known as the Firgower. Although actual paranormal events remain more implied than manifest, the brooding atmosphere of Carnglass and Logan's extreme trials lure the reader into a haunted venue that transcends the normal flow of time and space, in which reality itself seems suspended precariously between states of life and death defined by no conventional understanding of birth or mortality. All in all, a neglected Gothic treat.

lost boy lost girl
Peter Straub (born 1943)

In reviewing this 2003 novel, the well-regarded fantasist Michael Marshall Smith remarked that Peter Straub's work is "shot through with something unstable, an off-kilterness that can threaten to push the reader through the walls of the known." This teeter-totter atmosphere pervades *lost boy lost girl* (a title deliberately reminiscent of one of the most famous episodes from *The Twilight Zone*), sometimes literally, sometimes metaphorically.

To exploit what one chapter's title calls a "rip in the fabric" of familiar space-time and morality, Straub first establishes the quotidianness of his milieu with a vigorous exactitude, setting a contemporary scene replete with consumerist talismans much like those in a Ross Macdonald or Andrew Vachss crime novel. The reader is caught up in the strained dynamics of the Underhill family—crushed and sour father Philip, ill-fated mother Nancy, and adolescent questing son Mark—so as to render the supernatural doings that Mark uncovers in a neighbor's menacing house that much more believable. Straub provides alternate points of view on events past and present, further opening our understanding of his milieu and its denizens. Our "private eye" on all this is Philip's brother, novelist Tim Underhill, who must chart a path through family intransigence and official suspicion in his quest to find his nephew after Mark mysteriously disappears. Tim's search ends in a manner both more and less satisfactory than he had hoped for, capping a tale with an essential lesson that lingers with a ghostly persistence of its own: Life does not run to our dictates, and we must appreciate whatever it gives, to say nothing of what it takes away.

Topper
Thorne Smith (1892–1934)

Let's end our ghostly tour on a comic note. Steeped in the naughty high jinks of Prohibition, Thorne Smith's most famous novel, published in 1926, is a manic paean to hedonism and following one's bliss. So long as hidebound morality, stifled longings, and the pressures of consumerism and commercial demands exist, this book will hold vast appeal.

Two young and glamorous sybaritic socialites, George and Marion Kerby, perish in a drunken accident. Finding themselves celestially repurposed as ghosts, they whimsically attach themselves to a milquetoast businessman with the improbable name of Cosmo Topper. They beguile him to act less stuffy and to enjoy himself, with Marion an untouchable succubus, tempting Topper with ineffable delights that never quite materialize. Eventually Topper gives in and lets go, and bluenoses and minor tyrants of all stripes receive an ebullient rebuke in this forerunner to all classic screwball comedies.

The Travels of Marco Polo

Marco Polo (ca. 1254–1324)
As told to Rustichello da Pisa

Book of Wonders

....

Some books are better read with eyes closed, so to speak—with a blank mind, cleared of preconceptions. Imagine, then, an open sea, a barren landscape, a caravan. Slowly fill the picture with the author's words, one by one by one, like a discoverer seeing things for the first time. Across the water is a paradise of islands, around that ridge in the distance are fabulous cities, amid the caravan are jewels and spices and all the baggage of adventure, soon to be palpable, in a page or two. . . . Such books of wonder, of which Marco Polo's is perhaps the greatest, depend on the reader as well as the writer, for they were written when imagination was more powerful than information as a tool of knowledge.

Which is not to say that *The Travels of Marco Polo*, dictated by the titular explorer to a romance writer named Rustichello da Pisa when the two men shared a prison cell in Genoa at the end of the thirteenth century (that's another story), is spun from wholly invented cloth. Quite the opposite, in fact: Polo's chronicle of his expedition from Venice to the East, his nearly twenty-year sojourn at the court of Kublai Khan, and his travels with the emperor through the provinces of China is filled with largely verified reports on trade (the Chinese were pioneers in the use of paper money), technology (the burning of coal), and culture (the book's portrait of the admirable sophistication, curiosity, and erudition of the imperial retinue overturned previous European conceptions of the "barbarian" character of Mongol civilization). There are indeed marvels—lakes of fire, winds so persistent that people must submerge their bodies in water to escape their punishment, promiscuous hospitality—but where these are not credible, they are certainly delightful, and might easily be ascribed to the invention of Polo's literary partner (not for nothing was Rustichello a writer of romances).

Upon its publication, *The Travels of Marco Polo* became an international bestseller, or the nearest a book could get to that status before the invention of the printing press (in the

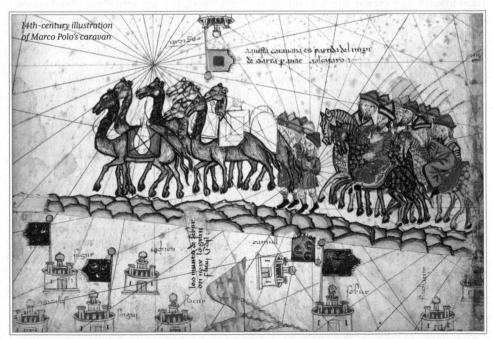

14th-century illustration of Marco Polo's caravan

French in which it was originally set down, it was known as *The Book of the Marvels of the World*). It has inspired merchants, cartographers, and literary voyagers from Coleridge, in his legendary poem "Kublai Khan," to Italo Calvino, in the exquisite fiction *Invisible Cities* (see page 120). But best of all, it has enchanted the mind's eye for generation upon generation of readers, and continues to do so today.

What: Travel. Adventure. *When:* ca. 1300. *Editions:* The translations by William Marsden and Ronald E. Latham are especially good. *Further Reading: Marco Polo: From Venice to Xanadu* by Laurence Bergreen. *Try: The Adventures of Ibn Battuta* by Ross E. Dunn (see page 239). *In Xanadu* by William Dalrymple (see page 193). *Adaptations:* There have been several film adaptations, including Hollywood's serenely ridiculous *The Adventures of Marco Polo* (1938), starring Gary Cooper, and a lavish Netflix series that premiered in 2014; most interesting is the 2008 PBS documentary, *In the Footsteps of Marco Polo*, about two friends from Queens, Denis Belliveau and Francis O'Donnell, who retrace the Venetian's itinerary.

The Collected Stories of Katherine Anne Porter
Katherine Anne Porter (1890–1980)

American Encounters with Time and Destiny

Born on a Texas farm, Katherine Anne Porter, whose mother died when she was two, was raised by her grandmother until the elder woman's death nine years later. Despite sparse formal education, Porter was savvy enough, by age fourteen, to take ownership with her sister of an acting school in a small Texas town. By age sixteen, she had embarked upon the first of her several marriages; as she approached thirty, having endured a bout of tuberculosis and abandoned her own theatrical ambitions, she turned to writing, publishing her first short story, "Maria Concepcion," in 1922. The rest of her long life would prove equally turbulent, and while her biography might provide the plot for a rich and dramatic novel, her art undoubtedly produced a body of work as accomplished and significant as that of any author in American literature.

That art found its fullest expression in the pieces collected in this invaluable volume; its twenty-seven stories and novellas are filled with the gravity and grace of a shelf of full-length works. *Collected Stories* contains three complete volumes—*Flowering Judas*; *Pale Horse, Pale Rider*; *The Leaning Tower and Other Stories*—as well as four stories that had been previously unpublished in book form. The precision and assuredness of Porter's prose and her uncanny knack for quickly probing the inner lives of her characters make every tale rewarding reading, but "Noon Wine" and the autobiographical Miranda cycle deserve special mention. The former, a short novel about a small-town murder, unfolds with the ineluctable logic of a Greek tragedy. The latter—beginning with the story "The Old Order" and continuing in "Old Mortality" before culminating in "Pale Horse, Pale Rider"—plumbs Porter's memories of her childhood, her grandmother, and her own near-death experience in the influenza epidemic of 1918, revealing an extraordinary sensitivity to the experience of time in all its tenses. Both exhibit Porter's art at its best, imbuing ordinary life with all the larger-than-life elements—love, death, eternity—that shadow it.

What: Short Stories. Novellas. *When:* 1965 (most of the contents written between 1922 and 1940). *Awards:* Pulitzer Prize for Fiction and National Book Award for Fiction, 1966. *Also By: Ship of Fools* (1962). *The Collected Essays and Occasional Writings of Katherine Anne Porter* (1970). *Letters of Katherine Anne Porter* (1990). *Further Reading: Katherine Anne Porter: The Life of an Artist* by Darlene Harbour Unrue. *Try: The Collected Stories of Eudora Welty* (see page 841). *Adaptation:* Sam Peckinpah directed a 1966 television adaptation of "Noon Wine" that stars Jason Robards. *Footnote:* Porter's last book, *The Never-Ending Wrong* (1977), is an account of the trial and execution of Sacco and Vanzetti in the late 1920s.

The World of Peter Rabbit
Beatrix Potter (1866–1943)

The Little Bunny Who Could—and Did

Toddlers revel in the culture of coziness, and one of the joys of parenthood (and, perhaps even more so, of grandparenthood) is the free pass we're given to return to its happy domain, very often in the pages of classic children's books. The dimensions of the cozy are nowhere more easily entered than through the gate of the lovely little books created by Beatrix Potter at the turn of the twentieth century. Beginning with *The Tale of Peter Rabbit* (first written in a picture letter to the young son of her last governess), and continuing in twenty-two additional books, Potter created an unsentimental yet tender world of mischievous creatures whose humorous adventures are a delight to share. The author's exquisite watercolor illustrations display her study of art and natural history (she was an accomplished mycologist—a student of mushrooms) while still conveying a singular imaginative whimsy. The physical smallness of the books (in their original and traditional format, the Potter hardcovers measure four-and-a-quarter by five-and-five-eighths inches) echo the snug charm of their contents.

Beatrix Potter, 1913

In the first book in the series, Potter introduces the resourceful and endearing title character, his mother Mrs. Rabbit, and his sisters Flopsy, Mopsy, and Cotton-tail. When Peter, against his mother's warning ("your Father had an accident there; he was put in a pie"), sneaks into a nearby garden to feast on vegetables, we also meet the fearsome Mr. McGregor, who threatens the bunny thief to within an inch of his life. After several close calls, Peter manages his escape, returning home having left his blue jacket, with its bright brass buttons, behind (it will be retrieved from the scarecrow McGregor has hung it on in the fourth book, *The Tale of*

Benjamin Bunny). Comforted by his mother and a cup of chamomile tea, Peter will soon be ready to make mischief another day, in the company of Potter's delightful cast of anthropomorphized animals, including Jemima Puddle-Duck, Squirrel Nutkin, and Cecily Parsley. To savor and share the Beatrix Potter library of imaginatively big littleness is one of a reading life's lasting joys.

What: Children's. **When:** Privately printed, 1901. Trade edition, 1902. **Edition:** A handsome boxed set, *The World of Peter Rabbit*, contains all twenty-three volumes—and is a marvelous gift for a newborn. **Also By:** Beatrix Potter: *A Journal* (2006; excerpts from the author's diaries, with her own illustrations). **Further Reading:** *Beatrix Potter: A Life in Nature* by Linda Lear. *At Home with Beatrix Potter* by Susan Denyer. **Try:** The Brambly Hedge books by Jill Barklem. **Adaptation:** The 2006 film *Miss Potter* stars Renée Zellweger in the title role. **Footnote:** A Peter Rabbit doll was on sale a year after the phenomenal publishing of his *Tale*, making Potter's creation one of the very first licensed characters.

Peter Rabbit with his mother and sisters

The Wicked Pavilion
Dawn Powell (1896–1965)

A Writer Still Not Rediscovered Enough

The Wicked Pavilion

In a 1940 *New York Times* article about author Dawn Powell, Robert Van Gelder wrote, "The books make a stir on publication but don't get much of anywhere in sales." Powell joked that she'd try to write longer, duller books, since "there is so great a premium on dullness," but she continued to write as only she could, producing books critic Michael Dirda describes as "bittersweet screwball comedies, where the characters all drink like maenads at a bacchanal and the race under the table is always to the wittiest." (Dorothy Parker comparisons abound, but Diana Trilling famously said it was Powell "who really says the funny things for which Dorothy Parker gets credit.") When she died in 1965, nearly all of Powell's many novels were out of print. She was buried in an unmarked grave.

Fortunately, that's not the end of her story. Following a generous 1987 Gore Vidal appraisal in the *New York Review of Books* (in which he calls Powell a better satirist than Mark Twain) and a 1991 Edmund Wilson tribute, music critic Tim Page was inspired to pick up a used copy of one of her books, and thus began something of a personal crusade. Instrumental in getting Powell's novels back into print, Page went on to edit her diaries and letters and to pen a biography. With each new venture—and with the ultimate compliment of a pair of Library of America volumes released in 2001—came a new wave of interest. Still, with a consistency that would no doubt have amused the sardonic Powell, "the books make a stir . . . but don't get much of anywhere in sales."

It may be Dawn Powell's fate to remain always a neglected genius—all the more reason for her impassioned advocates to share the pleasure of her work with fellow readers at every opportunity. Where does one begin? All of Powell's novels are good (though she disowned her first, *Whither*), and many of them are even better, so it would be hard to go wrong. Powell was born in Ohio and spent her adult life in Greenwich Village; both locales supplied settings and perspectives for her work, which is often divided into "Ohio novels" and "New York novels." Three of the latter—*The Locusts Have No King* (1948), *The Wicked Pavilion* (1954), and *The Golden Spur* (1962)—are among her most praised, and the best of these is the second.

The setting of *The Wicked Pavilion* is the Café Julien, modeled on Powell's favorite Manhattan hangout, the Café Lafayette. The characters are painters and writers, lovers and gold diggers, patrons and frauds. With razor-sharp precision, Powell inscribes a portrait of bohemian New York in which aspirations, ambitions, and infatuations are spent wildly, with no return other than the confusion of those possessed by them. Savagely perceptive, *The Wicked Pavilion*, like all of the author's best work, has a revelatory comic edge, fierce and fresh. Dirda said it best: "A writer like this deserves more than rediscovery: She deserves readers. Lots of them."

What: Novel. *When:* 1954. *Edition: The Wicked Pavilion, The Locusts Have No King,* and *The Golden Spur* can all be had in one Library of America edition, along with *My Home Is Far Away. Also By: Dance Night* (1930). *Turn, Magic Wheel* (1936). *Angels on Toast* (1940). *The Diaries of Dawn Powell, 1931–1965* (1995). *Selected Letters of Dawn Powell, 1913–1965* (1999). *Try: Vile Bodies* by Evelyn Waugh. *The Bachelors* by Muriel Spark.

Heisenberg's War

THE SECRET HISTORY OF THE GERMAN BOMB

Thomas Powers (born 1940)

Uncertain Hero

I n the middle of World War II, a British scientist told American officials that he considered physicist Werner Heisenberg "the most dangerous possible German in the field because of his brain power." As Thomas Powers writes, "Heisenberg's contributions to the revolution in theoretical physics of the 1920s and '30s— the invention of quantum mechanics and the 'uncertainty principle' attached to his name— had earned him a Nobel Prize in 1932, a place among the great names of science, and the respect of his colleagues." What his colleagues did not respect was Heisenberg's decision to stay in Germany even as the horror of the Nazi regime became apparent. While his fellow physicists, many of them Jewish, fled the country for jobs in the United States and elsewhere, Heisenberg bought a house and told everyone who asked that he "loved his country, but not its regime," and that his country needed him.

In the first month of the war, Powers relates, Heisenberg was appointed "chief theoretician" of Germany's atomic bomb project. Fear of Heisenberg's mental prowess—and the consequent possibility that the Nazis would be the first to build a nuclear weapon—played no small part in fueling the urgency of the Allies' Manhattan Project. But at the war's end, it was discovered that, in the words of one American diplomat, "The Nazis had not even reached first base" in their effort to construct the fearsome device, which only led to further puzzlement regarding Heisenberg's wartime motives and activities. To the question of why he remained in Germany was added another: Why had the world's greatest theoretical physicist failed so miserably?

In *Heisenberg's War*, Powers, a Pulitzer Prize–winning reporter, attempts to solve both mysteries with a single answer, making a case that Heisenberg purposely foiled the Germans' atomic program. Had he behaved heroically, despite his refusal to clarify matters even after the war was over? A suspenseful tale of science and espionage as well as military and moral drama, Powers's book is an important piece of historical detective work, a riveting literary narrative, and a compelling portrait of a man who was one of the most brilliant and enigmatic figures of the twentieth century.

What: History. War. Science. When: 1993. Also By: The Man Who Kept the Secrets: Richard Helms and the CIA (1979). Intelligence Wars: American Secret History from Hitler to al-Qaeda (2002). Further Reading: The Making of the Atomic Bomb by Richard Rhodes. Hitler's Uranium Club: The Secret Recordings at Farm Hall by Jeremy Bernstein. Try: American Prometheus: The Triumph and Tragedy of J. Robert Oppenheimer by Kai Bird and Martin J. Sherwin (see page 79). Adaptation: Heisenberg's War inspired Michael Frayn's Tony-winning drama, Copenhagen.

A Glastonbury Romance

John Cowper Powys (1872–1963)

The Magnum Opus of a Prodigious and Untamed Imagination

A ny moment is the sum of time's parts. From that kernel this novel sprouts, and how dizzying and exhilarating are its branches. John Cowper Powys's masterpiece, published in 1932, runs to more than 1,100 pages, and its sentences sow seeds of imagery, idea, and profound and crazy intuition that suggest another 1,100 pages of uncultivated invention lying just below the surface. What else can you expect from a novel that begins with a man getting off a train and proceeds to explore how all the forces of the past and present—cosmological, mythical, historical, economic, geographical, spiritual—are brought to bear on life in a given place?

The Glastonbury of Powys's novel is an immense canvas on which the figures and elements of a twentieth-century present—men, women, and children as well as animals and flowers, soil and stone and water—are haunted by the pentimento of storied centuries, from the ancient auras of King Arthur's Avalon and the legend of the Holy Grail, which have long haunted the Somerset town, to the newer actualities of capitalism, communism, and tourism. The enormous cast of characters includes a mayor obsessed with the Grail legend, a skeptic in his employ, a hated industrialist bent on electrifying the local cave, and assorted Bolsheviks, anarchists, sensualists, and mystics. Political intrigues and adulterous liaisons enliven the landscape, and Powys's pantheistic sensibility endows nature with an active intelligence that courses through the novel, culminating in the catastrophic flood—told from the flood's point of view, no less—that closes the book. Eternal impulses inform the public and private dramas that Powys depicts, giving his work a philosophical ambition and rhetorical scope that are breathtaking, bewildering, and pretty much beyond explication. Yet once you've entered the world of this novel, as George Steiner has put it, "almost everything else on your bookshelf will start looking thin."

What: Novel. *When:* 1932. *Reading Note:* The very first sentences will give you a fine sense of the bewildering reach of Powys's imagination: If your mind can move from a third-class carriage at the Brandon railway station to "the deepest pools of emptiness between the uttermost stellar systems" with a sense of both interest and humor, and without succumbing to vertigo, you're in for an uncommon, bewitching reading experience. *Also By: Wolf Solent* (1929). *Weymouth Sands* (1934). *Autobiography* (1934). *Maiden Castle* (1936). *Owen Glendower* (1940). *Porius* (1951). *Visions and Revisions* (1955). *Further Reading: A Glastonbury Reader*, edited by John Matthews. *Try: Little, Big* by John Crowley (see page 187). *The Cornish Trilogy* by Robertson Davies. *Strandloper* by Alan Garner.

"The realm of John Cowper Powys is dangerous. The reader may wander for years in this parallel universe, entrapped and bewitched, and never reach its end." —Margaret Drabble

The House of Life
Mario Praz (1896–1982)

Chambers of the Imagination

Mario Praz was an Italian critic with a penchant for English literature; he spent a decade between the wars teaching in British universities before returning to Rome to continue his professorial career. In addition to his command of literary scholarship (which produced *The Romantic Agony*, the best known of his many books), Praz was a connoisseur of antiques and domestic décor; indeed, he composed a quirky and magnificent *Illustrated History of Furnishing from the Renaissance to the Twentieth Century*. His intelligence seemed to find its true definition inside the suite of the apartment, in a palazzo on the Via Giulia in

Rome, in which he lived for many decades, beginning in 1934. Within and upon its walls he carefully set the pieces of furniture (much of it Empire), pictures, sculptures, and curios that together constellated his sensibility.

In form, *The House of Life* is a simple tour of the author's home—room by room, exquisite object by exquisite object—with learned digressions into a collector's recondite passions or a scholar's erudition. Each piece has its own history, as well as an added significance supplied by its place in Praz's memory, a value that is enhanced by the sophisticated style of the author's reminiscence. What seems at first a circumspect, dutiful survey of possessions grows into a many-layered narrative of intuition and serendipity in the pursuit of beauty and personal purpose, a tale as rich and subtle in psychology and expression as the later novels of Henry James. Through Praz's sketches of his past we inhabit Manchester and the English countryside, Rome at peace and war, and the intellectual landscapes of an aesthete's personal culture. We are introduced, through a packet of letters discovered tucked away in what was once his daughter's bedroom, to intriguing intellectual colleagues such as the novelist Italo Svevo, the philosopher Benedetto Croce, and the gifted English author Vernon Lee (the excerpts from her mentoring letters alone, tellingly illuminating her correspondent's "painful slow emergence out of the unreal self of first youth into the reality, prosaic but comfortable and let us hope *useful*, of mature age," are worth the price of Praz's book all by themselves).

We spend hours with the author in his quests through the catalogs of antique dealers and auction houses, enjoying vicariously what James himself called "the mysteries of ministrations to rare pieces." And we recognize at last in this house of life both the temper of genius and the soulfulness of taste, and see the apartment on the Via Giulia as what Praz himself, in writing this singular and original personal testament, proved it to be: "a mould of the spirit, the case without which the soul would feel like a snail without its shell."

What: Autobiography. *When:* Published in Italy in 1958; English translation by Angus Davidson, 1964. *Reading Note:* This is a slow book, requiring patience to reveal its aesthetic pleasures. *Also By: Unromantic Spain* (1928; Praz's own English translation published in 1929). *Try: A House in Bryanston Square* by Algernon Cecil. *The Lost Library: The Autobiography of a Culture* by Walter Mehring.

History of the Conquest of Mexico
William H. Prescott (1796–1859)

An American Epic to Rival Tales of Troy

Writing in *The New Yorker* more than 130 years after its original publication, Andrew Porter took the measure of this historical masterpiece, placing it in the same literary league as the tales of the Round Table and poems of Homer: "William H. Prescott's *History of the Conquest of Mexico* is the great American epic, as stirring as the Matter of Arthur or the Matter of Troy, as romantic and adventurous as Ariosto or *The Faerie Queene*, and with the added charm and interest of being true." Indeed, the events that Prescott chronicles—those surrounding Hernando Cortés's rapid, stunning conquest of the Aztec empire in the early sixteenth century—boast a scale, sweep, and swiftness that would be hard for any writer of fiction to conjure up.

To give the barest outline, the narrative relates the arrival in Mexico in 1519 of a small band of Spanish soldiers under the command of Cortés. Aided by a native woman who became his interpreter and mistress, the invader was quick to recognize and exploit political dissension among the Aztecs. In a matter of weeks, he marched on the capital, Tenochtitlan (modern Mexico City). Despite his modest force, Cortés quickly subjugated Montezuma's powerful empire, in no small part because the Aztec chief believed the Spaniards to be supernatural beings, descendants of the god Quetzalcoatl. It is a story of fierce battles, bloody losses on both sides, and fateful reversals of fortune.

Such a précis gives no adequate sense of the riveting strangeness of the incidents, characters, calamities, villainy, and heroism Prescott portrays. Based on prodigious research in Spanish archival documents and other primary sources, Prescott's work is historically accurate in its large details (although his view of the Aztecs is subject in some degree to the assumptions of his nineteenth-century

19th-century engraving of Cortés and Montezuma

New England background and perspective). Yet, for the common reader, the admirable diligence of his scholarship is secondary to what Daniel J. Boorstin has termed his genius for the epic: "Though Prescott has been called the nation's first 'scientific historian' for his use of manuscript sources," the longtime Librarian of Congress wrote, "he would live on as a creator of literature." Prescott's *History* remains a stirring and compelling account of an extraordinary conquest.

What: History. *When:* 1843. *Also By: The History of the Reign of Ferdinand and Isabella, the Catholic* (1837). *History of the Conquest of Peru* (1847). *Further Reading: The True History of the Conquest of New Spain* by Bernal Díaz del Castillo, a firsthand account of Cortés's campaigns and one of Prescott's sources. A fascinating biomedical perspective on the Aztecs' fall is presented in William McNeill's *Plagues and Peoples* (see page 539). *Try: The War with Hannibal* by Livy. *Footnote:* Prescott never actually saw Mexico. While attending Harvard College, he was virtually blinded in a freak accident. His vision may have been impaired, but his mind and motivation were not; inspired by his fascination with Spanish history, he embarked on a scholarly career. Secretaries would read relevant materials to him, and Prescott would construct whole chapters in his head before transcribing them via a special apparatus called a noctograph, a frame with parallel wires to guide a writer's hand.

A Palpable God
Reynolds Price (1933–2011)

Scripture Rescripted

" Thirty Stories Translated from the Bible, with an Essay on the Origins and Life of Narrative": the subtitle accurately describes the

contents of this book, but gives no hint of the profound surprises it delivers. Reynolds Price—best known for his novels of the American South—reinvigorates texts from the Old and New Testaments, dispensing with the bland

and bloodless language that is the legacy of translation-by-committee. In Frederick Buechner's words, "By removing centuries of stylistic varnish, he has stripped them down to something approaching their original rough-hewn and reckless power, making it possible for us to hear them almost as if for the first time."

Included are passages from Genesis, Exodus, Judges, Numbers, Kings, and all four Gospels—including an astounding version of the entire Gospel of Mark that reveals the bewilderment and fear that shadows faith. Price's introductory essay—speculating on the origins of mankind's unquenchable need to tell and hear stories ("second in necessity apparently after nourishment and before love

A PALPABLE GOD

REYNOLDS PRICE

THIRTY STORIES TRANSLATED FROM THE BIBLE
WITH AN ESSAY ON THE ORIGINS
AND LIFE OF NARRATIVE

and shelter")—is filled with provocative and fecund meditations on human nature, consciousness, and the enduring resonance of sacred story. His masterful, literal, spare, incisive renderings of the scriptural texts he has chosen are filled with revelations, reinvesting holy words with a sense of power and wonder.

What: Religion & Spirituality. *When:* 1978. *Also By:* Fiction: *A Long and Happy Life* (1962); *Kate Vaiden* (1986). Nonfiction: *Clear Pictures* (1989); *A Whole New Life: An Illness and a Healing* (1994); *Three Gospels* (1996). *Try:* The Bible (see page 76). *The Book of Job,* translated by Stephen Mitchell (see page 78). *The New Testament: A Translation* by David Bentley Hart.

Clockers
Richard Price (born 1949)

The Inner Life of the Inner City

Richard Price's novels pulse with urban life, sweeping us through neighborhoods in which the forces of crime and punishment are both unleashed and obscured. Like most of Price's mature works, *Clockers* features a plot that follows a police investigation, but the framework of law and order is no match for the confusion and drama of his characters' lives, whether those characters are cops, criminals, or others caught in the crossfire of the inner city. And it would be a mistake to categorize Price's work by the convenient labels the milieus of his tales might suggest: "I've always resisted my stuff being cubby-holed as 'Crime' or 'Thriller' or something like that," Price has said. "I certainly use elements of those kinds of books, but for me it's a matter of convenience. I'm just sort of glomming onto the investigation of a crime as the best horse for me to ride through a very complex landscape." That

complex landscape is the American inner city at the end of the twentieth century, and no one has traced its gritty trials and small-time tragedies better than Price.

In *Clockers*, the setting is the fictional locale of Dempsey, New Jersey, not far from Newark and Manhattan. Although the novel boasts a broad cast of vividly drawn characters, its two main protagonists are Strike, a drug dealer intent on climbing what might be called the management ladder of his trade, and Rocco Klein, a veteran detective in his early forties, yet nearing retirement. Strike deploys his posse of adolescent "clockers" (street-corner cocaine dealers) with a worry for detail that consumes him; like middle managers everywhere, he carries his job around in the pit of his stomach, in the form of an ulcer he calms by swigging vanilla Yoo-Hoo (the vanilla flavor, by the way, invented by Price). Klein is a young man with an old man's fatigue, desperate to start a new life but immured in the only one he knows. Both men navigate the heres-and-nows of their respective responsibilities beneath the looming—almost religious—specter of a different reality that each can sense but not quite grasp: a life not governed by the adrenaline-laced demands of dealing with homicides or the ad hoc alertness demanded by the world of the "two-minute clockers."

The plot hangs on a murder that, stunningly, Strike's upstanding half-brother, Victor, confesses to. Convinced Victor is protecting Strike, Rocco is determined to prove the latter's guilt. When the certainties of both Rocco and Strike are rendered moot by events, the two play cat and mouse as they struggle to invent a common language they don't quite realize they need. Their personal dramas unfold on a larger canvas of city experience that is colored with street-smart dialogue and alive with violence and humor. Price observes family

dynamics, police procedures, and neighborhood lassitudes and urgencies with unblinking attention, and sweeps them all into a fiction of page-turning intensity. Like Dickens and Zola, he is a storyteller whose eyes and ears naturally capture the fugitive emotions and details that can define characters and customs; he shares with them as well a novelistic intelligence that is magnanimous in the exact sense of the word.

What: Novel. *When:* 1992. *Also By: The Wanderers* (1974). *Freedomland* (1998). *Samaritan* (2003). *Lush Life* (2008). *Further Reading: The Corner* by David Simon and Edward Burns. *Try: Our Mutual Friend* by Charles Dickens. *The Young Manhood of Studs Lonigan* by James T. Farrell. *Manchild in the Promised Land* by Claude Brown. *Adaptation:* Spike Lee adapted *Clockers* for the screen in 1995. *Footnote:* Price has also won acclaim for his writing for film (*The Color of Money; Sea of Love*) and television (*The Wire*).

IN SEARCH OF LOST TIME

SWANN'S WAY • WITHIN A BUDDING GROVE • THE GUERMANTES WAY • SODOM AND GOMORRAH • THE CAPTIVE • THE FUGITIVE • TIME REGAINED

Marcel Proust (1871–1922)

A Voyage of Discovery

"For a long time I would go to bed early." So, modestly, begins Marcel Proust's enormous excursion into wonderlands of memory, time, consciousness, and love. Imagine sitting on a shore, contemplating a vast and placid sea; imagine the waves slowly coming up to lift you off the sand and pull you gently toward the unfathomable deep, as a steady current lures you into regions of new sensation and meaning. That's what reading Proust's ocean of words is like, for those with the patience and daring to let themselves be carried away.

In Search of Lost Time (known in earlier English translations as *Remembrance of Things Past*) comprises seven novels, originally published in France in seventeen volumes between 1913 and 1927. Each of the books is suffused with shifting colors of theme and mood as the narrator—we will call him Marcel, although the text itself is never quite definitive on this point,

Marcel Proust, ca. 1910

leaving him unnamed—weaves his expansive tapestry of sentiment and sensibility across roughly fifty years, beginning around 1870. Recurring characters appear throughout the work's three thousand pages in an elaborate choreography of social and sexual relations. Places, importantly, are given the same repeating presence, evoking Marcel's memories and aesthetic rumination.

The people animating Marcel's narrative include his immediate family of mother, father, grandmother, and great-aunt; their neighbor in the country, the cultivated Charles Swann, whose sophistication will be undone by his attachment to the former courtesan Odette de Crécy; Swann and Odette's daughter, Gilberte, the narrator's first infatuation; the Duchesse de Guermantes, another neighbor, whose name and nobility will introduce Marcel into a glittering circle; the Verdurins, minor socialites whose calibrated snobbishness makes their coterie a source of ongoing comedy; Robert de Saint-Loup, a glamorous soldier who fascinates Marcel; Albertine Simonet, the object of Marcel's desire and, ultimately, obsession; and the Baron de Charlus, an impolite aristocrat who shocks polite society with his immersion in the sexual underworld of the age. If Charlus becomes flagrant in this last regard, he has no shortage of furtive companions among Proust's characters; assuredly, the vagaries and varieties of erotic attachment the author skirts, suggests, and embraces in the course of his narrative are one of Proust's most sensitive legacies. As with desire, so with art: The examples of the writer Bergotte, the composer Vinteuil, and, especially, the painter Elstir infiltrate Marcel's aesthetic ambition with lasting effect.

What happens to fill three thousand pages? Well, from one point of view, not much: There are affairs and assignations, salons and soirées and balls, walks in the countryside, journeys to resorts at the sea, travel to Venice, the comings and goings of generations—births,

illnesses, death. But mostly, Marcel thinks, and broods, and daydreams, mapping his states of mind and measuring his feelings and anxieties, from superficial affections to intricate jealousies, and then turning them to a different angle and measuring them again. And again. He observes the emotions of others and how they are represented in society, be it intimate or public. He contemplates landscapes and meditates on music and art, always looking for ways of seeing that summon the sensation of past experience and thereby make Time an ally of consciousness, rather than its enemy. Miraculously, he gives Time itself a tangible being in the material world—in his childhood bedroom, in a hawthorn bush, in a chamber at a seaside resort, in a vista of trees on the horizon—that imbues it with the presence of a place or, deeper still, the pervasiveness of a dimension:

A feeling of vertigo seized me as I looked down beneath me, yet within me, as though from a height, which was my own height, of many leagues, at the long series of the years.

All of this unfolds slowly. The writing is slow, and so is the reading: Traversing all of *In Search of Lost Time* is not an easy expedition, for what the author does from the start is layer Time into what seem simple episodes, like the one that opens the book, in which the narrator is trying to fall asleep. Of course, it isn't really the narrator we're observing, but his younger self, upon whom the narrator is looking back in retrospect. Yet Proust does so with a variability of perspective that makes the Marcel on the page seem six years old in one clause and sixty in the next. The shifting of planes of Time within a single sentence is one of Proust's most pervasive innovations, and it allows him to render events with all the nuances that turn them, ultimately, into experience. It is a sleight of hand he repeats on nearly every page of the seven novels, and it is this steady translation of incidents from "this changing realm of fact to the steady realm of thought"—to use a phrase Henry James once applied to a different context—that makes *In Search of Lost Time* such a singular achievement. This continuous act of translation allows the author to articulate insights into memory, love, identity, social poise, and social poses—into Time and the art of living—with extraordinary fidelity to the reader's own inner life. For none of Proust's wisdom is unfamiliar, exactly; we encounter it again and again in his pages with a shock of recognition, because his perceptions echo with something we seem to know but have never given proper scrutiny. That makes the novelist's intelligence anything but common or easy to come by; indeed, what we come to realize is that quarrying these truths took someone with a miner's sense of labor as well as the artistic dedication to consider our passing pains and pleasures hard enough, and long enough, and slowly enough, to extract meaning from them.

Communing with Proust's intuition and discernment across the months it takes to read his masterpiece is its own kind of therapy. Especially in our present age of digital distraction, it can retune our attention in beneficial ways and enhance our appreciation of our days (it's delightful, but not, on reflection, surprising to know that contemporary philosopher Alain de Botton has written a book called *How Proust Can Change Your Life*; see page 200). But to reap any of this reward, one does have to dive into the water and make a considerable commitment to swim across its immensity. So: Read the "Overture," which begins with the boy in bed, on the border between sleep and waking, and closes, some fifty pages later, with the famous scene in which the form and substance of the narrator's past is conjured by the taste and smell of a madeleine dipped into a cup of tea. Even if you get no farther, you will have at least sampled the flavor of this exceptional work. If you want to continue in order to savor all its richness, set a regimen of ten pages a day, and keep to it (and if you can find a partner to read in parallel, so much the better; your conversations will be an extra bounty).

Except to say it is unlike any other reading experience you'll ever have, it's hard to describe the cumulative effect of reading all of *In Search of Lost Time*. Perhaps the best way is to invoke the words of the painter Elstir, who, a third of the way through the work, offers a lesson the narrator Marcel immediately ignores, but that the writer Marcel, by the end of this long novel whose real subject is the development of the knowledge needed to write it, comes to hold dear:

"We do not receive wisdom, we must discover it for ourselves, after a journey through the wilderness which no one else can make for us, which no one can spare us, for our wisdom is the point of view from which we come at last to regard the world. The lives that you admire, the attitudes that seem noble to you, have not been shaped by a paterfamilias or a schoolmaster, they have sprung from very different beginnings, having been influenced by everything evil or commonplace that prevailed round about them. They represent a struggle and a victory. I can see that the picture of what we were at an earlier stage may not be recognisable and cannot, certainly, be pleasing to contemplate in later life. But we must not repudiate it, for it is a proof that we have really lived, that it is in accordance with the laws of life and of the mind that we have, from the common elements of life . . . extracted something that transcends them."

What: Novels. *When:* 1913–27. *Edition:* D. J. Enright's 1992 revision of Terence Kilmartin's 1981 reworking of C. K. Scott Moncrieff's translation (originally published between 1922 and 1931) is the best choice for the work as a whole. *Also By: Pleasures and Regrets* (1896). *Jean Santeuil* (1952). *Letters of Marcel Proust,* edited and translated by Mina Curtiss (1949). *Further Reading: Proust's Way: A Field Guide to "In Search of Lost Time"* by Roger Shattuck. *Monsieur Proust* by Céleste Albaret. *Marcel Proust: A Life* by William C. Carter. *Try: Praeterita: The Autobiography of John Ruskin. The Waves* by Virginia Woolf. *Adaptations:* Volker Schlöndorff's 1984 film, *Swann in Love,* focuses on the relationship between Swann (Jeremy Irons) and Odette (Ornella Muti). Raoul Ruiz's 1999 adaptation, *Time Regained,* is more ambitious in scope and impressive in its achievement. Although never filmed, Harold Pinter's *Proust Screenplay* has been published in book form; it is a remarkable distillation of the source material.

The Golden Compass
Philip Pullman (born 1946)

Unparalleled Adventures in a Parallel World

A girl and a moth are stealing through an imposing dining hall on their way to the Retiring Room, the private chamber of the Scholars of Jordan College, Oxford. On a mission of mischievous espionage, they quickly discover more than they bargained for, stumbling on an assassination plot and eavesdropping on the explorer Lord Asriel's description of his researches into magnificent celestial, scientific, and metaphysical mysteries in the Far North.

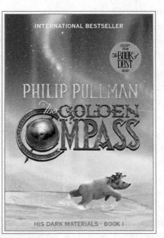

That's the opening of *The Golden Compass*, the start of a breathless adventure that soon has readers turning pages at a frantic pace. The girl is twelve-year-old Lyra Belacqua, a supposed orphan, and the moth is, for the moment, the shape taken by her "dæmon," Pantalaimon, in one of his myriad temporary incarnations. The most inspired creations in this transporting tale of a parallel universe resembling an enchanted version of our own, dæmons are manifestations of the inner life—embodiments of the soul—in animal form. For children and adolescents, the form a dæmon takes is constantly shifting, while for adults it is fixed in a single creature. Giving physical reality to ideas and states of mind through dæmons and other inventions, Pullman animates one of the most alluring imaginative worlds in modern literature.

The plot is a humdinger. Falling into the orbit of the alarming but seductive Mrs. Coulter and leaving Jordan College, Lyra learns more about the mysteries she overheard in the Retiring Room. However, intuiting Mrs. Coulter's role in nefarious experiments with children, Lyra plots a desperate escape. With the protection of a band of maritime nomads known as the gyptians, and the aid of the balloonist Lee Scoresby and the armored bear Iorek Byrnison, Lyra follows her destiny across a realm of ice in pursuit of Asriel.

Into the excitement of the action, Pullman weaves threads of religious and theological questioning that endow Lyra's journey with profound consequence (these made both the book and the film based on it controversial in some circles). And yet the ideas the book engages suggest a respect for the essential purposes of our existence that is filled with a curious and welcome reverence. "Why should a distant theological riddle interest a healthy, thoughtless child?" the Librarian of Jordan College asks about Lyra early on in the book. "Because she is alert to life and its sublime quandaries," is the answer her tale provides. Combining enduring themes with headlong storytelling, *The Golden Compass* is sure to leave you wanting more, no matter your age. Happily, its sequels, *The Subtle Knife* (1997) and *The Amber Spyglass* (2000), which complete the trilogy called His Dark Materials, stand ready to supply it.

What: Children's. Fantasy. *When:* First published in England as *Northern Lights* in 1995; in America as *The Golden Compass*, 1996. *Reading Notes:* Age 12 and up. Any adult with a taste for speculative fiction will also read it with reward. *Also By: The Book of Dust: La Belle Sauvage* (2017) is the first volume of an announced second trilogy set in the same world. Two small volumes offer footnotes to the saga: *Lyra's Oxford* (2003) and *Once Upon a Time in the North* (2008). *Try: A Wrinkle in Time* by Madeleine L'Engle (see page 473). *The Dark Is Rising* by Susan Cooper. *Adaptations:* The 2007 feature film stars Nicole Kidman, Daniel Craig, and Dakota Blue Richards. London's National Theatre mounted a two-part adaptation of the trilogy in 2003. Don't miss the superb unabridged audiobook, performed by the author and a full cast.

Eugene Onegin

A NOVEL IN VERSE

Alexander Pushkin (1799–1837)

The Crowning Masterpiece of Russia's Greatest Poet

Alexander Pushkin is Russia's greatest poet, and *Eugene Onegin* is his finest work, a dazzlingly clever creation that is also a compelling and deeply moving tale. Tatyana, an unsophisticated country girl, falls in love with Onegin, a bored cosmopolitan dandy who spurns her affection to immerse himself in a lonely life on the estate he has inherited from his uncle. Coaxed back into society, he offends Lensky, his best friend and the fiancé of Tatyana's sister, and kills him in a duel. (Pushkin himself would die of wounds sustained in a duel with his wife's alleged lover.) In the aftermath of this tragedy, the consequence of Onegin's petulance and Lensky's jealousy, Tatyana continues to nurse her unrequited love for Onegin while he wanders aimlessly, enveloped in ennui.

Time passes. On Onegin's return to Moscow he is stunned to discover that Tatyana has become the toast of Moscow society. Now it's Onegin who's smitten: "Deep in love, just like a boy," he woos her. But she has married, and the tables have turned: In the end she rejects him, her steadfastness and fidelity to her husband overcoming the ardor that still smolders in her and has at last inflamed Onegin. Love's hopes and heartbreaks have seldom been as poignantly conveyed as they are in Pushkin's drama of ill-fated romance.

In form, *Onegin* is a rarity—a novel written as a poem. It is divided into eight chapters, each of them containing several dozen stanzas. Devised by Pushkin, the "Onegin stanza" consists of fourteen lines, in iambic tetrameter, with the following rhyme scheme: *ababccddeffegg*. Remarkably, the effect of this formality is fleetness and brio: The verse's rhythm makes the telling swift, and the ordering of incident and commentary into discrete stanzas brings a snapshot sequencing to the narration that is modern and seductive. Here is an example from the final chapter:

Alas, *our* youth was what we made it,
something to fritter and to burn,
when hourly we ourselves betrayed it,
and it deceived us in return;
when our sublimest aspiration,
and all our fresh imagination,
swiftly decayed beyond recall
like foliage in the rotting fall.
It's agony to watch the hollow
sequence of dinners stretch away,
to see life as a ritual play,
and with the decorous throng to follow,
although one in no manner shares
its views, its passions, or its cares!

Sir Charles Johnston's 1977 translation, from which the above is taken, admirably captures the dash and effervescence of Pushkin's original, allowing English-only readers to fall under the spell of its singular combination of lyricism, wit, psychological insight, and narrative magic.

Illustration of Alexander Pushkin, ca. 1820

What: Literature. *When:* 1825–31. *Edition:* The Johnston translation is available in Everyman's Library Pocket Poet Series. *Also By:* Pushkin's other major works include *Ruslan and Lyudmila* (1820), *Boris Godunov* (1831), and *The Bronze Horseman* (1833). English readers are well served by *The Bronze Horseman: Selected Poems of Alexander Pushkin* translated by D. M. Thomas and *The Complete Prose Tales* translated by Gillon R. Aitken. *Further Reading:* *Pushkin: A Biography* by T. J. Binyon. *Try:* Vikram Seth's 1986 novel, *The Golden Gate* (see below), employs the Onegin stanza to tell a twentieth-century California tale. *Adaptations:* Tchaikovsky's opera *Eugene Onegin* was first performed in 1879. Ralph Fiennes stars in a 1999 film version of the novel. *Footnote:* Vladimir Nabokov's literal English translation is exhaustively annotated—and exhaustingly idiosyncratic. "To my ideal of literalism," Nabokov defiantly boasted, "I sacrificed everything (elegance, euphony, clarity, good taste, modern usage, and even grammar) that the dainty mimic prizes higher than truth." He said it.

|||||||||||||||||||||||||||||||||||||||||||||| B O O K N O T E ||||||||||||||||||||||||||||||||||||||||||||||

A NOVEL IN SONNETS

The Golden Gate
Vikram Seth (born 1952)

The Golden Gate (1986) is a novel about a group of worthy but unexceptional Bay Area people falling in and out of love on the path to middle age. There's John, a successful but lonely Silicon Valley exec; his ex-girlfriend Janet, a drummer in the band Liquid Sheep; Liz, a lawyer who responds to the personal ad Janet places on John's behalf; Liz's unsettled brother Ed; and John's friend Phil, adrift back east, having floated free of job and marriage. There's a cat named Charlemagne and some pet iguanas, as well as pleasant digressions into wine making, olive picking, and other aspects of 1980s California life. There are also serious forays, via rumination, conversation, and incident, into matters of the heart, celibacy and sexual identity, music and politics, families and friendships—even, from time to time, into the narrator's concern about the manner in which he's relating his tale: in fourteen-line tetrameter stanzas (690 of them!), rhymed *ababccddeffegg* to match the form of the novel's inspiration, Charles Johnston's translation of Alexander Pushkin's *Eugene Onegin* (see above).

You'd think the verse's intricate form would hinder Seth's storytelling, but you'd be wrong; his rhymes lead us so fleetly through the action that it is hard to put the book down (even the table of contents, summarizing the action of each chapter without breaking the Onegin stanza mold, is replete with interest and invention). The novelist's affectionate understanding of his characters is dispensed with the same generosity as his linguistic gifts, making the book a marvel of human sympathy as well as literary ingenuity. Amusing, clever, and artfully true to life, it's one of the most enticing novels you'll ever pick up. As Gore Vidal put it, "The Great California Novel has been written, in verse (and why not?): *The Golden Gate* gives great joy."

Excellent Women
Barbara Pym (1913–1980)

"A 20th-Century Jane Austen."
—*Harper's Queen*

Sometimes fiction can be way too loud: Stylistic effects and outrageous behavior are paraded before us as if it is only sensation a reader seeks. But there can be great literary pleasure in quietness, and few modern novelists have exuded that Austenite virtue with the effectiveness of Barbara Pym. Although her novels of unassuming gentlewomen, anthropologists, curates, and other members of the slightly distressed gentry have an immediate appeal by dint of their comedy, measured style, and sanity, it is Pym's sympathy for both the goodness and the loneliness of her characters that has made readers welcome her as a kind of confidante. It's comforting to know that someone as alert to human foibles as this author can recognize that the circumscribed experience of careful, patient people is as worthy of attention as the lives of adventurous or unscrupulous protagonists.

Excellent Women is the story of Mildred Lathbury, a clergyman's daughter and thirty-something spinster in 1950s England who occupies herself with churchgoing, jumble sales, and "oversight" of the comings and goings of her neighbors. Excitement arrives in the form of the anthropologist Helena Napier and her debonair husband, Rocky, who move into Mildred's world, broadening its society and its sense of romantic possibility. The amorous inclinations of the vicar, and of Mildred herself, move the plot along, yet it is not action but observation—suffused with psychological insight, gentle satire, and high comedy—that turns the pages.

Pym's second novel, *Excellent Women* appeared in 1952. She published four more books in the next decade before her career went into sudden eclipse, her deceptively modest creations deemed too tepid for the fervid energies of swinging London in the 1960s. It was not until 1977, when Lord David Cecil and Philip Larkin independently championed her work in a *Times Literary Supplement* feature on the most underrated novelists of the century, that Pym again found a publisher for new work and saw all her earlier books returned to print to wide popular and critical acclaim. As legions

Barbara Pym, 1979

of readers have since discovered, she certainly deserves both.

What: Novel. *When:* 1952. *Also By: Jane and Prudence* (1953). *Less Than Angels* (1955). *A Glass of Blessings* (1958). *Quartet in Autumn* (1977). *A Very Private Eye: An Autobiography in Diaries and Letters* (1984). *Further Reading: A Lot to Ask: A Life of Barbara Pym* by Hazel Holt. *Try: Cranford* by Elizabeth Gaskell (see page 310). *Pomfret Towers* by Angela Thirkell. *Hotel du Lac* by Anita Brookner.

Gravity's Rainbow
Thomas Pynchon (born 1937)

A Postmodern Baggy Monster

To crib from Walt Whitman: *Gravity's Rainbow* is large; it contains multitudes. From the opening line—"A screaming comes across the sky"—Thomas Pynchon's phantasmagoria of arcane knowledge, low humor, high anxiety, and pop culture leads the reader through a disorienting and exhilarating series of imaginative theaters in the waning days of the Second

World War. We move from London to the French Riviera and across Europe, following the misadventures of a US Army intelligence operative named Tyrone Slothrop. Slothrop possesses a peculiar gift of prophetic power: Locations of his erotic encounters in London precisely map the sites of imminent German V-2 rocket strikes (the rainbow of the book's title is the arced vapor trail of these deadly missiles). When the predictive accuracy of Slothrop's peccadilloes is discovered by a secret Allied psychological warfare agency, it sets off a series of events sufficiently elaborate and bizarre as to defy ready summarization—and nearly to defy the contours of the book itself. Traveling along the dozens of digressive byways of plot Pynchon concocts for his cast of hundreds, the reader is immersed in a landscape of detailed learning that encompasses engineering, mathematics, and the occult, to say nothing of a labyrinthine network of allusions literary, cinematic, and musical (there are also lots of silly songs, a Pynchon trademark). It's nearly eight hundred pages of comedy, science, history, psychology, and sexual shenanigans that portray the entropic unraveling of Western civilization as it might have been conceived by Hieronymus Bosch.

Although it has been hailed as a masterpiece of authorial ambition on a par with Joyce's *Ulysses* (see page 422), and has defeated as many intrepid readers, Pynchon's novel is more freewheeling than that modernist icon. *Gravity's Rainbow* is entirely postmodern—and groundbreakingly so—in its virtuosic orchestration of disparate materials into a kind of symphony of theme and variation that embodies rather than expresses its sense of paranoia and conspiracy about the ways of a disordered world (for what are paranoia and conspiracy but a desperate hope for an order that isn't apparent on the surface of things?). It may seem odd to say, but Pynchon's controlled, carefully calibrated mayhem calls to mind Henry James's instruction to aspiring novelists in "The Art of Fiction": "Try to be one of the people on whom nothing is lost." Whereas James applies his preternatural attention to the world of social relations and its private resonances, Pynchon applies his own to society itself, and even history, treating both as organisms with their own cryptic laws to be observed, dramatized, mocked, and mistrusted. Everything from bad jokes to thermodynamics is grist for his mill, and what that mill produced, in the case of *Gravity's Rainbow*, is among the most distinctive and influential works in American fiction.

What: Novel. *When:* 1973. *Award:* National Book Award, 1974. *Also By: V.* (1963). *The Crying of Lot 49* (1966). *Vineland* (1990). *Mason & Dixon* (1997). *Against the Day* (2006). *Bleeding Edge* (2013). *Further Reading: A "Gravity's Rainbow" Companion: Sources and Contexts for Pynchon's Novel*, edited by Steven C. Weisenburger, is a worthwhile investment. *Try: Pale Fire* by Vladimir Nabokov. *Infinite Jest* by David Foster Wallace. *White Noise* by Don DeLillo. *Footnote:* The famously reclusive Pynchon, who refuses to be photographed, has done three guest appearances on *The Simpsons*; his animated character appears with a paper bag over his head.

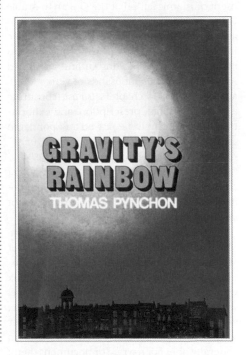

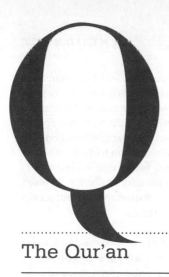

The Qur'an

"God is aware of all you do."

As the fundamental text of Islam, the Qur'an (or Koran) holds a revered place in the religious life of nearly two billion people around the globe. It also occupies a place in the ideological tumult of our age, where its messages are often distorted by fear, false assumptions, and misbegotten advocacy. It is a primary element of Islamic faith that the Qur'an in Arabic is the verbatim word of God, possessed of an authority no translation can convey. "We have made this (Qur'an) easy in your tongue," God assures the Arabic-speaking faithful (in Ahmed Ali's rendering). Its thousands of verses (*ayat*), arranged into 114 chapters (*suras*), constitute a body of wisdom, prescription, and exhortation that is meant to be prayed and pondered as much as read. In fact, the word "Qur'an" springs from the root meaning "to recite," and the intricate rhyme and rhythmic energy that characterize the original Arabic—difficult if not impossible to mimic in English—are no doubt an aid to recitation of the verses.

The Qur'an collects the divine guidance Muslims believe was revealed to the prophet Muhammad beginning in AD 609 and continuing until his death in AD 632. The book was given its canonical form and sequence, which is neither chronological nor thematic, two decades later. Although its verses refer to historical and religious events, the Qur'an generally does not narrate or document them; rather, it calls attention to them to explain their significance. Interpretation and devotional encouragement are privileged over storytelling. The distinctive structure, latticed on a framework of invocations and injunctions, can make the Qur'an daunting reading. What one gets in place of more familiar narrative is an interleaving of imagery and instruction enjoining obedience to God, righteous conduct, and acceptance of both human frailty and divine mercy. (When violence appears in the Qur'an, it strikes a dissonant chord, for the persistent music of the verses resounds with the need for compassion and forgiveness.)

In its first words, the Qur'an addresses God—"All praise be to Allah, / Lord of all the worlds, / Most beneficent, ever-merciful, / King of the Day of Judgement"—and from the outset, the import of His will and His relationship to the reader is clear, and settled. Most of the book that follows is His direct address to the faithful. Core to His message is the idea that Islam is the culmination of the religious history that began with the Pentateuch and continued through the Gospels (many familiar biblical stories are invoked and recast in the Qur'an's pages). Similarly, Muhammad is understood to be the final prophet in the genealogy of monotheistic faith that began with Abraham.

> Say: "We believe in God,
>   and in what has been revealed to us,
>   and in what had been sent down
>   to Abraham and Ishmael
>   and Isaac and Jacob and their offspring,
>   and what had been revealed
>   to Moses and to Jesus
>   and to all other prophets by their Lord.
>   We make no distinction between them,
>   and we submit to Him and obey."

Page from a 14th-century Qur'an written in Naskh script

Myriad beauties of expression and spiritual intention are inlaid in the intricate patterns of repetition and religious exposition we encounter on the page. The cavernous poetry of first and last things is intoned again and again in God's own voice:

Man prays for evil as he prays for good,
for man is hasty.
We have created night and day as two signs,
then We efface the sign of the night,
and make the sign of the day resplendent
that you may seek
the bounty of your Lord,
and know the computation of years and
    numbers.
We have expounded most distinctly every
    thing.
Round each man's neck We have hung his
    ledger of deeds,
and on the Day of Resurrection will present it
as a book spread out (and say):
"Read your ledger; this day
you are sufficient to take your own account."

Qur'an manuscript housed in the Lahore Archaeological Museum, attributed to Hamail Sharif

For the uninitiated, reading the Qur'an can at times feel like a march across deserts of strictures, cheered on by encouragements to right living and correct observance; along the way, welcome oases of imagery and eloquence refresh both mind and heart. (In fact, water itself is a predominant source of imagery in the Qur'an.) Contemplating any sacred work demands a kind of sacramental attention that leaves the world of common reading behind. God works in mysterious ways, and so, too, do the words in which His meanings are transcribed.

What: Scripture. *When:* Ca. AD 652. *Editions:* Ahmed Ali's *Al-Qur'ān: A Contemporary Translation* (revised definitive edition, 1988) is quoted here. See also *The Koran Interpreted* by A. J. Arberry (1955); M. A. S. Abdel Haleem's *The Qur'an: A New Translation* (2004), which exhibits the stately flavor of traditional scriptural renditions in English; and *The Study Quran: A New Translation and Commentary,* Seyyed Hossein Nasr, editor in chief (2015). *Further Reading: The Koran in English: A Biography* by Bruce B. Lawrence. *Approaching the Qur'an: The Early Revelations* by Michael Sells.

Old Glory

A VOYAGE DOWN THE MISSISSIPPI

Jonathan Raban (born 1942)

An Englishman Adrift on the Big Muddy

Jonathan Raban was born in Norfolk, England. When he was seven years old, he read *The Adventures of Huckleberry Finn* and began daydreaming about floating down the mighty Mississippi: "The only real river I knew was hardly more than a brook." Thirty years later, in the fall of 1979, Raban's childhood fantasy became a reality, though the craft in which he eventually set out wasn't like Huck's raft. Instead, it was a sixteen-foot aluminum motorboat that someone had christened *Raban's Nest*. That painfully punning name may be the only bit of inelegant expression in this marvelous account of his river journey.

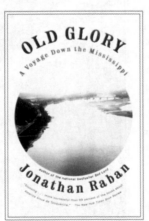

From Minneapolis all the way to New Orleans, Raban tries to go with the flow. "Everything would be left to chance. There would be no advance reservations, no letters of introduction. One would try to be as much like a piece of driftwood as one could manage." The Mississippi, however, turns out to be a lot less placid than expected, and the author a lot less prepared than he might have hoped; other vessels, as well as the river's "mercurial caprices," keep this particular piece of British driftwood spinning. All the while, as Raban explores the lives, past and present, of those who live along its banks, the Big Muddy rolls on.

There is quiet comedy in Raban's clear-eyed assessment of his ineptitudes and miscalculations, and a steady strain of satirical musing resonates from his close attention to the manners and foibles of the natives he encounters. His portraits of people and places are entirely unsentimental, keen to capture exactly what swims into view as he floats down the river or ventures ashore to observe barbecues and mayoral campaigns, meet bikers and bankers, bag catfish and raccoons, pursue amorous digressions, and follow the path of a mythic but moldering past as it wanders into the smaller confines of America's ever nostalgic present. Raban's alertness is winning and invigorating, his prose an instrument of extraordinary perception. Here he is describing a row of businesses propping up the Memphis riverbank: "The bar/restaurants, dotting the ruined waterfront, were working hard to restore a touch of forced glitter to the . . . abandoned city. They had taken on a job that was out of all proportion to their powers."

Like the very best travel writers, Raban lives inside his language in a way that makes it a vehicle for the reader's own reflective, ruminating inner life. In literary terms, he's good company, and *Old Glory* will leave you wanting to ride his sentences on further journeys.

What: Travel. *When:* 1981. *Also By: Hunting Mister Heartbreak: A Discovery of America* (1990). *Bad Land: An American Romance* (1996). *Passage to Juneau:*

A Sea and Its Meanings (1999). Driving Home: An American Journey (2011). Try: The Great Railway Bazaar by Paul Theroux (see page 779). Blue Highways by William Least Heat-Moon (see page 360). Life on the Mississippi by Mark Twain. Mississippi Solo by Eddy L. Harris.

Gargantua and Pantagruel
François Rabelais (ca. 1494–ca. 1553)

A Larger-Than-Life Epic of Learning and Laughter

Combining the ebullient inspirations of intoxication with the scope of an epic, *Gargantua and Pantagruel* is unlike any other book you'll ever read. In fact, its uniqueness has earned its creator a place among the few authors in the history of literature whose names have become adjectives in common parlance. Defined by one dictionary as "marked by or manifesting a gross robust humor, an extravagance of caricature, or a bold naturalism," *rabelaisian* may be the only adjective that begins to do justice to this capacious and irreverent volume. Salaciously funny and frank about the facts of life, *Gargantua and Pantagruel* is a sourcebook of both elaborate satire and earthy humor. As novelist Anthony Burgess once noted, "What Rabelais rubs our noses in is not dirt but the remarkable fact that man is a kind of sewer with a holy spirit hovering over it."

An episodic novel about the adventures of the giant Gargantua, his gigantic son, Pantagruel, the latter's companion, Panurge, and a broad cast of their friends, enemies, and foils, this sprawling mock-heroic romance is both an uninhibited celebration of the physical and an exuberant commendation of the values of Renaissance humanism over the strictures of scholasticism. From the moment that Gargantua is born from his mother's ear bellowing, "Drink, drink . . ." (it takes, we're told, 17,913 cows to satisfy the infant's thirst), we are swept up in outsize merriment. Rabelais, a one-time monk, a doctor, and a secular priest, was renowned for his learning, which leaps and lurches through these pages drunk on multilingual wordplay. Unforgettable set pieces—such as the one describing Pantagruel's servant's six-month wandering through his master's mouth (book 3, chapter 32)—are juxtaposed with scholarly, linguistic, legal, and scientific parodies, and there are numerous sightings of the author's famed creation, the "two-backed beast." Part tall tale, part picaresque, part satire of learning, politics, culture, and manners, *Gargantua and Pantagruel* is an encyclopedia of comic invention that embodies its author's belief that "writing should laugh, not weep, since laughter is of man the very marrow."

Gustave Doré illustration for Gargantua and Pantagruel

What: Novel. Humor. **When:** In French, 1532–52; first English language translation (books 1 and 2) by Thomas Urquhart, 1653. **Editions:** Modern readers should seek a recent translation—those by Donald Frame, M. A. Screech, and Burton Raffel are all superb. **Reading Note:** Browsers will be well rewarded: Dip in anywhere and let serendipity be your guide. **Further Reading:** *Rabelais and His World* by Mikhail Bakhtin. **Try:** *Don Quixote* by Miguel de Cervantes (see page 142). *The Life and Opinions of Tristram Shandy, Gentlemen* by Laurence Sterne (see page 756). *Three Trapped Tigers* by Guillermo Cabrera Infante.

Sparkle and Spin
Ann Rand (1918–2012) and Paul Rand (1914–1996)

A Picture Book That's Giddy with Words

> What are words?
> Words are how what you think inside
> comes out
> and how to remember what you might
> forget about.

The corporate identities that designer Paul Rand created for IBM, Westinghouse, ABC, and Steve Jobs's NeXT made him one of the most acclaimed and influential designers of the twentieth century. Between 1956 and 1970, he also used his gift for simple, colorful, and bold graphic brilliance to illustrate—"realize" is probably a better word—children's books written by his wife, Ann. Together, the couple created volumes that more than six decades later remain distinctive combinations of words and images. Remarkably, the two-dimensional displays of cutouts, collages, and spare representational forms that

Rand deploys across the pages convey an attentiveness that few picture books can match.

Sparkle and Spin celebrates the genius of words and their capacity to express all manner of meaning.

> Some words are gay and bright
> and full of light
> like tinsel and silver
> and sparkle and spin . . .

Inventive and exuberant fun, *Sparkle and Spin* is perfect for parents to share with the youngest kids. The Rands' *Little 1* (1962) works similar magic with numbers.

What: Children's. **When:** 1957. **Also By:** *I Know a Lot of Things* (1956). *Listen! Listen!* (1970). **Further Reading:** *Paul Rand: A Designer's Art* by Paul Rand. **Try:** *Ounce Dice Trice* by Alastair Reid and Ben Shahn. *What Pete Ate from A to Z* by Maira Kalman. *Opposites, More Opposites, and a Few Differences* by Richard Wilbur.

Atlas Shrugged
Ayn Rand (1905–1982)

Here's to the Winners

It is not too much of a stretch to suggest that Ayn Rand's magnum opus has had a more material effect on America in the late twentieth and early twenty-first centuries than any other novel. In literary circles, the work generally has elicited smirks and howls, but it has spoken revelation, if not truth, to power and its brokers. The book's pointed, merit-based reordering of conventional morality has inspired free-market champions and the technocratic elite, trickling down to straighten the intellectual posture of even ambitious politicians. Alan Greenspan, the chairman of the Federal Reserve from 1987 to 2006, first met Rand in the 1950s and became a member of her coterie, an early reader of *Atlas Shrugged*, and a lifelong proponent of her ideas, as his later monetary and regulatory policies would reflect. Paul Ryan, the 2012 Republican vice presidential candidate and subsequently Speaker of the House of Representatives, was once in the habit of giving copies of *Atlas Shrugged* to his interns as Christmas presents, and told one audience, "I think Ayn Rand did the best job of anybody to build a moral case of capitalism."

Is it fair to judge fiction by the real-world ripples it sets in motion through its readers? Not always, perhaps, but in this case, it's exactly its enormous political influence that makes this outsized novel fascinating (*Atlas Shrugged* runs to twelve hundred pages). Rand herself would no doubt have relished debating the book's merits on these terms, for she wrote it as a manifesto of her philosophy, which she called Objectivism and which, at its core, asserts that egoism is—and must be—the true measure of morality. Rand, a White Russian who emigrated from Saint Petersburg to New York in 1926, venerated the successful and spoke of the poor as "takers" and, more chillingly, "refuse." When she died, a six-foot-tall floral arrangement in the shape of a dollar sign was propped up next to her coffin, in—spoiler alert!—a poignant evocation of the last line of *Atlas Shrugged*.

Although she wrote several nonfiction explications of the Objectivist worldview, including *The Virtue of Selfishness* and *Introduction to Objectivist Epistemology*, Rand relied on fiction to promulgate its tenets to popular audiences (her earlier novel, *The Fountainhead*, was also a bestseller). That she succeeded with *Altas Shrugged* is measured not only by its enduring sales (running to many millions of copies),

Ayn Rand, 1957

but also by the frequency with which the book polls near the top of any crowd-sourced list of influential books.

The protagonist of *Atlas Shrugged* is a woman, Dagny Taggart, who runs a transcontinental railroad, but its real hero, and Rand's chief spokesman, is John Galt, a philosophically minded inventor at the center of a cadre of industrialists, scientists, and inventors that, in opposition to a meddlesome government, withdraws from society to a remote desert ranch and watches as the country collapses without its expertise. The resulting dystopia is strikingly portrayed, with a page-turning melodramatic flair that explains part of the narrative's appeal; imagine the classic film of *The Adventures of Robin Hood* turned upside down, with King John the hero, replete with grace, good looks, and all the best lines, and you'll get some idea of the emotional sweep of Rand's saga. Galt's bitterly merry band of industrialists, capitalists, heirs, and high achievers are depicted as dashing, handsome supermen, while politicians, workers, and journalists appear as spineless ingrates. In case readers have missed the ideological framework of the gleefully sensationalized action, the book concludes, more or less, with Galt's escape from hiding to deliver a lengthy radio broadcast—it's seventy-odd pages long—on the virtues of selfishness, the vices of egalitarian impulses and collectivist ideals, and the superiority of his self-appointed crew, "the men of the mind": "We are the *cause* of all the values that you covet," he lectures. "[. . .] We taught you to know, to speak, to produce, to desire, to love."

There is a sweeping extravagance to Rand's telling that is undeniably gripping, and the book's cultural force in our contemporary economic and political climate seems almost gravitational. Yet, all in all, reading *Atlas Shrugged* is something like watching a football game in which one team is so much stronger than the other that it remorselessly runs up the score at will. Which is fine if it is your team, or if you think that a football game takes the measure of life's meaning. Or better than fine, one can only assume, if you believe that such meaning can be captured for cash on the open market.

What: Novel. *When:* 1957. *Also By: We the Living* (1936). *Anthem* (1938). *The Fountainhead* (1943). *Further Reading: Objectivism: The Philosophy of Ayn Rand* by Leonard Peikoff. *Ayn Rand and the World She Made* by Anne C. Heller. *Try: Animal Farm* by George Orwell. *The Moon Is a Harsh Mistress* by Robert A. Heinlein. *Faith of the Fallen* by Terry Goodkind.

Citizen
AN AMERICAN LYRIC
Claudia Rankine (born 1963)

A Poet's Vigilance

" Yes, and this is how you are a citizen," we read as we approach the end of this book about race, identity, language, and memory: "Come on. Let it go. Move on." The phrases echo others sounded on earlier pages in their urging that the consciousness at work—the "you" being addressed—evade engagement with racial hostility, disregard insults and slights, swallow pride in the face of prejudice ignorant or intentional: "Then the voice in your head silently tells you to take your foot off your throat because just getting along shouldn't be an ambition."

Winner of the 2014 National Book Critics Circle Award in Poetry (in a sign of the book's multivalent singularity, it was also a finalist in the Criticism category), Claudia Rankine's remarkable book is about being a citizen in an uncivil union, a relationship that renders one's figure in the world alternatively ominous and invisible. Innovative in both structure and

substance, *Citizen* unfolds at the start in succinct and carefully composed paragraphs that evoke the discourtesies, aggressions, dismissals—call it the realities—that are inherent in both the private and the public lives of people of color in a society shaped by white priorities. The persistent "you" implicates the reader in the poet's recognitions, while Rankine's intimate voice, as if talking to itself, struggles to find meaning in a recurring daze of provocations. The litany of incidents Rankine recites begins in an elementary school classroom and continues into adulthood and professional life, when, for instance, a colleague complains, "his dean is making him hire a person of color when there are so many great writers out there." She distills the anguish of these recollected moments with keen awareness:

As usual you drive straight through the moment with the expected backing off of what was previously said. It is not only that confrontation is headache-

producing; it is also that you have a destination that doesn't include acting like this moment isn't inhabitable, hasn't happened before, and the before isn't part of the now as the night darkens and the time shortens between where we are and where we are going.

In a brilliant résumé of the career of tennis champion Serena Williams, Rankine contemplates the athlete's rare but powerful reactions to flagrant discrimination on the court:

. . . it is difficult not to think that if Serena lost context by abandoning all rules of civility, it could be because her body, trapped in a racial imaginary, trapped in disbelief—code for being black in America—is being governed not by the tennis match she is participating in but by a collapsed relationship that had promised to play by the rules.

Something like a gallery, *Citizen* is unconventional in form as well as force: Photographic images and paintings are juxtaposed with text, and a section of the volume presents scripts for "situation videos." Created with John Lucas, these are collage-like constructions of quotations and meditations on injustice, discrimination, and violence as reflected in specific instances, including Hurricane Katrina, the killings of Trayvon Martin and James Craig Anderson, the death of Mark Duggan at the hands of British authorities, and the policy of stop-and-frisk adopted by urban police forces.

Given such deadly serious subject matter, the book's subtitle—*An American Lyric*—might seem ironic, yet it holds the key to Rankine's most telling achievement: The composed space of reflection and repose that is the domain of lyric poetry provides a magnifying frame for everything *Citizen* examines, as the book's initial paragraph suggests: "When you are alone and too tired even to turn on any of your devices, you let yourself linger in a past stacked among your pillows. . . . [The moon's] dark light dims in degrees depending on the density of clouds and you fall back into that which gets reconstructed as metaphor." Exactly because Rankine is a lyric poet of such extraordinary gifts, she cannot comply with the forgetfulness her citizenship demands: "Come on. Let it go. Move on." In the pages of *Citizen*, she holds fast to what she's seen, brings close what others have felt and suffered, and breathes language into the deadened air of grief, forcing herself—and her readers—to scrutinize the pain that racism provokes, and to stand still and ponder its cumulative injury and sorrow.

What: Poetry. Essays. *When:* 2014. *Also By: Nothing in Nature Is Private* (1994). *The End of the Alphabet* (1998). *Plot* (2001). *Don't Let Me Be Lonely: An American Lyric* (2004). *Try:* Collected Essays by James Baldwin (see page 43). *Voyage of the Sable Venus and Other Poems* by Robin Coste Lewis.

Swallows and Amazons
Arthur Ransome (1884–1967)

Adventure Big as All Outdoors

Swallows and Amazons is the first in Arthur Ransome's classic series of books about the children of the Walker family. In their initial appearance, the Walkers—John (the oldest, at twelve), Susan (ten), Titty (eight), and Roger (seven)—are summering with their mother in England's Lake District, and the lakeland setting seems alive with the anticipation of a holiday. On the first day, Ransome writes,

. . . they had seen the lake like an inland sea. And on the lake they had seen the island. All four of them had been filled at once with the same idea. It was not just an island. It was the island, waiting for them. It was their island. With an island like that within sight, who could be content to live on the mainland and sleep in a bed at night?

When Mrs. Walker sends a letter informing her husband, an officer in the Royal Navy, of the children's desire to sail out and camp by themselves on the island called Wild Cat (a letter followed by separate communications in the same vein from each of his four kids), he responds with a terse but empowering telegram:

BETTER DROWNED THAN DUFFERS IF NOT DUFFERS WONT DROWN

That sets the tone for much of what follows in this enchanting book: children left to their own devices to manage their days and make their own fun.

After piloting the catboat *Swallow* to the island, the Walker children camp amidst the glories of the outdoors and the richness of their fancies. Having made friends with the Blackett sisters, Nancy and Peggy, who live locally and sail a dinghy named *Amazon*, they engage in friendly competition and join forces against the Blacketts' unfriendly uncle James, whom they nickname Captain Flint. Adventure ensues when the

Captain's boat is burgled, but all comes right in the end, setting the stage for ten delightful sequels that similarly celebrate the resourcefulness of young people allowed to get their hands dirty as they master real skills—boating, camping, fishing, and the like—in a delightfully imagined but recognizable natural world.

What: Children's. *When:* 1930. *Also By:* Sequels: *Swallowdale* (1931); *Peter Duck* (1932); *Winter Holiday* (1933); *Coot Club* (1934); *Pigeon Post* (1936); *We Didn't Mean to Go to Sea* (1937); *Secret Water* (1939); *The Big Six* (1940); *Missee Lee* (1941); *The Picts and the Martyrs* (1943); *Great Northern?* (1947). *Try: The Story of the Treasure Seekers* by E. Nesbit. *The Island of Adventure* by Enid Blyton. For additional children's series, see also More to Explore: Best Friends Forever, page 435. *Adaptation:* The 2016 feature film, directed by Philippa Lowthorpe, is the most recent cinematic version.

■ For Frederic Raphael and Kenneth McLeish's *The List of Books*, see page 209.

Period Piece
Gwen Raverat (1885–1957)

The Evolution of Charles Darwin's Granddaughter

This captivating volume—a recollection of an English childhood and youth at the end of the Victorian era—is everything a period piece should be: charming, imbued with both the familiarity of affectionate memory and the exoticism of manners no longer extant, luxuriant in its passage through reminiscence and custom, alertly observed and stylishly composed, suffused with the good humor a satisfied old age can bring. Gwen Raverat's book, first published in 1952, looks back sixty years to life

when her American mother and British father (son of Charles Darwin) brought her up lovingly within Cambridge's well-ordered university society.

"The best of these Darwins," wrote Virginia Woolf of Raverat, her sometime correspondent, "is that they are cut out of rock—three taps is enough to convince one how immense is their solidity." And winning, too, as this welcoming, warmly amusing volume proves:

I was only once spanked that I can remember. I had been put to rest after lunch on my mother's bed, under the muslin curtains, which fell down from the hanging canopy. Now resting is a foolish theory, from which many parents suffer. It is far too exhausting for children, it is really only suitable for the old.

Raverat's splendid drawings enhance her high-spirited narrative, which courses with puckish irreverence through chapters on education, propriety, ghosts and horrors, religion, sport, clothes, and society. Once she left childhood, she became an accomplished artist, earning deserved acclaim for her role in reviving and extending the medium of wood engraving (a story ably told in Frances Spalding's excellent biography).

What: Memoir. *When:* 1952. *Further Reading: Gwen Raverat: Friends, Family, and Affections* by Frances Spalding. *Virginia Woolf and the Raverats,* edited by William Pryor. *Try: A London Child of the 1870s* and *A London Girl of the 1880s* by M. V. Hughes.

The Long Walk
Slavomir Rawicz (1915–2004)

Impossible to Put Down—But Impossible to Believe?

Since its publication at the height of the Cold War, Slavomir Rawicz's account of his 1941 mid-blizzard escape from a Soviet labor camp in Siberia with six fellow prisoners has won legions of devoted readers. It is a chronicle of flight, endurance, and ultimate triumph against extraordinary odds: Poorly clothed, undernourished, on the brink of death, Rawicz and his companions braved the desolate Siberian tundra, icy rivers, the Himalayas, and the great Gobi desert on a four-thousand-mile trek to freedom that brought them to safety in India. They had no map and no compass, only an ax head, a homemade knife, and a fierce determination to survive; their suffering and courage dignify their astonishing, desperate adventure.

Although the veracity of the tale has been called into question based on recently released Soviet records and internal inconsistencies in the book itself (to say nothing of the party's sighting of a pair of Yeti), Rawicz's narrative remains an inspiring and unforgettable reading experience. Whether truth, fiction, or a little of both, *The Long Walk* is bound to be among the most amazing, heroic, and compelling stories you'll ever read.

What: Adventure. *When:* 1955. *Try: Endurance* by Alfred Lansing (see page 463). *We Die Alone* by David Howarth (see page 391). *Adaptation:* Peter Weir's 2010 film, *The Way Back,* is based on the book.

Village School
Miss Read (1913–2012)

The Charming Life and Times of a Country Schoolteacher

Calm is not a virtue much prized by literary critics, yet, as many readers are well aware, a wisely calm book can be both restful and, paradoxically, deeply stimulating. That is the case with the "Miss Read" books, a modest yet addictively absorbing series of novels by Dora Jessie Saint. Saint was a teacher herself, and her working knowledge—and patience with learners young and old—pervades these thoughtful and generous accounts of the vibrant though unspectacular life of an English country schoolmistress and the denizens of Fairacre, her village. Everyday animation fills her pages, and there's fine irony in the narrator's gentle but perspicacious eye as it roams over a slow, small, well-measured life that, like high adventure, is no doubt best experienced in books.

In addition to writing twenty Fairacre books, in which Miss Read narrates her career from her early years in the classroom through her retirement, Saint composed (also using the pen name Miss Read) another well-loved series set in the community of Thrush Green. Each sequence offers the reader the same restorative pleasure: escape into a friendly and familiar fictional landscape where the imagination can relax and happily linger.

What: Novel. *When:* 1955. *Also By: Village Diary* (1957). *Storm in the Village* (1958). *Thrush Green* (1959). *Winter in Thrush Green* (1961). *Try: August Folly* by Angela Thirkell. *Excellent Women* by Barbara Pym (see page 649). *At Home in Mitford* by Jan Karon.

Mumbo Jumbo
Ishmael Reed (born 1938)

What Goes Around Comes Around

M umbo Jumbo may be the most rambunctious novel you'll ever read, a noir mystery steeped in the lore of African American HooDoo, the social tumult and political corruption of the 1920s, Egyptian mythology, and the deep wells of Ishmael Reed's idiosyncratic imagination. Reed's amalgam of erudition, invention, and inspired satire follows ("chases" might be a better word, there being no straight lines in the plot) PaPa LaBas, a "detective of the metaphysical" based in Harlem, as he investigates a murder and attempts to recover a lost manuscript whose contents will provide keys to a bigger puzzle: the outbreak of a "psychic epidemic" called "Jes Grew" that has the nation on the edge of panic.

What's Jes Grew? A phrase Reed borrowed from James Weldon Johnson's preface to *The Book of American Negro Poetry* ("The earliest Ragtime songs, like Topsy, 'jes' grew,'" wrote Johnson, referring to the slave girl in Harriet Beecher Stowe's *Uncle Tom's Cabin*). For the author, Jes Grew represents the life-affirming energies of African American culture; the jazz of the 1920s was one embodiment. A threat to the repressive forces of the Wallflower Order, which in the novel represents the social and political powers that be, Jes Grew "is electric as life and is characterized by ebullience and ecstasy."

Like a learned DJ sampling the metaphorical beats of several traditions, Reed constructs a narrative—enlivened by photographs, drawings, charts, radio dispatches, and typographic variety—that disrupts the conventions of both fiction and scholarship, defying our expectations on nearly every page. In the process, he spins a tale that undermines assumptions of Western thought and questions its hegemony over the minds and bodies of the populace. The storytelling is episodic and polyphonic, larded with historical characters and incidents and spiced with anachronism; footnotes and intellectual digressions embellish the plot with ideas and conspiracy theories. Shrewdly synthetic in its creative logic, *Mumbo Jumbo* is simultaneously fierce and funny, jubilant and angry. Exploding across its own pages like illicit fireworks, the book is a startling and colorful illumination of the tangled history of black-white relations.

What: Novel. *When:* 1972. *Also By: Yellow Back Radio Broke-Down* (1969). *The Last Days of Louisiana Red* (1974). *Flight to Canada* (1976). *New and Collected Poems, 1964–2007* (2007). *Juice!* (2011). *Try: Vineland* by Thomas Pynchon. *I Am Not Sidney Poitier* by Percival Everett. *Big Machine* by Victor LaValle.

Tender at the Bone

GROWING UP AT THE TABLE

Ruth Reichl (born 1948)

___

A Flavorful Memoir of Family, Food, and More

Since Ruth Reichl would grow up to become a *New York Times* restaurant critic and the last editor of *Gourmet* magazine, we might assume she was nurtured in a family kitchen rich with culinary accomplishment. But nothing could be further from the truth. "I had three grandmothers and none of them could cook," she writes in this memoir. Reichl's mother, we soon learn, was even worse with food: Her kitchen misadventures earned her the epithet "the queen of mold."

But if Reichl's palate was acquired later rather than nurtured at home, her gifts as a storyteller were fostered from the start. "I learned early that the most important thing in life is a good story," she says at the outset, and she proceeds to serve up one after another. Her accounts of childhood with her bipolar mother and her reserved book-designer father (the pioneering, page-filling capital "S" that introduces "Stately, plump Buck Mulligan" at the opening of the iconic Random House edition of James Joyce's *Ulysses* is Ernst Reichl's inspiration) are engaging and affectionate even in exasperation. Her detailing of the fond, if eccentric, embrace of

grandparents, housekeepers, and other relations throughout her youth; of the training of her taste at the most unexpected tables; of restaurant work and the emotional aimlessness that followed her college studies—all are funny and magnanimous (and annotated, here and there, with recipes). She is especially good at describing how she learned, finally, to breathe deep when she found herself floating in the thin air of adulthood. Rare among memoirists, Reichl paints her coming-of-age in its brightest, most forgiving colors; if she has chosen to idealize her education, it is not to escape it, but better to use it, both imaginatively and emotionally. Since that is the goal toward which all education strives—is, indeed, the true meaning of "growing up"—her book is as wise as it is nourishing, and heartwarming in every sense.

What: Memoir. *When:* 1998. *Also By: Comfort Me with Apples* (2001). *Garlic and Sapphires: The Secret Life of a Critic in Disguise* (2005). *Not Becoming My Mother* (2009; also published as *For You, Mom, Finally*). *My Kitchen Year* (2015). *Try: The Art of Eating* by M. F. K. Fisher (see page 275). *Home Cooking: A Writer in the Kitchen* by Laurie Colwin. *Toast* by Nigel Slater.

NEW YORK TIMES BESTSELLER

TENDER AT THE BONE

Growing Up at the Table

RUTH REICHL
AUTHOR OF *DELICIOUS!*

___

All Quiet on the Western Front

Erich Maria Remarque (1898–1970)

___

One of the Most Powerful Antiwar Novels of All Time

Encouraged by their teachers and fueled by optimism, patriotism, and the promise of glory, Paul Bäumer and three friends volunteer for what would come to be known as World War I. But the reality of war in the trenches, as

they witness unimagined carnage, leaves them struggling to keep their sanity and to survive. Their hours are measured out in short rations of food and cigarettes, in wounded comrades and dead friends. Their endless battle has no name and is fought according to no plan or purpose. "We were eighteen and had begun to love life and the world;" Paul writes, "and we had to shoot it to pieces. The first bomb, the first explosion, burst in our hearts." Just as the war shatters the young soldiers' illusions, Remarque's novel shattered the mold of the war novel.

Published in Germany in 1929, *All Quiet on the Western Front* rapidly became an international bestseller. Remarque's groundbreaking book portrays the day-to-day horror and desperate futility of combat with searing and unprecedented force. Eschewing the idealized themes—nobility, nationalism, courage—that had been the conventional emphases of war literature, Remarque writes with relentless focus of the perils and privations of the soldiers' lot. Most tellingly, by putting the narration in the all-too-human voice of nineteen-year-old Paul, the author gives his antiwar message a poignancy few writers have equaled; his voice

Erich Maria Remarque, 1939

provides a breathing presence that makes the constant senseless murder it describes all the more real, and all the more appalling.

What: Novel. War. *When:* 1928 in German; first American edition translated by A. W. Wheen, 1929. *Also By:* A sequel, translated as *The Road Back* (1931), follows a different set of characters from the same company as they attempt to reintegrate into society. Also, *Three Comrades* (1937) and *Arch of Triumph* (1945). *Try: The Red Badge of Courage* by Stephen Crane (see page 184). *Good-bye to All That* by Robert Graves (see page 332). *The Naked and the Dead* by Norman Mailer. *Adaptation:* The 1930 film starring Lew Ayres won the Oscar for Best Picture. *Footnote:* Remarque fought for Germany in World War I. Despite its initial success in his homeland, his masterpiece was banned under Nazi rule, and he was stripped of his citizenship.

Lenin's Tomb
THE LAST DAYS OF THE SOVIET EMPIRE
David Remnick (born 1958)

Recovering the Memory of 20th-Century Russia

A s a correspondent for the *Washington Post*, David Remnick (now editor in chief of *The New Yorker*) was in the Soviet Union from 1988 through 1992, reporting the momentous events that marked a second Russian revolution. That tumultuous time culminated in the failed *putsch* of August 1991, when Mikhail Gorbachev fell and Boris Yeltsin and the people of Moscow blocked the path of the conservative resurgence. Remnick's gripping book bears unforgettable witness to that history.

Throughout his chronicle of these large political developments, Remnick surveys the past and present of Soviet society through the experiences of representative men and women, "some well known," he tells us, "others not." Again and again, the ghosts of Stalinist terror

haunt the tense struggles for power under way in Moscow. For instance, in the summer of 1991, the announcement that Gorbachev is "stepping down" for "reasons of health" is heard by a colonel in the Soviet Military Prosecutor's Office as he is on his way to his work site in a birch forest

David Remnick, 2000

twenty miles outside the city of Kalinin: There, half a century earlier, on Stalin's direct order, Soviet executioners "slaughtered fifteen thousand Polish military officers and threw the bodies into rows of mass graves."

We stand with Remnick as he knocks on the door of ninety-year-old Lazar Moiseyevich Kaganovich, the last living member of Stalin's inner circle. We meet Dima Yurasov, born in 1964, who, throughout his youth, with stealth and perseverance, collected the names of nearly 200,000 citizens—out of tens of millions—who had been imprisoned or executed by the Soviet regime (in many cases, the index cards Yurasov wrote on provided the only proof that a man or woman had ever lived or died). Deftly narrating these and many other encounters, Remnick unrolls a canvas of collective memory that was hidden for decades behind the Kremlin's curtain of forgetting. One might well call *Lenin's Tomb* as compelling as a novel, but when history is as accomplished and astonishing as this, most fiction can't hold a candle to it.

What: History. Journalism. *When:* 1993. *Awards:* Pulitzer Prize for General Nonfiction, 1994. *Also By: The Devil Problem, and Other True Stories* (1996). *Resurrection: The Struggle for a New Russia* (1997). *King of the World: Muhammad Ali and the Rise of an American Hero* (1998). *Reporting: Writings from* The New Yorker (2006). *The Bridge: The Life and Rise of Barack Obama* (2010). *Further Reading: The Harvest of Sorrow* by Robert Conquest. *CNN Reports—Seven Days That Shook the World: The Collapse of Soviet Communism* by Stuart H. Loory and Ann Imse. *Try: Secondhand Time* by Svetlana Alexievich.

A Judgement in Stone
Ruth Rendell (1930–2015)

A Chilling Psychological Novel from a Master of the Form

A Judgement in Stone begins with a startling first sentence: "Eunice Parchman killed the Coverdale family because she could not read or write." That statement introduces a two-page description of her "peculiarly literate" quartet of victims, shot down in their home in the space of a quarter hour on a violent St. Valentine's Day. Two weeks later, we're told as the prologue concludes, Eunice was arrested for the murders because, we're reminded, she could not read. "But there was more to it than that."

More to the plot, and more to the telling, for Ruth Rendell writes with a lapidary precision that gives her sentences a resonance both striking and sure. There is no posing in her prose, just an observant, declarative, relentless style in which lyrical impulses and literary allusions are concentrated with telegraphic concision and delivered with confidence. Rendell writes like Dashiell Hammett would have if he had been British, and less romantic; she tightens his wonderful and worldly tough-guy reticence by stripping the sentimentality it doesn't admit to but wears like a fedora. Narrating this tale of an evil housekeeper whose illiteracy spells inexorable doom for the happy family that employs her, Rendell creates an insidious atmosphere of terror, even though we know the outcome from the start. Her insight into the dilemmas of the isolated, afflicted, and socially at risk as well as her skill at probing the mentality of malefactors and their victims are on brilliant display.

A prolific writer, Rendell won many fans for her two dozen or so Chief Inspector Wexford mysteries. Fine as these are, and they are very fine indeed, her stand-alone psychological thrillers, of which *A Judgement in Stone* was her seventh, showcase her true distinction as a novelist. The fourteen novels she wrote under the pen name Barbara Vine treat similarly fraught circumstances of obsession, dysfunction, and deadly disadvantage with chilling effect on the reader. She was a modern tragedian, with something of the fatalistic perspicacity of the ancient Greek practitioners of that art, and nowhere more so than in the book at hand.

What: Novel. *When:* 1977. *Also By:* Psychological thrillers: *A Demon in My View* (1976); *Make Death Love*

Me (1979); *Live Flesh* (1986). Inspector Wexford novels: *From Doon with Death* (1964); *A Guilty Thing Surprised* (1970); *An Unkindness of Ravens* (1985). Writing as Barbara Vine: *A Dark-Adapted Eye* (1986); *A Fatal Inversion* (1987). *Try: A Taste for Death* by P. D. James (see page 411). *The Sculptress* by Minette Walters. *Adaptations:* Claude Chabrol's 1995 film *La Cérémonie* is a better treatment of the original material than the 1986 British version, *The Housekeeper*.

Wide Sargasso Sea
Jean Rhys (1890–1979)

A Prequel to *Jane Eyre*

" I n the deep shade, at the farther end of the room, a figure ran backwards and forwards. What it was, whether beast or human being, one could not, at first sight, tell: it grovelled, seemingly, on all fours; it snatched and growled like some strange wild animal: but it was covered with clothing, and a quantity of dark, grizzled hair, wild as a mane, hid its head and face." In Charlotte Brontë's *Jane Eyre*, that's how readers meet Bertha Mason, the first wife of Edward Rochester, the man Jane is about to marry. The revelation of her existence exposes Rochester's duplicity, disrupting his bigamous wedding to Brontë's heroine. The madwoman in the attic plays a larger role in the novel's plot—but that's another story.

This story, *Wide Sargasso Sea*, imagines the early life of Brontë's strange, benighted character, detailing her childhood and adolescence in the West Indies and tracing her tragic progress to her ultimate confinement in Rochester's Thornfield Hall. Set mostly in Jamaica and Dominica (its author's birthplace), Jean Rhys's book portrays a vulnerable girl caught in the dangerous racial and sexual currents of the slaveholding Caribbean society into which she is born. Far from the monster Rochester loathes and Jane describes with fascinated horror, Rhys's Bertha (known as Antoinette Crossway for most of *Wide Sargasso Sea*) is a sympathetic, tender, poignant figure. *There but for the grace of God*, the reader can't help but think, *goes Jane*. If *Jane Eyre* is the most brooding and beautiful of romantic ballads, lushly orchestrated and achingly sung, Rhys's compact and haunting tale is like a jazz improvisation on the same melody and themes: edgy, exploratory, startling, and unforgettable.

What: Novel. **When:** 1966. *Also By: After Leaving Mr. Mackenzie* (1930). *Voyage in the Dark* (1934). *Good Morning, Midnight* (1939). *Try: Grendel* by John Gardner. *The Autobiography of My Mother* by Jamaica Kincaid. *Foe* by J. M. Coetzee.

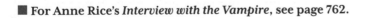

■ For Anne Rice's *Interview with the Vampire*, see page 762.

Selected Poetry
Rainer Maria Rilke (1875–1926)

A Modern Orpheus

P oetry, Rilke says in the first of the fifty-five sonnets he addresses to Orpheus, the mythic master of his art, builds a temple deep inside our hearing. More than most poetic voices, Rilke's—so urgent, intimate, and eerily familiar—seems to intone prayers from that sacred place, enthralling us with a blend of delicacy and strength both seductive and encouraging. We suspect he speaks for us, even when the intuitions his words evoke are not wed to any clear logic. He ennobles our longing with his lyrical evocation of his own. The two lines that conclude his "Portrait of My Father as a Young Man" imply volumes about memory, inheritance, and the transience of every human bond: "Oh quickly disappearing photograph / in my more slowly disappearing hand." Every gifted seventeen-year-old who turns his or her attention to poetry has a little trace of Rilke between the lines, even if the fledgling artist has no acquaintance with his work. As the American poet Robert Hass put it, "That voice of Rilke's poems, calling us out of ourselves, or calling us into the deepest places in ourselves, is very near to what people mean by poetry."

Rilke's masterpieces are *The Sonnets to Orpheus* and *The Duino Elegies*, both published in 1923 (although the former was composed in less than a month, the latter was the product of a decade's labor). Readers may find that lyrics

Rainer Maria Rilke, 1925 (above); 1901 Kolo Moser illustration for the poem "Early Spring" (left)

in *The Book of Hours* (1905), *The Book of Images* (1902–06), and *New Poems* (1907–08) offer somewhat easier entry into his creative realm, but once you've wandered into it, you'll want to linger.

Stephen Mitchell's translations, presented in a bilingual volume (noted below) of selections and accompanied by Hass's splendid introduction, are superb; of the myriad other English versions, Edward Snow's are also worth seeking out.

What: Poetry. When: 1905–26. Edition: Mitchell's *The Selected Poetry of Rainer Maria Rilke* was published in 1982. **Also By:** Rilke's prose is also eloquent: see *Stories of God* (1900), *The Notebooks of Malte Laurids Brigge* (1910), and *Letters to a Young Poet* (written 1902–08, published 1929). **Further Reading:** *Reading Rilke: Reflections on the Problems of Translation* by William H. Gass. **Try:** *Collected Poems* of Wallace Stevens. *The Apple Trees at Olema: New and Selected Poems* by Robert Hass.

Illuminations
Arthur Rimbaud (1854–1891)

The Teenage Genius of French Poetry

He wrote for only three or four years. By the age of twenty he was done with poetry, and he'd moved on to a series of shady jobs around the world, including a spell as a weapons dealer in Ethiopia. But Arthur Rimbaud, the wild and precocious genius of French verse, had already made his indelible mark: The eighty or so poems he wrote in his teenage years have given rise to more than a century's worth of praise, criticism, interpretation, and hero worship. Indeed, the short fuse and bright explosion of Rimbaud's gifts suggest descriptions that wouldn't become current until the era of rock star troubadours that arrived a hundred years after his birth: punk, misfit, drugged-out hippie, gay hero, revolutionary, spoiled brat—the elements of his legend can make him seem all too familiar. And yet his influential poetry retains its strange and thrilling pull.

Illuminations, his most important collection, offers the best introduction to his literary work. Most of its forty-three pieces look like prose; there are no line breaks, and some poems are laid out as a solid block of text. More polished than the erotic and scatological poems of his earliest days, the lines that light Illuminations are packed with an overwhelming wealth of imagery. They deal with love and anguish, the power of nature, the tension between creation and destruction, the delight and disgust Rimbaud felt for city life, and the joy of travel—indeed the French text is studded with words in English and

Young Arthur Rimbaud, 1870

German, which Rimbaud picked up on the road. Illuminations requires us to read slowly and let the poems unlock themselves over time.

Rimbaud wrote much of the work collected in Illuminations in 1871 and 1872, when he was traveling around Europe with Paul Verlaine, his older lover and a deeply inventive poet in his own right. But the visionary poems almost didn't make it into public view, because of plot turns that today would befit headlines of a celebrity-magazine exposé. While they were living in Brussels, Verlaine shot Rimbaud in the wrist and ended up in prison; after the older poet was released, Rimbaud handed Verlaine the manuscript and asked him to find a publisher for it. But Verlaine's estranged wife succeeded in blocking publication for nearly a decade. By the time the poems appeared in 1886, Rimbaud was long gone. But the poems endure, as does the mythic legacy of the tormented, tormenting teenage genius.

What: Poetry. *When:* 1886. *Editions:* In English, notable translations include those of Louise Varese, John Ashbery, and Wyatt Mason. *Also By:* *The Drunken Boat* (1871). *A Season in Hell* (1873). *Letters* (1870–91). *Further Reading: Arthur Rimbaud* by Enid Starkie. *Rimbaud: The Double Life of a Rebel* by Edmund White. *Try: The Flowers of Evil* by Charles Baudelaire (see page 55). The poems of Paul Verlaine. *The Time of the Assassins: A Study of Rimbaud* by Henry Miller.

Midnight in Sicily
ON ART, FOOD, HISTORY, TRAVEL, AND LA COSA NOSTRA
Peter Robb (born 1946)

The Hidden History of Modern Italy, with Meals

This terrifying, tantalizing chronicle of the true if hidden history of Italy from the end of the Second World War to the mid-1990s has all the intrigue of a complicated thriller—and a lot of the pleasure of a trip to Italy, too. Robb's brilliant book is an account of his experiences during sojourns in southern Italy and of his attempts, upon his 1995 return to Sicily from his native Australia, to make sense of the incredible developments that led to the indictment of Italy's longest-lived and preeminent power broker, former Prime Minister Giulio Andreotti. Robb's explication of the Andreotti affair is an exploration of a corruption so pervasive, so powerful, so fantastic, and so fatal that no novelist could have conceived it. It traces a murderous web spun by the Sicilian mafia over several decades, with the entangling complicity of the government, the Vatican, the CIA, and the national and international financial communities—a web that touched on nearly every element of Italian life.

Midnight in Sicily is a jewel of many facets, not the least sparkling of which is the author's astute appreciation of Italian character. His one-paragraph elucidation of the difference between Sicilian and Neapolitan tempers would provide a Henry James with enough human intelligence to inform several complex novels. Erudite enough to offer a wonderful digression on the history of the fork, Robb also knows his way around restaurants, markets, and kitchens, making his attentions to Italian cuisine especially delightful. And what a celebration of the glories of Naples he offers.

Part exploration of the political and social history of southern Italy, part exposition of the dangerous, brave, often subverted efforts of prosecutors and magistrates to loosen the knot of organized crime that strangled the country, *Midnight in Sicily* coheres around the drama of one man's attempt to make sense of patterns of events too large to comprehend by direct observation: "something big and hideous that was working itself out in the dark." To read this extraordinary book is to leave the edifices of fact and data that dominate our conception of modern history and to wander—through Italy's enchanted and romantic landscape— into grand, dangerous palaces of greed, brutality, evil, deceit, cunning, and violence that the Borgias could have built, and would certainly find familiar.

What: Journalism. Travel. History. *When:* 1996. *Also By: M: The Man Who Became Caravaggio* (2000). *A Death in Brazil: A Book of Omissions* (2004). *Further Reading: Excellent Cadavers: The Mafia and the Death of the First Italian Republic* by Alexander Stille. *Try: The Honoured Society* by Norman Lewis. *Falling Palace: A Romance of Naples* by Dan Hofstadter.

Gilead
Marilynne Robinson (born 1943)

Magnanimous Truths in a Small-Town Life

Marilynne Robinson writes slow novels. Her first, the highly acclaimed *Housekeeping*, was published in 1981; *Gilead*, her second, did not appear until nearly a quarter century later. But the slowness that characterizes her fiction is not of the calendar but on the page: It is so carefully composed, in precise language resplendent with illuminations of beauty, impermanence, domesticity, happiness, and spiritual apprehension, that one can imaginatively inhabit paragraphs for hours and never feel the weight of time. She restores to reading—indeed to our inner lives—a contemplative capacity that is rare, welcome, and, in the end, exhilarating.

When *Gilead* finally appeared, it was rapturously received, winning the Pulitzer Prize,

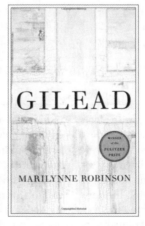

among many other accolades. But to call it the best novel of 2004 would not do justice to the timeless experience its story shapes. The Reverend John Ames, an Iowa preacher who is the son and grandson of preachers, ostensibly sets down these words in 1956, toward the end of his life, as he seeks to leave a legacy for his own young son, seven decades his junior. Knowing he will not survive to see his child grow up to adulthood, Ames is writing his way into the boy's memory: "I wish I could leave you certain of the images in my mind, because they are so beautiful that I hate to think they will be extinguished when I am. Well, but again, this life has its own mortal loveliness." He ponders the relationship between his own father, an ardent pacifist, and his violently abolitionist grandfather. ("He thought we should all be living at a dead run. I don't say he was wrong. That would be like contradicting John the Baptist.") He celebrates the curious satisfactions of his work:

When people come to speak to me, whatever they say, I am struck by a kind of incandescence in them, the "I" whose predicate can be "love" or "fear" or "want," and whose object can be "someone" or "nothing" and it won't really matter, because the loveliness is just in that presence, shaped around "I" like a flame on a wick, emanating itself in grief and guilt and joy and whatever else. But quick, and avid, and resourceful. To see this aspect of life is a privilege of the ministry which is seldom mentioned.

He celebrates as well the simplest pleasures, such as playing catch on a hot summer's day: "I think of leaping after a high throw and that wonderful collaboration of the whole body with itself and that wonderful certainty and amazement when you know the glove is just where it should be. Oh, how I will miss the world!"

In its ruminative examination of a family's disappearing past and an old man's diminishing future, *Gilead* unfolds with the inexorable, quiet majesty of daybreak, filled with the ever-present mysteries of light and grace and goodness.

What: Novel. *When:* 2004. *Awards:* National Book Critics Circle Award, 2004. Pulitzer Prize for Fiction, 2005. *Reading Note: Gilead* delivers its treasures without urgency: You can pick it up and put it down as the spirit moves you across weeks and even months. *Also By:* Fiction: Robinson's 2008 novel, *Home*, revisits characters and incidents in *Gilead* from a different perspective, as does *Lila* (2014). Nonfiction: *The Death of Adam: Essays on Modern Thought* (1998). *When I Was a Child I Read Books* (2012). *What Are We Doing Here? Essays* (2018). *Try: The Tree of Life* by Hugh Nissenson. *A Dresser of Sycamore Trees* by Garret Keizer (see page 436). *Adaptation:* There is a very good unabridged audiobook, read by Tim Jerome.

Hunger of Memory

THE EDUCATION OF RICHARD RODRIGUEZ

Richard Rodriguez (born 1944)

The Weight of the Word

Upon its initial publication in 1982, *Hunger of Memory* was read by many as a kind of policy statement about the schooling of minority students, bilingualism in the classroom, affirmative action, and related themes. It was even billed as such by the publisher; the flap copy of the original edition leads with an encomium from activist Bayard Rustin, which begins, "Mr. Rodriguez's book is must reading for those who wish to deal honestly with the disparities in our educational system and who wish to preserve and improve our public schools." The book was, and remains, controversial, reviled by progressives for its failure to assert the primacy of ethnic identity over a common public language, and championed by conservatives comforted by the author's refusal to accept the assumptions of affirmative action. Yet, while *Hunger of Memory* treats all of the subjects suggested by the above, to read it as a

book of advocacy, as the simple staking out of a set of positions, is to miss the drama of intimacy and eloquence at the core of this uneasy autobiography.

Rodriguez traces the contours of his life with a set of seven essays—meditations, really—on themes of upbringing, language, achievement, faith, ethnicity, academia, and secrecy. The biographical narrative he threads through them is simple enough, circumscribed by home and school; his parents were working-class Mexican immigrants in Sacramento, California, and his elementary teachers were Irish nuns of the Sisters of Mercy.

The boy who first entered a classroom barely able to speak English, twenty years later concluded his studies in the stately quiet of the reading room in the British Museum. Thus with one sentence I can summarize my academic career. It will be harder to summarize what sort of life connects the boy to the man.

Describing that connection is the work these essays do. They mark the milestones of Rodriguez's gradual distancing from the home that reared him and its native tongue, depicting his travels along the ever longer roads his education in English maps for him. After becoming a doctoral candidate in Renaissance literature, he abruptly turns down teaching offers from prestigious universities to avoid complicity in their delight at discovering a scholar who fits a minority profile. He rejects the academic path for a freelance life.

The story of how education can estrange a student from his origins and complicate the ease with which he embraces familial affection is, of course, nothing new (the same sorrows, for instance, are enacted in the pages of *Great Expectations*; see page 221). What's special about Rodriguez's version of the tale is its recognition that the language one's education provides can be not just a mode of learning and expression, but a mode of worry as well, fretful and brooding and aware that it can never—despite a writer's proficiency, even virtuosity—pin enough meaning to the page to make up for what's been left unsaid. Imbuing his prose with this quiet, almost prayerful sense of torment, Rodriguez weighs his themes on a sensitive but often equivocal scale, not avoiding the clear statement of truths so much as approaching truth, and life, with care and reverence. His concentrated, vigilantly composed sentences, their clauses setting off like gentle probes into the mysteries of self and experience, speak to

Richard Rodriguez visits his alma mater, 1982

a faith in words that defines the vocation he assumed in *Hunger of Memory* and has carried with him through three other volumes as striking and enigmatically beautiful as this one.

What: Autobiography. *When:* 1982. *Also By: Days of Obligation: An Argument with My Mexican Father* (1992). *Brown: The Last Discovery of America* (2002). *Darling: A Spiritual Autobiography* (2013). *Try: A Mass for the Dead* by William Gibson (see page 314). *Lost in Translation: A Life in a New Language* by Eva Hoffman.

The Tuscan Year
LIFE AND FOOD IN AN ITALIAN VALLEY
Elizabeth Romer (born 1941)

Savoring the Rhythms and Flavors of the Seasons

Elizabeth Romer's Tuscan adventure began when she and her husband, John, a fellow archaeologist, were in search of a home somewhere between their native England and their digs in Egypt. Fortune brought them to a valley in Italy and the farm of the Cerotti family, who showed them a house they had for sale, made room for them at the lunch table, and invited them into what would become years of friendship. As the Romers soon learned, each of those years followed the same rhythm of agricultural and kitchen observance and activity. This book details the author's education in the Tuscan annual round under the tutelage of *materfamilias* Silvana Cerroti.

Romer is a wonderful writer, relaxed but unfailingly articulate in her vivid descriptions of the sights, sounds, smells, and tastes she encounters as she traverses the culinary calendar in Silvana's footsteps, from the curing of prosciutto in the winter to cheese making in the spring and the gathering of wild mushrooms in the fall. As this family in Italy's heartland honors nature's unvarying course of birth, nurturing, bounty, and death with seasonal traditions, Romer treats us along the way to their accumulated recipes and lore. Life takes solace in the rhythms of such rituals, as Romer discovers to her enduring satisfaction—and as the reader does, too, in her transporting book.

What: Food & Drink. Travel. *When:* 1984. *Also By: Italian Pizza and Hearth Breads* (1988). With John Romer: *The Seven Wonders of the World* (1995). *Try: Leaves from Our Tuscan Kitchen* by Janet Ross and Michael Waterfield. *A Valley in Italy* by Lisa St. Aubin de Téran. *Under the Tuscan Sun* by Frances Mayes. *Footnote:* Do try the book's recipes; they're clearly written, easy to manage, and delicious.

The Walls Came Tumbling Down
Henriette Roosenburg (1916–1972)

An Inspiring True Tale of Nobility in the Wake of World War II

"This is the story of the liberation of four Dutch political prisoners at the end of World War II, and about their trek home to Holland after Russian soldiers had freed them from the prison in Waldheim, a small village in south-eastern Germany." Thus begins this first-hand account of the adventures of three women and one man in the hellish aftermath of the war in Europe.

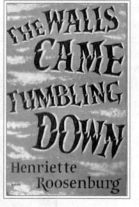

A graduate student at the University of Leiden at the outset of the war, Henriette Roosenburg served as a courier in the Dutch resistance, code name "Zip." In 1944, she was arrested and sent to the Waldheim camp to join the ranks of the condemned *Nacht und Nebel* (Night and Fog) prisoners, where she and many others languished without medical care, adequate meals, or communication with the outside world. Awakened from the nightmare of their confinement by the Russian army in May 1945, Roosenburg and her compatriots, after a series of delays and detours, begin their arduous journey toward the Netherlands. They are without food, funds, or papers; virtues—stripped of all pretense and tempered by the rigors of their trauma—are all that remain in their possession. It is these—nobility, friendship, honor, fortitude, pride in their bloodied but unbowed humanity—that guide them home through the dangerous war-ravaged landscape.

As Noel Perrin has aptly written: "Here is a book full of utterly unselfconscious heroism. Here is an author who shows in the most matter-of-fact way just how generous and brave human beings can be. She even shows, without particularly meaning to, that patriotism can be a solemn and lofty thing. It may be the last refuge of scoundrels, but under the right circumstances it is also the first thought of heroes."

Gripping and beautiful, Roosenburg's memoir is a tale of bravery that will make you care deeply about its protagonists, even make you weep at their ordeal and homecoming. It is one of the unjustly neglected gems of Second World War literature.

What: Autobiography. War. *When:* 1957. *Further Reading:* Noel Perrin's superb essay on *The Walls Came Tumbling Down* can be found in his collection *A Reader's Delight* (see page 209). *Try: The Diary of a Young Girl* by Anne Frank (see page 295). *We Die Alone* by David Howarth (see page 391). *Isabella: From Auschwitz to Freedom* by Isabella Leitner.

Explaining Hitler

THE SEARCH FOR THE ORIGINS OF HIS EVIL

Ron Rosenbaum (born 1946)

A Curious Inquiry into the 20th Century's Heart of Darkness

Adolf Hitler must be one of history's most thoroughly examined figures. Historians, political scientists, psychoanalysts, philosophers, theologians, novelists, and, not least, victims have explored the facts of his life and the facets of his character, the fears he inflamed, the methods of murderous evil he invoked and embodied. And yet, as we learn in this riveting look at attempts to explain this demonic creature looming over twentieth-century history, Hitler still somehow escapes definition, even by those who have studied him most closely. The pioneering Hitler biographer Alan Bullock maintains that the more he learns about his subject, "the harder I find it to explain."

How could such a monster prove so elusive to our understanding? That's the question Ron Rosenbaum poses again and again in *Explaining Hitler*, as he considers how "the search for Hitler has apprehended not one coherent, consensus image of Hitler but rather many different Hitlers, competing Hitlers, conflicting embodiments of competing visions." Indeed, one of the most engrossing aspects of this 1998 work is discovering just how different the myriad "Hitler theories" are. They range from the conviction that he consciously embraced mass murder as his "mission" to a belief that he was the pawn of "irresistible historical forces." There are suppositions of trauma both physical and psychological, as well as hypotheses of deviant sexuality, of encephalitis and syphilis, and of countless other motivations.

Relying on formidable scholarly work and his dynamic reportorial skills, Rosenbaum engages not only the explanations but the explainers in a series of fascinating, at times uneasy interviews. Through encounters with—among others—Daniel Goldhagen, the author of *Hitler's Willing Executioners*; revisionist historian David Irving; George Steiner, the esteemed literary critic and author of the controversial novel *The Portage to San Cristobal of A. H.*; and

Claude Lanzmann, director of the landmark film *Shoah*, an oral history of the Holocaust, Rosenbaum interrogates the past and those who have devoted their lives to exploring its darkness. His restless curiosity and intellectual energy propel us through a dense forest of ideas, mysteries, and recognitions, forcing us to think about the nature and meaning of evil, about determinism and personal responsibility, about the capacities of human nature, and, most tellingly, about the limits of our "faith in an explicable world."

What: History. **When:** 1998. *Reading Note:* Rosenbaum's propulsive, reflexive style can be off-putting at first, but the rewards of following the paths cut by his idiosyncratic energy are considerable. *Also By: The Secret Parts of Fortune: Three Decades of Intense Investigations and Edgy Enthusiasms* (2000). *The Shakespeare Wars* (2006). *Further Reading: Hitler: A Study in Tyranny* by Alan Bullock. *Hitler's Willing Executioners* by Daniel Goldhagen. *The War Against the Jews: 1933–1945* by Lucy S. Dawidowicz. *Try: The Hitler of History* by John Lukacs. *The Portage to San Cristobal of A. H.* by George Steiner.

Adolf Hitler addressing a rally, ca. 1934

Call It Sleep
Henry Roth (1906–1995)

A Bold and Brilliant Novel of Jewish Immigrant Life

. . . .

Standing before the kitchen sink and regarding the bright brass faucets that gleamed so far away, each with a bead of water at its nose, slowly swelling, falling, David again became aware that this world had been created without thought of him.

S o we meet, at the outset, this book's protagonist: David Schearl, six years old, whose consciousness we will follow through several hundred pages as he comes of age in New York City around 1910 and comes to uncertain grips with the slippery, violent, unsettling world of family and immigrant life. This world may have been created with no thought of him, but there can be no doubt that he is thinking of it—ceaselessly, troublingly, painfully. Within that contradiction, Henry Roth taps an imaginative well that makes *Call It Sleep* one of the most distinctive and powerful American fictions of the twentieth century.

Written in the trough of the Great Depression and set among the tenements of New York's Lower East Side two decades earlier, this ambitious, cantankerous, and profoundly autobiographical first novel is ripe with the sensuous realities of the urban setting it powerfully depicts. It is richer still with the ruminations of the young Jewish boy at its center, who attempts to make sense of his existence caught between a devoted mother and a vicious father ("Shudder when I speak to you," that father demands) as well as between the imprecations of urban life and the prayers of religious instruction. Most tellingly, the book is enlivened by David's continuous translation of experience between the mongrel language of the New York streets, presented in jagged dialect, and the Yiddish of his home, which Roth renders into luminous

English—a stunning vernacular that resonates with an almost biblical (in the King James sense) nobility, even when its message is anger or suspicion.

Call It Sleep is not a plucky, tale-of-two-cities immigrant novel, with heartwarming reminiscences of the old country and grandmother's kreplach in the midst of rough-and-tumble New World values. Roth set out to treat the immigrant experience in America with the freshness of literary modernism, and he brings to his fictional New York not a little of the rigor and verve that James Joyce brought to Dublin in *Ulysses*, impelled by a sense of writerly vocation similar to the one memorialized in Joyce's *A Portrait of the Artist as a Young Man*. That's exalted company for any novel, but Roth's debut would not earn such prestige until thirty years after its original release, when it was rediscovered and released as a paperback in 1964, thanks to the efforts of critic Alfred Kazin. It would be another three decades before Roth, at the age of eighty-eight, issued his second novel, having spent the sixty years in between as a tool and gauge maker, an attendant in the psychiatric ward of a New England hospital, and a poultry farmer. Very quickly, three other novels in the quartet *Mercy of a Rude Stream* appeared to acclaim (two were published posthumously). Another posthumous novel, *An American Type*, came out in 2010, putting the final punctuation on what was, in more ways than one, a remarkable career.

What: Novel. *When:* 1934. *Also By: Mercy of a Rude Stream: A Star Shines Over Mt. Morris Park* (1994). *A Diving Rock of the Hudson* (1995). *From Bondage* (1996). *Requiem for Harlem* (1998). *Further Reading: Redemption: The Life of Henry Roth* by Steven G. Kellman. *Try: Jews Without Money* by Michael Gold. *The Adventures of Augie March* by Saul Bellow (see page 66). *The Assistant* by Bernard Malamud.

PHILIP ROTH
(1933–2018)

P hilip Roth burst onto the literary scene in 1959 with *Goodbye, Columbus*, a story collection that won the young author a National Book Award and a reputation as a provocateur, especially when he engaged, with exuberant irreverence, the theme of Jewish life in contemporary America. *Portnoy's Complaint*, published a decade later, poured fuel on the fire lit by his early talent. A raunchy, ribald monologue of one Alexander Portnoy to his psychoanalyst, Dr. Spielvogel (replete with attention to Portnoy's masturbatory ingenuity), the novel unleashed a manic comedy the novelist could clearly no longer contain, and marked his literary celebrity with a sexual stigma it never shed. From the high-spirited celebration of baseball, *The Great American Novel* (1973), through his poignant and harrowing

Philip Roth, 1962

memorial to his father, *Patrimony* (1991) and his singular exploration of the nature of self and history, *Operation Shylock: A Confession* (1993), to *Everyman* (2006), a fierce naturalistic parable of life's diminishing returns, the abundance and variety of his work post-*Portnoy* find common ground in the impulsive verbal energy of his inspiration and the search for themes large enough to concentrate it.

The Ghost Writer
Portrait of the Writer as a Young Man

T en years after *Portnoy's Complaint*, Roth published *The Ghost Writer*, an exquisite short novel in which both irreverence and comedy (and, yes, masturbation, too) are subsumed into a tale that explores with an almost serene sense of creative control all of Roth's earlier themes. The narrator is a forty-three-year-old writer named Nathan Zuckerman, who looks back on his twenty-three-year-old self as he makes a pilgrimage to the Berkshire retreat of his literary master, E. I. Lonoff. The apprentice, whose early stories landed him

in the same sort of hot water that Roth had boiled with *Goodbye, Columbus*, is in search of an artistic father to offer wisdom and guidance now that his relationship with his real father, a podiatrist from Newark, has been strained by Nathan's artistic liberties with fictional family portraits.

Zuckerman's observation of the circumscribed daily life of his reclusive hero ("I don't know anybody. I turn sentences around, and that's it," says Lonoff) and his desperately unhappy wife ("I got fondled by more strangers on the rush-hour subway during two months in 1935 than I have up here in the last twenty years!" says Mrs. Lonoff) opens the young acolyte's eyes to the domestic terrors of artistic dedication. But it is the fantasy he spins around the lovely former student disrupting the Lonoffs' marriage ("It's just—that you bear some resemblance to Anne Frank," Zuckerman tells her) that transforms this short fiction from a simple tale into an intricate, almost perilously inventive imaginative work.

Roth has spent a half century turning sentences around themes of family and independence, ethnic identity and assimilation, artistic vocation and ordinary human pleasures, but he has never turned them quite so gracefully as he does in *The Ghost Writer*.

What: Novel. *When:* 1979. *Edition: The Ghost Writer* was later collected as the first of four sections in *Zuckerman Bound*, which also contains the "sequels" *Zuckerman Unbound* (1981), *The Anatomy Lesson* (1983), and *The Prague Orgy* (1985). *Also By: The Counterlife* (1986). *Sabbath's Theater* (1995). *Try: My Name Is Asher Lev* by Chaim Potok. *Humboldt's Gift* by Saul Bellow.

American Pastoral
Portnoy Meets Tolstoy

It's easy to begin talking about *American Pastoral* by noting its central place in the Zuckerman Saga, a series of nine novels that follow the fortunes of Nathan Zuckerman, a novelist who shares an awful lot of characteristics with his creator (make that ten fictions if you count *The Facts*, from 1988, an ostensible autobiography that opens with a letter from Roth to Zuckerman and closes with one from Zuckerman to Roth). But what's most memorable about this 1998 Pulitzer Prize winner is the way the author engages the subject of America with a fervor few novelists have dared since World War II.

Narrated by Zuckerman, *American Pastoral* relates the life of Seymour Lvov, hero of the schoolyards and playing fields of Nathan's childhood. Nicknamed "the Swede" because of his blond, blue-eyed looks, Lvov is an athlete whose prowess in football, basketball, and baseball make him a living legend in Newark's 1940s Jewish community. The evocation of that era is affectionate and funny, filled with unexpected warmth and generosity. As the Swede grows up, his education in the family glove trade—replete with his father's exacting tutelage in the tanning of leather and the arcana of stitching—is reported with an attention to detail even Balzac might admire. And the joy that he, having transplanted himself, his wife, and his daughter from city to suburb, feels in his personal "American pastoral" is poignantly captured in the image of the Swede walking home across fields imagining himself as Johnny Appleseed. No kidding.

The idyll doesn't last, however, for the Swede's dream turns into a nightmare when Merry, his only child, becomes an antiwar terrorist during the Vietnam era. As Zuckerman imagines his boyhood idol in middle age, struggling to comprehend "the American berserk" of the late 1960s, it becomes increasingly clear that the narrator is putting his protagonist's travails to his own novelistic uses (just as Roth is putting Zuckerman's narration to *his*), and the novel itself spins artfully out of control in a wild cry of bewilderment at all that has been lost since Nathan's and the Swede's shared childhood.

Passages of *American Pastoral*, especially those describing what was destroyed in the 1967 Newark riots, have a fierce and grieving majesty seldom matched in our literature. In telling the Swede's story, albeit in the voice of Nathan Zuckerman, Philip Roth embraces his past with an almost penitential reverence, honoring the world that made him—and is now forever gone—with nostalgic, rueful, angry tenderness.

What: Novel. *When:* 1997. *Award:* Pulitzer Prize for Fiction, 1998. *Also By: I Married a Communist* (1998). *The Human Stain* (2000). *The Plot Against America* (2004). *Exit Ghost* (2007). *Try: The Adventures of Augie March* by Saul Bellow (see page 66). *Independence Day* by Richard Ford (see page 288). *Adaptation:* There is a brilliant audiobook read by Ron Silver.

The Medical Detectives
Berton Roueché (1911–1994)

True Tales of Medical Detection

Nothing's more gripping than a true-life medical mystery. Take the one recounted in "Eleven Blue Men." On a September day in 1944, a ragged old man collapses on a New York City street. His nose, ears, lips, and fingers are a startling sky blue. Within hours of his being admitted to the hospital, other "blue men," all of them derelicts, are turning up. Doctors are understandably alarmed. Eventually the experts are able to determine that the blue men are victims "of a type of poisoning so rare that only ten previous outbreaks of it had been recorded in medical literature."

"Eleven Blue Men" is the first story in *The Medical Detectives*, an absorbing collection of twenty-five tales that were the lifeblood of the Annals of Medicine department of *The New Yorker*. In addition to the case of the unfortunate souls who changed hue (among other critical symptoms), Berton Roueché recounts bizarre fatal illnesses, odd contagions, and puzzling epidemics. Each weird ailment brings out the Sherlock Holmes in the doctors, health authorities, and epidemiological sleuths whose painstaking detective work Roueché skillfully shapes into suspenseful, fascinating, and informative case histories.

Dr. Lewis Thomas, author of *The Lives of a Cell* (see page 781), has pointed out that "Roueché's writings have become unofficial textbooks for medical students, interns, practitioners, scientists, and for that matter anyone interested in human illness. They are engrossing, instructive, accurate, and marvelous fun to read, and the present collection presents Roueché at his best." Why not turn off the television and take a break from forensic dramas with some reality reading?

What: Medicine. Science. Journalism. *When:* 1980 (collecting essays published from the 1940s on). *Also By: The River World and Other Explorations* (1978). *Special Places: In Search of Small Town America* (1982). *Try: Microbe Hunters* by Paul de Kruif (see page 203). *Napoleon's Glands* by Arno Karlen. *The Ghost Map* by Steven Johnson.

Classic Crimes
A SELECTION FROM THE WORKS OF WILLIAM ROUGHEAD
W. N. Roughead (1870–1952)

"The cornerstone of any library of crime."
—*New York Times*

In books with quaintly lurid titles such as *Mainly Murder*, *Malice Domestic*, *Rogues Walk Here*, and *Knaves' Looking-Glass*, Scottish criminologist William Roughead documented the most notorious murders and trials of eighteenth- and nineteenth-century Britain. His meticulously detailed and unfailingly dramatic accounts are among the classics of true crime writing; mystery master Dorothy Sayers called Roughead "the best showman who ever stood before the door of the chamber of horrors."

Containing the author's own choice of his best tales, *Classic Crimes* makes compelling reading. One of the cases it includes, "The West Port Murders," may be familiar in its outline: It tells the story of the infamous "body snatchers" Burke and Hare, who, in 1827 and 1828, murdered seventeen people to make money by selling their victims' corpses to Professor Robert Knox of Edinburgh Medical College. (The professor, it appears, had a purely scientific interest in these transactions; he needed the cadavers for classroom dissection and anatomical study.) The rest of Roughead's gallery of nefarious characters are less well known but no less enterprising. They are real-life archetypes for the shady and sinister protagonists murder enthusiasts have followed with fascination through mystery novels, films noirs, and macabre thrillers. "The Arran Murder," Luc Sante has written, even "suggests a great lost Hitchcock movie." Throughout, *Classic Crimes* testifies to what Joyce Carol Oates has called Roughead's "intelligence, skepticism, and flair for old-fashioned storytelling." It's a must for true crime aficionados.

What: True Crime. Mystery & Suspense. *When:* 1951; culled from more than two dozen earlier volumes. *Edition:* The 2000 New York Review Books Classics edition has an introduction by Luc Sante. *Try: Murder for Profit* by William Bolitho. *Studies in Murder* by Edmund Pearson. *Murder on Several Occasions* by Jonathan Goodman. *Footnote:* A Roughead piece was the inspiration for Lillian Hellman's play *The Children's Hour.*

....

The Confessions
Jean-Jacques Rousseau (1712–1778)

An Unprecedented and Influential Life

....

I have resolved on an undertaking that has no model and will have no imitator. I want to show my fellow-men a man in all the truth of nature; and this man is to be myself.

Myself alone ... I am not made like any that I have seen; I venture to believe that I was not made like any that exist. If I am not more deserving, at least I am different.

C ombining bravado with the invocation of a higher-order authenticity, the opening sentences of Rousseau's *Confessions* perfectly capture the animating spirit of the protagonist whose bold ideas and volatile personality will fascinate the reader for the several hundred pages that follow.

Covering the first fifty-three years of the author's life (and published only four years after his death, at age sixty-six), the book is a relentlessly open and thorough account of Rousseau's progress from orphan to composer, novelist, philosopher, and social and religious thinker of influence and international renown. Along the way, the autobiographer offers candid portrayals of himself as a sometime liar and petty thief, an amorous adventurer with a passion for prostration in the name of love, and a mercurial friend. His quarrel with fellow philosopher Denis Diderot, narrated—and documented by letters—in books 9 and 10, provides some of the most vivid reading in the book, not least because of the involvement of Madame d'Epinay, the brilliant and intriguing benefactress who

Sophie d'Houdetot, dressed as a man, visits Rousseau, a liaison described in the Confessions

allowed Rousseau use of the Hermitage, a cottage on her estate at Montmorency, as a retreat. Through the vagaries of fame and exile, Rousseau's sense of self seldom wavers, a fitting exhibition of his faith in an ineluctable identity that lies beneath the devitalizing accretions of social and cultural convention; indeed, it is his groundbreaking concept of selfhood that animated many of his most consequential philosophical, political, and educational theories and made him a prophet of the nineteenth-century Romantic movement in literature, art, and music. He embodied it with such fearless and unstinting energy that, even 250 years later, his

Confessions is an absorbing and vibrant reading experience.

What: Autobiography. **When:** 1782. **Edition:** There are many available translations; the one by Angela Scholar in the Oxford World's Classics series is eminently readable. **Also By:** *Discourse on the Arts and Sciences* (1750). *Discourse on the Origin and Basis of Inequality Among*

Men (1754). *Julie, or the New Héloïse* (1761). *Émile, or On Education* (1762). *The Social Contract, or Principles of Political Right* (1762). *Reveries of a Solitary Walker* (1782). *Further Reading: Jean-Jacques Rousseau: Restless Genius* by Leo Damrosch. For more on Madame d'Epinay, see Francis Steegmuller's *A Woman, A Man, and Two Kingdoms* (see page 748). *Try: Rameau's Nephew* and *Jacques the Fatalist* by Denis Diderot.

Harry Potter and the Sorcerer's Stone
J. K. Rowling (born 1965)

The Boy Who Lived, and Conquered the World

Mr. and Mrs. Dursley, of number four, Privet Drive, were proud to say that they were perfectly normal, thank you very much. They were the last people you'd expect to be involved in anything strange or mysterious, because they just didn't hold with such nonsense.

So, modestly, J. K. Rowling opens the saga that launched millions of readers around the world on a voyage across ten years and more than 4,000 pages, enthralled by the adventures of a boy named Harry Potter and the friends, mentors, and enemies he meets at Hogwarts School of Witchcraft and Wizardry. In their passage through Harry's magical education, fans young and old have been held spellbound by Rowling's compelling mix of boarding school camaraderie, delightfully arcane erudition as elaborated in the intricate traditions and curious curriculum of Hogwarts, recognizably adolescent instincts and uncertainties, heart-stopping exploits of derring-do, and, not least, the hopeful bravery of simple good versus complex evil.

Vernon and Petunia Dursley are "muggles" (that is, denizens of the nonwizarding world) who were unhappily surprised one day to find themselves guardians of the orphaned Harry. The boy's wizard parents, engaged in a struggle for the soul of the magical world, had been murdered by the malevolent Lord Voldemort (a force so fearsome, he is referred to by most of the characters as "You-Know-Who" or "He-Who-Must-Not-Be-Named"). Despite his terrifying powers and best efforts, however, the Dark Lord failed to kill the infant Harry, who will bear the sign of Voldemort's hatred for the rest of his life in a lightning-bolt-shaped scar on his forehead. This mark is the symbol of Harry's singularity and of the wizardly destiny he will pursue through every sort of trial, triumph, threat, grief, and danger as his thrilling, headlong story unfolds across the vast and varied canvas of Rowling's seven novels.

As first in the series, *Harry Potter and the Sorcerer's Stone* offers not only an entry to the larger story of Harry's contest with Voldemort, but, more tellingly, a testament to Rowling's gift for beguiling the reader with an endless stream of invention. Growing up with the Dursleys, Harry has believed himself an ordinary child, unspecial in every way (a conviction the Dursleys do everything to impress upon him). Upon his eleventh birthday, however, he receives an unexpected invitation to enroll at Hogwarts, and the moribund normalcy of his life on Privet Drive is swept away by that flood of delightful invention that Rowling unleashes as Harry assumes his magical inheritance. The book does have a wonderfully page-turning plot, but its excitement cannot compare to the sheer fun of discovering, with Harry, the enchantments of wizardry. The peculiar emporiums of Diagon Alley, where wizarding students go to shop for school supplies, buying their wands at Ollivanders and their magical textbooks at Flourish and Blotts, and to manage accounts at goblin-run Gringotts Bank; the hidden platform nine and three-quarters at Kings Cross Station that offers the only access to the Hogwarts Express, a train replete with candy trolleys proffering such treats as Chocolate Frogs, Cauldron Cakes, and Bertie Bott's Every Flavor Beans (every flavor indeed: spinach and tripe as well as peppermint!); the four houses of Hogwarts—Gryffindor, Hufflepuff, Ravenclaw, and Slytherin—and their rich troves of lore; the spells, potions, and courses (for example, Herbology and Defense Against the Dark Arts) that make up Harry's studies; and the comprehensively conjured game of Quidditch, which concentrates student passions as only a sport can do—all, and much more, are evoked by the author with lively attention, and the reader just can't get enough, as the wild popularity of the subsequent books proved beyond doubt.

Add to this the unforgettable characters—Harry's best friends Ron Weasley and Hermione Granger, his sinister enemy Draco Malfoy, the half giant Rubeus Hagrid, the professors Severus Snape and Minerva McGonagall, and the revered headmaster Albus Dumbledore, among dozens of others—whom we meet in these pages and who will share Harry's story through the years of his coming-of-age. It's clear that *Harry Potter and the Sorcerer's Stone* is a book whose richness belies its mere three

hundred pages (compared with the gargantuan Potter tomes that would later flow from Rowling's pen, it's a succinct effort). The progenitor of the most astonishing publishing phenomena in history, the first volume in the Harry Potter chronicle is happy evidence of the enduring magic and undiminished power of good storytelling—a magic and power that its sequels dispense with a more familiar but no less seductive lavishness.

What: Children's. Fantasy. *When:* First published in England as *Harry Potter and the Philosopher's Stone,* 1997; retitled US edition in the same year. *Also By:* The six sequels are *Harry Potter and the Chamber of Secrets* (1998); *Harry Potter and the Prisoner of Azkaban* (1999); *Harry Potter and the Goblet of Fire* (2000); *Harry Potter and the Order of the Phoenix* (2003); *Harry Potter and the Half-Blood Prince* (2005); and *Harry Potter and the Deathly Hallows* (2007). Rowling also wrote these companion books: *Fantastic Beasts and Where to Find Them* (2001; under the name Newt Scamander); *Quidditch Through the Ages* (2001; under the name Kennilworthy Whisp); and *The Tales of Beedle the Bard* (2007). With *The Cuckoo's Calling* (2013), Rowling began publishing mysteries under the pen name Robert Galbraith. *Try: The Lord of the Rings* by J. R. R. Tolkien (see page 795). *Charmed Life* by Diana Wynne Jones. *So You Want to Be a Wizard* by Diane Duane. *Adaptations:* The Warner Bros. films of the Harry Potter books star Daniel Radcliffe, Rupert Grint, and Emma Watson. The extraordinary Listening Library audiobooks, performed by the incomparable Jim Dale, are magnificent entertainments even if you've already read the novels.

The God of Small Things
Arundhati Roy (born 1961)

"The Big Things lurk unsaid inside."

Skittering between present and past, Arundhati Roy's intense novel of a shattered family is infused with the sights and smells of southern India; it's an indelible depiction of the struggles of women and of lower-caste Indians against the enduring constraints of traditional society. Yet the sensual and

social specificity of the tale only deepens the resonance of the book's grasp of a far-reaching truth: how human structures empower fate, turning essential yearnings for love and security into ineluctable tragedy.

At the heart of *The God of Small Things* are a boy named Estha and a girl named Rahel, fraternal twins whose mother, Ammu, has divorced their father and returned with them to Kerala, the religiously and politically diverse state at the tip of India where "the nights are clear, but suffused with sloth and sullen expectation." The social stigma of Ammu's divorce means that the twins find themselves unable to make friends, but they live in awe of Velutha, a carpenter in the family's employ who comes to fall in love with their mother. Although Velutha is an active Marxist, that's not all that sets him apart: He's also a Dalit—that is, a member of the caste formerly called Untouchable; as a consequence, his romance with Ammu must be kept secret. Meddling family members and meddlesome officials conspire to keep the two apart, with awful results: "They broke the Love Laws. That lay down who should be loved. And how. And how much."

Arundhati Roy, 1997

There is much more to Roy's multifarious creation than Ammu and Velutha's desperate love—everything from a pickle factory to communist rallies, from a trip to the cinema to see *The Sound of Music* to violations of the most intimate taboos. As fellow writer Pankaj Mishra observed, looking back on the novel's original publication when honoring Roy's selection by *Time* magazine as one of the world's most influential people for 2014, "The novel seemed, in its evocations of the beauty and terror of life, its radical distrust of power, reflexive hatred of injustice and effervescent humor, almost miraculous." It did, and still does. That *The God of Small Things* was its author's first—and for twenty years her only—novel makes its literary achievement and emotional wisdom all the more remarkable. And although Arundhati Roy's subsequent work as an essayist, documentarian, political activist, and fierce critic of the Indian government is what placed her among *Time*'s influential elite seventeen years after its publication, it's a good bet that *The God of Small Things* will prove to possess a timeless influence all its own.

What: Novel. *When:* 1997. *Award:* Booker Prize, 1998. *Also By:* Nonfiction: *The Cost of Living* (1999). *Walking with the Comrades* (2011). Fiction: *The Ministry of Utmost Happiness* (2017). *Try: Untouchable* by Mulk Raj Anand. *To Kill a Mockingbird* by Harper Lee (see page 469). *A Fine Balance* by Rohinton Mistry (see page 555). *The Lowland* by Jhumpa Lahiri.

Guys and Dolls
Damon Runyon (1880–1946)

The Bard of Broadway

"I am such a guy as will always listen to a tip on a horse if a story goes with the tip. In fact, I will not give you a nickel for a tip without a story, but it must be a first-class story, and most horse players are the same way." When it comes to a tip on a writer recommended for the idiosyncratic pleasure of his language, most readers are the same way: They'll take the tip on the prose if a story goes with it.

Damon Runyon, the bard of an imaginatively embellished Roaring Twenties Broadway peopled with gamblers, chorus girls, and other operators (and author of the sentence quoted above), is a case in point. As novelist William Kennedy once put it while describing the author's distinctive argot, "there is a comic fluency in this invented tongue, an originality of syntax, a fluidity of word and event that is a relentless delight." And the stories the tongue treats us to are indeed first-rate. Told by an unnamed but well-connected narrator who knows his way around racetracks, delicatessens, and assorted dens of high- and low-life, Runyon's tales travel from the street-smart to the sentimental with unrelenting attention to the human comedy. Their narrative charm has no better validation than the number of films based on them: to mention just a few, *Lady for a Day* (three versions); *Little Miss Marker* (four versions, beginning with the one that launched Shirley Temple's stardom); *The Lemon Drop Kid* (two versions). Runyon's world and characters were also the inspiration for one of the greatest American musicals, Frank Loesser's *Guys and Dolls*.

For all their cinematic and theatrical adaptation, the tales remain an undiluted pleasure when encountered on the page. The names of characters alone are a joy to savor—Brandy Bottle Bates, Nicely-Nicely Jones, Miss Florentine Fayette—and the epithets that regularly attach to them add a mock-epic wink to Runyon's delivery; the odds are pretty good that you'll smile each time "Regret, the horse player" makes an appearance. And it's a sure bet you'll be glad to make the acquaintance of the writer who devised the useful formula "All life is six-to-five against."

Marlon Brando and ensemble on the set of the 1956 film adaptation

What: Short Stories. Humor. *When:* 1932. *Edition:* The Penguin paperback, *Guys and Dolls and Other Writing*, is a good Runyon compendium. *Further Reading: Damon Runyon* by Jimmy Breslin. *Broadway Boogie Woogie: Damon Runyon and the Making of New York City Culture* by Daniel R. Schwarz. *Try: The Thin Man* by Dashiell Hammett. *Up in the Old Hotel* by Joseph Mitchell (see page 556). *Fame and Obscurity* by Gay Talese (see page 771). *Adaptations:* Too numerous to mention, but Frank Loesser's 1950 Broadway musical, *Guys and Dolls* (made into a 1956 film with Marlon Brando and Frank Sinatra), earns pride of place.

Midnight's Children
Salman Rushdie (born 1947)

Best of the Booker

Imagine a literary love child of Charles Dickens and *The Arabian Nights*, and you'll have some idea of the human interest and narrative ingenuity of Salman Rushdie's masterpiece, one of the most admired, acclaimed, and enjoyed novels of the second half of the twentieth century. Not only did *Midnight's Children* garner the Booker Prize in the year of its publication, but it was also proclaimed, more than a quarter-century later, "Best of the Booker" on the award's fortieth anniversary, prevailing over all previous winners of the prize in an international popular vote.

Like Dickens, Rushdie draws indelible characters and sets them in a swirling social context; he similarly shares a gift for exaggeration that gets closer to the truth about people than observational exactitude, illuminating his caricatures with a sense of justice and a sense of humor, often entwined. Like the tale spinning of *The Arabian Nights*, *Midnight's Children* leavens the world it depicts with magical capabilities and coincidences, thereby evoking the intense devotion our emotional lives demand of us, no matter our circumstances. Rushdie's unshakable belief in the regenerative power of telling stories, a faith given form in the unrelenting narrative energy of *Midnight's Children*, is a legacy of both forebears.

The midnight in question belongs to August 15, 1947; at its stroke the novel's twin protagonists—the nation of India and the narrator, Saleem Sinai—are born. "I had been mysteriously handcuffed to history," Saleem comments on this coincidence, "my destinies indissolubly chained to those of my country." Saleem's distinction is by no means singular: He is but one of a thousand babies who came into the world at the hour of his country's birth, each one possessing preternatural powers. Saleem exhibits an early ability to read the thoughts of others, and, later, because he is "possessor of the most delicately-gifted olfactory organ in history," to sniff out trouble as it is brewing. This proves to be a burden as much as a blessing.

Beginning his narrative three decades before the fabled midnight with a comic chronicle of his parents' courtship, Saleem leads us through a wild landscape of childhood memories, family lore, mistaken identities, misfired passions, and political upheaval as he wends his way toward the 1970s, inscribing along the way an astute imaginative history of India's own struggle to come of age. Violent tragedies of war and oppression shadow smaller losses of love, money, and dignity, all embodied in people and incidents that Rushdie animates

Salman Rushdie, 2005

with evocative particulars. From Saleem himself to Parvati-the-witch (another child of midnight who helps him overcome amnesia), from William Methwold, a scion of British colonialists, to the ill-starred poet Nadir Khan, from meddling midwives to dueling snake charmers, Rushdie inspirits his cast with personality. The adventures and misadventures they pursue plot enough twists and turns to enliven a dozen lesser novels.

Opening *Midnight's Children*, one enters a realm more variegated and teeming with reality than the world one sees when one looks up from its chapters. The force of Rushdie's prose is so propulsive, the currents of story-within-story so transporting, that each page is a further winding of the crank on an enormous jack-in-the-box that explodes again and again with the wonders of living that history can never contain.

What: Novel. *When:* 1981. *Awards:* Booker Prize, 1981; the Booker of Bookers, 1993; and Best of the Booker, 2008. *Also By:* *Shame* (1983). *The Satanic Verses* (1988). *The Moor's Last Sigh* (1995). *Fury* (2001). *Shalimar the Clown* (2005). *Two Years Eight Months and Twenty-Eight Nights* (2015). *Try: One Hundred Years of Solitude* by Gabriel García Márquez (see page 308). *The Famished Road* by Ben Okri (see page 602). *The God of Small Things* by Arundhati Roy (see page 681). *Adaptation:* A film version, directed by Deepa Mehta with screenplay by Rushdie, was released in 2012.

The Stones of Venice
John Ruskin (1819–1900)

A Genius in Love with a City and Its History

"Among the many strange things that have befallen Venice," wrote Henry James in tribute to the city's most ardent chronicler, John Ruskin, "she has had the good fortune to become the object of a passion to a man of splendid genius, who has made her his own, and in doing so has made her the world's." Ruskin's passion, and his genius, found their most comprehensive and eloquent expression in *The Stones of Venice*, his monumental appraisal of Venetian architecture, ornament, and culture.

Ruskin was an art critic, painter, collector, social commentator, and all-around gadfly of Britain's Victorian era. His most enduring work began as a rigorous treatise on the architecture of La Serenissima, with long discussions of the shapes of arches and the varieties of pediments. But over the course of its composition, the three-volume study expanded into a larger history of Venice as well as a disquisition on the state of contemporary Britain, which he saw as slipping into moral and social decay.

Many modern editions of *The Stones of Venice* are abridged, and that's fine; only specialists read all three volumes. If you want to get to the core of Ruskin, turn to his spirited defense of the Gothic style. Ruskin spends page after page praising the windows and columns of such Venetian monuments as the Doge's Palace in Piazza San Marco, which he anoints as "the central building of the world." Why? Because for Ruskin the Gothic expressed, as classical architecture did not, the talents and creativity of individual artisans, who combined thought and labor to thrilling effect. The subtext, at least for the nineteenth-century reader, was clear: In the midst of the Industrial Revolution, labor was increasingly alienated from the objects it produced; architecture, Ruskin implied, would suffer as a result. His concern for the material conditions of architectural production made him especially appealing to radicals and socialists, such as the artist William Morris—who published part of *The Stones of Venice* in a volume of his own design.

Ruskin was a massively influential figure in art criticism in the late nineteenth and early twentieth centuries. (Oxford University, his alma mater, now calls its art school The Ruskin.) His reputation declined precipitously in the wake of modernism, owing in part to the fustiness of his prose, and despite his profound influence on Marcel Proust, who translated Ruskin's *Sesame and Lilies* (1865) into French and was inspired by his autobiography, *Praeterita* (1885–89). In recent decades, Ruskin has been discovered by a new generation, which sees in his engaged criticism—especially his concern for labor and the environment—a model for writing about art today. More broadly, no visitor to Venice, by airplane or armchair, will enjoy the trip as much without this brilliant, bracing companion.

What: Art. Architecture. Culture. *When:* 1851–53. *Edition:* The one-volume abridgement edited by J. G. Links offers an astute redaction of the original. *Also By: Modern Painters* (five volumes; 1843–60). *The Seven Lamps of Architecture* (1849). *Unto This Last* (1862). *Further Reading: John Ruskin* by Tim Hilton. *Ruskin's Venice: The Stones Revisited* by Sarah Quill. *Try: Venice for Pleasure* by J. G. Links (see page 492). *The World of Venice* by Jan Morris.

The Longest Day

JUNE 6, 1944

Cornelius Ryan (1920–1974)

The Story of the Allied Invasion of Normandy

Now Eisenhower stood watching as the planes trundled down the runways and lifted slowly into the air. One by one they followed each other into the darkness. Above the field they circled as they assembled into formation. Eisenhower, his hands deep in his pockets, gazed up into the night sky. As the huge formation of planes roared one last time over the field and headed toward France, NBC's Red Mueller looked at the Supreme Commander. Eisenhower's eyes were filled with tears.

What a wealth of human drama these 350 pages contain. Less than fifteen years after the end of World War II, Cornelius Ryan constructed a fleet and intricate narrative of the maneuverings on both sides of the English Channel during the ambitious operation that would turn the tide of the battle against Hitler and the Third Reich. As he writes in his foreword, *The Longest Day* is "not a military history. It is the story of people: the men of the Allied forces, the enemy they fought and the civilians who were caught up in the bloody confusion of D Day."

From Eisenhower and the Allied high command to Field Marshal Erwin Rommel, overseer of Hitler's Atlantic wall; from the soldiers, pilots, and paratroopers who carried the fight across enemy lines to the German soldiers who struggled to repel them; from the meteorologists who gave the operation a twenty-four-hour window of opportunity on June 6 (after the invasion's initial postponement) to the German intelligence officers who knew that the broadcast of two lines of Verlaine's poetry over the BBC would announce the operation to the French underground, Ryan's swift, compelling chronicle weaves the stories of individuals into a tough fabric of suspense and history, honoring the private dimensions—the courage, fear, fortune, and faith—that shaped the fateful day. It is difficult to put this book down and impossible not to be awed by the scope of the events described.

What: War. History. *When:* 1959. *Also By: The Last Battle* (1966). *A Bridge Too Far* (1974). *Further Reading: Overlord* by Max Hastings. *Try: Six Armies in Normandy* by John Keegan. *Ike: An American Hero* by Michael Korda. *Adaptation:* A film version starring Eddie Albert, Jean-Louis Barrault, and Richard Burton appeared in 1962.

Home

A SHORT HISTORY OF AN IDEA
Witold Rybczynski (born 1943)

A Delightful Survey of the Progress of Domestic Comfort

"Home is where one starts from," wrote T. S. Eliot, and it is Witold Rybczynski's intention in this enlightening book to explain how very long it took us to arrive at that starting point. Privacy, domesticity, comfort, the concept of home and family we have inherited—these were all quite clearly invented in the course of the past five hundred years. Rybczynski traces their origins from roots in seventeenth-century Holland through development and refinement in Rococo France, Georgian England, and turn-of-the-century America, in each case illuminating happy confluences of economic development, social conditions, and national character.

What makes *Home* so engaging is the variety of thought it provokes. By making us see that the most familiar elements of our lives were once unfamiliar—were, indeed, once nonexistent—Rybczynski leads us to speculate on things we normally barely notice. His discussion of chairs, which runs throughout the book, is representative. First, he reminds us, not all cultures have them; mankind is split between sitters and squatters. The questions start there, and proceed from the general to the specific: Why chairs at all? Then, why a Windsor rather than a Louis XV *fauteuil*? What can we deduce from a Chippendale, or a stuffed Victorian armchair, a Wassily or a Barcelona? More than you'd imagine, and Rybczynski reveals it all.

An architect and professor of architecture and urbanism, Rybczynski is a winsome writer, clearheaded and without an ideological ax to grind—although he is very sharp on the naïveté of architectural modernism in the domestic realm. His text is strewn with information you don't need to know but are glad to learn: about the introduction of sash windows, the date of the first candles, the origin of spring cleaning, and other curiously compelling details. All in all, his *Home* is a splendid place to spend some time.

What: Culture. House & Garden. Sociology. *When:* 1986. *Also By: The Most Beautiful House in the World* (1989). *A Clearing in the Distance: Frederick Law Olmsted and America in the Nineteenth Century* (1999). *The Perfect House: A Journey with the Renaissance Master Andrea Palladio* (2002). *How Architecture Works: A Humanist's Toolkit* (2013). *Now I Sit Me Down: From Klismos to Plastic Chair: A Natural History* (2016). *Try: An Embarrassment of Riches: An Interpretation of Dutch Culture in the Golden Age* by Simon Schama. *At Home: A Short History of Private Life* by Bill Bryson.

S, T

S

HIS ODYSSEY

Rafael Sabatini (1875–1950)

The Greatest Swashbuckler of Them All

Rafael Sabatini's perennially popular adventure yarn opens on a tranquil scene: "Peter Blood, bachelor of medicine and several other things besides, smoked a pipe and tended the geraniums boxed on the sill of his window." The promise inherent in that teasing phrase about extracurricular qualifications is soon realized. Doctor Blood's quiet life in the seventeenth-century English countryside is shattered when he finds himself unjustly arrested for treason. Convicted, he's then transported on a slave ship to Barbados, where he eventually escapes from the clutches of a brutal plantation owner during a pirate attack. This sets the stage for Blood's own career as a pirate—and before long, he is the greatest buccaneer of them all. Raids, sea battles, sword fights, acts of gallantry and low cunning: The stuff of Blood's action-packed odyssey is recounted with zest and skill, in chapter after page-turning chapter, by a robust, natural-born storyteller. Filled with despicable enemies (in English, French, and Spanish flavors), an attractive romantic interest, and the inspiring élan of a dauntless hero, the book dares you to put it down. You won't.

Captain Blood and Rafael Sabatini have had millions of admiring readers through the years. According to George MacDonald Fraser, the author of the Flashman books (see page 297), it is

Rafael Sabatini, ca. 1937

"one of the great unrecognized novels of the twentieth century, and as close as any modern writer has come to a prose epic."

What: Novel. *When:* 1922. *Reading Note:* Don't be put off by Sabatini's at-times-ornate prose and rich vocabulary (for example, *armigerous, pannikin, pusillanimity*). Under the spell of his storytelling, you'll soon come to relish both. *Also By: The Sea-Hawk* (1915). *Scaramouche* (1921). *Bellarion the Fortunate* (1926). *Captain Blood Returns* (1931) and *The Fortunes of Captain Blood* (1936) document further twists and turns in the Blood saga. *Try: The Scarlet Pimpernel* by Baroness Orczy. *The Prisoner of Zenda* by Anthony Hope. *Captain from*

Castile by Samuel Shellabarger. *Adaptation: Captain Blood* (1935), one of the silver screen's grand old swashbucklers, was directed by Michael Curtiz; it features stirring music by Erich Wolfgang Korngold, and—unforgettably—stars Errol Flynn as Peter Blood.

"Some years ago I was asked by a magazine what were the ten most important books in my development. The book I listed first was *Captain Blood*. Then came *Das Kapital*." —Norman Mailer

The Man Who Mistook His Wife for a Hat

AND OTHER CLINICAL TALES

Oliver Sacks (1933–2015)

A Pensive Neurologist Explores the Mind

Imagine being a young man of nineteen in the year 1945. Imagine then living for the next thirty years believing you are still nineteen and the year is still 1945. Even as your body grows older, your mind is unaware of the passing decades.

Or imagine this: You lose the ability to recognize people and objects, although all of your senses remain intact. So you can describe a glove as "a continuous surface [with] five out-pouchings" but not have a clue about its use. At the end of your medical exam, you reach out for your hat. Taking hold of your wife's head as if it were the very thing you were searching for, you try to pick it up and put it on.

This last scenario, which describes the very real affliction of a very real musician, provides this surprising book—a phenomenal best-seller upon its publication in 1985—with its title

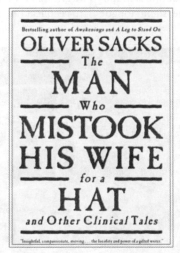

essay. Dr. Oliver Sacks, a clinical neurologist, collected two dozen such tales in this volume, each a compelling examination of a neurological disorder. The case histories, written in clear, sure prose, introduce us to people whose unusual ailments make up a gallery of curious experience, including twins who communicate with each other by exchanging twelve-digit prime numbers, a man who dreams that he's a dog and wakes with a canine's sensitivity to smell, and an autistic eight year old who is completely uncommunicative except for an uncanny talent for drawing. One cannot read these tales without feeling a mixed sense of terror and wonder before the human brain's unfathomable complexity and delicate balance. What other reaction can one have to the knowledge that less than a single milligram of Haldol daily can so alter the brain's chemistry that a tortured victim of Tourette's syndrome becomes well? Dr. Sacks provokes deep reflection on how our minds work, and on the sobering fact that they might not always work the way we take for granted they will.

What: Medicine. Psychology. Essays. *When:* 1985. *Reading Note:* Dr. Sacks wrote about arcane matters

with remarkable grace and acuity. No scientific learning is needed to enjoy his essays. *Also By: Migraine* (1970; revised 1992). *Awakenings* (1973). *A Leg to Stand On* (1984). *An Anthropologist on Mars* (1995). *Uncle Tungsten: Memories of a Chemical Boyhood* (2001). *On the Move: A Life* (2015). *Try: Phantoms in the Brain* by V. S. Ramachandran and Sandra Blakeslee.

....

All Passion Spent
Vita Sackville-West (1892–1962)

A Portrait of the Artist as an Old Woman

....

Readers know her first, probably, as a lover of Virginia Woolf and as the inspiration for that novelist's most buoyant work, *Orlando* (see page 870); second, as one-half of the couple so compellingly portrayed by their son in *Portrait of a Marriage* (see page 587); and third—if their tastes run to horticulture—as the spirit that cultivated the gardens at Sissinghurst Castle. Only last, it seems, do readers come to know Vita Sackville-West through her writing, but once they do, they won't forget her voice, which enters the ear with such a delicate balance of confidence and refinement that one is immediately enchanted. Before the silent tongue

has time to utter, "Tell me more," the ear is seduced by the sentences sounding out down the page.

This literary seduction is equally strong in her travel writing (*Passenger to Teheran*) as in her gardening books (*In Your Garden* and its sequels), her surprising explorations of the lives of saints (*Saint Joan of Arc* and *The Eagle and the Dove*, her dual biography of Saint Teresa of Avila and Saint Thérèse of Lisieux), and her fiction. The one book of hers that is not to be missed is *All Passion Spent*, a novel that tells the story of an octogenarian widow who abandons the family home—to the dismay of her children—and retires to a tiny house in Hampstead to recollect her life. Sackville-West's portrait of

The gardens at Sissinghurst Castle, Kent, England

an aged woman is both whimsical and serious, and altogether inspiring; the theme of personal freedom has seldom been put through such telling, elegant variations. And the measured grace of the prose is glorious.

What: Novel. *When:* 1931. *Also By: The Edwardians* (1930). *Further Reading: Vita: The Life of V. Sackville-West* by Victoria Glendinning. *Try: The Last September* by Elizabeth Bowen. *Mrs. Palfrey at the Claremont* by Elizabeth Taylor. *Adaptation:* The three-part 1986 BBC television series stars Dame Wendy Hiller.

The Dragons of Eden
SPECULATIONS ON THE EVOLUTION OF HUMAN INTELLIGENCE
Carl Sagan (1934–1996)

The Mind's Progress,
from Prehistory to the Present

Although he had not yet achieved the fame that was to come with his documentary television series *Cosmos*, Carl Sagan was already an astronomer of some renown when he published *The Dragons of Eden*, his first book to venture freely beyond the astronomical realm. Employing his celebrated gift for lucid explication of complex scientific matters, he produces a breathtaking overview of the nature and development of human intelligence.

Equally at ease with the scientific method and the literary imagination, with experiment and metaphor (myth being, in his deft description, "a metaphor of some subtlety on a subject difficult to describe in any other way"), Sagan is able to sketch a vision bold enough to engage the large question of what it means to be human. That he sees the evolution of human intelligence from a cosmological perspective gives his thinking a refreshing breadth, and his frequent segues from anatomical and biological detail to mythology—the expulsion from Eden, say, or St. George's battle with a dragon—entwine human and natural history in provocative and illuminating ways. Throughout, he spices his speculations with playful ideas and expressions that increase the reader's appetite for intellectual adventure. (His concentration of the history of the universe into the span of a single year, for instance, is itself worth the price of the book.)

In the more than four decades since the publication of *The Dragons of Eden*, some of Sagan's theorizing has surely been overtaken by

Carl Sagan visits the planets

new research. But the bold sweep of the book's perception still opens unforgettable vistas of knowledge and imagination.

What: Science. Anthropology. Culture. *When:* 1977. *Awards:* Pulitzer Prize for General Nonfiction, 1978. *Also By: The Cosmic Connection* (1973). *Broca's Brain: Reflections on the Romance of Science* (1979). *Cosmos* (1980). *Comet* (1985; with Ann Druyan). *Pale Blue Dot: A Vision of the Human Future in Space* (1994). *The Varieties of Scientific Experience: A Personal View of the Search for God* (2006). *Try: The Roots of Civilization* by Alexander Marshack (see page 527). *The Origin of Consciousness in the Breakdown of the Bicameral Mind* by Julian Jaynes (see page 414).

The Sagas of Icelanders

The Icelandic Discovery of a New World of Narrative

" Elaborate, various, strange, profound, and as eternally current as any of the other great literary treasures—the Homeric epics, Dante's *Divine Comedy*, the work of William Shakespeare or of any modern writer you could name." So novelist Jane Smiley writes in her preface to this peerless selection of medieval Icelandic prose narratives, drawn from a five-volume translation project published to commemorate the one thousandth anniversary of Leif Eriksson's voyage to Vinland. The eleven sagas and six shorter tales included here—set mostly around the turn of the first millennium AD (although written two to four centuries later)—charted new literary territory. While the rest of medieval literature was locked in lines of verse, the unknown authors of the sagas freely employed prose to fashion fictions of mythic roots and visionary scope that nonetheless portrayed, in realistic detail, the lives of the Norse families who first settled Iceland. To chronicle the deeds of the settlers' descendants, the sagas venture farther west to Greenland and even Vinland and North America. Long before the advent of the novel as a robust form, these tales of independent men and women—farmers, poets, warriors, adventurers, outlaws, and matriarchs—expanded the domain of storytelling in tales that remain both puzzling and compelling today.

Encompassing history and myth, the epic and the tragic, the comic and the sublime, these tales re-create a world of honor codes, feuds, and abiding obsessions in which the demands of agricultural work are treated with the same respect as heroic motives and burdens. They are filled with unforgettable characters, from the fierce and cunning Egil, a warrior-poet called upon to save his life with verse, to the formidable heroine Gudrid Thorbjarnardottir—born in Iceland, married in Greenland, she traveled to Vinland and there bore a son. Thrilling and mysterious, the sagas are—as one commentator has described them— "a sort of literary Stonehenge."

What: Literature. Mythology. *When:* Ca. 1220–ca. 1400. *Edition:* The Penguin Classics edition, published in 2000, is the best introduction to the sagas and their world. *Reading Note:* Episodic and often telescoping vast stretches of time, the sagas can be disconcerting on first acquaintance. They have a narrative method and logic all their own. *Try:* Additional sagas published in readily available editions: *Njal's Saga, The Saga of the Volsungs, King Harald's Saga. Footnote:* In its motifs, narrative architecture, and mythological foundations, J. R. R. Tolkien's *The Lord of the Rings* (see page 793) exhibits the influence of the sagas.

Statue of Leif Eriksson in Reykjavik

The Little Prince
Antoine de Saint-Exupéry (1900–1944)

Life Lessons from an Interplanetary Traveler

Antoine de Saint-Exupéry was an intrepid pilot, a pioneer in the early days of commercial aviation who flew mail routes and, later, military reconnaissance missions for the Allies until his plane disappeared in 1944 off the coast of Marseille. During his lifetime, Saint-Exupéry also earned an international reputation as an author, writing a handful of books inspired by his career in flight. By far the most famous of his literary works is a children's book, *The Little Prince*, illustrated with Saint-Exupéry's own drawings. Published a year before its author's death, this endearing philosophical fable became one of the most beloved books of the twentieth century.

It begins with a pilot who has crash-landed in the Sahara and hopes to repair his engine before his water supply runs out. On his first night in the desert, he is awakened by a "funny little voice" politely asking him to draw a sheep. The request comes from a small person attired in a royal cape with gold epaulets. Bit by bit over the next several days, the pilot learns the history of the little prince and his distant home, a planet so small that he can watch the sunset anytime he likes, simply by moving his chair a few feet. There the prince's daily routine includes weeding baobab sprouts before they become calamitously large "When you've finished washing and dressing each morning," he explains, "you must tend your planet"—and tending to a rose whom he loves despite her prickly personality. He has been traveling from one celestial body to another seeking the meaning of life, a task in which, as we learn from both his accounts of the eccentric characters he has met and the pilot's own remarks, grown-ups offer very little help.

"I am not sure I have lived since my childhood," the author once wrote to his mother, and *The Little Prince* is in many ways an attempt to resurrect a child's innocence and intuition. "In his last years especially," writes Saint-Exupéry's biographer Stacy Schiff, "he appeared a man with a stubborn faith in search of a place in which to invest it." That faith—in the imagination, in the magic of childhood, in the tenderness that must weather bruising life as best it can—found its final home in the wise and whimsical figure of the little prince, who continues to teach generation after generation to greet the world's infinite variety with wonder and with welcome.

What: Children's. *When:* 1943 in French; first English translation, 1943. *Edition:* A new translation by Richard Howard appeared in 2000, replacing, with some controversy, Katherine Woods's 1943 effort. *Reading Note:* A splendid family read-aloud. *Also By: Southern Mail* (1929). *Night Flight* (1931). *Wind, Sand, and Stars* (1939). *Flight to Arras* (1942). *Further Reading: Saint-Exupéry* by Stacy Schiff (see next page). *The Tale of the Rose: The Love Story Behind "The Little Prince"* by Consuelo de Saint-Exupéry, the aviator's wife. *Try: Skellig* by David Almond (see page 16). *Adaptations:* A 1974 live-action film, with songs by Lerner and Loewe, stars Richard Kiley as the Pilot and Bob Fosse as the Snake. Cliff Robertson narrates a 1979 animated version; another animation appeared in 2015, featuring the voices of Jeff Bridges, Rachel McAdams, and Marion Cotillard.

||||||||||||||||||||||||||||||||||| B O O K N O T E |||||||||||||||||||||||||||||||||||||||||

A HERO IN FLIGHT

Saint-Exupéry
A BIOGRAPHY

Stacy Schiff (born 1961)

"When a man dies," writes Antoine de Saint-Exupéry in *Wind, Sand, and Stars,* "an unknown world passes away." The hard bone of each skull, he continues, "is in a sense an old treasure chest": "what colored stuffs, what images of festivities, what vestiges" it might contain! The treasure a man carries inside him, even if he has carefully exposed it in his own writing, can be buried by a biographer intent on piling facts into a scholarly monument. Fortunately for readers, Stacy Schiff undertakes her 1994 life of the French aviator and author with a true appreciation of the imaginative riches her subject possessed, and the result is a riveting and illuminating life of one of the most romantic figures of the twentieth century.

Born into an aristocratic family in 1900, Saint-Exupéry became one of the legends of the early days of commercial aviation. His formidable gifts as a writer, first revealed in *Southern Mail* (1929),

a novel detailing the pioneering days of international postal flight, and then in the fiction and memoir of *Night Flight* (1931) and *Wind, Sand, and Stars* (1939), brought him earthbound celebrity as well. His philosophical fable *The Little Prince* (1943) would make him one of the most beloved authors of his time, and his disappearance in 1944, while on a reconnaissance mission tracking German troop movements in southern France, only added to the glamour that surrounded his name.

Schiff's generous understating of the courage, confusion, and creativity that marked Saint-Exupéry's life, from boyhood through his formative, exotic adventures in open cockpits, from his public dignified idealism to his private bewildered despair, makes her prose resonate with his own themes. The stylish composition of her narrative conveys the substance of her subject's imagination nearly as well—if not as lyrically and meditatively—as his works do, and her writing amplifies his exploration of the danger, isolation, and grandeur of flight with moving proof of the danger, isolation, and grandeur of a single remarkable life.

Memoirs
Duc de Saint-Simon (1675–1755)

An Insider's Report on Life at Versailles

Louis de Rouvroy was a French aristocrat known at court as the Duke of Saint-Simon. His posthumously published memoirs are an invaluable historical document—and one of history's most deliciously gossipy reads.

Louis XIV (1638–1715) ruled France for more than seventy-two years. He was known as *Le Roi Soleil*—"The Sun King"—and his reign has been called the Age of Magnificence. At the heart of that reign was his court at Versailles, a palace of unequaled splendor and a hotbed of intrigue where courtiers vied ceaselessly for power and influence. Saint-Simon, though frequently out of favor with the king, was on the scene for many years, and his memoirs, based on diaries he kept throughout his life, cover the period from 1691 to 1723.

Although his position at Versailles was often marginal—in part because he was a fierce opponent of the king's policy of relying on ministers from the bourgeoisie rather than the aristocracy—his deftness at depicting, through observation and anecdote, the character behind the public façade of his contemporaries, including the Sun King himself, gives his account a novelistic flair (aptly, Saint-Simon was a favorite of both Stendhal and Proust). His skill in this regard is especially compelling in describing an event such as the sudden death of the dauphin, the king's son and heir, in 1711; Saint-Simon's focus on the emotions of the court is insightful and revealing. In other, less dramatic times, he writes with relish of scandalous behavior and does not shy away from the intimate or the scatological.

Saint-Simon's memoirs, in addition to being an eyewitness account of events that shaped European history, are a human and very entertaining exposé of the lifestyles of the richest and most famous at the turn of the eighteenth century.

What: Memoir. History. *When:* Although fragments began to appear in the late 1780s, the first complete edition was not published until 1829. *Edition:* Saint-Simon's memoirs in French fill a bookshelf. The most readily available English version is the three-volume abridged translation that Lucy Norton prepared between 1967 and 1972. *Further Reading: The Sun King* by Nancy Mitford. *Try: The Princess of Clèves* by Madame de Lafayette (see page 458). *The Letters of Madame de Sévigné.*

The Catcher in the Rye

J. D. Salinger (1919–2010)

On Being Sixteen

...if I ever die, and they stick me in a cemetery, and I have a tombstone and all, it'll say "Holden Caulfield" on it, and then what year I was born and what year I died, and then right under that it'll say "Fuck you." I'm positive.

It's been considerably more than a half century since the first angst-ridden teenager cracked the spine of *The Catcher in the Rye* and felt he'd found a book—or more specifically, a character—that spoke for him. In the intervening years, millions of other self-anointed outsiders have felt the same way. For such receptive readers, J. D. Salinger's Holden Caulfield is the embodiment of everything it is to be sixteen, smart, directionless, skeptical, and on the brink of adult life in mass market America. Kicked out of his fourth prep school, wary of facing his "touchy" parents, Holden flees to New York City and embarks on a series of encounters—with nuns, taxi drivers, an ex-girlfriend, a former teacher, a prostitute—all of which just fuel his depression. Feeling everything too intensely, weighing everything too carefully, seeing everyone as a phony and a sellout, he wonders how to avoid the same fate. Only his beloved younger sister is able to remove a brick or two from the wall he's building around himself.

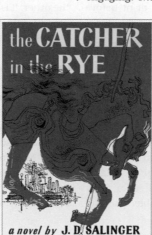

the CATCHER in the RYE

a novel by J. D. SALINGER

In creating a voice for his protagonist, Salinger reached back to *The Adventures of Huckleberry Finn* for a mode of address refreshing in its directness; to this he added a modern, sarcastic knowingness that was shocking in its day and even now remains conspiratorially engaging. *The Catcher in the Rye* was Salinger's first novel (he had previously published stories in *The New Yorker* and elsewhere), and his disaffected teenager felt almost too real to too many people. An immediate bestseller, the book faced charges of obscenity and immorality almost from the start, and the intense response, both positive and negative, was a shock to the author, who became the literary world's most famous recluse, publishing nothing after 1965. Meanwhile, *The Catcher in the Rye* continues to be one of the most assigned, most banned, and most cherished books in print.

What: Novel. *When:* 1951. *Also By: Nine Stories* (1953). *Franny and Zooey* (1961). *Raise High the Roof Beam, Carpenters* (1963). *Further Reading: Letters to J. D. Salinger,* a collection in which eighty authors, academics, and fans describe what *The Catcher in the Rye* has meant to them, was published in 2002. *Salinger* by David Shields and Shane Salerno. *Try: On the Road* by Jack Kerouac (see page 442).

Light Years
James Salter (1925–2015)

Illuminating a Marriage Shadowed by Time

James Salter is an interesting case. He graduated West Point in 1945 and flew more than a hundred combat missions in Korea. He published *The Hunters*, a novel based on those missions, in 1957 and resigned his commission to pursue writing. A second fighter pilot novel, *The Arm of Flesh*, appeared in 1961. Notwithstanding the positive reception of his first two novels, Salter remained dissatisfied with them (he would issue heavily revised versions of both four decades later), and he described his third as his "first acceptable book." *A Sport and a Pastime* (1967) is indeed a departure—in skill, style, and subject. Set in France, it's the story of an erotic affair between an eighteen-year-old French girl and a Yale dropout, as observed by an older man. Despite glowing reviews, it went out of print before resurfacing as a connoisseur's favorite. Eight years later came *Light Years*.

Portraying the progress of a marriage through two decades, *Light Years* unfolds in a series of exquisitely posed tableaux. Viri and Nedra Berland pass in and out of contentment and disenchantment in the company of children, friends, and lovers, their movements—from their big white house in the Hudson River valley to the beaches of Long Island's East End—dazzlingly reflected by the beautiful surfaces they cross with suppleness and style. Their lives are seductive yet recognizable, real and achingly within our own purview. "The only thing I'm afraid of are the words 'ordinary life,'" Nedra says at one point. As she and Viri grow apart, each retreating into a solitude they can neither share nor comprehend ("mysterious," Salter writes, "it is like a forest"), time drowns their desires at the same time as it deepens them, and the ordinary, with all its saving graces, slips away: "It happens in an instant. It is all one long day, one endless afternoon, friends leave, we stand on the shore."

As critic Michael Dirda has put it, Salter "can, when he wants, break your heart with a sentence." Indeed, no American novelist of the latter part of the twentieth century wrote with more care or keen emotional accuracy than Salter. "There are really two kinds of life," the narrator of *Light Years* tells us. "There is . . . the one people believe you are living, and there is the other. It is this other which causes the trouble, this other we long to see." Stunning in the exact sense, *Light Years* will leave you newly alert to the lives and loves within your grasp, and the ones that lie just beyond it.

What: Novel. When: 1975. Also By: Solo Faces (1979); Dusk and Other Stories (1988); Burning the Days: Recollection (1997). The Arm of Flesh was republished as Cassada in 2000. Try: Revolutionary Road by Richard Yates. The Maytrees by Annie Dillard. Footnote: Solo Faces, a novel about rock climbing, started out as a script for Robert Redford, who had starred in Salter's best-known screenplay, Downhill Racer.

Lost in Place
GROWING UP ABSURD IN SUBURBIA
Mark Salzman (born 1959)

A Connecticut Youngster in Kung Fu's Court

When I was thirteen years old I saw my first kung fu movie, and before it ended I decided that the life of a wandering Zen monk was the life for me. I announced my willingness to leave East Ridge Junior High School immediately and give up all material things, but my parents did not share my enthusiasm.

Mark Salzman is a graceful, winning writer, as the opening sentences of *Lost in Place* suggest. You want to keep going, and when you do, you'll likely find yourself halfway through this memoir of coming-of-age in Ridgefield, Connecticut, before you look up.

It's not only the easy assurance of the author's voice that leads us on. From an early age, Salzman was unconventional, supplying his older self with terrific material. His fascination with Chinese boxing and philosophy, for instance, leads him into all sorts of attempts at discipline and solemnity, such as wearing a bald wig in lieu of shaving off his hair, walking to school barefoot in the snow, and taking kung fu lessons from a sadist. Yet the very familiarity of the appointments of his suburban childhood and adolescence, and his more-or-less standard stumble toward adulthood, are what make this memoir so telling, and so funny. Salzman's appreciation of his younger self's adventures is complemented by his fond portrait of his father, a "good-natured pessimist" who survives on a steady diet of diminished expectations. (When asked by his son how the dust from the tail of a comet, blown out of the solar system, can drift forever, he answers, "Nobody knows, really. But you'll have a better idea once you get a job.") Nonetheless, the elder Salzman provides his son with the widest vistas of affection and sagacity, and the reader is glad to glimpse them in these pages, which prove delightfully that although all happy families may be alike, as Tolstoy averred, books about them don't have to be.

What: Memoir. *When:* 1995. *Also By:* Memoir: *Iron & Silk* (1986); *True Notebooks* (2003); *The Man in the Empty Boat* (2012). Fiction: *The Soloist* (1994); *Lying Awake* (2000). *Try: Tender at the Bone* by Ruth Reichl (see page 664). *Angry White Pyjamas* by Robert Twigger. *Don't Let's Go to the Dogs Tonight* by Alexandra Fuller.

Poems
Sappho (ca. 620 BC–ca. 550 BC)

The First Lyric Poet

> I confess
>
> I love that
> which caresses
> me. I believe
>
> Love has his
> share in the
> Sun's brilliance
> and virtue

Sappho in a 19th-century engraving

To trace the lineage of lyric poetry back to its roots is to describe, in fine lines, the memory of human feeling; it is an exercise by turns both exotic and familiar, as even a glance at Sappho's work reveals. We know little about the poet's life: She was born on the island of Lesbos in the latter part of the seventh century BC, and her poetic gifts were praised by Plato and honored throughout antiquity. In fact, much of the work that has come down to us (in essence, one complete poem and two-hundred-odd fragments) has survived as quotations in the works of other authors.

As Homer gave verse its bone, strength, and sinew, Sappho blessed it with flesh and bright senses, suppleness and grace. Even the bits and pieces that are her legacy are imbued with intimacy, marked by the touch and scent of pleasure and desire. Her celebration of eros in poems to both men and, more famously, women, echoes throughout the ensuing centuries of the lyric tradition.

Mary Barnard's pioneering 1958 translation (quoted here) presents Sappho's verses as shapely English poems. Faithful to the spirit of the originals, Barnard's renderings offer the best introduction to their beauty, proving the truth of the poet's claim, made more than 2,500 years ago:

Although they are

Only breath, words
which I command
are immortal

What: Poetry. *When:* Ca. sixth century BC. *Editions:*
Mary Barnard's *Sappho: A New Translation* was published
in 1958. Anne Carson's brilliant *If Not, Winter: Fragments
of Sappho*, published in 2002, gives all the extant texts in
their fragmentary form and thereby offers a very different
reading experience from the Barnard. *Further Reading:
Assault on Mount Helicon: A Literary Memoir* by Mary
Barnard. *Try: Sappho's Lyre: Archaic Lyric and Women
Poets of Ancient Greece*, translated by Diane J. Rayor.
Eros the Bittersweet by Anne Carson.

No Exit
Jean-Paul Sartre (1905–1980)

"Hell is—other people!"

A grand drawing room, done up in the style of Napoleon III's Second Empire, with a massive bronze statue standing on the mantel of the fireplace. It doesn't look like such a bad place to spend some time; in fact, it's a lot nicer than Garcin had expected. "Where are the red-hot pincers?" he asks the valet who's shown him in. "The racks and red-hot pincers and all the other paraphernalia?" No need for those, the valet explains. And he's right, as Garcin and his two new roommates, Inès and Estelle, will discover, for this small company of sinners is about to suffer misery more painful than any cartoon depiction of damnation could envision.

Jean-Paul Sartre, 1961

Welcome to hell, existentialist style.

No Exit is Jean-Paul Sartre's lean, mean one-act drama about our dire human condition (the French title, *Huis clos*, is tough to translate; it's the legal term for a closed hearing). The play distills and presents the ideas that Sartre explored at great length in his magnum opus, *Being and Nothingness*, published a year earlier. Despite a shelf of acclaimed novels and plays, Sartre was a man of ideas more than a man of letters. Nonetheless, he was awarded the 1964 Nobel Prize in Literature—an honor he refused on the grounds that he wanted to remain independent of all institutions. He was the best known of the French Existentialists, who believed that our lives are determined by our actions and our nonactions; there are no metaphysical defenses that can excuse our conduct. "We do not do what we want," as Sartre once succinctly put it, "and yet we are responsible for what we are—that is the fact." Yet the presence of others confuses the terms of our autonomy by objectifying who we are, even in our own eyes. Suffice it to say, it's complicated, which is why Sartre often turned to fiction and to the stage to give dramatic life to his intellectual formulations.

Which brings us back to the hell of *No Exit*, in which the three sinners pose for and provoke one another, powerless to escape the others' gaze. As it becomes clearer that they're stuck together for eternity, Garcin, Inès, and Estelle find themselves on a not-so-merry-go-round of accusations, cruelties, confessions, doubts, and humiliations. Each serves as both torturer and victim, unable to evade self-knowledge and its reflection in, and judgment by, the other two. Reduced to their dependence upon one another, they see no redemption in sight. As Garcin puts it in the play's most famous line, "Hell is—other people!" And a clever, gripping, living hell it is.

What: Drama. *When:* 1944; in English, 1946. *Also By:
Nausea* (1938). *The Age of Reason* (1945). *The Devil
and the Good Lord* (1951). *The Words* (1964). *Try: Six
Characters in Search of an Author* by Luigi Pirandello.
Waiting for Godot by Samuel Beckett (see page 64).
The Zoo Story by Edward Albee.

The Complete Memoirs of George Sherston
Siegfried Sassoon (1886–1967)

A Soldier-Poet's Searing Memoirs of the First World War

The first thing to know about the memoirs of George Sherston is that they are actually the thinly fictionalized memoirs of Siegfried Sassoon. Sherston is merely the name Sassoon adopts for himself as he narrates his story.

Who, then, was Siegfried Sassoon? Despite his Germanic first name, he was an Englishman, born in Kent and educated at Cambridge University, which he left in 1907 without obtaining a degree. He passed the next few years in leisured idleness. In 1914, with the First World War looming, he enlisted in the army, and a year later was posted to the Western Front in France, where his near-suicidal bravery earned him the nickname Mad Jack. In 1917, in protest against the war (it was, he would write, "a dirty trick which had been played on me and my generation"), he refused to return to duty after a convalescent leave. Rather than being court-martialed for his "knight-errantry about the War," as he describes it, he was declared unfit for service and was sent to "a shell-shock hospital," where he came under the care of Dr. W. H. R. Rivers, a renowned psychiatrist.

Sassoon tells his story in three volumes: childhood and the prewar years; combat and protest; hospitalization and postprotest experiences up to age thirty-two. Taken together, *The Complete Memoirs of George Sherston* is generally held to be, along with *Good-bye to All That* by Sassoon's friend and fellow soldier-poet Robert Graves, the finest autobiographical work to have come out of Britain about World War I. Sassoon's writing differs from Graves's

Siegfried Sassoon, ca. 1916

most notably in seeming to be the product of a fragile, war-damaged psyche: His narrative—eloquent, powerful, and unfailingly compelling—is eerie, fevered, told by someone who has looked too long into the mouth of hell, as this excerpt illustrates:

Wherever we looked the mangled effigies of the dead were our memento mori. Shell-twisted and dismembered, the Germans maintained the violent attitudes in which they had died. The British had mostly been killed by bullets or bombs, so they looked more resigned. But I can remember a pair of hands (nationality unknown) which protruded from the soaked ashen soil like the roots of a tree turned upside down: one hand seemed to be pointing at the sky with an accusing gesture. Each time I passed that place of protest those fingers became more expressive of an appeal to God in defiance of those who made the War. Who made the War? I laughed hysterically as the thought passed through my mud-stained mind.

What: Memoir. War. *When:* Originally published in individual volumes: *Memoirs of a Fox-Hunting Man* (1928); *Memoirs of an Infantry Officer* (1930); *Sherston's Progress* (1936). *Also By:* War Poems (1919). *The Old Century and Seven More Years* (1938). *The Weald of Youth* (1942). *Siegfried's Journey, 1916–1920* (1945). *Siegfried Sassoon Diaries, 1915–1925* (in three volumes, 1981–85), edited by Rupert Hart-Davis. *Further Reading:* Pat Barker's novel *Regeneration* (see page 51) is based on Sassoon's experiences in the Craiglockhart War Hospital. *Try: Good-bye to All That* by Robert Graves (see page 332). *The First Day on the Somme* by Martin Middlebrook (see page 548). *The Great War and Modern Memory* by Paul Fussell.

■ For Marjane Satrapi's *The Complete Persepolis*, see page 582.

Landscape and Memory
Simon Schama (born 1945)

Through the Woods to
the Well-Springs of Imagination

" Before it can ever be a repose for the senses, landscape is the work of the mind," writes Simon Schama. "Its scenery is built up as much from strata of memory as from layers of rock." Elaborating all the themes those sentences suggest, *Landscape and Memory* is a monumental yet thoroughly engaging historical examination of the myriad images of nature that Western culture has shaped to carry its elemental myths and memories.

Schama divides his massive work into three galleries—the first exploring "Wood," the second, "Water," and the third, "Rock"—creating a sort of museum to demonstrate how nature has informed the human imagination while that imagination, in turn, has projected itself onto nature. He leads us through fascinating landscapes of natural, historical, and folkloric inheritance; his trek through forests, for example, travels through time and space to visit the ancient woodland of Poland, Robin Hood's Sherwood, and the redwood kingdom of Yosemite. Putting his encyclopedic knowledge in the service of powerful intellectual enthusiasm, Schama instructively describes an astonishing range of exhibits: texts of Tacitus and Thoreau, the photographs of Ansel Adams and the paintings of Anselm Kiefer, the paths of pioneering naturalists, the Swiss Alps and Mount Rushmore, Old Father Thames and the fountains of Rome.

The author—and this is rare among scholars of Schama's ambition and achievement—is welcoming and generous to his readers; a page doesn't pass without a gift of perception or persuasion or an inviting image. The large pages, with illustrations integrated into the text, are seductive. You can open the book anywhere and, lured by a sentence or one of the brilliantly chosen reproductions of paintings, woodcuts, and etchings, happily fall into it for a few moments, or for hours at a time. "Nature is a wizard," wrote Thoreau, and so is the author of this book, conjuring spirits from wood, water, and rock in an expressive, original way. In short, despite its mammoth scope, *Landscape and Memory* is a friendly book, enriching our stores of learning, our meditations on history and memory, and, by no means least, our next walk in the woods.

What: Culture. Nature. *When:* 1995. *Also By: The Embarrassment of Riches* (1987). *Citizens* (1989). *Rembrandt's Eyes* (1999). *Rough Crossings* (2005). *Further Reading: Forests: The Shadow of Civilization* by Robert Pogue Harrison (see page 354). *Try: The Poetics of Space* by Gaston Bachelard (see page 39). *The Country and the City* by Raymond Williams.

■ For Stacy Schiff's *Saint-Exupéry*, see page 694.

Forms of Devotion
STORIES AND PICTURES
Diane Schoemperlen (born 1954)

A Playful Prayer Book of Puzzles
and Revelations

In this enchanting volume of inventive and unusual stories, Diane Schoemperlen arranges incidents, narratives, and philosophical speculations around wood engravings from the seventeenth, eighteenth, and nineteenth centuries to create fictional worlds of worship and wonder. The devotions she cleverly examines range from attachments to objects and daily rituals to romantic passions and anatomical attractions. She writes with a detachment that is not ironic but imaginatively analytical—classical reserve meets exuberant originality.

The title story, in which an essay by Emerson seems to have wandered into a story by Italo Calvino, is a lighthearted yet powerful celebration of faithfulness. Other tales explore the resonance of rooms and the innocence of objects, the shifting mysteries of perspective and love ("Love lets you loose in a part of the world where the atmosphere is too rare to sustain human life for long"). One story is constructed as a math word problem: "Train A and Train B are traveling toward the same bridge from opposite directions. . . ." Another, "Rules of Thumb," is an alphabet of imperatives

for the modern age, beginning with "Avoid the temptations of envy, pride, fast food, and day-time TV talk shows." Constructing her fictions with a comic, surprising, and deliciously odd formality, Schoemperlen manages to enhance our understanding of an astonishing range of everyday emotion and eternal perception. Her strangely told tales inform one's attention with a richness not often found in contemporary fiction. Opening this book is like uncovering an unconventional missal that is profoundly amusing and uncannily suggestive.

What: Short Stories. **When:** 1997. **Also By:** In the Language of Love (1994). Our Lady of the Lost and Found (2001). Red Plain Shirt (2002). This Is Not My Life: A Memoir of Love, Prison, and Other Complications (2016). **Try:** The Castle of Crossed Destinies by Italo Calvino. The Thin Place by Kathryn Davis.

The Last of the Just
André Schwarz-Bart (1928–2006)

A Novel of the Holocaust, Illumined by Legend

According to Jewish tradition, the equilibrium of the world rests upon thirty-six Just Men, the Lamed-Vov, who are born in every age to bear the weight of human grief. "[I]f just one of them were lacking, the sufferings of mankind would poison even the souls of the newborn, and humanity would suffocate with a single cry," writes André Schwarz-Bart in the opening chapter of The Last of the Just. The novel reaches back to this ancient legend through the lineage of Ernie Levy, whose family has known the grace of one Lamed-Vov-nik in each generation for three-quarters of a millennium. The book's narrator announces this at the outset:

Our eyes register the light of dead stars. A biography of my friend

Ernie could easily be set in the second quarter of the twentieth century, but the true history of Ernie Levy begins much earlier, toward the year 1000 of our era, in the old Anglican city of York.

Though the opening chapters trace the legacy of anguish and wandering across the centuries by European Jews and the Lamed-Vov of the Levy family, the heart of the book is an account of Ernie's suffering, desolation, and ultimate assumption of his destined role as "the last of the just" in a world overwhelmed by war and genocide. Recognizing his singularity, Ernie is daunted by its gravity and the fierce reality that engulfs him. He responds to the extermination of his family by escaping into a desperate hedonism, and is driven to attempt suicide in the face of Nazi violence. Yet he can escape neither the terror nor the blessing of his fate; a transforming love for a young woman rekindles his spiritual life, inspiring Ernie to embrace the magnanimity of his inheritance as he accompanies her and a group of children on their passage into the murderous chambers of Auschwitz.

Schwarz-Bart was born in France to Polish Jews who were deported to Auschwitz in 1941. By the age of fifteen, he was fighting in the French Resistance. Drawing on his personal experience and the wider tragedy of the Holocaust, as well as the longer history of Jewish persecution, Schwarz-Bart fashions a novel filled with vibrant characters and keen human sympathy. His detached realism is colored with moments of religious, at times almost magical, epiphany that deepen the indelible power and nobility of his tale.

What: Novel. *When:* 1959 in French; translated into English by Stephen Becker in 1960. *Award:* Prix Goncourt, 1959. *Also By: A Woman Named Solitude,* with Simone Schwarz-Bart (1972). *Try: Night* by Elie Wiesel (see page 851). *The Parnas* by Silvano Arieti. *Battlefields and Playgrounds* by János Nyiri. *Adaptation: The Last of the Just* inspired José Limón's 1967 ballet *Psalm.*

The Emigrants
W. G. Sebald (1944–2001)

Pictures of the Gone World

Winfried Georg Sebald was born in Bavaria in 1944. His father was a German soldier and World War II POW, and secrets ominous and unrevealed—not just paternal but historical—were a large part of his childhood inheritance: More was going on in the world than anyone was saying. As an adult, Sebald settled in England, where he taught literature for thirty years at the University of East Anglia. Yet he carried with him the sensibility of exile and a preoccupation with the nature of memory and the unseen but powerful influences of the past. In his midforties, he began writing distinctive novels that were published to great acclaim, first in Germany and then internationally. In December 2001 he was killed in a car accident; in the aftermath of his death, his literary reputation has only grown.

The book that introduced him to English-speaking audiences was his third, *The Emigrants,* and it's a good place to begin; as Susan Sontag wrote, "it seems perfect while being unlike any book one has ever read." Told by a narrator who shares much of Sebald's history, its four parts

are accounts of the dislocated lives of acquaintances and relatives—a Lithuanian doctor residing in the English countryside, a former schoolteacher whose suicide prompts investigation, an eccentric great-uncle, and a partner. Even as it evokes the violence and anti-Semitism of the larger history that convulsed twentieth-century Europe, Sebald's telling remains relentlessly small-scale and observable. His authorial voice combines narration, description, research, and erudition into a sort of serene but uneasy documentary reverie, leading the reader deeper into human anguish and emotion than any histrionics could.

Like all of Sebald's works, this prose narrative (a more apt description for his writing than "novel") incorporates elements of memoir and travelogue into something unique. His characters often share his interest in photographs and ephemera, and these, too, are presented to the reader, sometimes with explanation, sometimes not. What ties the disparate components of Sebald's art and the separate stories of *The Emigrants* together is the way that history and tragedy exert a tidal pull on sentences that recount the unremarkable surfaces of ordinary lives. The intimate force of his work has often been called uncanny, and that it is; it's unforgettable, too.

What: Novel. **When:** 1993. **Edition:** English translation by Michael Hulse, 1996. **Also By:** After Nature (1988).

Vertigo (1990). *The Rings of Saturn* (1995). *Austerlitz* (2001). *Further Reading: The Emergence of Memory: Conversations with W. G. Sebald,* edited by Lynne Sharon Schwartz. *Try: The Tongue Set Free* by Elias Canetti. *The Enigma of Arrival* by V. S. Naipaul. *Wittgenstein's Nephew* by Thomas Bernhard.

Where the Wild Things Are
Maurice Sendak (1928–2012)

A Picture Book Without Peer

"It is a constant miracle to me that children manage to grow up," Maurice Sendak once said, citing the unseen and inchoate dangers that well up from within—anxiety, pain, fear, anger, boredom, even love—that make kids' emotional survival such a prodigious feat. It is the slightly spooky magic of Sendak's picture books to depict the shifting weather of these states, and in no volume is his sorcery more spellbinding than in *Where the Wild Things Are*.

Maurice Sendak, 1982

The story is simple, told in 338 words: Mischievous Max, a boy of about five dressed in a wolf costume, chases his dog, threatens his mother ("I'll eat you up!"), and is sent to his room without supper. There a forest seems to sprout from the heat of his feelings, and he finds a boat that carries him—"in and out of weeks / and almost over a year"—to the land of the Wild Things. These monsters are portrayed with an indelible collective personality—once you've seen them, it is impossible to forget their huge yellow eyes or their menacing yet strangely childlike fearsomeness. Are they embodiments of Max's rage at his mother, phantoms of undirected frenzy? Sendak never tells us, and we don't need to know; the suite of distinctively colored and awkwardly gorgeous—there is no other apt description—illustrations carries us to a place where fantasy assumes all the presence and uncertainty of the real mysteries of living.

Max stares the monsters down, becomes their king, and leads them in a rumpus, only to be lured back home from his epic adventure by the smell of the dinner waiting for him—still hot.

Published in 1963 to both controversy ("It is not a book to be left where a sensitive child may come upon it at twilight," one librarian warned) and acclaim (it was awarded the Caldecott Medal as most distinguished American picture book of the year), *Where the Wild Things Are* has inspired an animated film, an opera by Oliver Knussen, a novel by Dave Eggers, and a 2009 feature film by Spike Jonze. Much more important, it has enlivened innumerable bedtimes, to say nothing of dreamtimes, for countless children and parents.

What: Children's. **When:** 1963. **Award:** Caldecott Medal, 1964. **Also By:** The Nutshell Library (1962). *In the Night*

Kitchen (1970). *Outside Over There* (1981). *Further Reading: The Art of Maurice Sendak* by Selma G. Lanes. *The Art of Maurice Sendak: 1980 to the Present* by Tony Kushner. *Making Mischief: A Maurice Sendak Appreciation* by Gregory Maguire. *Try: Jumanji* by Chris Van Allsburg.

■ **For Vikram Seth's *The Golden Gate*, see page 649.**

The Killer Angels
Michael Shaara (1928–1988)

The Best Civil War Novel

This is the story of the Battle of Gettysburg, told from the viewpoints of Robert E. Lee and James Longstreet and some of the other men who fought there.

Stephen Crane once said that he wrote The Red Badge of Courage *because reading the cold history was not enough; he wanted to know what it was like to be there, what the weather was like, what men's faces looked like. In order to live it he had to write it. This book was written for much the same reason.*

So writes Michael Shaara in a note prefacing this Pulitzer Prize–winning novel. And in the fleet, fierce narrative that follows, Shaara brilliantly shows "what it was like to *be*" at Gettysburg by recording the terrible butchery of the three days' fighting, switching among leaders' perspectives on both sides, including Confederates General Lee and his second in command, Lieutenant General Longstreet, and, for the Union, Colonel Joshua Chamberlain and Major General John Buford. Working from the combatants' own letters and other primary documents, Shaara has fashioned characters who live upon the page in a way that conveys the human drama of the epic battle that left fifty thousand soldiers dead, wounded, or missing. The fears and hopes,

memories and actions, of the protagonists in the face of Gettysburg's unrelenting carnage makes *The Killer Angels* one of the most deeply moving war novels ever written.

Ken Burns, who created the acclaimed television documentary *The Civil War*, calls Shaara's masterpiece "a book that changed my life." Burns's response to *The Killer Angels* mirrors the powerful effect the novel has had on countless readers since its publication three decades ago: "I had never visited Gettysburg, knew almost nothing about that battle before I read the book, but here it all came alive. . . . I wept. No book, novel or nonfiction, had ever done that to me before."

Robert E. Lee during the Civil War

What: Novel. War. *When:* 1974. *Award:* Pulitzer Prize for Fiction, 1975. *Also By: The Broken Place* (1968). *The Herald* (1981). *Soldier Boy* (1982). *For Love of the Game* (1991). *Try: Stars in Their Courses: The Gettysburg Campaign June–July 1863* by Shelby Foote. *Hallowed Ground: A Walk at Gettysburg* by James M. McPherson. *Andersonville* by MacKinlay Kantor (see page 429). *Adaptation:* The 1993 film *Gettysburg* was based on *The Killer Angels. Footnote:* Shaara's son, Jeff, is also a historical novelist. His *Gods and Generals* (1996) is a prequel to *The Killer Angels;* his *The Last Full Measure* (1998), a sequel.

WILLIAM SHAKESPEARE
(1564–1616)

A reader might well spend a lifetime exploring a single shelf, if that shelf is labeled "Shakespeare." On it are some three dozen plays, a sequence of 154 sonnets, plus a few odds and ends. Together these works compose as rich a portrait of human nature—and the fates that test, excite, exhaust, and exalt it—as has ever been penned. Shakespeare's art has such magic that this portrait evolves with us through the passages of time, so that even a familiar text will speak new truths to our hearts and minds at each stage of our experience.

From the ardent aspirations of young love (*Romeo and Juliet*) to the obdurate realities of old age (*King Lear*), Shakespeare parses the emotional grammar of living in ways that reveal its meaning even as they honor its mystery. As adept at the restorative silliness of low comedy as he is alert to the startling recognitions of high tragedy, he is a master of many registers of feeling and of myriad entertaining modes. With equal brilliance he explores the shadows cast on the public sphere by the dark energies of politics and power (*Julius Caesar, Macbeth*) and plumbs the private depths of searching consciousness (*Hamlet*).

The largest claims have been made for the scope of Shakespeare's achievement. The critic Harold Bloom credits Shakespeare, by virtue of his profound and original conception of personality, with "the invention of the human." By dint of his vision of the English past as a narrative of national inheritance transcending the discrete dramas of violence and valor that mark its progress (*Richard II, Henry IV, Henry V*), the playwright seems to invent our idea of history as well. Whatever Shakespeare's exact influence, his gallery of character, incident, metaphor, and reflection has supplied readers with the means to take the measure of humanity.

Despite an ever-growing stock of biographies, the documented facts of Shakespeare's life could fit on a few pages of the book you are holding in your hands. This only deepens the puzzle of his gifts. How did a provincial young man, who possessed at best a grammar school education, become the most esteemed author in the annals of literature? We know that he was born in 1564 in Stratford-upon-Avon to a family of some standing in the town, that he was married at eighteen to Anne Hathaway, and that he fathered three children. We know that in 1592, without explanation or fanfare, his name surfaced in the annals of the London stage, and that his reputation as actor and dramatist grew even while the archival record of his engagement with the repertory company of the Globe Theater remains spare. For all practical purposes, the Bard of Avon comes down to us as an artist more than as a man: His enormous reputation rests solely on his unparalleled achievements as a dramatist and poet.

His dramas draw from traditional sources of narrative and lore: Ovid, Plutarch's *Lives*, Holinshed's *Chronicles*, popular poems and plays, abiding legends. Yet the playwright is able, again and again, to imbue conventional forms—stories of love and of revenge, moral fables, historical pageants, comedies of mistaken identity—with an originality of expression that polishes the oldest pennies into ever valuable currency. Although his plots, stripped to their essential progression of entrances, exits, and events, are seldom unorthodox, they're viewed through a prism that refracts the subtlest colorings of human nature.

That prism, of course, is Shakespeare's language. Elegant, eloquent, rough-and-tumble, graceful, jocular, commanding, wise, delicate, muscular, frolicsome, inspired—English is a multifaceted marvel in his hands, revealing its potential without restraint, acknowledging no restriction on its ability to express every nuance and enigma of experience. The edifices Shakespeare builds with his blocks of verse and voices—from the castles-in-the-air of *A Midsummer Night's Dream* to the brooding battlements of *Othello*—hold, as Coleridge put it, "all the forms of human character and passion."

In his dramatic writing especially, Shakespeare exhibits what can best be described as a hands-on ingenuity for exploiting the exuberant irregularity and makeshift legacy of English, doubtless honed by the demands of theatrical deadlines and the always ad hoc nature of performance. In an essay exploring "the peculiar qualities of English," Robert Graves and Alan Hodge once compared the "apparent chaos" of our language to "the untidiness of a workshop in which a great deal of repair and other work is in progress: the benches are crowded, the corners piled with lumber, but the old workman can lay his hand on whatever spare parts or accessories he needs or at least on the right tools and materials for improvising them." No literary workman in the long history of our tongue has been as dexterous and versatile in this regard as Shakespeare. His toolbox, as inventoried by poet Ted Hughes, holds some 25,000

19th-century depiction of the Globe Theatre

words, "more than twice as many as Milton, his runner-up." A good number of them—*amazement, bedroom, dwindle, dishearten, clangor, watchdog, obscene, swagger*, to mention but a few—were, if not invented by Shakespeare, first recorded in his lines.

This stock of words served a peerless gift for turning phrases, and Shakespearean coinages by the hundreds have escaped their original confines to enter the language at large: *sound and fury; the dogs of war; the time is out of joint; something wicked this way comes; to thine own self be true; the better part of valor is discretion; screw your courage to the sticking place*—it's a *foregone conclusion* that the Bard was the *be-all and the end-all* of phrasemakers. His felicity *beggars description*. Although some of these constructions even a *blinking idiot* will remember as Shakespearean—*to be or not to be; neither a borrower nor a lender be; the winter of our discontent; what light through yonder window breaks*—others are by now so common that even the learned may be surprised to discover whose quill first inscribed them: *wild-goose chase; breathe life into a stone; strange bedfellows; fair play; he hath eaten me out of house and home; more in sorrow than in anger; a dish fit for the gods*. To read Shakespeare is to tour a veritable factory of the English language and watch its most beautiful and durable products being made.

This gives his texts a moment-by-moment energy that is exhilarating if you are intrepid in embracing it. *Ay, there's the rub*: How do you navigate the daunting seas of Shakespeare's soliloquies and sonnets? His diction is for-mal, his metaphors are complicated and often arcane, his syntax knotty, his vocabulary often obscure, and his metered verse uncongenial to readers bred on simpler sentences. You could bury yourself up to your ears in the abundant notes that accompany most editions of the Shakespearean canon, or you could resort to "translations" into modern, no-frills English (although this is akin to eating a steak substitute that provides some of the pro-tein while skipping all of the flavor). A better way is to throw caution to the wind and read the plays right through without worrying too much about comprehending every aspect of their meaning. You don't have to understand it all: If you're alert, you'll soon enough grasp the arc of the action and the contours of the characters.

The very best way to read the Bard is out loud, alone or in company. Letting the words lie silently upon the page misses a great deal of Shakespeare's power and playfulness, as well as much of the pleasure to be found in his work. Speaking his lines, following your voice through their intricate choreography of sound and sense, helps you grasp the glory of his inventions. He wrote for performance—no one has ever done so with more mastery—and until one plays the plays, however modestly, one doesn't know the half of Shakespeare.

In the act you'll be aided by the characters whom the words bring to life, for the plays are peopled with men and women whose heart-beats can always be heard through the dignified rhythm of the iambic pentameter that shapes their utterances. These indelible creations—Romeo and Juliet, Falstaff and Prince Hal, Ophelia and Hamlet, Iago and Othello, Cordelia and Lear, Ariel and Caliban, Prospero—are the flesh and blood Shakespeare's language con-jures out of the "airy nothing" of mere words. Larger-than-life, yet somehow never more than human scale, they are members of a cast with a depth and diversity of soul unrivaled in all of literature. Like us, they are, in the Bard's own formulation, "such stuff as dreams are made on," and they name in their persons the faiths and frailties of us all.

The entries that follow treat twelve of Shakespeare's plays—two early tragedies, a comedy, four histories, the quartet of mature tragedies that represents the pinnacle of his art, and a romance written as a kind of cur-tain call at the end of his career—as well as *The Sonnets*. This baker's dozen represents about a third of Shakespeare's extant output and dem-onstrates the variety and distinctive character-istics of his timeless art.

Although notes are appended to discus-sions of the individual works, a few general rec-ommendations for further reading are listed here.

Editions: There are many excellent annotated editions of Shakespeare. The layout and content of the notes in the Folger Library paperbacks of the individual plays are helpful and easy to use. Leslie Dunton-Downer and Alan Riding's *Essential Shakespeare Handbook* is an extraordinarily smart guidebook, with detailed synopses and considerations of each work. *Further Reading:* Anthony Burgess's *Shakespeare* is an inviting and accessible treatment of the life and work. Also of broad interest are Marjorie Garber's *Shakespeare After All* and Harold Bloom's *Shakespeare: The Invention of the Human. Adaptation: The Complete Arkangel Shakespeare* is a valuable audio set of all of the plays, unabridged and fully dramatized by first-rate actors. *Footnote:* The question of Shakespeare's literary and intellectual pedigree has proved so perplexing that it has provoked all sorts of theories positing some other figure—Edward de Vere, the 17th Earl of Oxford, for one, and Sir Francis Bacon for another—as the *real* author of the plays. These are intriguing, if ultimately unconvincing, hypotheses.

Romeo and Juliet
"But soft, what light through yonder window breaks?"

You know the story, as Shakespeare's Elizabethan audience no doubt did: Boy meets girl, and love at first sight transcends the enmity that fuels the bitter feud between their families, only to find its way to grief. In *Romeo and Juliet*, Shakespeare takes the trope of star-crossed lovers and, by setting their inter-ludes of youthful bliss within the swirling vio-lence incited by the stubborn anger of Verona's elders, creates a timeless drama of doomed romantic passion.

Olivia Hussey as Juliet in Franco Zeffirelli's 1968 film adaptation

One of Shakespeare's earliest tragedies, *Romeo and Juliet* exudes a keen theatrical intelligence: Its pacing is swift, its supporting players sharply drawn (especially memorable are Juliet's Nurse and Romeo's friend Mercutio). All of the characters, including the two principals, are dramatic as opposed to psychological figures, their roles determined by action and circumstance rather than by reflection or internal development. This simplicity gives the play a significant part of its power, as innocent ardor is pitted against petty political squabbles with no middle ground of ambiguity. If *A Midsummer Night's Dream* is the happiest literary expression of love's bewildering promise, *Romeo and Juliet* may well be the saddest; its tragic arc illustrates that the rapturous communion of souls is no match for the impetuous human inclination for misunderstanding.

For all the sorrow it delivers in its final act, what makes the play unrivaled as a love story is its lyrical intensity. From the moment of their first exchange, the poetry of Romeo and Juliet's love is set off from the prose of the strife-ridden world around them. In fact, the initial lines they address to each other at the Capulets' ball resolve themselves into the perfect harmony of a sonnet—and a kiss:

Romeo [To Juliet]
If I profane with my unworthiest hand
This holy shrine, the gentle sin is this,

My lips, two blushing pilgrims, ready stand
To smooth that rough touch with a tender
   kiss.
Juliet
Good pilgrim, you do wrong your hand too
   much,
Which mannerly devotion shows in this,
For saints have hands that pilgrims' hands do
   touch,
And palm to palm is holy palmers' kiss.
Romeo
Have not saints lips, and holy palmers too?
Juliet
Ay, pilgrim, lips that they must use in prayer.
Romeo
O, then, dear saint, let lips do what hands do:
They pray, grant thou, lest faith turn to
   despair.
Juliet
Saints do not move, though grant for prayers'
   sake.
Romeo
Then move not while my prayer's effect I take.

In the heat of the moment a second sonnet is begun, but it is thwarted by the interruption of the Nurse as the drama of desire and disjunction assumes its fateful pattern. Still, the music of their adoration remains, and returns, and survives in readers' minds to outlast even the plangent chords of mourning that close the play.

What: Drama. *When:* Written in 1594–96. *Also By: Love's Labour's Lost* (written in 1588–97). *Adaptations:* Leonard Bernstein's *West Side Story* brilliantly recasts the story with urban energy and musical genius. *Romeo and Juliet* has also inspired operas by Bellini and Gounod, as well as a ballet by Sergei Prokofiev. A 1968 film by Franco Zeffirelli is sumptuous. Baz Luhrmann's 1996 version, starring Leonardo DiCaprio and Claire Danes, translates the story to a gang-plagued modern California.

Julius Caesar

"Friends, Romans, countrymen, lend me your ears."

Like *Romeo and Juliet, Julius Caesar* is a good play with which to begin one's exploration of Shakespeare. Although the setting (ancient

Rome) and action (political assassination and its aftermath) make it different in kind from *Romeo and Juliet*, both share a clean narrative line in which the climactic elements of the tale are foretold. Shakespeare follows the historical record fairly closely in depicting both the murder of Julius Caesar at the hands of Brutus, Cassius, and their fellow republicans and the subsequent turning of the tables on the perpetrators by Mark Antony and Octavius.

The dramatist's literary art is here largely employed in the service of the plot; the language throughout is direct, stripped of metaphorical complexities and intricate wordplay. The fulcrum of the play is Antony's funeral oration for the slain Caesar in act 3, scene 2. Replete with a catalog of indelible phrases, from its famous invocation—"Friends, Romans, countrymen, lend me your ears. / I come to bury Caesar, not to praise him. / The evil that men do lives after them; / The good is oft interrèd with their bones"—through the echoing eloquence of "Ambition should be made of sterner stuff" and "This was the unkindest cut of all," the play gives a short but trenchant course in the varied arts of eulogy, rhetoric, and political spin.

The protagonists are richly drawn, and several vie for our attention; through their variety and complexity, the dramatist reveals how history is molded not just by the actions of men, but by their characters as well. Despite their emblematic stature, the major players are given the dignity of contradictory impulses: Caesar is a cunning and caring leader, dictatorially ruthless and humbly fatalistic; Antony is both idealistic and an opportunist; Brutus, something of a precursor to Shakespeare's later tragic heroes in his vacillations and regrets, turns from bold assassin to timorous penitent. One might say of any of them, as Antony says of Caesar at the conclusion of the last act, ". . . the elements [are] / So mixed in him that nature might stand up / And say to all the world 'This was a man.'"

What: Drama. *When:* Written in 1599–1600. *Also By:* *Macbeth* (written in 1606–07). *Antony and Cleopatra*

(written in 1606–07). *Further Reading: Plutarch's Lives* (see page 630). *Adaptations:* Joseph L. Mankiewicz's 1953 film stars Marlon Brando as Mark Antony, James Mason as Brutus, and John Gielgud as Cassius. In Stuart Burge's 1970 version, Charlton Heston plays Antony, Jason Robards portrays Brutus, and Gielgud is Caesar.

A Midsummer Night's Dream
"The course of true love never did run smooth."

Illustration for A Midsummer Night's Dream *by Sir John Gilbert, 1890*

Frequently turning on disguise and mistaken identity, and often demanding an extra-willing suspension of disbelief, Shakespeare's comedies are by and large better suited to stage than page. The actors' presences make the antics easier to follow, and good timing points up the humor of the rapid-fire wordplay, which may seem arcane in its intricate foolishness but bears a striking resemblance to the familiar pleasures of Abbott and Costello's "Who's on first?" routine, or some of the pun-driven volleys of the Marx Brothers' repartee.

Yet one comedy, *A Midsummer Night's Dream*, is so replete with intoxicating poetry that no reader should miss it. Set in a mythical ancient Greece, it begins in the court of Theseus, Duke of Athens, where a quartet of young, aristocratic Athenians is thwarted in its desires (Helena loves Demetrius who loves Hermia who loves Lysander—you get the idea). Meanwhile a group of commoners—the "rude mechanicals" led by the carpenter Peter Quince and the weaver Nick Bottom—are rehearsing a play for performance at the impending wedding of Theseus and Hippolyta. When lovers and laborers escape to a nearby wood to pursue their respective dalliances, they enter the realm of the fairies, whose king and queen, Oberon and Titania, are quarreling. Supernatural intrigue multiplies the romantic complications as errant spells cast by Oberon's page, the trickster Puck, spice the plot until it is dizzy with misdirected desire.

Throughout this comedic confection spun from confusion and enchantment, Shakespeare delights us with pure poetry of the highest order, assuming the role that Theseus himself describes at the opening of the play's last act:

> The poet's eye, in a fine frenzy rolling,
> Doth glance from heaven to earth, from earth
>   to heaven;
> And as imagination bodies forth
> The forms of things unknown, the poet's pen
> Turns them to shapes and gives to airy
>   nothing
> A local habitation and a name.

The transformations wrought by longing and magic under the influence of the midsummer moon are emblems of the capricious emotions that inspirit our lives and that, for all their lack of substance, embolden our actions and form our destinies, sometimes even conjuring from mere fancy, in Hippolyta's phrase, "something of great constancy." *A Midsummer Night's Dream* may well be the happiest tribute in all literature to the way love's fleeting promise not only haunts our dreams, but lingers to inhabit our hearts in the light of common day.

What: Drama. *When:* Written in 1595–96. *Also By: Much Ado About Nothing* (written in 1598–99). *As You Like It* (written in 1598–1600). *Twelfth Night* (written in 1600–02). *Adaptations:* Benjamin Britten's opera based on the play premiered in 1960. Several films have been made, including one of a Royal Shakespeare Academy performance in 1968, directed by Sir Peter Hall and featuring Helen Mirren, David Warner, Judi Dench, Ian Richardson, and Diana Rigg. Don't miss Max Reinhardt's 1935 Hollywood adaptation, with James Cagney as Bottom, Olivia de Havilland as Hermia, and a very young Mickey Rooney as Puck.

The Sonnets
"Not marble, nor the gilded monuments Of princes, shall out-live this powerful rhyme . . ."

The consummate exemplar of the Elizabethan love affair with the sonnet, Shakespeare's sequence of 154 fourteen-line poems is replete with luxurious, and lingering, literary melodies:

> Shall I compare thee to a summer's day?
>   (Sonnet 18)

> •

> When to the sessions of sweet silent thought
> I summon up remembrance of things past,
> I sigh the lack of many a thing I sought . . .
>   (Sonnet 30)

> •

> Let me not to the marriage of true minds
> Admit impediments. Love is not love
> Which alters when it alteration finds;
> Or bends, with the remover to remove.
>   (Sonnet 116)

Such music amply rewards any reader's attention, yet there is more to *The Sonnets* than a considerable catalog of lovely and quotable lines. Much has been made of the mysterious muses who incite the poet's fancy: The first 126 poems are addressed to a young man, and sonnets 127 to 152 address a woman who has become known as "the dark lady" (the last two sonnets draw portraits of Cupid). And yet, despite the fact that Shakespeare exploits every trope of amorous verse, the real extended subject of these rhymes is the triumph of verse over the vagaries of time:

> Yet, do thy worst, old Time: despite thy
>   wrong,
> My love shall in my verse ever live young.
>   (Sonnet 19)

Just as love transcends sexuality and ennobles passion, so poetry in its fixed measures can transcend the passing seasons, imbuing our affections with immortal echoes.

What: Poetry. *When:* Written ca. 1590; first published 1609. *Further Reading: The Art of Shakespeare's Sonnets* by Helen Vendler. *Try: Astrophel and Stella* by Sir Philip Sidney.

THE HENRIAD

T he Henriad comprises *Richard II, Henry IV, Part 1* and *Part 2*, and *Henry V*, and carries a thematic arc across the plays. The tetralogy traces the fortunes of the English crown as it is wrenched from the head of Richard II by Bolingbroke, then passed from that usurper's steady hands to his mercurial son, Prince Hal, who will at last merit its distinction after victory against the French on the battlefield of Agincourt. Together the dramas construct a purposeful narrative of the period from about 1399 through 1415, from the fits and starts of the royal, political, and military intrigues that made the era a turbulent one.

Although the four plays in sequence tell a coherent historical and dramatic tale, each is written in a different key: *Richard II* is elegiac, the two *Henry IV*s are alternately boisterously comic and fraught with themes of duty and regret, and *Henry V* is martial and triumphant. No other stretch of Shakespeare is quite so sweeping, and none so generous in its display of the playwright's insight into the conspiracy by which the historical imagination transforms the uncertain trials of personal souls into the convictions of patriotic myth.

Richard II
"For God's sake let us sit upon the ground And tell sad stories of the death of kings."

R ichard II is a history play distinguished by its poetry. In portraying the downfall of a monarch and the historic violation of the divine right of kings by Henry Bolingbroke, who usurped Richard's throne to launch the Lancastrian dynasty as Henry IV, Shakespeare gives his title character a lyric eloquence in speeches that are early explorations of the intimate meditative mode the dramatist would perfect in Hamlet's soliloquies.

At the outset of the play, Richard revels in his power, engendering scandal and political unrest by acting with despotic disregard toward his increasingly rebellious nobles. Having banished Bolingbroke from England, Richard seizes the exile's inheritance, provoking him into open revolt. Faced with Bolingbroke's bold rebellion, Richard's will is paralyzed, and he ultimately abdicates the throne, putting up no resistance to Bolingbroke's military threat. Imprisoned and isolated ("I have been studying how I may compare / This prison where I live unto the world"), the fallen king discovers his own humanity only by breaking faith with the idea of divine lineage that had once empowered him. In Bolingbroke's ascension, history seems to break free of heaven's hand, providing a new stage upon which the actions and emotions of men assume a graver, more uncertain power.

Initially filled with self-pity and equivocations, Richard's searching verbal reveries lead him to recognize the human measure of even a royal life, earning him a lonely but noble dignity. The knowledge of mortality that Richard acquires in despair is as bracing a lesson as Bolingbroke will soon be taught by the internecine realities of political intrigue.

What: Drama. *When:* Written in 1595–96. *Also By: Richard III* (written in 1592–94). *Further Reading: Richard II and the Revolution of 1399* by Michael Bennett. *Adaptation:* A 1978 BBC television production titled *King Richard the Second* stars Derek Jacobi, John Gielgud, and Wendy Hiller.

Henry IV, Part 1
"Thou seest I have more flesh than another man and therefore more frailty."

T oward the end of *Richard II*, Bolingbroke expresses his frustration with his "unthrifty son," Prince Hal, an offstage presence who will assume center stage—for as much time as his mentor in loose behavior, Sir John Falstaff, will allow—in the next installment of the Henriad.

"Inquire at London, 'mongst the taverns there," commands the new king. His intuition, we quickly learn in *Henry IV, Part 1*, is sound: The freshly minted heir to the throne is frequenting disreputable inns and leading a sporting life spiced with wine, wenches, and pranks. In such pursuits he is abetted and thoroughly educated by plump Jack Falstaff, one of the most endearing characters Shakespeare ever created. A large-hearted rogue, Falstaff has mischievous charm and a worldly sagacity that is often at odds with the sober obligations Henry would like to press upon Hal. The code of honor that motivates courtiers and soldiers, for instance, does little to satisfy Falstaff's sensible appetites:

Can honor set to a leg? No. Or an arm? No. Or take away the grief of a wound? No. Honor hath no skill in surgery, then? No. What is honor? A word. What is in that word "honor"? What is that "honor"? Air. A trim reckoning. Who hath it? He that died o' Wednesday. . . . Honor is a mere scutcheon. And so ends my catechism.

The play's scenes alternate between the tense setting of the royal chambers, where the king struggles to counter challenges to his legitimacy, especially from the upstart Hotspur, a paragon of bravery whose every virtue magnifies Prince Hal's faults, and the decidedly less stately haunts of Falstaff and his merry band, where ribaldry and high spirits vie for the audience's laughter. The court scenes are in blank verse, the tavern scenes in prose, and only Hal is at home in both verbal worlds, never losing sight of his duty despite his father's anxiety on that score. "I know you all, and will awhile uphold / The unyoked humor of your idleness," he declaims in a first-act soliloquy addressed to the rowdy reprobates who have just left the stage. "Yet herein will I imitate the sun," he continues, vowing to redeem his private sins upon the public stage. By the end of the play, Hal has made good on this promise, defeating the earnest Hotspur on the battlefield and earning, for the moment at least, his father's affection, while the wayward Falstaff holds fast to ours.

Shakespeare wrote no play more entertaining than *Henry IV, Part 1*. Its dynamic blend of broad comedy and fateful action, historical and familial strife, political intrigue and battlefield heroics give it an unmatched generosity of feeling and drama, evoking both the happy freedom of amiable indiscretions and the empowering gravity of large responsibilities. Several characters—Henry, Hal, Hotspur, and assorted supporting players both solemn and droll—light up the drama with vehement conflicts and playful pastimes, but Falstaff exudes an ineffable charm that outshines them all.

What: Drama. *When:* Written in 1596–97. *Also By: The Merry Wives of Windsor* (written in 1597–1601), a comedy also starring Falstaff, who has been transferred to Elizabethan England. *Try: Falstaff* by Robert Nye. *Adaptations:* Orson Welles's flawed but magnificent movie *Chimes at Midnight* (1965) concentrates the Henriad into a single, stunning film, with an emphasis on the two parts of *Henry IV* and *Henry V*; the director's performance as Falstaff is splendid. Giuseppe Verdi's wondrous final opera, *Falstaff*, is drawn largely from *Merry Wives*.

Henry IV, Part 2
"Uneasy lies the head that wears a crown."

No one who has made the acquaintance of Falstaff in *Henry IV, Part 1* has to ask why Shakespeare brought the stout knight back for a sequel. Indeed, legend—albeit largely unsupported by textual evidence—has it that even Elizabeth the queen was smitten by the character: Her call for a play on the theme of Falstaff in love allegedly prompted the Bard to compose *The Merry Wives of Windsor*. *Henry IV, Part 2* picks up where *Part 1* leaves off, but its tone is darker, for the play is dominated by the king's battles with illness and relentless political unrest. The crown Henry has usurped never sits easily on his brow: His struggle with rebellious nobles is mirrored by the turmoil of his own soul as he broods upon the consequences of his revolt against Richard II. Nevertheless, Falstaff again steals most of the show with his scheming antics; his seductive cleverness nearly scatters the dark shadows cast by the monarch's concerns of state and conscience.

Although Prince Hal is less of a presence than he was in the earlier play, leaving Falstaff and his cronies to their own delightful devices as they match wits with the law and extort favors from the hostess of their favorite inn, his scenes with the king enact a private drama of great power. Its psychological center is the scene in which Hal, thinking his sleeping father dead, dons the crown and bemoans the worries it brings its wearer. When Henry awakens, he upbraids the prince for his premature assumption of command. "I never thought to hear you speak again," the prince protests. "Thy wish was father, Harry, to that thought," retorts the king. In a scene of startling father-son intensity, filled with remonstrance and regret, the two bury their differences and are reconciled.

Kenneth Branagh (right) as Henry V in the 1989 film

Not so Hal and Falstaff. When Henry at last dies, Falstaff rushes to London to embrace his old friend the new king, only to be met with an unexpected regal iciness that foretells Henry V's pragmatic cruelty:

I know thee not, old man. Fall to thy prayers.
How ill white hairs becomes a fool and jester.

It may well be the saddest moment in all of Shakespeare, and Falstaff's disappointment is more poignant than many a tragic hero's fall. His larger-than-life vivacity, deemed so easily expendable by the new king, is the first casualty of Henry V's ruthless and triumphant reign.

What: Drama. **When:** Written in 1597–98. **Also By:** *Henry VI, Parts 1, 2,* and *3* (written in 1589–93). **Further Reading:** *The Fears of Henry IV* by Ian Mortimer.

Henry V

"We few, we happy few, we band of brothers . . ."

Once more unto the breach, dear friends, once more,
Or close the wall up with our English dead!
In peace there's nothing so becomes a man
As modest stillness and humility,
But when the blast of war blows in our ears,
Then imitate the action of the tiger:
Stiffen the sinews, summon up the blood,
Disguise fair nature with hard-favored rage. . . .
Follow your spirit, and upon this charge
Cry "God for Harry, England, and Saint George!"

I f the opening drama of the Henriad locates its emotional center in the quiet monologues of Richard II, the closing play finds its motive force in the stirring rhetoric Henry V declaims to rally his troops as they prepare to battle the French at Agincourt. Throughout, the patriotic pulse of *Henry V* is quickened by a military drumbeat.

Assuming his royal prominence, the king has left Falstaff—and the generous warmth and human frailty that Falstaff represents—behind to pursue the kind of glory his onetime mentor mocked: "[If] it be a sin to covet honor," the king confesses, "I am the most offending soul alive." And yet, while absent from the stage, plump Jack's skeptical spirit still haunts *Henry V.* Acting as a kind of comic chorus, his old accomplices Pistol and Bardolph interrupt the scenes of martial grandeur with their mercenary, scheming soldiering. Their self-protective cunning seems at times to represent the playwright's sardonic commentary on the earnest violence of the main action.

Yet the main action sweeps all before it: Inspiring his far-outnumbered troops to an astonishing victory, the once unworthy son of Henry IV—now a heroic amalgam of bravery, brutality, piety, and ruthlessness—unites his kingdom in nationalistic fervor. Historically, Henry V's achievements may be open to question; dramatically, his exploits are entirely satisfying, and conclude Shakespeare's Henriad with a rousing flourish.

What: Drama. *When:* Written in 1599. *Further Reading:* *Agincourt: Henry V and the Battle That Made England* by Juliet Barker. *Adaptations:* Laurence Olivier's World War II–era film trumpeted the play's patriotic music at a time when England desperately needed it. Kenneth Branagh's 1989 version offers a grittier, more complex interpretation.

Hamlet

"To be or not to be: that is the question."

The first of his mature tragedies, *Hamlet* is also Shakespeare's longest play. Animated with what seems an endless supply of indelible phrases—from "brevity is the soul of wit" and "to the manner born" to "the lady doth protest too much" and "to thine own self be true"—its more than four thousand lines plumb a bottomless well of human quandaries. Generations of actors, audiences, scholars, readers, critics, psychologists, and philosophers have attempted to fathom the meaning of the work and the motivations of its hero, yet both elude easy definition. So lively is the play's

Laurence Olivier as Hamlet in the 1948 film

language, so vital its characters, so cunning its drama, and so enigmatic its central figure that both play and protagonist increase in stature every time they escape our ready understanding. One of the pinnacles of literary art, *Hamlet* is inexhaustible.

To begin with, "Something is rotten in the state of Denmark": The king has died, and because the queen, Gertrude, has quickly married the deceased's brother, Claudius, the latter has assumed the Danish throne, disrupting Prince Hamlet's royal inheritance. The late king's ghost appears to Hamlet, revealing that Claudius poisoned him and commanding his son to avenge his murder. The stage is set for the sprawling drama that unfolds across the play's five acts: the bewildering antics of Hamlet's feigned madness, the play-within-a-play through which he taunts his guilty uncle, his escape from the entrapment Claudius plots for him, his confrontation with his mother, the fates that befall his childhood friends Rosencrantz and Guildenstern, the sycophantic royal counselor Polonius, and Polonius's daughter Ophelia, drowned in the rushing waters of the strange affection the prince demands.

But what happens in *Hamlet* is only a small portion of the play's living legacy, the better part of which resides in Hamlet's ruminations, given voice in the series of dazzling soliloquies Shakespeare composed for him. In these magnificent speeches, all the actions of the play, and every implication they suggest, are turned over in the hero's mind with an intense and intimate self-regard, as he stares into the abyss that his despair detects beneath the bustle of existence. In that dark uncertainty, Shakespeare probes the gravest matters: suicide, death, free will, responsibility, shame, expectation, the shackling hesitations not only of conscience, but of consciousness itself.

The central conflict of the drama is what gives this four-hundred-year-old work its decidedly modern currency. Hamlet realizes from the outset that he has been cast in a part in the revenge play life has written around him; what he vacillates about with such extraordinary eloquence is whether to join the work in progress on the stage. The drama's tension is created by the manner in which he stands outside the play, and outside of life, *thinking*:

Thus conscience does make cowards of us all;
And thus the native hue of resolution
Is sicklied o'er with the pale cast of thought,
And enterprises of great pith and moment
With this regard their currents turn awry,
And lose the name of action.

Hamlet would like to escape the plot of *Hamlet*, for to assume the role of avenging son—to engage all the messiness of emotion and commitment that exists beyond the brooding consolations of meditation—means, one way or another, to embrace death.

Which is just what he does, at last, leaping into the grave dug for Ophelia and setting in motion the lethal final act. The paradox of this greatest of English tragedies, in which Shakespeare grapples so bravely with the unsolvable mysteries of living, is that the prince is survived—for century upon century—by his soliloquies.

What: Drama. *When:* Written in 1599–1601. *Further Reading: What Happens in "Hamlet"* by John Dover Wilson. *Five and Eighty Hamlets* by J. C. Trewin. *Try: Rosencrantz and Guildenstern Are Dead* by Tom Stoppard. *Adaptations:* Most memorable among filmed versions of the play are those starring Laurence Olivier (1948), Nicol Williamson (1969), and Kenneth Branagh (1996).

Othello

"O, beware, my lord, of jealousy!
It is the green-eyed monster."

Except for the final, fatal scene, *Othello* is played out entirely in public spaces. The title character is a hero who dominates, with ease and assurance, any municipal or military situation. Despite being an outsider, Othello is honored as the defender of Venice, and he falls ardently in love with Desdemona, a patrician daughter of the city, who has been swept away by the romantic aura of exotic adventure the noble Moor exudes. At the outset, even their passion seems a public phenomenon, a point of contention between Desdemona's father and his fellow Venetian senators; it will remain, to its tragic end, a love starved of the confidences of intimacy.

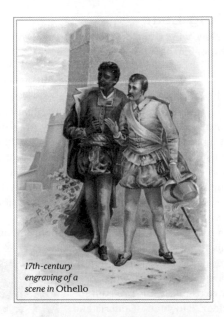

17th-century engraving of a scene in Othello

Although many of its scenes take place out of doors, the drama presents itself in psychologically claustrophobic close-up, our attention always zooming in to focus on Othello's villainous ensign, Iago, who manufactures a series of incidents to discredit Desdemona and to corrupt his commander's adoration of her. Othello's sure-footed decisiveness, a boon in battle (and, in a way, the very opposite of Hamlet's profound hesitation), leaves him awkward and uncertain in the sphere of private emotions. Iago preys upon this weakness, wielding words with lethal precision to transform his own envy into Othello's jealousy.

Relentlessly malign, Iago is a portrait of evil as sharply etched as any in literature. His insidious malevolence constricts the play's tragic ambitions to the mean dimensions of his own twisted heart, making *Othello* a work of intensely concentrated, breathtaking power.

What: Drama. *When:* Written in 1603–04. *Also By: Macbeth* (written in 1606–07). *Adaptations:* Giuseppe Verdi's penultimate opera, *Otello,* which premiered in 1887, is worthy of its source in every way. On screen, purely cinematic laurels go to Orson Welles's 1952 black-and-white masterpiece, which won the Palme d'Or at the Cannes Film Festival. Laurence Olivier's performance as the Moor was captured in 1965; more recently (1995) *Othello* was filmed with Laurence Fishburne in the title role.

King Lear

"Blow, winds, and crack your cheeks! Rage, blow!"

The most ambitious, inventive, and unconventional of Shakespeare's tragedies, *King Lear* is a towering work of imagination. Inspired by the legend of an early king of Britain, the realm of Shakespeare's *Lear* lies outside the reach of both the historical record and Christian theology, describing an almost mythic landscape of elemental forces. Indeed, the story is set in motion with the kind of plot device that might begin a fairy tale: An aged monarch decides to divide his kingdom among his three daughters, reserving the largest portion of inheritance to the one who "doth love us most." His two cunning elder daughters, Goneril and Regan, profess their boundless love, but when the youngest, Cordelia, the king's favorite, refuses to play along—"I cannot heave / My heart into my mouth"—she earns her father's wrath and is disinherited.

With fierce rapidity, the drama leaves the trappings of folklore behind to discover a new territory of the surreal. Wandering between the domains of the daughters he has favored, Lear is soon denied his fatherly prerogatives and his regal retinue, then locked out of the shelter of their castles. Wandering a barren heath, he rages across the boundaries between order and wildness, sanity and madness. Reduced to a voice in the wilderness, he calls the powers of wind and rain down upon his naked being, having been stripped, through his own agency, of the fragile clothing—literal and figurative—that protects human nature from nature's awful, reckless truths.

Nowhere else in Shakespeare does the author seem to disappear so completely: It is as if the Bard has set his words loose to engage the fundamental facts of life and death with whatever meaning they can sustain. No gods, no fates, no poetical or political structures afford any consolation in this bold, bleak view of our existence. We make our only mercies, *King Lear* tells us, and forsake them at our peril.

What: Drama. **When:** Written in 1605–06. **Try:** *The Book of Job* (see page 78). **Adaptations:** Peter Brook directed Paul Scofield in an excellent 1970 film. Akira Kurosawa's *Ran* (1983) is a stunning Japanese adaptation.

Macbeth

"Double, double toil and trouble; Fire burn, and cauldron bubble."

Orson Welles as Macbeth in the 1948 film

From the opening scene, in which three witches enter in thunder and lightning to invoke occult spirits in menacing rhymes, *Macbeth* inhabits a dark world of omens and hallucinatory visions. Impelled by the witches' prophecies, a military hero pursues a murderous course to the Scottish throne, only to be haunted by the victims of his violence and the depravity of his ambition. His bloody progress is prepared and abetted by the machinations of his wife, who curdles her husband's nature—"too full o' th' milk of human kindness," she claims—into a poisonous brew. Through the witches' auguries, supernatural forces seem to fuel the momentum of the couple's evil deeds, until their phantasmagoric guilt destroys them both.

Macbeth is shot through with bravura energy, the terrors of the tale supplying Shakespeare with sharp outlines to animate with the boldest colors of his poetry. Magnificent verse runs through the action like the dazzling camera movements of a film auteur lavishing visual invention on a ghost story or horror flick. Images electric with symbolism—the phantom dagger that lures Macbeth to his first victim; the ghost of Banquo, whom Macbeth alone perceives; the sleepwalking Lady Macbeth, futilely scouring her unclean hands—also have spellbinding power as narrative and theatrical effects. But for all of the drama's gruesome thrills and psychological acuity, what renders it timeless is the abiding genius of its language.

Tomorrow and tomorrow and tomorrow
Creeps in this petty pace from day to day
To the last syllable of recorded time,
And all our yesterdays have lighted fools
The way to dusty death. Out, out, brief candle!
Life's but a walking shadow, a poor player
That struts and frets his hour upon the stage
And then is heard no more. It is a tale
Told by an idiot, full of sound and fury,
Signifying nothing.

What: Drama. **When:** Written in 1606–07. **Also By:** *Titus Andronicus* (written in 1589–92). **Adaptations:** Verdi's *Macbeth* (1847) was the maestro's tenth opera. Orson Welles (1948) and Roman Polanski (1971) directed notable film versions, but the one that best captures the spirit of the play is Akira Kurosawa's *Throne of Blood* (1957).

The Tempest

"How beauteous mankind is! O,
   brave new world
That has such people in 't!"

Shakespeare's late romances—of which *The Tempest* is the culmination—are neither comedies nor tragedies, and they float far beyond the historical realm. They combine dramatic conflicts, fantastical ingredients, and theatrical spectacle into entertainments leavened by the promise of happy endings. What distinguishes *The Tempest* is the sense of creative repose from which it springs; a tranquil sensibility—lyrical, philosophic, and profound—is given its moment to strut upon the stage with playful energy, coloring each scene with a reflective and redemptive glow absent from all of Shakespeare's earlier works.

At the center of *The Tempest* is the sorcerer-philosopher Prospero, who, twelve years before the action of the play commences, had been deposed as Duke of Milan and set adrift in a decrepit boat ("the very rats / Instinctively have quit it") with his infant daughter, Miranda. Unbeknownst to his usurping brother, Antonio, Prospero and Miranda survived their sea-borne ordeal and alighted on a tropical

island. Once home to the witch Sycorax, this enchanted isle is still inhabited by her monster son, Caliban, and her former slave, the spirit Ariel, both of whom become Prospero's servants. When a ship bearing Antonio, along with the king of Naples and the king's son, Ferdinand, appears offshore, Prospero summons a storm that scuttles their vessel and washes them ashore.

What ensues, through scenes of comic confusion and magical contrivance, sets everything to rights: Miranda and Ferdinand fall in love, Prospero is restored to his rightful position, his brother's sins are forgiven, Ariel is liberated, and the once-savage Caliban vows to "be wise hereafter / And seek for grace." All the while Shakespeare muses—often in Prospero's voice, but with stunning eloquence in Caliban's as well—on life and love, freedom and slavery, treachery and forgiveness. Like Prospero casting spells upon his fellow characters, Shakespeare relishes his own artifice, transforming all the guile of his talents into a gift of wisdom and beauty, one that holds within it an elegy for his own unparalleled lifetime of literary invention:

Our revels now are ended. These our actors,
As I foretold you, were all spirits and
Are melted into air, into thin air;
And, like the baseless fabric of this vision,
The cloud-capped towers, the gorgeous palaces,
The solemn temples, the great globe itself,
Yea, all which it inherit, shall dissolve,
And, like this insubstantial pageant faded,
Leave not a rack behind. We are such stuff
As dreams are made on, and our little life
Is rounded with a sleep.

What: Drama. **When:** Written in 1611. **Also By:** *The Winter's Tale* (written in 1609–11). **Further Reading:** Robert Browning's "Caliban upon Setebos" and W. H. Auden's *The Sea and the Mirror*, both inspired by *The Tempest*. **Adaptations:** The most notable films are the science fiction classic *The Forbidden Planet* (1956), and Peter Greenaway's 1991 *Prospero's Books*, starring John Gielgud. *The Tempest* also inspired musicians, from Henry Purcell, who set songs and dances to the tale in 1695, to Thomas Adès, whose opera appeared in 2004.

Pygmalion
George Bernard Shaw (1856–1950)

The Inspiration for *My Fair Lady*

I n Greek mythology, Pygmalion was a sculptor who fell in love with a woman he had carved in stone. Taking pity on the lovesick artist, the gods brought the statue to life: Creator and creation married and had a child.

That's the legend that provides the title for George Bernard Shaw's play. Shaw's central character is not a sculptor, but a professor of phonetics by the name of Henry Higgins. He boasts that merely by changing the accent of Eliza Doolittle, a cockney flower girl, he can pass her off in polite society as a refined lady. In addition to inspiring pointed comedy, Higgins's arrogant project raises important questions about the cultural politics of the English language, a subject on which the Irish-born Shaw had particularly strong feelings (one of his most famous quips is that England and America are two countries "divided by a common language"). Shaw's prefaces to his plays always make provocative and rewarding reading, and in the substantial one that precedes *Pygmalion* he asserts that "it is impossible for an Englishman to open his mouth without making some other Englishman hate or despise him. . . . The reformer England needs today is an energetic phonetic enthusiast: that is why I have made such a one the hero of a popular play."

And popular *Pygmalion* has certainly been. Not only is it the prolific author's best-loved work, but it also inspired one of Broadway's

George Bernard Shaw, ca. 1930

Illustration of Eliza Doolittle

greatest triumphs, the 1956 Lerner and Loewe musical *My Fair Lady*. Despite Shaw's didactic specificity, his delightful confection transcends its English accents to inflect the tale of Eliza and the professor with insights into loss and love that are comic, compassionate, and universal. It ought to be noted, however, that the play is a bit less frothy than the better-known musical, in large part owing to their different endings. In *My Fair Lady*, it is suggested that Eliza may have a future with Higgins; in *Pygmalion*, there's no such possibility—a point reinforced by the vehement prose sequel that Shaw later appended to the text of the play. Less like Cinderella and more bracing than its glittering offspring, *Pygmalion* remains a masterpiece in its own right, and a perfect entrée into Shaw's rich oeuvre.

What: Drama. *When:* First produced in London in 1914; first published in 1920. *Award:* Nobel Prize in Literature, 1925. *Also By:* Man and Superman (1902). Major Barbara (1905). Saint Joan (1923). *Further Reading:* Bernard Shaw by Michael Holroyd. Bernard Shaw: Collected Letters, Volume 3: 1911–1925 (see page 505). *Try:* Zuleika Dobson by Max Beerbohm. The Importance of Being Earnest by Oscar Wilde (see page 854). *Adaptations:* Pygmalion was made into a fine movie in 1938, starring Leslie Howard and Wendy Hiller; Shaw wrote the screenplay. George Cukor directed Rex Harrison and Audrey Hepburn in the 1964 film of My Fair Lady. *Footnote:* Shaw won an Academy Award for his screenplay, making him the first person to win both a Nobel and an Oscar.

■ For George Bernard Shaw's *Bernard Shaw: Collected Letters, 1874–1950*, see page 505.

Frankenstein
Mary Shelley (1797–1851)

A Horror Story in a Class by Itself

"We will each write a ghost story," said Lord Byron, as detailed in Mary Shelley's introduction to her now legendary tale of Dr. Victor Frankenstein and his ungainly progeny. Two of the "we," the speaker and his fellow poet Percy Bysshe Shelley, took up but soon abandoned the assignment, while Mary, Shelley's nineteen-year-old wife, kept at it and sought a theme that "would speak to the mysterious fears of our nature and awaken thrilling horror—one to make the reader dread to look round, to curdle the blood, and quicken the beatings of the heart."

Some days later she heard the poets discussing the experiments of Erasmus Darwin (grandfather of Charles), "who preserved a piece of vermicelli in a glass case till by some extraordinary means it began to move with voluntary motion." That night, she lay in bed possessed by the idea that would animate her tale: "the hideous phantasm" of an assembled figure stirring to life through the machinations of a "student of unhallowed arts," mocking "the stupendous mechanism of the Creator of the world." She terrified herself, but had her story—one that has been frightening readers and audiences ever since.

And an intricate tale it is, told in interwoven voices. The first belongs to Robert Walton, recounting his expedition to the North Pole in letters to his sister. The second belongs to the desperate, half-mad man Walton discovers sledding across the ice, Dr. Victor Frankenstein, who relates the terrible history of his misbegotten project to create life on a laboratory table. The third and most haunting

Portrait of Mary Shelley, ca. 1840

voice belongs to the product of those experiments, the monstrous figure Frankenstein pursues across the Arctic, whose narrative of hope and disappointment, longing and violence, culminates in a passionate plea for a companion to share his solitude and redeem him from his murderous discontent. For he has learned what Dr. Frankenstein tragically realizes only too late: The spark of life, untended by sympathy and society, is just a breath away from flaring into horrifying savagery.

Shelley's novel is the work of a thinker, and not just the cheap thrill that countless sequels, spin-offs, and spoofs might lead one to expect. The philosophical, psychological, and ethical complexities in which she has tangled her tale deepen its strangeness and wonder. Strange and wonderful it remains, as suspenseful a monster yarn, and as absorbing a human one, as any reader could desire.

What: Novel. Horror. *When:* 1818. *Edition:* Currently available versions are typically reproductions of the third edition, from 1831, in which Shelley made changes to the language but not to the story. *Also By: Valperga* (1823). *The Last Man* (1826). *Lodore* (1835). *Falkner* (1837). *Further Reading: Mary Shelley: Her Life, Her Fiction, Her Monsters* by Anne K. Mellor. *The Monsters: Mary Shelley and the Curse of Frankenstein* by Dorothy and Thomas Hoobler. *Try: The Strange Case of Dr. Jekyll and Mr. Hyde* by Robert Louis Stevenson (see page 759). *Dracula* by Bram Stoker (see page 761). *Adaptations:* Countless, beginning soon after publication. The 1931 film starring Boris Karloff, which drastically alters Shelley's story, is the most famous. *Mary Shelley's Frankenstein,* made in 1994 and starring Kenneth Branagh, is a notable and worthwhile recent effort.

The Stone Diaries
Carol Shields (1935–2003)

A True Life Novel

The Stone Diaries is a sublime work of imaginative prose, a *matryoshka* of a book in which figures nest within figures, all exhibiting artistic and family resemblance.

The only novel ever to win both a Pulitzer Prize, America's most prestigious literary award, and Canada's Governor General's Award, Carol Shields's masterpiece recounts the life of one Daisy Goodwill Flett. Beginning with her birth on a kitchen floor in 1905, Daisy's life spans the twentieth century as it moves through adolescence and adulthood, two marriages, the rearing of children, a career in journalism, to old age and infirmity. "For a while I was worried because *The Stone Diaries* didn't seem to have a plot," Shields once explained. "And then I read an interview with [Australian Nobel Laureate] Patrick White . . . in which he says, 'I never worry about plot. I worry about life going on toward death.'"

As Daisy's life proceeds on that inevitable course, Shields presents it first through an invented autobiography, then through the remembrances of her friends, children, and other, more distant relations, whom the author positions for the reader on an elaborate family tree. The book even includes several glossy pages of photographs, such as one might find in a work of nonfiction. (For old photos of Daisy and her family, the author uses snapshots she found in archival collections and flea markets; the new photos, by intriguing contrast, picture Shields's own five children.)

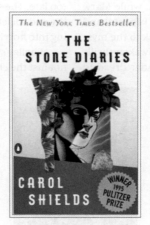

The New York Times Bestseller
THE STONE DIARIES
CAROL SHIELDS
WINNER 1995 PULITZER PRIZE

Neither Daisy's attempts to portray herself nor the reminiscences of those who know her provide any details dramatic enough to distinguish Shields's heroine from millions of others who have lived, loved, worked, raised families, and died, yet *The Stone Diaries* stunningly transforms the commonplace into the profound; it risks being true to life in a way few novels have attempted and fewer still have achieved. As in her other books, Carol Shields represents the difficult blessings of ordinary life as authentically as any novelist you're likely to read—and more cheeringly than you might imagine possible. Showing us how we piece together our prayer of being, she may even help us answer it.

What: Novel. *When:* 1993. *Awards:* National Book Critics Circle Award, 1994. Pulitzer Prize for Fiction, 1995. *Also By:* Swann (1987). *The Republic of Love* (1992). *Larry's Party* (1997). *Unless* (2002). *Collected Stories* (2004). Shields published a biography of Jane Austen in the Penguin Lives series in 2001. *Try: A Family Album* by David Galloway. *Lives of Girls and Women* by Alice Munro. *The Furies* by Janet Hobhouse.

Berlin Diary
THE JOURNAL OF A FOREIGN CORRESPONDENT, 1934–1941
William L. Shirer (1904–1993)

An Eyewitness Account of
Hitler's Rise to Power

Born in the American Midwest in 1904, William L. Shirer died in Boston nearly ninety years later, having seen at close range some of the most determinative events of the twentieth century. If, as Shirer believed, the luck of being in the right place at the right time was the cornerstone of a great journalistic career, then fate could not have been kinder to him. In the early 1930s he went to India, to cover the emergence and growing influence of an apostle of nonviolence, Mahatma Gandhi, and then to Paris, as European correspondent for the *New York Herald Tribune*; in 1935 he moved to Berlin, to report firsthand on the horrific events set in motion by a murderous avatar of evil, Adolf Hitler.

Berlin Diary begins in 1934, when Shirer was still in Paris. Once in Berlin, he was hired by Edward R. Murrow to join the pioneering CBS radio team. The Murrow-Shirer partnership's now legendary wartime broadcasts from London and the Continent heralded a new era of international reporting.

"The subject of this diary," Shirer tells us, ". . . is not, except incidentally, its keeper, but this Europe which he watched with increasing fascination and horror plunge madly down the road to Armageddon in the last half of the 1930's." For readers in 1941, *Berlin Diary* was the first uncensored account of Germany's march toward war, and it remains compelling reading today. Shirer's entries, animated by knowledge of contemporary German life as well as by his grasp of European politics, chart the rise of the Third Reich and the relentless approach of the coming conflict long before American involvement. We see the improvisatory, shifting nature of events as they unfold— before they've become history.

Shirer remained in Europe until December 1940. Sailing back to America from Portugal aboard the *Excambion*, he writes the following:

A full moon was out over the Tagus, and all the million lights of Lisbon and more across the broad river on the hills sparkled brightly as the ship slid down to sea. For how long? Beyond Lisbon over almost all of Europe the lights were out. This little fringe on the southwest corner of the Continent kept them burning. Civilization, such as it was, had not yet been stamped out here by a Nazi boot. But next week? Next month? The month after? Would not Hitler's hordes take this too and extinguish the last lights?

Reading this passage almost eight decades after it was written, we realize, after a moment, its import: Shirer's questions, despite their rhetorical eloquence, are not rhetorical at all. As he floated down the Tagus River that night, neither the author nor anyone else in the world knew the answers. He closes his *Berlin Diary* adrift in the midst of uncertain life, with history on the horizon, waiting to be written.

What: History. Diaries & Letters. *When:* 1941. *Also By: End of a Berlin Diary* (1947). *The Rise and Fall of the Third Reich* (1960). *Gandhi: A Memoir* (1980). *Twentieth Century Journey*, an autobiography in three volumes: *The Start, 1904–1930* (1976); *The Nightmare Years, 1930–1940* (1984); *A Native's Return, 1945–1988* (1990). *Try: I Will Bear Witness: A Diary of the Nazi Years, 1933– 1941* and *1942–1954* (two volumes) by Victor Klemperer. *Berlin Diaries 1940–1945* by Marie Vassiltchikov. *Inside the Third Reich: Memoirs* by Albert Speer.

···

The Pillow Book of Sei Shōnagon
Sei Shōnagon (ca. AD 966–ca. 1013)

**Sense and Sensibility
in Tenth-Century Japan**

··

While Europe still cowered in the shadows of the Dark Ages, a vibrant literary culture flourished at the court of the Japanese emperor in the capital city of Heian-kyō (the urban ancestor of present-day Kyoto). And although Japan had begun a period of isolation that would last nearly a thousand years,

the Heian era (AD 784–1185) produced two works that would earn a place among the masterpieces of world literature. Although many readers know Lady Murasaki Shikibu's *The Tale of Genji* (see page 575), a classic of Japanese literature, fewer are familiar with its contemporary, *The Pillow Book of Sei Shōnagon*, a work captivatingly original in form and content.

The daughter of a poet, Sei Shōnagon was a lady-in-waiting to the empress Sadako in the last decade of the tenth century. During her service she composed the *Pillow Book*, which remains an unrivaled source of detailed information on Heian court life, filled with descriptions of ceremonies and manners and with caustic judgments of people and pastimes. Yet the lasting appeal of the *Pillow Book* reaches beyond its historical importance, and modern readers will be rewarded—"entranced" may be a better word—by the book's revelation of its author's personality.

Written in 326 short (sometimes very short) chapters, the *Pillow Book* is a compendium of impressions and anecdotes, character sketches and observations of nature, ruminations and, most intriguing of all, delightfully surprising lists—"Things That Should Be Short," "Things That One Is in a Hurry to See or Hear," "People Who Seem to Suffer," "Things That Seem Better at Night than in the Daytime," "Things That Recall the Past but Serve No Useful Function." Sei Shōnagon's brilliant prose style is matched by her considerable poetic gifts, and both are complemented by her penchant for gossip and acerbic remarks. Across the gulf of more than a millennium, her wit and intelligence remain seductive, and her eloquence holds the reader rapt.

What: Diaries & Letters. Culture. History. *When:* ca. 1002. *Edition:* The 1967 translation by Ivan Morris is deft and erudite. *Try: The Diary of Lady Murasaki* by Murasaki Shikibu. *As I Crossed a Bridge of Dreams: Recollections*

Woodcut by Hokusai, portraying Sei Shōnagon

of a Woman in 11th-Century Japan by Lady Sarashina. *Footnote:* Sei Shōnagon's fellow author and rival, Murasaki Shikibu, was also a lady-in-waiting at the Heian court. In her memoirs, Lady Murasaki has sharp words for her colleague, condemning Sei Shōnagon's "extraordinary air of self-satisfaction" and belittling her writings—"which she so pretentiously scatters about the place"—as frivolous.

Bread and Wine
Ignazio Silone (1900–1978)

Fiction Against Fascism

Growing up in Abruzzo, a desolate region of Italy, losing his father when he was a boy and then his mother and many other family members in an earthquake when he was fifteen, Ignazio Silone was no stranger to hardship. He saw how the peasantry—already imprisoned, in Silone's words, by "the everlasting poverty handed down by fathers who inherited it from grandfathers, in the face of which honest toil

had never been any use"—was taken advantage of by those in power. "The harshest injustices were of such long standing that they had acquired the naturalness of the rain, the wind, and the snow," Silone wrote in 1930. He pledged himself to socialism and then to communism, and fought their hopeful battles passionately. Exiled under Mussolini for his anti-Fascist activities, he turned to writing fiction.

Silone's greatest work is his Abruzzo trilogy, comprising his first three novels—*Fontamara*

(1930), *Bread and Wine* (1936), and *The Seed Beneath the Snow* (1941)—the masterwork of which is the middle volume. *Bread and Wine* tells the story of Pietro Spina, an anti-Fascist revolutionary who, after fifteen years' exile, returns to his homeland posing as a convalescent priest. In the guise of being sick and with the police after him, Silone's protagonist is dependent on the town's peasants for more than he is comfortable with, and they begin to rely on him in ways suggested by the priestly role he has assumed. His purpose of empowering the powerless is complicated by his growing awareness that the human condition outlives any orthodoxy, be it fascist, communist, or religious. In one of the book's many political discussions, an old friend tells Pietro, "You too aspire to totalitarian power in the name of different ideas, which simply means in the name of different words and on behalf of different interests. If you win, which is a misfortune that will probably happen to you, we subjects will merely exchange one tyranny for another."

What sets Silone's political novel apart from others of its kind, and what makes it one of the most moving novels of the twentieth century, is his tender embrace of the human condition in all its poignant contradictions. His peasants are people, not avatars or messengers; they're flawed and funny and no purer than others, and his activists and priests are similarly perplexing—and perplexed. Their very humanity, like bread and wine, is the fruit of the harsh and unpredictable earth.

In recent decades, documents have come to light leading to accusations that Silone was a Fascist informer. The import of his correspondence with a police official, and the motivations for it (Silone's brother died while incarcerated in a Fascist prison), remain unclear, but the surrounding controversy has brought new attention to his work and a sharper focus on the moral turmoil of his characters. But morality, as literature knows in a way politics and religion can never seem to learn, is a messy business; like life itself, it transcends the boundaries of any doctrine—which is what *Bread and Wine* has told us all along.

What: Novel. *When:* The book's first publication was an English translation, in 1936; the first Italian edition appeared a year later. *Edition:* Steerforth Press released a paperback omnibus edition of Silone's Abruzzo Trilogy in 2000, with Eric Mosbacher's original translations revised by Darina Silone, the author's wife. *Also By: A Handful of Blackberries* (1952). *The Secret of Luca* (1956). *Emergency Exit* (1949). *Further Reading: Bitter Spring: A Life of Ignazio Silone* by Stanislao G. Pugliese. *Try: Christ Stopped at Eboli* by Carlo Levi (see page 480). *The Plague* by Albert Camus (see page 123).

City
Clifford D. Simak (1904–1988)

Dog Days of the Universe

" These are the stories that the Dogs tell when the fires burn high and the wind is from the north." This opening sentence of the "Editor's Preface" to *City* encapsulates all the wonders of this sad, savvy, and singular novel with a time span of twelve thousand years: change, heritage, art, love, loss, and, not least, story. The Dogs who do the telling ages and ages into the future are the inheritors of human sentience and sensibility, continuing to live fully without any irritable grasping after certainty, content with whatever miracles the universe will provide. The legends they relate around their fires rehearse the legacy of Man, a creature become myth, whose spiritual—there is no other word quite as apt—memory the canines sustain in their simple and desolate serenity.

The action of the stories proper, relating what happened before the Dogs began their mythologizing, begins in the year 1990 (far off from the 1940s, when the individual stories blended here into a seamless whole first appeared). Civilization is in the throes of a paradigm shift occasioned by new energy sources and something very much like the internet, a social media and information-delivery service, which allows humans to huddle in their scattered domiciles. Meanwhile, fully intelligent robots are being built; dogs are being engineered toward sapience; ogreish mutant humans are plotting; other dimensions are being sensed; and, to settle inhospitable Jupiter, colonists are being transformed into superior beings. (As the preceding sentence should make clear, the author is not a one-idea man, but rather a juggler of synergistic complexities.)

Simak follows generations of a single consequential family, the Websters, across twelve thousand years. Their surname even becomes a synonym for

"human" among the ever more relevant dogs; the family's domestic robot, Jenkins, persists through the millennia. He offers a wry perspective on the whole history of urban dissolution that *City* narrates, a process that ends not in apocalyptic drama but in an eerie, universal loneliness. A melancholy paean to mutability and longing, Simak's novel is elegiac and intoxicating. If the Ovid of the *Metamorphoses* (see page 609) had written twentieth-century speculative fiction, it might well read something like *City*.

What: Science Fiction. **When:** 1952. **Also By:** *Time and Again* (1951). *Way Station* (1963). *All Flesh Is Grass* (1965). **Further Reading:** *The World Without Us* by Alan Weisman. **Try:** *The City and the Stars* by Arthur C. Clarke. *Man Plus* by Frederik Pohl.

Maigret and the Man on the Bench
Georges Simenon (1903–1989)

Good Company for a (Reading) Life of Crime

French novelist Georges Simenon wrote hundreds of works of fiction, yet his most enduring creation remains the detective Jules Maigret. One of the most popular detectives in the annals of the mystery genre, Simenon's Parisian police inspector wends his way through the plots of seventy-five novels and a third as many stories, smoking his pipe, stopping here and there for a fortifying drink, enjoying the simple pleasure of a good meal, and untangling complex knots of murder and passion through the application of observation and intuition. The books are an addictive delight.

The first novel in the series, *Maigret and the Enigmatic Lett*, was published in 1931; the last, *Maigret and Monsieur Charles*, forty-one years later. *Maigret and the Man on the Bench* appeared a little more than midway through the run. It opens with a series of observations on a murder,

reflecting the ongoing mental processes of Simenon's protagonist—the kind of rumination that is an addictive source of pleasure to Maigret fans. We learn that the murder occurred on the inspector's sister-in-law's birthday, and on a Monday (although as everyone knows, "murders rarely take place on Mondays"). The case has "a flavor of winter about it," and soon Maigret and his wife are discussing their ever-unrepaired drafty windows and his need to don a coat before heading out into the chilly night.

The domestic details soon give way to the corpse's tale, the story of a quiet soul who breaks the predictable pattern of his days—and the grip of his domineering wife—to create a secret existence within the confines of his daily commute. By a canny focus on a puzzling pair of shoes, Maigret deciphers the mystery of Louis Thouret's life and death, with all kinds of insights and surprises and plenty of Parisian characters and atmosphere along the way.

You'll be sorry when you turn the last page, but happy that there are seventy-four more tales to enjoy: Reach for *Maigret and the Tavern by the Seine* (1931; also known as *The Two-Penny Bar*) or *My Friend Maigret* (1949) next. And don't miss *Madame Maigret's Own Case* (1950).

What: Mystery & Suspense. **When:** 1953, as *Maigret et l'homme du banc.* **Editions:** The most recent English translation is by David Watson (2017). Earlier versions have appeared as *Maigret and the Man on the Boulevard. Also By: The Strangers in the House* (1940), *Three Bedrooms in Manhattan* (1945), and *Dirty Snow* (1948) are among Simenon's many works of fiction that do not involve Inspector Maigret. *Try: Love in Amsterdam* by Nicolas Freeling. *Murder in the Marais* by Cara Black. *Adaptations:* Jean Gabin played Maigret in three French films (1958–63), and the character has inspired TV series in both France and Britain.

The Collected Stories
Isaac Bashevis Singer (1904–1991)

Translating the Human Condition into Tales—Across Centuries, Continents, and Tongues

Winner of the Nobel Prize in Literature, Isaac Bashevis Singer was born in Poland and lived there until 1935, when he immigrated to New York. A prolific writer who published dozens of novels, memoirs, and children's books, Singer is best known for his short stories. Although his tales reached their widest readership in their English versions, Singer wrote in Yiddish—"the tongue of martyrs and saints," as he once called it, "rich in humor and in memories that mankind may never forget. In a figurative way, Yiddish is the wise and humble language of us all, the idiom of frightened and hopeful humanity."

That idiom permeates Singer's stories, for whatever their setting, time period, or cast of characters, these deceptively simple narratives are steeped in the author's distinctive brew of faith, fable, and desire. Supernatural wonders appear amidst everyday realities, and slices of shtetl life are drawn as vividly as vignettes of life on Central Park West. The rigors and rewards of orthodoxy, the shelter of custom, the persistence and power of superstition, the grotesque and harrowing demands of history, and the pleasures and seductions of the present are woven into a tapestry that is both matter-of-fact and mysterious, as paradoxical as experience itself.

Singer chose the forty-seven stories in *Collected Stories*, which span his career from

Isaac Bashevis Singer, 1968

the 1950s to 1981. They include "Gimpel the Fool," in which the schlemiel who gives the tale its title has profound insight into the world's deceptions, and "The Spinoza of Market Street," in which a sophisticated man of learning is turned by love into a blessed fool. In these and the collection's other masterpieces—"A Crown of Feathers," "Yentl the Yeshiva Boy," "A Friend of Kafka," "The Letter Writer," "The

Power of Darkness"—comedy and tragedy of the largest human dimensions are played out in eight, twelve, or twenty pages. Singer's other selections range from reimagined folklore to portrayals of Jewish life in both the Old World and the New.

What: Short Stories. *When:* 1982; individual stories written between 1953 and 1981. *Award:* Nobel Prize in Literature, 1978. *Also By: The Family Moskat* (1950). *Satan in Goray* (1955). *The Magician of Lublin* (1960). *The Slave* (1962). *In My Father's Court* (1966). *The Manor* (1967). *The Estate* (1969). *Enemies: A Love Story* (1972). *Stories for Children* (1996). *Love and Exile: A Memoir* (1997). *Shadows on the Hudson* (1998). *Further Reading: World of Our Fathers* by Irving Howe (see page 391). *Try: Tevye the Dairyman and The Railroad Stories* by Sholem Aleichem. *The Dybbuk and Other Writings* by S. Ansky. *The Messiah of Stockholm* by Cynthia Ozick. *Adaptation:* Barbra Streisand directed and starred in *Yentl,* a 1983 musical film based on "Yentl, the Yeshiva Boy." Singer was not pleased.

The Three Golden Keys
Peter Sís (born 1949)

Magical Prague—and the Magic of Childhood

" Like a virtuoso poetic form, the interplay between few words and many pictures commonly called the picture book makes aesthetic demands that few have mastered," Maurice Sendak once wrote. "The best examples should rightfully take their place with comparably sophisticated 'grownup' works of art." In that company would certainly be the autobiographical works of Peter Sís, including *Tibet: Through the Red Box, The Wall,* and, especially, *The Three Golden Keys.* Picture books of enormous ambition, subtlety, beauty, intent, whimsy, and probity, they are telling conjurings of memory and experience; in them, Sís opens the private museum of his childhood to a public audience.

First published in 1994, *The Three Golden Keys* is addressed to the author's very young daughter:

By the time you can make sense of this note it will be the 21st century. You were born in New York, in the New World, and surely you will be wondering one day where your father came from. This book is to explain just that.

In the book's fairy-tale narrative, a young man's hot-air balloon is blown off course and lands him in an ancient town, which he recognizes as Prague, the city of his youth. He makes his way to his old home, but the house is dark, the door secured with three rusty padlocks.

A black cat appears to lead him through silent streets in search of the keys that will unlock the gate to his lost childhood.

Through the legends and landmarks of his native city, Sís revisits the wellsprings of his imagination in story and in sumptuous, eerie, evocative pictures. His images, crowded with detail and decoration, create an exhilarating cityscape that spreads like a map over the large pages. They are washed with colors both muted and luscious, colors that coat the illustrations with the mystic, tentative, tantalizing affections of remembrance. One falls into his marvelous memory palace like a thought tumbling into sleep—and dreams. Disguised as a children's book in format and style, *The Three Golden Keys* will nourish the imagination of any reader. It is a gift, humble and noble, and a loving legacy, which illustrates that the child is not only father to the man, but muse as well.

What: Children's. *When:* 1994. *Also By: Starry Messenger: Galileo Galilei* (1996). *Tibet: Through the Red Box* (1998). *The Wall: Growing Up Behind the Iron*

Curtain (2007). *Try: The Illustrator's Notebook* by Mohieddin Ellabbad. *The Arrival* by Shaun Tan.

The Immortal Life of Henrietta Lacks
Rebecca Skloot (born 1972)

A Singular Survival Story

At a fundamental level, Henrietta Lacks's contribution to the advance of medical science may be as great as that of anyone who has ever lived. Her cells, obtained without her permission or knowledge during treatment for terminal cancer in 1951, were the first human cells to be replicated and kept alive under controlled conditions in a laboratory. The cell line her tissue culture spawned enabled numerous breakthroughs, including the development of the polio vaccine, cloning techniques, chemotherapy drugs, AIDS medications, in vitro fertilization, and gene mapping, as well as tests for sensitivities to many medicines and products. The cell line is a critical component in more than ten thousand scientific patents, and the black woman from whom it was taken—a tobacco farmer and mother of five—would never know anything about her vast influence. She died at the age of thirty-one and was buried in an unmarked grave.

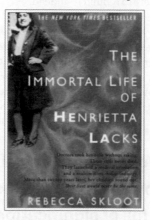

Rebecca Skloot initially learned of Lacks and the "HeLa" cells that are her legacy as a sixteen-year-old student in a community college biology class. Years later, Skloot said in a 2010 interview, "One of the first stories I imagined myself writing was hers. But it wasn't until I went to grad school that I thought about trying to track down her family." In the decade of sleuthing that she did for the book, Skloot uncovered the beginnings of HeLa research in the lab of George Otto Gey at Johns Hopkins, and she traced the offspring of Henrietta's cells as they powered multibillion-dollar initiatives in the biomedical industry. At the same time, Skloot struggled to win the trust of Lacks's descendants, first and foremost of her daughter Deborah, while they in turn struggled to come to terms with the strange idea that the cells of a deceased loved one were still alive—and of enormous medical and financial significance.

Told with a narrative fluency equal to the technical and emotional challenges of her subject—including profound ethical questions of patient consent and family privacy—Skloot's book is animated by voices that reveal, again and again, the shifting perspectives that make the story of Henrietta Lacks so compelling. A woman who worked as an assistant in Gey's lab told Skloot about the moment in the morgue when she noticed the bright red polish on Lacks's toes:

When I saw those toenails, I nearly fainted. I thought, Oh jeez, she's a real person. I started imagining her sitting in her bathroom painting those toenails, and it hit me for the first time that those cells we'd been working with all this time and sending all over the world, they came from a live woman. I'd never thought of it that way.

That Rebecca Skloot did think that way all along gives *The Immortal Life of Henrietta Lacks* a human interest and emotional resonance that deepen the relevance of the fascinating, many-layered story it explores.

What: Science. Medicine. *When:* 2010. *Try: The Spirit Catches You and You Fall Down* by Anne Fadiman (see page 263). *The Emperor of All Maladies* by Siddhartha Mukherjee (see page 572). *Adaptation:* A 2017 television film stars Renée Elise Goldsberry as Henrietta Lacks and Oprah Winfrey as her daughter Deborah.

Sailing Alone Around the World
Joshua Slocum (1844–1909)

A Nautical Solo of Historic Proportions

Talk about Yankee ingenuity: In 1892, having already had a prosperous career as a seaman, Captain Joshua Slocum was debating whether to apply for a new command or seek work at the shipyard. A friend said he had a boat to give him if he wanted, though she needed some repairs. "The next day I landed at Fairhaven . . . and found that my friend had something of a joke on me. . . . The 'ship' proved to be a very antiquated sloop called the *Spray*, which the neighbors declared had been built in the year 1. She was affectionately propped up in a field, some distance from salt water." Shocked when Slocum says he's there to rebuild her rather than tear her apart, the local gossips want to know if it will pay. "For a year or more I answered by declaring that I would make it pay." And so he did, not only for himself, but for generations of his readers as well.

Many men had sailed around the globe, but none had ever done it alone; determined to become the first, Slocum set sail from Boston in April 1895 on the restored *Spray*. Over the next three years, he piloted his thirty-six-foot wooden sloop on a historic voyage across 46,000 miles, and *Sailing Alone Around the World* tells the entire tale. Whether navigating storms and coral reefs, eating flying fish for breakfast, disguising his solitude at the approach of pirates, or calling at far-flung ports (once to meet the explorer Henry Stanley, and once to be mistaken for the Antichrist by zealous Christian converts), Slocum is delightful company. In a direct and unpolished voice, he relates his adventures—and his often valiant exertions—with a sly humor and flinty intelligence that make this classic a spirited journey indeed.

What: Adventure. Travel. *When:* 1900. *Also By: Voyage of the Liberdade* (1890). *Try: The Saga of Cimba* by Richard Maury. *Once Is Enough* by Miles Smeeton. *Gipsy Moth Circles the World* by Francis Chichester. *Footnote:* Slocum set sail again on the *Spray* in 1909 and was never heard from again. He was declared legally dead in 1924.

> **"Slocum has become the archetype of the American wanderer: creating himself on the page, he drew a classic hero, as resilient, as full of signification in his own rough-diamond way, as Huckleberry Finn."**
> —Jonathan Raban

Artful
Ali Smith (born 1962)

"Scotland's Nobel laureate-in-waiting"
—Sebastian Barry

"This book began life as four lectures given for the Weidenfeld Visiting Professorship in European Comparative Literature at St. Anne's College, Oxford," writes Ali Smith in a prefatory note to this exhilarating volume. "The lectures are published here pretty much as they were delivered."

This is not so much helpful as it is surprising—like everything else we are about to read. For nothing that the words "lectures," "comparative literature," or "Oxford" bring to mind suggests the character and richness of the author's subsequent musings "On Time,"

"On Form," "On Edge," and "On Offer and On Reflection." The first of these four pieces begins with an excerpt from the venerable English ballad "The Unquiet Grave," which ends with a young man's expression of his grief at his lover's death: "I'll sit and mourn all at her grave / For a twelvemonth and a day." Then Smith's voice starts in: "The twelvemonth and a day being up, I was still at a loss. If anything I was more at a loss." She goes on to describe herself picking up a battered copy of Dickens's *Oliver Twist* (see page 217) and trying to read it. She struggles to move her reading chair across the room. The ghost of her own deceased lover appears and sits down in front of the television, which is not turned on. "You came back from the dead to watch tv? I said."

An inspired amalgam of fiction, essay, and anecdote, *Artful* is part ghost story and part commonplace book, the author's invention crossing paths and joining hands with her wide reading. From *The Epic of Gilgamesh* (see page 255) and the Roman historian Sallust to Javier Marías (see page 525) and Margaret Atwood (see page 28), she displays a breadth of knowledge that will leave even the best-read among us feeling sheepish about the extent of our literary exposure. Yet her tone is so inviting and the connections she draws between disparate works are so natural that we are inspired rather than put off by her learning. Although this is not an easy book to read, it is an encouraging one, composed with such playfulness and ingenuity that we feel capable of approaching Smith's themes with something like her own alertness.

What are those themes? Loss and grief, the passing of time, writing and the making of meaning, memory. Smith's book is a celebration of the consolations of reading and of language, of the way the familiar patterns of a story or the rhythms of a phrase or sentence—or a line from a song—can become "a kind of dwelling place for us." Weird, wonderful, and stunning, *Artful* is like a book of commentary on a personal scripture that is shared here with generosity and love.

What: Literature. *When:* 2012. *Also By: Hotel World* (2001). *The Accidental* (2005). *There but for the* (2011). *How to Be Both* (2014). *Autumn* (2016). *Winter* (2017). *Try: Six Memos for the Next Millennium* by Italo Calvino. *The Beast in the Nursery* by Adam Phillips (see page 625). *Ongoingness* by Sarah Manguso (see page 521).

A Tree Grows in Brooklyn
Betty Smith (1896–1972)

On the Streets Where Childhood Lives

"I've never lived in Brooklyn, but someone must have told you the story of my life because that's what you wrote." So went a typical letter to Betty Smith in the aftermath of the publication of *A Tree Grows in Brooklyn* in 1943. That response to Smith's tale of a young woman's coming-of-age in the Williamsburg section of Brooklyn in the early twentieth century has been shared by countless readers since. An immediate popular success, the novel sold 300,000 copies in its first six weeks; by the time of Smith's death three decades later, more than six million copies had been sold, and the adventures of her protagonist, Francie Nolan, had been translated into more than a dozen languages.

It is easy to understand readers' identification with Francie's experience, even if their own lives have no ostensible common ground with that of the young girl collecting rags and copper, buying penny candy, stretching toward adulthood from the shadow of urban poverty.

For the alleys and avenues that the story leads us down are not specific to Smith's Brooklyn; they are the streets of childhood, the sidewalks of loneliness and yearning, the passageways of sentiment that carry us toward and away from home and family. They make up the neighborhood where the imagination grows up, and Smith's poignant book delivers it whole, whatever the details of time and place. Which is not to say the details of *A Tree Grows in Brooklyn* lack a compelling presence in themselves: The resilience of Francie's idealism in the face of the harsh realities of her privations, the drama inherent in the marriage of her romantic, irresponsible father and her practical, determined mother—these and the other essential elements of her story are drawn with such sympathy that Francie's family seems as real and important as our own.

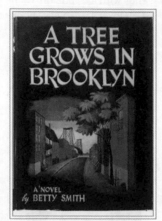

Best of all, the struggles and satisfactions of Francie's experience touch the life we live in our hearts, the life that surfaces only sporadically in our works and days. That's the joy and fierce power of the books that move us, as distinct from those that meet the colder gaze of critical analysis. A book like *A Tree Grows in Brooklyn* magically connects the dots of a reader's disparate selves into a coherent figure etched with deep emotion; that's why it has meant so much for readers in the first flush of youth, and stayed with so many of them so long.

What: Novel. *When:* 1943. *Reading Note:* For readers 12 and up. *Also By: Tomorrow Will Be Better* (1948). *Joy in the Morning* (1963). *Try: Angela's Ashes* by Frank McCourt (see page 536). *The House on Mango Street* by Sandra Cisneros. *Another Brooklyn* by Jacqueline Woodson. *Adaptations:* The 1945 movie was Elia Kazan's directorial debut. Less successfully, the story was turned, six years later, into a Broadway musical, with music by Arthur Schwartz and lyrics by Dorothy Fields. *Footnote:* Although she quit school after the eighth grade to help support her family, Betty Smith relentlessly pursued her dream of becoming a writer, eventually submitting a thousand-page autobiographical manuscript in a nonfiction contest announced by the publisher Harper and Brothers. The editors urged her to complete it as a novel, and, severely trimmed, it appeared as *A Tree Grows in Brooklyn*.

I Capture the Castle
Dodie Smith (1896–1990)

Too Hard to Classify, Too Delightful to Miss

From the first sentence—"I write this sitting in the kitchen sink"—Dodie Smith weaves a spell over her readers as she relates, in the voice of seventeen-year-old Cassandra Mortmain, the adventures of a remarkable family that lives, in impoverished eccentricity, in the ruins of a six-hundred-year-old castle (complete with moat) in England's Suffolk. In addition to Cassandra, there's Rose, her older sister, whose romantic intrigues much occupy our narrator; a younger brother; their stepmother, a sprite-like former artist's model; and the paterfamilias, James Mortmain, a once successful and lionized experimental writer whose creativity has been blocked for years. ("You can't trammel the creative mind," Cassandra tells her brother at one point, as they scheme to inspire their maddeningly unproductive dad. "'Why not?' said Thomas. 'His creative mind's been untrammelled for years without doing a hand's-turn. Let's see what trammelling does for it.'") There's also a young and handsome retainer smitten with Cassandra, and two young and eligible American men whose arrival sets the plot spinning. And spin the plot does, with intoxicating energy.

Yet it is the voice of the narrator, so unusual, alive, and imaginative, that makes the book so captivating. Cassandra's struggle to put her experience into words, to capture her feelings in sentences that reflect their depth, their strength, and their resourcefulness, is exhilarating to share. As Noel Perrin has put it, "*I Capture the Castle* is a hard book to classify. It is much too funny to be merely a teen romance, or merely any kind of romance. It's much too seriously romantic to be a spoof, a burlesque, or the kind of book they call 'rollicking.' In fact, it's much too individual and too well written

to be labeled at all." Let's just call it wonderful, then, and a book not to be missed.

What: Novel. *When:* 1948. *Also By: The New Moon with the Old* (1963). *Try: A Tree Grows in Brooklyn* by Betty Smith (see page 729). *The Greengage Summer* by Rumer Godden. *A Brief History of Montmaray* by Michelle Cooper. *Adaptation:* A movie, directed by Tim Fywell, appeared in 2003. *Footnote:* Despite an accomplished career as a playwright and the bestselling success of *I Capture the Castle*, Dodie Smith's most famous and best-loved work is certainly *The Hundred and One Dalmatians*, which inspired the popular Disney animated film (and its live-action sequels).

Polar Star
Martin Cruz Smith (born 1942)

A Hero of Our Time

Martin Cruz Smith's *Gorky Park* was a blockbuster when it appeared in 1981. It introduced readers to Arkady Renko, a Moscow homicide investigator caught in the twin grip of Russian soulfulness and Soviet bureaucracy. Renko is a compelling character: smart, tough, reflective, inured to the futility of his own sensitivity, yet sensitive nonetheless. He is a man of wit and learning condemned to the harsh realities of tawdry crime and state-sponsored spiritual disillusionment—which makes him, from a reader's point of view, very good company.

As satisfying as Renko's debut was, its sequel, *Polar Star*, proved every bit as compelling. Although *Gorky Park* is based in Moscow, it inscribes an international canvas of espionage, deceit, even heartbreak. In contrast, the second Renko novel is claustrophobic, its action largely confined to a commercial fishing trawler in the icy Bering Sea. There, in the wake of his *Gorky Park* exploits, the

officially disgraced Renko works the "slime line"—gutting fish by the thousands—in hopes that the job's anonymity and remoteness from Moscow will protect him from those seeking to either harm or, perhaps more frighteningly, "rehabilitate" him. When the body of a female crew member is hauled up in the ship's nets, Renko, against his better judgment, becomes entangled in the investigation of her death; he can't help but resist the authorities' attempts to write her death off as suicide. What ensues is part locked-room mystery, part exposé of the bleakness and brutality of Soviet existence despite the dawning of perestroika. ("Gogol's great vision of Russia was of a troika madly dashing through the snow, sparks flying, the other nations of the earth watching in awe," Renko tells a shipmate. "Yours is of a car trunk stuffed with stereo equipment.") Smith's prose is a delight, filled with striking images and memorable turns of phrase. But it's his hero who thrills us. Renko could be played by the Humphrey Bogart of *Passage to Marseille*: a man of honor, stubbornness, and intelligence who is endlessly watchable—or readable—as he navigates a world that refuses to live up to his melancholy hopes for it.

What: Mystery & Suspense. *When:* 1989. *Also By: Gorky Park* (1981). *Red Square* (1992). *Try: The Holy Thief* by William Ryan. *Adaptation:* Narrator Frank Muller recorded a superb audiobook.

A Simple Plan
Scott Smith (born 1965)

An Ingenious Thriller

C hasing their dog through the woods on a snowy night, three men come upon a crashed plane. In it they discover a dead pilot and a gym bag filled with money (more than four million in hundred-dollar bills, it turns out). Should they keep the money? Turn it over to the authorities? They arrive at "a simple plan" that promises them a big score without any risk. And that's when the trouble begins, as these regular guys are drawn to irregular extremes, their plan unraveling with increasing speed, menace, and violence, until—but let's not spoil it. Suffice it to say Scott Smith's sophisticated and macabre thriller is like a fun house of horrific surprise, in which every door that seems to let in light leads into a darker, more dangerous hallway.

What: Mystery & Suspense. *When:* 1993. *Also By: The Ruins* (2006). *Try: Mystic River* by Dennis Lehane. *Adaptation:* An excellent film, directed by Sam Raimi, appeared in 1998.

■ For Thorne Smith's *Topper*, see page 634.

White Teeth
Zadie Smith (born 1975)

London Calling

Z adie Smith burst onto the literary scene at the age of twenty-four with this roisterous first novel, a tour de force that sprawls across a quarter century of London life, beginning in 1975 (the year of the author's birth) and ending on New Year's Day 2000, the moment when the much-hyped Y2K bug was allegedly set to bring down our computers —to say nothing of civilization as we knew it. Tracing the lives of Caribbean and South Asian immigrants, Muslims and Jews, fancy Cambridge graduates and fundamentalists with a taste for marijuana, Smith's fiction is a comic portrait of a city at the turn of the millennium, and yet it's also a classic London story of adventures high, low, rich, and poor.

Descended from Dickens, *White Teeth* is alive with the same strains of energy, humor, and generosity that characterized the work of that distant literary forebear.

At the outset, Smith introduces us to two best friends: Archie Jones, a humble, indecisive white bloke, and Samad Iqbal, a waiter at a Bengali curry house. Having met while serving together in World War II, the men are each now raising a family in a changed and changing British capital. Archie has married Clara, a Jamaican-born Jehovah's Witness half his age. Samad and his wife, Alsana—betrothed in an arranged marriage before she was born—are the parents of twin boys; one of them is becoming worryingly serious about political Islam, and the other is desperate to be English, even giving himself a new name to fit in at the school chess club. The wages of assimilation are a central concern of Smith's novel, and throughout, she shows how thoroughly overlapping everyone's lives have become in a postcolonial, postmodern, post-everything London:

... it is still hard to admit that there is no one more English than the Indian, no one more Indian than the English. There are still young white men who are angry about that; who will roll out at closing time into the poorly lit streets with a kitchen knife wrapped in a tight fist.

But it makes an immigrant laugh to hear the fears of the nationalist, scared of infection, penetration, miscegenation, when this is small fry, peanuts, compared to what the immigrant fears— dissolution, disappearance.

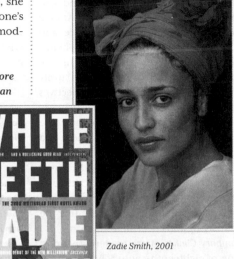

Zadie Smith, 2001

cosmopolitan, it is the great millennial novel.

Since her triumphant debut, Smith has gone on to write four other novels, among them *On Beauty* (2005), a postcolonial adaptation of E. M. Forster's *Howards End*, and the darker, ambitious *NW* (2012), which relies heavily on stream-of-consciousness narration. Still, *White Teeth* remains a touchstone, encapsulating a particular moment in British—indeed, in world—culture, when literary borders exploded and transnational promise finally found expression. Copious and

What: Novel. **When:** 2000. **Also By:** Fiction: *The Autograph Man* (2002). *Swing Time* (2016). Nonfiction: *Changing My Mind: Occasional Essays* (2009). *Feel Free* (2018). **Try:** *Brick Lane* by Monica Ali. *Small Island* by Andrea Levy. **Adaptation:** A four-part British television series aired in 2002. **Footnote:** Smith is a brilliant essayist: "Generation Why?" a 2010 piece on the meaning of Facebook, collected in *Feel Free*, offers a prescient analysis of the nascent—and now mature— digital distortion of experience.

The Expedition of Humphry Clinker
Tobias Smollett (1721–1771)

A Comic Tale-in-Letters from the English Novel's Earliest Days

One of the founding spirits of the English novel, Tobias Smollett was a man of many parts: novelist, physician, historian, poet and dramatist, translator (his rendering of *Don Quixote* is still in circulation today), editor and critic, medical writer, pioneering travel writer. Yet his primary place in literary history—as a writer of episodic humor populated with memorable characters—comes from having

imported into English the energies of French and Spanish picaresque fiction. *The Expedition of Humphry Clinker*, published in the year of his death, is his best novel.

Like several other early classics of English fiction, *Humphry Clinker* is an epistolary novel— written in the form of letters—but with an innovative twist. In contrast to Samuel Richardson's influential *Pamela* (1740) and *Clarissa* (1748), for instance, which consist almost entirely of letters written by the title characters, *Humphry Clinker* employs a group of correspondents, all of whom are accompanying Mr. Matthew Bramble as he travels through England and Scotland in pursuit of better health. Among them are his sister Tabitha, his niece and nephew, and the servant Winifred Jenkins. Although Mr. Bramble's letters make up the main part of the narrative, the others' lively contributions bring different perspectives to bear. Mrs. Jenkins's letters are particularly funny. She does her best—by, as she says, "the grease of God"—but her "spilling" is a mess, and she can hardly get through a single sentence without mangling the language hilariously. The title character is a servant who, although he contributes no letters of his own to the narrative, plays a pivotal role in precipitating the story's satisfying and cheerful resolution.

Humphry Clinker offers readers a vibrant depiction of eighteenth-century Britain, from the fashionable attractions of Bath to the filthy sprawl of London, from the newly popular pastime of beach-going to the disgusting food, foul water, and revolting accommodations that were the traveler's lot in the 1760s. Smollett's satirical bent is balanced by his sensitivity to the poverty and social injustice his characters witness. In this, as in his gift for creating unforgettable comic characters, he was both a precursor and an inspiration to Charles Dickens.

What: Novel. *When:* 1771. *Also By: The Adventures of Roderick Random* (1748). *The Adventures of Peregrine Pickle* (1751). *The Adventures of Ferdinand Count Fathom* (1753). *Travels Through France and Italy* (1766). *Try: Tom Jones* by Henry Fielding (see page 273). *Nicholas Nickleby* by Charles Dickens (see page 218). *The Sot-Weed Factor* by John Barth (see page 54). *Footnote: Travels Through France and Italy* shares with *Humphry Clinker* a focus on unpleasant and unsanitary conditions, prompting his contemporary Laurence Sterne, in *A Sentimental Journey Through France and Italy,* to mock Smollett with the moniker "Smelfungus."

Longitude
Dava Sobel (born 1947)

The Clockmaker Who Helped Sailors Find Their Way

On the night of October 22, 1707, Admiral Sir Clowdisley Shovell's fleet, returning home from Gibraltar, was wrecked on the Scilly Isles, only twenty miles off the southwest tip of England. The day before, Sir Clowdisley had been approached by a member of his flagship's crew, as Dava Sobel writes,

... who claimed to have kept his own reckoning of the fleet's location during the whole cloudy passage. Such subversive navigation by an inferior was forbidden in the Royal Navy, as the unnamed sailor well knew. However, the danger appeared so enormous, by his calculations, that he risked his neck to make his concerns known to the officers. Admiral Shovell had the man hanged for mutiny on the spot.

The admiral's refusal to listen combined with his miscalculating of his ships' position led to the death of his two thousand troops. The souls of these lost sailors, as Sobel elegantly puts it, precipitated (with all the speed a government can muster) the famed Longitude Act of 1714, in which Parliament promised a prize of £20,000 (well over ten million dollars in today's currency) for a comprehensive solution to the longitude problem, which, simply put, was this: How do you know where you are once you've lost sight of land?

Philip III of Spain had offered a similar bounty 136 years earlier, and every astronomer, mathematician, inventor, and crank, from Galileo and Newton to Sir Kenelm Digby (whose "powder of sympathy" inspired the remarkable "wounded-dog theory"—you have to read this to believe it), seems to have weighed in with a solution. It was not until the mid-eighteenth century that John Harrison— a self-taught watchmaker—invented the chronometer, "a clock that would carry the true time from the home port, like an eternal flame, to any remote corner of the world," thereby providing sailors a reliable means of finding their way.

This account of one of the most vexing dilemmas in scientific history is an intellectually adventurous narrative of exploration, experiment, trickery, and, not least, mechanical genius. Sobel's account of Harrison's forty years of struggle to improve his invention and to claim the prize, which George III finally awarded him in 1773, is a fine and fascinating journey.

What: Science. History. *When:* 1995. *Edition: The Illustrated Longitude* (1998) amplifies the text with more than 180 images. *Also By: Galileo's Daughter* (2000). *The Planets* (2005). *Further Reading: The Quest for Longitude,* edited by William J. H. Andrewes. *Try: The Riddle of the Compass* by Amir D. Aczel. *The Map That Changed the World* by Simon Winchester. *Adaptation:* Dramatized for television in 1999, with Michael Gambon as John Harrison.

···

River of Shadows

EADWEARD MUYBRIDGE AND THE TECHNOLOGICAL WILD WEST
Rebecca Solnit (born 1961)

The Reinvention of Time and Space

···

" In the spring of 1872 a man photographed a horse," writes Rebecca Solnit. The horse was Occident, one of the fastest in the country. The man was Eadweard Muybridge, a bookseller turned renowned landscape photographer who, among other commissions, documented the Modoc War, a fierce conflict between a Native American tribe and the United States Army; he also murdered his wife's lover (deemed "justifiable homicide" in court).

Occident belonged to Leland Stanford, a mastermind of the recently completed transcontinental railroad. The transportation magnate (and benefactor of the university that bears his name) had hired Muybridge to settle a debate about whether a trotting horse's four hooves are ever off the ground at the same time. With both imaginative and technological ingenuity, Muybridge answered Stanford's question by capturing multiple images of the horse as it was running.

He went on to do the same with other animals and with people. "By the end of the 1870s," Solnit writes, "these experiments had led to the photographer's invention of the essentials of motion-picture technology. He had captured aspects of motion whose speed had made them as invisible as the moons of Jupiter before the telescope, and he had found a way to set them back in motion. It was as though he had grasped time itself, made it stand still, and then made it run again, over and over. Time was at his command as it had never been at anyone's before."

Muybridge's innovations (and Stanford's, too, in bridging a continent with mechanical speed) would forever alter our experience of time and place, paving the way for both Hollywood and Silicon Valley. "A new world had opened up for science, for art, for entertainment, for consciousness," Solnit explains, "and an old world had retreated farther."

It's hard to imagine a more insightful guide to the "technological Wild West" that has shaped American modernity than Rebecca Solnit, whom critic Lawrence Weschler describes as "one of the most agile, protean, and consistently (jaw-droppingly) fascinating writers" at work today. She does a typically brilliant job here, weaving biography, history, landscape, and critical insight into a rare and provocative read.

What: Technology. *When:* 2003. *Award:* National Book Critics Circle Award, 2003. *Also By: Wanderlust: A History of Walking* (2000). *A Field Guide to Getting Lost* (2005). *A Paradise Built in Hell: The Extraordinary Communities That Arise in Disaster* (2009). *Try: A Clearing in the Distance* by Witold Rybczynski. *The Age of Wonder* by Richard Holmes.

ALEKSANDR SOLZHENITSYN
(1918–2008)

The central section in *The Gulag Archipelago*, Aleksandr Solzhenitsyn's mammoth "experiment in literary investigation," is called "The Soul and Barbed Wire." That juxtaposition of expansive spirit and captive flesh forms an emblem of the world the author explores in his writing, excavating fear and suffering—his own and that of millions of others subjected to the systematized brutality of the Soviet Union—from the forgetfulness of history. As a Red Army captain in World War II, Solzhenitsyn was imprisoned for insulting Joseph Stalin in a letter and served eight years in the camps (plus three more in enforced internal exile). Based on his experience in the gulag, his debut novel *One Day in the Life of Ivan Denisovich* was the first work to depict the monstrous realities of Stalin's rule; its 1962 publication in the Soviet literary journal *Novy Mir* was a result of Nikita Khrushchev's anti-Stalinist reforms. These reforms were short-lived, and despite the international acclaim his debut novel received, Solzhenitsyn's

Aleksandr Solzhenitsyn, 1975

later efforts were suppressed and had to be smuggled out for publication in the West—even after he was awarded the Nobel Prize in 1970. Expelled from the Soviet Union upon the publication in the West of *The Gulag Archipelago*, Solzhenitsyn lived in Vermont for nearly two decades. His Russian citizenship was restored in 1990, and he returned to his homeland in 1994. Through it all, he haunted the imagination of both East and West, like a recording angel conceived by Dostoevsky but possessing the patient concentration of Tolstoy, bearing witness to the terrors of ideology while never losing sight of the human nature that both enables and suffers them.

Gulag inmates constructing the White Sea–Baltic Canal, 1931–33

"If only there were evil people somewhere insidiously committing evil deeds and it were necessary only to separate them from the rest of us and destroy them," he wrote. "But the line dividing good and evil cuts through the heart of every human being. And who is willing to destroy a piece of his own heart?"

One Day in the Life of Ivan Denisovich
Grasping Dignity from a Brutal Destiny

A crucial book of the twentieth century, Solzhenitsyn's first novel chronicles a single day in the life of an inmate in a Soviet labor camp, beginning as "the hammer banged reveille on the rail outside camp HQ" at five o'clock on an inhumanly cold January morning—"too cold for the warder to go on hammering"— and ending that same night. In between, Ivan Denisovich Shukhov—wrongfully accused and imprisoned as a spy—and his fellow prisoners go about their daily rounds, struggling to make last the little warmth and food they have available to them, storing whatever scraps of dignity they still retain against the hope of some distant, almost unimaginable freedom.

The relentless brutality of Stalinist oppression is rendered all the more powerful by the author's focus—alternately fierce and tender—on the mundane dimensions of Ivan's experience.

In simple and recognizable sensory detail, Solzhenitsyn portrays the hunger Ivan and his comrades feel, the cold they suffer, the bodily fatigue and degradations that are their lot. The reader soon assumes the watchfulness of Solzhenitsyn's protagonist, becoming alert to the cunning necessary to cadge survival from a wintry Siberia bereft of any comfort, feeling Ivan's extreme delight when he discovers an unexpected bit of fish in his watery ration. Ivan observes the dignity of an old man—a prisoner for "as long as the Soviet state had existed"— unbowed as he eats his sparse meal: "instead of almost dipping his head in the bowl like the rest of them, he carried his battered wooden spoon up high." The author suffuses Ivan not only with sympathy but with simple, ineluctable nobility: He is the sort of man who cares whether the bricks he must work with are laid evenly, no matter the context of his labor. He is even able— time and again—to wring humor and joy from the bitter hours of his captivity.

In this spare, understated book, Solzhenitsyn puts a living face on the massive suffering and mortality that Stalin's cruel policies engendered. He would go on to document that suffering on a larger scale in his later works, but *One Day in the Life of Ivan Denisovich* remains the most vital, moving, and immediate expression of both the systemic degradation he witnessed and the individual decency it couldn't entirely extinguish.

What: Novel. *When:* 1962; English translation, 1963. *Editions:* The source for the first English translation was the text published in *Novy Mir*, which had been altered in anticipation of the Soviet censors. H. T. Willetts's translation in 1991 renders the complete work and is the only one Solzhenitsyn authorized and endorsed. *Award:* Nobel Prize in Literature, 1970. *Also By: The First Circle* (1968). *Cancer Ward* (1968). *The Red Wheel* (1971–91; multivolume novel including *August 1914* and *November 1916*). *Further Reading: Alexander Solzhenitsyn: A Century in His Life* by D. M. Thomas. *Try: Kolyma Tales* by Varlam Shalamov. *Journey into the Whirlwind* by Eugenia Ginzburg. *Adaptation:* The 1970 film stars Tom Courtenay.

The Gulag Archipelago 1918–1956

AN EXPERIMENT IN LITERARY INVESTIGATION

An Unparalleled Historical and Literary Testament

The first paragraph we read in Solzhenitsyn's three-volume, nearly two-thousand-page history of the Soviet state apparatus of repression and slave labor is a blackly comic anecdote. The author reports reading, in a 1949 scientific journal, of the discovery of a frozen subterranean stream in Siberia containing icebound specimens of prehistoric aquatic creatures. "Whether fish or salamander," Solzhenitsyn writes, "these were preserved in so fresh a state, the scientific correspondent reported, that those present immediately broke open the ice encasing the specimens and devoured them *with relish* on the spot." Only a fellow *zek* (political prisoner), he goes on to explain, would immediately understand, as he did, that the most revealing part of the story were the words captured in italic—not the freshness of the prehistoric flesh, but the hunger of the excavating laborers.

That image of a ravenous human present breaking through the expanse of ten thousand years of frozen time is the resonating opening chord of this enormous, courageous, and compelling history of the Soviet "prison industry"—the entire array of secret police operations, show trials, and labor camps subsumed in the acronym "Gulag," which abbreviates the Russian for "Chief Administration of Russian Labor Camps." Solzhenitsyn's detailed indictment of the state is drawn from his own bitter experience as well as from the reports, memoirs, and letters of 227 fellow *zeks*. With relentless realism and psychological acuity, he follows the course of arrest, interrogation, imprisonment, and oppression as suffered by millions upon millions of Soviet citizens. To unearth the roots of this endemic brutality and show how it grew from revolutionary seeds planted by Lenin (Solzhenitsyn repudiates any explanation of the Gulag as cultivated by Stalin alone), he uses reminiscence as well as sociological analysis, individual histories and documentary detail as well as political insight. The book's compassion is strengthened by the unblinking determination of its testimony, irrefutable in its abundance and its human density; and yet, as in *One Day in the Life of Ivan Denisovich*, Solzhenitsyn colors his narrative with threads of humor, deepening its hold on our hearts and minds. For all its reportorial breadth and intensity, it is the work of a writer whose words imbue the experiences he records with a poignancy and power that only literature can truly render.

aleksandr i. solzhenitsyn

THE GULAG ARCHIPELAGO

1918–1956

Winner of the Nobel Prize in Literature

Authorized Abridgment with a New Introduction by EDWARD E. ERICSON, JR.

But in every case, out of all the cells you've been in, your first cell is a very special one, the place where you first encountered others like yourself, doomed to the same fate. All your life you will remember it with an emotion that you otherwise experience only in remembering your first love. And those people, who shared with you the floor and air of that stone cubicle during those days when you rethought your entire life, will from time to time be recollected by you as members of your own family.

Solzhenitsyn's bravery in composing the work—and his cunning in keeping it hidden from the Soviet authorities throughout its decade of gestation—is worthy of a novel in itself, with climactic chapters devoted to the private and public effects of the hand-to-hand dissemination of *samizdat* copies within the USSR in the 1970s.

What: History. Literature. *When:* Written from 1958 to 1968, *The Gulag Archipelago* was published in English in three volumes, 1974–79. *Edition:* An authorized abridged single volume appeared in English in 1985. *Also By: The Oak and the Calf: Sketches of Literary Life in the Soviet Union* (1975; English version, 1980). *Try: Gulag: A History* by Anne Applebaum. *Hope Against Hope* by Nadezhda Mandelstam (see page 520).

SOPHOCLES
(ca. 496 BC–ca. 406 BC)

A man of means and a figure of civic stature as well as a dramatic genius, Sophocles lived through nine decades that coincided with the intellectual, political, and artistic flowering that made his native Athens the cultural seedbed of the Western world. He wrote more than 120 plays, only seven of which have come down to us complete. He won the theatrical competition at the city's annual festival of Dionysus twenty times, and never placed lower than second. His enigmatic but striking vision of the tragic hero has exerted a penetrating influence on the imaginations of readers, writers, and thinkers for more than two and a half millennia—including the good doctor Sigmund Freud, who would trademark Oedipus for his own purposes.

Younger than Aeschylus by some thirty years, Sophocles extended the reach of the stage tradition he inherited, adding characters and a more evocative sense of scene. Aeschylean tragedy mapped a course of progress from savagery to civilization under the guidance of the gods; Sophocles designed moral puzzles within a tighter and inescapably human frame. His protagonists act in fields of shifting moral forces that are often hidden from their view, and the irreconcilable realities of luck and fate define their circumstances. "How dreadful knowledge of the truth can be," says the prophet Tiresias to Oedipus, "When there's no help in truth."

The individual plays treated here—*Antigone, Oedipus the King*, and *Oedipus at Colonus*—belong to the same family of myths and are often grouped together as the "Three Theban Plays" or "The Oedipus Cycle," but they were neither conceived nor written as a trilogy. The first was written when Sophocles was in his midfifties, the second as he approached seventy, and the third, incredible as it may seem, twenty years later, shortly before his death at ninety (the play was performed posthumously). Despite their interlocking elements, each occupies its own circle of reverberating power.

Two single volumes collect all three plays in excellent translations: *The Oedipus Cycle* (Dudley Fitts and Robert Fitzgerald; quoted here) and *The Three Theban Plays* (Robert Fagles; with particularly informative introductions by Bernard Knox). Fitts's and Fitzgerald's version is more stately, whereas Fagles renders the plays in fleeter, more idiomatic language.

Antigone
An Unyielding Heroine

Although the events of *Oedipus the King* and *Oedipus at Colonus* precede those depicted in *Antigone*, Sophocles wrote *Antigone* first, sometime around 442 BC. Its title character is Oedipus's daughter, and its action unfolds in the aftermath of a bloody conflict between her brothers, Polynices and Eteocles, for the throne of Thebes. Their rivalry has proved fatal to both of them, and their uncle, Creon, has become king. Creon rules that because Polynices led an army against the city, he does not deserve the proper burial rites, and that anyone who disobeys this order will be put to death.

While the sentries guarding Polynices's body are sleeping, Antigone secretly inters him. The authorities quickly exhume the body, but Antigone is undeterred and again returns to rebury her brother. Not only is she caught, but in her confession she is unrepentant, accusing Creon of defying the gods by refusing to allow Polynices to be laid to rest. Creon invokes the primacy of civil order and civic duty over familial piety and—despite the pleas of his son Haemon, to whom Antigone is betrothed—sentences her to be walled up alive "in a vault of stone." Despite predictions by Tiresias that his stubborn cruelty will bring curses down upon Thebes, Creon will not be swayed from his stubborn righteousness.

It is easy to see the battle of wills between Antigone and Creon as a struggle between conscience and power, liberty and tyranny, individual courage and the brutality of the state. Many modern readings of the tale (including mid-twentieth-century restagings by Jean Anouilh and Bertolt Brecht) do so. Yet such an interpretation does not do justice to the complexity of Sophocles's drama, in which the importance of public allegiance over private fealty is strongly argued. Nevertheless, Antigone's bravery and the terrifying severity of her conviction make her tower over the calculating Creon, who at last yields to her resolve,

Cover of the score of Felix Mendelssohn's incidental music for Antigone

too late to prevent calamity for all concerned. In this, as in all of Sophocles's plays, virtue is as uncertain as circumstance, and no moral impulse is pure; the essence of his tragic figures is their human presence in the midst of incompatible and often overwhelming truths.

What: Drama. *When:* Ca. 442 BC. *Edition:* In addition to those noted above, see Seamus Heaney's 2004 translation in verse, *The Burial at Thebes. Also By: Ajax. The Women of Trachis. Electra. Philoctetes.* (None of these plays can be accurately dated.) *Try:* Plays by Aeschylus (see page 9) and by Euripides (see page 258). *The Island* by Athol Fugard. *Antigonick* by Anne Carson. *Adaptations:* The most notable among various screen adaptations stars Irene Pappas.

Oedipus the King
Aristotle's Perfect Tragedy

Nearly two centuries after Sophocles wrote *Oedipus the King*, Aristotle analyzed its extraordinary potency in his *Poetics*, concluding that the play defined the ideal qualities of tragedy. It's hard to quarrel with Aristotle's admiration for Sophocles's masterpiece; its fiendishly riveting plot unfolds with a horrifying, hypnotically inexorable logic unmatched by any drama before or since.

Oedipus the King (in Latin, *Oedipus Rex*) opens in a plague-stricken Thebes. Having appealed to the oracle at Delphi for guidance on how to alleviate the suffering of the city, Oedipus learns that his kingdom's fortune will turn only when the murderer of Laius, the former monarch, is discovered and exiled. Oedipus consults the blind prophet Tiresias, ultimately provoking him to assert that the present king himself is the culprit.

Sophocles's original audience would have known full well the entire tale of Oedipus, a tale of which Oedipus himself, through most of the play, knows only pieces: how he was sent away from Thebes as an infant because of a prophecy that he would prove dangerous to his father (Laius) and mother (Jocasta); how, after being raised as a prince in Corinth without knowledge of his true identity, the Delphic oracle warned him that he would kill his father and marry his mother; how he left Corinth and unknowingly killed Laius in a roadside confrontation; and how he became a hero—and then king of Thebes—by solving the riddle of the Sphinx ("What goes on four legs in morning, two legs at noon, and three in the evening?" The answer: Man, who crawls as a baby, walks upright in maturity, and uses a cane in old age), thereby dispelling an earlier curse on the city. It is a measure of the playwright's mastery that the suspense is screwed tighter by the irony created by the audience's foreknowledge.

And there is another level of irony that is even more striking: Oedipus is brought down not by a tragic flaw, but rather by his unrelenting application of his most commanding and commendable traits. An effective and civic-minded man of action, he fiercely pursues the truth about Laius's killer even as the evidence accumulates against him. Good intentions and a desire to escape the crimes and perils that have been prophesied impel every one of his actions. To no avail, alas: Recognizing at last the extent of his unwitting sins, he blinds himself and begs to be banished from Thebes.

Oedipus the King presents Sophocles's tragic sense of life with a fearsome and visceral clarity. Although fate is everywhere, not a god appears: Oedipus himself is the agent of his own undoing, and it is his fundamental honor that impels him toward his ruin. The faster we run from torment, the faster we may find it.

> Let every man in mankind's frailty
> Consider his last day; and let none
> Presume on his good fortune until he find
> Life, at his death, a memory without pain.

What: Drama. **When:** Ca. 426 BC. **Further Reading:** *Poetics* by Aristotle. *Tragedy* by Maurice Valency. *Sophocles's Tragic World* by Charles Segal. **Try:** *The Trial* by Franz Kafka (see page 425). **Adaptations:** Tyrone Guthrie and Pier Paolo Pasolini both made films of Sophocles's play. Jean Cocteau's *The Infernal Machine* is a modern dramatic adaptation; Cocteau also wrote the libretto for Igor Stravinsky's formidable oratorio, *Oedipus Rex*.

Oedipus at Colonus
A Stranger in a Strange Land

W ritten at the end of its author's long life, and as the golden age of Athens drew to a close, *Oedipus at Colonus* was destined to be a play about last things. Between the playwright's death and the play's first performance at the Festival of Dionysus in 401 BC, the city, weakened by internal strife, fell to Sparta; in the aftermath of the defeat, Athenian democracy gave way temporarily to oligarchy. It does not take a great deal of imagination to envision the original audience for one of Sophocles's final tragedies attending to it as they might heed a voice from beyond the grave.

The play opens in a grove on the outskirts of Athens, on ground sacred to the Eumenides, those spirits of watchfulness and vengeance who give their name to the last play of *The Oresteia* by Aeschylus (see page 9). Oedipus, now old and frail, has arrived there with his daughter Antigone and is convinced he has reached the burial place that has been prophesied for him. As the drama progresses, the aged wanderer will rehearse his sins and sad experience to the chorus and to Theseus, the Athenian ruler, yet his confessions are alert to the insoluble riddle of his fate:

Costume designs for Oedipus at Colonus, *1904*

And tell me this: if there were prophecies
Repeated by the oracles of the gods,
That father's death should come through his
    own son,
How could you justly blame it upon me?
On me, who was yet unborn, yet unconceived,
Not yet existent for my father and mother?

In this austere play, the cursed Oedipus assumes a strange grace, his imminent death promising a blessing, ordained by yet another oracle, on whatever city claims his burial place. Creon and Polynices arrive to escort him back to Thebes, but are cruelly rebuffed. Theseus at last embraces Oedipus and his posthumous legacy for Athens, escorting him off-stage to disappear into a forcefully evoked but mysterious sublime. He has transcended his fate, just as, in the infancy of his afterlife, Sophocles transcends the boundaries of his mortality.

What: Drama. *When:* Ca. 406 BC. *Try:* Plays by Aeschylus (see page 9) and by Euripides (see page 258). *King Lear* by Shakespeare (see page 716). *Adaptations:* A 1985 film of the reinvention of the play by theater director Lee Breuer and composer Bob Telson, *The Gospel at Colonus*, stars Morgan Freeman as the narrator and the Blind Boys of Alabama as Oedipus.

Aké
THE YEARS OF CHILDHOOD
Wole Soyinka (born 1934)

An African Nobel Laureate Conjures the Magic of Childhood

Aké is the town in western Nigeria where Wole Soyinka grew up in the late 1930s and 1940s. As readers make their way slowly through the opening pages, the setting may seem strange, the customs curious, the ubiquitous presence of the ancestral spirits disconcerting. Caught in the complex contradictions of British colonialism, Aké is also a place animated by the spirits of its native Yoruba folklore and religion. Despite what for many readers may be an unfamiliar setting, Soyinka's luminous memoir of his first eleven years is characterized by an uncanny fidelity to the sensations, uncertainties, and confidences of childhood—the continent on which inhabitants dwell in a landscape composed in equal parts of reality, faith, superstition, and personality. Like children everywhere, the young Soyinka accepts each day with a paradoxical combination of matter-of-factness and wonder. The unforgettable episode in which he, at four years old, is lured by the sound of a marching band out of his family's yard and all the way to the new world of a distant village before he realizes how far he has traveled, is as rich an evocation of the awakening of awareness as you're likely to come upon anywhere. Throughout, the warmth and nourishing peculiarities of the author's parents—his schoolmaster father, Essay, and his mother, a shopkeeper known to all as the "Wild Christian"—bless the book with a lovely, and loving, radiance.

The first black African to be awarded the Nobel Prize in Literature, Soyinka has met with acclaim as a playwright, novelist, poet, and critic. *Aké* stands on its own as his most magical book.

Wole Soyinka, 1969

What: Memoir. *When:* 1981. *Award:* Nobel Prize in Literature, 1986. *Also By: Death and the King's Horseman* (play; 1975). *Poems from Prison* (1969). *Myth, Literature, and the African World* (literary essays; 1976). Additional memoirs: *Isara: A Voyage Around Essay* (1989); *Ibadan* (1994); *You Must Set Forth at Dawn* (2006). *Try: The Famished Road* by Ben Okri (see page 602). *The Bride Price* by Buchi Emecheta. *Footnote:* Soyinka's outspoken political activism in Nigeria led to his arrest in 1967. His subsequent twenty-two-month imprisonment is documented in *The Man Died* (1972).

Memento Mori
Muriel Spark (1918–2006)

A Black Comedy in Deadly Dress

In this perfectly poised tale, wicked wit, artifice, and no little wisdom collude to produce a singular delight: a novel about mortality that is both unnerving and exuberant.

The title is Latin for "Remember, you must die." This is also what the anonymous caller says whenever seventy-nine-year-old Lettie Colson answers the phone: *"Remember, you must die."* Soon, other members of Lettie's set—a circle of upper-class English eccentrics that includes Lettie's brewing-magnate brother, Godfrey, and his wife, Charmian, a senile novelist; the poet and dreadful old fogey Percy Mannering; and the womanizing critic Guy Leet—are getting similar calls. As these mysterious warnings set the friends on edge, efforts at blackmail by Mrs. Pettigrew, the embittered companion of Guy's recently deceased ex-wife, bring all sorts of long-buried secrets and youthful indiscretions to light. There are yet further revelations that will unsettle Spark's characters—and surprise and amuse her readers.

Exhibiting the author's uncanny ability to infuse human affairs, no matter how petty or mundane, with an otherworldly gravity and inscrutable grace, *Memento Mori* portrays the fears, foibles, and vanities of old age in original and shocking ways. Quietly inventive and always a pleasure to read, Spark is a major writer who displays her mastery in deceptively modest and delightfully entertaining books.

What: Novel. *When:* 1959. *Also By: The Comforters* (1957). *Robinson* (1958). *The Ballad of Peckham Rye* (1960). *The Bachelors* (1960). *The Prime of Miss Jean Brodie* (1961). *The Girls of Slender Means* (1963). *The Mandelbaum Gate* (1965). *The Abbess of Crewe* (1973). *Territorial Rights* (1979). *Loitering with Intent* (1981).

A Far Cry from Kensington (1988). Symposium (1990). Curriculum Vitae: Autobiography (1992). Aiding and Abetting (2000). The Complete Short Stories (2001). The Finishing School (2004). Try: All Passion Spent

by Vita Sackville-West (see page 690). The Sin Eater by Alice Thomas Ellis. Ending Up by Kingsley Amis. Adaptation: The 1992 British television film features a cast of veteran British actors, including Maggie Smith.

The Complete Maus
A SURVIVOR'S TALE
Art Spiegelman (born 1948)

Mice, Men, and the Holocaust

Maus is a comic book about the Holocaust—or, if you prefer, a "graphic novel" or "graphic memoir." The shock is the same: Who would use a comic strip to document the Holocaust?

The answer is the American comics artist Art Spiegelman. His use of this improbable genre as a vehicle for reconstructing an unspeakable nightmare created one of the truly memorable books of the late twentieth century. Maus: A Survivor's Tale is startlingly original, singularly beautiful, and deeply moving.

At the center of the story is Spiegelman's prickly father, Vladek, who reached young adulthood in Czestochowa, Poland, about the time the Nazis came to power in Germany. As Maus takes up Vladek's tale, he is living in Rego Park, Queens, where his son regularly visits him and takes down his story: his marriage into a prosperous Jewish family, the gradual tightening of the Nazi noose, Vladek's imprisonment in Auschwitz, his survival, his postwar life in America. Juxtaposed with Vladek's scalding memories are his uneasy interactions in the present with his son and his second wife, Mala, who is also a survivor of Auschwitz. In outline, Vladek's story is familiar; presented in comic strip panels, however, it is anything but. Spiegelman's cartoons are daring, as is the artist's brilliant, unnerving, and powerful central conceit: He portrays all Jews—himself, his

father, and others—as mice, and Nazis as brutal leering cats. By stripping this survivor's tale of customary narrative structure, Spiegelman short-circuits conventional reaction to the horrors Vladek witnessed and jolts readers with unexpected emotional energy.

Maus—"an epic told in tiny pictures," as the New York Times succinctly put it—humbles all praise.

What: History. Memoir. *When: Maus I: My Father Bleeds History* (1986). *Maus II: And Here My Troubles Began* (1991). *Edition: The Complete Maus,* incorporating both parts, was published in 1997. *Award:* Pulitzer Prize Special Award, 1992. *Also By: In the Shadow of No Towers* (2004). *Try: A Contract with God* by Will Eisner. *The Complete Persepolis* by Marjane Satrapi (see page 582).

"The most affecting and successful narrative ever done about the Holocaust."
—The Wall Street Journal on Maus

Corinne, or Italy
Madame de Staël (1766–1817)

Passion, Politics, and Genius

A love story, a celebration of female agency and creativity, a seminal work of Romanticism, a sophisticated travelogue, and a study of European national characters and the political dynamics they set in motion, *Corinne, or Italy* is a remarkable novel written by an even more remarkable woman, whose company is the most compelling of the book's many attractions.

First, the story: Mourning his father's death, Oswald, Lord Nelvil, has traveled from Scotland to Italy, brooding over his failure to reconcile with the elder man before it was too late. In Rome, he encounters the beautiful and charismatic title character, a poet whose genius at extemporaneous composition has brought her not only acclaim but also a public presence rarely claimed by a woman at the time of the book's action (largely between 1794 and 1803). Corinne's artistic spirit and fearless nature mark her as one of the first embodiments of the Romantic hero in fiction, a model that would be picked up (and over-spiced with machismo) by Lord Byron in *Childe Harold's Pilgrimage* a few years later.

Staël details Oswald's and Corinne's developing infatuation as she takes them, and her readers, on a tour of Rome and its environs, one informed enough to become a travel guide used by the author's most sophisticated contemporaries. She suffuses the early parts of the slow-paced narrative with the pleasure of her own observational and psychological insight. Of Lord Nelvil's melancholy, for instance, she writes this:

Madame de Staël

... misfortune and repentance had made him afraid of destiny and he thought he could disarm it by making no demands on it. . . . He had been frightened by his past experiences, and nothing in this world seemed worth the risk of incurring such sorrows. But if you have the capacity to feel them, what kind of life can shield you from them?

Nearly every page of *Corinne* has an idea or expression to ponder. (This is delightfully true of all Staël's writing, including her non-fiction.) Entwined with the tale of her lovers' star-crossed entanglement are pioneering meditations on improvisation in art and nationalism in politics. In short, *Corinne* leads our attention from lovers to landscapes to history with an emotional and intellectual command that has few equals.

Which brings us to its author's unparalleled prominence in the turbulent age through which she lived. *Corinne* was her second novel; her first, *Delphine* (1802), played a part in Napoleon Bonaparte's decree that she be exiled from Paris for ten years. A French writer of the time succinctly captured her influence by saying there were three European powers vying against Napoleon: "England, Russia, and Madame de Staël." She is mentioned by Tolstoy in *War and Peace* (see page 798), and his consideration in that book of the influence of individual human wills upon history is much informed by her earlier expression of this idea. The biographer Richard Holmes put it best when he wrote, ". . . she was a truly extraordinary woman who courageously created a new role in society, one even larger than that of her irrepressible heroine Corinne. This role was that of the independent, freelance, female intellectual in Europe." Makes you want to know more, right? *Corinne* is the best place to start.

What: Novel. *When:* 1807. *Edition:* The translation by Sylvia Raphael in the Oxford World's Classics series is superb. *Also By: The Influence of the Passions Upon the Happiness of Individuals and of Nations* (1796). *The Influence of Literature Upon Society* (1800). *On Germany* (1810). *Ten Years of Exile* (1821). *Further Reading: Mistress to an Age: A Life of Madame de Staël* by J. Christopher Herold. *Try: Adolphe* by Benjamin Constant. *The Red and the Black* by Stendhal (see page 754). *Middlemarch* by George Eliot (see page 248).

The Valleys of the Assassins
Freya Stark (1893–1993)

An Englishwoman Among the Nomads

Freya Stark, who died in 1993 having lived a hundred years, journeyed where few European men had dared to go—through North Africa, the Levant, Turkey, Persia, Syria, Anatolia, and Kurdistan. She exemplified the bravery, stubbornness, and literary sensibility that characterized the intrepid English traveler.

"An imaginative aunt who, for my ninth birthday, sent a copy of the *Arabian Nights*, was, I suppose, the original cause of the trouble," Stark once wrote. Long before she was honored as a Dame Commander of the British Empire—a distinction that crowned her career as author of dozens of books, wartime emissary in Egypt, documentarian for the Royal Geographic Society, and star of BBC travel films—she was a bookish young woman who had read Homer's epics, toured exotic locales with her footloose parents, and spoke several languages, including Arabic ("I always had a feeling for learning languages, and Arabic covers the greatest number of countries with the most interesting history"). She dismayed friends and family by setting out in 1927 on the trip that was to become the basis for *The Valleys of the Assassins*. In addition to wanting to see an uncharted valley on the border of Iraq and Iran, she was in search of the legendary lost fortress of the Lords of Alamut, a band of hashish-fueled assassins that Marco Polo had described in his own *Travels*.

Stark had not intended to write a book about her exploits, but upon her return, her mother typed up the diaries she had kept and insisted she rewrite them for publication. The result is a beautifully rendered account of a world few Westerners had occasion to witness. On her mapless journey through lawless territory, dependent upon the knowledge and kindness of local guides, she is both patient and perceptive, drolly aware of the passing peril of her position and keenly observant of the landscapes, costumes, and customs she witnesses: "I spent a fortnight in that part of the country where one is less frequently murdered, and I saw the Lurs in their own medieval garb—the white tight-waisted coat with sleeves hanging in points from the elbow and white felt caps over the curls that hide their ears." Displaying her wise purchase on place, history, and people, *The Valley of the Assassins* is permeated with Stark's authorial genius—aphoristic, vigilant, exquisitely well mannered—that would articulate the heart and mind of the traveler in many subsequent books.

What: Travel. Adventure. *When:* 1934. *Also By:* Travel: *The Southern Gates of Arabia* (1936); *Baghdad Sketches* (1937); *A Winter in Arabia* (1940); *Alexander's Path* (1958). Autobiography: *Traveller's Prelude* (1950); *Beyond Euphrates* (1951); *The Coast of Incense* (1953); *Dust in the Lion's Paw* (1961). Also: *Perseus in the Wind* (brief, eloquent philosophical essays; 1948) and *Over the Rim of the World* (selected letters; 1988). *Further Reading: Passionate Nomad: The Life of Freya Stark* by Jane Fletcher Geniesse. *Traveller Through Time: A Photographic Journey with Freya Stark*, by Malise Ruthven, combines a gallery of Stark's own photos with a memoir by her godson. *Try: The Desert and the Sown* by Gertrude Bell. *Arabian Sands* by Wilfred Thesiger (see page 779).

Japanese Inn
A RECONSTRUCTION OF THE PAST
Oliver Statler (1915–2002)

A Four-Century Sojourn in Japanese History

In 1947, while serving in the army civil service during the American occupation of Japan, Oliver Statler jumped at the chance to spend a weekend at the Minaguchi-ya, a little inn about a hundred miles south of Tokyo that was one of the few public places not off-limits to

"Occupationaires." Enchanted by the place, Statler made many return trips, developing a powerful affection for both the inn and its proprietors, the Mochizuki family, who had maintained it for nearly twenty generations, beginning in the sixteenth century. The ultimate result was this 1961 bestseller, in which Statler weaves facts, traditions, history, and fictionalized narratives into a tapestry that brings four hundred years of Japanese culture to life.

Situated on the Tokaido Road, the ancient highway that linked Kyoto, the imperial capital, with Edo (now Tokyo), the shogunate's administrative center, the Minaguchi-ya literally and figuratively afforded a view of the pageant of Japanese history from the era of the feudal lords to the twentieth century. Statler deftly animates the warriors, concubines, sumo wrestlers, poets, pilgrims, and priests who traveled the Tokaido, yet what makes *Japanese Inn* a work to savor are the extended episodes in which he renders in high relief prominent figures and incidents. There is a fine retelling, for example, of the saga of the forty-seven *ronin*, the outlaw samurai whose vendetta to redeem the honor of the lord Asamo precipitates their ritual suicides. A superb biographical sketch of the renowned painter Hiroshige is replete with illuminating keen attention to his art. The most memorable chapter may well be "The Tokaido's Number One Boss," a delightful portrait of the gambler Jirocho, a wily brigand and genial Robin Hood who holds the busy thoroughfare in the embrace of his influence, protection, and scheming.

Statler's book is all told a marvelous collection of vignettes steeped in the color and character of Japanese tradition; it delivers the kind of pleasure Statler himself must have found so restorative at the Minaguchi-ya.

What: History. Travel. Culture. *When:* 1961. *Reading Note:* An ideal bedside book. *Also By: Modern Japanese Prints* (1956). *Japanese Pilgrimage* (1983). *Try: The Floating World* by James A. Michener. *Following the Brush* by John Elder.

The Man Who Loved Children
Christina Stead (1902–1983)

A Novel All Too Real— and Almost Too Original

"If all mankind had been reared in orphan asylums for a thousand years," wrote Randall Jarrell in an appreciative essay of rediscovery a quarter century after this book's publication, "it could learn to have families again by reading *The Man Who Loved Children*."

Christina Stead's singular novel is the kind of book that earns brilliant champions. Jarrell's 1965 quest to rescue the book from the edge of obscurity was echoed in the *New York Times Book Review* nearly forty-five years later by Jonathan Franzen. Angela Carter and Jane Smiley have also been ardent advocates, to say nothing of the thousands of common readers who pass the book along to friends with the kind of sacramental glee an especially treasured volume can inspire.

Lest Jarrell's encomium give you the wrong idea about the knowledge Stead's book might impart to future generations, you should know that no more than a few pages into *The Man*

Who Loved Children you'll begin to suspect the truth: This is a book about family life in all its ingenuous intimacy, greediness, neediness, and codependent nuttiness. Whoever first labeled the book "domestic Gothic" hit the nail on the head, for its depiction of a desperately unhappy marriage between a narcissistic and irresponsible idealist and an angry woman driven to the bitter edge by her husband's ridiculous schemes and relentless bidding for his children's adoration is, in a word, horrific.

And, in another word, hilarious. This is one of the most fiercely funny books you'll ever read. Louisa Pollit, Stead's eleven-year-old alter ego, grounds the book, if not the family, with the tender fury of her emerging intelligence. Mining her own childhood with an egotistical father—he loved small children because he could bend them to his will—and a stepmother nearly as abominable (if in different ways), Stead produces a tale that, in Jarrell's grateful assessment, "has one quality that, ordinarily, only a great book has: it does a single thing better than any other book has ever done it. *The Man Who Loved Children* makes you a part of one family's immediate existence as no other book quite does."

What: Novel. **When:** 1940. **Also By:** *House of All Nations* (1938). *For Love Alone* (1944). *Letty Fox: Her Luck* (1946). *I'm Dying Laughing* (1987). **Further Reading:** *Christina Stead: A Biography* by Hazel Rowley. **Try:** *Life Among the Savages* by Shirley Jackson (see page 404). *The Furies* by Janet Hobhouse.

A Woman, a Man, and Two Kingdoms
THE STORY OF MADAME D'ÉPINAY AND THE ABBÉ GALIANI
Francis Steegmuller (1906–1994)

An Enlightenment Friendship

Louise-Florence-Pétronille-Tardieu d'Esclavelles d'Épinay (1726–1783) was a lady of stature, sophistication, and accomplishment. A patron of Jean-Jacques Rousseau, who would come to scorn her (even among philosophers, it seems, no good deed goes unpunished), Madame d'Épinay held her own among the brightest intellects of the Enlightenment. Indeed, the reaction to being introduced to her in these pages is a desire to know more about her and her writings—letters, memoirs, articles— which are, fortunately, so copiously quoted here. What a remarkable mind she possessed, what astute yet unconventional instincts!

The same can certainly be said of Steegmuller's titular man, the Neapolitan priest-diplomat and economist Ferdinando Galiani (1728–1787). *A Man, a Woman, and Two Kingdoms* chronicles their friendship, allowing us to delight in the sparkling correspondence they began when Galiani was recalled from

Caricature of Madame d'Épinay

Paris to Naples in reprimand for diplomatic indiscretion. In their letters, mutual friends— including Diderot, Voltaire, Rousseau, and the fascinating Friedrich Melchior, Baron von Grimm—come to life as representatives of the ideas current in that intellectually electric age. Fashioning a narrative that is stimulating, amusing, even riveting, Steegmuller makes us feel the truth of Talleyrand's assertion— invoked at the outset of this book— that anyone who had not lived in pre-Revolutionary France could not fully know life's pleasure.

Celebrated as a biographer (his *Cocteau* won a National Book Award in 1971), translator (his version of Flaubert's *Madame Bovary* set the standard for decades), scholar, and versatile man of letters (he even penned a marvelous mystery, *The Blue Harpsichord*), Francis Steegmuller here combines his talents and erudition into a sophisticated entertainment of the highest order—a moving tale of human intimacy that is also a grand tour of history and ideas.

What: History. Biography. *When:* 1991. *Also By: Flaubert and Madame Bovary: A Double Portrait* (1939). *The Grand Mademoiselle* (1956). *Your Isadora: The Love Story of Isadora Duncan and Gordon Craig* (1974). *Try: Diderot* by P. N. Furbank. *Madame du Deffand and Her World* and *The Age of Conversation* by Benedetta Craveri.

Angle of Repose
Wallace Stegner (1909–1993)

A Novel of Family, Landscape, and History in the American West

Wallace Stegner's life work was the conservation—and celebration—of the American landscape. His famous "Wilderness Letter" was an instrument in the establishment of the National Wilderness Preservation System, and he worked for the Department of the Interior under JFK on the expansion of our national parks. He also, of course, honored the Western terrain he loved in a literary as well as a literal way, rendering it in detail in both his novels and his nonfiction. Though not all of his more than thirty books are concerned with the West, Stegner is often referred to as "the dean of Western writers," and the best of his books illustrate how much he merits the title.

Wallace Stegner, ca. 1970

Best of the best is the 1971 novel *Angle of Repose*. An intricately constructed, absorbing tale, it's narrated by Lyman Ward, a retired historian who has returned to his family home in Grass Valley, California, in the breathtaking Sierra Nevada. Suffering from a bone disease and using a wheelchair (he refers to himself as "battery operated"), Ward turns his historical training on his inherited past, embarking on a biography of his grandmother Susan Burling Ward, who left her promising life as a writer and artist in 1870s New York to venture into the West with her husband, Oliver, a mining engineer. (Stegner's fictional portrait

of Susan Burling Wade draws upon the life of California artist Mary Hallock Foote [1847–1938], from whose letters he sometimes quotes verbatim—a creative choice that sparked some controversy.)

As Lyman delves into his grandmother's past, Stegner uses the relationship between Susan and Oliver to reveal the unsettled arguments —between women and men, refinement and native force, society and the individual, culture and nature, East and West—on the fault lines of much American experience. Lyman's ruminations while researching his forebears and reflecting upon his own broken marriage and disillusioned parenthood bring those same questions into the turbulent era of the late 1960s, where they find their echo in the yawning gap between the generations— Lyman's son, a Berkeley professor, thinks his father's exploration of the past is a waste of effort while the issues of the day clamor for engagement.

The result is a human drama in which two stories span four generations, and one in which then and now are inextricably bound; the novel is at once a family saga, a Western quest, and a meditation on history. *Angle of Repose*, in the author's words, "reveals how even the most rebellious crusades of our time follow paths that our great-grandfathers' feet beat dusty." Stegner tells us that the past, like a vast landscape, must be settled into if it is to inform and enrich our lives. Even then, just off its beaten paths, an untamed, dangerous, vivifying wilderness looms.

What: Novel. **When:** 1971. *Award:* Pulitzer Prize for Fiction, 1972. *Also By:* Fiction: *Remembering Laughter* (1937); *The Big Rock Candy Mountain* (1943); *All the Little Live Things* (1967); *The Spectator Bird* (1976); *Crossing to Safety* (1987); *Collected Stories* (1990). Nonfiction: *Beyond the Hundredth Meridian: John Wesley Powell and the Second Opening of the West* (1954); *Where the Bluebird Sings to the Lemonade Springs: Living and Writing in the West* (1992). *Further Reading: A Victorian Gentlewoman in the Far West: The Reminiscences of Mary Hallock Foote*, edited by Rodman W. Paul. *Wallace Stegner and the American West* by Philip L. Fradkin. *Try: Gilead* by Marilynne Robinson (see page 670). *English Creek* by Ivan Doig. *Footnote:* Stegner founded the creative writing program at Stanford in 1964. His students included Edward Abbey, Ken Kesey, Thomas McGuane, and Larry McMurtry.

Abel's Island
William Steig (1907–2003)

A Small Fable About Big Virtues

A tale about a dapper mouse, whose civilized picnic with his wife is interrupted by the violence of a hurricane, this exquisite novel belongs on the small shelf of perfect books. Separated from his wife and stranded alone on an island as a result of the weather's whims, his comfortable existence horribly disrupted, Abel is forced to discover within himself a previously untapped resourcefulness. Steig elaborates his simple story, complemented by his marvelous drawings, with subtle and sophisticated beauty: Rarely has so compact a tale said so much so well about nobility, fortitude, steadfastness, love. The writing is a wonder throughout. (Have you ever read a better description of spring than this: "The sun seemed full of plans, less bored with the world than it had been, less aloof"?) This sparkling fable of civilization makes you glad to embrace the things you treasure, no matter how old you are.

Even though his career as a children's author did not begin until he was sixty years old, William Steig, who died in 2003 at the age of ninety-six, produced a large and beloved library of books for young readers, including *CDB!*, *Sylvester and the Magic Pebble*, and *The Amazing Bone* (to say nothing of the once modest, now famous *Shrek!*). Although his four decades of earlier artwork—*New Yorker* cartoons and covers, books of symbolic drawings and ingenious character studies—brought a new psychological acuity to the art of cartooning and proved their creator to be a dramatist, novelist, and poet in wordless images, Steig's children's books displayed his rich talents best, and none more so than *Abel's Island*.

What: Children's. **When:** 1976. *Reading Note:* For readers age 8 and up (younger if read aloud). *Also By: Gorky Rises* (1980). *Doctor De Soto* (1982). *Yellow and Pink* (1984). *Brave Irene* (1986). *Further Reading: The World of William Steig* by Lee Lorenz. *Try: The Mouse and His Child* by Russell Hoban (see page 378). *The Great Good Thing* by Roderick Townley (see page 802).

The Autobiography of Alice B. Toklas
Gertrude Stein (1874–1946)

A Playful Modernist Memoir—
with Plenty of Gossip, Too

Both Gertrude Stein and Alice B. Toklas (1877–1967) were born in America and moved to Paris in the early 1900s. They met there in 1907, became lovers, and remained partners till Stein's death. In the 1920s, their Parisian salon at 27 rue de Fleurus became the meeting place for what Stein herself christened the "Lost Generation." Pablo Picasso, Henri Matisse, Sherwood Anderson, and Ernest Hemingway were among the many artists and writers who frequented the women's painting-filled apartment—and who populate the pages of this book.

The bulk of Stein's writing is notorious for its difficulty. The ordinary reader is likely to feel that too much of it consists of riddling obscurity and maddening repetitiveness. For example, "Out of kindness comes redness and out of rudeness comes rapid same question, out of an eye comes research, out of selection comes painful cattle" is one of her signature sentences. "Rose is a rose is a rose is a rose" is another. *The Autobiography of Alice B. Toklas*, however, is not only easily accessible, but highly entertaining as well. Despite its title, it was written entirely by Stein ("as Defoe did the autobiography of Robinson Crusoe," she explains toward the end) in an extended act of literary impersonation. While playfully pretending to be her partner, Stein writes chiefly about her own life in Paris in the company of her celebrated friends, composing as she goes a gossipy (albeit highly selective and incomplete) account of the literary and artistic personalities who made Paris the capital of modernism in the 1910s and 1920s.

In the book's most remarked-upon passage, "Alice" describes her first meeting with Gertrude: "I was impressed by the coral brooch she wore and by her voice. I may say that only three times in my life I have met a genius and

each time a bell within me rang and I was not mistaken." In another famous passage, "Toklas" tells Picasso how much she likes his portrait of Stein: "'Yes,' he said, 'everybody says that she does not look like it but that does not make any difference, she will,' he said."

Gertrude Stein (left) with Alice B. Toklas, 1944

Spiced with anecdotes (including a few sharp enough to have earned the lasting displeasure of Matisse and Hemingway), Stein's reflections on her own life through the eyes of her confidante are a sparkling, amusing treat.

What: Memoir. Culture. *When:* 1933. *Also By: Three Lives* (1909). *Tender Buttons* (1914). *The Making of Americans* (1925). *How to Write* (1931). *Everybody's Autobiography* (1937). *Wars I Have Seen* (1945). *Brewsie and Willie* (1946). *Further Reading: What Is Remembered* by Alice B. Toklas. *The Third Rose: Gertrude Stein and Her World* by John Malcolm Brinnin. *A Movable Feast* by Ernest Hemingway. *Charmed Circle: Gertrude Stein and Company* by James R. Mellow. *Try: The Book of Salt* by Monique Truong. *Footnote:* A writer in her own right, Toklas is best known for *The Alice B. Toklas Cookbook*, which became something of a counterculture classic in the 1960s, in part because of its recipe for Hashish Fudge.

JOHN STEINBECK
(1902–1968)

John Steinbeck, ca. 1937

The natural resources of humanity—dignity, integrity, courage, compassion, nobility (and, of course, all their unattractive opposites)—characterize humble lives as well as grand ones, just as plain speech can express the most powerful, troubling, magnanimous emotions, and common experience can echo mythic themes. John Steinbeck learned these lessons early, and spent his career realizing them in books that remain immediately appealing and deeply affecting. He suffuses his best fiction with the strength of expression we find in folk songs and ancient ballads; simple on their surface, his novels and novellas sound deep wells of common humanity with a resonance both moving and haunting. In works such as *The Red Pony* (1937), *Of Mice and Men* (1937), *The Pearl* (1947), *East of Eden* (1952), and, most of all, *The Grapes of Wrath* (1939), he confronts elemental aspects of ordinary experience with an earthy acuity and an almost biblical earnestness, hammering archetypal themes into works of rough beauty and undeniable power.

The Grapes of Wrath
From Dust to Dust

It's hard to imagine now just how controversial a work *The Grapes of Wrath* was when it first appeared. And how popular: Published in March 1939, Steinbeck's saga of the havoc wreaked by the Great Depression was soon the country's number one bestseller, selling thousands of copies each week despite the difficult economic times. At the same time, communities from coast to coast found it obscene and banned (and even burned) it. The author's portrait of the poverty suffered by members of the Joad family, the Oklahoma sharecroppers the novel follows from the Dust Bowl to California's Salinas Valley, made the book politically suspect as well—its obvious sympathy for the victims of economic devastation called into question the virtues and verities of American capitalism.

Inspired by a series of newspaper articles Steinbeck had written, *The Grapes of Wrath* depicts the Joads' travails as they strap themselves and their meager belongings onto a jalopy—a boy on each running board, hanging on for dear life, the seats full of other siblings—and set off toward a hoped-for promised land. The Joads are a hard, funny, tenacious, colorful bunch, but the road they travel is strewn with death, hunger, social unrest, violence, and misfortune of every stripe. Still, the family endures, with a dignity distilled from survival, stripped of all material comfort or social adornment. Modern literature had no champion of that dignity more steadfast than

John Steinbeck, and *The Grapes of Wrath* is his masterpiece.

What: Novel. **When:** 1939. **Award:** Pulitzer Prize for Fiction, 1940. *Also By: Tortilla Flat* (1935). *Cannery Row* (1945). *The Winter of Our Discontent* (1961). *Further Reading:* Steinbeck's journal of writing the novel was published as *Working Days: The Journals of "The Grapes of Wrath,"* edited by Robert DeMott. *Obscene in the Extreme: The Burning and Banning of John Steinbeck's "The Grapes of Wrath,"* by Rick Wartzman. *Try: U.S.A.* by John Dos Passos (see page 229). *Out of the Dust* by Karen Hesse. *Adaptation:* John Ford directed the 1940 film adaptation, which stars Henry Fonda.

Travels with Charley
IN SEARCH OF AMERICA
A Writer's Road Trip

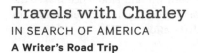

Steinbeck once described himself as "a lumbering soul . . . trying to fly." He even created a "Pigasus" logo for his personal correspondence, with a Latin epithet that translates as "To the stars on the wings of a pig." In 1960, when he was fifty-eight, his desire to take flight manifested itself in a cross-country journey in a customized truck—which he christened Rocinante, after Don Quixote's horse—with his dog Charley ("an old French gentleman poodle") at his side. He had his reasons:

I live in New York. But New York is no more America than Paris is France or London is England. . . . I, an American writer, writing about America, was working from memory, and the memory is at best a faulty, warpy reservoir. I had not heard the speech of America, smelled the grass and trees and sewage, seen its hills and water, its color and quality of light. I knew the changes only from books and newspapers. But more than this, I had not felt the country for twenty-five years.

Yet the itinerant author was looking back as much as forward; suffering from a heart condition, Steinbeck took to the road to say goodbye to the country he loved and to engage one more time with the American themes his imagination had brought to life in his fiction.

Travels with Charley is his account of the trip, which took him from New York to Maine to the Pacific Northwest, down the coast to his hometown of Salinas, California, then back east along the southern route. There is much nostalgia in these pages for a time when life was decidedly local and place was as powerful a determinant of character as mass media or governmental bureaucracy. Scorning sandwiches wrapped in plastic rather than served by hands, he bemoans his fellow citizens' pursuit of "cleanliness first, at the expense of taste," and senses more fear and bigotry than he cares to credit. Yet his interest in people and their passions and his keen eye for scenic beauties and social truths infuses his journey with an autumnal sense of satisfaction and grateful joy, making *Travels with Charley* this master's most companionable—and beloved—book.

What: Travel. **When:** 1962. *Also By:* More Steinbeck nonfiction: *Sea of Cortez* (1941); *A Russian Journal* (1948); *Journal of a Novel: The "East of Eden" Letters* (1969). *Further Reading: Long Way Home: On the Trail of Steinbeck's America* by Bill Barich. *Try: The Air-Conditioned Nightmare* by Henry Miller. *Blue Highways* by William Least Heat-Moon (see page 360). *The Lost Continent* by Bill Bryson. *Footnote:* In 2011, journalist Bill Steigerwald "fact-checked" *Travels with Charley* and found cause to question the veracity of some of the accommodations and adventures described in the book. Its hold on readers' imaginations is likely to outlast such scrutiny.

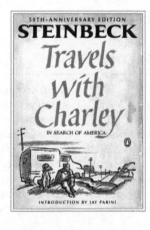

After Babel
ASPECTS OF LANGUAGE AND TRANSLATION
George Steiner (born 1929)

Speaking of Tongues:
The Mystery of Languages

I n the beginning, at least according to the book of Genesis, humanity spoke one common language—until the Babylonians had the presumption to try scaling the heavens via a tower. In his wrath at this audacity, God turned the builders' speech into a variety of different, mutually incomprehensible tongues, and the project fell victim to this divinely invoked failure to communicate.

The biblical story of the Tower of Babel offers the simplest, if not the most satisfying, explanation for what George Steiner calls "the bewildering multiplicity and variousness of languages spoken on this crowded planet." When you stop and think about it, it is truly puzzling. Human beings are essentially the same around the world; the digestive tract, for example, or the cerebral cortex, is identical from one end of the earth to the other. Yet humans speak thousands of languages. As Steiner asks, "Why does this unified, though individually unique mammalian species not use one common language?"

After Babel is a vastly learned, wide-ranging investigation of the "Babel problem." In the main, the book examines issues that arise from the theory and practice of translation. These lead in turn to a more general exploration of the central mysteries of language, for Steiner sees understanding as a process of translation: What goes on when we translate between languages parallels what happens when we communicate within one.

Steiner is one of the best-read and most influential critics of our era. He moves comfortably among several languages and seems to have at his command nearly all of world literature. This book, like his others, is riddled with an erudition so comprehensive that it can seem daunting page by page. Yet Steiner's ability to apply his acumen to fundamental human questions with wit and eloquence makes the rewards of following his intellectual ambitions well worth the effort.

What: Language. Philosophy. *When:* 1975. *Reading Note:* Take your time; Steiner's scholarship is dense but his thought is bold, lucid, and enormously stimulating. *Also By:* Tolstoy or Dostoevsky (1960). *The Death of Tragedy* (1961). *Language and Silence: Essays 1958–1966* (1967). *Real Presences* (1989). *No Passion Spent: Essays 1978–1996* (1996). *Errata: An Examined Life* (1997). *My Unwritten Books* (2008). *Try: The Language Instinct* by Steven Pinker. *Adaptation: After Babel* was the basis for the 1977 television documentary *The Tongues of Men.*

The Red and the Black
A CHRONICLE OF 1830
Stendhal [Marie-Henri Beyle] (1783–1842)

Hero and Villain:
The One and Only Julien Sorel

I n the pages of *The Red and the Black* (sometimes translated as *Red and Black* or *Scarlet and Black*), we meet one of literature's most memorable protagonists, Julien Sorel. The son of a sawmill owner, young Julien has Napoleonic dreams; handsome and clever, he has the gifts to pursue them. Recognizing that the path to glory for an ambitious youth in the France of the Bourbon Restoration runs through religious rather than martial channels, he dons the black robes of the clergy rather than the red uniform of the military. This decision reveals the scheming soul that animates Stendhal's hero's every action, even in the sphere of love. ("Julien's life," the author tells us, "was thus composed of a series of petty negotiations, and their success concerned him far more than the signs of special affection he could have read in Madame de Renal's heart, if only he had bothered.")

And love looms large in *The Red and the Black*, the plot charting first the course of Julien's passionate affair with Madame de Renal, the wife of the provincial mayor whose children the seminarian is tutoring, and then his tempestuous involvement with the daughter of a Parisian nobleman. Indeed, the story has all the elements of romantic melodrama: an ardent hero, a virtuous woman carried away by infatuation, a haughty lady humbled by desire, and episode upon episode of exile, assignation, escape, betrayal, revenge.

Stendhal is particularly deft at capturing the tumult of lovers' emotions, their prides and jealousies, anticipations and despairs. In fact, the psychological naturalism with which he

Portrait of Stendhal (pen name of Marie-Henri Beyle)

depicts Julien's conspiracy of one—his relentless opportunism in pursuing the unreachable triumphs he imagines are his due—undercuts the romantic sweep of the tale. The novelist's detached and realistic style combines with his wry intelligence to treat all that falls into its purview—from the hypocrisy of the church to the petty posturing of both provincial and Parisian society—to a worldly assessment both sardonic and shrewd, making *The Red and the Black* a pleasure to both read and ponder.

What: Novel. **When:** 1830. **Edition:** Burton Raffel's lively 2003 translation is superb. **Also By:** *On Love* (1822). *The Charterhouse of Parma* (1839). Published posthumously: *The Life of Henry Brulard* (1890). *Memoirs of an Egotist* (1892). *Lucien Leuwen* (1894). **Try:** *Vanity Fair* by William Makepeace Thackeray (see page 777). **Adaptation:** In the 1997 BBC production of *The Scarlet and the Black*, Ewan McGregor plays Julien Sorel.

Quicksilver
Neal Stephenson (born 1959)

A Capacious and Captivating Wonder-Cabinet

Neal Stephenson weaves threads of technological, scientific, historical, philosophical, economic, and cultural inquiry into brilliant tapestries of speculative fiction, virtual worlds of learning and invention that are both thought-provoking and addictively entertaining. Their complexity of incident and idea is made compelling by the author's stunning gift for narrative magic. Despite the gargantuan dimensions of his tomes (many of his novels push a thousand pages), the experience of reading his work is fleet and fun; chasing a Stephenson tale is an exhilarating exercise in enchantment.

Take *Quicksilver*. Even the briefest summary will be dizzying in its detail—and the book

represents only the first third of Stephenson's 2,700-page Baroque Cycle. Charting the adventures of Daniel Waterhouse, raised as a Puritan but matured into a mathematical philosopher and skeptical thinker; Jack Shaftoe, a street-smart London urchin who grows up to be the swashbuckling King of the Vagabonds; and the resourceful Eliza, rescued from a Turkish harem to become a woman of ways and means through her talents for royal intrigue, personal confidences, and savvy investment, *Quicksilver* begins in colonial Boston in 1713 and travels both backward and forward in time to present an astonishing panorama of the late seventeenth and early eighteenth centuries in England, France, and other parts of Europe. Daniel's time in Cambridge as Isaac Newton's roommate introduces scientific and mathematical investigations that develop further through his association with Robert Hooke, the Royal Society, and Gottfried Leibniz; Jack and Eliza's escapades enmesh them in court intrigues and the burgeoning network of financial markets, leading them—and us—from Vienna to Versailles. Historical figures like Samuel Pepys, the pirate Edward Teach (better known as Blackbeard), the cryptologist Rossignol, and assorted dukes and kings cross the paths of our protagonists, and Stephenson treats us to erudite descriptions of the Great Fire of London (1666), the Battle of Vienna (1683), the Pitchfork Rebellion (1685), and the Glorious Revolution (1688). Throughout, characters engage and debate the issues of the era (many of which still linger in our own)—from free will and determinism, physics and mathematics, experiment and alchemy, cognition and computation, politics, religion, to the meaning of money—with verve and intelligence, while myriad plot lines allow exciting diversions into episodes of theatrical high jinks and piracy on the high seas.

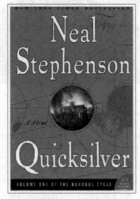

It is impossible to exaggerate the richness of this book or the thrilling pleasure of its nine-hundred-odd pages. *The Confusion* (2004) and *The System of the World* (2004) continue the Baroque Cycle in appropriately elaborate imaginative style. The trio is a prequel of sorts to Stephenson's earlier saga, *Cryptonomicon* (1999), in which Daniel Waterhouse's and Jack Shaftoe's descendants fight World War II in the company of Douglas MacArthur in the Pacific and Alan Turing at Bletchley Park. Original, expansive, immensely enjoyable, Stephenson's novels are beyond category.

What: Novel. *When:* 2003. *Also By: Snow Crash* (1992). *The Diamond Age* (1994). *Anathem* (2008). *Reamde* (2011). *Seveneves* (2015). *Further Reading: Civilization and Capitalism, 15th–18th Century* by Fernand Braudel. *Ingenious Pursuits: Building the Scientific Revolution* by Lisa Jardine. *Try: Lemprière's Dictionary* by Lawrence Norfolk. *A Case of Curiosities* by Allen Kurzweil.

The Life and Opinions of Tristram Shandy, Gentleman
Laurence Sterne (1713–1768)

A Postmodern Masterpiece—from the 1760s

"Nothing odd will do long. *Tristram Shandy* did not last," noted Dr. Samuel Johnson, eighteenth-century England's fiercest literary arbiter. But Johnson was uncharacteristically wrong: Laurence Sterne's comic masterpiece does last. This antic shaggy dog story firmly established itself during the twentieth century as one of the most admired books ever written. Virginia Woolf, for example, hailed it as "the greatest of all novels," and Czech writer Milan Kundera praised it for reaching "heights of playfulness, of lightness, never scaled before or since."

Tristram Shandy's levity is irrepressibly apparent even before you start reading: Flip through the book and you'll see black pages, marbled pages, blank pages, and typographic oddities that, you'll discover, are visual counterparts to specific moments in the story. In large part that story turns out to be about Tristram's difficulty telling it. You might say that his problems begin before he does. Tristram opens his account of his "life and opinions" at the moment of his conception—as it happens, a hilariously mismanaged moment. Though conception seems to be his starting point at first, Tristram soon discovers that "when a man sits down to write a history [. . .] he knows no more than his heels what lets and confounded hindrances he is to meet with in his way,—or what a dance he may be led, by one excursion or another, before all is over." As digression follows digression, and interruption interrupts interruption, Tristram leads the tale on such a merry dance that it proceeds in every direction but forward. His reflections on matters mundane and philosophical and his accounts of the lives of his father and of his eccentric and often incomprehensible uncle Toby are just a few of the detours that distract him from his own progress, which never gets much past his first three years. But his wayward narrative's energy

never flags, and Sterne's self-reflexive novel offers one of literature's first—and probably its funniest—portrayals of the errant urgencies of consciousness.

What: Novel. *When:* 1759–67. *Also By: A Sentimental Journey Through France and Italy* (1768). *Try: Gargantua and Pantagruel* by François Rabelais (see page 656). *At Swim-Two-Birds* by Flann O'Brien (see page 595). *If on a Winter's Night a Traveler* by Italo Calvino. *Adaptation:* Michael Winterbottom directed Steve Coogan in his film adaptation *Tristram Shandy: A Cock and Bull Story* (2005).

ROBERT LOUIS STEVENSON
(1850–1894)

Tuberculosis plagued Robert Louis Stevenson throughout the forty-four years of his short life. But the shadows his early illness cast on his imagination proved more deep than dark: The solitude of his sickly boyhood nourished powers of invention that later spun stories as captivating as clouds, transporting countless readers on voyages of exhilarating, riveting excitement.

Although Stevenson is remembered as the author of juvenile classics—adventure tales for boys, rhymes for children, a horror novella—his achievement has surprising scope and strength. If not seminal works in literary history, his books are seminal works in the annals of reading, from *Treasure Island* springs the pulse and energy of most modern thrillers; from *Kidnapped* the protagonist-driven passage through thickets of political intrigue that characterizes so much popular fiction; from *The Strange Case of Dr. Jekyll and Mr. Hyde* the ever-expanding realm of

psychological and paranormal horror; from *A Child's Garden of Verses* nearly the entire catalog of children's books we've come to know. The sheer pleasure of these volumes should not disguise the sophistication, ingenuity, and intelligence that animate all of Stevenson's output, which will reward the attentions of any reader who ventures beyond this renowned quartet into his many volumes of stories, essays, and travel writing.

Robert Louis Stevenson, 1889

Treasure Island
"Yo-ho-ho, and a bottle of rum."

....

O n any list of the best adventure stories ever written, *Treasure Island* deserves a place at the top. Hewing to a taut narrative line that ripples with ominous vibrations, it pulls the reader headlong into a fantastic realm of pirates and buried treasure. Read the first few pages and see if you can stop.

Young Jim Hawkins describes the arrival of an old salt at the Admiral Benbow, his parents' inn on the English coast. Peculiar, suspicious, and fond of rum, Bill Bones brays incessantly about "fifteen men on a dead man's chest" and terrifies the Benbow's taproom guests with tales of grisly exploits upon the high seas. Keeping constant lookout for a one-legged sailor and other pursuers, Bones is an intimidating guest, until his premonitions are made real in the form of yet two more threatening visitors, the buccaneers Black Dog and Blind Pew. Deadly developments follow fast, leaving Jim in possession of a treasure map that charts the way to the buried booty of bloody buccaneer Captain Flint. Soon enough, a ship—the *Hispaniola*—is outfitted by local eminences to retrieve the treasure, and Jim's on board.

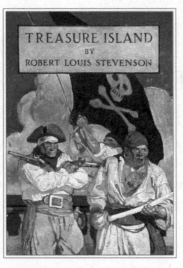

Now the fun really begins, for the crew of the *Hispaniola* has been surreptitiously seeded with Flint's former colleagues, courtesy of the ship's cook, Long John Silver. With a wooden leg (it was he who haunted Bill Bones's dreams) and a mind alive with a hundred tentacles, Long John Silver is a cunning blend of gruffness and sophistication, charm and menace, honor and brutality. Despite the danger he exudes, he forms a bond with Jim that is all the more powerful for its shifting, uncertain moral tenor. There is little time for Jim, or the reader, to worry about morality: So swift are the plot's suspenseful turnings through mutinies, murders, duplicities, and the like that all attention is focused on what happens next. This is part of the book's originality, for all of its considerable invention is in the service of the tale rather than in the interest of what the tale might teach. Its literary legacy is the exhilaration of pure adventure, and its imaginative one the romantic image of pirates that still animates popular culture (such as the *Pirates of the Caribbean* films), the essential elements of which—buried treasure, wooden legs, yo-ho-ho and all—made their first impression in *Treasure Island*.

What: Novel. Adventure. *When:* Serialized, 1881–82; first book publication, 1883. *Edition:* Look for the Scribner Illustrated Classics version, distinguished by N. C. Wyeth's magnificent illustrations. *Also By:* Novels: *The Black Arrow* (1888); *The Master of Ballantrae* (1889). Stories: *New Arabian Nights* (1882); *The Merry Men and Other Tales and Fables* (1887). Travel: *Travels with a Donkey in the Cévennes* (1879); *The Amateur Emigrant* (1895). *Further Reading: Under the Black Flag: The Romance and the Reality of Life among the Pirates* by David Cordingly. *Try: Captain Blood* by Rafael Sabatini (see page 688). *Adaptations:* Alfred Molina's award-winning 2007 audiobook reading is highly recommended. The 1950 Walt Disney feature, starring Robert Newton as Long John Silver, is the most memorable of dozens of film adaptations.

"I love Stevenson because he gives the impression he is flying." —*Italo Calvino*

Kidnapped
BEING THE MEMOIRS OF THE
ADVENTURES OF DAVID BALFOUR
IN THE YEAR 1751
Historical Adventure in the
Scottish Highlands

· ·

T reasure Island takes place in its own romantic time zone; the only date Stevenson supplies the reader is the deliberately unspecific
"17—." *Kidnapped*, in contrast, is fueled by similarly fleet storytelling but is very much fixed
in historical time. Although the heroics of the
book's two protagonists, the narrator David
Balfour and the dashing fugitive Alan Breck
Stewart, are captivating regardless of one's
knowledge of Scottish history, it does help
to know that their thrilling exploits are set in
the aftermath of the Battle of Culloden, when
English forces ruthlessly defeated Highlander
rebels and quelled the Jacobite uprising of
1745. Look what's possible, Stevenson is saying,
when Lowland loyalist (Balfour) and Jacobite
Highlander (Stewart) combine forces toward a
common goal.

The story begins with David's pursuit of
his family inheritance, which pits him against
his conniving uncle Ebenezer, one of the most
entertainingly nasty and unscrupulous villains you will ever come across. Owing to his
uncle's bad offices, David is kidnapped and
enslaved on a ship bound for America. An accident at sea lands him in the company of Alan, a
rebel on the run from the English authorities
and their Scottish enforcers. The two become
comrades as they conspire to win their freedom, weather shipwreck and separation, and
come together again in the Highlands, keeping one foot ahead of their pursuers as they
seek to find a safe haven, clear Alan's name,
and claim David's rightful legacy. Hiding by
day, traveling by night, enduring every kind of
hardship and close encounter with their enemies, they survive by their wits and their loyalty to each other. The historical context adds
a realistic texture to the fantastic excitement of
the pair's many escapes, and the human currency of their attachment transcends political
dogma. The same narrative framework would,
in due course, provide the plot for countless
thrillers and buddy movies, but it has seldom

been better realized than in this, its seminal
incarnation.

What: Novel. Adventure. *When:* Serial and first book
publication, 1886. *Edition:* Again, look for one with
N. C. Wyeth illustrations. *Reading Note:* The Scottish
vocabulary can sometimes prove nettlesome. *Also By:*
Stevenson's sequel, *Catriona* (also known as *David
Balfour*), was published in 1893. *Further Reading:*
*Myself and the Other Fellow: A Life of Robert Louis
Stevenson* by Claire Harman. *Footsteps: Adventures of
a Romantic Biographer* by Richard Holmes (see page
383). *Try: Rob Roy* by Sir Walter Scott. *Kim* by Rudyard
Kipling. *Adaptations:* Of the many movie versions,
best are the 1960 Walt Disney adaptation, starring
James MacArthur and Peter Finch, and Delbert Mann's
1971 film, starring Lawrence Douglas and Michael Caine.

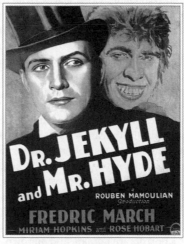
Poster for the 1931 film Dr. Jekyll and Mr. Hyde

The Strange Case of
Dr. Jekyll and Mr. Hyde
A Storyteller's Treatise on Human Nature

· ·

R are is the modern literary work that speaks
with the uncanny authority of folklore.
Stevenson's *The Strange Case of Dr. Jekyll and Mr.
Hyde*, published in 1886 to a popular acclaim
that has not diminished since, is just such a creation, a tale of tantalizing suspense that echoes
with disturbing and mysterious psychological
resonance. The figure at its core has become

an emblem of the duplicity of human nature: intellect and appetite, restraint and transgression, civility and brutality—Jekyll and Hyde.

It's hard to imagine a reader picking up Stevenson's novella today without an awareness that the genteel Dr. Jekyll and the bestial Mr. Hyde are one and the same, but in the telling Stevenson withholds this information until the story is quite far along. But foreknowledge does nothing to lessen our creepy delight in the unfolding horror, as Stevenson's narrative ingenuity—the tale is told in multiple voices—re-creates in the reader the apprehensive terror of Jekyll's friends. At the outset, we eavesdrop on the most gentlemanly of conversations, as a lawyer and his cousin, out on their usual Sunday stroll, ponder the reprehensible behavior of one Edward Hyde, whose strange cruelties make the respectable Dr. Jekyll's last will and testament, which leaves Hyde everything, inexplicable. Troubling connections between Jekyll and Hyde proliferate, and decorous Victorian dread creeps through the mystified narration of Jekyll's acquaintances. But when Hyde is implicated in cold-blooded murder, apprehension turns to alarm.

The ultimate revelation of Dr. Jekyll's double life, which began in indulgence of his taste for illicit pleasures and grew into an experimental quest, is not as haunting as the reflections it provokes. We cannot help but recognize that Jekyll is at every stage protective of his twin, and thus complicit in Hyde's vice and savage violence: Good cleaves to evil with appalling instinct. Stevenson's story tells us the world's horrors are human, and our own. That it remains compelling suggests the mysteries stories can summon and science cannot.

What: Novella. Horror. *When:* 1886. *Try: The Invisible Man* by H. G. Wells (see page 840). *Knots and Crosses* by Ian Rankin. *Adaptations:* The Jekyll-Hyde tale has been filmed countless times, from the earliest days of cinema. The most notable Hollywood versions—not counting Jerry Lewis's inspired *Nutty Professor* (1963)—are Rouben Mamoulian's 1931 version, starring Frederic March, and the 1941 remake, starring Spencer Tracy. But without question the best film adaptation is Jean Renoir's 1959 *Testament of Dr. Cordelier,* starring Jean-Louis Barrault.

A Child's Garden of Verses
The Rhymes and Seasons of Childhood

This little book of sixty-five poems is a necessary volume in any family library. On a roomy bed of comforting rhythm and rhyme, Robert Louis Stevenson invites us to join him as he explores in stanzas the reveries and longings of a child's imagination.

> When I was sick and lay a-bed,
> I had two pillows at my head,
> And all my toys beside me lay
> To keep me happy all the day.
>
> And sometimes for an hour or so,
> I watched my leaden soldiers go,
> With different uniform and drills,
> Among the bedclothes, through the hills . . .

That's from "The Land of Counterpane," one of the many unforgettable verses in *A Child's Garden*. Others include "Travel," "The Lamplighter," "The Land of Nod," and "My Shadow":

> I have a little shadow that goes in and out
>   with me,
> And what can be the use of him is more than
>   I can see.
> He is very, very like me from the heels up to
>   the head;
> And I see him jump before me, when I jump
>   into my bed.

Inspired no doubt by the author's memories of his own sickly youth, these small poems are suffused with a capacious, daydreaming ease. Perhaps for the first time in literature, the poet evokes the inner life of early childhood with tender attention and affection. If you are unfamiliar with Stevenson's exquisite musings, prepare yourself (be you child or adult) for one of the greatest, simplest pleasures in all reading.

What: Children's. Poetry. *When:* 1885. *Editions:* There are countless editions, illustrated by artists from Charles Robinson (1895) to Gyo Fujikawa (1957) and beyond. *Reading Note:* Ideal for reading aloud before bed and lights-out. *Try: Rhymes and Verses* and *Come Hither* by Walter de la Mare. *Talking Like the Rain,* edited by X. J. and Dorothy M. Kennedy (see page 440).

Letters of a Woman Homesteader
Elinore Pruitt Stewart (1876–1933)

Way Out West

In 1909, a young widow leaves Denver with her daughter and lights out for Burnt Fork, Wyoming. She corresponds—in lively, long conversational drafts—with her former employer, also a widow, back in the city, describing the life she makes out West. The hardships of the frontier are in these letters, as well as the curiously close community of ranchers and farmers she finds spread across great swaths of land. Yet what is most pleasurable is the sound of a warm, wise, and funny voice adding up its life, story by story.

In Denver I was afraid my baby would grow up devoid of imagination. Like all the kindergartners, she depended upon others to amuse her. I was very sorry about it, for my castles in Spain have been real homes to me. But there is no fear. She has a block of wood she found in the blacksmith shop which she calls her "dear baby." A spoke out of a wagon wheel is "little Margaret," and a barrel-stave is "bad little Johnny."

Stewart reports on chore-packed days, eccentric neighbors, holiday celebrations, and horse thieves, all with a plainspoken literary élan that makes the reader aware she is embellishing her experience for better reading while remaining true to its essential outlines. And what reader wouldn't fall for a writer who, in a tone that perfectly captures the pleasures of her book and her personality, acknowledges a "powerfully short" engagement but goes on to explain: ". . . although I married in haste, I have no cause to repent. That is very fortunate because I have never had one bit of leisure to repent in. So I am lucky all around."

What: Memoir. Diaries & Letters. **When:** 1914. **Edition:** Look for an edition containing the illustrations by N. C. Wyeth. **Also By:** *Letters on an Elk Hunt by a Woman Homesteader* (1915). **Further Reading:** *The Adventures of the Woman Homesteader: The Life and Letters of Elinore Pruitt Stewart* edited by Susanne George Bloomfield. **Try:** *Pioneer Women* by Joanna L. Stratton. *Women's Diaries of the Westward Journey* by Lillian Schlissel. **Adaptation:** Stewart's book was the inspiration for the 1979 film *Heartland*.

Dracula
Bram Stoker (1847–1912)

The Horrifying Count Who Just Won't Die

" I am Dracula, and I bid you welcome, Mr. Harker, to my house. Come in; the night air is chill."

You know the character, of course; you've seen him throughout your life—in cartoons, on cereal boxes, in countless movies and TV shows, and, later, teaming up with other creature-feature stars like Frankenstein and the Wolf Man, squaring off against good guys from Sherlock Holmes to Buffy the Vampire Slayer. But have you ever actually read

Bram Stoker, ca. 1906

Bram Stoker's Victorian horror classic, *Dracula*? Why not?

You're probably familiar with the outlines of the story: A centuries-old vampire lures an English visitor to his castle in Transylvania, then journeys to London to seek fresh blood from his visitor's paramour—with first mystified, then terrified, and finally horrified pursuers on his trail. But what you may not know is how the formal structure of Stoker's storytelling adds to the suspense. The initial chapters of the book are told through the journals of the Englishman who makes the trip to the count's eerie Transylvanian lair, and the rest of the novel portrays the growing fears and awareness of an extended circle of characters through letters, telegrams, newspaper stories, diary entries, and even transcriptions of early phonographic recordings. As episodes and revelations are pieced together, the reader's apprehension mounts with the discovery of each new wound, corpse, and coffin.

Stoker, an Irishman with a love for the stage (for years he managed the London theater company of celebrated actor Henry Irving), based the character of Dracula on elements of Eastern European vampire legends. Although he was not the first to turn such lore to literary profit, his addition of a veiled eroticism and a looming personality—along with a few new qualities, such as his vampire's lack of reflection in a mirror—created an undead villain for the ages, one who still runs rampant through a century of spin-offs.

What: Horror. *When:* 1897. *Also By: The Snake's Pass* (1890). *The Jewel of Seven Stars* (1903). *The Lady of the Shroud* (1909). *The Lair of the White Worm* (1911). *Try: Frankenstein* by Mary Shelley (see page 719). *The Strange Case of Dr. Jekyll and Mr. Hyde* by Robert Louis Stevenson (see page 759). *The Invisible Man* by H. G. Wells (see page 840). *Interview with the Vampire* by Anne Rice (see below). *Adaptations:* F. W. Murnau's 1922 *Nosferatu*, the first important film treatment of the Dracula tale, is still the most imaginatively ghoulish and unforgettable. In 1979, Werner Herzog remade *Nosferatu*, in a cinematic homage. Two other notable movie adaptations are the 1931 classic starring Bela Lugosi, and Francis Ford Coppola's *Bram Stoker's Dracula*, in 1992, which, despite its title, takes liberties with Stoker's story.

|||||||||||||||||||||||||||||||||||||| B O O K N O T E ||||||||||||||||||||||||||||||||||||||

UNDEAD MAN TALKING

Interview with the Vampire
Anne Rice (born 1941)

From Bram Stoker's *Dracula* (see above) to Stephenie Meyer's *Twilight* and Charlaine Harris's Sookie Stackhouse series, vampires have seduced generations of readers, their thirst for blood heralding love and death, themes as old as story itself. Forbidden love, untamed passion, otherworldly desire—when it comes to popular fiction, who could ask for anything more?

Anne Rice has been wildly prolific in the decades since *Interview with the Vampire*, her 1976 debut novel, catapulted her to fame, but her first book is still her most intriguing. Subverting convention in many ways, notably by making the vampire in question fallibly human and by presenting his story in his own words, Rice's tale also embraces the genre's Gothic-erotic roots with relish. The result is one of the best vampire novels ever written.

It begins in the present in a room in New Orleans, where a young reporter has secured an interview with Louis de Pointe du Lac, a man claiming to be a vampire. Louis asks the reporter if he has enough tape with him to record the story of a life. "Sure, if it's a good life," the reporter says, and a good life story is what he gets—two hundred years of it, beginning with the fateful night in 1791 when, on his family's Louisiana plantation, Louis first meets the vampire Lestat. Drunk and distraught over his younger brother's suicide, for which he feels responsible, Louis succumbs to Lestat's offer to make him an apprentice. What happens next, and next, and next is a page-turner of the first order, as Louis describes his opulent life with the sinister Lestat and the child, Claudia, whom the two of them "adopt," narrating their travels to Europe, their dark adventures in Paris among others of their kind, and their ultimate return to America. Imprisoned in immortality yet filled with regret, doubt, and grief, Louis reveals the tormented soul that survives his fiendish destiny, giving the first installment of Rice's Vampire Chronicles—nine more would follow—a human dimension that makes it as hard to forget as it is to put down.

Fer-de-Lance
Rex Stout (1886–1975)

At the Court of Nero Wolfe

Imperious, majestic, and possessed of unrivaled powers of ratiocination, the private investigator Nero Wolfe is mystery royalty. His cases, as recorded and narrated by Archie Goodwin, his assistant as well as his eyes and ears, are among the most entertaining in the annals of detective fiction.

Published in 1934, *Fer-de-Lance* was the first of Rex Stout's seventy-odd Nero Wolfe tales, and it establishes all the quirks and qualities of the hero's physique, character, and regimen. He is a large man: "Wolfe lifted his head," Goodwin reports just one paragraph into their first adventure, elaborating with typical insolence, "I mention that, because his head was so big that lifting it struck you as being quite a job. It was probably really bigger than it looked, for the rest of him was so huge that any head on top of it but his own would have escaped your notice entirely." Wolfe is loath to leave the comfortable confines of his brownstone on Manhattan's West Thirty-Fifth Street, less than a block from the Hudson River. Within its walls, he dedicates himself to an unchanging daily routine of tending his beloved orchids for four hours in the plant-rooms on the roof (aided by his private horticulturalist, Theodore Horstmann); indulging in the delights of the table prepared to his exacting standards by the live-in chef, Fritz Brenner; savoring bottle upon bottle of beer; and sampling the erudition encased in his library. In each tale, of course, iniquity, usually in the form of murder, intrudes upon Wolfe's den of serenity, and he sends Archie scurrying about town and country collecting clues, ferrying suspects and other concerned parties back to the brownstone for interrogation, and otherwise performing the nitty-gritty of detection.

Archie's reports on what he has seen and heard have an unfailing precision, and the sedentary fat man and his handsome, fit, and resourceful factotum share an obvious affection for each other, notwithstanding the constant caustic banter between them that is one of the delights of Stout's series. A recurring cast of characters rounds out Nero Wolfe's world, including the preternaturally gifted gumshoe Saul Panzer, the occasional operatives Orrie Cather and Fred Durkin, and the ever-exasperated representatives of the NYPD, Inspector Cramer and Sergeant Purley Stebbins.

In *Fer-de-Lance*, the genius must exert his mind as Archie exerts his body to unravel the serpentine connections between the murders of an immigrant laborer and a college president. The case Stout concocts is intricate enough to lend a compelling forward motion through the enchanted atmosphere of Wolfe's carefully constructed realm. Best of all, the author's brilliant combination of Wolfe's mental ingenuity and Goodwin's street-savvy sleuthing provides readers with the satisfactions of both the classic mystery of intellection and its more hardboiled cousin.

What: Mystery & Suspense. *When:* 1934. *Reading Note:* You can jump into the series at any point with pleasure, but some of Stout's best Wolfe tales, such as *Some Buried Caesar* (1939), depend upon familiarity with the routines the plots disrupt. So begin at the beginning. *Also By: The League of Frightened Men* (1935). *The Rubber Band* (1936). *Too Many Cooks* (1938). *Over My Dead Body* (1940). *Black Orchids* (1942). *The Silent Speaker* (1946). *In the Best Families* (1950). *The Golden Spiders* (1953). *The Black Mountain* (1954). *Further Reading: Nero Wolfe of West Thirty-Fifth Street* by William S. Baring-Gould. *Rex Stout: A Biography* by John McAleer. *Try: Hag's Nook* by John Dickson Carr. *Enter a Murderer* by Ngaio Marsh. *Adaptation:* Adapted by Hollywood in 1936 as *Meet Nero Wolfe*, starring Edward Arnold in the title role. *Footnote:* A mathematical prodigy, Rex Stout invented a school savings account system that ensured his financial independence. He published his first Wolfe tale at the age of forty-seven, and he would go on to write dozens more before he died.

■ For Peter Straub's *lost boy lost girl*, see page 634.

....

Alice James: A Biography
Jean Strouse (born 1945)

Portrait of a Lady

....

Alice James did not produce any significant body of work. She never married. She did not have children. She was not socially useful, particularly virtuous, or even happy. Her interests and talents might have led her to become . . . a historian, or a writer on politics, a pioneer in women's education, or the leader of a radical movement. Instead, she became an invalid.

So we read on the opening page of the author's introduction to her biography of Alice James. Although such a beginning might make you wonder about the pleasures to be found in continuing through the more than three hundred pages that follow, forge ahead and you'll quickly discover this remarkable volume to be the best of company on three counts.

The first is Alice James herself, a woman full of wit and fine intelligence. Despite a life dominated by mysterious and debilitating nervous ailments, she was articulate, politically astute, engagingly nettlesome, and intensely involved with those around her. These last included, of course, her own near relations, who provide a second focus for the reader's fascination. Led by Alice's famous brothers, novelist Henry (see page 408) and philosopher William (see page 412), the James family embodied its own peculiar genius: It was a small and vibrant country in the middle of the continent of the nineteenth century. Strouse explores this country and its natives with detail, discrimination, and insight. She knows her way around the continent as well, and rightly sees in Alice James an intensely private life that nevertheless "makes vivid the ideas, personalities, and social conditions of her time."

"The moral and philosophical questions that Henry wrote up as fiction and William as science," Strouse writes, "Alice simply lived." Thoughtfully tracing the hidden drama and destiny of that living through family archives and her subject's letters and diary, Strouse herself is the third party to the good company this book delivers. The initial sentence of chapter 1 reveals her acumen and command of expression, which never flag: "Interesting perceptions are preferable to marketable achievements only where there is enough money to go around." Biography gets no better than this.

What: Biography. *When:* 1980. *Award:* Bancroft Prize, 1981. *Also By:* Morgan: American Financier (see page 307). *Further Reading:* The Diary of Alice James, edited by Leon Edel. The Death and Letters of Alice James by Ruth Bernard Yeazell. *Try:* Henry James (five volumes) by Leon Edel. Alice in Bed by Susan Sontag.

....

■ For Jean Strouse's *Morgan: American Financier*, see page 307.

....

Sophie's Choice
William Styron (1925–2006)

Ensnared by History and Guilt, Love and Death

....

In 1954, after his first novel, *Lie Down in Darkness*, had been published to acclaim, but long before he would cause a stir with his 1967 novel about a slave rebellion, *The Confessions of Nat Turner*, William Styron sat at a Parisian café table with *Paris Review* founders Peter Matthiessen and George Plimpton for an interview. As Plimpton would explain years later, Styron, who had contributed a tone-setting "Letter to an Editor" to the magazine's inaugural issue a year earlier, "was the only contemporary the editors knew who actually had written a novel." Discussing influences and favorite books, Styron opined that "a great book should leave you with many experiences, and slightly exhausted at the end. You live several lives while reading it. Its writer should, too." In retrospect, he may have been describing his aim for the book he published a quarter century later: *Sophie's Choice*.

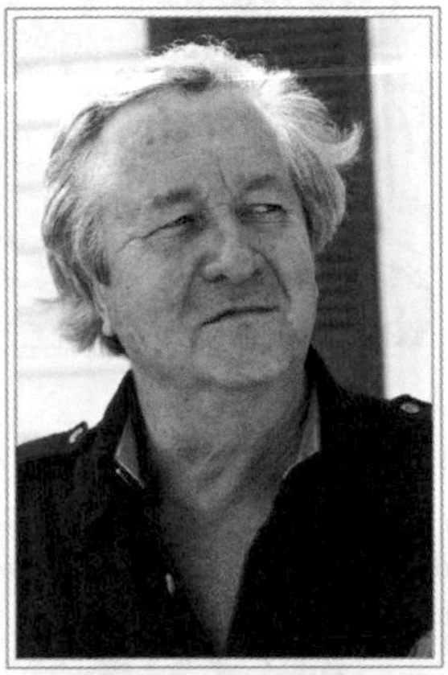

William Styron, 1982

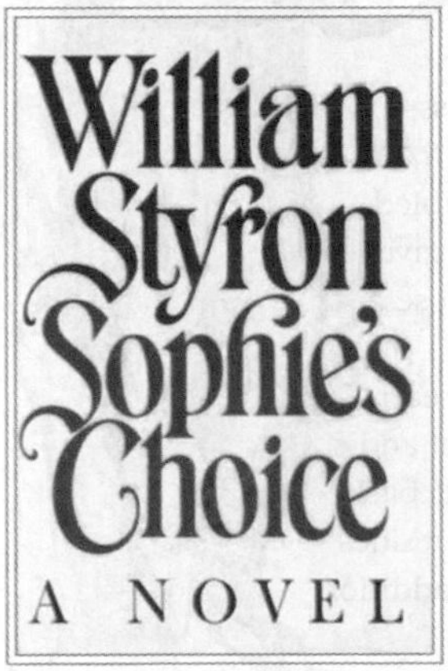

The novel is about history, coming-of-age, the Holocaust, survival, the legacy of slavery, guilt, lust, life's tantalizing and everlasting perishability, and—very much—writing. Stingo, the narrator, looks back three decades to the summer of 1947, when he was twenty-two years old. Dismissed from his forty-dollar-a-week junior editor job at McGraw-Hill, an occupation whose uninspired business he sends up with sardonic relish, Stingo moves to a boardinghouse in Brooklyn to focus on writing a novel—and losing his virginity. He soon becomes entangled with his audibly carnal upstairs neighbors: a moody but magnetic Harvard-educated Jewish biologist, Nathan, and Nathan's beautiful, blond Polish Catholic girlfriend, Sophie. Each member of the trio is fighting demons; Stingo reveals his own—he is living off a meager inheritance from his Southern family that he knows to be slave-trade revenue—while those of Nathan and Sophie are revealed slowly and sensationally in the course of the book, from the concentration camp number tattooed on Sophie's arm to the invisible but unending horror of her choice. Discursive, provocative, intellectually probing and emotionally wrenching, Styron's novel fits its author's youthful description of a great book, affording the reader, as it clearly afforded the writer, the chance to live several lives and be haunted by them ever after.

What: Novel. ***When:*** 1979. ***Award:*** National Book Award, 1980. ***Also By:*** *Lie Down in Darkness* (1951). *The Long March* (1957). *Set This House on Fire* (1960). *The Confessions of Nat Turner* (1967). *Darkness Visible: A Memoir of Madness* (1990). ***Further Reading:*** *Reading My Father* by Alexandra Styron. ***Try:*** *All the King's Men* by Robert Penn Warren (see page 834). *Angle of Repose* by Wallace Stegner (see page 749). ***Adaptation:*** The 1982 Alan Pakula film, which was nominated for five Academy Awards, stars Kevin Kline, Peter MacNicol, and Meryl Streep, who won the Best Actress Oscar.

The Twelve Caesars

Suetonius (ca. AD 69–ca. AD 125)
Translated by Robert Graves (1895–1985)

Lifestyles of the Rich and Imperial

Suetonius's portraits of the first twelve emperors of Rome are filled with anecdotes—from Julius Caesar's negotiations with pirates who held him captive to Nero's fiddling while the city burned—that are historically intriguing, deliciously entertaining, and, not least, indelibly emblematic of the personalities they present. Beginning with the ascendance of

Julius Caesar and the demise of the Roman Republic, and concluding with the tyrannical reign of Domitian, who was assassinated in AD 96, these biographical sketches encompass 150 years of eventful imperial history.

Suetonius served in Hadrian's retinue as an archivist and librarian, and his book reveals a gift for gossipy details— for example, Julius Caesar's embarrassment with his baldness, which prompted what may be the first documented comb-over—and an interest in the greed, delusions, and sexual proclivities (or depravities) of his subjects. Because the author is fond of eccentricity and stories of corruption great and small, his book is filled with lively narration of bizarre events (don't miss, for instance, the death of Nero, or the entire strange story of the troubled, and troubling, Caligula), which gives the matter-of-fact mask of his prose a pleasingly wry undercurrent.

The idea we've inherited of the early Roman Empire as a place of moral and political decadence can be traced back to Suetonius's focus on the darker sides of the Caesars (who include, in addition to those already mentioned, Augustus, Tiberius, Claudius, Galba, Otho, Vitellius, Vespasian, and Titus). In his characteristically and compellingly readable translation, Robert Graves proves the perfect interpreter. (Graves would plunder this source as material for his own marvelous novels, *I, Claudius* and *Claudius the God*.)

What: Antiquity. History. *When:* AD 121. *Edition:* The Latin title is *De Vita Caesurum* (*Lives of the Caesars*). Graves's translation, as *The Twelve Caesars*, appeared in 1957. *Also By:* *De Viris Illustribus* (AD 106–113). *Try: The Histories* and *The Annals* by Tacitus (see page 770). *The Letters of Pliny the Younger* (see page 630). *Memoirs of Hadrian* by Marguerite Yourcenar (see page 878). *I, Claudius* and *Claudius the God* by Robert Graves. *Adaptation:* The critically and popularly acclaimed 1976 television miniseries *I, Claudius*, starring Derek Jacobi, was based on Suetonius by way of Graves.

Augustus (above);
Julius Caesar (left)

....

Zeno's Conscience
Italo Svevo (1861–1928)

An Incurable Smoker Tries the Talking Cure

....

Zeno Cosini is a smoker. Like most smokers, he's always trying to quit. So he goes to a psychiatrist to make sense of his nicotine habit. The doctor advises him to keep a diary. Cigarettes, of course, are what Zeno starts writing about. He remembers his first one, and ponders his "last cigarette" hang-up, which began to afflict him just as he was entering his twenties. From there he goes on to discuss his rather plain-looking wife, his guilt-inducing extramarital affair, his late father, and his faltering business. The reader soon realizes that Zeno's monologue charts a course of rationalizations, exaggerations, and slight but suggestive deceptions, all in the service of vindicating the narrator in his own eyes. In other words, Zeno's story resembles the stream of consciousness in which every one of us makes narrative sense of our own life, constantly adjusting the stream's temperature to maintain our comfort.

Italo Svevo (the pen name of Aron Ettore Schmitz) was fascinated by the ideas of Sigmund Freud, and in *Zeno's Conscience* more than one critic has seen the birth of the psychoanalytic novel ("Our Freud is a great man," Svevo wrote in a letter, "far more for novelists than for the sick"). He has been placed in the company of such twentieth-century writers as James Joyce, Thomas Mann, Robert Musil, and Franz Kafka. But this book is a lot more fun than any of that sounds. Utterly charming in its wry reporting of everyday evasions and emergencies, it proves that a personality that might be exasperating to encounter in real life can be conspiratorially delightful on the page.

Although *Zeno's Conscience* is now acknowledged to be one of the masterworks of modern Italian fiction, Svevo published it himself in 1923 to little notice. The book might well have disappeared from literary history had it not been championed by James Joyce, who taught English to Schmitz at the Trieste branch of a language school. Some even consider Schmitz to be the model for Leopold Bloom, the wandering hero of Joyce's *Ulysses*, in which case the ledger of literary friendship is nicely balanced.

What: Novel. *When:* 1923. *Editions:* William Weaver translated *La coscienza di Zeno* as *Zeno's Conscience* in 2001. Others, such as Beryl de Zoete, have used the title *The Confessions of Zeno* (1930). *Also By: A Life* (1892). *As a Man Grows Older* (1898). *Further Confessions of Zeno* (unfinished; published in Italian 1957–59, in English 1969). *Further Reading: Italo Svevo: The Man and the Writer* by P. N. Furbank. *Try: Epitaph of a Small Winner* by Joaquim María Machado de Assis (see page 508). *Portnoy's Complaint* by Philip Roth.

Gulliver's Travels
Jonathan Swift (1667–1745)

Enthralling Adventure, Envenomed Satire, Immortal Invention

*G*ulliver's Travels* is a timeless and universal story, a narrative of bold invention that is laced with satire of a ferocity rarely equaled in the annals of literature. George Orwell, whose *Animal Farm* belongs to the same tradition as Swift's masterpiece, said it best: "Its fascination seems inexhaustible. If I had to make a list of six books which were to be preserved when all others were destroyed, I would certainly put *Gulliver's Travels* among them."

Like many readers before and since, Orwell was a child when he first fell under the spell of this tale of an Englishman, Lemuel Gulliver, who travels to fantastic lands. These strange places include Lilliput, where the inhabitants are small and Gulliver gigantic; Brobdingnag, where the reverse is true; Laputa, a flying island of highly educated, highly impractical men; and the country of the Houyhnhnms. This last is a utopia where gentle, rational horses rule over the vile Yahoos, dreadful humanlike

A. E. Jackson illustration of Gulliver among the giants of Brobdingnag

creatures whose unarguable physical resemblance to himself shames and disgusts Gulliver.

In each of Gulliver's adventures, Swift, an Irish-born priest whose other writings include poems and essays, satirizes foolishness and vice. His specific targets are now unfamiliar, but his mockery retains its bite because it addresses unchanging aspects of behavior. From the gigantic vanity of the pint-sized Lilliputians to the small-mindedness of the enormous Brobdingnagians, Swift skewers follies as recognizable to us as the faces we see in the mirror. Though the book is rife with page-turning pleasures, *Gulliver's Travels* contains some of the most savage criticism of humanity ever penned. That's especially true of the section devoted to the Houyhnhnms, in which Gulliver, having found an idyllic society of reason and intelligence among the horses, is unable on his return to England to reconcile himself to the proud unpleasantness of his Yahoo-like countrymen.

Fiercely funny and terrifically entertaining, *Gulliver's Travels* remains a storytelling feat in a class by itself.

What: Literature. Fantasy. *When:* 1726. *Also By:* Swift's other satirical masterpieces include *A Tale of a Tub* (1704), *The Battle of the Books* (1697), and *A Modest Proposal* (1729). *Try: Gargantua and Pantagruel* by François Rabelais (see page 656). *Adaptations:* Max Fleischer's 1939 animated film for children is a delight. An ambitious 1996 television version stars Ted Danson and Mary Steenburgen.

The Quest for Corvo
AN EXPERIMENT IN BIOGRAPHY
A. J. A. Symons (1900–1941)

The Biographer as Detective

" Have you read . . . ?" is a question that sends many readers off on bookish adventures. It sent A. J. A. Symons on a quest that resulted in this pathbreaking biography.

"Have you read *Hadrian the Seventh*?" a friend asked Symons in the summer of 1925. Not having done so, Symons borrowed and read his friend's copy. In Symons's opinion, the novel, published in 1904, was "one of the most extraordinary achievements in English literature [. . .]: a feat of writing difficult to parallel; original, witty, obviously the work of a born man of letters, full of masterly phrases and scenes, almost flabbergasting in its revelation of a vivid and profoundly unusual personality." So intrigued was Symons by that "unusual personality" that he set out to learn what he could about the author, who was listed as Fr. Rolfe. This turned out to be Frederick William Rolfe (1860–1913), a London-born artist and writer whose many pen names included Baron Corvo. The more deeply Symons looked into the life of Rolfe/Corvo, the weirder and more unnerving it became. No need here to spoil the pleasure of joining Symons in uncovering the bizarre truth; suffice it to say that you are unlikely to come across a more eccentric, self-destructive genius in literature's archives.

Traditionally, when biographers told the story of a life, they did not inject themselves into the narrative, nor did they describe the process of their research. *The Quest for Corvo* turned that approach on its head: Rolfe/Corvo's life story takes shape only as Symons recounts how, like a detective, he tracked down the truth about his mysterious subject. Since 1934, when Symons's daring "experiment in biography" was published, "in search of" biographies have become more common, but few of them have matched the ingenuity or thrilling allure of *The Quest for Corvo*. As the *New York Times* noted in 2005, it is still "the benchmark."

What: Biography. *When:* 1934. *Edition:* The 2001 New York Review Books Classics edition has an introduction by A. S. Byatt. *Also By: Essays and Biographies* (1969). *Further Reading: Hadrian the Seventh* and *The Desire and Pursuit of the Whole* by Fr. Rolfe (Baron Corvo). *A. J. A. Symons: His Life and Speculations* by Julian Symons. *Try: Hermit of Peking* by Hugh Trevor-Roper (see page 805).

Map
COLLECTED AND LAST POEMS
Wisława Szymborska (1923–2012)

Poems of Humor, Contemplation, and Compassion

There is no better defense of the power of poetry than the labors of the Polish poets of the twentieth century. The works of Wisława Szymborska, the 1996 Nobel Laureate, as well as those of her compatriots like Czeslaw Milosz and Zbigniew Herbert, prove that, even in the face of history's intractable brutalities, poetry still offers avenues of intense, intelligent engagement with the world.

Szymborska's appealing voice—personal but not private, droll, funny, experienced—makes her simple verses instant, invigorating companions for any reader. Spanning nearly sixty years of work, *Map* brings together more than two hundred of her poems, which have been translated by Clare Cavanagh and Stanisław Barańczak. Virtuosic in their playful simplicity and virtuous in their philosophical and ethical seriousness, her poems evoke the deep yet often unconscious contemplative spirit that hovers over the inconsequential details of our mundane activities. Whether writing about a bodybuilder's contest, a bird, or a birthday, her conversational voice captures the way the flotsam and jetsam of our days are caught in deep tides of time, fate, love, and individual morality. The mortal sentence we are all under does not daunt her. In "On Death, without Exaggeration," she chides her subject—"It can't take a joke, / find a star, make a bridge. / It knows nothing about weaving, mining, farming, / building ships, or baking cakes"—yet leaves us a little braver in the face of its inevitability:

There's no life
that couldn't be immortal
if only for a moment.

Death
always arrives by that very moment too late.

In vain it tugs at the knob
of the invisible door.
As far as you've come
can't be undone.

Wisława Szymborska, 1996

What: Poetry. *When:* 2015. *Edition:* Cavanagh and Barańczak are the best of Szymborska's several English translators. *Award:* Nobel Prize in Literature, 1996. *Also By: Nonrequired Reading: Prose Pieces* (1992). *Monologue of a Dog* (2002). *Try: New and Collected Poems: 1931–2001* by Czeslaw Milosz. *The Collected Poems: 1956–1998* by Zbigniew Herbert. *Sailing Alone Around the Room* by Billy Collins (see page 166).

HISTORIES OF ROME

HISTORIES • ANNALS

Tacitus (ca. AD 55–ca. AD 120)

**"Tacitus I consider the first writer in
the world without a single exception."
—*Thomas Jefferson***

An accomplished orator and public official
who rose to a consulship in AD 97, Tacitus
brought to the page both rhetorical mastery—
his are the most artfully composed of all extant
Roman histories—and an informed knowledge
of political tactics and intrigue. He also brought
a respect for the values of republican Rome that
colored his accounts of imperial excess and

corruption. The image of ancient turpitude
later encapsulated in the phrase "decline and
fall" was first sketched in the *Histories* and the
Annals. For Tacitus, moral degradation was
the inevitable result of the loss of freedom
that the autocratic rule of the emperors—to
say nothing of their personal depravities—
introduced into Roman governance.

Although written separately, these two
books together offer a coherent portrait of the
empire in the first century AD. The *Histories*, set
down first, begins in the confusion after the

Woodcut of Nero watching fire engulf Rome in AD 64

death of Nero and concludes with the reign of Domitian in AD 96. Although only a portion of the complete work survives, what remains—especially Tacitus's fleet, brilliantly structured, and dramatic description of the rampant civil warfare during the year of four emperors (AD 69)—exhibits a mastery of historical intelligence unequaled in the ancient world. Tacitus marches armies and mobs across his pages, then holds them still to hear the speeches of their leaders. In the *Annals*, which runs (again with gaps in the extant text) from the death of Augustus through the reign of Nero (AD 14–68), public history often cedes the stage to private (albeit imperial) scandal, recounted with no loss of attention or narrative skill. The cast of characters—including Claudius and Messalina, Tiberius, Nero and his wife, Octavia (and his husband, Pythagoras)—is horrid and gripping, their schemes in pursuit of pleasure and power incredible and quite often breathtakingly

ingenious. The final chapters relate not only the great fire at Rome through which Nero fiddled, but, just as memorably, the fiddler's increasingly intricate plots to kill off Agrippina, his politically minded mother. Tacitus's meticulous detailing of Nero's matricidal machinations constitutes one of the most blackly comic episodes in all literature. Lively, smart, stylish, the works of Tacitus remain, after two thousand years, hard to put down.

What: History. Antiquity. *When: Histories* (ca. AD 100–AD 110). *Annals* (ca. AD 116). *Edition:* The Modern Library Classics edition, edited by Moses Hadas, combines both works in one volume. *Also By: Agricola* (AD 98). *Germania* (AD 98). *Further Reading: A History of Histories* by John Burrow. *Try: The Twelve Caesars* by Suetonius (see page 765). *Plutarch's Lives* (see page 630). *The History of the Decline and Fall of the Roman Empire* by Edward Gibbon (see page 312). *I, Claudius* and *Claudius the God* by Robert Graves.

Fame and Obscurity
Gay Talese (born 1932)

"Frank Sinatra Has a Cold"—and Other Episodes Too Good to Miss

In the arts and athletics alike, the most accomplished performers blend originality, experience, and discipline into transparent virtuosity. Mining the deepest resources of popular song, Frank Sinatra exhibited such a talent; in his polishing of the baseball diamond, Joe DiMaggio was another. Gay Talese's celebrated portraits of both men are the centerpieces of this volume, and like them Talese is a virtuoso; his writing exhibits a poised command of the confidences and intuitions that distinguish mastery from competence. Both "Frank Sinatra Has a Cold" and "The Silent Season of the Hero," his account of the autumnal days of the retired baseball luminary, are legendary examples of what was labeled the New Journalism, a distinctive approach Talese perfected in the 1960s. Eschewing the stylistic and personal flamboyance of contemporary counterparts such as Tom Wolfe and Norman Mailer, Talese

observed his subjects with a detachment that allowed him to render the ordinary moments of conversation, mood, tension, and conflict that reveal subtle shadings of character.

Talese's journalism, especially as practiced in the pages of *Esquire* magazine, brought him wide acclaim and would prove uncommonly influential. The Sinatra piece in particular—in which the author offers a finely etched portrait of the mercurial singer despite the fact that Sinatra's cold (or the excuse it affords) keeps him from ever sitting for an interview—has earned an extraordinary reputation: Four decades after its original publication, *Esquire's* editors hailed it as "the best piece of writing ever to appear on its pages" and the *New York Times* called it "probably the most famous magazine profile ever written." Eyeing Sinatra only from a distance, yet measuring his relations with family, friends, and professional associates, Talese memorably captures the powerful, reserved, reckless, committed, impatient, and perplexing presence of the man.

Fame and Obscurity offers similarly insightful perspectives on figures theatrical (Joshua Logan and Peter O'Toole), pugilistic (Floyd Patterson and Joe Louis), criminal (Frank Costello), and journalistic (Diana Vreeland, George Plimpton and company, and Alden Whitman, fabled *New York Times* obituary writer). Although Talese would go on to write bestsellers such as *The Kingdom and the Power* and *Honor Thy Father*, the work collected here is what established him, in David Halberstam's words, as "the most important nonfiction writer of his generation, the person whose work most influenced at least two generations of other reporters."

What: Journalism. Culture. **When:** 1970, collecting pieces individually published throughout the 1960s. **Edition:** If you can't easily find a copy of *Fame and Obscurity*, look for *The Gay Talese Reader* (2003), which contains many of the earlier book's most important pieces. **Also By:** *The Kingdom and the Power* (1969). *Honor Thy Father* (1971). *Thy Neighbor's Wife* (1980). *Unto the Sons* (1992). *A Writer's Life* (2006). **Try:** *Up in the Old Hotel* by Joseph Mitchell (see page 556). *Piecework* by Pete Hamill.

··

This One Summer
Mariko Tamaki (born 1975)
Illustrated by Jillian Tamaki (born 1980)

A Summer Friendship in Words and Pictures

··

I n retrospect, the summers of childhood can seem sacred, our memories of them imbued with flavors of every sense. Even at the time, of course, they're pretty special, for the familiar sights and sounds of an annually visited resort are exotic enough—at least to a child—to add delight to the break from the rest-of-the-year routine. Such vacations create their own dimension of experience, one that slips away quickly each year but assumes a permanent aura of enchantment looking back.

The magic of Awago Beach, the vacation destination for the families of the two adolescent girls, Rose and Windy, whose friendship is at the heart of *This One Summer*, is pretty mundane. "My dad says Awago is a place where beer grows on trees and everyone can sleep in until eleven," Rose, the narrator, confides. Her summertime pal is a year and a half younger, less alert than Rose to the allure of boys or the enticing holiday freedom older teens enjoy. Yet the girls remain inseparable as they make their rounds in the humble, slightly ramshackle town, a lakeside agglomeration of cabins and conveniences.

During their regular trips to the variety store—where the jerky antics of the young clerk named Dunc both repel and attract—Rose and Windy try to unriddle the behavior of the teenagers before reverting to their habitual pleasures of games and horror movies. Through it all, Rose and Windy exchange thoughts, reactions, exclamations, nonsense—always sounding true to their respective ages and not like mouthpieces for adult sentiments. Their semisnarky, semi-serious, semi-confused idiolect, in which they express—or avoid—their own evolving feelings about life and family and love, is perfectly pitched. What's just beyond their ability to articulate—bewilderment, infatuation, anxiety, joy—is evoked nonetheless.

The writing is the work of Mariko Tamaki, and her cousin Jillian Tamaki draws the graphic novel's art. The naturalistic illustration, ever-so-slightly tinged with anime influences, has a captivating palette of blues. Glorious features of physical reality or human expression fill each page. Representational panels describing the clean lines of furniture and bicycles, store aisles and kitchens, alternate with natural panoramas, often making use of double-page spreads (the renderings of milkweed plants early on, and an overgrown hollow toward the end, are especially effective). The look of the characters completely matches the nature of the players. Windy is drawn with a trace of manga styling that symbolizes—and celebrates—her ebullience and naïveté. Rose's mom wears the thin, beaten-down look of a sufferer trapped in her own head, whereas her dad is big, bouncy, and exuberant; as a result, the struggles and sadness of their relationship, a powerful undercurrent in the book, is convincingly portrayed.

Seen from the point of view of the kids, the problems of the adults are nonetheless accorded full weight by the Tamakis. Indeed, all the characterizations are organic, sincere, drawn with subtlety to meet the eye when words might fail to catch a detail. The plotting is diffuse yet cumulatively powerful, and unpredictable as well. Although, as the title suggests, this is *one* summer, its focus frees it to represent the fleeting particularities of what becomes our most treasured experiences; it's the genius of the Tamakis' book to depict the desultory richness of a summer vacation as it's happening—long before the nostalgia that's waiting to happen kicks in. All told, *This One Summer* is a marvelous creation.

What: Graphic Novel. **When:** 2014. **Also By:** By Mariko and Jillian Tamaki: *Skim* (2008). By Jillian Tamaki: *Gilded Lilies* (2006) and *Indoor Voice* (2010). **Try:** *The Greatest of Marlys* by Lynda Barry. *Ghost World* by Daniel Clowes. *Unlovable* by Esther Pearl Watson. *Smile* by Raina Telgemeier.

The Joy Luck Club
Amy Tan (born 1952)

Mothers, Daughters, Memories, and Mah Jong

"**M**y father has asked me to be the fourth corner at the Joy Luck Club. I am to replace my mother, whose seat at the mah jong table has been empty since she died two months ago," narrator Jing-mei tells the reader. Her mother, Suyuan, had first formed her club in China more than forty years earlier. While China was under attack by the Japanese during World War II, the club gave the women a small way to take their minds off their fears: to eat as if everything were normal, to play mah jong for luck, and to tell stories into the night. When Suyuan escaped to America and settled in San Francisco, all she managed to take with her were "three shiny dresses" and this tradition.

As the book opens, thirty-six-year-old Jing-mei, also known as June, hasn't been to her mother's mah jong club since she was a teenager.

Arriving at the house of one of the "aunties" who occupy the other three corners of the Joy Luck Club, she is dismayed by the sameness—nothing has changed in the apartment; the aunties and uncles still follow their decades-old routines—and yet she feels completely out of place. Jing-mei has always been embarrassed by her mother and her friends and their persistence in their nostalgic ways. In this, she resembles her aunties' daughters, women of her own generation who are caught between cultures and are also estranged from their mothers' world. For their part, the mothers, who made unspeakable sacrifices to come to America, regret the distance between China and their daughters.

As Jing-mei takes her seat, her mother's stories come back to her, and as *The Joy Luck Club* progresses, Tan moves around the table, unfolding the lives of the aunties and their grown daughters. The deftly woven web of tales and tellers catches all the women's hopes and heartaches, dreams and disappointments, some especially Chinese American, others the lot of immigrants of any nationality, almost all familiar to mothers and daughters everywhere. Encouraged by the older women, Jing-mei travels to China to reconnect with those Suyuan left behind, allowing Tan to close a magical narrative circle that is warm and wonderful in its embrace of family, forgiveness, and the joy and luck that can redeem misfortune.

What: Novel. *When:* 1989. *Also By: The Kitchen God's Wife* (1991). *The Hundred Secret Senses* (1995). *The Bonesetter's Daughter* (2001). *The Opposite of Fate: A Book of Musings* (2003). *Try: Fifth Chinese Daughter* by Jade Snow Wong. *The Woman Warrior* by Maxine Hong Kingston. *Typical American* by Gish Jen. *Adaptation:* Tan wrote the screenplay for the acclaimed 1993 film directed by Wayne Wang.

Tao Te Ching

On the Way of Life

Ancient wisdom can seem mystical, detached as it is from the circumstances that define our days. But the reason texts written to capture such knowledge are often inscrutable has less to do with their antiquity than with the fact that wisdom itself is riddling and contradictory; words are never enough to capture what reality is trying to tell us. These are some of the paradoxes reflected in the Tao Te Ching, the foundational document of Taoism. One of the most translated works in history, it has had a powerful influence on religious and philosophical thinking across millennia and throughout the world. Most scholarship dates the Tao Te Ching to the mid–third century BC; its authorship has been traditionally ascribed to Lao Tzu (the name means "old philosopher"), but there is no certainty such a figure ever actually existed.

Epigrammatic in expression and enigmatic in substance, the Tao is composed with poetic economy, giving its instruction a confidence of expression that cuts into our attention.

> Great straightness seems crooked,
> Great cleverness seems clumsy,
> Great triumph seems awkward.

Its themes are the workings of the underlying cosmic order, or Way ("Tao" means "way" or "path"), and what this Way means for those who seek to follow it ("Te" means "integrity" or "inner power," and "Ching" translates as "book" or "scripture").

Lao Tzu rides a water buffalo in a Chinese engraving, ca. 1837

The Tao's eighty-one brief chapters fall into two parts. The first emphasizes the cosmic Way and applies it to the person (sections 1 through 37 in most translations); the second (sections 38–81) focuses on how individual character and virtue determine one's progress along the Way. The destination of this philosophical journey is a kind of stoicism that relies on serenity rather than strength, engendering a spirit that is poised rather than purposeful. Interestingly, the two parts are reversed in older manuscripts, which begin with personal behavior and then open out to a universal perspective, a sequence that may help the reader better grasp the cosmic concepts. Either way, the Tao is an uncanny distillation of the salient principles of living, abjuring the embellishments of moral strictures, law, and manners to reduce conduct to essential being rather than ephemeral doing.

> When the Way is lost,
>   afterward comes integrity.
> When integrity is lost,
>   afterward comes humaneness.
> When humaneness is lost,
>   afterward comes righteousness.
> When righteousness is lost,
>   afterward comes etiquette.

In those lines, the Tao presents a perfect précis of the stages of human development: from an infant's equanimity through the development of character, the recognition of ethics,

the tyranny of duty, and the consensus of convention. The path the book's teachings map out encourages us to dispense with habits that hold us hostage to individual will and social and cultural frameworks, so that we may learn again, quietly and without striving, to simply *be*.

What: Scripture. *When:* ca. mid-third century BC. *Editions:* Victor H. Mair's 1990 translation, quoted here, observes the reordering of parts mentioned above. Other translations worth study include those by Witter Bynner (1944), Gia-Fu Feng and Jane English (1972), Stephen Mitchell (1988), Ursula K. Le Guin (1997), and David Hinton (2013). *Try: Bhagavad Gita* (see page 75). *Wandering on the Way: Early Taoist Tales and Principles of Chuang Tzu* by Chuang Tzu, translated by Victor H. Mair. *The Four Chinese Classics: Tao Te Ching, Chuang Tzu, Analects, Mencius*, translated and with a commentary by David Hinton.

The Secret History
Donna Tartt (born 1963)

A Classical Education,
Laced with Psychological Suspense

In the prologue, we're shown the body, a testament to Donna Tartt's command. Despite this revelation at the outset, her story of a coterie of classics majors from an elite New England college delivers the satisfactions of a thriller—a thriller with a literary pedigree, but a thriller nonetheless. *The Secret History* is an evocation of lost friendship, lost promise, lost passion, and lost youth, in which the time before the losing is brilliantly conjured. There is plenty of lost learning as well, as the worldly unworldliness

of her protagonists is made dangerous by the intoxications of ancient rites and ideas. The group's cultish devotion to a priestly professor leads them into snares that hide in plain sight, like the traps foretold in Greek tragic drama. Yet the hypnotic horror of Tartt's tale has the seductiveness of tragedy's stepchild, melodrama; its allure casts a narrative spell that imbues callow lives with an eerie, uneasy attractiveness.

What: Novel. *When:* 1992. *Also By: The Little Friend* (2002). *The Goldfinch* (2013). *Try: Brideshead Revisited* by Evelyn Waugh. *The Likeness* by Tana French.

The Surprise of Cremona
Edith Templeton (1916–2006)

Armchair Italian Travel at Its Best

Splendid travel narratives of Italy are so abundant that to say *The Surprise of Cremona*

is in a class by itself is no small assertion. What makes it so special? Let's start with the fact that although a reader can rather easily assemble a sizable library of foreign visitors' excellently written accounts of sojourns in Venice, Florence, and Rome, books that wander off those deservedly beaten urban paths are fewer and farther between. The unexpected purview of Edith Templeton's 1954 travel diary—which its subtitle announces as "one woman's adventures in Cremona, Parma, Mantua, Ravenna, Urbino and Arezzo"—is just one of several qualities that sets it apart.

Alert to the local character—historical, artistic, gustatory—that each of the storied stops on her itinerary radiates, Templeton is a fine, fresh guide to both the sites and the flavors that infuse Italian culture with such pleasure. She is an astute (and often acerbic) guide to galleries and museums, able to convey the active engagement of looking at art rather than merely providing the checklist for categorizing it. Her considerable erudition is supported by a deep curiosity; the combination makes her an ideal companion (her passage through the galleries of the Gonzaga Palace in Mantua is marvelous to share). She is equally adept at directing our attention to the pageant of vegetables in an open market, or to the *dramatis personae* of the Italian table. (See her take-down of the bread served in Cremonese restaurants, or her ode to the profundity of the artichoke: "It has a melancholy flavour suggestive of mould and dust and of old books rotting away unread in the damp baronial libraries of old country manors. . . . He who does not take the time to conquer the artichoke by stages does not deserve to penetrate to its heart. There are no shortcuts in life to anything: least of all to the artichoke.") Templeton can capture the personal, social, and commercial tensions exhibited in the eye-rolls and not-so sotto voce mutterings of a husband-and-wife team

running a small hotel with the wit and reach of an accomplished novelist. Hers is an Italy in which every observation is an entrée to a wider story, whether she chooses to tell it or not.

The writing in *The Surprise of Cremona* is so good that one doesn't get too far into it before one wonders just who Edith Templeton was and what else she may have written. Born in Prague in 1916, she married an Englishman in 1938, then left England in the mid-1950s to live in India with her second husband. In that same decade she wrote several novels and began to publish stories in *The New Yorker* (which were collected more than four decades later in *The Darts of Cupid and Other Stories*; 2002). In 1966, under the nom de plume Louisa Walbrook, she wrote *Gordon*, a novel of a young woman's obsessive submission to a psychiatrist, which was lively enough to be banned in England and Germany. Rescued by Maurice Girodias's Olympia Press in Paris (the original publisher of Nabokov's *Lolita*), *Gordon* was finally issued under Templeton's own name in 2003, when its author was eighty-seven.

Even in the age of e-books and easy internet searches for forgotten volumes, *The Surprise of Cremona* is nearly impossible to find, but it is well worth seeking out—just like the best restaurants in strange provincial towns, which the author learns are usually discovered by heading down back streets and hidden alleys. How apt.

What: Travel. *When:* 1954. *Also By: Living on Yesterday* (1951). *The Island of Desire* (1952). *Gordon* (1966). *Further Reading: A Renaissance Tapestry: The Gonzaga of Mantua* by Kate Simon. *Try: A Time in Rome* by Elizabeth Bowen. *Rome and a Villa* by Eleanor Clark (see page 160). *Italy: The Places in Between*, also by Kate Simon. *Italian Ways* by Tim Parks.

The Daughter of Time
Josephine Tey (1896–1952)

Murder by the Book

Scotland Yard Detective Inspector Alan Grant is a sleuth whose consummate professionalism is all the more intriguing given

his particular mix of flaws and flair. Rather than placing him on a stage manufactured for murder, Josephine Tey's mysteries move him through complex political and social realities. He has an easy way with the wide range of characters his work introduces him to—and a hard-nosed, even obsessive way with the facts and evidence Tey concocts for him to puzzle out.

A triumph of ingenuity, *The Daughter of Time* finds Grant confined to a hospital bed but nevertheless investigating a couple of five-hundred-year-old homicides: the killing of the princes in the tower by the villainous Richard III. According to tradition and the damning pentameter of Shakespeare, Richard was motivated by monstrous ambition—yet when Grant studies a portrait of the malign king, he sees a sensitive face incapable of such atrocities. The detective inspector tracks his hunch through every historical source, beginning with children's history books, to arrive at a reversal of the verdict. Tey, who wears her own learning lightly, illustrates

Josephine Tey, 1934

along the way how historical truth "the daughter of time" in an old proverb—can become so tangled in legend that it becomes victim to the human imagination. It's a lesson most delightfully delivered.

What: Mystery & Suspense. *When:* 1951. *Also By:* Inspector Grant books: *The Franchise Affair* (1948); *The Singing Sands* (1952). Other mysteries: *Miss Pym Disposes* (1946); *Brat Farrar* (1949). *Further Reading:* For another perspective, read *The Princes in the Tower* by Alison Weir or *Royal Blood: Richard III and the Mystery of the Princes*, by attorney Bertram Fields. *Try: The Murders of Richard III*, a mystery by Elizabeth Peters. Nicola Upson's *An Expert in Murder*, the first in a series featuring the character of Josephine Tey as a sleuth. *Footnote:* Josephine Tey was a pseudonym of Elizabeth Mackintosh.

Vanity Fair

A NOVEL WITHOUT A HERO

William Makepeace Thackeray (1811–1863)

The Unforgettable Becky Sharp

Of all the celebrated nineteenth-century British novels, *Vanity Fair* is the most twenty-first century in scope and style. A gleeful satire of upper-class hypocrisy and every-class avarice in the early 1800s, during the era of the Napoleonic wars, Thackeray's panoramic comedy takes its title from *Pilgrim's Progress* by John Bunyan (1628–1688). In Bunyan's allegorical tale about living a Christian life, Vanity is the name of a town where worldly prizes and honors are sold at a fair rather than earned through good conduct. To Thackeray, the Vanity Fair is society itself, where greed, corruption, pride, and "dismal roguery" rule the mad scramble for temporal glory.

Fast paced and thoroughly entertaining, the story traces the fortunes of good but naïve Amelia Sedley, who is overshadowed in every way by her scheming and seductive friend Becky Sharp. Charming, clever, beautiful, and engagingly amoral, Becky is one of literature's great creations, a bad girl who makes for very good reading. While sentimental Amelia pines foolishly for a dashing but inconstant soldier, Becky climbs the social ladder with breathtaking enterprise. Ruthlessly opportunistic, she is also self-aware: "I'm no angel," Becky says at one point, leading Thackeray to comment, "And, to say the truth, she certainly was not."

Such authorial intervention—something of an innovation at the time—is one of the novel's distinctive charms. The vast canvas Thackeray

Portrait of William Makepeace Thackeray

and battlefields in Belgium, affords him every opportunity to comment upon the foibles of the age and the persistent follies of human nature, a role still being played with relish by social novelists today (Tom Wolfe's *The Bonfire of the Vanities* nods to Thackeray in more than its title). Few writers have been able to match Thackeray's flair for making an education in the ways of the world so engaging and instructive; his riveting, rollicking *Vanity Fair* remains in a class by itself.

What: Novel. *When:* 1847–48. *Also By: The Luck of Barry Lyndon* (1844). *The Book of Snobs* (1848). *The History of Pendennis* (1848–50). *The History of Henry Esmond, Esq.* (1852). *The Newcomes* (1853–55). *The Virginians* (1857–59). *Try: The Way We Live Now* by Anthony Trollope. *Gone With the Wind* by Margaret Mitchell (see page 557). *The Bonfire of the Vanities* by Tom Wolfe (see page 866). *Adaptations:* Filmed in 1935 as *Becky Sharp* by Rouben Mamoulian, and in 2004, as *Vanity Fair,* by Mira Nair, starring Reese Witherspoon as Becky.

creates, which leads from Miss Pinkerton's School for Girls to honeymoons at Brighton

How to Tell When You're Tired
A BRIEF EXAMINATION OF WORK
Reg Theriault (1924–2014)

Reflections on a Working Life

"There have been many volumes published on work," writes Reg Theriault, "but very little has been written by those who do it. What does it mean to work all your life at hard, physical labor?" The author, who worked as a fruit tramp in the western United States and then as a longshoreman on the San Francisco waterfront, answers his own question in a series of lithe chapters that are laced with wit and amplified by the author's wide reading.

His recollections of encounters with hand axes and forklifts—and of the "cruel, repetitious drudgery" that is often a laborer's lot—carry him toward measured and incisive consideration of public issues that have shaped the lives of workers and their place in economic and social history, but his writing always bears the stamp and the dignity of personal experience. Whether paying respect to "The Enchanted Hard Hat" or tackling the vexatious subject of "Bosses," Theriault has a knack for nailing—through well-drawn dialogue and apt anecdote—both the camaraderie and the contentiousness that course through any workplace. Anything but workmanlike, his essays on packing fruit, hauling sacks of coffee, work rules, unions, and Sisyphus, the laborer's patron saint, are elegant, funny, and wise. They add up to an engrossing, generous book.

What: Essays. Memoir. *When:* 1995. *Also By: Longshoring on the San Francisco Waterfront* (1978). *The Unmaking of the American Working Class* (2002). *Further Reading: The Working Life* by Joanne B. Ciulla. *Try: Working* by Studs Terkel. *Shop Class as Soulcraft* by Matthew B. Crawford.

The Great Railway Bazaar
BY TRAIN THROUGH ASIA
Paul Theroux (born 1941)

A Grand Tour by Train of Cultures and Characters

"Ever since childhood," the author begins, "when I lived within earshot of the Boston and Maine, I have seldom heard a train go by and not wished I was on it." In the three-hundred-odd pages that follow, Theroux indulges his lifelong desire on a grand scale, setting out from Victoria Station in London to travel across the Continent and through Asia on some of the world's greatest trains: the Orient Express, the Night Mail to Meshed, the Khyber Pass Local, the Golden Arrow, the Trans-Siberian Express. Luckily for us, we can ride along, entertained by his adventure and by his caustic views of the landscapes and people he encounters as he rides the rails.

"Anything is possible on a train," Theroux tells us early on, "a great meal, a binge, a visit from card players, an intrigue, a good night's sleep, and strangers' monologues framed like Russian short stories." He treats us to all of these in the course of his journey, especially the last. The passengers whose passing acquaintance Theroux records—from Misters Molesworth and Duffill, his companions leaving London on the Orient Express, to the Burmese Mr. Bernard, a septuagenarian hotel manager whose personal carriage seems to hold upright the last vestiges of British imperial tradition—form a novelist's gallery of satisfying portraits, quickly glimpsed and deftly drawn. Theroux's fleeting passage through terminals and across borders shows us squalor and splendor, enduring customs and postcolonial confusion, natural beauty and human truths. Sometimes, reality itself seems hard to reach, as if Theroux were journeying through the ominous plot of a thriller. One example is his comic, anxious, obstacle-strewn attempt to reach and ride over the legendary Gokteik Viaduct—a magnificent steel trestle bridge that spans a gorge on a never completed railroad line from northern Burma into China. Indeed, the Gokteik episode contains all the essential elements of a classic Graham Greene novel.

The first of the author's several successful books of journeys, *The Great Railway Bazaar* is, appropriately enough, transporting from beginning to end. Few books deliver the joy of armchair travel with such unfailing intelligence and entertainment—or with such easy and pleasing forward motion.

What: Travel. When: 1975. Also By: Travel: The Old Patagonian Express: By Train Through the Americas (1979); The Kingdom by the Sea: A Journey Around Great Britain (1985); Riding the Iron Rooster: By Train Through China (1988); Dark Star Safari: Overland from Cairo to Cape Town (2003). In Ghost Train to the Eastern Star (2008), Theroux returned thirty years later to retrace the tracks he traveled in The Great Railway Bazaar. Fiction: Saint Jack (1973); The Mosquito Coast (1981); Half Moon Street (1984); My Other Life (1989); Millroy the Magician (1993). Mother Land (2017). Try: The Big Red Train Ride by Eric Newby. Chasing the Monsoon by Alexander Frater.

Arabian Sands
Wilfred Thesiger (1910–2003)

A Journey Through the Last Unexplored Corner of the Earth

The Empty Quarter is one of the largest sand deserts in the world. Its 250,000 square miles in the southeast corner of the Arabian Peninsula include parts of Saudi Arabia, Oman, Yemen, and the United Arab Emirates. Although two Englishmen, Bertram Thomas (1892–1950) and H. St. John Philby (1885–1960), had previously crossed the *Rub' al Kahli* (as it is called in Arabic), Wilfred Thesiger was the first Westerner to thoroughly explore this forbidding and largely uninhabited "desert of deserts," with the help of the native, nomadic Bedouin, between 1945 and 1950.

As a twentieth-century adventurer, Thesiger was in a class by himself. Naturalist David Attenborough correctly described him as "one of the very few people who in our time could be put on the pedestal of the great explorers of the eighteenth and nineteenth centuries." An Oxford-educated descendant of a long line of British colonial aristocrats, Thesiger was averse to the character and comforts of the modern world, and was eager to escape its influence. "I knew instinctively," he writes, "that it was the very hardness of life in the desert which drew me back there—it was the same pull which takes men back to the polar ice, to high mountains, to the sea. To return to the Empty Quarter would be to answer a challenge, and to remain there for long would be to test myself to the limit."

His years in the Empty Quarter certainly offered the author the chance to truly test himself, as his many descriptions of thirst, hunger, and hostile conditions reveal. They also gave him the opportunity to become intimately familiar with the vanishing way of life of the Bedouin. This familiarity informs his narrative with fascinating details of the customs of his Bedu companions, as well as verbal portraits of the desert landscape, all rendered in well-made, watchful prose that shares the visual sensibility evidenced in Thesiger's excellent photographs (several of which appear in most editions of the book).

"The values of the desert have vanished," Thesiger would later write, "all over Arabia the

Wilfred Thesiger in Saudi Arabia, ca. 1947

transistor has replaced the tribal bard." This eloquent book is both an adventure and an elegy.

What: Exploration. Adventure. Travel. *When:* 1959. *Also By: The Marsh Arabs* (1964). *The Life of My Choice* (1987). *Among the Mountains: Travels Through Asia* (1998). A superb selection of Thesiger's photographs is gathered in *A Vanished World* (2001). *Further Reading: Wilfred Thesiger: The Life of the Great Explorer* by Alexander Maitland. *Try: Travels in Arabia Deserta* by Charles Montagu Doughty. *A Winter in Arabia* by Freya Stark. *Footnote:* The Pitt Rivers Museum in Oxford houses Thesiger's photographic archives—including some 38,000 negatives and seventy-five albums of prints; a sampling can be viewed on the museum's website.

Religion and the Decline of Magic

STUDIES IN POPULAR BELIEFS IN 16TH- AND 17TH-CENTURY ENGLAND

Keith Thomas (born 1933)

An Illuminating Study of the Years of Magical Thinking

When one thinks of the ever-present uncertainties that attend our existence, it's no wonder that belief in the supernatural has always held allure. In the 1500s and 1600s, before the emerging scientific outlook began to shape popular consciousness in England, systematized belief in the extramundane took two main, competing forms: religion and magic. Historian Keith Thomas's study of this turning point in the history of ideas reveals just how powerful, widespread, and richly developed the belief in astrology, witchcraft, and divination was at all levels of society, and how fragile organized religion's hegemony was in the face of magic's potent claims. (Not that the emergence of science closed the door completely on magical thinking; as Thomas perceptively notes, "if magic is defined as the employment of ineffective techniques to allay anxiety when effective ones are not available, then we must recognize that no society will ever be free from it.")

After a consideration of medieval Catholicism and the Protestant Reformation, Thomas examines in detail magical practices and the pervasive belief in ghosts and fairies as well as in ancient prophecies and omens. *Religion and the Decline of Magic* has had enormous influence in identifying new

RELIGION AND THE DECLINE OF MAGIC

'Still weaves its spell over successive generations of readers ... a great historical imagination' *Jonathon Barry*

Keith Thomas

kinds of material for scholarly research into the popular culture of the past, yet it is also a standout example of a "crossover": a work of serious scholarship that has found an audience among common readers because of the subject's inherent interest and the author's elegant and accessible style. The book is a genuinely absorbing journey down some forgotten byways of human thought, imagination, and credulity.

What: History. Anthropology. Religion & Spirituality. *When:* 1971. *Reading Note:* Despite Thomas's lucid style, the gravity of scholarship can be heavy. Yet even reading the book in segments over a long period of time is profitable and pleasurable. *Also By: Man and the Natural World* (1983). *Try: The Magical Universe: Everyday Ritual and Magic in Pre-Modern Europe* by Stephen Wilson. *Magic, Science and Religion and Other Essays* by Bronislaw Malinowski.

The Lives of a Cell
NOTES OF A BIOLOGY WATCHER
Lewis Thomas (1913–1993)

The Scientist as Man of Letters

Every genre has its native charms, and the allure of the essay is its easy way with rumination. In the best examples of the form, the essayist communicates not just learning, but *thinking*, inviting the reader to share the satisfactions of a mind at play on a field of observation or experience. When an essay's author is as masterful as Lewis Thomas, it can shine like a jewel, glittering with truths small and large.

The twenty-nine pieces collected in *The Lives of a Cell* have a distinguished scientific pedigree, for they first appeared in the *New England Journal of Medicine*. Dr. Thomas, the

biology watcher of the title, was an expert in immunology and microbiology as well as an esteemed medical administrator. Here, he brings literary eloquence to bear on subjects that start under the microscope and then travel around the cosmos on metaphoric flights that celebrate nature's interconnected, collaborative animation. The two essays that bookend *The Lives of a Cell*—the title piece and "The World's Biggest Membrane," a quietly stirring evocation of the grandeur and fragility of life on earth—reveal the author's empirical legerdemain. (He makes both the structure of a cell and the biological importance of a membrane intellectually and aesthetically thrilling.) And even a quick perusal of the pages in between reveals Thomas's curiosity and learning about language, music, and other humanistic themes. In short, the pleasures of this biology watcher's company are refreshingly varied. His brief reflections—each about five pages long—on cells, etymology, and other subjects are rewarding parcels of instruction and delight.

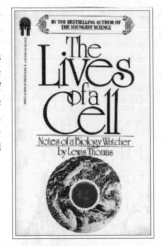

BY THE BESTSELLING AUTHOR OF THE YOUNGEST SCIENCE

The Lives of a Cell

Notes of a Biology Watcher by Lewis Thomas

What: Science. *When:* 1974. *Award:* National Book Award, 1975; nominated in two categories, Arts and Letters, and Sciences, it won

in the first. *Also By: The Medusa and the Snail* (1979). *Late Night Thoughts on Listening to Mahler's Ninth Symphony* (1984). *Et Cetera Et Cetera: Notes of a Word Watcher* (1990). *Try: On Being the Right Size* by J. B. S. Haldane. *Pluto's Republic* by Peter Medawar. *The Immense Journey* by Loren Eiseley (see page 247). *Footnote:* In addition to scientific research, Dr. Thomas was dean of the medical schools at New York University and Yale, and president of the Sloan-Kettering Institute.

On Growth and Form
D'Arcy Wentworth Thompson (1860–1948)

"The greatest work of prose in 20th-century science."—Stephen Jay Gould

A little more than a decade after D'Arcy Wentworth Thompson's death, British scientist and novelist C. P. Snow gave his famous lecture "The Two Cultures," in which he recognized an increasingly perilous gap between humanistic and scientific modes of thought. There is no better evidence that the divide can be bridged—that it is nothing more than a failure of imagination—than Thompson's 1917 masterpiece, *On Growth and Form*, described by biologist John Tyler Bonner as "good literature as well as good science; a discourse on science as though it were a humanity."

A zoologist, mathematician, and classicist, Thompson integrated intellectual approaches most often kept separate. His magnum opus—and at more than a thousand pages it is indeed magnum—springs from a mind conversant with natural philosophy from Aristotle to Darwin and with mathematical ideas from Pythagoras to Newton and beyond. Thompson writes about the development of form and structure in living organisms in prose that gracefully assimilates all the strands of his learning into a truly cultured whole, both

sonorous and substantive. Identifying mathematical patterns and mechanical forces where strict proponents of evolutionary theory would see only biological imperatives, *On Growth and Form* surveys a rich variety of specimens—cells, eggs, shells, jellyfish, skeletons—to reveal the abstract elegance and impulses of the physical world. Tracing his vision in the spiral of the nautilus, the geometry of spiderwebs and honeycombs, the arc of a flea's jump, even the curve of a raindrop and the concentric rings of water caused by a splash, Thompson's portrait of nature has inspired artists and architects as well as mathematicians and scientists for nearly a century. As Peter Medawar, the 1960 Nobel Laureate in Medicine, put it, *On Growth and Form* is "beyond comparison, the finest work of literature in all the annals of science that have been recorded in the English tongue."

What: Science. *When:* 1917. *Editions:* Dover Books publishes a complete and unabridged version, which runs to more than 1,100 pages. A smart abridgement is available in Cambridge University's Canto series. *Further Reading: The Two Cultures* by C. P. Snow. *Try: The Structure of Evolutionary Theory* by Stephen Jay Gould. *The Self-Made Tapestry* by Philip Ball.

Lark Rise to Candleford

Flora Thompson (1876–1947)

**A Celebration of Life in an
English Country Village**

....

B orn in Oxfordshire in 1876, Flora Thompson
was the daughter of a nursemaid and a
stonemason. From the age of fourteen she
worked in rural village post offices, educating
herself largely through her avid reading and
close observation of nature. After starting her
own family, she embarked upon a modest writing career, her first publication being an essay
on Jane Austen, which won a contest sponsored
by the *Ladies Companion* magazine.

   In the ensuing decades she composed
more essays, articles, and short stories, with
much of her work focusing on English literature and literary figures; she also formed a correspondence group offering writing instruction
and criticism to members. But it wasn't until she
was in her fifties that she produced the three
volumes of childhood reminiscence—*Lark Rise*
(1939), *Over to Candleford* (1941), and *Candleford
Green* (1943)—that made her famous, and on
which her lasting reputation rests. Soon after
its initial appearance, the trilogy was collected
in a single volume titled *Lark Rise to Candleford*.

   Detailing life in a country village in the
years before the Industrial Revolution, *Lark
Rise to Candleford* is a fictionalized autobiography. Its charming remembrance of local customs, crafts, and culture is distinguished by its

fidelity to the roaming curiosity of a child's eye,
as an early passage illustrates:

*One old woman once handed the little girl a leaf
from a pot-plant on her window-sill. "What's it
called?" was the inevitable question. "'Tis called
mind your own business," was the reply; "an' I think
I'd better give a slip of it to your mother to plant in a
pot for you."*

Farmers and traveling vendors, family and
schoolwork, seasonal festivals and the small
matters of community life are recalled, and
the natural beauty of the English countryside
is quietly honored by exact description. What's
most pleasing about Thompson's writing is
the easy confidence of her affectionate portrayal of times past. This is not only a book that
evokes a lost world, but one that transports us
to a simpler era with clarity and calm attention.
Novelist John Fowles wrote of Thompson that
our literature has no other observer "so genuinely endearing."

What: Memoir. Nature. *When:* 1945. *Also By: The
Peverel Papers: A Yearbook of the Countryside*
(composed 1921–27; published 1986). *Heatherley*
(written ca. 1944; published 1979). *Still Glides the
Stream* (1948). *Try: Our Village* by Mary Russell
Mitford. *Cider with Rosie* by Laurie Lee (see page 470).
Adaptation: A BBC television film was made in 2008.

....

Fear and Loathing in Las Vegas

A SAVAGE JOURNEY TO THE HEART OF THE AMERICAN DREAM

Hunter S. Thompson (1937–2005)

**The Crazed and Comic Genius of
an American Original**

....

W hacked out and drug crazed; riotous
and exuberant; immature and irresponsible; brilliantly original and more than
a little insane, *Fear and Loathing in Las Vegas*
chronicles the "bad craziness" that overtook

Hunter S. Thompson and a sidekick on a journalistic assignment in 1971. It's a book of headlong prose, reckless conduct, and delirious
inspiration.

   The backstory in brief: Thompson was
commissioned by *Sports Illustrated* to attend a
motorcycle race in Las Vegas and write a short
item about it. He went to Vegas as promised, but

that's where all resemblance to normal journalism ended. As described in *Fear and Loathing*'s first-person narrative, Thompson's pseudonymous alter ego Raoul Duke teams with "Dr. Gonzo," his "300-pound Samoan attorney," to cover not only the Mint 400 motorcycle race but also a convention of drug cops. From the very first sentence— "We were somewhere around Barstow on the edge of the desert when the drugs began to take hold"—Duke and his attorney find themselves in the grip of seriously mood- and mind-altering substances that induce hallucinations and Technicolor paranoia. On the page, though, their "savage journey to the heart of the American dream" is both a grand rhetorical celebration of acute sensitivities under the influence of relentless misbehavior and a merciless anatomy of mainstream American culture at the dawn of the Me Decade.

HUNTER S. THOMPSON
Fear and Loathing
in LAS VEGAS

flamingo
MODERN CLASSIC

Fear and Loathing in Las Vegas was first published as a two-part series in *Rolling Stone*, where British artist Ralph Steadman's bizarre slash-and-splatter illustrations proved the perfect visual counterpart to Thompson's compelling stylistic bravura. Thus was born the "gonzo journalism" that Thompson practiced for the rest of his influential writing career—although he would never again, frankly, "gonzo" anywhere near as memorably as he did in this outlandish tour de force.

What: Journalism. Memoir. Humor. *When:* 1971. *Edition:* The Modern Library edition includes Ralph Steadman's illustrations, as well as three companion pieces written and selected by Thompson. *Also By:* Hell's Angels: A Strange and Terrible Saga (1966). Fear and Loathing: On the Campaign Trail '72 (1973). The Great Shark Hunt (1979). The Proud Highway: The Saga of a Desperate Southern Gentleman, 1955–1967 (1997). Fear and Loathing in America: The Brutal Odyssey of an Outlaw Journalist, 1968–1976 (2000). *Try:* The Electric Kool-Aid Acid Test by Tom Wolfe. *Adaptation:* Johnny Depp and Benicio Del Toro star in the 1998 film adaptation of *Fear and Loathing in Las Vegas,* directed by Terry Gilliam.

Eloise
Kay Thompson (1909–1998)
Illustrated by Hilary Knight (born 1926)

A Fairy Tale of New York City

Incorrigible, imperious, inexhaustible, yet totally irresistible six-year-old Eloise is a child no parent would want to have in the house, but most grown-ups will enjoy introducing to youngsters at storytime, if only to commune with their own faraway childhoods (not for nothing did Kay Thompson subtitle her tale "A Book for Precocious Grown Ups"). Thompson's small heroine inhabits the ultimate urban wonderland: the swanky Plaza Hotel in Manhattan. With her mother perennially off in Paris, Eloise is ensconced in a penthouse suite at the Plaza with her Nanny, her dog, Weenie, and her turtle, Skipperdee. From her perch on the top floor, she commands the establishment with Napoleonic confidence and impish élan, venturing forth via elevator each day on a rigorous schedule of imaginary chores, errands, dramas, and pranks that take her up and down corridors and into the Persian Room, the Baroque Room, the Oak Room, the Terrace Room, the Grand Ballroom— in short, every corner of the splendid palace she calls home. Her English Nanny is "rawther" wonderful: She always says everything three times, and she graciously gives her young charge free rein. The result is a delicious romp through a world peopled with aristocrats and hotel staff, who all seem more or less oblivious to Eloise's revels. One minute she's pouring a pitcher of water down the mail chute; the next she might be crashing a wedding reception or pressing all the buttons on the elevator. Decades after its creation, Thompson's book retains its infectious allure, the humor and energy of its telling abetted and amplified on every page by Hilary Knight's marvelous illustrations.

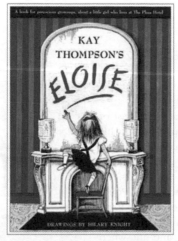

What: Children's. *When:* 1955. *Edition: Eloise: The Absolutely Essential 60th Anniversary Edition* was published in 2015. *Also By: Eloise in Paris* (1957). *Eloise at Christmastime* (1958). *Eloise in Moscow* (1959). *Try: Pippi Longstocking* by Astrid Lindgren. *Blueberries for Sal* by Robert McCloskey. *Adaptations:* Two 2003 made-for-television movies, *Eloise at the Plaza* and *Eloise at Christmastime,* star Julie Andrews as Nanny, Jeffrey Tambor as Mr. Salomone, and Sofia Vassileva as Eloise. *Footnote:* Kay Thompson started her career in show business as a singer, composer, and vocal coach. She famously stars as fashion editor Maggie Prescott alongside Fred Astaire and Audrey Hepburn in the musical film *Funny Face.* She lived at the Plaza Hotel. Thompson may have found the inspiration for Eloise in her young goddaughter, Liza Minnelli, who also resided at the Plaza with her mother, Judy Garland, when Garland was performing at the Persian Room.

||||||||||||||||||||||||||||||||||||||||||| B O O K N O T E |||||||||||||||||||||||||||||||||||||||||||

LAUGHTER AND LIFE LESSONS, IN COLOR AND RHYME

Madeline
Ludwig Bemelmans (1898–1962)

In an old house in Paris that was covered with vines lived twelve little girls in two straight lines.

So are young readers welcomed, in whimsy and rhyme spread across large pages of brightly hued illustrations, into one of the most delightful series of stories in children's literature. In this first of seven Madeline tales written and illustrated by Ludwig Bemelmans, our heroine, a French charmer whose special blend of moxie and mischief wins the hearts of all who meet her, proves her mettle. She is singularly unafraid of mice, she alone stands up to the (caged) tiger at the zoo, and she never fails to rally her fellow students to the cause of frightening their schoolmistress, Miss Clavel. When drama intrudes in the middle of one night, and Madeline is rushed to the hospital with appendicitis, she soon quells the alarm with such panache that all of her schoolmates want to have their appendixes out too.

Madeline and her world—including Pepito (the boy next door), the dog Genevieve, Miss Clavel, and Lord Cucuface, to say nothing of the books' grandest character, the city of Paris!—can't help but occupy a child's imagination in ways that foster resourcefulness and good cheer. Bemelmans's light-handed drawings and lighthearted verse make this 1939 book and its sequels memorable pleasures, particularly in their original large formats. Wonderful for reading aloud as early—and often—as possible.

Walden

OR, LIFE IN THE WOODS

Henry David Thoreau (1817–1862)

Retreat into Reality

Henry David Thoreau is the friendliest of philosophers, in no small part because his search for life's meaning was conducted with a first-person simplicity that gives his quest a narrative appeal: "I went to the woods," he writes of his famous sojourn at Walden Pond, "because I wished to live deliberately, to front only the essential facts of life, and see if I could not learn what it had to teach, and not, when I came to die, discover that I had not lived." His trek to the simple life did not cover a great distance—his destination was less than two miles from the center of his native Concord, to which he walked frequently to hear news and socialize—but the dwelling he constructed there, like the book he composed about his experiment in living, housed far-reaching ideas that would accrue influence as they traveled through time.

Henry David Thoreau, 1861

Walden begins with a long chapter, "Economy," which describes Thoreau's intended "business" of discovering the "necessaries of life," his building of "a tight shingled and plastered house, ten feet wide by fifteen long," and his planting of beans, potatoes, corn, peas, and turnips. Throughout the book, every aspect of his venture is subject to meticulous accounting, from the cost of the house ($28 and 12½ cents) to the money spent on food ($8.74) and clothing, oil, and household utensils ($10 and 40¼ cents). Every aspect is also subject to the expansive cast of his transcendentalist mind— "Heaven is under our feet as well as over our heads"—and to a literary genius that spins phrases with casual and unforgettable eloquence: "As if you could kill time without injuring eternity."

Culled from his copious journals, his thoughts are assembled into discrete chapters —"Where I Lived, and What I Lived For," "Reading," "Solitude," "Visitors," "The Bean-Field," "The Village," "Winter Animals," and "Spring," to name a sampling. His close observations of the world about him—take the catalog of noises, from train whistle to cock's crow, so faithfully rehearsed in "Sounds"— summon from his pen warnings about the conformist habits of society as well as rhapsodies about the liberating energies of nature. Whatever the theme, the smallest particular of plant or pond, light or land prompts an exhilarating song: "To him whose elastic and vigorous thought keeps pace with the sun, the day is a perpetual morning."

Despite the fact that it is now one of the best-known books in the American canon, *Walden* caused few ripples in its author's lifetime. Thoreau died a relatively unknown writer, distinguished mostly by his friendship with his mentor, Ralph Waldo Emerson. It was Emerson, in fact, who supplied the plot of land on which Thoreau built his cabin, and it was on Emerson's ground, literally and figuratively, that the younger man discovered an attitude toward life—earnest, alert, steeped in nature and in moral instinct—that would outlive him. The book spoke with special resonance in the 1960s, more than a century after his death, to a generation whose search for authenticity found encouragement and validation in Thoreau's words: "If a man does not keep pace with his companions, perhaps it is because he hears a different drummer. Let him step to the music which he hears, however measured or far away."

A profound influence on environmentalists, economists, rebels, and activists, *Walden* remains a tonic for any pensive reader trying to make sense of his or her own necessities. Many works can awaken our attention on first reading, but *Walden* has the inexplicable ability to startle us when we pick it up again, growing with us as we age. Thoreau's famous assertion that "The mass of men lead lives of quiet desperation" may be a challenge to a teenager, but it's a warning for a forty-year-old, and a rueful realization to a retiree. By conveying new meaning at every stage of our experience, the greatest books assure us that there is more to our lives than our daily grinds admit—which, of course, is Thoreau's message in a nutshell.

What: Philosophy. Nature. Memoir. *When:* 1854. *Also By: A Week on the Concord and Merrimack Rivers* (1849). *The Maine Woods* (1864). *Cape Cod* (1865). *Wild Fruits: Thoreau's Rediscovered Last Manuscript* (2000). The Library of America's *Collected Essays and Poems* (2001) includes Thoreau's seminal essay "Civil Disobedience," an important influence on Mohandas Gandhi and Martin Luther King Jr. *Further Reading: Henry Thoreau: A Life of the Mind* by Robert D. Richardson Jr. *The Thoreau Log: A Documentary Life of Henry David Thoreau* by Raymond R. Borst. *Try:* Essays by Ralph Waldo Emerson (see page 253). *Pilgrim at Tinker Creek* by Annie Dillard (see page 224). *Footnote:* Thoreau's given name was "David Henry"; he reversed it after graduating from Harvard because he thought "Henry David" sounded more authorial.

"An antidote to apathy and anxiety."
—John Updike on Walden

....

The History of the Peloponnesian War
Thucydides (ca. 455 BC–ca. 395 BC)

The Magnificent Chronicle of the Battle Between Athens and Sparta

Born a generation after Herodotus, Thucydides chose a different tack in his approach to writing history. His account of the epic struggle between Athens and the Peloponnesians (Sparta and its allies), a conflict that lasted nearly three decades (431 to 404 BC), focuses on political and military issues to the exclusion of the wandering curiosity and ethnographic concerns that characterized the *Histories* of Herodotus (see page 368). As one modern commentator put it, "Thucydides made a clean break with myths and legends and defined history as the pursuit of truth about the past," marshalling facts in a methodical and often disinterested fashion. Although himself an Athenian, and a one-time commander in the conflict he chronicles, Thucydides surveys both the failings and triumphs of each side with a critical eye. Exiled from his native city for his role in a failed rescue mission, he spent twenty years compiling materials and analyzing events, and his remove did much to inform his pioneering attempt at objectivity.

Thucydides begins his history of the war "at the moment it broke out," and his readiness to collect and compare eyewitness accounts of the various campaigns combines with his direct, incisive style to make his book lively reading. His reconstructions of speeches by generals of both camps contribute to the documentary feel of his narration; one of his most famous passages is Pericles's "Funeral Oration" for the Athenians who died in the first year of the conflict, recorded in book 2. It is a stirring celebration of the city's culture and its soldiers' courage and sacrifice, an abiding invocation of martial glory. To sample Thucydides at his best, go straight to his intricate account of the Athenians' invasion of Sicily and their ultimate defeat by the Spartans at Syracuse (books 6 and 7): "This was the greatest Hellenic achievement of any in this war, or, in my opinion, in Hellenic history; at once most glorious to the victors, and most calamitous to the conquered."

What: History. War. Antiquity. *When:* ca. 420–399 BC. *Editions:* Robert B. Strassler's extensively annotated revision of Richard Crawley's translation in *The Landmark Thucydides* (quoted here) includes useful maps and invaluable commentary. Rex Warner's Penguin Classics translation is also eminently readable. *Further Reading: The Peloponnesian War* by Donald Kagan. *A History of Histories* by John Burrow. *Try: Histories* by Herodotus (see page 368). *Histories* and *Annals* by Tacitus (see page 770). *The History of Rome from Its Foundations* by Livy.

The Thurber Carnival
James Thurber (1894–1961)

Thurber's World—and Welcome to It

Humorist James Thurber was a true American original. Born in Ohio and for decades on the staff of *The New Yorker*, he created in his stories and drawings a world uniquely his own.

Among the stories, the most famous is undoubtedly "The Secret Life of Walter Mitty." This brief tale reveals that even a meek and hen-pecked husband may harbor adventure-packed daydreams. Mitty-esque men are also much in evidence in Thurber's priceless drawings. One of the best-known Thurber cartoons, captioned "House and Woman," shows just such an unimposing fellow at the moment he reaches home and is startled to find that the house itself is actually becoming his scowling wife. In addition to harried, befuddled men and the women who loom over them, dogs and other animals are constant presences in the Thurber universe—as are, occasionally, other animals as well: In "The Pet Department," the author reluctantly dispenses advice to the owners of a stuffed cockatoo, a cast-iron lawn dog, and a wooden horse from a merry-go-round.

"Walter Mitty," "House and Woman," and "The Pet Department" are included in *The Thurber Carnival*, an anthology whose table of contents reads like a roster of the high points of modern American humor, for the volume generously proffers samples from seven of Thurber's books, including *My World and Welcome to It, The Middle-Aged Man on the Flying Trapeze,* and *Men, Women and Dogs.* It contains *My Life and Hard Times* complete, six previously uncollected stories, and "My Sixty Years with James Thurber," in which the author casts a skeptical eye over the work of "Thurber" and betrays exasperated amazement at the artist's unschooled style. Readers, however, have no doubts at all about Thurber's gifts and are happy to follow this one-of-a-kind author wherever—through words or pictures—his imagination leads.

What: Humor. *When:* 1945; revised and expanded, 1957. *Edition:* The 1957 Modern Library edition marked the first appearance of "My Sixty Years with James Thurber." *Also By: Is Sex Necessary?* (1929; with E. B. White). *Fables for Our Time and Famous Poems Illustrated* (1940). *The Beast in Me and Other Animals* (1948). *Alarms and Diversions* (1957). *The Years with Ross* (1959). *Credos and Curios* (1962). For children:

The 13 Clocks (1950); *The Wonderful O* (1957). *Try: The Benchley Roundup* by Robert Benchley. *Adaptations:* "The Secret Life of Walter Mitty" was filmed as a vehicle for Danny Kaye in 1947 and, in 2013, for Ben Stiller.

Prisoner Without a Name, Cell Without a Number
Jacobo Timerman (1923–1999)

The Harrowing Testament of a Political Prisoner

" The cell is narrow. When I stand at its center, facing the steel door, I can't extend my arms. But it is long, and when I lie down, I can stretch out my entire body. A stroke of luck, for in the cell I previously occupied—for how long?—I was forced to huddle up when seated and keep my knees bent while lying down." Nevertheless, Jacobo Timerman misses the smaller cell because it had a hole in the ground into which he could relieve himself. The new cell, in addition to its wet floor and total darkness, requires him to ask the guards (one wearing Timerman's watch, another using his cigarette lighter) to escort him to the latrine—providing each time a new opportunity for abuse and degradation. "I do it on myself. Which is why I miss the cell with the hole in it."

Timerman's family moved to Argentina from the Ukraine when he was five. With the newspapers he founded in Buenos Aires, most notably *La Opinión*, and his frequent presence on radio and television, he was one of the country's most vocal champions of human rights. Yet his visibility did not prevent him from becoming a victim of the military junta and its "Dirty War," the culmination of Argentina's frightful and tumultuous political climate in the 1970s. Despite the fact that he had originally supported the overthrow of the Perón regime, Timerman did not flinch from criticizing the military rulers' pervasive brutality and violence against citizens. The reliance on death squads and illegal imprisonments soon swelled the rolls of "the disappeared," which Timerman bravely published in his newspaper.

Early on the morning of April 15, 1977, Timerman was arrested by twenty armed men in civilian clothes. Without being charged, he was thrown into prison; for thirty months, he

Jacobo Timerman, 1982

underwent physical and psychological torture. His ordeal became the subject of international attention and ended not in death, as it did for thousands of others subjected to similar mistreatment, but in release and deportation. In the aftermath, he wrote this powerful account of his experience. From its description of the vistas of freedom seen through a peephole in his dark cell to its compelling account of the uncertain final hours of his captivity, this book's evocation of the plight of a prisoner—stripped not only of his human rights, but nearly of his very humanity—is unforgettable.

What: Memoir. History. *When:* 1981. *Edition:* Translated from the Spanish by Toby Talbot. *Also By: The Longest War: Israel in Lebanon* (1982). *Chile: Death in the South* (1987). *Cuba: A Journey* (1990). *Further Reading: A Lexicon of Terror: Argentina and the Legacies of Torture* by Marguerite Feitlowitz. *Try: Journey into the Whirlwind* by Eugenia Ginzburg. *The Man Died: Prison Notes* of Wole Soyinka. *Adaptation:* The 1983 TV movie stars Roy Scheider and Liv Ullmann.

Célestine
Gillian Tindall (born 1938)

**A Vivid Restoration of the
Life of a French Village**

What is the future of the past? Not the large past of wars and exploration, catastrophe and economy, but the small past, the intimate history of place and local tradition, of families and trades, of rituals and endeavors passed down by hand and by heart? If lucky, it falls under the gaze of a writer like Gillian Tindall, to be resurrected in the pages of a book like *Célestine*.

Tindall's engrossing, lovely book tells the story of a village—Chassignoles, in Berry, a traditional province in the heart of France—with remarkable intuition, sympathy, and eloquence. Herself a householder in Chassignoles, Tindall there came upon a cache of letters dating from the 1860s addressed to Célestine Chaumette (1844–1933), the village innkeeper's daughter.

The letters—saved by Célestine throughout her long life—were by different hands, and pressed the marriage proposals of a number of ardent but ultimately unsuccessful suitors. Intrigued by the letters and their recipient, Tindall employed her wiles as both historian and novelist to flesh out the history they intimated. The resulting volume not only remembers the life of Célestine, but movingly reveals the unrecorded destiny of Chassignoles as well, evoking the fate of thousands of places like it—places that house, within the silence of their modern aspects, the spirits of a vanished past.

What: History. Place. *When:* 1995.
Also By: The Fields Beneath (1977). *The Journey of Martin Nadaud* (1999). *Footprints in Paris* (2009). *Try: Akenfield* by Ronald Blythe (see page 84). *The Discovery of France* by Graham Robb.

Her Smoke Rose Up Forever
James Tiptree Jr. (1915–1987)

**The Remarkable Stories of
Alice Bradley Sheldon**

Most authors of fiction lead comparatively sedate, even humdrum lives. Seated alone at their desks for hours each day, or lecturing in snoozy classrooms, they seldom get a chance to venture out into the wide world of endeavor and adventure. Not so for Alice Bradley Sheldon, who wrote science fiction as James Tiptree Jr. Raised by globetrotting parents, she can be seen in vintage photographs as a toddler consorting with African wildlife. As an adult, she worked for the CIA (an occupation she shared with another science fiction master, Cordwainer Smith) and then got a doctorate in experimental psychology. Not content with

those achievements, she adopted a male pseudonym and loosed upon an unsuspecting genre a batch of truly revolutionary, brilliant stories, conducting a huge literary charade until she was ultimately exposed (after which she soldiered on, but with reduced enthusiasm). Finally, she wrought what was almost certainly a murder-suicide upon her ailing husband and herself, capping a life hard to duplicate for drama, accomplishment, and surprise.

Although she produced two novels, Tiptree's brilliance resides in the sharp shock of her short fiction, works that might be well described as clawed, fanged, and spitting. Deploying a sophisticated style in the service of deep characterizations, she was not afraid to embrace topics formerly taboo, adding a feminist slant deemed exceptional in a "male" writer, one whose tough-minded and sometimes brutal realism only strengthened the power of her disguise. As her career grew, she assembled a coterie of pen pals—Tiptree "himself" never went out in public—and a shelf of well-deserved awards.

Concerned with the essence and future of humanity, Tiptree dared to imagine us as much less worthy than our noblest self-conceptions assume. In "The Last Flight of Doctor Ain," the title character deliberately spreads a plague to wipe Gaia clean of the troublesome *Homo sapiens*. "I Awoke and Found Me Here on the Cold Hill's Side" postulates that upon meeting aliens, humans will succumb to fetishistic lusts and become the stage-door johnnies of the galaxy. And in "A Momentary Taste of Being," our species is proved to be nothing more than celestial "gametes," sperm-like carriers of only half an inheritance that fuses uncontrollably with the cosmic egg awaiting us in the stars.

With her flair for impersonation, Tiptree was adept at inhabiting hypothetical alien consciousness, as when she imagines the bizarre mating practices of behemoths in "Love Is the Plan, the Plan Is Death." She also exhibits keen techno-savvy, as we see in the story "The Girl Who Was Plugged In": With its jazzy cadences akin to the work of Alfred Bester (see page 73), this story came to influence a hundred cyberpunk descendants. Another Tiptree leitmotif was frustrated, yearning ghosts of various stripes, which eerily echoed her interest in the cultural politics of gender. In the classic, cleverly constructed tale "The Women Men Don't See," the earthbound, extraterrestrial-beseeching heroine longs to escape her male-dominated society, where to survive she and other women must "live by ones and twos in the chinks of your world-machine."

Although she published several story collections in her lifetime, the posthumous volume *Her Smoke Rose Up Forever* gathers much of her best work and is a stellar survey of her talent; its eighteen stories convey the hardheaded, despairing, compassionate, and even playful mind behind the mask.

What: Short Stories. Science Fiction. *When:* 1990. *Also By: Up the Walls of the World* (1978). *Brightness Falls from the Air* (1985). *The Starry Rift* (1986). *Further Reading: James Tiptree Jr.: The Double Life of Alice B. Sheldon* by Julie Phillips. *Try: Extra (Ordinary) People* by Joanna Russ. *The Collected Stories of Carol Emshwiller* by Carol Emshwiller. *The Story Until Now: A Great Big Book of Stories* by Kit Reed.

Democracy in America
Alexis de Tocqueville (1805–1859)

The Best Book Ever Written on America? *Oui!*

One of the most influential texts in the literature of political science, *Democracy in America*, as a team of recent translators put it, is "at once the best book ever written on democracy and the best book ever written on America." More important for the general reader, Alexis de Tocqueville conveys his insights with a forthright and companionable charm, rendering his masterpiece far more pleasurable than most volumes of such weighty reputation.

The book originated in a nine-month journey that Tocqueville made through the eastern United States in 1831. Accompanied by a fellow Frenchman, the young aristocrat (he was just turning twenty-six) was ostensibly investigating the country's prison system. The real point of the journey, however, was "to see what a great republic is." As he says, "I confess that in America I saw more than America; I sought the image of democracy itself, with its inclinations, its character, its prejudices, and its passions, in order to learn what we have to fear or hope from its progress." Tocqueville focused on the meaning and actual functioning of democracy, studying its effect on the social, political, and economic life of Americans. His intuitions as a thinker and his astute observations are apparent throughout his consideration of myriad topics, among them the philosophical under-pinnings of the democratic impulse, religion, the arts, language, the press, individualism, manners, the family, the military, and law and the judiciary. The result was—and remains—a more complete and insightful portrait of the United States than any observer has ever painted.

As critic Roger Kimball notes in a perceptive essay called "Tocqueville Today," first-time readers of *Democracy in America* "are almost always amazed by Tocqueville's contemporaneity, his relevance to America *now*." His eloquence is as incisive and enduring as his intellect; even his chapter titles seem stunningly prescient: "Why the Americans Show Themselves So Restive in the Midst of Their Well-Being"; "How Democratic Institutions and Mores Tend to Raise the Price and Shorten the Duration of Leases"; "Why One Finds So Many Ambitious Men in the United States and So Few Great Ambitions." In addition to Tocqueville's seemingly endless quotability, there's a more profound reason for *Democracy in America*'s continuing relevance. As Kimball notes, "What Tocqueville wrote was not a manifesto but an essential reflection on political life—which is to say our life in so far as we exist as social creatures. The questions he asks remain our questions." And his answers are still worthy of our attention.

What: History. Culture. *When:* First volume, 1835; the second, 1840. *Edition:* There are several excellent translations, including the one by Delba Winthrop and Harvey C. Mansfield for the University of Chicago Press quoted here. *Also By: The Old Regime and the Revolution* (1856). *Further Reading:* Kimball's book *Lives of the Mind* includes "Tocqueville Today." Hugh Brogan's *Alexis de Tocqueville: A Life* is an excellent 2007 biography. *Try: Domestic Manners of the Americans* by Frances Trollope. *Footnote:* At the turn of the twenty-first century, French philosopher Bernard-Henri Lévy followed his countryman's lead in *American Vertigo: Traveling America in the Footsteps of Tocqueville.*

J. R. R. TOLKIEN
(1892–1973)

I n the late 1920s, J. R. R. Tolkien, a professor of Anglo-Saxon at Oxford University, scribbled a sentence while correcting some student papers: "In a hole in the ground there lived a hobbit." Those ten words are the seed from which grew a complex and elaborate mythology that would captivate the imaginations of millions of readers throughout the world before spawning, some three decades after Tolkien's death, a movie and entertainment franchise of fantastic dimensions, in every sense that adjective conveys.

The first novel to flow from that inspiration, *The Hobbit*, is a much simpler tale than the one played out in the three novels of *The Lord of the Rings*, the sequels into which Tolkien put decades of loving labor—and more than a little philological magic. The initial spark of creation for the trilogy, in fact, was linguistic playfulness, as the author himself explained: "[My fiction] is not a 'hobby', in the sense of something quite different from one's work, taken up as a relief-outlet. The invention of languages is the foundation. The 'stories' were made rather to provide a world for the languages than the reverse." Thankfully, the invented grammars and vocabularies inspired the creation of a rousing epic packed with unforgettable characters, glamour-tinged amulets, suspenseful set pieces, and compelling moral quandaries.

The Hobbit
OR, THERE AND BACK AGAIN
The Enduring Enchantments of Middle-earth

Sir Ian McKellen as Gandalf in the film of The Hobbit

The hobbit Tolkien discovered at the end of his now famous scribbled sentence (it's the first line of this book) is named Bilbo Baggins. Like all hobbits, as is quickly explained, Bilbo is a stout little humanlike creature with pointy ears, furry feet, a taste for beer, and a preference for the quiet life. One day Bilbo's peaceful, lazy existence is interrupted by the arrival at his comfortable hobbit-hole of a wizard named Gandalf, who manages to lure the unassuming hobbit into an escapade being planned by thirteen dwarves. Their perilous quest: to regain possession of the Lonely Mountain and its fabulous treasure, which Smaug the dragon has seized from their ancestors. Bilbo reluctantly joins the daring band, and in the end, after harrowing encounters with an extraordinary assortment of invented creatures, including goblins, elves, wargs, trolls, sages, giant spiders, and the subterranean, riddling Gollum, he returns home with a modest fortune—and a piece of jewelry with dangerous powers: the One Ring. Like the readers who accompany him on his thrilling odyssey through the magical precincts of Tolkien's imagination, Bilbo will never be quite the same.

Introducing many important aspects of the lore of Middle-earth, the mythic world in which all of Tolkien's most celebrated stories unfold, *The Hobbit* serves as prologue to the epic exploits and intense battles of *The Lord of the Rings*. Yet its cozier dimensions and smaller-scaled excitements give *The Hobbit* a coherence and pleasure all its own; Bilbo's original saga

requires no further elaboration to be treasured for a lifetime.

What: Fantasy. *When:* 1937. *Editions:* The second (1951) and third (1966) editions contain revisions made by Tolkien to retrofit elements of *The Hobbit* to story developments detailed in its sequels. *Further Reading: J. R. R. Tolkien: A Biography* by Humphrey Carpenter. *The History of "The Hobbit"* by John D. Rateliff. *Try: The Princess and the Goblin* by George MacDonald. *A Wizard of Earthsea* by Ursula K. Le Guin (see page 468). *The Golden Compass* by Philip Pullman (see page 647). *Adaptations:* Peter Jackson directed *The Hobbit* as a film trilogy (2012–14), starring Martin Freeman as Bilbo Baggins and Ian McKellen as Gandalf.

The Lord of the Rings
A World of Narrative Wizardry

Appearing in three separate volumes between July 1954 and October 1955, *The Lord of the Rings* constitutes a single linear narrative that was segmented for publishing convenience rather than by authorial intent. Tolkien's hero, Frodo, is the adoptive heir of Bilbo Baggins, protagonist of *The Hobbit*. (Frodo would later be celebrated by late-1960s counterculture, to high-spirited if indeterminate purpose, in the graffiti-spread slogan "Frodo

Lives!") Bilbo bequeaths Frodo a ring, which, unbeknownst to both at first, actually belongs to the Dark Lord Sauron, who will do anything in his considerable power to repossess it. Exploits tied to the ring lead Frodo and his comrades across vast and dangerous landscapes of invented mythology, history, and culture, filled with supernatural elements of uncanny allure. A battle between good and evil has seldom been so extravagantly imagined.

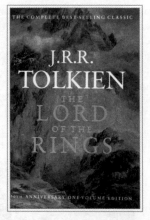

The narrative traverses many milieus and social strata, from the simplicity of the Hobbit Shire to the ethereal elegance of the Elvish pavilions at Rivendell, from the martial court of Gondor to the evil precincts of Sauron's Mordor (infused with the author's philological wizardry, the names of places and characters offer delights of their own). Contrasting camaraderie with selfishness, megalomania with humility, and tradition with destruction, the story maintains a dialectical tension throughout a series of rousing adventures, keeping the longed-for triumph of good hanging by a thread over a literal abyss of fire. Books in Tolkien's mold have emerged from the usual mix of commercial and aesthetic motives, but the breadth and depth of his trilogy's conception remains unmatched: *The Lord of the Rings* exists like a mountain transported from another dimension, cloaked in preexisting fauna and flora, with exotic and familiar forms of feeling animating its every crevice, cave, and peak.

What: Fantasy. *When: The Fellowship of the Ring* (1954); *The Two Towers* (1954); *The Return of the King* (1955). *Also By: Silmarillion* (1977; posthumous publication supervised by Tolkien's son Christopher). *The Letters of J. R. R. Tolkien*, edited by Humphrey Carpenter and Christopher Tolkien. *Further Reading: Tolkien's World from A to Z: The Complete Guide to Middle-earth* by Robert Foster. *Try: The Once and Future King* by T. H. White (see page 846). *Watership Down* by Richard Adams (see page 7). *The Eye of the World* by Robert Jordan. *Adaptations:* The three films directed by Peter Jackson—released in 2001, 2002, and 2003, respectively—have been popularly and critically acclaimed, with the last installment winning eleven Academy Awards, including Best Picture.

MORE TO EXPLORE

HEROIC FANTASY

One might argue that the idea of heroic fantasy can be traced back to tales of King Arthur and even beyond, yet in the past century the genre has taken on new luster, as writers of fantasy have explored brave worlds old and new, creating fully drawn secondary universes to serve as arenas in which good and evil are contested by warriors, wizards, halflings, goblins, dragons, and other exotic beings. The massive popularity enjoyed by J. R. R. Tolkien's *Lord of the Rings* and, more recently, George R. R.

Martin's *Game of Thrones* has proved that the appeal of the genre crosses compellingly from page to screen.

Inhabited by a panoply of humans and creatures derived from the default set of European and Norse legends, the modern literature of epic fantasy, born more or less with the novels of William Morris in Victorian times (for example, *The Story of the Glittering Plain*), exhibits much more variety than is commonly perceived and more nuanced psychological and even political insight than cinema's special effects, no matter how sensational, can convey. The genre's broad spectrum of style and substance is difficult to capture in a selection of titles, because its range of expression reaches from the primitive grunts of Robert E. Howard's character Conan the Barbarian to the "mannerpunk" politesse of Ellen Kushner's heroes (*Swordspoint*; *The Privilege of the Sword*). Still, the books and series listed here stand as talismans of heroic fantasy's special magic.

The Worm Ouroboros
E. R. Eddison (1882–1945)

C. S. Lewis (see page 484) called E. R. Eddison's heroic romances "irreplaceable" works of art. "Nowhere else," the author of *The Chronicles of Narnia* wrote, "shall we meet this precise blend of hardness and luxury, of lawless speculation and sharply realized detail, of the cynical and the magnanimous. No author can be said to remind us of Eddison." His extravagance of language and invention mark *The Worm Ouroboros* (1922), a precursor of *The Lord of the Rings*, as a landmark in high fantasy. Writing in an archaic style, Eddison canvases a lushly imagined natural world on the planet Mercury with singular grandeur: "Under the wings of night uplifted from the east, the unfathomable heights of air turned a richer blue; and here and there, most dim and hard to see, throbbed a tiny point of light: the greater stars opening their eyelids to the gathering dark."

Set in an environment surprisingly hospitable to life despite great kingdoms being at war, *Ouroboros* is a glorious cross between Norse sagas, *A Midsummer Night's Dream*, and interplanetary sagas still to be invented; it revolves, as Lewis rightly asserted, in a rarefied orbit of its own.

The Dying Earth
Jack Vance (1916–2013)

In this collection of connected tales, Jack Vance presents a vision of our familiar planet some millions of years hence, when the sun is guttering and red, the soil is littered with the ruins of ten thousand forgotten dynasties, and magic is indistinguishable from technology. His inspiration in *The Dying Earth* (1950) crystallized an imaginative framework that would afford himself and other writers a beautiful, melancholy playground for speculative expeditions. Through this etiolated yet surprisingly enthralling milieu, resourceful antiheroes strive to attain some measure of end-time comfort, while young-hearted adventurers, like Vance's Guyal of Sfere, persist in believing that even in the face of general extinction their lives can hold meaning and joy. Noted for his ornate yet inviting prose style, Vance opens up a window, in this and subsequent volumes, to a future we might hope will never come, framing a portrait of a senescent planet still animated by the hopes, schemes, and dreams of its inhabitants.

Two Sought Adventure
Fritz Leiber (1910–1992)

Modeling his two protagonists, Fafhrd and the Gray Mouser, on himself and his pal Harry Otto Fischer, Fritz Leiber brought the "buddy story" to heroic fantasy. He even coined the phrase "sword and sorcery" to name the subgenre he helped create—which would eventually evolve beyond the page into Dungeons and Dragons and other role-playing games.

The title story in this 1957 volume appeared in 1939, and Leiber would add to the Fafhrd and Gray Mouser canon for the next fifty years. His distinct yet utterly devoted mercenary heroes—one tall, muscular, blunt; the other short, wiry, and canny—were loyal to each other through thick and thin, whether encountering gods or demons, gorgeous temptresses or grasping wizards. Nehwon and its prize city of Lankhmar, the setting Leiber invented as the scene of the pair's exploits, have, like the stories themselves, both enchanted readers and influenced some of the most inspired science fiction and fantasy writers of later generations, such as Terry Pratchett and Joanna Russ.

The Book of Three
Lloyd Alexander (1924–2007)

The Book of Three (1964), the initial installment of The Chronicles of Prydain, a fabled five-volume series, was only Lloyd Alexander's second novel, yet it permanently established him as a writer for adolescents whose work could be enjoyed with uninhibited and even critical pleasure by adult readers as well. As such, it portended the success of J. K. Rowling's Harry Potter saga, to mention just one of the literary progeny that followed in Prydain's wake. With a most irregular juvenile hero, Taran the Assistant Pig-Keeper, and Princess Eilonwy, a vivacious and capable heroine to match him exploit for exploit, all the books in the series are replete with stirring escapades involving formidable supernatural foes. Deriving their uncommon template from Welsh legends, *The Book of Three* and its sequels offer not only thrills, but humor and romance in delightful measure, providing a sense of human scale amid the fantastical doings that makes the characters' extraordinary experiences relevant to the perilous real-life heroics of growing up.

Stormbringer
Michael Moorcock
(born 1939)

Michael Moorcock might well be the grand old *enfant terrible* of speculative fiction. From his teens through his maturity, his prodigious imagination has shaped an extraordinary oeuvre, as rich in revision as in original creation (it would take a dedicated librarian to sort through the intricacies of his bibliography). Although Moorcock has also turned with success to literary fiction (*Mother London*), it is in the realm of fantasy that he has left the largest footprint, especially with his Elric of Melniboné books.

Elric—plaything of the God of Chaos, cursed albino prince of a dying line, a hero troublingly addicted to the slaughtered souls fed to him through his sentient sword Stormbringer—is at the center of a saga, spread across many stories, novellas, and books,

conceived in deliberate reaction to the more culturally conservative fantasy of Tolkien and C. S. Lewis (in fact, Moorcock once penned an incendiary essay called "Epic Pooh," which decries the English coziness of such works, comparing them to A. A. Milne's tales of Christopher Robin and his bear). The author's rebellious attitude gives his work anarchic movement, in which the familiar elements of epic fantasy are turned upside down; friends are betrayed and enemies accommodated, and fuzzy ideas of nobility and courage are sharpened by satire and a sense of realpolitik. Nonetheless, *Stormbringer* (1965)—the best novel with which to begin—and Elric's other adventures tap an unanticipated level of pathos through Moorcock's skill at evoking his hero's Hamlet-like emotions as his duties confront, and constrain, his desires. Tying into Moorcock's massive Multiverse, where all the heroes are merely avatars of one Eternal Champion, the Elric stories are rakish romps across crepuscular terrain, in which terrors Frodo might never imagine seem present, palpable, and wholly unpredictable.

A Game of Thrones
George R. R. Martin
(born 1948)

In a 2005 review in *Time* magazine, critic Lev Grossman dubbed George R. R. Martin "the American Tolkien." The occasion was the publication of *A Feast for Crows*, the fourth volume in Martin's epic, *A Song of Ice and Fire*, which had been inaugurated in 1996 with the publication of *A Game of Thrones*. Since Grossman's encomium, Martin has published a fifth volume in the series, *A Dance of Dragons*, and his imaginative enterprise has achieved enormous popularity via the multiseason HBO television *Game of Thrones* franchise, which overtook Martin's progress toward

the work's literary conclusion.

Martin's hold on the popular mind derives from his ability to fill the bold outlines of epic fantasy with the gritty colors of historical fiction and from his narrative ruthlessness, which acknowledges that violence and sex are surer motivations than nobility and that circumstantial ambiguity determines more than a fixed moral compass. The plot revolves around a dynastic war among several families, but every step of the way the intricate story lines are personal and visceral. What's most compelling is that the reader's understanding of unfolding events is continually transformed by shifting narrative perspectives: *A Game of Thrones* details its action from nine different points of view, and *A Dance with Dragons* multiplies that by a factor of three. Many characters are given not only history, but agency as well, in a way fiction seldom realizes: The reader's judgment is suspended, then upended, again and again, as heroes shape-shift into villains or get caught in some uncertain liminal state. The network of connections the reader accrues must be constantly revised. It's no wonder that the time between books grew for the author as the story ramified; the world he created has taken on a life of its own.

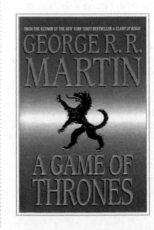

LEO TOLSTOY
(1828–1910)

"I f the world could write by itself, it would write like Tolstoy," said Isaac Babel. Certainly, Leo Tolstoy's twin masterpieces, *War and Peace* and *Anna Karenina*, seem as large as life and just as compelling: We immerse ourselves in them with an absorption that makes leaving their worlds—hundreds and hundreds of pages later—seem like a farewell to some signal era of our own experience. Tolstoy's literary legacy was to give a new and, in some ways, still unrivaled substance to the realism a book could hold.

The author's life had a dramatic arc commensurate with the imaginative genius animating his best work. Born in 1828 on his family's estate at Yasnaya Polyana, south of Moscow, he was carried along by his family's aristocratic pedigree through indifferent studies and a dissolute period of metropolitan indiscretion until signing up for military service. Soon after becoming a soldier, he became a writer as well; his autobiographical fictions, *Childhood* (1952), *Boyhood* (1854), and *Youth* (1857), reveal how he became aware of the walls his privilege had erected between himself and the general populace. This alertness to social and economic strata, and an attendant impulse to identify common human values deeper than class, became core elements of his mature fiction as well as of his later philosophical explorations. Although it eventually evolved into a complex and tumultuous battle of wills, his marriage to Sophia Andreyevna Behrs produced thirteen children and nourished the ambition that produced *War and Peace* and *Anna Karenina*. In his final years, he renounced his possessions and achievements in pursuit of a fierce ethical purity anchored in radical Christianity, political anarchism, and nonviolence (his writings of this period had profound influence on Mohandas Gandhi and Martin Luther King Jr.).

Tolstoy as a young officer, 1854 (left) and older man, ca. 1885 (above)

In all his work, but in his fiction especially, earnestness and worldliness, ferocity and tenderness combine to create a realism that is emotional as much as reportorial. The vast and complicated actualities he portrays are always shot through with feelings on a human scale. His true subject is how a spiritual being struggles—through love and action, history and family—to make a home in the material world.

War and Peace
An Epic of History and the Human Heart

A monument of world literature and a reader's rite of passage, *War and Peace* is among the longest works of fiction ever written. Its thirteen hundred pages blend private emotions and public events, love affairs and military campaigns, personality and history into a narrative that—as Tolstoy himself struggled to explain—is strictly speaking neither novel, nor epic, nor historical chronicle, nor philosophical inquiry; rather, it inherits characteristics of all four to embody an expressive life entirely its own.

This may sound more daunting than it proves to be once you surrender to the sweep of Tolstoy's panoramic vision. Filled with action, romance, and insight into the changing fortunes of families and nations, it is eminently, even obsessively, readable. The book opens at a grand ball in Saint Petersburg, where all the talk is of Napoleon and his triumphant progress across Europe: Everyone knows that the French army is headed for the Russian border. As Bonaparte's forces approach, Tolstoy follows five aristocratic families living in Saint Petersburg and in Moscow, some of them teetering on the edge of financial ruin. Although the massive narrative has no true central character, three stand out as nearly a decade of war and hardship ensues. One is Pierre Bezukhov, the illegitimate son of a count, who matures from a hard-drinking spendthrift to a sympathetic gentleman desperate to find meaning in his life. The second is Prince Andrei Bolkonsky, a brilliant but cynical prince who joins the campaign against Napoleon (whom both Andrei and Pierre actually idolize), only to suffer grave wounds in battle. And the third, Natasha Rostova, the daughter of a nobleman, discovers in herself a resilience as strong as the innate romanticism that attracts both Pierre and the prince.

A large part of the grandeur of *War and Peace* derives from two innovations. Not only does Tolstoy mix fictional characters with real-life figures drawn from scrupulous historical research, but he also shifts back and forth between bird's-eye-view narration of enormous events—military battles, lavish parties—and interior monologues of penetrating psychological awareness. In Tolstoy's hands, history is revealed not as a story of heroic generals and their strategic decisions, but as an almost inconceivably vast array of tiny, unpredictable events. Even Napoleon comes across as a minor figure in the overwhelming landscape of Tolstoy's imagination.

War and Peace is such a huge and extraordinary achievement that it is surprising to realize that it is the work of a young author. When it was first serialized in a Russian magazine (under the working title "The Year 1805"), Tolstoy was only in his late thirties. He completed the work at age forty-one; *Anna Karenina*, his brilliant shorter fiction, and his influential essays on nonviolence and Christianity still lay before him. Yet for all his later accomplishments, nothing he would write—not even the majestic *Anna Karenina*—compares to *War and Peace*. What's true of its form is true of the reading experience it creates: You live this book as much as you read it, and to recapture the engrossing sensation, you can only read it again.

What: Novel. *When:* 1863–69. *Editions:* The most recent English translation of note is by Richard Pevear and Larissa Volokhonsky (2007). Ann Dunnigan's 1968 translation is also recommended. *Also By:* *Sebastopol Sketches* (1855). *The Cossacks* (1863). *Further Reading: Tolstoy* by Henri Troyat. *Tolstoy and the Genesis of "War and Peace"* by Kathryn B. Feuer. *Try: The Charterhouse of Parma* by Stendhal. *Life and Fate* by Vasily Grossman (see page 337). *Doctor Zhivago* by Boris Pasternak (see page 618). *History: A Novel* by Elsa Morante (see page 565). *Adaptations:* The 1956 American film, directed by King Vidor, stars Audrey Hepburn, Henry Fonda, and Mel Ferrer. The four-part Soviet version, directed by Sergei Bondarchuk (1966–67), more successfully captures the scope of Tolstoy's vision. Sergei Prokofiev's epic opera premiered in 1955.

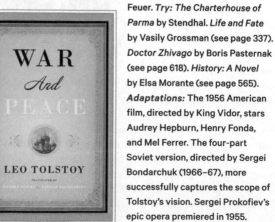
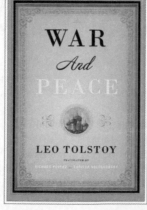

WAR
And
PEACE

LEO TOLSTOY

Anna Karenina
A Novel Without Peer

....

"All happy families are alike; each unhappy family is unhappy in its own way."

So reads the famous first line of Leo Tolstoy's masterpiece of love and society. Its juxtaposition of universal verity with particular insight sets the tone for the eight hundred pages that follow. Unlike *War and Peace*, which crisscrosses Europe and swallows armies, populations, and history itself, *Anna Karenina* is intimate—a tale of families and lovers, their obligations to one another, the costs of both betraying and upholding unspoken codes of behavior. The novel is a gloriously detailed and absorbing portrait of the lives of the nineteenth-century Russian aristocracy, but that's not why it's so popular: Its power over readers endures because Tolstoy's sympathy for men and women and his stunning psychological acuity are without rival. He crafts an entire world out of nothing, peopled with fictional counts and princesses who seem so real, we feel we know them, and in a way we do; like all the greatest fiction— even though this novel is in a class by itself—*Anna Karenina* reveals truths that are as real, as contradictory, as fully present as life itself. If only while we're reading it, and in the profound consolation of its afterglow, it gives us a sixth sense that intuits human nature as fully, and as mysteriously, as smell can evoke forgotten milieus.

Anna Arkadyevna Karenina, a Saint Petersburg princess married to an older, ambitious politician, has no shortage of virtues: She's charming and beautiful, a voracious reader, an art lover, a fierce protector of her family. But by chance, at a train station, she meets the man who will upend her life: the young and dashing Count Alexei Kirillovich Vronsky. Their long affair, for which she abandons her husband and her beloved son, defies both social and religious proprieties; following a dozen or more characters in Moscow and Saint Petersburg, Tolstoy registers how Anna's transgression ripples through society. We meet Stepan, Anna's brother and the father of the unhappy family that prompts the novel's first line; Karenin, Anna's cuckolded husband, a pious man who tries to maintain some semblance of respectability; and the three Shcherbatsky sisters, particularly Kitty, the youngest, whose innocence in the ways of love nearly undoes her. (At one point Tolstoy even enters the mind of a dog for two whole chapters.)

All of these breathtakingly complex creations, especially Anna, are indelible. But the hero of *Anna Karenina* is not the tragic title character. It's Konstantin Dmitrievich Levin, the sincere, slightly awkward country landowner whose love for Kitty seems hopeless at first. Anna and Levin meet only once, very late in the novel, but their lives are bound together by the social set they both occupy (one character, Dolly, is both Levin's and Anna's sister-in-law) and by their defiance of convention. They're opposites but they're also twins, and although Levin's final fate could not be more different from Anna's, there's an invisible thread throughout the novel that binds the two.

Living largely outside the glitter and whirl of Anna's Saint Petersburg, Levin isn't a recluse—he's engaged with his time, often arguing at length about the controversial political issues of 1870s Russia—but he doesn't meet society's expectations. His life comes to fruition only when he finds his own way to live it, recognizing—as dramatized in his perplexed and humbled feelings on the birth of his first child—that our experience is made sacred by the griefs and joys that "were equally outside all ordinary circumstances of life, were like holes in this ordinary life, through which something higher showed." You'll find no better encapsulation of Tolstoy's own faith and wisdom.

Anna Karenina was written after *War and Peace*, but curiously the author called it his first novel. He thought of its sweeping predecessor as a historical drama, whereas *Anna Karenina* was something else: a tighter, more probing, and, oddly enough, perhaps even more universal story of happy and unhappy fates. Legend has it that when he was asked to name the three greatest novels of all time, William Faulkner, whose fiction could not be less like Tolstoy's, answered, "*Anna Karenina. Anna Karenina. Anna Karenina.*" You'll see why.

What: Novel. *When:* 1875–77. *Edition:* Translation by Richard Pevear and Larissa Volokhonsky (2000). *Also By: Family Happiness* (1859). *Master and Man* (1895). *Further Reading: Tolstoy: A Biography* by A. N. Wilson. *Tolstoy: A Russian Life* by Rosamund Bartlett. *Try: Madame Bovary* by Gustave Flaubert (see page 282). *The Age of Innocence* by Edith Wharton (see page 844). *Adaptations:* Among the multiple adaptations for the screen, Greta Garbo stars in the 1935 film; Vivien Leigh leads the cast of the 1948 British version; and Keira Knightley is Anna in the 2012 adaptation written by Tom Stoppard.

The Death of Ivan Ilych

In the Mirror of Mortality

As circumscribed in its focus as *War and Peace* and *Anna Karenina* are sweeping, Tolstoy's late novella *The Death of Ivan Ilych* concentrates on a single man who is neither especially interesting nor all that likable. Ivan Ilych Golovin, the person in question, is a petty bureaucrat of small mind and pedestrian tastes who is never quite satisfied with the privileges of his position as a judge and the affections bestowed on him as husband and father. His appraisal of his own distinction is at odds with the world's sense of his unrelenting normality.

The story begins with the announcement at the law courts of Ivan Ilych's death; his former colleagues greet the news with rote expressions of grief, keen attention to what the news might mean for their own advancement, and no little annoyance at the disruption to their routines caused by the demands of condolence and funeral services. Tolstoy then gives a compressed description (the entire novella is roughly eighty pages long) of the deceased's personal life and professional

career, a familiar narration of youthful enthusiasms diffused by the demands of workplace and family until they've faded into a colorless and unfulfilling middle age in which a "new apartment is always one room too small, and a new income always 50 rubles short." The onset of his illness at first seems like an outgrowth of Ivan Ilych's dissatisfactions, but as he broods upon the progression of his disease, deeper thoughts begin to trouble him. He remembers a syllogism he had studied in logic, and the memory reveals—for the reader as well as for Ivan Ilych—the way mortality strips from every life the illusion of personal destiny that has sustained it:

"Caius is a man, men are mortal, therefore Caius is mortal," had always seemed to him correct as applied to Caius, but certainly not as applied to himself. That Caius—man in the abstract—was mortal, was perfectly correct, but he was not Caius, not an abstract man, but a creature quite, quite separate from all others. He had been little Vanya, with a mamma and a papa, with Mitya and Volodya, with the toys, a coachman and a nurse, afterwards with Katenka and with all the joys, griefs, and delights of childhood, boyhood, and youth. What did Caius know of the smell of that striped leather ball Vanya had been so fond of? Had Caius kissed his mother's hand like that, and did the silk of her dress rustle so for Caius? Had he rioted like that at school when the pastry was bad? Had Caius been in love like that? Could Caius preside at a session as he did? "Caius really was mortal, and it was right for him to die; but for me, little Vanya, Ivan Ilych, with all my thoughts and emotions, it's altogether a different matter. It cannot be that I ought to die. That would be too terrible."

Such was his feeling.

Thus the last act of the life of Ivan Ilych is introduced. In the agony of his final hours, consoled only by the tender attention of his servant, Gerasim, he falls toward death with a transcendent inevitability that is first painful and then breathtakingly serene. Thinking neither about the laws of history nor the romantic passions that can turn private lives upside down, but rather brooding upon the determined loneliness and utter commonness of a single fearful man, Tolstoy paradoxically hones in on the most universal questions: Why must we suffer the horror of mortality? What's the right way to live in the face of our ultimate extinction? What's it all *for*? His severe yet sacramental attention to these mysteries makes the eighty-odd pages of *The Death of Ivan Ilych* as riveting

and unforgettable as the hundreds upon hundreds of pages that compose his larger-than-life masterpieces.

What: Novella. *When:* 1886. *Also By: The Kreutzer Sonata* (1890). *A Confession* (1884). *Resurrection* (1899). *Hadji Murad* (1912). *Try: The Book of Job,* translated by Stephen Mitchell (see page 78). *Tell Me a Riddle* by Tillie Olsen (see page 603). *Adaptation:* Akira Kurosawa's 1952 film *Ikiru* is drawn from Tolstoy's tale.

The Sea and the Jungle
H. M. Tomlinson (1873–1958)

A Commuter Escapes to the Amazon, circa 1910

The best book by the best travel writer you've never read, *The Sea and the Jungle* is a narrative, in the author's words, "of the voyage of the tramp steamer *Capella* from Swansea to Pará in the Brazils, and thence 2,000 miles along the forests of the Amazon and Madeira Rivers."

Tomlinson's masterpiece of armchair travel begins on a dreary winter morning in 1909: "You know those November mornings with a low, corpse-white east where the sunrise should be, as though the day were still-born." The absence of sunlight is metaphorical as well as real, for Tomlinson, at the time a reporter on the London *Morning Leader*, is despondent about the constraints of his daily prospects: "on my way to catch the 8.35 that morning—it is always the 8.35—there came to me no premonition of change." Indeed, the opening pages, suffused with a commuter's restlessness within his perfectly predictable routine, are bound to resonate with suburban fellow travelers even a century on: "Where that morning train starts from is a mystery; but it never fails to come for us, and it never takes us beyond the city, I well know."

But then, to Tomlinson's surprise and the reader's ultimate reward, unexpected opportunity knocks, and almost before he knows it, he is on a train to Swansea in Wales, ready to board a freighter bound for the upper reaches of the Amazon. No longer resigned to "dutifully and busily climbing the revolving wheel like the squirrel," he is off the treadmill for the next two years: "I saw an open door. I got out. It was as though the world had been suddenly lighted, and I could see a great distance." The rest of the book tells the exhilarating story of his adventure on sea and land: It is both exciting and hilarious, and brilliantly written. Tomlinson's voice, so engaging in the opening chapter, only gains dimension and perspective when confronted with the liberating exertions of a voyage and the natural wonders of the equatorial jungle. Describing flora, fauna, landscape, and native companions with unerring alertness and élan, he composes a narrative that is itself refreshing and spirit-lifting. Don't miss it.

What: Travel. Adventure. *When:* 1912. *Also By: London River* (1920). *Tide Marks* (1924). *Out of Soundings* (1931). *Try: The Mirror of the Sea* by Joseph Conrad. *The Valleys of the Assassins* by Freya Stark (see page 746). *The Traveller's Tree* by Patrick Leigh Fermor.

Small Talk at Wreyland
Cecil Torr (1857–1928)

Local History of Lasting Appeal

Reading, like life, can be filled with parochial as well as cosmopolitan pleasures, and a good part of the joy to be found in books is the way they make other people's neighborhoods our own. Cecil Torr's *Wreyland* is a perfect example. "Wreyland," wrote Britain's Lord Birkett some eight decades after the book's first appearance, "is a small estate at Lustleigh in Devon. But the small talk of the village, as reported by one Cecil Torr in the 1920s, manages to encompass half the known world, and more subjects than were ever chattered about over the brightly-lit dinner tables of the metropolis."

The Cambridge-educated Torr was a classical scholar who wrote two volumes on the history of Rhodes, as well as one on *Ancient Ships*, which is still consulted. He was an avid, observant traveler who made an annual trip abroad for forty-six consecutive years, commencing when he was ten and ending as the First World War loomed over the Continent. He spent much of his life in Devon, where he came to inhabit his grandfather's house at Wreyland. There he listened to his neighbors, considered their customs, consulted the copious diaries and letters left to him by his father and grandfather, and mined his own travel journals to catalog, in poised paragraphs and circumscribed vignettes, whatever occupied his mind. His eye for the comic, together with his affection for both his shared locality and his private legacies of family lore and worldly learning, make *Small Talk at Wreyland* an ideal and engaging personal testament to the passing pageant of the years—and a desultory reader's delight.

What: Diaries & Letters. **When:** Published in three volumes, 1918–23. **Reading Note:** Dip in anywhere. **Also By:** *Rhodes in Ancient Times* (1885). *Ancient Ships* (1894). **Try:** *Kilvert's Diary* by Francis Kilvert (see page 445). *Word from Wormingford* by Ronald Blythe. *My Pamet* by Tom Kane.

The Great Good Thing
Roderick Townley (born 1942)

What Happens When a Tale Escapes the Page

We first meet Sylvie, the princess heroine of the book-within-this-book, as she is rushing back to page three, summoned by the attention of the first reader to crack the covers of her fairy tale in a very long time. Didn't you know that the life of storybook characters goes on even once their books are closed? Well, as we learn in this ingenious novel, such characters are just as surprised to find out that readers have a life apart from their reading. "You mean you don't *know* how your own story turns out?" Sylvie asks Claire, the young girl who becomes entranced by Sylvie's tale, then rescues the princess and her fellow characters when the volume they have inhabited for eight decades—since Claire's grandmother possessed it as a child—is threatened by fire. As the resourceful Sylvie escapes the borders of her book to enter Claire's dreams and take up sometimes perilous residence in the girl's imagination, real young readers—and their parents, if they're lucky—are bound to become lost in one of the most inventive and exhilarating narratives they'll ever discover. Filled with surprise and magnanimous wisdom, *The Great Good Thing* is a marvelous invocation of the power of books to transcend time and pass enchantments across generations.

What: Children's. **When:** 2001. **Reading Note:** Age 9 and up. **Also By:** Two sequels in the Sylvie Cycle: *Into the Labyrinth* (2002) and *The Constellation of Sylvie* (2006). Also: *Sky* (2004) and *The Red Thread* (2007). **Try:** *The Return of the Twelves* by Pauline Clarke. *Inkheart* by Cornelia Funke. **Adaptation:** The unabridged audiobook, read by Blair Brown, is just about perfect and an ideal family listening experience.

Centuries of Meditations
Thomas Traherne (1637–1674)

"Very near to being the happiest thing in English Christianity." —Ronald Blythe

The discovery of the writings of Thomas Traherne is one of the most remarkable tales in literary history, for most of the seventeenth-century clergyman's poetry—as well as the entirety of the *Centuries of Meditations*—came to light by chance in the early part of the twentieth century, when William T. Brooke purchased for a few pence two manuscripts that he found at a London bookstall. Their astonishing contents were subsequently published, edited by Bertram Dobell, as Traherne's *Poetical Works* (1903) and *Centuries of Meditations* (1908).

A worthy addition to the Anglican mystical tradition that reached its peak in the verse of George Herbert and Henry Vaughan, Traherne's poetry seems to foreshadow that of Blake and Wordsworth and even Walt Whitman, none of whom could have read the work of their predecessor ("There are invisible ways of conveyance," Traherne writes at the outset of *Centuries*, "by which some great thing doth touch our souls"). But it is Traherne's prose that is truly distinctive: Visionary and magnificent, it has no parallel in the annals of English literature.

A collection of four sets of one hundred meditations (plus a fifth that is only partially complete), *Centuries of Meditations* is a devotional work consisting of brief passages—in most instances less than a page—that focus on Christian belief and ethics and on the nature of God and divine love. Throughout, they display the author's dedication to a philosophy of "felicity." No one but Wordsworth has evoked with such passionate invention the joy of childhood, or written with such faith that the wonder of its innocence could be approached and experienced again despite the disenchantments of experience.

The pleasures the book offers are by no means entirely dogmatic, for Traherne's meditations send forth waves of well-being that welcome readers into a realm in which the soul seems as sensitive and receptive as the five senses. The resulting incantatory praise has a mysterious glory all its own; in a letter written at the end of 1941, C. S. Lewis called Traherne's *Centuries* "almost the most beautiful book (in prose, I mean, excluding poets) in English," and its sonorous contemplative magic lives up to that description.

What: Religion & Spirituality. *When:* Most likely written late in Traherne's life, the manuscript was discovered in 1896; published in 1908. *Reading Note:* Like all devotionals, Traherne's is best pondered in daily installments; even in strictly literary terms, the prose is too rich for lengthy immersion. *Also By: A Serious and Patheticall Contemplation of the Mercies of God* (1699). *Try: Revelations of Divine Love* by Julian of Norwich. The poetry of Wordsworth. The poems and prose of Gerard Manley Hopkins. *Adaptation:* British composer Gerald Finzi (1901–1956) set Traherne's evocations of childhood in *Dies Natalis*, a gorgeous piece for tenor solo and string orchestra. *Footnote:* As late as 1997, previously unknown Traherne manuscripts were still being discovered.

Garibaldi and the Thousand
George Macaulay Trevelyan (1876–1962)

The Middle Act of a Heroic Life

George Macaulay Trevelyan's three-volume narrative of the life of Giuseppe Garibaldi (1807–1882), "the most poetically minded of the world's famous warriors," is gripping as military history, stirring as the chronicle of the creation of the Italian nation, stylish as literature, and thrilling as sheer adventure. As Trevelyan writes, "Garibaldi had, perhaps, the most romantic life that history records, for it had all the trappings as well as the essence of romance," and the biographer does full justice to his singular subject. Tracing the patriot's career as buccaneer and guerrilla, as exile and campaigner in South America, and as the charismatic, bold, brilliant revolutionary hero of the Risorgimento, Trevelyan welcomes readers into the thick of historical exploit, and nowhere with more sweeping excitement than in the middle installment of his trilogy, *Garibaldi and the Thousand*, which can be enjoyed—if you must—without reference to its companions.

Beginning with the great man's return from his stint as a candlemaker in New York to his craggy home base on Caprera, an inhospitable island off the coast of Sardinia, *Garibaldi and the Thousand* culminates with Garibaldi's successful expedition to Sicily in 1860, a turning point in the formation of modern Italy. With one thousand volunteers, he wrested Palermo, the Sicilian capital, away from much larger Bourbon forces with a combination of boldness, bravery, and military genius.

Garibaldi's legendary ability to inspire devotion in his often ragtag troops (and, as the reader of Trevelyan soon becomes aware, in at least one erudite English historian) is wonderfully conveyed, as are the moral reserves and pragmatic intelligence that checked the hero's personal and political ambitions. Indeed, Garibaldi's character is so complex that he would have been a perfect protagonist for an opera by his contemporary, Giuseppe Verdi. Although the preceding volume, *Garibaldi's*

Giuseppe Garibaldi in Naples, 1861

Defense of the Roman Republic, 1848–49, and the subsequent one, *Garibaldi and the Making of Italy, June–November 1860*, are well worth your attention, the intervening book's ultimate focus on the extraordinary events of May 1860 gives it a rapturous dramatic arc.

What: History. Biography. War. **When:** 1909. **Also By:** *History of England* (1926). *England Under Queen Anne* (1930–34). **Further Reading:** *My Life* by Giuseppe Garibaldi. *Garibaldi* by Jasper Ridley. **Try:** *The Leopard* by Giuseppe Tomasi di Lampedusa (see page 462). *The Rise of Napoleon Bonaparte* by Robert Asprey.

The Collected Stories
William Trevor (1928–2016)

A Trove of Tales That Know Their Way Around the Heart

William Trevor's output of book-length fiction was somewhat unintentional, even though he wrote more than a score of acclaimed novels. "I start writing away, and sometimes I find myself, to my considerable horror, in the midst of a novel," William Trevor told an interviewer in 1990. The "horror" stems no doubt from the fact that stories never stopped presenting themselves to him, insisting on being set down—as his unstinting output in the shorter form reveals.

Born in County Cork, Trevor lived in England for much of his life, but never cut the cord of Irish storytelling that marked him as an heir to Sean O'Faolain, Frank O'Connor, and the Joyce of *Dubliners*. While Trevor's wide-ranging tales encompass everything from American expatriates to Italian innkeepers and the English upper class, his best rehearse the yearnings and regrets of ordinary Irish men and women, trapped by circumstance—and the poignant comfort of their own habituation to their fate—into lives of want in all the ample meanings of that word. His small portraits of spinsters and priests, students, tradesmen, farmers, shopgirls, and desperately fumbling lovers are closely observed and undramatic, yet suffused with emotional truths that endow them with the gravity of lifetimes. "The Ballroom of Romance," one of Trevor's most memorable stories, is emblematic; the protagonist, an unmarried woman approaching middle age, has no respite from the loneliness of caring for her crippled father except a weekly visit—via a seven-mile bicycle ride—to the local dance hall, where her hope for love slips through the hands of time for a few hours of made-up promise.

In his understated yet exact descriptions of the sorrows that define the days of nondescript yet often honorable people, Trevor plots the boundless and bewildering capacity of the human heart, no matter how faint its beating. Sound bleak? Perhaps. But taken one at a time, Trevor's stories are stunning in the shared sadnesses they evoke, and heartwarming in strange, startling ways.

What: Short Stories. *When:* 1992, collecting stories from individual volumes published between 1967 and 1989. *Also By: Selected Stories* (2009) gathers forty-eight tales published after *The Collected Stories*. His novels include *Elizabeth Alone* (1973), *Fools of Fortune* (1983), *Nights at the Alexandra* (1987), *Felicia's Journey* (1994), *Death in Summer* (1998), and *The Story of Lucy Gault* (2002). *Try: Dubliners* by James Joyce (see page 420). *Collected Stories* of Frank O'Connor (see page 598). *Adaptations:* Several of the stories have been adapted for the big or small screen. "The Ballroom of Romance" was filmed by Pat O'Connor in 1982.

Hermit of Peking

THE HIDDEN LIFE OF SIR EDMUND BACKHOUSE

Hugh Trevor-Roper (1914–2003)

The Riveting Tale of a Fraudulent Scholar

In the summer of 1973, under cloak-and-dagger circumstances, distinguished historian and Oxford don Hugh Trevor-Roper came into possession of two remarkable manuscripts by Sir Edmund Trelawny Backhouse (1873–1944). Backhouse, a China scholar long resident in Peking, was known as coauthor of a couple of standard works on Chinese history and as a singular benefactor of Oxford's Bodleian Library, to which he had presented a magnificent collection of some 27,000 Chinese books and manuscripts. It was not, however, this

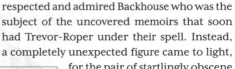

respected and admired Backhouse who was the subject of the uncovered memoirs that soon had Trevor-Roper under their spell. Instead, a completely unexpected figure came to light, for the pair of startlingly obscene manuscripts recorded in detail an extraordinary life, one that "touched, at so many points, the literary and social history of late Victorian England and late Manchu China" and included intimate acquaintance with the likes of French poet Paul Verlaine, Oscar Wilde, and the Dowager Empress of China. Trevor-Roper, amazed and abashed, found that he couldn't help but undertake a quest to discover the truth about

the libertine who had composed such scandalous self-portraits.

Or rather, had fabricated them. For as Trevor-Roper came to learn in the course of his extensive research, the *Backhouse* memoirs were a "glittering theatre of fantasy—fantasies of literature, politics and high life." Into these fictions, which were carefully constructed "out of real evidence, meticulously observed or selected in order to evade easy disproof," Backhouse had introduced himself, as either "the protagonist, or at least a major actor in the drama."

The "elusive and preposterous character" who emerged from Trevor-Roper's investigations into Backhouse's real and imagined lives turns out to have been one of the most outrageous frauds of the age. As recounted by the often perplexed but always fascinated Trevor-Roper, this true story within a story within a story makes, in the words of novelist Robert Nye, for "one of those rare books which, once begun, you have to finish in a single night."

What: Biography. History. *When:* 1976. *Edition:* Also published as *A Hidden Life. Also By: The Last Days of Hitler* (1947). *Try: The Quest for Corvo* by A. J. A. Symons (see page 768). *The Secret Lives of Trebitsch Lincoln* by Bernard Wasserstein.

The Warden
Anthony Trollope (1815–1882)

The Way We Live, Then and Now

One summer evening in the 1850s, while Anthony Trollope sauntered on the grounds of Salisbury Cathedral, the story of *The Warden* suggested itself to him. The title character, the Reverend Septimus Harding, is a good and gentle man who runs a hospital for pensioners in a provincial town. The institution is supported by a charitable trust that comes under the scrutiny of a young reformer, outraged by the unequal distribution of proceeds between Mr. Harding's living and the hospital itself. The kerfuffle is complicated by the fact that Mr. Harding is both beloved by his neighbors and diligent in discharging his responsibilities, and all the more entangled because the energetic reformer is in love with the warden's daughter.

The Warden was Trollope's fourth novel, but his first popular success (he would go on to write more than forty more). In it he discovered his singular ability to evoke, through an inveterate focus on small characters and circumscribed behaviors, an entire world shaped by the forces that condition social life everywhere: personal motivations,

A sketch of Anthony Trollope

the malleable but determining power of public perception and various forms of prestige, and the influence of entrenched institutions. Although the squabbles of a cathedral town and its clerics may seem remote from our twenty-first-century lives, the core drama (and comedy) of *The Warden* could be easily transported to an American college campus, as critic Adam Gopnik has astutely written in describing Trollope's method, adding, "His subject is always politics and his material gossip."

Trollope famously set down 250 words every fifteen minutes, and registered his progress like clockwork. Indeed, if he finished a novel in the middle of one of his daily three-hour writing sessions, he would begin another. To read his books is like following a storyteller who is out for a stroll: Slowly, steadily, he leads us down the roads, avenues, alleys, and lanes of his fictional domain, careful to leave no path untrod, no plot unturned. The small path on which *The Warden* sets out leads the reader into an expanding network of characters in the five subsequent novels in the Chronicles of Barsetshire; two of these, *Barchester Towers* (1857) and

A Small House at Allington (1864), which Virginia Woolf paired with *Pride and Prejudice* as "perfect" novels, are especially recommended. Despite the fuller pleasures of the later books, *The Warden* is the place to begin one's exploration of the large canvas on which Trollope explores, with empathy and irony, the complex relations of people, property, and position that transcend their local settings to both delight and instruct us. His later set of Palliser novels move from countryside to metropolis, and from church politics to the Parliamentary sort, with equal reward for the reader.

What: Novel. *When:* 1855. *Also By:* Also in the Barsetshire series: *Doctor Thorne* (1858); *Framley Parsonage* (1861); *The Last Chronicle of Barset* (1867). The Palliser novels, beginning with *Can You Forgive Her?* (six volumes, 1864–80). *The Way We Live Now* (1874–75). *Further Reading: The Gentleman in Trollope: Individuality and Moral Conduct* by Shirley Robin Letwin (see page 479). *Try: Cranford* by Elizabeth Gaskell (see page 310). *Adam Bede* by George Eliot. *Adaptation:* A 1982 BBC series, *The Barchester Chronicles*, adapted both *The Warden* and *Barchester Towers* in a single narrative.

Within the Context of No Context
George W. S. Trow (1943–2006)

The Media Age Through a Gimlet Eye

This elegant, astonishing polemic explores the infectious malaise of the television epoch with fierce insight, savage humor, and ruthless focus; it remains relevant— even revelatory—in the era of the internet. As novelist John Irving put it, *Within the Context of No Context* "is essential reading for anyone interested in the demise, the terminal silliness, of our culture." First published as the centerpiece of a special issue of *The New Yorker*, then issued in book form in 1981, it was reissued sixteen years later with a substantial new introduction by the author elaborating upon the original essay's wise and withering assessment of television's baleful power. Although we have progressed into the realm of another electronic kingdom, the book's insights may be even more pertinent for the digital age.

Trow's anatomy of American melancholy is cranky, passionate, poignant, knotty, and brilliant: He dissects our public destiny since the 1940s with unrelenting verve, as if he were the ghostwriter for some postmodern revival of the Old Testament books of prophecy. Arguing that television has reduced the wide world to

a single scale and frame of reference, and that celebrity and fashion ("the aesthetic of the hit") have become the only cultural markers, he ponders the inarguable evidence that history has been replaced by demographics as a lens of understanding, diminishing both erudition and sagacity along the way:

In the New History, nothing was judged—only counted. The power of judging was then subtracted from what it was necessary for a man to learn to do. In the New History, the preferences of a child carried as much weight as the preferences of an adult, so the refining of preferences was subtracted from what it was necessary for a man to learn to do.

Invoking an extraordinary range of intuitions and references, this small, singular book leads us through "the decline of adulthood" and "the adolescent orthodoxy," from the World's Fair of 1964 to the defining force of *People* magazine to—not last and not least—the faded fortune of the fedora. Everything that passes before Trow's gaze is illuminated, as the reader's intelligence and experience will be, by the author's rage and rue. One can only imagine what he would have made of Facebook.

What: Culture. Essays. *When:* First published in *The New Yorker,* November 17, 1980. *Edition:* The 1997 paperback edition contains Trow's significant new introductory essay, "Collapsing Dominant." *Also By: My Pilgrim's Progress: Media Studies, 1950–1998* (1999). *The Harvard Black Rock Forest* (2004). *Try: The Culture of Narcissism* by Christopher Lasch. *Amusing Ourselves to Death* by Neil Postman. *The Cult of the Amateur* by Andrew Keen.

The Guns of August
Barbara W. Tuchman (1912–1989)

The First Month of World War I: Thirty Days That Changed the World

Of the many satisfactions to be gained from *The Guns of August*, the first to greet readers is the pleasure of its prose. The book begins with a majestic opening paragraph whose composition reportedly claimed eight hours of the author's concentration:

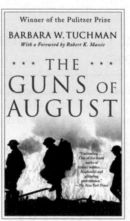

Winner of the Pulitzer Prize

BARBARA W. TUCHMAN

With a Foreword by Robert K. Massie

★★★ THE ★★★

GUNS OF

AUGUST

So gorgeous was the spectacle on the May morning of 1910 when nine kings rode in the funeral of Edward VII of England that the crowd, waiting in hushed and black-clad awe, could not keep back gasps of admiration. In scarlet and blue and green and purple, three by three the sovereigns rode through the palace gates, with plumed helmets, gold braid, crimson sashes, and jeweled orders flashing in the sun. . . . The muffled tongue of Big Ben tolled nine by the clock as the cortege left the palace, but on history's clock it was sunset, and the sun of the old world was setting in a dying blaze of splendor never to be seen again.

This is what used to be called the "pageant of history," yet Barbara Tuchman's evocation of it sets the stage not for a saga of spectacle but rather for an insightful account of the prejudices and collective myopia that combined to launch the catastrophe of World War I—and bring history's pageant crashing into disordered modernity.

With keen attention to the personalities of leaders in London, Berlin, Paris, and Saint Petersburg, Tuchman organizes the elements of a complex, multifaceted reality into a compelling drama of national ambitions and individual egos (among them General Joseph Joffre of France; Lord Kitchener, the British war minister; and the German generals von Moltke and von Kluck). As she charts the opening gambits of the war and the strategies and tactics of the early encounters, she offers incisive, illuminating accounts of the frontline advances and back-channel maneuverings that led to the Allied pursuit of the German battle cruiser *Goeben* through the Mediterranean, the German invasion of Belgium, the Battle of Liège, the burning of the city of Louvain, and, eventually, the tragedy of the Marne.

Winston Churchill characterized the first thirty days of World War I as "a drama never surpassed." *The Guns of August* tells us why.

What: History. War. *When:* 1962. *Award:* Pulitzer Prize for General Nonfiction, 1963. *Also By: The Proud Tower: A Portrait of the World Before the War, 1890–1914* (1966). *Stilwell and the American Experience in China, 1911–1945* (1971). *A Distant Mirror: The Calamitous Fourteenth Century* (1978). *Practicing History: Selected Essays* (1981). *Further Reading: The First World War* by John Keegan. *Try: Dreadnought* by Robert K. Massie. *Adaptation:* A documentary film based on the book was made in 1965. *Footnote:* The book was a favorite of John F. Kennedy, who reportedly gave copies to his ambassador to France, General James M. Gavin, and to British Prime Minister Harold Macmillan. For her part, Tuchman told the *New York Post:* "I'm not for sitting back in 1962 and saying, Look what fools they were. Anyone who wants to talk of the stupidity of 1914 has only to remember the Bay of Pigs in 1961."

Presumed Innocent
Scott Turow (born 1949)

A Compelling Literary Legal Precedent

This is how I always start:
    "I am the prosecutor.
    "I represent the state. I am here to present to you the evidence of a crime. Together you will weigh the evidence. You will deliberate upon it. You will decide if it proves the defendant's guilt.
    "This man—" And here I point.*

So begins this breakthrough novel, which, in bringing a new depth of intelligence and literary acumen to the courtroom drama, not only redefined that genre, but expanded the depth and breadth of commercial fiction generally by showing how complex characters and motives could enhance spellbinding plots. The narrator is Rusty Sabich, a prosecuting attorney in the American Midwest, who will end up being the one pointed at when the case he is pursuing—the murder of a colleague and ex-lover in a brutal sex crime—reaches the courtroom.

Scott Turow's inspired plotting continually reveals fresh and shifting perspectives on familiar aspects of the murder mystery, and his deft handling of subplots both political and personal makes *Presumed Innocent* an extraordinarily satisfying, psychologically acute novel. Although it has spawned many imitations (including Turow's own later, excellent but less innovative works), it remains a standout.

What: Novel. *When:* 1987. *Also By: The Burden of Proof* (1990). *Innocent* (2010). *Try: Anatomy of a Murder* by Robert Traver. *Adaptation:* The 1990 film stars Harrison Ford.

IIIIIIIIIIIIIIIIIIIIIIIIIIIIIIIIIIIIIIIIIIIII B O O K N O T E IIIIIIIIIIIIIIIIIIIIIIIIIIIIIIIIIIIIIIIIIIIIII

THE FINE POINT OF LEGAL SUSPENSE

The Firm
John Grisham (born 1955)

There are times in our reading lives when turning the page is more important than what's on it, when the headlong rush toward what happens next overwhelms reflection—and sometimes even reason. John Grisham has made a career creating plots that deliver just such pleasure to readers. In his writing, he clearly knows how to enjoy himself, as the crime fiction columnist in the *New York Times* noticed early in his career, flagging the "relish" with which he writes about the deadly and devious antics of the Memphis

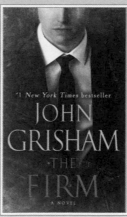

law partnership of Bendini, Lambert & Locke in *The Firm*, his second novel (1991). No matter how dark—or even far-fetched—the misdeeds Grisham has described in his shelf of legal thrillers, his vivid sketches of settings and personalities are made addictively entertaining as the writer's relish becomes the reader's. *The Firm* relates the education of Harvard Law–minted first-year associate Mitch McDeere while he uncovers—and scrambles to escape—the Mob-entangled web of malfeasance at the heart of B, L & L. Where does it all lead? To you turning pages faster and faster, until you're sorry you've run out.

MARK TWAIN
(1835–1910)

A fter apprenticeships as a printer, newspaperman, Mississippi riverboat pilot, and miner, Samuel Langhorne Clemens discovered his enduring occupation under the guise of what would become one of the most famous pen names in history: Mark Twain (in river parlance it means a depth of two fathoms as measured on the sounding line used to ensure a boat's safe passage through shallow water). Twain's first success as an author came with a story called "The Celebrated Jumping Frog of Calaveras County." The humorous sketch's combination of down-home anecdote, tall tale, and gently satiric assessment of human nature would evolve through the decades as Twain added length and literary polish to his work, even as he subtracted some of the gentleness from his authorial persona. That

persona, perhaps his greatest creation, inhabits American culture with a presence both amiable and acerbic; he's like an old uncle who is funny, wise, and genial, but committed to deflating the pretensions of every niece or nephew who crosses his path. His natural skill as a raconteur provided him with a living in the lecture hall that complemented the success of his books, and it more lastingly created in all his writing— stories, novels, and delightful travelogs such as *The Innocents Abroad* (1869), *Roughing It* (1872), and *A Tramp Abroad* (1880)—a bond between storyteller and reader that has seldom been matched and is still somehow magical.

Mark Twain, ca. 1900

The Adventures of Tom Sawyer
Boys Will Be Boys

T wain's first extended fictional narrative, *The Adventures of Tom Sawyer*, begins with its hero already in trouble, or at least on the verge

of it, under the watchful eye of his suspicious aunt Polly. "Well, I lay if I get hold of you I'll—" she exclaims as she searches for him under the bed and around the house, until at last he appears, asserting his innocence but no doubt hiding something, as readers as well as Aunt Polly can surely tell. The battle lines between youthful high spirits and the sober strictures of adult society are quickly drawn, and we know immediately whose side we're on.

The book is based on the author's recollections of his own youth in Hannibal, Missouri, although these are embellished, naturally, with imaginative flair. Tom's escapades are at first benign—playing hooky from school and the like—and recognizable, albeit ingenious, as in the famous scene in which he tricks his buddies into whitewashing a fence for him by pretending the labor is a privilege rather than a chore. But as the plot progresses, Tom's exploits escalate to include the kinds of adventures a boy would invent for himself and his friends if he were braver than he really is, and the world more dangerous and interesting: Tom and various conspirators (including, most notably, his love interest, Becky Thatcher, and his rascally companion, Huckleberry Finn) come upon body snatchers in a graveyard, witness a murder, explore a haunted house, get lost for days in a cave, uncover a buried treasure, escape to an island as self-appointed pirates, and have the remarkable experience of attending their own funeral after they are believed to have drowned in the Mississippi.

All in all, Twain's debut novel is a delightful evocation of the spirit that drives precocious youngsters to set themselves against the stultifying routines of the grown-up world, wrapped up in a plot that is filled with humor and suspense in equal measure. It is a joyful book that aptly meets the twin objective Twain describes in his preface: not only entertaining boys and girls, but also reminding adults of "what they once were themselves."

What: Children's. *When:* 1876. *Also By: The Prince and the Pauper* (1881). *A Connecticut Yankee in King Arthur's Court* (1889). *Tom Sawyer Abroad* (1894). *Tom Sawyer, Detective* (1896). *Further Reading: Mr. Clemens and Mark Twain: A Biography* by Justin Kaplan. *Dangerous Water: A Biography of the Boy Who Became Mark Twain* by Ron Powers. *Try: Swallows and Amazons* by Arthur Ransome (see page 660). *Adaptations:* First adapted as a silent movie in 1917, Tom Sawyer's story has been the source of a constant stream of film, television, and theatrical adaptations, with the 1938 film directed by Norman Taurog being especially memorable. The audiobook performed by Garrick Hagon is superb.

The Adventures of Huckleberry Finn
Tapping the Vernacular

T he Adventures of Huckleberry Finn was published eight years after *The Adventures of Tom Sawyer,* and from its first sentences we know by the writing that we are in a different world. While the former is told from the perspective of an anodyne third-person narrator, the latter is recounted by the protagonist himself, and the language is like a live wire of vernacular energy:

You don't know about me, without you have read a book by the name of "The Adventures of Tom Sawyer," but that ain't no matter. That book was made by Mr. Mark Twain, and he told the truth, mainly. There was things which he stretched, but mainly he told the truth. That is nothing. I never seen anybody but lied, one time or another, without it was Aunt Polly, or the widow, or maybe Mary. Aunt Polly—Tom's Aunt Polly, she is—and Mary, and the Widow Douglas, is all told about in that book—which is mostly a true book; with some stretchers, as I said before.

"All modern American literature comes from one book by Mark Twain called *Huckleberry Finn,*" Ernest Hemingway famously proclaimed in *Green Hills of Africa,* and it is the idiomatic

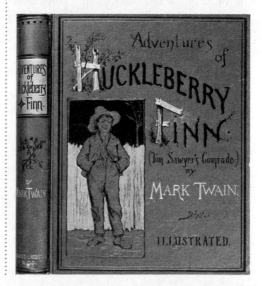

immediacy of Huck's voice—to say nothing of the speech rhythms of the several other spoken dialects Twain mimics in his novel—that delivers the innovation that would prove an inspiration for novelists across the generations. No novel before it in English had overthrown with such verve and abandon the strictures of linguistic decorum, and its influence was profound; Saul Bellow's *The Adventures of Augie March* (see page 661) and J. D. Salinger's *The Catcher in the Rye* (see page 695) are just two prominent examples in the American vein.

Twain's originality would have been academic, of course, if the technique was not perfectly matched to the character it represents. As Huck continues at the start of his *Adventures*, describing the ending of *Tom Sawyer*:

Now the way that book winds up, is this: Tom and me found the money that the robbers hid in the cave, and it made us rich. We got six thousand dollars apiece—all gold. . . . The Widow Douglas, she took me for her son, and allowed she would sivilize me; but it was rough living in the house all the time, considering how dismal regular and decent the widow was in all her ways; and so when I couldn't stand it no longer, I lit out.

What ensues in his own book is a series of incidents that invoke themes of capture and escape, race and identity, individual conscience and conventional morality. Kidnapped by his alcoholic and abusive father, Huck fakes his own death and flees to an island, where he meets up with Jim, a slave on the run toward his own freedom. The pair's adventures on a raft on the Mississippi and their encounters with various threatening characters and circumstances provide the heart of the book. The frequent use of contemporary slurs and racial epithets can distract readers today from the complexity and even sensitivity of the novel's attention to the cultural themes it embodies in its narrative. The friendship between Huck and Jim is both unsettled and unsettling in its implications, but human in its import—and therefore often several things at once. Huck's sense of emergent personal responsibility—"All right, then, I'll *go* to hell," he tells himself on deciding to break the law

and help Jim escape—is matched by Jim's fidelity to ideals that reach beyond his own circumstances.

Notably, Tom Sawyer, in a small but pivotal role late in *The Adventures of Huckleberry Finn*, is both unfeeling and self-absorbed, as if Twain is contrasting the way a character from a children's book—*The Adventures of Tom Sawyer*—is ill equipped for the serious matters of freedom and slavery, and life and death, that are at the core of this very different book. Whereas *The Adventures of Tom Sawyer* was an idyll of remembered childhood, *The Adventures of Huckleberry Finn* is a novel of real and present dangers: violence, abuse, oppression, greed, murder, fear. That Twain's telling is charming as well as troubling is a measure of the author's skill at spinning tales.

What: Novel. **When:** 1884. **Also By:** *Life on the Mississippi* (1883). *Pudd'nhead Wilson, A Tale* (1894). **Further Reading:** *Lighting Out for the Territory: Reflections on Mark Twain and American Culture* by Shelley Fisher Fishkin. *Searching for Jim: Slavery in Sam Clemens's World* by Terrell Dempsey. **Try:** *The Unvanquished* by William Faulkner. *To Kill a Mockingbird* by Harper Lee (see page 469). *Flight to Canada* by Ishmael Reed. **Adaptation:** An excellent audiobook is read by Grover Gardner.

Letters from the Earth
UNCENSORED WRITINGS
Edited by Bernard DeVoto
The Afterlife of a Satirist

That Twain was cagier than the white-suited folksiness of his public image would suggest is fully apparent in both the history and content of his posthumous publications, including *Letters from the Earth*, an incendiary collection of pieces on religious themes written toward the end of his life. The title story, for instance, takes the form of Satan's correspondence with the archangels in heaven after he has been sent to Earth by the deity as punishment for his irreverence. His reports are filled with wry commentary on God's "Human-Race experiment."

Man is a marvelous curiosity. When he is at his very very best he is a sort of low grade nickel-plated angel; at his worst he is unspeakable, unimaginable; and first and last and all the time he is a sarcasm. . . .

Moreover . . . he thinks he is the Creator's pet. He believes the Creator is proud of him; he even believes the Creator loves him; has a passion for him; sits up nights to admire him; yes, and watch over him and keep him out of trouble. He prays to Him, and thinks He listens. Isn't it a quaint idea? . . . He prays for help, and favor, and protection every day . . . although no prayer of his has ever been answered. The daily affront, the daily defeat, do not discourage him, he goes on praying just the same.

Cataloging stupidity, self-deception, and all manner of human frailty, the letters set the stage for the other short works gathered between these covers, which express disdain and derision for the Christian pieties of Twain's time and for conventional religious thinking generally. Emboldened by a despair exacerbated by age, debt, and the loss of his wife and a daughter, the Mark Twain on display in these writings is ready to question any received wisdom with vigorous skepticism. Dark humor has seldom been so mordant, incisive, and thought-provoking.

What: Essays. Humor. *When:* Written ca. 1909; published in book form, 1962. *Also By:* Other posthumous collections: *No. 44, The Mysterious Stranger* (1969); *A Pen Warmed-Up in Hell: Mark Twain in Protest,* edited by Frederick Anderson (1972); *The Bible According to Mark Twain,* edited by Howard G. Baetzhold and Joseph B. McCullough (1995). *Try: The Devil's Dictionary* by Ambrose Bierce. *A Mencken Chrestomathy* by H. L. Mencken (see page 545).

Dinner at the Homesick Restaurant
Anne Tyler (born 1941)

The Inner Lives of Ordinary People

Don't let the cute title fool you: Anne Tyler is a writer to be reckoned with. Her earliest influence was Eudora Welty (see page 841), who would eventually pay the younger novelist the highest compliment after reading this, Tyler's ninth novel: "If I could have written the last sentence in *Dinner at the Homesick Restaurant,*" Welty said, "I'd have been happy for the rest of my life."

Like Welty, Tyler writes books about the inner lives of regular folk. Yes, they are a bit eccentric. "People are always saying we understand you write about quirky characters, and I think, isn't everybody quirky?" she once explained to an interviewer. "If you look very closely at anybody you'll find impediments, women and men both." For Tyler, our obstacles are

always close to home, for marriages and familial relationships are her core subject, and never so vitally as in this novel.

Pearl Tull is old and dying. Her vision is mostly gone, but she still has her memories and her children. As the book opens, her son Ezra is sorting through her things, describing photos to her that send her thoughts back to the 1940s, when her traveling-salesman husband up and left her. It took her several years to tell the children he was not just away on business, and she recalls struggling to provide for them while hiding the truth, toiling as a grocery cashier to keep them fed, even as they never appreciated her sacrifices. But as the story shifts from Pearl's recollections to the children's, all three now middle-aged and struggling with the vicissitudes of their own adulthoods, we find they remember her not as a saint but as something of a monster, their young selves not always nurtured but sometimes lastingly scarred. There is Ezra, who has become Pearl's caregiver and the proprietor of the restaurant in the book's title; he is nostalgic for childhood and preternaturally nice, sometimes annoyingly so, especially in the mind of his brother Cody, who, although successful in business, is resentful toward life in general and his brother in particular. The third sibling, a busy physician, is on her third marriage and her first happiness. In what in other hands might be a cliché, but in Tyler's becomes a kind of resonant, organic wisdom, the Tulls can't manage to get through a meal together without old wounds becoming the main course.

It sounds simple, but it's not. Tyler calibrates the dearness of family in both senses, illustrating how the deepest affections are both the sweetest and the most costly. Her keen sensitivity to this duality is what gives her books their singular flavor; she knows that the real impediments we face are the circularities, the stuck-in-place-ness, of our lives. In this, she is at odds with the more romantic impulses of many novelists. Other writers may cover the same terrain of family with a more unforgiving scrutiny, which can make their work seem more ambitious than Tyler's. Or perhaps it just reveals that they know a little less about life.

Anne Tyler, 1985

What: Novel. *When:* 1982. *Also By: Morgan's Passing* (1980). *The Accidental Tourist* (1985). *Breathing Lessons* (1988). *Saint Maybe* (1991). *A Spool of Blue Thread* (2015). *Try: Selected Stories, 1968–1994* by Alice Munro (see page 573). *The Stone Diaries* by Carol Shields (see page 720). *Independence Day* by Richard Ford (see page 288). *Footnote:* Tyler's personal essay, "Still Just Writing," collected in *The Writer on Her Work*, edited by Janet Sternburg, is a shrewd, casually eloquent portrayal of the artist as a young mother: "Sitting on the bleachers in the school gymnasium, I told myself I could always use this in a novel someplace, but I couldn't really picture writing a novel about twenty little girls in leotards trying to walk the length of a wooden beam without falling off."

U, V, W
X, Y, Z

Life in Code

A PERSONAL HISTORY OF TECHNOLOGY

Ellen Ullman (born 1949)

Decrypting the Digital Age

This book collects seventeen essays written between 1994 and 2017, largely in the aftermath of Ellen Ullman's career as a software engineer in the 1980s and 1990s. Their subjects include the programming life, the first internet bubble, artificial intelligence, and broader cultural effects of the digital revolution. Although they were composed over more than two decades, the pieces coalesce into one absorbing and surprising conversation with a mind characterized by integrity and empathy. More importantly, despite the fact that their purview is technical, these essays reveal an author alert to nuance and on good terms with the literary graces. Imagine Virginia Woolf setting out to write "A Machine of One's Own" and you won't be far off the scent.

Of course, the machine in question has come to belong to all of us, shaping our experience in ways both hidden from view and as obvious as the phones in our hands. Ullman's singular gift (here as in her 1997 cult classic, *Close to the Machine: Technophilia and Its Discontents*) is her ability to bring human and social context to the digital sphere, whether she's writing about the peculiar workspace pathologies of programmers, the effects of technology boom-bust-and-reboom on her San Francisco neighborhood, the conundrums of memory, or the blessings of narrative. "The Dumbing Down of Programming," on the surface a hard-nosed professional's lament for the simplification of coding's syntax via graphical icons and prebuilt modules—"the consumerization of the computer, its curtseying and dumbing down and bullet-proofing behind dialogue boxes"—is at its depth about how we make meaning and the tools we need to do it. In the prescient "The Museum of Me," Ullman writes:

I fear for the world the internet is creating. Before the advent of the Web, if you wanted to sustain a belief in far-fetched ideas, you had to go out into the desert, or live on a compound in the mountains, or move from one badly furnished room to another in a series of safe houses.

That was written, astonishingly, in 1998. "The internet ideal," Ullman continues in the same essay, "represents a retreat not only from political life but also from culture—from that tumultuous conversation in which we try to talk to one another about our shared experiences." Making the recent history of technology a shared experience is precisely what Ullman does brilliantly in these pages, which are filled with impressions, ideas, and sentences that will stop your mind in its tracks, then set it going again with new energy and intelligence. You'll learn a lot about code in her book, but you'll learn even more about life.

What: Essays. Technology. Memoir. *When:* 2017. *Also By:* Fiction: *The Bug* (2003); *By Blood* (2012). *Try: Within the Context of No Context* by George W. S. Trow (see page 807). *You Are Not a Gadget* by Jaron Lanier. *The Four-Dimensional Human: Ways of Being in the Digital World* by Laurence Scott.

Kristin Lavransdatter

Sigrid Undset (1882–1949)

A Modern Epic of Medieval Norway

Sigrid Undset's archaeologist father instilled in her a fascination with the past, and her meticulous reconstruction of the customs of medieval Norway in this massive and magnificent saga—as in her equally impressive tetralogy, *The Master of Hestviken* (1925–27)—reflects that paternal legacy. Yet she brought a very modern sensibility to her material by virtue of her realistic, unromantic view of the fourteenth century, her frankness regarding sexuality, and her attention to the ordinary and passionate consciousness that gives coherence, if not fulfillment, to a life.

Telling the story of its title character, *Kristin Lavransdatter* comprises three novels: *The Wreath, The Wife,* and *The Cross.* As the trilogy opens, Kristin is a young girl devoted to her father and admired by her fellow townspeople. Betrothed by her family to a local landowner's son, she falls in love with a disreputable man and, sacrificing her family's affection and the respect of her neighbors, runs away with him. Undset brilliantly portrays the struggle between Kristin's ardent desire and the compromises, both practical and moral, it engenders. The story progresses across a broad canvas of medieval life as the couple lives through harmony and discord, raises seven sons, confronts issues of religion, politics, and status, and eventually returns to Kristin's home to face rejection and estrangement.

A summary does not do justice to Undset's achievement, nor to the singularity of her central character, who maintains a riveting identity in the midst of her struggles with family, community, and convention. Next to Kristin Lavransdatter, Emma Bovary is bloodless. In her book *13 Ways of Looking at the Novel*, Jane Smiley astutely describes Kristin's—and Undset's—originality:

> Perhaps the biggest difference between Undset's protagonist and most other female protagonists is that she is never without work to do. . . . Life is arduous in a way that is never true in novels about women of the middle and upper classes in France and England. Undset writes about work and weather and famine and accidents, illnesses, pregnancy, animals, and the natural world with immediacy and ease. Though Undset, too, explores the classic conflict between female virtue and female desire, she sets it into the context of female usefulness.

The result is a work of more than a thousand pages that richly imagines a world, and a woman, one is loath to leave behind.

What: Novel. *When:* Originally published in three volumes, 1920–22. *Edition:* Tiina Nunnally's award-winning 1997 translation is stylistically true to Undset's text and also restores scenes cut from the venerable 1920s translation, which had left out the sex and imposed a "Ye Olde English" diction on the language. *Award:* Nobel Prize in Literature, 1928. *Reading Note:* At first the number of characters can be challenging. *Also By: Gunnar's Daughter* (1909). *Jenny* (1911). *Try: Independent People* by Halldór Laxness (see page 466). *Adaptation:* Liv Ullman directed a 1995 Norwegian film.

The Maples Stories

John Updike (1932–2009)

The Marrying Kind

It is hard to name a major twentieth-century American writer more constant than John Updike. His commitment to his art, his puzzling over the knottiness and nobility (and inconstancy) of ordinary love, his apparent wonder at every subject he embraced, and his delight in the vocabulary at his command to describe them—in every aspect, Updike was a paragon of dedication and productivity. His sentences seem to smile with his pleasure in his vocation, and the uniform physical design and typographic consistency of the many volumes he published over a half century demonstrate how he cherished and groomed his appearance as an author in the world. He treated the output of other writers with commensurate respect; the reviews and essays collected in his several volumes of criticism, including *Picked-Up Pieces* (1975), *Hugging the Shore* (1983), and *Odd Jobs* (1991), are thoughtful, erudite, and enlightening.

The Maples Stories, a collection of eighteen tales written between 1956 and 1994 about a married, then divorced, couple named Joan and Richard Maples, may seem too modest to single out from Updike's generous oeuvre. Yet considered together, these short stories offer a probing, astute, and often poignant anatomy of a marriage that is remarkable both as a literary testament and a cultural portrait of a tumultuous period in American domestic life. Although Updike portrays the same themes on a much grander scale in his justly acclaimed sequence of Rabbit Angstrom novels, *The Maples Stories*, in their fleeting intimacy and atmosphere of amorous regret, distill the author's gift for evoking emotional uncertainty into an exquisitely moving testament.

John Updike, 1978

In his foreword, Updike writes, "A tribe segregated in a valley develops an accent, then a dialect, and then a language all its own; so does a couple," and the shared landscape of a marriage has seldom been so affectingly depicted. The titles alone suggest the Maples's passage from newly-wedded happiness through parenthood, dependence, routine, disillusion, and estrangement: "Snowing in Greenwich Village," "Wife-Wooing," "Giving Blood," "Twin Beds in Rome," "Your Lover Just Called," "Plumbing," "Sublimating," "Separating." The book is like a family album of high-resolution snapshots, mementos of both passing fancy and dramatic crises. Here's

a shot of the Maples's son John, tipsy and reacting to his father's announcement of the couple's separation:

"Why didn't you tell us?" he asked, in a large round voice quite unlike his own. "You should have told us you weren't getting along."

Richard was startled into attempting to force words through his tears.

"We do get along, that's the trouble, so it doesn't show even to us—" That we do not love each other *was the rest of the sentence; he couldn't finish it.*

Joan finished for him, in her style. "And we've always, *especially, loved our children."*

John was not mollified. "What do you care about us?" he boomed. "We're just little things you had."

Had and held, as best they could, like all the other memories these stories celebrate and eulogize. The last one, "Grandparenting," finds the divorced couple welcoming their first grandchild; as Richard holds the newborn baby, Updike puts a tender period on the long sentence of life and love the book records: "And the child's miniature body did adhere to his chest and arms, though more weakly than the infants he had presumed to call his own. Nobody belongs to us, except in memory."

What: Short Stories. **When:** 1956–94. *Editions:* Originally collected as *Too Far to Go* in 1979; reissued, with the addition of "Grandparenting," as *The Maples Stories*, in 2009. *Also By:* The Rabbit Angstrom Series: *Rabbit, Run* (1960); *Rabbit Redux* (1971); *Rabbit Is Rich* (1981); *Rabbit at Rest* (1990); *Rabbit Remembered* (2000). Other novels: *Couples* (1968); *The Coup* (1978); *The Witches of Eastwick* (1984). *Try:* The Stories of John Cheever (see page 152). *Selected Stories, 1968–1994* by Alice Munro (see page 573). *Adaptation:* The 1979 television film *Too Far to Go* stars Blythe Danner and Michael Moriarty.

V

The Letters of Vincent van Gogh

Vincent van Gogh (1853–1890)

A Portrait of the Artist in His Own Words

Sometimes I regret that I cannot make up my mind to work more at home and extempore. The imagination is certainly a faculty which we must develop, one which alone can lead us to the creation of a more exalting and consoling nature than the single brief glance at reality—which in our sight is ever changing, passing like a flash of lightning—can let us perceive.

A starry sky, for instance—look, that is something I should like to try to do, just as in the daytime I am going to try to paint a green meadow spangled with dandelions.

—Van Gogh to Émile Bernard, 1888

1888 letter with sketch for The Sower

V an Gogh's letters are among the most remarkable documents in the history of both art and literature. They chart, over a period of eighteen years (nearly half the painter's life span), the exertions, enthusiasms, disappointments, and ecstasies of a troubled and inspired mind.

The piercing virtue of Van Gogh's art—the fierce yet sympathetic energies of attention that he lavished on flowers, fields, and figures—is apparent, too, in his vivid letters to family (especially and predominantly his brother Theo), friends, and fellow painters such as Gauguin and Bernard. The several hundred pieces of correspondence he penned (often with accompanying illustrations; look for an edition that reproduces at least some of these) are the primary source of our knowledge of his life; they also provide a kind of real-time witness to his thinking about his work. Together they constitute the dramatic and compelling autobiography of a strong, sorrowful, sensitive vision searching for sustenance from life's daily bread.

What: Diaries & Letters. *When:* 1893. *Editions:* The pioneering three-volume set from the New York Graphic Society (quoted here) was published in 1958. In 2009, a six-volume, newly translated complete edition, with reproductions of two thousand works of art, was published by Thames and Hudson. Numerous smaller volumes offer satisfying alternatives to the deluxe sets. All the letters are also archived online. *Further Reading: Lust for Life* by Irving Stone. *Try: The Journal of Eugène Delacroix.*

■ For Jack Vance's *The Dying Earth*, see page 795.

Lives of the Most Excellent Painters, Sculptors, and Architects

Giorgio Vasari (1511–1574)

Artists as Models

Cimabue and Giotto; Duccio and Uccello; Masaccio, Brunelleschi, and Donatello; Piero della Francesca, Fra Angelico, and Leon Battista Alberti; Ghirlandaio, Botticelli, Mantegna, and Andrea del Sarto; the "divine trio" of Leonardo, Raphael, and Michelangelo— the glory of Renaissance art is evoked by this roster of sonorous names. Although these artists may get star billing in a modern reader's mind, there are eight score more whose biographies Giorgio Vasari saw fit to portray in his pioneering *Lives*, where the history of art was for the first time seen as the stories of the painters, sculptors, and architects who made it.

The stories are told by an author who was nearly contemporary with many of his subjects, and a colleague (Vasari was apprenticed to Andrea del Sarto and became an accomplished if ultimately minor painter himself); this seeds the text with a working knowledge that has kept it good reading for more than four centuries. His ear for gossip helps, too; just as one can call his *Lives* the first great work of serious art history, one can also identify in more than a few of his portraits the stirrings of the celebrity profile—the potent headline-generating potential of genius tinged with eccentricity. "Speak, speak, or be damned!" shouts Donatello at his statues: It's not hard to imagine this as a pull quote on a photo spread in *Vanity Fair*. And a cool Hollywood anti-hero has nothing on Giotto: When an emissary from Pope Benedict IX showed up and requested a sample of his work for a possible commission, the artist dipped his brush in red, "pressed his

The Sermon to the Birds *by Giotto, ca. 1300*

arm to his side to make a compass of it, and with a turn of his hand made a circle so even in its shape and outline that it was a marvel to behold. After he had completed the circle, he said with an impudent grin to the courtier: 'Here's your drawing.'" The pope's messenger thought he was being ridiculed; the pope, infallible in this instance at least, saw the import of the artist's calling card and summoned him to Rome.

Although Vasari's biographies are more journalistic than scholarly, two important innovations run through them and, by virtue of his work's influence, through much of the art history that followed him. The first, easy to take for granted today, represents an enormous achievement. With no illustrations in the earliest editions of his book, Vasari had to find a vocabulary to discuss the momentous art produced by his subjects: *disegno*, for example, meaning the capacity to combine skill in drawing with a larger sense of design; *grazia*, or grace; and, in acute appreciation of Michelangelo's intensity of execution and expression, *terribilità*. Second, he traced a progressive arc from Cimabue to Michelangelo in sophistication and expression that exalted the Florentine artistic legacy and has governed most people's appreciation of Renaissance art ever since. He had a very good eye, and a very agile pen.

What: Art. Biography. *When:* First edition, 1550; revised and enlarged, 1568. *Editions:* Translated by Julia Conaway Bondanella and Peter Bondanella (and quoted above), the Oxford World's Classics edition, titled *The Lives of the Artists,* offers an abundant selection. The Everyman's Library two-volume, 2,200-page set is complete. *Further Reading: The Collector of Lives: Giorgio Vasari and the Invention of Art* by Ingrid Rowland and Noah Charney. *Try: The Autobiography of Benvenuto Cellini* (see page 141).

Twenty Thousand Leagues Under the Sea
Jules Verne (1828–1905)

A Timeless Voyage from a Sci-Fi Pioneer

Before submarines were actually invented, Jules Verne, a prolific French pioneer of science fiction and one of the most widely read authors in history, dreamed of what it would be like to use one to travel around the world underwater. And although *Twenty Thousand Leagues Under the Sea* is now considerably more than a hundred years old, it is still a thrilling and wonderfully entertaining fantasy of deep-sea adventure.

The story opens with the sighting of a mysterious sea monster. An expedition is mounted to hunt it down, and the novel's narrator, marine biologist Pierre Aronnax, joins the crew. The search extends into the Pacific, where the creature is finally found and attacked. During the fight, Professor Aronnax, his assistant Conseil, and harpooner Ned Land are thrown overboard. They end up right on top of the beast—which, they discover, is in fact an underwater vehicle. Brought inside, the trio meets the ship's inventor and commander, Captain Nemo. Brilliant, odd, slightly crazed, and with a name that is Latin for "No One," Nemo teaches his guests about his amazing electrically powered submarine, which he has christened the *Nautilus.* Off they all set, through the underwater world, seeing its marvels as no one has before. (Twenty thousand leagues, incidentally, is the distance the *Nautilus* travels, not the depth to which it descends.) Eventually, after feasting their eyes on awe-inspiring wonders as well as surviving the onslaught of a giant squid, Aronnax and his two pals escape from the *Nautilus* and make it back to land.

When it comes to describing life beneath the waves, Verne mixes reported fact with his own luxuriant imaginings; it's the latter that keep the book fresh. And although Verne was prophetic in some ways, including about the

The crew of the Nautilus *fights a giant squid. Illustration by Henri Théophile Hildibrand, 1877*

military use of submarines, the real reason to read *Twenty Thousand Leagues Under the Sea* is to be on board as a master storyteller sounds the watery deep.

What: Children's. Science Fiction. *When:* 1870. *Also By: Paris in the Twentieth Century* (1863). *Journey to the Center of the Earth* (1864). *From the Earth to the Moon* (1865). *Around the Moon* (1870). *Around the World in Eighty Days* (1873). *The Mysterious Island* (1874). *Further Reading: The World of Jules Verne* by Gonzague Saint Bris. *Try: The Time Machine* and *The Island of Dr. Moreau* by H. G. Wells. *The Maracot Deep* by Sir Arthur Conan Doyle. *Adaptations:* From a 1916 silent movie right up to the present day, Verne's underwater saga has attracted numerous filmmakers, TV producers, and animators. Perhaps the most famous adaptation is the 1954 Disney version starring James Mason as Captain Nemo, with Kirk Douglas and Peter Lorre along for the ride. *Footnote:* Captain Nemo is a major figure in the graphic novel *The League of Extraordinary Gentlemen* by Alan Moore and Kevin O'Neill.

Burr
A NOVEL

Gore Vidal (1925–2012)

History as a Novel, the Novel as History

A scion of American aristocracy (such as it was), Gore Vidal was also its scourge. No writer took greater pleasure in skewering the pieties in which we wrap our founding myths, our imperial ambitions, or our cultural righteousness, and none was as gleeful in exposing the corruptions and peccadilloes that from time to time debase our democracy and spice our public life. His considerable oeuvre ranged from the provocative to the erudite to the elegant. Into the first category fall *The City and the Pillar* (1948), with its unapologetic treatment of homosexuality, and *Myra Breckinridge* (1968), with its comically apocalyptic treatment of gender-bending; into the second, his novels of the ancient world, including *Julian* (1964) and *Creation* (1981), both entertaining and deliciously informative performances; into the last, many of his essays, such as "The Oz Books" or "Homage to Daniel Shays" (at their best, Vidal's essays on subjects literary, historical, and personal stand equal in eloquence and alertness to any penned in the past century).

Gore Vidal, 1968

Vidal's signal achievement is the series of seven novels that trace our political life from the epoch of the Revolution to the era of JFK. Written out of chronological sequence and gathered together after the fact under the rubrics "Narratives of Empire" or "The American Chronicle," these lively, fact-based fictions—*Burr* (1973); *Lincoln* (1984); *1876* (1976); *Empire* (1987); *Hollywood* (1990); *Washington, D.C.* (1964); *The Golden Age* (2000)— are an astonishingly engaging course in our nation's past. The author's urge to debunk with insider's insight the personalities of the powerful adds piquancy to his portraits of grandees from Washington and Jefferson to Henry Adams, William Randolph Hearst, and Franklin Roosevelt. Fortunately, the history is as good as the gossip—often, as in *Lincoln*, grippingly so.

But the book devoted to the exploits of Aaron Burr (1756–1836) is in a class by itself. Most famous for killing Alexander Hamilton in an 1804 duel, Burr served as third vice president of the United States (a post he assumed after tying Jefferson in the presidential electoral vote). During Jefferson's second administration, Burr was tried for treason for an alleged conspiracy to create an independent empire in the unsettled American West. The auras of both distinction and disgrace he carries with him into old age—he is seventy-seven when the novel begins—make him a perfect protagonist for Vidal. As the young journalist who narrates the tale, Charlie Schuyler, puts it about his elderly friend, "He makes even a trip to the barber seem like a plot to overthrow the state."

In Vidal's depiction, Burr is charming (marrying a rich widow despite his advanced years), savvy (leveraging his connection to the current occupant of the office of vice president, Martin Van Buren, who may or may not be his illegitimate son), and scheming (he still has eyes for a large parcel of land in Texas). Best of all, he is wholly fascinating as he shares his memories with Schuyler, replete with unflattering intelligence regarding his legendary comrades in the early years of our federal government (none of whom impressed Burr). Witty and enlivened with intrigue throughout, *Burr* is, quite simply, a joy to read.

What: Novel. *When:* 1973. *Also By: Two Sisters* (1970). *United States: Essays 1952–1992* (1993). *Palimpsest: A Memoir* (1995). *Further Reading: Duel: Alexander Hamilton, Aaron Burr, and the Future of America* by Thomas Fleming. *Try: I, Claudius* by Robert Graves. *Ragtime* by E. L. Doctorow (see page 226).

The Aeneid
Virgil (70 BC–19 BC)

The Grandeur That Was Rome and the Griefs That Haunt Our Lives

Epics are powerful magnets, drawing close the values and qualities a culture prizes, extracting from myth, history, and time itself the character and vision of a people. The most literary of antiquity's epics and the most noble and formidable work of Latin literature, Virgil's *Aeneid* encompasses the fall of Troy; Aeneas's wanderings from Troy to Sicily to Carthage; his ill-fated liaison with Dido, Carthage's queen; his journey to the underworld; and his final arrival in Italy, where fierce warfare with native tribes paves the way for the completion of the task he has been assigned by Jupiter: the founding of Rome.

Virgil's celebration of the great city and the grandeur of Aeneas's civilizing mission is tempered by his sensitivity to the human price such greatness exacts. His rendering of Dido's heartbreaking love for Aeneas, for example, and of the enemy warrior Turnus's death, color his epic with profound, elegiac sympathy for the private griefs great events engender. In the first of the poem's twelve books, Aeneas is moved to tears by a painting of the Trojan war—a war he had survived. In what may be the poem's most telling line—*sunt lacrimae rerum et mentem mortalia tangunt*—he laments the sorrows that surround experience and how mortality touches the heart; the hero's invocation of "tears of pity for a mortal world" (in Sarah Ruden's translation; see page 824) are emblematic of the poem's distinctive emotional tenor.

Written in the reign of the emperor Augustus during the last decade of the author's life, the work, although nearly complete in twelve books, was unfinished at the time of Virgil's death in 19 BC. It remains a whole and satisfying reading experience nonetheless. Although it sings of arms and the man—as its first words (*Arma virumque cano*) famously announce—and of acts of courage and heroism, Virgil's epic is notable for its veneration of Aeneas's Roman virtues: devotion to family, loyalty to homeland, piety, duty.

Line by line, the long poem is intricately composed, yet the sweep of the narrative is stirring as Aeneas overcomes all obstacles to fulfill the imperial destiny he has been divinely charged to enact. The conflict between fate and free will that torments him as he struggles to reconcile his duty to the gods with his private desires underlies the drama of the poem's most famous episodes, such as the anguish of Dido at the hero's departure from Carthage, or the final farewell between Aeneas and his father in

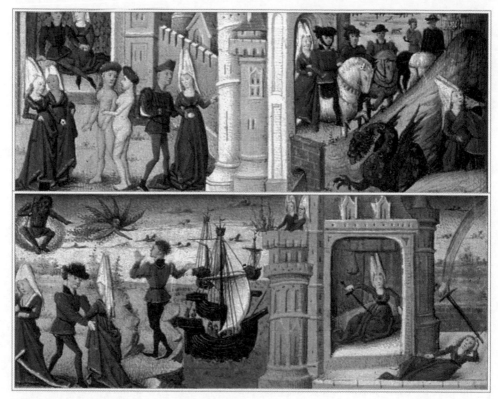

Late medieval depictions of scenes from The Aeneid

the underworld. These unforgettable scenes remain among the most moving in the history of literature, and they endow Virgil's ancient Roman tale with timeless and universal truths.

What: Literature. Antiquity. *When:* Begun ca. 30 BC; unfinished at the author's death. *Editions:* There are many excellent English translations, beginning with John Dryden's (1697) and culminating in a quartet of superb modern renderings by Allen Mandelbaum (1971), Robert Fitzgerald (1983), Robert Fagles (2006), and Sarah Ruden (2008). Any of these four will serve the contemporary reader well, although Ruden's decision to keep to a single metrical line for each line of Latin gives her work a concentration that—combined with her verbal ingenuity and narrative lucidity—makes her version especially pleasing. *Also By: Eclogues* (ca. 37 BC). *Georgics* (ca. 30 BC). *Further Reading:* *Virgil's Aeneid: A Reader's Guide* by David O. Ross. *Virgil: A Study in Civilized Poetry* by Brooks Otis. *Virgil* by David R. Slavitt. *Try:* Homer's *Iliad* and *Odyssey* (see page 386). Dante's *The Divine Comedy* (see page 194). Ariosto's *Orlando Furioso. Adaptations:* Henry Purcell's 1689 opera *Dido and Aeneas* is based upon the fourth book of the *Aeneid.* Hector Berlioz's opera *Les Troyens* also draws from Virgil's epic.

Candide, or Optimism
Voltaire (1694–1778)

The Best of All Possible Worlds

Voltaire, the nom de plume of François-Marie Arouet, was in many ways the guiding spirit of the eighteenth-century European Enlightenment. Through many decades of literary achievement, philosophical argument, and political intrigue, including long periods of exile from Paris, he turned his native irreverence toward all institutions of authority into an enduring legacy that championed the exposure of injustice, the advocacy of toleration, and the advancement of human rights. His collected works run to 150 volumes. But *Candide*, for all its brevity, is his magnum opus.

This darkly comic narrative reads like a surreal version of a medieval book of marvels, in which all the signs and wonders the hero encounters in his travels are calamities, each one more gruesome than the last. At the outset, we are introduced to the innocent young man who gives the book its name. Despite being illegitimately born, Candide lives in a castle in Westphalia in the company of nobility. We soon make the acquaintance of the princess Cunégonde and a tutor named Pangloss. The latter is a master of "metaphysico-theologico-cosmo-nigology" who espouses the principle that we live in the best of all possible worlds. Such teaching, emanating from the theological optimism advanced by Voltaire's contemporary, the philosopher Gottfried Wilhelm Leibniz, was in intellectual

Portrait of Voltaire. 1754

vogue at the time of *Candide*'s writing and is the primary target of the book's scathing and sustained satire. Voltaire's ridicule of this "all's right with the world" thinking was prompted in large measure by the earthquake that struck Lisbon in 1757, resulting in the loss of more than thirty thousand lives. How could such suffering exist in the best of all possible worlds?

Throughout the novella's thirty brief chapters, Candide is taught over and over a lesson strikingly at odds with Pangloss's optimistic instruction, starting with his expulsion from the castle for canoodling with the willing Cunégonde. Thus commences the whirlwind picaresque that leads him around the world—from Germany to Portugal to England to the Americas to Constantinople and beyond—to discover one locus of misery after another. He is conscripted into the army and beset by tempests, shipwreck, and earthquake; he is flogged,

robbed, and tortured by the Inquisition. At first separated from Cunégonde, Pangloss, and other Westphalians, Candide is reunited with them again and again through a series of coincidences and reversals of fortune in which characters left for dead in one country turn up alive, if not so well—one loses a nose, another a buttock—halfway around the globe. As many readers have pointed out, the Monty Python crew would be right at home in the scenes Voltaire portrays.

The novella is more like a musical composition of theme and variation than a conventional literary work: Recurring motifs of hope and despair color but never slow the piece's brisk, brilliant tempo. Although the tale's one hundred or so pages are a catalog of catastrophes, the style is always sprightly. As one critic wrote of Voltaire's prose in general, "His great work is always scored allegro vivace." Made to dance and dangle like a puppet on a string, Candide suffers indignity upon indignity until, at

Illustration from an 1809 edition of Candide

last, reunited with Cunégonde and the others on a modest farm, he surrenders to his small fate. No matter what larger plots history, theology, and nature may devise, Voltaire suggests, our only solace resides in a private plot of our own, as the tale's famous closing line, spoken by Candide, concludes: "We must cultivate our garden."

What: Novella. *When:* 1759. *Editions:* Three English translations appeared in the year of the work's original publication in French, including one by novelist Tobias Smollett; countless others have appeared since. *Also By: Letters Concerning the English Nation* (1733). *Zadig* (1747). *Micromégas* (1752). *Treatise on Toleration* (1763). *Philosophical Dictionary* (1764). *Try: Rasselas* by Samuel Johnson. *Gulliver's Travels* by Jonathan Swift (see page 767). *Jacques the Fatalist* by Denis Diderot. *Adaptation:* Leonard Bernstein's glittering operetta, *Candide,* premiered in 1956 and was revised several times with the help of a stellar cast of writers and lyricists, including Lillian Hellman, Richard Wilbur, Dorothy Parker, and Stephen Sondheim; its music is sheer delight.

Elizabeth and Her German Garden
Elizabeth von Arnim (1866–1941)

Cultivating Friendship

There are writers who conjure a voice so easygoing that the reader is seduced into a kind of literary conversation that feels a lot like friendship. When that chord of intimacy has been struck, any book the author pens can seem like a letter filled with news, gossip, and the consolations of a companionship more restorative than any real-life connection—fraught with the demands and duties of reciprocal attention—could ever be.

With her first book, Elizabeth von Arnim struck such a chord with countless readers. *Elizabeth and Her German Garden* is a slightly fictionalized, comic diary of a woman's year on an estate in Pomerania, delighting in the refuge her private landscape affords.

May 16th. — The garden is the place I go to for refuge and shelter, not the house. In the house are duties and annoyances, servants to exhort and admonish, furniture, and meals; but out there blessings crowd round me at every step.

Inside, too, is her upright Teutonic husband, whom she drolly dubs "The Man of Wrath,"

and for whom she evinces a mixture of irritation, affection, and irreverence. Outdoors, she can escape routine, read favorite books, play with her babies, and revel in the natural allure of flowers, trees, and even weeds. Through Elizabeth's eyes we watch the seasons change, each one bringing in its turn new incidents and personalities—all material for the amused personal journey she portrays with a disarming combination of mockery and gentleness.

Von Arnim's debut created such a sensation and found such a large audience that the character Elizabeth became what today would be called a brand. She went on to write some twenty books, including the beloved novel *The Enchanted April* (1922) and her marvelous autobiography, *All the Dogs of My Life* (1936), but she, and her readers, first found her captivating voice in her cultivated German refuge.

What: Memoir. *When:* 1898. *Also By: The Solitary Summer* (1899). *The Adventures of Elizabeth in Rügen* (1904). *Mr. Skeffington* (1940). *Try: Diary of a Provincial Lady* by E. M. Delafield (see page 206). *Perfume from Provence* by Winifred Fortescue.

Slaughterhouse-Five
Kurt Vonnegut (1922–2007)

The Genre-Blending Antiwar Classic of the 1960s

Kurt Vonnegut, 1972

Many thousands died when Allied planes firebombed Dresden, Germany, in February 1945. Kurt Vonnegut, an American soldier being held there as a prisoner of war, survived because he was confined to *Schlachthof-fünf*—slaughterhouse number five, an airtight, impregnable underground meat locker. When the future author and his fellow prisoners emerged from their shelter, they found a landscape of unimaginable destruction and were put to work unearthing corpses from the ruins.

This strange and compelling novel is the tale that Vonnegut eventually crafted from the horror of his Dresden experience. Its main character, Billy Pilgrim, resembles Vonnegut in that he, too, is a POW who survives Dresden's immolation thanks to the protection of the slaughterhouse. Although the laying waste of the city is described in just a few sentences, it is the central event of the book; the profound effect *Slaughterhouse-Five* had on its first generation of readers—and its continuing resonance—stems from the elaborate phantasmagorical web that Vonnegut weaves around this gruesome reality.

Before the publication of *Slaughterhouse-Five*, Vonnegut had made a name for himself as a science fiction writer, but the genre's constraints were never really able to contain his imagination. To tell the story of Billy Pilgrim, he juxtaposes the harrowing historical and autobiographical aspects of its inspiration with outrageous—and brilliantly effective—sci-fi elements. One of these is time travel: Billy Pilgrim, we're told early on, is "unstuck in time," and throughout the novel a force beyond his control pulls him from one era of his life to another in chronologically disjointed episodes. From childhood to army service, optometry school to mental hospital (where he receives electroshock treatments), from marriage and suburban prosperity to abduction by aliens in flying saucers, the progress of this pilgrim is most peculiar.

Throughout, the casual, insinuating authorial voice holds the reader rapt as Vonnegut combines the disparate components of his plot into a vivid indictment of the insanity of war and the absurdity of modern ways of life that corrupt both private and public rules of human engagement. The quiet tolling of the phrase "So it goes," which punctuates every death in the novel, expresses Vonnegut's tragic sense of life with a characteristically offhand knowingness.

In *Slaughterhouse-Five*, Vonnegut created an uncompromisingly idiosyncratic, intensely affecting work that not only reflected but also helped shape antiwar and counterculture sentiments of the late 1960s; it remains offbeat and eloquent today.

What: Novel. *When:* 1969. *Also By: Player Piano* (1952). *The Sirens of Titan* (1959). *Mother Night* (1961). *Cat's Cradle* (1963). *God Bless You, Mr. Rosewater* (1965). *Breakfast of Champions* (1973). *Slapstick* (1976). *Jailbird* (1979). *Deadeye Dick* (1982). *Galapagos* (1985). *Bluebeard* (1987). *Hocus Pocus* (1990). *Timequake* (1997). *A Man Without a Country* (2005). *Armageddon in Retrospect* (2008). *Try: Catch-22* by Joseph Heller (see page 362). *War with the Newts* by Karel Capek. *Adaptation:* Michael Sacks, Ron Leibman, and Valerie Perrine star in the 1972 film, directed by George Roy Hill. *Footnote:* The asteroid "25399 Vonnegut" is named in the author's honor.

Girl in Hyacinth Blue

A NOVEL

Susan Vreeland (1946–2017)

A Fiction Faithful to the Spirit of Vermeer

How little of our life makes it out into the world. Hour by quiet hour, we sail seas of desire and dread, expectation and anxiety, wish and disillusion, as we go through the undistinguished motions that describe us publicly to our friends and neighbors, our colleagues and coworkers, even the members of our family. The drama of our private voyage is seldom made manifest in a way that envisions the value we attach to it. It was the genius of the Dutch master Johannes Vermeer to capture such modest yet intense meaning on his canvases, in household scenes of unremarkable events that nonetheless portray the hopes and hesitations of the heart.

In this lovely and absorbing book, Susan Vreeland traces a putative Vermeer creation—*Girl in Hyacinth Blue*—backward in time through three centuries, from its theft by a Nazi officer through the hands of several owners to the studio of the artist himself. In a series of linked stories, Vreeland conveys the private lives and inscrutable emotions for which the mysterious, evocative figure of the painting stands as an emblem. Each story details a domestic drama in which "the momentous ordinary," in the author's phrase, is honored and ennobled, even as its characters—a family of Dutch Jews celebrating Passover the year before their deportation; a devoted couple consoled by the embrace of their long marriage; Vermeer's daughter Magdalena, the model for the girl in the portrait—fall under the sway of history's calamities and time's indifference. What remains, Vreeland tells us, of their "loneliness or suffering or grief," or, in the end, their love, is what has been, as Magdalena realizes, "borrowed by an artist to be seen by other people throughout the years who would never see them face to face." Like the real paintings that are its inspirations, *Girl in Hyacinth Blue* is a quietly astonishing articulation of the evanescent emotions that convey enduring human truths.

What: Novel. *When:* 1999. *Also By: The Passion of Artemesia* (2002). *The Forest Lover* (2004). *Luncheon of the Boating Party* (2007). *Further Reading: Johannes Vermeer* by Arthur K. Wheelock Jr. *A Study of Vermeer* by Edward Snow. *Try: A Coin in Nine Hands* by Marguerite Yourcenar. *Girl with a Pearl Earring* by Tracy Chevalier. *Adaptation:* A Hallmark Hall of Fame adaptation, titled *Brush with Fate* and starring Ellen Burstyn and Glenn Close, appeared in 2003.

Holy Land

A SUBURBAN MEMOIR

D. J. Waldie (born 1948)

The Consolation of Tract Housing

This book is a remarkable paradox: One of the quirkiest, most original, most poignant books published in the 1990s, its inspiration springs from the blandest of muses—the American suburb. And not the affluently disenchanted sort of community whose emotional tangles have been so lovingly conjured by Cheever and Updike, but rather Lakewood, California, at "the extreme southeast corner of Los Angeles County"—an example of the mass-produced, mid-twentieth-century "new" suburb that's older than all of them but the original, Levittown, New York. Born in Lakewood, D. J. Waldie still lived there at the time of the writing of *Holy Land* some four decades later, "in a 957-square-foot house of wood frame and stucco"—"a tract house on a block of other tract houses in a neighborhood of even more."

Composed in 316 short bits, some only a sentence or two long, none more than a page, the book details the history of Lakewood's development, from the financing of the land purchase to the clearing of the plots, the marking off of streets, and the erection of houses in a frenzy of construction efficiency. It tells us, glancingly, about Waldie's neighbors (conformity of architecture doesn't eliminate personal eccentricity), his boyhood, parking lots, the shopping center, his father's death, his career in Lakewood's public administration, his Catholic faith. The puzzle pieces cohere in a nearly tactile configuration as a strange and mysterious immanence.

"There was very little that distinguished any of us living here," Waldie writes toward the end of *Holy Land*, a book that belies the truth of his statement. Although it's labeled as such, to call it a memoir does not quite do justice to the magic it works, invoking the numinous in the anonymous through an almost sacramental act of attention. It is that rarest of testaments, a summoning of spirits both happy and humble, or, as Waldie put it after its publication, "It's about longing for what you already have."

What: Memoir. Culture. *When:* 1996. *Also By: Where We Are Now: Notes from Los Angeles* (2004). *Try: Landscape in Sight: Looking at America* by John Brinckerhoff Jackson. *Where I Was From* by Joan Didion.

The Color Purple
Alice Walker (born 1944)

Spirit from Flesh

Dear God,
I am fourteen years old. I am I have always been a
good girl. Maybe you can give me a sign letting me
know what is happening to me.

Those words belong to Celie, a poor African American girl in rural Georgia in the 1930s. Her letters, first to God and then to her younger sister, Nettie, make up the largest portion of *The Color Purple* (letters to Celie from Nettie, who escapes from the South and finds work with a missionary group in Africa, make up the rest). From the outset, the epistolary form of the book creates an intimacy that allows the reader to experience the intense emotions of this searing novel through Celie's voice, by which she marks off in her letters the only space she can claim as her own within the brutal reality of her life.

Repeatedly beaten and raped by her father, by whom she bears two children, Celie is married off to another man who is just as violent. As she makes her way into her twenties, she haltingly begins to take some solace from the circumstantial kinship with other women in her orbit. Chief among these are Sofia, wife to Celie's stepson, whose fearless self-assertion puts her in harm's way again and again but who never falters for long, and Shug Avery, a glamorous, seductive singer—longtime mistress to Celie's husband—whose fortitude and loyalty draw from a deep well of personal resourcefulness.

Not the least of Alice Walker's achievements in this remarkable book is the vividness with which these people are brought to life by the words of the unschooled Celie. Slowly, through the hesitant articulation of her letters, she discovers a world in which comfort and compassion are present in the influence of these other women. Nettie, absent from her sister's life for years, joins the circle as well

Alice Walker, 1989

when Shug leads Celie to a large packet of correspondence her husband had hidden from her. Through her sister's distant but loving intercession, Celie learns unsuspected truths about her past and her identity, prompting her, about two-thirds of the way through the book, to indict the indifference of providence:

My daddy lynch. My mama crazy. All my little
half-brothers and sisters no kin to me. My children
not my sister and brother. Pa not pa.
You must be sleep.

That's her last letter to God until the very end of the novel, when the sign she prayed for at the start seems to at last be coming into view.

Published in 1982, *The Color Purple* won the Pulitzer Prize and the National Book Award, and became a cultural phenomenon beyond the literary realm through a feature film and a Broadway musical, both broadly acclaimed. Although it's often rightly celebrated for its forthright attention to racism and violence against women, Walker's book has a moral and emotional power that is not defined solely by specific issues, for Celie's experience in forging her character in threatening and often terrible situations is as perilous and profound as any soldier's baptism by fire in a different kind of novel. Harrowing and revelatory, *The Color Purple* fulfills the intent the author described for it: "to explore the difficult path of someone who starts out in life already a spiritual captive, but who, through her own courage and the help of others, breaks free into the realization that she, like Nature itself, is a radiant expression of the heretofore perceived as quite distant Divine."

What: Novel. *When:* 1982. *Awards:* Pulitzer Prize for Fiction, 1983. National Book Award for Fiction, 1983. *Also By:* Fiction: *The Third Life of Grange Copeland* (1970); *Meridian* (1976); *The Temple of My Familiar* (1989); *Possessing the Secret of Joy* (1992). Nonfiction: *In Search of Our Mothers' Gardens: Womanist Prose* (1983). *Try: Their Eyes Were Watching God* by Zora Neale Hurston (see page 397). *I Know Why the Caged Bird Sings* by Maya Angelou (see page 20). *Beloved* by Toni Morrison (see page 569). *Adaptations:* The 1985 film, directed by Steven Spielberg, stars Whoopi Goldberg, Oprah Winfrey, and Danny Glover. The Broadway musical, with book by Marsha Norman and music and lyrics by Stephen Bray, Brenda Russell, and Allee Willis, premiered in 2005.

The Compleat Angler

OR, THE CONTEMPLATIVE MAN'S RECREATION

Izaak Walton (1593–1683)

A Treatise on How to Fish—and How to Live

In the 350 years since it was first published, *The Compleat Angler* has rarely if ever been out of print. It has been said to be the third most frequently reissued book in the English language (after the Bible and the works of Shakespeare). It is an excellent instruction manual, offering timeless how-to fishing advice, but could there possibly be enough aspiring fishermen and fisherwomen to account for its phenomenal popularity? Probably not. The explanation for its enduring appeal must lie elsewhere, and perhaps no one has expressed it better than novelist (and ardent fisherman) Thomas McGuane: "The Compleat Angler is not about how to fish but about how to be. [Walton] spoke about an amiable mortality and rightness on the earth that has been envied by his readers" throughout the centuries.

Walton casts his book in the form of conversations. It begins on the first day of May when three sportsmen meet while walking on a road through the English countryside. As the hunter (Venator), the fowler (Auceps), and the angler (Piscator), compare their recreations, the latter expounds on the merits of fishing in a way that ties the character of his pastime to the quality of his tranquil nature. Later, Piscator talks with a novice fisherman and describes how he catches and prepares various types of fish. In addition to angling lore, the book is laced with songs and poems, recipes and moral prescriptions, anecdotes and quotations. With Piscator as his spokesman, Walton sings the praises of quiet country living and explains how a true angler is an ideally contemplative and indeed virtuous individual: "He that hopes to be a good Angler must not only bring an inquiring, searching, observing wit, but he must bring a large measure of hope and patience . . . ; but having once got and practiced [the art], then doubt not . . . it will prove to be so pleasant, that it will prove to be like virtue, a reward to itself."

By trade, Walton was proprietor of a London ironmonger's shop. Yet he associated with learned men, including the poet John Donne, who, in addition to being the vicar of

Walton's church, also became his friend and fishing companion. *The Life and Death of Dr. Donne* (1640), written to appear with a collection of Donne's sermons, launched Walton's career as one of the first English biographers, a career forever overshadowed by his literary celebration of the angling life.

What: Sports. Nature. Philosophy. *When:* 1653. *Edition:* The 1997 Ecco Press edition features Arthur Rackham's illustrations and an introduction by Thomas McGuane. *Further Reading:* In *The Complete Angler: A Connecticut Yankee Follows in the Footsteps of Walton*, James Prosek recounts his modern pilgrimage to England to fish the same waters Izaak Walton fished. *Try: To Know a River* by Roderick Haig-Brown. *The River Why* by David James Duncan. *The Longest Silence: A Life in Fishing* by Thomas McGuane. *Little Rivers: Tales of a Woman Angler* by Margot Page.

"*The Compleat Angler* is about how to dream, and that is why we love it."

—*Howell Raines, author of* Fly Fishing Through the Midlife Crisis

Among Others
Jo Walton (born 1964)

A Book That Loves You Back

Jo Walton's tale of a fifteen-year-old Welsh girl whose imagination is animated by fairies, haunted by her dead twin, and nourished by her prodigious reading of fantasy and science fiction transcends every stereotype that description might suggest. Even readers unfamiliar with the novels and authors the young narrator engages in these pages will find her voice beguiling, her passionate affirmation of reading inspiring, and the stubborn nobility with which she stands off to the side of her peers admirable. Like the most resonant coming-of-age stories, this novel in the form of a diary—covering several months as 1979 turns into 1980—transforms solitude into life-enhancing fictional tidings.

Her name is Morwenna Phelps Markova, and she attends an English boarding school named Arlinghurst, to which she has been sent to escape the baleful influence of her half-mad mother. Morwenna is known as Mori to her friends and "Commie" (by dint of her Russian-tinged surname) and "Crip" or "Hopalong" (because of the permanent leg injury she suffered in the accident that killed her sister) to the more unfriendly of her schoolmates.

Longing for home and the affection of her aunt and grandfather, what Mori misses most is the Welsh countryside, where she and her sister communed with the fairies who enchanted their childhood. The spirit of Arlinghurst is neither magical nor familiar. "There's no chance for anything to become imbued, to come alive through fondness," she remarks of the anonymity of the school's institutional furnishings and matter-of-fact routine. "Nothing here is aware, no chair, no cup. Nobody can get fond of anything."

What saves her are her books. "If you love books enough, books will love you back," she writes. The volumes she is enamored of are largely classic works of science fiction and fantasy—novels by Robert Heinlein (see page 360) and Frank Herbert (see page 367), Susan

Cooper and Anne McCaffrey, Ursula K. Le Guin (see page 468) and C. S. Lewis (see page 484), Robert Silverberg and James Tiptree Jr. (see page 790), Roger Zelazny and J. R. R. Tolkien (see page 792). Although her literary voraciousness also extends to Mary Renault and Josephine Tey (see page 776), the dialogues of Plato (see page 627) and T. S. Eliot's *Four Quartets* (see page 249), it's her appetite for speculative fiction that leads her, through the good offices of two librarians, to a circle of like-minded readers who provide sympathetic points of connection.

Like Wordsworth's *Prelude* (see page 871), *Among Others* details the growth of an imagination, showing how it is impaired, restored,

and strengthened by experience. And like the Welsh landscape Mori cherishes, Walton's book is infused with a bit of magic—the kind by which a fictional character becomes a friend for life as her struggles, both great and small, become our own.

What: Novel. *When:* 2010. *Also By: Tooth and Claw* (2003). *Farthing* (2006). *Ha'penny* (2007). *Half a Crown* (2008). *Further Reading:* The story provides dozens of suggestions, but Mori's enthusiasm is sure to make you want to consider these two: *Pilgrimage* by Zenna Henderson and *The Wind's Twelve Quarters* by Ursula K. Le Guin. *Try: I Capture the Castle* by Dodie Smith (see page 730). *Unexplained Laughter* by Alice Thomas Ellis. *The Fortress of Solitude* by Jonathan Lethem.

■ For Gertrude Chandler Warner's *The Boxcar Children*, see page 435.

The Element of Lavishness
LETTERS OF SYLVIA TOWNSEND WARNER & WILLIAM MAXWELL, 1938–1978
Sylvia Townsend Warner (1893–1978) and William Maxwell (1908–2000)

Two Writer's Writers Write to Each Other

The novelist William Maxwell was for decades the fiction editor of *The New Yorker*. During his tenure at the magazine, one of his favorite authors was Sylvia Townsend Warner, an estimable woman of English letters, famous for the novel *Lolly Willowes*, whose stories became a staple of the periodical. Maxwell and Warner's happy and profound literary friendship is chronicled in their copious correspondence, collected here in a feast of perception and expression that will delight any devoted reader, even one unfamiliar with the works of the authors. From descriptions of hurricanes, blackouts, and other dramatic occurrences to accountings of mundane matters of domestic aggravation, from rites of private passage to passages of exquisite writing, from details of familial relationships to painstaking tinkerings with the nuts and bolts of literary work, this marvelous volume is an extraordinary testament to the powers and passions of the written word. Its episodic unfolding and the seductive

cadence of its conversation—a polite ping-pong of works and days—make it an ideal bedside book.

The Element of Lavishness (the title comes from Maxwell's characterization of the artistry Warner layered into her personal correspondence) is edited by Michael Steinman, who also supplies an excellent introduction. Steinman performed the same tasks in putting together *The Happiness of Getting It Down Right*, twenty years of letters between Maxwell and another of his *New Yorker* short story virtuosos, the Irishman Frank O'Connor. That volume is every bit as rewarding as this one: What starts as a book about words and writing grows into one about friendship and families, exuding all kinds of joy—not least, of course, the one its title celebrates. Both books of correspondence are inspiring, clever and wise, life enhancing.

What: Literature. Writing. *When:* 2001. *Also By: The Diaries of Sylvia Townsend Warner* (1994). *I'll Stand By You: Selected Letters of Sylvia Townsend Warner and Valentine Ackland* (1998). *What There Is to Say We*

Have Said: The Correspondence of Eudora Welty and William Maxwell (2011). *Try: Holmes-Laski Letters: The Correspondence of Mr. Justice Holmes and Harold J.* *Laski, 1916–1935* (see page 504). *The Habit of Being: Letters of Flannery O'Connor* (see page 505). *One Art: Letters* by Elizabeth Bishop.

Beautiful Swimmers

WATERMEN, CRABS AND THE CHESAPEAKE BAY

William W. Warner (1920–2008)

The Surprising Life and Culture of the Atlantic Blue Crab

"A book about crabs? Don't go away quite yet," began this book's original review in the *New York Times*. Since the title does sound like it could belong to a speech at a particularly boring Chamber of Commerce luncheon, the advice to linger is well placed, for *Beautiful Swimmers: Watermen, Crabs and the Chesapeake Bay* is wonderfully good reading. Indeed, in 1977, this entertaining, observant, and elegantly composed volume won a Pulitzer Prize and has remained a cult favorite ever since.

Officially dubbed *Callinectes sapidus* (the first word combines the Greek roots for "beautiful" and "swimmer," and the second is Latin, aptly enough, for "tasty"), the Chesapeake blue crab is the lifeblood of a huge commercial fishing industry. Lifelong proximity to its practitioners left Warner with a desire to understand the lore layered into their distinctive lingo, as in "That's where the doublers are at, hiding in the stumps," or "Get the Jimmy, but not the sook." Immersing himself in his subject, Warner rose at 2:00 AM to work with Bay watermen on their boats, learned how they pick a place to set wire-mesh traps, studied the rationale behind the trap's ingenious design, and picked up just about everything there is to know about the crabs and their habitat. Combining an environmentalist's respect for the intricacies of ecosystems, a naturalist's wonder at curious creatures, and a raconteur's sense of character and tale-telling (think Rachel Carson meets Annie Dillard meets Joseph Mitchell), Warner's book is a marvelous account of natural history, human resourcefulness, and the lore and tradition that enhances both.

What: Nature. *When:* 1976. *Edition:* An introduction by novelist John Barth, also a Maryland native, was added in 1987; a new afterword by the author in 1994. *Award:* Pulitzer Prize for General Nonfiction, 1977. *Also By: Distant Water: The Fate of the North Atlantic Fisherman* (1983). *Into the Porcupine Cave and Other Odysseys* (1999). *Try: Spartina* by John Casey (see page 136). *The Log from the Sea of Cortez* by John Steinbeck. *Pilgrim at Tinker Creek* by Annie Dillard (see page 224). *Oranges* by John McPhee (see page 540).

All the King's Men

Robert Penn Warren (1905–1989)

Personal and Political

All the King's Men has long been regarded as the finest novel about American politics, and rightly so. Robert Penn Warren's account of the rise and fall of Willie Stark is an absorbing portrait of a self-made populist whose early idealism is corrupted by his gift for getting power and his skill at leveraging it. That Stark's transformation is as necessary as it is relentless is part of the book's ruthless intelligence. On his path to the governorship of an unnamed southern state, Stark, whose character and career resemble those of the historical Huey "Kingfish" Long of Louisiana, learns to complement his larger-than-life charms with every opportunistic weapon that his henchmen can point at political enemies (and sometimes friends).

This absorbing tale is narrated by a cynical but deeply thoughtful political reporter named Jack Burden, whose training as a historian makes him an especially valuable Stark operative, research skills being helpful in digging up relevant dirt.

It all began, as I have said, when the Boss, sitting in the black Cadillac which sped through the night, said to me (to Me who was what Jack Burden, the student of history, had grown up to be), "There is always something."

And I said, "Maybe not on the Judge."

And he said, "Man is conceived in sin and born in corruption and he passeth from the stink of the didie to the stench of the shroud. There is always something."

Jack's story runs in counterpoint to Willie's throughout the novel, and his investigations into the life of a nineteenth-century ancestor enrich his meditations on the consequences of his own action in the present. His long and unresolved relationship with his childhood sweetheart, Anne Stanton, daughter of Governor Stark's predecessor, adds both narrative and emotional complexity.

The private intricacy of Jack's moral education adds to the resonance of the novel. Like Shakespeare, Warren understands that the loyalties and betrayals of politics are not functions of government but manifestations of human nature, and, as such, are fertile ground for insights into it. Indeed, one of the abiding pleasures of the novel is its rich store of memorable wisdom—not only from Jack, but from Willie and others—on everything under the sun, from the particular virtue of old friendships to the nature of love, from the transformative nature of love to the character of laughter and toothaches. Here's the governor on the law: "It's like a single-bed blanket on a double bed and three folks in the bed and a cold night. There ain't ever enough blanket to cover the case, no matter how much pulling and

Poster for the 1949 film

hauling, and somebody is always going to nigh catch pneumonia."

Warren's novel is at its core not just about how power reveals the character of those who wield it, but also about the fickleness of those who cede to them the right to do so. As such, it is a chilling reminder of the precariousness of the commonweal, for Willie Stark, in his charisma as well as his carelessness, represents—as the author himself would put it several years after the novel's writing—"the kind of doom that democracy may invite upon itself." Which makes *All the King's Men* as relevant now as it's ever been.

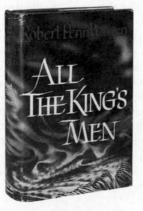

What: Novel. *When:* 1946. *Award:* Pulitzer Prize for Fiction, 1947. *Also By:* Novels: *Night Rider* (1939); *At Heaven's Gate* (1943); *World Enough and Time* (1950); *A Place to Come To* (1977). Poetry: *The Collected Poems of Robert Penn Warren* (1998). *Further Reading: Huey Long* by T. Harry Williams. *Try: The Last Hurrah* by Edwin O'Connor. *The Years of Lyndon Johnson: Means of Ascent* by Robert A. Caro (see page 131). *The Earl of Louisiana* by A. J. Liebling. *Adaptations:* Although not completely faithful to the novel, Robert Rossen's 1949 film won three Oscars, including Best Actor for Broderick Crawford in the role of Willie Stark. The 2006 remake, starring Sean Penn, was not as successful with audiences or critics.

Up from Slavery
Booker T. Washington (1856–1915)

A Study in Self-Reliance

There is a plaque on a bronze statue on the grounds of Tuskegee University, the institution Booker T. Washington built, that reads, "He lifted the veil of ignorance from his people and pointed the way to progress through education and industry." A renowned educator and orator, he lifted that veil not just by ideas and eloquence, but in large degree by hand.

"My life had its beginning in the midst of the most miserable, desolate, and discouraging surroundings," he writes on the first page of his remarkable life story. Born into slavery on a Virginia plantation a few years before the Emancipation Proclamation, Washington would eventually, and improbably, become Tuskegee's guiding light, shaping its growth, between its founding in 1881 and his death some three decades later, from a one-room shanty into a vibrant, well-endowed campus on which hundreds of staff served thousands of students. *Up from Slavery* recounts his stops along the way: his work in salt furnaces and coal mines; his valuable employment in the household of Mrs. Viola Ruffner; his struggle for an education, including his five-hundred-mile trek, a good part of it by foot, to the Hampton Institute, where he worked as a janitor to pay his way, and where he joined the staff when his schooling was complete. As teacher, president of Tuskegee, and increasingly prominent public figure, Washington preached that blacks should work toward self-improvement and strive for economic independence before social equality. His focus on industry and vocational skills—carpentry, printing, and the like—and his attention to manners and personal hygiene—he memorably invokes "the gospel of the tooth-brush"—put him at odds with intellectuals like W. E. B. Du Bois, who viewed Washington's programs as accommodating existing power structures rather than challenging them. Yet Washington's embrace of the pragmatic over the utopian gave his message a purchase on reality the pronouncements of his detractors often lacked: "No race can prosper

Booker T. Washington, ca. 1910

till it learns that there is as much dignity in tilling a field as in writing a poem."

Despite the mythic arc of his autobiography, it is told simply, almost conversationally, and never loses sight of essential tasks. As novelist Ishmael Reed (see page 663) writes, introducing one edition of the book, "Washington was a practical man. *Up from Slavery* is full of practical advice about everything from growing vegetables to selling bricks." Still, beneath its veneer of common sense and its varnish of experience, his life story evokes a previously unimaginable future for a people whose present was a prison erected by the past. It continues to teach the lesson that its author learned firsthand: There is no more potent fuel for the engine of idealism than getting things done in the world, and no greater freedom than being ready, willing, and able to get them done on one's own account.

What: Autobiography. *When:* 1901. *Also By: The Story of My Life and Work* (1900). *My Larger Education* (1911). *The Man Farthest Down* (1912). *Further Reading: Up from History: The Life of Booker T. Washington* by Robert J. Norrell. *Try: Narrative of the Life of Frederick Douglass, an American Slave* by Frederick Douglass (see page 233). *The Souls of Black Folk* by W. E. B. Du Bois (see page 235).

The Double Helix

A PERSONAL ACCOUNT OF THE DISCOVERY OF THE STRUCTURE OF DNA

James D. Watson (born 1928)

A Candid, Exciting Chronicle of Ambition and Discovery

Deoxyribonucleic acid—DNA—is the building block of life. Found in the nucleus of every cell, it carries an organism's genetic instructions, and since it enables the transmission of those instructions from one generation to the next, DNA is often called "the molecule of heredity." In 1953, English zoologist James Watson, who was only twenty-four years old at the time, and Francis Crick, twelve years his senior, discovered that the DNA molecule is shaped like a double helix—that is, like a twisted ladder or a spiral staircase. This turned out to be one of the most important scientific accomplishments in history, and it earned Watson and Crick a Nobel Prize in 1962 (a third scientist who had done related research, Maurice Wilkins, shared the award).

In 1968, Watson published this candid, page-turning account of his and Crick's momentous discovery. Exuding the author's brash ego, unrelenting drive, and often unchecked opinions, The Double Helix eschews the scholarly decorum readers might expect; nonetheless—or perhaps because of these qualities—it is among the best and most influential books ever written about science. As Nobel Prize–winning physicist and bestselling author Richard P. Feynman (see page 272) observed, Watson's narrative admirably captures "how it feels to have that frightening and beautiful experience of making a scientific discovery." In Watson's own view, that frightening and beautiful experience was an "adventure characterized both by youthful arrogance and by the belief that the truth, once found, would be simple as well as pretty." Involving numerous personality conflicts and controversies, and, in Watson's apt assessment, "complicated by the contradictory pulls of ambition and the sense of fair play," The Double Helix is both the documentary of an invaluable discovery and a riveting human drama.

What: Science. Memoir. *When:* 1968. *Also By: Genes, Girls, and Gamow: After the Double Helix* (2002). *Avoid Boring People: Lessons from a Life in Science* (2007). *Further Reading: What Mad Pursuit: A Personal View of Scientific Discovery* by Francis Crick. *Try: Rosalind Franklin: The Dark Lady of DNA* by Brenda Maddox. *The Eighth Day of Creation* by Horace Freeland Judson. *Adaptation: The Race for the Double Helix* was a 1987 BBC dramatization of Watson's book and related events. *Footnote:* In 1999 *The Double Helix* placed seventh on the Modern Library's list of the 100 best nonfiction works published in English since 1900.

The Loved One

Evelyn Waugh (1903–1966)

A Macabre Masterpiece

Evelyn Waugh was one of the leading British novelists of the twentieth century. His early works, such as Decline and Fall (1928) and Vile Bodies (1930), made him famous as a satirist of London's "Bright Young Things." He later used his experiences during World War II as the basis of his Sword of Honour Trilogy (1952–61). Nowadays, because of the acclaimed early 1980s television series, he is probably best known as the author of Brideshead Revisted (1945).

Waugh's comic novels are generally distinguished by their combination of hilarity and craftsmanship: They are savagely funny, impeccably well written, and flawlessly plotted. One of the best examples of his artistry is The Loved One, a perfect little macabre concoction that lampoons what was once famously called "the American way of death." Two cemeteries are at the heart of the action. One is Whispering Glades Memorial Park, Hollywood's "great necropolis." The other is the Happier Hunting Grounds, a pet cemetery that neighbors Whispering Glades. Dennis Barlow, a poet and newly arrived member of the British ex-pat film colony that is another target of the book's satire, ends up working as a pet mortician after he gives up his job as a scriptwriter at the all-powerful Megalopolitan Studios. Dennis has fallen for Aimée Thanatogenos, crematorium cosmetician at the Glades. But Aimée is the "honey-baby" of Mr. Joyboy, embalmer extraordinaire. Their love triangle raises the ultimate question: Who will end up "The Loved One"?

Evelyn Waugh as a young man

Waugh's black comedy received a notable rave from Wolcott Gibbs, who wrote in *The New Yorker*, "Never before that I can remember has a talent of such austere and classic design been applied to such monstrous vulgarities. . . . It is certainly a work of art, as rich and subtle and unnerving as anything its author has ever done."

What: Novel. *When:* 1948. *Also By: A Handful of Dust* (1934). *Scoop* (1938). *Put Out More Flags* (1942). *The Ordeal of Gilbert Pinfold* (1957). *Further Reading: Fathers and Sons: The Autobiography of a Family,* by Waugh's grandson Alexander Waugh. *Try: The Day of the Locust* by Nathanael West. *The American Way of Death* by Jessica Mitford. *Adaptation:* Tony Richardson's 1965 film stars Robert Morse and Jonathan Winters.

A Coffin for King Charles
THE TRIAL AND EXECUTION OF CHARLES I
C. V. Wedgwood (1910–1997)

The Unhappy End of "the Happiest King in Christendom"

On a cold afternoon in 1649, after many years of civil war and several days of chaotic judicial proceedings, King Charles I of England laid his neck across the executioner's block and was beheaded in a single stroke. It was an event so unimaginable, it left Britain, and indeed the whole of Europe, thunderstruck. Kings had been murdered before, but none had ever been brought to trial by his own people, and, as king still crowned, executed.

How had it come to that? Only a decade earlier Charles had described himself as "the happiest King in Christendom," ruling over what then seemed a singularly blessed dominion. But everything had changed swiftly as religious controversy led to defiance and defiance to armed rebellion, ending finally with the forty-eight-year-old king a prisoner of the rebel army. Even then, however, the murder of the king seemed unthinkable. Only the few most radical agitators had ever dared hint at taking such a course. But during the ten tumultuous weeks leading to the day of execution, what Oliver Cromwell, leader of the opposition to Charles, was to call "providence and necessity" shaped events to their staggering conclusion.

Dame Cicely Veronica Wedgwood focuses her thrilling book on just those two and a half momentous months. The remarkable central participants (chief among them, the inscrutable Cromwell and the unshakably dignified, suddenly eloquent monarch); the exciting sequence of events, including, especially, the unprecedented, ill-considered, yet awe-inspiring trial; the shifting hopes and fears of the key factions; the trembling astonishment

Depiction of the 1649 execution of Charles I

that seemed to grip the time: These are the elements that Wedgwood brilliantly crafts into a powerful and unforgettable work of narrative history.

What: History. *When:* 1964. *Edition:* Published in Britain as *The Trial of Charles I. Also By: The Thirty Years War* (1938). *Oliver Cromwell* (1939). *Velvet Studies: Essays on Historical and Other Subjects* (1946). *The Great Rebellion, Volume 1: The King's Peace, 1637–1641* (1955); *Volume 2: The King's War, 1641–1647* (1958). *Try: The Century of Revolution, 1603–1714* and *The World Turned Upside Down,* both by Christopher Hill. *Footnote:* Wedgwood translated from the German the first English edition of Nobel Laureate Elias Canetti's enormous novel, *Auto-da-Fé.*

Simone Weil: An Anthology
Simone Weil (1909–1943)
Edited by Siân Miles

The Devotions of a Modern Saint

Albert Camus considered her "the only great spirit of our time." T. S. Eliot felt she was possessed by "a kind of genius akin to that of the saints." Flannery O'Connor called her "a mystery that should keep us all humble." Simone Weil brought together in one short life political and mystical yearnings that make her seem an emblem of the soul in the midst of the twentieth century's tumult of doubt and brutality. Born in Paris to Jewish parents, she combined physical frailty with spiritual determination as a student of philosophy, a secondary school teacher, a workers' advocate, a laborer, a pacifist, an ineffectual combatant in the Spanish Civil War, and a near-convert to Roman Catholicism. No label does justice to the fierce intelligence she trained on passing circumstance and enduring truths. Here's a sample:

At the bottom of the heart of every human being, from earliest infancy until the tomb, there is something that goes on indomitably expecting, in the teeth of all experience of crimes committed, suffered, and witnessed, that good and not evil will be done to him. It is this above all that is sacred in every human being.

Her voluminous writing, a generous portion of which is collected in Siân Miles's superbly edited *Simone Weil: An Anthology*, engages politics, religion, literature, factory work, and metaphysics in sharp and surprising ways. Weil's essays, letters, and prose meditations are illuminating, enigmatic, and troubling, for they stir up the questions that haunt our own lives, but which, drowned by the business of our days, seldom break the surface of our attention. Reading her brilliant consideration of Homer's *Iliad*, "The Poem of Force," might just change your conception of life, so revelatory is her vision of how violence distorts the mind and constrains its very notion of reality; its consideration of the epic's

Simone Weil, ca. 1935–1940

moral dimension is profoundly moving, penetrating the mists of antiquity that enshroud the poem to reveal how human strength and cunning first came face-to-face with the ethical imperatives that entwine mortality and morality.

What: Philosophy. Religion & Spirituality. *When:* Collecting works originally published in French beginning in 1934. *Edition:* English language anthology, edited by Siân Miles, 1986. *Also By: Gravity and Grace* (1947). *Waiting for God* (1950). *The Notebooks of Simone Weil* (two volumes, 1951–56). *Further Reading: Simone Weil: A Modern Pilgrimage* by Robert Coles. *Simone Weil* by Francine du Plessix Gray. *Try: A Testament to Freedom: The Essential Writings of Dietrich Bonhoeffer.*

The Invisible Man
H. G. Wells (1866–1946)

A Seminal and Spellbinding Science Fiction Classic

Among the most prolific authors in the history of English letters (he is alleged to have written more words than Shakespeare and Dickens combined), H. G. Wells is best remembered for the groundbreaking quartet of science fiction tales he published in rapid succession in the last decade of the nineteenth century: *The Time Machine* (1895), *The Island of Doctor Moreau* (1896), *The Invisible Man* (1897), and *The War of the Worlds* (1898). Each is a penetrating novel of ideas dressed in a thrilling story of experiment gone awry.

"My fantastic stories," Wells once wrote, "do not pretend to deal with possible things. They aim indeed only at the same amount of conviction as one gets in a gripping good dream." That's certainly an accurate description of the target hit by *The Invisible Man*—although, by the end of the book, deliciously

entertaining as it is, the word "nightmare" might seem more appropriate than "dream."

H. G. Wells, 1896

It begins on a wintry day one February when an irritable stranger arrives in the English village of Iping. He makes his way to an inn called Coach and Horses and takes a room. At first all bundled up, he eventually discards his hat and coat, only to reveal that his whole head is bandaged. It's enough to give the inn's owner a shock. "The poor soul's had an accident or an op'ration or something." Soon enough the invisible mystery behind the stranger's dressing is revealed, as is the "strange and evil experiment" that has trapped him—a young scientist named Griffin—in a terror of his own creation.

Who hasn't imagined what it would be like to roam the world unseen? Like Griffin, we find it easy to imagine "all that invisibility might mean to a man—the mystery, the power, the freedom." Also like Griffin—"Drawbacks I saw none"—we are apt to underestimate the downside. Yet drawbacks there are, from the annoyance of pursuing dogs who can still discern his scent to the futility of his physical desires. After the initial exhilaration of its novelty wears off, Griffin's invisibility grows from liability to curse, while the author shapes a plot that elaborates the clever conceit of an invisible man into a crackerjack cautionary tale of grim and desperate horror.

What: Science Fiction. *When:* 1897. *Also By: The First Men in the Moon* (1901). *The Shape of Things to Come* (1933). *Tono-Bungay* (1909). *Try: The Strange Case of Dr. Jekyll and Mr. Hyde* by Robert Louis Stevenson (see page 759). *Memoirs of an Invisible Man* by H. F. Saint. *Adaptation:* The classic film adaptation of *The Invisible Man* was made in 1933 and stars Claude Rains.

The Collected Stories of Eudora Welty
Eudora Welty (1909–2001)

A Love of Storytelling

No one should close the book on a reading life without having enjoyed Eudora Welty's most famous story, "Why I Live at the P.O.," a rollicking monologue in the voice of Sister, the postmistress of China Grove, Mississippi ("Of course, there's not much mail," she admits). In a dozen pages or so, Sister explains her Fourth of July exit from the family home, prompted by the fireworks set off by the unexpected return of her spoiled sibling, Stella-Rondo, with a previously unannounced child in tow. The reception afforded the prodigal daughter by Mama, Papa-Daddy, and Uncle Rondo fuels the outrage that culminates in Sister's self-imposed exile to her workplace. Imagine a Carol Burnett sketch calibrated by Chekhov and you'll have some idea of the story's revelatory human comedy.

Although she is often stereotyped as a genteel Southern lady who wrote comical yarns,

Eudora Welty, ca. 1945

there's more to Welty than the ample delights of "Why I Live at the P.O." and its ilk. As the forty-one stories in this volume demonstrate, she is an artist of varied gifts and vivid imagination, capable of depicting the quiet tremblings of the inner life, the uncertain consolations of family relations, the manners and matters of small-town society, and the universal relevance of ordinary emotions and experience. Her characters are black and white, young and old, mad and sane; hairdressers, jazz pianists, and traveling salesmen; envious sisters and uncles with questionable impulses; crooks, doctors, and historical figures. One tale is hilarious, the next heart-rending; what they have in common is a magnanimity born of listening closely. There may be no truer description of Welty's genius than the title of Carol S. Manning's 1985 book: *With Ears Opening Like Morning Glories: Eudora Welty and the Love of Storytelling*.

What: Short Stories. **When:** 1980, collecting works written from the mid-1930s to the 1970s. **Edition:** The Library of America's *Eudora Welty: Stories, Essays & Memoir* complements the stories with some choice nonfiction, including her slim but stellar (and bestselling) autobiography, *One Writer's Beginnings.* **Award:** National Book Award, 1983. **Also By:** Welty's novels include *Delta Wedding* (1946), *The Ponder Heart* (1954), and *The Optimist's Daughter* (1972), for which she received a Pulitzer Prize. **Try:** *Collected Stories of William Faulkner. The Collected Stories of Katherine Anne Porter* (see page 636). **Footnote:** The early e-mail software Eudora, developed by Steve Dorner, was named after Welty, who is said to have been flattered and amused by the electronic homage.

....

Boggs: A Comedy of Values
Lawrence Weschler (born 1952)

A Merry Look at a Mischievous Artist—and the Meaning of Money

....

J. S. G. Boggs with a real $20 bill and one of his own creations

Cultural critic, journalist, and intellectual explorer Lawrence Weschler's portrayal of the antics and artistry of J. S. G. Boggs is a beguiling true story that poses fascinating questions about the nature of money, our perception of value, and the character of the trust upon which economic transactions are based. Boggs, you see, is a "money artist": He draws replicas of genuine currency with remarkable facility and considerable precision. He then uses these drawings to pay for services—meals, hotel rooms, and so on. But Boggs is not a counterfeiter: Whenever he initiates a transaction, he explains exactly what his artworks are to the person involved, and if they're not accepted as payment, Boggs happily forks over real dough. If the artist's barter is accepted, however, Boggs insists on receiving exact change—for example, if he offers a drawing of a $100 bill in payment for an $87 dinner, he must receive $13 back (with a receipt!). "It's incredibly difficult to make something that's worth a dollar," Boggs says. "As much as a dollar, only a dollar, exactly a dollar."

A superb reporter and a gifted storyteller with a knack for being in the right place to "[watch] the humdrum suddenly take flight," Weschler narrates how Boggs's money mischief has gotten him into serious trouble with the United States Treasury, the Bank of England, and the Australian Federal Currency Squad. The court actions that have resulted raise questions whose answers prove slippery indeed. Once you begin asking what a dollar is, what paper money really represents, and what its exchange for value signifies, the stakes become considerable, both practically and philosophically. And comically, too: The juxtaposition of bureaucracy's solemnity with Boggs's high spirits is a delight to savor. As Ira Glass, host of *This American Life*, said of this offbeat and witty chronicle, "One thing that makes Lawrence Weschler different from most writers is the sheer glee he communicates. This book is a complete pleasure. It's also a perfect mix of funny and serious."

What: Art. Economics. **When:** Published in book form in 1999, *Boggs* collects several pieces written between 1987 and 1998. **Reading Note:** Skip the preface until you've read the book, then return to it for further leads into this author's intriguing oeuvre. *Also By: Mr. Wilson's Cabinet of Wonder* (1995). *A Wanderer in the Perfect City* (1998). *Vermeer in Bosnia* (2004). *True to Life: Twenty-Five Years of Conversations*

with David Hockney (2008). *Seeing Is Forgetting the Name of the Thing One Sees: Over Thirty Years of Conversations with Robert Irwin* (2008). *Try: Newton and the Counterfeiter* by Thomas Levenson. *The Ransom of Russian Art* by John McPhee.

Black Lamb and Grey Falcon
A JOURNEY THROUGH YUGOSLAVIA
Rebecca West (1892–1983)

An Epic and Eloquent Journey Through History, Politics, Culture, and Human Nature

In the library of monumental works of twentieth-century literature, Marcel Proust's *In Search of Lost Time*, James Joyce's *Ulysses*, Thomas Mann's *The Magic Mountain*, and a handful of others have assumed unassailable positions on the top shelf. You might be surprised to learn that there is a travel book that deserves a place up there with them. Yet by virtue of its scope, its literary artistry, and its profound grasp of the roots and branches of European culture, Rebecca West's account of her journeys through Yugoslavia in the 1930s unquestionably does. At more than a thousand pages, it is an imaginative, keenly intelligent exploration of history, politics, landscape, philosophy, and human nature; it is also an unparalleled personal narrative in which memory and learning are woven into a tapestry of eloquence that is both compelling and magnanimous.

To call it a travel book isn't quite fair: *Black Lamb and Grey Falcon* is in a class by itself, and the country that is its subject no longer exists as such. (Carved out of the defunct Austro-Hungarian Empire in 1918, Yugoslavia, or "The Kingdom of Serbs, Croats, and Slovenes," as it was originally called, subsequently—and violently—broke apart along ethnic and religious lines into half a dozen states.) While West amply conveys the enduring character of the countryside she explores and the cities she visits, including Zagreb and Sarajevo, she also imbues each destination with the "dark waters" of the region's past. Roiled as they are by ancient ethnic animosities and centuries of political oppression from outside forces, these waters run through West's pages,

bringing "the past side-by-side with the present," whether she is describing the personalities and attitudes of her Bosnian and Croatian friends, the dresses being sold in an outdoor market, or the image of Archduke Franz Ferdinand, not long before his 1914 assassination, surveying a hall crammed with thousands of stuffed beasts he has killed as a hunter. West composes novelistic set pieces to explore historical events, only to bring us around again to a startling recognition of her present moment—and, even more startlingly, to reveal to twenty-first-century readers a prophetic sense of the future that would unfold in the decades after the book was composed, not only during World War II, but right through the siege of Sarajevo in the 1990s.

She writes at one point,

Were I to go down into the market-place, armed with the powers of witchcraft, and take a peasant by the shoulders and whisper to him, "In your lifetime, have you known peace?" wait for his answer, shake his shoulders and transform him into his father, and ask him the same question, and transform him in his turn to his father, I would never hear the word "Yes," if I carried my questioning of the dead back for a thousand years.

Throughout this long and brilliant book, and across the hundreds of years that fall into its purview, West shares her own perceptions as they are taking shape, giving her writing the quality of the most stimulating and exhilarating conversation one could ever wish to have.

What: History. Culture. Memoir. *When:* 1941. *Editions:* Originally published in two volumes, West's magnum opus is now available—complete—in a single Penguin paperback. Novelist's Geoff Dyer's introduction to the British Canongate edition is worth seeking out. *Reading Note:* Capacious yet conversational, animated with all sorts of interesting characters, *Black Lamb* can be read in fits and starts across several years with no diminution in its rewards. *Also By:* Fiction: *The Return of the Soldier* (1918); *Harriet Hume* (1929); *The Thinking* Reed (1936); *The Fountain Overflows* (1957). Nonfiction: *St. Augustine* (1933); *The Meaning of Treason* (1949); *The New Meaning of Treason* (1964). Rebecca West: *A Celebration* (1977) is a generous sampler of the remarkable variety of her work. *Try: A Time of Gifts* (see page 269) and *Between the Woods and Water* by Patrick Leigh Fermor. *Danube* by Claudio Magris.

The Hot Rock
Donald E. Westlake (1933–2008)

The Best-Laid Plans

Pure pleasure. That's what you'll find in the pages of Donald Westlake's Dortmunder novels. Comic crime capers featuring a genial, recurring cast of benignly larcenous characters, led by the "dogged but doomed" thief John Dortmunder, they're filled with schemes, mischief, mishaps, and over-the-top plot twists that will surprise even the most imaginative reader. *The Hot Rock*, which charts the theft, re-theft, theft again—there's more, but you get the idea— of a large emerald belonging to a small African nation, was the first in the series and sets the stage for the laugh-out-loud delights that follow.

Joining the dour Dortmunder in his carefully planned, never-quite-perfectly executed exploits—always hatched in the back room of the O. J. Bar and Grill on Manhattan's Amsterdam Avenue—are the inexhaustibly upbeat Andy Kelp, a gifted car thief and technological wizard, and Stan Murch, driver extraordinaire, who is always mentally mapping an itinerary. Through the course of the series, readers will also get to know other recurring characters, such as the inaptly nicknamed enforcer "Tiny" Bulcher,

Murch's cab-driving mom, the fence Arnie Albright, and Dortmunder's winningly sardonic paramour, a supermarket cashier named May.

In a long career, Westlake's output was prodigious—so much so that the tally of his pen names (including, most famously, "Richard Stark" for his celebrated Parker novels) is considerably longer than most authors' list of works. A three-time Edgar Award winner, he was named a Grand Master by the Mystery Writers of America in 1993. Many of his novels (including *The Hot Rock*) have been made into films, and he earned an Academy Award nomination for his script for *The Grifters*, an adaptation of Jim Thompson's novel of that name. But if Dortmunder and company were his only legacy, it would be more than enough. The last book in the series, *Get Real*, was published posthumously in 2009.

What: Mystery & Suspense. *When:* 1970. *Also By: Bank Shot* (1972). *Jimmy the Kid* (1974). *Nobody's Perfect* (1977). *Drowned Hopes* (1990). *Try: Burglars Can't Be Choosers* by Lawrence Block. *Stick* by Elmore Leonard. *Adaptation:* Robert Redford stars as Dortmunder in the 1972 film.

The Age of Innocence
Edith Wharton (1862–1937)

The Secret Agent of Society

Edith Wharton's best fiction is a form of intelligence, a gathering of detailed information that turns revelatory under her persistent and insightful gaze. She wrote about the world she knew—New York high society at the turn of the century, where rules were unbreakable, money

Edith Wharton, ca. 1885

a scion of Manhattan gentry, and both couldn't be happier. But soon May's cousin Ellen arrives from Europe, having left her husband, a Polish aristocrat, and Ellen's failure to abide by the strictures of New York society upsets the elite's delicate balance. Newland's admiration for Ellen's defiance of convention deepens into love, and he wonders if he should break off his engagement to May. The painful paradox Newland faces is one common to Wharton's heroes and heroines: To be free to follow your heart, you have to abandon society—or, more importantly, be abandoned by it. Only a social novelist of the first order understands the meaning of loneliness as well as Wharton does.

Compared with her earlier novel, *The House of Mirth* (1905), in which Wharton exposes the cruelty and capriciousness of old money (it's silent, yes, but demands attention nonetheless), *The Age of Innocence* paints a more nuanced and sympathetic portrait of the upper crust, both ackowledging and exposing the machinations that take place behind its genteel façade. It's a brilliant social critique as well as a sweeping love story; alongside *The House of Mirth*, it stands among the best novels ever written about the unraveling of individual destinies in the seductive—and enduring—bear pit of New York society.

was silent, and retribution for social transgression was severe. Her novels are both art and espionage.

Wharton's maiden name was Jones; all her family members were listed in the very first Social Register, and although it's certainly debatable, the phrase "keeping up with the Joneses" has been said to refer to the wealth of her own father. In *The Age of Innocence*, one of her most enduring novels, the Archers are a family much like the Joneses: well established, influential, spectacularly rich. Newland Archer, a successful lawyer, is engaged to May Welland,

What: Novel. *When:* 1920. *Award:* Pulitzer Prize for Fiction, 1921. *Also By: Ethan Frome* (1911). *The Custom of the Country* (1913). *Old New York* (1924). *Further Reading: Edith Wharton* by R. W. B. Lewis. *Try: Middlemarch* by George Eliot (see page 248). *Washington Square* and *The Portrait of a Lady* by Henry James (see page 409). *Rules of Civility* by Amor Towles. *Adaptation:* Martin Scorsese's 1993 film stars Daniel Day-Lewis, Michelle Pfeiffer, and Winona Ryder.

Charlotte's Web
E. B. White (1899–1985)

"Some Pig!"

Someone once called E. B. White the most companionable of writers, and the adjective fits him like a glove. His conversational genius set the enduring tone of *The New Yorker* in the magazine's formative years, and his unassumingly authoritative personal essays gave the genre a genuine American accent (see "Death of a Pig" or "Here Is New York," for starters).

White's command of literary etiquette was so sure, he could even make entertaining a book of grammar and usage instruction (*The Elements of Style*). In person as in prose, his mastery was modestly worn, and one might easily imagine his taking pleasure in the fact that his legacy will likely rest on the books he wrote for children: *Stuart Little* (1945), *The Trumpet of the Swan* (1970), and, especially, *Charlotte's Web*, which, like the spider at the center of its enchanting narrative, is in a class by itself.

White's book begins with a jarring question: "Where's Papa going with that ax?" It's asked by eight-year-old Fern Arable, who is distressed by her mother's answer: Mr. Arable is on his way to the hoghouse to do away with the runt of the litter born the night before, because, as he will explain, "A weakling makes trouble." After much cajoling, Fern persuades her father to let her raise the pig, whom she names Wilbur. Soon enough, making good on a promise she made to her dad, Fern sells Wilbur to her uncle Homer Zuckerman, and the pig takes up residence down the road in the Zuckerman barn.

There the realities of farm life fall under the spell of the author's invention, as hard facts—the hardest being, of course, that Wilbur's likely destiny is summed up in the words "pork chops"—are transformed into a lovely, funny, and deeply moving fable. The agent of this transformation is a spider named Charlotte A. Cavatica, who uses her gift for words to weave "SOME PIG!" and other messages into her webs, causing a commotion on Zuckerman's farm and saving Wilbur by making him a local celebrity. The collaborative ingenuity of the denizens of the barn—even the rat, Templeton, has his innate greed turned to good use—drives the tale to its satisfying conclusion, while the natural cycle of death and renewal is closely observed. White's attention to nature's truths is surpassed only by his allegiance to the human virtues—friendship, constancy, love—that can temper them. Deservedly beloved, *Charlotte's Web* is both winning and wise, just like its heroine. "After all, what's a life, anyway?" Charlotte says to Wilbur in response to his gratitude.

We're born, we live a little while, we die. A spider's life can't help being something of a mess, with all this trapping and eating flies. By helping you, perhaps I was trying to lift up my life a trifle. Heaven knows anyone's life can stand a little of that.

What: Children's. When: 1952. Award: Newbery Honor, 1953. Also By: One Man's Meat (1942). The Second Tree from the Corner (1954). Letters of E. B. White (1976; revised edition, 2006). Further Reading: E. B. White: A Biography by Scott Elledge. The Annotated Charlotte's Web, introduction and notes by Peter F. Neumeyer. Try: Freddy Goes to Florida by Walter R. Brooks. The Cricket in Times Square by George Selden. Quentin Corn by Mary Stolz. Adaptations: Paramount released an animated film version in 1973; the 2006 live-action film, directed by Gary Winick, features an all-star cast, including Julia Roberts as the voice of Charlotte, and Dakota Fanning as Fern. Best of all is the charming audiobook version, read by the author. Footnote: White was awarded a Pulitzer Prize special citation for the body of his work in 1978.

The Once and Future King
T. H. White (1906–1964)

King Arthur—and Camelot—Come of Age

King Arthur and his court have provided our literature with what may be its richest vein of story. A simple list of the names it encompasses—Arthur and Merlyn, Guenever and Lancelot, Avalon and Camelot—conjures a magical spell of adventure, intrigue, and nobility. No narrative enchanter has made more of its power than T. H. White. In the four novels—*The Sword in the Stone* (1938), *The Queen of Air and Darkness* (1939), *The Ill-Made Knight* (1940), and *The Candle in the Wind* (1958)—collected under the title *The Once and Future King*, White mined the ore of Arthurian tradition and infused it with both erudition and imagination to create a fresh treasury of humor, romance, fantasy, and tragedy.

The spirited comedy of *The Sword in the Stone* is pure pleasure, as the young and less-than-regal Arthur (an adopted orphan in the household of Sir Ector, he is unceremoniously known as "the Wart") grows up in the shadow of Ector's heir, Kay, the future knight whom the Wart expects to serve as squire. The Wart's unforeseen destiny begins to show itself with the appearance of Merlyn, an ancient magician growing younger through time, who becomes the boys' tutor. Knowing Arthur's eventual fate, Merlyn prepares him for it surreptitiously through a series of transformations, turning the Wart into bird, fish, ant, owl, and badger to instruct him in leadership, governance,

and compassion. These metamorphoses—some of the most charming episodes you will ever read—are just one aspect of the series of fantastic quests and encounters that Merlyn orchestrates for Arthur and Kay. Although the author's vast knowledge of medieval customs and culture is lightly worn, it permeates every page of the narrative, delivering a singular mix of history, fantasy, and fun (the last enhanced by White's judicious use of anachronism). When Arthur at last pulls the fabled sword—Excalibur—from the stone, his royal fortune is fully revealed.

Subsequent novels in the quartet depict the new king's attempts to apply Merlyn's lessons about might and right, the founding of the Round Table and the adventures of its knights, Arthur's marriage to Guenever and Guenever's passion for Lancelot, Lancelot's travails, and Arthur's tragic entanglement with his vengeful son Mordred, born of an incestuous union with his cruel and beautiful estranged half-sister Morgause. As we follow Arthur from joyful youth to sorrowful age, the lightheartedness of *The Sword in the Stone* gives way to the

Painting of the Knights of the Round Table by Évrard d'Espinques, ca. 1475

darker currents of the Arthurian—indeed, the human—saga, and the glow of Camelot's glittering aspiration is tarnished with grief. Like a sorcerer worthy of Merlyn's mantle, White has created a book that grows up before our eyes, imbued with all the wonder and emotions a life can hold.

What: Children's. *When:* Published in a single volume as *The Once and Future King*, 1958. *Also By:* White's coda to his quartet, *The Book of Merlyn*, was published posthumously in 1977. Other books include the

autobiography *England Have My Bones* (1936), the wondrous fantasy *Mistress Masham's Repose* (1946), and a translation of a medieval bestiary, *The Book of Beasts* (1957). *Try: Le Morte D'Arthur* by Thomas Malory. *The Crystal Cave* by Mary Stewart. *The Mists of Avalon* by Marion Zimmer Bradley. *Adaptations: The Sword in the Stone* inspired Disney's 1963 animated film of the same name. Lerner and Loewe's Broadway (1960) and Hollywood (1967) musical *Camelot* was drawn from White's complete saga. *Footnote:* The influence of *The Once and Future King* can be felt in much of J. K. Rowling's Harry Potter series.

The Making of the President 1960
Theodore H. White (1915–1986)

The Groundbreaking Chronicle of American Politics in Action

Published little more than a half year after the culmination of the events it narrates, Theodore White's account of the 1960 electoral contest between John F. Kennedy and Richard Nixon was a groundbreaking work of political journalism. Offering unusual insight into campaign strategy, demographic trends, and policy issues, and exhibiting zeal for the political process as well as sympathetic appreciation for the personalities of politicians, White's Pulitzer Prize–winning chronicle was both comprehensive and dramatic.

White once described his Harvard history professors as "a colony of storytellers," and he would ultimately make it his profession to be, in his own words, a "storyteller of elections." Certainly, his reportorial rigor was matched to an artistry that shaped facts into stories with riveting effect, never more than in his study of the Kennedy-Nixon battle, the first of his four *Making of the President* volumes. From the outset, one is captivated by the sheer momentum of his telling. Even though we know the outcome, there is real suspense as we follow the candidates from the first primary in New Hampshire to the long night of uncertainty on November 8. Folding astute forays into history, statistics, and interpretation into his journey along the campaign trail, White creates a narrative that is animated with anecdote, deft characterization, and close observation of—as he aptly puts it—"the mood and the strains, the weariness, elation and uncertainties of the men who sought to lead America in the decade of the sixties."

The author seems ubiquitous, and he brings the passions of the people who pursue the presidency to life in a way no one had previously managed. From the deployment of the extensive Kennedy organization across

Candidate John F. Kennedy and his wife Jacqueline meet Richard Nixon, 1959

the continent to the late-hour revival of Adlai Stevenson's support at the Democratic convention in Los Angeles, from Richard Nixon's mysterious Fifth Avenue rendezvous with fellow Republican Nelson Rockefeller to the televised debates that gave powerful credibility to the vice president's opponent, White charts the path to the presidency with unfailing industry, skill, and intuition. It didn't hurt that the storyteller was blessed by history with a cliffhanger—or with a victor who possessed more than a few of the characteristics of a leading man.

What: History. Politics. *When:* 1961. *Award:* Pulitzer Prize for General Nonfiction, 1962. *Also By:* Three additional *Making of the President* volumes, covering the elections of 1964, 1968, and 1972. *Breach of Faith: The Fall of Richard Nixon* (1975). *In Search of History: A Personal Adventure* (1978). *America in Search of Itself: The Making of the President 1956–1980* (1982). *Try: Report of the County Chairman* by James A. Michener. *Some Honorable Men: Political Conventions 1960–1972* by Norman Mailer. *The Boys on the Bus* by Timothy Crouse.

The Underground Railroad
Colson Whitehead (born 1969)

Reimagining America

A notion crept over her like a shadow: that this station was not the start of the line but its terminus. Construction hadn't started beneath the house but at the other end of the black hole. As if in the world there were no places to escape to, only places to flee.

Colson Whitehead, 2004

The "her" is Cora, a slave who has fled captivity on a Georgia plantation, and she is pondering a ghost tunnel—no one knows when it was dug, or where it leads, or even if it has ever been used—of the underground railway that has carried her, in several stages, toward liberty. Although her rumination here runs to the metaphorical, the railroad in Colson Whitehead's novel is not metaphorical at all: It's an actual network of underground tracks, trunk lines, and spurs, with real locomotives and train cars and conductors. Its workings are mysterious, as is its extent, but it carries passengers like Cora, and various companions, beneath the countryside and across state lines.

If Whitehead's conceit sounds whimsical, the uses to which he puts it are anything but: The stations on Cora's way to freedom lead her from one horrific manifestation of the evils of slavery and racism to another, and Whitehead rivets our attention to them. Overseers and owners brutally batter slaves, and the corpses of tortured runaways—and of the people who conspired to help them run—are hung from trees to decorate what local residents call the Freedom Trail. Cora's passage is like Dante's through the depravities of Hell.

The fear of recapture by vicious slave catchers pursues Cora and her fellow passengers everywhere, and the author summons other unexpected specters just as terrifying. The savage grasping of eugenic experimentation reaches out from beneath the surface benevolence of institutions; perverse museum exhibits of Living History portray "Scenes from Darkest Africa" and "Life on the Slave Ship" (including Cora as part of the displays) for the edification of white patrons. Again and again, Whitehead illuminates the pernicious hatred that runs like a current through even the ostensibly civilized order of the nonplantation society.

The pervasive pain—physical, emotional, psychological—experienced by Cora, and often shared with the wide cast of characters whose stories entwine with hers, grounds Whitehead's ambitious narrative in human truths. This is a book about griefs and longings and the fleeting tenderness of people in sorrow. Through its brave combination of empathy and invention, it brings a new dimension to the tradition of the slave story, summoning from the atrocities and sufferings of the past the enduring presence that literature can create. History needs fiction to transform it into stories that can speak across generations, rather than remain locked in time. No surprise, then, that *The Underground Railroad* is also a book about the power of language and the powerlessness that accompanies its loss.

They had been stolen from villages all over Africa and spoke a multitude of tongues. The words from across the ocean were beaten out of them over time. For simplicity, to erase their identities, to smother uprisings. All the words except for the ones locked away by those who still remembered who they had been before. "They keep 'em hid like precious gold," Mabel said.

Through his own gifts of expression, Whitehead mines such hidden words, fashioning them into a novel that gives voice to the humanity silenced by servitude.

What: Novel. *When:* 2016. *Awards:* National Book Award for Fiction, 2016. Pulitzer Prize for Fiction, 2017. *Also By: The Intuitionist* (1999). *John Henry Days* (2001). *Sag Harbor* (2009). *Zone One* (2011). *Try: The Known World* by Edward P. Jones. *One Hundred Years of Solitude* by Gabriel García Márquez (see page 308).

"This night the feeling settled on her heart again. It grabbed hold of her and before the slave part of her caught up with the human part of her, she was bent over the boy's body as a shield." —*from* The Underground Railroad

Leaves of Grass
Walt Whitman (1819–1892)

He Heard America Singing

Having been a printer's assistant, teacher, and newspaperman in New York and New Orleans, in 1855 a largely self-taught and unknown man named Walt Whitman self-published—not just footing the bill but designing the cover and setting the type—a small book called *Leaves of Grass*. Containing twelve untitled poems and a preface, it caused little stir, except in a reader named Ralph Waldo Emerson, who sent Whitman a letter of high praise. A year later Whitman released a second edition, this time with thirty-three poems (and, unbeknownst to its composer, Emerson's epistolary endorsement). The poet would continue revising and republishing *Leaves of Grass* over the next thirty-odd years; the final edition, printed in 1892, by which time the "Good Gray Poet" had become a national treasure, contained 383 poems.

Leaves of Grass captures a new American voice—bold, relaxed, exultant, shameless—in long, breath-fueled lines that exude an organic energy traditional stanzas could never contain:

I hear America singing, the varied carols I hear,
Those of mechanics, each one singing his as it should be
blithe and strong,
The carpenter singing his as he measures his plank or beam,
The mason singing his as he makes ready for work,....

"(I am large, I contain multitudes)," Whitman writes in "Song of Myself," and his poetry

Walt Whitman, ca. 1890

life, love, spirituality, slavery and the war it provoked, democracy and its discontents, the joys of sensual and sexual reality—all are absorbed and transformed by his verses into unforgettable utterance. His lines live ("I sing the body electric") and his rhythms endure ("Out of the cradle endlessly rocking") with an undimmed native vitality. His best poems are life-affirming hymns that strike what Abraham Lincoln—whom Whitman mourns in "When Lilacs Last in the Dooryard Bloom'd"—once called "the mystic chords of memory." Few poets have had his influence, and fewer still have so urgently charged the common language of their countrymen.

What: Poetry. *When:* 1855, with six subsequent revised and expanded editions prepared by the author before his death in 1892. *Edition:* The Library of America Whitman volume features both the original 1855 texts and the final, complete collected poems. *Also By: Drum-Taps* (1865). *Democratic Vistas* (1871). *Specimen Days* (1882). *Further Reading: Walt Whitman: A Life* by Justin Kaplan. *Walt Whitman's America: A Cultural Biography* by David S. Reynolds. *Try: The Prelude* by William Wordsworth (see page 871). *Howl and Other Poems* by Allen Ginsberg (see page 315). *Adaptations:* "When Lilacs Last in the Dooryard Bloom'd" has been set to music by both Paul Hindemith and Roger Sessions.

follows suit, embracing in its ruminative waves both country and cosmos, swelling to flights of soulful grandeur, then rushing back to earth to celebrate and bear witness to the tenderness and violence of the physical world. Labor,

······

Night
Elie Wiesel (1928–2016)

A Holocaust Testament

As a teenager in the town of Sighet in Transylvania, Elie Wiesel was pious and deeply observant: "By day I studied Talmud and by night I would run to the synagogue to weep over the destruction of the Temple." Still he yearned for more, to enter the world of Jewish mysticism—"a world fraught with peril" for a young man, his father warned him. The determined youth found a guide to the Kabbalah's revelations in the figure of Moishe the Beadle, "the poorest of the poor of Sighet." "I became convinced," Wiesel recollects of his thirteen-year-old self, "that Moishe the Beadle would

help me enter eternity, into that time when question and answer would become ONE."

So opens this slim but powerful testament to the horrors of the Holocaust. First Moishe is expelled from Sighet as a foreigner, only to return to warn his former neighbors of the Gestapo's deportation and murder of Hungarian Jews. In a world turned upside down, it is the mystic rather than the statesman who bears first witness to the evil onslaught of history. Wiesel and his father, mother, and sisters Hilda, Beatrice, and Tzipora are remanded to a ghetto within Sighet, their former lives encircled in barbed wire; then they are transported to the concentration camp at Birkenau, where the men are separated from the women (Wiesel's mother and youngest sister would be killed in the gas chambers there; his two older sisters would survive). Father and son begin a captive odyssey of terror and torment—forced labor, beatings, unrestrained brutality in Auschwitz, the Buna, Gleiwitz, Buchenwald. Wiesel sees bodies burned and a child writhing from an executioner's rope, too light to be easily complicit in his own hanging.

> Behind me, I heard [a] man asking:
> "For God's sake, where is God?"
> And from within me, I heard a voice answer:
> "Where He is? This is where—hanging here from this gallows . . ."
> That night, the soup tasted of corpses.

On other nights, there are other horrors, from small degradations to the extinguishing of his father's soul, which Wiesel attends in these pages with both the anguish of a boy's savaged innocence and the fierce devotion of a man's need to hold fast to memory once he has learned that eternity is nothing but a void without it.

Night ends soon after the liberation of Buchenwald in April 1945. Subsequently, Wiesel went into a French orphanage. As a young man, he studied at the Sorbonne and then worked as a journalist, going ten years

without speaking about his harrowing experience, unable to summon the words to do it justice. At last he produced, in Yiddish, a massive manuscript that was published in shorter form in Buenos Aires. A meeting with the writer François Mauriac inspired Wiesel to send him a French translation, and, after some difficulty, the work was published as *La Nuit* in 1958. Two years later an American edition, *Night*, appeared, and slowly found an enormous audience not only in the United States but internationally; it has been translated into more than thirty languages.

Once Wiesel began speaking, of course, he kept going: Forty books and a Nobel Peace Prize later, his memory became an emblem of what was suffered, lost, and endured in the Holocaust. Nowhere is that commemoration more eloquent than in the pages of *Night*.

What: Memoir. History. *When:* 1958. *Edition:* In 2006, a new translation from the French, by the author's wife, Marion Wiesel, was published. It also contains a new preface by the author. *Also By: Night* is the first book in what became a trilogy. The next two books are *Dawn* (1961) and *Day* (originally published as *The Accident*, 1961). *Further Reading: The War Against the Jews* by Lucy S. Dawidowicz. *The Lost: A Search for Six of Six Million* by Daniel Mendelsohn. *Try: Survival in Auschwitz* by Primo Levi. *All But My Life* by Gerda Weissmann Klein.

....

Kaddish
Leon Wieseltier (born 1952)

A Son's Mourning Prayer

In the year after his father's death in 1996, longtime literary editor of *The New Republic* Leon Wieseltier said the prayer known as the mourner's kaddish three times daily (during the morning, afternoon, and evening services in a synagogue in Washington, or when away

from home, in synagogues elsewhere). His dutiful embrace of Jewish ritual—"It looks after the externalities, and so it saves me from the task of improvising the rituals of my bereavement, which is a lot to ask"—would inspire a soulful journey through the chambers of learning in which the consolations of spiritual legacies are stored. As Wieseltier came to discover, those shared treasures can also illuminate both the grief and glory of personal inheritance: "Now I find it hard to imagine my father dying long ago. But one day his death will be old, and I will stand at the head of the congregation, and I will be old. —Stepping into another person's place, or: tradition."

In addition to the rounds of prayer, Wieseltier embarks on a bookish voyage through Jewish lore, story, exegesis, and analysis, searching for the history of the mourner's kaddish in ancient, medieval, and modern sources: "I was fixed in my obligation, but I was a rover in my tradition. The texts led me around, pointing me in many directions, establishing lines of filiation, referring to each other in a great chain of custom and consciousness." His scholarship is dedicated and assiduous, filled with "the charisma of learning": "Back and forth from my desk to my shelves, ten, twenty, thirty

times a day. The sources swirl around me. I am drugged by books. The sweet savor rises from the pages. A delirium of study."

His journal of a year of reading and prayer is a remarkable document, made all the more so for its plethora of eloquent aphorisms: "You can squander a lot of your soul not doing your duty." "Spirit may be the opposite of matter, but it is matter's loyal opposite." "Tradition is not reproduced. It is thrown and it is caught. It lives a long time in the air." *Kaddish* is a brilliant, dense, lyrical, provocative, powerful volume, a *vade mecum* for matters of life and death.

What: Religion & Spirituality. Memoir. *When:* 1998. *Also By: Against Identity* (1996). *Further Reading: Saying Kaddish* by Anita Diamant. *Try: A Grief Observed* by C. S. Lewis (see page 486). *Living a Year of Kaddish: A Memoir* by Ari L. Goldman.

Collected Poems 1943–2004
Richard Wilbur (1921–2017)

A Connoisseur's Garden of Verse

Richard Wilbur is a glorious anomaly among modern American poets, for he combines breathtaking technical mastery with syntactical clarity. Intricate as they are, his poems are never difficult to follow; his lines chime with wit and grace while encompassing intellectually engaging arguments and experiential truths. Their acquaintance with happiness is profound and invigorating, and their pursuit of beauty a reward when the exigencies of life and time push happiness beyond the poet's grasp.

To open Wilbur's *Collected Poems* is to enter a garden of words as refreshing and restorative as any wanderer could wish. The artfulness of the gardener's arrangements will certainly repay study if you are so inclined, but lovely flowers will seduce attention without any especially rigorous effort. The poet's intellectual reach ramifies from a detailed observation of the natural world, and his prodigious senses of paradox and irony are balanced by an eloquent human sympathy, all set in perfectly poised stanzas of sound and sense. The path finds fountains ("A Baroque Wall Fountain in the Villa Sciarra"), budding plants ("Seed Leaves"), lyrical bursts of pleasure ("A Late Aubade"), intricately trellised correspondences (as in "The Proof," a metaphorical entwining of proofreading and religious belief), epiphanies of cunning insight ("Love Calls Us to the Things of This World"), and one of the loveliest love poems you will ever read, "For C.," a celebration of romantic commitment set against the upset of more dramatic passions:

We are denied, my love, their fine tristesse
And bittersweet regrets, and cannot share
The frequent vistas of their large despair,
Where love and all are swept to nothingness;
Still, there's a certain scope in that long love
Which constant spirits are the keepers of,

And which, though taken to be tame and staid,
Is a wild sostenuto of the heart,
A passion joined to courtesy and art . . .

In these pages, readers can also savor Wilbur's masterful translations of French verse from Molière to Baudelaire, Villon to Mallarmé, as well as samplings from Spanish, Russian, and Italian poets. As a bonus, there are more than one hundred pages of his wonderful poems for children. These allow us to appreciate the poet at play as he puts the precision of his meters and the resourcefulness of his rhymes to work—making words jump, dance, and pose arrestingly; they are pure joy for readers young and old and ideal for reading aloud.

What: Poetry. *When:* 2004. *Awards:* Wilbur won the Pulitzer Prize for Poetry twice (1957 and 1989). He was US Poet Laureate in 1987–88. *Also By: Responses: Prose Pieces 1953–1976* (1976). *The Catbird's Song: Prose Pieces 1963–1995* (1997). *Further Reading: Conversations with Richard Wilbur,* edited by William Butts. *Try: Collected Poems* by Anthony Thwaite. *A Gilded Lapse of Time* by Gjertrud Schnackenberg. *Footnote:* Wilbur's lyrics to Leonard Bernstein's operetta, *Candide,* some of which are collected here, are dazzlingly good.

The Importance of Being Earnest
Oscar Wilde (1854–1900)

"I hope you have not been leading a double life, pretending to be wicked and being really good all the time. That would be hypocrisy."
—Cecily to Algernon

Oscar Wilde's unparalleled wit outweighs the stature of any of his individual works. His entirely deserved reputation for perfectly pitched comic utterance precedes him, and can, paradoxically, cast a shadow on a reader's pleasure. Not so with *The Importance of Being Earnest,* the sparkling play that asks for nothing but a willing suspension of disbelief—the plot piles absurdity upon absurdity as the characters trade names and identities with imaginary offstage figures—and greets it with a fusillade of epigrammatic humor that blends farce, parody, and comedy of manners into a sprightly attack on the poses that prop up social conventions.

From the pun of its title to the twist at its end, *The Importance of Being Earnest* presents itself as a lighthearted romp. It's the story of two friends—Algernon Moncrieff and Jack Worthing, whom Algernon knows as "Ernest." When Algernon finds Ernest's lighter, inscribed "young Cecily" to her "uncle Jack," he becomes

Oscar Wilde, 1882

suspicious. After a bit of taunting, Jack tells Algernon the truth: He is a country landowner who has invented a miscreant younger brother named Ernest; when he wants to escape his responsibilities, he claims Ernest has gotten into trouble and needs him, at which point he goes to live in the city as Ernest, making himself appear even more responsible in the process. Cecily is Jack's young ward. Algernon says he has long suspected something to that effect, since he, likewise, has created an invalid friend named Bunbury upon whose failing health he relies for his own escape to the country. Jack is in love with Algernon's cousin Gwendolen, who knows and loves him as Ernest, while Algernon, eager to meet Cecily, goes to Jack's home in the guise of Ernest, not knowing Cecily has long fantasized about marrying Jack's phantom brother. Confusion—and hilarity—ensues, all watched over by the domineering stare of Lady Bracknell, Algernon's aunt and Gwendolen's mother, who forbids Jack's marriage to her daughter because of the orphaned Jack's uncertain lineage: "To lose one parent, Mr. Worthing, may be regarded as a misfortune; to lose both looks like carelessness."

The plot careens through its perplexities toward a happy resolution, but not before

Wilde has, with almost geometrical clarity, plotted an uproariously accurate graph of the lies of convenience and connivance that describe Victorian ideas of propriety, romance, gender, identity, and—not least—earnestness. Originally subtitled "A Trivial Comedy for Serious People," the play opened on Valentine's Day, 1895, just three months before Wilde's fateful arrest for homosexuality. His subsequent trial would lead to imprisonment with hard labor, bankruptcy, exile, and the end of his career. *The Importance of Being Earnest* was the last comedy he wrote.

What: Drama. *When:* First produced in London, England, at St. James's Theatre, February 14, 1895; first published in 1899. *Also By: The Happy Prince and Other Tales* (1888). *The Picture of Dorian Gray* (1891). *An Ideal Husband* (1895). *The Complete Letters of Oscar Wilde* (2000). *Further Reading: Oscar Wilde* by Richard Ellmann. *Try: The Comedy of Errors* by William Shakespeare. *She Stoops to Conquer* by Oliver Goldsmith. *Adaptations:* The play has been adapted for movies and television numerous times; the 1952 movie directed by Anthony Asquith, starring Michael Redgrave and Edith Evans, is particularly good.

■ For Laura Ingalls Wilder's *Little House in the Big Woods*, see page 435.

The Bridge of San Luis Rey
Thornton Wilder (1897–1975)

A Haunting Moral Fable

Thornton Wilder's 1927 novel begins with the announcement of a tragedy: "On Friday noon, July the twentieth, 1714, the finest bridge in all Peru broke and precipitated five travelers into the gulf below." Witnessing the disaster, a Franciscan cleric named Brother Juniper wonders, "Why did this happen to *those* five?" In the hope of shedding light on the question of whether we live and die by accident or—as he

believes—by divine plan, Brother Juniper resolves to inquire into the secret lives of the victims. For six years, he knocks "at all the doors in Lima, asking thousands of questions, filling scores of notebooks, in his effort at establishing the fact that each of the five lost lives was a perfect whole." The stories he unravels become the threads that Wilder weaves into a haunting fabric of fact, fate, and faith.

Each of the interlocking tales—about the Marquesa de Montemayor and her companion

Pepita, the former on the verge of redeeming her life with newfound courage, inspired by the quiet bravery of the latter; about Estaban, inconsolable after losing his twin brother; and about Don Jaime and Uncle Pio, a fragile youngster and a world-weary old man, starting anew after deep sadness—is inconclusive with regard to Brother Juniper's quest, yet poignantly evokes the valiant struggle of human feeling against the vagaries of fortune. Alert with paradox and sorrow and suffused with a strange and consoling serenity, Wilder's small novel is an exquisitely-proportioned drama, "as close to perfect a moral fable," novelist Russell Banks has written, "as we are likely to get in American literature."

What: Novel. **When:** 1927. **Edition:** The Harper Perennial Modern Classics edition contains Russell Banks's introduction along with Wilder's notes and other documents. **Award:** Pulitzer Prize for Fiction, 1928. **Also By:** Famous for his two Pulitzer Prize–winning plays, Our Town (1938) and The Skin of Our Teeth (1942), Wilder is less appreciated for several excellent novels, including The Cabala (1926), The Ides of March (1948), The Eighth Day (1967, National Book Award), and Theophilus North (1973). **Try:** Death Comes for the Archbishop by Willa Cather. The Plague by Albert Camus (see page 123). **Adaptations:** The book has been thrice filmed: in 1929 (an early "talkie"), 1944, and 2004.

Stoner
John Williams (1922–1994)

Life Lessons

A summary of what happens in *Stoner* might well prompt even the most devoted book lover to consider a movie instead. A young farm boy named William Stoner goes off to an agricultural college where he develops a passion for poetry. He embarks on an undistinguished career as an assistant professor of English; his colleagues hold him in no particular esteem. He marries and has a daughter, but his home life becomes a long estrangement from his wife, and fatherhood is fraught with hesitations and mistakes. The hope he discovers in an affair with a colleague is scuttled by university politics. *Stoner* is "about work, the hard unyielding work of the farms; the work of living within a destructive marriage and bringing up a daughter with patient mutability in a poisoned household; the work of teaching literature to mostly unresponsive students," writes Irish novelist John McGahern in an introduction to its 2006 reissue. On the face of it, this doesn't sound inviting.

And yet: In plain prose that eschews sensation and dramatic emphases, with a modesty that seems to mirror that of his protagonist, John Williams portrays a life as meaningful as any you'll encounter in fiction. Published with little success in 1965, *Stoner* came in subsequent decades to be regarded with a kind of reverence by a growing coterie of enthusiastic readers around the world; sooner or later, likely as not, one of them is bound to recommend it to you.

The unexpected power of this unassuming tale is rooted in the way in which the author depicts the concentration of Stoner's inner being despite the diffusion of his outer life. His gradual self-possession provides the book's true narrative arc. When Stoner is called upon, in an English class he is taking merely to fulfill a requirement, to explicate two lines of Shakespeare's Sonnet 73, "This thou perceivest, which makes thy love more strong, / To love that well which thou must leave ere long," he is silent, stunned into a kind of soulfulness he hadn't known previously. In that moment, the agricultural student is converted to a revelatory faith in literature. He has found his vocation and, unbeknownst to himself, begun a rumination on the nature of love that will evolve through the decades toward wisdom despite his failure to master the wayward realities of his domestic and professional life. That he learns about love in loneliness helps him to see that it is more mysterious, and less requitable, than we normally believe:

He had, in odd ways, given it to every moment of his life, and had perhaps given it most fully when he was unaware of his giving. It was a passion neither of the mind nor of the flesh; rather, it was a force that comprehended them both, as if they were but the matter of love, its specific substance. To a woman or to a poem, it said simply: Look! I am alive.

The cumulative effect of Williams's unflinching attention to Stoner's ordinary life is strangely exhilarating—breathtaking, really—in its recognition that our inward selves embrace so much more than our outward lives appear to hold.

What: Novel. *When:* 1965. *Also By:* *Butcher's Crossing* (1960). *Augustus* (1972). *Try:* *The Professor's House* by Willa Cather. *A Month in the Country* by J. L. Carr (see page 132). *Larry's Party* by Carol Shields.

A Streetcar Named Desire
Tennessee Williams (1911–1983)

Acting Out

I n New Orleans at the time in which Tennessee Williams set his classic play, there really was a streetcar running through the French Quarter, where the drama unfolds, to Desire Street, which gave the transit line its name. A more romantic or fitting title for the play is hard to conceive: Its juxtaposition of the prosaic and the poetic characterizes both the playwright's heroine and his theme.

The heroine, Blanche DuBois, arrives unbidden at the cramped, dingy apartment of her sister, Stella, in a run-down section of the city. A fading Southern belle, she has been dispossessed of her home and possessed by indiscretions that have disrupted both her ill-starred marriage and her career as a teacher. Blanche's pronounced if somewhat shabby gentility is contrasted immediately by the earthy vigor of Stella's husband, Stanley Kowalski. The airs Blanche puts on, especially in her promiscuous flights of fancy about her past and her undisguised but nevertheless flirtatious disdain for Stanley, worry Stella and aggravate her husband. The carnal magnetism of the married couple's relationship, its palpable presence on the stage, contrasts with the wispy yearnings and, as we come to discover, desperate assignations that have left Blanche unmoored.

Marlon Brando and Jessica Tandy in the 1947 Broadway production

BLANCHE: What you are talking about is brutal desire—just— Desire!—the name of that rattle-trap street-car that bangs through the Quarter, up one old narrow street and down another . . .

STELLA: Haven't you ever ridden on that street-car?

BLANCHE: It brought me here.—Where I'm not wanted and where I'm ashamed to be . . .

From the moment she sets foot in the Kowalskis' apartment, Blanche commands the stage (until, in the drama's climactic act of violence, Stanley takes it back). She is very much a performer, and consciously so, whether sneering at Stanley or clutching at the attentions of his friend Mitch. Her desire is an attempt to redeem her distressed circumstances through sentiment, to gain admittance to a wider world than the one at hand through the only resource available to her imagination. "People don't see you—*men* don't—don't even admit your existence unless they are making love to you," she explains to her sister. "And you've got to have your existence admitted by someone." Although Stanley's—and, to some degree, Stella's—desire is uncomplicated, greedy, and grasping, the object of Blanche's is forever out of reach, for she wants more than she can express, and the ineffable wanting makes her reckless.

When he began his career as a playwright, Williams said he wanted to create works that would be "a picture of my own heart," and his best plays are certainly autobiographical. *Streetcar* is deeply personal, dramatizing an imaginative sensibility struggling to muster the resilience (and cleverness) to survive the brutalities of the reality surrounding it, but the play is also suffused with a tragic sense of life that anyone can feel. Both melodramatic and recognizable, its characters are haunting, and Blanche's ultimate fate harrowing and heartbreaking.

What: Drama. *When:* 1947. *Award:* Pulitzer Prize for Drama, 1948. *Also By: The Glass Menagerie* (1944). *The Rose Tattoo* (1951). *Cat on a Hot Tin Roof* (1955). *Orpheus Descending* (1957). *Suddenly Last Summer* (1958). *Sweet Bird of Youth* (1959). *The Night of the Iguana* (1960). *Further Reading: Tennessee Williams: Mad Pilgrimage of the Flesh* by John Lahr. *Try: Long Day's Journey into Night* by Eugene O'Neill (see page 604). *Death of a Salesman* by Arthur Miller (see page 549). *Adaptations:* The original Broadway production, directed by Elia Kazan, premiered on December 3, 1947, starring Jessica Tandy and Marlon Brando. Kazan's 1951 film stars Vivien Leigh and Brando. Brando's sensational performances as Stanley made him famous, obscuring for many that Blanche is both *Streetcar*'s central role and Williams's most enduring character.

....

Tarka the Otter

HIS JOYFUL WATER-LIFE AND DEATH IN THE COUNTRY OF THE TWO RIVERS

Henry Williamson (1895–1977)

An Enchanting, Lushly Written Nature Classic

In a famous 1974 essay, philosopher Thomas Nagel wondered, "What Is It Like to Be a Bat?" His answer, ultimately, was that we can't objectively know what the subjective experience of another creature is like. *Tarka the Otter* asks a similar question—namely, what is it like to be an otter?—but comes up with a rather different answer; to readers, it's a glorious one. Adopting the methods of imaginative literature rather than those of philosophical analysis, British novelist Henry Williamson provides a vivid, dramatic, and detailed account of the life of an otter in Devon in the west of England. Although the author had rescued the otter cub who inspired the book, *Tarka* is decidedly not of the "a person and his pet" school of animal writing. In fact, it's hard to exaggerate how different *Tarka* is from typical animal stories. Such tales usually emphasize the ways in which animal activities resemble human pursuits; they tend to sanitize the animal world and bring it, all tidied up, into the reader's study. By contrast, Williamson invites us to abandon our usual surroundings and plunge into a radically unfamiliar world.

The author works his magic in two principal ways. First, through his uncanny powers of observation: As naturalist Robert Finch has written, "Williamson knows this otter-country in his bones," and puts this familiarity to good use in providing the reader with an otter-eyed view of stream and bank as Tarka goes about his business, evading a persistent enemy like the dog Deadlock, or following a trail in his search for otter companionship:

He had been travelling for an hour, searching the uvvers of the banks for fish as he had learned in cubhood, when on a sandy scour he found the pleasing scent of otter. He whistled and hurried upstream, following the scent lying wherever the seals had been pressed. Soon he heard a whistle, and a feeling of joy warmed his being.

Second, through his lush prose and singular vocabulary: The narrative teems with strange, lovely words drawn from the English countryside: words like *uvver* in the passage just quoted, and—to mention just a few more—*scriddick, turves, ackymal,*

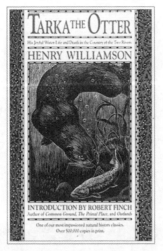

vair, leat, and *oolypuggers.* These verbal specimens of natural history startle and inform, giving the narrative a wondrous strangeness that is wholly apt and beguiling.

What: Nature. Animals. Novel. *When:* 1927. *Also By: Salar the Salmon* (1935). *The Story of a Norfolk Farm* (1941). A Chronicle of Ancient Sunlight (a series of fifteen novels, 1951–69). *A Clear Water Stream* (1958; revised 1975). *Try: Ring of Bright Water* by Gavin Maxwell (see page 533). *Adaptation:* A live-action movie of *Tarka the Otter* was released in 1979. Naturalist Gerald Durrell wrote the screenplay; Peter Ustinov is the film's narrator.

> **"*Tarka the Otter* is a thrilling story written in a prose style as rich as a river. It has been a favorite of such diverse readers as T. E. Lawrence, Rachel Carson, and Thomas Hardy, and for good reason. It is a masterpiece of natural observation and inspired language."** —John Casey

---

Lincoln at Gettysburg
THE WORDS THAT REMADE AMERICA
Garry Wills (born 1934)

How Lincoln Became Our "Redounding" Father

On November 19, 1863, four and a half months after the fighting on the Gettysburg battlefield had ended, a new cemetery was consecrated there. Among those who gave speeches was President Abraham Lincoln. He wasn't the main speaker, and he kept his remarks short: 272 words in all, which took no more than three minutes to deliver. (By contrast, the principal "oration" at the ceremony, given by Edward Everett, a former secretary of state, lasted about two hours.) And yet, as Garry Wills declares in this Pulitzer Prize-winning study of Lincoln's address, "The power of words has rarely been given a more compelling demonstration." For what Lincoln said ranks with the Declaration of Independence and the Bill of Rights as a quintessential formulation of America's democratic ideals.

"Four score and seven years ago," Lincoln began, and that much of what he said is familiar to the majority of Americans—it is, after all, a memorably different way of saying "back in

First page of the second draft of the Gettysburg Address, delivered November 19, 1863

1776." But as Wills develops the full story of the speech—its historical moment and its cultural background; its sources, composition, delivery, meaning, and abiding significance—many readers will discover that they don't know much at all about the words following the first six (some may even be mildly shocked to learn that "Gettysburg" is never mentioned in the Gettysburg Address). Beyond refuting the cherished myth that Lincoln scribbled the address on the back of an envelope on the spur of the moment, the analysis of text and context by the polymathic Wills is so erudite and profound that he justifies his assertion that Abraham Lincoln's "stunning verbal coup" launched in those few minutes on a November day a second American Revolution.

What: History. *When:* 1992. *Award:* Pulitzer Prize for General Nonfiction, 1993. *Also By: Inventing America: Jefferson's Declaration of Independence* (1978). *Explaining America: The Federalist* (1981). *Cincinnatus: George Washington and the Enlightenment* (1984). *Certain Trumpets: The Nature of Leadership* (1994). *Henry Adams and the Making of America* (2005). *Try: Abraham Lincoln: Speeches and Writings, 1859–1865* (see below). *A New Birth of Freedom: Lincoln at Gettysburg* by Philip B. Kunhardt Jr. *Abraham Lincoln and the Second American Revolution* by James M. McPherson.

|||||||||||||||||||||||||||||||||||||||||||||||| B O O K N O T E ||||||||||||||||||||||||||||||||||||||||||||||||

VOICE OF AMERICA

Abraham Lincoln: Speeches and Writings

VOLUME 1: 1832–1858; VOLUME 2: 1859–1865

Abraham Lincoln (1809–1865)

If the Gettysburg Address is the pinnacle of Abraham Lincoln's oratorical achievement in terms of expressiveness and influence, it is still but one exhibit from our sixteenth president's considerable legacy as speaker and author. Any collection of his speeches, letters, proclamations, and miscellaneous writings—the best is the two-volume set published by the Library of America (1989), which includes complete transcripts of his celebrated 1858 debates with Stephen A. Douglas during their Illinois senate race—reveals his keen political mind, his capacity for embracing and/or deflecting opposition, and his talent for pragmatic leadership, to say nothing of his wit and insight into human behavior. No other president has had such a spare, strong, inspired way with words: His felicity of expression is both personal and timeless. As Edmund Wilson

Abraham Lincoln as a lawyer, 1832

wrote in *Patriotic Gore,* "[Lincoln's] style was cunning in its cadences, exact in its choice of words, and yet also instinctive and natural; and it was inseparable from his personality in all of its manifestations." Of particular note is the power of his phrases to carry, with both a scriptural resonance and an uncanny sense of consolation, the purposes and destiny of our republic, from "the mystic chords of memory" and "the better angels of our nature" that animate his First Inaugural Address, to the magnanimity that concludes his second:

With malice toward none, with charity for all, with firmness in the right as God gives us to see the right, let us strive on to finish the work we are in, to bind up the nation's wounds, to care for him who shall have borne the battle and for his widow and his orphan, to do all which may achieve and cherish a just and lasting peace among ourselves and with all nations.

Reading Lincoln reminds us that eloquence, and all the lore and learning it encodes, not only nourishes a nation of laws, but also shines a light on the liberty that sustains it.

Israel and the Dead Sea Scrolls

Edmund Wilson (1895–1972)

A Scholar Adventurer in the Holy Land

Edmund Wilson was the preeminent literary journalist of mid-twentieth-century America. Fed by a voracious appetite for literature and ideas, his reportage and book reviews in *The New Republic* and *The New Yorker* were models of informed cultural criticism. His early book *Axel's Castle* was an insightful introduction to modernism, and his astute essays, collected in works such as *The Wound and the Bow*, offered incisive perspectives on texts from Sophocles to Hemingway. His ambitious study of confluences of historical and literary forces—yielding *To the Finland Station*, an exploration of ideas of history and revolution from France in 1789 to Russia in 1917, and *Patriotic Gore*, a deep consideration of the writings engendered by the American Civil War—can be compared only to the best college courses you never managed to take.

Opening any book by Edmund Wilson is to step into an ongoing education. When the subject is as compelling as the scrolls from the Dead Sea, the ancient and obscure Hebrew and Aramaic manuscripts that Bedouin boys unearthed in the late 1940s, it is a joy to linger there. His pioneering reports—both journalistic and scholarly—on the discovery, import,

and intrigue of the scrolls tell, in Leon Edel's phrase, "a modern Sherlock Holmes story," replete with religious, archaeological, political, and cultural clues. Wilson's consideration of each aspect of his subject—the content of the scrolls, the religious implications of their existence, the subterfuges surrounding their provenance and dissemination, the shadowy traffic in antiquities through which such valuable treasures often make their way into modernity—is characteristically stimulating, and his style of composing sentences, ideas, and impressions honors the reader's intellect by assuming its capability.

Originally published in the mid-1950s (and revised in 1969), Wilson's work on the Dead Sea Scrolls was one of the first to proclaim their importance. Although research, translation, new discoveries, and scholarly skullduggery in the decades since have added to our knowledge about these artifacts, Wilson's book remains an informative and engrossing intellectual adventure and a delight to read. Recent editions have prefaced the book with Wilson's superb essay "Israel," which begins with a fascinatingly detailed account of the author's efforts, as he entered his seventh decade, to master Hebrew in order to read the Book of Genesis in the original.

The Dead Sea Scrolls at excavation, 1947

What: Antiquity. Archaeology. *When:* First edition, 1955; revised and expanded, 1969; issued with "Israel," 1978. *Also By: Axel's Castle* (1931). *To the Finland Station* (1940; revised edition 1972). *The Wound and the Bow* (1941). *Patriotic Gore* (1962). *Upstate* (1971). *Letters on Literature and Politics 1912–1972* (1977). *Further Reading: Edmund Wilson: A Life in Literature* by Lewis M. Dabney. *The Complete World of the Dead Sea Scrolls* by Philip R. Davies, George J. Brooke, and Phillip R. Callaway. *The Complete Dead Sea Scrolls in English* by Geza Vermes. *Try: Cultural Cohesion: The Essential Essays* by Clive James. *Metaphor and Memory* by Cynthia Ozick.

Naturalist
Edward O. Wilson (born 1929)

"Most children have a bug period. I never grew out of mine."—*Edward O. Wilson*

What happened, what we think happened in distant memory, is built around a small collection of dominating images. In one of my own from the age of seven, I stand in the shallows off Paradise Beach, staring down at a huge jellyfish in water so still and clear that its every detail is revealed as though it were trapped in glass. The creature is astonishing. It existed outside my previous imagination.

For the best writers, words are tools for apprehending meaning. How those tools are shaped and sharpened by enthusiasm and experience; how their use matures from awkwardness to grace through study, labor, and luck; how they weather circumstance and setback, inspiration and inhibition—these are tales that can make, for book lovers, vivid reading. Science no less than literature is a field of imaginative activity, and the senses of formidable scientists are tools for apprehending reality as strong and refined, as clever and compelling, as odd and original as those of first-rate writers.

Edward O. Wilson—entomologist extraordinaire, master myrmecologist, theorist of sociobiology and champion of biodiversity, twice winner of the Pulitzer Prize—is such a scientist, and a first-rate writer, too. This exceptional autobiography details the shaping of his senses from earliest boyhood. Without literary artifice, but with no lack of style or expressiveness, Wilson brings the scientific imagination to life in a manner both personal and profound. We follow his passion for nature from the beaches of Pensacola and the swamps of Alabama to the cloud forests of the South Pacific, all the while surprised and enlightened by the insights empowered by one man's attention to insects. His memoir's intrinsic interest is magnified by the civility, intelligence, and character of its author, qualities that emanate from every page.

What: Autobiography. Science. *When:* 1994. *Also By: Sociobiology: The New Synthesis* (1975). *On Human Nature* (1978). *The Ants* (with Bert Hölldobler; 1990). *The Diversity of Life* (1992). *Journey to the Ants* (with Hölldobler; 1994). *Consilience: The Unity of Knowledge* (1998). *The Superorganism* (with Hölldobler; 2008). *Try: The Voyage of the* Beagle by Charles Darwin (see page 197). *The Insect World of J. Henri Fabre* by Jean-Henri Fabre. *The Song of the Dodo* by David Quammen.

April 1865
THE MONTH THAT SAVED AMERICA
Jay Winik (born 1957)

The Climactic Weeks of the Civil War

As Jay Winik sees it (and as you are likely to see it, too, once you've reached the end of his gripping narrative history), April 1865 was "a month that could have unraveled the American nation. Instead, it saved it." The darkest moment in its calendar of crises was the death of Abraham Lincoln. Since no president had ever been assassinated, there had never been a transfer of presidential power under such precarious circumstances. Further complicating the situation was the fact that the new chief executive, former Vice President Andrew Johnson, had a reputation as a drunkard; he had been so little regarded by Lincoln that the two had met only once since their inaugurations nearly six weeks earlier.

The momentous events justify Winik's assertion that this fateful April was "a month as dramatic and as devastating as any ever faced in American history." He vividly describes Confederate General Robert E. Lee's surrender at Appomattox to Union General Ulysses S.

Grant as well as Grant's remarkably generous treatment of the defeated foe, offering fresh insight into the culmination of the bloody conflict. With analytical acumen, he considers the South's collective decision not to continue the Civil War by means of guerrilla tactics, as was well within its power. He also examines the looming question of how the severed nation—"two separate political, social, and cultural entities that had been bitter military enemies"—was to be reunited. These thirty days—"marked by tumult and bloodshed, heroism and desperation, freedom and defeat, military prowess and diplomatic magnanimity, jubilation and sorrow, and, finally, by individual and national agony and joy"—provide material as weighty as any writer could wish, and Winik does it justice in his engrossing and richly detailed work.

What: History. **When:** 2001. **Also By:** *The Great Upheaval: America and the Birth of the Modern World, 1788–1800* (2007). **Try:** *The Civil War: A Narrative* by Shelby Foote (see page 286). *The Killer Angels* by Michael Shaara (see page 704). *Battle Cry of Freedom* by James M. McPherson.

....

■ For Lynne Withey's *Dearest Friend: A Life of Abigail Adams*, see page 251.

....

Pigs Have Wings
P. G. Wodehouse (1881–1975)

"The greatest comic writer ever."
—Douglas Adams

....

Lord Emsworth is a kindly dunderhead who makes his home at Blandings Castle. The apple of his eye is the peerless sow named Empress of Blandings, "twice in successive years winner in the Fat Pigs class at the Shropshire Agricultural Show." But will the Empress make it three in a row? Maybe not: Lord Emsworth's fiendish rival, Sir Gregory Parsloe-Parsloe of Matchingham Hall, has come up with a prodigious new challenger in the Queen of Matchingham. Enter Lord Emsworth's crafty brother, the Hon. Galahad Threepwood, who plots the abduction of the new Parsloe sow. This in turns leads Sir Gregory's pigman, George Cyril Wellbeloved, to pig-nap the Empress! Which in turn leads—but wait!—a complicated romance is unfolding back at the castle.

A dizzyingly convoluted and deliciously silly plot unfolds,

P. G. Wodehouse, ca. 1917

with clockwork precision, in *Pigs Have Wings*. It's the kind one expects in the happily unworldly world of Pelham Grenville Wodehouse (pronounced "Wood-house"), who once described the kind of writing he did as "musical comedy without music, and ignoring real life altogether." Evelyn Waugh once described Wodehouse's imaginary realm as "a world that cannot become dated, because it has never existed"—except, of course, on the page, where the author's prose mastery and lighthearted but accomplished literary invention invites the reader to enter his blissful comic kingdom.

Generally regarded as one of the bright lights of the Wodehouse canon, the irresistibly giddy *Pigs Have Wings* is an installment in a loosely connected series of novels and stories that center on Blandings Castle. This series, though not as well known as the one that features dim-witted Bertie Wooster and his ever-resourceful valet Jeeves, deserves wider recognition.

(The first Blandings volume, *Something Fresh*, was published in 1915; the fourteenth, *Sunset at Blandings*, was in progress when the author died in 1975.)

Wodehouse's prolific work—including more than one hundred books—has drawn raves from writers as disparate in style and time as Hilaire Belloc, who, in 1934, called him "the best writer of English now alive," and Douglas Adams, author of *The Hitchhiker's Guide to the Galaxy* (see page 6), who sighted Wodehouse "up in the stratosphere of what the human mind can do, above tragedy and strenuous thought, where you will find Bach, Mozart, Einstein, Feynman and Louis Armstrong, in the realms of pure, creative playfulness." Even there, no doubt, he is surrounded by people giggling.

What: Humor. Novel. *When:* 1952. *Also By:* The Blandings Saga: *Leave It to Psmith* (1923); *Summer Lightning* (1929); *Heavy Weather* (1933); *Blandings Castle* (1935); *Galahad at Blandings* (1965). Jeeves and Wooster: *The Inimitable Jeeves* (1923); *Carry On, Jeeves* (1925); *Thank You, Jeeves* (1934); *The Code of the Woosters* (1938); *Joy in the Morning* (1946). *Further Reading: Wodehouse: A Life* by Robert McCrum. *Try: Three Men in a Boat* by Jerome K. Jerome. *Queen Lucia* by E. F. Benson. *Footnote:* As a young man, Wodehouse had a successful career in the theater, writing more than 200 song lyrics for dozens of musicals. His best-known song? "Bill," from Jerome Kern's *Show Boat*.

Look Homeward, Angel
Thomas Wolfe (1900–1938)

The Boy Wonder of American Letters

A major literary figure in the first half of the American century, Thomas Wolfe wrote only four novels in his short life, two of which were published posthumously. In its ambition, not to mention its length, Wolfe's fiction equaled the efforts of authors whose careers were twice as long. *Look Homeward, Angel*, his pioneering autobiographical first novel, is set in a town called Altamont, a thinly disguised version of Asheville, North Carolina; it follows the fortunes of Eugene Gant from his difficult birth through childhood, adolescence, sexual awakening, university days, to finally a career as a writer. In ornate, often breathtaking, sometimes unbearably intense prose—in which "the minute-winning days, like flies, buzz home to death, and every moment is a window on all time"—Wolfe spins an almost mythic tale about hating a home you will long for only after you leave, and about forging a career as an artist in defiance of family expectation. In so doing, he

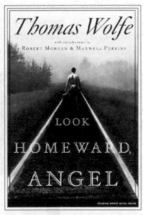

fueled the fantasies and consoled the doubts of generations of aspiring writers.

When *Look Homeward, Angel* was published to acclaim in 1929, Wolfe cut a confident, even bombastic figure on the cultural stage. He believed he was destined to become the greatest writer of the age. "I don't know what I am doing, but, by God, I have genius," Wolfe wrote—the sort of thing you can say without shame when you're only twenty-three. That brashness led Wolfe to write with abandon: The editor of *Look Homeward, Angel*, Maxwell Perkins, cut sixty thousand words from the manuscript, and it still runs to more than five hundred pages in most editions. His subsequent novels were equally eloquent and prolix. All the same, it's unfair to dismiss Wolfe as a "young man's author," as many critics have done since his early death from tuberculosis. In his debut, as well as in later efforts such as *You Can't Go Home Again*, Wolfe gave voice to an American experience that had not yet been put down in prose, driven by a sense of purpose both quixotic and noble. As his fellow Southerner William

Faulkner said after Wolfe's death, "Among his and my contemporaries, I rated Wolfe first because we had all failed but Wolfe had made the best failure because he had tried hardest to say the most."

What: Novel. *When:* 1929. *Edition:* In 2000, Wolfe's original, considerably longer version of the novel was published as *O Lost: A Story of the Buried Life.* *Also By: Of Time and the River* (1935). *The Web and the Rock* (1939). *You Can't Go Home Again* (1940). *Further Reading: Look Homeward: A Life of Thomas Wolfe* by David Herbert Donald. *Try: A Tree Grows in Brooklyn* by Betty Smith (see page 729). *The Town and the City* by Jack Kerouac. *A Death in the Family* by James Agee.

The Bonfire of the Vanities
Tom Wolfe (1930–2018)

A Scathing Social Satire of 1980s New York

Sherman McCoy is an investment banker with a fourteen-room Park Avenue apartment, a wife and child, a mistress, and a sense of self-worth so large, it insulates him from the rough-and-tumble realities of the metropolis that he and his colleagues look down upon from their lofty and lucrative Wall Street perches. "He was of that breed," explains Tom Wolfe, "whose natural destiny it was . . . to have what they wanted!"

Sherman moves in circles small but shiny enough to create the illusion that he is—as he likes to style himself—a "Master of the Universe." Until the day, that is, when, having picked up his mistress at the airport, he takes a wrong turn into the Bronx, and fear and fate propel his Mercedes into an accident that will cost him not just his mastery but his universe, too.

What's most impressive about Wolfe's rollicking fictional tour of New York in the 1980s is its vigor. He depicts so many facets of the city's life: Park Avenue and Wall Street and their social and financial scheming; inner city housing projects and their attendant miseries and machinations; the personal and political confusions of the criminal courts; the vapid, venal power of the media. Each slice of life is drawn and quartered with a wicked pen. Give Wolfe a shoe, an architectural detail, or a verbal inflection and he'll turn it into a satiric weapon sharpened by insight. This is the novel as comic romp, riffing on observable reality with an intelligence that is both precise and completely over the top. There may be no psychological depth here, but that, in part, is the author's very subject. His furiously paced, hilariously funny novel is an ideal witness to the sad comedy of a metropolis cowering behind the shattering glass of its glittering and glowering façades.

What: Novel. *When:* 1987. *Also By:* Nonfiction: *The Kandy-Kolored Tangerine-Flake Streamline Baby* (1963); *The Electric Kool-Aid Acid Test* (1968); *The Painted Word* (1975); *The Right Stuff* (1979). Fiction: *A Man in Full* (1998); *I Am Charlotte Simmons* (2004). *Try: Liar's Poker* by Michael Lewis (see page 488). *Money* by Martin Amis. *Footnote: Rolling Stone* magazine serialized an earlier, very different version of the novel—"as it was being written, without a safety net," Wolfe has said.

Tom Wolfe, 1988

VIRGINIA WOOLF
(1882–1941)

V irginia Woolf's work has been viewed through many lenses— feminist, psychoanalytic, and modernist, to name three—as has the social, artistic, and intellectual phenomenon known as Bloomsbury. She has been celebrated and excoriated for her liaisons, her pacifism, her snobbery, and her brilliantly experimental novels ("If this sort of thing doesn't indicate degeneration and perversion, what does it indicate?" editorialized the *New York Times* in 1923 about *Jacob's Room*). Numerous popular and scholarly tomes have anatomized her life and probed her death, by suicide, at age fifty-nine. The quicksilver presence of her prose renders all such attempts senseless. Read the

Virginia Woolf, ca. 1927

essay "Street Haunting: A London Adventure," in which a trip to the stationer's to buy a pencil inspires a stunning evocation of the wanderings of consciousness through the wonders of a city, or her description of a glimpse of the sea and its restorative effects that leaps from an early page of *To the Lighthouse*, or any random sequence from her voluminous diaries and letters, and you will know that no category can capture the strength and sparkle of her imagination. Her multifaceted oeuvre constitutes one of the most valuable literary legacies of the twentieth century.

The Common Reader
"How Should One Read a Book?"

One of the most articulate and enjoyable essayists of the modern era, Virginia Woolf makes literary criticism personal, private musing universal, and social commentary both particular and purposeful. Her gift for encompassing expansive themes in what seems a mere creative glance always animates her serious import; for instance, all the ramifications of her astute appraisal of the oppression of women's imaginative lives sprout from the title of her marvelous book-length essay on the subject, *A Room of One's Own*.

Woolf's essays are legion, and they have been collected and regrouped in any number of individual volumes. Start with the pieces the author gathered in two volumes and called *The Common Reader*. "The common reader," Woolf explains, taking her cue from Samuel Johnson, " . . . differs from the critic and scholar. . . . He reads for his own pleasure rather than to impart knowledge or correct the opinions of others. Above all, he is guided by an instinct to create for himself, out of whatever odds and cnds he can come by, some kind of whole—a portrait of a man, a sketch of an age, a theory of the art of writing."

In *The Common Reader*, Woolf assembles a refined personal library. Scholarship takes a back seat to serendipity, education seems—as it should—a circuit of enthusiasms, and a serious mind finds its shape among the sentences and sentiments that speak most directly to it. In these engaging volumes, Woolf develops her understanding while the reader learns valuable lessons about Chaucer and the Elizabethans, Montaigne and Defoe, Joseph Addison and Jane Austen, the Brontës and George Eliot. Of special note are the essays "On Not Knowing Greek" and "How It Strikes a Contemporary" (in the first volume), and "How Should One Read a Book?" (in the second). Making their acquaintance, one gains insight not only into reading, but into thinking and being as well.

Virginia Woolf and her friend Lytton Strachey, 1923

What: Essays. Books. **When:** *The Common Reader*, 1925. *The Common Reader: Second Series*, 1932. **Also By:** *A Room of One's Own* (1929). *Three Guineas* (1938). *The Death of the Moth and Other Essays* (1942). **Further Reading:** *Virginia Woolf: A Biography* by Quentin Bell. *Virginia Woolf* by Hermione Lee. **Try:** The essays of William Hazlitt. *Readings* by Michael Dirda.

A Moment's Liberty
THE SHORTER DIARY OF VIRGINIA WOOLF

Abridged and edited by
Anne Olivier Bell

Genius and Domesticity, Day by Day

" There were two Virginia Woolfs: the rather gorgeous artist and the busy, observant, ironical, everyday woman. We're lucky to have books by both of them," Anatole Broyard once wrote. While the gorgeous artist takes center stage in works such as *To the Lighthouse* and *Orlando*, the everyday woman displays her astonishing vitality and her intermittent but fateful anguish across the five

installments of her complete diary, here admirably abridged into a single volume.

Woolf began her diary in 1915, while recovering from a breakdown and her first suicide attempt, and she continued it until four days before drowning herself in the River Ouse, in March 1941. She wrote through the births and deaths of friends and relations, and through bouts of her own madness. She recorded details of weather and war, of her own writing and the shared work with which she and her husband, Leonard, built their Hogarth Press, of househunting, of who said what at dinner. Woolf was the brightest star in the constellation known as Bloomsbury, and the "who" that came to dinner encompassed John Maynard Keynes, E. M. Forster, Vita Sackville-West, and Lytton Strachey. Many other luminaries pass through these pages, including Sigmund Freud, who, with Freudian slipperiness, presents Woolf with a narcissus.

Most memorable in these diary entries is the alertness with which Woolf perceives all about her, from mundane domestic arrangements to dramatic personal doubts and crises. Literary struggles and triumphs take their place between caustic assessments of her contemporaries and sympathetic concern for friends and relations. The elegiac power of her best fiction is matched here by her awareness of life's fleeting presences: "Occupation is essential," she writes in her penultimate entry, three weeks before her death. "And now with some pleasure I find that its [sic] seven; & must cook dinner. Haddock & sausage meat. I think it is true that one gains a certain hold on sausage & haddock by writing them down."

What: Diaries & Letters. **When:** 1990. **Editions:** Anne Olivier Bell, the editor of *A Moment's Liberty*, drew pieces from her five-volume edition of Woolf's complete diary, published between 1977 and 1984. Leonard Woolf edited an earlier selection, published as *A Writer's Diary* in 1953. *Also By: Congenial Spirits: The Selected Letters of Virginia Woolf* edited by Joanne Trautmann Banks. *Further Reading: Snapshots of Bloomsbury: The Private Lives of Virginia Woolf and Vanessa Bell* by Maggie Humm. *Try: Diaries 1939–1972* by Frances Partridge. *Adaptation:* Domenick Argento's song cycle, *From the Diary of Virginia Woolf*, won the 1975 Pulitzer Prize for Music.

To the Lighthouse

"One of the greatest elegies in the English language, a book which transcends time."
—Margaret Drabble

In the 1924 essay "Character in Fiction," Woolf encourages readers to demand more from novelists' depiction of personality than the reductive portraits wrought through realism's "enormous stress upon the fabric of things"—upon houses and dress and disease and other discrete, describable circumstances. "You have gone to bed at night bewildered by the complexity of your feelings," she reminds her audience. "In one day thousands of ideas have coursed through your brains; thousands of emotions have met, collided, and disappeared in astonishing disorder." This complexity, Woolf believes, is "the spirit we live by, life itself," and it is this spirit that she seeks to capture in her novels. In *To the Lighthouse* she succeeds with a keen and miraculous grace.

The novel's story is simple, told in three parts. In "The Window," set at a summer home on the Isle of Skye, we are introduced to the Ramsay family and their guests, including the painter Lily Briscoe. Mrs. Ramsay assures her young son James that an outing to the lighthouse will indeed be possible on the morrow, but Mr. Ramsay insists the weather will thwart the plan; a dinner party is held. "Time Passes" is an interlude in which events of the subsequent decade—encompassing World War I and the death of Mrs. Ramsay—are sketched. In the final section, "The Lighthouse," which takes place ten years after "The Window," some of the family returns to the summer home, James's childhood wish to visit the lighthouse is finally realized, and Lily Briscoe completes a long-unfinished painting.

But "story," of course, is the wrong word, for the book unfolds not so much by the author's telling of events as by her seamless movement from the mind of one character to that of another, then another, then another, passing like a benevolent ghost between the prompts of perception and the chaotic and redemptive reveries of consciousness. From one paragraph to the next, Woolf animates the volatile emotions of a young boy, the thwarted ambitions of his fearful philosopher father, and the poignant wisdom of Mrs. Ramsay, who hears, in the fall of waves upon the shore, the remorseless beating of the measure of life, warning "her whose day had slipped past in one quick doing after another that it was all as ephemeral as a rainbow."

The reader who gives in to the pull of Woolf's prose enters a realm in which words transcend both plot and description to communicate with an unparalleled directness the beauties and sorrows of time, loss, love, friendship, custom, art. Unlike James Joyce, her contemporary adventurer on the stream of consciousness, who mapped his routes with a scholastic rigor that held art, in the end, aloof from life, Woolf places her faith in "the spirit that we live by"—striking, again and again, the chords of fleeting emotions. To read *To the Lighthouse* is as close as we may ever come to reading a living thing.

What: Novel. **When:** 1927. *Also By: Mrs. Dalloway* (1925). *The Waves* (1931). *The Years* (1937). *Between the Acts* (1941). *Try: Near to the Wild Heart* by Clarice Lispector. *The Dead of the House* by Hannah Green (see page 333). *The Leper's Companions* by Julia Blackburn. *Adaptation:* Rosemary Harris stars as Mrs. Ramsay in the 1983 film.

Orlando
Who's Afraid of Virginia Woolf?

The intricacies of Woolf's narrative innovations have combined with the shadow cast by her afflictions to darken her image in the minds of many who have yet to explore her work. This is not only unfortunate but also profoundly misleading, for there are few modern masters who are more fun to read. Woolf's words invariably dance across her pages with an enthusiasm that engenders delight.

None of her books is more joyful than *Orlando*, a mock-biography that follows the fortunes of its protagonist across four centuries, from the era of Elizabeth I to the stroke of midnight on the eleventh of October, 1928. Orlando grows up as a young nobleman in thrall to love and literature, travels as an ambassador to the Ottoman court in Constantinople, returns to the England of Pope and Dryden, and enters and exits the Victorian era, having achieved in the end the ripe old age of thirty. Traversing more than the borders of nations and centuries, Orlando is transformed along the way from hero to heroine, a willing victim of the author's exuberant invention as Woolf engages, with playful abandon, themes of gender, biography, writing, and desire. Written in tribute to her friend and lover Vita Sackville-West (see page 690), Woolf's biographical fantasy is a delicious celebration of the exhilarating powers of infatuation and imagination.

What: Novel. *When:* 1928. *Also By:* Flush: A Biography (1933). *Further Reading: Vita: The Life of V. Sackville-West* by Victoria Glendinning. *Portrait of a Marriage* by Nigel Nicolson (see page 587). *Try: The Passion* by Jeanette Winterson. *Adaptation:* Tilda Swinton stars as Orlando in Sally Potter's 1992 film.

IIIIIIIIIIIIIIIIIIIIIIIIIIIIIIIIIIIIIIIIII   B O O K N O T E   IIIIIIIIIIIIIIIIIIIIIIIIIIIIIIIIIIIIIIIIII

HOMAGE TO A MODERN CLASSIC—AND A MASTERPIECE ITSELF

The Hours
Michael Cunningham (born 1952)

Virginia Woolf's 1925 novel *Mrs. Dalloway*, set on a single June day in London, is punctuated by the tolling of Big Ben, the bell inside the clock tower at the Houses of Parliament. Its regular marking of the time—"First a warning, musical; then the hour, irrevocable"—reminds Clarissa Dalloway of both the day's passage and the evanescence of all things. This indelible symbol provided Woolf's novel with its working title: *The Hours*. Seven decades on, Michael Cunningham, a writer of uncommon sensitivity and an unabashed Woolf lover, retrieved it for his best novel, a stunning invocation of *Mrs. Dalloway* and a masterful fiction in its own right. *The Hours* (1998) is a book that leaves the reader feeling hopeful and blessed, suffused with the ever-present, ineffable wonder of life. Really.

Cunningham refracts Clarissa into three women at three different historical moments. There is Clarissa Vaughan, an urbane literary editor in late-twentieth-century New York who is preparing to throw a party, just like her namesake. "What a thrill," she thinks, "what a shock, to be alive on a morning in June, prosperous, almost scandalously privileged, with a simple errand to run." Then there is Laura Brown, a young mother living in post–World War II Los Angeles, who is reading *Mrs. Dalloway* in bed and trying to cope with the pressures of an unhappy marriage. And then, most daringly, there is Virginia Woolf herself, trying to hold on to her sanity as she struggles to write:

This morning she may penetrate the obfuscation, the clogged pipes, to reach the gold. She can feel it inside her, an all but indescribable second self, or rather a parallel, purer self. If she were religious, she would call it the soul.

Cunningham braids the three strands of his narrative so adroitly that they flow unimpeded. Sentences with the solid, faceted allure of precious stones delineate his finely calibrated themes of sympathy, tenderness, desire, and regret. His characters' loyalty to their own emotional core—as elusive and mutable as that core may be—fills the reader with magnanimous empathy. The author invites us "to inhabit the world; to understand the promises implied by an order larger than human happiness, though it contained human happiness along with every other emotion." At the end of *The Hours*, we're wiser than we were before we read it, and the wisdom it gives us seems magically drawn from the fabric of our own lives.

The Prelude and Other Poetry
William Wordsworth (1770–1850)

The Invention of Solitude

In the first stanza of his lovely lyric "I Wandered Lonely as a Cloud," William Wordsworth recounts his vision of

> a crowd,
> A host, of golden daffodils;
> Beside the lake, beneath the trees,
> Fluttering and dancing in the breeze.

It's a clear vision, clearly expressed, available not only to other poets but to any walker lucky enough to stumble upon a flourishing field of flowers. Only in the fourth and final stanza of the poem does Wordsworth's true genius raise its head, immortalizing the poem and its daffodils by the poet's remembering their glory.

> For oft, when on my couch I lie
> In vacant or in pensive mood,
> They flash upon that inward eye
> Which is the bliss of solitude . . .

In poem after poem—from his lyrical ballads and eloquent sonnets to his magnificent longer poems, such as "Tintern Abbey" and "Ode: Intimations of Immortality"—Wordsworth enriches his experience by reflecting upon it in solitude. Retrospect is Wordsworth's medium, and he may well be said to have invented it, and perhaps solitude itself, as a dimension of the literary imagination. His achievement is so large, so pervasive in its influence, that we are in danger of barely noticing it today. But much of the most inventive literature created in the nineteenth and twentieth centuries, aptly enough, looks back to him.

Although "Ode: Intimations of Immortality" may be the most beautiful expression of the poet's ethos (and no reading life is complete without a dive into its deep, bracing, and soothing waters), Wordsworth paints his most complete picture in The Prelude, a book-length autobiographical poem on the "growth of a poet's mind." It follows him from early childhood and school through studies at Cambridge and residence in London to France during the Revolution. Whether describing the looming, numinous presence of nature he feels while skating as a boy on a lake, or the pageant of passing faces on a London street, or the passions with which he and other enthusiasts greeted the early days of France's rebellion ("Bliss was it in that dawn to be alive, / But to be young was very heaven!"), Wordsworth writes with an eager, earnest energy that integrates experience into the stream of consciousness that is the true, emergent medium of all our lives. In The Prelude's thousands of pentameters, Wordsworth charts the fears and fabrications, the habits and the intuitions, the shaping processes and private emanations of the self, in a way that no seer had previously envisioned; in his pages the human imagination comes to life as a natural resource worth the work and wonder of cultivation. The vast poem is dense and lyrical and at times slow-going, but it need not be read all at once; it remains a rich reading landscape to wander in, and wandering is the best way to navigate its riches, for serendipity will bring you face to face, again and again, with qualities of your own solitude that you have forgotten or never paused before to recognize.

What: Poetry. *When:* Wordsworth's poetry was first published in 1793. Although The Prelude was not titled or published until after his death, he first sketched its contents in 150 lines in 1798, expanded the text to more than 500 lines the following year, then composed two complete versions, the first in 1805 and the final revision in 1850. The 1805 text is usually given pride of place. *Editions:* A sumptuous annotated, illustrated edition of the 1805 Prelude was published by David R. Godine in 2016. *Selected Poetry of William Wordsworth,* edited by Mark Van Doren, includes The Prelude as well as an extensive selection of shorter poems. *Further Reading: The Grasmere Journals* by Dorothy Wordsworth. *William Wordsworth: A Life* by Stephen Gill. *Try:* The poetry of Samuel Taylor Coleridge, Rainer Maria Rilke (see page 667), and W. H. Auden.

Native Son
Richard Wright (1908–1960)

The Shock of Recognition

" The day *Native Son* appeared," wrote critic Irving Howe, "American culture was changed forever." Richard Wright's searing portrait of a young black man's crime and punishment indicts both the book's protagonist, Bigger Thomas, and the society that incubated him. What fuels the enduring power of *Native Son* is the bruising ugliness of the story it tells, and its recognition that the ugliness cannot be mitigated by goodwill. In the brutality of Bigger Thomas and his experience, Wright gives ominous reality to the present horror of America's tragic past of oppression.

The setting is Chicago in the 1930s. Twenty-year-old Bigger dwells with his mother and his younger siblings in a rat-infested ghetto apartment. Offered a job as chauffeur to a real estate magnate, he is aware that even opportunity mocks the constraints of his circumstance: "Yes, he could take the job . . . and be miserable, or he could refuse it and starve. It maddened him to think that he did not have a wider choice of action." Swept into a world of easygoing privilege and possibility, Bigger's sensitivity to the dangers of his position as a black man in a white world is heightened to a pitch of uneasy apprehension. He inadvertently kills a white woman and then, in the frenzied aftermath of his misdeed, murders his girlfriend. As events spin out of control, Bigger acknowledges a paradoxical sensation:

He had done this. He had brought this all about. In all of his life these two murders were the most meaningful things that had ever happened to him. . . . Never had he had the chance to live out the consequences of his actions; never had his will been so free as in this night and day of fear and murder and flight.

Despite Wright's understanding—explication, even—of society's complicity in creating the hopelessness and hatred that envelops Bigger, the author does not invoke the reader's sympathy or seek to excuse his viciousness. For Wright, Bigger Thomas is not a symbol, but a *fact*, and that's what makes this fiction so powerful. Bigger's yearning for "a wider choice of action" is the desire for a story different from the one he is allowed to imagine for himself. *Native Son* tells us that, given the injustice and deprivation that have shaped black experience in America, there may be no other story available to him. Bigger's fate may be man-made, but, in the Chicago of the 1930s—and not only there and then—it is fate nonetheless, implacable and without mercy.

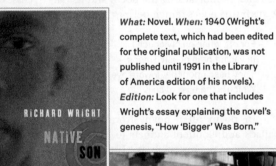

What: Novel. *When:* 1940 (Wright's complete text, which had been edited for the original publication, was not published until 1991 in the Library of America edition of his novels). *Edition:* Look for one that includes Wright's essay explaining the novel's genesis, "How 'Bigger' Was Born."

Richard Wright, 1950

Also By: Fiction: Uncle Tom's Children (1938); The Outsider (1953). Autobiography: Black Boy (1945); American Hunger (1977). Further Reading: Collected Essays by James Baldwin (see page 43). Try: Invisible Man by Ralph Ellison (see page 252). Beloved by Toni Morrison (see page 569). A Lesson Before Dying by Ernest J. Gaines (see page 305). Adaptation: The 1986 film version stars Victor Love, Matt Dillon, Geraldine Page, and Oprah Winfrey.

The Invention of Nature
Andrea Wulf (born 1972)

Lost Hero of Science

In 1802, Alexander von Humboldt climbed Chimborazo, the inactive volcano that is the highest mountain in Ecuador; it rises to nearly 21,000 feet. On that expedition, the great naturalist experienced an epiphany that coalesced his evolving vision of nature in "a single glance"—a glance that has, gradually but surely, come to shape our understanding of the natural world ever since. As Andrea Wulf makes clear in this marvelous biography, Humboldt's holistic view of nature "as a network of forces and interrelationships" played a significant role in advancing ecological thinking and thereby gave rise to modern conceptions of the environment. Detailing with verve and erudition Humboldt's exploits as an explorer in far-flung corners of the world, Wulf also reveals the extraordinary extent of his reputation in his own lifetime. In his day (born in 1769, he died ninety years later), he was the most famous scientist in the world and an international celebrity.

On the one hundredth anniversary of his birth, Wulf informs us,

There were festivities in Moscow where Humboldt was called the 'Shakespeare of sciences', and in Alexandria in Egypt where guests partied under a sky illuminated with fireworks. The greatest commemorations were in the United States, where from San Francisco to Philadelphia, and from Chicago to Charleston, the nation saw street parades, sumptuous dinners and concerts. In Cleveland some 8,000 people took to the streets and in Syracuse another 15,000 joined a march that was more than a mile long. President Ulysses Grant attended the Humboldt celebrations in Pittsburgh together with 10,000 revellers who brought the city to a standstill.

Fifteen thousand people in a parade in Syracuse—for a scientist! In 1869! How times have changed: Today it's a news story when an American presidential candidate asserts faith in science. In addition to such passing hoopla, Humboldt made quieter if more lasting claims on human memory: Nearly three hundred plants and more than one hundred animals are named for him, and there are more places on earth and in the heavens—from Humboldt, South Dakota, to Pico Humboldt in Venezuela; from the Humboldt Current off the west coast of South America to Humboldt Falls in New Zealand; from the Humboldt Sink, a dry lake bed in Nevada, to the equally dry Mare Humboldtianum on the moon—named after Alexander von Humboldt than after any other person.

Wulf adeptly portrays the excitement, dangers, and discoveries of his expeditions, and her accounts of his personal relationships with renowned figures of his time such as Goethe, Thomas Jefferson, and Simón Bolívar are fascinating. She is particularly good at explaining the cultural context that fueled Humboldt's prodigious curiosity and elucidating the influence of his work—in particular Views of Nature (1808), Personal Narrative of a Journey to the Equinoctial Regions of the New Continent (1814–31), and Cosmos (1845–62)—on the next generation of natural philosophers, including Charles Darwin (who carried Humboldt's books with him on the Beagle), Ernst Haeckel, Henry David Thoreau, and John Muir.

This long, rich, information-packed biography repays leisurely attention at the same time as it stimulates one's thinking about fundamental issues. "Humboldt was not so much interested in finding new isolated facts but in connecting them," Wulf writes. A reader can thankfully say the same of the author of this delightful book.

What: Biography. Nature. Science. *When:* 2015. *Also By:* The Brother Gardeners: Botany, Empire and the Birth of an Obsession (2008). Founding Gardeners: The Revolutionary Generation, Nature and the Shaping of the American Nation (2011). Chasing Venus: The Race to Measure the Heavens (2012). *Try: The Voyage of the Beagle* by Charles Darwin (see page 197). *The Age of Wonder: How the Romantic Generation Discovered the Beauty and Terror of Science* by Richard Holmes.

The Day of the Triffids
John Wyndham (1903–1969)

Global Shop of Horrors

British master of science fiction Brian Aldiss called John Wyndham's most famous book a "cozy catastrophe," and it's a brilliant characterization. For just as Agatha Christie's Miss Marple novels bring an agreeable coziness to murder, so Wyndham brings a satisfying comfiness to global cataclysm. Yes, in *The Day of the Triffids* the human race does go blind and people die in immense numbers from sheer sensory incapacity—to say nothing of the genetically engineered predatory plants given star billing in the book's title. Yet, as Aldiss rightly conveyed, the novel exudes a holiday air, a sense of liberation from artificial constraints and social falsities, and seemingly welcomes the prospect of a fresh relaunch of civilization and its contents. The fate of the masses might be horrific, but the plucky survivors on whom the narrative instinctively focuses will inherit a planet full of treasures, both natural and man-made, and—just maybe—find beyond the dark days of collapse a new Golden Age.

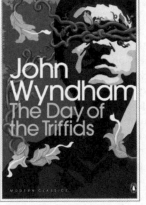

The story begins as our protagonist, Bill Masen, observes something strange. "When a day that you happen to know is Wednesday starts off by sounding like Sunday, there is something seriously wrong somewhere." Masen has had his eyes bandaged during a London hospital stay and consequently has escaped the global blinding-by-celestial-fireworks that affected the other 99 percent of the planet's citizenry. He exits the hospital to a scene of utter chaos, as the newly sightless multitude seeks help, fights, scrambles, and dies. He eventually rescues a sighted woman named Josella, and they encounter a band of seeing survivors who have a plan for escape and sustainable living. But antagonistic forces intervene, and the pair, in the midst of becoming enamored of each other, is separated. The narrative then follows Bill's adventures until, near the close, he and Josella are reunited. Up to this point, the book has filled a few weeks of subjective time with a lucidly envisioned, intensely conveyed particularity of danger, but when the couple begin managing their own little farm haven, the days speed by and the inescapable eternality of the situation dawns upon both the participants and us, the readers. Bill returns to London to find a city aging, rapidly and ineluctably, from metropolis to wilderness:

The gardens of the Parks and Squares were wildernesses creeping out across the bordering streets. Growing things seemed to press out everywhere, rooting in the crevices between the paving stones, springing from cracks in concrete, finding lodgement even in the seats of abandoned cars.

And, of course, over all looms the menace of the rampant triffids, carnivorous plants with an urgent hunger that gives their energy what appears to be a malevolent intelligence. These inspired inventions give Wyndham's book a creepily delightful, uncannily titillating appeal.

What: Science Fiction. *When:* 1951. *Also By: The Chrysalids* (1955). *The Midwich Cuckoos* (1957). *Chocky* (1968). *Try: The Long Tomorrow* by Leigh Brackett. *Greybeard* by Brian W. Aldiss. *The Crystal World* by J. G. Ballard. *The Night of the Triffids* by Simon Clark. *Adaptation:* The 1962 film plays fast and loose with Wyndham's text (and the flailing arms of the triffids tend to resemble prickly vacuum cleaner hoses). *Footnote:* Audrey Jr., the carnivorous plant in Roger Corman's 1960 film *The Little Shop of Horrors*, no doubt has a triffid lineage.

The Zoom Trilogy
Story by Tim Wynne-Jones (born 1948)
Pictures by Eric Beddows (born 1951)

Picture-Perfect Picture Books

A picture book should be an "Open, Sesame," opening a child's mind to riches in the same way that the fabled phrase opened the treasure-laden cave of the forty thieves to Ali Baba in the famous tale from *The Thousand and One Nights*. These riches, which often glitter with fun and fancy, soon become creative resources to nourish and enhance all the lessons later education will deliver. Tucked away deep in the folds of a reader's earliest memories, the imaginative magic of beloved picture books can shape and color all that he or she will come to learn.

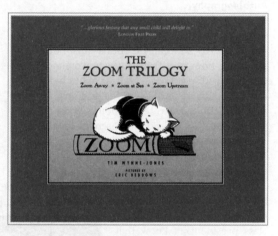

Especially when the books in question are as wonderful as the three Zoom tales of Tim Wynne-Jones and Eric Beddows, which relate the adventures of a cat in search of his mysterious, seafaring Uncle Roy. Zoom's search leads him to his uncle's friend Maria, a woman whose house holds not only the ocean (as we discover in *Zoom at Sea*), but also—up near the attic—the North Pole (as we learn in *Zoom Away*), and—behind the books in the library—Egypt and the Nile (*Zoom Upstream*). With a gentle mix of wisdom and whimsy, the author and the illustrator take us by the hand and lead us, easily and gracefully, into the heady atmosphere of imagination's chamber.

If you ever find better picture books to share—and share again, and again—with your children, you're a lucky family indeed.

What: Children's. *When: Zoom at Sea* (1983). *Zoom Away* (1985). *Zoom Upstream* (1993). *Edition: The Zoom Trilogy*, an omnibus volume with a preface by yours truly, and an afterword by Tim Wynne-Jones, was issued in 1997. *Reading Note:* Ages 3 to 7. *Also By:* Wynne-Jones: *The Maestro* (1995); *Some of the Kinder Planets* (1993). Beddows: *Joyful Noise* (1988) and *Shadow Play* (1990), both written by Paul Fleischman. *Try: Gorky Rises* by William Steig. *The Three Golden Keys* by Peter Sís (see page 726). *Flotsam* by David Wiesner.

X

The Autobiography of Malcolm X
Malcolm X (1925–1965) as told to Alex Haley (1921–1992)

An Urgent American Life, and a Seminal Autobiography

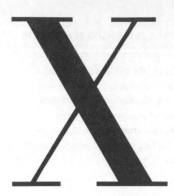

"Malcolm, one of life's first needs is for us to be realistic. Don't misunderstand me, now. We all here like you, you know that. But you've got to be realistic about being a nigger. A lawyer—that's no realistic goal for a nigger. You need to think about something you *can* be." So a junior high school English teacher advised the ambitious Malcolm Little, who, despite the deprivations of a desperate childhood, had become a top academic student, popular enough to have been elected class president. "I know that he probably meant well," the man who became Malcolm X comments in his *Autobiography*; yet the effect of the disillusioning words was profound: "It was then that I began to change—inside."

In some ways, though, he can be said to have followed the advice, for he did become "realistic," and with a vengeance, dropping out of school and leaving Lansing, Michigan, for Boston and New York to pursue a high life of hustling, drugs, and burglary, until, at the age of twenty, he was arrested. In jail, he changed again, widening his education through a rigorous course of reading, embracing the beliefs of Elijah Muhammad's Nation of Islam, and adopting its militant black separatist ideology. As a result, his life after prison was as

Alex Haley, 1966

focused as his previous life had been undirected. His realism turned visionary, and the strength of that conversion fueled a new life of commitment, increasing influence, and no little drama before it was cut short by murderers in 1965.

In the year before his assassination, Malcolm enlisted journalist Alex Haley, who had interviewed him for *Playboy* in 1963, to write his autobiography. Haley crafted the book from extensive taped conversations. "A writer is what I want," Haley quotes Malcolm as saying, "not an interpreter," and the first-person voice of the narrative is electric, unflinching, unforgettable in its honesty, fraught with the power that made Malcolm the Nation of Islam's most effective speaker and organizer for a decade before his acrimonious split with Elijah Muhammad in 1964. On every page, one man's struggle toward a higher calling is given vivid context by reference to the ordinary and extraordinary attentions of the narrator's life: the pain of prejudice both passing and violent, the joys of dancing the Lindy, the logistics of a street hustle or a robbery, the liberating vistas of a library (even in prison), the pride inherent in the careful refiguring of Jackie Robinson's batting average "up through his last turn at bat."

In March 1964, Malcolm X left the Nation of Islam and, one month later, made a pilgrimage to Mecca, embracing the orthodox Muslim faith. He modified his views on black separatism and acknowledged the possibility of positive relations between races. His thinking continued to evolve, and his role as a leader of his own growing group of followers was blossoming before he was gunned down in February 1965. (Three members of the Nation of Islam were convicted of his murder.) His autobiography, as Taylor Branch writes in *At*

Canaan's Edge: America in the King Years 1965–1968 (see page 93), was pulled from the presses by a fearful publisher within days of the assassination, and "a dozen major publishing firms subsequently spurned the orphaned manuscript." Grove Press finally published the book to great acclaim in the fall of 1965. More than three decades later, *Time* magazine, which had disparaged Malcolm X at his death, listed the *Autobiography* as one of the ten most important nonfiction books of the twentieth century. In the reading, it remains riveting—as intense, honest, alert, dangerous, provocative, surprising, and complex as the man whose life it tells.

What: Autobiography. History. *When:* 1965. *Further Reading: Malcolm X Speaks: Selected Speeches and Statements,* edited by George Breitman. *Malcolm X: A Life of Reinvention* by Manning Marable. *Try: Invisible Man* by Ralph Ellison (see page 252). *Manchild in the Promised Land* by Claude Brown. *Soul on Ice* by Eldridge Cleaver. *Adaptation:* The 1992 Spike Lee film *Malcolm X* was based on *The Autobiography. Footnote:* Alex Haley is best known for his second book, the Pulitzer Prize–winning *Roots.*

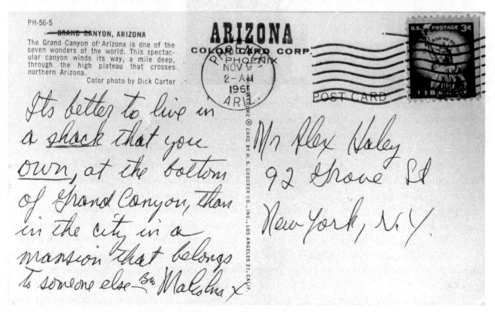

1961 postcard from Malcolm X to Alex Haley

Memoirs of Hadrian

Marguerite Yourcenar (1903–1987)

The Intimate "Autobiography" of a Roman Emperor

Publius Aelius Traianus Hadrianus (AD 76–AD 138) was emperor of Rome from AD 117 to AD 138. Hadrian, as he is known in English, is generally regarded as the most intellectual and cultivated of all the Roman emperors. His reign was largely peaceful, thanks in part to his enlightened acceptance of cultural differences within the empire and in part to a policy of securing borders with fortifications (Hadrian's Wall in the north of Britain, for instance). He traveled the Roman world, made many reforms in law and administration, and was a refined patron of the arts. With a special interest in architecture and beauty, he is responsible for the Pantheon, which sits to this day in the middle of Rome, a brooding and arresting presence, as well as a villa constructed at Tivoli that remains breathtaking even in its ruins. A complex of more than thirty buildings covering some 250 acres, Hadrian's Villa was a symphony of stone and plants and water. The emperor is said to have died uttering the Latin words *"animula, vagula, blandula"*—a poem, addressed to his soul, which translates as "little breath of life, wandering, enticing."

In her celebrated *Memoirs of Hadrian*, Marguerite Yourcenar reinforces the impression that Hadrian's fascinating life had the shape and substance of a work of art. Drawn with scholarly exactitude and imaginative

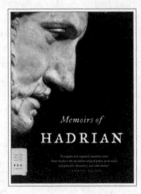

Memoirs of
HADRIAN

sympathy from extant writings by Hadrian as well as by his contemporaries (both friends and enemies) and from the work of latter-day historians, this marvelous "autobiography" is, in Yourcenar's words, both a "psychological novel and meditation on history." Written in the form of a letter from Hadrian to his eventual successor, Marcus Aurelius, the emperor looks back over his formative decades and his years in power, recalling both personal affections (his love for the boy Antinous) and public actions (the destruction of Jerusalem). Ranked among the most adroit and persuasive evocations of antiquity, *Memoirs of Hadrian* is a learned, compelling, and credible reconstruction of the life of emperor and era, written in prose of measured majesty.

What: Novel. History. *When:* 1951; translated from the French by Grace Frick in collaboration with the author, it was first published in English in 1954. *Edition:* The Modern Library edition contains the author's "Reflections on the Composition of *Memoirs of Hadrian." Also By:* Fiction: *A Coin in Nine Hands* (1934); *Coup de Grâce* (1939); *The Abyss* (1968). Essays: *The Dark Brain of Piranesi and Other Essays* (1962). *Further Reading: Hadrian's Villa and Its Legacy* by William L. MacDonald and John A. Pinto. *Try: I, Claudius* by Robert Graves. *Julian* by Gore Vidal. *Augustus* by John Williams. *Footnote:* In 1980, at the age of seventy-seven, Marguerite Yourcenar was the first woman elected to the Académie Française. She lived a large part of her adult life on Mount Desert Island, Maine.

Swallowing Clouds
A. Zee (born 1945)

A Theoretical Physicist on Chinese Food, Language, and Culture

A culture, like an army, marches on its stomach, and in this sly, deft, wise book, physicist Tony Zee examines the long march of Chinese culture by studying the language of its food. Zee begins with the characters on a restaurant menu: These striking graphic symbols, alluring even to the untrained eye, cache tradition, folklore, and history. They create a visual poetry unknown in alphabetic scripts, a mysterious encoding that Zee explicates by revealing the ancient pictographs at their root. You'll never look at Chicken Ding in Brown Sauce or Hot and Sour Soup (not to mention Woman Song's Fish Broth or Buddha Jumping Over the Wall) in the same way again; more important, you'll never look at language in quite the same way either. Throughout this delectable meal, Zee amuses,

charms, and educates readers with his intelligent diversions through two millennia of Chinese civilization. "I will consider the book a success," the author confides, "if I manage to confuse bookstore owners and librarians about where to put the book. The only solution, ladies and gentlemen, is to put it in all three sections—culture, language, and food." He's absolutely right.

What: Food & Drink. Language. Culture. *When:* 1990. *Also By: Fearful Symmetry: The Search for Beauty in Modern Physics* (1986). *An Old Man's Toy: Gravity at Work and Play in Einstein's Universe* (1989). *Quantum Field Theory in a Nutshell* (2003). *Further Reading: The Eater's Guide to Chinese Characters* by James D. McCawley. *Try: Speaking of Chinese* by Raymond Chang and Margaret Scrogin Chang. *Shark's Fin and Sichuan Pepper* by Fuchsia Dunlop. *Footnote:* The literal meaning of "wonton," the Chinese dumpling, gives Zee's book its title.

Within This Wilderness
Feenie Ziner (1921–2012)

The Adventure of a Mother's Love

Events sometimes conspire to let true life assume the shape and significance of a fable, as this lovely and affecting book makes plain. The author's son left home at sixteen (a member of that "whole band of children [who]

fell out of the world in 1969"), and, by the time Feenie Ziner's chronicle begins seven years later, he had settled into a solitary life in the untracked Canadian wilderness, three thousand miles from home. "Ben was on perfectly safe ground when he asked me to come out to British Columbia to see where he was living.

Any kid who had gone to the trouble of putting a whole continent between himself and his family could count on their never showing up at his doorstep."

Any mother who would make the trip—a transcontinental flight, a six-hour bus ride to the end of the line, then a journey by bush plane into a densely forested nowhere—is clearly a force to be reckoned with, and the reckoning between parent and child that *Within This Wilderness* witnesses takes on, because of its remote setting, an archetypal resonance. Indeed, both the awesome natural charms of the surroundings and the hard manner of living that isolation dictates engage and even relax our attention, protecting us for a time from the climate of deep emotion in which the protagonists dwell.

The narrative moves swiftly, its emotional power the current of a swift, transporting stream that describes Ben's rigorous existence, his few wilderness colleagues, and their sporadic negotiations with the local logging industry. Ziner's deft portrayal of the elaborate, often comic diplomacy of the relations between parents and grown children, her sensitivity to the alarming innocence of the toughest youth ("Starting every process from scratch, taking nothing on outer authority, he behaved as if he had a century in which to grow to maturity"), and her splendid writing ("I was unwilling to be a lone figure in so vast and open a landscape. I lacked the protective coloration") reward the reader throughout, and her unstinting appraisal of her own noble confusion—a spell of love, worry, wonder, guilt, loss, pride, anxiety, anger, obligation, yearning—is both moving and magnanimous. As we ride with her through the eddies of instinct and will that mark her journey toward her son, we recognize the familiar waters of experience—deep, dancing, startling, dangerous—that the heart, with hope if never certainty, must teach itself to navigate.

What: Memoir. *When:* 1978. *Also By: A Full House* (1967). *Try: A Mass for the Dead* by William Gibson (see page 314). *Fierce Attachments* by Vivian Gornick. *The Florist's Daughter* by Patricia Hampl.

Germinal
Émile Zola (1840–1902)

The Novelist as Witness and Provocateur

You don't write a cycle of twenty novels unless you're an uncommonly ambitious writer. And Émile Zola, the engineer of literary naturalism in nineteenth-century France, was nothing if not ambitious. He wanted to capture in prose the entirety of French society—rich and poor, urban and rural—under the Second Empire. Each of the works in his Rougon-Macquart cycle (named after the extended family whose members appear in most of the books) stands on its own, however, and the enduring power of a few—such as *Le Ventre de Paris* (*The Belly of Paris*), set in the food market of Les Halles, or *Nana*, a tale about a high-class prostitute who inspired Flaubert and Manet—has come to overshadow the stature of the series as a whole.

The outstanding novel of Zola's cycle is *Germinal*, a gritty portrayal of a coal miners' strike in northern France in the 1860s. Its hero is Étienne Lantier, a homeless migrant worker who journeys from Paris to an unlovely mining town and gets a job pushing carts loaded with coal. The labor is backbreaking, and all the workers who slave away hundreds of feet under the earth—including Catherine, another cart-pusher with whom Lantier falls in love—complain that even after their relentless exertions they can barely make ends meet. Lantier, impulsive and inspired by the socialist arguments of the day, organizes a strike, which is met with violent suppression. The conflict inspires some of Zola's most powerful writing; he is a master of crowd scenes, and the heaving battles at the mine are drawn as intricately and as compellingly as a history painting. His

An announcement of the publication of Zola's Germinal *in 1885 (left); Émile Zola and his mistress, Jeanne Rozerol, ca. 1892 (right)*

treatment of these scenes portends a new kind of storytelling, both panoramic and documentary, which cinema technology would enable a few decades hence.

Germinal, with its unsparing look at lives and labors of the working class, is an exceptionally gripping novel. In the darkness of the coal pits it illuminates signal battles of the coming age: between labor and capital, between nature and industry, and between the promise of socialism and the hazards of its practice. The author's contemporaries certainly bore witness to its impact: When Zola died in Paris in 1902, crowds followed his coffin as a parade carried it to the Montmartre cemetery. As the cortège passed, they shouted one word: "Germinal!"

What: Novel. *When:* 1885. *Also By: Thérèse Raquin* (1867). *Le Ventre de Paris* (1873). *L'Assommoir* (1876). *Nana* (1880). *La Bête Humaine* (1890). *Further Reading: Zola: A Life* by Frederick Brown. *Try: Lost Illusions* by Honoré de Balzac (see page 47). *In Dubious Battle* by John Steinbeck. *God's Bits of Wood* by Ousmane Sembène. *Adaptation:* The 1993 film, directed by Claude Berri, stars Gérard Depardieu and Miou-Miou. *Footnote:* Zola may be best known today as the author of "J'accuse," a landmark of journalism that turned the tide in the Dreyfus Affair, the anti-Semitic military and political scandal that convulsed French society for more than a decade as the nineteenth century gave way to the twentieth.

A Part of Myself

PORTRAIT OF AN EPOCH

Carl Zuckmayer (1896–1977)

A 20th-Century Life

Some books arrive in our lives out of the blue, when a fellow reader launches a hopeful enthusiasm in our direction. "Have you ever read Carl Zuckmayer's *A Part of Myself*?" we may find ourselves being asked, and such questions, and the spirit that provokes them, can lead us into volumes in which our native interest may be slight, but in whose pages we discover unsuspected rewards.

This moving, magnificent autobiography is just the kind of book one likes to pass on to friends. Carl Zuckmayer was one of the finest playwrights (*The Captain of Köpenick*) and screenwriters (*The Blue Angel*) of Weimar Germany, whose literary, theatrical, and cinematic achievements met with accolades and awards throughout the middle decades of the twentieth century. You may at first wonder what the story of his life has to offer. You won't be many pages into *A Part of Myself* before you stop asking. His book is a beautiful narrative of childhood and youth, of the horrors of the First World War, of heady early success in the theater, of the encroaching terror of World War II as it destroyed a world of great human substance and dignity. Forced by the Nazis to flee

his homeland, he became an exile in America, working first as a Hollywood screenwriter and later as a Vermont farmer. He returned to Europe after the defeat of Hitler.

Filled with culture and compassion, and with noble friendships (celebrated ones, too: Bertolt Brecht, Marlene Dietrich, Ernest Hemingway, and theater impresario Max Reinhardt are among the notables summoned by Zuckmayer's recollections), this portrait of an epoch is also one of its more exquisite monuments.

What: Autobiography. *When:* 1966; English translation by Richard and Clara Winston, 1970. *Further Reading: The Farm in the Green Mountains* by Alice Herdan-Zuckmayer. *Before the Deluge: A Portrait of Berlin in the 1920s* by Otto Friedrich. *Try: Diana Cooper: Autobiography,* by Diana Cooper.

Acknowledgments

This book is the product of fourteen years' labor: reading, writing, revising, reading more, rewriting again and again. All the while, new books were swimming into my ken. That it has finally arrived between covers is largely due to the editorial attention, organizational energy, and generosity of Margot Greenbaum Mustich, without whose dedication it might have been *213 Books to Read Before You Die* or something equally unimpressive. Her tireless support in helping me to turn reading into thought and ideas into words, and her perseverance in holding those words to her own high standards once I got them on a page, have been essential to the making of this book. I am grateful for the intelligence and effort she has lavished on this undertaking, but not nearly as much as I am grateful for what she has brought to our shared life outside it.

The early days of this project benefited from significant contributions from Thomas Meagher, a collaborator in books from our high school days in the Bronx through our work together on the book catalog *A Common Reader*, and Karen Templer, foundress of Readerville.com, which, while long gone, remains the most vibrant representation of the reading life ever to have graced the internet. Editorial insight has also been provided at various stages of the project by Jason Farago, whose literary acumen is as developed as the eye that is making him a prominent art critic, and the science fiction magus Paul Di Filippo. In the past year, the scholar and critic Thomas DePietro added an unexpected but welcome clause to the sentence of our nearly fifty-year friendship by taking on a close reading of the entire text, commenting on it with erudition and brio. I would also like to voice a sincere but appropriately quiet shout-out to the public library in New Fairfield, Connecticut, particularly to reference librarian Margaret Golden and interlibrary loan facilitator Jill Tandy.

Fourteen years is in truth only the short-term measure of the making of *1,000 Books*. Whether arranged on shelves or set down on pages, a record of a reading life told through books is a tangible autobiography in which one can trace the stages of one's growth, the evolution of one's education, even the nature and quality of one's relationships. Every book I've written about summons to memory a network of associations: the teacher who unlocked its meaning, the fellow reader who recommended it, the bookstore I discovered it in, the bookseller or publisher who pressed it upon me. Mapping all of these connections would require another, more discursive book, but I would like to acknowledge here a few such personal attachments with special significance for me.

Among teachers: Geraldine Schaechter Bloch, Fernand Beck III, Charles W. DaParma, Arthur K. McCormack, and Maria DiBattista opened doors in books through which I entered a larger life. Among fellow readers, I salute the customers of *A Common Reader*, the mail-order catalog I founded with Alex Goulder in 1986 and which I ran for the next two decades. The company of books that *A Common Reader* fostered was animated with the curiosity of countless book mavens, whose correspondence—in those days it came via handwritten or typed letters delivered through the postal service—still fills a bank of large file cabinets in my basement, a library of shared annotations from solitary reading sent across time and space by people I seldom met.

Among booksellers, let my thanks to Charles and Diane Newman, who gave me my first job in a bookstore ($2.30 an hour), signal my boundless gratitude to booksellers everywhere. Steve Riggio has enriched my reading and thinking through more than three decades of friendship; he also provided welcome opportunity for me at Barnes & Noble, especially in commissioning the *Barnes & Noble Review* with the best kind of direction: "Make something you and I will find interesting." My literary horizons were expanded through my work with scores of gifted writers in the early days of the *Review*, and by constant collaboration with my partner in shaping it, Bill Tipper.

Among publishers, my debt to those who shared their knowledge with me is incalculable.

In particular, I thank David R. Godine and Herman Graf, titans of the trade, for the years of kinship we've shared. Two other giants in my book, J. P. Leventhal and Paul Feldstein (now my agent), have been the best of friends both personally and professionally.

Which brings me to Workman, publishers of the book you are holding. I am grateful to the entire Workman team for its patience through the many years of composition, and their professionalism in this last one, as the enormous manuscript made its way to press. Pride of place goes to my editor, Margot Herrera, whose forbearance through nearly a decade and a half has been appreciated, as has her line-by-line persistence in untangling convoluted thinking and knotty expression; equally persistent has been her unfailing good cheer in the face of authorial crankiness. I'm especially pleased I got to work with Alison Humes—called in from the bullpen like an editorial Mariano Rivera to safeguard the game—whose acuity was bracing, fortifying every passage she touched. Laurel Robinson provided precise and perspicacious copy editing.

Publisher and editorial director Susan Bolotin should run for office; the republic could use her good sense, sagacity, and pragmatic effectiveness. I'd vote for her for anything. Dan Reynolds, Page Edmunds, David Schiller, and James Wehrle have been ardent and creative supporters of this project; I am glad to have the benefit of their care, skill, and ingenuity—likewise Lathea Williams and Moira Kerrigan.

Production of a book of this length and complexity is an enormous project, which Kim Daly has managed with grit and grace. Doug Wolff has adeptly arranged every element of the book's manufacture, while Aaron Clendening artfully researched and—abetted by an expert photo department—summoned hundreds of images across time, space, and style to enliven our pages. Most especially: No project was ever better served by a typesetter than this one has been by Barbara Peragine;

I'm more grateful than I can say for the dedication she brought to the task. And that a manuscript of nearly half-a-million words has been turned into a book of such graphic delight and visual allure is due to the consummate gifts and extraordinary devotion of Janet Vicario: Thank you, thank you, thank you.

Carolan and Peter Workman have been stalwart friends to the Mustich family for many years. My appreciation for their generosity and warmth extends far beyond the margins of these pages or the dimensions of this project. I am glad Carolan can celebrate the occasion of its completion with us, and I am deeply sorry Peter has not lived to see *1,000 Books* make its way into the world. Like the books he published with such success, Peter was innovative, quirky, one-of-a-kind. His approach to books was the epitome of a passion that many of us share. He took pleasure in the traffic in books and everything that fueled it: from an idea and the author who could deliver it through the design and art direction, from controlling the costs of paper, printing, and binding to setting the press runs, from the in-house sales conferences with his merry band of reps to sales calls on key accounts. There is no part of the whole complicated equation that Peter did not embrace with energy, expertise, and exuberance. His inspiration was endless, and relentless: It let no detail go by. You could almost call his method an ethic, one built on the collaboration of good people, smart products, and, not least, a pride in commerce.

Quite simply, Peter knew better than any other publisher I've ever met how to make a book take on a life of its own—thereby enriching the lives of everyone who touched it along the way to the reader. He delighted in his books, and sharing that delight—whether it was in *Oh, Yuck!* or *The French Laundry Cookbook*—was for him the ultimate joy of the work. No one ever walked out of Peter's office without being handed a book to take home, and I regret that I can only imagine, but not witness, the joy with which he would have passed along this one.

A Miscellany of Special Lists

Read in a Sitting

- *Love, Loss, and What I Wore*, Ilene Beckerman, page 62
- *The Uncommon Reader*, Alan Bennett, page 67
- *Memorial*, Ferdinando Camon, page 120
- *A Month in the Country*, J. L. Carr, page 132
- *The Chemical History of a Candle*, Michael Faraday, page 264
- *The Little Virtues*, Natalia Ginzburg, page 316
- *The Third Man*, Graham Greene, page 335
- *The All of It*, Jeannette Haien, page 344
- *84, Charing Cross Road*, Helene Hanff, page 350
- *Ill Met by Moonlight*, W. Stanley Moss, page 570
- *Within the Context of No Context*, George W. S. Trow, page 807
- *Candide*, Voltaire, page 824

A Long Climb, but What a View

- *The Civil War*, Shelby Foote, page 286
- *Les Misérables*, Victor Hugo, page 394
- *Zibaldone*, Giacomo Leopardi, page 475
- *The Golden Notebook*, Doris Lessing, page 477
- *The Magic Mountain*, Thomas Mann, page 521
- *The Tale of Genji*, Lady Murasaki Shikibu, page 575
- *The Man Without Qualities*, Robert Musil, page 578

- *In Search of Lost Time*, Marcel Proust, page 644
- *On Growth and Form*, D. W. Thompson, page 782
- *War and Peace*, Leo Tolstoy, page 798
- *Kristin Lavransdatter*, Sigrid Undset, page 817
- *Black Lamb and Grey Falcon*, Rebecca West, page 843

12 Books to Read Before You're 12

- *Skellig*, David Almond, page 16
- *Tuck Everlasting*, Natalie Babbitt, page 37
- *The Wonderful Wizard of Oz*, L. Frank Baum, page 56
- *Matilda*, Roald Dahl, page 192
- *Harriet the Spy*, Louise Fitzhugh, page 280
- *The Wind in the Willows*, Kenneth Grahame, page 328
- *The Mouse and His Child*, Russell Hoban, page 378
- *From the Mixed-Up Files of Mrs. Basil E. Frankweiler*, E. L. Konigsburg, page 452
- *Anne of Green Gables*, L. M. Montgomery, page 564
- *Abel's Island*, William Steig, page 750
- *The Great Good Thing*, Roderick Townley, page 802
- *Charlotte's Web*, E. B. White, page 845

LOL

- *The Hitchhiker's Guide to the Galaxy*, Douglas Adams, page 6
- *The Ascent of Rum Doodle*, W. E. Bowman, page 90

- *A Bullet in the Ballet*, Caryl Brahms and S. J. Simon, page 92
- *A Walk in the Woods*, Bill Bryson, page 104
- *The Decline and Fall of Practically Everybody*, Will Cuppy, page 190
- *Cold Comfort Farm*, Stella Gibbons, page 313
- *Life Among the Savages*, Shirley Jackson, page 404
- *the lives and times of archy and mehitabel*, Don Marquis, page 526
- *At Swim-Two-Birds*, Flann O'Brien, page 595
- *The Portable Dorothy Parker*, Dorothy Parker, page 615
- *The Bogey Man*, George Plimpton, page 629
- *Pigs Have Wings*, P. G. Wodehouse, page 864

Cities in Fact and Fiction

- *Invisible Cities*, Italo Calvino, page 120
- *The Piano Shop on the Left Bank*, Thad Carhart, page 128
- *The Power Broker*, Robert A. Caro, page 130
- *Rome and a Villa*, Eleanor Clark, page 160
- *Bleak House*, Charles Dickens, page 220
- *The Death and Life of Great American Cities*, Jane Jacobs, page 405
- *Ulysses*, James Joyce, page 422
- *Venice for Pleasure*, J. G. Links, page 492
- *Life: A User's Manual*, Georges Perec, page 623

- *American Pastoral*, Philip Roth, page 677
- *The Stones of Venice*, John Ruskin, page 684
- *The Bonfire of the Vanities*, Tom Wolfe, page 866

A Garden of Verse

- *The Flowers of Evil*, Charles Baudelaire, page 55
- *The Complete Poems, 1927–1979*, Elizabeth Bishop, page 80
- *The Poems of Catullus*, Gaius Valerius Catullus, page 139
- *Sailing Alone Around the Room*, Billy Collins, page 166
- *Poems*, Emily Dickinson, page 222
- *The Poetry of Robert Frost*, Robert Frost, page 301
- *Howl and Other Poems*, Allen Ginsberg, page 315
- *Selected Poetry*, Rainer Maria Rilke, page 667
- *A Child's Garden of Verses*, Robert Louis Stevenson, page 760
- *Map: Collected and Last Poems*, Wisława Szymborska, page 769
- *Collected Poems 1943–2004*, Richard Wilbur, page 853
- *The Prelude and Other Poetry*, William Wordsworth, page 871

Listen Up! 12 Terrific Audiobooks

- *Ender's Game*, Orson Scott Card (read by Stefan Rudnicki and others), page 126
- *Great Expectations*, Charles Dickens (read by Martin Jarvis), page 221
- *The Iliad*, Homer (Fagles translation read by Derek Jacobi), page 385

- *The Portrait of a Lady*, Henry James (read by Juliet Stevenson), page 409
- *Dubliners*, James Joyce (read by Frank McCourt and others), page 420
- *Moby-Dick*, Herman Melville (read by Frank Muller), page 542
- *Lolita*, Vladimir Nabokov (read by Jeremy Irons), page 579
- *The Little Red Chairs*, Edna O'Brien (read by Juliet Stevenson), page 595
- *The Golden Compass*, Philip Pullman (read by the author and a full cast), page 647
- *Gilead*, Marilynne Robinson (read by Tim Jerome), page 670
- *American Pastoral*, Philip Roth (read by Ron Silver), page 677
- *Treasure Island*, Robert Louis Stevenson (read by Alfred Molina), page 758

Family Read-Alouds

- *Peter and Wendy*, J. M. Barrie, page 53
- *The Secret Garden*, Frances Hodgson Burnett, page 113
- *The Phantom Tollbooth*, Norton Juster, page 424
- *Talking Like the Rain*, X. J. and D. M. Kennedy, page 440
- *Just So Stories for Little Children*, Rudyard Kipling, page 449
- *The Lion, the Witch and the Wardrobe*, C. S. Lewis, page 485
- *The Voyages of Doctor Dolittle*, Hugh Lofting, page 494
- *Betsy-Tacy*, Maud Hart Lovelace, page 436

- *Swallows and Amazons*, Arthur Ransome, page 660
- *The Little Prince*, Antoine de Saint-Exupéry, page 693
- *Twenty Thousand Leagues Under the Sea*, Jules Verne, page 821
- *Little House in the Big Woods*, Laura Ingalls Wilder, page 435

Offbeat Escapes

- *Laughing in the Hills*, Bill Barich, page 51
- *No Picnic on Mount Kenya*, Felice Benuzzi, page 68
- *The Outermost House*, Henry Beston, page 74
- *The Wilder Shores of Love*, Lesley Blanch, page 83
- *Tracks*, Robyn Davidson, page 198
- *The Auberge of the Flowering Hearth*, Roy Andries de Groot, page 202
- *Brazilian Adventure*, Peter Fleming, page 285
- *West with the Night*, Beryl Markham, page 525
- *A Short Walk in the Hindu Kush*, Eric Newby, page 585
- *The Valleys of the Assassins*, Freya Stark, page 746
- *The Sea and the Jungle*, H. M. Tomlinson, page 801

Singular Self-Portraits

- *The Education of Henry Adams*, Henry Adams, page 6
- *Memoirs of a Dutiful Daughter*, Simone de Beauvoir, page 60
- *Earthly Paradise*, Colette, page 165
- *The Diary of a Young Girl*, Anne Frank, page 295
- *If This Is a Man*, Primo Levi, page 481
- *Tristes Tropiques*, Claude Lévi-Strauss, page 482

- *Autobiography of John Stuart Mill*, John Stuart Mill, page 548
- *Speak, Memory*, Vladimir Nabokov, page 580
- *Hunger of Memory*, Richard Rodriguez, page 671
- *The Confessions*, Jean-Jacques Rousseau, page 679
- *Aké: The Years of Childhood*, Wole Soyinka, page 742
- *The Autobiography of Malcolm X*, Malcolm X and Alex Haley, page 876

Novel Pleasures

- *Half of a Yellow Sun*, Chimamanda Ngozi Adichie, page 8
- *Cat's Eye*, Margaret Atwood, page 28
- *The Sweet Hereafter*, Russell Banks, page 49
- *The Feast of Love*, Charles Baxter, page 58
- *Possession*, A. S. Byatt, page 118
- *Spartina*, John Casey, page 136
- *Clear Light of Day*, Anita Desai, page 210
- *The Game of Kings*, Dorothy Dunnett, page 240
- *A Visit from the Goon Squad*, Jennifer Egan, page 245
- *An Infamous Army*, Georgette Heyer, page 373
- *Epitaph of a Small Winner*, Joaquim María Machado de Assis, page 508
- *The Wicked Pavilion*, Dawn Powell, page 638

War Stories

- *Slightly Out of Focus*, Robert Capa, page 124
- *The Red Badge of Courage*, Stephen Crane, page 184

- *Good-bye to All That*, Robert Graves, page 332
- *I Was a Stranger*, Sir John Winthrop Hackett, page 343
- *Dispatches*, Michael Herr, page 369
- *We Die Alone*, David Howarth, page 391
- *The Face of Battle*, John Keegan, page 433
- *Kaputt*, Curzio Malaparte, page 515
- *Goodbye, Darkness*, William Manchester, page 519
- *War in Val d'Orcia*, Iris Origo, page 605
- *The Walls Came Tumbling Down*, Henriette Roosenburg, page 673
- *The Killer Angels*, Michael Shaara, page 704

From the 21st Century

- *Fun Home*, Alison Bechdel, page 61
- *Can't We Talk About Something More Pleasant?*, Roz Chast, page 148
- *Between the World and Me*, Ta-Nehisi Coates, page 162
- *Those Who Leave and Those Who Stay*, Elena Ferrante, page 270
- *Ten Years in the Tub*, Nick Hornby, page 210
- *11/22/63*, Stephen King, page 448
- *The Story of My Teeth*, Valeria Luiselli, page 509
- *Ongoingness*, Sarah Manguso, page 521
- *Citizen: An American Lyric*, Claudia Rankine, page 659
- *This One Summer*, Jillian Tamaki and Mariko Tamaki, page 772

- *Life in Code*, Ellen Ullman, page 816
- *The Underground Railroad*, Colson Whitehead, page 849

Soul Food

- *Meditations*, Marcus Aurelius, page 31
- *Journal of a Disappointed Man*, W. N. P. Barbellion, page 50
- *The Diary of a Country Priest*, Georges Bernanos, page 72
- *The Long Loneliness*, Dorothy Day, page 31
- *Four Quartets*, T. S. Eliot, page 249
- *Time and the Art of Living*, Robert Grudin, page 339
- *The Seven Storey Mountain*, Thomas Merton, page 547
- *Dakota*, Kathleen Norris, page 591
- *The Book of Tea*, Kakuzo Okakura, page 601
- *Zen and the Art of Motorcycle Maintenance*, Robert M. Pirsig, page 626
- *Gilead*, Marilynne Robinson, page 670
- *Artful*, Ali Smith, page 728

Mysterious Matters

- *The Big Sleep*, Raymond Chandler, page 147
- *The Murder of Roger Ackroyd*, Agatha Christie, page 159
- *The Moonstone*, Wilkie Collins, page 168
- *The Complete Sherlock Holmes*, Sir Arthur Conan Doyle, page 171
- *The Moving Toyshop*, Edmund Crispin, page 186
- *The Maltese Falcon*, Dashiell Hammett, page 346
- *A Taste for Death*, P. D. James, page 411

General Index of Books and Authors

P

1,000 Books Checklist

A

☐ **Desert Solitaire,** Edward Abbey

☐ **Flatland,** Edwin A. Abbott

☐ **Things Fall Apart,** Chinua Achebe

☐ **My Dog Tulip,** J. R. Ackerley

☐ **The Hitchhiker's Guide to the Galaxy,** Douglas Adams

☐ **The Education of Henry Adams,** Henry Adams

☐ **Watership Down,** Richard Adams

☐ **Half of a Yellow Sun,** Chimamanda Ngozi Adichie

☐ **The Oresteia,** Aeschylus

☐ **Let Us Now Praise Famous Men,** James Agee

☐ **Who's Afraid of Virginia Woolf?,** Edward Albee

☐ **Little Women,** Louisa May Alcott

☐ **The Book of Three,** Lloyd Alexander

☐ **The Absolutely True Diary of a Part-Time Indian,** Sherman Alexie

☐ **Voices from Chernobyl,** Svetlana Alexievich

☐ **The House of the Spirits,** Isabel Allende

☐ **Skellig,** David Almond

☐ **A Coffin for Dimitrios,** Eric Ambler

☐ **Lucky Jim,** Kingsley Amis

☐ **Fairy Tales,** Hans Christian Andersen

☐ **I Know Why the Caged Bird Sings,** Maya Angelou

☐ **The Arabian Nights**

☐ **The Clouds,** Aristophanes

☐ **Nicomachean Ethics,** Aristotle

☐ **Old Herbaceous,** Reginald Arkell

☐ **Study Is Hard Work,** William H. Armstrong

The Foundation Trilogy, Isaac Asimov
☐ Foundation
☐ Foundation and Empire
☐ Second Foundation

☐ **Instead of a Letter,** Diana Athill

☐ **Cat's Eye,** Margaret Atwood

☐ **Aubrey's Brief Lives,** John Aubrey

☐ **Confessions,** Saint Augustine

☐ **Meditations,** Marcus Aurelius

● **JANE AUSTEN:**
☐ Emma
☐ Mansfield Park
☐ Northanger Abbey
☐ Persuasion
☐ Pride and Prejudice
☐ Sense and Sensibility

B

☐ **Tuck Everlasting,** Natalie Babbitt

☐ **The Baburnama,** Zahiruddin Muhammad Babur

☐ **The Poetics of Space,** Gaston Bachelard

☐ **The Ideological Origins of the American Revolution,** Bernard Bailyn

☐ **The Birthday Boys,** Beryl Bainbridge

☐ **The Mezzanine,** Nicholson Baker

☐ **Growing Up,** Russell Baker

☐ **Collected Essays,** James Baldwin

☐ **Slaves in the Family,** Edward Ball

☐ **The Drowned World,** J. G. Ballard

● **HONORÉ DE BALZAC:**
☐ Lost Illusions
☐ Père Goriot
☐ The Wild Ass's Skin

☐ **The Sweet Hereafter,** Russell Banks

☐ **The Journal of a Disappointed Man,** W. N. P. Barbellion

☐ **Laughing in the Hills,** Bill Barich

The Regeneration Trilogy, Pat Barker
☐ Regeneration
☐ The Eye in the Door
☐ The Ghost Road

☐ **Flaubert's Parrot,** Julian Barnes

☐ **Peter and Wendy,** J. M. Barrie

☐ **The Sot-Weed Factor,** John Barth

☐ **The Narrow Road to the Deep North,** Matsuo Bashō

☐ **Samuel Johnson,** W. Jackson Bate

☐ **The Flowers of Evil,** Charles Baudelaire

☐ **The Wonderful Wizard of Oz,** L. Frank Baum

☐ **The Feast of Love,** Charles Baxter

☐ **Vacuum Diagrams,** Stephen Baxter

● **SIMONE DE BEAUVOIR:**
☐ The Coming of Age
☐ Memoirs of a Dutiful Daughter
☐ The Second Sex

☐ **Fun Home,** Alison Bechdel

☐ **Love, Loss, and What I Wore,** Ilene Beckerman

● **SAMUEL BECKETT:**
☐ Company
☐ Molloy
☐ Waiting for Godot

☐ **The Hills is Lonely,** Lillian Beckwith

☐ **The Adventures of Augie March,** Saul Bellow

☐ **Madeline,** Ludwig Bemelmans

☐ **The Uncommon Reader,** Alan Bennett

☐ **No Picnic on Mount Kenya,** Felice Benuzzi

☐ **Beowulf**

☐ **Midnight in the Garden of Good and Evil,** John Berendt

☐ **A Fortunate Man,** John Berger

☐ **The Memoirs of Hector Berlioz,** Hector Berlioz

☐ **The Diary of a Country Priest,** Georges Bernanos

☐ **All the President's Men,** Carl Bernstein and Bob Woodward

☐ **The Stars My Destination,** Alfred Bester

☐ **The Outermost House,** Henry Beston

☐ **Bhagavad Gita**

☐ **The Bible**

☐ **The Book of Job**

☐ **American Prometheus,** Kai Bird and Martin J. Sherwin

☐ **The Complete Poems, 1927–1979,** Elizabeth Bishop

☐ **Friday Night Lights,** H. G. Bissinger

☐ **The Emperor's Last Island,** Julia Blackburn

☐ **Songs of Innocence and of Experience,** William Blake

☐ **The Wilder Shores of Love,** Lesley Blanch

☐ **Are You There, God? It's Me, Margaret.,** Judy Blume

☐ **Akenfield,** Ronald Blythe

❑ **The Decameron,**
Giovanni Boccaccio

❑ **2666,** Roberto Bolaño

❑ **The Book of Common Prayer**

❑ **Ficciones,** Jorge Luis Borges

❑ **The Life of Samuel Johnson,**
James Boswell

❑ **The Death of the Heart,**
Elizabeth Bowen

❑ **The Sheltering Sky,** Paul Bowles

❑ **The Ascent of Rum Doodle,**
W. E. Bowman

❑ **Fahrenheit 451,** Ray Bradbury

❑ **The Chaneysville Incident,**
David Bradley

❑ **A Bullet in the Ballet,**
Caryl Brahms and S. J. Simon

America in the King Years,
Taylor Branch
 ❑ Parting the Waters
 ❑ Pillar of Fire
 ❑ At Canaan's Edge

❑ **How Buildings Learn,**
Stewart Brand

❑ **The Mediterranean and the
Mediterranean World in the
Age of Philip II,** Fernand Braudel

❑ **Navigator of the Flood,**
Mario Brelich

❑ **The Physiology of Taste,**
Jean Anthelme Brillat-Savarin

❑ **Jane Eyre,** Charlotte Brontë

❑ **Wuthering Heights,** Emily Brontë

❑ **The Da Vinci Code,** Dan Brown

❑ **Bury My Heart at Wounded
Knee,** Dee Brown

● **MARGARET WISE BROWN:**
 ❑ Goodnight Moon
 ❑ Little Fur Family

❑ **The Major Works,**
Sir Thomas Browne

❑ **The Story of Babar,**
Jean de Brunhoff

❑ **A Walk in the Woods,** Bill Bryson

❑ **The Thirty-Nine Steps,**
John Buchan

❑ **The Good Earth,** Pearl S. Buck

❑ **Bulfinch's Mythology,**
Thomas Bulfinch

❑ **The Master and Margarita,**
Mikhail Bulgakov

❑ **The Civilization of the
Renaissance in Italy,**
Jacob Burckhardt

❑ **A Clockwork Orange,**
Anthony Burgess

❑ **Reflections on the Revolution
in France,** Edmund Burke

● **FRANCES HODGSON BURNETT:**
 ❑ A Little Princess
 ❑ The Secret Garden

❑ **The Anatomy of Melancholy,**
Robert Burton

❑ **Independent Spirit,** Hubert Butler

❑ **The Way of All Flesh,**
Samuel Butler

❑ **The Tartar Steppe,** Dino Buzzati

❑ **Possession,** A. S. Byatt

C

❑ **The Marriage of Cadmus and
Harmony,** Roberto Calasso

❑ **Invisible Cities,** Italo Calvino

❑ **Memorial,** Ferdinando Camon

The Masks of God, Joseph Campbell
 ❑ Primitive Mythology
 ❑ Occidental Mythology
 ❑ Oriental Mythology
 ❑ Creative Mythology

● **ALBERT CAMUS:**
 ❑ The First Man
 ❑ The Plague

❑ **Slightly Out of Focus,**
Robert Capa

❑ **In Cold Blood,** Truman Capote

❑ **Ender's Game,** Orson Scott Card

❑ **Eyewitness to History,**
John Carey

❑ **True History of the Kelly Gang,**
Peter Carey

❑ **The Piano Shop on the Left
Bank,** Thad Carhart

❑ **Papa, Please Get the Moon
for Me,** Eric Carle

❑ **The Power Broker,** Robert A. Caro

❑ **The Years of Lyndon Johnson,**
Robert A. Caro

● **ROBERT A. CARO:**
 ❑ Master of the Senate
 ❑ Means of Ascent
 ❑ The Passage of Power
 ❑ The Path to Power

❑ **A Month in the Country,** J. L. Carr

Alice in Wonderland, Lewis Carroll
 ❑ Alice's Adventures in
 Wonderland
 ❑ Through the Looking-Glass

❑ **Silent Spring,** Rachel Carson

❑ **The Horse's Mouth,** Joyce Cary

❑ **History of My Life,**
Giacomo Casanova

❑ **Spartina,** John Casey

❑ **The Book of the Courtier,**
Baldassare Castiglione

❑ **O Pioneers!,** Willa Cather

❑ **The Poems of Catullus,**
Gaius Valerius Catullus

❑ **Melbourne,** David Cecil

❑ **Journey to the End of the
Night,** Louis-Ferdinand Céline

❑ **The Autobiography
of Benvenuto Cellini,**
Benvenuto Cellini

❑ **Don Quixote,** Miguel de Cervantes

❑ **The Amazing Adventures of
Kavalier & Clay,** Michael Chabon

❑ **Clémentine in the Kitchen,**
Samuel Chamberlain

❑ **Products of the Perfected
Civilization,** Sébastien-Roch
Nicolas Chamfort

❑ **The Big Sleep,** Raymond Chandler

❑ **Can't We Talk About
Something More Pleasant?,**
Roz Chast

❑ **The Songlines,** Bruce Chatwin

❑ **The Canterbury Tales,**
Geoffrey Chaucer

❑ **Dawn of Art: The Chauvet
Cave,** Jean-Marie Chauvet,
Eliette Brunel Deschamps, and
Christian Hillaire

❑ **The Stories of John Cheever,**
John Cheever

● **ANTON CHEKHOV:**
 ❑ The Cherry Orchard
 ❑ The Seagull
 ❑ Stories
 ❑ Three Sisters
 ❑ Uncle Vanya

❑ **Alexander Hamilton,**
Ron Chernow

❑ **The Worst Journey in the
World,** Apsley Cherry-Garrard

❑ **The Man Who Was Thursday,**
G. K. Chesterton

❑ **The Riddle of the Sands,**
Erskine Childers

❑ **The Awakening,** Kate Chopin

❑ **The Murder of Roger Ackroyd,**
Agatha Christie

❑ **Their Finest Hour,**
Winston Churchill

❑ **The Hunt for Red October,**
Tom Clancy

❑ **Rome and a Villa,** Eleanor Clark

❑ **Childhood's End,** Arthur C. Clarke

❑ **Between the World and Me,** Ta-Nehisi Coates

❑ **A Classical Education,** Richard Cobb

❑ **Life & Times of Michael K,** J. M. Coetzee

❑ **Earthly Paradise,** Colette

❑ **Sailing Alone Around the Room,** Billy Collins

❑ **Carrying the Fire,** Michael Collins

❑ **The Hunger Games,** Suzanne Collins

❑ **The Moonstone,** Wilkie Collins

❑ **The Worm Forgives the Plough,** John Stewart Collis

❑ **Memoirs of a Medieval Woman,** Louise Collis

❑ **The Fringes of Power,** John Colville

❑ **The Complete Sherlock Holmes,** Sir Arthur Conan Doyle

❑ **Son of the Morning Star,** Evan S. Connell

❑ **Enemies of Promise,** Cyril Connolly

● JOSEPH CONRAD:
  ❑ Heart of Darkness
  ❑ A Personal Record

❑ **The Road from Coorain,** Jill Ker Conway

❑ **Memories of the Great and the Good,** Alistair Cooke

❑ **Talleyrand,** Duff Cooper

❑ **The Last of the Mohicans,** James Fenimore Cooper

❑ **Torregreca,** Ann Cornelisen

❑ **Cronopios and Famas,** Julio Cortázar

❑ **Conversations with Glenn Gould,** Jonathan Cott

❑ **Stravinsky,** Robert Craft

❑ **The Red Badge of Courage,** Stephen Crane

❑ **The Andromeda Strain,** Michael Crichton

❑ **The Moving Toyshop,** Edmund Crispin

❑ **Little, Big,** John Crowley

❑ **Complete Poems, 1904–1962,** E. E. Cummings

❑ **Rebellion in the Backlands,** Euclides da Cunha

❑ **The Hours,** Michael Cunningham

❑ **The Decline and Fall of Practically Everybody,** Will Cuppy

D

❑ **Memoirs of Lorenzo Da Ponte,** Lorenzo Da Ponte

❑ **Matilda,** Roald Dahl

❑ **In Xanadu,** William Dalrymple

The Divine Comedy, Dante Alighieri
  ❑ Inferno
  ❑ Purgatorio
  ❑ Paradiso

❑ **The Dew Breaker,** Edwidge Danticat

❑ **The Voyage of the *Beagle*,** Charles Darwin

❑ **The Geography of the Imagination,** Guy Davenport

❑ **Tracks,** Robyn Davidson

The Deptford Trilogy, Robertson Davies
  ❑ Fifth Business
  ❑ The Manticore
  ❑ World of Wonders

❑ **The Selfish Gene,** Richard Dawkins

❑ **The Long Loneliness,** Dorothy Day

❑ **How Proust Can Change Your Life,** Alain de Botton

❑ **The Complete War Memoirs of Charles de Gaulle,** Charles de Gaulle

❑ **The Auberge of the Flowering Hearth,** Roy Andries de Groot

❑ **Microbe Hunters,** Paul de Kruif

❑ **Giants and Heroes,** Dianne Tittle de Laet

❑ **Robinson Crusoe,** Daniel Defoe

❑ **Diary of a Provincial Lady,** E. M. Delafield

❑ **Nova,** Samuel R. Delany

❑ **Great Books,** David Denby

❑ **Clear Light of Day,** Anita Desai

❑ **The Brief Wondrous Life of Oscar Wao,** Junot Diaz

● PHILIP K. DICK:
  ❑ Do Androids Dream of Electric Sheep?
  ❑ The Man in the High Castle
  ❑ The Three Stigmata of Palmer Eldritch

● CHARLES DICKENS:
  ❑ Bleak House
  ❑ A Christmas Carol
  ❑ David Copperfield
  ❑ Dombey and Son
  ❑ Great Expectations
  ❑ The Life and Adventures of Nicholas Nickleby
  ❑ A Tale of Two Cities
  ❑ Oliver Twist

❑ **Poems,** Emily Dickinson

❑ **The Year of Magical Thinking,** Joan Didion

❑ **Pilgrim at Tinker Creek,** Annie Dillard

❑ **Winter's Tales,** Isak Dinesen

❑ **Bound to Please,** Michael Dirda

❑ **Ragtime,** E. L. Doctorow

❑ **This House of Sky,** Ivan Doig

❑ **Poems and Sermons,** John Donne

U.S.A., John Dos Passos
  ❑ The 42nd Parallel
  ❑ 1919
  ❑ The Big Money

● FYODOR DOSTOEVSKY:
  ❑ The Brothers Karamazov
  ❑ Crime and Punishment
  ❑ Notes from Underground

❑ **Narrative of the Life of Frederick Douglass, an American Slave,** Frederick Douglass

❑ **Sister Carrie,** Theodore Dreiser

❑ **The Souls of Black Folk,** W. E. B. Du Bois

❑ **Rebecca,** Daphne du Maurier

❑ **"Bequest of Wings,"** Annis Duff

❑ **The World As I Found It,** Bruce Duffy

● ALEXANDRE DUMAS:
  ❑ The Count of Monte Cristo
  ❑ The Three Musketeers

❑ **The Adventures of Ibn Battuta,** Ross E. Dunn

❑ **The Game of Kings,** Dorothy Dunnett

❑ **My Family and Other Animals,** Gerald Durrell

The Alexandria Quartet, Lawrence Durrell
  ❑ Justine
  ❑ Balthazar
  ❑ Mountolive
  ❑ Clea

❑ **Darwin Among the Machines,** George Dyson

E

❑ **The Name of the Rose,** Umberto Eco

❑ **The Worm Ouroboros,** E. R. Eddison

❑ **Bright Air, Brilliant Fire,** Gerald M. Edelman

❑ **The Book of Ebenezer Le Page,** G. B. Edwards

❑ **A Visit from the Goon Squad,**
Jennifer Egan

❑ **Travels with Lizbeth,**
Lars Eighner

❑ **The Immense Journey,**
Loren Eiseley

❑ **Middlemarch,** George Eliot

❑ **Four Quartets,** T. S. Eliot

❑ **Founding Brothers,** Joseph J. Ellis

❑ **Invisible Man,** Ralph Ellison

❑ **Essays and Lectures,**
Ralph Waldo Emerson

❑ **Crazy Salad,** Nora Ephron

❑ **The Epic of Gilgamesh**

❑ **Praise of Folly,** Desiderius Erasmus

❑ **The Virgin Suicides,**
Jeffrey Eugenides

● **EURIPIDES:**
❑ Alcestis
❑ The Bacchae
❑ Medea
❑ The Trojan Women

❑ **A Fan's Notes,** Frederick Exley

F

❑ **The Spirit Catches You and You Fall Down,** Anne Fadiman

❑ **The Chemical History of a Candle,** Michael Faraday

● **WILLIAM FAULKNER:**
❑ Absalom, Absalom!
❑ As I Lay Dying
❑ Light in August
❑ The Sound and the Fury

❑ **A Time of Gifts,**
Patrick Leigh Fermor

The Neapolitan Novels,
Elena Ferrante
❑ My Brilliant Friend
❑ The Story of a New Name
❑ The Story of the Lost Child
❑ Those Who Leave and Those Who Stay

❑ **Coming of Age in the Milky Way,** Timothy Ferris

❑ **QED,** Richard P. Feynman

❑ **The History of Tom Jones, A Foundling,** Henry Fielding

❑ **Time and Again,** Jack Finney

❑ **The Art of Eating,** M. F. K. Fisher

● **F. SCOTT FITZGERALD:**
❑ The Great Gatsby
❑ Tender Is the Night

❑ **Offshore,** Penelope Fitzgerald

❑ **Harriet the Spy,** Louise Fitzhugh

● **GUSTAVE FLAUBERT:**
❑ Madame Bovary
❑ Sentimental Education

❑ **From Russia with Love,**
Ian Fleming

❑ **Brazilian Adventure,**
Peter Fleming

❑ **Gone Girl,** Gillian Flynn

❑ **The Civil War,** Shelby Foote

❑ **Johnny Tremain,** Esther Forbes

❑ **The Good Soldier,**
Ford Madox Ford

❑ **Independence Day,** Richard Ford

❑ **Flour Water Salt Yeast,**
Ken Forkish

❑ **A Passage to India,** E. M. Forster

❑ **The Day of the Jackal,**
Frederick Forsyth

❑ **A Dictionary of Modern English Usage,** H. W. Fowler

❑ **The French Lieutenant's Woman,** John Fowles

❑ **The Diary of a Young Girl,**
Anne Frank

❑ **My Brilliant Career,**
Miles Franklin

❑ **Flashman,** George MacDonald Fraser

❑ **My Father's Fortune,**
Michael Frayn

❑ **The Interpretation of Dreams,**
Sigmund Freud

❑ **The Feminine Mystique,**
Betty Friedan

❑ **The Poetry of Robert Frost,**
Robert Frost

❑ **Critical Path,** R. Buckminster Fuller

G

❑ **The Recognitions,** William Gaddis

❑ **A Lesson Before Dying,**
Ernest J. Gaines

❑ **The Great Crash, 1929,**
John Kenneth Galbraith

❑ **One Hundred Years of Solitude,**
Gabriel García Márquez

❑ **The Spare Room,** Helen Garner

❑ **Cranford,** Elizabeth Gaskell

❑ **The Glass Palace,** Amitav Ghosh

❑ **The History of the Decline and Fall of the Roman Empire,**
Edward Gibbon

❑ **Cold Comfort Farm,**
Stella Gibbons

❑ **A Mass for the Dead,**
William Gibson

❑ **Pattern Recognition,**
William Gibson

❑ **Howl and Other Poems,**
Allen Ginsberg

❑ **The Little Virtues,** Natalia Ginzburg

❑ **Passing the Time in Ballymenone,** Henry Glassie

● **JOHANN WOLFGANG VON GOETHE:**
❑ Faust
❑ Italian Journey
❑ The Sorrows of Young Werther

❑ **Dead Souls,** Nikolai Gogol

❑ **Lord of the Flies,** William Golding

❑ **Darwin's Dreampond,**
Tijs Goldschmidt

❑ **Oblomov,** Ivan Goncharov

❑ **The Goncourt Journal,**
Edmond de Goncourt

❑ **There Is a World Elsewhere,**
F. González-Crussi

❑ **The Panda's Thumb,**
Stephen Jay Gould

❑ **Personal History,**
Katharine Graham

❑ **The Wind in the Willows,**
Kenneth Grahame

❑ **Personal Memoirs of U. S. Grant,** Ulysses S. Grant

❑ **The Tin Drum,** Günter Grass

❑ **Good-Bye to All That,**
Robert Graves

❑ **Autobiography of a Face,**
Lucy Grealy

❑ **The Dead of the House,**
Hannah Green

● **GRAHAM GREENE:**
❑ The End of the Affair
❑ The Power and the Glory
❑ The Third Man

❑ **Grimms' Tales for Young and Old,** Jacob and Wilhelm Grimm

❑ **The Firm,** John Grisham

❑ **Life and Fate,** Vasily Grossman

❑ **Time and the Art of Living,**
Robert Grudin

❑ **The Little World of Don Camillo,** Giovanni Guareschi

H, I

❑ **Hiroshima Diary,** Michihiko Hachiya

❑ **I Was a Stranger,**
Sir John Winthrop Hackett

❑ **The All of It,** Jeannette Haien

☐ **The Best and the Brightest,** David Halberstam

☐ **String Too Short to Be Saved,** Donald Hall

☐ **A Drinking Life,** Pete Hamill

☐ **The Maltese Falcon,** Dashiell Hammett

☐ **A Romantic Education,** Patricia Hampl

☐ **Hunger,** Knut Hamsun

☐ **A Sorrow Beyond Dreams,** Peter Handke

☐ **84, Charing Cross Road,** Helene Hanff

☐ **Sleepless Nights,** Elizabeth Hardwick

☐ **Jude the Obscure,** Thomas Hardy

☐ **The Silence of the Lambs,** Thomas Harris

☐ **Forests,** Robert Pogue Harrison

☐ **Act One,** Moss Hart

☐ **The Essential Haiku,** Robert Hass

● **NATHANIEL HAWTHORNE:**
  ☐ The Scarlet Letter
  ☐ Tales and Sketches

☐ **Adam's Task,** Vicki Hearne

☐ **Blue Highways,** William Least Heat-Moon

☐ **Stranger in a Strange Land,** Robert A. Heinlein

● **JOSEPH HELLER:**
  ☐ Catch-22
  ☐ Something Happened

● **ERNEST HEMINGWAY:**
  ☐ A Farewell to Arms
  ☐ The Old Man and the Sea
  ☐ In Our Time

☐ **Dune,** Frank Herbert

☐ **Histories,** Herodotus

☐ **Dispatches,** Michael Herr

☐ **Zen in the Art of Archery,** Eugen Herrigel

☐ **All Creatures Great and Small,** James Herriot

☐ **My Past and Thoughts,** Alexander Herzen

☐ **The Glass Bead Game,** Hermann Hesse

☐ **An Infamous Army,** Georgette Heyer

☐ **Kon-Tiki,** Thor Heyerdahl

☐ **The Destruction of Lord Raglan,** Christopher Hibbert

☐ **The Talented Mr. Ripley,** Patricia Highsmith

☐ **Goodbye, Mr. Chips,** James Hilton

☐ **A Rage in Harlem,** Chester Himes

☐ **The Mouse and His Child,** Russell Hoban

☐ **Alan Turing: The Enigma,** Andrew Hodges

☐ **Mr. Blandings Builds His Dream House,** Eric Hodgins

☐ **Gödel, Escher, Bach,** Douglas R. Hofstadter

☐ **The Private Memoirs and Confessions of a Justified Sinner,** James Hogg

☐ **One Hundred Views of Mt. Fuji,** Katsushika Hokusai

☐ **Holmes-Laski Letters,** Oliver Wendell Holmes Jr.

☐ **Dr. Johnson and Mr. Savage,** Richard Holmes

☐ **Footsteps,** Richard Holmes

● **HOMER:**
  ☐ The Iliad
  ☐ The Odyssey

☐ **The Poetry of Gerard Manley Hopkins,** Gerard Manley Hopkins

☐ **The Odes of Horace,** Horace

☐ **Great River,** Paul Horgan

☐ **Ten Years in the Tub,** Nick Hornby

☐ **Rogue Male,** Geoffrey Household

☐ **We Die Alone,** David Howarth

☐ **World of Our Fathers,** Irving Howe

☐ **A High Wind in Jamaica,** Richard Hughes

☐ **The Fatal Shore,** Robert Hughes

☐ **Les Misérables,** Victor Hugo

☐ **The Autumn of the Middle Ages,** Johan Huizinga

☐ **Their Eyes Were Watching God,** Zora Neale Hurston

☐ **Brave New World,** Aldous Huxley

☐ **In the Vineyard of the Text,** Ivan Illich

☐ **The World According to Garp,** John Irving

☐ **The Berlin Stories,** Christopher Isherwood

☐ **The Remains of the Day,** Kazuo Ishiguro

J

☐ **The Haunting of Hill House,** Shirley Jackson

☐ **Life Among the Savages,** Shirley Jackson

☐ **The Death and Life of Great American Cities,** Jane Jacobs

☐ **Beyond a Boundary,** C. L. R. James

☐ **Cultural Amnesia,** Clive James

● **HENRY JAMES:**
  ☐ The Aspern Papers
  ☐ The Portrait of a Lady

☐ **The Collected Ghost Stories of M. R. James,** M. R. James

☐ **A Taste for Death,** P. D. James

● **WILLIAM JAMES:**
  ☐ The Selected Letters of William James
  ☐ The Varieties of Religious Experience

☐ **The Origin of Consciousness in the Breakdown of the Bicameral Mind,** Julian Jaynes

☐ **Heat and Dust,** Ruth Prawer Jhabvala

☐ **Harold and the Purple Crayon,** Crockett Johnson

☐ **A Johnson Reader,** Samuel Johnson

☐ **A False Spring,** Pat Jordan

● **JAMES JOYCE:**
  ☐ Dubliners
  ☐ A Portrait of the Artist as a Young Man
  ☐ Ulysses

● **Memories, Dreams, Reflections,** C. G. Jung

☐ **The Phantom Tollbooth,** Norton Juster

K

● **FRANZ KAFKA:**
  ☐ The Complete Stories
  ☐ The Trial

☐ **The Boys of Summer,** Roger Kahn

☐ **When French Women Cook,** Madeleine Kamman

☐ **Andersonville,** MacKinlay Kantor

☐ **The Liars' Club,** Mary Karr

☐ **The Perfect Stranger,** P. J. Kavanagh

☐ **Palm-of-the-Hand Stories,** Yasunari Kawabata

☐ **The Greek Passion,** Nikos Kazantzakis

☐ **Letters of John Keats,** John Keats

☐ **The Face of Battle,** John Keegan

☐ **The Secret of the Old Clock,** Carolyn Keene

❑ **A Dresser of Sycamore Trees,**
Garret Keizer

❑ **The Story of My Life,** Helen Keller

❑ **Part of Our Time,** Murray Kempton

❑ **A Boy at the Hogarth Press,**
Richard Kennedy

❑ **Talking Like the Rain,**
X. J. Kennedy

❑ **The Pound Era,** Hugh Kenner

❑ **On the Road,** Jack Kerouac

❑ **The Living Thoughts of
Kierkegaard,** Søren Kierkegaard

❑ **Kilvert's Diary,** Francis Kilvert

❑ **Why We Can't Wait,**
Martin Luther King Jr.

● STEPHEN KING:
  ❑ Carrie
  ❑ 11/22/1963

❑ **The Poisonwood Bible,**
Barbara Kingsolver

❑ **Just So Stories for Little
Children,** Rudyard Kipling

❑ **Old House of Fear,** Russell Kirk

❑ **Death of My Aunt,** C. H. B. Kitchin

❑ **The Oldest Dead White
European Males,** Bernard Knox

❑ **From the Mixed-Up Files of
Mrs. Basil E. Frankweiler,**
E. L. Konigsburg

❑ **Into Thin Air,** Jon Krakauer

❑ **A Hole Is to Dig,** Ruth Krauss

❑ **The Structure of Scientific
Revolutions,** Thomas S. Kuhn

❑ **The Book of Laughter and
Forgetting,** Milan Kundera

❑ **Angels in America,** Tony Kushner

L

❑ **Dangerous Liaisons,**
Pierre Choderlos de Laclos

❑ **The Princess of Clèves,**
Madame de Lafayette

❑ **The Dwarf,** Pär Lagerkvist

❑ **Interpreter of Maladies,**
Jhumpa Lahiri

❑ **Notes on a Cowardly Lion,**
John Lahr

❑ **The Leopard,** Giuseppe Tomasi
di Lampedusa

❑ **Endurance,** Alfred Lansing

❑ **Sons and Lovers,**
D. H. Lawrence

❑ **Gardening for Love,**
Elizabeth Lawrence

❑ **Independent People,**
Halldór Laxness

❑ **The Spy Who Came In from
the Cold,** John le Carré

❑ **A Wizard of Earthsea,**
Ursula K. Le Guin

❑ **To Kill a Mockingbird,** Harper Lee

❑ **Cider with Rosie,** Laurie Lee

❑ **Another Self,** James Lees-Milne

❑ **Two Sought Adventure,**
Fritz Leiber

❑ **The Cyberiad,** Stanislaw Lem

❑ **Book of Ages,** Jill Lepore

❑ **A Wrinkle in Time,** Madeleine
L'Engle

❑ **Friends in High Places,**
Donna Leon

❑ **LaBrava,** Elmore Leonard

❑ **Zibaldone,** Giacomo Leopardi

● DORIS LESSING:
  ❑ The Grass Is Singing
  ❑ The Golden Notebook
  ❑ Re: Colonised Planet 5, Shikasta

❑ **The Gentleman in Trollope,**
Shirley Robin Letwin

❑ **Christ Stopped at Eboli,**
Carlo Levi

❑ **If This Is a Man,** Primo Levi

❑ **Rosemary's Baby,** Ira Levin

❑ **Tristes Tropiques,**
Claude Lévi-Strauss

● C. S. LEWIS:
  ❑ A Grief Observed
  ❑ The Lion, the Witch and
    the Wardrobe

❑ **The Journals of Lewis and
Clark,** Meriwether Lewis and
William Clark

❑ **Liar's Poker,** Michael Lewis

❑ **Voices of the Old Sea,**
Norman Lewis

❑ **Main Street,** Sinclair Lewis

❑ **Between Meals,** A. J. Liebling

❑ **Einstein's Dreams,** Alan Lightman

❑ **Abraham Lincoln: Speeches
and Writings,** Abraham Lincoln

❑ **Venice for Pleasure,** J. G. Links

❑ **Complete Stories,**
Clarice Lispector

❑ **The Voyages of Doctor Dolittle,**
Hugh Lofting

❑ **The Call of the Wild,** Jack London

❑ **The Art of the Personal Essay,**
Phillip Lopate

❑ **Arctic Dreams,** Barry Lopez

❑ **Man Meets Dog,** Konrad Lorenz

❑ **The Case of Charles Dexter
Ward,** H. P. Lovecraft

❑ **Betsy-Tacy,** Maud Hart Lovelace

❑ **Under the Volcano,** Malcolm Lowry

❑ **The Way Things Are,** Lucretius

❑ **The Bourne Identity,**
Robert Ludlum

❑ **The Story of My Teeth,**
Valeria Luiselli

❑ **Five Days in London,** John Lukacs

❑ **Adventures on the Wine Route,**
Kermit Lynch

❑ **The Undertaking,** Thomas Lynch

❑ **The Lyttelton Hart-Davis
Letters,** George Lyttelton and
Rupert Hart-Davis

M

❑ **Leo Africanus,** Amin Maalouf

❑ **The Towers of Trebizond,**
Rose Macaulay

❑ **Anybody Can Do Anything,**
Betty MacDonald

❑ **Epitaph of a Small Winner,**
Joaquim María Machado de Assis

❑ **The Prince,** Niccolò Machiavelli

❑ **Whisky Galore,**
Compton Mackenzie

❑ **Eastern Approaches,**
Fitzroy Maclean

❑ **Confessions of a Philosopher,**
Bryan Magee

● NORMAN MAILER:
  ❑ The Armies of the Night
  ❑ The Executioner's Song

❑ **Kaputt,** Curzio Malaparte

❑ **In the Freud Archives,**
Janet Malcolm

❑ **A Book of One's Own,**
Thomas Mallon

❑ **The Voices of Silence,**
André Malraux

❑ **Goodbye, Darkness,**
William Manchester

❑ **Hope Against Hope,**
Nadezhda Mandelstam

❑ **Ongoingness,** Sarah Manguso

❑ **The Magic Mountain,**
Thomas Mann

❑ **A Place of Greater Safety,**
Hilary Mantel

❑ **Mystery Train,** Greil Marcus

❑ **The Infatuations,** Javier Marías

☐ **West with the Night,**
Beryl Markham

☐ **the lives and times of archy and mehitabel,** Don Marquis

☐ **The Roots of Civilization,**
Alexander Marshack

☐ **Life of Pi,** Yann Martel

☐ **A Game of Thrones,**
George R. R. Martin

☐ **The Eighteenth Brumaire of Louis Bonaparte,** Karl Marx

☐ **Nicholas and Alexandra,**
Robert K. Massie

☐ **Tales of the City,** Armistead Maupin

☐ **A Genius in the Family,**
Hiram Percy Maxim

☐ **Ring of Bright Water,**
Gavin Maxwell

☐ **A Year in Provence,** Peter Mayle

☐ **The Road,** Cormac McCarthy

☐ **Make Way for Ducklings,**
Robert McCloskey

☐ **Angela's Ashes,** Frank McCourt

☐ **The Heart Is a Lonely Hunter,**
Carson McCullers

☐ **Truman,** David McCullough

☐ **Lonesome Dove,** Larry McMurtry

☐ **Plagues and Peoples,**
William H. McNeill

☐ **Oranges,** John McPhee

☐ **The Rainbabies,** Laura Krauss
Melmed

● HERMAN MELVILLE:
  ☐ Moby-Dick
  ☐ The Piazza Tales

☐ **The Metaphysical Club,**
Louis Menand

☐ **A Mencken Chrestomathy,**
H. L. Mencken

☐ **On the Shoulders of Giants,**
Robert K. Merton

☐ **The Seven Storey Mountain,**
Thomas Merton

☐ **The First Day on the Somme,**
Martin Middlebrook

☐ **Autobiography of John Stuart Mill,** John Stuart Mill

☐ **Death of a Salesman,** Arthur Miller

☐ **Black Spring,** Henry Miller

☐ **A Canticle for Leibowitz,**
Walter M. Miller Jr.

The World of Winnie-the-Pooh,
A. A. Milne
  ☐ Winnie-the-Pooh
  ☐ The House at Pooh Corner

☐ **Paradise Lost,** John Milton

☐ **Little Bear,** Else Holmelund Minarık

☐ **A Fine Balance,** Rohinton Mistry

☐ **Up in the Old Hotel,**
Joseph Mitchell

☐ **Gone With the Wind,**
Margaret Mitchell

☐ **Hons and Rebels,** Jessica Mitford

☐ **The Pursuit of Love,** Nancy Mitford

☐ **House Made of Dawn,**
N. Scott Momaday

☐ **Essays,** Michel Eyquem de
Montaigne

☐ **Anne of Green Gables,**
L. M. Montgomery

☐ **Stormbringer,** Michael Moorcock

☐ **Judgment Night,** C. L. Moore

☐ **History: A Novel,** Elsa Morante

The Bookshop Novels,
Christopher Morley
  ☐ Parnassus on Wheels
  ☐ The Haunted Bookshop

☐ **The Rise of Theodore Roosevelt,** Edmund Morris

☐ **Pax Britannica,** Jan Morris

☐ **Beloved,** Toni Morrison

☐ **Ill Met by Moonlight,**
W. Stanley Moss

☐ **My First Summer in the Sierra,**
John Muir

☐ **The Emperor of All Maladies,**
Siddhartha Mukherjee

☐ **The Hunger Angel,** Herta Mùller

☐ **Selected Stories, 1968–1994,**
Alice Munro

☐ **The Wind-Up Bird Chronicle,**
Haruki Murakami

☐ **The Tale of Genji,**
Lady Murasaki Shikibu

☐ **The Sea, the Sea,** Iris Murdoch

☐ **The Man Without Qualities,**
Robert Musil

N

● VLADIMIR NABOKOV:
  ☐ Lolita
  ☐ Speak, Memory

☐ **Reading Lolita in Tehran,**
Azar Nafisi

☐ **A House for Mr. Biswas,**
V. S. Naipaul

☐ **A Beautiful Mind,** Sylvia Nasar

☐ **The Women of Brewster Place,**
Gloria Naylor

☐ **A Short Walk in the Hindu Kush,** Eric Newby

☐ **The Reckoning,** Charles Nicholl

☐ **Merry Hall,** Beverley Nichols

☐ **Portrait of a Marriage,**
Nigel Nicolson

☐ **The Birth of Tragedy,**
Friedrich Nietzsche

☐ **Ringworld,** Larry Niven

☐ **The 9/11 Commission Report**

☐ **Mutiny on the Bounty,**
Charles Nordhoff and
James Norman Hall

☐ **Dakota,** Kathleen Norris

O

☐ **Dreams from My Father,**
Barack Obama

☐ **Master and Commander,**
Patrick O'Brian

☐ **The Little Red Chairs,** Edna O'Brien

☐ **At Swim-Two-Birds,** Flann O'Brien

☐ **Mrs. Adams in Winter,**
Michael O'Brien

☐ **The Things They Carried,**
Tim O'Brien

● FLANNERY O'CONNOR:
  ☐ The Complete Stories
  ☐ The Habit of Being

☐ **Collected Stories,** Frank O'Connor

☐ **Are You Somebody?,**
Nuala O'Faolain

☐ **Into the Heart of Borneo,**
Redmond O'Hanlon

☐ **The Book of Tea,**
Kakuzo Okakura

☐ **The Famished Road,**
Ben Okri

☐ **Tell Me a Riddle,** Tillie Olsen

☐ **Long Day's Journey into Night,**
Eugene O'Neill

☐ **The Origins of European Thought About the Body, the Mind, the Soul, the World, Time, and Fate,** R. B. Onians

☐ **War in Val D'Orcia,** Iris Origo

● GEORGE ORWELL:
  ☐ 1984
  The Collected Essays, Journalism, and Letters:
    ☐ An Age Like This
    ☐ My Country Right or Left
    ☐ As I Please
    ☐ In Front of Your Nose

☐ **Metamorphoses,** Ovid

P, Q

❑ **The Village of Waiting,**
George Packer

❑ **The Gnostic Gospels,**
Elaine Pagels

❑ **The Cosmic Code,**
Heinz R. Pagels

Memoirs of a Provençal Childhood, Marcel Pagnol
❑ My Father's Glory
❑ My Mother's Castle

❑ **The Portable Dorothy Parker,**
Dorothy Parker

❑ **France and England in North America,** Francis Parkman

❑ **Pensées,** Blaise Pascal

❑ **Doctor Zhivago,** Boris Pasternak

❑ **Cry, the Beloved Country,**
Alan Paton

❑ **Kiss the Girls,** James Patterson

❑ **Medieval in LA: A Fiction,**
Jim Paul

The Gormenghast Trilogy,
Mervyn Peake
❑ Titus Groan
❑ Gormenghast
❑ Titus Alon

❑ **Book Lust,** Nancy Pearl

❑ **The Diary of Samuel Pepys,**
Samuel Pepys

❑ **Life: A User's Manual,**
Georges Perec

❑ **Most of the Most of S. J. Perelman,** S. J. Perelman

❑ **A Reader's Delight,** Noel Perrin

❑ **Giving Up the Gun,** Noel Perrin

❑ **The Beast in the Nursery,**
Adam Phillips

❑ **Zen and the Art of Motorcycle Maintenance,** Robert M. Pirsig

❑ **The Book of the City of Ladies,**
Christine de Pizan

❑ **Collected Dialogues,** Plato

❑ **The Bogey Man,** George Plimpton

❑ **Letters of Pliny the Younger,**
Pliny the Younger

❑ **Plutarch's Lives,** Plutarch

❑ **Poetry and Tales,** Edgar Allan Poe

❑ **The Travels of Marco Polo,**
Marco Polo

❑ **The Collected Stories of Katherine Anne Porter,**
Katherine Anne Porter

❑ **The World of Peter Rabbit,**
Beatrix Potter

❑ **The Wicked Pavilion,**
Dawn Powell

❑ **Heisenberg's War,**
Thomas Powers

❑ **A Glastonbury Romance,**
John Cowper Powys

❑ **The House of Life,** Mario Praz

❑ **History of the Conquest of Mexico,** William H. Prescott

❑ **A Palpable God,** Reynolds Price

❑ **Clockers,** Richard Price

● MARCEL PROUST:
  In Search of Lost Time:
  ❑ Swann's Way
  ❑ Within a Budding Grove
  ❑ The Guermantes Way
  ❑ Sodom and Gomorrah
  ❑ The Captive
  ❑ The Fugitive
  ❑ Time Regained

❑ **The Golden Compass,**
Philip Pullman

❑ **Eugene Onegin,** Alexander Pushkin

❑ **Excellent Women,** Barbara Pym

❑ **Gravity's Rainbow,**
Thomas Pynchon

❑ **The Qur'an**

R

❑ **Old Glory,** Jonathan Raban

❑ **Gargantua and Pantagruel,**
François Rabelais

❑ **Sparkle and Spin,** Ann Rand and Paul Rand

❑ **Atlas Shrugged,** Ayn Rand

❑ **Citizen,** Claudia Rankine

❑ **Swallows and Amazons,**
Arthur Ransome

❑ **The List of Books,** Frederic Raphael and Kenneth McLeish

❑ **Period Piece,** Gwen Raverat

❑ **The Long Walk,** Slavomir Rawicz

❑ **Village School,** Miss Read

❑ **Mumbo Jumbo,** Ishmael Reed

❑ **Tender at the Bone,** Ruth Reichl

❑ **All Quiet on the Western Front,**
Erich Maria Remarque

❑ **Lenin's Tomb,** David Remnick

❑ **A Judgement in Stone,**
Ruth Rendell

❑ **Wide Sargasso Sea,** Jean Rhys

❑ **Interview with the Vampire,**
Anne Rice

❑ **Selected Poetry,** Rainer Maria Rilke

❑ **Illuminations,** Arthur Rimbaud

❑ **Midnight in Sicily,** Peter Robb

❑ **Gilead,** Marilynne Robinson

❑ **Hunger of Memory,**
Richard Rodriguez

❑ **The Tuscan Year,** Elizabeth Romer

❑ **The Walls Came Tumbling Down,** Henriette Roosenburg

❑ **Explaining Hitler,** Ron Rosenbaum

❑ **Call It Sleep,** Henry Roth

● PHILIP ROTH:
  ❑ American Pastoral
  ❑ The Ghost Writer

❑ **The Medical Detectives,**
Berton Roueché

❑ **Classic Crimes,** W. N. Roughead

❑ **The Confessions,** Jean-Jacques Rousseau

❑ **Harry Potter and the Sorcerer's Stone,** J. K. Rowling

❑ **The God of Small Things,**
Arundhati Roy

❑ **Guys and Dolls,** Damon Runyon

❑ **Midnight's Children,**
Salman Rushdie

❑ **The Stones of Venice,**
John Ruskin

❑ **The Longest Day,** Cornelius Ryan

❑ **Home,** Witold Rybczynski

S

❑ **Captain Blood,** Rafael Sabatini

❑ **The Man Who Mistook His Wife for a Hat,** Oliver Sacks

❑ **All Passion Spent,**
Vita Sackville-West

❑ **The Dragons of Eden,** Carl Sagan

❑ **The Sagas of Icelanders**

❑ **The Little Prince,** Antoine de Saint-Exupéry

❑ **Memoirs,** Duc de Saint-Simon

❑ **The Catcher in the Rye,**
J. D. Salinger

❑ **Light Years,** James Salter

❑ **Lost in Place,** Mark Salzman

❑ **Poems,** Sappho

❑ **No Exit,** Jean-Paul Sartre

❑ **The Complete Memoirs of George Sherston,**
Siegfried Sassoon

❑ **The Complete Persepolis,**
Marjane Satrapi

❑ **Landscape and Memory,** Simon Schama

❑ **Saint-Exupéry,** Stacy Schiff

❑ **Forms of Devotion,** Diane Schoemperlen

❑ **The Last of the Just,** André Schwarz-Bart

❑ **The Emigrants,** W. G. Sebald

❑ **Where the Wild Things Are,** Maurice Sendak

❑ **The Golden Gate,** Vikram Seth

❑ **The Killer Angels,** Michael Shaara

● **WILLIAM SHAKESPEARE:**
❑ Hamlet
❑ Henry IV, Part 1
❑ Henry IV, Part 2
❑ Henry V
❑ Julius Caesar
❑ King Lear
❑ Macbeth
❑ A Midsummer Night's Dream
❑ Othello
❑ Richard II
❑ Romeo and Juliet
❑ The Sonnets
❑ The Tempest

❑ **Pygmalion,** George Bernard Shaw

❑ **Bernard Shaw: Collected Letters, 1874–1950,** George Bernard Shaw

❑ **Frankenstein,** Mary Shelley

❑ **The Stone Diaries,** Carol Shields

❑ **Berlin Diary,** William L. Shirer

❑ **The Pillow Book of Sei Shōnagon,** Sei Shōnagon

❑ **Bread and Wine,** Ignazio Silone

❑ **City,** Clifford D. Simak

❑ **Maigret and the Man on the Bench,** Georges Simenon

❑ **The Collected Stories,** Isaac Bashevis Singer

❑ **The Three Golden Keys,** Peter Sís

❑ **The Immortal Life of Henrietta Lacks,** Rebecca Skloot

❑ **Sailing Alone Around the World,** Joshua Slocum

❑ **Artful,** Ali Smith

❑ **A Tree Grows in Brooklyn,** Betty Smith

❑ **I Capture the Castle,** Dodie Smith

❑ **Polar Star,** Martin Cruz Smith

❑ **A Simple Plan,** Scott Smith

❑ **Topper,** Thorne Smith

❑ **White Teeth,** Zadie Smith

❑ **The Expedition of Humphry Clinker,** Tobias Smollett

❑ **Longitude,** Dava Sobel

❑ **River of Shadows,** Rebecca Solnit

● **ALEKSANDR SOLZHENITSYN:**
❑ One Day in the Life of Ivan Denisovich
❑ The Gulag Archipelago 1918–1956

● **SOPHOCLES:**
❑ Antigone
❑ Oedipus at Colonus
❑ Oedipus the King

❑ **Aké,** Wole Soyinka

❑ **Memento Mori,** Muriel Spark

❑ **The Complete Maus,** Art Spiegelman

❑ **Corinne, or Italy,** Madame de Staël

❑ **The Valleys of the Assassins,** Freya Stark

❑ **Japanese Inn,** Oliver Statler

❑ **The Man Who Loved Children,** Christina Stead

❑ **A Woman, a Man, and Two Kingdoms,** Francis Steegmuller

❑ **Angle of Repose,** Wallace Stegner

❑ **Abel's Island,** William Steig

❑ **The Autobiography of Alice B. Toklas,** Gertrude Stein

● **JOHN STEINBECK:**
❑ The Grapes of Wrath
❑ Travels with Charley

❑ **After Babel,** George Steiner

❑ **The Red and the Black,** Stendhal

❑ **Quicksilver,** Neal Stephenson

❑ **The Life and Opinions of Tristram Shandy, Gentleman,** Laurence Sterne

● **ROBERT LOUIS STEVENSON:**
❑ A Child's Garden of Verses
❑ Kidnapped
❑ The Strange Case of Dr. Jekyll and Mr. Hyde
❑ Treasure Island

❑ **Letters of a Woman Homesteader,** Elinore Pruitt Stewart

❑ **Dracula,** Bram Stoker

❑ **Fer-de-Lance,** Rex Stout

❑ **lost boy, lost girl,** Peter Straub

❑ **Alice James: A Biography,** Jean Strouse

❑ **Morgan: American Financier,** Jean Strouse

❑ **Sophie's Choice,** William Styron

❑ **The Twelve Caesars,** Suetonius

❑ **Zeno's Conscience,** Italo Svevo

❑ **Gulliver's Travels,** Jonathan Swift

❑ **The Quest for Corvo,** A. J. A. Symons

❑ **Map: Collected and Last Poems,** Wisława Szymborska

T

Histories of Rome, Tacitus
❑ The Histories
❑ The Annals

❑ **Fame and Obscurity,** Gay Talese

❑ **This One Summer,** Mariko Tamaki and Jillian Tamaki

❑ **The Joy Luck Club,** Amy Tan

❑ **Tao Te Ching**

❑ **The Secret History,** Donna Tartt

❑ **The Surprise of Cremona,** Edith Templeton

❑ **The Daughter of Time,** Josephine Tey

❑ **Vanity Fair,** William Makepeace Thackeray

❑ **How to Tell When You're Tired,** Reg Theriault

❑ **The Great Railway Bazaar,** Paul Theroux

❑ **Arabian Sands,** Wilfred Thesiger

❑ **Religion and the Decline of Magic,** Keith Thomas

❑ **The Lives of a Cell,** Lewis Thomas

❑ **On Growth and Form,** D'Arcy Wentworth Thompson

❑ **Lark Rise to Candleford,** Flora Thompson

❑ **Fear and Loathing in Las Vegas,** Hunter S. Thompson

❑ **Eloise,** Kay Thompson

❑ **Walden,** Henry David Thoreau

❑ **The History of the Peloponnesian War,** Thucydides

❑ **The Thurber Carnival,** James Thurber

❑ **Prisoner Without a Name, Cell Without a Number,** Jacobo Timerman

❑ **Célestine,** Gillian Tindall

❑ **Her Smoke Rose Up Forever,** James Tiptree Jr.

❑ **Democracy in America,** Alexis de Tocqueville

● **J. R. R. TOLKIEN:**
❑ The Hobbit
❑ The Lord of the Rings

- **LEO TOLSTOY:**
  - ☐ Anna Karenina
  - ☐ The Death of Ivan Ilyich
  - ☐ War and Peace
- ☐ **The Sea and the Jungle,** H. M. Tomlinson
- ☐ **Small Talk at Wreyland,** Cecil Torr
- ☐ **The Great Good Thing,** Roderick Townley
- ☐ **Centuries of Meditations,** Thomas Traherne
- ☐ **Garibaldi and the Thousand,** George Macaulay Trevelyan
- ☐ **The Collected Stories,** William Trevor
- ☐ **Hermit of Peking,** Hugh Trevor-Roper
- ☐ **The Warden,** Anthony Trollope
- ☐ **Within the Context of No Context,** George W. S. Trow
- ☐ **The Guns of August,** Barbara W. Tuchman
- ☐ **Presumed Innocent,** Scott Turow
- **MARK TWAIN:**
  - ☐ The Adventures of Huckleberry Finn
  - ☐ The Adventures of Tom Sawyer
  - ☐ Letters from the Earth
- ☐ **Dinner at the Homesick Restaurant,** Anne Tyler

U, V

- ☐ **Life in Code,** Ellen Ullman
- ☐ **Kristin Lavransdatter,** Sigrid Undset
- ☐ **The Maples Stories,** John Updike
- ☐ **The Dying Earth,** Jack Vance
- ☐ **The Letters of Vincent van Gogh,** Vincent van Gogh
- ☐ **Lives of the Most Excellent Painters, Sculptors, and Architects,** Giorgio Vasari
- ☐ **Twenty Thousand Leagues Under the Sea,** Jules Verne
- ☐ **Burr: A Novel,** Gore Vidal
- ☐ **The Aeneid,** Virgil
- ☐ **Candide, or Optimism,** Voltaire
- ☐ **Elizabeth and Her German Garden,** Elizabeth von Arnim
- ☐ **Slaughterhouse-Five,** Kurt Vonnegut
- ☐ **Girl in Hyacinth Blue,** Susan Vreeland

W

- ☐ **Holy Land,** D. J. Waldie
- ☐ **The Color Purple,** Alice Walker
- ☐ **The Compleat Angler,** Izaak Walton
- ☐ **Among Others,** Jo Walton
- ☐ **The Boxcar Children,** Gertrude Chandler Warner
- ☐ **The Element of Lavishness,** Sylvia Townsend Warner and William Maxwell
- ☐ **Beautiful Swimmers,** William W. Warner
- ☐ **All the King's Men,** Robert Penn Warren
- ☐ **Up from Slavery,** Booker T. Washington
- ☐ **The Double Helix,** James D. Watson
- ☐ **The Loved One,** Evelyn Waugh
- ☐ **A Coffin for King Charles,** C. V. Wedgwood
- ☐ **Simone Weil: An Anthology,** Simone Weil
- ☐ **The Invisible Man,** H. G. Wells
- ☐ **The Collected Stories of Eudora Welty,** Eudora Welty
- ☐ **Boggs: A Comedy of Values,** Lawrence Weschler
- ☐ **Black Lamb and Grey Falcon,** Rebecca West
- ☐ **The Hot Rock,** Donald E. Westlake
- ☐ **The Age of Innocence,** Edith Wharton
- ☐ **Charlotte's Web,** E. B. White
- ☐ **The Once and Future King,** T. H. White
- ☐ **The Making of the President 1960,** Theodore H. White
- ☐ **The Underground Railroad,** Colson Whitehead
- ☐ **Leaves of Grass,** Walt Whitman
- ☐ **Night,** Elie Wiesel
- ☐ **Kaddish,** Leon Wieseltier
- ☐ **Collected Poems 1943–2004,** Richard Wilbur
- ☐ **The Importance of Being Earnest,** Oscar Wilde
- ☐ **Little House in the Big Woods,** Laura Ingalls Wilder
- ☐ **The Bridge of San Luis Rey,** Thornton Wilder

- ☐ **Stoner,** John Williams
- ☐ **A Streetcar Named Desire,** Tennessee Williams
- ☐ **Tarka the Otter,** Henry Williamson
- ☐ **Lincoln at Gettysburg,** Garry Wills
- ☐ **Dearest Friend: A Life of Abigail Adams,** Lynne Withey
- ☐ **Israel and the Dead Sea Scrolls,** Edmund Wilson
- ☐ **Naturalist,** Edward O. Wilson
- ☐ **April 1865,** Jay Winik
- ☐ **Pigs Have Wings,** P. G. Wodehouse
- ☐ **Look Homeward, Angel,** Thomas Wolfe
- ☐ **The Bonfire of the Vanities,** Tom Wolfe
- **VIRGINIA WOOLF:**
  - ☐ The Common Reader
  - ☐ A Moment's Liberty
  - ☐ Orlando
  - ☐ To the Lighthouse
- ☐ **The Prelude and Other Poetry,** William Wordsworth
- ☐ **Native Son,** Richard Wright
- ☐ **The Invention of Nature,** Andrea Wulf
- ☐ **The Day of the Triffids,** John Wyndham
- **The Zoom Trilogy,** Tim Wynne-Jones
  - ☐ Zoom at Sea
  - ☐ Zoom Away
  - ☐ Zoom Upstream

X, Y, Z

- ☐ **The Autobiography of Malcolm X,** Malcolm X
- ☐ **Memoirs of Hadrian,** Marguerite Yourcenar
- ☐ **Swallowing Clouds,** A. Zee
- ☐ **Within This Wilderness,** Feenie Ziner
- ☐ **Germinal,** Émile Zola
- ☐ **A Part of Myself,** Carl Zuckmayer

Excerpt Permissions

Photo Credits